Encyclopedia of Television Subjects, Themes and Settings

Encyclopedia of Television Subjects, Themes and Settings

VINCENT TERRACE

McFarland & Company, Inc., Publishers
Jefferson, North Carolina, and London

LIBRARY OF CONGRESS CATALOGUING-IN-PUBLICATION DATA

Terrace, Vincent, 1948–
Encyclopedia of television subjects, themes and settings / Vincent Terrace.
p.   cm.
Includes index.

ISBN-13: 978-0-7864-2498-6
(illustrated case binding : 50# alkaline paper) ∞

1. Television programs — Plots, themes, etc.— Encyclopedias.   I. Title.
PN1992.18.T38   2007   791.45'75 — dc22   2006100495

British Library cataloguing data are available

On the cover: TV ©2006 Stockbyte; Screen image ©2006 PhotoSpin

Manufactured in the United States of America

*McFarland & Company, Inc., Publishers
Box 611, Jefferson, North Carolina 28640
www.mcfarlandpub.com*

Contents

Preface 1

Adolescence 5
"Adult Film" Actresses (*see also* Nudity and Sexuality) 16
Adventurers 18
Africa 20
African American Performers and Characters 20
After-School Hangouts *see* Teen After-School Hangouts
Aliens 24
American Indian Performers and Characters 28
Angels 32
Animals (*see also* Talking Animals and Machines) 34
Arizona 37
Asian American Performers and Characters 37
Australia 40
Aviators *see* Pilots
Babies 40
Ballet 41
Baltimore 42
Bars (*see also* Restaurants) 42
Beaches and Islands 46
Biblical *see* Religious Characters
Blind *see* Visually Impaired Characters
Boston 49
Broadway and Stage Shows 50
Butlers *see* Housekeepers
Café *see* Bars; Restaurants
California 59
Camps 61
Canada 62
Cars (*see also* Gadgets; Talking Animals and Machines; Taxi Cabs; Truckers) 62
Cartoons 64
Chicago 68
Children — Extraordinary 69

Children's Programs — Pioneering Years, 1941–1969 (*see also* Adolescence; Cartoons; Children — Extraordinary; Fairy Tales; Puppets; Teenagers) 71
Christmas *see* Holiday Specials
Circus and Carnivals (*see also* Clowns) 72
The Civil War 73
Clowns (*see also* Circus and Carnivals) 74
Clubs and Lodges 75
Color Broadcasting 77
Comedies *see* Sitcoms
Computers — Extraordinary (*see also* Talking Animals and Machines) 77
Con Artists 79
Connecticut 81
Cooking — Pioneering Years, 1945–1970 81
Country Folk 82
Cross Dressers 83
Cuban American Performers and Characters (*see also* Latino Performers and Characters; Mexican American Performers and Characters; Puerto Rican Performers and Characters) 85
Detectives *see* Men — Law Enforcers; Women — Law Enforcers
The Devil (for God-related programs *see also* Religious Programs) 86
Diners *see* Restaurants
District Attorneys (*see also* Lawyers; Judges) 86
Doctors (*see also* Women — Nurses) 88
Drama (*see also* Drama — Repeat Series) 92
Drama — Repeat Series 99

"Dumb Blondes" *see* Women — "Dumb Blondes"

Dwarves *see* Little People

Elderly *see* Senior Citizens

Espionage 100

Fairy Tales 102

F.B.I. Agents (*see also* Espionage; Government Agents; Men — Law Enforcers; Women — Law Enforcers) 104

Films Based on Television Series 105

Florida 106

Forensics 106

Gadgets 107

Game Shows — Pioneering Years, 1941–1960 110

Gays (Male) (*see also* Cross Dressers; Lesbians; Transsexuals) 116

Genies 118

Geniuses (*see also* Children — Extraordinary; Men — Extraordinary; Women — Extraordinary) 119

Ghosts 121

God *see* Religious Characters; Angels

Government Agents (*see also* Espionage; F.B.I. Agents) 124

Hawaii 126

Hearing Impaired Characters 126

Historical Settings (*see also* The Civil War; War — Korea, Vietnam, Iraq; War — World War II; Westerns) 127

Holiday Specials 129

Horror *see* Ghosts; Supernatural; Vampires; Werewolves; Witches

Hospitals *see* Doctors; Women — Nurses

Hotels (*see also* Lodges) 135

Housekeepers 139

Immigrants 142

Iraq War *see* War — Korea, Vietnam, Iraq

Islands *see* Beaches and Islands

Judges (*see also* District Attorneys; Lawyers) 143

Korean War *see* War — Korea, Vietnam, Iraq

Las Vegas 145

Latino Performers and Characters (*see also* Cuban American Performers and Characters; Mexican American Performers and Characters; Puerto Rican Performers and Characters) 145

Law Enforcement *see* Men — Law Enforcers; Women — Law Enforcers

Lawyers (*see also* District Attorneys; Judges) 149

Lesbians 153

Little People 157

Lodges *see* Clubs and Lodges

London 159

Look-alikes (*see also* Twins) 160

Los Angeles (*see also* California) 161

Love 163

Magazines *see* Newspapers and Magazines; Reporters

Magicians 165

Maids *see* Housekeepers

Martial Arts 167

Matchmakers *see* Love

Mediums 168

Men — Extraordinary (*see also* F.B.I. Agents; Men — Law Enforcers; Pilots; Space; Truckers) 170

Men — Gays *see* Gays (Male)

Men — Law Enforcers (*see also* District Attorneys; F.B.I. Agents; Forensics) 172

Mentally Disabled Characters 186

Mermaids 187

Mexican American Performers and Characters (*see also* Cuban American Performers and Characters; Latino Performers and Characters; Puerto Rican Performers and Characters) 188

Midgets *see* Little People

Ministers *see* Religious Characters

Morphing 192

Native Americans *see* American Indian Performers and Characters

New Jersey 194

New York 194

News Broadcasts — Pioneering Years, 1927–1958 196

Newspapers and Magazines (*see also* Reporters) 198

Nightclubs (*see also* Hotels) 201

Nudity and Sexuality (*see also* "Adult Film" Actresses) 202

Nuns *see* Religious Characters

Nurses *see* Women — Nurses (*see also* Doctors)

Opera 210

Philadelphia 211

Physically Disabled Performers and Characters 212

Pilot Film Series 215

Pilots (Aviators; for space ship pilots *see* Space) 216

Politics (*see also* Presidential Appearances) 218

Presidential Appearances 221

Priests *see* Religious Characters

Prison 222

Prostitutes 223

Psychiatrists (*see also* Doctors; Women — Nurses) 224

Psychics *see* Mediums

Puerto Rican Performers and Characters (*see also* Cuban American Performers and Characters; Latino Performers and Characters; Mexican Rican Performers and Characters) 226

Puppets and Marionettes (*see also* Children's Programs) 228

Rabbis *see* Religious Characters

Reality Programs 234

Religious Characters (God, ministers, nuns, priests, rabbis) (*see also* Angels; Devil; Religious Programs) 237

Religious Programs (*see also* Angels; Devil; Holiday Specials [e.g., for Christmas and Easter programs]; Religious Characters) 239

Reporters (*see also* Newspapers and Magazines) 240

Restaurants (*see also* Bars) 244

Rescue 247

Ringmasters *see* Circus and Carnivals

Robots (*see also* Computers — Extraordinary) 249

San Francisco (*see also* California) 252

Scatterbrained Women *see* Women — "Dumb Blondes"; Women — Scatterbrained

Schools *see* Teachers

Secret Agents *see* Espionage

Senior Citizens 253

Series Based on Films (*see also* Films Based on Television Series; Series Based on Radio Programs) 261

Series Based on Radio Programs 262

Sex *see* Nudity and Sexuality

Shakespeare 264

Shows Within Shows 265

Sitcoms — Pioneering Years, 1936–1960 267

Soap Operas — Pioneering Years, 1945–1970 273

Space 276

Spectaculars *see* Variety and Drama Spectaculars

Speech Impaired Characters 279

Stage Shows *see* Broadway

Stock Car Racers 280

Super Heroes (*see also* Children — Extraordinary; Men — Extraordinary; Women — Extraordinary) 280

Supernatural 284

Talking Animals and Machines (*see also* Animals; Computers — Extraordinary; Puppets) 286

Taxi Cabs 287

Teachers 288

Teen After-School Hangouts (*see also* Adolescence; Teenagers) 292

Teenagers (*see also* Adolescence; Twins) 294

Television Firsts 310

Time Travel 312

Transsexuals (*see also* Gays; Lesbians) 313

Truckers 314

Twins (*see also* Look-alikes) 314

Vampires 317

Variety and Drama Spectaculars (*see also* Broadway and Stage Shows; Variety Programs) 318

Variety Programs — Pioneering Years, 1930–1960 (*see also* Broadway and Stage Shows; Variety and Drama Spectaculars) 322

Ventriloquists *see* Puppets and Marionettes

Vietnam War *see* War — Korea, Vietnam, Iraq

Visually Impaired Characters   328
War — Civil War see The Civil War
War — Korea, Vietnam, Iraq   330
War — World War II   331
Washington, D.C.   334
Werewolves   334
Westerns   335
Witches   342
Women — "Dumb Blondes" (see also
    Women — Scatterbrained)   344

Women — Extraordinary (see also F.B.I.
    Agents; Mediums; Robots; Witches;
    Women — Law Enforcers)   347
Women — Law Enforcers (see also
    District Attorneys; F.B.I. Agents;
    Forensics; Lawyers)   350
Women — Nurses   355
Women — Scatterbrained (see also
    Women — "Dumb Blondes")   357

Index   361

Preface

Over the last 80 years television has generated a remarkable body of work, providing one of the best records of our historical, sociological and cultural heritage as well as entertaining generations of Americans and now people all over the world. For good or ill, television has influenced people in big and small ways.

This is the first work of its kind. Chronologies are as complete as possible covering series, pilots, specials and experimental program information. This information provides scholars and fans a new way to approach subjects of interest. This book allows television broadcasts on subjects of interest to be identified and will allow in-depth study, if a reproduction of the show is available. The timeline presentation provides insight into changing and developmental patterns.

For some users of this book, having the facts (e.g., what and when the first color broadcasts were or descriptions of the shows about women) may be sufficient. For some users, access to the shows themselves may be desirable.

It is an unfortunate but many of the 1920s, '30s, '40s and early '50s programs listed in this book no longer exist. Sources like the Museum of Broadcasting in New York and Los Angeles and the Library of Congress in Washington, D.C., have what few remnants remain from these early eras. Those fortunate enough to live near such institutions will find viewing some of these programs very helpful in uncovering long lost information.

There are positive developments toward increasing the availability of television broadcasts. With the continuing growth of the DVD, many older television series are being released — programs that never saw the light of day on VHS.

For those interested in acquiring old (and even new) TV series, there are two collector papers: *The Big Reel* and *Toy Shoppe*. These publications list individuals and companies that sell (and trade) such programs. Video Yesteryear, Radio Spirits, Shokus Video and Critic's Choice Video offer a wide range of TV series for sale (mostly public domain programs). Prices range from $10 to $20 per hour on VHS. The companies mentioned above are reliable and offer excellent quality programs (usually first generation from a master). If any problems should arise, such as a defective tape, exchanges can be made.

Dealing with individuals can be a bit of a headache. Most are honest and reliable. Most of these people are collectors and have the original 16mm prints of old TV series. Because the equipment to transfer film to video is quite expensive, many cannot afford top of the line units. Transfers of film to video tape can be quite good; however, when you purchase a tape you receive a very good to fair second generation copy (made from the master tape). Reproduction quality aside, these programs offer excellent research possibilities. While this writer has not personally experienced any dishonest dealers, be prepared for the possibility of very poor reproduction quality, long waiting periods and missing material (usually openings or closings; original commercials in some cases). Remember also that many of the programs obtainable from private dealers are not public domain programs and remain under copyright.

Purchasing from individuals offers a great (and money saving) advantage — you can pick and choose the shows you want (as opposed to buying a pre-recorded set). Each tape is custom made and it does take time. The wait can well be worth the anxiety. When dealing with individuals, request a catalogue. The more obscure programs you are seeking may not be listed in their ad. It is also more reassuring to purchase from a catalogue as opposed to an ad when you are not familiar with a collector. For industry people looking for clips, these individual collectors are a gold mine of material. Although clearances for broadcast will have to be made on non–public domain material, you can, for minimal costs (as opposed to approaching production companies), view clips, save the producing companies the hassle of finding what you want, and pay only for the rights for broadcast.

When purchasing VHS tapes always order at the SP (2 hour) speed. This assures the best quality and readable credits; ordering at the slower EP (6 hour) speed makes a fair quality original a bad quality copy (very white and unclear). And, if after searching catalogue after catalogue, you still can't find what you need, try eBay on the Internet. You never know what TV show will turn up for sale here.

As a television writer who sometimes has information in my books that is not available in any other published source, I have often been asked, "Where do you get your information?" My main source is actually the shows themselves. As anyone who has done research on a television show knows, the basic information you find is the same. What began as an interest in collecting old time radio programs gradually became collecting old television shows for research. This has proved to be a wealth of information and I try to reflect this in my work.

TV Guide, newspaper reviews, library files (specifically the New York Public Library at Lincoln Center) and network records serve well for basic information. With this project I needed to go beyond the basics and with the advent of VCRs, I have been able to watch and tape (and compile notes at my leisure) in addition to mining my personal historical collection of shows. For the topics, I tried to pick subjects that I felt would have historical or other research interest.

For example, if you are from Chicago or you are researching about Chicago or need to depict Chicago, this book can be a unique information source. You would be able to see how the skyline of Chicago is depicted from *Stud's Place* in 1949 and then in 1982's *Crime Story* to compare to today. A show like *Life with Luigi* might offer insight into how life in Chicago was perceived during the earlier decades.

A person interested in social issues, like the themes explored in the feature film *Brokeback Mountain*, is able to identify and possibly view series of the 1950s and later that precursed outright depictions and broke new ground with their characters. The evolutions revealed by the chronological presentation allow a new way to track changing perspectives.

People in the industry may want to research previous subject treatment to develop their own ideas. In addition, this book can be a tool to find public domain material or material available for licensing clips that are needed to add a certain element to a project.

Devotees of a particular genre, like entertainment related to vampires, may want to know about every offering going back to the beginning, either as collectors or to master the subject.

This project is a distillation of thousands of hours of watching shows over the last thirty years. It gave me an opportunity to become reacquainted with shows I had seen much earlier but half forgotten as well as to use a lot of information that I have accumulated naturally because of the nature of my work. It is my hope that this book will fill some of the needs that I envisioned as I compiled it.

The Encyclopedia

Adolescence

While children are adorable and sweet, television's devotion to them is primarily as secondary or background characters. This listing comprises those programs that star or feature pre-teen children. See also *Extra Ordinary Kids, Teenagers, Twins.*

1949. Sharon, Chuck, Donna and Donald (Margaret Kerry, Tommy Bernard, Judy Nugent, Jimmy Hawkins) are the children of Charlie Ruggles and his wife Margaret on *The Ruggles* (ABC). Donald Devlin plays the mischievous 12-year-old Wesley Eggleston on *Wesley* (CBS).

1950. Donnie Henderson (Clifford Sales, Stuffy Singer) is the son of attorney Harry Henderson and his wife Alice on *Beulah* (CBS). Sheila James plays Jackie Erwin, the resourceful daughter of school principal Stu Erwin and his wife June on *Trouble with Father* (ABC).

1951. Gene O'Donnell plays Randolph Foster, the younger brother of Judy Foster on *A Date with Judy* (ABC).

1952. Richard Eyer plays Bobby Peterson, the ten-year-old nephew of scatterbrained secretary Irma Peterson on *My Friend Irma* (CBS).

1953. Little Ricky Ricardo (Richard Keith) is the son of bandleader Ricky Ricardo and his wacky wife Lucy on *I Love Lucy* (CBS). Brandon DeWilde pitches the sponsor's product (Sunsweet Prune Juice) while playing the mischievous Jamieson Francis John McHummer on *Jamie* (ABC). Rusty and Linda Williams (Rusty Hamer, Angela Cartwright) are the children of nightclub comedian Danny Williams and his wife Kathy on *Make Room for Daddy* (ABC/CBS). Kevin Acton (Ronnie Walker) is a young boy whose experiences with his family in Ludlow, Kentucky (1919) are recalled on *Wonderful John Acton* (ABC; the title refers to Kevin's father, John, a court clerk and general store owner).

1954. Corporal Rusty (Lee Aaker) and his dog, Rin Tin Tin, help the 101st Cavalry maintain the peace on *The Adventures of Rin Tin Tin* (ABC). Jimmy Hawkins plays Tagg Oakley, the brother of Old West sharpshooter Annie Oakley on the syndicated *Annie Oakley*. Alexander and Cookie (Stuffy Singer, Ann Barnes) are the children of the dim-witted Dagwood Bumstead and his levelheaded wife Blondie on *Blondie* (NBC). Kathy Anderson (Lauren Chapin) faces the problems of growing up on CBS's *Father Knows Best*. Jeff

Miller (Tommy Rettig) encounters adventures as the owner of a beautiful collie on *Lassie* (CBS). Emily and Peter (Susan Strasberg, Malcolm Broderick) are the children of Ben and Liz Marriott on *The Marriage* (NBC). Butch Russell (David Saber) is the mischievous nephew of Thomas Russell, the mayor of Springdale on the syndicated *Mayor of the Town*. A whirlwind of energy named Jeep Allison (Martin Houston) finds life adventurous in a small town on ABC's *My Son Jeep.*

1955. "Like a streak of lightning flashing across the sky" describes Champion, the stallion of Ricky North (Barry Curtis) on CBS's *The Adventures of Champion*. Keena Nomkeena plays Keena, the son of Cheyenne Indian Chief Brave Eagle on *Brave Eagle: Chief of the Cheyenne* (CBS). Nancy Gilbert plays Calamity, the mischievous sister of Buffalo Bill, Jr., the marshal of the town of Wileyville on the syndicated *Buffalo Bill, Jr.* Cullen Crabbe plays Cuffy Sanders, the son of a slain French Foreign legionnaire, who is now the ward of Captain Michael Grant on *Captain Gallant of the Foreign Legion* (NBC/ABC. Also known as *Foreign Legionnaire*). "The story of a horse and the boy who loves him" introduces Joey Newton (Bobby Diamond), the owner of NBC's *Fury*. Cubby O'Brien, Sharon Baird, Cheryl Holdridge and Karen Pendleton are the youngest of the children who sing, dance and entertain children as Mouseketeers on *The Mickey Mouse Club* (ABC). Eleven-year-old Diane and her six-year-old brother Hank (Susan Holloran, Evan Elliott) are the children of First National Bank vice president Pearson Norby and his wife Helen on *Norby* (NBC). Kit and Twig (Beverly Washburn, Ted Marc) are the children of child psychologist Thomas Wilson and his wife Helen on *Professional Father* (CBS).

1956. Elizabeth, Candy and Buster (Patricia Morrow, Susan Hawkins, Jimmy Hawkins) are the children cared for by actress Carolyn Daniels on the NBC pilot *Carolyn*. NBC's *Circus Boy* finds Corky (Mickey Braddock), water boy to Bimbo the elephant, traveling with the 19th century Champion Circus. Small town girl Corky Brady (Darlene Gillespie) helps her sheriff father, Matt uphold the law on ABC's *Corky and White Shadow*. Jeri Lou James plays Josie, the daughter of Jan Stewart, a widow struggling to become a nightclub singer on CBS's *It's Always Jan*. Ken McLaughlin (Johnny Washbrook) learns responsibility as the owner of a horse on *My Friend Flicka* (CBS).

1957. Michael Carr Hartley plays Boy, the young, orphaned survivor of a plane crash, who has made Africa his home on *The Adventures of a Jungle Boy* (Syn.). Bobby Clark is Casey Jones, Jr., the son of famed railroad engineer Casey Jones on the syndicated *Casey Jones*. Gail Stone and Karen Greene play Jenny and Mary Hammond, the twin daughters of Liza Hammond, a widowed traveling lecturer on *The Eve Arden Show* (CBS). Amateur sleuths Frank and Joe Hardy (Tim Considine, Tommy Kirk) solve crimes in the small town of Bayport on ABC's *The Hardy Boys*. Wally and Theodore Cleaver (Tony Dow, Jerry Mathers) learn valuable lessons about life in the small town of Mayfield on *Leave It to Beaver* (CBS/ABC).

1958. Jody O'Connell (Tommy Nolan), the young son of Annie O'Connell, helps his mother, a widow, run a Montana hotel in the 1880s on *Buckskin* (NBC). Orphaned sisters Cassie and Midge Beamer (Jacklyn O'Donnell, Sherry Alberoni) encounter misadventure living with their retired grandfather, John, on NBC's *The Ed Wynn Show*. Mary and Jeff Stone (Shelley Fabares, Paul Petersen) find help in facing life's problems from their wise mother, Donna on *The Donna Reed Show* (ABC). Patty Petersen later joins the cast as Tricia, the young girl adopted by Donna and Alex. Eugene Martin is Joey Drum, the son of Jefferson Drum, a widowed and embittered newspaper publisher in the town of Jubilee during the 1850s on NBC's *Jefferson Drum*. Mark McCain (Johnny Crawford) is the son of Lucas McCain, the fastest man with a .44–40 hair trigger action rifle on *The Rifleman* (ABC). Alice Holliday (Patty Ann Gerrity), a bubbly girl with untapped energy, finds mishaps in everything she does on the syndicated series *This Is Alice*.

1959. Patricia, Nicky and Roy (Gigi Perreau, Richard Miles, Dennis Joel) are the children cared for by Goldie Appleby, a vivacious ex-showgirl on *The Betty Hutton Show*. The mischievous Dennis Mitchell (Jay North) hits the airwaves to cause pandemonium for his parents and next-door neighbor Mr. Wilson on CBS's *Dennis the Menace*. Barbara Beaird plays Teeny, the little girl who lives next door to Fibber McGee, the world's greatest liar, and his understanding wife Molly on *Fibber McGee and Molly* (NBC). Robert Crawford, Jr. plays Andy, the kid brother of Slim Sherman who, with his friend Jess Harper, operates a stage depot for the Great Overland Mail Stage Lines in 1880s Wyoming on *Laramie* (NBC).

Twelve-year-old Tory Peck (Patty McCormack) prefers her life as a tomboy rather than face the world as a young lady on CBS's *Peck's Bad Girl*.

1960. Young Opie Taylor (Ronny Howard) is the respectful but slightly mischievous son of Sheriff Andy Taylor on *The Andy Griffith Show* (CBS). Diane Mountford plays Patty Greer, the daughter of Bill Greer, an ex-marine turned owner of a charter boat for hire on *Assignment: Underwater* (Syn.). Pebbles Flintstone (voice of Jean VanderPyl) is the daughter of Fred and Wilma Flintstone on *The Flintstones*. Also on the ABC series, Bamm Bamm (Don Messick) is the adopted son of Barney and Betty Rubble. Brook Hooten (Flip Mark) is the son of Bill and Babs Hooten, a city couple who now operate a ranch in New Mexico on *Guestward Ho* (ABC). Chip Douglas (Stanley Livingston) is the youngest of three boys, the sons of aeronautical engineer Steve Douglas on *My Three Sons* (ABC/CBS). Mike (Tim Considine), the eldest son, leaves the series in 1965; Ernie Thompson (Barry Livingston), an orphan adopted by Steve, replaces Mike. Small town farm girl Velvet Brown (Lori Martin) strives to achieve a dream: train her horse, King, for competition in the Grand National Steeplechase on *National Velvet*. Also on the NBC series, Joey Scott plays Donald Brown, Velvet's younger brother. Merry Martin and Gil Smith play Leslie and Steve, the children of Peter Lind Hayes and Mary Healy, a show business couple who move from New York to Connecticut to find a quieter life on *Peter Loves Mary* (NBC). Carol, Debbie and Cissy (Cindy Robbins, Sherry Alberoni, Eileen Chesis) are the obedient but slightly mischievous children of real estate agent Tom Potter on *The Tom Ewell Show* (CBS).

1961. Ritchie Petrie (Larry Matthews) is the son of TV comedy writer Rob Petrie and his wife Laura on *The Dick Van Dyke Show*. Bobby Buntrock plays Harold Baxter, the son of attorney George Baxter and his wife Dorothy on *Hazel* (NBC). In 1965, when the series switched to CBS, Julia Benjamin joined the cast as Susie, the daughter of George's brother Steve and his wife Barbara. Gina Gillespie plays Pippi Longstocking, a magical young girl who lives in a strange house with a horse and a monkey on the ABC pilot *Pippi Longstocking*.

1962. Judy and Elroy Jetson (voices of Janet Waldo, Daws Butler) are the children of the futuristic George and Jane Jetson on *The Jetsons* (ABC).

Vickie (Beverly Washburn), Maria (Tracy Stratford), Marnie (Celia Kaye) and Binkie (Carol Sydes) are the younger children of Christine Massey on *The New Loretta Young Show* (CBS). Regina Groves, Ricky Kelman and K.C. Butts play Joanne, Tommy and Dinghy, the children of Duncan and Alice MacRoberts, a family cared for by an English butler on *Our Man Higgins* (ABC). Butch Patrick plays Gregg, the young son of Louise Howard, the widow who dates widower Luke McCoy on the last season episodes of *The Real McCoys* (CBS). A loving married couple (George and Anna Rose) with two natural children (Laurie and Flip) and two adopted children (Mary and Jeff) have a home where there is always *Room for One More* (ABC).

1963. Steve and Danny (Mickey Sholdar, Rory O'Brien) are the children of widowed Washington, D.C. congressman Glen Morley on *The Farmer's Daughter* (ABC). Westfield Military Academy Cadet Gary McKeever (Scott Lane) does things his way (or tries to) on NBC's *McKeever and the Colonel*. Twelve-year-old Jaimie McPheeters (Kurt Russell) experiences the hardships of a wagon train journey destined for California on *The Travels of Jaimie McPheeters* (ABC).

1964. Wednesday and Pugsley Addams (Lisa Loring, Ken Weatherwax) are the gloomy children of the eccentric Gomez Addams and his beautiful wife Morticia on *The Addams Family* (ABC). Tabitha (Erin and Diane Murphy) and Adam (David and Greg Lawrence) are the witch and warlock children of Samantha and Darrin Stevens on *Bewitched* (ABC). Veronica Cartwright and Darby Hinton play Jemima and Israel Boone, the children of frontiersman Daniel Boone and his wife Rebecca on *Daniel Boone* (NBC). Sandy and Bud (Luke Halpin, Tommy Nordon) are the sons of Florida park ranger Porter Ricks, who have a pet dolphin named *Flipper* (NBC). Gina Gillespie plays Mimi Scott, the sister of vivacious teenager Karen Scott, and the daughter of Steve and Barbara Scott on NBC's *Karen*. Dwight Eisenhower Wong (Ricky Der) is a 10-year-old orphan who is cared for by Kentucky Jones, a widowed rancher on *Kentucky Jones* (NBC). Timmy Martin (Jon Provost) becomes the new owner of *Lassie* (CBS) when Jeff Miller moves to the city. Edward Wolfgang Munster (Butch Patrick) is the werewolf son of a Frankenstein-like father (Herman) and his vampire wife Lily on *The Munsters* (CBS). Jason

Marsden plays Eddie as 16-year-old on the syndicated update, *The Munsters Today*.

1965. Katie Sweet plays Tina, the sister of enterprising businessman Hank Dearborn on NBC's *Hank*. Will Robinson (Billy Mumy) is the youngest child of John and Maureen Robinson, a family of explorers who are *Lost in Space* (CBS). Cindy and Randy (Cindy Eilbacher, Randy Whipple) are the children of Dave Crabtree, the man whose mother has been reincarnated as a car, and his wife Barbara, on *My Mother the Car* (NBC). Kyle and Joel Nash (Kim Tyler, Brian Nash) are the children of Jim and Joan Nash on *Please Don't Eat the Daisies* (NBC).

1966. Orphaned twins Buffy and Jody Davis (Anissa Jones, Johnny Whitaker) find a home and love in New York with their Uncle Bill (Brian Keith) on CBS's *Family Affair*. In 2002, the WB revised the series with Sasha Pieterse and Jimmy Pinchak as Buffy and Jody Davis. Young Cindy Fenton (Donna Butterworth) has a dream to become a marine — right now on the ABC pilot *Little Leatherneck*. Jefferson, Fennimore and Amy (Keith Schultz, Kevin Schultz, Tammy Locke) are the younger members of the Monroes, a family of children struggling to establish a home in 1875 Wyoming on *The Monroes* (ABC). Christopher Shea is Joey, the young son of 1880s Wyoming rancher Marion Starrett, who befriends the wandering cowboy Shane on ABC's *Shane*. Manuel Padilla, Jr. plays Jai, the orphaned jungle boy befriended by Tarzan, the Lord of the Jungle, on NBC's *Tarzan*. Seven-year-old Chris Williams (Billy Mumy) prefers the world of fantasy created from his mother's book illustrations to that of making real friends on the CBS pilot *The Two of Us*.

1967. Eve Plumb is Bonnie Braids, the adopted daughter of police detective Dick Tracy and his wife Tess Trueheart Tracy, on the pilot *Dick Tracy*. Jay Blood plays the Tracy's natural son, Junior Tracy. Young Mark Wedloe (Clint Howard), the son of Florida game warden Tom Wedloe and his wife Ellen, has a most unusual pet — a black bear named Ben on CBS's *Gentle Ben*. Parents Kate and Bill Wallace struggle to cope with their son Googie (Teddy Eccles), a problem eight-year-old child, on the CBS pilot *My Boy Googie*. Also on the series is Googie's 12-year-old sister Frannie (Pamela Dapo).

1968. Pamelyn Ferdin and Peter Robbins play Cookie and Alexander Bumstead, the children of architect Dagwood Bumstead and his wife Blondie on *Blondie* (CBS). Billy and Toby (Philip Brown, Tod Starke) are the children of San Francisco magazine reporter Doris Martin on *The Doris Day Show* (CBS). Candy and Jonathan Muir (Kellie Flanagan, Harlen Carraher) are the children of Carolyn Muir and live in a cottage haunted by the ghost of Captain Daniel Gregg on *The Ghost and Mrs. Muir* (NBC/ABC). Marc Copage is Corey, the young son of recently widowed nurse Julia Baker on NBC's *Julia*. Barry Lockridge (Stefan Arngrim) is the only child (with six adults) marooned on a world parallel to earth on *Land of the Giants* (ABC). Mike Jones (Buddy Foster) is the son of Sam Jones, the widowed city councilman of Mayberry, North Carolina, on *Mayberry, R.F.D.* (CBS).

1969. The NBC pilot *Anderson and Company* revolves around Marshall Anderson, the owner of a turn-of-the-century department store, his wife, Augusta, and their eight children: Amanda (Cynthia Eilbacher), Alfa (Heather Harrison), Adrienne (Robin Eccles), Anstruther (Nick Beauvy), Amory (Ray Dimas), Ansford (Teddy Eccles), Artanza (Sean Kelly) and Apollo (Leig Nervik). A widow with three daughters, Marcia, Jan and Cindy (Maureen McCormick, Eve Plumb, Susan Olsen) marries a man with three sons, Greg, Peter and Bobby (Barry Williams, Christopher Knight, Michael Lookinland) to form ABC's *The Brady Bunch*. Six-year-old Eddie Corbett (Brandon Cruz) attempts to find a wife for his widowed father, Tom (Bill Bixby) on ABC's *The Courtship of Eddie's Father*. Lisa Gerritsen plays Lydia, the daughter of cartoon artist John Monroe and his wife Ellen on *My World and Welcome to It* (NBC). Sonny Hammond (Gary Pankhurst), the son of Waratah National Park Ranger Matt Hammond, shares adventures with Skippy, his pet kangaroo, on *Skippy, the Bush Kangaroo* (Syn.). Also on the series is Liza Goddard as Clancy Merrick, the pretty teenage girl who resides with the Hammonds. Allison (Joyce Menges), Penny (Susan Neher) and Pokey (Melanie Fullerton) are the children of Michael Endicott, a widowed teacher living in Rome, Italy, on *To Rome with Love* (CBS).

1970. Two boys, Jud and Billy (Mitch Vogel, Mark Kearney), growing up in a small Wisconsin town, is the basis for the NBC pilot *Two Boys*. A clubhouse located in a double decker London bus and a group of kids headed by Scooper (Peter Firth) and Billie (Gillian Bailey) are the elements of ABC's *Here Come the Double Deckers*. The friendship between a white boy named Homer (Tony Frazer) and a black boy named Benjy (Kevin Herron) becomes the focal point of the NBC pilot *Me and Benjy*. Dawn Lyn joins the cast of *My Three Sons* (CBS) as Dodie, the daughter of Barbara Harper, a schoolteacher the widowed Steve Douglas marries. Hal, Jr., Prudence and Butch (David Doremus, Kim Richards, Trent Lehman) are the children of college professor Harold Everett and are looked over by the mystical Phoebe Figalilly on *Nanny and the Professor* (ABC). Ten-year-old Danny Partridge (Danny Bonaduce) organizes his family into the singing sensation, *The Partridge Family* (ABC).

1971. Susan Neher is Jenny Conway, the sister of Bobby Conway, a struggling songwriter on ABC's *Getting Together*. Butch Patrick plays Mark, a boy who falls into an enchanted well and reappears in a magic land of living hats on ABC's *Lidsville*. Michael Hughes plays Michael Johnson, the six-year-old son of Terry, the daughter of nightclub comedian Danny Williams and his wife Kathy on *Make Room for Granddaddy* (ABC). Annie Preston (Angela Powell) is the nine-year-old daughter of Arizona TV talk show host Dick Preston and his wife Jenny on *The New Dick Van Dyke Show* (CBS).

1972. Mitch Vogel plays Jamie, the adopted son of Ben Cartwright, the owner of the Ponderosa Ranch in Nevada on *Bonanza* (NBC). The ABC animated series *Kid Power* is set at the Rainbow Club where children of all ethnic backgrounds share thoughts on prejudice, teamwork and responsibility. Melora Hardin plays Cindy Prescott, a young girl who owns Thunder, a fabulous, semi-wild black stallion on *Thunder* (NBC). Kitty and Scott Reynolds (Kami Colter, Scott Kolden) are the children of Michael and Liz Reynolds and the owners of Buttons, a mischievous chimp they found, on *Me and Buttons* (CBS). Jodie Foster plays Henrietta Bennett, a pretty tomboy who prefers to be called Hank, and who fears becoming a girl and liking "girlie things" on the CBS pilot *My Sister Hank*. Lori and T.J. (Lori Ann Rutherford, Marty McCall) are the children of Andy Sawyer, mayor of Greenwood, North Carolina, and his wife Lee, on *The New Andy Griffith Show* (CBS).

1973. Jodie Foster plays Elizabeth, the 12-year-old daughter of Ted and Alice Henderson, and Bradley Savage is the six-year-old son of Bob and

Carol Sanders on ABC's *Bob & Carol & Ted & Alice*. Widower Bob Randall (Eddie Albert) struggles to raise his vibrant daughter, Flossie (Dawn Lyn) on the CBS pilot *Daddy's Girl*. Cindy and Jan (Leslie Graves, Kim Richards) are the children of Susan Evans, a divorced career woman on ABC's *Here We Go Again*. Gina, Jimmy and Al (Ellen Sherman, Jack David Walker, Albert Anderson) are the children of Herbert Koska, an unemployed aerospace engineer, and his wife Isabel on the NBC pilot *Koska and His Family*. Johnny and Scott Stuart (Johnny Whitaker, Scott Kolden) are brothers with a most unusual pet, a sea monster named Sigmund on NBC's *Sigmund and the Sea Monsters*.

1974. Helen Hunt is Jill Prentiss, the daughter of San Francisco Police Chief Amy Prentiss on NBC's *Amy Prentiss*. Widower Fess Hamilton (Fess Parker) faces the dilemma of raising his mischievous daughters, Susie (Cynthia Eilbacher), Beth (Dawn Lyn) and Holly (Michelle Stacy) on the CBS pilot *The Fess Parker Show*. Michael Evans (Ralph Carter) is the youngest child of Florida and James Evans on *Good Times*. Also on the CBS series, Janet Jackson plays Penny Gordon, the adopted daughter of Willona Woods. Joanie Cunningham (Erin Moran) is a young girl growing up in 1950s Milwaukee on ABC's *Happy Days*. Susan Neher played Joanie in the original pilot, "Love and the Happy Days," which aired on *Love, American Style* in 1972. Matt, Steve and Dwayne (Todd Lookinland, Carey Wong, William Attmore) are the adopted children of Ken and Kathy Kelly on the ABC pilot *Kelly's Kids*. Holly Marshall, the daughter of forest ranger Rick Marshall, is marooned with her family in a world forgotten by time on *Land of the Lost* (NBC). The hardships of frontier life confront young Laura Ingalls (Melissa Gilbert) and her sister, Mary (Melissa Sue Anderson) on *Little House on the Prairie*. Also on the NBC series are Laura's sisters, Carrie (Lindsay and Sidney Greenbush) and Grace (Wendi and Brenda Turnbaugh) and Alison Arngrim and Jonathan Gilbert as Nellie and Willie Oleson, Laura and Mary's friends. Robbie Rist plays Glendon Farrell, the young neighbor of English teacher Lucas Tanner on NBC's *Lucas Tanner*. Anneliese and Tuliff (Debbie Lytton, Todd Lookinland) are the children of Christian and Ann Larsen, a Scandinavian family struggling to carve a new life for themselves on the Minnesota frontier of the 1880s on *The New Land*

(ABC). Taylor and Tim Reed (Mark Slade, Johnny Doran) are brothers who live in Nassau and have a most unusual pet, a sea lion named *Salty* (Syn.). Pamelyn Ferdin, Jackie Haley and Andrew Parks provide the voices for Cathy, Danny and Ben, the children of Martha Day, a widow in the town of Elmsville during the early 1900s on the animated *These Are the Days* (ABC).

1975. Quinn Cummings is Ginger Smith, the granddaughter of Eddie Smith, a gambler turned owner of the Big E Sports Arena on *Big Eddie* (CBS). Bachelor police officer Frank Murphy (Charles Durning) struggles to raise Lucas Adams (Tierre Turner), a black orphan who is now his ward on NBC's *The Cop and the Kid*. Laurie and Haywood (Rosanne Katon, Haywood Nelson) are the children of Hal and Ellie Marshall on NBC's *Grady* (a spinoff from *Sanford and Son*). Single cartoonist Mac McLeish (Dick Van Dyke) attempts to raise Augie (Jimmy Baio), the 12-year-old son of a late friend on the ABC pilot *McLeish and the Kid*. Eleven-year-old Addie Loggins (Jodie Foster) helps Bible salesman Moses Prey con people on ABC's *Paper Moon*. Lisa Gerritsen plays Dess Lindstrom, the daughter of Phyllis Lindstrom, a commercial photographer's assistant on *Phyllis* (CBS. The character first appeared on *The Mary Tyler Moore Show*, from which *Phyllis* is a spinoff). Elizabeth Cheshire plays Jill, the daughter of Sam Hayden, a widowed, happy-go-lucky musician on NBC's *Sunshine*. Fred and Ernie (Willie Aames, Eric Olson) are the children of Karl and Lottie Robinson, members of a family shipwrecked on a deserted island on *Swiss Family Robinson* (ABC).

1976. Robbie Rist is Little John Martin, the 12-year-old version of Big John Martin (Herb Edelman), a high school teacher who can change his age when he drinks from a fountain of youth he discovered on *Big John, Little John* (NBC). Michelle Stacy plays Kimmy, the sister of Calvin Campbell, a veterinarian whose life is hampered by McDuff, the ghost of a sheep dog on *McDuff, the Talking Dog* (NBC). Anthony Perez and Dennis Vasquez are Abraham, Jr. and Luis, the children of Abraham Rodriquez, Sr., a widowed Puerto Rican handyman on *Popi* (CBS). Quinn Cummings plays Annie Cooper, the adopted daughter of Doug and Kate Lawrence on ABC's *Family*. Claudia Lamb plays Heather Hartman, the seemingly normal daughter of the neurotic housewife, Mary Hartman on *Mary Hartman,*

Mary Hartman (Syn.). Sachi and Aki (June Angela, Gene Protanata) are the children of widowed Japanese businessman Taro Takahashi and cared for by Tina, a dizzy American governess, on *Mr. T and Tina* (ABC). Hallie Morgan and Debbie Leyton play Emma and Martha, the daughters of Martha Higgins, the owner of a boarding house in the town of Independence, Colorado, on *Sara* (CBS).

1977. Scott Baio plays Anthony DeLucca, the brother of Joey, the assistant to Las Vegas choreographer Nancy Blansky on ABC's *Blansky's Beauties*. Melora Hardin, Tara Talby and Poindexter Yothers play themselves as members of a kids club on *The Cliffwood Avenue Kids* (Syn.). Nicholas Bradford is the youngest son of Tom and Joanie Bradford on ABC's *Eight Is Enough*. Jilly (Denise Miller), Diane (Sarah Natoli), Mike (Lenny Bari) and Loomis (Todd Bridges) are among the street-wise Brooklyn kids being cared for by retired police officer Phil Fish and his wife Bernice on *Fish* (ABC). Liz and Robbie (Wendy Fredericks, Brad Wilken) are the children of Clifford Bean. Kevin, Ernie and Alexander (Jeff Harlan, Robbie Rist, Sparky Marcus) are the offspring of Frank Boyle. Single fathers Clifford and Frank pool their resources, move in together and form an *Instant Family* (NBC pilot). Jill Whelan plays Vicki, the sweet daughter of Merrill Stubing, the captain of the *Pacific Princess* on *The Love Boat* (ABC). Incidents in the life of a precocious boy named Mason Bennett (Mason Reese) became the plot of the ABC pilot *Mason*. Also on the series is Lee Lawson as Joyce, Mason's 13-year-old sister. Lisa Whelchel, Kelly Parsons, Julie Piekarski, Mindy Feldman, Curtis Wong and Allison Fonte are among the children who perform in songs, dances and skits as the merry Mouseketeers on *The New Mickey Mouse Club* (Syn.). David (Eric Cohen) is the son of real estate agent Jeffrey Brooks III and his wife Anne, the neighbors of Stanley and Helen Roper on *The Ropers* (ABC). Angie and Nat Wheeler (Tina Andrews, John Earl) are the children of Phil Wheeler, a widower who runs the Sanford Arms rooming house on NBC's *Sanford Arms*.

1978. Kelly and Mark Gardner (Lisa Lindgren, Al Eisenman) are the children of a busy married couple, Don and Ginny Gordon, on *Another Day* (CBS). Angie and Jordan (Kim Fields, Tony Holmes) are the children of Olivia Ellis and her estranged husband, Ray (who is trying to reestab-

lish himself) on *Baby, I'm Back* (CBS). Black orphans Arnold and Willis Jackson (Gary Coleman, Todd Bridges) find a home with white millionaire Philip Drummond (Conrad Bain) and his daughter Kimberly (Dana Plato) on NBC's *Diff'rent Strokes*. Seven Ann McDonald plays Jennie Brown, the 11-year-old daughter of Lacey Brown, a receptionist at the law form of Devlin, Linkman and O'Brien on *The Eddie Capra Mysteries* (NBC). Willie (Olivia Barash), Jerome (Bobby Ellerbee) and Tony (Cosie Costa) are among the street-wise kids who frequent a mission for children on *In the Beginning* (CBS). Lauri Hendler plays the mischievous *Little Lulu* (ABC pilot), a resident of the town of Rocky River. Susan, David and Ricky (Darian Mathias, Stephen M. Schwartz, Bryan Scott) are the children of Frank and Carol Lambert, a couple who run the world's smallest TV station (KRDA) from their garage on *Please Stand By* (Syn.). Tammy Lauren plays Melissa Turner, the nine-year-old sister of Las Vegas nightclub entertainer Stacy Turner on *Who's Watching the Kids?* (NBC).

1979. Twelve-year-old Amanda Wurlitzer (Tricia Cast) pitches for the Wendell Weaver School Bears, a rowdy Little League team on CBS's *The Bad News Bears*. Other members of the team include Tanner Boyle (Meeno Peluce), Rudi Stein (Billy Jacoby), Regi Tower (Corey Feldman) and Ahmad Rahim (Kristoff St. John). Missy Gold plays Katie, the adorable daughter of Governor Gene Gatling on *Benson* (ABC). Dawn Lyn is Flossie, the adorable eight-year-old daughter of widowed Boston newspaper columnist Bob Randall on the CBS pilot *Daddy's Girl*. Jet Yardum is Lisa Hudson, the young daughter of Kate Hudson, a divorced undercover woman with the L.A.P.D. on *Dear Detective* (CBS). Cissy (Elissa Leeds), Meredith (Susan Brecht), Frankie (Linda Manz) and Margo (Michele Greene) are the featured students at the Hannah Huntley School for Girls in Connecticut on *Dorothy* (CBS). The friendship between eleven-year olds Nancy, Pete and Randy (Jill Whelan, Charles Aiken, Jarrod Johnson) becomes the focal point of *Friends* (ABC). Househusband Charlie Featherstone (Ken Berry) attempts to care for daughters Kelly and Courtney (Susan Swift, Dana Hill) while his wife attends law school on *Featherstone's Nest* (CBS pilot). Lili Haydn plays Jenny, the daughter of famed police lieutenant Columbo and his wife Kate on NBC's *Mrs. Columbo* (later titled *Kate*

Loves a Mystery). Stacey and Laura Richards (Tammy Lauren, Olivia Barash) are children watched over by an angel named Random on *Out of the Blue* (ABC). Tony, a pony endowed with special powers by the *Book of Magic*, and a young boy named Jonathan (Poindexter Yothers) share adventures on the syndicated *Tony the Pony*.

1980. Rori King is Rebecca, the daughter of Diana Cassidy, a young divorcee struggling to rebuild her life on ABC's *I'm a Big Girl Now*. Natasha Ryan plays Amy, the daughter of Alan Thackeray, the token male writer for *Women's Life* magazine on *Ladies' Man* (CBS). Eleven-year-old Maxx Davis (Melissa Michaelsen) begins life with her estranged father Norman (Joe Santos) on NBC's *Me and Maxx*. Dylan and Nicky (Rosie Harris, Justin Dana) are the children of Richard and Libby Chapin, a talkative married couple on the very talkative series *United States* (NBC).

1981. Casey, Todd and Jennifer (Tim Waldrip, Michael Hershewe, Andrea Smith) are the children of Danny and Donna Novack, a white couple who move to an interracial inner city on *The American Dream* (ABC). Eleven-year-old Chris Mason (Christopher Gardner) learns aspects of the sights and sounds that surround him from Drip, a magical drop of water that comes to life (in animation) on the syndicated *Chris and the Magical Drip*. Samantha Kanisky (Lara Jill Miller) is the adorable daughter of gruff police captain Carl Kanisky on NBC's *Gimme a Break*. Lynette Paradise and Kirk Brennan host *Kids 2 Kids*, a syndicated pilot that explores the world of children. Kelly and Keith (Amy Linker, David Hollander) are the children of Stewart Lewis, the owner of the Nassau County Café in Texas, and his wife, Alicia, on *Lewis and Clark* (NBC). Kaleena Kiff plays Patti Morgan, the young daughter of Laurie Morgan, a single mother who lives with Sidney Shorr, a homosexual, on NBC's *Love, Sidney*. Gabrielle (Dana Hill) is the delightful, slightly mischievous daughter of Nan Gallagher, host of the TV show "Mid-Morning Manhattan" on *The Two of Us* (CBS). Heather McAdam and Rad Daly play Dwana and Michael Pusser, the children of Buford Pusser, a widowed Tennessee lawman who battles injustice with fearless determination and a large club on *Walking Tall* (NBC).

1982. *The Adventures of Pollyanna* (CBS pilot) charts the life of Pollyanna Harrington (Patsy Kensit), a pretty 12-year-old girl who brings out the best in people. Tia and Tony (Tracey Gold,

Andy Freeman) are alien children seeking to find their way back home to Witch Mountain after they become lost on the CBS pilot *Beyond Witch Mountain*. Nona and Little Big Jim (Heather Hobbs, Corey Feldman) are the children of Cass Malloy, the sheriff of Burr County, Indiana on the CBS pilot *Cass Malloy* (Cass inherited the job from her late husband, Big Jim). Betsy, Roxie, Dakota and Q.P. (Sarah Torgow, Sydney Penny, Roberto Ramon, Barrett Oliver) are the children of Hearst Circle, a widower who runs the Circle Family Motor Court on the NBC pilot *The Circle Family*. Tina Yothers is Jennifer Keaton, the pretty, bright younger daughter of Steven and Elyse Keaton on NBC's *Family Ties*. Paula McFadden (Karen Valentine) is a single mother struggling to raise her young daughter, Lucy (Lili Haydn) on the NBC pilot *Goodbye Doesn't Mean Forever* (based on the feature film *The Goodbye Girl*). The relationship between Willie James (Brian Kerwin), a divorced construction company worker, and his young son Sam (Eric Coplan) is the focal point of the NBC pilot *The James Boys*. Princess (Jennifer George), Cricket (Erin Nicole Brown), Sparky (Joey Lawrence) and Daisy (Marissa Mendenhall) are among the kids who attend a day care center run by a struggling writer on the NBC pilot *Scamps*. *Silver Spoons* (NBC) explores the life of Ricky Stratton (Ricky Shroder), the son of eccentric millionaire Edward Stratton. Celia and Clovis (Sara Abeles, Keith Mitchell) are orphans won in a poker game by gambler Russell Donovan and now his responsibility on the CBS pilot *Tales of the Apple Dumpling Gang* (based on the feature film. A limited run series called *Gun Shy*, based on the pilot, ran on CBS with Bridgette Andersen replacing Sara Abeles as Celia). Eleven-year-old Jeffrey Jones (Meeno Peluce) is a Voyager, a traveler in time who helps correct history's mistakes on *Voyagers!* (NBC).

1983. Brandy Gold, Emily Moultrie and Andre Gower play Annie, Laurie and Michael, the children of Eddie and Jennie Riddle, a couple struggling to make ends meet on *Baby Makes Five* (ABC). The tomboyish Melissa Scott (Maia Brewton) becomes a member of a fifth grade club called *The Big Five* (NBC pilot). Young Gussie Mapes (Dana Hill) helps her widowed father raise her sister Theresa and brother Logan on the CBS pilot *Brannigan and Mapes*. Stacy Ferguson, Connie Law and Rene Sands are the main members of a pre-teen rock band on the Disney Channel's *Kids*

Incorporated. The NBC pilot *Little Shots* presents a modern-day version of "The Little Rascals" with Keri Houlihan (Griddy) and Joey Lawrence (Pete) in leading roles. Philip and Jamie (Paul Stout, Greg Morton) are the young sons of Amanda King, a housewife who is secretly an undercover agent for the government on *Scarecrow and Mrs. King* (CBS). Shelby (Lou Ann Ponce) and Eric (Kirk Cameron) are the children of Janet and Michael Armstrong, a suburban Iowa couple on ABC's *Two Marriages.* A black orphan named Webster Long (Emmanuel Lewis) finds a home and love with a white couple on ABC's *Webster.*

1984. Natalie Klinger and Corey Feldman play Lori and Keith Schneider, the niece and nephew of Dwayne Schneider (from *One Day at a Time*) who moves to Florida to care for them after their parents' death on the CBS pilot *Another Man's Shoes.* Lila (April Lerman), Douglas (Jonathan Ward) and Jason (Michael Pearlman) are the children of Stan and Jill Pembroke and cared for by Charles (the college student with no last name) on *Charles in Charge* (CBS). Rudy Huxtable (Keshia Knight Pulliam) is the very obedient child of Dr. Cliff Huxtable and his wife Clair on *The Cosby Show* (NBC). Harold Crane (Christian Brackett-Zika) is a 10-year-old near genius and the son of TV commentator Martin Crane and his wife Candy on *Domestic Life* (CBS). Kelly and Stacy (Dana Kimmell, Shannen Doherty) are the children of Barbara, a single mother who marries playboy newspaper columnist Jimmy McCabe on the CBS pilot *His and Hers.* Frederick Koehler plays Chip Lowell, the son of single mother Allie Lowell on CBS's *Kate and Allie.* Six-year-old Penelope Brewster, better known as Punky (Soleil Moon Frye), finds a home with a gruff photographer when her mother abandons her on NBC's *Punky Brewster.* Also on the series are Cherie Johnson (herself) and Ami Foster (as Margaux Kramer), Punky's friends. Samantha Micelli (Alyssa Milano), the daughter of Tony Micelli, grew from pretty tomboy to gorgeous young woman on ABC's *Who's the Boss?* Also featured on the series is Danny Pintauro as Jonathan, the son of ad agency owner Angela Bower.

1985. A ten-year-old Drew Barrymore plays Con Sawyer on the ABC pilot *The Adventures of Con Sawyer and Hucklemary Finn*, a role reversal retelling of the Mark Twain stories. Brandy Ward plays her friend, Mary Finn. The syndicated *Clue You In* follows the activities of pre-teen sleuths Paula Hoffman and Tripper McCarthy (themselves). Chrissy Seaver (Ashley Johnson) is the daughter of Jason and Maggie Seaver on ABC's *Growing Pains.* A group of talented children form a rock group and seek stardom on the syndicated *Kids Incorporated.* Stacy Ferguson and Renee Sands star. Brice Beckham plays Wesley, the mischievous young son of George and Marsha Owens on *Mr. Belvedere* (ABC). Vicki Lawson (Tiffany Brissette) is no ordinary 10-year-old girl. She is a robot learning how to become a real girl on the syndicated *Small Wonder.* Also on the series, Jerry Supiran plays Vicki's real brother, Jamie, and Emily Schulman is Harriet Brendel, the girl who suspects Vicki is anything but a real girl but can't prove it.

1986. Jason Late plays Lanny, the son of Buddy Landau, the coach at the Charles Lindberg Elementary School on NBC's *Fathers and Sons.* The prehistoric adventures of ABC's *The Flintstones* main characters (Fred, Wilma, Barney and Betty) are seen at a time when they were youngsters on the animated *Flintstone Kids.* Young Stacy Scott hosts *Kids' Biz*, a syndicated pilot wherein she offers music, fashion advice and other entertainment geared to children. The *Leave It to Beaver* update, *The New Leave It to Beaver* (TBS), presents the children of the show's former children. Kip and Ollie (Kipp Marcus, John Snee) are the children of Beaver Cleaver and his wife Kimberly; Kelly (Kaleena Kiff) is the daughter of Wally Cleaver and his wife Mary Ellen; Freddie and Bomber (Eric and Christian Osmond) are the sons of Eddie Haskell and his wife Gert; and J.J. Rutherford (Keri Houlihan) is the daughter of Lumpy Rutherford. June (Barbara Billingsley), the mother of Wally and Beaver Cleaver, is now a widow and a member of the Mayfield City Council. Ernie Reyes, Jr. plays Ernie, a ten-year-old karate master who helps police detective Jake Rizzo solve crime on *Sidekicks* (ABC). Paul W. Cooper plays Jeremy, the son of Sandy Betty, a young divorcee who works as an assistant at Throb Records on *Throb* (Syn.).

1987. Skye Bassett is Kelly, the daughter of Rick Armstrong. Eddie Castrodad and Jason Naylor are Kenny and Allan, the children of Louis Mangott. Rick and Louis are single fathers who move in together to save on expenses on *Duds* (CBS). Nicole Stoffman (Stephanie), Stacie Mistysyn (Caitlin), Sarah Ballingall (Melanie) and Pat Mastraianni (Joey) are among the students on the syndicated *Degrassi Jr. High*. A syndicated pilot for an updated version of *Dennis the Menace* airs with Victor DiMattia as the mischievous Dennis Mitchell. Ginger Orsi plays Amanda, the adorable four-year-old daughter of patio furniture sales man Richard Phillips and his wife Linda on *Duet* (Fox). Incidents in the lives of sisters D.J., Stephanie, and Michelle Tanner (Candace Cameron, Jodie Sweetin, Mary Kate and Ashley Olsen) become the subplot of ABC's *Full House*. A group of children turn an abandoned TV studio into their clubhouse and form their own station, Kidsongs, on *The Kidsong TV Show* (Syn.). Nicole Mandich, Julie Gourson, David Chan and Tiffany Johnson are among the kids who perform songs for children. Twelve-year-old Nicole Bradford (Staci Keanan) struggles to cope with life and the two single men who are raising her on NBC's *My Two Dads*. Allison (Nicky Rose) and Kenny (Taliesin Jaffe) are the children of Hildy Grainger, the sheriff of Lakes County, Nevada on *She's the Sheriff* (Syn.). Edan Gross is Bart Holden, the son of Georgia and Ken Holden, a young Philadelphia couple, on *Sweet Surrender* (NBC).

1988. Roseanne, Martin and Frank (Samantha Mathis, Erin Chase, Scott Curtis) are the children of Aaron and Sarah Miller, an Amish couple living in California on *Aaron's Way* (NBC). Sarah and Charley Cobb (Alyson Croft, Danny Gerard) become part of a blended family when their father, Frank, marries Annie Pfeiffer, a widow with a 12-year-old daughter named Zoe (Kim Hauser) on *Blue Skies* (CBS). Brandy Gold plays Lindsay, the nine-year-old daughter of voice impersonator Frank Dutton on *First Impressions* (CBS). Zack Morris (Mark Paul Gosselaar), Lisa Turtle (Lark Voorhies), Screech Powers (Dustin Diamond) and Nikki Coleman (Heather Hopper) are the featured students at J.F.K. Junior High School in Indiana on *Good Morning, Miss Bliss* (Disney). Ex gunfighter Ethan Allen Cord finds he is now the guardian of Claire, Joseph, Ben and George (Jenny Beck, Matthew Newmark, Brian Lando, Michael Patrick Carter) his sister's children after her death on *Guns of Paradise* (CBS). Sherry (Heidi Zeigler) and J.R. (Matt Shankman) are the pre-teen children of high school coach Graham Lubbock and his wife Elizabeth on ABC's *Just the Ten of Us*. Juliette Lewis and Mayim Bialik play Terry Rankin and Jennifer Cole, students at the Eastland School for Girls, which now allows boys when Blair Warner from *The Facts of Life* becomes

its new headmaster on the NBC pilot *The Lisa Whelchel Show*. Marsha Moreau plays Erin Clemens, the daughter of Stephanie and the sister of Andrew, the teen who battles evil as his hero Ultraman on *My Secret Identity* (Syn.). Carrie Heim is Pippalotta Longstocking, called Pippi, a feisty red-haired girl who lives in Villa Villekula (her house) without adults on the ABC pilot *Pippi Longstocking*. Sarah Polley plays Ramona Quimby, a nine-year-old girl who believes in helping people — even if they don't want her help on the syndicated *Ramona*. Michael Fishman plays D.J. Tanner, the youngest child of Dan and Roseanne Conner, an argumentative couple living in Lanford, Illinois, on *Roseanne* (ABC). The adventures of a group of kids who are members of the super secret Juniper Knights are the premise of the CBS pilot *Wildest Dreams*. Lizzie Joy (as P.J) and Danny Girard (Tommy) starred. A young Kevin Arnold (Fred Savage) and his girlfriend Winnie Cooper (Danica McKellar) learn about life on ABC's *The Wonder Years*.

1989. Judy Winslow (Jaimee Foxworth) and Richie Crawford (Bryton McClure) are the youngest members of the Winslow household on *Family Matters* (ABC). Chelsea Hertford plays Casey Cooper, the youngest daughter of Polly Cooper and her new husband, Major John MacGillis on *Major Dad* (CBS). Megan McCullough (Wendy Cox) becomes the new owner of Lassie, the beautiful collie on *The New Lassie* (Syn.).

1990. Eleven-year-old Molly Newton (Candace Hutson) is the daughter of Wood and Ava Newton on *Evening Shade* (CBS). Ashleigh Blair Sterling plays Allison and Matthew Brooks is Brian, the young children of fire captain Jack Taylor on *The Family Man* (CBS). Karen Valentine plays Jeannie Kelvin, the mother of Sam (Ben Savage), an energetic child with a high I.Q. on the CBS pilot *Hurricane Sam*. Tracy Clarke (Alexis Caldwell) is the very bright and knowledgeable 10-year-old daughter of the not-so-bright Lenny Callahan and his wife Shelly on *Lenny* (CBS). Ten-year-old Caroline Gidot (Rebecca Harrell) offers opinions as she observes life on CBS's *Room for Romance*. The child every parent dreads comes to light in the guise of Bart Simpson (voice of Nancy Cartwright), a ten-year-old wisecracking brat on *The Simpsons* (Fox). His younger sister, Lisa (Yeardley Smith) is the dream child — respectful, obedient and kind. Tucker, Cory and

Maggie (Stephen Dorff, Joshua Rudoy, Jeanna Michaels) are the children of Ed and Polly Brannigan, a couple who own Buzz, a ventriloquist's dummy who has come to life and is full of wise cracks and stale vaudeville jokes on *What a Dummy* (Syn.). Molly Marshall (Kyndra Joy Casper) is the nine-year-old daughter of Sarah Marshall, the assistant manager of the Bennington Hotel in Manhattan on *Working It Out* (NBC).

1991. Nicole Finnegan (Heidi Zeigler), Willie Trancus (Jason Biggs) and Kenny Sanders (Damian Cagnolatti) are the principal students of teacher Otis Drexell on Fox's *Drexell's Class*. Marshall Teller (Omri Katz) and his friend Simon Holmes (Justin Shenkarow) collect evidence to prove that all is not normal in the small town of *Eerie, Indiana* (NBC). Beauty Weed (Meghan Andrews) is, as her name indicates, a beautiful 12-year-old girl who happens to be the daughter of Arlo Weed, a divorced con artist who lives off scams on *Flesh 'n' Blood* (NBC). Randy, Mark and Brad (Jonathan Taylor Thomas, Taran Noah Smith, Zachery Ty Bryan) are the sons of Tim "The Tool Man" Taylor and his wife Jill on ABC's *Home Improvement*. Eleven-year-old Rose Haber (Shanelle Workman) is a girl with attitude, street smarts and a hood-like personality on the ABC pilot *Howie and Rose*. Mark Foster (Christopher Castile) and Brendon Lambert (Josh Byrne) are the youngest members of the recently blended Foster and Lambert families on ABC's *Step by Step*. Ruth Ann (Anna Slotky), Mary Sue (Rachel Duncan), Steven Floyd (Aaron Michael Metchik) and Chuckie Lee (Lee Norris) are the pre-teen children of Millicent Torkelson, a divorcee who is devoted to raising her children on *The Torkelsons* (NBC). A cast of children headed by Heather Gottlieb, Lisa Gay Hamilton and Spencer Barrows perform skits relating aspects of the world to kids on the syndicated *Way Cool*. Two fun-loving brothers, Larry and Ozzie (Mark Simmin, Billy Sullivan) try to outsmart their parents on the ABC pilot *What's Going on Down There?*

1992. Tina Majorino plays Sophie, the daughter of ER nurse Ricky Wilder on ABC's *Camp Wilder*. Elementary school students Tina Nuen (Tram-Ahn Tran) and Gaby Fernandez (Mayteana Morales) help their older friends solve crimes on *Ghostwriter* (PBS). The antics of nine-year-old "demon child" Mercy (Ashley Johnson) became the basis for the CBS pilot *Have Mercy*. Zachary and Matthew (Adam Wylie, Justin Shenkarow) are the youngest children of Rome, Wisconsin, sheriff Jimmy Brock and his wife Jill on *Picket Fences* (CBS). Noley Thornton plays Teresa, the young daughter of police officer Angela Garcia on *Tequila and Bonetti* (CBS). Talented six-year-old Violet Fields (Raven Symone) attempts to break into show business on the NBC pilot *Violet*.

1993. Frontier doctor Michaela Quinn becomes the guardian of Colleen (Erika Flores, Jessica Bowman), Matthew (Chad Allen) and Brian Cooper (Shawn Toovey) after the death of their mother on *Dr. Quinn, Medicine Woman* (CBS). Julie and Nicki (Ashley Sterling, Nicki Vannice) are the children of Cathy Hale, a single mother who works for the Chicago Welfare Office on *Getting By* (NBC). Raven Symone plays Nicole, the adorable daughter of single mother Geneva Lee, a music teacher at Oakridge College on *Hanging with Mr. Cooper* (ABC). Kaitlin Cullum plays Libby Kelly, the pre-teen daughter of single mother Grace Kelly on ABC's *Grace Under Fire*. NBC's *The Mommies* presents the children of Caryl Kellogg and her husband Paul: Blake and Danny (Sam Gifaldi, Ryan Merriman) and Caryl's best friend Marilyn and her husband Jack: Casey (Ashley Peldon) and teenager Adam (Shiloh Strong). Gracie Sheffield (Madeline Zima) is the adorable six-year-old daughter of Maxwell Sheffield, a Broadway show producer, on *The Nanny* (CBS).

1994. A cartoon character named McGhee comes to life in animated form to guide the life of 12-year-old Nicholas Martin (Joseph Dammann) on *McGhee and Me* (ABC pilot). Eleven-year-old Claudia Salinger (Lacey Chabert) finds becoming an adult difficult on Fox's *Party of Five*. Pretty, vibrant and fun-loving eleven-year-old Gaby Stepjack (Gaby Hoffman) finds misadventure on *Someone Like Me* (NBC). Also on the series, Reagan Kotz plays Gaby's friend, Jane Schmidt. Claudine (Kelly Vint), Jenny (Lindsay Felton) and Harry (Haley Joel Osment) are the children of Bobbi Turner, a divorcee who works as the bookkeeper for her father, the owner of a garage on *Thunder Alley* (ABC). Ashley Gorrell plays Jessica, the nine-year-old daughter of Megan Whitaker, the owner of the Paradise Beach Hotel in Florida on *Thunder in Paradise* (Syn.).

1995. Sweet and adorable eight-year-old twins Mary Kate and Ashley Olsen (themselves) attempt to solve crimes on the ABC pilot *The Adventures* *of Mary Kate and Ashley.* Reagan Kotz plays Danielle Clayton, the very independent 12-year-old daughter of postal worker Burt Clayton and his wife Alice on *Bless This House* (CBS). "The scariest little brother you can have — Farley Drexel Hatcher," better known as Fudge (Luke Tarsitano), is the premise of ABC's *Fudge.* Tiffany and Austin (Maia Campbell, Jeffrey Wood) are the children of Jackie Warren, a divorcee who works as a lawyer at the firm of Comstock, Nathan and Smythe on *In the House* (NBC). Matt and Justin (Haley Joel Osment, Jonathan Lipnick) are the children of Jeff Foxworthy and his wife Karen on *The Jeff Foxworthy Show* (ABC/NBC). Phoebe (Taylor Frye), Corey (Will Estes) and Russell (Courtland Mead) are the siblings of (and now his responsibility after their parents death in a car accident) Kirk Hartman, a graphic artist, on *Kirk* (WB). Ashley Johnson plays Gracie, the 11-year-old daughter of single mom Julia Wallace (divorced) on *Maybe This Time* (ABC).

1996. Madlyn Sweeten plays Ally, the sweet and obedient daughter of newspaper columnist Raymond Barone and his wife Debra on *Everybody Loves Raymond* (CBS). Her twin brothers, Jeffrey and Michael are played by Sawyer and Sullivan Sweeten. Alexandra Purvis plays Katherine, the 10-year-old daughter of psychologist Rachel Corrigan, who shows potential of extraordinary psychic abilities on *Poltergeist: The Legacy* (Showtime/Sci Fi). Chloe (Caitlin Wachs, Evan Rachel Wood) is the daughter of Samantha Waters, a widowed FBI profiler for the V.C.T.F. (Violent Crimes Task Force) on *Profiler* (NBC). Five-year-old Ruthie Camden (Mackenzie Rosman), the daughter of a minister and his wife, finds growing up in the shadow of four older siblings a bit challenging on the WB's *7th Heaven* (over the course of the series run Ruthie grew into a beautiful teenage girl). Lorenzo and Nicholas Brino play Sam and David, Ruthie's younger twin brothers in later episodes.

1997. Amanda Bynes hosts *The Amanda Show*, a series of skits involving children on Nickelodeon. Ted Hiller and Ned Diller are TV writers on ABC's *Hiller and Diller.* Ted is married to Jeannie and the father of Lizzie and Josh (Faryn Einhorn, Johnathan Osser). Ned is single (his wife left him) and the father of Zane (Kyle Sabihy) and Brooke (Allison Mack). Nicholas and Ce Ce (Curtis Williams, Ashli Amari Adams) are the youngest children of New York University professor Robert Townsend and his wife Geri on *The Parent'Hood* (WB).

1998. Sydney and Michael Hughley (Ashley Monique Clark, Dee Jay Daniels) are the children of Darryl and Yvonne Hughley, a suburban California couple on *The Hughleys* (ABC/UPN). Nicole Fugere plays 11-year-old Wednesday Addams and Brody Smith is her eight-year-old brother, Pugsley, the somber children of the eccentric Gomez Addams and his wife Morticia on *The New Addams Family* (Fox Family). Tahj Mowry plays T.J. Henderson, a 12-year-old genius who is attempting to cope with life, especially high school, on *Smart Guy* (WB). Identical 12-year-old twins Mary Kate and Ashley Olsen star as the tomboyish Mary Kate Burton and her studious sister Ashley on ABC's *Two of a Kind.*

1999. Angela Anaconda (voice of Susan Rose) is a young girl who finds misadventure in everything she does on the animated *Angela Anaconda* (ABC Family). Bess (Rachel Skarsten), Nan (Brittney Irvin) and Dan (Cory Sevier) are among the students who attend the Plumfield School (run by Jo Bhaer) in 1860s Massachusetts on *Little Men* (PAX). Apache and Moonglow (Zack Hopkins, Rachel David) are the children of action film star Reese Harden and his wife Jacey Wyatt, "a chick who makes classy flicks" on the WB's *Movie Stars.* A mischievous pre-teen witch named Amanda (Emily Hart) causes problems for all concerned when she uses her magical powers on *Sabrina, the Teenage Witch* (ABC/WB).

2000. Erik Per Sullivan plays Dewey, the youngest, seemingly less troublesome son of Hal and Lois on Fox's *Malcolm in the Middle.* Dominic and Logan (Joel Homan, Christopher Berry) are the children of Jimmy and Christine Hughes. Sam and Emily (Anthony LaMar, Marissa Poer) are the offspring of Greg and Kim Warner. They are friends who live together to save on expenses on *Yes, Dear* (CBS).

2001. Gracie, Ruby and Kyle (Billie Bruno, Taylor Atelian, Conner Rayburn) are the children of building contractor Jim and his wife Cheryl on *According to Jim* (ABC). Twins Mary Kate and Ashley Olsen play Special Agents Misty and Amber on *Mary Kate and Ashley in Action,* an ABC animated series in which the girls fight evil to save the world. Parker McKenna plays Cady Kyle, the youngest and most obedient child of Michael and Jay Kyle on *My Wife and Kids* (ABC). Eleven-year-old Emily Stewart (Brie Larson) takes on the responsibility of helping to care for the house and "raise" her widowed father, Matt, on the WB's *Raising Dad*. Mitch Holleman plays Jake, the youngest child of Reba Hart and her ex-husband Brock on *Reba* (WB).

2002. Debi Derryberry provides the voice of James Isaac "Jimmy" Neutron, a not-so-typical kid who invents gadgets that seldom work on the computer animated series *The Adventures of Jimmy Neutron: Boy Genius* (NIK). His robotic dog Goddard (Frank Welker) assists him.

2003. Tuga (Damani Roberts) is the young son of Anthony Anderson, a divorced, hopeful actor who has fallen on hard times and has moved back with his parents, Joe and Flo, on *All About the Andersons* (WB). Khamani Griffin plays Bobby, the young son of Robert and Neesee, divorced parents who share custody of him on *All of Us* (UPN). Eleven-year-old Oliver Beene (Grant Rosenmeyer) is the son of dentist Jerry Beene and his wife Charlotte on *Oliver Beene* (Fox). Bernie Mac and his wife Wanda are the guardians of Vanessa, Jordan and Bryann Tompkins (Camille Winbush, Jeremy Suarez, Dee Dee Davis), Bernie's sister's children on *The Bernie Mac Show* (Fox). Soleil Borda plays Tina, the adorable younger child of bathroom fixtures salesman Bill Miller and his wife Judy on *Still Standing* (CBS). Jake Harper (Angus T. Jones) lives with his divorced father, Alan, at the home of his womanizing uncle Charlie Harper on *Two and a Half Men* (CBS).

2004. Julianna Rose Mauriello plays Stephanie, a very pretty pink-haired girl who lives in Lazy Town, "the laziest town you'll ever visit," on *Lazy Town* (NIK). Stories revolve around Stephanie's efforts to foil the foul deeds of Robbie Rotten (Stefan Karl Steffansson), the town grump. Malcolm David Kelley is Walt, the son of a divorced father (Michael) and the only child survivor of a plane crash, who is now marooned on a mysterious island with 47 others on *Lost* (ABC). Jack and Bo (Oliver Davis, Matthew Josten) are the children of Rodney and Trina Carrington, a couple struggling to make ends meet on *Rodney* (ABC).

2005. Regina King provides the voices for Huey and Riley Freeman, youngsters who move from the congestion of Chicago to its suburbs to live with their grandfather (Robert) on *The Boondocks* (Cartoon Network). ABC's *Little House on the Prairie* updates the 1974 series with a harsher

look at frontier life as seen through the eyes of young Laura Ingalls (Kyle Chavarria) and her older sister Mary (Danielle Chuchran). Sofia Vassillieva and Maria Lark play Ariel and Bridget, the children of Allison DuBois, a medium who helps the police solve crimes on NBC's *Medium*. Carole, Lisa and Stevie (Keenan MacWilliam, Sophie Bennett, Lara Jean Marshall) are friends who also share a love of horses on *The Saddle Club* (Discovery Kids).

2006. Miley Cyrus plays Miley Stewart, a 'tween who is secretly Hannah Montana, a superstar pop singer on *Hannah Montana* (Disney).

"Adult Film" Actresses

Actresses who star in Triple X adult films but who have also appeared on television are profiled here. Also chronicled are movie and television actresses who, by accident or on purpose, have made an X-rated film. See also *Nudity and Sexuality*.

1948: Marilyn Monroe. *Gentlemen Prefer Blondes*, *The River of No Return* and *Bus Stop* are a few of the films that starred the ultimate sex symbol, Marilyn Monroe. She made her TV debut on *Yer Ole Buddy*, a local Los Angeles series in 1948 (for which she was paid $10). She next appeared on *The Jack Benny Program* in 1953 and created a sensation in 1962 when she sang a sultry version of "Happy Birthday" in a sexy gown on the TV special *President Kennedy's Birthday Salute*.

In 1948 the struggling starlet was said to have made several "nudie films," the most famous of which is *The Girl, the Coke Bottle and the Apple*. It has been rumored that the girl in the film is not Marilyn, but possibly then famous stripper/stag film star Juanita Slusher (better known as Candy Barr). Although existing prints are scratchy and a bit blurred, the girl in the film has the high eyebrows of Candy, not the lower set ones of Marilyn. Marilyn did appear nude, however: for the famous 1949 "Golden Dreams" calendar and as Miss December, the very first *Playboy* Playmate in 1953.

1954: Jayne Mansfield. Like Marilyn, Jayne Mansfield struggled to achieve her sex symbol status of the 1950s and 60s. Before she made a name for herself in such films as *Will Success Spoil Rock Hunter* and *The Girl Can't Help It*, Jayne appeared totally nude in an 16mm soft-core film wherein she bathes and prepares for bed. She was next a 1955 *Playboy* Playmate. Jayne lit up TV screens in 1956 when she starred in the musical special, *The Bachelor*. Her only attempt at a TV series was an unaired 1961 NBC pilot called *Monte Carlo*.

1967: Candy Samples. The voluptuous Candy Samples (48DD-27–38) is perhaps best known for her series of "Big Bust" films as well as a string of hard-core shorts. Candy acted on TV's *Peyton Place* in 1968 but returned to adult films shortly after.

1969: Linda Lovelace. Linda, the most famous porn star of all time, is best known for her role as Nurse Lovelace in the 1971 film *Deep Throat* (the film that took porn out of the sleazy theater and put it into the mainstream). Linda began her career in 1969 and appeared on a number of TV shows: *The 1974 Academy Awards*, talk shows (explaining how she was forced to star in adult films) and on the E! Channel special, *Linda Lovelace: The E! Hollywood Story* in 2000.

1971: Marilyn Chambers. Marilyn is perhaps most famous as the cover girl on Ivory Soap boxes (where she posed holding a baby). Before appearing in adult films (her first was *Behind the Green Door* in 1971) Marilyn played the role of Evelyn Lang in *The Owl and the Pussycat* in 1970. Her TV roles include the CBS series *Women of the House* (1995), *Blood Brothers—Jim and Artie Mitchell: The E! True Hollywood Story* (2003), the documentary *Thinking XXX*, and on various pay cable services where edited versions of her films can be seen.

1974: Vanessa Del Rio. The seductive Vanessa Del Rio is of Cuban and Puerto Rican descent and measures 42DD-26–30. She made her first film, *China Doll,* in 1974 and her last one, *Dr. Lust,* in 1987. She appeared on TV's *N.Y.P.D. Blue* in the episode of February 27, 1996 ("Head Case").

1977: Kay Parker. English-born adult actress Kay Parker made three now classic films in her first year: *The Erotic Adventures of Casanova, Seven Into Snowy* and *Sex World*. However, she is best known for her role as Barbara Scott in the 1980 film *Taboo*. Edited versions of Kay's early films can be seen on cable (the latter ones are too explicit) and she appeared on TV in 1984 on the series *Midnight Blue*.

1978: Joan Collins. Before achieving fame as Alexis Carrington on ABC's *Dynasty*, English-born actress Joan Collins appeared in two steamy, soft-core films, *The Bitch* and *The Stud* (Joan is to-

tally nude and in some provocative sexual situations). She also paraded around in her bra and panties in *The Terror from Under the House* and lost her life to a lovesick tree in *Tales That Witness Madness*.

1982: Angelique Pettyjohn. Angelique is perhaps best known for her role as Shahna, the sexy alien on "The Gamesters of Triskellion" episode of *Star Trek* in 1968. She also appeared on *Love, American Style, The Felony Squad, Batman, Mr. Terrific* and *Get Smart*. However, when she was unable to succeed on TV or in motion pictures, Angelique turned to X-rated films, where she made *Body Heat* (with Kay Parker) and *Titillation*.

1982: Ginger Lynn Allen. *N.Y.P.D. Blue, Sunset Beat, Silk Stalkings* and *Super Force* are some of the TV series on which adult film actress Ginger Lynn Allen has appeared. Ginger was born in 1962 and has appeared in such X-rated films as *I Dream of Ginger, Those Young Girls, The Pink Lagoon* and *The Ginger Effect*. She made her last adult film in 2002 (*Sunset Strippers*) and also appeared as herself on E! *True Hollywood Story* and in seven episodes of the E! Channel's *101 Biggest Celebrity Oops!*

1984: Nina Hartley. Blonde, blue-eyed Nina Hartley measures 35-24-35 and is considered one of the most beautiful and seductive of the adult film actresses. She was born Marie Louise Hartman and has a bachelor's degree in nursing. She made her film debut in *Educating Nina* and her last eight films in 2004 (including *Head Nurse, Baby Doll Lesbian Orgies* and *Nina Hartley's Guide to Sensual Submission*). Nina has talked about her life in adult films on *Oprah* and *Phil Donahue* (defending the X-rated film industry) and appeared on an MTV documentary on the adult film industry as well as on *Traci Lords: The E! True Hollywood Story* in 1998.

1984: Traci Lords. Fifteen-and-a-half-year old Traci Lords (born on May 7, 1968) made her first adult film (*What Gets Me Hot*) in early 1984. In total she made 100 Triple X films, 99 of which are illegal (she was under the age of 18); her only legal film is 1987's *Traci, I Love You* (Traci lied about her age, saying she was born on November 17, 1962). On July 11, 1986 the TV newsmagazine *A Current Affair* broke the story of a minor appearing in adult films and Traci's movies were pulled from distribution (Traci claims she made the films to support her then cocaine habit). Traci managed to bounce back. She made legit feature films (such as *Not of This Earth, Intent to Kill* and *Epicenter*) and has also made her mark on television. She played Sharon Lasher on *The Profiler* in 1996 and Jordan Radcliff on *The First Wave* in 2000. Traci has also guest starred on numerous TV shows, including *The Dream Team, Super Force, Wiseguy, Gilmore Girls, Married ... With Children* and *Roseanne.*

1987: Dana Plato. Sweet and adorable Dana Plato (Kimberly Drummond on *Diff'rent Strokes*) grew up all too fast when she played a lesbian in the racy film *Different Strokes* (no apostrophe between the *f* and *r*). Dana appears nude and her love scene is quite explicit.

1999: Tonya Harding. Figure skating champion Tonya Harding became an unwitting adult star when a video of her wedding night was sold to a magazine and released on home video as *Tonya and Jeff's Wedding Night.* The rather short (25 minutes) badly photographed (from a distance) video was a best seller. The 1994 champion appeared on a number of TV shows, including *Arliss, Celebrity Boxing, The Weakest Link* and *The 100 Most Shocking Moments in Entertainment.*

2000: Pamela Anderson. The ultra sexy *Baywatch* star found herself in the adult section of video stores when a home movie of her and hubby Tommy Lee was apparently stolen and released on tape. While hyped for more than it actually showed, it was a best seller and a top rental. A second such tape was later released. A third tape with Pamela and singer Bret Michaels was seen on the Internet.

2003: Jaimee Foxworth. At the age of five Jaimee Foxworth was starring in McDonald's commercials; at the age of nine she landed the role of Judy Winslow on *Family Matters.* At 12 she was written out and she and her family fell on hard times. Jaimee became depressed and eventually turned to alcohol. She posed nude for a photographer and appeared in three XXX-rated films (after which she quit, reunited with her family and got her life back together again).

2003: Paris Hilton. The Hilton Hotel heiress and the star of *The Simple Life* TV series made two X-rated home movies that found their way to the market place: *The Paris Hilton Home XXX Video* and *One Night in Paris.*

2004: Jenna Lewis. Jenna Lewis, one of the contestants on CBS's *Survivor*, became an Internet porn star when a sexually explicit home video played on the Internet.

2005: Gena Lee Nolin. The sexy star of *Baywatch* and *Sheena* performed explicit sex acts in a late 1990s tape she made with her now ex husband called *The Gena Lee Nolin Home Video Sex Tape* that appeared on the Internet in 2005.

Note: Beginning in the early 1960s, a young Barbra Streisand was rumored to have made a hard core 16mm loop. This has since been disproved. In 1977, a Farrah Fawcett look-alike was promoted in the film *Little Orphan Dusty.* Two years later, the film *Taxi Girls* boasted a Cheryl Ladd look-alike. As home videos became more and more popular, actresses resembling Brooke Shields, Nikki Cox and even super model Tyra Banks have appeared on the scene.

Adventurers

Restless individuals seeking to satisfy some uncontrollable urge could describe an adventurer. On television adventurers could also be described as people who pursue that dream — but also become heroes as they help people in distress they meet along the way.

1952. Three syndicated series air: *The Adventures of Captain Hartz* with Philip Lord as jungle explorer Captain Hartz (sponsored by Hartz Mountain pet food), *The Affairs of China Smith* wherein American soldier of fortune China Smith (Dan Duryea) finds intrigue in Singapore; and *Ramar of the Jungle* wherein the mysteries of Africa become a challenge for research scientist Dr. Thomas Reynolds (Jon Hall).

1953. Robert Newton plays Colin Glencannon, the skipper of a freighter called *Inchcliff Castle* on the ABC pilot *Mr. Glencannon Takes All.*

1954. Three additional syndicated series air. *The Adventures of Noah Beery, Jr.* features the film actor's various adventures; *I Search for Adventure* has Jack Douglas narrating films depicting man's quest for adventure; and *Passport to Danger*, where U.S. diplomatic courier Steve McQuinn (Cesar Romero) becomes the unwitting decoy of the Hungarian Secret Police.

1955. CBS airs *Captain Safari of the Jungle Patrol* with Randy Knight in the title role. Forrest Tucker plays Crunch Adams and Sandy Kenyon is his partner, Des Smith, the owners of the *Poseidon*, a charter boat for hire on the syndicated *Crunch and Des.* Free-lance magazine reporter Matt Anders (Brian Keith) finds intrigue on CBS's

The Crusader. Syndication again rules with Charles McGraw as *The Falcon*, a troubleshooter for the U.S. Army. Alex Raymond's comic strip character, *Jungle Jim* comes to life with Johnny Weissmueller as the intrepid jungle guide. Tim Kelly (John Russell) and Toubo Smith (Chick Chandler) become *Soldiers of Fortune* as they battle injustice throughout the world.

1956. Mild mannered proofreader Hiram Holliday (Wally Cox) travels around the world helping people in trouble on NBC's *The Adventures of Hiram Holiday*. Bowie knife inventor Jim Bowie (Scott Forbes) was "a fighter, a fearless, a mighty adventurin' man" on ABC's *The Adventures of Jim Bowie*. CBS invited us to go "a roamin' across the seas" with Dan Tempest (Robert Shaw) on *The Buccaneers*.

1957. Syndication gave us David Grief (Maxwell Reed), the skipper of a sloop in the West Indies on *Captain David Grief*. American motor freighter captain Grant Mitchell (Lorne Greene) found danger in the Mediterranean on *Sailor of Fortune*. Ex-navy frogman turned underwater troubleshooter Mike Nelson (Lloyd Bridges) found danger beneath the surface on *Sea Hunt*.

1958. A series based on the 1953 pilot, *Mr. Glencannon Takes All*, sails into view with Thomas Mitchell as Colin Glencannon on the syndicated *Glencannon*.

1959. The schooner *Tiki*, captained by Adam Troy (Gardner McKay), was our ticket to tour the South Pacific on ABC's *Adventures in Paradise*. In syndication John Hawk (John Howard) captained the *Sea Hawk*, a floating electronics lab, on *The Adventures of the Sea Hawk*. Rocky Shaw, Silky Harris and Reno McKee (Dorothy Provine, Roger Moore, Jeff York) were ABC's *The Alaskans*, adventurers searching for gold during the 1890s.

1960. Ex-marine turned charter boat captain Bill Greer (Bill Williams) and his young daughter Patty (Diane Mountford) take on assignments as owners of *The Lively Lady* on the syndicated *Assignment: Underwater*. Alaska of the 1890s again becomes the backdrop as Kathy O'Hara (Marie Blanchard) struggles to operate a hotel on NBC's *Klondike*. The NBC pilot *Renegade* charts the escapades of Rory O'Neill (Steve Cochran) and Burton Smythe (Richard Ney) as they help people in trouble. A 1960 Chevrolet becomes the co-star as Tod Stiles (Martin Milner) and Buzz Murdock (George Maharis) wander along the highway of CBS's *Route 66*.

1961. Do-gooders Gregg Miles (James Coburn) and Patrick Malone (Ralph Taeger) help distressed people in Mexico on NBC's *Acapulco*. Salvage divers Drake Andrews (Keith Larsen) and Larry Lahr (Jeremy Slate) encounter underwater dangers on CBS's *The Aquanauts* (the series was revised as *Malibu Run* when Larry Lahr and his new partner, Mike Madison [Ron Ely] become diving instructors in Malibu Beach, California). Hawaiian-based magazine writers Ben Gregory and Paul Templin (Barry Coe, Brett Halsey) find adventure and intrigue on ABC's *Follow the Sun*. In syndication John King (Broderick Crawford) battles the unscrupulous as an investigator for the diamond industry on *King of Diamonds*.

1962. Troubleshooter Carlos Borella (Carlos Thompson) finds intrigue as an investigator for an import-export company on *The Sentimental Agent* (Syn.).

1963. For reasons that are known only to him, the suave and sophisticated Simon Templar (Roger Moore), alias the Saint, sets out to right the world's wrongs on *The Saint* (Syn/NBC).

1965. Moss Andrews (Ty Hardin) finds dangerous assignments as the captain of the charter boat *Riptide, Inc.* on the syndicated series *Riptide*.

1967. A bumbling plantation owner (Wally Cox) fights injustice in his spare time on the CBS pilot *Alfred of the Amazon*. Another CBS pilot, *Sinbad*, finds the Ulysses of Persia (Michael Stefan) sailing the Arabian Seas in search of adventure. Chris, Alan and Simon (Larry Pennell, Alejandro Rey, Charles Carlson) are soldiers of fortune on the ABC pilot *Three for Danger*.

1968. Australian writer John Wells (Walter Brown) captained the schooner *Seaspray* while roaming the South Pacific seeking story material on the syndicated *The Adventures of the Seaspray*.

1971. Troubleshooters Hank Brackett and Johnny Reach (Rod Taylor, Dennis Cole) roam America's Southwest in a 1914 Stutz Bearcat on CBS's *Bearcats!* Sam Elliott portrays dare devil Evel Knievel on the CBS pilot *Evel Knievel*. The thought of finding long-lost treasures motivates Andrew Bass, Arleigh Marley and Milovan Drumm (James Stacy, Ben Cooper, Bo Svenson) to become treasure hunters on the CBS pilot *Lost Treasure*. Quarrelsome playboys Brett Sinclair (Roger Moore) and Danny Wilde (Tony Curtis) help a retired judge bring criminals to justice on ABC's *The Persuaders!* Nassau becomes the backdrop for Carter Primus (Robert Brown), a global underwater troubleshooter on the syndicated *Primus*.

1975. NBC's pilot, *The Log of the Black Pearl*, charts the adventures of Chris Sand (Keil Martin) as he captains a three-mast sailing ship. Steve Andrews (Van Williams) his wife Kate (Niki Dantine) and their children Robin and Tom (Kimberly Beck, Steve Burns) explore the various Hawaiian Islands on their yacht *The Westwind* (NBC).

1979. CBS casts Ian Ogilvy as Simon Templar in *Return of the Saint*, an update of the 1963 series *The Saint*.

1981. Vagabond cowboys J.D. Reed and Will Ewbanks (Jerry Reed, Geoffrey Scott) explore America on CBS's *Concrete Cowboys*. Key Tortuga, Florida, is the setting as John Tyree (Scott Thomas), captain of the charter boat *Hemingston*, hires out his services on the CBS pilot *Key Tortuga*.

1984. Felicity Ryan (Kelbe Nugent), Andy Coles (Woody Brown) and Bo Wallace (Jerry Dinome) roam the South Pacific on their boat *Paradise* on the CBS pilot *Welcome to Paradise*.

1985. True wild life stories based on the experiences of explorer Stan Brock (himself) becomes the basis for the syndicated *Expedition: Danger*.

1987. Ron Ely becomes the new Mike Nelson, underwater troubleshooter, on the syndicated *Sea Hunt* with Kimber Sissons as his daughter Jennifer Nelson. When he feels there is no sense or reward as a trauma surgeon, John Dockery (James Naughton) quits and hits the road seeking adventure on the CBS pilot *Traveling Man*.

1993. A red and white 1961 Corvette becomes the co-star as Nick Lewis and Andrew Clark (James Wilder, Dan Cortese) travel along the highway on NBC's *Route 66*.

1998. The era of ancient myths and legends is the setting for the syndicated *Adventures of Sinbad* wherein Sinbad (Zen Gesner), captain of the *Nomad*, sails the Seven Seas battling evil. The beautiful Sydney Fox (Tia Carrere) risks her life to battle thieves who prey on ancient artifacts on the syndicated *Relic Hunter*.

2002. Judson Cross (Michael Biehn) and Mackenzie Previn (Karen Cliche) are treasure hunters and underwater explorers who battle evil on the syndicated *Adventure, Inc.*

Africa

A listing of series set in and around Africa.
1952. *Ramar of the Jungle* (Syn.).

1955. *Jungle Jim* (Syn.).
1956. *Sheena, Queen of the Jungle* (Syn.).
1957. *The Adventures of a Jungle Boy* (Syn.); *The African Patrol* (Syn.); *White Hunter* (Syn.).
1966. *Daktari* (CBS); *Tarzan* (NBC).
1967. *Cowboy in Africa* (ABC).
1974. *Born Free* (NBC).
2000. *Sheena* (Syn.).

African American Performers and Characters

Before the advent of the UPN network, which devotes a generous portion of its schedule to programs starring African Americans, black shows, as they were also called, were present but not abundant, especially during the 1940s and 50s. This listing comprises programs that starred and featured African Americans during their pioneering years, 1939 to 1977 (when *Roots* aired and placed black shows on the same level as other ethnic groups).

1939. NBC airs *Variety Over the Air* on June 14th. The program, a potpourri of variety acts, features Ethel Waters performing a dramatic scene from the Broadway play *Mamba's Daughters*. The program is also known as *The Ethel Waters Show*. On September 6th NBC airs *Total Eclipse* with Howard Reed, a singer who provided his own ukulele accompaniment.

1946. Talley Beatty plays "the colored slave" Joe (and sings "Ol' Man River") on a mini adaptation of the Broadway show *Showboat* on the CBS experimental program *Choreotones* (February 22nd). On June 2nd CBS airs *Legend* with Pearl Primus and her troupe of singers and dancers performing the tale of an African witch doctor's triumph over an evil sorceress.

1949. Singer-pianist Bob Howard becomes the star of his own show, *Sing It Again* on CBS. Black performers are spotlighted on CBS's *Sugar Hill Times* (also known as *Uptown Jubilee*) and NBC begins airing *The Three Flames Show* starring Tiger Haynes, Roy Testamark and Bill Pollard as the popular black trio.

1950. Ethel Waters, Hattie McDaniel and Louise Beavers each play the role of Beulah, the wise, understanding maid to attorney Harry Henderson and his family on CBS's *Beulah*. *The Jack Benny Program* moves from radio to CBS TV with Eddie Anderson continuing his role as Rochester,

Jack's faithful, wisecracking valet. Willie Best takes on the role of Willie, the janitor at Hamilton High School on ABC's *Trouble with Father* (also known as *The Stu Erwin Show*).

1951. "Radio's all time favorites, Amos and Andy" come to television on CBS's *The Amos 'n' Andy Show*. Andrew H. Brown (Spencer Williams, Jr.) and Amos Jones (Alvin Childress) struggle to run a cab company under the watchful eye of George "Kingfish" Stevens (Tim Moore), an inept con artist who sees Andy as his meal ticket.

1952. Willie Best takes time off from *Trouble with Father* to moonlight as Charlie, the elevator operator at the Carlton Arms Hotel, the home of CBS's *My Little Margie*.

1953. Louise Beavers begins the role and Amanda Randolph takes over as Louise, the sassy maid to nightclub comedian Danny Williams and his family on ABC's *Make Room for Daddy*.

1954. Black entertainers perform from the historic Apollo Theater in Harlem on the syndicated *Showtime at the Apollo*. Willie Bryant hosts.

1956. Singer Nat King Cole and NBC team up to present a weekly half-hour of songs on *The Nat King Cole Show*.

1960. Harry Belafonte hosts *Belafonte, New York*, an hour of folk songs, on CBS. Singer Barbara McNair hosts and performs on the syndicated *Circle*

1961. Singer Leslie Uggams becomes a regular on NBC's popular *Sing Along with Mitch*.

1965. Kenneth Washington and Ivan Dixon are Richard Baker and James Kinchloe, American POW's on *Hogan's Heroes* (CBS). Bill Cosby becomes Alexander Scott, a U.S. undercover agent who poses as a trainer to fellow spy, tennis pro Kelly Robinson (Robert Culp) on NBC's *I Spy*. Sammy Davis, Jr. stars in two variety specials: *Sammy and His Friends* on ABC (November 25th; with Count Basie, Frank Sinatra and Joey Heatherton) and *The Sammy Davis, Jr. Special* on NBC (February 18th; with Billy Daniels and Lola Falana).

1966. Wayne Grice is Detective Dan Carter, the partner of police detective John Hawk on *Hawk* (ABC). Electronics expert Barney Collier (Greg Morris) is a member of the Impossible Missions Force on *Mission: Impossible* (CBS). The variety series, *The Sammy Davis, Jr. Show*, airs on NBC. Nichelle Nichols becomes a role model for black girls as Lieutenant Uhura on *Star Trek* (NBC).

1967. Don Mitchell is Mark Sanger, aide to crippled police chief Robert Ironside on *Ironside*.

1968. Bill Cosby becomes the host of six variety specials: *The Bill Cosby Special* (March 20, 1968; NBC), *Bill Cosby Does His Own Thing* (a.k.a *The First Bill Cosby Special*, February 9, 1969; NBC), *The Second Bill Cosby Special* (March 11, 1969; NBC), *The Third Bill Cosby Special* (April 1, 1970; NBC), *The Bill Cosby Special Or?* (March 2, 1971; NBC), and *Cos: The Bill Cosby Special* (November 10, 1975; CBS). Nurse Julia Baker (Diahann Carroll) struggles to raise her young son Corey (Marc Copage) after the death of her husband on NBC's *Julia*. Don Marshall is Dan Erickson, one of humans marooned in a world of giants on ABC's *Land of the Giants*. Gail Fisher is Peggy Fair, secretary to Joe Mannix on *Mannix* (CBS). Clarence Williams III is Linc Hayes, a member of ABC's police unit *The Mod Squad*. Earl Corey (Don Murray), an uprooted Virginian aristocrat, and Jemal David (Otis Young), an ex-slave freed by the Proclamation, form an alliance of survival as bounty hunters on ABC's *The Outcasts*.

1969. Della Reese hosts ... *And Beautiful*, a syndicated variety program that features Redd Foxx and Wilson Pickett. Singer Barbara McNair hosts *The Barbara McNair Show*, an entertaining, syndicated variety series. Bill Cosby returns to TV as Chet Kincaid, athletic coach at Richard Allen Holmes High School on NBC's *The Bill Cosby Show*. Diana Ross stars on the NBC special *Diana Ross and the Supremes and the Temptations on Broadway*. Dionne Warwick hosts an hour of music and song on her CBS special *The Dionne Warwick Show*. Singer Eartha Kitt performs a solo concert on *The Eartha Kitt Special*, a syndicated special. The relationship between black D.A. William Washburn (Hari Rhodes) and white police chief Sam Danforth (Leslie Nielsen) forms the basis for NBC's *The Law Enforcers*. Leslie Uggams heads her own CBS variety series, *The Leslie Uggams Show*. *The Pigeon*, an ABC pilot features Sammy Davis, Jr. as Larry Miller, an L.A. based private detective. Lloyd Haynes is teacher Pete Dixon and Denise Nicholas is the guidance counselor at Walt Whitman High School on *Room 222* (ABC). Former football star Rosey Grier becomes host of *The Rosey Grier Show*, a syndicated chat fest. *Sammy Davis, Jr. in Europe* is a syndicated variety outing that features highlights of Sammy's overseas concert tour.

1970. The special *... And Beautiful II* (see 1969) features performances by Louis Armstrong, Count Basie, Duke Ellington and Billie Holliday. Paul and Corey Bratter (Scoey Mitchlll, Tracy Reed) are struggling newlyweds on ABC's *Barefoot in the Park*. Singer Della Reese and comedian Flip Wilson host their own variety series — *The Della Reese Show* (Syn.) and *The Flip Wilson Show* (NBC). ABC teams Harry Belafonte and Lena Horne for the special *Harry and Lena*. Hal Frederick is Cal Barrin, an intern at New North Hospital in *The Interns* (CBS). Percy Rodrigues is Jason Hart, a government agent on *The Silent Force* (ABC). Louis Gossett is Isaac Poole, a man protecting the Colonies from the British in 1777 Pennsylvania on *The Young Rebels* (ABC).

1971. Mike Evans is Lionel Jefferson, Archie Bunker's neighbor on *All in the Family* (CBS). Isabel Sanford is his mother, Louise, and Mel Stewart his uncle, Henry. Sherman Hemsley is later Louise's husband, George. Diana Ross and Dihann Carroll host NBC specials: *Diana* and *The Diahann Carroll Show*. Michael, Randy, Jackie, Tito and Marlon Jackson appear in animated form on *The Jacksons* (ABC). *Our Street* is a PBS series about the Robinsons, a black family living on any street in any town searching for dignity and respect. Barbara Mealy and Gene Cole star as the parents, Mae and Bull, with Curt Stewart, Howard Rollins and Sandra Sharp as their children Jeff, Slick and Kathy. Singer Pearl Bailey brings her unique style to ABC on *The Pearl Bailey Show*. Black singers entertain on the syndicated (and still current in 2007) *Soul Train*. Don Cornelius hosts.

1972. Walt and Liz Jones (John Amos, Teresa Graves), a black couple living in a New York brownstone, become the focus of the NBC pilot *Keeping Up with the Joneses*. Louis Gossett plays Doug Newman, a defensive end for the Chicago Cherokees football team on the CBS pilot *The Living End*. A sassy maid named Florida Evans (Esther Rolle) cares for the Findlays on CBS's *Maude* before acquiring a husband, James (John Amos) and three children, J.J., Thelma and Michael (Jimmie Walker, BernNadette Stanis, Ralph Carter) and her own CBS series *Good Times* in 1974. A Manhattan brownstone becomes the setting for music and songs on CBS's *The Melba Moore-Clifton Davis Show*. Music, songs and comedy are also the fare for CBS's *The New Bill Cosby Show*. Georg Stanford Brown is rookie police officer Terry Webster on ABC's *The Rookies*. Junk dealers Fred and Lamont Sanford (Redd Foxx, Demond Wilson) begin their five-year run on NBC's *Sanford and Son* while on ABC Dr. Jerry Noland (Cleavon Little) creates havoc at Capitol General Hospital in Washington, D.C. on *Temperature's Rising*.

1973. Richard Roundtree becomes fireman Shelly Forsythe on the ABC pilot *Firehouse*. One time football hero Rosey Grier hosts a TV cooking show on the CBS pilot *Big Daddy*. Oscar Furst (Godfrey Cambridge) and his mother, Eloise (Theresa Merritt) are *The Furst Family of Washington*, the owners of Oscar's Barber Shop on this ABC pilot. L.A.P.D. detectives Francis Buchanan (Louis Gossett) and Luther Prince (Felton Perry) find mishaps as *The Fuzz Brothers*, an ABC pilot. North Robin Hood Road in San Fernando's Sherwood Forest Estates becomes home to Ferguson and Jackie Bruce (Harrison Page, Janet McLachlan), an efficiency expert and his wife on ABC's *Love Thy Neighbor*. The medical profession is spoofed via the antics of Dr. Jerry Noland (Cleavon Little) on ABC's *The New Temperature's Rising Show*. A bumbling, soft touch disciple from Hell named Sammy (Sammy Davis, Jr.) is given a chance to redeem himself by securing souls for Satan on the NBC pilot *Poor Devil*. Stu Gilliam and Hilly Hicks are Carter "Sweet" Williams and Jed Brooks, World War II soldiers with the 5050th Quartermaster Trucking Company on CBS's *Roll Out!* John Shaft, the hip black detective, comes to television in the guise of Richard Roundtree on *Shaft* (CBS). Los Angeles based detective Harry Tenafly (James McEachin) solves crimes for Hightower Investigations on NBC's *Tenafly*. A remake of the 1972 pilot *The Living End* called *Two's Company* appears on CBS with John Amos as Charlie Travis, a running back for the Chicago Cherokees football team. Diana Sands plays his wife, Diana.

1974. John Morse (Ron Glass), a black Harvard graduate, finds work in an all white banking firm on the CBS pilot *Change at 125th Street*. Della Reese is Della Rogers, garage owner Ed Brown's landlady, and Scatman Crothers is Louie, the garbage man, on NBC's *Chico and the Man*. A black range cook named Mr. Nightlinger (Moses Gunn) helps a widow run her ranch on ABC's *The Cowboys*." You're under arrest, Sugah!" becomes the catch phrase of Christie Love (Teresa Graves), a sexy detective with the L.A.P.D. on

ABC's *Get Christie Love*. Gladys Knight and her backup group, the Pips, perform on the NBC special *Gladys Knight an the Pips Midnight Train to Georgia. Good Times* becomes part of CBS's prime time schedule while basketball stars the Harlem Globetrotters host the Saturday morning kids show, *The Harlem Globetrotters Popcorn Machine*. William Atmore (as Dwayne) becomes one of the adopted children of different ethnic backgrounds on the ABC pilot *Kelly's Kids*. Oscar's Barber Shop in Washington, D.C., becomes the setting for ABC's *That's My Mama*, wherein Clifton Curtis (Clifton Davis) attempts to run his late father's business. Theresa Merritt plays his mother Eloise. Idealistic American teacher Paul Cameron (Hari Rhodes) finds life a challenge when he becomes a faculty member of a British high school on the CBS pilot *To Sir with Love*.

1975. Michael D. Roberts plays Rooster, Tony Baretta's snitch on ABC's *Baretta*. Ron Harris (Ron Glass) becomes an officer with the Manhattan 12th Precinct on ABC's *Barney Miller*. Louis Gossett plays Black Bart, an Old West black sheriff in the bigoted town of Paris, Arizona, on the CBS pilot *Black Bart*. Carl Franklin is Miami-based police agent Mark Walters on ABC's *Caribe*. Tierre Turner is Lucas Adams, an orphan who becomes the ward of a white police officer (Frank Murphy) on NBC's *The Cop and the Kid*. Ray Charles, Billy Daniels, Redd Foxx, Cleo Laine and Jimmie Walker are among the guests who recreate the comedy and music of the famed Cotton Club on the NBC special *Cotton Club '75*. Gladys Knight and her group the Pips host the CBS summer series *Gladys Knight and the Pips*. The *Sanford and Son* spinoff, *Grady* finds Fred's neighbor Grady Wilson (Whitman Mayo) leaving Los Angles to move in with his daughter Ellie (Carol Cole) and her husband, Hal (Joe Morton) in Santa Monica. The prospect of an interracial marriage is explored on the ABC pilot *Guess Who's Coming to Dinner?* when a white girl, Joanna Drayton (Leslie Charleston) marries a black man, John Prentiss (Bill Overton). *The Jeffersons* joins the CBS schedule (see 1971, *All in the Family*) and Adam Wade becomes the first black to host a game show, CBS's *Musical Chairs*. Mel Stewart is Mr. Gibson, a correctional officer, and Hal Williams is Lester DeMott, a prisoner at the Alamesa State Minimum Security Prison on ABC's *On the Rocks*. Black street hustler Curtis

Brown (Art Evans) struggles to care for his adopted son, Leonard Brown (Todd Bridges) on the ABC pilot *The Orphan and the Dude*. Can two retired senior citizens live together without killing each other? That was the plot of *Rosenthal and Jones*, a CBS pilot with George Kirby as Henry Jones and Ned Glass as his white roommate Nate Rosenthal. A prejudiced black widow (Mel Stewart) struggles to adjust to his daughter's (Dorothy Meyer) marriage to a Puerto Rican (Frank LaLoggia) on the NBC pilot *Salt and Pepe*. Sammy Davis, Jr., hosts the syndicated variety series *Sammy and Company*. Antonio Fargas is Huggy Bear, the enterprising snitch to *Starsky and Hutch* (ABC). Lawrence-Hilton Jacobs is Freddie Washington, one of ABC's Sweathogs on *Welcome Back, Kotter*.

1976. Two dim-witted private detectives are the subjects of the NBC pilot *Adventuring with the Chopper*. Harrison Page was Arnold "The Chopper" Jackson and Antonio Fargas his partner, Leonard Jones. Singer Diahann Carroll headlines her own CBS summer series, *The Diahann Carroll Show* while Della Reese attempts to run her own dockside hotel and restaurant on the NBC pilot *Flo's Place*. Bill Cosby hosts his own variety series, *Cos* on ABC. A ghost named Freeman (Stu Gilliam) attempts to live in a house with its white residents on the ABC pilot *Freeman*. The Jackson brothers (Michael, Marlon, Randy, Jackie and Tito) as well as their sisters (Maureen, LaToya and Janet) perform on *The Jacksons* (CBS). A rugged bounty hunter became the subject of *Salanthiel Harris*, a CBS pilot starring Rosey Grier. Ted Ross became lawyer Sawyer Dabney, the defense attorney, on NBC's *Sirota's Court*. Teenagers Roger Thomas (Ernest Thomas), Dwayne Clemens (Haywood Nelson) and Freddie Stubbs (Fred Berry) find life a challenge on *What's Happening!!* (ABC).

1977. Kene Curtis is Sgt. Curtis Baker, an urban black officer on *Carter Country* (ABC). Redd Foxx and Richard Pryor headline their own variety series — *The Redd Foxx Hour* on ABC; *The Richard Pryor Show* on NBC. Retired army man Phil Wheeler (Theodore Wilson) purchases the Sanford and Son junkyard and turns it into a rooming house on NBC's *Sanford Arms. Soap*, the ABC spoof of soap operas, finds Robert Guillaume as Benson DuBois, the butler to the wealthy Tate family (the character was spun off into his own show, *Benson*, in 1979). J.T. Cumbuka is Hawk, an ex-slave on *Young Dan'l Boone* (CBS). Walkin' Walter (Spo-De-Odee), a free-spirited ex-vaudeville songwriter, freeloads off his long lost brother's wife and two children on the ABC pilot *Walkin' Walter*. ABC's presentation of *Roots*, a dramatization of the Alex Haley novel that traces his family history from 18th century tribal Africa to their emancipation to the Post Civil War South, becomes a landmark TV event (acquiring the largest viewing audience ever to view a dramatic TV program). Many African American performers appeared but LeVar Burton as the slave Kunta Kinte is perhaps the best known. In 1979 ABC aired the sequel, *Roots: The Next Generations*, which picked up where the original miniseries left off.

After-School Hangouts see *Teen After-School Hangouts*

Aliens

A listing of series on which aliens — those from outer space — are the stars or regulars.

1949. *Captain Video and His Video Rangers* becomes the first series to feature aliens. The DuMont series, set in the 21st century, deals with the mysterious Captain Video (Richard Coogan, Al Hodge), the man known as "The Guardian of the Safety of the World." While there were no regular aliens, there was the evil Dr. Pauli who ruled from the manmade metallic planet of Dr. Pauli and sought to conquer the universe. The Video Ranger (Don Hastings) assisted the Captain.

1950. Tonga (Nina Bara), a beautiful reformed outer space thief, assists Buzz Corry (Ed Kemmer) as a member of ABC's 30th century *Space Patrol*. The CBS (then ABC, NBC, DuMont) series *Tom Corbett, Space Cadet* features Astro (Al Markim), the Venusian member of Space Academy, U.S.A.

1953. The lone survivor of the planet Krypton, Kal-El, grows up on Earth to become Clark Kent (George Reeves), the Man of Steel on the syndicated *Adventures of Superman*. The character would also appear on the 1961 pilot *The Adventures of Superboy* (John Rockwell as Clark Kent); 1988's syndicated *Superboy* (John Haymes Newton then Gerard Christopher as Clark Kent); ABC's 1993

Lois and Clark: The New Adventures of Superman (Dean Cain as Clark Kent); and finally in 2001 with Tom Welling as Clark Kent on the WB's *Smallville*. Aliens are seen but not regulars on the syndicated *Flash Gordon* with Steve Holland in the title role. Earthling Ernest P. Duckweather (Wright King) invents interplanetary television and is able to see and speak to the people (puppets) of Jupiter on the DuMont (then ABC) series *Johnny Jupiter*.

1954. Rocky Jones (Richard Crane) and his assistant Vena Ray (Sally Mansfield) battle aliens on the syndicated *Rocky Jones, Space Ranger*. Here, Dian Fauntelli played Yarra, ruler of the planet Medina; Walter Coy was Zorvac, King of the moon Fornax, and Patsy Iannone was Volaca, Zorvac's daughter.

1955. Commando Cody (Judd Holdren) battles the evil alien Retik (Gregory Gray) on NBC's *Commando Cody, Sky Marshal of the Universe*.

1963. Stranded Martian Exatitious 12 1/2 (Ray Walston) finds life on Earth a burden when he adopts the alias of Uncle Martin and moves in with newspaper reporter Tim O'Hara on CBS's *My Favorite Martian*.

1965. The Robinson family becomes *Lost in Space* on CBS as they set out on a mission to explore the planet Alpha Centauri. While encountering numerous aliens, only several appeared more than once: Athena, the Green Alien Lady (Vitina Marcus), Nancy Pi Squared, the Space Beauty (Dee Hartford), Mr. Zumdish, the space entrepreneur (Fritz Feld) and Farnum the Great (Leonard J. Stone).

1966. NBC launches *Star Trek* with William Shatner at the helm of the Starship *U.S.S. Enterprise*. The Vulcan, Mr. Spock (Leonard Nimoy), assists Kirk as the science officer. Everett, an invisible baby, becomes the responsibility of an Earth couple, Alan and Sylvia Barker (Alan Alda, Patricia Smith) when his parents abandon him on their doorstep on the CBS pilot *Where's Everett?*

1967. Architect David Vincent (Roy Thinnes) uncovers a plot by aliens to take over the Earth but can't seem to convince anyone of its reality on ABC's *The Invaders. Ultraman*, the 400-foot tall alien robot sent to protect the Earth from outer space monsters, premiered in syndication. Over the course of 31 years (1967–2001) eleven incarnations of the Japanese series are produced. Three versions appear in the U.S.: *Ultraman*

(1967), *The Ultraman* (1979) and *Ultraman: Towards the Future* (1992).

1968. Gary Seven (Robert Lansing), a human trained by aliens to protect mankind, begins his assignment when teamed with a beautiful alien named Roberta Lincoln (Teri Garr) on the NBC pilot *Assignment: Earth.* Four aliens led by the beautiful Dr. Aphrodite (Shirley Jones) from the planet Kurzon land on Earth in an attempt to study its culture on the CBS pilot *Out of the Blue.*

1972. SHADO, the Supreme Headquarters Alien Defense Organization, is established in England to battle UFO's on the syndicated *UFO.* Ed Bishop stars as its commander, Edward Stryker.

1973. The long running British series, *Doctor Who,* finds a home on American television via syndication. Tom Baker portrays the Doctor, a Time Lord from the planet Gallifrey, who travels through time and space to battle evil.

1975. Bumbling NASA crewmen Barney and Junior (Chuck McCann, Bob Denver) accidentally launch a rocket and are propelled into outer space on CBS's *Far Out Space Nuts.* The beautiful alien Lantana (Eve Bruce) and her pet Honk (Patty Maloney) travel with them. Futuristic androids Fi and Fum (Ruth Buzzi, Jim Nabors) from the planet ZR-3 become lost in space when their ship malfunctions on ABC's *The Lost Saucer.* A radioactive chain reaction blasts the moon out of orbit and strands 300 astronauts on *Space: 1999.* The syndicated series features Catherine Schell as Maya, a beautiful alien from the planet Psychon, who is capable of changing her form.

1977. Liana (Katie Saylor), a beautiful alien from the planet Atos, is one of the beings trapped on a mysterious island in the Bermuda Triangle where the past, present and future coexist on NBC's *Fantastic Journey.* Believed to be the lone survivor of the lost city of Atlantis, Mark Harris (Patrick Duffy) opts to help mankind rather than return to the sea on NBC's *The Man from Atlantis.* Milwaukee high school teacher Eric Smith (Bob Neill) is not who he appears to be. He is the scion of an alien father and an Earth mother who uses his unique psychokinetic powers to help the government on the NBC pilot *The Man with the Power.* John Dorsey (Lewis Smith) is *The Man Who Fell to Earth,* the surviving alien of a space ship crash, who is marooned and seeking a way to return to his home planet (Athena) on this ABC pilot. The alien Loki (Eric Greene) is a member of the Nova Blue Team, a futuristic group of space cadets on *Space Academy* (CBS). The beautiful female members of the planet Medusa meet Earthmen for the first time when their planet locks onto Earth's orbit on the syndicated *Star Maidens.*

1978. Sophisticated robots patterned after the human form called Cylons (from the planet Cylon) threaten the humans aboard the battle ship *Galactica* on ABC's *Battlestar Galactica.* Lorne Greene heads the cast as Commander Adama. An alien explorer named Mork (from the planet Ork) lands on Earth, befriends a human named Mindy McConnell (Pam Dawber) and sets out to learn all he can about Earthlings on ABC's *Mork and Mindy.* UFO incidents investigated by the U.S. Air Force and chronicled in its Project Blue Book became the basis for NBC's *Project UFO* with William Jordan as the chief investigator, Major Jake Gatlin. Adam Quark (Richard Benjamin) pilots a United Galaxy Sanitation Patrol garbage ship with the assist of twins Betty I and Betty II, a transmute (Jean/Gene) and science officer Ficus Panderato (Richard Kelton), a plant from the planet Vegeton on *Quark* (NBC).

1979. American astronaut William "Buck" Rogers (Gil Gerard) finds himself in the 25th century after leaking gases on a rocket place in a state of suspended animation on NBC's *Buck Rogers in the 25th Century.* The beautiful Princess Ardella (Pamela Hensley), the daughter of the king of the planet Draconia, and her aide, Kane (Michael Ansara), are first season aliens. Hawk (Thom Christopher), the man-bird, replaces them.

1982. Stranded alien youngsters Tia and Tony (Tracey Gold, Andy Freeman) search for the other members of their Earth colony with the help of Jason O'Day (Eddie Albert), the human who befriends them, on the CBS pilot *Beyond Witch Mountain.* A government agent named Conrad (Joseph Campanella) seeks to prove that Zef (Christopher Connelly), Lara (Meredith MacRae) and Teva (Elissa Leeds) are an alien family on the NBC pilot *Earthbound.* A marooned Earth space shuttle, the *Destiny,* becomes lost in space and the home to two aliens: Jaza (Leonard Frey) and Zet (Debbie Carrington) on the ABC pilot *The Earthlings.* Earthling Arthur Dent (Simon Jones) and Ford Prefect (David Dixon), an alien from the Betelgeuse system, become marooned in space after the Earth is destroyed to make way for a hyperspace bypass on PBS's *The Hitchhiker's Guide* *to the Galaxy.* Aliens pose as evangelists He and She (John Forsythe, Priscilla Pointer) to recruit humans for their cause of serenity (New Tomorrow) on the NBC pilot *The Mysterious Two.* An ancient astronaut named Bennu of the Golden Light (Judson Scott) awakens in modern times to search for his destiny on *The Phoenix* (ABC). Matthew Star (Peter Barton) appears to be a normal high school student. In reality he is Ehawk, prince of the planet Quadris, who has been sent to Earth under the guidance of Walt Shepherd (Louis Gossett) to develop his abilities on *The Powers of Matthew Star* (NBC).

1983. Benji, the famous movie dog, helps Ubi (Chris Burton), prince of the planet Antaz, and his android Zax, escape the clutches of the evil Zanu (Ken Miller) on CBS's *Benji, Zax and the Alien Prince.* Dan Aykroyd, Jane Curtin and Laraine Newman recreate their *Saturday Night Live* skit roles as Beldar, Prymaat and Connie Conehead, the aliens from the planet Remulak who are living on Earth on the NBC pilot *The Coneheads.*

1984. TV newsman Mike Donovan (Marc Singer) and scientist Julie Parrish (Faye Grant) lead the battle against the Visitors (aliens from the planet Sirius) on *V* (NBC). Here, Elizabeth Maxwell (Jenny Beck, Jennifer Cooke), the Star Child (the daughter of an Earth mother and alien father) possesses amazing powers and becomes Earth's hope for survival.

1985. Mary (Belinda Bauer) is the name taken by an alien after she escapes from her once utopian planet to find safety on Earth. The U.S. government and agents of her planet (to show her people there is no escape) search for her on the ABC pilot *Star Crossed.*

1986. A furry brown alien from the planet Melmack with an enormous appetite and a knack for causing trouble finds Earth a bit uncomfortable on NBC's *ALF* when he crash lands and becomes the permanent house guest of the Tanner family. Aliens Tivia, Lord Beathan and Uncle Pike (Loretta Haywood, Graham Ravey, Kazuhisa Kahamaru) recruit exceptional Earthling Bhodi Li (Christopher Lockwood) to battle the evil Warlord of Arr on the syndicated series *Photon.* Fourteen years after fathering a child with a human woman, an alien named Paul Forrester (Robert Hays) returns to Earth to find his son Scott and wife Jenny on ABC's *Starman.*

1987. A pretty teenage girl named Evie Garland (Maureen Flannigan) finds coping with life

a bit disarming being the daughter of an Earth mother (Donna) and an alien father (Troy of Anterius) on the syndicated *Out of This World.* Deanna Troi (Mariana Sirtis), the daughter of a human mother and Betazoid father, possesses telepathic powers and serves as the counselor on the syndicated *Star Trek: The Next Generation.* Also on board is Natasha Yar (Denise Crosby), the Chief of Security who is also an expert in the martial arts.

1988. Ta'ra (Maryam D'Abo), an alien from an unknown planet, helps Detective Jack Breslin (Joe Cortese) solve bizarre crimes on NBC's *Something Is Out There.* The Earth's battle against aliens from the planet Mortex is depicted on *War of the Worlds.* The syndicated series features Jared Martin as Harrison Blackwood, the leader of the government's Omega Squad. Franklin Smith and Patricia Adams (Chris Makepeace, Hilary Edson) are aliens from the planet Ovaten who seek to learn more about the Earth on the ABC pilot *Why on Earth?*

1989. Beings from the planet Tencton establish an Earth colony in Los Angeles on Fox's *Alien Nation* when they are stranded and unable to return home. Eric Pierpont (as George) and Michelle Scarabelli (his wife, Susan) head the large cast. A violent warrior named Jesse (Martin Cove) with no regard for laws is banished from his home planet (Anterius) to help people and reform his ways on CBS's *Hard Time on Planet Earth.* Intergalactic law enforces Nardo and Bida (William Bumiller, Shanti Owen) of the planet Ich find they are microscopic compared to Earthlings on the CBS pilot *Microcops.*

1990. Carefree aliens Abe and Bo (Stuart Fratkin, Dean Cameron) of the planet Crouton begin an automobile tour of the Earth (in a red 1957 Corvette) to discover the wonders of a new world on the syndicated *They Came from Outer Space.*

1993. Teenagers who are able to transform themselves into Power Rangers to protect the Earth from aliens is the premise of Fox's *Mighty Morphin Power Rangers.* Many aliens appear on this long-running series. Most notable are Rita Repulsa (Barbara Goodson), Lord Zedd (Robert Axelrod), Divatox (Hilary Shepard Turner) and Astronomus (Melody Perkins). Jo Jo Thornton (Marjorie Monaghan), a tall and beautiful woman from a planet where men are wimps, and Zylyn (Cary-Hiroyuki Tagawa), a super-strong man from the planet Grakka, are the alien Federal Space Rangers who battle evil throughout the universe on *Space Rangers* (CBS). Three aliens are represented on the syndicated *Star Trek: Deep Space Nine*: Ezri Dax (Nicole de Boer), a station commander (born on the planet Trill); Jadzia Dax (Terry Farrell), a helm officer on the *U.S.S. Defiant*, is like Ezri, a combination of two life forms — a Trill and a Symbian Dax; and Kira Nerys (Nana Visitor), a Bajorian Militia Colonel on the *Defiant*. Dana Scully (Gillian Anderson) and Fox Mulder (David Duchovny) are agents for the X-Files Bureau, a government organization that investigates strange happenings, including UFO sightings on Fox's *The X-Files*.

1995. Aric (Sinbad), an alien from the planet Ganu, teams with young Richard Bickerstaff (Ben Savage), to save the Earth from the Drunes — beings who plan to conquer it through charm (their smiles put humans under their spell) on *Aliens for Breakfast* (ABC pilot). Part human, part Borg, the beautiful Seven of Nine (Jeri Ryan) assists Kathryn Janeway, captain of the *U.S.S. Voyager* on UPN's *Star Trek: Voyager*. Also on board: Tuvok (Tim Russ), the Vulcan Security Chief, Neelix (Ethan Phillips), the Talaxian Morale Office, and B'Elanna Torres (Roxann Dawson), the half Klingon, half Earthling Chief Engineer.

1996. Alien DNA scientist Cookie (Margaret Trigg) marries Earthling Doug Brody (John Bedford Lloyd) and together they attempt to live a normal life on Earth on ABC's *Aliens in the Family*. John Lonegard (Eric Close) and Kimberly Sayers (Megan Ward) find themselves on the run from the U.S. government after they uncover Majestic 12, a concealed hive of aliens on NBC's *Dark Skies*. Four aliens pose as the Solomon family and take up residence in Rutherford, Ohio, to study Earth life on NBC's *Third Rock from the Sun*. John Lithgow plays Dick Solomon and Kristen Johnston his sister, Sally.

1997. Meego Smith Triangle Not to Scale (Bronson Pinschot), an alien from the planet Marmazon Four Point 0, crash lands on Earth to become a nanny to the Parker children on CBS's *Meego*. Teal'c (Christopher Judge), a warrior from a society called Jaffa, battles evil on distant worlds as part of the Stargate Team on the Sci Fi Channel's *Stargate SG-1*.

1999. The space ship *Moya* is spotlighted on the Sci Fi Channel's *Farscape*. Its alien crew members are Chiana (Gigi Edgely), a skilled thief born on the planet Nabari; Aeryn Sun (Claudia Black), a woman raised to be a soldier; and Ka D'Argo (Anthony Simcoe), an aggressive warrior who has characteristics of a lizard, dog and elephant. A group of teenagers who are also part alien (born in Roswell, New Mexico, the sight of a supposed UFO landing) struggle to survive as humans and conceal their alien identities on UPN's *Roswell*. Emilie de Ravin (as Tess Harding), Shiri Appleby (Liz Evans), Jason Behr (Max Evans) and Katherine Heigl (Isabelle Evans) head the cast.

2000. Laura Bertram plays Trance Gemini, a member of the space ship *Andromeda*, who is actually the Avatar of the Sun (a balance between light and dark) on the syndicated *Andromeda*. Alien bounty hunter Ethaniel (Cameron Bancroft) teams with earth scientist Laura Keating (Ingrid Kavelaars) to stop an evil alien from taking over the Earth to make it his world on *Code Name: Eternity* (Syn.). Eve Habern (then Xenia Seeberg) plays Zev Bellringer, part woman, part cluster lizard; and Kai (Michael McManus), an undead assassin from a society called the Brunnen-G, are crewmembers aboard the Sci Fi Channel's *Lexx*.

2001. UPN launches *Star Trek Enterprise* with the beautiful Vulcan, T'Pol (Jolene Blalock) as the science officer to Jonathan Archer, captain of the *U.S.S. Enterprise*. Phlox (John Billingsley) is the ship's doctor, an alien who requires only six hours of sleep a year. Back on Earth, Cole (Adrian Paul), an alien from the Migor Solar System, seeks to capture escaped alien fugitives on the syndicated *Tracker*.

2004. Keeping track of 4,400 humans who were abducted by aliens then returned to Earth becomes the job of Diana Skouris (Jacqueline McKenzie) and Tom Baldwin (Joel Gretsch), agents for the National Threat Assessment Committee on *The 4400* (USA).

2005. The alien Cylon robots return to plague the inhabitants of the star ship *Galactica* in an update of the 1978 series called *Battlestar Galactica (2005)*. Edward James Olmos heads the cast as Commander Adama. The ABC series *Invasion* uses body possession aspects when the people of a small Florida community become the subjects of an invasion by unknown beings. Kari Matchett and William Fichtner head the cast. Molly Anne Caffrey (Carla Gugino) is a government contingency analyst and head of a team of scientists who are seeking to find the purpose of an extraterrestrial craft that has landed on Earth on *Threshold* (CBS).

American Indian Performers and Characters

This entry chronicles the programs that have starred or featured Native Americans. Also included are those series on which non Native Americans have played roles relating to the subject.

1947. *Howdy Doody* airs on NBC. Here the puppet Howdy Doody and his guardian Buffalo Bob Smith run a circus in the town of Doodyville, Texas. Living on the outskirts of town were several Indian tribes, the most famous being the Ooragnak (kangaroo spelled backwards) and their leader, Chief Thunderthud (Bill LeCornec). The other tribes were the Tinka Tonka and the Sycapoose. Chief Thunderthud is best known by his catchphrase "Kowa-bunga." Princess Summerfall Winterspring (Judy Tyler, Linda Marsh) was the Tinka Tonka tribal representative; and Chief Featherman, head of the Sycapoose tribe, was played by Bob Keeshan (who also played the role of Clarabell the Clown).

1949. Jay Silverheels, a Mohawk Indian, plays Tonto on ABC's *The Lone Ranger*. Tonto, a Potawatomi Indian, became the companion to John Reid, the masked rider of the Plains in the early 19th century who fights injustice. Tonto called the Ranger "Kemo Sabe" (translated as both "Faithful Friend" and "Trusted Scout").

1950. Indian culture and cowboy folklore are explained to children by host Rex Bell on ABC's *Cowboys and Injuns*.

1951. Nino Marcel plays Little Fox, a Sioux Indian brave on the Storybook Time segments of NBC's *Smilin' Ed McConnell and His Gang* (Nino also plays Gunga, the East Indian Boy, in other Storybook segments). While he does not play an Indian on TV, Roy Rogers is, in real life, part Choctaw Indian and on *The Roy Rogers Show* (NBC) he and his wife, Dale Evans, uphold the law in Mineral City.

1953. A real Native American, Little Beaver, plays Little Beaver, a Navaho Indian who is the companion to Red Ryder, cattle rancher and unofficial lawman on the pilot *Red Ryder* (Little Beaver's catch phrase is "You betchum, Red Ryder." He rides a horse named Papoose).

1954. In 1954 (to 55), ABC created a nationwide sensation when it aired *Davy Crockett* on its *Disneyland* series. The first episode, *Davy Crockett, Indian Fighter*, features Pat Hogan as Red Stick, the leader of the Creeks Indian Tribe. The third episode (of five), *Davy Crockett at the Alamo* features Nick Cravat as Bustedluck, a wandering Indian who attaches himself to Davy (Fess Parker) and his friend Georgie Russell (Buddy Ebsen).

1955. Keith Larsen plays *Brave Eagle: Chief of the Cheyenne* on CBS. Brave Eagle lived in the Black Mountain region of Wyoming (1860s) and it was through his eyes that the Indian viewpoint of the West was seen. Keena Nomkeena plays Keena, Brave Eagle's adopted son (Keena was rescued by Brave Eagle after his tribe was attacked by the Comanche); Kim Winona is Morning Star (Brave Eagle's romantic interest) and Burt Wheeler is Smokey Joe, "a man born of white man's blood" who, after serving with the U.S. Cavalry, choose to live with his mother's people. Clint Walker plays Cheyenne Bodie, a man of many occupations who roams the West of the 1860s on ABC's *Cheyenne*. Cheyenne is believed to be the son of the wealthy Lionel Abbott. He was kidnapped as an infant by White Cloud (Richard Hale), Chief of the Cheyenne, when his braves attacked a wagon train. White Cloud raised the boy and gave him the Indian name Grey Fox. When Grey Fox became of age, he chose to go the way of the white man and took the name Cheyenne Bodie.

1956. Michael Ansara plays Cochise, leader of the Apache Indians (Arizona, 1870s) on ABC's *Broken Arrow* (Ricardo Montalban played the role in the pilot film). On the series, Army Indian Agent Tom Jeffords (John Lupton) and Cochise worked together to maintain peace between the Indian and white man (the title refers to the Indian symbol for peace, friendship and understanding; an arrow is seen being broken by Cochise in the opening theme). Stirring up trouble was Geronimo (Charles Horvath), the chief who opposed the peace. Red Ryder (Rocky Lane) and his Indian companion Little Beaver (Louis Letteri) struggle to maintain law and order in the West of the 1860s on the syndicated *Red Ryder*.

1957. A young Indian boy named Pow Wow learns about life on the animated *Adventures of Pow Wow* (Syn.). Lon Chaney, Jr. plays Chingachgook, a Mohican Indian who assists Nat Cutler (John Hart), a fur trapper of the 1750s (at the time of the French and Indian Wars) on the syndicated *Last of the Mohicans* (also known as *Hawkeye and the Last of the Mohicans*).

1958. NBC's *Northwest Passage* features Larry Chance as Black Wolf, the Native American Indian who became involved with explorer Major Robert Rogers (Keith Larsen) as he sought the fabled waterway between New York State and Eastern Canada. Lisa Davis plays Natula, a member of Black Wolf's tribe. X Brands plays Pahoo-Ka-Ta-Wah ("Wolf Who Stands in Water"), the Pawnee American Indian who watches over Yancy Derringer (Jock Mahoney) on CBS's *Yancy Derringer* (Pahoo went against his faith and saved the life of a white man. He is now responsible for Yancy's life).

1959. Michael Ansara plays Sam Buckhart, an Apache Indian who, to help his people maintain the peace, becomes a Deputy U.S. Marshal in Santa Fe, New Mexico (1880s) on NBC's *Law of the Plainsman* (the pilot episode, "The Indian," aired on ABC's *The Rifleman*). Abel Fernandez plays Agent William Youngfellow, a Cherokee Indian who works with Eliot Ness (Robert Stack) as a member of *The Untouchables* (ABC), elite Treasury Department agents out to end organized crime in Chicago (1930s).

1960. Chief Hawkeye (J. Carrol Naish) is a scheming American Indian who runs the trading post and souvenir stand opposite Guestward Ho, a dude ranch near Santa Fe, New Mexico on ABC's *Guestward Ho!* Hawkeye is assisted by the beautiful Pink Cloud (Jolene Brand) and orders his "genuine" Indian souvenirs from Hong Kong.

1962. Burt Reynolds plays Quint Asper, a half-breed Indian who worked as the blacksmith in Dodge City, Kansas, on CBS's *Gunsmoke*.

1964. Ed Ames plays Mingo, an Oxford educated Cherokee Indian who is a friend of frontiersman Daniel Boone (Fess Parker) on NBC's *Daniel Boone*. Also on the series, Rosey Grier plays Gabe Cooper, a runaway slave who became Chief Canawahchaguaoo of the Tuscarora Indians (in Kentucky, the series setting) and Don Pedro Colley plays Gideon, a Negro Indian. The syndicated *Forest Rangers* features Michael Zenon as Joe Two Rivers, an Indian who, with the Junior Ranger Club, assists the forest rangers of the Canadian North Woods.

1965. Frank DeKova plays Wild Eagle, Chief of the Hekawi Indians on ABC's *F-Troop*. The Hekawis are a peaceful tribe and live in the hills surrounding Fort Courage (Kansas, 1860s). They earn money by making souvenirs for army sergeant Morgan O'Rourke's illegal O'Rourke Enterprises and he and his tribe live a good life (so much so that they have forgotten the hard times they once lived). Crazy Cat (Don Diamond) is the assistant chief. Other Indians are Bald Eagle (Don Rickles), Wild Eagle's renegade son (wants to go on the warpath); Roaring Chicken (Edward Everett Horton), the medicine man; Flaming Arrow (Phil Harris), the 147-year-old Indian who wants to kill the white man; Wise Owl (Milton Berle), the deceitful Indian detective; Papa Bear (Ben Frommer), a tribe member; Laurie Sibbald as Wild Eagle's daughter, Silver Dove; Cathy Lewis as Whispering Dove, Wild Eagle's sister; and Paul Petersen as Johnny Eagle Eye, Wild Eagle's nephew.

1966. Burt Reynolds plays John Hawk, an Iroquois Indian who works as a detective lieutenant with the N.Y.P.D. on ABC's *Hawk*. Ron Soble plays Jim, a renegade Sioux Indian who befriends the pioneering Monroe family in Wyoming (1870s) on ABC's *The Monroes*. Lon Chaney, Jr. plays Eagle Shadow, Chief of the Kiowa Indians (Colorado, 1870s) on CBS's *Pistols 'n' Petticoats*. Also appearing are Marc Cavell as Grey Hawk, Eagle Shadow's son; Jay Silverheels as Great Bear, chief of the Atona Indians; and Alex Henteloff as Little Bear, Great Bear's son. On the unaired pilot version of ABC's *That Girl*, Ted Bessell plays Don Blue Sky, part Cherokee Indian and the artist representative for aspiring actress Ann Marie (Marlo Thomas). On the actual series Ted became Don Hollinger, a reporter for *Newsview* magazine.

1967. John Henry (Tom Nardini) is a Navaho Indian who helps Jim Sinclair (Chuck Connors) round up animals for a game preserve in Kenya on ABC's *Cowboy in Africa*. Michael Dante plays Crazy Horse, Chief of the Sioux Indians who personally confronted George Armstrong Custer (Wayne Maunder) in 1860 on ABC's *The Legend of Custer*. Michael Pate plays Vittoro, an Apache Chief (Arizona Territory, 1860s) on ABC's *Hondo*. Pink Cloud (Guy Marks) is a "modernized" Indian who lives among savages but sees no need to go native on ABC's *Rango*. Pink Cloud is somewhat of a coward and helps Texas Ranger Rango (Tim Conway) outwit the bad guys.

1968. Ruffled Feathers and Running Board (voices of Sandy Becker, George S. Irving) are animated gophers who resemble Indians and struggling to protect their land from Kit Coyote (Kenny Delmar), an army colonel seeking to rid the West of gophers on CBS's *Go Go Gophers*. Ted Cassidy provides the voice for Injun Joe, the vengeful Indian who pursues the live action Tom Sawyer, Becky Thatcher and Huck Finn on NBC's *The New Adventures of Huck Finn*. Chief Irontail (Ben Blue) is a 149-year-old Indian and the last member of the Manhattan Tribe (of New York) who claims to own Manhattan Island on the CBS pilot *We'll Take Manhattan* (it appears that over 100 years ago, the original buyer failed to pay the chief for the land and it has since reverted back to him. Leslie Perkins and Allan Melvin play the Chief's children, Laughing Rock and Eagle Eye).

1970. United Council Church member Prudence MacKenzie (Sally Ann Howes) attempts to establish a school on a Cheyenne Reservation against the wishes of its Chief, Snow Eagle (Rick Jason) on the ABC pilot *Prudence and the Chief*.

1971. Sandra Ego plays Joanie Little Bird, the American Indian dispatcher for Sheriff Sam Cade in Madrid County on CBS's *Cade's County* (Betty Ann Carr replaced Sandra as Kitty Ann Sundown). NBC airs two pilots called *Cat Ballou*. The first one (September 5th) stars Lesley Ann Warren as Catherine "Cat" Ballou, a schoolteacher struggling to establish a school in Wolf City, Wyoming. Tom Nardini plays Jackson Two Bears, the Indian foreman of her ranch. In the second pilot (September 6th), Jo Ann Harris is Cat Ballou and Lee. J. Casey plays Jackson Two Bears. Chief Iron Eyes Cody, a Cherokee Indian, appears in a series of TV commercials called "Keep America Beautiful." The P.S.A.'s (Public Service Announcements) show the Chief, seated on his horse, surveying the wonders of Nature, but saddened (a tear comes to his eye) when he sees the pollution man has caused. The spots did, in fact, stop some Americans from polluting the landscape by tossing trash out their car windows.

1974. Abner Biberman plays Abraham Lincoln Imhook, friend to Alaska State Patrol officer Cal McKay (Clint Walker) on ABC's *Kodiak*. Robert Forster plays Nakia Parker, an American Indian who is the Deputy Sheriff of Davis County, New Mexico on ABC's *Nakia*. Also in the cast are Indians John Tenorio, Jr. as Half Cub, and Victor Jory as Ben Redearth.

1975. An Apache brother and sister, Ebon and

Melody (Oscar Valdez, Melody Strong) gain a new perspective on what it means to be a Native American when they receive a visit from their great grandfather, a medicine man who is called the Shaman (Dehl Berti) on the ABC special *The Shaman's Last Raid*.

1976. Morgan "Two Persons" Baudine (Kurt Russell), a young boy captured by the Cheyenne and freed eight years later by the army, joins his brother, Quentin Baudine (Tim Matheson) in a search to find their sister, Patricia, also captured by Indians (but by a different tribe) on NBC's *The Quest*.

1977. Shirley Kirkes plays Gladys "Cochise" Littlefeather, a Native American dancer who works at the Oasis Hotel in Las Vegas on ABC's *Blansky's Beauties*. Don Shanks plays Nakuma, the Native American blood brother to mountain man Grizzly Adams (Dan Haggerty) on NBC's *The Life and Times of Grizzly Adams*. The ABC special *The Nunundaga* presents a dramatic look at a fictional Indian tribe (the Nunundaga) as they struggle for survival in a hostile world. Ned Romero stars as Painted Bear with Monika Ramirez (Wind Song), Guillarmo San Juan (Snake Eyes), Victoria Racimo (Star Fire) and John War Eagle (One Feather). Will Sampson plays Sam Watchman, a Navaho Indian and Arizona State Trooper who uses his Indian skills to track criminals on the CBS pilot *Relentless*. *You Gotta Start Somewhere* is a true CBS special about Philip Gilbert (Panchito Gomez), an 11-year-old Indian boy who established a school for Indian children in Rapid City, Iowa, when his grammar school curriculum ignored his Indian heritage. Eloy Phil Casados plays Tsiskwa, a Cherokee Indian and friend of Daniel Boone (Rick Moses) at the age of 25 before he became a legend on CBS's *Young Dan'l Boone*.

1978. Shirley Kirkes reprises her role of Gladys "Cochise" Littlefeather, the role she played on *Blansky's Beauties* (see 1977), on the NBC pilot *Legs* (where she worked at the not-so-plush Las Vegas Hotel) and on the NBC series *Who's Watching the Kids* (where she danced at the seedy Club Sandpile). Marilyn Tokuda plays Shana "Pipeline" Akira, an Eskimo American who was a member of the roller derby team, the Pittsburgh Pitts, on NBC's *The Roller Girls*. Harlan Two Leaf (Will Sampson) is a Native American who helps private detective Dan Tanna on ABC's *Vegas*.

1979. Sandra Griego then Victoria Racimo plays

Kewerinok, the Indian wife of Will Chisholm (Ben Murphy), one of the pioneering Chisholm family as they travel by wagon train from Wyoming to California on CBS's *The Chisholms*.

1980. Will Sampson plays Sergeant Cheney, a Native American soldier stationed at Pearl Harbor in Hawaii just after the attack in 1941 on NBC's *From Here to Eternity*.

1982. The NBC series *Born to the Wind* is set in 1825 and follows the lives of a tribe of Plains Indians who call themselves "The People." Will Sampson stars as Painted Bear with A Martinez (Lone Wolf), Dehl Berti (One Feather), Rose Portillo (Star Fire) and Henry Darrow (Lost Robe).

1983. Will Sampson plays John Stronghart, a Native American who works as a ranch hand on the 200,000-acre West Texas ranch, *The Yellow Rose* (NBC).

1985. Billy Night Eyes (Michael Horse) is a Native American police informant who also owns a Los Angeles newspaper stand on ABC's *Hollywood Beat*.

1987. Dehl Berti plays Vittorio, an elderly Native American who is a friend to renowned Texas surgeon *Buck James* (ABC).

1988. Tony Acieto plays White Eagle, a Shoshone Indian who works with Jesse Hawkes (Robert Conrad), head of the *High Mountain Rangers* (CBS), a rescue group in the Sierra Nevada near Lake Tahoe. Thomas McAllister (Steve Inwood) is a tough attorney who is half Apache and who fights for the underdog on the ABC pilot *McAllister*. John Taylor (Dehl Berti) is the American Indian friend of ex gunfighter Ethan Allen Cord (Lee Horsley) and the only person in town (*Paradise*) who appears to have medical knowledge on CBS's *The Guns of Paradise* (also titled *Paradise*). Richard Chaves plays Colonel Paul Ironhorse, a member of the Blackwood Project, a secret U.S. agency designed to battle aliens on *War of the Worlds* (Syn.).

1989. Tom Jackson plays Billy Two Feathers, the Native American handyman (and former railroad engineer) at *Shining Time Station* (PBS). Gregg Rainwater plays Buck Cross, the half-breed who works with the pony express riders on ABC's *The Young Riders*.

1990. Beau Jack Bowman (Miguel Ferrer) is a former New Orleans police detective (part Chickasaw Indian) who now works for the Bay City, California Police Department on CBS's *Broken Badges*. Darren E. Burrows plays Ed Chigliak, a

Native American who assists Dr. Joel Fleischman (Rob Morrow) in the town of Cicely, Alaska on CBS's *Northern Exposure*. Also seen is Marilyn Whirlwind (Elaine Miles), the Eskimo woman who helps Joel run his office. On ABC's *Twin Peaks* Michael Horse plays Tommy Hill (called "The Hawk"), a Deputy Sheriff in the town of Twin Peaks.

1991. The CBS children's series, *Riders in the Sky*, features Dwanna Murcell as Princess, the Indian girl who lived on a reservation near Tumbleweed City. She was a friend to the cowboys of Harmony Ranch and her full name is Princess Little Running Bear.

1992. Bryan Brightcloud plays Zac, the Native American who works at Little Innocents Hospital on *Rachel Gunn, R.N.* (Fox). Branscombe Richmond plays Bobby Sixkiller and Kathleen Kinmont is his half-sister Cheyenne Phillips, bounty hunters of Indian descent on the syndicated *Renegade*.

1993. Nick Ramus plays Black Kettle, Chief of the Cheyenne Indians (Colorado, 1860s) who gave the white woman, Dr. Michaela Quinn (Jane Seymour) the name "Medicine Woman" after she saved his life on CBS's *Dr. Quinn, Medicine Woman*. Also featured was Larry Sellers as Cloud Dancing, a Cheyenne Indian living near the town of Colorado Springs. Saginaw Grant is Auggie Velasquez, the Native American who ran the general store in Sholo, Nevada (near the Flying Tumbleweed Ranch) on CBS's *Harts of the West*. Also featured was Talisa Soto as Cassie, Auggie's granddaughter. Wes Studi is One Horse, the "crazy" Indian who lives outside the town of Plum Creek, Texas, and who carries a bag he will not allow anyone to touch on CBS's *Ned Blessing: The Story of My Life and Times*. Michael Horse plays George Steelman, a full-blooded Cherokee Indian who becomes one of the elite group of Treasury agents designed to end organized crime in Chicago (1930s) on *The Untouchables* (Syn.; see also 1959). Cordell Walker (Chuck Norris) is a Texas Ranger who uses his upbringing as a Cherokee Indian to battle crime on *Walker, Texas Ranger* (CBS). Cordell's Uncle Roy (Floyd "Red Crow" Westerman then by Indian actor Apesanahkwat) raised him on the reservation after racists killed his parents (who objected to Elizabeth [Kathleen Steele] being married to full blooded Cherokee John Firewalker [Don Brook]). Cordell was given the Indian name War-shaw (Lone Eagle) and raised in both the ways of the white man and the Indian.

1994. Rodney A. Grant plays Chingachgook, a Mohican Indian and friend of fur trapper Natty "Hawkeye" Bumppo (Lee Horsley) during the time of the French and Indian Wars (1775) on the syndicated *Hawkeye*.

1995. Nick Crowfoot (Jim Davidson) is a Cheyenne Indian who works as an undercover agent for the Maui, Hawaii Police Department on the CBS pilot *Crowfoot*. Robert Beltran plays Chakotay, First Officer on the Starship *Voyager* who is a descendant of a North American tribe that became known as the Rubber Tree People on UPN's *Star Trek: Voyager* (Chakotay wears a symbol of his people as a tattoo over his left eye).

1997. Jonathan Joss provides the voice of John Redcorn, the neighbor of Hank Hill (Mike Judge), who works as an American Indian new age healer in the town of Arlen, Texas, on Fox's *King of the Hill*.

2001. On ABC's *According to Jim*, Jim (Jim Belushi), a construction company owner, claims to be one-sixteenth Cherokee Indian.

2002. Navaho folklore comes into focus on *Skinwalkers*, a series of PBS films about Lt. Joe Leaphorn (Wes Studi), a city bred Native American who returns to his native roots to uphold the law as a tribal cop. The title refers to the spirits of murdered Indians who return to seek revenge upon those who disrespect the land. The second film, *Coyote Waits*, aired in 2003; *A Thief of Time*, the third film, aired in 2004.

2003. A large American Indian cast appears on ABC's *Dream Keeper*, the story of a grandfather (August Schellenberg) who believes in the traditions of his ancestors, and his teenage grandson Shane (Eddy Spears), who believes only what he knows about in today's world (Shane learns to respect his heritage through the stories he hears from his grandfather — which are seen in flashbacks). Chad Michael Murray stars as Luke Hartman, alias the Lone Ranger, on the WB pilot *The Lone Ranger* that follows, for the most part, the original 1949 series concept (character names are different). Here Tonto (Nathaniel Archand) finds Luke (not John Reid) and nurses him back to health after his group of Texas Rangers are ambushed by outlaws. Luke becomes the Lone Ranger (the one ranger who survived the attack) to avenge their deaths by bringing outlaws to justice.

2005. The Disney Channel movie *Buffalo Dreams* is a look at the life, culture and land of the Navaho Indian. Reiley McClendon, Jane Sibbett, Tessa Vonn and Graham Greene head a large cast. TNT's *Into the West* follows two multi generational families, one the pioneering Wheeler family (see *Westerns*) the other, Native Americans from the Lakota Tribe (each side tells dramatic events in the development of the West). Heading a very large cast are Nathaniel Arcand (Brings Horse), Sean Wei Mah (Heavy Shield), Zahn McClarnon (Running Fox), Jay Tavarel (Chief Prairie Fire) and Travis Dugas (Bear Blood).

Angels

Angels are thought of as beautiful celestial beings dressed in white and possessing wings. Television's concept of angels, for the most part, is anything but. Television angels come in all shapes and sizes and the following list represents the programs that star or feature characters as angels.

1954. The DuMont network presents the first concept of an angel in a series called *The Stranger*. Robert Carroll plays the Stranger, a mysterious man who suddenly appears to help people threatened by evil.

1959. Six-year-old Barnaby Baxter (Ronny Howard) wishes upon a star for a fairy godmother who can make his dreams come true. What he gets is Mr. O'Malley (Bert Lahr), a cigar smoking, jovial, pink-winged fairy godfather on the CBS pilot *Mr. O'Malley*. A disreputable soul named Finch (Walter Slezak) enters Heaven and becomes an angel by clerical error. He tries to live up to that honor by performing good deeds on Earth on the NBC pilot *The Slightly Fallen Angel*.

1960. A guardian angel named J. Hardy Hempstead (Henry Jones) is assigned to help deserving earthlings on the CBS pilot *Mr. Bevis* (a proposed spinoff from *The Twilight Zone*).

1962. Harmon Cavender (Jesse White), a bumbling apprentice angel with the Third Celestial Division, Angel Placement, is assigned to help deserving earthlings to earn his wings on the CBS *Twilight Zone* spinoff pilot *Cavender Is Coming*. Angel First Class Charlie Angelo (James Komack) attempts to promote good and discourage evil on the CBS pilot *Charlie Angelo*.

1965. In 1963 Tom Smothers (himself) "was lost at sea without his water wings." Two years later he returns as Probationary Angel Agent 009, a wingless apprentice angel, who helps people in trouble to earn full-fledged angel status on CBS's *The Smothers Brothers Show.* A beautiful wood sprite named Sybil (Suzy Parker) commits the sin of vanity and is banished from her native habitat to Earth to help people and atone for her sin on the CBS pilot *Sybil.*

1969. A young boy named Michael (Johnnie Whitaker) attempts to adjust to Heaven on the NBC *Hallmark Hall of Fame* special *The Littlest Angel.*

1973. A mysterious woman, known only as Laura (Valerie Perrine), magically appears to help people who are in need of guidance on the NBC pilot *Lady Luck.*

1976. Varying stories in which a celestial messenger named Mr. Angel (Carl Reiner) helps people fulfill their fantasies becomes the premise of ABC's *Good Heavens.*

1977. Kevin Leahy (James Farentino), an ex-minister fallen from the grace of God and expelled from the church, is brought back to life after a fatal car accident by celestial forces to ferret out evil and gain salvation on the NBC pilot *The Possessed.*

1978. Lydia (Eva Gabor) and Danny (Jay Leno) are deceased souls regulated to the Heavenly Crisis and Conscience Center, a place where they have to remain until they can earn their wings by performing good deeds on Earth on the ABC pilot *Almost Heaven.* Mr. Roarke (Ricardo Montalban) is a mysterious man who dresses in while, appears to be immortal and grants people's wishes. The series is ABC's *Fantasy Island* and Mr. Roarke is assumed to be a celestial messenger.

1979. A celestial blunder causes a car accident that claims the lives of Roxy and Karen (Carol Wayne, Donna Ponterotto). The girls are returned to Earth in their former status and under the watchful eye of celestial messenger Sebastian Parnell (William Daniels) help deserving people on the NBC pilot *Heaven on Earth.* When Boss Angel (Eileen Heckert) feels the Richards family requires help she sends Random (James Brogan), a somewhat inept angel to watch over them on ABC's *Out of the Blue.*

1981. The Wings Through Rehabilitation Program is the Almighty's way of allowing deserving souls into Heaven by performing good deeds. Katie Fredericks (Ilene Graff), Douglas Sheehan (Jerry Davidson) and Ron Contreras (Luis Padia) are three such souls attempting to redeem themselves on the NBC pilot *Heaven on Earth* (also known as *Heaven Sent*).

1982. Amy Watson (Helen Slater) is a girl with low self-esteem. Oliver (Albert Macklin) is the angel assigned to watch over her. When Amy's condition worsens and she wishes she had never been born, Oliver grants her wish to let her see how much she contributes to the lives of her friends and family on the ABC special *Amy and the Angel.* A prankish angel named Andy LeBeau (Gary Coleman) is sent back to Earth to help people and redeem himself on the NBC pilot *The Kid with the Broken Halo* (which led to the 1982 animated series *The Gary Coleman Show*).

1984. Earth-bound angel Jonathan Smith (Michael Landon) and his human assistant Mark Gordon (Victor French) perform good deeds for "The Boss" on NBC's *Highway to Heaven.*

1986. *The Last Chance Café* (ABC pilot) is situated in the middle of nowhere and allows weary travelers to enjoy a meal before continuing their journey. The mysterious owner, Virgil (Henry Jones), allows troubled customers to "see" crucial moments from their pasts with themselves as they were many years ago. A mysterious old man (Jack Gilford) who is actually an angel, grants deserving people their wish to become *Young Again* (ABC pilot).

1987. Ida Early (Jackee Harry) dresses in outlandish attire and appears to be an angel who uses her magical charm to help people in need on the NBC pilot *The Incredible Ida Early.* When Charles Russell (Keil Martin) is judged unfit for Heaven or Hell he is sent back to Earth to relive his own past and right his wrongs on Fox's *Second Chance* (Matthew Perry plays his 15-year-old self, whom he now watches over as a Guardian Angel).

1992. Michael Price (Joel Grey) is a mysterious man who runs an equally mysterious retreat called Whisper Mountain. Here, he and his assistant Amy (Jane Leeves) are assigned by celestial powers to see that evil is punished on the ABC pilot *Just Desserts.* The All Night Café is an eatery near the docks. The mysterious Blackie (Robert Englund) runs the eatery for a higher authority. People who wander into the café and wish they could change their pasts are given that chance on NBC's *Nightmare Café.*

1993. Steve Matrix (Nick Mancuso) is a deceased hit man suspended between Heaven and Hell. He is given a chance to make up for his past misdeeds by helping people in need on *Matrix* (USA).

1994. Following a plane crash that claims the lives of newlyweds Doug and Lexy Monroe (John Schneider, Melinda Clarke) their souls are sent to limbo. Mr. Shepherd (Ricardo Montalban), a heavenly messenger, grants them apprentice angel status. To earn their way into Heaven Doug and Lexy must perform good deeds on the syndicated *Heaven Help Us*. Under the supervision of her superior angel, Tess (Della Reese), apprentice angel Monica (Roma Downey) answers the prayers of deserving people on CBS's *Touched By an Angel*.

1996. Nash Bridges (Don Johnson) is the only police detective on TV with a personal guardian angel — Angel (Tracey Walter), an apparent homeless man who dresses in white with a pair of wings. He came from out of nowhere to save Nash's life and has now taken it upon himself to watch over him on CBS's *Nash Bridges*.

1997. On a dare to eat an eight-month old hamburger Marty DePolo (Mike Damus) takes a bite and dies. He becomes an apprentice angel and is sent back to Earth to help his friend Steve Beauchamp (Corbin Allenda) and prove himself worthy of Heaven on *Teen Angel* (ABC).

1998. The WB's *Charmed* introduces Leo Wyatt (Brian Krause) as a White Lighter, a guardian angel of witches. In this case to Prue, Piper and Phoebe Halliwell, three sisters who are known as the Power of Three. In 2005 episodes, half-sister Paige Matthews (Rose McGowan) becomes a White Lighter.

1999. "Seamless lingerie with a heavenly fit" was the slogan for the Victoria's Secret line of bras and panties. To further enhance the product, Victoria's Secret Angels were created. Models adorned with wings and sexy lingerie stepped out of the pages of the catalogue and into real life when *The Fourth Annual Victoria's Secret Fashion Show* was web cast on Valentine's Day. Tyra Banks was the most notable of the models. Model Heidi Klum joined Tyra on the sequel web cast in May of 2000. ABC (2001) and CBS (2002) also broadcast lingerie fashion shows starring the Victoria's Secret Angels. The mysterious Mr. Jones (Gordie Brown) is a heavenly messenger who guides the lives of people who are given a second chance to change the course of their lives on *Twice in a Lifetime* (PAX). Mr. Smith (Paul Popowich) is the guide in second season episodes.

2003. Sixteen-year-old Arcadia high school student Joan Girardi (Amber Tamblyn) becomes a somewhat reluctant earth-based angel God has chosen to carry out His assignments on CBS's *Joan of Arcadia*.

Animals

This entry concerns itself with the animals that go beyond the call of duty and become the stars or featured players on a program. See also *Talking Animals and Machines*.

1949. A white stallion named Silver becomes the companion to John Reed (Clayton Moore), the mysterious Masked Rider of the Plains on ABC's *The Lone Ranger*.

1951. Champion, the horse of western hero Gene Autry, performs on *The Gene Autry Show* (Syn.).

1952. A mischievous chimpanzee named Bingo becomes the pet of Lou Costello on the syndicated *Abbott and Costello Show*. Roy Rogers, King of the Cowboys, rides Trigger, a golden Palomino; Dale Evans, his wife, Queen of the West, rides her horse, Buttermilk. Assisting them in upholding the law on CBS's *The Roy Rogers Show* is "Roy's wonder dog," Bullet. NBC's *Today Show* adds an unusual regular to the cast in the persona of J. Fred Muggs, a somewhat mischievous chimpanzee.

1954. A young boy, an unofficial member of the 101st Cavalry, named Corporal Rusty (Lee Aaker) and his German Shepherd, Rin Tin Tin, help preserve the law on ABC's *The Adventures of Rin Tin Tin*. The adventures of a beautiful collie and her various masters begin as CBS launches *Lassie*. Her masters: Tommy Rettig as Jeff Miller (1954–57), Jon Provost as Timmy (1957–64) and Robert Bray as Forest Ranger Corey Stuart (1964–68). Lassie wanders on her own helping people in trouble (1968–71) and in syndication (1972) finds a home on the California ranch of the Holden family. Lassie reappears in 1978 on the ABC pilot *Lassie: The New Beginning* where youngsters Samantha and Chip Stratton (Sally Boyden, Shane Sinatko) become her masters. Megan McCulloch (Megan Cox) becomes Lassie's next master on the 1989 syndicated series *The New Lassie*.

1955. Horses are featured. Twelve-year-old Ricky North (Barry Curtis) rides Champion, the Wonder Horse, on *The Adventures of Champion* (CBS). Young Joey Newton (Bobby Diamond) of the Broken Wheel Ranch shares adventures with a black stallion on *Fury* (NBC). Tamba is the chimpanzee of *Jungle Jim* (Syn.). William Preston (Richard Simmons), a sergeant with the Canadian Northwest Mounted Police, upholds the law with the help of his horse (Rex) and dog Yukon King on the syndicated *Sergeant Preston of the Yukon.*

1956. The Goose Bar Ranch in Coulee Springs, Montana, is the setting for the adventures shared by young Ken McLaughlin (Johnny Washbrook) and his black stallion Flicka on the CBS (then ABC) series *My Friend Flicka.* Chim is the chimpanzee of *Sheena, Queen of the Jungle* (Syn.).

1957. The work of veterinarians Sam Rinehart and Noah McCann (Paul Burke, Vic Rodman) is spotlighted on the NBC series *Noah's Ark.*

1958. A takeoff on the Superman legend called *The Adventures of Superpup* (pilot) finds actors dressed as dogs to relate the exploits of Bark Bent, alias Superpup, a reporter for the *Daily Beegle.* Pamela Poodle was the always in distress reporter and Perry Bite was the newspaper editor. The people and animals of Africa are explored by marrieds George and Marjorie Michaels on *The Michaels in Africa* (Syn.).

1960. Twelve-year-old Velvet Brown (Lori Martin) trains her chestnut horse King for competition in the Grand National Steeplechase on NBC's *National Velvet.* Anthropologist professor Rashford Wallington III (Gil Stratton) attempts to prove animals are as intelligent as humans by civilizing a headstrong chimpanzee on the CBS pilot *Waldo.*

1961. Walter and Elinor Hathaway (Jack Weston, Peggy Cass) find their hands full as the managers of Enoch, Charlie and Candy, three talented theatrical chimpanzees on ABC's *The Hathaways.*

1963. Marlin Perkins narrates documentary-style films about animals on NBC's *Mutual of Omaha's Wild Kingdom.* Arthur Jones hosts films depicting the capture of wild animals for zoos on the syndicated *Wild Cargo.*

1964. Coral Key Park Ranger Porter Ricks (Brian Kelly) receives help in protecting the Florida marine preserve from a dolphin on NBC's *Flipper.* In 1995 PAX aired *Flipper: The New Adventures.* Flipper, now a resident of the Bal Harbor Marine Research Center in Florida, helps Drs. Keith Ricks (Brian Wimmer) and Pam Blondell (Colleen Flynn) safeguard the center. London, a wandering German shepherd helps people he finds in trouble on the syndicated *The Littlest Hobo.* A revised version of the series, also titled *The Littlest Hobo,* aired again in syndication in 1980.

1965. Bill Williams and Arthur Jones narrate films depicting the capture of wild animals on the syndicated *Capture.* A talented pig named Arnold Ziffel is featured on CBS's *Green Acres.* Raised by Fred and Doris Ziffel, who consider him the son they never had, Arnold attended school, watched TV, played cricket, predicted the weather with his tail, and could carry on a conversation with anyone in his hometown of Hooterville.

1966. Loren Eisley narrates wild life films on NBC's *Animal Secrets.*

1967. Chuck Connors plays Jim Sinclair, a rodeo rider who helps game rancher Howard Hayes establish a game preserve in Kenya on ABC's *Cowboy in Africa.* An orphaned bear cub named Ben bonds with Mark Wedlow, the boy who raises him on *Gentle Ben* (CBS). Young Terry Bowen (Jay North), searching for his missing father in India, befriends Raji (Sajid Kahn), an orphaned Indian boy, and his pet elephant on NBC's *Maya.*

1968. Bill Burrud hosts and narrates wild life films on NBC's *Animal Kingdom.*

1969. CBS's *Animal World* features wild life films narrated by Bill Burrud. Marshall Thompson and his assistant Judy the Chimp host stories of African wild life on NBC's *Jambo.* A kangaroo named Skippy helps Australian park ranger Matt Hammond (Ed Devereaux) protect the Waratah National Park on the syndicated *Skippy, the Bush Kangaroo.* Animal behaviorist Don MacMasters (Peter Jason) attempts to cope with life as the owner of a pet tiger named Sultan on the NBC pilot *Tiger! Tiger!* Philip Carey explores the people and animals of the remote regions of the world on NBC's *Untamed World.*

1970. Chimpanzees speak via voice-over dubbing on ABC's *Lancelot Link, Secret Chimp,* the story of a fumbling secret agent for A.P.E. (the Agency to Prevent Evil).

1971. Bill Davidson narrates wild life films on the syndicated *Audubon Wild Life Theater.* Betty White and her guests (animal and human) light up the stage on the syndicated *Pet Set.* A seeing eye dog named Pax (German shepherd) helps blind insurance investigator Michael Longstreet (James Franciscus) continue working on ABC's *Longstreet.* Dentist Mike Reynolds (Ted Bessell) attempts to cope with the antics of his kid's pet chimpanzee, Buttons, on CBS's *Me and the Chimp.*

1972. The adventures shared by young Victoria Gordon (Judi Bowker) and her horse Black Beauty is the essence of the syndicated *The Adventures of Black Beauty*.

1973. Kiddie show host Pete Richards (Soupy Sales) uses a talking bear named Barney (Janos Prohaska) to boost his faltering ratings on the NBC pilot *Barney and Me*. William Conrad narrates films about wild life on the syndicated *Wild, Wild World of Animals*.

1974. The relationship between man and animal is explored through African Game Warden George Adamson and his wife, Joy (Gary Collins, Diana Muldaur) on NBC's *Born Free*. Lorne Greene is the host and narrator of wild life films on the syndicated *Last of the Wild*. Joe, an army trained German shepherd falsely accused of attacking his master, escapes before being destroyed to become a fugitive (but help people in trouble) on NBC's *Run, Joe, Run*. A sea lion becomes the pet of youngsters Taylor and Tim Reed (Mark Slade, Johnny Doran) on the syndicated *Salty*.

1975. Doc Coolidge (Leslie Nielsen) heads *905-Wild*, an NBC pilot about the Los Angeles Bureau of Animal Control.

1976. Hal Linden hosts *Animals, Animals, Animals*, a series that attempts to explain the relationship of animals to man in history, art, music, mythology and literature.

1977. Max, a bionically enhanced German shepherd helps Jaime Sommers (Lindsay Wagner) battle evil on the NBC version of *The Bionic Woman*. Junior high school teacher Cliff Sellers (Fred Grandy) becomes the owner of *Duffy* (CBS pilot), a nondescript dog with human qualities. Mountain man Grizzly Adams (Dan Haggerty) is fond of all animals and has a pet bear named Ben on *The Life and Times of Grizzly Adams* (NBC). The relationship between animals and humans is again explored on the syndicated pilot, *Keeper of the Wild* with Denny Miller as Jim Donaldson and Pamela Susan Shoop as Holly James, the operators of an animal preserve in Africa. Fourteen-year-old Gillie Walker (Joey Green), the owner of a horse named Little Vic, dreams of becoming a jockey on the syndicated *Little Vic*. L.A.P.D. Officer Mike Breen (Mark Harmon) and his partner Sam, a specially trained Labrador Retriever battle crime on CBS's *Sam*. The adventures shared by young Cindy Prescott (Melora Hardin) and her horse Thunder, a semi-wild stallion, is the basis of NBC's *Thunder*.

1978. John Stevens (Don Pascoe), a veterinary surgeon near the town of Gottens Creek, treats the animals of the Australian Outback on the syndicated *Woobinda — Animal Doctor*.

1979. Trucker Billie Jo McKay (Greg Evigan) and his simian traveling companion Bear find adventures on the highways of America on NBC's *B.J. and the Bear*. Man as seen through the eyes of his best friend (actors dressed as dogs) was the premise of the NBC pilot *A Dog's Life*.

1980. Private detective Alexander Parker (Jack Stauffer) solves crimes with the help of five smart Doberman pinchers (Duke, Harlow, Little Bogie, Gabel and Rocky) on the NBC pilot *Alex and the Doberman Gang* (revised as *Nick and the Dobermans* with detective Nick Luchese [Michael Nouri] solving crimes with the help of Doberman pinschers Duke, Erskine and Pee Wee). New York photographer Eugene Henderson (Todd Susman) finds life a bit overwhelming when a stray baby elephant takes a liking to him and becomes his responsibility on the CBS pilot *Ethel Is an Elephant*. Tender stories about the impact a stray, roaming dog has on the lives of the people he meets becomes the premise of *Here's Boomer* (NBC).

1982. Animal talent scout Ginny Provost (Lauralee Bruce) finds her life overrun with animals on the NBC pilot *Kangaroos in the Kitchen*. Clinical psychologist Carrie Jessup (Karen Valentine) uses her dog, Skeezer, as a therapeutic aid for emotionally disturbed children in the heartwarming NBC pilot *Skeezer*.

1984. Youngsters James and Louise Cole (Tim Topper, Emily Moultrie) and Roxanna Banana, an orangutan zapped by a ray from outer space and endowed with super powers, battle evil on NBC's *Going Bananas*.

1983. Bill Burrud and Loretta Swit host *Animals Are the Funniest People*, an ABC pilot that takes a lighthearted look at the crazy things animals do.

1985. Doris Day chats with celebrity guests about their pets on *Doris Day's Best Friends* (CBN).

1987. Amusing films of animals are coupled with a game show for charity on the ABC pilot *Animal Crack-Ups* with Alan Thicke as the host (the format has players answering questions based on animals seen in tape clips). Martin Wilde and his wife Melanie (Joseph Bottoms, Jennifer Hetrick) are *The Doctors Wilde* (CBS pilot), veterinarians who treat wild animals wherever they are needed. Various aspects of the animal kingdom are seen through films and the narration of John Forsythe on the syndicated *John Forsythe's World of Survival.*

1988. Tabloid reporter Sid Barrows (Robert Wuhl) finds help in solving crimes from his dog, Sniff, a bloodhound with a super enhanced sense of smell who believes he is a detective on the CBS pilot *Sniff.* Police officer Hank Katz (Jesse Collins) and his German shepherd, Rin Tin Tin of the K-9 Corps, solve crimes on *Rin Tin Tin, K-9 Cop* (CBN).

1989. Niner, a cloned German shepherd with a computer-enhanced brain, becomes the partner of L.A.P.D. detective Eddie Monroe (Chris Mulkey) on the Fox pilot *K-9000.* Lindsay Wagner plays Rebecca Cafferty, director of the Los Angeles County Zoo on CBS's *Peaceable Kingdom.*

1990. In Cypress, "a small town with small crime," police officer Scott Turner (Tom Wilson) finds himself burdened with Hooch, a mischievous dog on the NBC pilot *Turner and Hooch.*

1991. A German shepherd named Jerry Lee and his human partner, L.A.P.D. officer Jack Bergen (Robert Carradine) ferret out criminals on the ABC pilot *K-9.*

1995. Flipper, the intelligent dolphin from the 1964 series *Flipper*, returns to Florida (this time Bal Harbor) to help research scientist Alexandra Parker-Hamilton (Tiffany Lamb) on *Flipper: The New Adventures* (Syn.).

1999. Ruh (a tiger), Koto and Poto (ferrets) and Sharak (an eagle) help Dar (Daniel Goddard) protect the innocent from evil on the syndicated *BeastMaster.*

2002. Alan Thicke hosts *Miracle Pets*, a PAX series of inspirational stories of the relationship between people and their pets. Hearing impaired FBI agent Sue Thomas (Deanna Bray) receives help from Levi, a golden retriever who becomes her ears on *Sue Thomas, F.B.Eye* (PAX).

2003. Pet expert Marc Morrone offers tips on pet care on the syndicated *Pet Keeping with Marc Morrone.* A transplanted New York girl named Scout (Anastasia Baranova) struggles to adjust to a world of animals she never knew existed in South Africa on *Scout's Safari* (Discovery Kids on NBC).

2004. Films that explore the world of animals from Africa to Asia "and every interesting place in between" are narrated by Eric Schwartz on the syndicated *Animal Atlas.* Jeff Corwin explores the world of animals and insects on *Jeff Corwin Unleashed* (Discovery Kids on NBC). Mariette Hartley hosts *Wild About Animals*, a fascinating look at animals and the amazing things they do.

2005. Blinded when shot during a case, N.Y.P.D. detective Jim Dunbar (Ron Eldard) returns to the force with the help of Duke, his seeing eye dog on ABC's *Blind Justice.*

2006. The wonders of the animal world are explored in depth on *Safari Tracks*, a syndicated series filmed in Africa and hosted by Ushaka (credited name).

Arizona

A listing of series set in and around Arizona.
1951. *Sky King* (CBS;).
1954. *Annie Oakley* (Syn.).
1955. *The Life and Legend of Wyatt Earp* (ABC).
1956. *Broken Arrow* (CBS); *The Sheriff of Cochise* (Syn.).
1957. *Tombstone Territory* (ABC); *U.S. Marshal* (Syn.).
1958. *Frontier Doctor* (Syn.); *26 Men* (Syn).
1959. *The Deputy* (NBC); *Johnny Ringo* (CBS).
1960. *The Brothers Brannigan* (Syn.).
1967. *The High Chaparral* (NBC); *Hondo* (ABC).
1971. *The New Dick Van Dyke Show* (CBS.); *Nichols* (NBC).
1976. *Alice* (CBS).
1981. *Bret Maverick* (NBC).
1988. *Coming of Age* (CBS).
1989. *Hey Dude* (NIK).
2002. *Greetings from Tucson* (WB).
2005. *Medium* (NBC).

Asian American Performers and Characters

While there are few programs that star Asian Americans, there are many that feature such actors in major supporting roles. This list reflects the American actors portraying Asians coupled with Asian programs broadcast from 1949–2005.
1949. Marvin Miller portrays Dr. Yat Fu, an amateur crime sleuth and owner of a curio shop

in San Francisco on ABC's *Mysteries of China-town*. Gloria Saunders portrays his daughter and assistant, Ah Toy.

1950. The evil Chinese physician Dr. Fu Manchu (John Carradine) sets out to destroy mankind on the NBC pilot *The Adventures of Fu Manchu*. In 1956 the syndicated series, *Dr. Fu Manchu*, featured Glenn Gordon as the evil physician who tries to provoke tensions between East and West.

1951. The sultry Anna May Wong becomes the first Asian to actually star in a program about an Asian on DuMont's *The Gallery of Mme. Liu Tsong*. The program, later called simply *Mme. Liu Tsong*, first told of Liu Tsong as an art gallery proprietor, then as an exporter battling evildoers.

1952. Lai Choi San (Gloria Saunders), alias the Dragon Lady, and her band of pirates wreck havoc in the Orient on the syndicated *Terry and the Pirates*.

1957. Swinging bachelor Bentley Gregg and his orphaned niece Kelly are cared for by Peter Tong (Sammee Tong), the resourceful housekeeper on *Bachelor Father* (CBS/NBC/ABC). Paladin, the man with the fast gun for hire on CBS's *Have Gun—Will Travel* finds his leisure time at the Carlton Hotel a bit more comfortable being cared for by Hey Boy (Kam Tong). Lisa Lu, as Hey Girl, appeared often. The courteous, shrewd and philosophical Chinese detective Charlie Chan came to TV for the first time with J. Carrol Naish as the lead in *The New Adventures of Charlie Chan* (Syn.). James Hong played his son and assistant, Barry Chan.

1959. Ponderosa ranch cook Hop Sing (Victor Sen Yung) finds that his meals are thoroughly enjoyed by the Cartwrights, especially Hoss, on NBC's *Bonanza*.

1960. ABC's *Hong Kong* presents Mai Tai Sing as Ching Mei, the sultry waitress at the Golden Dragon Café; Harold Fong as Ahting, houseboy to Glenn Evans, foreign correspondent for World Wide News; and Gerald Jann as Mr. Ling, an assistant police inspector. Daria Massey plays Naja, a 20-year-old Balinese dancer at the American Bar on ABC's *The Islanders*. In syndication, Yuki Shimoda plays Aki, houseboy to *Johnny Midnight*, an actor turned detective. On CBS it is learned that the elderly Po Chang (Philip Ahn) was responsible for raising an orphaned boy who would one day become a financial wizard named *Mr.*

Garland. Kam Tong plays Po's natural son, Kam Chang, the owner of a curio shop in San Francisco.

1963. Fuji Kobiaji (Yoshio Yoda) is a captured, unreported prisoner of World War II who enjoys the easy life as the cook for Quinton McHale and his crew on ABC's *McHale's Navy*.

1964. Ten-year-old orphan Dwight Eisenhower Wong (Ricky Der) finds a home with ranch owner *Kentucky Jones* (NBC). Also featured are Cherylene Lee and Keye Luke. Sammee Tong is Sammy Ling, the manager of the Newport Arms Hotel on *Mickey* (ABC). A homeless sister and brother (Cherylene Lee, Douglas Moe) find a home with U.S. Army entertainer Mike Parker on the CBS pilot *Papa G.I.* Jack Soo is Rocky Sin, the valet to playboy Valentine Farrow on ABC's *Valentine's Day*.

1966. He poses as the houseboy to Britt Reid, publisher of the *Daily Sentinel*. In reality Kato (Bruce Lee) is the masked assistant to Britt's crime fighting alter ego, *The Green Hornet* (ABC). Hikaru Sulu (George Takei) is the helm officer under James T. Kirk, captain of the starship *U.S.S. Enterprise* on NBC's *Star Trek*.

1968. Wo Fat, the clever nemesis of Detective Steve McGarrett, is played by Khigh Dhiegh on *Hawaii Five-0* (CBS).

1969. Miyoshi Umeki becomes Mrs. Livingston, housekeeper to Tom Corbett and his son Eddie on ABC's *The Courtship of Eddie's Father*.

1971. Yul Brynner plays the King of Siam and Samantha Eggar is Anna Owens, the American teacher who instructs his children on *Anna and the King* (CBS). Keye Luke plays Prince Kralahome; Lisa Lu is Lady Thiang; and Rosalind Chao is Princess Serena. Bruce Lee appears as Li Tsung, martial arts instructor to Michael Longstreet, the blind insurance investigator on ABC's *Longstreet*.

1972. Kwai Chang Caine (David Carradine) is a Shaolin priest who wanders across the American frontier of the 1870s on ABC's *Kung Fu*. Keye Luke and Philip Ahn appear in flashback sequences as Master Po and Master Kan, Caine's teachers at a temple in China.

1973. Carey Wong plays Steve, one of the adopted children of ethnic backgrounds on the ABC pilot *Kelly's Kids*.

1974. Sergeant Nick Yemana (Jack Soo) signs on for duty at Manhattan's 12th police precinct on ABC's *Barney Miller*. Arnold Takahashi (Pat

Morita) finds himself enjoying the company of the kids who hang out at his hamburger joint, Arnold's Drive-In on ABC's *Happy Days*. Khigh Dhiegh plays Judge Dee, a seventh century Chinese magistrate turned detective on the ABC pilot *Judge Dee in the Monastery Murders*.

1975. Khigh Dhiegh takes on the role of Detective Khan (but refuses screen credit) on CBS's *Khan!* Irene Yah-Ling Sun plays his daughter, Anna Khan, and Evan Kim his son, Kim Khan.

1976. Evan Kim plays Shimokawa, a recruit at the San Diego Naval Training center on NBC's *C.P.O. Sharkey*. Student criminologist Lester Hodges (Les Lannom) finds help in solving crimes from his college mentor, Dr. Fong (Keye Luke) on the ABC pilot *Lester and Dr. Fong*. Pat Morita is Taro Takahashi, the American branch head of Moyati Industries who finds his life complicated by the antics of Tina Kelly (Susan Blanchard), the nanny who cares for his children Sachi and Aki (June Angela, Gene Profanata) on ABC's *Mr. T and Tina*. Dr. Sam Fugiyama (Robert Ito) finds that, like his mentor Dr. Quincy, detective work is a part of his job as a medical examiner on NBC's *Quincy, M.E.*

1977. The character of Arnold Takahashi (Pat Morita) travels from 1950s Milwaukee (*Happy Days*) to 1977 Las Vegas as the owner of a coffee shop on ABC's *Blansky's Beauties*.

1979. Ross Martin becomes the famous Oriental sleuth Charlie Chan on the ABC pilot *The Return of Charlie Chan* with Virginia Ann Lee and Rocky Gunn as his children Doreen and Peter Chan. T.K. Yu (Johnny Yune) is a Korean police sergeant assigned to study crime detection methods with the L.A.P.D. on the NBC pilot *Sergeant T.K. Yu.*

1980. Japan's top-rated singers, Mie and Kei, better known as Pink Lady, star with American comic Jeff Altman on NBC's *Pink Lady*. A realistic look at feudal Japan is seen through the eyes of shipwrecked Dutch navigator John Blackthorne (Richard Chamberlain) on *Shogun*, a 12-hour NBC miniseries that also stars Toshiro Mifune, Yoko Shimada and Frankie Sakai. The comical problems of a mixed marriage are seen when an American girl named Cindy (Judith-Marie Bergan) marries Korean comic Johnny Quan (Johnny Yune) on the NBC pilot *The Son-in-Law.*

1982. The romance between an American tourist, Susan (Diana Canova), and the Chinese musician, Tony (Teneyck Swackhamer) she meets while visiting Peking becomes the plot of the syndicated special *Peking Encounter*.

1983. Rosalind Chao becomes the wife of former *M*A*S*H* regular Maxwell Klinger (Jamie Farr) on CBS's *AfterMASH*.

1984. Major Taro Oshira (Mako) oversees the criminal investigation unit of the Hawaiian Police Department on ABC's *Hawaiian Heat*. Mac Robinson (Charles Robinson), an African American court clerk, and Quan Le Duc (Denice Kumagai), a Vietnamese girl, marry and attempt to make a new life together on *Night Court* (NBC).

1985. Pat Morita plays Kenji Sato, a bitter and disillusioned Japanese-American on the syndicated special *Blind Alleys*. After a three-year absence Kenji returns to his American wife, Fran (Cloris Leachman) to attend the wedding of his daughter, Amy (June Angela) only to discover that his prejudice has hindered his life.

1986. Police detective Jake Rizzo (Gil Gerard) becomes the guardian of Ernie (Ernie Reyes, Jr.), a ten-year-old karate master on ABC's *Sidekicks*. Sam (Ke Hu Quan) is the adopted Oriental child of David and Lori Randall on CBS's *Together We Stand* (revised as *Nothing Is Easy* in 1987).

1987. Japanese foreman Kazuhiro (Gedde Watanabe) oversees the American branch of Assan motors of Japan on ABC's *Gung Ho*. Pat Morita returns to TV as Lieutenant Ohara, a compassionate L.A.P.D. detective who solves crimes through mental abilities on ABC's *Ohara*.

1988. Ken Hakuta explores items that become overnight sensations on *Dr. Fad* (CBS). Kimiko Fannuchi (Maggie Han) is a beautiful Eurasian model whose claim to fame is the calendar girl for Morgan Power Tools. She is also the love interest for insurance investigator Patrick Murphy on ABC's *Murphy's Law*.

1990. John Henderson (Jason Scott Lee), a Korean teenager adopted as an infant by an American couple, struggles with his cultural identity on the CBS special, *American Eyes*.

1991. Tamayo Otuski plays Elaine Yamagami, the mother of a young daughter named Nikki (Kristi Murakami), who works as the assistant principal of Pomahac Elementary School on ABC's *Davis Rules*. Ty Nuygen (Keith Cooke), the son of an American father and Vietnamese mother, embarks on a *Noble Quest* (ABC pilot) to find his missing father. Lauren Tom plays Judy

Song, a liaison to San Francisco politician Philip Harte on the CBS pilot *Our Song*. Also on CBS, *Teech* features Maggie Han as Cassie Lee, the assistant headmaster at the Winthrop Academy Boarding School.

1992. Super Dave Osborne (Bob Einstein), the world's most incompetent stuntman, receives help in potential stunts that will kill him from Fuji Akido (Art Irizawa) on Fox's *Super Dave*.

1993. Maggie Han plays Cookie, a gorgeous Eurasian girl who helps amateur detective and used record shop owner Dave Brodsky solve crimes on NBC's *Black Tie Affair*.

1994. Margaret Cho is Margaret Kim, the daughter of strict Korean parents who lives in San Francisco, works as a cosmetics counter salesgirl and tempts fate by dating American boys on ABC's *All American Girl*. Samantha Woo (Jennie Kwan) is a foreign high school girl from Hong Kong who finds life a challenge when she becomes a member of NBC's *California Dreams*, a soft rock band.

1995. Lauren Tom is Kim, a sassy manicurist at a beauty salon called *The Chatterbox* (CBS pilot). HBO's *Arliss* presents Sandra Oh as Rita Wu, the girl Friday at Arliss Michaels Management. Ming-Na Wen plays Trudy Sloan, the childhood friend of hopeful writer Jonathan Eliot on NBC's *The Single Guy*.

1998. Ling Woo (Lucy Liu) becomes a ruthless lawyer with the firm of Cage and Fish on Fox's *Ally McBeal*. Sammo Hung plays Sammo Law, a detective with the L.A.P.D. who uses martial arts as his weapon on CBS's *Martial Law*. Sue Blake (Michelle Krusiec) is the adopted Oriental daughter of Karen and Dave Blake, a 16-year-old South Beach High School girl who dreams of becoming a member of the Women's Olympic Soccer Team on NBC's *One World*.

2000. Laine Kim (Keiko Agena), a Korean girl raised by a strict mother, tries to break her family tradition and enjoy life like her American girlfriend, Rory Gilmore on the WB's *Gilmore Girls*.

2001. A beautiful Japanese girl named Kami (Sung Hi Lee) is a warrior from a cult called Shurinji Kimpo. She battles evil with a ceremonial sword, "The Blade of the Samurai," on the syndicated pilot, *The Dragon*. Hoshi Sato (Linda Park) becomes an ensign and communications officer under Jonathan Archer, captain of the *U.S.S. Enterprise* on UPN's *Star Trek: Enterprise*.

2003. Lindsay Price is Jane, the Asian-American friend on NBC's *Coupling*. Christina Chang plays Sandy Chang, an assistant D.A. of Los Angeles County on *L.A. Dragnet* (ABC).

2004. *Joey*, the NBC spinoff from *Friends*, features Lucy Liu as Lauren Beck, Joey's producer on his TV series *Deep Powder*. Kim and Jim (Yunjin Kim, Daniel Dae Kim) are among the survivors of a devastating plane crash now struggling for survival on ABC's *Lost*.

2005. Sandra Oh plays Christina Yang, an intensely competitive intern at Seattle Grace Hospital on *Grey's Anatomy* (ABC). Ming-Nu plays Rachel Lu, a therapist and co-founder of the Family Option Fertility Clinic on NBC's *Inconceivable*. Brenda Song plays London, the beautiful, rich and spoiled daughter of the manager of the posh Tipton Hotel on *The Suite Life of Zack and Cody* (Disney Channel).

2006. Ivan Shaw is Adam Webster, the adopted son of a minister on *The Book of Daniel* (NBC). Smith Glo is Glitter, a book editor on *Emily's Reasons Why Not* (ABC). Brenda Song plays Wendy Wu, a high school girl who battles evil as a martial arts expert on *Wendy Wu: Homecoming Warrior* (Disney pilot).

Australia

A listing of series set in and around Australia.
1959. *The Flying Doctor* (Syn.).
1961. *Whiplash* (Syn.).
1968. *The Adventures of the Seaspray* (Syn.); *Hunter* (Syn.).
1969. *Skippy, the Bush Kangaroo* (Syn.).
1971. *Barrier Reef* (NBC).
1973. *The Evil Touch* (Syn.).
1978. *Woobinda—Animal Doctor* (Syn.).
1980. *Prisoner: Cell Block H* (Syn.).
1989. *Dolphin Cove* (CBS).
2003. *Pirate Islands* (Fox).
2005. *McLeod's Daughters* (WE).

Aviators see *Pilots*

Babies

A listing of programs that star or feature infants as an integral part of a family.

1952. *I Love Lucy* premieres on CBS and becomes the first series to deal with the issues of an expectant mother (the word pregnancy was taboo), childbirth and raising an infant. Lucille Ball was actually with child at the time and her pregnancy was written into the series. She and hubby Desi Arnaz (Lucy and Ricky Ricardo) became real life parents in 1953 and on TV, the birth of their son, Little Ricky, became an important aspect of the program (he was rarely neglected by the writers) and stayed with the series until it ended in 1957. The Mayer Twins, James John Gauzer, Richard Lee Simmons and Richard Keith played Little Ricky over the years. A five-minute syndicated program called *Oh, Baby!* aired with host Jack Barry talking to infants who respond via voice-over dubbing.

1960. Christopher Hapgood Day (David and Steven Born) is the infant son of Sally and Chris Day (Yvonne Lime, Ronnie Burns) on NBC's *Happy*. Sally and Chris run the Desert Palms Hotel in Palm Springs and Happy, as the infant is called, comments on adult activities via voice-over dubbing.

1966. Single pediatrician Peter Cooper (James Stacy) struggles to cope with young mothers and their infants on the ABC pilot *Baby Crazy*.

1967. ABC airs *The Baby Game*, wherein contestants must predict the reactions of infants to specific situations in order to win prizes. Richard Hayes hosts.

1979. Commercial artist and single mother Susan Winslow (Darleen Carr) struggles to readjust her life after the birth of her son Edmund on *Miss Winslow and Son* (CBS).

1987. Mary Kate and Ashley Olsen play a single role — Michelle Tanner, the baby of the Tanner family on ABC's *Full House*.

1988. High powered executive J.C. Wiatt (Kate Jackson) struggles to rearrange her life and care for Elizabeth (Michelle and Kristina Kennedy), the infant she inherited from a distant cousin, on NBC's *Baby Boom*. Career-oriented couple George and Sally Collier (Lawrence Pressman, Jane Galloway) adapt to life as the parents of an infant girl named Abigail (Abigail and Emily Simpson) on the CBS pilot *Baby on Board*.

1990. Quietly observing life while sucking on her pacifier can best describe Baby Maggie, the animated, forever infant of Homer and Marge Simpson on Fox's *The Simpsons*.

1991. Single mother Maggie Campbell (Julia

Duffy, Mary Page Keller) finds life a challenge trying to raise her son Mickey on ABC's *Baby Talk*. Mickey's thoughts (voice of Tony Danza) are heard as he comments on life. Baby Sinclair (voice of Kevin Clash) is a mischievous infant dinosaur (electronic puppet) whose motto "I'm the baby, gotta love me," excuses him from all the trouble he causes on ABC's *Dinosaurs*. Baby's parents are Earl and Fran; Charlene and Robbie are his older siblings.

1996. Electronic puppet Bobut is the bug-eyed, fish-faced son of a beautiful alien mother (Cookie) who believes he is the center of the universe on ABC's *Aliens in the Family*.

2003. Six-month-old Bob, the son of Walter and Liz Spencer (Adam Arkin, Jocly Fisher) finds he can talk (voice of Ken Campbell) but must keep his ability amongst his family on CBS's *Baby Bob*.

Ballet

The following list comprises stand-alone ballet performances that have been broadcast from 1945 to 2005. Excerpts of ballet productions, such as those broadcast on *Omnibus* and *Great Performances*, are not included.

1945. CBS presents *Folksay*, an adaptation of the modern ballet by Sophie Maslon that explores the simple folk music and humor of America's remote regions. William Bales, Jane Dudley and Pearl Primus performed. Balladeers Woody Guthrie and Tony Kruber provided commentary. Dancer-choreographer Leonide Massine of the Ballet Theater stages *Massine's Ballet* for NBC. Katharine Lee, Ivan Kirov, Anne Istomin and Serge Ismailoff perform. The Nayla Dancers perform the Rimsky-Korsakov ballet *Scheherazade* that is danced to recordings by the Cleveland Symphony Orchestra.

1946. Three short ballet sequences built around the theme of "Young Love on a Park Bench" is presented on *Choreotones* (CBS). Pauline Koner, Joseph Hahn and Betty Lind perform. A second presentation of *Choreotones* presented tunes from the Broadway musical *Showboat* set to ballet music to tell the story of the Mississippi. Bambi Linn and Robert Pagent play the young couple in love.

1948. Shakespeare's story of ill-fated lovers Romeo and Juliet (Douglas Moppert, Eleanor

Chapin) is adapted to a ballet performance by NBC on *Romeo and Juliet*.

1954. Two mini ballets are presented by NBC on *Sunday in Town*. Janet Reed and Jacques D'Amboise star in "The Filing Station" (about one day's incidents at a gas station); Judy Holliday is a waitress who dreams of joining a ballet troupe on the second story, "The Waitress."

1955. The Sadler Wells Ballet Company of England (now called The Royal Ballet) performs the story of *Sleeping Beauty* on NBC. David Wayne (as Harlequin) narrates the story of a beautiful princess (Margot Fonteyn) who is put under a spell by a wicked fairy (Frederick Ashton). Michael Somes plays the prince whose kiss awakens Sleeping Beauty.

1957. The Royal Ballet of Great Britain performs the story of *Cinderella* (NBC). Margot Fonteyn plays Cinderella, the belittled girl whose dream to become beautiful and attend a lavish ball is granted by her fairy godmother (Julia Farrow).

1958. A young girl's journey through a fantasy world of fairies, toy soldiers and an army of mice is the basis of *The Nutcracker*, which was adapted to television in six ballet performances: *1958:* Margot Fonteyn (Sugar Plum Fairy), Michael Soames (Nutcracker); *1965:* Melissa Hayden (Sugar Plum Fairy), Edward Villella (Nutcracker); *1977:* Mikhail Baryshnikov (Nutcracker), Gesley Kirkland (Sugar Plum Fairy); *1985:* Lesley Collier (Sugar Plum Fairy), Anthony Dowell (Nutcracker); *1995:* Peggy Fleming (Sugar Plum Fairy), Todd Eldridge (Nutcracker); *1998:* Alina Cojocaru (Girl); Miyako Yoshida (Sugar Plum Fairy), Ivan Putrov (Nutcracker).

1972. A young Scottish nobleman's (Michael Denard) love for a captured woodland sprite (Ghislaine Thesmar) is the basis of *La Sylphide* (PBS).

1976. Louisa May Alcott's *Little Women* is presented as a ballet by NBC. Anna Aragno (Meg), Susan Hendl (Jo), Susan Pilarre (Beth) and Judith Fugate (Amy) play the March sisters.

1980. *Baryshnikov on Broadway* (ABC) features Russian-born ballet star Mikhail Baryshnikov performing to songs from the American Musical Theater.

1981. Leslie Collier is Cinderella and Anthony Dowell plays Prince Charming in a lavish production of *Cinderella* that was taped at the Royal Opera House in 1979 and first presented in America via syndication in 1981. Monica Mason plays the Fairy Godmother.

1982. Mikhail Baryshnikov returns to TV (CBS) for a ballet performance of the silent film *The Sheik* on *Baryshnikov in Hollywood*. Bernadette Peters plays the harem maiden he rescues.

1983. CBS airs *Dorothy Hamill in Romeo and Juliet on Ice*. The ice skating star plays Juliet with Brian Pocker as her ill-fated lover, Romeo, in an elaborate ice ballet.

1987. PBS presents *Sleeping Beauty* as an ice ballet based on Charles Perrault's classic fairy tale about a handsome prince (Robin Cousins) who awakens Sleeping Beauty (Rosalynn Summers) with a kiss.

1998. Tchaikovsky's classic fantasy, *Swan Lake* (PBS) comes to life with Adam Cooper as the Swan and Fiona Chadwick as the Queen.

2000. Suitors seeking the coveted hand of wealthy widow Anna Glawari (Yvonne Kenny) is the basis of *The Merry Widow* (PBS) by Franz Lehar.

2001. Cervantes classic tale about the great lover Don Quixote comes to life on the PBS production of *Don Quixote* with Rudolf Nureyev as Don Quixote and Lucette Aldous as Kitri.

2005. The classic ballet, *Swan Lake,* is presented by PBS with Gillian Murphy as the Snow Queen and Angelo Corellara as her suitor, Prince Siegfried.

Baltimore

A listing of series set in Baltimore, Maryland.
1975. *Hot l Baltimore* (ABC).
1986. *The Ellen Burstyn Show* (ABC).
1990. *True Colors* (Fox).
1991. *Flesh 'n' Blood* (NBC); *Roc* (Fox).
1993. *Homicide: Life on the Street* (NBC).
2000. *Thieves* (ABC).
2001. *One on One* (UPN).
2002. *The Wire* (HBO).

Bars

Bars, or local watering holes as they are also called, are a part of many series, mostly as a talked about place to go or seen infrequently. This listing concerns itself with those programs on which a bar (or bar-café) is a regular part (or even "the star") of a program. See also *Restaurants*.

1945. Louie's Bar became the hangout to World War II servicemen stationed in Europe on the NBC experiment *Beachhead at Louie's*. Crusading newspaper crime photographer Casey (Oliver Thorndike) finds relaxation at the Blue Note Café on the NBC pilot *Diary of Death*.

1951. When John Bickerson (Lew Parker) needs to cool down after his daily argument with wife Blanche (Virginia Grey) he finds solace at Murphy's Bar and Grill on *The Bickersons* (Syn.). The Blue Note Café provides a place of refuge for Casey (Richard Carlyle, Darren McGavin), a crusading newspaper photographer on CBS's *Crime Photographer*.

1954. The free lunch costs 15 cents with a beer. The owner is never seen; a confidence man named Archie (Ed Gardner) runs the bar. This bar, on Third Avenue in New York is *Duffy's Tavern* (NBC).

1955. Rick Blaine (Charles McGraw) retreats to *Casablanca* (ABC) to open a bar called Rick's Café Americain. The Long Branch Saloon, operated by Kitty Russell (Amanda Blake), provides refreshment for Matt Dillon (James Arness), the Marshal of Dodge City on *Gunsmoke* (CBS).

1957. Criminal attorney Perry Mason (Raymond Burr) takes time off from defending clients to enjoy a meal at McQuade's Bar and Grill. Old West newspaper editor Harris Clayton (Richard Eastman) enjoys a drink at the Crystal Palace on ABC's *Tombstone Territory*.

1958. Dan Troop (John Russell), Marshal of Laramie, Wyoming, enjoys a drink at the Birdcage Saloon on ABC's *Lawman*. The Last Chance Saloon provides a drink for thirsty travelers on ABC's *The Rifleman*.

1959. Lupo's, a speakeasy at 14 Cherry Street in Kansas City, is where Pete Kelly (William Reynolds) and his band, The Big Seven, earn a living on NBC's *Pete Kelly's Blues*.

1960. Foreign correspondent Glenn Evans (Rod Taylor) talks more than he drinks at Tully's Bar on ABC's *Hong Kong*. Shipwreck Callahan's American Bar is the watering hole for the regulars on ABC's *The Islanders*. Newspaper reporters for the *Daily Record* enjoy a drink at the neighboring bar (first called Chauncey's then The Pit) on ABC's *The Roaring 20s*.

1962. The character of Joe the Bartender (Jackie Gleason) and his conversations with Crazy Guggenheim (Frank Fontaine) become a featured skit on *Jackie Gleason and His American Scene Magazine* (CBS).

1970. In addition to the bottle of booze he keeps in his office desk drawer, the Happy Hour Bar provides that extra nip Lou Grant (Ed Asner) needs to cope with his staff at WJM-TV on *The Mary Tyler Moore Show* (CBS).

1971. The bigoted Archie Bunker (Carroll O'-Connor) enjoys a beer at Kelsey's Bar on CBS's *All in the Family*. Several years later he purchases Kelsey's and turns it into a bar he (and CBS) call *Archie Bunker's Place*. The Slater House Bar in Nichols, Arizona, is the hangout for the regulars on NBC's *Nichols*.

1972. Harry Grant (Gabriel Dell) owns Grant's Toomb, a bar on Amsterdam Avenue in New York City on ABC's *The Corner Bar*. The battle-weary doctors and nurses of CBS's *M*A*S*H* find a break from the Korean War at Rosie's Bar.

1973. ABC's *The Corner Bar* returns with Mae and Frank (Anne Meara, Eugene Roche) as the co-owners of a bar that is now called The Corner Bar.

1975. Ginny Wroblinki (Mary Louise Wilson) is the sexy waitress at the Alibi Room Bar on CBS's *One Day at a Time*.

1976. Medical examiner Quincy (Jack Klugman) takes a break from his duties at Danny's Place, a bar-restaurant on NBC's *Quincy, M.E.*

1977. The Capri Lounge, a bar in Fernwood, Ohio, provides a gathering place for the auto plant workers on the syndicated *Mary Hartman, Mary Hartman*. The Regal Beagle, a British-styled pub, becomes the gathering place for the regulars on ABC's *Three's Company*.

1978. The spaced-out Jim Ignatowski (Christopher Lloyd) enjoys the company of friends at Mario's (a bar) so much that he purchases it and renames it Jim's Mario's on *Taxi* (ABC/NBC).

1979. Retired boxer turned private detective Duke Ramsey (Robert Conrad) is also part owner of the Chicago bar Duke and Benny's Corner on *The Duke* (NBC). Gorgeous waitress Daisy Duke (Catherine Bach) draws customers to the Boar's Nest Bar on CBS's *The Dukes of Hazzard*.

1980. Florence Jean Castleberry (Polly Holliday) leaves her job as a waitress at Mel's Diner (CBS's *Alice*) to open her own bar, Flo's Golden Rose on CBS's *Flo*. The King Kamehameha Club in Hawaii becomes a place of refuge for harried private detective Thomas Magnum (Tom Selleck) on *Magnum, P.I.* (CBS). East Pittsburgh steel workers find relaxation at the Fat Lady's Bar on NBC's *Skag.*

1981. Bret Maverick (James Garner) is the owner of the Red Ox Saloon in Sweetwater, Arizona, on *Bret Maverick* (NBC). Bounty hunter Colt Seavers (Lee Majors) relaxes (when he can) at the Palomino Club on ABC's *The Fall Guy.* Stewart Lewis (Gabriel Kaplan) and Roscoe Clark (David Hollander) are partners in the Nassau County Café, a bar in Texas on NBC's *Lewis and Clark.*

1982. Sam Malone (Ted Danson) runs *Cheers* (NBC), the Boston bar "where everybody knows your name." A swinging singles bar in Cleveland, Ohio, is the gathering place for an exchange of conversation on the CBS pilot *I'd Rather be Calm.* While mentioned often (but rarely seen), the Bigger Jigger is the bar Vinton Harper (Ken Berry) frequents on NBC's *Mama's Family.* Cargo plane pilot Jake Cutler (Stephen Collins) frequents the Monkey Bar on the South Pacific Island of Bora Gora on *Tales of the Gold Monkey* (ABC).

1983. Rick Blaine (David Soul) returns to run Rick's Café Americain on a new version of *Casablanca* (NBC; see also 1955). New Orleans-based detective Johnny Blue (Gil Gerard) runs Johnny Blue's, a bar-restaurant on the CBS pilot *Johnny Blue.*

1984. Hard-boiled detective Mike Hammer (Stacy Keach) enjoys a drink at the Lite 'n' Easy Bar on CBS's *Mike Hammer.* Racecar driver Brewster Baker (Don Johnson) frequents The Pitstop Bar on the NBC pilot *Six Pack.* The Pleez All Tavern is a place of refuge for magazine editor Maggie Briggs on CBS's *Suzanne Pleshette Is Maggie Briggs.*

1985. The pressures of the medical profession prompt OR Nurse Kaye Brenner (Kelly Bishop) and intern Steve Griffon (Mark-Linn Baker) to open Kaye and Steve's Recovery Room, a bar, on the CBS pilot *The Recovery Room.*

1987. The students at Hillman College in Georgia relax for an occasional drink at the campus pub, The Pit, on NBC's *A Different World.* Dixie's Bar in Costa Del Mar, California, is the favorite watering hole of D.A. J.L. McCabe (William Conrad) on CBS's *Jake and the Fatman.* College professor Frank Parrish (Tim Reid) inherits and struggles to run the Chez Louisianne, a Creole bar-restaurant in New Orleans on *Frank's Place* (CBS). The Jiggly Room of the Nudie Bar

is the only refuge Al Bundy (Ed O'Neill) has from life on Fox's *Married ... With Children.*

1988. An after hours New York bar called Lulu's becomes the gathering place for a group of people each week on the CBS pilot *After Midnight.* Jonelle Allen plays Lulu, the bar owner. The regulars on NBC's *Dear John* frequent Clancy's Bar after a meeting of their singles club. Ex-cop turned radio personality Jack Killian (Gary Cole) hosts the call-in show *Midnight Caller* (NBC) and enjoys a drink at Carmen's Bar. Phil's Bar (which also serves food) is the second home to Murphy Brown (Candice Bergen) and her fellow TV reporters on CBS's *Murphy Brown.* Siobhan (Eileen Brennan), a cop's widow, opens the bar Off Duty to cater to the men and women in blue on the CBS pilot *Off Duty.* Roseanne Conner works for a short time as a bartender at the Lobo Lounge before opening her own luncheonette on ABC's *Roseanne.*

1989. The Touchdown Club (bar and grill) is the hangout of college football coach Hayden Fox (Craig T. Nelson) on ABC's *Coach.* Dr. Mike Stratton (Matt Frewer) finds Johnny's Bar and Grill a place of refuge on CBS's *Doctor, Doctor.* FBI agent Nick Mancuso (Robert Loggia) finds time for a drink or two at Gertie's Bar on *Mancuso, FBI* (NBC). The doctors and nurses of 13 East Hospital find relaxation at Jake's Pub on NBC's *13 East.* Ex-CIA agent Charlie Gordon (Beau Bridges) retreats to the south of France to open a bar called Charlie's on the ABC pilot *Three of a Kind.*

1990. Frankie Fanelli (Christopher Meloni), one of NBC's *The Fanelli Boys,* works as a bartender at Caggiano's Bar. The Brick Bar in Cicely, Alaska, provides a form of relaxation to the regulars on CBS's *Northern Exposure.* The animated Homer Simpson overindulges on beer at Moe's Tavern on *The Simpsons* (Fox). Gorgeous private eye Sydney Kells (Valerie Bertinelli) enjoys a drink and conversation at the Blue Collar Bar on CBS's *Sydney.* While waiting for a flight at Sandpiper Air in Nantucket, passengers can enjoy a drink at the nearby King Arthur's Bar and Grill on NBC's *Wings.*

1991. The Meteor Tiki Lounge is the watering hole of Earl Sinclair, a dinosaur struggling to raise a family on ABC's *Dinosaurs.* Pilot Sally Monroe (Shannon Tweed) relaxes between flights at the Bomber's Bar on *Fly by Night* (CBS). Magazine fact checker Herman Brooks (William Ragsdale) frequents McNally's Pub after a day's work on *Herman's Head* (Fox). Nick Williams (Ray Aranha), one of ABC's *Married People*, hangs out at Morry's Pool Hall in Harlem. Kay Lochman (Nancy Everhard) owns the Setup Bar, the watering hole for the regulars on *Reasonable Doubts* (NBC). Sanitation engineer Roc Emerson (Charles S. Dutton) enjoys a drink at Charlene's Bar on *Roc* (Fox). Chicago police sergeant Adam Beaudreaux (Carl Weathers) and a mysterious woman named Molloy (Charlene Fernetz) are partners in Molloy's Bar on the syndicated *Street Justice*. The Tropical Heat Bar on Key Mariah in Florida is run by former rock star Ian Stewart (David Bland) on *Sweating Bullets* (Syn.). C.D.'s Bar and Grill is the favorite hangout for Cordell Walker (Chuck Norris) and his co-workers on CBS's *Walker, Texas Ranger*.

1992. The Roll Call is the local bar for the detectives attached to the Homicide Division of the Violent Crimes Unit of the Chicago Police Department on CBS's *Angel Street*. Bonnie Kennedy (Bonnie Hunt) and her friends frequent the Firescape Bar in Chicago on *The Building* (CBS). The bodyguards of the all female Personal Touch in Dallas, Texas, enjoy an after work drink at the Blue Cat Blues Bar on *Dangerous Curves* (CBS). Delta Bishop (Delta Burke) is a hopeful singer working as a waitress at the Green Lantern, a country bar on ABC's *Delta*. Former jazz musician Jack Evans (Hal Linden) owns Jack's Bar and Restaurant (famous for its chocolate fudge cake) on *Jack's Place* (ABC). World famous chef Wally Porter (Susan Dey) struggles to keep the Blue Shamrock Bar afloat on *Love and War* (CBS). Riff 'o Bar is the getaway for Jamie and Paul Buchman (Helen Hunt, Paul Reiser) on NBC's *Mad About You*. The regulars on Fox's *Melrose Place* find drink and conversation at Upstairs, a jazz club. Big Kahuna's Bar in Hawaii is home to Ski Jablonski (Lee Majors), a hard-drinking security analyst on *Raven* (CBS). In pre-Revolutionary Philadelphia, the Procter family runs the Cock and Doberman, a bar on the CBS pilot *1775*.

1993. McGinty's Bar is the occasional watering hole for the regulars on NBC's *Frasier*. The Rain Check is the bar in the bus terminal in St. Louis, Missouri on NBC's *The John Larroquette Show*. Seamus O'Neill (Fisher Stevens) is the man who lives in Key West, hopes to follow in Hemingway's footsteps and has a drink at Gumbo's Bar

and Grill on *Key West* (Fox). Jamaica's Bar is the hangout for the regulars on Fox's *The Sinbad Show*.

1994. Nasty New York cabbie George O'Grady (George Carlin) finds refreshment and talk at the Molin Tavern on *The George Carlin Show* (Fox). Natalie's Bar in Harlem is the hangout for the police officers on Fox's *New York Undercover*. The Scuttlebutt Bar and Grill on Paradise Beach in Florida is owned by Kelly LaRue (Carol Alt) on the syndicated *Thunder in Paradise*.

1996. The Steinway Pub is the favorite hangout of former airport baggage handler Hilton Lucas (Bill Cosby) on *Cosby* (CBS). Gary Hobson (Kyle Chandler), the man who gets tomorrow's newspaper today, runs McGinty's Bar in Chicago on CBS's *Early Edition*. It started out as Kelly's Pub, the hangout of Malcolm McGee (Malcolm-Jamal Warner) on UPN's *Malcolm and Eddie*. Malcolm later purchases it and renames it Malcolm McGee's Sports Bar. When it fails, it becomes a jazz club called The Fifty/Fifty Club. The Mayor of New York and his staff frequent The Landmark Tavern on ABC's *Spin City*. Glamorous San Francisco magazine columnist Susan Keane (Brooke Shields) finds relief from the pressures of work at Bucky's Tavern (later called O'Malley's Bar then Murphy's Bar) on NBC's *Suddenly Susan*.

1997. Private investigator Anthony Dellaventura (Danny Aiello) is a man who likes a happy ending to all his cases and a good beer at the Knickerbocker Bar and Grill on CBS's *Dellaventura*. Miami's Banana Bar is the favorite watering hole of the regulars on UPN's *Head Over Heels*. The Tailwind, a military bar, caters to the pilots and personnel of the Sea Dragons squadron on the syndicated *Pensacola: Wings of Gold* (the bar is later called Kate's; sometimes Kate's Bucket).

1998. A bar called House of Jugs (referring to bottles of beer, not a girl's breasts) is the hangout for soldiers on the WB's *The Army Show*. The Quake (named so after it was damaged by an earthquake) is a San Francisco bar owned by Piper Halliwell (Holly Marie Combs), a good witch on the WB's *Charmed*. Piper later opens a bar nightclub called P-3. Jesse Warner (Christina Applegate) is a young divorcee struggling to become a nurse while working at the family pub, Der Biergarten, on NBC's *Jesse*. Vallery Irons (Pamela Anderson) and her employees at Vallery Irons Protection enjoy a drink at a bar called Foam on *V.I.P.* (Syn.).

1999. Before the Bar is the hangout of Norm (Norm McDonald), a frustrated social worker on ABC's *Norm*. The men and women of the WB's *Rescue 77* find the Fireman's Bar a place to unwind after a grueling days work.

2000. The teachers at Winslow High School find Doyle's Pub a relaxing bar to visit on Fox's *Boston Public*. Washington, D.C. Police Chief Jack Mannion (Craig T. Nelson) enjoys a drink at a bar called Teddy R's on *The District* (CBS). The Drunken Pig is the bar frequented by Jack Stiles (Bruce Campbell), a hero who battles evil as the Daring Dragoon on *Jack of All Trades* (Syn.). The After Hours, a bar located opposite a cemetery in New Jersey, is the workplace of Lydia DeLucca (Heather Paige Kent) on *That's Life* (CBS).

2001. The medical staff attached to the spooky All Souls Hospital find The Salty Cod a place of refuge on UPN's *All Souls*. Hell's Kitchen, a bar with a tame reputation, is the hangout for the police officers of CBS's *Big Apple*. Crime fighter Helena Kyle, alias the Huntress (Ashley Scott), works as a bartender at the Dark Horse Bar in New Gotham City on *Birds of Prey* (WB). Professional speaker Bob Patterson (Jason Alexander) frequents a bar called The Tip Top Bar and Grill on ABC's *Bob Patterson*. Jordan Cavanaugh (Jill Hennessy) is a medical examiner that frequents but rarely has a drink at her father's bar, Cavanaugh's on *Crossing Jordan* (NBC). Retired fireman Pop Fitzgerald (Brian Dennehy) hangs out at Gibson's Tavern on *The Fighting Fitzgeralds* (NBC). A.J. Langer plays Annie Bernstein-Flynn, a bartender at the Canteen on Sunset Boulevard in Los Angeles on *Three Sisters* (NBC). Mel Porter (Amy Price-Francis) owns the Watchfire, a bar in the Chicago Criminal Courts District on *Tracker* (Syn.).

2002. George Lopez (himself), plant manager of Powers Brothers Aviation, enjoys a beer at Thirsty's Bar on *The George Lopez Show* (ABC). Sean Finnerty (Donal Logue) runs a bar called The Red Boot Pub on Staten Island in New York on *Grounded for Life* (WB). Ex-cop turned Philadelphia cab driver Mike Olshansky (David Morse) enjoys a drink at a bar called Bernie's Tap.

2003. The Z Lounge is the classy bar hangout for the regulars on UPN's *Eve*. Mace and Audrey O'Neill (Lenny Clarke, Harriet Sanson Harris) are a married couple that run O'Neill's, a bar on *It's All Relative* (ABC). Deputy Sheriff Rico Amonte (Danny Nucci) frequents Fontane's Bar in Los Angeles on *10-8: Officers on Duty* (ABC).

2004. Niagara Falls sales girl Jaye Tyler (Caroline Dhavernas) hangs out at a bar called The Barrel on *Wonderfalls* (Fox).

2005. Beginning with 2005 episodes, Joan Clayton (Tracee Ellis Ross) opens a trendy bar called The J Spot on UPN's *Girlfriends* (the series began in 2000). Rachel Nichols (Rebecca Locke), a profiler with the FBI in Los Angeles, frequents Dugan's Pub with her co-workers on *The Inside* (Fox).

2006. George Wendt is Tug Clark, the owner of The Tug House, a bar hangout, on *Modern Men* (WB).

Beaches and Islands

Whether man-made (*Gilligan's Island*) or real (*Survivor*) television has presented its fair share of programs set on beaches and islands. This listing comprises the programs where the water and sand are as much the star as the performers who inhabit them.

1945. NBC's experimental drama, *Victory*, follows incidents in the lives of a group of people who frequent a small hotel on an island in the Java Sea.

1957. It could be the waters off a popular beach or those off a remote island that underwater troubleshooter Mike Nelson (Lloyd Bridges) needs to do his job on the syndicated *Sea Hunt*.

1959. The various islands of the South Pacific provide adventure for Adam Troy (Gardner McKay), skipper of the schooner *Tiki* on ABC's *Adventures in Paradise*. The Hawaiian Islands first became a regular on TV with ABC's private detectives Tracy Steele (Anthony Eisley) and Tom Lopaka (Robert Conrad) on *Hawaiian Eye*.

1960. Drake Andrews and Larry Lahr (Keith Larsen, Jeremy Slate) are professional divers based in Hawaii on CBS's *The Aquanauts*. Ex-marine turned underwater troubleshooter Bill Greer (Bill Williams) hires out his experiences on the syndicated *Assignment: Underwater*. Ben Gregory and Paul Templin (Barry Coe, Brett Halsey) are freelance magazine writers based in Hawaii on ABC's *Follow the Sun*. Ambowina is a small island off the coast of Sumatra where Sandy Wade (William Reynolds) and Zack Malloy (James Philbrook) operate an airline on ABC's *The Islanders*. Three handsome bachelors who are also private detectives live on a houseboat moored on Indian Creek in Miami Beach, Florida, on ABC's *SurfSide 6*.

1961. When society gets the best of businessman John Lackland (Cameron Mitchell) he retreats to Amura, a small island in the South Pacific to become *The Beachcomber* (Syn.). Ron Hayes plays Lincoln Vail, law enforcement officer with the Everglades County Police Patrol in Florida on *The Everglades* (syndicated). Mike Madison (Ron Ely) and Larry Lahr (Jeremy Slate) are diving instructors based on Miami Beach in Florida on CBS's *Malibu Run*.

1962. *Chalk One Up for Johnny* (ABC) was the working title for a pilot about a dissatisfied politician named Johnny Pace (Lee Tracy) who retreats to the small island of Kauai in Hawaii to open a hotel. The South Pacific island of Taratupa during World War II provides the backdrop for a comical look at combat for Quinton McHale (Ernest Borgnine) and his crew on *McHale's Navy* (ABC).

1964. Charter boat captain Sam Bailey (Paul Ford) attempts to operate his decrepit vessel, *The Island Princess*, on Balboa Beach in California on *The Baileys of Balboa* (CBS). The male-dominated island of Ranakai is the setting for *Broadside* (ABC), a *McHale's Navy* spinoff about four WAVES, led by Lt. Anne Morgan (Kathleen Nolan) assigned to the motor pool. The waters surrounding Coral Key Park in Florida are home to *Flipper* (NBC), the dolphin who helps Ranger Porter Ricks (Brian Kelly) protect the preserve. Seven castaways stranded on an island in the South Pacific forms the basis of perhaps the most famous series ever to be set on an island on CBS's *Gilligan's Island*. Alan Hale, Jr. and Bob Denver head the cast as the Skipper and Gilligan. Three NBC updates also aired: *Rescue from Gilligan's Island* (1978), *The Castaways on Gilligan's Island* (1979) and *The Harlem Globetrotters on Gilligan's Island* (1981). A shipwrecked Englishman struggles for survival on a deserted island from which there is no escape on the syndicated *Robinson Crusoe*. Robert Hoffman stars.

1965. The beaches of Santa Monica, California, are the second home of teenager Frances Lawrence (Sally Field), better known as *Gidget* (ABC).

1966. Passengers en route to Mexico City from Florida become marooned on a deserted island when their plane develops engine trouble on the pilot *Stranded*. Richard Egan, Julie Adams and Peter Graves star.

1967. The top names in rock music perform on Malibu Beach in California, on ABC's *Malibu U*. Rick Nelson plays the dean of the mythical college. Eunice (Lori Martin) and Norm (Tony Dow) are two of the teenagers who flock to the beach on the ABC pilot *Weekend*.

1968. The schooner *Seaspray* roams the South Pacific islands as writer John Wells (Walter Brown) seeks story material on *The Adventures of the Seaspray* (Syn.). Bert and Claudia Gramus (Herb Edelman, Joyce Van Patten) run Bert's Place, a California beach eatery on CBS's *The Good Guys*. Detective Steve McGarrett (Jack Lord) keeps the peace as a member of the Hawaiian Police Department on CBS's *Hawaii Five-0*.

1969. Visits to various tropical islands via the sailing ship *Islanda* are narrated by Bill Burrud on the syndicated *Islands in the Sun*. Forty American college students are stranded on a remote island called Bormano when their plane crashes during a storm on ABC's *The New People*. The forbidding Caribbean island of Maljardan finds a beautiful young woman named Holly Marshall (Sylvia Feigel) battling sinister forces on the syndicated *Strange Paradise*.

1970. Three men plagued by life's endless problems pool their resources and head for Tahiti to purchase a hotel on the ABC pilot *Three for Tahiti*.

1972. Dr. Sean Jamison (Brian Keith) and his daughter Anne (Shelley Fabares) treat children at their clinic in Kahala, Hawaii, on NBC's *The Brian Keith Show* (originally called *The Little People*). Various tropical islands are visited with host Lloyd Bridges on the syndicated *Lloyd Bridges Water World*.

1973. The cave at Deadman's Point on Cypress Beach in California is home to Sigmund Ooz (Billy Barty), a sea monster unable to scare humans on NBC's *Sigmund and the Sea Monsters*.

1975. Martin Milner and Pat Delany are Karl and Lottie Robinson, the parents of a family shipwrecked on a deserted tropical island on ABC's *Swiss Family Robinson*. The various Hawaiian Islands are the setting as underwater photographer Steve Andrews (Van Williams) seeks material on *The Westwind* (NBC).

1976. A new version of *The Swiss Family Robinson* airs in syndication with Chris Wiggins and Diana Leblanc as Johann and Elizabeth Robinson, the parents of a family shipwrecked on a deserted island in the year 1881. Kevin Dobson, Lara

Parker and Marie Windsor are among the survivors stranded on a remote island after their plane crashes on the CBS pilot *Stranded*.

1977. John Dehner is Barrett Fears, the owner of the Paradise Ranch in Hawaii on NBC's *Big Hawaii*. California's San Pedro Beach is the setting for four young men who live on an old fishing boat called *Our Boat* on ABC's *The San Pedro Beach Bums*.

1978. The mysterious Mr. Roarke (Ricardo Montalban) grants dreams to people on *Fantasy Island* (ABC). Retired lawyer Gabe McQueen (Dennis Weaver) struggles to operate a hotel on the CBS pilot *The Islander*. Jeff and Barbara Wild (Chris Robinson, Julie Gregg) are animal behaviorists working in the wetlands of Western Florida along the Gulf of Mexico on the CBS pilot *The Wilds of Ten Thousand Islands*.

1979. Jan Plummer (Christine DeLisle) and Marty Green (Jonathan Frakes) are two of the members of the Beach Patrol Unit of the San Gabriel Police Department on the ABC pilot *The Beach Patrol*. Westside High School students Vince Butler (James Vincent McNichol) and Laurie (Michele Tobin) hangout together on California's Sunset Beach on *California Fever* (CBS). A reluctant sea-going fisherman named Cuda Weber (Clu Gulager) becomes the substitute uncle to the five-orphaned MacKenzie children on ABC's *The MacKenzie's of Paradise Cove*.

1980. Pearl Harbor in Hawaii just after the attack in 1941 is the setting for a look at the lives of the civilians and personnel on NBC's *From Here to Eternity*. Barbara Hershey and William Devane head the large cast. The work of oceanographer Dana Ryan (Jared Martin) off the coast of Hawaii is the focal point of the CBS pilot *M Station: Hawaii*. Tom Selleck stars as Thomas Magnum, a private detective based in Hawaii on CBS's *Magnum, P.I.* A mysterious woman named Madge (Janis Paige) makes romance happen on the NBC pilot *Valentine Magic on Love Island*. Reckless private detectives Ronnie Browning and David King (Dack Rambo, Steve Marachuk) help policewoman Cassie Howard (Donna Mills) of the Oahu, Hawaii, Police Department solve crimes on the CBS pilot *Waikiki*.

1981. Debbie Reynolds plays Sydney Chase, the manager of Paradise Village, a secluded resort for lovers in Hawaii on ABC's *Aloha Paradise*. A group of school children are marooned with several adults on a deserted island when their plane crashes into the ocean on the NBC pilot *Crash Island*. Gregg Mullavey and Meadowlark Lemon star.

1982. Ex-CIA agent Robert Gavilan (Robert Urich) works as a consultant for the DeWitt Oceanographic Institute on Malibu Beach in California on NBC's *Gavilan*. Jake Cutler (Stephen Collins) attempts to run a one-cargo plane business on the South Pacific island of Bora Gora on ABC's *Tales of the Gold Monkey*.

1984. Ex-Chicago police officers Mac Riley and Andy Senkowski (Robert Ginty, Jeff McCracken) now work as undercover officers for the Oahu Police Department on *Hawaiian Heat* (ABC). The activities of a group of spirited high school students who live in the ocean front community of Southern California is the focal point of the CBS pilot *Summer*.

1986. The lives of the people who vacation at the Club Med resort in Ixtapa, Mexico, was the premise of the ABC pilot *Club Med*. *The New Gidget* premieres in syndication with Caryn Richman as Gidget. She is now married (to Jeff) and works as a real estate agent. She still loves to hang out at the beach, this time with her teenage niece Danni (Sydney Penny). Mike Nelson (Ron Ely) returns to battle evil in a new, syndicated version of *Sea Hunt* (see 1957).

1987. Timothy, Joseph, Samuel and Benjamin Bottoms plays Tim, Joe, Sam and Ben Farraday, brothers struggling to operate the Farraday Cattle Ranch in Hawaii on the ABC pilot *Island Sons*.

1988. Peter Roman (Frank Langella) is a morally detestable millionaire who runs the Dr. Paradise Resort and Health Clinic on the remote Olympus Isle on the CBS pilot *Dr. Paradise*. A year after its premiere in 1987, CBS's *Jake and the Fatman* switched locales from California to Hawaii to focus on J.L. McCabe (William Conrad) as a prosecuting attorney for the Honolulu Police Department. The new format ran until 1990 (at which time it switched back to California).

1989. Mitch Buchannon (David Hasselhoff) and the beautiful lifeguards of Malibu Beach, California, are the focal point of *Baywatch* (NBC then syndicated). Alyssa Milano and Alan Hunter host the syndicated pilot *Malibu Beach Party* wherein teenagers dance to music on California's Malibu Beach. Jodi Lambert (Tasia Valenza) and Bob Bailey (Phill Lewis) are members of the Westside Police Department who also share Surf House, a beach residence in Santa Monica, California on the ABC pilot *Protect and Surf*. Caribbean-based government agents headed by Ben Bishop (Chad Everett) stop the flow of contraband into the U.S. on the ABC pilot *Thunder Boat Row*.

1990. Richard Chamberlain plays Dr. Daniel Kulani, staff physician at the Kamehameha Medical Center in Honolulu on CBS's *Island Son*.

1992. A beachside eatery on California's Pacific Coast called Sharkey's is the hangout for a group of high school students who are also members of a soft rock band on NBC's *California Dreams*. Heidi Noelle Lenhart and Kelly Packard head the cast. Six young people searching for sun and fun at the New Jersey Shore forms the basis for Fox's *Down the Shore*. Pamela Segall and Anna Gunn star as Miranda and Arden.

1993. Marshall Fisher and his wife Karen (Adam Arkin, Jane Kaczmarek) move from Chicago to Hawaii to open *Big Wave Dave's* (CBS), a surf shop.

1994. College professor Sam Byrd (Timothy Busfield) struggles to make a new life for his children in Hawaii after the death of his wife on ABC's *The Byrds of Paradise*. Incidents in the lives of the guests who vacation at the Hotel Malibu on Malibu Beach in California are the focal point of CBS's *Hotel Malibu*. Joanna Cassidy heads the cast as hotel owner Ellie Mayfield. The work of Dawn Holliday (Cheryl Ladd), a medical examiner for the Hawaiian Police Department, is the basis of CBS's *One West Waikiki*. Randolph Spencer (Hulk Hogan) and Martin Brubaker (Chris Lemmon) are friends who operate Thunder, a troubleshooting service off Paradise Beach in Florida on the syndicated *Thunder in Paradise*.

1995. Girls dressed in very revealing bikinis and dancing to music on various beaches forms the basis of *Caliente* (Spanish for *Hot*) on Univision. Bal Harbor in Florida provides the setting for an updated version of *Flipper* (see 1964) called *Flipper: The New Adventures* (PAX).

1996. Oahu, Hawaii-based private detective Jonathan Raven (Jeffrey Meek) finds his former training as a ninja beneficial to fighting evil on *Raven* (CBS).

1999. The California-based *Baywatch* moves to the North Shore to become *Baywatch Hawaii* (syndicated) with Mitch Buchannon (David Hasselhoff) establishing a lifeguard-training center.

2000. The FX cable channel premieres *Son of the Beach*, a spoof of *Baywatch* that stars Timothy Stack as Notch Johnson, an out-of-shape lifeguard who heads the SPF-30 female lifeguards on Malibu Adjacent Beach in California. The busty, in-shape lifeguards are B.J. Cummings (Jaime Bergman), Kimberlee Clark (Kim Oja) and Jamaica St. Croix (Leia Arcieri). Sixteen to twenty real life people are abandoned on some of the most god-forsaken islands on earth, divided into teams and struggle for survival on CBS's harsh reality series *Survivor*. Jeff Probst hosts and the lone survivor wins $1 million.

2003. Kate (Brooke Harman), a resourceful teenage girl, her younger sister, Sarah (Eliza Taylor-Cotter) and brother Nicholas (Nicholas Donaldson) are magically swept into a dangerous video game involving mysterious islands on Fox's *Pirate Islands*.

2004. Max Harrison (Michael Biehn) heads an elite team of police detectives who investigate bizarre murders on the North Shore on NBC's *Hawaii*. Survivors of a plane crash (Oceanic Flight 815) struggle for survival on a mysterious, apparently uncharted island in the South Pacific on *Lost* (ABC). Real people who resemble the characters on *Gilligan's Island* (see 1964) are placed on a deserted island and must work together to find a way back home on TBS's reality series *The Real Gilligan's Island*. Ava Gregory (Lori Loughlin) struggles to make a life for herself as a fashion designer on Payla Beach in California on the WB's *Summerland*.

2005. The Lifetime series *The Beach Girls* explores the lives of three teenage girls who spend their summers together in the sleepy beach town of Hubbard's Point. Chelsea Hobbs, Kristin Adams and Kristin Hager star as Nell, Claire and Skye.

Biblical see *Religious Characters*

Blind see *Visually Impaired Characters*

Boston

A listing of series set in Boston, Massachusetts.
1959. *21 Beacon Street* (NBC).
1970. *The Young Lawyers* (ABC).

1972. *Banacek* (NBC); *Paul Sand in Friends and Lovers* (CBS).

1975. *Beacon Hill* (CBS).

1977. *James at 15* (NBC).

1978. *James at 16* (NBC).

1982. *Cheers* (NBC).

1983. *Goodnight, Beantown* (CBS).

1985. *Spenser: For Hire* (ABC.

1986. *The Cavanaughs* (CBS).

1987. *Frank's Place* (CBS); *The Law and Harry McGraw* (CBS).

1990. *Against the Law* (Fox).

1993. *It Had to Be You* (CBS).

1995. *The Great Defender* (Fox).

1996. *Boston Common* (NBC).

1997. *Ally McBeal* (Fox); *The Practice* (ABC).

1998. *Two Guys, a Girl and a Pizza Place* (ABC).

2000. *Boston Public* (Fox), *Gideon's Crossing*.

2001. *All Souls* (UPN).

2003. *It's All Relative* (ABC).

2004. *Boston Legal* (ABC).

2005. *The Suite Life of Zack and Cody* (Disney).

Broadway and Stage Shows

In 1907 Florenz Ziegfeld changed the look of Broadway when he introduced a show called simply *The Follies*. Based on the *Folies Bergère* of France, the show introduced the American public to chorus girls who were not only beautiful but who could sing and dance (these shows would later become famous as *The Ziegfeld Follies*). Prior to this Broadway shows were a mix of entertainment acts — novelty, skits and songs and dances. Others followed Ziegfeld's lead and glamorous and dazzling productions that sang the promise of America would see Times Square in New York City become "The Great White Way" and "The Street of Dreams."

Television, especially in its early years, capitalized on Broadway and stage productions to keep their audiences captivated. It was, of course, impossible for the new medium to capture the ambiance of the stage, but it could, at least, give the viewing audience a taste of Broadway with its glamour, music and songs. The following listing comprises stand-alone TV adaptations of Broadway and stage shows broadcast from 1928 through 2005 (series that presented excerpts of Broadway shows, like *Omnibus*, have been excluded). See also *Variety and Drama Spectaculars*.

1928. Station WGY in Schenectady, New York, airs the first stage play, *The Queen's Messenger* by J. Hartley Masters. Joyce Evans, Izetta Jewell and Maurice Randall star.

1931. Performers from the Great White Way appeared on TV's first musical variety series, *Half-Hour on Broadway*.

1936. NBC airs *If Men Played Cards As Women Do*, an adaptation of the play by George S. Kaufman. Alan Bunce, Arthur Maitland and Alvin Simmons star.

1939. *Another Language*, a play by Rose Franken, stars Ann Revere, Robert Allan and Jack Rose. Benn Levy's play, *Art and Mrs. Bottle*, features Katherine Emery, Ann Revere and Jabez Gray in leading roles. Lyle Bettger, Marjorie Davies and Juliet Forbes appear in George Abbott's play *Brother Rat*. *The Butter and Egg Man* by George S. Kaufman stars Helen Twelvetrees, Ted Leavitt and Florence Sundstrom. Owen Davis's play, *The Donovan Affair*, features Laura Baxter and William Harrigan. Gloria Blondell and Lowell Gilmore star in *The Fortune Hunter*, a play by Winchell Smith. Thornton Wilder's *The Happy Journey* stars Elizabeth Goddard, Perry Wilson and Jane Rose. The play *Hay Fever* by Noel Coward features Dennis Hoey, Isobel Elsom and Virginia Campbell. Helen M. Clark's play, *May Eve*, stars Florence Edney and Henry Castle. The 1934 stage play, *The Cheese Champ*, is adapted to TV as *The Milky Way* with Fred Stewart and June Blossom in leading roles. Elizabeth Paige, Lee Patrick and Janet Fox star in an adaptation of the 1936 play *Stage Door* by George S. Kaufman. All of the above titles aired on NBC.

1940. Vicki Cummings and Julie Grant star in *June Moon* an NBC adaptation of the George S. Kaufman play. *Mady Christians' Ode to Liberty* (NBC), a play by Gilbert Miller, stars Ian Claire and Walter Slezak. Anton Chekov's *The Marriage Proposal* (NBC) stars Frieda Allen and Robert Allen. *When We Are Married*, a British play by J.P. Priestley, airs on NBC with Ann Andrews, Robert Henderson and Alice Fleming in leading roles.

1942. *To the Ladies*, a play by George S. Kaufman, airs on NBC with Marjorie Clark, Maurice Wells and Richard Jones as the stars.

1945. Robert E. Sherwood's three-act play, *Abe Lincoln in Illinois*, is adapted by NBC over the course of seven weeks. Act one airs on April 15,

1945 (Lincoln campaigns for U.S. Senator); Act two on May 20, 1945 (his personal life with Mary Todd); and the final act (May 27, 1945) deals with his Presidency. Stephen Courtleigh plays Abraham Lincoln with Mary Michaels as Mary Todd. Judy Blake and John Dudley star in *The Bourgeois Gentleman*, an adaptation by NBC of the Mollere play. *The Copperhead*, a play by Augustus Thomas, airs on NBC with Richard Keith and Douglas Dick in leading roles. The 1928 play *The Front Page* by Ben Hecht comes to NBC and stars Vinton Hayworth, Helene Reynolds and Matt Crowley. Leo G. Carroll, Neil Hamilton and Sidney Blackmer star in George S. Kaufman's play *If Men Played Cards As Women Do* (NBC). *Nettie*, George Ade's play about a beautiful nightclub singer, airs on NBC with Leila Ernst as Nettie. The 1935 play, *Petticoat Fever*, comes to NBC and stars Ann Burr and John McQuade. Maxwell Anderson's *Winterset* airs on NBC with John McQuade and Eva Langbord in leading roles. *You Can't Take It with You*, the 1936 play by George S. Kaufman, stars Robert Ober, Mabel Taliaferro and Diane Clement and airs on NBC.

1946. Grace Carney and David Durston star in *Angels Don't Marry*, an NBC adaptation of the play by Florence Byerson and Colin Clemens. Rose Franken's play, *Another Language*, is again adapted by NBC (see 1939) with Jean Adair and Richard Barrows as the stars. *Blithe Spirit*, the 1941 play by Noel Coward, airs on NBC with Carol Goodner and Philip Tonge in leading roles. The 1920 play *The First Year* comes to NBC with Grace Livingston and Michael Road as its stars. Retired private detective Jerry North (John McQuade) and his zany but shrewd wife Pamela (Maxine Stuart) attempt to solve a murder on *Mr. and Mrs. North* (NBC), a stage play by Frances and Richard Lockridge. George M. Cohan's mystery play *Seven Keys to Baldpate* (based on the story by Earl Derr Biggers) airs on NBC and stars David Andrews, Helen Jerome and Vinton Hayworth. Philadelphia is the setting for *The Showoff* a 1920 play by George Kelly and starring Lillian Foster and Alan Bunce.

1948. *Stage Door*, a 1936 play by George S. Kaufman and Edna Ferber, airs on NBC with Elizabeth Paige, Janet Fox and Lee Patrick in leading roles (see also 1939).

1949. *Arsenic and Old Lace*, Joseph Kesserling's comical play about two spinster sisters who delight in poisoning elderly men, airs for the first time on CBS (see also 1955, 62, 69). Josephine Hull, Ruth McDevitt and Boris Karloff star. A second-rate comic named Skid Johnson (Bert Lahr) attempts to make a comeback in *Burlesque*, an NBC adaptation of the Broadway play. Vicki Cummings co-stars as Skid's wife, Bonny. NBC adapts the 19th century play *Vanity Fair* to TV on *Philco Television Playhouse* as *Becky Sharpe* with Claire Lucas playing the amoral adventuress. Burgess Meredith (Biff), Francesca Bruning (Amy) and Hume Cronyn (Hugo) star in *One Sunday Afternoon* on *The Ford Theater Hour* (NBC) adaptation of the play by James Hogan.

1950. *Anything Goes*, an adaptation of the 1934 play, airs on NBC and stars Martha Raye as nightclub singer Reno Sweeney. The people of Grover's Corners, a small New Hampshire town, come to life on both ABC and NBC in separate presentations of Thornton Wilder's *Our Town*. On ABC (December 1, 1950), Edward Arnold plays the Stage Manager and Betty Caulfield is Emily Webb. NBC's adaptation on April 10, 1950 finds Burgess Meredith as the Stage Manager and Jean Gillespie as Emily. Leslie Nielsen and Barbara Bel Geddes star in Philip Barry's play *The Philadelphia Story* on NBC.

1951. *Prudential Playhouse* (CBS) airs *One Sunday Afternoon* with Richard Carlson and June Lockhart in the title roles.

1952. Condensed versions of Broadway plays are presented locally in New York on *Broadway TV Theater*. **Productions**: *The Acquittal* (Judith Evelyn), *Adam and Eva* (Katherine Bard, Hugh Riley), *Angel in the Pawnshop* (Sylvia Field, Ernest Truex), *Angel Street* (Sylvia Sidney), *The Barker* (Virginia Gilmore, Sidney Blackmer), *The Bat* (Jay Jostyn), *The Bishop Misbehaves* (Gene Lockhart, Alice Pearce), *Blind Alley* (Beverly Roberts, Ernest Graves), *Burlesque* (Buddy Ebsen, Jean Bartel), *Candlelight* (Ian Keith), *Climax* (Sylvia Sidney), *Craig's Wife* (Mildred Dunnock), *Criminal at Large* (Basil Rathbone), *Dark Victory* (Christopher Plummer), *Death Takes a Holiday* (Wendy Drew, Nigel Green), *The Enchanted Cottage* (Judith Evelyn), *The Farebrand* (Benvenuto Cellini), *For Love or Money* (Vicki Cummings, Buddy Ebsen), *The Fortune Hunter* (Peter Cookson), *The Front Page* (Edward Everett Horton), *George and Margaret* (Ernest Truex, Sylvia Field), *The Golddiggers* (John Newland, Olivia McGehee), *The Gramercy Ghost* (Veronica Lake), *Guest in the House* (Bonita Granville), *The Hasty Heart*

(Hurd Hatfield), *I Like It Here* (Bert Lytel), *It Pays to Advertise* (Roddy McDowall), *It's a Boy* (Hope Miller, Michael Higgins), *The Jazz Singer* (Lionel Ames, Celia Adler), *Janie* (Marjorie Gatson), *Jenny Kissed Me* (Christine White), *The Kick-In* (Meg Mundy), *Kind Lady* (Sylvia Sidney), *The Last of Mrs. Cheney* (Vicki Cummings), *The Letter* (Gene Raymond), *Mrs. Moonlight* (Beverly Whitney), *The Nervous Wreck* (Buddy Ebsen), *Night Cap* (Melville Cooper), *Night Must Fall* (Ruth Gates), *The Night of January 16th* (Virginia Gilmore), *Nothing But the Truth* (Orson Bean, Sylvia Field), *One Sunday Afternoon* (Gloria McGehee, Jack Warden, Mimi Kelly), *Outward Bound* (Jean Adair), *The Patsy* (Christine White, Luella Gear), *Rebecca* (Patricia Breslin), *Room Service* (Lara Parker), *R.U.R.* (Dorothy Hart), *Seven Keys to Baldpate* (Buddy Ebsen), *Seventh Heaven* (Geraldine Brooks), *Smilin' Through* (Beverly Whiting, Wesley Addy), *Suspect* (Florence Reed), *Theater* (Sylvia Sidney), *The 13th Chair* (Claire Luce), *This Thing Called Love* (Ruth Warrick), *Three Cornered Moon* (Bethel Leslie, William Post, Jr.), *Three Men on a Horse* (Ann Thomas, Orson Bean), *The Trial of Mary Dugan* (Ann Dvorak, Richard Derr), *The Twentieth Century* (Constance Bennett), *The Two Mrs. Carrols* (Signe Hasso), *The Velvet Glove* (Richard Derr, Lola Monte), *The Village Greene* (Marc Connelly), *Whistling in the Dark* (Edward Everett Horton), *The Witching Hour* (Ian Keith, Sarah Burton), *Within the Law* (Lola Montes, Cara Williams), *Wuthering Heights* (Meg Mundy), *Your Uncle Dudley* (Edward Everett Horton).

1954. The 1934 play *Anything Goes* is adapted to TV by NBC for a second time (see 1950) with Ethel Merman as nightclub singer Reno Sweeney. Also in the cast: Frank Sinatra, Sheree North and Bert Lahr. CBS launches *The Best of Broadway* a monthly series that recreates Broadway shows. **Productions**: *Arsenic and Old Lace* (Orson Bean, Helen Hayes), *Broadway* (Joseph Cotton, Piper Laurie), *The Guardsman* (Claudette Colbert, Franchot Tone), *The Man Who Came to Dinner* (Joan Bennett, Merle Oberon, Monty Woolley), *Panama Hattie* (Art Carney, Ethel Merman), *The Philadelphia Story* (Mary Astor, Dorothy McGuire, Richard Carlson), *The Royal Family* (Fredric March, Claudette Colbert), *The Showoff* (Jackie Gleason, Thelma Ritter) and *Stage Door* (Rhonda Fleming, Peggy Ann Garner). Marilyn Maxwell plays Gale Joy, a fading movie star who finds she has not been forgotten in *Best Foot For-*

ward (NBC). Moss Hart's play *Lady in the Dark* (NBC) stars Ann Sothern as Liza Elliott, an insecure editor who dreams propel her into a world where she is in charge of her life. Monty Woolley plays Sheridan Whiteside, *The Man Who Came to Dinner* in the NBC adaptation of the George S. Kaufman and Moss Hart play. Frank Albertson, Valerie Cossart and John Shellie star in a *Kraft Television Theater* (NBC) adaptation of *One Sunday Afternoon* by James Hogan. Social differences are explored when sassy singer Panama Hattie (Ethel Merman) meets Nick Bullett (Ray Middleton), the son of a wealthy family, in *Panama Hattie* (NBC). *The Philadelphia Story* by Philip Barry comes to CBS with Neva Patterson and Dorothy McGuire in leading roles. Claudette Colbert, Helen Hayes, Fredric March and Nancy Olson are the Cavendishes, "America's number one family of the theater" on *The Royal Family* by George S. Kaufman and Edna Ferber (CBS). Ginger Rogers makes her television debut as Lily Pepper, a petulant, caustic-tongued housewife on the NBC production of Noel Coward's *Tonight at 8:30*.

1955. A young girl's adventures in Wonderland forms the basis of *Alice in Wonderland* (NBC) with Gillian Barber as Alice and Martyn Green as the White Rabbit. Helen Hayes, Billie Burke and Boris Karloff star in a second adaptation of the Joseph Kesselring play *Arsenic and Old Lace* on CBS (see 1949). The 1930 play *The Barretts of Wimpole Street* (CBS), tells the tale of the courtship of Elizabeth Barrett (Geraldine Fitzgerald) and Robert Browning (Robert Douglas). Nightclub dancer Billie Moore (Piper Laurie) becomes involved with a murder in CBS's adaptation of the 1926 play *Broadway*. A second-rate comic named Skid Johnson (Dan Dailey) attempts to make a comeback on the CBS adaptation of *Burlesque*. *Dearest Enemy* (NBC) stars Anne Jeffreys and Robert Sterling in a musical about a group of American women who helped the Continental Army. George Bernard Shaw's play *The Devil's Disciple* (NBC) tells the story of Dick Dudgeon (Maurice Evans), a sinner who helps a servant girl (Judith, played by Teresa Wright) when no one else will. Georgina Allerton (Vivian Blaine) is a bored bookstore manager who daydreams herself into exciting adventures on *Dream Girl* (NBC). An actor (Franchot Tone) poses as a dashing guardsman to test his wife's (Claudette Colbert) fidelity on *The Guardsman*

(CBS). The 1940 play *Johnny Belinda* by Elmer Harris comes to CBS and explores the life of a deaf girl named Belinda MacDonald (Katherine Bard). Detective Mark McPherson (Robert Stack) attempts to protect Laura Hunt (Dana Wynter) from a killer on the CBS presentation of *Laura*. The statue of Venus (Janet Blair) comes to life to win the love of reluctant Rodney Hatch (Russell Nype) on the NBC presentation of *One Touch of Venus*. Thornton Wilder's play *Our Town* is dramatized for the third time (see 1950) with Frank Sinatra as the Stage Manager, Eva Marie Saint as Emily and Paul Newman as George Gibbs. James Barrie's 1904 play *Peter Pan* comes to NBC with Mary Martin as the boy who never grows up. Escaped convicts take over an Arizona diner in *The Petrified Forest*, an NBC adaptation of the Robert Sherwood play. Henry Fonda, Lauren Bacall and Humphrey Bogart star. An egotistical, loud-mouthed showoff named Aubrey Piper (Jackie Gleason) attempts to impress people with his ambitions on *The Showoff* (CBS), a play by George Kelly. Helen Hayes and Mary Martin star in *The Skin of Our Teeth* (NBC), Thornton Wilder's play about a family beset with problems. A look at backstage Broadway life is presented on *Stage Door* (CBS). Diana Lynn and Peggy Ann Garner star in the George F. Kaufman and Edna Ferber play. The effect a rumor has on a happily married housewife is the basis of *The Women* (NBC), a play by Claire Boothe Luce. Shelley Winters, Paulette Goddard and Ruth Hussey star.

1956. Noel Coward stars as Charles Condomine, a novelist with two wives, in an adaptation of the 1941 play *Blithe Spirit* (CBS; see also 1946). Claudette Colbert plays Ruth, his second wife; Lauren Bacall is Elvira, the spirit of his first wife. Elvinia Applegate (Barbara Cook) crusades for women's rights in *Bloomer Girl* (NBC). Wealthy junk dealer Harry Brock (Paul Douglas) tries to educate his sassy girlfriend, Billie Dawn (Mary Martin) in *Born Yesterday* (NBC), a play by Garson Kanin. George Bernard Shaw's play *Caesar and Cleopatra* comes to NBC with Sir Cedric Hardwicke and Claire Bloom in leading roles. Emlyn Williams's play *The Corn Is Green* (NBC) stars Eva LaGallienne as a schoolteacher in a Welch mining town in the early 1900s. Spinster librarian Addie (Betty Field) attempts to make a banker named Paul (Harry Nelson) notice her on *Happy Birthday* (NBC), a play by Anita Loos. The ghost of a 17th century Dutch girl named Lise

(Julie Andrews) helps a man named Van Dorn (Bing Crosby) keep his mountain, High Thor from being sold on the Maxwell Anderson play *High Thor* (CBS). Greer Garson and Franchot Tone star in *The Little Foxes* (NBC), a taut drama about a desperate Southern family in the post-Civil War days. Bachelor John Tanner (Maurice Evans) struggles to remain single in *Man and Superman* (NBC), an adaptation of the George Bernard Shaw play. Mary Martin recreates her role as *Peter Pan* (NBC) in a live, color, restaged version of the James Barrie play (see also 1955, 60, 76). A bankrupt theatrical producer named Oscar Jaffe (Orson Welles) tries to recoup his loses by signing a famous movie star, Lily Garland (Betty Grable), to an exclusive contract on *The Twentieth Century* (CBS).

1957. Events in the life of sharpshooter Annie Oakley (Mary Martin) are the basis of the musical *Annie Get Your Gun* (NBC) by Irving Berlin and Dorothy and Herbert Fields. *The Lark* (NBC), a dramatic retelling of the story of Joan of Arc, stars Julie Harris as Joan. The true-life story of Helen Keller (Patty McCormack), the deaf, mute and blind child who learns to communicate through her teacher Annie Sullivan (Teresa Wright) is the basis of *The Miracle Worker* (CBS). Requiring more time to raise his grandson, a grandfather (Ed Wynn) chases death away on NBC's *On Borrowed Time*. The Lux Video Theater (NBC) airs *One Sunday Afternoon*, an adaptation of the James Hogan play, with Gordon MacRae (Biff), Mary Healey (Amy) and Peter Lind Hayes (Hugo). The struggles of an Hungarian family caught up in the 1956 Soviet invasion comprise the story for *There Shall Be No Light* (NBC). Charles Boyer, Ray Walston and Katherine Cornell star.

1958. NBC airs a second adaptation of *Johnny Belinda* (see 1955) with Julie Harris and Christopher Plummer in leading roles. Dedicated drinker Elwood P. Dowd (Art Carney) receives advice from an invisible six-foot tall white rabbit on *Harvey* (CBS). Shrewish ex-wife Lili Vanessi (Patricia Morison) seeks to win back the love of former hubby Fred (Alfred Drake) on *Kiss Me, Kate* (NBC). *The Member of the Wedding* (CBS) tells of 12-year-old Frankie Adams (Collin Wilcox), a girl who can't wait to grow up and become a woman. The romance that develops between John Kent (Howard Keel), the owner of a fashion boutique called Roberta's, and Stephanie (Anna Maria

Alberghetti), an exiled Russian princess, is the plot of *Roberta* (NBC). *Wonderful Town* (CBS) tells of the romantic adventures of Ruth and Eileen Sherwood (Rosalind Russell, Jacqueline McKeever), sisters who have come to New York from Ohio seeking fame and fortune.

1959. Connecticut newspaperman Lee Kinsolving (Richard Miller) attempts to court Abigail Kellogg (Muriel McComber) against the wishes of her father on *Ah! Wilderness* (NBC). Childlike woman Nora Helmer (Julie Harris) searches for her own identity in *A Doll's House* (NBC). In the NBC special, *Merman on Broadway*, Ethel Merman recalls the music and songs associated with her Broadway career. Art Carney plays the Stage Manager and Kathleen Widdoes is Emily Webb in an NBC production of Thornton Wilder's *Our Town* (see also 1950, 55, 77). *The Philadelphia Story* is adapted by NBC (see also 1954) with Diana Lynn as Tracy Lord, Christopher Plummer as Mike Connor and Ruth Roman as Liz Imbrie. The play *One Sunday Afternoon* becomes *The Strawberry Blonde* for NBC with dentist Biff Grimes (David Wayne) seeking to get even with Hugo Barnstead (Eddie Bracken), the man who stole his sweetheart, Virginia Brush (Dolores Dorn-Heft). NBC airs *Winterset*, the Maxwell Anderson play about Milo Romagna (Don Murray) and his attempts to clear the name of his father, who was executed for a murder he did not commit.

1960. Greer Garson plays Lady Cicely, a woman who tries to reform the feared Captain Brassbound (Christopher Plummer) in the George Bernard Shaw play *Captain Brassbound's Conversion* (NBC). Greedy relatives try to drive young heiress Annabelle West (Collin Wilcox) insane to disqualify her from a will in *The Cat and the Canary* (NBC). Lawyer Daniel Webster's (Edward G. Robinson) battle against the Devil (David Wayne) to save the soul of Jabez Stone (Tim O'Connor) is the basis of the 1939 play, *The Devil and Daniel Webster* (NBC). Mary Martin again plays *Peter Pan* (see 1955), the boy who never grows up, in a color and videotape production (NBC).

1961. Two married people (Laura and Alec) meet by chance and fall in love in Noel Coward's *Brief Encounter* (NBC). Dinah Shore and Ralph Bellamy star. A prince (Christopher Plummer) grieves over the loss of his love, a beautiful ballerina who died three years earlier on *Time Remem-*

bered (NBC). Nineteenth century amoral adventuress Becky Sharpe (Diane Cilento) is brought to life on the CBS production of *Vanity Fair* (see also 1949). Vignettes trace the life of England's Queen Victoria (Julie Harris) in the Laurence Houseman play *Victoria Regina* (NBC).

1962. *Arsenic and Old Lace* comes to TV in a new NBC production (see 1949) with Dorothy Stickney (Abby Brewster), Mildred Natwick (Martha Brewster) and Boris Karloff (Jonathan Brewster). Richard Burton, Robert Goulet and Stanley Holloway pay tribute to Broadway composers Alan Jay Lerner and Frederick Loewe on the NBC special *The Broadway of Lerner and Loewe*. American soldiers try to introduce their culture to the natives of a Japanese village at the end of World War II on *Teahouse of the August Moon* (NBC). John Forsythe, David Wayne and Yuki Shimoda star.

1963. Ingrid Bergman plays a woman seeking to find a life of excitement in NBC's adaptation of the Ibsen play *Hedda Gabler*. The 1790s period play *The Patriots* (NBC) pits Thomas Jefferson (Charlton Heston) against Alexander Hamilton (John Fraser) as they clash over the new Constitution. Phonetics professor Henry Higgins (James Donald) struggles to transform cockney London flower girl Eliza Dolittle (Julie Harris) into a refined woman on the NBC adaptation of the George Bernard Shaw play *Pygmalion*.

1964. Carol Burnett plays Winifred Woebegone, a girl who lives in a bog and seeks to win the heart of Dauntless the Drab (Joe Bova), a prince whose mother, Queen Aggravain (Jane White) strives to keep him from marrying on *Once Upon a Mattress* (CBS; see also 1972 and 2005).

1965. A reenactment of the famous 1925 Scopes Trial (Clarence Darrow defending a schoolteacher accused of teaching Darwin's theory of evolution) is the plot of *Inherit the Wind* (NBC). Melvyn Douglas and Ed Wynn star. Emmet Lavery's play *The Magnificent Yankee* (NBC) traces the Washington years of Supreme Court Justice Oliver Wendell Holmes (Alfred Lunt).

1966. The ghost of a novelist's first wife threatens his new marriage on *Blithe Spirit* (NBC; see also 1946). Dirk Bogarde, Rachel Roberts and Rosemary Harris star. Two Americans lost in the Scottish moors find *Brigadoon* (ABC), a strange village that appears for one day every 100 years. Robert Goulet, Peter Falk and Sally Ann Howes star in the Lerner and Loewe musical. Arthur Miller's play *Death of a Salesman* (CBS) tells of Willie Loman (Lee J. Cobb), a salesman who comes to realize his life has been a failure. *The Glass Menagerie* (CBS) by Tennessee Williams focuses on Laura Wingfield (Barbara Loden), the crippled daughter of a once glamorous mother, Amanda (Shirley Booth), who lives in a dream world of the small glass animals she collects.

1967. Conspirators persuade an amnesiac woman to pose as Anastasia (Julie Harris), the daughter of the Czar of Russia to collect the money she will inherit on *Anastasia* (NBC). Ethel Merman plays Annie Oakley and Bruce Yarnell is Frank Butler in a second adaptation of the play about the rivalry between the two sharpshooters on *Annie Get Your Gun* (NBC; see also 1957). Robert Goulet plays carnival barker Billy Bigelow in the ABC production of *Carousel*. Three escaped convicts hold a middle class family hostage on the ABC adaptation of the Joseph Hayes play *The Desperate Hours*. Arthur Hill, Teresa Wright and Yvette Mimieux star. The diary kept by a 13-year-old girl hiding from Nazis in occupied Amsterdam during World War II is *The Diary of Anne Frank* with Diane Davilla in the title role. A street beggar in ancient Baghdad falls in love with a princess in *Kismet* (ABC). Jose Ferrer, Anna Maria Alberghetti and Barbara Eden star. Mia Farrow is Belinda and Ian Banner the doctor who teaches her to speak through sign language on the ABC production of *Johnny Belinda* (see also 1955, 58). The citizens of the Ozark community of Dog Patch come to life in Al Capp's *Li'l Abner*. The NBC comedy stars Sammy Jackson as Li'l Abner and Jeannine Riley as Daisy Mae.

1968. A group of people set up a community on a tropical island after a shipwreck on *The Admirable Crichton* (NBC). Bill Travers and Virginia McKenna star. Edmond O'Brien and Kim Stanley star in *Flesh and Blood* (NBC), a play about an American family that was intended for Broadway but made its debut on TV. *A Hatful of Rain* (ABC) tells the story of Johnny Pope (Michael Parks), a war veteran hooked on drugs. *Kiss Me Kate* airs on ABC with Robert Goulet as Fred Graham and Carol Lawrence as Lilly. Robert Stack and Lee Bouvier star in *Laura* (ABC), a second adaptation of the play by Vera Caspary and George Sklar (see 1955).

1969. *Arsenic and Old Lace* airs for the last time on ABC with Helen Hayes (Abby Brewster), Lillian Gish (Martha Brewster) and Fred Gwynne (Jonathan Brewster); see 1949. *Roberta* airs for a second time (NBC; see 1958) with John Davidson, Michele Lee and Bob Hope.

1970. The relationship between newspaper editor Walter Burns (Robert Ryan) and ace reporter Hildy Johnson (George Grizzard) is the focal point of the 1928 play *The Front Page* (ABC). The life and songs of George M. Cohan, Broadway's "Yankee Doodle Dandy," are celebrated on *George M!* (NBC). Joel Grey, Bernadette Peters and Red Buttons star.

1971. *Harvey*, the play by Mary Chase, airs on NBC (see also 1958) with James Stewart as Elwood P. Dobbs, a drinker who hallucinates Harvey, a six-foot tall white rabbit. The characters of Dog Patch again come to life on ABC's *Li'l Abner* (see also 1967). Ray Young plays Li'l Abner with Nancee Parkinson as Daisy Mae. After 16 years of separation two brothers (George C. Scott, David Burns) gather at a condemned Manhattan brownstone to sell off family heirlooms in the Arthur Miller play *The Price*.

1972. Orson Welles plays Sheridan Whiteside, *The Man Who Came to Dinner,* on the NBC adaptation of the George S. Kaufman and Moss Hart play. Carroll O'Connor plays John P. Wintergreen, a presidential candidate who runs on a platform of silver linings and love on *Of Thee I Sing* (CBS) by George Gershwin. Carol Burnett reprises her role as Winifred Woebegone on *Once Upon a Mattress* (CBS), a spoof of the Hans Christian Andersen fairy tale, "The Princess and the Pea." Ken Berry plays the role of Dauntless the Drab and Jane White also reprises her role as Drab's mother, Queen Aggravain (see also 1964 and 2005).

1973. *Applause* (CBS) by Betty Comden and Adolph Green, tells the story of Eve Harrington (Penny Fuller), an aspiring actress who schemes her way into the life of Broadway star Margo Channing (Lauren Bacall). The CBS special *Ed Sullivan's Broadway* looks at the history of the Great White Way with such guests as Frank Sinatra, Ethel Merman, Julie Andrews and Gwen Verdon. Joanna Miles is Laura Wingfield, the crippled girl sheltered by her mother Amanda (Katharine Hepburn) on *The Glass Menagerie* (ABC; see also 1966). The Eugene O'Neill play *Long Day's Journey into Night* (ABC) relates one long, hot August day in the life of the Tyrone family in 1912. Sir Laurence Olivier and Constance

Cummings star. A waiting room for the afterlife is the subject of *Steambath* (PBS). Bill Bixby, Herb Edelman and Valerie Perrine star (Valerie made history by exposing her breasts in what would become TV's first staged nude scene).

1974. Two married people meet by chance and fall in love in *Brief Encounter*, an NBC adaptation of the Noel Coward play. Sophia Loren (her American TV debut) and Richard Burton star (see also 1961). Clifford Odets *The Country Girl* comes to NBC with Shirley Knight Hopkins as Georgia Dodd, the long-suffering wife of Frank Elgin (Jason Robards, Jr.) a self-pitying matinee idol. Strangers Anne Miller and Paul Freeman (Carol Burnett, Alan Alda) meet in an empty apartment and have an affair on *6 RMS RIV VU* (real estate talk for a six room Manhattan apartment with a Riverside Drive view) on CBS. Colleen Dewhurst (as Josie Hogan) and Jason Robards (Phil Hogan) star in *A Moon for the Misbegotten*, an NBC adaptation of the Eugene O'Neill play.

1975. The vulnerability of Superman is spoofed when the Man of Steele (David Wilson) is psyched out of his powers by a mad scientist on *It's a Bird, It's a Plane, It's Superman* (ABC). Lesley Ann Warren plays Lois Lane and Allen Ludden is Perry White. Carol Burnett plays three sisters and their elderly Irish Catholic mother in *Twigs* (CBS).

1976. The George Bernard Shaw play *Caesar and Cleopatra* (NBC) examines Caesar's (Sir Alec Guinness) role as instructor to Cleopatra (Genevieve Bujold), the fledgling ruler of Egypt in 48 B.C. (see also 1956). Laurence Olivier is Big Daddy, Natalie Wood is Margaret and Robert Wagner is Brick on the NBC adaptation of the Tennessee Williams play *Cat on a Hot Tin Roof*. *Peter Pan* comes to TV for a fourth time (see 1955, 56, 60) with Mia Farrow as Peter Pan and Danny Kaye as Captain Hook.

1977. Hal Holbrook is the Stage Manager and Glynnis O'Connor is Emily Webb in the final adaptation of Thornton Wilder's play *Our Town* (NBC; see also 1950, 55, 59).

1978. The Ozark community of Dog Patch again comes to life with the NBC musical *Li'l Abner in Dog Patch Today* (see also 1967, 71). Stephan Burns plays Li'l Abner with Debra Feuer as Daisy Mae. Graduates of an exclusive women's college meet seven years later to discuss their life and loves on *Uncommon Women and Others* (PBS). Swoosie Kurtz, Jill Eikenberry and Meryl Streep star.

1979. Patty Duke plays Annie Sullivan and Melissa Gilbert is Helen Keller, the blind, mute and deaf girl Annie tries to teach on *The Miracle Worker* (NBC). *You Can't Take It with You* (CBS), a play by Moss Hart and George S. Kaufman, relates the story of two people who fall in love and the night their families meet for the first time. Art Carney, Blythe Danner and Jean Stapleton star.

1980. Liza Minnelli plays Lillian Hellman in the Showtime production of *Are You Now or Have You Ever Been* by Eric Bentley (about the infamous House of Un-American Activities Committee investigation of Communism in the movie industry). A comical view of marriage is the basis of *The Cheaters* (Showtime); Peggy Cass and Patricia Barry star. *A Conflict of Interest* (Showtime) stars Barnard Hughes and Roland Winters in a story about the balance of power in the American government. Melissa Gilbert plays Anne Frank, the girl who hid from the Nazis in occupied Amsterdam during World War II on *The Diary of Anne Frank* (NBC). Gerri Dean, a member of the original stage version, stars in the Showtime adaptation of *The Me Nobody Knows*. A musical review based on the works of Noel Coward is presented on *Oh Coward!* (Showtime) starring Jamie Ross, Roderick Cook and Pat Galloway. Christopher Bernau plays the title role in the Showtime production of *The Passion of Dracula*. *The Robber Bridegroom* airs on Showtime with Marjoe Gortner as a charming rogue who leads a double life.

1981. Broadway musicals are celebrated by Showtime with Gwen Verdon hosting *The American Dance Machine Presents a Celebration of Broadway Dance*. Elliott Gould and Alice Ghostley star in *Come Blow Your Horn* (Showtime), a Neil Simon comedy about a family ruled by a domineering father. D.L. Coburn's play *The Gin Game* (Showtime) tells of two elderly people (Hume Cronyn, Jessica Tandy) trapped in an old age home. The instability of urban life is explored in *Hold Me*, a Showtime adaptation of cartoonist Jules Feiffer's play, starring Paul Dooley. A second-rate con man (Jason Robards) finds his confidence bolstered by a hotel night clerk (Jack Dodson) in Eugene O'Neill's *Hughie* (Showtime). Figure skating is coupled with classical and modern dance on *John Curry's Ice Dancing* (Showtime), an adaptation of the Broadway production *Ice Dancing*. Peggy Fleming co-stars. An American jockey journeys to England to ride in the Derby in *Lit-*

tle Johnny Jones (Showtime). Eric Weitz stars in the George M. Cohen musical. A look at British society is presented in *Look Back in Anger* (Showtime) starring Malcolm McDowell. Charles Nelson Reilly and Darryl Hickman star as Felix Unger and Oscar Madison in Neil Simon's *The Odd Couple* (Showtime). Melba Moore and Robert Guillaume star in *Purlie*, the story of an aspiring black preacher's attempts to gain a flock for his church. Hit numbers from the Broadway plays *Finian's Rainbow, South Pacific, Sweet Charity* and *Lady in the Dark* are restaged on PBS's *Musical Comedy Tonight*. Sylvia Fine Kaye is the host. Shelley Hack, Meredith Baxter and Annette O'Toole are friends who recall their times in high school as cheerleaders (1963) to their post-college reunion (1974) in HBO's *Vanities*. A look at the working class from a hooker to a housewife is the basis of *Working* (Showtime). Didi Conn, Rita Moreno, Vernee Watson and Patti LaBelle star.

1982. The career of blues and bop performer Thomas "Fats" Waller is recreated in the musical *Ain't Misbehavin'* (NBC) with Nell Carter, Andre DeShields and Ken Page. Newlyweds Paul and Corie Bratter (Richard Thomas, Bess Armstrong) struggle to make a life for themselves in New York City on Neil Simon's *Barefoot in the Park* (HBO). Richard Harris is King Arthur and Meg Bussert is Queen Geneviere in the Lerner and Loewe musical *Camelot* (HBO). Grace's Diner (30 miles from Kansas City) is the setting for the romance between Cherie (Margot Kidder), a saloon singer, and Bo (Tim Matheson), the lovesick cowboy who pursues her on *Bus Stop* (HBO). *The Drunkard*, a play first staged in 1844, tells of one man's bout with alcoholism and his attempts to save his soul. Tom Bosely stars in the now defunct Entertainment Channel production. Scott Baio, Sheree North and Danny Aiello star in *Gemini* (Showtime), the story of a Harvard student coming of age on his 21st birthday. CBS modernizes the Elmer Harris play *Johnny Belinda* with Rosanna Arquette as Belinda McAdam and Richard Thomas as the Vista volunteer who helps her speak through sign language (see also 1955, 58, 67). Twelve-year-old Frankie Adams (Dana Hill) is a girl who can't wait to grow up on the NBC production of *The Member of the Wedding* (see also 1958). A dramatic retelling of the life of Edith Piaf (Jane Lapotaire) called France's "Little Sparrow" is the subject of *Piaf* (The Entertainment Channel). The lives of three couples who, at

different times, stayed at the same suite (709) of the Plaza Hotel in New York City is the basis of Neil Simon's *Plaza Suite*. Lee Grant and Jerry Orbach head the cast (HBO). A man promises to make it rain and save a drought-stricken farm on *The Rainmaker* (HBO). Tommy Lee Jones and Tuesday Weld star. George Hearn plays *Sweeney Todd* (The Entertainment Channel), a London barber who delights in killing his customers. Angela Lansbury plays Mrs. Lovett, the pastry chef who helps him dispose of the evidence as "meat pies." Cloris Leachman plays three sisters and their feisty mother in *Twigs* (The Entertainment Channel; see also 1975). Katharine Ross is a blind girl terrorized by convicts seeking a musical doll filled with drugs on *Wait Until Dark* (HBO).

1983. A clever woman (Joanne Woodward) is caught in a comic love triangle between her macho husband (Ron Paraday) and a fanciful young poet (Eugene Marchbanks) on *Candida* (The Entertainment Channel). Charles Grodin plays a man who poses as his friend's aunt on The Entertainment Channel's production of *Charley's Aunt*. The problems of growing up and growing old are seen through a family spending one last summer together on *Close Ties* (The Entertainment Channel). Shelley Hack, Kim Darby and Ann Dusenberry star. Sandy Dennis, Cher and Karen Black are the women whose lives revolve around the death of James Dean on *Come Back to the Five and Dime, Jimmy Dean, Jimmy Dean* (Showtime). *The Hasty Heart* (Showtime) tells the story of a man with only a few weeks to live (Gregory Harrison) and of the nurse (Cheryl Ladd) who cares for him. Life in the trenches of World War II forms the story of *Journey's End* (Showtime) with Andrew Stevens and Maxwell Caulfield in leading roles. A man (Robert Klein) struggles to conceal his gorgeous mistress (Pia Zadora) from his unsuspecting wife (Susan George) on *Pajama Tops* (Showtime). The musical *Pump Boys and Dinettes* airs on NBC as *Pump Boys and Dinettes on Television*. The story, set along Highway 57 in North Carolina, follows the lives of four pump boys (at the L&M Gas Station) and two sisters who run the Double Cupp Diner. Jim Wann, Lisa Morgan, Debra Monk and Mark Hardwick star. Bittersweet relationships at an English seaside resort are explored on *Separate Tables* (HBO). Julie Christie and Alan Bates star.

1984. A Mississippi Delta plantation house is the setting for a look at a decaying Southern family on *Cat on a Hot Tin Roof* (Showtime) by Tennessee Williams. Jessica Lange, Tommy Lee Jones and Rip Torn star. Douglas Roberts (Robert Hays) is a World War II lieutenant stationed aboard a cargo vessel who longs to see action on *Mr. Roberts* (NBC). Ann-Margret plays the seductive Blanche DuBois in Tennessee Williams's *A Streetcar Named Desire* (ABC).

1985. Tony Randall hosts *Curtain's Up*, a syndicated special that compares the stages of Broadway and London with clips of shows that played in both cities. Rex Harrison is a retired, slightly mad sea captain who finds his house anything but shipshape in *Heartbreak House* (Showtime).

1986. Broadway tackles the AIDS issue in *As Is*, and Showtime adapts it with Robert Carradine as Rich Farrell, a homosexual stricken with the disease. The story of the French artist Georges Seurat (Mandy Patinkin), who created the celebrated canvas "A Sunday Afternoon on the Island of La Grande Jaffe" (shows Parisians enjoying a day in the park) is the subject of *Sunday in the Park with George* (Showtime). Bernadette Peters co-stars.

1987. Tom Conti and John Travolta play hit men who receive a series of baffling food orders via a dumb waiter as clues to their next target on *The Dumb Waiter* (ABC). Incidents in the lives of three couples are again presented (see 1982) on *Plaza Suite* (ABC) with Carol Burnett and Dabney Coleman in leading roles.

1988. A woman (Glenda Jackson) is haunted by the memories of the untimely death of her husband in World War II on *Strange Interlude* (PBS). The Peanuts characters reveal their secrets, hopes and dreams on the animated *Snoopy—the Musical* (CBS). Cameron Clark (Snoopy), Sean Colling (Charlie Brown) and Tiffany Billings (Lucy) head the cast.

1989. Carol Channing, Diahann Carroll, Chita Rivera, Vic Damone and Hal Linden are among the celebrities who pay tribute to composer Jule Styne by performing his songs on *Broadway Sings the Music of Jule Styne* (PBS).

1992. PBS airs *Guys and Dolls: Off the Record*, a behind-the-scenes look at the cast album recording of the 1992 Broadway revival of the Frank Loesser musical. Josie DeGuzman, Peter Gallagher, Nathan Lane and Faith Prince perform.

1993. PBS airs *On the Town in Concert*. Adolph Greene and Betty Comden host a special that celebrates the music and songs of the Broadway play *On the Town*. Tyne Daly, Frederica Von Stade and Cleo Laine are among the performers.

1995. Songwriter Albert J. Peterson (Jason Alexander) and his secretary Rose Alvarez (Vanessa L. Williams) attempt to arrange a final farewell performance for rock idol Conrad Birdie (Marc Kudrisch) on *Bye Bye Birdie* (ABC). Julie Andrews plays out of work singer Victoria Grant who pretends to be a man (Victor) to get a job in early 1920s Paris on *Victor/Victoria* (PBS).

1996. *Passion* (PBS) is a Stephen Sondheim musical about Giorgio (Jere Shea), a young soldier torn between two loves — Clara (Marin Mazzie), a married woman, and Fosca (Donna Murphy), an unhappy and unhealthy girl who develops a strong passion for him.

1998. Elaine Paige, John Mills, Ken Page, Rosemarie Ford and Michael Gruber star in *Cats* (PBS), an adaptation of "The World's best-loved musical," wherein Jellicle cats rejoice with their leader Old Deuteronomy at a ball where one cat will be chosen to go to the Heavyside Layer and be reborn.

1999. The life of an adorable orphan named Annie (Alicia Morton) is the subject of the musical *Annie* (Disney). Kathy Bates plays Miss Hannigan, head of the orphanage. Stacey Logan, Jane Connell, and Larry Linville star in *Crazy for You* (PBS), an adaptation of the George and Ira Gershwin 1930 hit *Girl Crazy* (about the escapades of a stage struck playboy in a Nevada mining town). The Rodgers and Hammerstein musical *Oklahoma* comes to TV (ABC) with Hugh Jackman (Curly), Josephina Gabrielle (Laurey) and Shuler Hensley (Jud).

2000. *Kiss Me Kate* recounts the backstage and onstage antics of the cast of the touring company of Shakespeare's *Taming of the Shrew*. Rachel York, Brent Barnett and Nancy Anderson star in the PBS production. Nathan Lane stars as Sheridan Whitehead, a critic who slips and falls and becomes the seemingly permanent houseguest of the Stanley family on *The Man Who Came to Dinner* (PBS). ABC airs *The Miracle Worker* with Hallie Kate Eisenberg as Helen Keller and Alissa Elliott as Annie Sullivan, the teacher who helps the blind, mute and deaf girl communicate with people.

2001. *Anne Frank: The Whole Story* airs on ABC with Hannah Taylor Gordon as Anne Frank, the 13-year-old girl who hid from Nazis in occupied Amsterdam during World War II. *Jesus*

Christ, Superstar (PBS) is a rock opera that tells of the last seven days in the life of Jesus (Glen Carter) from his arrival in Jerusalem to his crucifixion. Glenn Close, Harry Connick, Jr., Ilene Graff and Lori Tan Chinn star in *South Pacific*, the Rodgers and Hammerstein musical about a young nurse who falls in love with an older French plantation owner.

2003. Carol Channing hosts *Broadway's Lost Treasures*, a clip filled PBS special that highlights the golden years of the annual *Tony Awards* TV presentations (1967–1986). Dick Van Dyke and Mary Tyler Moore appear as two elderly people trapped in a retirement home on the PBS production of *The Gin Game*. Matthew Broderick stars as Professor Harold Hill and Kristen Chenoweth is Marian on the ABC production of *The Music Man*.

2004. Julie Andrews hosts *Broadway: The American Musical*, a lavish six-part history of the Broadway musical that is rich with film clips (PBS).

2005. The Pay Per View service Broadway Television Network tapes actual Broadway plays and airs them on a pay basis. The following Broadway plays have thus far aired: *Duke Ellington's Sophisticated Ladies* (Paula Kelly, Phyllis Hyman, Lorraine Fields), *Jekyll and Hyde* (David Hasselhoff as Dr Jekyll and Edward Hyde, Colleen Sexton as Lucy and Andrea Rivette as Emma), *Smokey Joe's Café* (DeLee Lively, Brenda Braxton, Matt Bogart, Deb Lyons), *Stephen Sondheim's Putting It Together: A Musical Revue* (Carol Burnett, George Hearn, Ruthie Henshall, Bronson Pinchot), *Tintypies* (Carolyn Migrini, Jerry Zacks, Lynne Thigpen, Trey Wilson). Kristen Johnston, Rue McClanahan, Cynthia Nixon and Jennifer Tilly star in *The Women*, a play by Clare Booth Luce that depicts the lives of a group of 1930s women. ABC revises *Once Upon a Mattress* (see 1964 and 1972) with Carol Burnett as Queen Aggravain (originally played by Jane White), the mother who clings to her son, Prince Dauntless (Denis O'Hare), and refuses to let him marry. Seeking his heart is Winifred Woebegone (Tracey Ullman; the role was originally played by Carol Burnett), a girl who lives in a bog.

Butlers see *Housekeepers*

Café see *Bars; Restaurants*

California

A listing of series set in California (excluding Los Angeles and San Francisco, which are listed as separate entries). When a specific locale was indicated on the program, it is indicated here after the network.

1950. *The George Burns and Gracie Allen Show* (CBS; Beverly Hills); *The Jack Benny Program* (CBS; Beverly Hills).

1952. *The Abbott and Costello Program* (Syn; Hollywood); *Boss Lady* (NBC).

1953. *My Favorite Husband* (NBC).

1954. *The Whirlybirds* (Syn.); *Waterfront* (Syn.).

1955. *Love That Bob* (NBC; Hollywood); *So This Is Hollywood* (NBC).

1956. *The Charlie Farrell Show* (CBS; Palm Springs).

1957. *Bachelor Father* (CBS; Beverly Hills).

1958. *77 Sunset Strip* (ABC; Hollywood).

1959. *Hennessey* (CBS; San Diego); *Zorro* (ABC).

1960. *Bringing Up Buddy* (CBS); *The Tab Hunter Show* (NBC; Malibu); *Dan Raven* (NBC).

1961. *The Bob New Cummings Show* (CBS); *Malibu Run* (CBS; Malibu).

1962. *The Beverly Hillbillies* (CBS; Beverly Hills); *Oh, Those Bells!* (CBS; Hollywood).

1963. The *Lieutenant* (NBC; Oceanside).

1964. *The Baileys of Balboa* (CBS; Balboa Beach); *Harris Against the World* (NBC; *Mickey* (ABC; New Port Beach); *Karen* (NBC); *90 Bristol Court* (NBC); *Tom, Dick and Mary* (NBC).

1965. *The Big Valley* (ABC; Stockton); *Gidget* (ABC; Santa Monica); *The John Forsythe Show* (NBC); *O.K. Crackerby* (ABC; Palm Springs).

1966. The *Jean Arthur Show* (CBS; Beverly Hills).

1967. *Accidental Family* (NBC; San Fernando); *Malibu U.* (ABC; Malibu Beach); *The Second Hundred Years* (ABC; Woodland Oaks).

1968. *The Doris Day Show* (CBS; Mill Valley).

1969. *Bracken's World* (NBC; Hollywood); *Marcus Welby, M.D.* (ABC; Santa Monica).

1970. *Dan August* (ABC; Santa Luisa); *The Storefront Lawyers* (CBS).

1971. *Men at Law* (CBS; Century City); *Owen Marshall, Counselor at Law* (ABC; Santa Barbara); *Sarge* (NBC; San Diego).

1973. *Here We Go Again* (ABC; Encino); *Love Thy Neighbor* (ABC; San Fernando); *The Six Million Dollar Man* (ABC; Ojai).

1974. *Chopper One* (ABC); *Sons and Daughters* (CBS).

1975. *Bronk* (CBS; Ocean City); *Grady* (NBC; Santa Monica); *Isis* (CBS; Larkspur); *S.W.A.T.* (ABC).

1976. *The Bionic Woman* (ABC; Ojai); *C.P.O. Sharkey* (NBC; San Diego); *Family* (ABC; Pasadena); *The Nancy Walker Show* (ABC; Hollywood); *Spencer's Pilots* (CBS).

1977. *CHiPs* (NBC); *Code R* (CBS); *Eight Is Enough* (ABC; Sacramento); *The Kallikaks* (NBC; Nowhere, Ca.); *Lanigan's Rabbi* (NBC; Cameron); *Mulligan's Stew* (NBC); *Three's Company* (ABC; Santa Monica).

1978. *Husbands, Wives and Lovers* (CBS; San Fernando).

1979. *Knots Landing* (CBS); *The Ropers* (ABC; Chevia Hills); *Stockard Channing in Just Friends* (CBS; Beverly Hills); *240-Robert* (ABC).

1980. *Laverne and Shirley* (ABC; Burbank); *The Life and Times of Eddie Roberts* (Syn; Anaheim); *The Stockard Channing Show* (CBS; Hollywood).

1981. *Falcon Crest* (CBS; Napa Valley); *Gimme a Break* (NBC; Glenlawn); *McClain's Law* (NBC; San Pedro); *Open All Night* (ABC; Englewood); *Simon and Simon* (CBS; San Diego); *Strike Force* (ABC); *240-Robert* (ABC).

1982. *Gavilan* (NBC; Malibu); *King's Crossing* (ABC); *Knight Rider* (NBC); *Madame's Place* (Syn; Hollywood); *Seven Brides for Seven Brothers* (CBS); *Star of the Family* (ABC); *T.J. Hooker* (ABC); *Tucker's Witch* (CBS).

1983. *Bay City Blues* (NBC); *Emerald Point NAS* (CBS); *Jennifer Slept Here* (NBC; Beverly Hills); *Just Our Luck* (ABC; Venice); *Trauma Center* (ABC); *Zorro and Son* (CBS).

1984. *Airwolf* (CBS); *Half Nelson* (NBC; Beverly Hills); *It's Your Move* (NBC; Van Nys); *Riptide* (NBC; King Harbor); *Three's a Crowd* (ABC; Santa Monica).

1985. *I Had Three Wives* (CBS; Brentwood).

1986. *Easy Street* (NBC; Beverly Hills); *Fortune Dane* (ABC; Bay City); *Leo and Liz in Beverly Hills* (CBS).

1987. *Beverly Hills Buntz* (NBC); *The Charmings* (ABC; Burbank); *The Dom DeLuise Show* (Syn.); *Hard Copy* (CBS); *Jake and the Fatman* (CBS); *Out of This World* (Syn; Marlowe); *Second*

Chance (Fox; Venice); *Shell Game* (CBS; Santa Ana).

1988. *Just the Ten of Us* (ABC; Eureka); *Malibu, Ca.* (Syn.).

1989. *Ann Jillian* (NBC; Marvel); *Brand New Life* (NBC); *Doogie Howser, M.D.* (ABC; Brentwood); *Knight and Daye* (NBC; San Diego); *Major Dad* (CBS; Oceanside); *Saved by the Bell* (Palisades).

1990. *Beverly Hills, 90210* (Fox); *Broken Badges* (CBS); *The Fresh Prince of Bel Air* (NBC); *Molloy* (Fox; Beverly Hills); *Family Man* (CBS; Eagle Ridge); *Parker Lewis Can't Lose* (Fox); *Sugar and Spice* (CBS); *The Trials of Rosie O'Neill* (CBS; Santa Monica).

1991. *Blossom* (NBC); *Pacific Station* (NBC); *P.S.I. Luv U* (CBS; Palm Springs); 2000 *Malibu Road* (CBS; Malibu).

1992. *Bill and Ted's Excellent Adventures* (Fox; San Demas); *California Dreams* (NBC); *Camp Wilder* (NBC; Santa Monica); *Hanging with Mr. Cooper* (ABC; Oakland).

1993. *Bakersfield, P.D.* (Fox).

1994. *The Secret World of Alex Mack* (Nik).

1995. *Baywatch Nights* (Syn; Santa Monica); *First Time Out* (WB); *Unhappily Ever After* (WB).

1996. *Aliens in the Family* (ABC; Sherwood Hills); *Clueless* (ABC; Beverly Hills); *7th Heaven* (WB; Glean Oak).

1997. *Buffy the Vampire Slayer* (WB; Sunnydale); *Jenny* (NBC; Hollywood); *Total Security* (ABC; Culver City).

1998. *The Hughleys* (ABC; West Hills).

1999. *Family Law* (CBS); *Ladies' Man* (CBS; Van Nys); *Movie Stars* (WB; Malibu); *Pacific Station* (NBC; Venice); The Parkers (UPN; Santa Monica); Snoops (ABC; Santa Monica).

2000. *M.Y.O.B.* (NBC); *The Queen of Swords* (Syn.).

2001. *The Bernie Mac Show* (Fox; Encino); *Even Stevens* (Disney; Sacramento); *Kate Brasher* (CBS; Santa Monica).

2002. *Baby Bob* (CBS; Santa Monica); Hidden Hills (NBC); *That 80s Show* (Fox; San Diego).

2003. *Arrested Development* (Fox); *The O.C.* (Fox; Orange County); *Two and a Half Men* (CBS; Malibu).

2004. *The Stones* (CBS; Sherman Oaks); *Veronica Mars* (UPN; Neptune).

2006. *Hannah Montana* (Disney; Malibu); *Love Spring International* (Lifetime).

Camps

The following list represents the programs that were set at camps for children, the military and prisoners of war.

1952. Alan Hale, Jr. plays Roger Stone, director of the North Oak Boys Camp in *The Trailblazers*, a pilot that became the first attempt to set a series as a camp.

1955. *The Mickey Mouse Club* (ABC) serial *Spin and Marty* finds Spin Evans (Tim Considine) and Marty Markham (David Stollery) attending the Triple R Summer Boys Camp. In 1957, girls were added to the cast when the serial returned as *The Further Adventures of Spin and Marty*. Annette and Darlene (Annette Funicello, Darlene Gillespie) were campers at the Circle H Girl's Ranch who stole the hearts of Spin and Marty. Further adventures in the lives of Spin, Marty, Annette and Darlene continued in the final chapter, *The New Adventures of Spin and Marty* in 1958. Master Sergeant Ernest Bilko (Phil Silvers) manipulates the establishment for his own benefit at the Camp Freemont Army base in Roseville, Kansas, on *The Phil Silvers Show*.

1963. The Camp Pendleton Marine Base in Oceanside, California is the setting for the personal and professional lives of officers on *The Lieutenant* (NBC).

1964. Naïve Marine recruit Gomer Pyle (Jim Nabors) finds military life challenging at Camp Henderson in California on CBS's *Gomer Pyle, U.S.M.C.*

1965. NBC's *Camp Runamuck* presents Arch Johnson as Commander Wivenhoe, the harassed head of the slipshod run Camp Runamuck for Boys, and the gorgeous Caprice Yeudelman (Nina Wayne), a counselor at the impeccably maintained Camp Divine for Girls (across the lake from Runamuck). Stalag 13, a World War II P.O.W. camp is more of a leisure camp than a prison camp for U.S. colonel Robert Hogan (Bob Crane) and his inmates as they outwit their German captors on *Hogan's Heroes* (CBS).

1967. If Germans could hold Americans prisoners, why not Italy? NBC tried with *Campo 44*, a pilot wherein the World War II prisoners of Campo 44 live the good life outsmarting their captors. Philip Abbott and Vito Scotti star.

1972. The military personnel attached to the 4077th Mobile Army Surgical Hospital in Korea during the war call their camp "a hellhole" on CBS's *M*A*S*H*.

1980. Uncle Bernie (Carl Ballantine) is the head of Uncle Bernie's Camp Grizzly on the NBC pilot *Camp Grizzly*. Like Camp Runamuck, Camp Grizzly is rundown and badly run. Its only saving grace is Missy (Hilary Thompson), a gorgeous counselor who made everything seem all right. Teenagers explore the natural wonders of the U.S. on the syndicated *Camp Wilderness*. Franci Hogle and Stefan Hayes play the counselors. Leslie (Jacqueline Allen), Ann (Taisha Washington), Tom (Richard Levey), Cathy (Emily Wagner) and Ken (Robert Y.R. Chung) are among the children who attend the High Feather Summer Camp on *High Feather* (PBS).

1981. Pampered Judy Benjamin (Lorna Patterson) struggles to adjust to army life at Fort Bradley in Hobart, California on CBS's *Private Benjamin*.

1982. Angel Bright (Pamela Segall) and Farris Whitney (Tammy Lauren) are tough teenage girls who excel in mischief, so naturally they attend a camp (Camp Little Wolf) on the pilot *Little Darlings* (based on the feature film).

1983. Conniving Sergeant Tyrone Valentine (Jimmie Walker) seeks to profit from his hitch in the army at Camp Tar Creek, Texas, on ABC's *At Ease*.

1985. Camp Pinewood in Clifton, Maine, is the setting for the NBC pilot *Poison Ivy*. "Big" Erv Klopper (Robert Klein) and his wife Margo (Caren Kaye) run the camp. The harsh treatment of a group of British and Dutch women taken prisoner by the Japanese during World War II and placed in a decrepit camp on a hot and desolate island is *Tenko* (Syn.). Louise Jameson and Ann Bell star.

1989. White collar criminals live the good life at Club Fed, the nickname for a minimum-security prison in Santa Ramona, California, on the ABC pilot *Camp California*. Lorraine Toussaint stars as warden Cheryl Woodrich. Benjamin Ernst (David Brisben) is the owner of the Bar None, a dude ranch for children in Tucson, Arizona on *Hey Dude* (NIK).

1991. A group of children at a summer camp called Camp Anawanna find more mischief than fun by not obeying the rules on *Salute Your Shorts* (NIK). Ben Stiller plays the camp owner, Dr. Kahn; Kirk Bailey is the counselor, Kevin Lee; and among the kids are Heidi Lucas (Dina), Danny Cooksey (Bobby), Michael Bower (Eddie) and Megan Berwick (Z.Z.).

1993. While not exactly a camp in the traditional sense, the home at 1115 Fairlawn Avenue in Los Angeles is the residence of Ricky Wilder (Mary Page Keller), a mother who allows her children's friends to hang out at what she calls *Camp Wilder* (ABC).

2005. Nine real-life troubled teens are sent to Sage Walk, a wilderness school in Oregon to straighten out on ABC's reality series *Brat Camp*. Tony Randazzo is the narrator.

Canada

A listing of series set in Canada.

1953. *Renfrew of the Mounted* (Syn.).

1955. *Sergeant Preston of the Yukon* (Syn.).

1960. *Royal Canadian Mounted Police* (Syn.).

1965. *Forest Rangers* (Syn.); *Seaway* (Syn.).

1971. *Dr. Simon Locke* (Syn.); *Trouble with Tracy* (Syn.).

1972. *Police Surgeon* (Syn.).

1975. *Sunshine* (NBC).

1977. *King of Kensington* (Syn.), *Search and Rescue: The Alpha Team* (NBC).

1983. *Seeing Things* (Syn.).

1985. *Night Heat* (CBS).

1986. *Check It Out* (Syn.); *Anne of Green Gables* (PBS).

1987. *Degrassi Junior High* (PBS).

1988. *Anne of Avonlea* (PBS); *Ramona* (syndicated); *My Secret Identity* (Syn.).

1991. *Fly by Night* (CBS); *Urban Angel* (CBS).

1992. *Forever Knight* (CBS).

Cars

What type of cars do television characters drive? The following entry is a selective look at the characters and their cars from the more popular series over the years. See also *Gadgets, Talking Animals and Machines, Taxi Cabs, Truckers*.

1950. Jack Benny (*The Jack Benny Program*): 1920s Maxwell (badly in need of an overhaul).

1951. Pat Brady (*The Roy Rogers Show*): Jeep he calls Nellybelle.

1957. Bentley Gregg (*Bachelor Father*): Sedan convertible. Ward Cleaver (*Leave It to Beaver*):

Dodge sedan; Lumpy Rutherford: "Sickly green" convertible. Amos McCoy (*The Real McCoys*): 1920s Model T Ford. Nick Charles (*The Thin Man*): 1957 Ford Convertible.

1960. Andy Taylor (*The Andy Griffith Show*): Black and white Ford squad car. Fred Flintstone (*The Flintstones*): Foot powered car of stone. Wilbur Post (*Mister Ed*): 1961 Studebaker. Buzz Murdock and Tod Stiles (*Route 66*): 1960 Corvette.

1962. Jed Clampett (*The Beverly Hillbillies*): 1920s Oldsmobile truck.

1963. Amos Burke (*Burke's Law*): Rolls Royce. Simon Templar (*The Saint*): White Volvo 1800S. Rob Petrie (*The Dick Van Dyke Show*): Tarantula sports car.

1964. Darrin Stevens (*Bewitched*): Chevy Malibu convertible. Napoleon Solo (*The Man from U.N.C.L.E.*): Metallic blue Piranha.

1965. Maxwell Smart (*Get Smart*): Red Sunbeam Tiger Sport Convertible.

1966. John Steed (*The Avengers*): Yellow 1926 Rolls-Royce Silver Ghost; dark green 1929 4.5 liter Bentley; white Rolls-Royce "That I usually keep in moth balls." Emma Peel (*The Avengers*): 1966 Lotus Élan. Tara King (*The Avengers*): Red Lotus Europa MK1. Bruce Wayne (*Batman*): The Batmobile. Britt Reid (*The Green Hornet*): 1966 Chrysler Imperial (the Black Beauty). The Monkees (*The Monkees*): The Monkey Mobile.

1967. Joe Mannix (*Mannix*): Blue-green convertible.

1968. Officers Pete Malloy and Jim Reed (*Adam-12*): Plymouth Squad Car. Steve McGarrett (*Hawaii Five-0*): Black Mercury sedan. Julie, Pete and Linc (*The Mod Squad*): 1950 Mercury station wagon (a "Woodie"). Number 6 (*The Prisoner*): Green Lotus 7 sports car (before his arrest).

1970. Shirley Partridge (*The Partridge Family*): 1957 yellow school bus (psychedelically painted).

1971. Lt. Columbo (*Columbo*): 1950 purple Peugeot. Hank Brackett and Johnny Reach (*Bearcats!*): White Stutz Bearcat. Sally McMillan (*McMillan and Wife*): Yellow MG roadster.

1972. John Walton (*The Waltons*): 1930s Dodge pickup truck.

1973. Anthony Blake (*The Magician*): White convertible (The Spirit).

1974. Howard Cunningham (*Happy Days*): Black DeSoto; Richie Cunningham: 1952 Ford convertible (The Love Bandit). Moses Pray (*Paper Moon*): 1931 Roadster. Jim Rockford (*The Rockford Files*): Bronze Pontiac Firebird.

1975. Dave Starsky (*Starsky and Hutch*): Red and white 1974 Ford Torino; Ken Hutchinson: Scratched, dented, gas eating, muffler-smoking gray sedan. Tony Baretta (*Baretta*): Sedan he calls the Blue Ghost. Matt Helm (*Matt Helm*): Red Ford Thunderbird and a Rolls-Royce.

1976. Jaime Sommers (*The Bionic Woman*): Blue Datsun 280Z sports car. Kris Monroe (*Charlie's Angels*): White Cobra. Dr. Quincy (*Quincy, M.E.*): Black coroner's station wagon.

1977. J.Z. Kane (*Dog and Cat*): Volkswagen with a Porsche engine. Abby Bradford (*Eight Is Enough*): MG sedan she calls Gwendolyn.

1978. Bobby Ewing (*Dallas*): Red Mercedes convertible. Dan Tanna (*Vegas*): Red 1956 Ford Thunderbird convertible. Mindy McConnell (*Mork and Mindy*): Dark blue-gray Jeep.

1979. Bo and Luke Duke (*The Dukes of Hazzard*): Orange 1969 Dodge Charger (The General Lee); Daisy Duke: White AMC Golden Eagle Jeep she calls Dixie. Jonathan Hart (*Hart to Hart*): Mercedes sedan. Gary Ewing (*Knots Landing*): Black Jaguar XJ-S. Harry Broderick (*Salvage 1*): Antique Rolls-Royce.

1980. Thomas Magnum (*Magnum P.I.*): Red Ferrari 308 and an Audi 5000. Lionel Whitney (*Tenspeed and Brown Shoe*): Green Triumph TR-7 sports car.

1981. Colt Seavers (*The Fall Guy*): GMC Pickup Truck.

1982. Jim Douglas (*Herbie, the Love Bug*): Volkswagen Bug. Michael Knight (*Knight Rider*): Black Pontiac Trans-Am (KITT). Madame (*Madame's Place*): White antique Rolls-Royce. Ellen Jackson (*Mama's Family*): 1982 Cadillac Seville. Matt Houston (*Matt Houston*): Rolls-Royce. Remington Steele (*Remington Steele*): 1936 Auburn and a blue Mercedes.

1983. B.A. Baracus (*The A-Team*): Black with red trim GMC van; Templeton Peck: Sedan. Lee Stetson (*Scarecrow and Mrs. King*): 1953 Porsche 350.

1984. Mark Gordon (*Highway to Heaven*): Gray Ford sedan. Mike Hammer (*Mike Hammer*): Blue Mustang convertible. Dan Fielding (*Night Court*): Mercedes he calls The Dan Mobile. Tony Micelli (*Who's the Boss?*): 1967 blue Chevy Van (then a 1989 blue Jeep Cherokee); Samantha Micelli: Yellow 1968 Oldsmobile.

1985. Robert McCall (*The Equalizer*): Black 1985 XJ6 Jaguar. Mike Seaver (*Growing Pains*): Red Volkswagen convertible. Father Noah Rivers (*Hell Town*): 1940s Chevy woodie station wagon. Katy Mahoney (*Lady Blue*): Bronze Ford Bronco. Angus MacGyver (*MacGyver*): Jeep Wrangler (later a 1957 Chevy Nomad station wagon, then a yellow 1946 Ford pickup truck). Spenser (*Spenser: For Hire*): 1965 Black Mustang, then a 1986 Ford.

1986. Deacon Ernest Frye (*Amen*): Oldsmobile Regency. L.K. McGuire (*Easy Street*): Blue Rolls-Royce. Ray (*Stingray*): Black 1965 Corvette Stingray.

1987. Jesse (*Full House*): Yellow Ford Mustang he calls Sally; Joey: Red 1963 Rambler he calls Rosie. Claire McCarron (*Leg Work*): Silver Porsche. Al Bundy (*Married … With Children*): 1974 brown Dodge sedan.

1988. Murphy Brown (*Murphy Brown*): White Porsche. Jack Arnold (*The Wonder Years*): Chevy Impala sedan; Kevin Arnold: Blue Oldsmobile.

1989. Steve Urkel (*Family Matters*): BMW Isetta minicar.

1990. George Costanza (*Seinfeld*); 1976 Chevy Impala. Jerry Seinfeld (*Seinfeld*): Black Saab convertible. Maxwell Beckett (*Over My Dead Body*): Rolls-Royce. Rosie O'Neill (*The Trials of Rosie O'Neill*): Mercedes.

1991. Dylan Del'Amico (*Undercover*): Vintage Corvette. Frank Lambert (*Step by Step*): GMC pickup truck. Tim Taylor (*Home Improvement*): 1933 blue Ford Roadster; Jill Taylor: Red Chevrolet Nomad station wagon.

1992. Detective Nicholas Knight (*Forever Knight*): 1962 Cadillac. Duncan MacLeod (*The Immortal*): Classic Thunderbird.

1993. Cordell Walker (*Walker, Texas Ranger*): Dodge 4×4. Dr. Mark Sloan (*Diagnosis Murder*): Jaguar. Grace Kelly (*Grace Under Fire*): Blue Pontiac GTO.

1994. Tess (*Touched by an Angel*): Red Cadillac. Joe Astor (*Viper*) drives a red Dodge Viper RT/10 Roadster that morphs into the silver Defender (in later episodes the car is a blue Dodge Viper GTS Coupe). In 1996 episodes of *Viper*, Cameron Westlake drives a 1996 Dodge Avenger (then a 1998 Jeep Grand Cherokee Limited); Frankie Waters drives a 1971 Plymouth Barracuda then a Dodge Challenger.

1995. Cybill Sheridan (*Cybill*): 1964 Dodge

Dart. Drew Carey (*The Drew Carey Show*): White Volkswagen Bug.

1996. Nash Bridges (*Nash Bridges*): Yellow 1971 Plymouth Barracuda. Jim Ellison (*The Sentinel*): Ford Sedan. Steve Hightower (*The Steve Harvey Show*): Ford Taurus.

1998. Darryl Hughley (*The Hughleys*): Lexus. Jesse Warner (*Jesse*): Orange Volkswagen. Vallery Irons (*V.I.P.*): Blue Mustang; Nikki Franco: White Mustang (later a Dodge); Kay Simmons: Ford minivan; Tasha Dexter: Mustang.

2000. Lorelai Gilmore (*Gilmore Girls*): Silver Jeep. Cassie, D.D. and Shane (*She Spies*): Share a yellow Jeep convertible.

2001. Darcy Walker (*Black Scorpion*): Orange Corvette (later said to be a red Stingray) that morphs into her crime fighting Scorpion Mobile. The Lone Gunmen (*The Lone Gunmen*): Rusty green and white Volkswagen Van.

2002. George Lopez (*The George Lopez Show*): SUV.

2004. Veronica Mars (*Veronica Mars*): Midnight blue sports convertible.

2005. Professor Harold March (*Stacked*): 1965 Dodge Dart.

Cartoons

Before the advent of Saturday morning cartoons (which became a full morning tradition for ABC, CBS and NBC in 1970 with Fox, the W.B. and kid-oriented cable stations following suit years later) there were few made-for-television cartoons (*The Mighty Mouse Playhouse* became the first animated series to air on Saturday morning in 1955).

Saturday morning TV in the early 1950s was a strange mix of programming. There were some kid shows (*Smilin' Ed's Gang, Saturday at the Bronx Zoo, The Big Top, Foodini the Great*) but there were also live and filmed comedy series (*Two Girls Named Smith, A Date with Judy*), space shows (*Tom Corbett, Space Cadet, The Secret Files of Captain Video*), adventure and western series (*Fury, The Roy Rogers Show*), anthology series (*Faith Baldwin's Theater of Romance*) and even old theatrical serials mixed in with cartoons (*Kiddie Showtime*).

Cartoons were regulated mostly to the early evening hours (4 P.M. to 6 P.M.) and consisted of such theatrical favorites as *Popeye the Sailor, Oswald*

the *Rabbit, Farmer Alfalfa, Bugs Bunny, Little Lulu, Casper the Friendly Ghost* and *Woody Woodpecker*. In 1957 William Hanna and Joseph Barbera created *The Ruff and Reddy Show* and within the months and years that followed would change the course of animated TV history with such shows as *Huckleberry Hound, Quick Draw McGraw, The Flintstones* and *The Jetsons*.

The listing that follows charts the progression of cartoons (including theatrical firsts) of the animated series that appeared on TV from the first known program in 1939 to 1970.

1920s. Experimental TV stations broadcast images of Felix the Cat as a means of testing their transmissions.

1939. *Donald's Cousin Gus*, a Walt Disney theatrical cartoon, is the first known cartoon to be broadcast in its entirety (NBC on May 19).

1940. The Disney cartoon *The Ugly Duckling* airs on *A Milestone in Television* (May 15), a variety program on which NBC celebrated its first year of regular programming.

1946. Live action is mixed with animation very early in TV history on *Shorty* (CBS). The mischievous Shorty is a cartoon character whose adventures unfold as artist Syd Hoff sketches a story for his friend Patty Foster, a real-life skating star.

1948. Artist Charles Luchsinger draws line sketches to illustrate the yarns spun by Jack Luchsinger on ABC's *Cartoon Theater*.

1949. The serial-like adventures of Crusader Rabbit and his friend Rags the Tiger came to life on the syndicated *Crusader Rabbit*. Non-animated cartoon strips are viewed and narrated panel by panel on *The Telecomics* (Syn; on NBC in 1950 as *The NBC Comics*). Stories included *Brother Goose; Joey and Jug; Rick Rack, Special Agent* for syndication. On NBC they were *Danny March; Johnny and Mr. Do-Right; Kid Champion* and *Space Barton*.

1950. Cartoon strips drawn by Cousin Kibb follow the adventures of Billy Boone on *Billy Boone and Cousin Kibb* (CBS). The animated adventures of a young boy and girl air on ABC's *Lois and Looey*.

1953. A ghost who longs to befriend people is the focus of the syndicated *Casper the Friendly Ghost*. Two youngsters find adventure on the animated series *Jim and Judy in Teleland* (Syn.). Jack Barry hosts *Winky Dink and You* (NBC), the second program to combine live action with animation (see also 1946). Children participated at home via "Winky Dink and You Home Kits." A clear plastic screen was placed over the TV screen and with crayons, the child drew essential elements to help the animated boy Winky Dink and his pal Woofer the Dog out of dangerous situations. As a child drew a rope, for example, it would appear on the TV screen and allow Winky Dink to use it to escape some perilous situation.

1955. The mischievous talking magpies Heckle and Jeckle come to TV via syndication on *The Heckle and Jeckle Show*. When a mouse scientist invents a potion called "Atomic Energy" he becomes the heroic Mighty Mouse on CBS's *The Mighty Mouse Playhouse*.

1956. Dick Van Dyke hosts a series of theatrical cartoons including *Heckle and Jeckle, Gandy Goose* and *Little Roguefort* on *The CBS Cartoon Theater*. CBS also airs *Gerald McBoing Boing*, a series about a young boy who speaks in sound effects ("Boing! Boing!") rather than words.

1957. A young Native American boy learns about life on *The Adventures of Pow Wow* (NBC). When the evil Dr. Destructo begins to wreck havoc in outer space, Colonel Bleep and his Space Deputies Squeak the Puppet and Scratch the Caveman, attempt to stop him on the syndicated *Colonel Bleep*. Serial-like stories about Ruff the cat and Reddy the dog comprise *The Ruff and Ready Show* (NBC). A young boy acquires amazing powers from his funnel-like hat on *Tom Terrific* (CBS). The world's most beloved (and mischievous) bird comes to ABC on *The Woody Woodpecker Show*.

1958. A dog tackles various jobs on *The Huckleberry Hound Show*. Also seen on the syndicated series: *Pixie and Dixie* (mice who plague Mr. Jinks the cat) and *Hokey Wolf* (about a conniving wolf). The fantasy-like adventures of a young boy and his come to life teddy bear are the basis of the syndicated *Spunky and Tadpole*. Jellystone Park residents Yogi Bear and his sidekick Boo Boo Bear scheme to get picnic lunch baskets on *Yogi Bear*. Other segments on the syndicated series: *Snagglepuss* (a trouble prone lion) and *Yakky Doodle Duck* (a mischievous duckling).

1959. A young boy and girl travel throughout the world on the syndicated *Bob and Betty in Adventure Land*. Adventurer Clutch Cargo and his pals Spinner (a boy) and Paddlefoot (a dog) battle evil on the syndicated *Clutch Cargo*. ABC airs *Matty's Funday Funnies*, a series of Harvey theatrical cartoons sponsored by Mattel toys and

hosted by the animated Matty and Sisterbelle. Dim-witted horse sheriff Quick Draw McGraw and his deputy, the donkey Baba Looey, attempt to maintain the peace on *The Quick Draw McGraw Show* (Syn.). Other segments: *Snooper and Blabber* (cat and mouse crime fighting team) and *Augie Doogie and Doggie Daddy* (a father attempts to control the antics of his potentially juvenile delinquent son). Rocky the Flying Squirrel and his dim-witted friend Bullwinkle J. Moose battle the evils of Boris Badenov and his companion Natasha Fataly on ABC's *Rocky and His Friends*. Other segments: *Aesop's Fables, Fractured Fairy Tales* and *Peabody's Improbable History*.

1960. Elmer Fudd and Yosemite Sam are two of the characters struggling to cope with the antics of that mischievous rabbit, Bugs Bunny on *The Bugs Bunny Show* (ABC/CBS). A simple minded Mississippi lawman attempts to uphold the peace on the syndicated *Deputy Dawg*. Felix the cat battles evil with his magic bag of tricks on the syndicated *Felix the Cat*. Prehistoric marrieds Fred and Wilma Flintstone and their neighbors Barney and Betty Rubble come to life on ABC's *The Flintstones*. King Leonardo, the ruler of Bongoland, and his assistant Odie Colognie, are the featured segments of *King Leonardo and His Short Subjects* (also known as *The King and Odie*). Other segments on the NBC series: *The Hunter* (a beagle detective attempts to capture the cunning Fox) and *Tutor the Turtle* (who becomes anything he wishes through the magic of Mr. Wizard the Lizard). The legendary hero of mythology, Hercules protects the Learien Valley from the evil wizard Deadalus on *The Mighty Hercules* (Syn.). Fumbling private detective Q.T. Hush, his dog Shamus, and his shadow Quincy (able to operate independently of Q.T.) form the elements of the syndicated *Q.T. Hush*.

1961. Dave Saville manages Theodore, Simon and Alvin, the singing chipmunks on *The Alvin Show* (CBS). Other segments: *Clyde Crashcup* (a wacky inventor) and *Sinbad, Jr.* (a mighty sailor). The young boy Beany and his sidekick, Cecil the Seasick Sea Serpent, star on the syndicated (later ABC) *Beany and Cecil Show*. Animation and live action mix when cartoon brothers Butch and Billy host edited theatrical westerns on the syndicated *Butch and Billy and Their Bang Bang Western Movies*. The antics of a not-too-bright bear (Calvin Burnside) and his friend, a cunning fox (Montgomery J. Klaxon), are the elements of

Calvin and the Colonel (ABC). Upholding the law in crime-ridden Empire City becomes the job of Courageous Cat and his assistant Minute Mouse on the syndicated *Courageous Cat*. The beloved characters from L. Frank Baum's *The Wizard of Oz* find new adventures in the Land of Oz on the syndicated *Tales of the Wizard of Oz*. Twelve-year-old Tin Tin and his dog Snowy attempt to solve crimes on the syndicated *Tin Tin*. Arnold Stang provides the voice for *Top Cat* (ABC), a master con artist (patterned after the Sergeant Bilko character created by Phil Silvers) who schemes to live the good life.

1962. The title tells it all — *The Adventures of Hoppity Hopper from Foggy Bogg* (Syn/ABC). Space-age comedy comes to TV via George Jetson, his wife Jane and children Judy and Elroy on ABC's *The Jetsons*. The syndicated *Lippy the Lion* follows the antics of a trouble prone lion. Popeye, Olive Oyl, Brutus and Swee'pea are adapted to TV from the theatrical cartoons on the syndicated *Popeye the Sailor*. Interplanetary Space Force agent Scott McCloud battles evil on *Space Angel* (Syn.). A turtle that believes he is a modern-day knight battles injustice on *Touche Turtle* (Syn). A bon vivant alligator-about-town is the hero of the syndicated *Wally Gator*. Live action and animation mix when the animated Wally Western and his pal Skeets host edited theatrical westerns on the syndicated *Wally Western*.

1963. The first Japanese produced (and dubbed in English) cartoon comes to America as *Astro Boy*. The syndicated series tells of a robot boy (Astro Boy) and his sister (Astro Girl) as they battle evil. Paul Winchell hosts *Cartoonsville*, an ABC series of theatrical cartoons (*Sheriff Saddle Head, Goodie the Gremlin, Jeepers Creepers* and *Scat Cat*). A scientist uses a time machine to investigate the major events of the world on *The Hector Heathcote Show* (NBC). The King Features comic strips *Barney Google, Beetle Bailey* and *Krazy Kat* come to life on the syndicated *King Features Trilogy*. The nearsighted Quincy Magoo comes to TV via syndication on *Mr. Magoo*. Don Adams provides the voice of Tennessee Tuxedo, a penguin who, with his friend Chumley the Walrus, attempts to improve living conditions at the Megopolis Zoo on *Tennessee Tuxedo and His Tales* (Syn.).

1964. Young Jonny Quest assists his father, Dr. Benton Quest, as he searches for the answers to scientific mysteries on *The Adventures of Jonny Quest* (ABC). A young boy explores the mysteries of the planets on *The Big World of Little Adam* (Syn.). Rocky the Flying Squirrel and Bullwinkle J. Moose return to ABC (and run until 1973) on *The Bullwinkle Show* (see 1959). Legendary tales and figures of past history are adapted to TV and star the nearsighted Quincy Magoo (voice of Jim Backus) on *The Famous Adventures of Mr. Magoo* (NBC). Sheldon Leonard provides the voice for Linus, the gentle ruler of animals in Africa on CBS's *Linus the Lionhearted*. The fun-loving Magilla Gorilla, the permanent resident of Mr. Peebles Pet Shop, comes to TV on *The Magilla Gorilla Show* (Syn.). Purple hippo Peter Potamus and his friend So So the Monkey travel around the world in an air balloon on *The Peter Potamus Show*. Other segments on the syndicated series: *Breezly and Sneezly* (Breezly the polar bear and Sneezly the seal seek warmth at Camp Frostbite in the North Pole) and *Yippie, Yappie and Yahooey* (mischievous dogs attempt to guard their king). The stuttering Porky Pig comes to TV in his own series, *The Porky Pig Show* on ABC. "There's no need to fear, Underdog is here," says Shoeshine Boy, a humble dog who becomes a daring crime fighter on NBC's *Underdog*. Wally Cox provides the voice.

1965. *The Atom Ant/Secret Squirrel Show* (NBC) presents the adventures of the world's mightiest insect and a daring secret agent squirrel. The songs of John Lennon, George Harrison, Ringo Starr and Paul McCartney are seen in animated form on ABC's *The Beatles*. *Dodo — The Kid from Outer Space* (Syn.) tells of Dodo, a boy from the planet Hena Hydro who is sent to Earth to assist Professor Fingers with his important research. Police agent Peter Brady's life force is embodied into Tobor, an indestructible crime-fighting robot on *The Eighth Man* (Syn.). The incompetent feline Klondike Kat seeks to apprehend the notorious rodent Savior Faire on the syndicated *Klondike Kat*. The Marvel comic book characters *Captain America, Incredible Hulk, Iron Man, Mighty Thor* and *Sub Mariner* are animated in serial-like stories on the syndicated *Marvel Super Heroes*. Several cartoons comprise *The Milton the Monster Cartoon Show* (ABC): *Milton the Monster* (a lovable Frankenstein-type creature), *Fearless Fly* (insect who fights crime), *Flukey Luke* (cowboy doubles as a private eye), *Muggy Doo* (con artist) and *Penny Penguin* (mischievous child). The Peanuts characters come to TV for the first time in *A Charlie Brown Christmas* (CBS).

Charlie Brown, Snoopy, Lucy, Linus and the other Charles Schulz characters would appear in many specials over the years. A scientist who discovers a power pill that endows him with the power of 20 atom bombs for 20 seconds is the premise of *Roger Ramjet* (Syn.).

1966. Movie comedians Bud Abbott and Lou Costello become animated for *The Abbott and Costello Cartoon Show* (Syn.). Bud Abbott provides his own voice; Stan Irwin is Lou. A daring bat and his pal Karate battle evil on the syndicated *Batfink*. Stringer and Tubby are the canines that comprise the rock group, *The Beagles* (ABC). A dashing secret agent wages a war against crime on NBC's *Cool McCool*. A 30-foot tall robot (Frankenstein Jr.) and the Impossibles (Coil Man, Fluid Man and Multi Man) battle evil on CBS's *Frankenstein Jr. and the Impossibles*. Gigantor, an indestructible space-age robot, and his 12-year-old master Jimmy Sparks, battle interplanetary evil on the syndicated *Gigantor*. A rare and brave white lion struggles to protect his kingdom of Africa on the syndicated *Kimba, the White Lion*. The legendary gorilla King Kong helps his young master, Bobby Bond battle the evil Dr. Who on ABC's *The King Kong Show*. The Ocean Patrol and its number one agent, Marine Boy, battle evil beneath the sea on the syndicated *Marine Boy*. With the aid of an incredible baby bottle and working out of a crib, Diaper Man battles evil on *The Mighty Heroes* (Syn.). An animated Moe, Larry and Curly come to TV in ten minute syndicated cartoons called *The New Three Stooges*. The Universal Peace Corps of the planet Radian attempts to keep the peace in space through its unique agent *Prince Planet* (Syn.). CBS's *Space Ghost* relates the adventures of an interplanetary crime fighter. Youngsters battle evil in outer space on NBC's *Space Kiddettes*. Magneto Man, Elevator Man, Super Scuba, Granite Man, Captain Wammy and Super Bowing are crime fighters for Super Services, Inc. who are known as *The Super Six* (NBC). Theatrical cartoons mix with made-for TV cartoons on *The Tom and Jerry Show* (CBS; about the antics of Tom the cat and Jerry the mouse).

1967. Earthling Kenny Carter battles evil with the help of three celestial beings on *The Amazing Three* (Syn.). Ray Randall, alias Birdman, and the Galaxy Trio (Galaxy Girl, Vapor Man, Meteor Man) battle evil on NBC's *Birdman and the Galaxy Trio*. Scientists Reed Richards, Sue Richards,

Ben Grimm and Johnny Storm battle evil as *The Fantastic Four* on ABC. Tree-crashing prone, simple-minded George battles evil in the jungle on ABC's *George of the Jungle*. Other segments: *Super Chicken* (Henry Cabot Henhouse III battles evil) and *Tom Slick* (naïve race car driver). Animals struggle to protect their utopian planet from evil on CBS's *The Herculoids*. Explorers seek the unknown mysteries of the earth's core on ABC's *Journey to the Center of the Earth*. The legendary white whale, Moby Dick, struggles to protect his human foundlings Tom and Tub on CBS's *Moby Dick and the Mighty Mightor*. A futuristic Robin Hood battles injustice in the year 3000 on the syndicated *Rocket Robin Hood*. A young boy becomes Samson and his dog the mighty Goliath on NBC's *Samson and Goliath*. Twins Nancy and Chuck and their genie Shazzan battle evil in the age of the Arabian Knights on *Shazzan!* (CBS). The adventures of a young and daring racing car driver are explored on the syndicated *Speed Racer*. James Norcross, the President of the U.S., uses the powers he acquired from a cosmic storm to battle evil on NBC's *Super President*.

1968. Live action hosts the Banana Splits (Fleegle, Bingo, Drooper and Snorky) host cartoons (*The Three Musketeers, The Arabian Knights* and *The Hillbilly Bears*) on *The Banana Splits Adventure Hour* (NBC). Four people are reduced to microscopic size to fight the unseen enemies of the free world on ABC's *Fantastic Voyage*. Ruffled Feathers and Running Board, gophers who resemble Indians, struggle to safeguard their domain from army colonel Kit Coyote on *The Go Go Gophers* (CBS). Live characters Tom Sawyer, Huck Finn and Becky Thatcher (Kevin Schultz, Michael Shea, Lu Ann Haslam) travel through strange animated fantasy lands to escape the clutches of the animated Injun Joe on *The New Adventures of Huck Finn* (NBC). Wile E. Coyote's fruitless attempts to capture the elusive Road Runner and have himself a decent meal are depicted on *The Road Runner Show* (CBS). A cross-country auto race is held to find the world's wackiest racer on *The Wacky Races* (CBS).

1969. Archie Andrews and his gang from Riverdale (Betty Cooper, Veronica Lodge and Jughead Jones) jump from the comics to TV on *The Archie Comedy Hour* (CBS). Chessie, Kitty Jo, Scootz, Groovy and Country are a feline rock group on ABC's *The Cattanooga Cats*. Dick Dastardly, an evil World War I air ace, and his fumbling assistant Muttley the dog, seek to win the war for their unnamed superior by intercepting the vital messages of the courier Yankee Doodle Pigeon on *Dastardly and Muttley in Their Flying Machines*. A dim-witted North Canadian Mounted Policeman attempts to uphold the law on *The Dudley Do-Right Show* (ABC). A young boy seeks to find the Crystal Key and lift the Curse of Gloom an evil Grump has placed on a kingdom on NBC's *Here Comes the Grump*. Responsible young drivers who are also members of the Hot Wheels Racing Club in Metro City are the subjects of ABC's *Hot Wheels*. The vulnerable Penelope Pitstop seeks to escape the clutches of the evil Hooded Claw on *The Perils of Penelope Pitstop* (CBS). The non-talking, non-conformist Pink Panther comes to TV on NBC's *The Pink Panther Show*. The cowardly dog Scooby-Doo and his human friends Freddy, Daphne, Shaggy and Velma solve mysteries on *Scooby-Doo, Where Are You?* (CBS). The Wilson family, operators of the air rescue unit Skyhawks, Inc., come to the aid of people in need on *The Skyhawks* (ABC). Smokey the Bear as both a cub and bear emphasize forest fire safety on *The Smokey Bear Show* (ABC). Peter Parker is bitten by a spider, acquires amazing abilities and battles evil on ABC's *Spider-Man*. A jungle boy acquires powers from a radioactive tree to battle evil on the syndicated *Taro, Giant of the Jungle*. A syndicated version of *Winky Dink and You* (see 1953) allows children to again help the main characters out of trouble via their "Winky Dink Home Kits."

1970. A veterinarian's ability to talk to animals becomes the basis of NBC's *Doctor Dolittle*. Basketball wizards the Harlem Globetrotters are seen in animated form as they help good defeat evil on CBS's *The Harlem Globetrotters*. Josie, Melody and Valerie are the all-girl rock group *Josie and the Pussycats* on CBS. Auto Cat attempts to beat Motor Mouse in a car race on ABC's *Motor Mouse*. Sir Malcolm struggles to protect a 400-year-old fire-breathing dragon from a little girl who delights in making him sneeze and breathe fire on ABC's *The Reluctant Dragon and Mr. Toad*. Sketches, songs and poetry based on children's literature comprise NBC's *Tomfoolery*. Disorganized football players Ed Huddles and Bubba McCoy are the stars of CBS's *Where's Huddles?* Comedian Jerry Lewis (voice of David L. Lander) works as a fumbling janitor for the Odd Job Employment Agency on *Will the Real Jerry Lewis Please Sit Down* (ABC).

Chicago

A listing of series set in Chicago, Illinois.
1949. *Chicago Land Mystery Players* (DuMont); *Stud's Place* (NBC).
1952. *Life with Luigi* (CBS).
1957. *M Squad* (NBC).
1959. *The Untouchables* (ABC).
1971. *The Chicago Teddy Bears* (CBS).
1972. *The Bob Newhart Show* (CBS).
1974. *Good Times* (CBS); *Kolchak: The Night Stalker* (ABC).
1976. *Mr. T and Tina* (ABC).
1979. *The Duke* (NBC), *Out of the Blue* (ABC).
1981. *American Dreams* (ABC).
1982. *Chicago Story* (NBC).
1983. *Joanie Loves Chachi* (ABC).
1984. *E/R* (CBS), *Punky Brewster* (NBC).
1985. *Charlie and Company* (CBS); *Lady Blue* (ABC).
1986. *Crime Story* (NBC); *Jack and Mike* (ABC); *Perfect Strangers* (ABC); *Tough Cookies* (CBS).
1987. *Married ... With Children* (Fox); *Nothing in Common* (NBC); *Sable* (ABC); *A Year in the Life* (NBC).
1989. *Anything But Love* (ABC); *Family Matters* (ABC); *Father Dowling Mysteries* (NBC).
1990. *Uncle Buck* (CBS); *Gabriel's Fire* (ABC).
1991. *Reasonable Doubts* (NBC); *Sisters* (NBC); *Top of the Heap* (Fox).
1992. *Angel Street* (CBS); *Bob* (CBS); *Vinnie and Bobby* (Fox).
1993. *The Building* (CBS); *Getting By* (NBC); *Missing Persons* (NBC); *The Second Half* (NBC); *The Untouchables* (Syn.).
1994. *Chicago Hope* (CBS); *ER* (NBC); *The Good Life* (NBC); *Viper* (NBC); *Wild Oats* (Fox).
1995. *The Bonnie Hunt Show* (CBS); *The Home Court* (NBC); *The Pursuit of Happiness* (NBC).
1996. *Early Edition* (CBS); The *Steve Harvey Show* (WB).
1997. *Between Brothers* (Fox); *Nothing Sacred* (ABC).
1998. *Two of a Kind* (ABC).
2001. *Special Unit 2* (UPN); *Tracker* (Syn.); *What About Joan* (ABC).
2003. *Andy Richter Controls the Universe* (Fox). *My Big Fat Greek Life* (CBS).
2005. *The Bad Girl's Guide* (UPN), *Freddie* (ABC).
2006. *The Loop* (Fox); *Modern Men* (WB); *Pepper Dennis* (WB).

Children — Extraordinary

This entry lists kids (pre-teen and teenage) who either possess extraordinary skills or are placed in situations that would not normally involve a child. See also *Adolescence, Teenagers.*

1957. Michael Carr plays Boy, the orphaned survivor of a plane crash, as he helps a research scientist (Ronald Adams) battle evil in Africa on *The Adventures of a Jungle Boy* (Syn.).

1961. Pippilotta Delicatessa Windowshade Mackrelmint Ephraim Longstocking (Gina Gillespie) is a brilliant young girl (the daughter of a cannibal king) who lives in a strange house with a horse and a monkey on the ABC pilot *Pippi Longstocking.*

1966. Dick Grayson (Burt Ward) is an orphaned teenage boy (adopted by Bruce Wayne) who is secretly Robin, the Boy Wonder, Batman's aide on ABC's *Batman.*

1974. Teenager Billy Batson (Michael Grey) is chosen by the immortal elders (Mercury, Atlas, Zeus and Achilles) to battle evil as Captain Marvel on CBS's *Shazam.*

1977. A young boy, lost in the woods, is found by the legendary Big Foot (Ray Young) and raised to become Wild Boy (Joseph Butcher), a protector of the forests on ABC's *Big Foot and Wild Boy.*

1978. Sixteen-year-old Molly Foster (Linda Purl) marries 18-year-old David Benton (Roger Kern) and the two struggle to establish a life for themselves in the rugged Dakota Territory of the 1870s on ABC's *The Young Pioneers.*

1981. Teenager Zack Rogers (Clark Brandon) is chosen by the modern-day Merlin the Magician (Barnard Hughes) to become his sorcerer's apprentice on CBS's *Mr. Merlin.*

1985. Courteney Cox plays Gloria Dinallo, a 17-year-old girl with amazing telekinetic powers on NBC's *The Misfits of Science.* Carrie Heim plays Pippi Longstocking, a feisty, courageous, red-haired girl who lives without adults (in Villa Villekulva), spins tall tales and enjoys exciting adventures on the ABC pilot *Pippi Longstocking* (see also 1961).

1987. Royana Black plays Molly McCue, a very pretty 14-year-old girl with the mind of Sherlock Holmes, who helps her friend, Detective Jack Wilder (Paul Sorvino) solve crimes on the kid-friendly PBS pilot *Almost Partners.* Jonathan Ward is Beans Baxter, a Washington, D.C. high school student who secretly works as a spy courier for the government on Fox's *The New Adventures of Beans Baxter.*

1988. Fourteen-year-old Andrew Clements (Jerry O'Connell) is hit by blue rays from an experimental machine, acquires amazing powers and uses his new found ability to battle evil as his hero Ultraman on the syndicated *My Secret Identity.*

1989. Scott Bremner plays Leroy Brown, a brainy kid named "Encyclopedia" for his vast knowledge, who solves crimes as an amateur detective on HBO's *Encyclopedia Brown — The Boy Detective.*

1992. A group of grammar school children become amateur sleuths with the help of a friendly entity they call Ghost Writer on the PBS series *Ghost Writer.* Blaze Berdahl and Sheldon Turnipseed head the cast as Lenni Frazier and Jamal Jenkins.

1993. Teenagers in Angel City are chosen by alien forces to safeguard the world with super powers on Fox's *Mighty Morphin Power Rangers.*

1994. Exposure to a leaking chemical endows 13-year-old Alexandra Mack (Larissa Oleynik) with amazing powers on *The Secret World of Alex Mack* (NICK). While working at his computer teenager Sam Collins (Matthew Lawrence) is zapped by a light that links his brain to the computer and enables him to enter the digital world (as Servo) to battle evil on the syndicated *Super Human Samurai Syber Squad.*

1996. Jubilee (Heather McComb), Buff (Suzanne Davis) and Refrax (Randall Slavin) are among the teenagers who possess a mutant X-factor that endows them with special powers on the Fox pilot *Generation X*

1997. Camela (Charlotte Sullivan), Emily (Erica Luttrell) and Strick (Kristian Ayre) are the 13-year-olds who solve crimes with the help of an entity they call Ghost Writer on CBS's *The New Ghost Writer Mysteries.*

2000. Michelle Trachtenberg joins the cast of *Buffy the Vampire Slayer* as Dawn Summers, Buffy's mysterious 14-year-old sister. Dawn was created from the energy of a powerful source called the Key by its guardians to safeguard it from the evil seeking to control it. She was given to Buffy (as a sister) to protect.

2001. Zack Greenberg (Robert Clark) is a student at the Horace Hyde White School for Boys who is like no other — wherever he goes strange things happen on Fox's *The Zack Files.*

2002. Sixteen-year-old Dinah Lance (Rachel

Skarsten) is a crime fighter with telekinetic powers on the WB's *Birds of Prey*. Emma Taylor-Isherwood plays Josie Trent, a student at Blake Holsey High School, who investigates the strange phenomena that occur there on *Strange Days at Blake Holsey High* (Discovery Kids on NBC).

2003. Kate (Brook Harman), her sister Sarah (Eliza Taylor-Cotter) and their brother Nicholas (Nicholas Donaldson) are transported to (and seek a way to escape) a series of mysterious islands inhabited by pirates while playing a new video game on Fox's *Pirate Islands*.

Children's Programs — Pioneering Years, 1941–1969

The need to address children with special programming has been a part of television since its earliest days. While most were just meant to entertain via cartoons and games, others tried to educate children or relate aspects of life to them. This listing chronicles children's programs from 1941 to 1969 (when *Sesame Street* premiered and showed that TV could entertain and educate at the same time). See also: *Adolescence, Cartoons, Children — Extraordinary, Extra Ordinary Kids, Fairy Tales, Puppets, Teenagers.*

1941. CBS airs the first series for children, *Jack and the Beanstalk*. A young girl (Anne Francis) kneels by her mother (Lydia Perera) to hear the story of "Jack and the Beanstalk." As she listens, an artist draws the pictures that follow the narration (the camera switches back and forth between the child, the mother and the ever-expanding panel of drawings).

1945. NBC airs a similar format on *The Amazing Adventures of Tumblin' Tim*. As young Timothy Taylor (Robert Ellis) retires to bed, his mother (Betty Babcock) reads him stories from the book "Tumblin' Tim Joins the Circus." As Timothy falls asleep the viewer sees his dream adventures in the Land of In-Between. Singer Ireene Wicker sings and relates stories for children on ABC's *Tele Tales for Children*.

1946. Ireene Wicker returns to ABC for an informal program of stories for children on *The Ireene Wicker Show*.

1947. A pre-selected child's birthday is celebrated on the air on *Happy Birthday*, a DuMont series hosted by Ted Brown. Buffalo Bob Smith and the puppet Howdy Doody set up a circus in Doodyville to entertain kids on *Howdy Doody* (NBC). Five smart children answer difficult questions submitted by home viewers on NBC's *Juvenile Jury*. Music, songs, game contests, magic tricks and audience participation are the elements of *The Small Fry Club* (DuMont).

1948. Ireene Wicker hosts a program of music, songs and fairy tales on *The Singing Lady* (ABC).

1949. Talented youngsters perform on *The Children's Hour*, an NBC series hosted by Ed Herlihy. John Kiernan explains scientific principles to children on *Kiernan's Kaleidoscope* (Syn.). Madge Tucker reads stories for children on NBC's *The Lady Next Door*. Zovella, a clever magician, hosts an NBC series of songs, games and magic tricks for children on *The Magic Clown*. Stories, fairy tales, games and art instruction is presented by Pat Meikle on *The Magic Cottage* (DuMont). Dramatizations of past historical events are coupled with music and stories on *Mr. Imagination*, a CBS series starring Paul Tripp. Popular children's fables are dramatized on *Through the Crystal Ball* (CBS) with Anita Alvarez as the host.

1950. Sketches of a dog-named Chester are drawn by an artist and narrated by Art Whitfield on ABC's *Chester the Pup*. Stories for children are told by Edith Skinner and illustrated by Lisa Weil on NBC's *Children's Sketch Book*. Musical acts are coupled with sketches on *Crash Corrigan's Ranch*, an ABC series with a western motif hosted by film star Ray "Crash" Corrigan. Baseball legend Joe DiMaggio chats with youngsters, answers their questions and interviews guests on *The Joe DiMaggio Show* (Syn.). Classic and contemporary stories are dramatized on *The Magic Slate* (NBC). As an eight-year-old girl named Sandy (Rose Marie Iannone) drifts off to sleep her dreams of a magic land where children sing, dance and perform in sketches are shared with viewers on ABC's *Sandy Dreams*. Smilin' Ed McConnell hosts an NBC series of music, songs, stories and skits called *The Buster Brown TV Show with Smilin' Ed McConnell and His Buster Brown Gang* (later changed to *Smilin' Ed McConnell and His Gang*). Todd Russell hosts *Rootie Kazootie* (NBC), a series of music, songs and puppet antics set against the background of the Rootie Kazootie Club. Facts about wild life are related to children through drawings of animals on the syndicated *Unk and Andy*.

1951. Actress Maureen O'Sullivan hosts a program of films for youngsters on *The Children's Hour* (Syn.). Six children compete in various athletic contests on ABC's *Hail to the Champ* (hosted by Herb Allen). Al Gannaway hosts *Half-Pint Party*, an ABC series of music and songs for children. Two children compete in a series of thirty-second boxing bouts for prizes on *Kid Gloves* (CBS). Western film star Lash LaRue demonstrates his cowboy skills on the syndicated *Lash of the West*. Aspiring child talent performs on DuMont's *Kids and Company* with host Johnny Olsen. Fairy tales, songs and feats of magic are presided over by Geraldine Larsen on *The Magic Lady* (Syn.). Mary Hartline, "Queen of the Super Circus," presents music, songs and games for children on *The Mary Hartline Show* (ABC). Don Herbert explains scientific principles to children on *Mr. Wizard* (NBC).

1952. *Ding Dong School* (NBC) presents educational entertainment for pre-school children with Dr. Frances Horwich as Miss Frances. Sketches are coupled with film shorts as Warren Wright hosts *Junior High Jinks* on CBS. Bob Archer presents western variety acts on ABC's *Junior Rodeo*. The Story Princess (Katherine Heger) spins yarns for children on NBC's *Once Upon a Fence*. Nonprofessional children compete for the title "The Most Talented Child of the Week" on *Pud's Prize Party* (ABC) with host Todd Russell. Various entertainment acts geared to children is the format of ABC's *Tootsie Hippodrome* (hosted by John Reed King).

1953. Ireene Wicker sings and relates stories to children on *Ireene Wicker's Story Time* (ABC). Entertainment geared to preschool children is presented on the syndicated *Romper Room*.

1954. Children compete for prizes in a question-and-answer session on NBC's *Funny Boners* with host Jimmy Weldon. Cartoons are coupled with game contests on DuMont's *The Funny Bunny*. Dick Noel is the host; Dick West plays the Funny Bunny.

1955. Andy Devine hosts *Andy's Gang*, a program of music, skits and stories on NBC. Bob Keeshan helps children understand their rapidly changing world on CBS's *Captain Kangaroo*. The adventures of jungle explorer Captain Safari (Randy Knight) unfold through a magic TV screen on CBS's *Captain Safari of the Jungle Patrol*. Music, songs and puppet adventures are presented by hostess Josie Carey and puppeteer Fred Rogers on *The Children's Corner* (NBC). Children learn about various aspects of their world as they visit places on interest with host Sonny Fox on *Let's Take a Trip* (CBS). Jimmie Dodd and a group of Mouseketeers (Annette Funicello being the most famous) entertain children on a daily basis on *The Mickey Mouse Club* (ABC). Paula Stone hosts a mix of music, songs and stories set against the background of a toy store on *Paula Stone's Toy Shop* (Syn.).

1956. Children compete in various game contests on NBC's *Choose Up Sides* with Gene Rayburn as the host. Bert Parks hosts *The Giant Step* (NBC), a game in which children answer questions of increasing difficulty to win a college education.

1957. Twelve-year-old Susan Heinkel hosts *Susan's Show*, a CBS series of songs, stories and "Popeye" theatrical cartoons. Galen Drake presents music and songs for children on ABC's *This Is Galen Drake*.

1958. Music, songs, puppet antics and adventure stories are presented for children with host Al Lewis on *The Uncle Al Show* (ABC).

1959. Game contests, cartoons and circus acts set under a big top is the format of *Bozo the Clown* (also known as *Bozo's Circus* and *Bozo's Big Top Circus*), a format that was syndicated to allow local stations to supply their own hosts as Bozo.

1960. Magician Mark Wilson hosts *The Magic Land of Allakazam*, a CBS series set against a magical kingdom of music, cartoons and feats of magic.

1961. Cliff Norton portrays various characters (such as Police Mann, Milk Mann, Post Mann) on the skit comedy *The Funny Manns* (Syn.). Jack Lescoulie is the host of *One, Two, Three — Go!* an NBC series that explores places of interest to children. Pip the Piper (Jack Spear) and Miss Merrynote (Phyllis Spear) lead children in a series of fantasy adventures on ABC's *Pip the Piper*. Children compete on a large stage game board for prizes on CBS's *Video Village Junior* (a kid version of the adult game show *Video Village*).

1962. Dr. Albert Hobbs hosts *Exploring*, an NBC series that relates various aspects of the world to children via films, songs and sketches.

1963. Pom Pom, the trained stallion, and Dixie, "the world's smartest Doberman," are part of *Buckaroo 500*, a western-accented, syndicated variety series for children hosted by Buck Weaver. The various cultures and events of the world are explored for children on ABC's *Discovery*. Virginia Gibson, Frank Buxton and Bill Owen are the hosts.

1964. Bob Keeshan takes time off from *Captain Kangaroo* to host the Saturday morning CBS series *Mr. Mayor* (who relates aspects of the adult world to children). A child must either answer a question or perform a stunt for prizes on *Shenanigans*, an ABC series hosted by Stubby Kaye.

1967. The emotional development of children is the focal point of *Mr. Rogers' Neighborhood*, an NET (then PBS) series hosted by Fred Rogers, a kind man who invited everyone to be his friend and join him for a half-hour of educational fun.

1969. Stories of African wildlife are geared to children on NBC's *Jambo* ("Hello"). Marshall Thompson hosts. Preschool children are taught to recognize letters of the alphabet, reinforce their reading skills and learn to count from one to twenty on *Sesame Street* (NET, then PBS), the anywhere street in an anywhere town where learning becomes fun. Jim Henson's Muppets, led by Kermit the Frog, star. Adult actors dressed as characters from children's literature are the X's and O's on a large nine-square board where children play the game of Tic Tac Toe on *The Storybook Squares* (NBC; Peter Marshall hosts).

Christmas see *Holiday Specials*

Circus and Carnivals

From the very first known presentation of a circus on television in 1940 to the latest incarnation in 2003, circuses and carnivals have been a major attraction to people of all ages. This listing chronicles the circus and carnival themed programs that have, for the most part, followed the tradition of being "The Greatest Show on Earth" (slogan of the Ringling Brothers and Barnum & Bailey Circus). See also *Clowns*.

1940. CBS broadcasts the Ringling Brothers and Barnum & Bailey Circus from Madison Square Garden in New York City on April 25th.

1944. World famous clown Emmett Kelly is the featured performer on *Side Show*, a series of three NBC broadcasts (April 15, 22, 29) of the Ringling Brothers and Barnum & Bailey Circus from Madison Square Garden.

1946. The entire 2½-hour presentation of the Ringling Brothers and Barnum & Bailey Circus is telecast by CBS on May 3rd.

1947. Buffalo Bob Smith and his wooden marionette pal, Howdy Doody, invite kids to the Doodyville Circus on NBC's *Howdy Doody*.

1948. Gil Fates provides the commentary for two compete CBS broadcasts of the Ringling Brothers and Barnum & Bailey Circus from Madison Square Garden (April 7, 11). A magician named Zovella hosts circus variety acts on *The Magic Clown* (NBC).

1950. Jack Stillwell (as the Ringmaster, Uncle Tim) presents circus variety acts on ABC's *Acrobat Ranch*. Ringmaster Jack Sterling introduces foreign and American circus acts on CBS's *The Big Top*.

1951. Hollywood Candy sponsors *Hollywood Junior Circus* on NBC (then ABC) with Art Jacobson (then Paul Barnes) and the Ringmaster.

1952. Circus variety acts are coupled with the story of an aging clown (Joe E. Brown) and his attempts to help a young singer (Dolores Gray) who has joined his troupe on *The Buick Circus Hour* (NBC). Frank Gallop is the Ringmaster. Undiscovered talent performs against a carnival background on *The M&M Candy Carnival* (CBS) with Barry Cassell as the Ringmaster. John Reed King hosts the circus attractions on ABC's *Tootsie Hippodrome*.

1954. NBC airs *Contest Carnival*, a variety series that presents performances by aspiring circus acts.

1956. Mickey Braddock stars as Corky, water boy to Bimbo the elephant on the first circus adventure series *Circus Boy*. Robert Lowery plays Big Tim Champion, owner of the 19th century Champion Circus. Paul Winchell hosts *Circus Time*, an ABC series of circus variety acts. Although broadcast locally in New York (over WOR-TV), *Terrytoon Circus* is known both far and wide. Ringmaster Claude Kirchner, assisted by his clown puppet, Clownie, presented stories, guests and Terrytoon theatrical cartoons set against the backdrop of a traveling circus.

1961. The saga of the traveling 19th century one ring Thompson and Travis Combined Circus is the basis of *Frontier Circus* (CBS). Chill Wills stars as Colonel Casey Thompson with John Derek as Ben Travis. Don Ameche hosts NBC's

International Showtime a weekly series that spotlights circus variety acts.

1962. Ringmaster Claude Kirchner introduces circus acts from around the world on NBC's *Magic Midway.*

1963. A behind-the-scenes look at circus life is seen via the Ringling Brothers and Barnum & Bailey Circus on *The Greatest Show on Earth* (ABC). Jack Palance stars as Johnny Slade with Stu Erwin as Otto King.

1971. Bert Parks hosts *Circus,* a syndicated series featuring circus variety acts.

1974. Life in the circus world is seen through the experiences of Peter "Punch" Travers (Glenn Ford), a jack-of-all-trades with Charney's Great American Circus on the NBC pilot *Punch and Jody.* Pam Griffin plays Punch's daughter, Jody.

1977. *Little House on the Prairie* co-stars Melissa Gilbert (Laura Ingalls) and Melissa Sue Anderson (Mary Ingalls) host *Circus, Lions, Tigers and Melissa's Two,* an NBC special that presents circus acts from around the world. CBS airs the first of 17 *Circus of the Stars* specials. Celebrities perform circus acts under the supervision of professionals. William Conrad and Shirley Jones host *The World Famous Moscow Circus* (CBS) that presents highlights of the Moscow Circus in the USSR.

1978. Dan Haggerty, star of *The Life and Times of Grizzly Adams,* hosts a series of circus acts on NBC's *Dan Haggerty Goes to the Circus.*

1979. Sherisse Laurence and Cal Dodd host *Circus of the 21st Century,* a syndicated series of circus variety acts.

1981. Tony Randall presents highlights of Sweden's Stockholm International Circus on *Tony Randall's All Star Circus* (NBC).

1982. Circus entertainers perform and clown around on the syndicated *Mr. Moon's Magic Circus.* John Sarantos plays the circus owner, Mr. Moon.

1987. A behind-the-scenes look at circus life is presented through the experiences of Conrad and Leonora Simpson (Tony Jay, Margaret Hall), owners of the Traveling Simpson Circus on the CBS pilot *Circus.* Max Galpin (James Eckhouse) is a former CPA who buys a near-bankrupt circus and struggles to make it a success on the CBS pilot *Sawdust.* The circus at Epcot Center at Walt Disney World in Florida is spotlighted on *Walt Disney World's Celebrity Circus.* Tony Randall hosts the NBC special.

1988. Harry Anderson (of NBC's *Night Court*) hosts circus highlights from around the world on *The Seven Wonders of the Circus World* (CBS).

2003. HBO's *Carnivale* is a supernatural-based series that follows a traveling carnival during the 1930s Dust Bowl era. Nick Stahl stars as Ben Hawkins, a mysterious man who appears to be the focus in the battle between good and evil.

The Civil War

The Civil War was a conflict that pitted brother against brother, state against state and divided our nation for four years (1861–65). Television's coverage of the Civil War is quite limited but still an important aspect of its history. See also *The Korean, Vietnam and Iraqi Wars, World War II.*

1957. John Mosby (Tod Andrews), a Confederate major known as the Gray Ghost, conducts cunning raids against the Union Army in hopes of fostering a Confederate victory on *The Gray Ghost* (Syn.).

1960. *The Sounds of Home,* an ABC musical special, is set against the backdrop of the Civil War and tells of the love of a Southern belle (Dorothy Collins) for her beau (James Hurst) who has gone off to war.

1961. Brother is pitted against brother as Ben Canfield (Darryl Hickman) becomes a Union Loyalist and Jeff Canfield (Dick Davalos) joins the Confederacy (the Virginia Militia) on NBC's *Americans.*

1982. The Civil War from its ramblings in 1859 to the assassination of President Abraham Lincoln is the focus of *The Blue and the Gray,* an eight-hour miniseries broadcast by CBS. Stacy Keach, Kathleen Beller, Diane Baker and Lloyd Bridges head the large cast.

1985. Kirstie Alley, David Carradine and Georg Stanford Brown head the large cast of the 12-hour ABC miniseries *North and South* (which focuses on the friendship and hatred between two families, the Mains and the Hazards).

1986. The Main family of South Carolina and the Hazard family of Pennsylvania are embroiled in the Civil War conflict in *North and South, Book II,* ABC's 12-hour sequel to *North and South.* Kirstie Alley and David Carradine reprise their roles.

1990. Colleen Dewhurst, Jeremy Irons and Jason Robards, Jr. star in *Ken Burns' Civil War,* an elaborate nine-part PBS documentary that begins with the causes of the Civil War in 1861 and concludes with the effects of its aftermath in 1865.

1992. Devin O'Neill (Clive Owen) and Shelby Preston (Dan Futterman) are 1861 graduates of West Point who soon find themselves enemies when Devin sides with the North and Shelby the South on the ABC pilot *Class of '61.*

Clowns

Ronald McDonald, the mascot of the McDonald's hamburger chain, is probably the first name that comes to mind when someone mentions a clown. Emmett Kelly is the most famous clown of all time (with the Ringling Brothers and Barnum & Bailey Circus) and Clarabell and Bozo are perhaps the most famous TV clowns. This entry chronicles the TV clowns that have appeared on the medium from 1944 to 2005. See also *Circus and Carnivals.*

1944. Emmett Kelly is featured on *Side Show,* an NBC series of three live 20-minute telecasts showcasing side show attractions from the Ringling Brothers and Barnum & Bailey Circus at Madison Square Garden in New York City (Emmett is famous for his Depression-ear hobo clown Weary Willie).

1945. Pudgy Nose the Clown (Joe Kelly) lives in the Land of In-Between, a world that becomes real when Timothy Taylor (Robert Ellis) falls asleep and dreams on *The Amazing Adventures of Tumblin' Tim* (NBC).

1946. CBS telecasts the Ringling Brothers and Barnum & Bailey Circus featuring Emmett Kelly and other circus clowns.

1947. Clarabell Hornblow the Clown, who never speaks but answers by honking a yes or no horn on a utility belt he wears, entertains kids on NBC's *Howdy Doody.* Bob Keeshan (then Henry McLaughlin, Bobby Nickerson and Lew Anderson) played the role. He spoke only once on the last show in 1960 to say "Goodbye kids."

1949. Bonomo Turkish Taffy sponsors *The Magic Clown* on NBC. A magician named Zovella plays the Magic Clown and entertains kids in a circus atmosphere (Richard DuBois took over the role in 1952). Family man Roscoe Karns (himself) finds help in solving problems from Inky Poo (Curtis Wheeler), a clown projected by his conscience on the DuMont test film *Roscoe Karns*

and Inky Poo. Cliffy (Cliff Sobier), Scampy (Brady Patton) and Nicky (Nicky Francis) are the clowns on ABC's *Super Circus.*

1950. Ed McMahon (then Chris Keegan) plays the Clown to Ringmaster Jack Sterling on CBS's *The Big Top* (which presents live circus acts).

1951. Boffo the Clown (Carl Marx) keeps the festivities moving for Hollywood Candy, the sponsor of *Hollywood Junior Circus* (NBC/ABC). Joe E. Brown plays a clown who tries to help a circus newcomer (Dolores Gray) on the musical drama *The Buick Circus Hour* (NBC).

1955. A biography of Emmett Kelly is presented on *The General Electric Theater* (CBS) with Henry Fonda in the title role. Before becoming *Captain Kangaroo,* Bob Keeshan played Corny the Clown on *Time for Fun,* a local New York program (WABC-TV) wherein Corny chatted with kids between cartoons.

1956. Noah Beery, Jr. plays Joey the Clown on *Circus Boy* (NBC/ABC), a member of the 19th century traveling Champion Circus. Claude Kirchner and his clown puppet Clownie, host Terrytoon theatrical cartoons locally in New York on WOR-TV's *Terrytoon Circus.*

1958. Keds Sneakers introduces Kedso the Clown in TV commercials to help sell their sneakers to kids (the animated Kedso was superimposed with live action children).

1959. A syndicated circus format with local stations providing their own clown hosts is the essence of *Bozo the Clown.* In 1966–67 Frank Avruch played Bozo in a syndicated, complete in itself version called *Bozo's Big Top Circus Show* (he repeated the role in 1972 for a new version called *Bozo's Place.* In 1974, the series reverted to its original format and ran until 2001).

1960. Whether it was the East Side or the West Side, "all the kids love Tommy Seven because he's our favorite TV clown." Ed Bakey played Tommy Seven, a tramp clown on *The Tommy Seven Show,* a local New York program (WABC-TV) wherein he hosted cartoons, sang songs, told stories and performed in skits. Prior to this, Ed played *Pop Pop the Clown* on WJZ-TV in Baltimore (1957–60).

1961. Koko the Clown, his girlfriend Kokette and their dog Kokonut battle the evil Mean Moe on the syndicated cartoon *Out of the Inkwell.*

1965. Ronald McDonald, the clown who lives in McDonald Land, first comes to life at a local hamburger franchise in Washington, D.C. By

1970 he begins appearing in TV commercials as the mascot for the McDonald's hamburger chain. McDonald's has two sets of commercials: those with Ronald McDonald normally only appear on children's programs (like Saturday morning cartoons) and adult-themed commercials without Ronald air on prime time TV.

1966. Red Skelton hosts *Clown Alley*, a CBS tribute to circus clowns with guests Billy Barty, Amanda Blake, Vincent Price and Martha Raye.

1970. Members of the Ringling Brothers and Barnum & Bailey Circus perform on *The Klowns*, an ABC special hosted by Charlie Callas, Sammy Davis, Jr. and Juliet Prowse. He was rarely seen but Chuckles the Clown was one of the most beloved performers at the fictitious WJM-TV in Minneapolis on *The Mary Tyler Moore Show*. Chuckles, real name George Bowerchuck was played at various times by Richard Schaal and Mark Gordon (he was killed off when he dressed as Peter Peanut for a parade and a rogue elephant tried to shell him).

1972. Ed Sullivan hosts *Clownaround*, a CBS special that pays tribute to circus clowns and comedians.

1984. Richard Kiley hosts *Those Fabulous Clowns* (HBO), a look at the history of clowns from real life circus clowns to the vaudeville and movie comedians of yesteryear.

1987. A teenage girl named Amy Fisher (Kim Hauser) struggles to hide the fact that her father works as a circus clown from her friends on the syndicated special *My Father the Clown*.

1988. The world of clowns is explored on *The Ringling Brothers and Barnum & Bailey Clown College 20th Anniversary*, a CBS special that celebrates the world famous circus clown college. Dick Van Dyke hosts.

1990. Damon Wayans plays Homey the Clown on Fox's *In Living Color*. Here ex convict Herman Simpson became the nasty Homey D. Clown as part of his prison work release program (he worked the streets and did kid parties). Clowns are not all cute and nice. On *Stephen King's IT* (ABC) Tim Curry plays the white-faced Pennywise the Dancing Clown, an evil, alien clown who feeds on children in a small Maine town. Krusty the Clown is the hero of Bart Simpson on Fox's *The Simpsons*. Krusty is nasty, illiterate and believes violence can solve all problems. Krusty (voice of Dan Castellaneta) is actually Herschel Krustofski, the son of a rabbi who became a clown (to make people laugh) against his father's wishes.

1992. Loonette the Clown (Alyson Court) and her doll Molly Dolly conduct activities for children on an oversized green and floral print couch on PBS's *The Big Comfy Couch*.

2004. Darph Bobo (voice of Terrence Schammell) is a computer-animated clown on the Sci Fi Channel's *Tripping the Rift*. Darph is an evil clown who rejected the peace and love teachings of the great warrior clown Ben Dover to use his powers to take over the universe. He enjoys crushing his enemies under his big floppy clown shoes and exterminating his own witless storm troopers.

2005. Tom Poston plays a former vaudeville clown on NBC's *Committed*. Clown (no other name) lives quietly in the closet of an apartment rented by Marni Fliss (Jennifer Finnegan), a young woman who inherited the homesteading clown (he came packaged with the Manhattan apartment). Clown and Marni find the arrangement comfortable and Clown relishes his former work as a clown. Bob Newhart made a cameo appearance as Blinkey, Clown's former partner in vaudeville.

Clubs and Lodges

Series characters who belong to a lodge or social club are the subjects of this entry.

1951. On *The Amos 'n' Andy Show* (CBS), Amos Jones (Alvin Childress), Andy H. Brown (Spencer Williams, Jr.) and George Stevens (Tim Moore) are members of Harlem's (New York) Mystic Knights of the Sea Lodge (of which George was the Kingfish).

1953. On *The Life of Riley* (NBC), Brooklyn born Chester A. Riley (William Bendix) establishes a lodge called the Brooklyn Patriots of Los Angeles when he moves to the West Coast to remember the old days with friends from the old neighborhood.

1954. On *The Great Gildersleeve* (Syn.), Throckmorton P. Gildersleeve (Williard Waterman), the Water Commissioner of Summerfield, is a member of the Jolly Boys Club ("All for one and one for all"; the weekly meeting is called Jolly Boys Night). Birdie Lee Coggins (Lillian Randolph), Throckmorton's maid, is a member of the Daughters of Cleopatra Society.

1955. On *The Honeymooners* (CBS), Ralph

Kramden and Ed Norton (Jackie Gleason, Art Carney) are members of the Raccoon Lodge (also called The International Order of Friendly Sons of the Raccoons, The International Order of Loyal Raccoons and The Royal Order of Raccoons; Ralph was the treasurer).

1957. On *Blondie* (NBC), bumbling architect Dagwood Bumstead (Arthur Lake) was a member of a lodge called The Caribou Club. On *The Real McCoys* (CBS), Amos McCoy (Walter Brennan) is a member of the Royal Order of the Mystic Nile Lodge (where he is the Grand Imperial Mummy).

1959. On *The Many Loves of Dobie Gillis* (CBS), Herbert T. Gillis (Frank Faylen), the father of teenage Romeo Dobie Gillis, is a member of the Benevolent Order of the Bison Lodge.

1960. On *The Andy Griffith Show* (CBS), Sheriff Andy Taylor and Deputy Barney Fife (Andy Griffith, Don Knotts) are members of the Regal Order of the Golden Door to Door Fellowship Lodge. Andy's Aunt Bee (Frances Bavier) is a member of the Greater Historical Society and Tourist Bureau. On *The Flintstones* (ABC), Fred Flintstone and Barney Rubble (voices of Alan Reed, Mel Blanc) are members of the Royal Order of the Water Buffalo Lodge (originally called the Loyal Order of Dinosaurs).

1961. On *Car 54, Where Are You?* (NBC), Bronx police officers Francis Muldoon and Gunther Toody (Joe E. Ross) are members of the Brotherhood Club for officers of the 53rd Precinct. Francis was also a member of the Bronx Stamp Club. On *Hazel* (NBC/CBS), domestic engineer Hazel Burke (Shirley Booth) is a member of the Sunshine Girls, a society of local neighborhood maids.

1962. On *Jackie Gleason and His American Scene Magazine* (CBS), Crazy Guggenheim (Frank Fontaine) is a member of a lodge called the Smiling Sons of the Friendly Shillelaghs on "Joe the Bartender" skits.

1963. On *Petticoat Junction* (CBS), Joe Carson (Edgar Buchanan) is a member of the Royal Order of Camels in the rural community of Hooterville.

1971. On *All in the Family* (CBS), dock foreman Archie Bunker (Carroll O'Connor) is a member of the Queens, New York lodge the Kings of Queens.

1974. On *Happy Days* (ABC), hardware store owner Howard Cunningham (Tom Bosley) is a member of the Leopard Lodge (of which he became the Grand Puba).

1976. On *Laverne and Shirley* (ABC), beer truck drivers Lenny Kosnoski and Squiggy Squigman (Michael McKean, David L. Lander) are members of the Fraternal Order of the Bass. On *Mary Hartman, Mary Hartman* (Syn.), auto assembly line worker Tom Hartman (Greg Mullavey) is a member of a lodge called the Glorious Guardians of Good.

1982. On *Cheers* (NBC), talkative, know-it-all mailman Cliff Clavin (John Ratzenberger) is a member of the Boston branch of a lodge called the Knights of the Scimitar. On *Newhart* (CBS), Vermont handyman George Utley (Tom Poston) is a member of the Beaver Lodge.

1983. On *Mama's Family* (NBC/Syn), Raytown locksmith Vinton Harper (Ken Berry) is a member of the Mystic Order of the Cobra Club. Thelma Harper (Vicki Lawrence) is a member of the Raytown Church Ladies League.

1985. On *Mr. Belvedere* (ABC), butler Lynn Belvedere (Christopher Hewett) is a member of the Happy Guys, a neighborhood crime watch.

1987. On *Married ... With Children* (Fox), shoe salesman Al Bundy (Ed O'Neill) establishes NO MA'AM (The National Organization of Men Against Amazonian Masterhood) as a way of opposing his wife's domination over him. His neighbor, Marcy Rhoades (Amanda Bearse) counter attacks with FANG (Feminists Against Neanderthal Guys).

1990. On *The Simpsons* (Fox), the animated and dim-witted Homer Simpson is a member of the Sacred Order of the Stonecutters (its motto: "Let's get drunk and play ping pong").

1991. On *Step by Step* (ABC), Frank Lambert (Patrick Duffy) is a member of the Mallard Lodge.

1992. On *Northern Exposure* (CBS), former astronaut Maurice Minnifield (Barry Corbin) is a member of the Sons of Tundra, a lodge in the town of Cicely, Alaska.

1997. On *Buffy the Vampire Slayer* (WB), Buffy Summers (Sarah Michelle Gellar) and her fellow demon slayers were called the Scooby Gang in early episodes set at Sunnydale High School (named after the characters from the animated series *Scooby-Doo, Where Are You?*).

1998. On *That 70s Show* (Fox), Red Forman (Kurtwood Smith) is a member of the Viking Lodge.

2000. On *Gilmore Girls* (WB), Connecticut society hostess Emily Gilmore (Kelly Bishop) is a member of the DAR (Daughters of the American Revolution).

Color Broadcasting

Prior to 1966 (when the networks switched to all color programming) TV was, for the most part, an eye that saw virtually everything in black and white. On rare occasions the NBC peacock was seen in color with these words "The following program is brought to you in living color on NBC." Although there were very few color sets in homes NBC pioneered color broadcasting throughout the 1950s. The following entry chronicles the first known color broadcast through the pioneering years before full color broadcasting.

1941. On July 17 CBS accomplished a TV first: a 20-minute over-the-air color transmission demonstrating its mechanical color wheel developed by Peter Goldmark (the system eventually lost out to RCA's development of the tri-color picture tube). Prior to this telecast the Country Dance Society and Ukrainian Costume Dancers were seen in black and white. The transmission from the Chrysler Tower then switched to color.

1945. NBC experiments with its color picture tube and transmits a view of the New York skyline.

1950. The syndicated series *The Cisco Kid* is filmed in color but shown in black and white. On February 20th ABC airs *The Rainbow Review*, its experimental attempt to market color TV with C.T.I. (Color Television, Inc.), a small San Francisco company that also lost out when the FCC approved of NBC's color picture tube system (CBS had the color wheel). Here, the C.T.I. technicians used a standard black and white RCA TV set that was modified to receive color images. The color was sharp but facial features and fine details were not very distinguishable. The tests were made against a variety show background and were transmitted from the Statler Hotel in Washington, D.C. Singer Lanny Ross was the host and Eileen Christopherson appeared as the C.T.I. "Color Video Girl." CBS attempts a second color wheel experiment (see 1941) on January 8th with the drama *Sorry, Wrong Number* (Meg Mundy plays an invalid woman who overhears a murder plot on the telephone then seeks to get help — unaware that she is the intended victim).

1951. On June 25th CBS inaugurates commercial broadcasting with a five-city hookup (New York, Philadelphia, Baltimore, Washington, D.C. and Boston). Top CBS performers appear but the CBS Color Wheel just doesn't catch on (it shows brilliant color but plays havoc with faces and hair, giving a two-tone look). Patty Painter appeared as "Miss CBS Color" and among the pioneering sponsors were General Mills, Pepsi-Cola, Revlon, Toni Home Permanents and Wrigley's Gum. Later that year NBC broadcasts the opera *Carmen* in color, using its tri color picture tube (The FCC approved of the system on December 17, 1953).

1954. NBC broadcasts several specials in living color: *Fanfare* (music and songs with Steve Allen, Judy Holliday and Frank Sinatra), *The Follies of Suzy* (French ballerina Jean Marie performs in a series of romantic vignettes) and *Satins and Spurs* (Betty Hutton and Guy Raymond in a story about a magazine reporter who falls in love with a rodeo queen). The NBC children's series *Howdy Doody* is broadcast in color as is the syndicated *Amazing Tales of Hans Christian Andersen*.

1955. On March 27th NBC's *Entertainment 1955* becomes the first color program to be broadcast from its new $3.7 million Burbank Studios. Fred Allen hosted. The syndicated western series *Judge Roy Bean* is produced in color.

1956. A live color presentation of *Peter Pan* airs on NBC with Mary Martin in the title role. CBS and ABC also air color series: *My Friend Flicka* and *The Lone Ranger*.

1957–1965. NBC leads the pack with color series. Among the series being broadcast on a weekly basis in color are: *Bonanza, Club 60, The Dinah Shore Show, The Eddie Fisher Show, The George Gobel Show, Hazel, The Kraft Suspense Theater, Northwest Passage, The Perry Como Show, The Virginian, Walt Disney's Wonderful World of Color, Your Hit Parade* and, on a daily basis, *Matinee Theater*.

1966. The era of full color broadcasting arrives. Among those pioneering shows: *Family Affair, The Felony Squad, Gilligan's Island, I Dream of Jeannie, I Spy, Jericho, Love on a Rooftop, The Man from U.N.C.L.E., My Three Sons, The Tammy Grimes Show, That Girl* and *T.H.E. Cat.*

Comedies see Sitcoms

Computers — Extraordinary

This entry deals with computers that go beyond all that is possible or even imaginable by today's technology. Only computers that are a regular part of a program are listed. See also *Talking Animals and Machines*.

1965. On *Get Smart* (NBC/CBS), a computer named Aardvark One controls the functions of CONTROL, the super secret spy agency at 123 Main Street in Washington, D.C.

1966. On *Batman* (ABC), although seemingly simplistic (only a handful of controls on the front panel) and rather small (as computers at this time filled whole rooms) the Batcomputer was ahead of its time. It had the ability to identify objects or substances, translate messages, analyze data and do anything else imaginable. On *The Time Tunnel* (ABC), Tic Toc Base is a secret location in the middle of the Arizona desert that houses the Time Tunnel. Here, a seven-and-one-half billion-dollar computer has been developed to send a man through time. The computer is capable of tracking a person through time and picking up audio and visual images from a past or future time. The computer is also capable of freezing time to remove a traveler from a dangerous situation.

1972. On *Search* (NBC), Probe is a super computerized detective agency run by B.C. Cameron (Burgess Meredith) that operates out of World Securities Corporation in Washington, D.C. Probe Control One is the main computer and allows Cameron access to any transmission signal in the world as well as the ability to monitor any agent in any part of the world. See *Gadgets* for more information.

1976. On *Electra Woman and Dyna Girl* (ABC), Crime Scope is an ultramodern computer complex designed to battle evil. It uses the power of electricity to transform Laurie and Judy (Deidre Hall, Judy Strangis) from ordinary women into Electra Woman and Dyna Girl. See *Gadgets* for additional information.

1977. *Marlo and the Magic Movie Machine* (CBS), Marlo Higgins (Laurie Faso) is an engineer for the L. Dullo Computer Company who secretly develops the Magic Movie Machine, a computer that can talk, tell jokes and show a variety of films. Mert Hoplin provides the computer voice. On *Wonder Woman* (CBS), Ira (voice of Tom Kratichzil), the computer at the Inter Agency Defense Command in Washington, D.C., directs the operations for the cases handled by Diana Prince, alias Wonder Woman, and her superior, Steve Trevor, Jr.

1981. On *The Hitchhiker's Guide to the Galaxy* (PBS), Deep Thought (voice of Valentine Dyall) is a computer built by a race of advanced beings that was designed to think and provide the answers to impossible questions.

1982. On *Voyagers!* (NBC), the History Surveillance Unit, a highly sophisticated computer complex, keeps track of Voyagers (travelers in time who right history's wrongs). Phineas Bogg (Jon-Erik Hexum) is such a Voyager. He is from the planet Voyager and carries a compass-like computer called the Omni, which allows him to travel through time. When it flashes red it indicates history is wrong; a green light means all is normal in an historical period.

1983. On *After George* (CBS pilot), Susan Roberts (Susan Saint James) is a recent widow who must contend with her late husband George's alter ego — their house. Before his death, George rigged his personality into the house via a computer that is an extension of his life. The house now looks out for Susan's well being. Richard Schaal provides the computer voice. On *Automan* (ABC), L.A.P.D. computer department head Walter Nebecher (Desi Arnaz, Jr.) creates a computer generated holographic image called Automan (Chuck Wagner) that he programs with all the knowledge of sleuthing from Sherlock Holmes to James Bond. Although Automan is an electronic display, he appears human and can use the power of the computer to create whatever he needs to help Walter battle evil.

1989. On *Quantum Leap* (NBC), Ziggy (voice of Deborah Pratt) is a massive computer complex that is responsible for Quantum Leap, a time machine that enables Dr. Sam Beckett to travel back in time (within thirty years of his own life) to right the wrongs of people he has never known. A miniature hand-held Ziggy is used by Al Calavicci, a project observer, to communicate with Sam (Al appears as a holographic image and can only be seen and heard by Sam).

1993. On *Time Traxx* (Syn.), Darien Lambert (Dale Midkiff) is a traveler in time who seeks fugitives from the future (2192) who have made a new life of crime for themselves in 1993. He is assisted by SELMA (Specified Encapsulated Limitless Memory Archive), a microcomputer that contains all information ever printed since Guttenberg's Bible. SELMA is specifically designed for Darien and the command "Visual Mode" brings her into view as a hologram (Elizabeth Alexander).

1994. On *RoboCop* (Syn.), Neuro Brain is a master computer run by a human brain (harvested by deranged scientist Craig Mallardo from the body of Diana Powers [Andrea Roth], a secretary at Omni Consumer Products). Diana, as Neuro Brain, now commands all functions in the futuristic Delta City. On *Thunder in Paradise* (Syn.), Russ Wheeler provides the deep voice for "The Thunder Computer," an advanced computer created by ex Navy SEAL Martin Brubaker to run Thunder, his super high tech boat.

1996. On *Homeboys in Outer Space* (UPN), Loquatia (voice of Rhona Bennett) is the sexy, sassy computer that controls the *Space Hoopty*, the intergalactic ship of jack of all trades Ty Walker and Morris Clay.

1997. On *Team Knight Rider* (Syn.), Sky (voice of Linda McCullough) is a sexy-voiced computer that controls *Sky One*, a large, black cargo plane that serves as the base of operations for Team Knight Rider, a squad of special cars (see *Talking Animals and Machines* for more information) that are used to battle evil. Although the series *Viper* (Syn.) first appeared on NBC in 1994, the computer aspect was not introduced until 1997. Viper is a futuristic car designed to battle crime. Dr. Allie Farrow (Dawn Stern) controls the car from a secret location called the Viper Complex (which contains all known crime detection information). The complex has the ability to monitor all areas of the city and call up crime files or track any vehicle via the Crime Analysis Tracking System.

1998. On *Algo's Factory* (Syn.), Main Brain is a supercomputer that turns ideas into facts. It is represented by Alpha Rhythm, called Algo, a talking computer that its programmer, Al (Alan Westbrook) and his four kid assistants, Whitney (Angelica Chitwood), Erin (Bethany Santiago), Brian (James Sorbel, Jr.) and Robert (Adam Ward) use to learn about all aspects of science.

2000. On *Andromeda* (Syn.), Rommie (Lexa Doig) is a very beautiful and very sexy computer hologram that runs the *Andromeda Ascendant*, a battle star ship captained by Dylan Hunt. Rommie (real name Andromeda) thinks of herself as a real person and her official designation is Artificial Intelligence GRA 112, Serial Number XMC-10–182.

Con Artists

If there is something you have that somebody else wants a con artist will find a way to relieve you of that burden. In the opening to the series *Racket Squad*, Captain John Braddock says, "What you are about to see is a real life story taken from the files of police racket and bunco squads … all over the country. It is intended to expose the confidence game, the carefully worked out frauds by which confidence men take more money from the American public than all the bank robbers and thugs with their violence." This entry chronicles the programs on which confidence men (and women) are the heroes — not always, however, working for self-gain but helping the government with their skills. And, as Captain Braddock would say at the close of each show: "I'm closing this case now but there'll be others because that's the way the world is built. Remember, there are people who can slap you on the back with one hand and pick your pocket with the other — and it could happen to you."

1939. *The Saturday Evening Post* story, "A Spot of Philanthropy," comes to NBC with George Taylor as Colonel Humphrey J. Flack, a kind confidence man who fleeces the bad to help the good.

1947. Dramas exposing "the tricks of the tricky traders" are the basis of *Rackets Are My Racket*, A DuMont series with Sgt. Audley Walsh (of the Ridgefield, N.J. Police Department) as the host.

1950. Captain John Braddock (Reed Hadley) exposes the step-by-step methods used by confidence men on *Racket Squad* (Syn/CBS). Red Skelton switches from radio to TV and brings his array of characters with him, including con artist San Fernando Red on *The Red Skelton Show* (NBC/CBS).

1953. Humphrey J. Flack (Alan Mowbray), the retired army colonel who uses cons to help people in need returns to TV on DuMont in *The Adventures of Colonel Flack*. Frank McHugh played the Colonel in an ABC pilot that aired earlier in the year called *Colonel Humphrey J. Flack*.

1955. Phil Silvers plays Ernest Bilko, a master sergeant who is also the army's greatest con artist on *You'll Never Get Rich* (CBS; later titled *The Phil Silvers Show*).

1957. Brothers Bret and Bart Maverick (James Garner, Jack Kelly) are untrustworthy gentlemen gamblers who find that pulling cons helps them out of tight situations on ABC's *Maverick*.

1959. Silky Harris (Roger Moore) is a suave con artist seeking gold in 1898 Alaska on *The Alaskans* (ABC).

1960. A count (Walter Slezak) and his son Leo (Leo Slezak) try to live the good life by conning people into believing they are of European nobility on the CBS pilot *Slezak and Son*.

1962. Doc (Ernie Kovacs), a fast-talking con man, his silent Indian partner Junior (Buster Keaton) and Doc's son Chris (Kevin Brodie) roam the West seeking rich prey on the pilot *Medicine Man*.

1963. Phil Silvers plays con artist Harry Grafton, maintenance man for Osborne Industries, on *The New Phil Silvers Show* (CBS). Gifford Tyler (Bobby Rydell) is a young schemer who seeks to profit from his hitch in the army on the pilot *Rockabye the Infantry*.

1964. Con artists Clint Hightower and Claudie Hughes (Jerry Lanning, Ross Martin) devise unique schemes to make money on the CBS pilot *I and Claudie*. A stylish family of con artists steals from those who can afford to be robbed or deserve to be on NBC's *The Rogues*. David Niven, Charles Boyer and Gig Young star.

1965. Pat Buttram plays Mr. Haney, a dealer of junk who uses his wares to con the people of Hooterville, especially farm owner Oliver Douglas, on *Green Acres* (CBS). A crooked wagon peddler named Luke Herkimer (Edgar Buchanan) and his tenderfoot partner Pete Queen (Carleton Carpenter) fleece people as they sell their wares on the CBS pilot *Luke and the Tenderfoot*.

1968. Sophisticated and cunning thief Alexander Mundy (Robert Wagner) uses his skills to help the government on ABC's *It Takes a Thief*.

1969. Mordecai Jones (Forrest Tucker) is a Robin Hood-like confidence man who cheats only the greedy, dishonest and gullible on the NBC pilot *The Flim-Flam Man*. Charles Duffy (Larry Storch) is a master schemer and first mate of a decrepit ocean liner (*The Amsterdam Queen*) who uses his skills to save his floating paradise from the scrap heap on CBS's *The Queen and I*.

1970. Phil Silvers again plays a con artist, this time Eddie Skinner, a private patrolman at the posh El Dorado Estates in Bel Air on the CBS pilot *Eddie*. Dudley Jericho (Patrick Macnee) is a dapper con man that travels the world to acquire other people's wealth on the ABC pilot *Mr. Jericho*.

1974. Moses Pray (Christopher Connelly) is a fast-talking con artist who uses the cover of salesman for the Dixie Bible Company to fleece people on ABC's *Paper Moon*. Inept con men Quince

Drew and Jason O'Rourke (Larry Hagman, Lou Gossett, Jr.) travel the post Civil War West seeking prey on the ABC pilot *Sidekicks*.

1975. An engaging private detective named McCoy (Tony Curtis) uses his unique skills as a con artist to solve crimes on *McCoy* (NBC). Retired bunco cop Frank MacBride (Eddie Albert) teams with confidence man Pete Ryan (Robert Wagner) to beat swindlers at their own game on CBS's *Switch*.

1977. Ben Gordean (Tom Selleck), Frankie Dawson (Donna Mills) and Ed Walker (Robert Urich) are L.A.P.D. Bunco Squad cops who devise schemes to bring swindlers to justice on the NBC pilot *Bunco*. Ex con man Harry Danton (Harold Gould) uses his skills to help his daughter, lawyer Feather Danton (Stefanie Powers) solve crimes on ABC's *The Feather and Father Gang*.

1979. Master confidence man Boss Hogg (Sorrell Booke) lives the good life by swindling the people of Hazzard County, Georgia, on CBS's *The Dukes of Hazzard*.

1980. Street-wise con scam artist E.L. "Tenspeed" Turner (Ben Vereen) teams with demure stockbroker Lionel Whitney (Jeff Goldblum) to solve crimes as detectives on ABC's *Tenspeed and Brown Shoe*.

1981. Assembly line worker Harry Crockett (Jay Kerr) quits his job to live off scams on the NBC pilot *A Rock and a Hard Place*.

1983. Tyrone Valentine (Jimmie Walker) is a conniving sergeant who attempts to profit from his hitch in the army on ABC's *At Ease*.

1984. Harry Fox (Jack Warden) is a detective who uses the art of the con on *Crazy Like a Fox* (CBS). Charming ex con Howard Bender seeks an easy life through elaborate schemes on the CBS pilot *The Bounder*.

1985. Sophisticated thief Billy Diamond (Billy Dee Williams) elects to work with the police and use his skills to help them rather than spend time in jail on CBS's *Double Dare*. Ann Dusenberry and Nana Visitor star as Kelly Myerson and Bonnie Dalton, members of the L.A.P.D. Fraud Squad who apprehend con artists on the ABC pilot *Fraud Squad*. Country bumpkin Gus Brown (John Schneider) and his beautiful but dim-witted girlfriend Raylene (Teri Copley) team with slick con artist Midnight Brewster (Ron Glass) to get what they want through elaborate schemes on the NBC pilot *Gus Brown and Midnight Brewster*. P. Oliver Pendergast (Charles Durning) is a lovable con artist who uses his skills to help people on the NBC pilot *P.O.P.*

1986. Madeline Kahn plays Violet Kingsley, an investigator for a TV station who goes undercover to expose rackets on the ABC pilot *Chameleon*. Willie Goode (Sherman Hemsley) is a slick con artist trying to straighten out his life without much luck after serving time in jail on UPN's *Goode Behavior*. Patricia Finley (Carol Potter) and Bernie Rollins (Bernie Casey) are members of the Fraud and Bunco Division of the Los Angeles County Sheriff's Office who devise schemes to apprehend swindlers on the ABC pilot *Pros and Cons*.

1987. Heart-of-gold scam artist Harry Porschak (Alan Arkin) finds his job in the purchasing department of New York's North Street Community General Hospital the perfect cover for his scams on ABC's *Harry*. Gorgeous con artist Jennie Jerome (Margot Kidder) helps TV show host John Reid (James Read) acquire stories by conning the con men on CBS's *Shell Game*.

1988. Kirk Morris (Jere Burns) is a master schemer who tries not to con friends, only strangers on NBC's *Dear John*. Slick schemer Tommy (Anthony Starke) and his naïve brother Nick (John Pinette) struggle to survive on cons on the NBC pilot *Smart Guys*.

1991. Chris Nizzle (Tim Curry) and Dash Ryan (Corey Parker) are con artists who hope to one day turn one of their schemes into a money making venture on the ABC pilot *Big Deals*. Jim Doyle (James Garner) is a city councilman who pulls off scams to survive "because I can't survive on what they pay me" on NBC's *Man of the People*. Dani Powell (Connie Sellecca) is a beautiful con artist who helps police detective Joey Pociorek (Greg Evigan) solve crimes on *P.S.I. Luv U* (CBS).

1991. Freddie Paddington (Trevor Eve) is a charming English con man who worms his way into the household of Iris Cloverdale (June Lockhart) as a front for his schemes on the ABC pilot *Up to No Good*.

1993. Kate Patrick (Yancy Butler), a slick con artist who thought she was beyond capture, finds herself stealing for the government when she is captured on NBC's *South Beach*.

1994. Fred Roggin hosts *Too Good to Be True*, an NBC pilot that exposes, through dramatizations, the schemes con men use to cheat people.

1998. David Anthony Higgins plays Dave Hopkins, a sergeant at Fort Baxter who manipu-

lates the system to get what he wants on *The Army Show* (WB). Amanda Webb (Julie Brown), Jonathan Vance (Edward Atterton) and Marcus Miller (Bumper Robinson) are expert thieves who are recruited by the FBI to solve crimes on the WB's *Three*.

2001. Johnny (John Stamos), an expert pick pocket, and Rita (Melissa George), a highly skilled thief, are recruited by the Inter Agency Task Force to "steal things that were stolen from us" on ABC's *Thieves*.

2002. A mysterious woman known only as the Director (Jennifer Doyle) recruits Lee Anne (Sandrine Holt), an expert thief with a sense of morals, Victor (Nicholas Leo), an intelligence agent, and Mac (Ivan Sergri), an ex con, to use their combined skills to help her enforce the law on the syndicated *Once a Thief*.

Connecticut

A listing of series set in Connecticut.

1960. *Peter Loves Mary* (NBC).
1962. *The Lucy Show* (CBS), *The New Loretta Young Show* (CBS).
1964. *Bewitched* (ABC).
1969. *My World and Welcome to It* (NBC).
1975. *The Montefuscos* (NBC).
1977. *Soap* (ABC).
1979. *Dorothy* (CBS).
1984. *Who's the Boss?* (ABC).
1989. *Free Spirit* (ABC).
1992. *Scorch* (CBS).
1999. *Judging Amy* (CBS).
2000. *Gilmore Girls* (WB).
2001. *My Wife and Kids* (ABC).
2006. *Crumbs* (ABC).

Cooking — Pioneering Years, 1945–1970

Why pick up a cookbook when it is so much more fun to see how a meal is prepared? This is on of the reasons why cooking shows have become so popular. But this wasn't always so. This entry chronicles the pioneering programs that paved the way for the numerous cooking shows that not only appear on PBS but on cable channels like the Food Network.

1945. The DuMont Network airs *The Queen*

Was in the Kitchen, an experiment sponsored by the American Central Manufacturing Company (makers of American Kitchens). Skits, narration and films were used to show housewives what kitchens will look like following World War II and how to prepare meals in the busiest place in the house. Allen Prescott was the host.

1946. A program aimed at housewives (*Radio City Matinee*) presented instructional information including a cooking segment with Ben James. The test program aired on NBC.

1947. Alma Kitchell shows housewives how to prepare meals in a spacious kitchen (provided by the sponsor, Nash Kelvinator Appliances) on NBC's *In the Kelvinator Kitchen*.

1948. CBS airs *To the Queen's Taste* (later titled *Dione Lucas' Cooking School*) with Dione Lucas offering cooking advice and demonstrations to housewives. Broadway restaurant owner Vincent Sardi was the host of *Home on the Range*, a cooking show that used actors to prepare meals for the home audience.

1949. An unknown chef offers step-by-step cooking instructions on NBC's *Mystery Chef* (the chef was later identified as John McPherson).

1950. Betty Crocker (Adelaide Hawley), the General Mills homemaking expert, demonstrates kitchen techniques and answers questions submitted by viewers on CBS's *The Betty Crocker Show*. Cooking is coupled with shopping advice and household tips on *Homemaker's Exchange*. Louise Leslie hosted the CBS series.

1951. Simple American meals to elaborate foreign dishes was the idea behind *Creative Cookery*, a CBS program hosted by Bob and Francois Pope.

1952. Fedora and Pino Bontempi prepare Italian meals, interview guests and even sing songs on *The Bontempis* (Syn.). Jean Holt prepares foreign and American meals for housewives on ABC's *Video Chef*.

1953. Chef Josephine McCarthy instructs housewives on the preparation of international meals on the NBC series *Josephine McCarthy*. Chatter, songs and cooking tips mix on *Breakfast Time* (Syn.) with hosts Fedora and Pino Bontempi.

1958. Dione Lucas returns to TV (see 1948) to prepare gourmet meals on *The Gourmet Club* (Syn.).

1963. *The French Chef* comes to educational TV (NET stations) with Julia Child preparing elaborate meals. Syndication produces a program

of cooking, decorating ideas and subjects of interest to women with gourmet chef and cook book author James Beard on a show titled simply *James Beard*.

1966. Fedora and Pino Bontempi host the syndicated *Continental Cookery* and again combine cooking with songs and interviews.

1969. Humor is spiced with cooking instruction as international culinary expert Graham Kerr prepares meals on *The Galloping Gourmet* (Syn.). David Wade, "The Rembrandt of the kitchen, the Edison of the cookbook," prepares meals on *The Gourmet* (Syn.).

1970. Julia Child as *The French Chef* comes to PBS and sets the standard for future cooking shows (such as PBS's *Chan-Ese-Way, The Frugal Gourmet, Daisy Cooks* and *Jacques Pepin: Fast Food My Way*; and the Food Network's *Thirty Minute Meals with Rachael Ray, Emeril Live, Iron Chef* and *Food 911*).

Country Folk

When one thinks of country folk on TV, shows like *The Beverly Hillbillies* and *Green Acres* probably come to mind. This entry chronicles the programs on which the main characters are rural, rural taken out of their natural environment, or transplanted city dwellers who move to rural locations to find a new way of life.

1948. CBS airs a simple test program called *Colonel Stoopnagle's Stoop*. Here Southern Colonel Lemuel Stoopnagle (F. Chase Taylor) converses with friends and neighbors who just happen to drop by.

1949. CBS adapts the radio show *Lum and Abner* to TV with Chester Lauck and Norris Goff as Lum Edwards and Abner Peabody, the simple country folk who own the Jot 'Em Down General Store in Pine Ridge, Arkansas.

1951. City dwellers Betty and Bob MacDonald (Patricia Kirkland, Frank Craven) move to Cape Flattery in upstate New York to operate a chicken farm on *The Egg and I* (CBS). Doris Rich and Frank Twedell play their neighbors, the ambitious Ma Kettle and her lazy husband Pa. Red Skelton brings his character of farm boy Clem Kaddiddlehopper to TV from radio on *The Red Skelton Show* (NBC/CBS).

1957. A poor farm family from West Virginia relocates to California's San Fernando Valley in

California to operate a farm on ABC's *The Real McCoys*. Walter Brennan stars as Amos McCoy with Richard Crenna and Kathy Nolan as Luke and Kate McCoy.

1960. A simple, gentle life in Mayberry, North Carolina, is seen on CBS's *The Andy Griffith Show* with Andy Griffith as Sheriff Andy Taylor and Don Knotts as Deputy Barney Fife. The ABC pilot *Cissie* follows the life of Cissie Shanks (Molly Bee) an Ozark girl with a heart of gold as she helps people in trouble.

1962. Ozark hillbilly Jed Clampett (Buddy Ebsen) strikes oil and moves his family from the backwoods to the plush life on CBS's *The Beverly Hillbillies*. Donna Douglas, Max Baer, Jr. and Irene Ryan co-star. Simple backwoods Iowa veterinarian Judson McKay (Josh Peine) joins the army, is transferred to France and refuses to let the sophistication of European life change his square but innocent ways on NBC's *Don't Call Me Charlie*. Country politician Eugene Smith (Fess Parker) struggles to adjust to the norms of political life in Washington, D.C., on ABC's *Mr. Smith Goes to Washington*.

1963. Hillbilly outlaw Bella McKavitch (Jeanette Nolan) and her two inept sons, Esdras and Clel (L.Q. Jones, Morgan Woodward), seek to make a name for themselves in the Old West in an untitled pilot that ran as "Charlie Wooster, Outlaw" on ABC's *Wagon Train*. The simple pleasures of country living are seen through the eyes of loafer Joe Carson (Edgar Buchanan), a permanent resident of the Shady Rest Hotel on CBS's *Petticoat Junction*.

1964. Naïve country boy Gomer Pyle (Jim Nabors) leaves Mayberry, North Carolina, to join the Marines and create chaos on CBS's *Gomer Pyle, U.S.M.C.* Naïve Georgia farm boy Will Stockdale (Sammy Jackson) is drafted into the Air Force and causes chaos on ABC's *No Time for Sergeants*.

1965. Aggravated writer Tom Dutton (Walter Matthau) moves from New York to rural Bucks County, Pennsylvania, and into a decrepit farmhouse to find a better life on the CBS pilot *Acres and Pains*. "Green Acres is the place to be, farm living' is the life for me" says Oliver Wendell Douglas (Eddie Albert), a successful New York attorney who moves to rural Hooterville to operate a decrepit farm on CBS's *Green Acres*. Eva Gabor plays his glamorous wife, Lisa. Louisiana bayou girl Tammy Tarleton (Debbie Watson) struggles to shed her backwoods ways and become sophisti-

cated when she acquires a job as a secretary on ABC's *Tammy*.

1967. Al Capp's comic strip rural community of Dog Patch, U.S.A., comes to life on the NBC pilot *Li'l Abner*. Sammy Jackson plays Li'l Abner with Jeannine Riley as Daisy Mae and Judy Canova as Mammy Yokum.

1969. Simple country gentleman Longfellow Deeds (Monte Markham) inherits the multi million dollar Deeds Enterprises in New York City and proceeds to run it his way on ABC's *Mr. Deeds Goes to Town*.

1970. A hillbilly feud is the basis of the ABC pilot *The Murdocks and the McClays*. Here family leaders Angus McClay (Dub Taylor) and Calvin Murdock (Noah Beery, Jr.) seek ways to keep their feud going by discouraging the marriage of their children Julianna McClay and Junior Murdock (Kathy Davis, John David Carson), which could end the fighting.

1971. Ray Young is Li'l Abner, Nancee Parkinson is Daisy Mae and Billie Hayes is Mammy Yokum in *Li'l Abner*, a second NBC pilot about the residents of Al Capp's Dog Patch, U.S.A.

1973. CBS's *Dirty Sally* tells the tale of Sally Ferguson (Jeanette Nolan) an aging hillbilly collector of prairie junk and her outlaw friend Cyrus Pike (Dack Rambo) as they head for the gold hills 1880s California.

1977. A poor Appalachian family migrates west to Nowhere, California, to operate a rundown gas station on NBC's *The Kallikaks*. David Huddleston stars as Jasper Kallikak with Edie McClurg as his wife Venus.

1978. The residents of Al Capp's Dog Patch, U.S.A., again come to life in the NBC pilot *Li'l Abner in Dog Patch Today*. Stephan Burns (Li'l Abner) and Debra Feuer (Daisy Mae) star.

1982. Larry, Darryl and Darryl (William Sanderson, Tony Papenfuss, John Volstadt) are three unkempt, rural Vermont brothers who run the Minuteman Café on CBS's *Newhart*.

1994. Christy Huddleston (Kellie Martin) is a 19-year-old girl who leaves her wealthy family in Nashville to teach the poor, backwoods children of Cutter Gap, Tennessee, on CBS's *Christy*.

Cross Dressers

This entry lists the programs on which cross dressers are regularly featured. Single episode cases on series (which number in the hundreds) are not included. Some examples of these are: *The Munsters* (Herman is struck by lightning and turned into a woman), *Saved by the Bell* (Zack poses as his female cousin to supply a date for the girl-shy Screech), *F Troop* (Agarn dresses as an Indian maiden to lure the renegade Loco brothers out of hiding), *Diagnosis: Murder* (Dick Van Dyke plays a female cousin of Dr. Mark Sloan), *Car 54, Where Are You?* (Toody dresses as a woman to catch a purse-snatcher), *The Suite Life of Zack and Cody* (Cody poses as a girl to win a beauty contest).

1948. Milton Berle, the first star of television ("Uncle Miltie"), dresses frequently as a woman for skits on NBC's *The Texaco Star Theater* (later titled *The Milton Berle Show*).

1966. Sid Caesar plays several roles, including Duchess Gloriana XIII on the CBS pilot *The Mouse That Roared*.

1967. Harvey Korman becomes a woman when needed for skits on CBS's *The Carol Burnett Show*.

1968. Timothy Blair (Peter Kastner) poses as a girl (Timmie) for some hippie pictures and finds his life turned upside down when he continues the masquerade and becomes *The Ugliest Girl in Town* (ABC).

1970. Flip Wilson is the sassy Geraldine — "What you see is what you get" on *The Flip Wilson Show* (NBC).

1972. Hoping to show the army "that I'm nuts" and get a Section 8 psycho discharge, Corporal Maxwell Klinger (Jamie Farr) parades around as a woman on CBS's *M*A*S*H*.

1976. Female impersonator Don McClain plays Beverly La Salle, a friend of Archie Bunker's on CBS's *All in the Family*.

1978. The NBC science fiction comedy *Quark* features Tim Thomerson as Jean/Gene, a transmute who possesses a full set of male and female chromosomes. Jean/Gene always appears physically as a male but unpredictably switches genders (via voice and actions) to alert the viewer to which sex she/he is.

1980. In order to afford a decent apartment in Manhattan, ad agency employees Henry Desmond and Kip Wilson (Peter Scolari, Tom Hanks) pose as women (Hildegarde Desmond, Buffy Wilson) to live at the Susan B. Anthony, a hotel for women only on ABC's *Bosom Buddies*.

1990. Jamie Fox plays Wanda, the busty woman with the exaggerated lips on Fox's *In Living Color*.

1991. David Dukes plays Wade Halsey, the husband of Georgie and the father of two children who has a most unusual leisure time activity — dressing as a woman on NBC's *Sisters*. As Georgie said, when she discovered her husband's secret, "You're not the man I thought you were."

1992. Martin Lawrence plays three roles on Fox's *Martin*: radio broadcaster Martin Payne; his mother; and his neighbor, the outrageous Sheneneh.

1995. John Carroll Lynch plays Steve Carey, the cross dressing brother of Drew Carey on ABC's *The Drew Carey Show*. Steve gave up his dual life style when he married Drew's co-worker, Mimi Bobeck.

1996. In addition to his role as Cedric, a school athletic coach on *The Steve Harvey Show* (WB), Cedric the Entertainer plays his nosey Aunt Puddin.

1997. Mark Davis plays Ashley, a female impersonator on NBC's *Fired Up*. Chandler (Matthew Perry) discovers that his estranged father is a cross dresser and performs on stage at a gay club on NBC's *Friends* (a recurring storyline that is talked about more than it is seen).

2000. In order to fool the enemy and carry out assignments on behalf of President Thomas Jefferson, Jack Stiles (Bruce Campbell) often dresses as a woman on the syndicated *Jack of All Trades*.

2002. Michael Cerveris plays Gary Forbush, the cross dressing neighbor of Emma Brody, vice counsel at the U.S. Embassy in London on Fox's *The American Embassy*.

2003. Kelly Lynch plays drag king Ivan, the woman who identifies as a man on Showtime's *The L-Word*.

2004. In Paris in 1652, Jacqueline Roget (Karen Cliche) kills the man who murdered her father. She becomes a wanted woman but escapes capture by dressing as a man. She takes the name of Jacques LaPont and joins D'Artagnan, Jr. to become one of the king's musketeers on PAX's *Young Blades*.

2005. On *The War at Home* (Fox) a question is raised as to whether 15-year-old Larry (Kyle Sullivan) is gay (like his father, sister and friends believe). He dresses in girls' clothes, listens to Broadway soundtracks and has sleepovers. Larry says he is normal, but the program never actually admits to that fact.

Cuban American Performers and Characters

This entry chronicles the programs that feature Cuban-Americans in starring or regular roles. See also *Latino Performers and Characters; Mexican American Performers and Characters;* and *Puerto Rican Performers and Characters.*

1951. Desi Arnaz plays Ricky Ricardo, a bandleader and singer who is married (in real life) to Lucy (Lucille Ball), a scatterbrained woman who yearns for a career in show business on *I Love Lucy* (CBS). Desi (and Lucy) continued their roles on *The Lucy-Desi Comedy Hour* (CBS, 1957–60). In a change of heritage, Desi Arnaz played Raphael Del Gado, a Mexican bullfighter on several episodes of NBC's *The Mothers-in-Law* in 1967.

1974. Desi Arnaz is Juan Domingo, a doctor in a small town who has a knack for stumbling upon murder on the NBC pilot *Doctor Domingo.*

1975. Steven Bauer (under the name Rocky Echevarria), Velia Martinez and Margarita Mendez are among a large cast of Cuban-Americans who appear on *Que Pasa, U.S.A.?,* a PBS sitcom about families living in an American community called Little Havana.

1976. Manuel Martinez plays Raoul, a Cuban immigrant on *Ivan the Terrible* (CBS). Raoul lives with the nine-member Petrovsky family in a 3½ room apartment in Moscow, Russia.

1978. Home repair expert Bob Vila becomes the host of *This Old House* (PBS). Bob hosts the show until 1989 and a year later begins his own series, *Bob Vila's Home Again* in syndication (the series is also known as *Home Again*). Bob can also be seen on PBS stations on *Classic This Old House* (repeats of his early work).

1981. NBC's *Flamingo Road* features Gina Gallego and Fernando Allende as Alicia and Julio, a sister and brother who lived in the Barrio in Truro, Florida.

1984. Edward James Olmos plays Martin Castillo, an Hispanic detective with the Miami Police Department on NBC's *Miami Vice.* The series also features Saundra Santiago as Gina Calabrese, an undercover police woman with the narcotics division of the department.

1989. Maria Navarro plays Maria Conchita Alonzo, the manager of the Lukowski Construction Company in Queens, New York on *One of the Boys* (CBS). Amy Aquino plays her sister, Bernice.

1990. Liz Torres plays Anna Maria Batista, a Cuban-born clerk for the Department of City Services in a locale referred to only as "The City" on CBS's *City.* Steven Bauer (a.k.a. Rocky Echevarria) plays Miguel, the disbarred federal prosecutor who now works with the Justice Department on *Wiseguy* (CBS).

1992. Diana Uribe plays Lorena Costa, the sexy, sassy and beautiful teenage girl who helps manage the soft rock group California Dreams on NBC's *California Dreams.* Daisy Fuentes hosts *The MTV Top 20 Countdown* (until 1997). Daisy, at age 19, began her career as a newscaster for WXTV, Channel 41, the local Univision station in New York City. She was discovered by MTV a year later. Daisy also played Tess on *Loving* (ABC, 1992) and was the host of *Daisy Fuentes* (a 1994 talk show), *The Latino Laugh Festival* (1997), *House of Style* (1997), *America's Funniest Home Videos* (1997–2000), *I Was an MTV V.J.* (1998), *Take Two: Living the Movies* (2002) and *Color Vision* (2004). Miriam Margulyes is Frannie and Tomas Milian her husband Joseph Escobar on *Frannie's Turn* (CBS). Frannie worked as a seamstress from her apartment and was the mother of two children, Olivia and Eddie (Phoebe Augustine, Stivi Paskoski).

1993. Geno Silva is Hector Allegria, the powerful (and influential) Cuban on Fox's *Key West.*

1996. NBC's *Suddenly Susan* features Nestor Carbonell as Luis Rivera, a photographer for *The Gate,* a trendy San Francisco magazine.

1998. Alisa Reyes plays Marci Blake, a Cuban-born teenager who is adopted by Dave and Karen Blake, a Caucasian couple, on NBC's *One World.*

2001. Tessie Santiago plays Lucia Rojas-Klein, the sexy newscaster on NBC's *Good Morning, Miami.* The character, however, was dropped shortly after the premiere.

2002. Adam Rodriquez plays Erik Delko, a member of Horatio Caine's Crime Scene Investigation unit for the Miami Police Department on *C.S.I.: Miami* (CBS).

Detectives see Men—Law Enforcers; Women—Law Enforcers

The Devil

This entry chronicles the programs on which the Devil himself or servants of the Prince of Darkness are the featured characters. See also *Religious* (for God-related programs).

1962. Seventeen-year-old Satanya (Karen Kadler) is given a chance to escape Hell after committing suicide over a lovers' quarrel by becoming a messenger of the Devil (Lon Chaney, Jr.) on the syndicated *Number 13 Demon Street*. Her mission: deliver a special invitation called a "Passport," which contains the necessary evil to make people candidates for Hell.

1964. A mysterious, nameless man (Ray Walston), assumed to be Satan, meddles in people's lives to tempt them on the CBS pilot *Satan's Waitin*.

1973. Sammy Davis, Jr. plays Sammy, a bumbling soft-touch disciple from Hell who is given a chance to redeem himself by securing souls for Satan on the NBC pilot *Poor Devil*.

1975. Three forgotten singers make a pact with Rick, the Devil's son (Don Scardino) for a year at the top in the music world on the NBC pilot *Hereafter*.

1977. Three aging and disorganized performers sell their souls to Dee Dee, the Devil's daughter (Kelly Bishop) in exchange for youth and a year in the music world as the group Top on the CBS pilot *A Year at the Top*. During the summer of 1977 CBS ran a four episode series called *A Year at the Top* wherein unknown singers Greg and Paul (Greg Evigan, Paul Shaffer) sell their souls to Paragon Records president Frederick J. Hanover (Gabriel Dell)—the Devil's son, in return for a year at the top in the music world.

1978. Roddy McDowall plays Satan, who is seeking the mysterious Mr. Roarke's immortal soul on ABC's *Fantasy Island*.

1981. A celestial courtroom is the setting where deceased souls are judged for either Heaven or Hell on the NBC pilot *Judgment Day*. Victor Buono plays Mr. Heavener and Roddy McDowall is Mr. Heller.

1985. A covenant of evil presided over by a woman named Ranada (Judy Parfitt) is used by the Noble family to maintain their fabulous wealth on the ABC pilot *Covenant*.

1987. Micki Foster (Louise Robey) and Ryan Dallion (John D. LeMay) seek to retrieve antiques cursed by the Devil before their owners commit murders on *Friday the 13th: The Series* (Syn.).

1989. The Messenger of Death (Ian McShane) believes humans are greedy and tempts them with a chain letter. His assistant, Miss Smith (Leslie Bevis), believes people are basically good. The ABC pilot *Chain Letter* explores what happens when people receive a mysterious chain letter and must choose which path to take.

1995. Lucas Buck (Gary Cole) is a demonic sheriff who keeps the town of Trinity in a grip of fear on CBS's *American Gothic*.

1998. Peter Horton plays Ezekiel Stone, a deceased cop who is returned to earth by the Devil to recapture 113 escaped evil spirits on Fox's *Brimstone*.

2000. Can one person make the world a better place before God destroys it? When God (James Garner) becomes fed up with the world he asks the Devil (Alan Cummings) to choose who that one person should be. His choice: Bob Alman (French Stewart), a lazy auto plant worker. Without help from God, Bob sets out to do what he can on NBC's *God, the Devil and Bob*.

2003. Grim Reapers Georgia Cass (Ellen Muth), Daisy (Laura Harris), Roxy (Jasmine Guy) and Rube (Mandy Patinkin) seek the souls of people moments before they are destined to die on Showtime's *Dead Like Me*.

2005. Christina Nickson (Elisabeth Harnois) is a very unusual teenage girl. She is the daughter of the Devil and a mortal woman. Good and evil live inside her and when she comes to realize who she really is, the town of Point Pleasant, New Jersey, becomes the battleground for her soul on Fox's *Point Pleasant*.

Diners see Restaurants

District Attorneys

The job of a District Attorney, at least on TV, is to be "a champion of the people, a defender of truth and a guardian of our fundamental rights to life, liberty and the pursuit of happiness" (the opening theme narration from the very first such series, *Mr. District Attorney*). While there are many crime drama series on television, not every one is represented by a regularly cast D.A. This entry provides a look at the programs on which a District Attorney or an Assistant D.A is a major part of a program.

1951. The long-running radio series *Mr. District Attorney* is adapted to TV (via syndication) with Jay Jostyn (then David Brian) in the role of Paul Garrett, an anywhere D.A. in an anywhere city or town.

1957. The shrewd state prosecuting attorney Hamilton Burger (William Talman) of the Los Angeles District Attorney's office gives defense attorney Perry Mason a reason to worry on CBS's *Perry Mason*. In the series revival, *The New Perry Mason* (CBS, 1973), Harry Guardino plays the role of Hamilton Burger.

1959. A private detective known only as Shannon (John Compton) works anonymously under the auspices of the New York District Attorney's office on *The D.A.'s Man* (Syn.). Ralph Manza plays Al Bonacorsi, Shannon's contact at the D.A.'s office.

1961. Glenn Wagner (Richard Anderson) is the D.A. of Sunrise, Colorado, a place where troubled people bring their problems on ABC's *Bus Stop*.

1964. A district attorney with senatorial ambitions was the basis of *Arena*, an NBC pilot with Lloyd Bochner as D.A. Joseph Campbell.

1965. Howard Da Silva plays Anthony Chase, a New York D.A. on *For the People* (CBS). Paul Maytric (Leslie Nielsen) is a small town D.A. who has waged a personal war on crime to avenge the death of his wife (killed in a bombing meant for him) on the NBC pilot *The Green Felt Jungle*.

1966. Leslie Nielsen plays Gregg Collier, an A.D.A. who will not rest until he gets the goods on criminals on the NBC pilot *Guilty or Not Guilty*.

1971. Robert Conrad is Paul Ryan, a Los Angeles D.A. who functions as both a detective and prosecutor on *The D.A.* (NBC). Pat Harrington, Jr. plays Assistant D.A. Charlie Gianetta and Russell Johnson is D.A. Grant on ABC's *Owen Marshall, Counselor at Law*. Jim Hutton plays Doug Selby, a small town D.A. on the NBC pilot *They Call It Murder* (filmed in 1969 and slated to be called *Doug Selby*). Travis Logan (Vic Morrow) is a D.A. in Camino County who puts his work before everything on the CBS pilot *Travis Logan, D.A.*

1973. Lawyer Amanda Bonner (Blythe Danner) and her husband Adam (Ken Howard), a Los Angeles D.A., find themselves on the opposite sides of legal issues on ABC's *Adam's Rib*.

1976. Susan Clark plays Laurel McNaughton, the daughter of a D.A. who works as the Deputy D.A. of Los Angeles on NBC's *McNaughton's Daughter*.

1977. Dan Corcy (John Rubinstein) is a Los Angeles A.D.A. with a sincere drive to help people in trouble on the NBC pilot *Corey for the People*.

1980. William Daniels is Walter Cruikshank, a San Francisco D.A. on *Freebie and the Bean* (CBS). Kathleen Lloyd plays D.A. Carol Baldwin on *Magnum, P.I.* (CBS).

1981. Craig T. Nelson plays Kenneth A. Dutton, the District Attorney on NBC's *Chicago Story*. Bryce Landis (Michael Shannon), the Deputy D.A. of San Francisco, receives help in solving crimes from Frank Riker (Josh Taylor), his hard-nosed special undercover investigator on CBS's *Riker*.

1982. Patty Duke plays Molly Quinn, a Manhattan Assistant D.A. who struggles to balance a career with family on ABC's *It Takes Two*.

1986. Susan Dey plays Grace Van Owen, a Los Angeles D.A., on NBC's *L.A. Law*. Margaret Colin plays Alexandra Harrigan, an A.D.A. working out of the Criminal Courts Building in New York City on CBS's *Foley Square*. James L. McShane (William Conrad) is a former cop turned-D.A. (of Atlanta, Georgia) who has vowed to break the back of organized crime on the NBC pilot *McShane*.

1987. William Conrad's McShane character becomes J.L. "Fatman" McCabe, a tough, cagey D.A. (of an unnamed Southern California city) on CBS's *Jake and the Fatman*.

1988. Terry Donahoe plays D.A. Carolyn Gilder. Salvatore "Sonny" Spoon (Mario Van Peebles) is the smooth-talking private eye who helps her solve crimes on NBC's *Sonny Spoon*.

1989. New Orleans Assistant D.A. Jessica Filley (Alfrie Woodard) struggles to do her job while caring for her troubled son on the NBC pilot *Orleans*.

1990. George DiCenzo is Pittsburgh D.A. Arnold Bach and Cotter Smith is the Deputy D.A. Gene Rogan on ABC's *Equal Justice*. Claire Kincaid (Jill Hennessy), Jack McCoy (Sam Waterston) and Abbie Carmichael (Angie Harmon) are Assistant D.A.'s on NBC's *Law and Order*. The relationship between Kate, McKenzie and Ruth, three sisters living in New York City, is the focal point of the CBS pilot *Sisters*. Kate (Rita Wilson) works as an Assistant D.A.

1991. District Attorney Kate Ward (Lauren Holly) and defense attorney Jack Scarlett (David Andrews) clash over cases on CBS's *The Antagonists*. Assistant D.A. Rachel Brennan (Lisa Darr) struggles to do her job while catering to long lost relatives who have made her home their home on NBC's *Flesh 'n' Blood*.

1993. Sharon Lawrence plays Sylvia Costas, a New York A.D.A. on ABC's *N.Y.P.D. Blue*. Alexandra Cahill (Sheree J. Wilson) is the A.D.A. on CBS's *Walker, Texas Ranger*.

1996. Stacey Bridges (Angela Dohrman), the sister of San Francisco police inspector Nash Bridges, works as an A.D.A on CBS's *Nash Bridges*.

1997. Bill Smitrovich plays D.A. Kenneth Walsh and Lara Flynn Boyle is Assistant D.A. Helen Gamble on ABC's *The Practice*.

1999. Diane Neal plays Casey Novak, the compassionate Manhattan D.A. on NBC's *Law and Order: Special Victims Unit*.

2001. Assistant D.A. Ron Carver (Courtney B. Vance) lends a hand when needed to the detectives of NBC's *Law and Order: Criminal Intent*.

2003. Christine Chang plays Sandy Chang, a Los Angeles County A.D.A. on ABC's *L.A. Dragnet*.

2005. NBC's *Law and Order: Trial by Jury* features Fred Thompson as Manhattan D.A. Arthur Branch, Bebe Neuwirth and Amy Carlson as A.D.A.'s Tracy Kibre and Kelly Gaffney, and Scott Cohen as D.A. investigator Chris Ravell. Manny Devalos (Miguel Sandoval), the D.A. of Mariposa County, Arizona, receives help in solving crimes from Allison DuBois (Patricia Arquette) on NBC's *Medium*.

2006. Alexandra Cabot (Stephanie March), Brian Peluso (Eric Balfour), Christina Finn (Julianne Nicholson) and Billy Desmond (J. August Richards) are among the Manhattan D.A.'s on NBC's *Conviction*.

Doctors

This entry chronicles doctors from their very first appearance on TV in 1945 to their latest ap-

pearance in 2005. Hospital affiliations are listed on applicable programs. See also *Women—Nurses*.

1945. Vinton Hayworth (Dr. Ferguson), Rupert LaBelle (Dr. Cavanaugh) and Robert Rhoades (Dr. Gordon) become TV's first doctors on *Men in White*, an NBC medical drama that aired on January 24th.

1951. Barton Crane (Melvin Ruick) and Kate Murrow (Ann Burr) are doctors at New York Hospital on *City Hospital* (ABC/CBS).

1952. Edward Dowling and Robert Preston play doctors who help people with neglected health problems on ABC's *Anywhere, U.S.A.* Dramas of people confronted with mentally disturbing situations are seen through the eyes of a general practitioner (Warner Anderson) on NBC's *The Doctor*.

1954. John Howard plays Wayne Hudson, a doctor at Memorial Hospital (later called Center Hospital) on the syndicated *Dr. Hudson's Secret Journal*. Authentic and sophisticated approaches to medical problems are seen through the eyes of Dr. Konrad Styner (Richard Boone) on NBC's *Medic*.

1955. The kindly Galen Adams (Milburn Stone), fondly referred to as "Doc," does the best he can with what medicine has to offer in the 1880s on CBS's *Gunsmoke*.

1956. The problems faced by Mark Christian (Macdonald Carey), a young doctor in River's End, Minnesota, is the basis of the syndicated *Dr. Christian*.

1958. Fran Mitchell (Frances Bergen) is a doctor trying to balance her medical career with her duties as a wife and mother on the NBC pilot *The Doctor Was a Lady*. Rex Allen plays Bill Baxter, a doctor in Rising Springs, Arizona, in the early 20th century on the syndicated *Frontier Doctor*.

1959. A young doctor's experiences in a large metropolitan hospital are the basis of the CBS pilot *Dr. Mike*. Keith Andes stars as Dr. Mike Grant.

1960. Patrick O'Neal plays Dr. Daniel Coffee, head of a pathology unit of New York Hospital who uses scientific technology to solve crimes on CBS's *Diagnosis Unknown*.

1961. Neurosurgeon Ben Casey (Vince Edwards) takes up residency at County General Hospital on ABC's *Ben Casey*. Sam Jaffe plays his mentor, Dr. David Zorba. Over at NBC, Richard Chamberlain becomes Dr. James Kildare at Blair

General Hospital on *Dr. Kildare*. Raymond Massey plays his mentor, Dr. Leonard Gillespie.

1962. Donald May plays Paul Larson, a doctor at County General Hospital in Colorado on the ABC pilot *County General*. A young wife is the hero of *For the Love of Mike*, a CBS pilot about Betty Stevens (Shirley Jones) who performs with the Emil Sinclair Society Orchestra as a means of supplementing her husband, Mike's (Burt Metcalf) $98 a month salary as an intern at New York's Hudson General Hospital. Jim Barkley (Don Porter), a doctor with a large city practice, moves to a small suburban community to begin a new life on the CBS pilot *I Love My Doctor*.

1963. Michael Ansara plays Adam MacKenzie, a doctor who travels throughout the Old West to assist where he is needed on the NBC pilot *Adam MacKenzie, Frontier Doctor*. A young doctor struggling to establish a practice in the country, having just relocated from the city, is the plot of the CBS pilot *Come a Running*. Linden Chiles stars as Dr. David Latham. Michael Parks plays Daniel Dana, a doctor with the County Health Service of a large metropolitan hospital on the CBS pilot *Diagnosis: Danger*.

1964. The series *The Nurses* adds Joseph Campanella (Dr. Ted Steffin) and Michael Tolan (Dr. Alex Tazinski) to the cast to become *The Doctors and the Nurses* (CBS).

1965. Sam Cody (Gary Lockwood) is a medical student at Johns Hopkins. Sally Marten (Cynthia Pepper) is a young career woman. They meet, fall in love and struggle to balance their careers and make a relationship work on the CBS pilot *Sally and Sam*.

1966. Peter Piper (Jefferson Davis) is a mother-dominated doctor whose total dedication to work leaves him little time to spend with his wife Barbara (Julie Gregg) on the CBS pilot *My Son the Doctor*.

1969. Jason Fillmore (Forrest Tucker) is an elderly doctor plagued by a bumbling assistant, Dr. Orville Truebody (Rick Lenz) on the NBC pilot *Doc*. The work of Dr. Benjamin Craig (E.G. Marshall), founder of the Craig Medical Research Center in Los Angeles, is the focal point of NBC's *The Doctors* segment of *The Bold Ones*. The elderly Marcus Welby (Robert Young) and his youthful assistant Steven Kiley (James Brolin) are doctors in private practice who also work at Lang Memorial Hospital in Santa Monica on ABC's *Marcus Welby, M.D.* The work of Paul Lochner

(James Daly), administrative surgeon at University Medical Center in Los Angeles, and Joe Gannon (Chad Everett), a professor of surgery, are featured on CBS's *Medical Center*.

1970. The interns at New North Hospital in Los Angeles are featured on CBS's *The Interns*. Christopher Stone, Sandra Smith and Mike Farrell are interns Pooch Hardin, Lydia Thorpe and Sam March.

1971. Andrew Sellers (Jack Albertson) and Simon Locke (Sam Groom) are doctors helping people in Dixon Mills, Canada, on the syndicated *Dr. Simon Locke*. A young female doctor named Michael Griffin (Rosemary Forsythe) struggles to win over the people of a small town on the NBC pilot *Is There a Doctor in the House?*

1972. Jane Wyman plays pediatrician Amanda Fallon in the first of two pilots for NBC called *Amanda Fallon* (the second one appeared on NBC in 1973). Jon Cypher and Craig Littler star as John Ogden and Pat Loeb, doctors with the Emergency Medical Division of the U.C.L.A. Medical Center on the pilot *Code 3*. Alan Alda heads a large cast of doctors attached to the 4077th Mobile Army Surgical Unit in Korea during the war on CBS's *M*A*S*H*. Calvin Briggs and Jonathan Martin (Robert Foxworth, Jonathan Lippe) are ex Vietnam medics who join with nurse Michelle Johnson (Kate Jackson) to help the people of a rural California community on the ABC pilot *The New Healers*. Dr. Simon Locke (Sam Groom) leaves private practice to become a doctor with the Canadian Medical Unit of the Metro Police Force on the syndicated *Police Surgeon*. Dr. James Kildare (Mark Jenkins) returns to Blair General Hospital in a new version of the 1961 series called *Young Dr. Kildare* (Syn.). Gary Merrill is his mentor, Dr. Leonard Gillespie.

1973. Dr. Sean Jamison (Brian Keith) and his daughter Dr. Anne Jamison (Shelley Fabares) are pediatricians based at the Jamison Clinic in Hawaii on NBC's *The Brian Keith Show* (originally titled *The Little People*). Hoping to find the true meaning of being a doctor, Benjamin Elliot (James Franciscus) leaves Bellevue Hospital in New York and retreats to the Alora Valley in Colorado on ABC's *Doc Elliot*. The ABC pilot *D.H.O.* follows the work of Sam Delaney (Frank Converse), a doctor who runs a District Health Office. The work of eccentric diagnostician Justin Fable (W.B. Brydon) is the focal point of the ABC pilot *The Fabulous Dr. Fable*. Tim O'Connor plays

Zach Clinton, a doctor turned attorney who works for a firm that specializes in medical cases on the ABC pilot *Rx for the Defense*. The physically and emotionally exhausting routine of a harried medical staff is the plot of the CBS pilot *Stat!* Frank Converse stars. The antics of Jerry Noland (Cleavon Little), a doctor at Capitol General Hospital in Washington, D.C., are the basis of ABC's *Temperature's Rising*.

1974. Small town physician Juan Domingo (Desi Arnaz) has a knack for finding trouble on the NBC pilot *Doctor Domingo*. The work of Dr. Robert Kier (John Forsythe), the director for the Institute for Medical Research, is the focal point of the NBC pilot *The Healers*. Medical series are satirized by the antics of the staff at Capitol General Hospital in Washington, D.C. on ABC's *The New Temperature's Rising Show*. Paul Lynde and Cleavon Little star.

1975. Forty-two-year-old insecure salesman Bob Wilcox (Bob Crane) quits his job to pursue a medical career at the City Medical School of University Hospital in Los Angeles on NBC's *The Bob Crane Show*. George Peppard is Dr. Jake Goodwin, chief of neurosurgery at Lowell Memorial Hospital on NBC's *Doctors Hospital*. A human approach to the problems of medicine is seen on the NBC anthology, *Medical Story*.

1976. Barnard Hughes stars in two CBS series titled *Doc*. In the first one, which begins in 1975, Hughes plays Joe Bogart, a G.P. in a rundown New York neighborhood. In the revised version, Joe becomes the medical director of the New York Westside Community Clinic. The experiences of an army doctor are explored through Major Annie Malone (Lois Nettleton) on the CBS pilot *Major Annie, M.D.* ABC produces two anthology oriented medical anthologies called *The Oath*. The first (August 24th) stars Hal Holbrook; the second (August 26th) features Jack Albertson. The gruff Jules Bedford (Danny Thomas) is a caring doctor who practices on New York's Lower East Side on NBC's *The Practice*. L.A. County medical examiner Dr. R. Quincy (Jack Klugman) comes to NBC to solve crimes on *Quincy, M.E.*

1977. Larry Linville plays Jim Storm, a resident surgeon at All Fellows Hospital on the NBC pilot *Calling Dr. Storm, M.D.* The CBS pilot *Mobile Medics* depicts the work of doctors who operate a mobile medical unit, mini lab and operating room to provide immediate assistance. Ellen Weston and Jack Stauffer star. Former army doc-

tor Sid Rafferty (Patrick McGoohan) turns diagnostician at L.A. City General Hospital on CBS's *Rafferty*. Dr. Sam Lanagan (James Sloyan) and Dr. Janet Cottrell (Linda Carlson) are physicians at California's Westside Memorial Hospital on ABC's *Westside Medical*.

1978. The antics of the medical staff of the poorly equipped Adult Emergency Services Hospital on the Lower East Side of New York City are spotlighted on ABC's *A.E.S. Hudson Street*. Gregory Sierra stars as Dr. Tony Menzies. Obstetrician Julie Farr (Susan Sullivan) deals with the joys and traumas of childbirth at City Memorial Hospital on ABC's *Julie Farr, M.D.* A harddrinking ambulance driver named Mother (Ray Vitte), a gorgeous and busty doctor nicknamed Juggs (Joanne Nail) and an embittered ex cop turned paramedic named Speed (Joe Penny) are a danger to the public but get the job done on the ABC pilot *Mother, Juggs and Speed*.

1979. John Gavin plays Jeffrey Latimer, one of the doctors attached to the cardiovascular unit of California's City Hospital on ABC's *Doctors' Private Lives*. Ed Nelson (Dr. Michael Wise) and Gwen Humble (Dr. Sheila Castle) co-star. Wayne Rogers, Lynn Redgrave and Sharon Gless are on staff at fictional Kensington General Hospital on CBS's *House Calls*. No nonsense Webster Memorial Hospital cardiologist MacArthur St. Clair (Louis Gossett, Jr.) finds he is a victim of ABC's *The Lazarus Syndrome* (a situation where a patient believes a doctor is a miracle worker). Barrie Tucker (Leah Ayres) is a young doctor that begins her internship at a hospital where her mother, Lil (Rue McClanahan), is a nurse on the NBC pilot *Mother and Me, M.D.* The NBC pilot *Operating Room* deals with the antics of the doctors at L.A.'s Memorial Hospital. David Spielberg and Oliver Clark star. Pernell Roberts becomes John McIntyre, a surgeon at San Francisco's Memorial Hospital on the *M*A*S*H* spinoff *Trapper John, M.D.* Forbesy Russell plays Liz Spencer, one of the medical students at Manhattan General on the ABC pilot *Who's on Call?*

1980. Richard Crenna plays Joshua Torrance, a doctor in the small town of Strawee, Arkansas, during the 1930s on the CBS pilot *Joshua's World*. The money comes first, the patient somewhere down the line to the doctors of *Scalpels*, an NBC pilot starring Rene Auberjonois and Charles Haid.

1981. Dr. Judith Bergstrom (Maud Adams) is a Chicago-based doctor who helps the police solve crimes on NBC's *Chicago Story*.

1982. Richard Crenna plays Sam Quinn, a doctor at the Rush-Thornton Medical Center on ABC's *It Takes Two*. William Daniels heads the large cast of the doctors and nurses at Boston's St. Eligius Hospital on NBC's *St. Elsewhere*.

1983. Beth Gilbert (Shelley Hack), Andy Fenton (Jim Metzler) and Alec Baldwin (Hal Wexler) are the young doctors battling disease in a small Texas town on CBS's *Cutter to Houston*. Tom Skerritt plays Thomas Ryan, the director of interns at Wilshire Memorial Hospital in Los Angeles on ABC's *Ryan's Four*. Michael Royce (James Naughton), John Six (Lou Ferrigno) and Nate Baylor (Dorian Harewood) are among the medical personnel attached to the Medstar Trauma Center of McKee General Hospital in Los Angeles on *Trauma Center* (ABC).

1984. Bill Cosby plays Dr. Cliff Huxtable, a pediatrician who works out of his home in Brooklyn, New York, and at both Corinthian Hospital and the Children's Hospital on NBC's *The Cosby Show*. Ear, nose and throat specialist Howard Sheinfeld (Elliott Gould) moonlights as a doctor in the emergency room of Chicago's Clark Street Hospital on CBS's *E/R*. Kind-hearted Marcus Welby (Robert Young) returns as a resident doctor at Coast Community Hospital in California on ABC's *The Return of Marcus Welby* (see also 1969).

1986. Attractive second year surgical resident Kay O'Brien (Patricia Kalember), called "Kayo," begins her TV duties at Manhattan General Hospital on CBS's *Kay O'Brien*.

1987. Frank "Buck" James (Dennis Weaver) is a no-nonsense surgeon who heads the trauma center of Holloman Hospital in Texas on ABC's *Buck James*. Vince Edwards returns to the role of Ben Casey (see 1961), the gruff but caring neurosurgeon, after a 12-year absence to become the chief of surgery at County General Hospital on the syndicated pilot *The Return of Ben Casey*.

1988. Widowed pediatrician Harry Weston (Richard Mulligan) practices at the Community Medical Center in Miami Beach on NBC's *Empty Nest*. The personal and professional lives of the doctors at the Women's Medical Arts, a progressive practice that caters to patients, is the focal point of ABC's *Heart Beat*. Kate Mulgrew (Dr. Joanne Springsteen), Laura Johnson (Dr. Eve Autry) and Gail Strickland (Dr. Marilyn McGrath) star. Following the death of his wife, Dr. Cyrus Beekman (Scoey Mitchell) quits his job as chief of surgery at Mid-Mercy Hospital in New York to open an inner city clinic for the needy on the NBC pilot *Miracle at Beekman's Place*

1989. Eccentric practitioner Dr. Mike Stratford (Matt Frewer) uses unusual but effective tactics to deal with patients at Northeast Medical Partners on CBS's *Doctor, Doctor*. Sixteen-year-old Doogie Howser (Neal Patrick Harris) is a second-year resident physician at the Eastman Medical Center who can prescribe drugs but can't buy beer on ABC's *Doogie Howser, M.D.* ABC revises *Heart Beat* (see 1988). The series is now set at Bay General Hospital and Gail Strickland is dropped. Kate Mulgrew plays Dr. Joanne Halloran and Laura Johnson, Dr. Eve Calvert.

1990. Harlan Eldridge (Charles Durning) is a doctor in the small town of Evening Shade, Arkansas, who works at City Hospital on CBS's *Evening Shade*. Daniel Kulani (Richard Chamberlain), the adopted son of Hawaiian parents, practices medicine at the Kamehameha Medical Center in Honolulu on CBS's *Island Son*. Freshly minted New York doctor Joel Fleischman (Rob Morrow) must set up practice in quirky Cicely, Alaska, in CBS's *Northern Exposure*.

1991. Elizabeth Newberry (Allison LaPlaca) and Tony Menzies (Dennis Boutsikaris) are doctors at Hudson Memorial Hospital whose sense of humor gets them through a day on ABC's *Stat!*

1992. The U.C.I. Inner City Teaching Hospital provides the setting for CBS's *The Human Factor*. John Mahoney and Allan Miller star as Drs. Alec McMurty and Walter Burke. Housewife and mother Laurie Hill (DeLane Matthews) is a doctor at the Weisman, Kramer and Hill Family Medical Clinic who struggles to balance all three careers on ABC's *Laurie Hill*.

1993. Dick Van Dyke plays Mark Sloan, a doctor with the mind of a detective at Community General Hospital in Los Angeles on CBS's *Diagnosis Murder*. Dr. Michaela Quinn (Jane Seymour) struggles to establish a medical practice in the Colorado Territory of the 1860s on CBS's *Dr. Quinn, Medicine Woman*. Aging doctor Harlan Davidson (Jack Warden) takes on three young doctors to help him treat the people of his community on the ABC pilot *Partners*. Carol Huston, Dan Gauthier and Jeff Yagher co-star.

1994. Chicago's Hope Hospital provides the setting for the work of Doctors Aaron Shutt (Adam Arkin) and Philip Watters (Hector Elizondo) on CBS's *Chicago Hope*. Cook County General Hospital in Chicago is the setting for

NBC's *ER*, TV's longest running prime time medical drama (current in 2006). Members of the large cast include Noah Wyle (Dr. John Carter), George Clooney (Dr. Doug Ross) and Anthony Edwards (Dr. Mark Greene). Cheryl Ladd plays Dr. Dawn Holliday, a medical examiner for the Hawaiian Police Department on CBS's *One West Waikiki*.

1995. The work of doctors at Bayview Medical Center in Seattle, Washington, is the focus of Fox's *Medicine Ball*. Jensen Daggett and Sam McMurray star.

1998. Nasty Bronx, New York, based physician John Becker (Ted Danson) cares little about his own health but worries for his patients on CBS's *Becker*.

2000. The lives of the female doctors at the Rittenhouse Women's Health Clinic in Philadelphia provides the setting for Lifetime's *Strong Medicine*. Janine Turner (Dr. Dana Stowe) and Rosa Blasi (Dr. Luisa Delgado) head a large cast.

2001. Nicole DeBrae (Serena Scott Thomas) and Mitchell Grace (Grayson McCouch) are doctors at an eerie Boston Hospital where the dead have powers on UPN's *All Souls*. Dr. Clint Cassidy (Billy Ray Cyrus) is a doctor at the Woodbury Clinic of Manhattan Memorial Hospital on PAX's *Doc*. Medical intern John Dorian (Zach Braff) faces an oddball staff of doctors and nurses at Sacred Heart Hospital on NBC's *Scrubs*.

2002. Dr. Isaac Braun (Peter Strauss) and Dr. Rachel Griffen (Larissa Laskin) are doctors with Century Hospital in Columbus, Ohio, on PAX's *Body and Soul*. The lives of patients, as well as doctors, are explored at the Presidio Medical Group Hospital on CBS's *Presidio Med*. Blythe Danner (Dr. Harriet Lanning) and Dana Delany (Dr. Rae Brennan) star.

2004. Billy Grant (Rob Lowe) is a highly skilled physician with an office in the Metro Hotel and Casino in Las Vegas, Nevada, on CBS's *Dr. Vegas*. Diagnostician Gregory House (Hugh Laurie) prefers to treat the illness, not the patient at the Princeton-Plainsboro Teaching Hospital in New Jersey on Fox's *House*. Ed Begley, Jr. plays Jesse James, a doctor on staff at the eerie Kingdom Hospital in Maine on ABC's *Stephen King's Kingdom Hospital*

2005. First year surgical intern Meredith Grey (Ellen Pompeo) struggles to have a life while performing a tough residency at Seattle Grace Hospital on ABC's *Grey's Anatomy*. Sandra Oh,

Katherine Heigl and Justin Chambers co-star. Henry Winkler and Stockard Channing play Stewart and Lydia Barnes, doctors whose children are also in the medical profession on CBS's *Out of Practice*. Paula Marshall is Regina, an ER surgeon; Oliver (Ty Burrell) is a plastic surgeon; and Ben (Christopher Gorham) is the black sheep of the family, a psychologist.

Drama

Drama series, especially those that present different stars and stories each week, have been a part of television from the very beginning. This entry lists the anthology type drama series from their struggling beginnings in the 1930s to their last attempts at a comeback in the 1990s. Information on the drama series that rebroadcast episodes can be found on the entry that follows this one.

1931. CBS premieres *The Television Ghost,* the first dramatic anthology series with George Kelty as the host and narrator.

1932. CBS airs three additional anthology series: *CBS Tele-Talkie, Character Slants* and *Dramatic Moments.*

1944. *Crime Quiz* airs on DuMont. Host Ted Cott plays a detective and attempts to solve a crime from a skit that is enacted onstage.

1945. Students from the American Academy of Dramatic Arts perform acts from well-known plays on NBC's test program *Actors in the Making*. A cast of regulars performs stories related by kindly Aunt Jenny (Eve Spencer) and her husband Calvin (Bill Adams) on the CBS test program *Aunt Jenny's Real Life Stories*. Dramatizations based on stories published in *Look* magazine is the basis of *Photocrime*, a CBS test program.

1946. CBS airs *Brief Pause for Murder*, a test program for a weekly series of murder mysteries. Reenactments of jury trials are the basis for *Famous Jury Trials*, an ABC test film. NBC adapts the radio program *Light's Out* to TV for a test of live suspense dramas. The DuMont test program, *Stories in One Camera* presents one act plays in simplistic style with the use of one television camera. A cast enacts a story narrated by the host (Milton Bacon) on the CBS test program *Tales to Remember*. Sweetheart Soap sponsors *Write Me a Love Scene*, a four week DuMont series of romantic dramas.

1947. The Borden Company attempts a weekly series of dramas on *The Borden Television Theater*. The NBC test program ran for only one night (May 25th). Long time radio sponsor Kraft Foods ventures into the new medium with *The Kraft Television Theater* on NBC (later ABC). Known and lesser known actors appear in quality dramas.

1948. Live dramas air on NBC's *Chevrolet Tele-Theater*. Young hopefuls appear with established stars on ABC's *Hollywood Screen Test*. Bert Lytell hosts *The Philco Television Playhouse*, a series of quality dramas on NBC. Quality dramas are also broadcast on CBS via its dramatic anthology *Studio One*.

1949. Kim Hunter, George Reeves and Cloris Leachman are among the recurring performers who appear on *Actor's Studio* (ABC/CBS). Robert L. Ripley hosts *Believe It or Not*, an NBC series of dramas based on Ripley's newspaper column of the same name. William Sloane (then Ben Grauer and Burgess Meredith) narrates dramas based on newspaper reporters on NBC's *Big Story*. People attempt to overcome a crisis before time runs out on *The Clock* (CBS/ABC). Actual murder cases are reenacted through flashbacks on DuMont's *Famous Jury Trials*. A cozy fireplace sets the mood for the first of the filmed drama series, *Fireside Theater* on NBC. Unsuspecting individuals seek a way out of a web of supernatural intrigue on DuMont's *Hands of Murder* (also called *Hands of Destiny* and *Hands of Mystery*). Jack LaRue (then Frank Gallop) hosts eerie mystery and suspense dramas on *Light's Out* (NBC). Anthony Clark (as the host, Mr. Black) presents mystery stories wherein the bad guys get their just desserts on *Mr. Black* (ABC). ABC's *Quiet, Please* presents mystery and suspense stories narrated by Ernest Chappel. Horror film star Boris Karloff hosts an ABC series of mysteries on *Starring Boris Karloff* (also known as *The Boris Karloff Mystery Playhouse*). *Story Theater* becomes the first syndicated anthology and features such stars as Marjorie Lord, Eva Gabor, Evelyn Ankers and Melville Cooper. Paul Frees narrates "well calculated tales to keep you in suspense" on CBS's *Suspense*. Ernest Chappel narrates eerie stories of horror and suspense on ABC's *Volume One*. Arthur Fields is the host of *Your Show Time*, an NBC series of filmed dramas.

1950. Robert St. John becomes the host of NBC's *Believe It or Not*, which switches formats to that of horror yarns based on true incidents. Dramas that explore the art of murder are the basis

of CBS's *Danger*. William Conrad narrates live dramas in which people are caught in life and death situations on CBS's *Escape*. Lux soap products sponsor *The Lux Video Theater*, a series of quality dramas. James Mason, Otto Kruger, Gordon MacRae and Ken Carpenter hosted the CBS (then NBC series). The Magnavox Corporation sponsors a short-lived series of comedies and dramas on CBS's *Magnavox Theater*. Well-known literary works are adapted to TV in live presentations on NBC's *Masterpiece Playhouse*. Stories from *My True Story* magazine are adapted to TV on ABC's *My True Story*. Prudential Life Insurance sponsors a live series of dramatic presentations on CBS's *Prudential Family Playhouse*. Elmer Davis hosts adaptations of Pulitzer Prize winning stories on *Pulitzer Prize Playhouse* (ABC). Lucky Strike Cigarettes sponsors *Robert Montgomery Presents*, a series of quality NBC dramas hosted by Robert Montgomery and also known as *Robert Montgomery Presents Your Lucky Strike Theater*. Mystery and suspense stories are situated around the number 13 and broadcast live from New York on *Stage 13* (CBS). Established actors appear in romantic stories on CBS's *Starlight Theater*. The first Hollywood-based dramatic anthology, *Stars Over Hollywood*, premieres on NBC. Francis L. Sullivan hosts *Sure as Fate*, dramas about people caught in situations that are not of their own doing, on CBS. Thanatopsis, a black cat, assists host James Monks to introduce stories of mystery and suspense on the syndicated *Tales of the Black Cat*. William Somerset Maugham hosts adaptations of his own stories on the CBS (then NBC) series *Teller of Tales*. Tales of people who are suddenly confronted with uncertain situations are narrated by Joe DeSantis on CBS's *The Trap*. Stories of people suddenly trapped in perilous situations unfold on *The Web* (CBS).

1951. Dramas based on the newspaper column "Pitching Horseshoes" appear on NBC's *Billy Rose's Playbill*. Live dramas are broadcast from New York and sponsored by the Celanese Corporation of America on *Celanese Theater* (ABC). Stories from *Cosmopolitan* magazine are adapted to TV on DuMont's *Cosmopolitan Theater*. The problems faced by people in their everyday lives are dramatized on *Faith Baldwin's Theater of Romance* (ABC). Guest police chiefs host and narrate *Gangbusters* (NBC), dramas based on true crime stories. Fantasy presentations are aired alongside comedies and dramas on the Gruen watches sponsored *Gruen Guild Playhouse* (ABC/DuMont). Prestigious presentations are the hallmark for television's longest running anthology program, *The Hallmark Hall of Fame* (NBC; later ABC, CBS, PBS). Sarah Churchill was the original host. CBS airs the second anthology to originate from the West Coast — *Hollywood Opening Night* (When the series aired on NBC the following year, it switched from filmed to live dramas). Filmed special effects are integrated into live science fiction stories for the first time on *Out There* (CBS). Schlitz becomes the first beer company to sponsor an anthology series on *The Schlitz Playhouse of Stars*. Irene Dunne hosted the CBS series in 1952. ABC's *Tales of Tomorrow* presents science fiction stories culled from classic and modern stories. Adolph Menjou hosts *Target*, a syndicated series of high-tension dramas that depict the conflicting forces that drive men and women. The Westinghouse Corporation sponsors a summer series of original dramas on CBS's *Westinghouse Summer Theater*.

1952. Dramas based on the people and events that shaped America are presented on NBC's *Cavalcade of America*. Live suspense dramas set against the background of New York City are presented on *Dark of Night* (DuMont). Western dramas based on the lives of the people who lived, worked and journeyed throughout Nevada and California during the 1880s is the basis of the syndicated *Death Valley Days*. Stanley Andrews (as the Old Ranger, 1952–64), Ronald Reagan (1964–67), Robert Taylor (1967–69) and Dale Robertson (1969–72) were the hosts. Guests select their own stories to be dramatized on the syndicated *Favorite Story* with Adolph Menjou as the host. Original dramas are aired during the summer on CBS's *Footlight Theater*. Dick Powell, Charles Boyer, Rosalind Russell and Joel McCrea form Four Star Studios and venture into television with *Four Star Playhouse*, a series of quality dramas broadcast by CBS and "Filmed by Four Star." Chester Morris hosts *Gangbusters*, stories based on the files of local and federal law enforcement authorities. Live dramas are sponsored by the Gulf Oil Corporation and broadcast on NBC as *Gulf Playhouse*. People caught in sudden, unexpected situations are the subject of dramas on ABC's *Hour Glass*. The syndicated *Magic Vault* relates the plight of people caught in unusual happenings. Burton Turkus hosts *Mr. Arsenic*, an ABC series of dramas based on actual criminal cases. Irene Dunne hosts dramatic presentations on CBS's *Playhouse of Stars*. Norman Rose narrates live dramas based on the files of the Nashville, Tennessee Police Department on *Police Story* (CBS). Live mystery presentations air on ABC's *Projection Room* with Ruth Gilbert as the host. Dramas set against the background of New York City air on DuMont's *Pulse of the City*. Bonita Granville, Natalie Wood, Lynn Bari and Billy Gray are among the stars to appear on the syndicated Schaefer beer sponsored *Schaefer Century Theater*. Ruth Warrick hosts *Short, Short Drama*, an NBC series of 15-minute stories. In syndication one act-plays written especially for TV are hosted by Mary Kay on *Short Story Theater*. Carmen Andrews and Eugene Lee perform dramas based on past American history on CBS's *Story for Americans*. Supernatural-based tales are syndicated as *Terror*. People trapped in sudden, unexpected situations are the basis for the syndicated *The Unexpected*. Phyllis Coates, Sheldon Leonard, Celeste Holm, Ellen Corby and Ruth Warrick are among the stars of dramas on *Your Jeweler's Showcase* (CBS).

1953. Donald Cook hosts *ABC Album*, a series of comedy and drama presentations that is also known as *Plymouth Playhouse*. Arlene Dahl hosts a series of quality dramas on *Arlene Dahl's Playhouse* (ABC). Charles Boyer is the host and frequent star of dramas on *The Charles Boyer Theater* (Syn.). Dramas based on the experiences of the men of the clergy are presented on ABC's *Crossroads*. Gloria Swanson hosts the drama series *Crown Theater with Gloria Swanson* (Syn.). People trapped in uncertain situations as the result of emotional problems are the subject of ABC's *Dark Adventure*. Douglas Fairbanks, Jr. hosts and stars in stories that feature mostly unknown performers on the syndicated *Douglas Fairbanks, Jr. Presents*. Live dramas about people who witness accidents and come forward to testify are hosted by Richard Carlson on NBC's *Eye Witness*. Dramas of people involved with the supernatural are presented on *Fear and Fancy* (ABC). *First Person Singular* on DuMont presents stories in which the TV camera becomes the eyes of the main character; an unseen voice sets the emotional tone. Ronald Reagan hosts *General Electric Theater*, a CBS series of comedies and dramas sponsored by the General Electric Corporation. Original dramas air for the summer on ABC's *Half-Hour Theater*. Actress Loretta Young answers letters from viewers in the form of dramatic stories on NBC's *A*

Letter to Loretta. Original dramas called *Montgomery's Summer Stock* replaces *Robert Montgomery Presents* during the warm weather months on NBC. Dramas set against the background of the Old East set the scene for ABC's *The Orient Express.* Anita Colby (then Polly Bergen) hosts a series of dramatic presentations on *The Pepsi Cola Playhouse* (ABC). Philip Morris Cigarettes is the sponsor and Charles Martin the host of dramas on CBS's *Philip Morris Playhouse.* Revlon Cosmetics sponsors a summer series of NBC dramas on *Revlon Mirror Theater* with spokeswoman Robin Chandler. Sir Cedric Hardwicke hosts a proposed series of vignettes based on stories by famous authors on ABC's *Sketch Book.* Author Ben Hecht hosts dramas based on his own stories on the CBS summer series *Tales of the City.* John Newland plays Morpheus, the host of *Tales of Morpheus,* an NBC pilot based on real dreams people are said to have had. People facing unexpected situations are the focal point of ABC's *The Turning Point.* NBC airs original dramas for the summer on *TV Sound Stage.* United States Steel sponsors a long running series of dramas and comedies under the title *The U.S. Steel Hour* (CBS). Historical dramatizations that place modern-day newsmen in America's past are the subject of CBS's *You Are There* with host Walter Cronkite. The series was revised on CBS in 1971 with Walter Cronkite again serving as the host.

1954. Gene and George Sheldon perform stories based on fables on *The Amazing Tales of Hans Christian Andersen* (Syn.). Mary Costa and William Lundigan host *Climax!,* a CBS series of suspense dramas. Live dramas are broadcast from New York and sponsored by Elgin watches on NBC's *The Elgin Hour.* The problems faced by the U.S. Postal Service in the handling of mails are the source for dramas on ABC's *Handle with Care.* Henry Fonda hosts dramas based on the selections of guest stars on the syndicated *Henry Fonda Presents the Star and the Story.* The unseen Raymond (Paul McGrath) narrates stories in which people are confronted with perilous situations on *The Inner Sanctum* (Syn.). Joseph Schildkraut hosts a series of filmed dramas on DuMont's *Joseph Schildkraut Presents.* Loretta Young is the host and frequent star of *The Loretta Young Theater* (NBC). DuMont's *Love Story* presents dramas that emphasize the goodness in nature and the kindness in man. Martha Scott (then Mel Brandt) hosts serialized dramas based on modern romance stories on NBC's *Modern Romances.* Lavish productions of stories by noted authors are presented on *Producer's Showcase* (NBC). *Spotlight* premieres in syndication and adapts stories from all fields. Each play stars three actors and uses no sets and few props. Although premiering in 1954, DuMont titles its series of dramatic presentations *Studio '57* (which ran until 1956). Stories of people confronted with the supernatural are the subject of the syndicated *Tales of Mystery.* A single actor or actress appears to enact a science fiction story on the syndicated *Tales of the Unknown.* Ron Rondell hosts stories of people caught in a web of their own misdeeds on ABC's *The Vise.* A man who walks by night and knows many strange things hidden in the hearts of men and women who have stepped into the shadows tells their tales of mystery on *The Whistler* (Syn.). Bill Forman narrates the syndicated series. CBS airs original dramas during the summer on *Your Play Time.*

1955. The Alcoa Corporation sponsors top quality dramas on *The Alcoa Hour* (NBC). It became *The Alcoa-Goodyear Theater* in 1958 and *Alcoa Premiere* in 1961 with Fred Astaire as the host. Master suspense filmmaker Alfred Hitchcock brings his theater magic to TV on *Alfred Hitchcock Presents* (NBC, then CBS; later titled *The Alfred Hitchcock Hour*). David Susskind produces *Appointment for Adventure,* a CBS series of dramas based on the experiences of ordinary people. Donald Woods hosts *The Damon Runyon Theater,* a CBS series of stories based on the colorful underworld characters of writer Damon Runyon. Live dramas based on Broadway plays and works by noted authors are the basis of *Front Row Center* on CBS. Walter Coy hosts western dramas that relate the struggles of pioneers who journeyed west during the 1880s on NBC's *Frontier.* John Conte hosts a daily series of dramatic productions from Hollywood on *Matinee Theater* (NBC). Marvin Miller plays Michael Anthony, secretary to the mysterious billionaire John Beresford Tipton, who hands unsuspecting individuals a check for $1 million on CBS's *The Millionaire.* Allyn Edwards hosts *Mr. Citizen,* an ABC series of dramas that detail the unselfish acts of ordinary people. People suddenly confronted with unknown danger are the basis of the syndicated *Pitfall.* Pontiac Automobiles sponsors *Playwrights '55,* an NBC series of live adaptations of stories by famous authors. Rheingold Beer is the sponsor and Henry Fonda (then Douglas Fairbanks, Jr.) hosts dramatic presentations on NBC's *Rheingold Theater*. An insight into the problems man faces as he attempts to unravel the mysteries of science and nature are explored on *Science Fiction Theater*. Truman Bradley hosts the syndicated series. Well-known Hollywood directors select stories for NBC's *Screen Director's Playhouse*. CBS airs filmed dramas from Hollywood on *Stage 7*. An unknown performer is teamed with an established actor on ABC's *Star Tonight*. Stories are adapted from *Reader's Digest* magazine for *TV Reader's Digest*. Hugh Riley (then Gene Raymond) hosts the ABC series. Feature films produced by 20th Century-Fox are adapted to TV on CBS's *20th Century-Fox Hour*. Walter McGraw hosts dramas based on incidents in the lives of criminals wanted by the FBI on CBS's *Wanted*. Gloria Lucas appears as Linda Porter in stories adapted from leading women's magazines on NBC's *Way of the World*. Dramas about people confronting real problems air on the CBS summer series *Windows*.

1956. Barbara Stanwyck hosts *Barbara Stanwyck Presents*, a pilot for a proposed series of dramas. People whose lives are suddenly changed by unexpected circumstances are seen on *Conflict*, a segment of ABC's *Warner Bros. Presents*. Veteran actress Ethel Barrymore hosts a DuMont series of dramas on *The Ethel Barrymore Theater*. General Electric sponsors a warm weather series of first run dramas on ABC's *G.E. Summer Originals*. Ida Lupino is the host and frequent star of *The Ida Lupino Theater* (Syn.). Jane Wyman hosts highly dramatic productions on CBS's *The Jane Wyman Theater*. Virtually unknown performers star in quality productions on *The Lilli Palmer Theater*. Actress Lilli Palmer hosts the syndicated series. Top name guest stars join top name producers (Fred Coe, John Houseman, Martin Manulis) for a series of outstanding 90-minute dramas on CBS's *Playhouse 90*. Edward Arnold hosts supernatural-based tales on the syndicated *Strange Stories*. John Nesbitt (then Dr. Frank Baxter) hosts a series of historical dramas on *Telephone Time* (CBS/ABC). NBC airs *The Unexplained*, a proposed series of chilling fantasy stories that failed to become a series. Donald May plays Cadet Charles C. Thompson and Clint Eastwood appears in a number of dramas based on the training periods of West Point Academy cadets on *The West Point Story* (CBS/ABC). Dick Powell hosts a well-produced series of western dramas for CBS on *Zane Grey Theater*.

1957. True stories of Americans in combat are presented on the syndicated *The Big Attack*. Desi Arnaz hosts *The Desilu Playhouse*, a series of highly dramatic presentations for CBS. The DuPont Corporation teams with producer David Susskind to present varying presentations (drama, musical, comedy) for CBS on *The DuPont Show of the Month* (later *The DuPont Show of the Week*). Actor Errol Flynn is the host and frequent performer on the DuMont series *The Errol Flynn Theater*. Amanda Blake plays Margo, a socialite who hosts *Female of the Species*, a proposed series of dramas about women. Frank Sinatra hosts and stars in various presentations that capitalize on his many talents on ABC's *The Frank Sinatra Show*. George Sanders hosts a summer series of NBC mysteries on *The George Sanders Mystery Theater*. Art Gilmore narrates stories based on incidents in the training of cadets at Annapolis, the U.S. Naval Academy, on the syndicated *Men of Annapolis*. An unsold series of mysteries called *Midnight Mystery* airs on NBC on June 5th. Thomas Mitchell hosts *The O. Henry Playhouse*, a syndicated series based on the stories of William Sidney Porter who, while in prison, wrote under the penname of O. Henry. Stories of people confronting unexpected situations are the subject of *Panic*, an NBC series narrated by Westbrook Van Voorhis. How did a song come to be written? That was the idea for *The Story Behind the Song*, an interesting ABC pilot that failed to become a series. Dennis O'Keefe (then Walter Abel) hosts *Suspicion*, an NBC series of dramas that focus on people's fears and suspicions. Kathy Norris hosts *True Story*, an NBC series of dramas based on real life incidents. Dramas of people who are suddenly propelled into unexpected and perilous situations are the idea behind NBC's *Turn of Fate*. Walter Winchell hosts ABC's *The Walter Winchell File*, adaptations of stories covered by newspaper columnist Walter Winchell. Stories of people who attempt to overcome problems that are caused by their own doing are the idea behind NBC's *The Web*.

1958. American and Canadian actors appear together on ABC's *Encounter*. Vincent Price hosts *E.S.P.*, an ABC summer series of dramas about people endowed with extrasensory perception. The syndicated *Nightmare* presents stories of people who are suddenly involved in perilous situations. Westbrook Van Voorhis narrates stories of people who are suddenly placed in peril by an unexpected crisis on NBC's *No Warning*. Tense stories of people being pursued by others are the format of CBS's *Pursuit*. NBC's *Turning Point* presents stories of people who face sudden circumstances that force them to make a decision. Boris Karloff hosts *The Veil*, dramatizations based on true but incredible phenomena.

1959. ABC's *Behind Closed Doors* presents Bruce Gordon as the host and narrator (as Commander Matson) of stories based on the files of Admiral Zacharies, a World War II Naval Intelligence Chief. Carolyn Jones, Fay Wray, Frank Lovejoy and Anne Francis are among the stars to appear on NBC's *The David Niven Theater* with host and occasional star David Niven. Paul Stewart hosts *Deadline*, a syndicated series of dramas based on the work of newspapermen. The series is also known as *Front Page Story*. Stories written especially for host June Allyson are a major part of CBS's *The June Allyson Show*. Songs by Florence Henderson and Bill Hayes are coupled with dramas on *The Oldsmobile Music Theater* (NBC). "Have you ever been certain the phone would ring in the next 10 seconds? Or have you ever walked down a strange street and knew what lay beyond the unturned corner? Yes? Then you've taken a small step beyond. Now take a giant one." Host John Newland spoke these words to prepare viewers for stories that are strange, frightening and true — and "unexplainable in terms of normal human experience" on ABC's *One Step Beyond*. Rod Serling hosts CBS's *The Twilight Zone*, fascinating stories of people confronted with the mysterious regions of the fifth dimension, a place that is everywhere yet nowhere, a place that lies beyond what is known and beyond understanding.

1960. Barbara Stanwyck is the host and occasional star of NBC's *The Barbara Stanwyck Theater*. Intriguing mystery presentations are presented on NBC's *Dow Hour of Great Mysteries*. Joseph N. Welch hosts. Dramas based on the experiences of members of the Overseas Press Club of America are presented on the syndicated *Exclusive*. *The Play of the Week* airs in syndication and becomes the first two-hour drama series. Top name guests appear in quality productions. Adaptations of short stories and plays are presented on CBS's *Robert Herridge Theater*. The CBS Symphonic Orchestra conducted by Alfredo Antonini provides the music for *Theater '60*, a CBS series of varying dramatic and musical productions. Boris Karloff hosts *Thriller*, an NBC series of dramas about people trapped in unexpected situa-

tions. Author Roald Dahl hosts *Way Out*, a CBS series of supernatural stories.

1961. Dick Powell hosts an NBC series of dramas on *The Dick Powell Show*. Frank Gallop hosts mystery and suspense dramas on *Great Ghost Tales* (NBC). Suspense dramas produced in England air on NBC for the summer on *The Kraft Mystery Theater* with Frank Gallop as the host. Eerie horror stories based on the premise of man delving into areas that are shocking and forbidden was the idea behind *Tales of Frankenstein*, a pilot that failed to produce a series.

1962. Jack Webb hosts *General Electric True*, a CBS series of adaptations of stories appearing in *True* magazine. Dramas depicting the events that spark the lives of interesting individuals is the premise of the syndicated *The Story Of—*. John Willis hosts.

1963. The Chrysler Corporation is the sponsor and Bob Hope is the host and occasional star of varying productions on *The Bob Hope Chrysler Theater* (NBC). Actual newsreel footage is coupled with documented accounts to tell the stories of international undercover agents on NBC's *Espionage*. Van Heflin hosts *Great Adventure*, a CBS series of dramas based on past American events. The Kraft Foods Company sponsors *The Kraft Suspense Theater*, an NBC series of mystery and suspense presentations. Lee Marvin hosts adaptations of real criminal cases on the syndicated *Lawbreaker*. Lloyd Bridges plays free-lance journalist Adam Shepherd on *The Lloyd Bridges Show*, a CBS series that recounts his stories through dramatizations. The Control Voice (Vic Perrin) tells us "there is nothing wrong with your television set ... we are controlling all that you see and hear. You are about to experience the awe and mystery which reaches from the inner mind to *The Outer Limits*," an ABC series of science fiction dramas. Richard Boone is the host and regular performer of NBC's *The Richard Boone Show*.

1964. John F. Kennedy's book, *Profiles in Courage*, is adapted to NBC and dramatizes the valor of political figures that risked everything to defend unpopular causes. Jack Warden plays Jack Fleming, a Hemingway-like writer whose observations of people are seen in stories on the NBC pilot *Second Look*. Sebastian Cabot hosts "tales well calculated to keep you in *Suspense*" on CBS. Lavish science fiction stories were to be the basis of *The Unknown*, an ABC pilot that failed to generate a series.

1966. Original musicals and dramas air on the ambitious but short-lived *ABC Stage '67*.

1967. Danny Thomas is the host and occasional star of varying productions on NBC's *The Danny Thomas Hour*. Animated characters from the film *The Wizard of Oz* host *Off to See the Wizard*, an ABC series of dramas geared to young adults. Stories about chilling events that could happen to anyone comprise *Thriller*, a British produced series that was first televised in the U.S. on *ABC's Wide World of Entertainment*.

1968. A leading American actor appears with British supporting players on ABC's *Journey to the Unknown*, a series of mystery and suspense stories that focus on the slender thread between nightmares and reality.

1969. The world's oldest subject, love, is satirized in comedy stories on ABC's *Love, American Style*.

1970. PBS airs *Hollywood Television Theater*, a series of quality productions featuring top name guest stars. Alistair Cook is the host of *Masterpiece Theater*, a PBS series of British-produced dramas. Rod Serling takes viewers to an art gallery where each canvas hides a twisted tale of another dimension on NBC's *Night Gallery*. Christopher Lee hosts a British produced series of horror yarns on the syndicated *Theater Macabre*.

1971. Author Norman Corwin is the host of dramatic stories on the syndicated *Norman Corwin Presents*.

1972. Sensitive dramas aimed at teenagers are the focus of *The ABC Afterschool Special*. Sebastian Cabot plays Winston Essex, a mysterious gentleman who introduces stories of people confronted with the supernatural on NBC's *Ghost Story*. NBC airs *Lights Out*, a proposed series of suspense stories that failed to become a series.

1973. A monthly series of dramas designed for housewives is the basis of *The ABC Afternoon Playhouse*. Supernatural based tales air on NBC's *Circle of Fear*. Jack Webb narrates *Escape*, true stories of people caught in life and death situations. Anthony Quayle hosts *The Evil Touch* (syndicated), an Australian produced series of stories about people driven to evil through frustration. People are chosen from a phone book to receive an anonymous check for $1 million on the NBC pilot *If I Had a Million*. Adult and contemporary variations on the theme of love are presented on NBC's *Love Story*. Orson Welles hosts *Orson Welles' Great Mysteries*, a British produced series of

mystery stories that airs in syndication. Realistic, hard-hitting dramas covering the day-to-day activities of law enforcement officers are dramatized on NBC's *Police Story*.

1974. Rex Harrison hosts *Rex Harrison's Short Stories of Love*, an NBC pilot that failed to become a series.

1975. NBC's *Medical Story* presents an open, human approach to the problems of medicine as seen through the eyes of the doctor rather than the patient.

1976. NBC's *Best Seller* presents adaptations of best-selling novels. Dramatizations of American plays are presented on PBS's *Visions*.

1977. Writer P.G. Wodehouse hosts humorous adaptations of his stories on the syndicated *Wodehouse Playhouse*. William Conrad hosts a series of mystery and suspense presentations on NBC's *Tales of the Unexpected*.

1978. John Newland returns to TV (see 1959) with an update of his *One Step Beyond* series with a new syndicated version called *The Next Step Beyond*, true stories of psychic happenings.

1979. Roald Dahl (then John Houseman) hosts *Tales of the Unexpected*, a syndicated series of dramas that depict how certain, unexpected events can alter the destinies of people.

1980. Vincent Price (then Diana Rigg) hosts *Mystery*, a PBS series of British-produced mystery stories.

1981. James Coburn hosts *Darkroom*, an ABC series of supernatural tales. For syndication James Coburn hosts the pilot *Escape*, dramas based on famous escapes, that failed to become a series. Chuck Connors is the host of *The Great Mysteries of Hollywood*, a proposed series that was to explore the various mysteries surrounding the films and stars of Hollywood. Another pilot, *Suspense Theater on the Air*, plays in syndication but fails to produce a weekly series of suspense dramas. Christopher Lee also hosts a pilot, *Tales of the Haunted*, an unsold series of supernatural tales. Regis Philbin and Mary Hart host *True Life Stories*, a pilot based on the problems faced by real people, that also fails to become a series.

1982. Shelley Duvall is the host for a series of elaborate adaptations of fairy tales on Showtime's *Fairy Tale Theater*. Alexander Scourby is the host of *Strange True Stories*, a syndicated series of dramas based on mystical experiences and parapsychology.

1983. Nudity, adult situations and strong language are a part of *The Hitchhiker*, an HBO series about the effects a mysterious hitchhiker (Nicholas Campbell, Page Fletcher) has on the people he meets.

1984. The syndicated *Tales from the Darkside* presents stories of people who enter the opposite side of reality — a dark-sided world of evil and death.

1985. NBC airs *Alfred Hitchcock Presents,* a revised version of the 1955 program, that presents new adaptations of stories that appeared on the original series. Top name performers appear on *Amazing Stories*, an NBC series developed by Steven Spielberg that combines elements of fantasy, amazement, irony and comedy. George Burns hosts a weekly series of comedies on CBS's *George Burns Comedy Week*. ABC airs *The New Love, American Style*, an update of stories that parody love and marriage (see 1969). Shelley Duvall is the host for a series of folk tale adaptations on *Shelley Duvall's Tall Tales and Legends* (Showtime). Guests tell their favorite stories on *The Teller and the Tale*, a syndicated pilot with Sally Struthers as the host. *The Twilight Zone* returns with Charles Aidman as the host of eerie stories that delve into the uncharted dimensions of the mind (see 1959).

1986. Adaptations of stories by Ray Bradbury appear on HBO (then USA and in syndication) on *The Ray Bradbury Theater* with the author acting as the host. Joe Flaherty hosts comical tales of people confronted by strange situations on *Really Weird Tales* (HBO). Mario Ruccuzzo hosts *Scary Tales*, a proposed series of horror yarns that produced only a syndicated pilot. Bill Bixby is the host of *True Confessions*, a daily syndicated series of dramas based on stories appearing in *True Confessions* magazine.

1987. John Hurt plays a medieval storyteller who relates tales based on European folklore on *The Storyteller*, an NBC pilot that features Jim Henson's Muppets. Gritty stories based on the actual experiences of Vietnam vets are the basis of HBO's *Vietnam War Story*.

1988. Robert Englund plays Freddie Kruger, an evil spirit who haunts the dreams of people on the syndicated *Freddy's Nightmares: A Nightmare on Elm Street the Series*. Stories of the supernatural and unearthly beings are elements of *Monsters*, a syndicated horror anthology.

1989. Shelley Duvall produced *Nightmare Classics*, a Showtime series of adaptations of famous horror stories. John Kassir provides the voice of the Crypt Keeper (an electronic marionette), the host of HBO's *Tales from the Crypt*, a series of eerie horrors tales based on the comic book of the same title.

1992. A group of children gather in the woods around a campfire to tell ghost stories on *Are You Afraid of the Dark?* (NIK). Rachel Blanchard, Jodie Resther, Ross Hull and Raine Pare-Coull star (see also 1999). Jake Webster (David Duchovny) is a man who reads the personal diaries of women to understand their mysterious ways on *Red Shoe Diaries* (Showtime). Shelley Duvall presents animated stories for children on *Shelley Duvall's Bedtime Stories* (Showtime).

1993. Lynette Walden is Fay Friendly, the host of mystery stories on *Fallen Angels* (Showtime). Stories set against the background of New York City are seen on Fox's short-lived *Tribeca*.

1995. Horror stories geared to (and starring) children are the subject of *Goosebumps* (Fox). *The Outer Limits* returns to TV (see 1963) via the USA network in a new series of science fiction stories that are also seen in syndication.

1998. Inspirational stories about people whose lives are changed as the result of supposed miracles are the basis of *It's a Miracle*. Richard Thomas (then Roma Downey) hosts the PAX series.

1999. *Are You Afraid of the Dark?* is revived by NIK with the Midnight Society, a group of kids who gather around a camp fire in the woods, telling ghost stories. Vanessa Lengies, Daniel DeSanto and Elisha Cuthbert star (see also 1992). Heartwarming stories about people whose lives are touched by the kindness of others are the essence of PAX's *Chicken Soup for the Soul*. Scott Whyte (then Michael Tucker) is the host.

2001. Henry Rollins hosts *Night Visions*, a Fox series of supernatural tales coupled with stories about twisted human nature. Creatures of urban legends terrify teenagers on *Nightmare Room* (WB).

2002. Forest Whitaker is the host of UPN's *The Twilight Zone*, an updated version of the 1959 and 1985 versions of the Rod Serling series.

2006. Adaptations of stories by Stephen King are seen on *Nightmares and Dreamscapes: Short Stories by Stephen King* (TNT).

Drama — Repeat Series

This entry lists the network and syndicated anthology series that used episodes from the various series listed on the prior entry as their programming source.

1952. *Counterpoint* (Syn.).

1953. *Carnival* (ABC), *Demi-Tasse Tales* (CBS), *Paragon Playhouse* (CBS), *Return Engagement* (ABC).

1954. *The Best in Mystery* (NBC), *Center Stage* (ABC), *Counterpoint* (Syn.).

1955. *Kodak Request Performance* (NBC), *Pall Mall Playhouse* (ABC), *Romantic Interlude* (ABC), *Spotlight Playhouse* (CBS), *Undercurrent* (CBS).

1956. *Celebrity Playhouse* (Syn.), *Encore Theater* (NBC), *Festival of Stars* (NBC), *Goodyear Theater* (NBC), *Key Club Playhouse* (ABC), *The Pendulum* (Syn.).

1957. *Action Tonight* (NBC), *Moment of Decision* (ABC), *Playhouse of Mystery* (CBS), *S.R.O. Playhouse* (CBS), *Theater Time* (ABC).

1958. *Adorn Playhouse* (CBS), *Award Theater* (Syn.), *Comedy Playhouse* (ABC), *The Don Ameche Theater* (Syn.), *Frontier Justice* (CBS), *Hour of Stars* (Syn.), *Opening Night* (NBC), *Spotlight on the Stars* (CBS), *Theater '58* (CBS), *Trails West* (Syn.), *Twilight Theater* (ABC), *Western Theater* (NBC).

1959. *Cameo Theater* (Syn.), *Fanfare* (CBS), *Reckoning* (CBS), *Theater '59* (Syn.).

1960. *Chevy Mystery Show* (NBC), *Moment of Fear* (NBC), *Playhouse of Stars* (NBC).

1961. *Adventure Theater* (CBS), *Comedy Spotlight* (CBS), *Sunday Mystery* (NBC).

1963. All air in syndication: *Star for Today*, *Star Theater*, *Times Square Playhouse*, *Western Hour*, *Western Star Theater*.

1964. *The Pioneers* (Syn.).

1965. *Cloak of Mystery* (NBC), *Face of Danger* (Syn.), *The Westerners* (Syn.).

1966. *Hollywood Showcase* (Syn.).

1969. Both syndicated: *Call of the West*, *Suspense Theater*.

1971. *NBC Action Playhouse*, *NBC Adventure Theater*, *NBC Comedy Theater*, *Crisis* (Syn.), *Suspense Playhouse* (CBS).

"Dumb Blondes" see Women — "Dumb Blondes"

Dwarves see Little People

Elderly see Senior Citizens

Espionage

This entry concerns itself with programs that are built around intrigue, espionage or spying. Single episode occurrences from other types of programs are not included.

1951. Melville Ruick plays John Randolph, chief of NBC's *The Door with No Name*, a secret Washington, D.C. agency through which the government battles international intrigue. The U.S. government's battle against espionage rings is seen through the cases of Peter House (Helmut Dantine), Chief of International Security, on *Shadow of the Cloak* (DuMont).

1952. Biff and Louise Baker (Alan Hale, Jr., Randy Stuart) are a husband-and-wife who pose as export buyers for their undercover work for the U.S. government on CBS's *Biff Baker, U.S.A.* Pat Gallagher and Stoney Crockett (Russell Hayden, Jackie Coogan) are U.S. government undercover agents who patrol the West of the 1880s on the syndicated *Cowboy G-Men*. NBC revises *The Door with No Name* (1951) as *Doorway to Danger* with Roland Winters as Chief John Randolph, head of an agency that battles international intrigue. Barry Nelson (then Keith Larsen) play Bart Adams, a mysterious U.S. government agent known as the Hunter who uses unorthodox methods to corrupt the forces of Communism in the Western World on CBS's *The Hunter*.

1953. Richard Carlson plays Herbert Philbrick, a man who led three lives (private citizen, undercover agent, FBI counterspy) on the syndicated *I Led Three Lives*.

1954. Gerald Mohr plays Christopher Storm, a hotel owner in Vienna who helps people in trouble with the international underworld on the syndicated *Foreign Intrigue*. American espionage agent Bill Morgan (Robert Alda) and Colonel Custer (Lois Hansen) investigate situations that pose a threat to the U.S. on *Secret File, U.S.A.* (Syn.).

1956. Raymond Massey hosts (as Anton the Master Spy) tales of intrigue and espionage that span time from the 16th to the 20th centuries on the syndicated *I Spy*. Barry Sullivan plays Ken Thurston, a U.S. Intelligence agent who operates under the code name X on *The Man Called X* (Syn.).

1958. Bruce Gordon plays Commander Matson, the host of tales of international intrigue on NBC's *Behind Closed Doors*. Don Megowan plays

David Harding, U.S. government counter intelligence agent on the syndicated *Counterspy*.

1959. Victor Sebastian (David Hedison) and Simone Genet (Luciana Paluzzi) are U.S. counterintelligence agents based in Europe on NBC's *Five Fingers*.

1961. Patrick McGoohan plays John Drake, special investigator for NATO on CBS's *Danger Man*.

1962. The ABC pilot *The Reluctant Spy* fails to produce a series about international intrigue.

1963. Herbert Brodkin produces *Espionage*, an NBC series about the activities of international undercover agents.

1964. Napoleon Solo and Illya Kuryakin (Robert Vaughn, David McCallum) are agents for the United Network Command for Law Enforcement, an international organization responsible for the welfare of peoples and nations against the evils of THRUSH on NBC's *The Man from U.N.C.L.E.*

1965. Amos Burke (Gene Barry) is a former millionaire police captain (from the series *Burke's Law*) turned U.S. government undercover agent on ABC's *Amos Burke, Secret Agent*. The fumbling Maxwell Smart (Don Adams) and the beautiful 99 (Barbara Feldon) are CONTROL agents that battle the evils of KAOS on NBC's *Get Smart*. Kelly Robinson and Alexander Scott (Robert Culp, Bill Cosby) are U.S. government undercover agents that battle the enemies of freedom on NBC's *I Spy*. In the last season of *Mister Ed* (CBS), Wilbur Post (Alan Young) and his horse, Mister Ed (who believes he is a secret agent), solve cases of espionage for the National Intelligence Agency. Patrick McGoohan plays John Drake, a British intelligence agent on CBS's *Secret Agent*. Government Secret Service agents James T. West (Robert Conrad) and Artemus Gordon (Ross Martin) battle the enemies of the U.S. in the 1870s on CBS's *The Wild Wild West*.

1966. John Steed (Patrick Macnee) and his partners, Emma Peel (Diana Rigg) and Tara King (Linda Thorson) avenge crimes committed against the British government on *The Avengers* (ABC). Henry Phyfe (Red Buttons) is an accountant who happens to resemble a spy named U-31. When U-31 is killed by a hit and run, the CIA convinces a reluctant Henry to replace him and carry out his assignments on ABC's *The Double Life of Henry Phyfe*. April Dancer (Stefanie Powers) and Mark Slate (Noel Harrison) join the United Net-

work Command for Law Enforcement to stop the evils of THRUSH on NBC's *The Girl from U.N.C.L.E.* (The pilot episode, broadcast on *The Man from U.N.C.L.E.*, features Mary Ann Mobley as April Dancer and Norma Fell as Mark Slate). American espionage agent Peter Murphy (Robert Lansing) becomes millionaire Mark Wainwright to protect his cover when Mark (his exact double) takes a bullet meant for Peter on ABC's *The Man Who Never Was*. Dan Briggs (Steven Hill) then Jim Phelps (Peter Graves) heads the IMF (Impossible Missions Force), a government organization that tackles sensitive international assignments on CBS's *Mission: Impossible*.

1967. Stanley Baker plays U.S. government agent Frank Wheatley on the NBC pilot *Code Name: Heraclitus*.

1971. Harry Guardino is Monty Nash, a U.S. government special investigator that handles top-secret White House affairs on the syndicated *Monty Nash*.

1972. Gene Barry plays Gene Bradley, a wealthy businessman turned U.S. government undercover agent on *The Adventurer* (Syn.). Robert Conrad plays Jake Webster, a U.S. government agent who poses as the owner of Jake's Bar and Grill on ABC's *Assignment: Vienna*. Roy Scheider played the role in the pilot film, *Assignment: Munich*. Glenn Garth Gregory (Laurence Luckinbill) is an investigator for the Delphi Bureau and is responsible only to the President of the United States on ABC's *The Delphi Bureau*.

1975. Michael Jayston plays Quiller, a British intelligence agent in two pilots that aired on ABC but failed to become a series: *Quiller: The Price of Violence* and *Quiller: Night of the Father*.

1976. Comedy mixes with intrigue as Peter Davlin (Henry Gibson) sets out to solve cases no other government agency wants on the NBC pilot *The Bureau*. Ray Danton is Derek Flint, a daring U.S. government undercover agent on the ABC pilot *Our Man Flint*.

1977. Johnny Paul (Roy Thinnes) is a U.S. intelligence agent based on Hawaii's Diamond Head who poses as a womanizing beachcomber on the NBC pilot *Diamond Head*. James Hunter (James Franciscus) and Marty Shaw (Linda Evans) are U.S. government special intelligence agents who cover the world of counter espionage on CBS's *Hunter*.

1978. U.S. government secret agents Joshua Rand (Granville Van Dusen) and Suzy (Morgan

Fairchild) operate on orders from a computer named Oz on the CBS pilot *Escapade.* Patrick Macnee returns as British government agent John Steed on CBS's *The New Avengers,* where he is teamed with agents Purdy (Joanna Lumley) and Mike Gambit (Gareth Hunt).

1979. Thomas Remington Sloane (Robert Conrad) is a Priority One Agent for Unit, a select counter espionage team on NBC's *A Man Called Sloane.* Guy Christian (Barry Bostwick) is a playboy who battles international evil in his spare time on the ABC pilot *Young Guy Christian.*

1980. Jack Chenault and Paige Tannehill (Ted Danson, Mary Louise Weller) are agents for the Organization and operate under orders from "The Lady" (Eleanor Parker) on the ABC pilot *Once Upon a Spy.* Lavinia Kean (Cornelia Sharpe) is a beautiful agent for S*H*E (Security Hazards Expert), a division of U.S. Intelligence on the CBS pilot *S*H*E.*

1981. Jet-set socialite Marcus Cabot (Craig Stevens) is a U.S. government agent who receives help from his daughters, Olivia and Muffin (Catherine Shirriff, Jane Actman) on cases on the CBS pilot *The Cabot Connection.*

1982. Former criminal attorney turned mysterious adventurer Modesty Blaise (Ann Turkel) uses her skills to assist Gerald Tarent (Keene Curtis), head of the Special Intelligence Bureau, on the ABC pilot *Modesty Blaise.*

1983. Average housewife turned spy Amanda King (Kate Jackson) teams with agent Lee Stetson (Bruce Boxleitner), code name "Scarecrow," to keep America safe on CBS's *Scarecrow and Mrs. King.*

1984. Dani Reynolds (Jennifer O'Neill) is a beautiful U.S. government espionage agent who poses as a fashion photographer to carry out assignments on *Cover Up* (CBS). Parker Stevenson plays Nick Larabee, a U.S. government secret agent who operates under the code name "Rock Hopper" for the National Security Agency on the CBS pilot *Rock Hopper.* Cass Daton (Leah Ayres), Julie Rhodes (Shari Belafonte), Lauren Dawes (Mary-Margaret Humes) and Ellen Stockwell (Sheree J. Wilson) are agents for Velvet International, a U.S. government intelligence agency that uses a health spa chain as its cover on the ABC pilot *Velvet.*

1985. Elizabeth Towne (Joanna Cassidy) is a gorgeous CIA agent who works directly for the President of the U.S. (although he is represented

by his brother, Larry Hutchins [John McCook]) on NBC's *Code Name: Foxfire.*

1986. Robert Conrad plays Henry Stanton, a secret operative for the Agency, a U.S. government intelligence unit, on the CBS pilot *Assassin.*

1987. Jonathan Ward plays Beans Baxter, a 17-year-old high school student who is also a spy courier for the Network, a U.S. government agency, on Fox's *The New Adventures of Beans Baxter.* Ian Stone (George Hamilton) is a dashing master spy for the Company who constantly defies rules and regulations on CBS's *Spies.* Tony Curtis played Ian in the unaired pilot film.

1988. Peter Graves returns as Jim Phelps (see 1966) to once again lead the Impossible Missions Force on extremely dangerous assignments on ABC's *Mission: Impossible.*

1991. James Coburn plays Robert Fox, an aging secret agent called "The Silver Fox," who tries to balance his activities as a spy with his personal life on the ABC pilot *Silver Fox.* Kate and Dylan Del'Amico (Linda Purl, Anthony John Denison) are a married couple that work for the National Intelligence Agency on ABC's *Undercover.*

1995. The battle against the evils of KAOS continue as secret agent Maxwell Smart (Don Adams) takes over the reins of CONTROL on Fox's *Get Smart.*

2000. Costas Mandylor plays Monk, a highly skilled, womanizing operative for the Agency on UPN's *Secret Agent Man.*

2001. Jennifer Garner plays Sydney Bristow, a beautiful spy for the CIA who really finds the game of espionage a threat to her life on ABC's *Alias.*

Fairy Tales

While fairy tales and folk legends have been around for countless decades, television was not the medium to exploit these timeless tales and very little airtime has been devoted to them. Because there are so few programs devoted to this topic, the episodes that comprise the major series have been included with the entry.

1941. CBS airs *Jack and the Beanstalk,* a daily series in which drawings are used to tell the tale of boy, some magic beans, a beanstalk and a terrifying giant. Each episode opens with a young girl (Anne Francis) kneeling beside her mother

(Lydia Perera). As the mother reads the story, artist John Rupe illustrates the action.

1946. Ireene Wicker sings songs and relates fairy tales to children on ABC's *The Singing Lady*.

1954. The stories of Hans Christian Andersen are adapted to TV on *The Amazing Tales of Hans Christian Andersen*. Gene and George Sheldon play all the roles on the syndicated series. Tommy Tucker (Dennis Day) attempts to court the lovely Jane Piper (Barbara Cook) in the magical Toyland against the wishes of the evil Silas Barnaby (Jack E. Leonard) who seeks her hand in marriage on *Babes in Toyland* (NBC).

1955. A young girl's adventures in a magical fantasyland come to life on *Alice in Wonderland*, an NBC special starring Gillian Barber as Alice. Mary Martin becomes Peter Pan, the boy who never grows up in four TV adaptations of *Peter Pan*: 1955, 1956 and 1957 (all NBC) and in 1976 with Mia Farrow as Peter Pan.

1957. The story of Cinderella, the young girl dominated by her evil stepsisters, comes to television in three adaptations (all titled *Cinderella*). Julie Andrews plays Cinderella in 1957 (CBS); Lesley Ann Warren becomes Cinderella in 1967 (CBS); Leslie Collier plays the role in 1981 (Syn.) and Brandy Norwood plays Cinderella in a 1997 all-black version.

1958. Red Buttons is Hansel and Barbara Cook Gretel, the brother and sister who become lost in the woods and face danger from a witch (Hans Conried) on the NBC special *Hansel and Gretel. Shirley Temple's Storybook* premieres on NBC. Actress Shirley Temple hosts a series of 16 fairy tales broadcast over the course of eleven months. **The Fables:** *Ali Baba and the 40 Thieves* (Nehemiah Persoff); *Beauty and the Beast* (Claire Bloom, Charlton Heston); *Dick Wittington and His Cat* (Jack Diamond, Sebastian Cabot); *The Emperor's New Clothes* (Sebastian Cabot, Pernell Roberts, Eli Wallach); *Hiawatha* (John Ericson, J. Carrol Naish, Pernell Roberts); *The Land of Green Ginger* (Sue England, Jack Albertson); *The Legend of Sleepy Hollow* (Jules Munshin, Shirley Temple, John Ericson); *The Little Lame Prince* (Lorne Greene, Anna Lee); *The Magic Fishbone* (Leo G. Carroll, Lisa Daniels); *Mother Goose* (Elsa Lanchester, Shirley Temple); *The Nightingale* (Thomas Mitchell, Lisa Lu); *Rapunzel* (Carol Lynley); *Rip Van Winkle* (E.G. Marshall, Leora Dana); *Rumpelstiltskin* (Shaike Ophir); *The Sleeping Beauty* (Anne Helm, Nancy Marc-

hand); *The Wild Swans* (Olive Deering, Phyllis Love).

1960. *The Shirley Temple Theater* premieres on ABC. Shirley Temple is the host for a series of 25 stories that are adapted from both fairy tales and classic stories. **The Programs:** *Babes in Toyland* (Shirley Temple, Jonathan Winters, Angela Cartwright); *The Black Arrow* (Carroll O'Connor, Marshall Reed); *The Black Sheep* (Gloria Vanderbilt, Geraldine Fitzgerald); *Emmy Lou* (Frankie Avalon, Bernadette Withers); *The Fawn* (Jena Engstrom, Charles McGraw); *The House of Seven Gables* (Shirley Temple, Agnes Moorehead, Martin Landau); *The Indian Captive* (Cloris Leachman, Steve Cochran); *Kim* (Michael Rennie, E.J. Andre); *King Midas* (Wally Cox, Paul Ford, Anne Helm); *The Land of Oz* (Shirley Temple, Frances Bergen, Jonathan Winters); *Little Men* (Shirley Temple, Fernando Lamas); *The Little Mermaid* (Shirley Temple, Nina Foch, Ray Walston); *Madeline* (Gina Gillespie, Imogene Coca); *Onawandah* (Shirley Temple, David Kent); *The Peg Leg Pirate* (Claude Akins, Miriam Colon); *Pippi Longstocking* (Gina Gillespie, Willard Waterman); *The Prince and the Pauper* (Gig Young, Peter Lazer); *The Princess and the Goblins* (Shirley Temple, Mary Wickes, Jack Ging); *Rebel Gun* (Jackie Coogan, Christopher Dark); *The Reluctant Dragon* (Shirley Temple, Jonathan Harris); *The Return of Long John Silver* (Walter Burke, James Westerfield); *The Terrible Clocksman* (Shirley Temple, Jacques Aubuchon, Sam Jaffe); *Tom and Huck* (David Ladd, Teddy Rooney, Ruthie Robinson); *Two for the Road* (Richard Eyer, Robert Emhardt); *Winnie the Pooh* (Shirley Temple, Bil and Cora Baird).

1967. Live action mixes with animation to tell the tale of a poor farm boy, Jack (Bobby Rhea), who buys magic beans from a peddler (Gene Kelly) that grow into a beanstalk and lead him to an evil giant on the NBC special *Jack and the Beanstalk*.

1971. A cast of regulars performs improvisational adaptations of classic fairy tales on PBS's *Masquerade*. Avery Schreiber, Barbara Sharma, Louise Lasser, Phil Bruns and Alice Playten are among the performers. Paul Sills is the host of *Story Theater*, a syndicated series that presents tales by Aesop and the Brothers Grimm.

1974. Richard Chamberlain narrates *The Little Mermaid*, an animated CBS special based on the Hans Christian Andersen fable about a beautiful mermaid who gives up her immortal soul for human love.

1977. CBS airs *Once Upon a Brothers Grimm*, a special that adapts eight of the Wilhelm and Jack Grimm fairy tales to TV. The fables are: *The Bremen Town Musicians* (Don Correra, Gary Morgan); *Cinderella* (Stephanie Steele, John Mc-Cook); *The Frog Prince* (Teri Garr, Ken Olfson); *Hansel and Gretel* (Mia Bendixsen, Chita Rivera); *The King with Eight Daughters* (Dan Tobin, Clive Revil); *Little Red Riding Hood* (Susan Silo, Cleavon Little); *The Mazurka* (performed by the Los Angeles Ballet Company); *Sleeping Beauty* (Joanna Kirkland, John Clifford).

1982. Shelley Duvall is the host of lavish adaptations of fairy tales on Showtime's *Fairy Tale Theater*. **The Fables:** *Aladdin and His Wonderful Lamp* (Leonard Nimoy, Valerie Bertinelli, James Earl Jones); *Beauty and the Beast* (Susan Sarandon, Klaus Kinski); *The Boy Who Left Home* (Dana Hill, Peter MacNichol, Christopher Lee); *Cinderella* (Jennifer Beals, Matthew Broderick); *The Dancing Princesses* (Maryedith Burrell, Lesley Ann Warren); *The Emperor's New Clothes* (Art Carney, Dick Shawn); *Goldilocks and the Three Bears* (Tatum O'Neal, Hoyt Axton); *Hansel and Gretel* (Joan Collins, Bridgette Andersen, Ricky Schroder); *Jack and the Beanstalk* (Dennis Christopher, Jean Stapleton, Elliott Gould); *The Little Mermaid* (Pam Dawber, Treat Williams); *Little Red Riding Hood* (Mary Steenburgen, Diane Ladd, Malcolm McDowell); *The Nightingale* (Mick Jagger, Barbara Hershey); *The Pied Piper* (Eric Idle); *Pinocchio* (Paul Reubens, Lainie Kazan, James Coburn); *The Princess and the Pea* (Liza Minnelli, Tom Conti); *The Princess Who Had Never Laughed* (Ellen Barken, Howard Hesseman); *Puss 'n' Boots* (Gregory Hines, Ben Vereen); *Rapunzel* (Shelley Duvall, Jeff Bridges); *Rip Van Winkle* (Harry Dean Stanton, Talia Shire); *Rumpelstiltskin* (Shelley Duvall, Ned Beatty, Herve Villechaize); *Sleeping Beauty* (Bernadette Peters, Christopher Reeve); *The Snow Queen* (Melissa Gilbert, Lance Kerwin); *Snow White and the Seven Dwarfs* (Elizabeth McGovern, Vincent Price, Vanessa Redgrave); *The Tale of the Frog Prince* (Robin Williams, Teri Garr); *The Three Little Pigs* (Billy Crystal, Valerie Perrine, Jeff Goldblum); *Thumbelina* (Carrie Fisher, William Katt).

1985. *Shelley Duvall's Tall Tales and Legends*

presents adaptations of well-known folk tales and legends with Shelly Duvall as the host. Stories on the Showtime series include: *Annie Oakley* (Jamie Lee Curtis, Brian Dennehy); *Casey at the Bat* (Elliott Gould, Carol Kane); *Johnny Appleseed* (Martin Short, Molly Ringwald, Rob Reiner); *The Legend of Sleepy Hollow* (Beverly D'Angelo, Ed Begley, Jr.); *Pecos Bill, King of the Cowboys* (Martin Mull, Rebecca DeMorney).

1987. ABC's *The Charmings* presents a modern adaptation of the Snow White legend. Here Snow White (Caitlin O'Heaney, Carol Huston) and her husband Prince Charming (Christopher Rich) live in modern-day Burbank, California as the result of an evil spell that backfired (placed on them by the evil queen Lillian [Judy Parfait] when she was told by her Magic Mirror [Paul Winfield] that not she, but her stepdaughter Snow White, was the fairest of all. The spell was to put Snow White to sleep for 1,000 years. Instead all were put to sleep and awoke in the modern world).

F.B.I. Agents

Programs devoted to agents of the Federal Bureau of Investigation are the subjects of this entry. Agents who appear in single episodes (guest roles) of a series are excluded. See also *Espionage, Government Agents, Men — Law Enforcers, Women — Law Enforcers*.

1949. Edward E. Conroy, former Chief of the FBI in New York City, narrates stories based on bureau files on the DuMont pilot *Federal Agent*.

1955. Walter McGraw narrates *Wanted*, a CBS series that depicts how the FBI captures criminals.

1961. Former underworld attorney Nicholas Caine (Peter Mark Richman) teams with federal authorities to bring the nation's top 100 criminals to justice on NBC's *Cain's Hundred*. FBI agent Jach Flood (Robert Harland) teams with racket reporter Paul Marino (Stephen McNally) to infiltrate organized crime on ABC's *Target: The Corrupters*.

1962. Edward Fox (William Reynolds) and LeRoy Gifford (Philip Carey) are FBI agents united in "a total war against crime with every hideout a battlefield" on the pilot *FBI Code 98*.

1965. Widowed FBI agent Inspector Lew Erskine (Efrem Zimbalist, Jr.) leads an elite team of Washington, D.C.-based agents on ABC's *The F.B.I.*

1970. Amelia Cole (Lynda Day), Jason Hart (Percy Rodrigues) and Ward Fuller (Ed Nelson) are the Silent Force, a special unit of the FBI that is designed to disrupt organized crime on ABC's *The Silent Force.*

1982. Ben Slater (Mike Connors), Maggie Clinton (Carol Potter) and Al Gordean (Richard Hill) are an elite team of FBI agents who investigate cases based on actual bureau files on *Today's F.B.I.* (ABC).

1984. FBI agent David Dalton (Charles Taylor) teams with Joanna St. John (Joanna Pettet), the widow of a murdered lawyer, to bring criminals to justice on the NBC pilot *All That Glitters.*

1987. Ken Wahl plays Vinnie Terranova, an agent with the Organized Task Force of the FBI who infiltrates the underworld on CBS's *Wiseguy.*

1989. Nick Mancuso (Robert Loggia) is a no nonsense agent with the FBI Metro Bureau Field Office on NBC's *Mancuso, FBI.*

1996. Annie Morrison (Andrea Roth) and Nicky Farrell (Adam Trese) are agents with the FBI's Behavioral Science Unit in Virginia on the ABC pilot *The Bureau.* Samantha Waters (Ally Walker) is a gifted young woman who possesses highly developed intuition that allows her to feel for the victims of crime as a Profiler for the FBI's Violent Crimes Task Force on NBC's *Profiler.* Rachel Burke (Jamie Luner), an equally gifted Profiler, replaced Samantha in 1999. Their superior is Bailey Monroe (Robert Davi), an agent who is totally dedicated to his job.

1997. Amanda Reardon (Angie Harmon), John Olansky (Eric Roberts), Scott Stoddard (D.B. Sweeney) and Dennis Grassi (Michael Cavanaugh) are agents with C-16, a special criminal investigation unit of the FBI on ABC's *C-16: F.B.I.*

2000. Annie Price (Kate Hodge) is an FBI agent with a remarkable arrest record who heads Level 9, an agency that solves the cases no one else can on UPN's *Level 9.*

2002. Deanne Bray plays Sue Thomas, a deaf FBI agent who uses her ability to read lips to solve cases on *Sue Thomas, F.B.Eye* (PAX). Jack Malone (Anthony LaPaglia), Samantha Spade (Poppy Montgomery) and Vivian Johnson (Marianne Jean-Baptiste) are agents for the Missing Persons Squad of the FBI on CBS's *Without a Trace.*

2003. Joe Pantoliano plays Joe Renato, an FBI Handler (sets up agents for cases) on CBS's *The Handler.* Leslie Hope plays Lisa Cohen, an FBI agent at the Richmond Center who leads a battle against organized crime (namely the Malloy Crime Syndicate) on ABC's *Line of Fire.* FBI agents track missing persons on Lifetime's *1–800-Missing* (later titled *Missing*). Gloria Reuben (as Brooke Haslett), Vivica A. Fox (Nicole Scott) and Jess Mastriani (Caterina Scorsone) play the agents.

2005. David Boreanaz plays Seeley Booth, a special FBI agent who investigates gruesome crimes on Fox's *Bones.* Special Agent Aaron Hotchner (Thomas Gibson) heads an elite squad of profilers in the FBI's Behavioral Analysis Unit on *Criminal Minds* (CBS). Rebecca Locke (Rachel Nichols) is a Profiler for the Violent Crimes Section of the FBI on *The Inside* (Fox). Peter Coyote plays her superior, Virgil Webster. FBI Agent Don Eppes (Rob Morrow) solves complex cases with the help of his brother, Charlie (David Krumholtz), a math genius who believes numbers hold the key to solving crimes on NUMB3RS (CBS).

Films Based on Television Series

This entry concerns itself with theatrical films that have been based on television series. The concept is actually not new. Motion pictures started the premise back in 1930 when *Check and Double Check* was adapted from the radio series *Amos 'n' Andy.* Other radio programs, such as *My Friend Irma, Duffy's Tavern, The Goldbergs* and *The Adventures of Ozzie and Harriet* (as *Here Come the Nelsons*), were also adapted from radio programs.

1949. *Captain Video and His Video Rangers* (theatrical serial).

1954. *Dragnet* (with Jack Webb; see also 1987).

1956. *Our Miss Brooks; The Lone Ranger and the City of Gold* (based on *The Lone Ranger*).

1965. *McHale's Navy Joins the Air Force* (based on *McHale's Navy*).

1966. *Batman; A Man Called Flintstone* (based on *The Flintstones*); *Munster Go Home* (based on *The Munsters*).

1967. *Gunn* (based on *Peter Gunn*).

1970. *What Do You Say to a Naked Lady?* (based on *Candid Camera*).

1979. *Star Trek: The Motion Picture.*

1980. *The Gong Show Movie* (based on *The Gong Show*). *The Nude Bomb* (based on *Get Smart*).

1981. *The Legend of the Lone Ranger.*

1983. *Twilight Zone: The Movie.*

1984. *Sheena* (based on *Sheena, Queen of the Jungle*).

1987. *Dragnet* (with Dan Aykroyd).

1988. *The Naked Gun: From the Files of the Police Squad.* (Based on *Police Squad*).

1990. *Jetsons: The Movie.*

1991. *The Addams Family; Sergeant Bilko* (based on *The Phil Silvers Show*).

1992. *Boris and Natasha* (based on *Rocky and His Friends*); *Twin Peaks: Fire Walks with Me* (based on *Twin Peaks*).

1993. *The Beverly Hillbillies; Dennis the Menace; The Fugitive.*

1994. *Car 54, Where Are You?; The Flintstones; Maverick; Richie Rich.*

1995. *The Brady Bunch; Mighty Morphin Power Rangers: The Movie.*

1996. *Mission: Impossible.*

1997. *George of the Jungle; Leave It to Beaver; The Saint; Turbo: A Power Rangers Movie.*

1998. *The Avengers; The Mark of Zorro* (based on *Zorro*); *The X-Files.*

1999. *Dudley Do-Right; Inspector Gadget; The Mod Squad; The Wild Wild West.*

2000. *The Adventures of Rocky and Bullwinkle* (based on *Rocky and His Friends*); *Charlie's Angels.*

2001. *Josie and the Pussycats.*

2002. *Scooby-Doo* (based on *Scooby-Doo, Where Are You?*).

2003. *S.W.A.T.*

2004. *Starsky and Hutch; Thunderbirds.*

2005. *Bewitched; The Dukes of Hazzard; The Honeymooners.*

2006. *Miami Vice.*

Note: There are several other movies, such as *Batman* (1989) and *Superman* (1978), which are based on the comic strip, not the TV series (the 1966 *Batman* listed above features the stars of the TV series).

Florida

A listing of series set in Florida.

1960. *Michael Shayne* (NBC); *SurfSide 6* (ABC).

1961. *The Everglades* (Syn.); *Miami Undercover* (Syn.); *Tallahassee 7000* (Syn.).

1964. *Flipper* (NBC).

1965. *I Dream of Jeannie* (NBC).

1967. *Gentle Ben* (CBS).

1975. *Caribe* (ABC).

1981. *Flamingo Road* (NBC).

1984. *Miami Vice* (NBC).

1985. *The Golden Girls* (NBC).

1988. *Empty Nest* (NBC).

1989. *B.L. Stryker* (ABC).

1991. *Clarissa Explains It All* (NICK); *Nurses* (NBC); *Silk Stalkings* (CBS); *Sweating Bullets* (CBS).

1992. *The Golden Palace* (NBC).

1993. *Dave's World* (CBS); *Key West* (Fox); *Moon Over Miami* (NBC).

1994. *Thunder in Paradise* (Syn.).

1995. *Coach* (ABC); *Flipper: The New Adventures* (PAX); *Out of the Blue* (Syn.).

1996. *Pensacola: Wings of Gold* (Syn.).

1997. *Alright Already* (WB); *Head Over Heels* (UPN).

1999. *Odd Man Out* (ABC).

2001. *One World* (NBC).

2002. *C.S.I.: Miami* (CBS); *Good Morning, Miami* (NBC).

2003. *Eve* (UPN); *Karen Sisco* (ABC); *Nip/Tuck* (FX).

2004. *The Help* (WB).

2006. *South Beach* (UPN).

Forensics

Programs dealing with the science of forensics to solve crimes and showing (reconstructing) gruesome events gained popularity after the introduction of *C.S.I.: Crime Scene Investigation* in 2000. Many prior series talk about the use of forensics but stop there. This entry chronicles the programs that provide the viewer with all the unsettling and often gruesome visuals that real life pathologists face in their everyday lives.

1976. On *Quincy, M.E.* (NBC), what is implied is often as disturbing as a visual. While tame compared to *C.S.I.*, *Quincy, M.E.* presented Jack Klugman as a Los Angeles County medical examiner whose search for clues led to his use of forensics. Gruesome crime scenes and lab autopsies were part of the show but not presented in a way that could literally upset a viewer. The focus was on the doctor's investigation, not the gruesome visuals of a killing.

1989. On *Unsub* (NBC), David Soul plays Wes Grayson, the head of the Behavioral Sciences unit of the U.S. Department of Justice who leads a team of forensic investigators that use the latest in scientific technology to solve baffling crimes. The title refers to an unknown subject. The program was ahead of its time for what is common in the 2000's (although it was more implication than actual gore).

1994. On *One West Waikiki* (CBS), Cheryl Ladd plays Dr. Dawn Holliday, TV's first female medical examiner (for the Hawaiian Police Department). While Holli, as Dawn is called, is a forensic scientist, she does investigate gruesome crime scenes and perform autopsies (camera angles prevent the viewer from seeing gruesome details; implication is used but far less than before).

1999. On *The Happy Face Murders* (Showtime TV Movie), Marg Helgenberger plays Jen Powell, a forensic detective searching for the brutal killer of a retarded girl in what set the pace for the broadcast networks (especially CBS) to show what would normally only be seen on pay cable channels. CBS did, however, refuse to incorporate the nudity and foul language of the TV movie (another aspect of cable programs that are beginning to work their way onto broadcast television).

2000. On *C.S.I.: Crime Scene Investigation* (CBS), Gil Grissom (William Petersen) and his team of forensic experts, Catherine Willows (Marg Helgenberger), Sara Sidle (Jorja Fox), Warrick Brown (Gary Dourdan) and Nick Stokes (George Eads), solve gruesome murders as part of the Criminalistics Division of the Metropolitan Las Vegas P.D. The use of computer animation (to reveal how a weapon caused death) and studio created body parts add to the visual impact of the unsettling series.

2001. On *Crossing Jordan* (NBC), Jill Hennessy plays Dr. Jordan Cavanaugh, a gutsy medical examiner for the Commonwealth of Massachusetts, Office of the Chief Medical Examiner. While not as gruesome as *C.S.I.*, Jordan's own words sum up the series: "I cut up dead people for a living." And like Dr. Quincy, she has extraordinary skills and strives to solve crimes.

2002. On *C.S.I.: Miami* (CBS), Horatio Caine (David Caruso) investigates Florida's gruesome crimes as the head of the Crime Investigation Team of the Miami Dade County Crime Lab. His team members are Calleigh Duquesne (Emily Procter), Tim Speedle (Rory Cochrane) and Eric Delko (Adam Rodriquez).

2003. On *Navy NCIS* (CBS), a forensics team called the Naval Criminal Investigative Service investigates crimes associated with the military. Agent Leroy Gibbs (Mark Harmon) heads the team and his investigators are Abby Sciuto (Pauley Perrette), Anthony DiNozzo (Michael Weatherly) and Caitlin Todd (Sasha Alexander). While crime scenes are often unsettling, the lab scenes with David McCallum as Dr. Donald "Ducky" Mallard are even more so.

2004. On *C.S.I.: New York* (CBS), Mac Taylor (Gary Sinise) and Stella Bonasera (Melina Kanakaredes) are forensic detectives with the N.Y.P.D. who investigate very gruesome and unsettling cases.

2004. On *Medical Investigation* (NBC), Natalie Durant (Kellie Williams) and Stephen Conner (Neal McDonough) are doctors with the National Institute of Health who battle unexplained and frightening diseases, hoping to prevent an epidemic, plague or contagious outbreaks.

2005. On *Bones* (Fox), Dr. Temperance Brennan (Emily Deschanel) is a doctor who takes forensic programs one-step further. She is a forensic anthropologist who solves crimes using evidence supplied by skeletal remains.

Gadgets

Every series has some sort of gadget, gimmick or weapon that it uses to dazzle viewers. This entry looks at some of the more popular shows that incorporate these aspects in a major way.

1949. On *Captain Video and His Video Rangers* (DuMont), Captain Video, the Guardian of the Safety of the World (22nd century), is a scientific genius that invented many items to help battle evil from outer space. Among his creations were the Atomic Rifle, the Atomic Collector Screen, the Cathode Ray Gun, the Cosmic Vibrator, a TV-like device called the Opticon Scillometer Astro Viewer, and a pocket radio (much like today's transistor radios).

1950. In the world of the 24th century, women wear short skirts (something daring for TV at the time) and men have one piece suits on *Tom Corbett, Space Cadet* (CBS/ABC/NBC/DuMont). Astrogators have replaced navigators and pilots use Tele-Transceivers for visual communications. A TV set called the Strato-Screen allows for visual exploration of space. The most common weapon is the Paralo-Ray (which causes temporary paralysis). Medicine has also advanced. Blood pills heal the deepest wounds. Personal telephones have been developed (worn on a belt and capable of interplanetary use). Light sticks (which contain a constantly glowing material) have replaced flashlights. And children have it the best of all. Study machines allow a child to learn while he sleeps.

1964. On *The Man from U.N.C.L.E.* (NBC), Napoleon Solo and Illya Kuryakin are agents for the United Network Command for Law Enforcement whose espionage work requires unique gadgets and weapons. The weapon of choice is a P-38 pistol that fires sleep darts and is capable of converting to a rifle when a 12-inch breakaway barrel is added. Also of use is a flip top cigarette lighter that doubles as a .32 caliber pistol. Agents communicate with headquarters via their Pen Communicator (set on Channel D). Also used are guns that fire gas pellets, a portable mine detector and a miniature reel-to-reel tape recorder (the cassette recorder had not yet been invented in real life). Agents were often threatened by the evils of THRUSH and faced many of their deadly weapons: High frequency sound machines, fear gas, earthquake machines, brain altering rays, mind reading devices, a communications jammer, miniature atomic bombs and heat-activated explosives.

1965. On *Get Smart* (NBC/CBS), Maxwell Smart is a secret agent for CONTROL, a government agency based in Washington, D.C. Max is most famous for his shoe phone, a device by which he communicates with headquarters. He also carried a revolver, an exploding wallet and drove a red sports car equipped with a machine gun, ejector seat, a smoke screen and a cigarette lighter that was actually a telephone. Max's apartment is booby-trapped and he needs to use the password "Bismark" for safe entry. At headquarters there is the seldom-working Cone of Silence (which is supposed to enable secure communication).

1965. On *Honey West* (ABC), Honey West is a shapely (36–24–34) blonde who operates the H. West and Company Detective Agency in Los Angeles. She works out of her lavish apartment at 6033 Del Mar Vista and uses a TV repair truck as her mobile base of operations. Honey has a black belt in karate and uses the latest in scientific detection equipment. Her lipstick, earrings and makeup compact double as transmitters. Her earrings double as miniature gas bombs and the innocent looking ball point pen Honey gives to certain clients is actually a miniature transmitter she uses for tracking purposes. She also carries a gun and is not afraid to use it.

1965. On *The Wild Wild West* (CBS), James T. West is a Secret Service Agent in the West of the 1870s. Jim travels by train and lives in an 1860s passenger coach called the Nimrod. He has pop-out guns up his sleeves, a tiny derringer concealed in the heel of his boot, a skeleton key hidden behind his jacket lapel, a sword in his pool cue, and smoke bombs concealed under his holster.

1966. On *Batman* (ABC), the Batcave beneath stately Wayne Manor in Gotham City is the secret headquarters of Batman, a mysterious crime fighter who is actually millionaire Bruce Wayne. Of all the Bat gadgets used on the series, the Batmobile is without a doubt the most famous. The sleek black atomic-powered car has a Bat Ram, Bat Parachute (to stop the car at high speeds), the Bat Projector Ray and the Bat Homing/Receiving Scope. Next in line is the Bat Computer (seen in virtually every Batcave scene), a remarkable machine capable of virtually any task (it was modified from an actual U.S. Air Force surplus computer). The blue and silver computer was 55 in. tall, 47 in. wide and 36 in. deep. Other Bat gadgets are the Bat Signal (a red and black bat-shaped sky spotlight), Batgas pellets, the Batrope, the Batboat, the Batcopter, the Batspeech Imitator, the Batalert (a buzzer sound), the Bat Sound Analyzer and the Batscope. When Yvonne Craig joined the cast in 1968 as Batgirl, the Batgirl Cycle came into being.

1966–2005. From the original *Star Trek* (NBC) to all its syndicated incarnations (*Star Trek: Deep Space Nine, Star Trek: Enterprise, Star Trek: The Next Generation* and *Star Trek: Voyager*) hundreds of gadgets have been used. The most famous of all is perhaps the Phaser (emitted an energy beam similar to a laser that could be set to stun or kill). There were four types: hand held pistol, the uniform clip on, the rifle-like Phaser and the ship-mounted Phaser (set alongside the Photon Torpedoes). The Phaser (as well as many of the components on the various Starfleet ships) are powered by dilithium crystals. There were also a number of other Phaser types: The alien Trill Phaser, the Breen Disruptor (17in. long Phaser), the Cardassian Phaser, the Boomerang Phaser, the Dax Phaser, the Bajoran Phaser, the Phaser Rifle (23 in. long), the Dolphin Phaser (resembles a dolphin). Other gadgets are the Tricorder (all one piece), the Hinged Tricorder (fold-down mouthpiece) the Star Fleet PADD (communication link), the Wrist Tricorder, the Holographic Transmissions Panel, the Klingon Pain Stick, the Medical Scanner, the Phase II Communicator (cricketlike sound when activated) the Transporter (rearranged molecules to transport people and objects) and last but not least those cuddly furry lovable Tribbles. See *Space* for the *Star Trek* ships and their captains.

1966. On *The Girl from U.N.C.L.E.* (NBC), April Dancer, like Napoleon Solo, is an agent for the United Network Command for Law Enforcement. In addition to incorporating much of what Napoleon uses, April is fashion conscious and incorporates weapons into her wardrobe. Her coat buttons double as explosives; her makeup case conceals gas capsules; her lipstick can be used as a dart gun and a communicator. April is also fond of using X-757, a liquid nail polish that when dry can be peeled off and used like plastic explosives.

1972. On *Search* (NBC), the agents for Probe, a super computerized detective agency, are equipped with special devices that allow them to complete assignments. Most notable of the agents are Hugh Lockwood, Nick Bianco and Christopher R. Grover. A super miniaturized transmitter-receiver is surgically implanted in their ears (called an Ear Check). The agents also have a sensory device implanted in their bodies and an ultra miniaturized and ultra sensitive scanner (a dime-sized TV camera that can transmit a signal from any point of the world; it also has a Spy Scope to X-ray items). For non-verbal communication, field agents use their Dental Contact Switch (implanted in the upper jaw and activated by pressing the lower teeth against the upper teeth. Beeps are sent to Probe Control. One beep means affirmative; two mean negative). The Medical Telepathy Body Implant monitors vital body functions twenty-four hours a day. An enemy of all this technology is a cold (it disrupts communication by the agents to Probe Control). All agents carry a bottle of biohystodine, which they take when they feel a cold coming on.

1975. On *Wonder Woman* (ABC/CBS), Diana Prince, alias Wonder Woman, is a beautiful Amazon who lives in tranquility on Paradise Island but uses her amazing abilities to fight evil in the outside world. Diana possesses a set of gold bracelets, made from a metal called Feminum that allows her to deflect bullets. Her magic lariat compels people to tell the truth. She travels via her invisible plane (unable to be detected by radar; once inside Diana is also undetectable). Diana also possesses the ability to impersonate any voice, jump to great heights and run at an incredible speed. She also performs a twirling striptease that allows her to change from her street clothes into her sexy Wonder Woman outfit.

1976. On *Electra Woman and Dyna Girl* (ABC), newspaper reporters Laurie and Judy are secretly Electra Woman and Dyna Girl, crime fighters who use the power of electricity to battle evil. Laurie and Judy are based at a computer complex called Crime Scope (Electra Base is its headquarters). They travel in either the Electra Car or the Electra Plane and use such devices as the Electra Comp (their wrist-worn, portable link to Electra Base), Electra Strobe (allows them to perform anything at 10,000 times normal speed), Electra G (adds gravity to their bodies when activated) and Electra Power (a sudden burst of power to help in difficult situations). The Electra Change is perhaps the most unique gadget of all: Laurie and Judy go from their street clothes to their crime fighting outfits in a matter of seconds.

1982. On *Knight Rider* (NBC), the Knight Industries 2000 is a black Trans Am car, called KITT that is driven by Michael Knight as an agent for the Foundation for Law and Government. KITT is able to talk via its ultra sophisticated and elaborate micro circuitry. Micro sensors make it the world's safest car (it is also programmed with a chip to protect human life). KITT has long-range tracking scopes, turbo boost, normal and auto driving and a pursuit mode. It is programmed to avoid collisions and is equipped with a mini-lab and a third stage aquatic synthesizer that allows it to ride on water. In the 1991 pilot *Knight Rider 2000* (NBC), KITT is upgraded to the Knight Industries 4000 and is said to cost $10 million. It is a three-liter, 300 horsepower red car that can go from zero to 300 mph in a matter of seconds. It runs on nonpolluting hydrogen fuel that is refined from gasses emitted by algae fields. KITT has an odor detector and sonic beams to immobilize the enemy. A collision factor tells Michael when it is safe to run a red light or speed through traffic. Digital sampling allows KITT to analyze voice patterns and duplicate them exactly. It also has a thermal expander that heats the air in the tires of fleeing cars and explodes them.

1984. On *Airwolf* (CBS), Airwolf is an awesome attack helicopter piloted by Stringfellow Hawke that he uses on missions for the U.S. government. Airwolf is a black with white underbelly Bell 222 helicopter with a cruising speed of 300 knots and a maximum speed of 662 plus miles (it can travel to a height of 82,000 feet). Airwolf has radar scanners, turbos for fast flight and movie and infrared cameras. It also has a number of armaments: 30mm wing chain guns; 40mm wing cannons and missiles. The missiles include Sidewinder and Sparrow (radar homing), Redeye (short range) and Phoenix (programmable radar homing). Air-to-surface missiles include: Copperhead (long range), Hellfire (short range), Maverick (infrared radio imaging) and Shrike (electromagnetic homing). Airwolf also has two warheads: the Bullpup (radio command) and Harpoon (radio homing, anti sky).

1985. On *Street Hawk* (ABC), Street Hawk is a motorcycle of the future designed for law enforcement. It is driven by Jesse Mach of the L.A.P.D. and has a cruising speed of 200mph (by incorporating four high volume air boxes and hyper thrust, the speed approaches 300mph). Street Hawk has an aerodynamic co-efficient of 0.05; thus friction is non traceable. It has a hydraulic suspension system that adjusts to off-road or street use. It uses negative airflow for braking (it can stop on a dime) and a press of the button on the handlebars activates compressed air that can propel Jesse 30 meters into the air. Street Hawk has a high-energy particle beam with two settings: Maximum charge (which can immobilize a ten ton truck) and reduced power (used to stun a suspect). The helmet Jesse wears is his nerve center. There are digital readouts in each corner. The left computes speed and RPM's; the right calibrates distance. It also has infrared detectors and light amplification for all-weather and night-fighting capabilities.

1994. On *Viper* (NBC/Syndicated), Viper is a crime-fighting car of the future. It was originally a red (then blue) 1992 Dodge Viper RT/10 Roadster that morphs into the indestructible silver Defender at the touch of a button. It is made of "an armor skin" and can withstand temperatures of up to 1500 degrees. It has four-wheel drive with raised suspension and tire enlargers, a grappling hook, static pulse, a holographic projector and a tunneller missile. Viper also has a 50-caliber machine gun and a flame-thrower. The final season

kept the abilities of the prior car but incorporated them into a stock blue Dodge Viper GTS Coupe. It had the added capabilities of a hovercraft and a torpedo launcher and also carried cluster and canister bombs.

1997. On *Stargate SG-1* (Sci Fi Channel), a Stargate is a mysterious portal through which members of the U.S. Air Force's Stargate Command travel from one planet to another. It was said that the Stargates were created millions of years ago by the Ancients and scattered throughout the universe. Each Stargate is a circular structure that sits atop a base. It is accessed by a unique address. By pushing several of 39 symbols called glyphs a Stargate can be opened. The Stargates are made of an alien metal called Naquadah and when opened it forms a silvery liquid wormhole that connects to another Stargate. The DHD (Dial Home Device) activates the Stargate. A hand-held remote control (like for a TV) called the GDO (Garage Door Opener) opens the Stargate Iris. Stargate teams use Zatn'Kitel energy pistols (developed from the alien Goa'uld technology) that has three functions: one shot will stun; two shots will kill; a third shot will vaporize. Teal'c, a member of the featured Stargate team (SG-1), was a former member of the Goa'uld Jaffa Guard and often uses a Jaffa Staff Weapon (a long ornate pole that fires energy blasts).

2003. On *Stripperella* (Spike TV), Pamela Anderson provides the voice for the animated Erotica Jones, an extremely intelligent woman who poses as a stripper for her cover as a crime fighter for T.H.UG.G. The busty Erotica calls herself "a Double-D cup superhero" and possesses a number of amazing abilities. She is impervious to all temperatures and weather conditions. She rides a motorcycle and can cut glass with her finger nails. Her navel jewelry is actually a control device used to contact her superior (or vice versa). Erotica has enhanced blonde hair that enables her to float to safety from tall buildings. She conceals a lie detector in her bra and a digital scanner, placed under her tongue, allows her to download information into a computer.

Game Shows — Pioneering Years, 1941–1960

Game (or quiz and audience participation) shows have been and still are a major part of television. This entry chronicles the genre from its early beginnings through its definite impact as major programming source.

1941. Dr. Henry Zorbaugh hosts *Play the Game*, a NBC experiment based on the game of charades. Ralph Edwards brings his popular radio program *Truth or Consequences* to NBC (see also 1944, 49, 50). Players who fail to answer a nonsense question must perform a stunt for prizes. Bill Slater (as Uncle Jim) hosts *Uncle Jim's Question Bee*, a video version of the radio series wherein players attempt to answer questions for prizes (NBC).

1943. DuMont airs a 15-minute game show called *Let's See* on its experimental series *DuMont Varieties*. Here host Charlie Taylor and his opponent (Lee Morrison) attempt to answer questions based on tunes heard from records. CBS adapts *The Missus Goes-a-Shopping* radio program to TV with John Reed King as the host. The format involves contestants performing stunts for prizes. NBC simulcasts its radio series *Truth or Consequences* on May 27th. Ralph Edwards hosted the live telecast, which proved to be a minor disaster when a female contestant was asked to identify her disguised husband from a TV set, displayed on stage. The wife, as well as the studio audience had never seen TV before and its amazement caused the stunt to fail when the wife couldn't identify him.

1945. ABC attempts its first game show called *King's Record Shop*. Host John Reed King plays a record. Viewers call in and attempt to identify the singer or the song. The DuMont Network airs *Ladies Be Seated* with hosts Johnny and Penny Olsen overseeing stunts performed by women. DuMont also airs *The Quiz Kids*, a TV version of the radio series with Joe Kelly asking bright children to answer very difficult questions.

1946. DuMont adapts the radio program *The Answer Man* to TV with host Herbert Mitchell responding to questions asked of him by members of the studio audience. Dennis James hosts *Cash and Carry* on DuMont. Here players answer questions that are attached to labels of the sponsor's product (Libby Foods). Female players answer questions based on shopping on the CBS test program *Consumer Quiz* (Fred Uttal hosts). Lew Lehr hosts *Detect and Collect*, a DuMont test program wherein players answer questions for prizes. Players are racecar drivers and advance one state (from New York to California) with each question they

answer on *DuMont Beepstakes*, a DuMont program hosted by Dennis James (the first driver to reach L.A. wins). *Face-to-Face* (NBC) has players identifying celebrities from verbal clues (Eddie Dunn hosts). Warren Hull hosts *Fare Enough* on ABC. Here players answers questions to win a trip to a destination of their choice. John Reed King hosts and players answer questions for prizes on CBS's *It's a Gift*. The CBS test program, *King's Party Line* (hosted by John Reed King) allows viewers to call in an attempt to answer questions for prizes. ABC presents the test program *Ladies Be Seated* with Johnny Olsen as the host and female players competing in outrageous stunts for prizes. Frances Scott is the editor of a newspaper (the host) of ABC's *Let's Play Reporter*. Cub reporters (players) are involved in a situation that must be reported to the editor. The player who most accurately describes the incident wins. *Let's Dance*, an ABC test program hosted by Walter Herlihy, has players attempting to identify dances performed by members of the Arthur Murray Dance Studios. NBC adapts its radio series *People Are Funny* to TV with Art Linkletter as the host. Players perform stunts for prizes. ABC airs *Play the Game*, a live test program wherein contestants play the game of charades in return for prizes. Ireene Wicker performs songs between the games. The host (Dick Eastman) reads a newspaper story that contains several factual errors to players on the CBS test program *Right or Rewrite*. The player who finds the most errors wins a year's subscription to a daily newspaper. Bennett Cerf hosts *See What You Know*, a CBS game wherein players display their knowledge of objects for prizes. The NBC test program *Stump the Authors* has three guests attempting to weave a plot around props suggested by the studio audience (Sydney Mason hosts). Players attempt to break or tie records on the DuMont test program *Tie This* hosted by Bill Slater. ABC's interesting test, *Topsy Turvey Quiz* does everything backwards. It opened with the show's closing, closed with the program opening and gave contestants money — which they had to return if thy failed to answer questions correctly. Frances Scott hosted.

1947. High school students compete in an American History quiz on NBC's *Americana* (hosted by John Mason Brown then Ben Grauer). Players have to identify charades performed by a stock company on DuMont's *Charade Quiz* (Bill Slater hosts). Women shoppers compete in contests for prizes on CBS's *The Missus Goes a Shopping* (John Reed King then Bud Collyer hosts). Bert Parks hosts *Party Line* on NBC. Here viewers are telephoned (postcard selection) and asked a question in return for money. NBC's test program *Seven Arts Quiz* has players answering questions based on the Seven Lively Arts. Bill Slater was the host.

1948. Bert Parks (then Bud Collyer) hosts *Break the Bank* (ABC/NBC/CBS) wherein players win a jackpot by answering eight difficult questions in a row. On NBC's *The Eyes Have It*, players have to identify a famous performer from portions of a picture. Douglas Edward hosts. Couples perform stunts for prizes on *Messing Prize Party*. Bill Slater hosts the CBS series sponsored by Messing Bakeries. Players have to identify film titles and stars on ABC's *Movie Land Quiz* (Arthur Q. Bryan then Ralph Dumke hosts). A crime is dramatized on the CBS test *The Old Nickerbocker Music Hall*. Patrons of the New York club win prizes if they identify the culprit. Panelists attempt to identify news events through an artist's sketchings on *Quizzing the News* (ABC; Alan Prescott hosts). An incomplete joke submitted by a viewer is read. A panel of three comedians attempt to complete it with an original punch line on NBC's *Stop Me If You've Heard This One*. Ted Brown, Roger Bower and Leon Janney served as the hosts. Johnny Bradford is the host of NBC's *Tele Pun*. Here a contestant performs a pun representing a person, place or thing. If the studio audience likes his pun he wins a prize; if not he is charged with "punning in public places" and loses. Contestants perform stunts for prizes on NBC's *Try and Do It* with Jack Bright as the host. NBC's *What Will They Think of Next?* has amateur inventors demonstrating their gadgets with the hope of interesting a manufacturer. Ed Herlihy is the host. Players have to identify news stories from quotations on NBC's *Who Said That?* Robert Trout, Walter Kiernan and John Daly were the hosts. Players answer questions based on sketches on CBS's *Winner Take All*. Bud Collyer then Bill Cullen hosts.

1949. Players have to solve criminal cases based on partial reenactments on CBS's *Armchair Detective*. A girl, concealed from two men, chooses one for a date based on a series of questions on *Blind Date* (ABC/NBC/DuMont; Arlene Francis hosts). Players have to identify geographical locations through stills or rhyming clues on ABC's *Bon Voy-*

age (John Weigel hosts). Adrian Spies hosts *Crisis* on NBC. Here actors ad lib an ending to a story told by a person who faced a real crisis. Prizes are awarded to the person for participating. On DuMont's *Cut*, an operator places a random phone call. If the viewer can guess the person, place or object being performed on stage, he wins a prize (Carl Caruso hosts). A player attempts to draw a gag line funnier than an artist's on ABC's *Draw Me a Laugh* (Walter Herlihy hosts). Players attempt to identify a merchandise item hidden behind "The Magic Curtain" on ABC's *Fun for the Money* (Jack Lescoulie then Johnny Olsen hosts). On CBS's *Hold It Please*, a random telephone call is placed to a viewer (who wins a prize if he gives the correct response; Gil Fates hosts). A player can win a prize if he can extract a response from a panel who evade answering questions like "What color was George Washington's white horse?" on *It Pays to Be Ignorant* (CBS/NBC; Tom Howard hosts). Bandleader Kay Kyser hosts *Kay Kyser's Kollege of Musical Knowledge* on NBC. Players have to identify song titles to win. Ed Prentiss hosts *Majority Rules*, an ABC game wherein answers to questions must be a majority decision (at least two of the three players per game; Mike Stokey hosts). Five intelligent children answer difficult questions on *Quiz Kids* (NBC/CBS; Joe Kelly then Clifton Fadiman hosts). Celebrity teams compete in a game of charades on *Say It with Acting* (DuMont/NBC/ABC; Bill Cullen, Maggi McNellis and Bud Collyer host). Walter Kiernan hosts *Sparring Partners*, a CBS game in which male vs. female teams compete in question and answer sessions. Carl Caruso (then Eddie Dunn and Kathi Norris) hosts DuMont's *Spin the Picture*, wherein a phone call is placed to a home viewer who must identify the subject of a rapidly spinning picture. While an orchestra plays a song, a phone call is placed to a viewer. When a call is completed, "Stop the Music" is yelled and the viewer must identify the song. Bert Parks (then Jimmy Blaine) hosts ABC's *Stop the Music*. Players answer questions based on newsreel footage of horse races on DuMont's *They're Off* (Tom Shirley hosts). Ralph Edwards (then Jack Bailey and Bob Barker) hosts the CBS (then NBC) game *Truth or Consequences* (wherein players perform stunts for prizes). A player has to identify a subject by asking indirect questions (20 the maximum) on *Twenty Questions* (NBC/ABC/DuMont; Bill Slater then Jay Jackson hosts).

1950. A celebrity panel must predict whether or not a player would involve himself in a specific situation on NBC's *Answer Yes or No* (Moss Hart hosts). Contestants win prizes by performing a stunt before time on a sixty-second ticking clock runs out on *Beat the Clock* (CBS/ABC; Bud Collyer hosts). A panel of three comedians tries to beat the score of a joke sent in by a home viewer on ABC's *Can You Top This?* (Ward Wilson hosts). Players have to guess song titles based on an artist's clues on *Cartoon-O* (DuMont; Holland Engle hosts). Denise Darcell hosts *Chance of a Lifetime*, an ABC game wherein players answer questions based on clues provided by singers or comics. Jimmy Blaine and Kyle McDonnell host *Hold That Camera* (DuMont). Here a player is paired with a viewer (via telephone). The viewer directs the studio player through a series of shenanigans. The team (of two that compete) that performs the best time wins. A "Brain Panel" answers questions submitted by home viewers on CBS's *Information Please* (Clifton Fadiman hosts). Players must match numbers on dollar bills to win on NBC's *Lucky Letters* (Carl Cordell hosts). The game of charades is played on *Say It with Acting* (DuMont/NBC/ABC; Bill Cullen hosts, then Maggi McNellis and Bud Collyer). Kay Westfall hosts *Sit or Miss*, an ABC game wherein musical chairs is played. Ralph Edwards (then Jack Bailey and Bob Barker) hosts *Truth or Consequences*, a CBS (then NBC) game wherein contestants perform stunts for prizes. Celebrities have to supply definitions for words submitted by viewers on CBS's *We Take Your Word* (John Daly then John K.M. McCaffrey hosts). A celebrity panel must identify the occupations of guests on CBS's *What's My Line?* (John Daly hosts). Groucho Marx first interviews then quizzes ordinary people on NBC's *You Bet Your Life*.

1951. Disc jockeys, playing for home viewers, attempt to answer questions based on songs on *The Art Ford Show* (NBC; Art Ford hosts). Selected studio audience members perform stunts for prizes on *The Big Payoff* (NBC/CBS; Bert Parks and Bess Myerson are among the hosts). Players have to guess phrases or slogans by suggesting letters that may appear in a line of dashes on *Down You Go* (DuMont/CBS/ABC/NBC; Dr. Bergen Evans then Bill Cullen hosts). Contestants have to identify common phrases from skits on *Go Lucky* (CBS; Jan Murray hosts). Mike Wallace hosts *Guess Again*, a CBS game wherein players answer questions based on skits. A player has to determine which celebrity panelist is relating a true news story on CBS's *It's News to Me* (John Daly, Walter Cronkite then Quincy Howe hosts). A female must defend the woman's point of view on topical issues against a panel of men on DuMont's *Ladies Before Gentlemen* (Ken Roberts hosts). A celebrity panel must guess the birth names of guests who have the same names as famous personalities on ABC's *The Name's the Same* (Robert Q. Lewis hosts, then Dennis James and Bob Elliott and Ray Goulding). Celebrity panelists have to solve mystery stories submitted by viewers on *Q.E.D.* (ABC; Fred Uttal then Doug Browning hosts). Contestants with the saddest hard luck stories receive cash prizes on CBS's *Strike It Rich* (Warren Hull hosts). Hal Block hosts *Tag the Gag*, an NBC game in which players have to supply funny endings to jokes. A panel has to identify news stories from skits on DuMont's *What's the Story?* (Walter Kiernan and John K.M. McCaffrey are among the hosts). The CBS pilot *Who's Whose?* has a celebrity panel attempting to discover which three women are married to which three men. Phil Baker hosts.

1952. Players have to identify sports figures through indirect questions on *Ask Me Another* (NBC; Joe Boland hosts). Players can win their yearly household budgets by answering questions on CBS's *Balance Your Budget* (Bert Parks hosts). Show business veterans compete against young hopefuls in a series of talent contests on *Battle of the Ages* (DuMont/CBS; John Reed King then Morey Amsterdam hosts). Players wager money on their ability to answer questions on CBS's *Double or Nothing* (Bert Parks hosts). Henry Morgan hosts *Draw to Win*, a CBS game wherein players have to identify persons, places or things from an artist's sketches. Players have to guess words by suggesting letters on NBC's *Ghost* (later titled *Super Ghost*; Dr. Bergen Evans hosts). Five male contestants compete in stunts to be named *The Greatest Man on Earth* (ABC; Ted Brown hosts). Panelists must identify famous persons, places, or objects from statements revealed by the host (Richard Kollmar) on DuMont's *Guess What?* Panelists have to guess the news story in which a guest was involved on NBC's *Guess What Happened?* (John Cameron Swayze hosts). Garry Moore (then Steve Allen) hosts *I've Got a Secret*, a CBS game wherein a celebrity panel has to discover (through indirect questions) the secret of a guest. Celebrity panelists must guess the identities of elaborately disguised guests on *Masquerade Party* (NBC/CBS/ABC; Bud Collyer and Bert Parks were among the hosts). Jan Murray hosts *Meet Your Match*, an NBC game that pits players against one another in a question-and-answer session. Contestants identify phrases suggested by cartoon drawings on DuMont's *Quick on the Draw* (Robin Chandler hosts). Players compete in a game based on the five senses on NBC's *Sense and Nonsense* (Bob Kennedy then Ralph Paul hosts). Dennis James and Sam Levinson are among the hosts on *Two for the Money*, an NBC (then CBS) game wherein the money a player wins in the first round doubles for each question he correctly answers in the second round. A celebrity panel must determine the newspaper story in which a guest appeared on the syndicated *What Happened?* (Ben Grauer hosts). Players must determine the "why" of a situation on ABC's *Why?* (John Reed King hosts). Basil Rathbone hosts *Your Lucky Clue*, a CBS game wherein players must solve criminal cases based on the facts of a dramatic skit. Players can select merchandise from a "Surprise Store" if they answer questions correctly on CBS's *Your Surprise Store* (George Fenneman hosts).

1953. Panelists must identify celebrities whose identities are concealed by makeup on CBS's *Anyone Can Win* (Al Capp hosts). Players have to have proof of the facts they are stating during interviews on ABC's *Back the Fact* (Joey Adams hosts). Studio audience members have to answer questions posed to them by Dr. I.Q., the Mental Banker (James McLain, Jay Owen, Tom Kennedy) on ABC's *Doctor I.Q.* On *Dollar a Second* (DuMont/NBC/ABC), players compete in rapid-fire question and answer rounds with silver dollars being awarded for each correct response (Jan Murray hosts). On CBS's *Follow the Leader* hostess Vera Vague performs a skit; the player who best duplicates her performance wins. A female contestant has to suggest a solution for a household crisis that is suggested by a skit on CBS's *Freedom Rings* (John Beal hosts). Home viewers are called (post card selection) and asked to answer questions from clues that appear on the screen on the pilot *Look Photo Quiz* (Hugh James hosts). Red Benson, Bill Cullen then George DeWitt hosts *Name That Tune*, an NBC (then CBS) game wherein players win prizes by identifying song titles. Players compete in question-and-answer

rounds on the DuMont (then ABC) series *On Your Way* (Bud Collyer hosts, then John Reed King and Kathy Godfrey). Players flash light signals for first chance to identify a person, place or object on ABC's *Quick as a Flash* (Bobby Sherwood then Bud Collyer hosts). A player indirectly questions a celebrity panel to determine a mystery phrase known only to them on CBS's *Take a Guess* (John K.M. McCaffrey hosts). Contestants attempt to win a needed item by relating sad stories on ABC's *Turn to a Friend* (Dennis James hosts). Viewers bid (via mail) on merchandise items displayed on stage on ABC's *TV General Store* (Dave and Judy Clark host). Players have to determine the identity of white elephant objects on ABC's *What Have You Got to Lose?* (John Reed King hosts). Studio audience members use their own money to bid on merchandise items on *What's Your Bid?* (ABC/DuMont; John Reed King then Robert Alda hosts). Panelists have to determine where contestants had been at certain times on DuMont's *Where Was I?* (Dan Seymour hosts, then Ken Roberts and John Reed King). Players must identify mystery guests through props and apparel clues on CBS's *Who's There?* (Arlene Francis hosts).

1954. Nonsense drawings have to be identified by players on NBC's *Droodles* (Roger Price hosts). Players answer questions of ascending difficulty to win their dream vacation on CBS's *Earn Your Vacation* (Johnny Carson hosts). Players have to find feathers in merchandise articles then answer their associated questions to win that prize on NBC's *Feather Your Nest* (Bud Collyer hosts). Denise Darcell and Ernie Kovacs host *Gamble on Love*, a DuMont series wherein players vie to answer "The Cupid Question" to win a mink coat. People who have never met but have something in common must determine what it is on CBS's *In Common* (Ralph Story hosts). Incidents from the past have to be identified by players on ABC's *It's About Time* (Dr. Bergen Evans hosts). Players with sad stories to tell attempt to win money by being the most desperate on CBS's *On Your Account* (Eddie Albert hosts, then Win Elliott and Dennis James). Panelists must talk for one minute on a topic without repeating themselves on DuMont's *One Minute Please* (John K.M. McCaffrey then Allyn Edwards host). Art Linkletter hosts *People Are Funny*, an NBC game wherein players perform stunts for prizes. *The Sky's the Limit* on CBS also has players performing stunts for prizes with Gene Rayburn as the host. Sid Stone hosts *TV Auction*, an ABC game wherein home viewers bid (via mail) for merchandise items that are displayed on stage. Married or engaged couples win money by predicting how long (in seconds) it will take for them to answer a question on *Two in Love* (Bert Parks hosts). Ralph Story hosts *What Do You Have in Common?*, a CBS game wherein specially selected players must determine their common denominator. A team based in the studio must determine (through questions with host Lee Bowman) what a team outside the studio is doing on CBS's *What's Going On?* Single rhymes (for example, "Red Bed") have to be identified by a celebrity panel on ABC's *What's in a Word?* (Mike Wallace then Clifton Fadiman hosts). A secretary can win money if a celebrity panel can identify her employer through indirect clues on ABC's *Who's the Boss?* (Walter Kiernan hosts).

1955. John Reed King hosts *Have a Heart*, a DuMont series in which players donate their winnings from a question-and-answer session to their favorite charities (they are reimbursed by the show for their kindness). Married couples compete in a series of question-and-answer rounds on NBC's *It Pays to Be Married* (Bill Goodwin hosts). A celebrity has to determine how his path crossed with a layman guest on NBC's *Make the Connection* (Gene Rayburn then Jim McKay host). Bill Leyden hosts *Musical Chairs*, an NBC game wherein players must answer questions regarding singers by impersonating the singer to whom the question refers. Players compete in a spelling bee wherein each correctly spelled word doubles a penny from one to a million ($10,000) on ABC's *Penny to a Million* (Bill Goodwin hosts). A contestant selects a category then proceeds to answer its questions (that begin at one dollar. Each correct response doubles the previous amount to a maximum of $64,000) on CBS's *The $64,000 Question* (Hal March hosts).

1956. *Break the Bank* (see 1948) gets a higher jackpot ($250,000) and allows a player to have an expert assist in answering very difficult questions on NBC's *Break the $250,000 Bank* (Bert Parks hosts). Contestants are quizzed on items from their local newspapers on CBS's *High Finance* (Dennis James hosts). Three people appear on stage and claim to be the same person. A celebrity panel must determine who the real person is on CBS's *To Tell the Truth* (Bud Collyer hosts. The program premiered as *Nothing But the*

Truth and aired as such for the first three weeks with John Cameron Swayze as the host). Players seek to win $100,000 by answering increasingly difficult questions in a category of their choice on CBS's *The $100,000 Big Surprise* (Jack Barry then Mike Wallace hosts). Players have to guess the retail value of merchandise items on *The Price Is Right* (NBC/ABC; Bill Cullen then Jack Clark hosts. Bob Barker became host in 1972; the show is still current in 2006). Women bear their souls, hoping to tell the saddest story to win prizes and be treated like royalty on *Queen for a Day* (NBC/ABC; Jack Bailey hosts). A winner from *The $64,000 Question* can double his earnings by answering questions on CBS's *The $64,000 Challenge* (Sonny Fox hosts). Player X and Player O answer questions to acquire a square on a large board on NBC's *Tic Tac Dough* (Jack Barry then Gene Rayburn hosts). Players answer questions to select one of 30 treasure chests on *Treasure Hunt* (ABC/NBC; Jan Murray hosts). Jack Barry hosts *Twenty-One*, a CBS game wherein players answer questions by point values to score an exact 21 to win. A husband can answer a question himself or trust his wife to do so on *Who Do You Trust?* (CBS/ABC. Edgar Bergen hosts, then Johnny Carson and Woody Woodbury). Steve Dunne hosts *You're on Your Own*, a CBS game wherein incorrect answers to questions force a player to perform humiliating stunts.

1957. A player can win $1500 by answering more questions in a "High" category or $500 less in a "Low" category on NBC's *High Low* (Jack Barry hosts). Players win money by identifying song titles in as few notes as possible in NBC's *Hold That Note* (Bert Parks hosts). Two five-member families compete in a question-and-answer session on ABC's *Keep It in the Family* (Keefe Brasselle hosts). A celebrity panel has to identify the purpose of a gadget registered by the U.S. Patent Office on NBC's *What's It For?* (Hal March hosts).

1958. George Fenneman hosts *Anybody Can Play*, an ABC game wherein players identify objects possessed by celebrities. Players bid for clues to the identity of unknown objects on CBS's *Bid 'n' Buy* (Bert Parks hosts). Tom Kennedy hosts NBC's *Big Game*. Here a correctly answered question allows a player to "shoot" the animals his opponent has hidden on a board by calling a position (as in the game of Battleships). The first player to shoot his opponent's animals wins. On

NBC's *Brains and Brawn* hosts Fred Davis and Jack Lescoulie oversee two contests: a difficult question-and-answer session with the Brain and physical dexterity stunts with the Brawn. The team that is best at solving its portion wins. Players select two of 30 numbered squares that reveal two prizes. If the prizes match, they revolve to reveal two puzzle parts; if not, they return to numbers. Players have to recall what numbers match what prizes on NBC's *Concentration*. The player who identifies the puzzle wins what prizes he uncovered. Hugh Downs then Ed McMahon and Jack Barry host. Players connect dots to uncover the identity of a person, place or object on CBS's *Dotto* (Jack Narz hosts). Bill Nimmo hosts *For Love or Money*, a CBS game wherein players win a prize by answering questions associated with it. Contestants have to identify concealed photos by answering questions to remove portions of it on NBC's *Haggis Baggis* (Jack Linkletter then Dennis James hosts). Intelligence and reasoning powers are tested on CBS's *How Do You Rate?* (Tom Reddy hosts). Married couples relate personal situations that were brought on as the result of popular songs on NBC's *It Could Be You* (Bill Quinn hosts). One celebrity is given a secret phrase and must work it into a conversation. His partner must guess what it is on *Keep Talking* (CBS/ABC; Monty Hall then Carl Reiner and Merv Griffin host). Players chosen from the studio audience compete in a question-and-answer session on NBC's *Lucky Partners* (Carl Cordell hosts). Mothers compete in games based on the operation of a household on ABC's *Mother's Day* (Dick Van Dyke hosts). Contestants have to determine which factor distinguishes one object from a set of three on *Play Your Hunch* (CBS/NBC; Richard Hayes hosts, then Gene Rayburn, Merv Griffin and Robert Q. Lewis). Players suggest letters that are contained in an unknown word on CBS's *Top Dollar* (Toby Reed hosts). Players stand before a starting post (like in a horse race) and answer questions to reach the finish line on NBC's *Win with a Winner* (Sandy Becker then Win Elliott hosts). Answering very difficult questions is the basis of CBS's *Wingo* (Bob Kennedy hosts).

1959. College students compete in a series of question-and-answer rounds on *The G.E. College Bowl* (CBS/NBC; Allen Ludden then Robert Earle hosts). Dick Van Dyke hosts *Laugh Line*, a CBS game wherein celebrities supply comic cap-

tions for cartoons. Guest comics attempt to make a contestant laugh on ABC's *Make Me Laugh* (Robert Q. Lewis hosts). Players must guess the identity of a celebrity from two sets of clues on NBC's *Split Personality* (Tom Poston hosts). A celebrity panel attempts to identify a mystery guest from skits that are performed on stage on ABC's *Take a Good Look* (Ernie Kovacs hosts). Celebrity panelists have to identify a mystery guest by indirectly questioning two of his employees on NBC's *Who Pays?* (Mike Wallace hosts).

1960. Ben Alexander hosts *About Faces*, an ABC game in which players must unravel clues that relate to incidents in their past lives. Players win money to buy merchandise prizes by making the most words from sixteen letter words on NBC's *Charge Account* (Jan Murray hosts). The NBC pilot *Head of the Class* has players answering questions based on skits or musical numbers. Gene Rayburn hosts. The roll of two dice determines the move a player makes on a large game board on CBS's *Video Village*. Jack Narz then Monty Hall hosts the program as the Mayor of Video Village.

Gays (Male)

This entry is an overall review of the programs on which gay characters are featured (regulars or semi-regulars). Single guest appearances on a series are excluded. See also *Cross Dressers*, *Lesbians* and *Transsexuals*.

1955. One of the many characters created by comic genius Ernie Kovacs was Percy Dovetonsils, a lisping, soused poet (NBC's *The Ernie Kovacs Show*). His drinking (not sexual preferences) and dress made him appear gay (mustache, curly bangs, smoking jacket and reading glasses with sleepy painted on eyelids).

1972. Select PBS stations air the controversial *La Route Est Dure* (*The Roads to Freedom*), a British produced series about life in pre-World War II France. Daniel Massey plays Daniel, a homosexual who is unable to act or think definitively. Vincent Schiavelli plays Peter Panama, a gay male fashion designer who frequents ABC's *The Corner Bar*.

1975. George (Lee Bergere) and Gordon (Henry Calvert) are homosexuals who live together at the *Hot l Baltimore* (ABC; the *e* in the neon sign has burned out).

1976. Ken Olfson plays Terry Folsom, the apparently gay assistant to theatrical agent Nancy Kitteridge on ABC's *The Nancy Walker Show*.

1977. The syndicated satire *Mary Hartman, Mary Hartman*, features the gay couple Ed and Howard (Larry Holden, Beeson Carroll). Billy Crystal plays Jodie Dallas, the gay son of Bert and Mary Campbell on ABC's *Soap*. Bob Seagren plays Jodie's boyfriend, Dennis Phillips. John Ritter plays Jack Tripper, a straight man who pretends to be gay (to please his landlord) and lives with two beautiful girls (Janet and Chrissy) on *Three's Company* (ABC).

1981. Steve Carrington (Al Corley, Jack Coleman), the gay son of wealthy Blake Carrington, first dated Chris Deegan (Grant Goodeve) then Bart (Kevin Conroy, Cameron Watson) on ABC's *Dynasty*. The TV movie *Sidney Shorr* (NBC) features Tony Randall as a 40-year-old homosexual. It lead to the TV series *Love, Sidney* but references to his homosexuality were toned down.

1982. Richard Thomas plays Ken Talley, Jr., a homosexual Vietnam vet struggling to cope with a family he loves and fears on the Showtime special *Fifth of July*.

1984. Showtime airs the first series to revolve around a gay — *Brothers*. Here Paul Regina plays Cliff Waters, the youngest of three brothers who is gay.

1987. Joseph Gian plays Rick Silardi, a gay police officer with the San Francisco P.D. on ABC's *Hooperman*. Fourteen-year-old Francesca (Tracey Ullman) lives with her two gay fathers, David and William (Dan Castellaneta, Sam McMurray) on *The Tracey Ullman Show* (Fox). *What if I'm Gay?* is a CBS *Schoolbreak Special* that stars Richard J. Paul as Todd Bowers, a teenager whose sexuality is questioned when he is found to have a male porno magazine. Scott Baio stars in *The Truth About Alex*, an HBO special in which a teenager discovers his best friend is gay.

1988. Martin Mull plays Leon Carp, a gay who first dated Terry Gimble (Michael Des Barres) but later married Scott (Fred Willard) on ABC's *Roseanne*.

1990. Jeffrey Alan Chandler plays Ray Rodbart, the gay mayor's aide on ABC's *Cop Rock*. The sketch comedy *In Living Color* (Fox), presents a segment called "Men on Film" with gay movie reviewers Blaine Edwards (Damon Wayans) and Antoine Meriwether (David Alan Grier). Ron and Eric (Doug Ballard, Don McManus) are gays who

buy a bed and breakfast in Cicely, Alaska, on CBS's *Northern Exposure*. Peter (Peter Frechetti) and Russell (David Marshall Grant) are gay lovers on ABC's *thirtysomething*.

1992. Doug Savant plays Matt Fielding, a resident of *Melrose Place* (Fox) who is also gay. Liberty High School student Ricky Vasquez (Wilson Cruz) is half black, half Hispanic — and gay on ABC's *My So-Called Life*. Also on the series is Jeff Perry as Richard Katimski, a closet gay English teacher.

1994. Vondie Curtis Hall plays Dennis Hancock, a gay doctor on CBS's *Chicago Hope*.

1995. When Ellen Morgan (Ellen DeGeneres) admitted to being a lesbian, her friends Peter and Barnett (Patrick Bristow, Jack Plotnick) also came out of the closet on ABC's *Ellen*. Bob and Ray (Yul Vazquez, John Paragon) are the "tough" gays Jerry and Kramer encounter on NBC's *Seinfeld*. Anthony Kalloniatis, better known as Ant, plays Barry, the gay high school student on *Unhappily Ever After* (WB).

1996. Although he is not gay, San Francisco police detective Joe Dominiquez (Cheech Marin) owns a gay bar, the Tender Loin, on CBS's *Nash Bridges*. The sophisticated Carter Sebastian Heywood (Michael Boatman) is a gay black activist who works as the head of Minority Affairs for the Mayor of New York on ABC's *Spin City*.

1997. Patrick Bristow plays Ian, the bisexual romance counselor at the Miami dating service *Head Over Heels* (UPN). Wallace Langham plays Joshua, a man who finally realizes he is gay after everyone (including his mother) thought he was on NBC's *Veronica's Closet*. Lee Tergesen and Charles Busch play gay prisoners Tobias Beecher and Nat "Natalie" Ginsberg on HBO's *Oz*.

1998. Louis Antonio Ramos is Billy Hernandez, the gay Hispanic TV weatherman on *The Brian Benben Show* (CBS). Joseph Maher is Mr. John, a gay interior decorator on *Style and Substance* (CBS). Ian Gomez plays Javier Quintata, the gay manager of Dean and DeLuca's Restaurant in New York City on *Felicity* (WB). Will Truman (Eric McCormick) is a conservative gay who lives with his straight friend Grace (Debra Messing); Jack McFarland (Sean Hayes) is an outrageously proud gay on NBC's *Will and Grace*. Will works as a lawyer; Jack is, after many jobs, an employee of Out TV, a gay network.

1999. Bumper Robinson plays Bradley, college student Kim Parker's (Countess Vaughn) gay roommate on UPN's *The Parkers*. John Ducey plays Ford Vandemear, a gay lawyer who was married but didn't realize he was different until he tied the knot on ABC's *Oh Grow Up*.

2000. James Dreyfus plays Oscar, the apparently gay pianist (to singer Bette) on CBS's *Bette*. Middle-aged construction company owner Butch Campbell (John Goodman) comes out of the closet because he wasn't happy living a lie on Fox's *Normal, Ohio*. Bill Brochtrup plays John Irvin, a gay police officer (a secretary) on *N.Y.P.D. Blue* (ABC). The life, loves and ambitions of a group of gay men and lesbians living in Pittsburgh are the focal point of Showtime's *Queer as Folk*. Gabe Howard, Scott Lowell and Hal Parks head a large cast.

2001. Michael C. Hall plays David Fisher, a middle child who works at the family mortuary (Fisher and Sons) and who is also gay on HBO's *Six Feet Under*.

2002. Alex Mapa plays Adam Bennett, the gay Delicious Records company employee on UPN's *Half and Half*. Robot Head 790 (voice of Jeffrey Hirschfield) is a gay robot (zapped by a love machine) that is in love with Kai, an undead assassin on *Lexx* (Sci Fi Channel).

2003. Shawn Harrison plays Peaches, a hair stylist who doubles as Joan Clayton's office receptionist (law firm) on UPN's *Girlfriends*. Schoolteacher Simon Banks (Christopher Siber) and art gallery owner Philip Stoddard (John Benjamin Hickey) are lovers on ABC's *It's All Relative*. Pete Peterson (Daniel Roebuck) and Lou Peterson (Garret Dillahunt) are married (Lou took Pete's last name) and run the Peterson Boys Diner in Waterford Falls, Wisconsin on *A Minute with Stan Hooper* (Fox). Five gay male stylists attempt to make over straight men on *Queer Eye for the Straight Guy* (Bravo). Ted Allen, Kyan Douglas, Thom Filicia, Caron Kressley and Jai Rodriquez star. Gay actor Ant is a regular judge of weird acts on *Steve Harvey's Big Time Challenge* (WB).

2004. Lamont Johnson plays Ronnie, Maya Wilkes gay hair stylist on UPN's *Girlfriends*.

2005. Eric Mabius plays Chris Didion, a gay Primary Investigator for Judd Risk Management on ABC's *Eyes*. Ryan Carnes plays Ryan, the gay gardener for housewives on Wisteria Lane on ABC's *Desperate Housewives*. Tim Meadows plays Greg Peters, the gay, black friend of Fran (Fran Drescher) on the WB's *Living with Fran*. Four gay male fashion experts attempt to make over straight

women on *Queer Eye for the Straight Girl* (Bravo). Robbie Laughlin, Danny Teeson, Damon Pease and Honey Labrador star. Chris Fitzgerald plays Neil, a designer at Arnold Under Garments (for females) who is gay and seeking the right man on *Twins* (WB).

2006. Peter Webster (Christian Campbell) is the 23-year-old gay son of Episcopal minister Rev. Daniel Webster on *The Book of Daniel* (NBC). Ben Savage plays Mitch Crumb, a gay Hollywood writer who returns to his hometown to help run the family restaurant on *Crumbs* (ABC). Andrew Van De Kamp (Shawn Pyfrom), the rebellious teenage son of gorgeous housewife Bree Van De Kamp, is revealed to be gay on ABC's *Desperate Housewives*. Khary Payton plays Josh, the gay friend of book editor Emily Sanders on *Emily's Reasons Why Not* (ABC).

Genies

Thanks to the wonderful world of TV reruns, the NBC series *I Dream of Jeannie* will forever be thought of as the only TV show about a genie. This entry disputes that suggestion and provides all the programs that starred genies — both male and female.

1955. On *Al Haddon's Lamp* (Pilot), Al Haddon (Robert Hutton) is a salesman at Booth Real Estate. One day at an auction he buys a strange-looking brass lamp for $8. At home he begins polishing it and out pops a male genie (Buddy Ebsen) that can grant his any wish.

1957. On *Sabu and the Magic Ring* (Pilot), Sabu (himself), a stable boy to the Caliph in India, finds a magic ring that when rubbed, makes him the master of Uda (William Marshall), a powerful, giant genie. This pilot is actually a combination of two unsold pilots that were edited together, released theatrically then placed into TV syndication.

1963. One day while in the basement of her uncle's antique shop, Annie Brenner (Diane Jergens) stumbles upon a dusty old lamp on *Three Wishes* (Pilot). As Annie examines it, she rubs it and out pops a genie (Gustavo Rojo), who can grant her any wish.

1965. On *I Dream of Jeannie* (NBC), astronaut Tony Nelson (Larry Hagman) becomes stranded on a deserted island (as the result of a failed space flight) finds a strange bottle, rubs it and out pops a puff of smoke that materializes into a beautiful genie named Jeannie (Barbara Eden). While Tony can have anything he wants, he asks for very little, mainly struggling to keep Jeannie a secret from the rest of the world.

1967. On *Shazzan!* (CBS cartoon), twins Nancy and Chuck (Janet Waldo, Jerry Dexter) find two halves of a ring that when placed together spell the world "Shazzan." Instantly they are transported to the age of the Arabian Knights and become the masters of Shazzan (Barney Phillips), a powerful, sixty-foot genie.

1971. In Lidsville, a land of living hats, the evil magician Whoo Doo (Charles Nelson Reilly) controls Weenie the Genie (Billie Hayes), who is friendly but magically inept on *Lidsville* (ABC). Weenie is seeking to retrieve her magic ring, which Whoo Doo possesses, and free herself of his control.

1973. On *Jeannie* (CBS cartoon), while surfing, Central High School student Corey Anders (Mark Hamill) is overcome by a wave and washed ashore. There the finds a bottle in the sand and opens it. A gorgeous young genie named Jeannie (Julie McWhirter) and her inept genie friend Babu (Joe Besser) become his slaves. Corey now struggles to live a normal life while Jeannie and Babu enjoy life in the 1970s.

1973. On *Sigmund and the Sea Monsters* (NBC), Rip Taylor plays Sheldon the Sea Genie, a fun-loving genie who resides in the ocean near Dead Man's Point at Cypress Beach in California. Also appearing is his nephew Shelby (Sparky Marcus), an apprentice genie.

1977. On *Magic Mongo* (ABC), while walking on the beach Donald Connelly (Paul Hinckley) finds a strange looking bottle that produces a mischievous genie named Magic Mongo (Lennie Weinrib) when he opens it. While Donald becomes Mongo's master, Mongo finds life a ball — and nothing but trouble for Donald.

1979. On *The Seven Wishes of a Rich Kid* (ABC Special), a genie (Butterfly McQueen) magically appears to a rich boy named Calvin (Robbie Rist) through his TV set to teach him responsibility by offering him seven wishes (all of which he uses in the wrong manner to impress a girl).

1983. On *Just Our Luck* (ABC), while jogging TV weatherman Keith Barrow (Richard Gilliland) bumps into a souvenir stand and cracks a strange looking green bottle (which he is forced to buy). At home Keith's cat knocks over the bottle and

breaks it. A black genie, Sabu (T.K. Carter), emerges from the rubble and becomes Keith's slave.

1986. On *Pee Wee's Playhouse* (CBS), in a dazzling magic playhouse there exists a purple box that is owned by Pee Wee (Paul Reubens). Inside the box lives Jambi (John Paragon), a mystical but sarcastic genie who can grant Pee Wee any wish.

1994. On *Weird Science* (USA), Lisa (Vanessa Angel) is a computer genie that resulted when a computer program went awry. High school students Wyatt Donnelly and Gary Wallace (Michael Manasseri, John Mallory Asher) set out to design the ultimate woman: Wyatt wanted intelligence; Gary sought beauty. A bolt of lightning struck the computer and out popped the gorgeous and exceptionally intelligent Lisa (who possesses the power to take her creators through time and space).

1997. On *You Wish* (ABC), while looking for a rug, Gillian Apple (Haley Jane Kozak) finds an old rug in a curio shop that when unfolded produces a 2,000-year-old genie named Genie (John Ales). Gillian is divorced, a single mother and owner of a genie who can grant her any wish. Alex McKenna and Nathan Lawrence plays Gillian's daughter Mickey and son Travis.

2005. While not a genie show in the traditional sense, *Three Wishes* (NBC) borrows the concept with Amy Grant (herself) leading a team of experts to grant wishes to make the hopes and dreams of deserving people come true.

Geniuses

Characters who are distinguished by exceptional intelligence are the subjects of this entry. See also *Children — Extraordinary; Men — Extraordinary and Women — Extraordinary.*

1949. Jack Diamond plays Tommy Howard, a child prodigy on DuMont's *Family Genius.*

1954. Jack Jackson, Jr. (Gil Stratton, Jr.) is near-sighted, prone to hay fever and sinus attacks and averse to sports. He is a big disappointment to his father, Jack, Sr. (Eddie Mayehoff), a former college athlete who can't understand how he acquired an academic genius instead of an athlete on CBS's *That's My Boy.*

1955. Tommy Adams (Tommy Terrell) is a

young boy who was born with one of the highest I.Q.'s ever known. He is so advanced that the government has designed a crime-fighting robot named Tobor with an ESP detector that allows Tommy's mind to control it on the pilot *Here Comes Tobor*.

1959. Zelda Gilroy (Sheila James) is an exceptionally bright high school girl who knows she is not beautiful. She is pretty but not the type of girl her dream man, Dobie Gillis (Dwayne Hickman), craves. She feels her genius hampers her and would give it up in an instant for Dobie on CBS's *Dobie Gillis*.

1963. Lester Bishop (Frank Aletter) is a mechanical genius who can visualize an idea but when it comes to perfecting it what can go wrong does on the CBS pilot *The Big Brain*.

1964. Roy Hinkley (Russell Johnson) is a high school science teacher who finds his vast knowledge essential to his and his fellow castaways' survival on CBS's *Gilligan's Island*.

1965. Alec Tate (Dean Jones) is a brilliant scientist who has developed a computer that is capable of solving any problem. He is also the guardian of his 15-year-old sister Bunny (Robyn Millan) and a swinging bachelor whose genius often comes between him and a date on the CBS pilot *The Dean Jones Show*. Angela Cartwright plays Penny Robinson, the exceptionally bright daughter of John and Maureen Robinson on CBS's *Lost in Space*. Penny has an I.Q of 147 and is interested in zoology. Her brother, Will (Billy Mumy), is also a genius. He graduated from the Campbell Canyon School of Science at the age of nine and held the highest average in the school's history. His field of expertise is electronics.

1966. Donald O'Connor plays Benjamin Boggs, an exceptionally brilliant research scientist who is plagued by life's misfortunes on the NBC pilot *Brilliant Benjamin Boggs*.

1968. Warren Springer (Fred Gwynne) is an ingenious amateur inventor who concocts weird inventions that seldom work as he planned on the NBC pilot *Guess What I Did Today?*

1972. Glenn Garth Gregory (Laurence Luckinbill) is a man with an exceptional I.Q. who also possesses a photographic memory and total recall abilities who works for *The Delphi Bureau* (ABC) and is responsible only to the President of the United States.

1981. Dick Clark hosts *The Krypton Factor* on ABC, a game in which people with exceptional I.Q.'s or abilities compete in ultimate physical or mental tests.

1982. Peter Billingsley is Christopher Massarati, a 12-year-old with an I.Q. of 180 who helps his uncle Mas (Daniel Pilon), an international soldier of fortune, solve crimes on the ABC pilot *Massarati and the Brain*. Sam Waterston plays Quentin E. Deverill, a science professor at Harvard and ingenious inventor who quits to pursue his own research on *Q.E.D.* (CBS).

1983. Michael Richards plays Herndon P. Pool, a clumsy computer genius that works for the Judico Computer Company on the ABC pilot *Herndon and Me* (the "me" refers to Jeff [Ted McGinley], Pool's friend). Tom Swift (Willie Aames) is a genius that puts his knowledge of science to work to solve crimes on the ABC pilot *The Tom Swift and Linda Craig Mystery Hour*. Richie Adler (Matthew Laborteaux), Alice Tyler (Andrea Elson) and Jeremy Saldino (Jeffrey Jacquet) are teenage computer geniuses that help the police solve crimes on CBS's *Whiz Kids*. Murray Bozinsky, called "Boz," (Thom Bray) is an electronics genius that earns money for his inventions by working as a private detective on NBC's *Riptide*.

1985. Richard Dean Anderson plays Angus MacGyver, a survival expert and computer genius who uses his extraordinary skills to solve cases for the Phoenix Institute on ABC's *MacGyver*.

1986. An accidental overexposure to a direct beam of sunlight while photographing an eclipse endows astronaut Jack North (Greg Evigan) with an I.Q. of 1000 on the ABC pilot *North Star*. Jack uses his abilities to investigate cases for Operation North Star. Simon McKay (David Rappaport) is an electronics genius who uses his special skills to help the government solve complex cases on CBS's *The Wizard*.

1987. Matthew Wiggins (Corey Haim) is a whiz kid who entered high school at the age of eleven and now, at 14, is a college freshman on NBC's *Roomies*.

1988. Austin James (Parker Stevenson), the greatest scientific mind of the century, uses his genius to solve complex cases on ABC's *Probe*.

1989. Steven Q. Urkel (Jaleel White) is a nerd who is also a genius on ABC's *Family Matters*. Urkel claims, "I'm 98 percent brain, two percent brawn" and has the ability to create robots, duplicating machines and whatever else seems impossible. At 16 years of age Doogie Howser (Neal Patrick Harris) is a second year resident physician at the Eastman Medical Center on ABC's *Doogie Howser, M.D.* He completed high school in nine weeks and graduated from Princeton at the age of 14.

1990. Ben Savage plays Sam Kelvin, a young boy with a high I.Q. who is also a whirlwind of mischief for his parents on the CBS pilot *Hurricane Sam.*

1991. Logan Murphy (Steve Hytner) is a brilliant scientist who once worked for NASA but now prefers to develop things he thinks the world needs on NBC's *The 100 Lives of Black Jack Savage.*

1994. Annie Mack (Maryedith Bishop) is a brilliant 16-year-old high school girl who believes "genius is lonely" on *The Secret World of Alex Mack* (NICK). Annie has maintained a 4.0 grade average since pre-school and takes advanced science classes hoping to one day win the Nobel Peace Prize.

1995. Peter Scolari plays Warren Mosby, a genius software developer who establishes his own company (Cyberbite) on CBS's *Dweebs.* Lori Singer plays Sydney Bloom, a TeleCal Telephone Company lineman and computer genius who discovers the unknown realm of virtual reality five on Fox's *VR-5.* Sydney can enter VR-5 but can't control its events.

1997. Wayne Szalinski (Peter Scolari) is an ingenious inventor who incorporates a strange alien power source he found in a cave to make his weird inventions work on *Honey I Shrunk the Kids: The TV Series.*

1998. Tahj Mowry plays T.J. Henderson, a 12-year-old boy with an I.Q. of 180 who is struggling to adjust to high school on the WB's *Smart Guy.* Kay Simmons (Leah Lail) is a brilliant (and sexy) computer expert who works for V.I.P. (Vallery Irons Protection). Kay was an exceptionally bright child who, at the age of seven, attended Neo Tech, "a school for brainy kids."

2000. Malcolm (Frankie Muniz) could read before he could walk. He taught his father how to change the car's transmission at age five and a year later was solving algebraic problems. Unfortunately he lives with a truly weird family on *Malcolm in the Middle* (Fox).

2001. Christy Carlson Romano plays Ren Stevens, a 16-year-old girl who is beautiful and exceptionally bright on *Even Stevens* (Disney). Ren

strives for perfection and enjoys being looked up to by others. Adam Kane (John Shea) is considered the smartest man alive for his work in genetic research. He created Mutant X, a society of enhanced DNA agents, and battles evil on *Mutant X* (Syn.). Brenda Chenowith (Rachel Griffiths) was declared a genius at the age of six. She was placed in care of psychiatrists and manipulated (she became the subject of a book called *Charlotte Light and Dark*). She is highly intelligent and skeptical and has prospects of someday finding happiness on HBO's *Six Feet Under.*

2002. Debi Derryberry is the voice of boy genius Jimmy Neutron on the computer animated *The Adventures of Jimmy Neutron: Boy Genius* (NIK). A man, known only as John Doe (Dominic Purcell), is an amnesiac who, after an accident he can't recall, acquires exceptional intelligence on Fox's *John Doe* (he can, for example, watch the game show *Jeopardy* and give the questions before the answers are given). Seven-year-old Franklin Aloysius Mumford (Noah Grey-Cabey) has degrees from Harvard and MIT but attends Crestview Elementary School with his girlfriend, seven year old Cady Kyle on ABC's *My Wife and Kids.*

2003. Lauren and Danny O'Keefe (Tania Raymonde, Joseph Cross) are home-schooled geniuses totally dedicated to learning who must leave home and attend an actual high school on the WB's *The O'Keefe's.* It's book smarts vs. street smarts.

2005. David Krumholtz plays Charlie Epps, a brilliant mathematician and college professor who believes numbers hold the key to everything on CBS's *NUMB3RS.*

Ghosts

This entry chronicles the programs on which ghosts (or spirits) play a major role. Single episode occurrences on a series are excluded.

1944. An NBC experiment called *The Favor* (June 30th) is the first evidence of a ghost on TV. A girl (Lesley Woods) is ready to buy a fur coat when a visit by the ghost of a soldier killed in World War II persuades her to use the money to buy war bonds. A short time later (August 22nd) NBC broadcasts *Miracle at Blaize*, a World War II story about a mysterious American woman (Claire Luce) who receives the help from the spirit of a girl killed in the war (Tabitha) to complete a dangerous mission for the Allies in France.

1945. An experimental drama, called *Untitled* and written by Norman Corwin for radio in 1944, tells of the ghost of a deceased soldier who appears before the viewing audience to tell of his horrifying war experiences and how he came to be killed.

1946. A husband (Philip Tonge) struggles to live with two wives — his second wife Ruth (Carol Goodner) and the ghost of his first wife, Elvira (Lenore Corbett) who appears and speaks only to him on the NBC special *Blithe Spirit*. Lawrence Dobkin and Oliver Thorndike play brothers, one of whom is a ghost, seeking to make up for past grievances on the NBC experiment *Laughter in Paris*.

1950. Joseph Boland and Susan Shaw play George and Marian Kerby, ghosts who haunt the henpecked Cosmo Topper (Jack Sheehan) on the CBS pilot *Topper*.

1952. Banker Cosmo Topper (Leo G. Carroll) finds his life changing when the ghosts of George and Marian Kerby (Robert Sterling, Anne Jeffreys) decide to bring some fun into his dull life on CBS's *Topper*.

1953. *Casper the Friendly Ghost* theatrical cartoons play on TV for the first time in syndication. In 1963 ABC airs the first made for TV Casper cartoons on *The New Casper Cartoon Show*.

1956. A second version of *Blithe Spirit* (see 1946) airs on NBC. Noel Coward is married to Ruth (Claudette Colbert) but is haunted by the ghost of his first wife Elvira (Lauren Bacall).

1961. Frank Gallop hosts a series of twelve suspense stories on the NBC summer series *Great Ghost Tales*.

1966. Dirk Bogard is Charlie, the man with two wives — Ruth (Rachel Roberts) and the ghost of his first wife, Elvira (Rosemary Harris) on the NBC special *Blithe Spirit*. Sarah Collins (Sharon Smythe) died of a high fever in 1795. She returns as a ghost in modern times to protect her brother, Barnabas Collins, from the evil witch Angelique on ABC's *Dark Shadows*. Also haunting the Collinwood Estate in Maine is the spirit of Josette Collins (Kathryn Leigh Scott; studio special effects at times), the girl Barnabas loved in the 1790s. Ten-year-old Annabelle Thompson (Pamela Dapo) conjures up the ghost of Henry Thompson (Bert Lahr), a 470 year old ancestor, while experimenting with formulas from a book on black magic on the ABC pilot *Thompson's Ghost*.

1967. Kerwin Matthews plays Barnaby Cross,

a university professor who dabbles in the occult on the NBC pilot *Ghost Breaker*. Dick Cameron (Barry Nelson) is a magazine editor whose life is complicated by the spirit of his wife, Marge (Joanna Moore), who has come back to find him a new mate on the CBS pilot *Heaven Help Us*.

1968. Edward Mulhare plays the ghost of Daniel Gregg, a 19th century sea captain living with a modern day family (the Muirs) in a house he built on *The Ghost and Mrs. Muir* (NBC/ABC).

1969. Kerwin Matthews again plays a ghost hunter (see 1967), this time Jonathan Fletcher on ABC's gothic pilot *In the Dead of Night*. Cowardly Great Dane Scooby-Doo (voice of Don Messick) and his human friends Freddy, Daphne, Shaggy and Velma (Frank Welker, Heather North, Casey Kasem, Nicole Jaffe) battle ghosts and other creatures of the supernatural on the animated *Scooby-Doo, Where Are You?* (CBS).

1971. A Revolutionary War coward named Jonathan Muddlemore hides in a grandfather clock to escape British soldiers and becomes trapped. Three hundred years later teenagers April, Skip and Augie open the clock and release his spirit (whom they call Musty) on the ABC cartoon *The Funky Phantom*.

1973. Winston Essex (Sebastian Cabot) is a mysterious man who hosts *Ghost Story*, an NBC series of gothic yarns. Deceased private detective Marty Hopkirk (Kenneth Cope) returns as a ghost to keep an eye on his wife Jean (Annette Andre) and help his former partner Jeff Randall (Mike Pratt) solve crimes on *My Partner the Ghost* (Syn.). Cosmo Topper, Jr. (Roddy McDowell) finds his life complicated by the ghosts of George and Marian Kerby (John Fink, Stefanie Powers) when he inherits his late uncle's possessions on the NBC pilot *Topper Returns*. Michele Carey plays Elaine, the ghost of a wife who returns to help her husband raise their son on the pilot *What's Happened to Elaine?*

1974. Madge and Artie (Cloris Leachman, Dick Van Patten) are a married couple haunted by the ghost of Ernie (Frank Sutton), Madge's first husband, on the ABC pilot *Ernie, Madge and Artie*.

1975. Kong (Forrest Tucker), Spencer (Larry Storch) and their gorilla Tracy (Bob Burns) dematerialize ghosts on CBS's *The Ghost Busters*.

1976. Stu Gilliam plays Freeman, a ghost who refuses to leave the home he loves when a new family (the Wainwrights) purchases it on the ABC pilot *Freeman*. The NBC pilot *Jeremiah of Jacob's Neck*, finds the spirit of Jeremiah Starbuck (Keenan Wynn) refusing to leave the home he loves when a sheriff and his family move in and try to make it their home.

1977. College bound student Sharon Adams (Lauren Tewes) buys a used motor home and then seeks to rid it of the ghosts who haunt it (by finding them a new place to haunt) on the ABC special *The Haunted Trailer*.

1979. Twelve-year-old James Harrison (Shane Sinutko) suddenly finds his life plagued by the ghost of Thomas Kemp, a 17th century sorcerer on the ABC special *The Ghost of Thomas Kemp*. The CBS special, *Once Upon a Midnight Dreary*, presents two ghost stories for children: "The Legend of Sleepy Hollow" (about a schoolteacher who encounters the headless horseman) and "The Ghost Belonged to Me" (about the spirit of a young girl who comes back from the dead to save a bus load of children headed for a disaster). Andrew Stevens and Kate Jackson play George and Marian Kerby, the ghosts who haunt the henpecked Cosmo Topper (Jack Warden) on the ABC pilot *Topper*.

1980. Jenny Clifford (Shelley Long) finds her life haunted by the ghost of her first husband, Tom Chance (Steven Keats), when she marries Wayne Clifford (Barry Van Dyke) on the ABC pilot *Ghost of a Chance*. Private detectives Holly and Nick Landon (Nancy Dolman, Daren Kelly) find help in solving crimes from the ghost of their father, Ben (William Windom), on the CBS pilot *Landon, Landon & Landon*.

1981. Celena McKenna (Cyndi Girling) is a governess at a mysterious farm called Castle Rock that appears to be haunted by the spirit of a murdered woman (Elizabeth) whose body was never found on the CBS gothic pilot *Castle Rock*. The ghost of a beautiful woman (Ivana Moore) haunts and protects the innocent and pure of heart at Beacon House, a small honeymoon hotel in North Carolina, from evil on the CBS pilot *Comedy of Horrors*. Fourteen-year-old Polly Ames (Dominique Dunne) attempts to solve the mysterious happenings at a spooky hotel on the CBS special *The Haunting of Harrington House*. The spirit of actor Humphrey Bogart (Robert Sacchi) in the role of movie detective Philip Marlowe helps fledging private detective Steve Pryor (Philip Levien) solve crimes on the ABC pilot *Hard Knocks*. Deceased private detective T.C. Cooper

(William Windom) returns as a ghost to help his son Elliott (Rick Lohman) solve crimes on the CBS pilot *Quick and Quiet*.

1982. Skip Midler (Jeff Altman) and Donovan Scott (Harold Van Couver) are investigators for B.O.O.O. (the Beardsely Office of Occult Occurrences) on the ABC pilot *Scared Silly*.

1983. The spirit of Jennifer Farrell (Ann Jillian), a beautiful movie actress who died before her time, returns to earth to guide the life of a 14-year-old boy who has moved into her former home with his family on NBC's *Jennifer Slept Here*.

1984. When a celestial computer malfunctions and keeps the spirit of the late Herkie Burke (Paul Provenza) earthbound, he decides to haunt his close friends, Anne and Elliott Harrington, on the CBS pilot *Back Together*. A Civil War ghost named Henry Hamilton (Steve Nevil) appears to a modern-day family to teach them to believe in themselves and their dreams on the ABC special *Henry Hamilton, Graduate Ghost*.

1985. When Scooby-Doo, the cowardly Great Dane (voice of Don Messick), opens a mysterious chest, he releases thirteen of the most terrifying ghosts in the universe on *The 13 Ghosts of Scooby-Doo*, an ABC animated series that follows his efforts to return the ghosts to the Chest of Demons.

1986. Howard Witt plays William Hanover, the ghost of a 17th century man called "Mr. Boogedy" for his habit of scaring children, who returns 300 years later to haunt the new home built on his land on the ABC pilot *Mr. Boogedy*. An animated version of the 1975 series *The Ghost Busters* is seen in syndication with Jake Kong, Eddie Spencer and Tracy the Gorilla battling the ghosts of Prime Evil, a diabolical spirit. To avoid confusion with titles, ABC airs *The Real Ghost Busters*, an animated adaptation of the 1984 feature film *The Ghost Busters* that continues to relate the adventures of Pete, Ray, Winston and Egon as they capture ghosts.

1988. Rebecca Smart plays Elly Locket, the ghost of a 15-year-old girl who was murdered in the 19th century and whose spirit remains earthbound on the syndicated *Elly and Jools*. Elly now haunts an inn and shows herself only to Jools (Clayton Williamson), the 13-year-old son of the inn's owner, in the hope that he can help her solve the mystery of her death and move on. Although deceased, Justin Case (George Carlin) decides to remain in his capacity as a detective (ghostly) and help his secretary Molly Hagan (Jennifer Spalding) solve crimes on the ABC pilot *Justin Case*.

1989. Grant Pritchard and his wife Claire (Eric Idle, Caroline McWilliams) are a married couple who perish in a rock slide while on vacation then return as ghosts to haunt their home, now in the hands of the Dooley family, on *Nearly Departed* (NBC). Three ghosts from the American Revolution — highwayman Jack Marlowe (Mark Lindsay Chapman), his woman, Cassandra (Lesley-Anne Downe) and a pig slopper named Silas (Courtney Gains) haunt a rebuilt 200-year-old inn on the CBS pilot *Shivers*.

1990. Horror novelist Anthony Strack (Anthony Perkins), his wife Elizabeth (Leigh Taylor Young) and their children Cindy and Edgar (Juliet Sorcey, Josh Miller) find ghosts and other phenomena are also residents in a house with a mind of its own on the Fox pilot *The Ghost Writer*. After being shot, L.A.P.D. detective Michael Burton (John D. Aquino) is able to see ghosts on the syndicated series *Shades of L.A.* The Shades, as Michael calls ghosts, have unfinished business and seek his help.

1991. Veronica Lauren plays Sarah Collins, the ghost of a nine-year-old girl who died in 1795 who watches over her brother, the vampire Barnabas Collins, on NBC's update of *Dark Shadows* (see 1966). The ghost of Black Jack Savage (Steven Williams), a 17th century pirate, haunts Blackbird Castle on the island of San Pietro in the Caribbean, hoping to redeem himself for the 100 people he killed on NBC's *The 100 Lives of Black Jack Savage*.

1992. A group of pre-teen children solve mysteries with the help of an entity they call *Ghost Writer* (PBS); Blaze Berdahl stars as Lenni Frazer. The spirit of Moe Baker (Deon Richmond), a 12-year-old boy who was a victim of street violence, returns to look over his family on the ABC pilot *Moe's World*.

1995. Sarah Paulson plays Merlyn Temple, the ghost of a 16-year-old girl who has come back to protect her younger brother, Caleb (Lucas Black) from Lucas Buck (Gary Cole), an evil sheriff who rules the town of Trinity, on CBS's *American Gothic*. Stacy Keach hosts *Real Ghosts*, a UPN pilot that recreates stories of ghostly sightings. Stephanie Hodge plays housewife Jennie Malloy on the WB's *Unhappily Ever After*. In what was explained as "the writer's mistake," Jennie fell asleep in a tanning salon and was "turned into beef jerky remnants." She returned as a ghost to help guide her family but the storyline didn't work and Jennie was returned to the living.

1997. A new group of children inherit Ghost Writer, the entity that helps them solve crimes on CBS's *The New Ghost Writer Mysteries*. Charlotte Sullivan stars as Camela Gorrick.

2001. Will Yunlee plays Danny Woo, the ghost of a police detective who watches over his former partner, Sara Pezzini (Yancy Butler) on *Witchblade* (TNT).

2002. After an operation to save his life, private detective Frank Taylor (Matthew Fox) acquires the ability to see spirits (and uses them to help him solve crimes) on UPN's *Haunted*.

2005. Jason Hawes and Grant Wilson are plumbers who seek real life spirits on *Ghost Hunters* (Sci Fi). Jennifer Love Hewitt is Melinda Gordon, a woman who sees spirits on *Ghost Whisperer* (CBS). Allison DuBois' visions of ghosts help her solve crimes on *Medium* (NBC). Brothers Dean and Sam Winchester (Jensen Ackles, Jared Padalicki) encounter ghostly elements on *Supernatural* (WB/CW).

God see *Angels; Religious Characters*

Government Agents

Agents of the U.S. government, other than those involved with espionage or the F.B.I., are the subjects of this entry. See also *Espionage* and *F.B.I. Agents*.

1950. *Treasury Men in Action* (ABC/NBC) presents stories based on the files of the U.S. Customs and Treasury departments. Walter Greaza plays the Chief.

1952. Brian Donlevy plays Steve Mitchell, a U.S. government agent whose cases take him to the trouble spots of the world on the syndicated *Dangerous Assignment*. Agents Brand and Powell (Paul Stewart, Gena Rowlands) investigate cases for the Bureau of Scientific Information on the syndicated *Top Secret*.

1959. Elliot Ness (Robert Stack) leads the Federal Special Squad, a team of U.S. Treasury agents who battle organized crime in Chicago (1930s) on ABC's *The Untouchables*.

1961. U.S. Treasury Department agent Robert

Hale (Lloyd Nolan) recruits citizens with special abilities to solve crimes on the CBS pilot *Call to Danger*.

1963. Suzanne Pleshette plays Anita King, a seductive U.S. government undercover agent on the NBC pilot *Expose*.

1965. David Matthews (Karl Held) is a special U.S. government undercover agent who investigates cases that involve strange happenings on the NBC pilot *The 13th Gate*.

1966. Jack Lord plays Don Owens, an agent for B.O.S.S. (Bureau of Secret Services) on the NBC pilot *The Faceless Man*.

1968. Jim Kingsley (Peter Graves) is the Chief of Natural Resources, a U.S. government organization that recruits ordinary people with special skills to solve highly complex crimes on the CBS pilot *Call to Danger*.

1971. Farrah Fawcett plays Patricia Boulion, a museum tour guide who also works for Ron Hart (Bill Daily), the director of O.U.T. (Office of Unusual Tactics), a government agency that handles cases nobody else wants, on the NBC pilot *Inside O.U.T.* Treasury Agent James O'Hara (David Janssen) investigates crimes committed against Customs, Secret Service and Internal Revenue on CBS's *O'Hara, United States Treasury*.

1972. Daring undercover agent Pete King (Christopher George) tackles hazardous assignments on the CBS pilot *Man on a String*.

1973. Douglas Warfield (Peter Graves) is an inspector for the Department of Justice who recruits people with special skills for hazardous assignments on the CBS pilot *Call to Danger*. Steve Austin (Lee Majors) is a former astronaut turned agent for the O.S.I. (Office of Scientific Intelligence) who uses his bionic arm and legs to solve cases on ABC's *The Six Million Dollar Man*.

1976. Jeff Cable (William Shatner) is a U.S. government undercover agent of the 1880s who uses his mastery of makeup and impersonation to solve crimes in San Francisco on ABC's *The Barbary Coast*. Jaime Sommers (Lindsay Wagner) is a former tennis pro who repays the government for saving her life (replacing her arm and legs with bionic substitutes) as an agent for the O.S.I. on *The Bionic Woman* (ABC/NBC). Ray Danton plays Derek Flint, an agent for the U.S. government who tackles dangerous international assignments on the ABC pilot *Our Man Flint*.

1977. Linda Allen (Cornelia Sharpe) and Monique Lawrence (Jayne Kennedy) are agents for the C.I.U. (Criminal Intelligence Unit) of the U.S. government who pose as models on the NBC pilot *Cover Girls*. Richie Martinelli (Ron Leibman) is *The Outside Man* (CBS pilot), a streetwise federal agent who goes undercover to apprehend dangerous criminals.

1978. Bill Cosby is Aaron Strickland and Tracy Reed his beautiful partner McGee, U.S. government agents who solve sensitive cases on the NBC pilot *Top Secret*.

1979. Claire Bryant and Maggie David (Debbie Allen, Martha Smith) are singers known as Ebony and Ivory. Nick Jade (Bert Convy) is their manager, a song and dance man. Secretly they are Central Intelligence agents who work the nightclub circuit as their cover on the CBS pilot *Ebony, Ivory and Jade*.

1980. Country singer Lorette Peach (Tanya Tucker), her sister, auto mechanic Sue Lynn Peach (Terri Nunn), and stock car racer Dusty Tyree (Dirk Benedict) are undercover Treasury Department agents on the CBS pilot *The Georgia Peaches*.

1981. Willy Dymes (Robin Strand) and Buck Nichols (Rocky Bauer) are special government agents who assist local law enforcement agencies to get the job done on the NBC pilot *Nichols and Dymes*. Max Catlin (Nick Mancuso), Martin Farnum (Ben Murphy), Tori Lysdahl (Zina Brandt) and Deke Thomas (William Allen Young) are the military's best commandos who are organized into a strike force by the U.S. government's Security Bureau on the CBS pilot *Unit 4*.

1983. Rod Taylor plays Mr. Lavender, head of the National Intelligence Agency, who recruits ordinary people with special skills for missions on ABC's *Masquerade*. Kirstie Alley and Greg Evigan play agents Casey Collins and Danny Doyle.

1984. Cass Daton (Leah Ayres), Julie Rhodes (Shari Belafonte), Lauren Dawes (Mary-Margaret Humes) and Ellen Stockwell (Sheree J. Wilson) work as aerobic instructors for Velvet International, a front for their work with the National Security Intelligence Agency on the ABC pilot *Velvet*.

1985. Elizabeth Towne (Joanna Cassidy) is a CIA agent who performs high-risk missions for the President of the United States (represented by his brother, Larry Hutchins) on NBC's *Code Name: Foxfire*.

1986. Cab driver Jeffrey Wilder (Scott Bakula) is accidentally exposed to an alien substance that makes him indestructible on the ABC pilot *I-*

Man. He is immediately recruited by the International Security Agency to solve high-risk cases. David Rappaport plays Simon McKay, an ingenious toy maker who uses his unique inventions as an agent for the U.S. government on CBS's *The Wizard.*

1987. Michael McKean plays Dr. Warren Starbinder, a veterinarian who takes the place of his twin brother, Jason, a secret agent for the U.S. government who is presumed dead, on the ABC pilot *Double Agent.*

1988. A beautiful young woman known only as Nicole (Linda Blair) runs a ritzy nightclub (Nicole's) on Manhattan's fashionable East Side as her cover for a U.S. government agency that recruits ordinary people with unique skills for hazardous cases on the syndicated pilot *Call to Danger.* Scott Glenn plays Alexander Crawford, an American undercover intelligence agent who poses as a cultural attaché at the U.S. Embassy in Brussels on the CBS pilot *Intrigue.* Jack Stuart (Roger Wilson) is the anti-authoritarian, down on his luck twin brother of flamboyant undercover agent Nick Stuart. When Nick is killed during an assignment, the government recruits Jack to take his place and teams him with the beautiful Alexandra Greer (Amanda Pays) on the CBS pilot *The Pretenders.* Tough N.Y.P.D. cop Remo Williams (Jeffrey Meek) is recruited by a U.S. government agency called CURE for special assignments on the ABC pilot *Remo Williams.*

1990. David Wohl plays Phil Jacobs, head of the D.E.A. (Drug Enforcement Administration) Special Task Force, on Fox's *D.E.A.* Tom Mason and Jenny Gago play agents Bill Stadler and Teresa Robles.

1991. Kate and Dylan Del'Amico (Linda Purl, Anthony John Dennison) are a married couple who work for the National Intelligence Agency on ABC's *Undercover.*

1993. A mysterious man, known only as Mr. Smith (John Vernon) and head of a special government organization called C-5, incorporates the Hemisphere Emergency Action Team (H.E.A.T.) to solve complex crimes on the syndicated *Acapulco H.E.A.T.* Ashley Coddington (Catherine Oxenberg) leads the team, which is based in Acapulco, Mexico. Federal Special Squad agent Elliot Ness (Tom Amandes) returns to battle organized crime in the Chicago of the 1930s on *The Untouchables* (Syn.).

2001. John Keller (Grant Show) leads a Justice Department Special Operations unit designed to

fight crime on *U.C.: Undercover* (NBC). Also in the cast are Vera Formiga, Gabrielle Miller and John Seda.

2006. Jonas Blane (Dennis Haysbert) heads an elite team of specially trained agents who battle terrorism on *The Unit* (CBS).

Hawaii

A listing of series set in Hawaii.
1959. *Hawaiian Eye* (ABC).
1960. *Follow the Sun* (ABC).
1966. *Hawaii Calls* (Syn.).
1968. *Hawaii Five-0* (CBS).
1972. *The Brian Keith Show* (NBC).
1975. *The Diamond Head Game* (Syn.).
1976. *The Don Ho Show* (ABC).
1977. *Big Hawaii* (NBC).
1979. *The MacKenzies of Paradise Cove* (ABC).
1980. *From Here to Eternity* (NBC); *Magnum, P.I.* (CBS).
1981. *Aloha Paradise* (ABC).
1984. *Hawaiian Heat* (ABC.
1988. *Jake and the Fatman* (CBS).
1990. *Island Son* (CBS).
1993. *Big Wave Dave's* (CBS).
1994. *The Byrds of Paradise* (ABC); *One West Waikiki* (CBS).
1996. *Raven* (CBS).
1999. *Baywatch Hawaii* (Syn.).
2004. *Hawaii* (NBC); *The North Shore* (Fox).

Hearing Impaired Characters

Characters who appear as regulars and are capable of partial hearing or are totally deaf are the subjects of this entry. Characters who are mentioned as being deaf or who appear in only one episode of a series (guest role) are excluded.

1955. Katherine Bard plays Belinda McDonald, a deaf mute girl who learns how to speak through sign language on the CBS special *Johnny Belinda.*

1957. Gene Sheldon plays Bernardo, the deaf mute servant of Don Diego de la Vega, alias Zorro, the defender of the oppressed in Old California on ABC's *Zorro.*

1958. NBC airs a *Hallmark Hall of Fame* presentation of *Johnny Belinda* with Julie Harris as the deaf girl who learns to speak through sign language.

1961. Gena Rowlands plays Teddy Carella, the deaf mute wife of N.Y.P.D. detective Steve Carella on NBC's *The 87th Precinct*.

1965. Kimberly Beck plays Kim Schuster, the six-year-old deaf daughter of Doris and David Schuster on ABC's *Peyton Place*.

1967. Mia Farrow plays Belinda McDonald on *Johnny Belinda*, an ABC special based on the Broadway play about a deaf girl who learns to speak through sign language.

1973. Tony Hart hosts *Vision On*, a syndicated program of total visual entertainment (cartoons, sketches and songs) that relate aspects of the adult world to hearing impaired children.

1975. Emily Litella (Gilda Radner) is an elderly, hard-of-hearing woman, who appears on "The Weekend Update" skits on NBC's *Saturday Night Live*.

1976. Ed Begley, Jr., plays Steve Fletcher, the deaf mute boyfriend of Cathy Schumway (Debralee Scott), the sister of Mary Hartman (Louise Lasser) on the syndicated *Mary Hartman, Mary Hartman*. Linda Bove joins the cast of PBS's *Sesame Street* as Linda, the deaf librarian.

1978. Real life hearing-impaired actor Lou Ferrigno plays the green Hulk, the alter ego of Dr. David Banner on CBS's *The Incredible Hulk*. Rosanna Arquette plays Charlotte Meredith, a beautiful 15-year-old girl with many friends, who is the daughter of deaf parents on the ABC special *Mom and Dad Can't Hear Me*. Charlotte communicates with them through sign language and fears she will be ridiculed if her friends find out (they do and accept them as they do her).

1982. Gil Gerard plays Bill Dragon, a deaf San Francisco police detective who lost his hearing as the result of a car bombing that was meant to kill him on the CBS pilot *Hear No Evil*. Now, with the help of his hearing dog Bozo, Bill uses his other senses to their best advantage to solve crimes.

1983. Toby Benjamin (Jonathan Hall Kovacs) plays the deaf son of Annie and Sam Benjamin on NBC's *Family Tree*. Bill Dana plays Bernardo, the deaf mute servant to an aging Don Diego de la Vega, and his son, Don Carlos, the youthful Zorro and defender of rights in Old California on CBS's *Zorro and Son*.

1986. *Have You Ever Tried Talking to Patty?* is a CBS special about Patty Miller (Mary Vreeland), a pretty but deaf high school girl struggling to be

accepted by others. The McDonald's Corporation begins airing a bittersweet hamburger commercial in which real life deaf people, Beth Ann Bull and Andrew Rubin, converse in sign language while enjoying a hamburger.

1991. Marlee Matlin plays Tess Kaufman, a gorgeous hearing-impaired prosecuting attorney for the Chicago District Attorney's office on NBC's *Reasonable Doubts*.

1994. Heather Whitestone, a deaf beauty contestant (representing Alabama), is crowned Miss America and becomes the first woman with a disability to win the crown (NBC's *Miss America Pageant*).

1995. Marlee Matlin plays Laurie Bey, a hearing-impaired, modern-day Robin Hood on the CBS pilot *The Dancing Bandit* (a proposed spinoff from *Picket Fences*).

2000. Las Vegas Crime Scene Investigator Gil Grissom (William Petersen) suffers from an inherited (from his mother) hearing loss on *C.S.I.: Crime Scene Investigation* (CBS). Lou Ferrigno joins the cast of *The King of Queens* (CBS) as the hearing-impaired neighbor of Carrie and Doug Heffernan.

2002. Deanne Bray plays hearing-impaired FBI agent Sue Thomas on *Sue Thomas, F.B.Eye* (PAX). Sue can read lips and is helped by her hearing dog Levi. Also on the series, Sammi Bourgeois plays Amanda Duffman, a deaf teenage girl Sue befriends.

Historical Settings

The following entry lists the series that are set in eras other than the one in which they are filmed (for example, *That 70s Show* is filmed in 2005 but set in the 1970s). Space shows and war and western series have been excluded from this list. For additional settings see *The Civil War; War—Korea, Vietnam, Iraq; War—World War II* and *Westerns*. The era in which the series is set follows the network indication.

1949. *Mama* (CBS; San Francisco, 1910).

1953. *Life with Father* (CBS; Turn-of-the-century New York); *Wonderful John Acton* (ABC; Kentucky, 1919).

1954. *Davy Crockett* (ABC; Tennessee to Texas, 1813–1836); *Sherlock Holmes* (Syn; London, 1890s).

1955. *The Adventures of Robin Hood* (CBS; England, 1191); *King's Row* (ABC; Turn-of-the-century small town); *Sergeant Preston of the Yukon* (Syn; Canada, 1890s).

1956. *The Adventures of Jim Bowie* (ABC; New Orleans, 1830s); *The Adventures of Long John Silver* (Syn; 18th century); *The Count of Monte Cristo* (Syn; 18th century France); *The Three Musketeers* (Syn; France, 1620s).

1957. *The Adventures of William Tell* (Syn; 14th century Switzerland); *Ivanhoe* (Syn; England, 1190s); *The Last of the Mohicans* (Syn; 1750s America); *The Sword of Freedom* (Syn; 15th century Italy); *Tomahawk* (Syn; America's Northeast, 1700s).

1958. *Northwest Passage* (NBC; 1750s America).

1959. *The Alaskans* (ABC; Alaska, 1890s); *The Lawless Years* (NBC; New York City, 1920s); *Pete Kelly's Blues* (NBC; Kansas City, 1920s); *Riverboat* (NBC; Mississippi to Missouri, 1840s); *The Untouchables* (ABC; Chicago, 1930s); *Yancy Derringer* (CBS; New Orleans, 1880s); *Zorro* (ABC; Monterey, California, 1820s).

1960. *The Flintstones* (ABC; Prehistoric Age); *Klondike* (NBC; Alaska, 1890s); *The Roaring 20s* (ABC; New York City, 1920s); *Tales of the Vikings* (Syn; Scandinavia, 1000 A.D.).

1961. *Margie* (ABC; 1920s small town); *Whiplash* (Syn; 1850s Australia); *Whispering Smith* (NBC; Denver, 1870s).

1962. *The Adventures of Sir Francis Drake* (NBC; 16th century England).

1964. *Daniel Boone* (NBC; 19th century Kentucky).

1966. *It's About Time* (CBS; Prehistoric era); *Mickie Finn's* (NBC; 1890s nightclub).

1967. *Hurdy Gurdy* (Syn; Gay 90s nightclub).

1968. *Here Come the Brides* (ABC; Seattle, 1870s); *The New Adventures of Huckleberry Finn* (NBC; Missouri, 1845).

1970. *Happy Days* (CBS; 1930s).

1971. *The Bearcats!* (CBS; America's Southwest, 1914); *The Chicago Teddy Bears* (CBS; Chicago, 1920s); *Little Women* (Syn; New England, 1880s); *Nichols* (NBC; Arizona, 1914).

1972. *The Waltons* (CBS; Virginia, 1930s-1950s).

1974. *Happy Days* (ABC; 1950s Milwaukee); *Korg, 70,000 B.C.* (ABC; Prehistoric era); *Little House on the Prairie* (NBC; Minnesota, 1870s); *Manhunter* (CBS; Idaho, 1934); *Paper Moon* (ABC; 1930s Midwest).

1975. *Beacon Hill* (CBS; Boston, 1920s); *Ellery*

Queen (NBC; New York City, 1947); *The Family Holvak* (NBC; Tennessee, 1933); *Swiss Family Robinson* (ABC, 1860s); *When Things Were Rotten* (ABC; 12th century England).

1976. *City of Angels* (NBC; Los Angeles, 1930s); *Gibbsville* (NBC; Pennsylvania, 1940s); *Laverne and Shirley* (ABC; Milwaukee, 1960s); *The Swiss Family Robinson* (Syn; 1860s).

1977. *Banyon* (NBC; Los Angeles, 1937); *The Life and Times of Grizzly Adams* (NBC; America's wilderness, 1850s); *What Really Happened to the Class of '65?* (NBC; Los Angeles, 1965–1977); *Young Dan'l Boone* (CBS; 19th century Kentucky).

1978. *Apple Pie* (ABC; Kansas City, 1933); *The Young Pioneers* (ABC; Dakota, 1870s).

1979. *Delta House* (ABC; Faber College, 1962); *Little Women* (NBC; Concord, Massachusetts, 1880s).

1980. *From Here to Eternity* (NBC; Pearl Harbor, Hawaii, 1941); *Goodtime Girls* (ABC; Washington, D.C., 1942); *Palmerstown, U.S.A.* (CBS; Tennessee, 1935).

1982. *Bring 'Em Back Alive* (CBS; The Far East, 1939); *Q.E.D.* (CBS; London, 1912); *Tales of the Gold Monkey* (ABC; Bora Gora, 1938); *Zorro and Son* (CBS; Monterey, California, 1850s).

1983. *Boone* (NBC; Tennessee, 1953).

1984. *Call to Glory* (ABC; 1960s).

1985. *Our Time* (NBC; 1960s).

1986. *Crime Story* (NBC; Chicago, 1960s).

1987. *Private Eye* (NBC; Los Angeles, 1956); *Rags to Riches* (NBC; Los Angeles, 1961).

1990. *Elvis* (ABC; 1950s).

1991. *Dinosaurs* (ABC; Prehistoric era); *The Home Front* (ABC; early 1940s).

1992. *Brooklyn Bridge* (CBS; New York City, 1956); *Covington Cross* (ABC; 14th century England).

1993. *A League of Their Own* (CBS; Illinois, 1940s); *The Untouchables* (Syn; Chicago, 1930s).

1996. *Remember WENN* (AMC; Pittsburgh, 1930s-40s).

1998. *The Lost World* (Syn; Lost Plateau, 1920s); *That 70s Show* (Fox; Wisconsin, 1970s).

1999. *Little Men* (PAX; Concord, Massachusetts, 1860s)

2000. *The Queen of Swords* (Syn; Old California, 1817).

2001. *The Secret Adventures of Jules Verne* (Sci Fi; Europe, 1860s).

2002. *American Dreams* (NBC; Philadelphia, 1960s); *That 80s Show* (Fox; San Diego, 1980s).

2004. *Oliver Beene* (Fox; Queens, New York, 1960s).

2005. *Little House on the Prairie* (ABC; 1870s Prairie).

Holiday Specials

Holiday specials have been a part of television since 1947. This entry is an overall review of the Christmas, Easter, New Year's and Thanksgiving specials broadcast from 1945 to 1990 (at about which time the entertainment specials, as chronicled below, were replaced mostly by cartoon repeats and Christmas-themed TV movies).

1945. House Jameson narrates *The Story of Easter,* an Easter Sunday evening program that tells the religious story of Easter through narration (over religious paintings), scripture readings and songs (NBC). NBC also airs *The Strange Christmas Dinner* on December 9th. John Souther plays Herman Grubb, a miserly man who refuses to let his employees have Christmas Eve off. Suddenly a man, dressed as if he stepped out of the 1870s, appears and talks with Grubb. As the stranger exists Grubb has a change of heart and gives his staff the day off. In the closing curtain, it is revealed that the stranger was Charles Dickens (Grandon Rhodes), author of *A Christmas Carol.*

1947. DuMont presents *A Christmas Carol.* The miserly Ebenezer Scrooge comes to see his faults on Christmas Eve, when the ghosts of Christmas Past, Present and Future visit him. John Carradine, Eva Marie Saint and Barnard Hughes star. A group of children meet Santa Claus, see store decorations and visit a fairyland candy castle on NBC's *Merry Christmas Land.*

1948. NBC airs its version of *A Christmas Carol* with Dennis King as Ebenezer Scrooge (Bing Crosby made his TV debut on this program singing "Silent Night"). Jan Murray hosts *A Christmas Present* (CBS), a program of holiday songs. Wendell Niles hosts *The R.C.A. Thanksgiving Show,* a live, two-hour program of music and songs.

1949. Rudy Vallee hosts *Hotpoint Holiday,* a musical celebration of Thanksgiving sponsored by Hotpoint Appliances.

1950. Harold Brown, Gordon Dilworth and Beverly Hanis star in *A Christmas Song,* a DuMont

musical play about how the Christmas spirit affects the people who live in an apartment house on New York's Lower East Side. CBS airs *Fun for '51,* a 1950 New Year's Eve program of music and comedy hosted by Ed Sullivan. Walt Disney hosts *One Hour in Wonderland,* a Christmas Day special featuring holiday songs and segments from classic Disney cartoons (NBC). Milton Berle hosts *Uncle Miltie's Christmas Party* on NBC with guest Martha Raye.

1951. *Amahl and the Night Visitors* airs for the first time on Christmas Eve (restaged in 1952–56; 1963 and 1978). The Christmas opera, broadcast on *The Hallmark Hall of Fame,* was written especially for TV by Gian-Carlo Menotti and tells of Amahl, a crippled boy who joins the Three Wise Men as they journey to Bethlehem on the eve of the first Christmas. *A Christmas Carol* by Charles Dickens airs on NBC with Ralph Richardson as Scrooge. Milton Berle hosts NBC's celebration of Easter on *Uncle Miltie's Easter Party.* Walt Disney hosts the Disney studio's first Christmas program, *The Walt Disney Christmas Show* on CBS.

1952. Pabst Blue Ribbon Beer sponsors *The Blue Ribbon Christmas Eve Musical,* a CBS program of music and songs hosted by Gene Lockhart. Bob Hope hosts his first Christmas special, *The Bob Hope Show,* on NBC (Dec. 7th).

1953. Gale Storm guests on *The Bob Hope Christmas Show* (NBC). NBC's *Christmas with the Stars* features performances by Bob Hope, Eddie Fisher, Helen Hayes and Rosemary Clooney.

1954. The magical world of Toyland comes to life as Tommy Tucker (Dennis Day) struggles to romance Jane Piper (Barbara Cook) against the wishes of Silas Barnaby (Jack E. Leonard), who seeks the girl for himself on the NBC musical *Babes in Toyland.* The *Bob Hope Christmas Show* airs on NBC with guests Anita Ekberg and William Holden. Fredric March plays Scrooge in a CBS presentation of *A Christmas Carol.* Robin Chandler, Irene Dunne, Eva Gabor and Phyllis Kirk are among the performers on CBS's *Easter Parade of Stars.* Bandleader Guy Lombardo begins a television tradition when he hosts *Guy Lombardo's New Year's Party* (also called *A New Year's Eve Party with Guy Lombardo and His Royal Canadians*). The program premiered on CBS and ran yearly on New Year's Eve until 1977. NBC's *My Three Angels* tells the story of three ex-convicts who try to provide a merry Christmas for a destitute family. Walter Slezak, Barry Sullivan and George Grizzard star. Gwen Verdon performs an Easter parade dance number and Bobby Clark plays a boy who eats a forbidden Easter egg and is transported to a magical fantasy land on CBS's *Once Upon an Easter Time*.

1955. Betty Grable guests on *The Bob Hope Christmas Show* (NBC). Fran Allison hosts and Burr Tillstrom provides the puppet movement and voices for *The Kuklapolitan Easter Show*, an NBC program wherein the Easter Bunny gives a tour of the Easter Bunny candy-making plant. Thomas Mitchell plays Kris Kringle, a man who believes he is the real Santa Claus on CBS's *Miracle on 34th Street*.

1956. *The Bob Hope Christmas Special* airs on NBC with guest Ginger Rogers.

1958. Gordon MacRae is Jim and Sally Ann Howes his wife, Delia, on CBS's *Gift of the Magi*. The O. Henry story follows the poor couple as they seek to give each other the perfect Christmas gift. The story of a young girl's trip through a magic fantasyland of fairies and toy soldiers comes to life on the Christmas story, *The Nutcracker*. Six versions appeared. *1958:* Margot Fonteyn (Sugar Plum Fairy), Michael Soames (Nutcracker); *1965:* Melissa Hayden (Sugar Plum Fairy), Edward Villella (Nutcracker); *1977:* Gesley Kirkland (Sugar Plum Fairy), Mikhail Baryshnikov (Nutcracker); *1985:* Lesley Collier (Sugar Plum Fairy), Anthony Dowell (Nutcracker); *1995:* Peggy Fleming (Sugar Plum Fairy), Todd Eldridge (Nutcracker); *1998:* Miyako Yoshida (Sugar Plum Fairy), Ivan Putrov (Nutcracker).

1959. Gina Lollobrigida guests on *The Bob Hope Christmas Show* on NBC (which was filmed at ten military bases as a tribute to U.S. GIs). NBC's *Christmas Star Time with Leonard Bernstein* features holiday music and readings. *The Hallmark Hall of Fame Christmas Special* (NBC) presents four segments: an ice skating fantasy ("The Ice Princess"); a performance by the Obernkirchen Children's Choir; a story about a man's efforts to overcome his cynicism about Christmas on "The Borrowed Christmas"; and a reading of "The Nativity." Ed Wynn plays Kris Kringle, the man who believes he is the real Santa Claus on NBC's *Miracle on 34th Street*. Claude Rains, Kate Smith and Patty Duke star in *Once Upon a Christmas Time*, an NBC musical about a group of people who try to provide a merry Christmas for the children of an orphanage.

1960. Jayne Mansfield guests on *The Bob Hope Christmas Show* (NBC).

1961. Zsa Zsa Gabor guests on *The Bob Hope Buick Christmas Show* (NBC).

1962. Mary Martin joins Bing Crosby on ABC's *The Bing Crosby Christmas Show*. On NBC, Jayne Mansfield and Dorothy Provine guest on *The Bob Hope Christmas Show*.

1963. Fred MacMurray guests on *The Andy Williams New Year's Eve Special* on NBC. *The Arthur Godfrey Thanksgiving Special* (NBC) spotlights guests Shari Lewis, Tony Bennett and Liza Minnelli. *The Bob Hope Christmas Special* (NBC) is filmed at U.S. military bases in the Orient. The story of "The Nativity" is seen in animated form and holiday songs from many lands are performed on *The Story of Christmas* with host Tennessee Ernie Ford (NBC).

1964. Anne Bancroft and Janet Leigh guest on *The Bob Hope Christmas Show* (NBC). The ABC drama, *Carol for Another Christmas*, restages the Charles Dickens story, "A Christmas Carol," with Sterling Hayden as Daniel Grudge, a modern-day isolationist who sees through the Christmas ghosts that the world is headed for H-Bomb annihilation. *The Perry Como Christmas Show* (NBC) airs with guest Angela Lansbury. NBC airs *Rudolph, the Red-Nosed Reindeer* and begins a tradition that is still current in 2006. Burl Ives, as Sam the Snowman, tells the story of how Rudolph helped guide Santa's sleigh through a fierce snow storm one Christmas Eve.

1965. A holiday tradition, *A Charlie Brown Christmas*, comes to TV for the first time on CBS. Here Charlie Brown (voice of Peter Robbins) puts a damper on the holiday season by trying to relate the commercialism of Christmas to his friends. Liza Minnelli plays Little Red Riding Hood on the ABC musical *The Dangerous Christmas of Red Riding Hood*. Here, as the animals in the zoo are preparing for Christmas, Mr. Lone T. Wolf finds he cannot join them because of his role in the story of "Little Red Riding Hood." Music and songs relate Mr. Wolf's efforts to set the record straight: he was trying to befriend Red not harm her. Angela Lansbury and Bob Newhart are the guests on *The Perry Como Thanksgiving Special* (NBC).

1966. Anita Bryant guests on *The Bob Hope Christmas Show* (NBC). Truman Capote narrates *A Christmas Memory* (ABC), a story he wrote in 1954, that relates a Christmas he shared with his eccentric but gentle Aunt Sookie (Geraldine Page). Host Lorne Greene and the UNICEF Children's Choir reflect on the meaning of Christmas on NBC's *Christmas with Lorne Greene*. Boris Karloff narrates *Dr. Seuss' How the Grinch Stole Christmas* (CBS), a tradition in which a crotchety creature who hates Christmas (the Grinch) tries to erase the holiday from the town of Whoville by stealing all the material symbols of the season. Dick and Tom Smothers guest on *The Jack Benny Christmas Special* (NBC). Anne Meara and Jerry Stiller guest on *The Perry Como Christmas Show* (NBC). Angela Lansbury guests on *The Perry Como Thanksgiving Special* (NBC).

1967. Claudine Longet guests on *The Andy Williams Christmas Show* (NBC). Wally Cox and Ernest Borgnine are among the guests on *The Bob Hope Christmas Show* (NBC). *The Little Drummer Boy* (NBC) follows Aaron (voice of Teddy Eccles) as he journeys with the Three Wise Men on the eve of the birth of Christ. The Rockettes appear on NBC's *Radio City Music Hall at Christmas Time*, a program of holiday music, songs and dances.

1968. Claudine Longet and the Osmond Brothers guest on *The Andy Williams Christmas Show* (NBC). *The Bob Hope Christmas Show* (NBC) features guests Janet Leigh and Stella Stevens. *The Burl Ives Thanksgiving Special* (syndicated) presents holiday music and songs. *The Legend of Silent Night* (ABC) relates how Franz Gruber (James Mason) came to write "Silent Night." Don Adams and Carol Burnett guest on *The Perry Como Christmas Show* (NBC). Truman Capote's story, *The Thanksgiving Visitor* (ABC) tells of Truman as a boy (Michael Kearney) and how he and his Aunt Sookie (Geraldine Fitzgerald) prepared for Thanksgiving in rural Alabama.

1969. *The Bob Hope Christmas Show* (NBC) airs with guest Elke Sommer. Singer Frankie Avalon celebrates Easter on the syndicated *Frankie Avalon's Easter Special*. The holiday tradition *Frosty the Snowman* airs for the first time on CBS. Jackie Vernon provides the voice of Frosty, a snowman who comes to life when a magic hat is placed on his head. A young boy (Johnnie Whitaker) struggles to adjust to Heaven on NBC's *The Littlest Angel*. Singer Mike Douglas celebrates Christmas with guest Patti Page on the syndicated *Mike Douglas Christmas Special*.

1970. *The Bing Crosby Christmas Show* airs on NBC with guest Melba Moore. Jack Benny,

Dorothy Lamour and Elke Sommer guest on *The Bob Hope Christmas Show* (NBC). ABC begins another tradition with *Santa Claus Is Comin' to Town* wherein the origins of Santa Claus (Mickey Rooney) are explained.

1971. Andy's wife, Claudine Longet and the Lennon Sisters guest on *The Andy Williams Christmas Show* (NBC). Robert Goulet joins Bing and his family on *Bing Crosby and the Sounds of Christmas* (NBC). *The Bob Hope Christmas Special* features guest Barbara Eden (NBC).

1972. Elke Sommer guests on *The Bob Hope Christmas Special* (NBC). *Christmas with the Bing Crosbys* airs on NBC with guest Sally Struthers. Dick Clark begins a yearly tradition on ABC with *Dick Clark's Rockin' New Year's Eve*, a program of music and song that ran until 2003. The sentimental drama *The House Without a Christmas Tree* (CBS) tells of young Addie Mills (Lisa Lucas) and her efforts to convince her unsentimental father that their house needs a Christmas tree. Lynn Anderson and Mac Davis guest on *Tennessee Ernie Ford's White Christmas* (NBC).

1973. *The Andy Williams Christmas Special* airs on NBC (which also airs *Bing Crosby's Sun Valley Christmas* and *The Bob Hope Christmas Show*). Charlie Brown (voice of Todd Barbee) attempts to organize a holiday feast on CBS's *A Charlie Brown Thanksgiving*. Merv Griffin celebrates the holidays with children on the syndicated *Merv Griffin and the Christmas Kids*. Sebastian Cabot plays Kris Kringle, the man who believes he is the real Santa Claus on the CBS production of *Miracle on 34th Street*. Holiday music, songs and readings are presented on NBC's *The Sounds of Christmas Eve* with host Doc Severinsen. Lisa Lucas plays Addie Mills, an 11-year-old girl who tries to mend a feud between her father and a gruff neighbor in time for Thanksgiving on CBS's *The Thanksgiving Treasure*. Chester, a cricket who can make any song sound like a violin solo with his wings, attempts to provide a happy holiday for his friends Harry the cat and Chester the mouse on the animated ABC special *A Very Merry Cricket*.

1974. NBC airs *The Andy Williams Christmas Show* (with Claudine Longet), *The Bob Hope Christmas Show* (with Barbara Eden) and *Christmas with the Bing Crosbys*. The Peanuts gang eagerly awaits the arrival of the Easter Beagle, a magical dog that hands out candy on *It's the Easter Beagle, Charlie Brown* (CBS). Karen and Richard Carpenter guest on *The Perry Como Christmas*

Show (CBS). The citizens of Junctionville await a visit from St. Nicholas on the animated *'Twas the Night Before Christmas* (CBS). Mickey Rooney provides the voice for Santa Claus on ABC's *The Year Without a Santa Claus* (Santa considers canceling his annual sleigh ride due to a lack of Christmas spirit). A letter written by eight-year-old Virginia O'Hanlon to a newspaper editor in 1897 asking "Is There a Santa Claus?" is the basis of the heartwarming *Yes, Virginia, There Is a Santa Claus* (ABC).

1975. *Merry Christmas from the Bing Crosbys* airs on CBS. NBC airs *Bob Hope's Christmas Party* (with Donny and Marie Osmond) and *Dean Martin's Christmas in California*. Actress Constance Payne (Jean Simmons) struggles to keep a promise she made to 12-year-old Addie Mills (Lisa Lucas)—to spend time with her on Easter on CBS's *The Easter Promise*. Olivia Newton-John guests on *John Denver's Rocky Mountain Christmas* (ABC). Peggy Fleming guests on *The Mac Davis Christmas Special* (NBC). The Captain and Tennille guest on *Perry Como's Christmas in Mexico* (CBS).

1976. Bernadette Peters guests on *Bing Crosby's White Christmas* (CBS). Dyan Cannon guests on *Texaco Presents Bob Hope's Comedy Christmas Special* (NBC). Various Christmas traditions are explained on NBC's *Christmas Around the World*. A Scrooge-like character finds the true meaning of Christmas at Disneyland on ABC's *Christmas in Disneyland* (Art Carney stars). In *Frosty's Winter Wonderland* (CBS), an animated sequel to *Frosty the Snowman* (see 1964), the children build Frosty (Jackie Vernon) a Mrs. Frosty (Crystal the Snow Girl; voiced by Shelley Winters) as a companion when Frosty returns to the North Pole for the summer. The Lennon Sisters (Diane, Janet, Kathy and Peggy) are guests on *The John Davidson Christmas Show* (NBC). Aaron, the Little Drummer Boy (see 1967), journeys with the Three Wise Men to tell the world of a new savior after the birth of Christ on *The Little Drummer Boy, Book II* (NBC). Raquel Welch guests on *The Mac Davis Christmas Special ... When I Grow Up* (NBC). Sid Caesar guests on *Perry Como's Christmas in Australia* (NBC). On *Rudolph's Shiny New Year* (ABC), Rudolph the Red-Nosed Reindeer (voice of Billie Richards) must find the Baby New Year who has run away from Father Time.

1977. NBC airs *Bing Crosby's Merrie Olde Christmas* and *The Bob Hope Special*. Bugs Bunny

seeks a replacement for a bed-ridden Easter Rabbit on *The Bugs Bunny Easter Special* (CBS). Kristy McNichol joins Karen and Richard Carpenter for holiday music and songs on *The Carpenter's at Christmas* (ABC). *Dean Martin's Christmas in California* airs on NBC. Doc Severinsen and Gladys Knight host a three-hour program of holiday music celebrating the New Year (1978) on *Doc and Gladys Celebrate*. How the tradition of the Easter Bunny came into being is explored on ABC's *The Easter Bunny Is Comin' to Town*. A modern-day, black version of the Nativity is presented on the animated *Fat Albert Christmas Special* (CBS). Bill Cosby provides the voice of Fat Albert. Several Jewish people substitute for Christians on a job to allow them to celebrate Christmas with their families on NBC's *Have I Got a Christmas for You*. Milton Berle and Adrienne Barbeau star. *The John Davidson Christmas Show* (ABC), *The Johnny Cash Christmas Show* (CBS), *Mac Davis ... I Believe in Christmas* (NBC) and *Perry Como's Olde English Christmas* (ABC) air. *Nestor, the Long-Eared Christmas Donkey* (ABC) tells the story of a long-eared donkey that takes Mary and Joseph to the little town of Bethlehem on the eve of the first Christmas. A small whispering pine tree and several forest animals attempt to make a joyous Christmas for a crippled girl and her family when a storm isolates them from town (and the girl's presents) on the animated *The Tiny Tree* (CBS). ABC's *'Twas the Night Before Christmas* looks at how an American family celebrated Christmas in the 1890s. Paul Lynde and Anne Meara star.

1978. Barbi Benton celebrates Christmas in music and song on the syndicated *A Barbi Doll for Christmas*. NBC airs *Bob Hope's All-Star Christmas*. The animated *First Easter Rabbit* (CBS) explains how the traditions of Easter, including the Easter Bunny came into being. NBC airs *Mac Davis's Christmas Odyssey: Two Thousand and Ten*. The rag dolls, Raggedy Ann and Andy, attempt to save Christmas from a mean wolf that seeks to turn Santa's workshop into a modern factory on the animated *Raggedy Ann and Andy in the Great Santa Claus Caper* (CBS). Beau Bridges plays Stubby Pringle, a lonesome cowboy whose generous heart brings some Christmas happiness to an impoverished family on NBC's *Stubby Pringle's Christmas*.

1979. Angie Dickinson and Bonnie Franklin guest on *The Bob Hope Christmas Special* (NBC).

Porky Pig is Bob Cratchit and Yosemite Sam is Ebenezer Scrooge in "A Christmas Carol" told rabbit style on the animated *Bugs Bunny's Looney Christmas Tales* (CBS). Bugs Bunny and his friends seek a way to avoid unwanted holiday pounds on the animated *Bugs Bunny Thanksgiving Diet* (CBS). Casper the Friendly Ghost seeks a new home to celebrate Christmas when he is evicted from his old haunt on the animated *Casper's First Christmas* (NBC). Donny and Marie Osmond celebrate the holidays on ABC's *The Donny and Marie Christmas Special.* The youngsters who made Frosty the Snowman (see 1969), create a Mrs. Frosty on the animated *Frosty's Winter Wonderland.* CBS airs *A Johnny Cash Christmas.* Dolly Parton guests on *Christmas Special ... With Love, Mac Davis* (NBC). Loni Anderson and Robert Urich host *Merry Christmas from the Grand Ole Opry* on ABC. *Merry Christmas ... with Love, Julie* (syndicated) stars Julie Andrews in a program of music and song. Rosemary Clooney guests on ABC's *The Pat Boone Family Christmas Special.* Also airing on ABC is *The Pat Boone and Family Easter Special.* A country version of "A Christmas Carol" is presented on NBC's *Skinflint,* the story of s stingy banker (Hoyt Axton) who comes to see his faults on Christmas Eve.

1980. Angie Dickinson guests on *Alan King's Thanksgiving Special* (ABC). *The Bob Hope Christmas Special* (NBC) features guests Loni Anderson and Loretta Swit. Minnie Pearl hosts *A Country Christmas* (CBS) with guests Tanya Tucker, Glen Campbell and Loretta Lynn. Daffy Duck celebrates two animated holiday specials on NBC: *Daffy Duck's Easter Show* and *Daffy Duck's Thanks-for-Giving Special.* NBC airs *The Dean Martin Christmas Special.* Buddy Hackett narrates NBC's *Jack Frost,* the story of the sprite winter elf as he attempts to rescue his girlfriend, Elissa, from a wicked king. ABC airs *John Denver and the Muppets: A Christmas Together.* Jeannie C. Riley guests on *A Johnny Cash Christmas* (CBS). NBC airs *Mac Davis—I'll Be Home for Christmas.* Loretta Swit and Toni Tennille guest on ABC's *Perry Como's Christmas in the Holy Land.* James Stewart stars as Willie Kruger, a lonely and aging widower who discovers the true meaning of Christmas on the syndicated *Mr. Kruger's Christmas.* Pinocchio, the wooden boy who came to life, searches for the perfect gift for his Papa Gepetto on the animated *Pinocchio's Christmas* (ABC).

1981. Olivia Newton-John guests on *The Bob Hope Christmas Special* (NBC). Christmas is celebrated country style on *A Country Christmas* (CBS). Ann-Margret guests on *George Burns Early, Early, Early Christmas Show* (NBC; broadcast on Nov. 16th). CBS airs *Johnny Cash's Christmas in Scotland* while on NBC *The Mac Davis Christmas Show* airs. Carole Demas and Paula Janis host the syndicated *A Magic Garden Christmas* (wherein they and puppets Sherlock the Squirrel and Flap the Bird celebrate the holidays in music and song). Singer Anne Murray celebrates the yuletide season on CBS's *A Special Anne Murray Christmas.*

1982. CBS airs *Andy Williams' Early New England Christmas.* *The Bob Hope Christmas Special* is broadcast by NBC. Richard Hilger plays Scrooge, the man who comes to see his faults on Christmas Eve on the Entertainment Channel production of *A Christmas Carol.* NBC begins a yearly December tradition with *Christmas in Washington.* Diahann Carroll hosts the first program of music and songs from the lawn of the White House. Pat Boone and Dottie West host *Christmas Legends of Nashville,* a syndicated program that salutes country stars of the past. CBS airs *Johnny Cash—A Merry Memphis Christmas.* *The Juggler of Notre Dame* (syndicated) tells of Barnaby Stone (Carl Carlsson), a poor street performer who has only his talents as a juggler to offer as a Christmas present to the statue of the Virgin Mary. The 12th century folk tale, on which the story is based, reveals that when Barnaby offered his only gifts, the statue came to life and presented him with the red rose she was holding. Cast members from various NBC series celebrate the holidays on *The NBC Family Christmas Party.* Debby Boone guests on *Perry Como's French-Canadian Christmas* (ABC). Freddy the Freeloader (Red Skelton) struggles to raise money for a Christmas dinner on HBO's *Red Skelton's Christmas Dinner* special. Yogi Bear and his buddy Boo Boo Bear leave Jellystone Park to celebrate the holidays in the big city on the animated *Yogi Bear's All-Star Christmas Caper* (CBS).

1983. Loretta Swit plays Grace Bradley, a housewife who attempts to overcome a number of obstacles as she produces *The Best Christmas Pageant Ever* (ABC) for her local Sunday school. Brooke Shields is the guest on *Bob Hope's Merry Christmas Show* (NBC). President Ronald Reagan and his wife Nancy appear on NBC's *Christmas in Washington.* John Schneider welcomes guest Debbie Allen on *John Schneider's Christmas Holiday* (CBS). Also on CBS is *A Johnny Cash Christmas 1983*. Barbara Mandrell guests on *The Mac Davis Special: The Music of Christmas* (NBC). *Perry Como's Christmas in New York* (ABC) features Michele Lee as a guest.

1984. Brooke Shields and Shirley Jones guest on *Ho Ho Hope's Christmas Hour* (NBC). A sidewalk Santa (Mr. T) tries to rekindle the Christmas spirit in a depressed latchkey youngster (Emmanuel Lewis) on *A Christmas Dream* (NBC). Hal Linden hosts *A Christmas in Washington* (NBC). CBS airs *Johnny Cash: Christmas on the Road*. Kenny Rogers and Dolly Parton celebrate the holidays on *Kenny and Dolly: A Christmas to Remember* (CBS). Ann-Margret joins singer Perry Como for *Perry Como's Christmas in England* (ABC). A young girl (Lee Benton) tries to help a Scrooge-like character (Jack Elam) see the meaning of Christmas on the syndicated *Scrooge's Rock 'n' Roll Christmas*.

1985. Soleil Moon Frye, Joey Lawrence and Lisa Bonet are among the children on NBC's *Andy Williams and the NBC Kids Search for Santa*. Brooke Shields, Barbara Eden and Raquel Welch guest on *The Bob Hope Christmas Show* (NBC). Newsman Tom Brokaw hosts *Christmas in Washington*. Martin Sheen stars as Artaban, a man who sets out on his own to find the Christ child on the eve of the first Christmas on ABC's *The Fourth Wise Man*. CBS airs *The Johnny Cash 10th Anniversary Christmas Special*. Marie Osmond is the guest on *Perry Como's Christmas in Hawaii*.

1986. Drew Barrymore plays Jane Piper, a girl who is magically transported to a world of storybook characters on the NBC production of *Babes in Toyland*. Barbara Mandrell and her sisters, Louise and Irlene gather for *Barbara Mandrell's Christmas ... A Family Reunion* (CBS). Brooke Shields, Donna Mills and Crystal Gayle guest on *Bob Hope's Bagful of Christmas Cheer* (NBC). John Forsythe hosts *Christmas in Washington* (NBC). A kind-hearted widow (Katherine Helmond) and her adopted children face eviction on Christmas from a Scrooge-like landlord (Reginald Synder) on NBC's *Christmas Snow*. Robert Guillaume plays John Grin, a Scrooge-like character who is visited by three ghosts on Christmas Eve, in a modern retelling of "A Christmas Carol" on *John Grin's Christmas* (ABC). A group of toys contemplate the joys they will bring to a group of children on Christmas morning on *Kraft Presents Jim Hen-*

son's "*The Christmas Toy*" (ABC). Angie Dickinson guests on *The Perry Como Christmas Special* (ABC). Kelly McGillis narrates *Santa Bear's First Christmas*, the animated story of a bear who helps Santa Claus deliver toys to woodland animals. Gene Autry and Crystal Gayle guest on *Christmas Present*, a syndicated program of yuletide songs by the Statler Brothers.

1987. Kim Fields, Tina Yothers and Joey Lawrence guest on *Andy Williams and the NBC Kids: Easter in Rome*. James Stewart hosts a program of yuletide songs on *A Beverly Hills Christmas* (Fox). Brooke Shields and Morgan Fairchild guest on *The Bob Hope Christmas Show — A Snow Job in Florida* (NBC). An old man (Denholm Elliott) recalls the memories of his Christmases as a youth in a small Welch town on *A Child's Christmas in Wales* (PBS). Barbara Mandrell hosts NBC's *A Christmas in Washington*. Singer Crystal Gayle celebrates the holiday season in Sweden on the syndicated *A Crystal Christmas*. Garfield the cat and his owner, Jon, spend the holidays with his family on the animated *A Garfield Christmas* (CBS). Singer Julie Andrews celebrates the holidays in Austria on *Julie Andrews ... The Sound of Christmas* (ABC). Philip Michael Thomas hosts a Motown salute to Christmas on *A Motown Merry Christmas* (NBC). Jim Henson's Muppets celebrate the holidays on *A Muppet Family Christmas* (ABC). A Jewish girl (Megan Follows) and a Catholic boy (Mark Davis) learn to accept each other's views of Christmas when a public controversy erupts over a Nativity display on *Seasonal Differences* (ABC).

1988. Barbara Eden is a guest on *Bob Hope's USO Christmas from the Persian Gulf: Around the World in Eight Days* (NBC). The history of Christmas, which is believed to have begun in Germany over 750 years ago, is traced on *Christmas Calendar* (PBS). James Stewart hosts *Christmas in Washington* (NBC). Orchestra leader Robert Shaw celebrates the holidays on *Robert Shaw's Christmas* (PBS). Pop stars perform holiday songs on *A Rock 'n' Roll Christmas* (Fox). Yuletide songs are heard on NBC's *Season's Greetings — An Evening with John Williams and the Boston Pops Orchestra*. How the Christmas song "Silent Night" came to be written is explored on PBS's *Silent Mouse*. Lynn Redgrave narrates the legends and myths that surround Christmas on *The True Meaning of Christmas* (syndicated).

1989. *Bob Hope's Christmas in Hawaii* (NBC)

features guest Barbara Eden. President George Bush and his wife Barbara appear on NBC's *Christmas in Washington*. Garfield attempts to lose weight just when Thanksgiving approaches on the animated *Garfield's Thanksgiving Special* (CBS). The history of Easter is traced on the syndicated *Glory of Easter*.

1990. Loni Anderson guests on *Bob Hope's 1990 Christmas Show* (NBC). Bob appeared on three additional Christmas shows before retiring: *Bob Hope's Christmas Cheer from Saudi Arabia* (his USO themed show in January of 1991), *Bob Hope's Cross Country Christmas Show* (in December of 1991) and his final special in December of 1992, *Bob Hope's Four Star Christmas Fiesta*. John Denver hosts *Christmas in Washington* (NBC). Ice skaters Peggy Fleming and Katarina Witt star in a yuletide celebration on *Disney's Christmas on Ice*.

Horror see *Ghosts; The Supernatural; Vampires; Werewolves; Witches*

Hospitals see *Doctors; Women — Nurses*

Hotels

Programs set at or revolving around a hotel, motel, apartment house, boarding house or inn is the subject of this entry. Many series are set at hotels. When an establishment is not identified by a name, but an address is given, the program is included here. If, however, there is no establishment name or address given, the program has been excluded.

1945. The NBC experimental drama, *Victory* is set at a hotel on a small island in the Java Sea that is run by a German innkeeper (E.A. Krumschmidt).

1949. Molly Goldberg (Gertrude Berg) and her family live in an unnamed apartment house at 1030 East Tremont Avenue in the Bronx on CBS's *The Goldbergs*. The Hotel Broadway, a mythical establishment in New York City, is the backdrop for music and songs on *Hotel Broadway* (DuMont).

1951. Cab driver Amos Jones and his wife Ruby

(Alvin Childress, Jane Adams) live in a small apartment at 134 East 145th Street in Harlem on CBS's *The Amos 'n' Andy Show*.

1950. Entertainment acts are set against the background of the Pelican Room of the Holiday Hotel on New York's Park Avenue on ABC's *Holiday Hotel*.

1952. Comedians Bud Abbott and Lou Costello reside at the Fields Rooming House at 214 Brookline Avenue in Hollywood on *The Abbott and Costello Show* (Syn.). Bandleader Ricky Ricardo and his wife Lucy (Desi Arnaz, Lucille Ball) live in the Mertz's Apartment Building at 623 East 68th Street in Manhattan on CBS's *I Love Lucy*. Secretary Millie Bronson (Elena Verdugo) resides in Apartment 3B of an unnamed building at 137 West 41st Street in Manhattan on CBS's *Meet Millie*. Mrs. O'Reilly's Boarding House on West 73rd Street in Manhattan is home to Irma Peterson (Marie Wilson) on *My Friend Irma* (CBS). The Carlton Arms Hotel in Manhattan serves as the residence for Margie Albright (Gale Storm) and her father, Vern (Charles Farrell) on *My Little Margie* (CBS/NBC). Madison High School teacher Connie Brooks (Eve Arden) resides at Mrs. Davis's Boarding House on CBS's *Our Miss Brooks*.

1953. Nightclub comedian Danny Williams (Danny Thomas) and his family live at the Parkside Apartments in Manhattan on *Make Room for Daddy* (ABC/CBS). Secretary Susie McNamara (Ann Sothern) lives at the Brockhurst Apartments on East 92nd Street in New York City on CBS's *Private Secretary*.

1955. Sarah Selby plays Ma Smalley, the owner of the Dodge City Boarding House in 1880s Kansas on CBS's *Gunsmoke*. Bus driver Ralph Kramden and his wife Alice (Jackie Gleason, Audrey Meadows) live in a less-than-desirable apartment at 728 Chauncey Street in Brooklyn, New York, on CBS's *The Honeymooners*. Singer Janis Stewart (Janis Paige) lives in an unnamed apartment building at 46 East 50th Street in Manhattan on CBS's *It's Always Jan*.

1956. The NBC pilot *Calling Terry Conway* stars Ann Sheridan as a public relations director at a Las Vegas hotel. Incidents in the lives of people who stay at the Wayward Inn, an off–Broadway theatrical hotel in New York City, were to be the focal point of the NBC pilot *One Minute from Broadway*. Stanley Peck (Buddy Hackett) is a disorganized newsstand owner in the lobby of the Sussex Hotel in New York City on *Stanley* (NBC).

1957. Hired gun Paladin (Richard Boone) calls the Carlton Hotel in San Francisco (1880s) home on CBS's *Have Gun— Will Travel*. Conal F. Mc-Connell (Gary Merrill) runs the Fisherman's Bend Hotel and Sportsman Lodge in Northern California on the CBS pilot *Hey Mack*. Incidents in the lives of the people who frequent the Hotel Cosmopolitan are the subjects of CBS's *Hotel Cosmopolitan*.

1958. Katy O'Connor is the assistant manager of the Bartley House Hotel in New York City on *The Ann Sothern Show* (CBS). Annie O'Connell (Sallie Brophy) operates the Buckskin Hotel in Montana (1880s) on NBC's *Buckskin*. The Tower Apartment House on Park Avenue in New York City is the residence of Mike, Loco and Greta (Merry Anders, Barbara Eden, Lori Nelson), three beautiful girls seeking rich husbands on the syndicated *How to Marry a Millionaire*. The Hotel Laramie is the residence for visitors on ABC's *Lawman*. Eddie Holstead (John Harmon) runs the Madera House Hotel in North Fork, New Mexico, on ABC's *The Rifleman*.

1959. The Hotel DuJor was an establishment owned by Trader Penrose (George Tobias) on ABC's *Adventures in Paradise*. He changed the name to the Bali Miki Hotel shortly after. When Clay Baker (James Holden) became the owner, he renamed it the Bali Miki Baker Hotel. Nora Travis (Anna-Lisa) operates the Marathon Hotel in Latigo, New Mexico, on ABC's *Black Saddle*. Adventurer Slate Shannon (Dane Clark) owns Shannon's Place, a hotel in Trinidad, on the syndicated *Bold Venture*. Cricket Blake (Connie Stevens) sings at the Shell Lounge of the Hawaiian Village Hotel on ABC's *Hawaiian Eye*. A former gunfighter known only as Sundance (Earl Holliman) operates the Hotel De Paree in Georgetown, Colorado (1870s), on CBS's *Hotel De Paree*. Martha Cominter (Nora Marlowe) runs the Santa Fe Boarding House in the New Mexico of the 1880s on NBC's *Law of the Plainsman*.

1960. Bill Hooten (Mark Miller) operates Guestward Ho, a dude ranch in New Mexico on ABC's *Guestward Ho*. Sally and Chris Day (Yvonne Lime, Ronnie Burns) operate the Desert Palms Hotel on NBC's *Happy*. Kathy O'Hara (Marie Blanchard) struggles to operate the Golden Nugget Hotel in Skagway, Alaska (1890s) on NBC's *Klondike*. Sisters Ruth and Eileen Sher-

wood (Shirley Boone, Elaine Stritch) live at the Appopolous Arms in New York's Greenwich Village on *My Sister Eileen* (CBS). Cha Cha O'Brien (Margarita Sierra) sings in the Boom Boom Room of the Fontainebleau Hotel in Miami Beach on ABC's *SurfSide 6*.

1961. Johnny Miller and Frank Boone (Johnny Wayne, Frank Shuster) are social directors at the Holiday Lodge in Upper New York State on CBS's *Holiday Lodge*. Jeff Thompson (Lee Bowman) is a troubleshooter for the Miami Hotel Association on the syndicated *Miami Undercover*.

1963. Bewildered Latin American bellboy Jose Jimenez (Bill Dana) struggles to cope with life at the Park Central Hotel in New York on *The Bill Dana Show* (NBC). TV star Alan Brady (Carl Reiner) lives at the Temple Towers on East 61st Street in Manhattan on *The Dick Van Dyke Show* (CBS). Stranded Martian Uncle Martin (Ray Walston) lives with newspaper reporter Tim O'Hara (Bill Bixby) at Mrs. Brown's Rooming House in Los Angeles on CBS's *My Favorite Martian*. Kate Bradley (Bea Benaderet) operates the Shady Rest Hotel in Hooterville on CBS's *Petticoat Junction*. Elena Verdugo plays Gerry Gold, the manager of the Gran Quivera Hotel in Mesa, New Mexico, on NBC's *Redigo*.

1964. Mickey Grady (Mickey Rooney) operates the Newport Arms, a California hotel fraught with problems on ABC's *Mickey*.

1965. Private detective Honey West (Anne Francis) lives in a luxurious apartment in an unnamed building at 6033 Del Mar Vista in Los Angeles on ABC's *Honey West*.

1966. Woody Banner (Will Hutchins) is a recent college graduate who owns a ten-room apartment house in Manhattan on NBC's *Hey Landlord!*

1969. American English professor Michael Endicott (John Forsythe) resides at the Rome Hotel and Apartments (a.k.a. Mama Vitale's Boarding House) on *To Rome with Love* (CBS).

1970. Mary Richards (Mary Tyler Moore), associate producer of the WJM-TV "Six O'clock News" program in Minneapolis, resides at 119 North Weatherly in an unnamed apartment building on CBS's *The Mary Tyler Moore Show*. Felix Unger and Oscar Madison (Tony Randall, Jack Klugman) are mismatched roommates who live in Apartment 1102 at 1049 Park Avenue in Manhattan on ABC's *The Odd Couple*.

1971. Student teacher Sandy Stockton (Sandy

Duncan) lives at the Royal Weatherly Hotel (Apartment 2A) in Los Angeles on *Funny Face* (CBS; later titled *The Sandy Duncan Show*).

1973. Incidents in the lives of couples who stay in Room 300 of the Honeymoon Suite of the Beverly Hills Hotel are the focal point of the ABC pilot *Honeymoon Suite*.

1974. Hard-working parents Florida and James Evans (Esther Rolle, John Amos) and their children live in Apartment 17C of the Cabrini Housing Project on North Gilbert in Chicago on CBS's *Good Times*. Michele Lee plays Michele Burton, a newsstand clerk at the Beverly Wiltshire Hotel in Beverly Hills on the CBS pilot *The Michele Lee Show*. Department store window designer Rhoda Morganstern (Valerie Harper) lives in an unnamed apartment building at 332 West 46th Street in Manhattan on CBS's *Rhoda*.

1975. Eleven people reside in a decaying residence called the Hot l Baltimore (the *e* in the neon sign has burned out) on ABC's *Hot l Baltimore*. A young woman named Sue Burton (Libby Stevens) struggles to operate the Imperial Grand, a Canadian hotel that she inherited on the ABC pilot *The Imperial Grand Band*. The liberated Ann Romano (Bonnie Franklin) and her daughters live in an unnamed apartment house at 1344 Hartford Drive in Indianapolis on CBS's *One Day at a Time*. L.A.P.D. detective Ken Hutchinson (David Soul) lives at the Venice Place Apartments on ABC's *Starsky and Hutch*. Brooklyn schoolteacher Gabe Kotter and his wife Julie (Gabriel Kaplan, Marcia Strassman) live in Apartment 3C at 711 East Ocean Parkway (later in Apartment 409 at 1962 Linden Boulevard) on ABC's *Welcome Back, Kotter*.

1976. Ivan Petrovsky (Lou Jacobi) is a waiter at the Hotel Metropole in Moscow, Russia, on CBS's *Ivan the Terrible*. Brewery workers Laverne DeFazio and Shirley Feeney (Penny Marshall, Cindy Williams) live in Apartment A of a building at 730 Knapp Street in Milwaukee on ABC's *Laverne and Shirley*.

1977. The Las Vegas Oasis Hotel and Casino provides the setting for the dance girls of Nancy Blansky (Nancy Walker) on ABC's *Blansky's Beauties*. The inept and henpecked Basil Fawlty (John Cleese) attempts to operate an inn called Fawlty Towers in England on the syndicated *Fawlty Towers*. Retired army man Phil Wheeler (Theodore Wilson) purchases the Sanford and Son Junkyard and turns it into a rooming house called the *San-*

ford Arms (NBC). Helen and Stanley Roper (Audra Lindley, Norman Fell) own the Roper's Apartment House in Santa Monica, California, on ABC's *Three's Company*.

1978. Phoenix waitress Alice Hyatt (Linda Lavin) resides at the Desert Sun Apartments (then the Phoenix Arms) on CBS's *Alice*. Millionaire Philip Drummond (Conrad Bain) lives in the penthouse of an unnamed building at 679 Park Avenue in Manhattan on NBC's *Diff'rent Strokes*. Gabe McQueen (Dennis Weaver) is a retired lawyer who purchases the Queen Kulani, an Hawaiian Hotel fraught with problems on the CBS pilot *The Islander*. Roger Miller plays Cotton Grimes, a semi-retired country and western singer who opens a motel in Alabama on the CBS pilot *King of the Road* (refers to Miller's hit song). Colorado talk show host Mindy McConnell (Pam Dawber) resides with the alien Mork (Robin Williams) in an apartment in an unnamed building at 1619 Pine Street on ABC's *Mork and Mindy*. Rita Moreno plays Marie Costanza, the social director of a rundown hotel in Pennsylvania on CBS pilot *The Rita Moreno Show*. The loud mouthed and totally incompetent Henry Snavely (Harvey Korman) struggles to run the Snavely Manor Hotel on the ABC pilot *Snavely*. The Desert Inn Hotel and Casino in Las Vegas provides the backdrop for private detective Dan Tanna (Robert Urich) on ABC's *Vegas*. Showgirls Stacey and Angie (Caren Kaye, Lynda Goodfriend) perform at the seedy Las Vegas casino and hotel Club Sandpile on NBC's *Who's Watching the Kids?*

1979. Arnie Sutter (Brian Dennehy) is the house detective at the Ansonia Hotel in Atlantic City, New Jersey, on CBS's *Big Shamus, Little Shamus*. Michael Lerner and Gail Collins (Larry Breeding, Stephanie Faracy) are college students working as waiters at *The Last Resort* (CBS), a mountain hotel for the summer. James Murtaugh plays Henry Sinclair, the manager of the Xavier Hotel's Pleasure Cove resort on the NBC pilot *Pleasure Cove*. Wally Grainger (Bill Daily) manages the Rendezvous Hotel, a resort in California on the CBS pilot *Rendezvous Hotel*. Ben Callister and his family run McCallister's Midway Inn on an orbiting way station between Earth and Pluto in the 22nd century on the CBS pilot *Starstruck*.

1980. Henry Wilson and Kip Desmond (Peter Scolari, Tom Hanks) pretend to be women to afford an apartment at the Susan B. Anthony, a hotel for women only on ABC's *Bosom Buddies*.

1981. Florence Johnston (Marla Gibbs) is the executive housekeeper at the St. Frederick Hotel in New York City on CBS's *Checking In*. Ivana Moore plays a female spirit who haunts Beacon House, a honeymoon hotel in North Carolina, on the CBS pilot *Comedy of Horrors*.

1982. Hearst Circle (Max Baer, Jr.) runs the twelve-story Circle Family Motor Court on the NBC pilot *The Circle Family*. Bob Loudon and his wife Joanna (Bob Newhart, Mary Frann) run the Stratford Inn in Vermont on CBS's *Newhart*. Brianne Leary plays Sharon, desk clerk at the Hotel Pelican in Atlantic City on ABC's *No Soap, Radio*. Private detective Laura Holt (Stephanie Zimbalist) lives in Apartment 3A of a building owned by the Commercial Management Corporation in Los Angeles on *Remington Steele* (NBC). Bon Chance Louie (Ron Moody, Roddy McDowall) owns the Monkey Bar and Hotel on the island of Bora Gora on ABC's *Tales of the Gold Monkey*.

1983. Beatrice Arthur plays Amanda Cartwright, the owner of Amanda's By the Sea, a hotel fraught with problems on ABC's *Amanda's*. Peter McDermott (James Brolin) is manager of the fashionable St. Gregory Hotel in San Francisco on ABC's *Hotel*.

1986. Larry Appleton (Mark Linn-Baker) and his cousin Balki (Bronson Pinchot) share a room at the Caldwell Hotel in Chicago on ABC's *Perfect Strangers*. Sylvan Sprayberry (Jim Nabors) is an inept bell captain at the Hotel Linda Lana in Hawaii on the NBC pilot *Sylvan in Paradise*.

1987. Alex West (Bud Cort) is a friend of Norman Bates (from the film *Psycho*) who inherits the Bates Motel and its haunted reputation on the NBC pilot *Bates Motel*. Architect Peter Farrell (Daniel Hugh Kelly) and his family live in an unnamed apartment building at 46 La Paloma Drive in Los Angeles on ABC's *I Married Dora*. Isabel Scott (Isabel Sanford) runs Isabel's Honeymoon Hotel, a debt-ridden inn on the syndicated pilot *Isabel Sanford's Honeymoon Hotel*. Richard Lewis plays Joey, doorman at an unnamed hotel at 731 Park Avenue in New York City on the CBS pilot *King of the Building*. Mona Robinson (Katherine Helmond) invests her life savings in the seedy Hotel Nottingham then tries to make it a success on the ABC pilot *Mona*. Former Secret Service agent Jonathan Kelly (Ben Masters) retreats to the French Riviera to open a chateau once run by his father on the ABC pilot *Riviera*.

1989. Reginald J. Tarkington (Harvey Korman) is the manager of the Nutt House, a New York Hotel that has fallen on hard times on NBC's *The Nutt House*.

1990. Whoopi Goldberg plays Brenda, a feisty woman who runs the Bagdad Café, a rundown diner, hotel and truck stop in the one building town of Bagdad on CBS's *Bagdad Café*. Comedian Jerry Seinfeld lives in Apartment 3A (later 5A) in an unnamed apartment house at 129 West 81st Street in Manhattan on NBC's *Seinfeld*. Jane Curtin plays Sarah Marshall, assistant manager of the Bennington Hotel in Manhattan on NBC's *Working It Out*.

1991. Julie Van Buren (Robin Bartlett) runs the Van Buren Hotel next to the Coconut Downs Race Track on the ABC pilot *Coconut Downs*. Thomas Logan (D.W. Moffett) is the security chief for the Palace Hotel chain on CBS's *Palace Guard*.

1992. *The Golden Girls* spinoff *The Golden Palace* finds Blanche (Rue McClanahan), Rose (Betty White) and Sophia (Estelle Getty) attempting to run the Golden Palace Hotel in Florida (CBS). Thirty-six-year old Jack Thorpe (David Beecroft) owns the Caesar's Palace Hotel and Casino in Las Vegas on CBS's *Hearts Are Wild*. Jeremy Proctor and his wife Annabelle (Ryan O'Neal, Lesley-Anne Down) own the Cock and Doberman Inn in pre–Revolutionary Philadelphia on the CBS pilot *1775*. Construction worker Vinnie Verducci (Matt LeBlanc) lives in Apartment 3B of an unnamed building at 623 Cypress Avenue in Chicago on *Vinnie and Bobby* (Fox).

1993. Bonnie Kennedy (Bonnie Hunt) is a single woman who lives in Apartment 5 of a building across the street from Wrigley Field in Chicago on *The Building* (CBS).

1994. Joanna Cassidy plays Ellie Mayfield, the owner of the fashionable Hotel Malibu on Malibu Beach in Southern California on CBS's *Hotel Malibu*. The Melrose Place Apartments in Los Angeles is the setting for Fox's *Melrose Place*. Drego's Oasis is a roadside diner and motel in Michigan that is run by Madeline Cooper (Jennifer Aniston) and her mother Connie Drego (Stephanie Hodge) on CBS's *Muddling Through*. Edward Whitaker (Patrick Macnee) oversees operations at the Paradise Beach Hotel in Paradise

Beach, Florida, on the syndicated *Thunder in Paradise*.

1996. Aspiring actor Jamie King (Jamie Foxx) works at his aunt and uncle's hotel, the King's Tower Hotel, while waiting for his big break on *The Jamie Foxx Show* (WB). Magazine columnist Susan Keane (Brooke Shields) lives in an apartment at 3235 Washington Street in San Francisco on NBC's *Suddenly Susan*.

1998. Will Truman and Grace Adler (Eric McCormack, Debra Messing) live in Apartment 9C in an unnamed apartment building at 155 Riverside Drive in Manhattan on *Will and Grace* (NBC). The gorgeous Vallery Irons (Pamela Anderson), head of Vallery Irons Protection, resides in an apartment at 9100 Sunset Boulevard in Beverly Hills on the syndicated *V.I.P.*

1999. John Larroquette plays Royal Payne, owner of the Whispering Pines Hotel in California on CBS's *Payne*. Cameron Greene (Joe Viterelli) is the owner of the Caesar's Palace and Hotel and Gambling Casino in Las Vegas on *The Strip* (UPN).

2000. Nikki Whyte (Nikki Cox) is a gorgeous showgirl at the Golden Calf Hotel and Casino in Las Vegas on *Nikki* (WB).

2003. Former singer Mavis Raye (Whoopi Goldberg) owns the somewhat fashionable LaMont Hotel in Manhattan on NBC's *Whoopi*. The Montecito Hotel and Resort is the setting for action and romance on NBC's *Las Vegas*.

2004. The Metro Casino and Hotel in Las Vegas provides an office for Dr. Billy Grant (Rob Lowe) on *Dr. Vegas* (CBS). The Grand Waimea, a lush tropical hotel in Hawaii, is the backdrop for romance on Fox's *North Shore*.

2005. Zack and Cody Martin (Dylan and Cole Sprouse) are mischievous twins who reside at the luxurious Hotel Tipton in Boston on the Disney Channel's *The Suite Life of Zack and Cody*.

2006. Vanessa Williams is Elizabeth Bauer, the owner of the swanky Hotel Soleil in Florida on *South Beach* (UPN).

Housekeepers

People who are hired to keep house, cook and clean are the subjects of this entry.

1948. Ann Sullivan plays Birdie, maid to insurance salesman John Payne and his family on DuMont's *Growing Paynes*.

1950. Beulah (Ethel Waters, Hattie McDaniel, Louise Beavers) is the maid to attorney Harry Henderson and his family on CBS's *Beulah*. Eddie Anderson plays Rochester, the valet, housekeeper, cook and confidant to comedian Jack Benny on *The Jack Benny Program* (CBS/NBC).

1953. Mary Wickes plays Martha, housekeeper to opera singer Babbo Bonino and his six children on NBC's *Bonino*. Nora (Marion Ross) is the maid to the Day family in turn-of-the-century New York on *Life with Father* (CBS). Louise (Louise Beavers, Amanda Randolph) is the housekeeper to nightclub comedian Danny Williams and his family on *Make Room for Daddy* (ABC/CBS). Kathleen Freeman plays Katie, the first maid to Cosmo and Henrietta Topper on *Topper* (CBS). Edna Skinner as Maggie later replaced her.

1954. Birdie Lee (Lillian Randolph) is the housekeeper to Throckmorton P. Gildersleeve, Water Commissioner of Summerfield on *The Great Gildersleeve* (Syn.). Mary Wickes plays Alice, housekeeper to Ivy College president William Todhunter Hall and his wife Vicky on CBS's *The Halls of Ivy*. Marilly (Kathleen Freeman) is the housekeeper to Thomas Russell, the mayor of Springdale on *Mayor of the Town* (Syn.).

1955. Jane Moutrie plays Maude, the housekeeper to Homer Bell (Gene Lockhart), justice of the peace in Spring City, on *His Honor, Homer Bell* (Syn.).

1957. Sammee Tong plays Peter Tong, houseboy to attorney Bentley Gregg on *Bachelor Father* (CBS/NBC/ABC). Frances Bavier plays Nora, the housekeeper and babysitter for Liza Hammond, a widow and traveling lecturer with twin daughters (Jenny and Mary) on *The Eve Arden Show* (CBS).

1958. Katie (Mary Wickes) is the maid to the McCleod family on ABC's *Annette* (*Mickey Mouse Club* serial).

1959. Hop Sing (Victor Sen Yung) is the cook and housekeeper to the Cartwrights, owners of the Ponderosa Ranch on NBC's *Bonanza*. Sarge (Hope Emerson) is the maid to newspaper columnist Hal Towne on *The Dennis O'Keefe Show* (CBS).

1960. Aki (Yuki Shimoda) is the houseboy to private detective *Johnny Midnight* (Syn.). Michael Francis O'Casey (William Frawley), called "Bub," then Charlie O'Casey (William Demarest), called

"Uncle Charlie," cares for Steve Douglas and his family on *My Three Sons* (ABC/CBS).

1961. Hazel Burke (Shirley Booth) is the enterprising maid to attorney George Baxter and his family on NBC's *Hazel.* Mary Grace Canfield plays Amanda Allison, maid to Walter and Elinor Hathaway on ABC's *The Hathaways.* Reta Shaw plays Aunt Lavinia, the housekeeper to Bob Major, the publisher of the Phippsboro *Bulletin* on *Ichabod and Me* (CBS).

1962. Nadia Westman plays Mrs. Featherstone, the rectory housekeeper to Father Charles O'Malley on *Going My Way* (ABC). Hilda (Mary Treen) is the maid to comedian Joey Barnes and his wife Ellie on *The Joey Bishop Show* (NBC/CBS). Stuffy English butler Higgins (Stanley Holloway) cares for the MacRoberts, a disorganized American family on ABC's *Our Man Higgins.*

1963. Leon Lontoc is Henry, the houseboy and chauffeur to millionaire police captain Amos Burke on *Burke's Law* (ABC). In the 1994 CBS update (also called *Burke's Law*), Danny Kamakona plays Henry, houseboy and chauffeur to police captain Amos Burke. Inger Stevens plays Katy Holstrom, a governess and housekeeper to Congressman Glenn Morley and his children on ABC's *The Farmer's Daughter.* Imogene Coca plays Grindl, a fumbling maid with the Foster Temporary Employment Service on NBC's *Grindl.* Margaret Hamilton plays Mrs. MacDonald, maid to the Lane family on ABC's *The Patty Duke Show.*

1964. Lurch (Ted Cassidy) is the tall, zombielike butler to Gomez Addams and his family on ABC's *The Addams Family.* Rocky Sin (Jack Soo) is the valet, housekeeper, cook and confidant of playboy Valentine Farrow on *Valentine's Day* (ABC).

1965. Silas (Napoleon Whiting) cares for the house and cooks for the Barkleys, ranchers on ABC's *The Big Valley.* Hazel Burke (Shirley Booth) becomes the maid to Steve Baxter, the brother of her former employer George Baxter (see 1961), on *Hazel* (CBS). Margaret Malloy (Mercedes McCambridge) is the housemother at Kappa Phi, a college sorority on the CBS pilot *Young in Heart.*

1966. Alfred Pennyworth (Charles Napier) is the ever-faithful butler to millionaire Bruce Wayne on ABC's *Batman.* Sebastian Cabot is Giles French, the gentleman's gentleman to bachelor Bill Davis on CBS's *Family Affair.* Kato

(Bruce Lee) appears to be the valet for newspaper publisher Britt Reid. In reality he is crime-fighting assistant on ABC's *The Green Hornet.*

1968. Naomi Stevens is Juanita, the housekeeper to Buck Webb, the father of Doris Martin, a widow with two sons, on *The Doris Day Show* (CBS). Reta Shaw is Martha Grant, housekeeper to magazine writer Carolyn Muir and her children on *The Ghost and Mrs. Muir* (NBC/ABC). Bee Taylor (Frances Bavier) begins the role as housekeeper to councilman Sam Jones on CBS's *Mayberry, R.F.D.* Alice Ghostley (as Alice) replaces her.

1969. Alice Nelson (Ann B. Davis) cares for the eight-member Brady family on ABC's *The Brady Bunch.* Mrs. Livingston (Miyoshi Umeki) cares for young Eddie and "Mr. Eddie's Father" (as she calls magazine editor Tom Corbett) on ABC's *The Courtship of Eddie's Father.* Sara (Nora Marlowe) is the housekeeper to Governor William Drinkwater and his daughter J.J. on CBS's *The Governor and J.J.*

1970. Juliet Mills plays Phoebe Figalilly, governess and housekeeper to college professor Harold Everett and his children on ABC's *Nanny and the Professor.*

1971. Albert and Jane Miller (Larry Hagman, Donna Mills) pose as a butler and cook to live what they consider *The Good Life* (NBC). Mildred (Nancy Walker) is the housekeeper to San Francisco Police Commissioner Stewart McMillan and his wife Sally on NBC's *McMillan and Wife.*

1972. Angie Bianco (Connie Stevens) is an ex-waitress who works as the housemother at Alpha Rho Epsilon, an all male frat house on the ABC pilot *Call Her Mom.* Florida Evans (Esther Rolle) is the maid to the liberal and outspoken Maude Findlay on CBS's *Maude.* Joanna Pettet plays Kate Stewart, teacher, coach and housemother at an exclusive boys school on the CBS pilot *Miss Stewart, Sir.*

1976. Mary Grace Canfield plays Mrs. Canfield, housekeeper for the six-member Lawrence family on ABC's *Family.* Marla Gibbs plays Florence Johnston, maid to the snobbish George Jefferson and his tolerant wife Louise on CBS's *The Jeffersons.* Aggie Thornton (Martha Raye) is the housekeeper for Police Commissioner Stewart McMillan on NBC's *McMillan.* Rachel Roberts plays Mrs. McClellan, housekeeper to Judge Walter Franklin on *The Tony Randall Show* (ABC/CBS).

1977. Connie Booth plays Polly Sherman, housekeeper at the incompetently run British inn, *Fawlty Towers* (Syn.). Gertrude Hardy (Edith Atwater), the sister of detective Fenton Hardy, cares for him and his sons Frank and Joe on ABC's *The Hardy Boys Mysteries*. Benson DuBois (Robert Guillaume) is the housekeeper to the wealthy Jessica Tate and her family on ABC's *Soap*.

1978. Edna Garrett (Charlotte Rae) then Adelaide Brubaker (Nedra Volz) and Pearl Gallagher (Mary Jo Catlett) were the housekeepers to millionaire Philip Drummond on *Diff'rent Strokes* (NBC/ABC). Annette Funicello plays Dee Dee, a sorority housemother at Malibu University on the NBC pilot *Frankie and Annette: The Second Time Around*. Deborah Zon plays Connie, housekeeper at Snavely Manor on the ABC pilot *Snavely*.

1979. Edna Garrett (Charlotte Rae) becomes the housemother for a group of high school girls at the Eastland School on NBC's *The Facts of Life*. Max (Lionel Stander) cares for Jonathan and Jennifer Hart, a married couple who like to solve murders on ABC's *Hart to Hart*. Nedra Volz plays Pinky Nolan, housekeeper to Braddock University professor Louis Harper on CBS's *Hanging In*. Jenny O'Hara plays Rebecca, the housekeeper for the eccentric residents of the Blacke Foundation on NBC's *Highcliffe Manor*. Mickey Deems plays Nails Doyle, butler to Michael Cooper, a kindhearted mayor on *Hizzoner* (NBC). Hannah Dean plays Gladys, housekeeper to the five orphaned Richards children and their aunt, Marion, on *Out of the Blue* (ABC).

1980. Carmen Zapata is Mrs. Chavez, housekeeper to investigator Paul Hagen on CBS's *Hagen*. Mary Alice plays Donie, housekeeper to Dr. Joshua Lawrence on the CBS pilot *Joshua's World*. Jonathan Higgins (John Hillerman) is the major domo to pulp fiction writer Robin Masters on CBS's *Magnum, P.I.* Cindy Snow (Jenilee Harrison) is a college student who earns money by hiring herself out as a maid on ABC's *Three's Company*.

1981. Chao-Li (Chao-Li Chin) is the housekeeper for the powerful Channing family on CBS's *Falcon Crest*. Peter Cook is Robert Brentwood, a spit and polish British butler who seeks to organize the life of New York TV show host Nan Gallagher on *The Two of Us* (CBS).

1982. Walter Pinkerton (Johnny Haymer) is the butler to Madame, a once famous movie star who now hosts a TV talk show on *Madame's Place* (Syn.).

1983. Mickey McKenzie (Teri Copley) is a beautiful live-in maid to sloppy bachelors David and Jay on NBC's *We Got It Made*.

1984. Scott Baio plays Charles, live-in helper for the Pembroke family on CBS's *Charles in Charge*. The series returned in syndication in 1987 with Charles as the helper to the Powell family. Tony Micelli (Tony Danza) is the housekeeper to ad agency president Angela Bower on ABC's *Who's the Boss?*

1985. Raoul (Chick Vinnera) is the housekeeper to Julia Mansfield, the first woman president of the U.S. on ABC's *Hail to the Chief*. Lynn Belvedere (Christopher Hewett) is a prim and proper English butler who cares for the totally disorganized Owens family on ABC's *Mr. Belvedere*. Henry Jones plays Phillips, butler to Larry Hutchins, the brother of the President of the U.S. on *Code Name: Foxfire* (NBC). Lisa Antelle is Lisa Flores, the young Mexican housekeeper to Ted and Muriel Knight on *The Ted Knight Show* (Syn.).

1986. Toinette (Mary Louise Wilson) is the maid to Sloan Thorn and his family on ABC's *The Thorns*.

1987. Sonny Barnes (Jimmie Walker) is an ex con who works as the housekeeper to social worker Mimi Shaw on the syndicated *Bustin' Loose*. April Ortiz is Carmen, the housekeeper to clothes hanger tycoon Dave Whiteman and his family on *Down and Out in Beverly Hills* (Fox). Elizabeth Pena is Dora Calderon, the El Salvadorian housekeeper to architect Peter Farrell and his children, Kate and Will on *I Married Dora* (ABC). Dyana Ortelli plays Lupe Lopez, a sexy cook and maid to the wealthy Randolph and Hilary Stonehill on the syndicated *Marblehead Manor*.

1988. Elden Benecky (Robert Pastorelli) is a house painter hired by newscaster Murphy Brown who eventually became her jack-of-all-trades helper on CBS's *Murphy Brown*.

1989. Mary Wickes plays Marie, the rectory cook at St. Michael's Parish in Chicago on *The Father Dowling Mysteries* (NBC/ABC). Winnie Goodwin (Corinne Bohrer) is a witch who cares for the house and children of widower Thomas Harper on ABC's *Free Spirit*. Lisa Patrick (Lisa Wells) is a live-in helper for the Matthews family on CBS's *Live-In*. Arlene Sorkin plays Geneva, housekeeper to Richard and Linda Phillips on *Open House* (Fox).

1990. Joseph Marcell plays Geoffrey, butler to

Philip Banks and his family on NBC's *The Fresh Prince of Bel Air*. Patsy Cole (Diana Canova) is a housemother at Buckley University on the NBC pilot *Social Studies*.

1992. Bernice Farrell, called Bernie (Laurel Cronin), is the housekeeper to veterinarian Sam McGuire on ABC's *Julie*. Elizabeth Berridge plays Charlotte, the maid to Senator Bill Franklin and his dysfunctional family on *The Powers That Be* (NBC).

1993. Millicent Torkelson (Connie Ray) is the mother of three children (Dorothy Jane, Mary Sue and Chuckie) who works as the housekeeper and nanny to attorney Brian Morgan and his two mischievous children (Molly and Gregory) on *Almost Home* (NBC). Daphne Moon (Jane Leeves) is the caretaker to Martin Crane, the father of psychiatrist Frasier Crane on NBC's *Frasier*.

1994. Oona Dowd (Alice Playten) is the housekeeper for N.Y.P.D. forensic scientist Guy Hanks on *The Cosby Mysteries* (NBC). Rita Moreno replaces Oona in later episodes as Angie Corea.

1996. Fran Fine (Fran Drescher) is the nanny to the children of widower Max Sheffield; Niles (Daniel Davis) is his butler on CBS's *The Nanny*.

1998. John DeSantis plays Lurch, the tall, morbid, zombie-like butler of Gomez Addams and his family on *The New Addams Family* (Fox Family Channel).

2000. Emily Gilmore is a rich woman who each week has a different maid on the WB's *Gilmore Girls* (much in the same manner as Murphy Brown each week has a different secretary). Shelley Morrison plays Rosario, the constantly belittled maid to the snobbish Karen Walker on NBC's *Will and Grace*.

2002. Tim Curry plays Giles French, the gentleman's gentleman to bachelor Bill Davis on the WB's *Family Affair*.

2003. Berta (Conchata Ferrell) is the housekeeper to Charlie Harper, a womanizing composer of TV commercial jingles on *Two and a Half Men* (CBS). Gordana Rashovich plays Jadwiga, housekeeper at the LaMont Hotel in New York City on NBC's *Whoopi*.

2004. Anna (Mindy Cohn), Molly (Tori Spelling) and Maria (Camille Guaty) are among the servants to the wealthy Ridgeway family of Florida on the WB's *The Help*.

2005. Dolly (Patricia Belcher) is the house-

keeper to Alan and Lee Arnold, the founders of the Arnold Undergarment Company on *Twins* (WB).

Immigrants

This entry concerns itself with people from other countries who have come to America in the hope of finding a new or better life.

1949. Peggy Wood and Judson Laire play Marta (Mama) and Lars (Papa) Hanson, Norwegian immigrants who have settled in San Francisco (1910) and are now struggling to raise a family on *Mama* (CBS; also known as *I Remember Mama*).

1952. Luigi Basco (J. Carrol Naish, Vito Scotti) is an Italian immigrant, newly arrived in the U.S. who attempts to operate an antique store in Chicago's Little Italy on CBS's *Life with Luigi*.

1963. Eric Tegman (William Shatner) and John Reardon (Robert Brown) are immigrants struggling to begin new lives in California's San Fernando Valley, 1912, on the NBC pilot *Colossus*.

1974. Scott Thomas and Bonnie Bedelia head a family of Scandinavian immigrants attempting to build a new life for themselves in Minnesota, 1858, on ABC's *The New Land*.

1976. Four immigrant families begin a new life on New York's Lower East Side during the early 1900s on the CBS pilot *Land of Hope*. Marian Winters, Richard Liberman and Roberta Wallach head a large cast.

1977. Lupe (Maria O'Brien), Yosef Ari (Harvey Jason), Chuma (Freeman King) and Yoko (Suesie Elene) are among the students learning English on the ABC pilot *The Primary English Class*.

1978. The lives of Lithuanian immigrants Joseph and Anna Bresner (Rob Reiner, Judy Kahan) are traced from 1909 to 1978 on ABC's *Free Country*. The strange Latka Gravas (Andy Kaufman), a mechanic for the Sunshine Cab Company in New York, is an immigrant from an unknown land on ABC's *Taxi*. Carol Kane plays his equally strange girlfriend (then wife), Simka Dabhlitz.

1981. Ming-Lee Chang (Rosalind Chao), Kwame Botulo (Ernie Hudson) and Milosh Dubrowski (Bob Ari) are among the immigrant students preparing for their naturalization tests on the NBC pilot *Almost American*.

1985. Enci Shagula (Keith Szarabajka) is a Russian immigrant who has come to America to make his mark on the NBC pilot *Big Shots in America*.

1986. Yung Lee (Leila Hee Olsen), Nikolai Rospovitz (Yakov Smirnoff) and Laslo Garbo (George Murdock) are among the immigrants studying for their citizenship tests on the syndicated *What a Country*.

1987. Dora Calderon is a girl from El Salvador working as a housekeeper (to widower Peter Farrell) while hoping for a marriage to keep her in the U.S. on ABC's *I Married Dora*.

Iraq War see War—Korea, Vietnam, Iraq

Islands see Beaches and Islands

Judges

Programs starring or revolving around judges are the subjects of this entry. See also *District Attorneys* and *Lawyers*.

1948. New York Supreme Court Judge Ferdinand Pecora appears in reenactments of actual court cases on the ABC pilot *On Trial*.

1949. Frankie Thomas, Sr., plays the judge on NBC's *The Black Robe*, dramas based on actual police night court cases. Real judges appear on *They Stand Accused*, dramas based on actual court cases.

1952. Jim Backus plays Bradley Stevens, a Los Angeles domestic relations court judge on NBC's *I Married Joan*.

1953. The ABC pilot *Justice* is a proposed series based on actual cases from the files of the Legal Aid Society (John Lehine plays the judge in the pilot story about a wife who seeks help after she discovers her husband is being blackmailed).

1954. NBC adapts the ABC pilot *Justice* to a series that presents guests as judges in cases based on Legal Aid files.

1955. Lamar Kendall (Jack Carson) is a self-appointed judge who attempts to uphold the law in Arroyo, New Mexico, on the NBC pilot *Arroyo*. Edgar Buchanan plays Roy Bean, the self-appointed judge of Langtry, Texas, on the syndicated *Judge Roy Bean*. Robert Warwick plays the Judge in *On Trial*, an NBC pilot for a series based on actual court cases.

1956. Margaret Lindsay plays TV's first female judge, Carrie Williams, on the pilot *Carrie Williams, Justice of the Peace*. Carrie is a judge in the town of Palmerdale who helps the people of her community with their problems. John Cooper (Leon Ames) is a circuit-riding judge of the Old West on the pilot *Frontier Judge*. Gene Lockhart plays Homer Bell, justice of the peace in Spring City on the syndicated *His Honor, Homer Bell*. John McIntire plays Judge Cardiff on *Justice*, an NBC pilot for a series based on actual court cases.

1957. Cases based on actual divorce hearings are the basis of the syndicated *Divorce Court*. The judges: Voltaire Perkins (1957–69), William B. Keene (1984–99), Mablean Ephriam (1999–Current). Actual court cases are dramatized on CBS's *On Trial* (Joseph Cotten hosts; various judges appear).

1958. Judge Edgar Allan Jones, Jr., presides over actual criminal and civil cases on ABC's *Day in Court*. Divorce hearings are restaged on the syndicated *Divorce Hearing* (various judges appear). Actual small claims court hearings are reenacted on *The People's Court of Small Claims*, a syndicated series with Judge Orrin B. Evans. Judge Edgar Allan Jones, Jr., presides over reenactments of actual cases on *Traffic Court* (ABC). Guest judges appear on *The Verdict Is Yours*, a CBS series that reenacts actual court cases.

1959. Judge James Gehrig presides over a domestic relations court on NBC's *The House on High Street*. Dan Duryea plays Mark Johnston, a small town judge on the NBC pilot *Justice of the Peace*.

1960. Andy Taylor (Andy Griffith) is the justice of the peace in the small town of Mayberry, North Carolina, on CBS's *The Andy Griffith Show*. Frank Lovejoy plays Judge Parker in Fort Smith, Kansas, 1870s, on the NBC pilot *The Hanging Judge*. Judges William Gwinn and Georgiana Hardy preside over actual court case reenactments on ABC's *Morning Court*.

1961. A comical look at the life of a judge is seen through the experiences of Cyrus Dunn, a Beverly Hills judge on the CBS pilot *My Darling Judge*.

1963. Life in a small American town is seen through the eyes of kindly Judge Fairweather (Charlie Ruggles) on the NBC pilot *Adamsburgh, U.S.A.* Newly appointed Supreme Court Judge Daniel Zachary (Richard Basehart) begins his duties on the NBC pilot *The Judge*.

1965. Jay Jostyn plays the judge on *Night Court*, a syndicated series based on New York and Los Angeles night court hearings.

1971. Laurence Naismith plays Judge Fulton, a retired magistrate who teams with playboys Brett Sinclair and Danny Wilde to bring criminals to justice on ABC's *The Persuaders*.

1972. Darren McGavin is Mike Bryan, a widowed judge with five children on the NBC pilot *Father on Trial*. The retired, eccentric Judge Meredith (Bette Davis) and ex con Jake Wyler (Doug McClure) open a detective agency to help people on the NBC pilot *The Judge and Jake Wyler*.

1974. Khigh Dhiegh plays Judge Dee, a seventh-century Chinese magistrate who solves crimes on the ABC pilot *Judge Dee in the Monastery Murders*.

1976. Anthony Newlands plays the judge on *Crimes of Passion*, a syndicated series of cases based on French criminal records of crimes of passion. Michael Constantine is Matthew Sirota, a compassionate but harassed night court judge on NBC's *Sirota's Court*. Walter O. Franklin (Tony Randall) is a less-than-magisterial judge of the Court of Common Pleas in Philadelphia on *The Tony Randall Show* (ABC/CBS). Diana Muldaur plays his romantic interest, Judge Eleanor Hooper.

1978. Actual courtroom cases are dramatized on the syndicated *On Trial* (guests appear as the judges).

1981. Barry Sullivan plays the judge, the celestial being who must decide where to send a soul—to Heaven or Hell—on the NBC pilot *Judgment Day*. Real cases before real judges are aired on the syndicated *People's Court*. The judges: Joseph Wapner (1981–93), Ed Koch (1997–99), Jerry Sheindlin (1999–2001), Marilyn Milian (2001-Current).

1983. Retired Judge Milton C. Hardcastle (Brian Keith) teams with two-time loser Mark McCormick (Daniel Hugh Kelly) to bring criminals to justice on ABC's *Hardcastle and McCormick*.

1984. Harry J. Stone (Harry Anderson) is an unorthodox New York night court judge on NBC's *Night Court*. The lives of the judges who preside over the Hall of Justice at 100 Centre Street in New York are the focal point of the ABC pilot *100 Centre Street*. Dee Wallace and Henry Darrow star as judges Nell Hartigan and Ramon Robledo.

1986. Judge Robert F. Shield presides over actual cases involving family disputes on *The Judge* (Syn.). William D. Burns is the judge in cases based on criminal justice issues on the syndicated *Superior Court*.

1989. Raymond Burr plays former judge Gordon Duane who guides viewers through legal procedures and explains legal terminology during case reenactments on the syndicated *Trial by Jury*.

1990. Philip Banks (James Avery) is a lawyer turned judge on NBC's *The Fresh Prince of Bel Air*.

1991. Nicholas Marshall (Ramy Zada, Bruce Abbott) is a superior court judge who avenges crimes within the law on CBS's *Dark Justice*.

1994. Attorney F. Lee Bailey hosts *On Trial*, an NBC pilot for a series based on real life trials. Guest judges preside.

1995. Judge Sydney J. Solomon (Pamela Reed) is a family court judge and a single mother with four children on NBC's *The Home Court*.

1996. Judge Judith Sheindlin hears the real cases of real people on the syndicated *Judge Judy*.

1997. The non-nonsense Mills Lane conducts a very strict courtroom as he hears real cases on the syndicated *Judge Mills Lane*. Real cases involving animal disputes are heard by retired judge Joseph Wapner on *Judge Wapner's Animal Court* (Animal Planet).

1998. Real people argue their own cases in small claims court on the syndicated *Judge Joe Brown*.

1999. Judge Greg Mathis hears real small claims court cases on the syndicated *Judge Mathis*. Amy Brennerman is a former New York corporate lawyer turned family court superior judge on CBS's *Judging Amy*.

2002. Sally Field plays Kate Nolan, a superior court judge on ABC's *The Court*. James Garner plays Chief Justice Branken and Charles Durning, James McEachin and Gail Strickland are justices Henry Hoskins, Jerome Morris and Deborah Swark on CBS's *First Monday*. Judge Larry Joe Doherty hears real testimonies on the syndicated *Texas Justice*.

2003. Jack Moran (Oliver Platt) is an unorthodox judge of the Queens Supreme Court in New York on CBS's *Queen Supreme*.

2004. Judge Glenda Hatchett hears real cases on the syndicated *Judge Hatchett*.

2005. Alex Ferrer, a cop turned criminal lawyer turned judge, hears real cases on the syndicated *Judge Alex*.

Korean War see War—Korean, Vietnam and Iraq

Las Vegas

A listing of series set in Las Vegas, Nevada.
1967. *The Las Vegas Show* (United Network).
1977. *Blansky's Beauties* (ABC).
1978. *Vegas* (ABC); *Who's Watching the Kids?* (NBC).
1980. *Las Vegas Gambit* (NBC).
1987. *The Tortellis* (NBC).
1992. *Hearts Are Wild* (CBS).
1999. *The Strip* (UPN).
2000. *C.S.I.: Crime Scene Investigation* (CBS); *Nikki* (WB).
2003. *Las Vegas* (NBC).
2004. *Dr. Vegas* (CBS).

Latino Performers and Characters

This entry chronicles the program on which Latin (and Spanish) Americans are the stars or featured regulars. See also *Cuban American Performers and Characters; Mexican American Performers and Characters* and *Puerto Rican Performers and Characters.*
1949. Latin singer Delora Bueno hosts her own musical variety series, *Flight to Rhythm* on Du-Mont.
1955. Lloyd Berrell plays Mendoza, a Spanish sailor of the 17th century on *The Adventures of Long John Silver* (Syn.).
1956. Bill Dana appears as a regular on *The Steve Allen Show* (NBC) in skits featuring his bewildered Latin character, Jose Jimenez.
1957. Manuel Rojas plays Elfego Baca, the Spanish-American sheriff who strives to uphold the peace without gunplay in the Old West on the ABC pilot *Elfego Baca*. Latin bandleader Xavier Cugat headlines his own musical variety series, *The Xavier Cugat Show*, on NBC. Guy Williams plays Don Diego de la Vega, a Spanish nobleman who is secretly Zorro, a hero of Old California, on *Zorro* (ABC). In 1983, CBS aired *Zorro and Son* with Henry Darrow as Don Diego and Paul Regina as his son Don Carlos, the new Zorro. In 1990 the Family Channel aired *Zorro* with Duncan Regehr

as Don Diego, alias Zorro. In 1997 *The New Adventures of Zorro* aired in syndication with Michael Gough II as Don Diego/Zorro.
1958. Robert Loggia is Elfego Baca, the Spanish-American sheriff turned lawyer who battles for justice in Socorro County, New Mexico (1880s) on *Elfego Baca* (ABC; as a segment of *Frontierland* on *Walt Disney Presents*). Elena Barra plays Tina, the assistant to Joe Joes, an American private detective based in Spain who helps American tourists on *It Happened in Spain* (Syn.).
1959. Ross Martin plays Andamo, the Latin assistant to Mr. Lucky, the owner of the gambling yacht *Fortuna* on *Mr. Lucky* (CBS).
1960. Arthur Batanides plays Lupo Olivera, a sergeant with the N.Y.P.D. on the syndicated *Johnny Midnight*. Margarita Sierra plays Cha Cha O'Brien, the Latin singer and dancer at the Boom Boom Room of the Fontainebleau Hotel in Miami Beach on *SurfSide 6* (ABC).
1961. Bill Dana plays Jose Jimenez, the Latin doorman at the Parkside Apartments in Manhattan (the home to night club comic Danny Williams and his family) on *The Danny Thomas Show* (CBS; syndicated as *Make Room for Daddy*).
1962. Roger Delgado plays Ambassador Mendoza, an official of the Spanish Court (16th century) on *The Adventures of Sir Francis Drake* (NBC).
1963. Bill Dana switches networks (to NBC) as the star of *The Bill Dana Show* wherein Jose Jimenez is now the bewildered Latin bellhop at the Park Central Hotel in Manhattan.
1964. Paul Geary is John Ramos, the Hispanic political aide to James Slattery, a minority leader in the State Senate on *Slattery's People* (CBS).
1965. John Astin becomes Gomez Addams, the wealthy eccentric on ABC's *The Addams Family*. Gomez is of Spanish ancestry (although he also states his heritage dates back to ancient Egypt).
1966. Robert Carricart plays Pepe, the Spanish owner of the Casa Del Gato, a San Francisco nightclub frequented by professional bodyguard Thomas Hewitt Edward Cat on *T.H.E. Cat* (NBC).
1969. Emilio Delgado and Sonia Manzano play Luis and Maria, the Spanish repair shop workers on *Sesame Street* (PBS).
1970. Vito Scotti plays Mr. Velasquez, the landlord of the Manhattan brownstone where

newlyweds Paul and Corie Bratter live on ABC's *Barefoot in the Park*.

1973. Jose Perez is Ramon Gonzalez, an employee of the New York State Department of Unemployment on *Calucci's Department* (CBS).

1974. Rafael Campos plays Ramon Diaz, Jr., the assistant to Rhoda Morganstern at the Doyle Costume Company on *Rhoda* (CBS).

1975. Richard Beauchamp plays Rodriquez, the Hispanic recruit at the U.S. Navy's San Diego Training Center on NBC's *C.P.O. Sharkey*. Lisa Mordente is Teresa Ortega, the Hispanic employee of the Westside Medical Clinic in New York City on *Doc* (CBS). Liz Torres plays Julie Erskine, the Hispanic owner of Erskine's Commercial Photography Studio (the company for which Phyllis Lindstrom works in first season episodes) on *Phyllis* (CBS).

1976. Charo plays herself, a beautiful Spanish entertainer on the ABC pilot *Charo and the Sergeant* (wherein she marries a U.S. Marine sergeant). Rita Moreno plays Googie Gomez, an Hispanic singer-dancer hoping to make it into the big time on the ABC pilot *The Rita Moreno Show*.

1977. Charo plays April Lopez, the sexy Spanish singer who entertained on the *Pacific Princess* in a recurring role on *The Love Boat* (ABC). J. Victor Lopez plays Jimmy, the Hispanic crewmember of the *Citation*, a submarine used by the Oceanic Research Foundation on *The Man from Atlantis* (NBC). Gino Conforti is Felipe Gomez, the Hispanic kitchen aide (to Jack Tripper) at Angelino's Italian Restaurant on *Three's Company* (ABC).

1978. Gregory Sierra is Dr. Tony Menzies, an Hispanic chief resident at the poorly equipped Adult Emergency Services Hospital on Hudson Street in Manhattan on *A.E.S. Hudson Street* (ABC). Also featured are Rosana Soto as Nurse Rosa Santiago and Susan Peretz as Foshko, an E.M.T. Priscilla Lopez is Sister Agnes, the streetwise Hispanic nun who works with Father Dan Cleary at an inner city youth mission on *In the Beginning* (CBS). Bert Rosario is Hector Ramirez, the Hispanic ex-con who helps his former cellmate, Jack Cole apprehend white-collar criminals on NBC's *Sword of Justice*.

1979. Rocky Echevarria (a.k.a. Steven Bauer) plays Ignacio Carmona, an Hispanic private stationed at Pearl Harbor at the time of the Japanese attack on NBC's *From Here to Eternity*.

1979. Taylor Negron is Silvio Galindez, an Hispanic student at the Nick Hannigan Detective School and Agency on ABC's *Detective School*. Luis Avalos plays Dr. Sanchez, the Hispanic researcher seeking to take control of the wealthy Blacke Foundation on NBC's *Highcliffe Manor*.

1980. ABC's *Soap* features Gregory Sierra as Carlos Valdez, the South American revolutionary (called "El Puerco") who finds refuge with the wealthy Tate family of Connecticut.

1981. Liz Torres plays Elana Beltran, the assistant housekeeper at the St. Frederick Hotel in Manhattan on *Checking In* (CBS). Rene Enriquez is Ray Calletano, an Hispanic lieutenant with the Hill Street Police Station on NBC's *Hill Street Blues*.

1982. A Martinez is Benny Silva, the manager of a gym and the legman for private detective Cassie Holland on NBC's *Cassie and Co.* Hector Elias is Rollin Espinoza, the musical conductor (of the Madame's Place All-Divorced Orchestra) for the puppet Madame on her TV show *Madame's Place* (Syn.). Rita Moreno plays Violet Newstead, a Latin widow who works as the secretarial supervisor at Consolidated Industries on *9 to 5* (ABC). Violet, maiden name Fernandez, is the mother of a 12-year-old Tommy (Tony LaTorre). Danny Mora plays Max Hernandez, an Hispanic fireman in sequences dealing with Buddy Krebs, a fire captain and the father of Jennie, an aspiring singer on ABC's *Star of the Family*.

1983. Luis Avalos is Jesse Rodriquez, an Hispanic businessman on ABC's *Condo*. Jesse, his wife Maria (Yvonne Wilder) and their daughter Linda (Julie Carmen) live next door to James Kirkridge, an insurance salesman, his wife Kiki and their children Scott and Billy. Eddie Velez is George Lucas, an Hispanic private with the peacetime army's 88th Airborne, a military unit stationed at Fort Geller, Texas, on *For Love and Honor* (NBC). Fernando Lamas is Cesar de Portago, the scheming Hispanic who shares a Malibu Beach house with Robert Gavilan, a consultant for the DeWitt Institute on NBC's *Gavilan*. Fausto Bara is Gaucho, the Hispanic leader of the Wild Cats, a street gang that helps the police uphold the law on *Renegades* (ABC).

1984. Luis Avalos is Dr. Thomas Esquivel and Conchata Ferrell is Nurse Joan Thor on the CBS comedy *E/R*. Richard Yniquez is Father Jose Silva, an Hispanic priest on CBS's *Mama Malone*. Edward James Olmos is Martin Castillo, an Hispanic lieutenant with the Miami Vice Squad on NBC's *Miami Vice*. Henry Darrow plays Ramon Robledo, an Hispanic judge on the ABC pilot *100 Center Street*. NBC's *Berringer's* features Eddie Velez as Julio Morales, an apprentice Hispanic clothes designer. Israel Juarbe plays Angel Gomez, an Hispanic ex-con who works as a messenger for the Manhattan D.A.'s office on *Foley Square* (CBS). Hispanic actor Hector Elizondo stars on *Foley Square* but in the role of Jesse Steinberg, a Jewish A.D.A. Chick Vennera is Raoul, the Latino butler to Julia Mansfield, the first woman president of the U.S. on *Hail to the Chief* (ABC). Luis Avalos plays Lieutenant Gomez, the L.A.P.D. detective who comes to the rescue of private eye Jackson Beaudine, the man with three ex-wives on *I Had Three Wives* (CBS). Ricardo Guiterrez is Harvey, an Hispanic information man (snitch) for private detective Katy Mahoney on ABC's *Lady Blue*.

1986. Robert Hegyes joins the cast of *Cagney and Lacey* (CBS) as Manny Esposito, the seemingly disorganized Hispanic detective with the 14th Precinct of the N.Y.P.D. Robert Beltran is Hector Martinez, an Hispanic lawyer who, in his youth was a gang member, on the CBS pilot *The Family Martinez*. Also in the cast are Anne Betancourt as his mother, Anita (a widow) and Karla Montana as his 16-year-old sister Rainbow. Leslie Bega and Michael DeLorenzo play Maria Borges and Alex Torres, Hispanic students in the Individual Honors Program at Fillmore High School in New York City on ABC's *Head of the Class*. Elizabeth Pena plays Connie Rivera, an Hispanic Chicago police woman on *Tough Cookies* (CBS).

1987. Efrain Figueroa is Estaban Gutierre, an Hispanic lieutenant with the Houston, Texas, P.D. on *Houston Knights* (CBS). Elizabeth Pena plays Dora Calderon, the El Salvadorian housekeeper to architect Peter Farrell and his children Kate and Will on ABC's *I Married Dora*. Dyana Ortelli is Lupe Ortiz, the sexy Hispanic maid and cook to the stuffy Randolph Stonehill and his wife Hilary on the syndicated *Marblehead Manor*. In the original pilot (which aired as the last episode) Charo played the role of Cookie, the sexy maid (she was replaced by Dyana Ortelli). Wanda de Jesus is Leda Cervantes, the Hispanic corrections officer at Mariah State Prison on ABC's *Mariah*.

1988. Constance Marie is Penny Rivera, the Latin dancer (and partner to dance instructor Johnny Castle) at Kellerman's Summer Resort in the Catskill Mountains on CBS's *Dirty Dancing*. Mateo Cordero (Pepe Serna), his wife Lupe (Evelyn Guerrero) and their daughter Xochia (Marisol Rodriquez) are an Hispanic family who live at Fort Figueroa, a decrepit Los Angeles building on the CBS pilot *Fort Figueroa*. Benjamin Bratt is Tony Maldonato, an Hispanic ex-gang member who heads the Knights of the City, a volunteer group that helps the police patrol the streets of New York on *Knight Watch* (CBS). Tasia Valenza is Yeoman Rosie Henriques and Gerardo Mejia is Airman Luis Cruz, Hispanics stationed on the USS *Georgetown*, an aircraft carrier on ABC's *Super Carrier*.

1989. The ABC episodes of *Kojak* feature Kario Salem as Paco Montana, a detective with the N.Y.P.D.'s 74th Precinct. Roxana Biggs is Yolanda Puente, a Latino student nurse at Wiltshire Memorial Hospital in L.A. on *Nightingales* (NBC).

1990. Jenny Gago is Teresa Robles, an Hispanic undercover agent with the DEA (Drug Enforcement Agency) on *DEA: Special Task Force* (Fox). Benjamin Bratt plays Eduardo Cruz, the Latino member of the Northern Narcotics Bureau of the Las Vegas Police Department, an undercover unit that busts drug rings, on NBC's *Nasty Boys*. Nia Peeples played Eduardo's wife, Serena. On NBC's *Shannon's Deal*, Elizabeth Pena plays Lucy Acosta, the Hispanic secretary to criminal lawyer Jack Shannon. Steven Bauer plays Miguel Santana, a disbarred federal prosecutor working undercover for the Organized Crime Unit of the FBI on *Wiseguy* (CBS).

1991. Maria Rangel is Maria Trent, an Hispanic schoolteacher and battered wife who killed her husband and is now serving time at the Women's State Prison on *Dangerous Women* (Syn.). NBC's *Nurses* features Ada Maris as Gina Cuevas, the Latino nurse at the Community Medical Center in Florida. Bert Rosario is Abel Vasquez, the corrupt governor general of the Caribbean island of San Pietro on *The 100 Lives of Black Jack Savage* (NBC). Julio Oscar Mechosa plays Julio Oscar, the Hispanic orderly at the Hudson Memorial Hospital in Manhattan on *STAT* (ABC). Justin Louis plays Victor Torres, an investigative reporter for the Montreal *Tribune* on *Urban Angel* (CBS).

1992. Mayteana Morales and David Lopez are

Gabriella and Alejandro Fernandez, a sister and brother who are among a small group of children who solve minor crimes with the help of an entity called *Ghost Writer* (PBS). *Going to Extremes* (ABC) presents Camillo Gallardo as Kim Shelby, an Hispanic student at the Croft University Medical School (on the Caribbean island of Jantique). Costas Mandylor is Kenny Locos, a deputy to Sheriff Jimmy Brock in the town of Rome, Wisconsin, on *Picket Fences* (CBS).

1993. Tony Plana is Luke Ramirez, an Hispanic police detective with the Bakersfield, California, Police Department on *Bakersfield, P.D.* (Fox). Rachel Ticotin is Annette Rey, an Hispanic detective with the L.A.P.D. on NBC's *Crime and Punishment.* Maria Celedonio plays Annette's daughter, Tonya. Lupe Ontivera is Marta, the Hispanic maid to Dudley Bristol, a divorced New York nightclub entertainer on *Dudley* (CBS). Juan Ramirez plays Carlos Marrone, an Hispanic detective with the Department of Missing Persons in Chicago on *Missing Persons* (NBC). On NBC's *Sea Quest DSV* Mario Sanchez plays Miguel Ortiz, an Hispanic naval crewman aboard the futuristic submarine *Sea Quest.* John Mendoza is John Palmero, the off-the-wall Hispanic sportswriter (for the *Chicago Daily*) on *The Second Half* (NBC). Also in the cast is Jessica Lundy as John's sister, Denise Palmero. Salma Hayek plays Gloria Contreras, the Hispanic babysitter for Zana and L.J., the adopted children of TV show host David Bryan on *The Sinbad Show* (Fox).

1994. The syndicated series *Babylon 5* features Silvana Gallardo as Dr. Maya Hernandez, an Hispanic physician aboard the space station *Babylon 5. Chicago Hope* (CBS) features Hector Elizondo as Dr. Philip Watters, a chief of surgery at Chicago Hope Hospital. Ricardo Montalban is Mr. Shepherd, an angel (Hispanic accent) who helps apprentice angels acquire their wings on *Heaven Help Us* (Syn.). Wilson Cruz is Enrique Vasquez, an Hispanic student at Liberty High School in Pittsburgh on ABC's *My So-Called Life.*

1995. *The Drew Carey Show* (ABC) features Ian Gomez as Larry Almada, the Hispanic "yes man" to Winford-Louder department store owner Mrs. Louder. Fox's *The Great Defender* features Carlos Sanchez as Jerry Perez, the assistant district attorney. John Leguizamo (Columbian) hosts (and stars in skits) on *House of Buggin,* a Fox series that features a Latino supporting cast (including Rosie Perez, Luis Guzman and Jorge Luis

Abreu). Benjamin Bratt joins the cast of NBC's *Law and Order* as Reynoldo Curtis, an Hispanic detective with the N.Y.P.D. Joanna Sanchez is Lupe, the Hispanic cashier at Pop's Joint, a diner in New York City on *The Wayans Bros.* (WB).

1996. ABC's *Common Law* features Greg Giraldo as John Alvarez, an Hispanic lawyer (educated at Harvard) in a Manhattan law firm. Gregory Sierra plays John's father, Luis, the owner of a barbershop, and Diana-Maria Riva is Maria Marquez, the office manager.

Jackie Guerra plays herself, the Hispanic owner of a hair salon called Tudor on *First Time Out* (WB). John Ortiz plays Nelson Marquez (nicknamed "Margarita"), the bartender at a shabby bar on *Life* (Fox). The CBS series *Matt Waters* features Cyndi Cartegena as Angela Perez, a student at Bayview High School in New Jersey.

1997. Adam Rodriquez is Hector Villanueva, an Hispanic police officer with the 74th Precinct of the N.Y.P.D. on *Brooklyn South* (CBS). Dion Bosco is Alberto Ramos, a scheming Hispanic teen who can get you what you need for a price on NBC's *City Guys* (he is a student at Manhattan High School). NBC's *Crisis Center* features Clifton Gonzalez Gonzalez as Nando Taylor, an Hispanic counselor at a youth center (Fox's *413 Hope Street* has the same format with Vincent Laresca as Carlos Martinez, an Hispanic counselor at a teen center in Manhattan). Roselyn Sanchez is Lili Arquedo, a young Latino woman seeking to become a professional dancer on the syndicated *Fame L.A.* HBO's *Oz* features several Hispanic prisoners confined to the Emerald City center of the Oswald State Penitentiary: David Zayas as Enrique Morales; Luiz Guzman as Raoul Hernandez and Kirk Acevedo as Miguel Alvarez. Costas Mandylor is Alphonse Royo, an Hispanic ex-con who works undercover for the FBI on NBC's *Players.* Mariska Hargitay is Nina Echeverria, a Latino undercover cop with the Intelligence Unit of the N.Y.P.D. on NBC's *Prince Street.* The syndicated *Soldier of Fortune* features Billy Gallo as Rico Valesquez, an Hispanic Navy SEAL who is also a medic. Maria Canals plays Carmen Cruz, an Hispanic sportswriter on *The Tony Danza Show* (NBC). Constance Marie is Gabriella Diaz, an aspiring actress who frequents Union Square, a Manhattan diner on NBC's *Union Square.*

1998. Louis Antonio Ramos is Billy Hernandez, a gay TV weatherman on CBS's *The Brian Ben-*

ben Show. Ian Gomez plays Javier Quintata, the Hispanic manager of a restaurant (Dean and DeLuca's) on *Felicity* (WB). Randy Vasquez is Paolo Kaire, the bar manager on the *Sun Princess*, the cruise ship seen on *The Love Boat: The Next Wave* (UPN). Glenn Taranto plays Gomez Addams, the eccentric investor and head of a spooky family on *The New Addams Family* (Fox Family Channel).

1999. Ian Gomez plays Danny Sanchez, an Hispanic who works for the Department of Social Services in New York City on *Norm* (ABC; also known as *The Norm Show*). Rick Batalla plays Mo, the bumbling Hispanic bellhop at the Whispering Pines Hotel on *Payne* (CBS). Tamera Mello is Lily Esposito, the featured Hispanic student at Kennedy High School in Los Angeles on *Popular* (WB). Beside aliens, who look human, UPN's *Roswell* features Adam Rodriquez as Jesse Rodriquez, an Hispanic attorney in Roswell, New Mexico. Anthony Ruivivar is Carlos Nieto, a rookie patrolman with the 55th Precinct of the N.Y.P.D. on NBC's *Third Watch* (the 3 P.M. to 11 P.M. shift).

2000. Tessie Santiago plays Dona Maria Teresa Alvarado, a beautiful young Spanish aristocrat living in Old California (1817) who is secretly the Queen of Swords (a female Zorro) who defends the people from the corrupt Luise Rivera Montoya (Valentine Pelka) on *The Queen of Swords* (Syn.).

2001. NBC's *Battery Park* features Jacqueline Obradors as Elena Vera, an Hispanic police detective with the Battery Park Division of the N.Y.P.D. *Gideon's Crossing* (ABC) features Ruben Blades as Max Cabranes, an Hispanic psychiatrist at a Boston teaching hospital. *Philly*, on NBC, features Diana-Maria Riva as Patricia, the office assistant to lawyer Kathleen McGuire. NBC's *Scrubs* features Judy Reyes as Carla Espinosa, an Hispanic nurse at Sacred Heart Hospital. *Six Feet Under* on HBO features Freddy Rodriguez as Rico Diaz, the Latino cosmetologist at the Fisher and Sons Funeral Home. Vanessa, Rico's wife, is played by Justina Machada. Diana-Maria Riva joins the cast of *Sabrina, the Teenage Witch* (WB) as Annie, the editor of *Scorch*, the music magazine for which Sabrina Spellman works. *The Tick* (Fox) features Nestor Carbonell as the Latino super hero Batmanuel, who helps the Tick uphold the law in the city.

2002. Casper Martinez hosts *Urban Latino TV*

(Syn.), a program of news and information geared to the Latin community.

2003. Hector Elizondo plays Father "Poppi" Calero, a consultant to Paul Callan, a man who investigates modern miracles on *Miracles* (ABC). Assisting Paul is Evelyn Santos (Marisa Ramirez), a former police investigator.

2004. The Latino community is spotlighted by Christina Fernadez and Liza Quinn on *American Latino TV* (Syn.). Latino sex symbol Eva Longoria is Gabrielle, one of ABC's *Desperate Housewives*. Eva also appeared as a regular on *The Young and the Restless* (CBS; 2002–03) as Isabella; and on *L.A. Dragnet* (ABC) as Det. Gloria Duran. *Lati Nation* (Syn.), hosted by Desi Sanchez, focuses on the fusion of Latin American culture in the U.S.

2005. Sofia Vergara plays Lola Hernandez, an extremely beautiful and sexy real estate agent with Summerlin and Associates on ABC's *Hot Properties*.

Lawyers

This entry chronicles the men and women who serve the legal profession as either a defense lawyer or a prosecutor. See also *District Attorneys* and *Judges*.

1951. Lee Tracy plays John J. Malone, a criminal attorney on CBS's *The Amazing Mr. Malone*.

1953. Unjustly disbarred attorney turned private detective Steve Randall (Melvyn Douglas) seeks to regain his right to practice law by finding those responsible for framing him on *Hollywood Off Beat* (Syn/DuMont/CBS).

1954. Matthew Considine (Edward G. Robinson) is a former police captain turned criminal defense lawyer on the pilot *For the Defense*. Reed Hadley plays Bart Matthews, a public defender of indigent people on CBS's *Public Defender*. Gary Merrill and William Prince are Walter and Peter Guilfoyle, brothers who are also New York based lawyers on *The Mask* (ABC). June Havoc plays Willy Dodger, TV's first female attorney, who works out of her hometown of Renfrew, New Hampshire, on CBS's *Willy*.

1955. CBS revises the concept of its 1954 series *Willy* with Willy Dodger (June Havoc) as the legal counsel for the Bannister Vaudeville Company in New York City.

1956. Zachary Scott plays Reno English, a barrister with a knack for winning cases (called "the magical touch") on the ABC pilot *Reno English*.

1957. Bentley Gregg (John Forsythe) is a suave and sophisticated Beverly Hills lawyer on *Bachelor Father* (CBS/NBC/ABC). Attorney Erle Stanley Gardner (Paul Birch) and detective Sam Larsen (Lyle Bettger) team to solve crimes on NBC's *The Court of Last Resort*. Raymond Burr plays Perry Mason, the shrewd criminal attorney on CBS's *Perry Mason*. Tom Brewster (Will Hutchins) is a student of law who wanders across the frontier of the 1860s helping people on ABC's *Sugarfoot*.

1958. Elfego Baca (Robert Loggia) is a sheriff (the man who was said to have nine lives) turned lawyer in Socorro County, New Mexico, 1880s, on *Elfego Baca* (ABC). Dan Garrett (Darren McGavin) is a young lawyer who battles crime through the legal system on the NBC pilot *Man Against Crime*. Walter Brennan plays Mr. Tutt, a respected small town New York State lawyer on the NBC pilot *Mr. Tutt*.

1959. Clay Culhane (Peter Breck) is gunfighter turned lawyer who practices out of Latigo, New Mexico, on ABC's *Black Saddle*. Herbert L. Maris (Macdonald Carey) is a Philadelphia based lawyer who defends unjustly accused people on the syndicated *Lock Up*. Ray Milland plays Ray Markham, a Los Angeles based criminal attorney on CBS's *Markham*.

1960. The father and son legal team of James Harrigan, Sr. and James Harrigan, Jr. (Pat O'Brien, Roger Perry) defend clients on ABC's *Harrigan and Son*. Abraham Lincoln Jones (James Whitmore) is a tough but honest criminal attorney working out of New York City on ABC's *The Law and Mr. Jones*. Torin O'Connor (John Payne) is a yachtsman and lawyer for a marine firm who tackles cases involving crimes on the high seas on the NBC pilot *O'Connor's Ocean*. DeForest Kelley plays Jake Brittin, a criminal attorney who resides at 333 Montgomery in San Francisco on the NBC pilot *333 Montgomery*.

1961. The father and son legal team of Lawrence and Kenneth Preston (E.G. Marshall, Robert Reed) defend clients in New York City on CBS's *The Defenders*. In the 1957 pilot, *The Defender*, Ralph Bellamy and William Shatner are father and son lawyers Walter and Kenneth Pearson.

1962. Barry Morse plays Max McIntyre, a famous criminal attorney working out of San Francisco on the ABC pilot *All My Clients Are Innocent*.

Edmond O'Brien is a defense attorney working out of San Francisco on NBC's *Sam Benedict*.

1963. Chuck Connors plays John Egan, a defense counselor on ABC's *Arrest and Trial*. Keith Granville (Keith Andes) is a criminal attorney who is married to Glynis (Glynis Johns), a woman who loves to solve crimes on CBS's *Glynis*. Jeffrey Hunter plays Temple Houston, a circuit-riding attorney of the Old West on NBC's *Temple Houston*.

1964. The eccentric Gomez Addams (John Astin) is a defense lawyer who is responsible for putting more men behind bars than any other lawyer in the U.S. on ABC's *The Addams Family*.

1965. Jarrod Barkley (Richard Long), the eldest son of ranch owner Victoria Barkley, is a lawyer (1860s) with offices in Stockton, California, and San Francisco on ABC's *The Big Valley*. Peter Falk plays Daniel J. O'Brien, an untidy and disorganized criminal attorney working out of New York City on CBS's *The Trials of O'Brien*.

1966. Patricia and Paul Marshall (Jean Arthur, Ron Harper) are a mother and son team of legal eagles on CBS's *The Jean Arthur Show*.

1967. A British trail-riding barrister known only as Dundee (John Mills) and his partner, the Culhane (Sean Garrison), defend people in the Old West on *Dundee and the Culhane* (CBS). Carl Betz is Clinton Judd, a free-wheeling Texas-based defense lawyer on ABC's *Judd for the Defense*.

1968. Liz and John Higher (Sally Kellerman, John McMartin) are a married team of defense lawyers who do their own investigative work on the CBS pilot *Higher and Higher, Attorneys at Law*.

1969. Burl Ives plays Walter Nichols, a prestigious Los Angeles attorney on *The Bold Ones: The Lawyers* (NBC). Joseph Campanella and James Farentino play his protégés, brothers Brian and Neil Darrell.

1970. David Henson (Robert Foxworth) and Deborah Sullivan (Sheila Larken) are lawyers with the Neighborhood Legal Services in Los Angeles on CBS's *The Storefront Lawyers* (later titled *Men at Law*). Aaron Silverman and Pat Walters (Zalman King, Judy Pace) are Berkel University law students who work part time at the Boston-based Legal Aid Service (The Neighborhood Law Office) on ABC's *The Young Lawyers*.

1971. Arthur Hill plays Owen Marshall, a Santa Barbara-based criminal attorney on ABC's *Owen Marshall, Counselor at Law*.

1972. Jessica Fitzgerald (Susan Hayward) is a prominent Los Angeles attorney who tackles controversial cases on the CBS pilot *Heat of Anger*. Paul Simms (Paul Lynde) is a lawyer plagued by life's endless problems on ABC's *The Paul Lynde Show*.

1973. Amanda Bonner (Blythe Danner) is a prosecuting attorney with the Los Angeles firm of Kipple, Kipple and Smith who is married to Assistant D.A. Adam Bonner (Ken Howard) on ABC's *Adam's Rib*. Ben Sikes (John Ritter) is a recent law school graduate who is just beginning his law practice on the CBS pilot *Bachelor at Law*. James Stewart plays Billy Jim Hawkins, a shrewd criminal attorney working out of West Virginia on *Hawkins* (CBS). Monte Markham plays the brilliant criminal attorney Perry Mason on *The New Perry Mason* (CBS; see 1957). Zach Clinton (Tim O'Connor) is a doctor turned attorney who solves cases involving the medical field on the ABC pilot *Rx for the Defense*.

1974. Tony Petrocelli (Barry Newman) is a Harvard-educated attorney working out of San Remo, a Southwestern cattle town, on NBC's *Petrocelli*.

1975. Anne Meara plays Kate McShane, an uninhibited and unorthodox lawyer working out of Los Angeles on CBS's *Kate McShane*. Claire Kronski (Laraine Stephens) is a private practice attorney who works with Matt Helm (Anthony Franciosa), a private detective who calls her "the most honest lawyer who ever lived, but one of the sneakiest people I have ever known," on ABC's *Matt Helm*.

1976. Doug Lawrence (James Broderick) is a private practice attorney working out of Pasadena, California, on ABC's *Family*. John Hazzard (John Houseman) is a renowned criminal attorney whose style and flair sets him apart from his peers on the CBS pilot *Hazzard's People*. Julius V. Hickey (Jack Weston) is an unorthodox lawyer who will take any case in which there is money to be made on the NBC pilot *Hickey vs. Anybody*. Allen Burnett (Joel Fabiani) is a lawyer who uses ex con Joe Risko (Gabriel Dell) as his legman on the CBS pilot *Risko*. NBC's *Sirota's Court* features Kathleen Miller as public defender Gail Goodman and Ted Ross as defense attorney Sawyer Dabney.

1977. Janet McCarther (Joan Prather), the girlfriend of David Bradford, is a lawyer with the firm of Goodman, Saxon and Tweedy on ABC's *Eight Is Enough*. Stefanie Powers plays Toni "Feather"

Danton, a lawyer with the Los Angeles firm of Huffaker, Danton and Binkwell, on ABC's *The Feather and Father Gang*. Joseph Rosetti (Tony Roberts) and Frank Ryan (Squire Fridell) are girl chasing criminal attorneys in Los Angeles on NBC's *Rosetti and Ryan*.

1978. Eddie Capra (Vincent Baggetta) is an attorney with the Los Angeles firm of Devlin, Linkman and O'Brien, who does things his own way on *The Eddie Capra Mysteries* (NBC). John Houseman plays Professor Charles Kingsfield, Jr., a brilliant contract lawyer who now teaches aspiring law students at a Northwestern university on CBS's *The Paper Chase*. John Houseman would repeat his character on Showtime's *The Paper Chase: The Second Year* (1983), *The Paper Chase: The Third Year* (1985) and *The Paper Chase: The Graduation Year* (1986).

1979. Sara James (Shelley Smith), Tucker Kerwin (Martin Short) and Leslie Dunn (Ally Mills) are members of the legal staff of the Bass and Marshall Law Offices in New York on ABC's *The Associates*.

1980. David Ross (Harold Gould) and Jo Keene (Mary Elaine Monti) are lawyers with the Legal Assistance Bureau in New York City on CBS's *Park Place*.

1982. Elizabeth Farrell (Valerie Harper) is a prosecutor for the Manhattan D.A.'s office who has set her goal to become the D.A. on the NBC pilot *Farrell: For the People*.

1983. Martin Barry and Grace Harmon (Wilford Brimley, Anne Twomey) are a father and daughter criminal law team based in New York City on the NBC pilot *The Firm*. Ben Walker (Ralph Waite) is a lawyer who lives on a tugboat (*The Mississippi*) and helps the people who live by the river on CBS's *The Mississippi*.

1985. Geena Davis plays Sara McKenna, an idealistic attorney working for the Bay Area Legal Group (later Cooper and Associates) in San Francisco on NBC's *Sara*.

1986. Michael Kuzak (Harry Hamlin), Arnold Becker (Corbin Bernsen), Ann Kelsey (Jill Eikenberry), Abby Perkins (Michele Greene) and Douglas Brackman, Jr. (Alan Rachins) head a large cast of lawyers at the Los Angeles firm of McKenzie, Brackman, Chavey and Kuzak on NBC's *L.A. Law*. Christine Sullivan (Markie Post) is the prosecuting attorney and Dan Fielding (John Larroquette) the defense attorney on NBC's *Night Court*. Ben Matlock (Andy Griffith) is an Atlanta based attorney whose high fees ($100,000 a case) also mean successful defenses on *Matlock* (NBC/ABC). Ben first worked with his daughter Charlene Matlock (Linda Purl) then attorney Michelle Thomas (Nancy Stafford). He was most often pitted against Julie March (Julie Sommars), the prosecuting attorney for the D.A.'s office.

1987. Mickey Travis (Ted Wass) is a former CIA agent turned lawyer whose past always comes back to haunt him on the CBS pilot *Mickey and Nora* (Barbara Truetelaar plays his wife Nora).

1988. Bud Lutz, Jr. (Scott Bakula) is a graduate of the Las Vegas School of Law and Acupuncture who opens a law office in Palm Springs with a fake partner (to give the firm class) on CBS's *Eisenhower and Lutz*. Amanda Taler (Alex Amini) is a tough criminal attorney on the syndicated *T&T*.

1989. Jaclyn Smith plays Christine Cromwell, a lawyer with the San Francisco firm of Blair and Knapp, who solves crimes of the rich and famous on ABC's *Christine Cromwell*. Ving Rhames plays Charles Hazard, a Baltimore based criminal attorney on ABC's *Men*.

1990. Unorthodox Boston attorney Simon McHeath (Michael O'Keefe) does what is necessary to win a case on Fox's *Against the Law*. Claudia Reese (Joanna Cassidy) and Melanie Rosten (Marcy Walker) are bickering attorneys who open their own law firm (Reese and Rosten) on the CBS pilot *Bar Girls*. Ava Newton (Marilu Henner), the wife of high school coach Wood Newton (Burt Reynolds) is the town of Evening Shade's (Arkansas) first female prosecuting attorney on CBS's *Evening Shade*. Victoria Heller (Laila Robbins) is a dedicated attorney who will fight for any cause she believes in on ABC's *Gabriel's Fire*. Lesley Ann Warren plays Lola Baltic, a Connecticut based attorney who struggles to divide her time between a family, a home and a job on the CBS pilot *Lola*. Elizabeth Meyers (Bess Armstrong) is a Yale Law School graduate who works for the Manhattan firm of Michaelson & Michaelson on ABC's *Married People*. John Francis Shannon (Jamey Sheridan) is a former corporate lawyer turned independent criminal lawyer who is divorced, addicted to gambling and in serious debt to bookies on NBC's *Shannon's Deal*. Fiona Rose O'Neill, called Rosie (Sharon Gless), is a lawyer with the Central Felonies Division of the Los Angeles County

Public Defender's Office on CBS's *The Trials of Rosie O'Neill*.

1991. Sydney Guilford (Mariel Hemingway) is a gorgeous divorce lawyer and senior partner in the firm of Guilford, Levinson and Howell in New York City on ABC's *Civil Wars*. Eddie Dodd (Treat Williams) is a tough defense attorney who tackles the cases nobody else wants on ABC's *Eddie Dodd*. Althea Jones (Christine Ebersole) is a lawyer who tackles the cases of sports figures on the ABC pilot *Miss Jones*. Thelma Todd Fagori (Teri Hatcher) is a beautiful 30-year-old environmental lawyer who believes she has a direct line to God (whom she calls "Chief") on *Sunday Dinner* (CBS).

1994. Carrie Grace Battle (Cicely Tyson) and her young protégé Kate Delacroy (Melissa Gilbert) are lawyers who tackle controversial cases on NBC's *Sweet Justice*.

1995. Steve Landesberg plays Steve Best, a deputy public defender with the Seattle Public Defender's Office on the ABC pilot *The Best Defense*. Lou Frischetti (Michael Rispoli) is a fast talking Boston lawyer who represents clients from hookers to bookies on *The Great Defender* (Fox). Jake Lassiter (Gerald McRaney) is a former football player turned New Orleans lawyer who handles controversial cases on the NBC pilot *Jake Lassiter: Justice on the Bayou*. Alicia Sundergard (Maria Pitillo) is the only female partner in a law firm she calls "White, Saxonhouse and the one with breasts" on Fox's *Partners*. Tom Amandes plays Steve Rutledge, a good-natured Chicago attorney on NBC's *The Pursuit of Happiness*. British barrister Charles Wright (Tom Conti) is a respected member of the legal community who uses outrageous antics to achieve his goals on *The Wright Verdicts*.

1997. Ally McBeal (Calista Flockhart) is a young, intelligent and beautiful (but very thin) lawyer with the Boston firm of Cage and Fish on *Ally McBeal* (Fox). Other members of the law firm include John Cage (Peter MacNichol), Elaine Vassal (Jane Krakowski), Richard Fish (Greg Germann), Georgia Thomas (Courtney Thorne-Smith) and Ling Woo (Lucy Liu). Greg Montgomery (Thomas Gibson) is first a lawyer for the Justice Department, then a private practice attorney in San Francisco on ABC's *Dharma and Greg* (the title refers to Greg's wife Dharma, played by Jenna Elfman). Diane Szlinski (Barbara Alyn Woods) is married to a research scientist and works as a lawyer with the firm of Coleman and Associates in Colorado on the syndicated *Honey I Shrunk the Kids: The TV Series*. Jimmy Berluti (Michael Badalucco), Ellenor Frutt (Camryn Manheim), Eugene Young (Steve Harris) and Jamie Stringer (Jessica Capshaw) are among the Boston-based lawyers on ABC's *The Practice*.

1998. Will Truman (Eric McCormack) is a gay lawyer who lives with a straight woman, Grace (Debra Messing), on NBC's *Will and Grace*.

1999. Randi King (Dixie Carter), Rex Weller (Christopher McDonald) and Patricia Dumar (Merrilee McCommas) are attorneys who tackle cases in the field of family law on CBS's *Family Law*. John Ducey plays Ford Vandemer, a lawyer with the firm of Tattleman and Keeler on ABC's *Oh Grow Up*.

2000. Ed Stevens (Tom Cavanaugh) is a lawyer who operates from a former bowling alley in the small town of Stuckyville on NBC's *Ed*. Tracee Ellis Ross plays Joan Clayton, an intelligent, sophisticated and dedicated lawyer on the first four seasons of UPN's *Girlfriends* (she quit over a dispute and later opened her own restaurant, the J-Spot). Nick Fallin (Simon Baker) is a lawyer, arrested for possession of drugs, who is fined and ordered to serve 1500 hours' community service as a lawyer for children at the Children's Legal Services on CBS's *The Guardian*. Kathleen Maguire (Kim Delaney) is a middle-aged divorcée who begins practicing criminal law at a small Philadelphia firm on ABC's *Philly*.

2002. Lynne Camden (Gretchen Mol), Jeannie Falls (Kathleen Robertson) and Sarah Mickle (Chyler Leigh) are friends who graduated Stanford Law School and now work in the San Francisco law firm of Berry, Cherry and Fitch, LLD on Fox's *Girls Club*. Hamilton Whitney (Richard Thomas) is a dedicated lawyer and a senior partner in the prestigious San Francisco law firm of Burdick, Whitney and Morgan on *Just Cause* (PAX).

2003. Scott Foley plays Adam Sullivan, an assistant U.S. attorney based in New York on NBC's *A.U.S.A.*

2004. Denny Crane (William Shatner), Paul Lewiston (Rene Auberjonois), Shirley Schmitt (Candice Bergen) and Alan Shore (James Spader) are among the lawyers at Boston's Crane, Poole and Schmitt law firm on ABC's *Boston Legal*. Taye Diggs plays Kevin Hill, a 28-year-old self-made, hot shot New York entertainment lawyer on UPN's *Kevin Hill*.

2005. A look at the justice system in action is seen through the eyes of Annabeth Chase (Jennifer Finnigan), a young wife and mother who is also a prosecuting attorney on *Close to Home* (CBS). Leslie Towne (Laura Leighton) is a slick Los Angeles attorney with the firm of Sacco, Kemper and Pratt on ABC's *Eyes*. Don Johnson plays Grant Cooper, a once great lawyer who has fallen on hard times, and Jay Baruchel is David "Skip" Ross, an enthusiastic young lawyer who joins Grant to help clients on the WB's *Just Legal*.

2006. Brianna Brown (Constance Zimmer), David Swayne (Kyle MacLachlan), Charles Conti (Jason O'Mara) and Sonya Quintano (Marisol Nichols) are lawyers with the National Justice Project (defend people with no where else to turn) on *Injustice* (ABC).

Lesbians

This entry chronicles the programs on which a lesbian character is the star or a featured regular. Also included are the historic lesbian kisses that have occurred on TV from 1977 to 2005.

1955. NBC airs a program called *So This Is Hollywood*. Kim Tracy (Virginia Gibson) and Queenie Dugan (Mitzi Green) are roommates who share a small apartment in Hollywood. They are also seen sleeping in the same bed. This is quite rare as two adults in the same bed was taboo at the time. The characters, however, are not lesbians.

1976. Pamela Bellwood plays Amy and Frances Lee McCain is her lover, Jenny, on the PBS drama, *The War Widow*.

1977. While not lesbians, the first lip kiss between two girls appeared on ABC's *Laverne and Shirley* in the episode "Airport '59" (September 20th). Laverne (Penny Marshall) kisses Shirley (Cindy Williams) full on the lips when they are aboard a plane (which Shirley is piloting) and Laverne believes they are not going to make it. After the kiss Shirley turns to Laverne to say, "We'll have to talk about that." Gloria DeHaven plays Annie Wylie, TV's first lesbian character on the syndicated *Mary Hartman, Mary Hartman*. Annie was a resident of the small town of Fernwood, Ohio, and had the nickname "Tippytoes." Randee Heller plays Alice, a lesbian on ABC's satire *Soap*.

1978. Elizabeth Montgomery and Jane Seymour play Sayward and Genny Luckett, sisters who lip kiss to experience a kiss on *The Awakening Land* (NBC).

1980. Carol Burns plays Franky Doyle, a woman sentenced to life at the Wentworth Women's Detention Center in Australia, for murder and robbery on the syndicated *Prisoner: Cell Block H.* Franky is a lesbian with eyes for straight fellow inmate Karen Travers (Peita Toppano).

1983. Donna Pescow plays Lynn Carson, a lesbian doctor on the ABC soap opera *All My Children.*

1986. Michele Greene and Amanda Donohoe play attorneys Abby Perkins and C.J. Lamb on NBC's *L.A. Law.* The women are also lesbians. In 1991 they shared a prolonged kissing scene in a parking lot that became TV's first lesbian kiss. Elizabeth Kemp also played a lesbian, C.J.'s ex lover, Maggie.

1987. Antoinette Byron plays Bonnie Harper, a coquettish lesbian (arrested for soliciting) and serving time at the Bass Women's Prison in Wisconsin on Fox's *Women in Prison.* Bonnie has eyes for straight inmate Vicki Springer (Julia Campbell).

1988. Gail Strickland plays Marilyn McGrath, a lesbian doctor who is in love with a girl named Patty (Gina Hecht) on ABC's *Heart Beat.* Although Wanda Cannon and Marsha Moreau play mother and daughter (Stephanie and Erin), they share a camera close up lip kiss on the syndicated *My Secret Identity. Roseanne* premieres on ABC. In 1992, Nancy (Sara Bernhard), the friend of Roseanne's sister Jackie, reveals that she is a lesbian (her lover is Marla [Morgan Fairchild], a cosmetics salesgirl at Rodbell's Department Store in Lanford, Ohio. They frequent the lesbian bar Lips). In 1995, Roseanne's mother, Beverly (Estelle Parsons) announces she has found a female lover — Joyce Levine (Ruta Lee), a famous lounge singer. It was also at this time that Sharon (Mariel Hemingway), a lesbian Nancy once dated, took a fancy to Roseanne and the two kissed.

1990. Christine Belford plays Samantha Sanders, Steve's lesbian mother on *Beverly Hills, 90210* (Fox). In 1994 on this series, Sara Melson portrays the lesbian character Allison Lash. CBS's *Northern Exposure* is set in the small town of Cicely, Alaska. It was revealed that two lesbians, Rosalyn (Jo Anderson) and Cicely (Yvonne Suher), founded the town. Although not a lesbian, Elaine Benes (Julia Louis-Dreyfus) was

"best man" at a lesbian wedding on NBC's *Seinfeld.* Her friend, George Costanza (Jason Alexander) had dated Susan Ross (Heidi Swedeberg). When they broke up she turned to women (she eventually went back to George and gave up her lesbian lover, Mona [Viveca Davis]).

1991. While she does not admit to being bisexual, Heddy Newman (Jane Sibbett) let it slip that she once made love to another woman on Fox's *Herman's Head.*

1992. On CBS's *Hearts Afire*, Diandra, the wife of senatorial aide John Hartman (John Ritter) left him for her female lover, Ruth.

1993. Meredith Baxter plays Paula and Joanna Cassidy is Linda, the lesbian mothers of Will (Justin Whalin), a high school student on "Other Mothers," a segment of *The CBS Schoolbreak Special.* Sixteen-year-old Kimberly Brock (Holly Marie Combs) and her girlfriend Lisa Fenn (Alexondra Lee) erotically kiss when they each wonder what it would be like to kiss another girl on CBS's *Picket Fences.* Nora Dunn plays Norma Lear, a lesbian friend of the Reid sisters on NBC's *Sisters.*

1994. Ellen DeGeneres plays Ellen Morgan, a bookstore owner on ABC's *These Friends of Mine.* When the titled switched to *Ellen*, Ellen declared that she was a lesbian. She shared her first kiss with her best friend Paige Clark (Joely Fisher) and in 1997 she and guest star Lisa Darr (as Laurie) kiss. The lesbian characters of Drs. Maggie Doyle (Jorja Fox) and Carrie Weaver (Laura Innes) and psychiatrist Kim Legaspi (Elizabeth Mitchell) are introduced on NBC's *ER.* In 2000 Carrie and Kim share a kiss. On NBC's *Friends*, it is revealed that Carol (Anita Baron, Jane Sibbett) left her husband Ross (David Schwimmer) for her lesbian lover Susan Bunch (Jessica Hecht). Two years later, Susan and Carol are married in prime time TV's first lesbian wedding. In 2001 (on *Friends*), Rachel (Jennifer Aniston) kisses her sorority sister, Melissa (Winona Ryder) to prove to her friend Phoebe (Lisa Kudrow) that they did kiss once before in college. Later, in the episode "The One with Rachel's Big Kiss," Phoebe surprises Rachel with a kiss — "To see what all the fuss is about." She then adds, "I've had better" (but never reveals the name of the girl). In last season episodes of *Friends* it is apparent that Phoebe is sexually attracted to Monica, especially when she says, "Monica has the breasts of a Greek goddess." Paige Turco plays Abby Sullivan, a lesbian police officer on ABC's *N.Y.P.D. Blue*. Also on the series, Detective Andrea Lesnick (Justine Micelli) has doubts about her sexuality and fantasizes about making love to another woman.

1995. Jenifer Lewis is Rosetta Reide, TV's first African-American lesbian on CBS's *Courthouse*. Alyssa Milano and Sarah Strange share a passionate kiss as Hannah and Lisa on the "Caught in the Act" episode of *The Outer Limits* (USA). Paige Turco is Abby Sullivan, a lesbian police officer on ABC's *N.Y.P.D. Blue*. Lesbians Rhonda (Lisa Edelstein) and Suzanne (Kristin Datillo) kiss on ABC's *Relativity*. Terry Farrell as Jadzi Dax shares a kiss with guest star Suzanne Thompson (as Lenora) on the syndicated *Star Trek: Deep Space Nine*. Also on this series, Nana Visitor (as Kira Nerys) and Nicole de Boer (as Ezra Dax) kiss. Stephanie Hodge plays Jennie Malloy, a housewife and mother on the WB's *Unhappily Ever After*. When Stephanie wanted to leave the series in 1998, her character left husband Jack to be with her lesbian lover (although Jack claims she was abducted by aliens). *Xena: Warrior Princess* premieres in syndication. Xena (Lucy Lawless) and her traveling companion Gabrielle (Renee O'Connor) are beautiful warriors who shared a close relationship as they battled evil. They kissed on several occasions but it was only hinted that they were lesbians.

1996. Susan Gibney and Felicity Huffman play Liz and Donna, a lesbian couple on Showtime's adult series *Bedtime*. Debbie Buchman (Robin Bartlett), the sister of filmmaker Paul Buchman, reveals she is a lesbian and had been dating Dr. Joan Golfinos (Suzie Plakson) on NBC's *Mad About You*. Jeri Ryan is Valerie Madison, the lesbian resident of Fox's *Melrose Place*.

1997. Calista Flockhart plays Boston lawyer Ally McBeal on Fox's *Ally McBeal*. While Ally is not a lesbian she believes other women are attracted to her. She is troubled by erotic gay dreams and she did share three passionate kisses with other women over the course of the series, all her co-workers: Georgia Thomas (Courtney Thorne-Smith), Elaine Vassal (Jane Krakowski) and Ling Woo (Lucy Liu). Willow Rosenberg (Alyson Hannigan) is a witch who battles evil on *Buffy the Vampire Slayer* (WB/UPN). As the series progressed, Willow revealed she was a lesbian and bonded with (and kissed) Tara (Amber Benson), a lesbian who is also a witch. In a later episode Willow shares a kiss with Kennedy (Iyari Limon).

Nina Van Horne (Wendie Malick) is a former super model turned magazine fashion editor on NBC's *Just Shoot Me*. She confessed that in the past she made love to another woman but is not a lesbian. Stacy Bridges (Angela Dohrman), the sister of *Nash Bridges* (CBS), is an assistant D.A. who became attracted to other women and bonds with and kisses Samantha (Tamara Mark).

1998. On USA's *La Femme Nikita*, the seemingly heartless killer Nikita (Peta Wilson), finds a brief attraction to Jenna (Gina Torres) and kisses her. Megan Mullally plays Karen Walker, the rich and snobbish straight friend of gays Will Truman and Jack McFarland on NBC's *Will and Grace*. Karen is also a friend of Grace Adler (Debra Messing), her straight friend with whom she shared a kiss (in 2002). In a 2001 episode Karen revealed that she was once in love with tennis star Martina Navratilova. Based on dialogue, Martina was straight until she met Karen (who never admitted to being a lesbian). Karen and Martina had planned to marry but Karen broke it off—"I've found someone else" (the someone else was most likely her second husband, the wealthy but grossly overweight Stan Walker). Although it is assumed Karen made love to Martina (she never actually says it) she does admit in a later episode that she is attracted to beautiful women and did experiment with making love to another girl. She smiles but never reveals whether she liked it or not. As for Grace, she reveals that although she is not a lesbian, she did make love to another woman — "But it wasn't my thing." On *Sex and the City* (HBO) Samantha Jones (Kim Cattrall) experimented with making love to another girl but gave her up when she couldn't handle the commitment and intimacy her lover wanted.

1999. Soleil Moon Frye plays Robin Carlucci, the lesbian roommate of Internet entrepreneur Calvin Frazer (Jaleel White) on UPN's *Grownups*. Julia Salinger (Neve Campbell), the eldest daughter on Fox's *Party of Five*, begins to question her sexuality when she becomes fascinated with an older woman (Perry) at college. Julia and Perry (Olivia D'Abo) begin a relationship and kiss. Ally Mills plays Robin, the lesbian mother of high school student Harrison John on *Popular* (WB). Azure Skye plays Jane Cooper, a girl who studies other girls to see what makes them sexy on the WB's *Zoe, Duncan, Jack and Jane*. While Jane is not an admitted lesbian, she does have deep feelings for her friend Zoe (Selma Blair) and becomes extremely jealous if Zoe befriends another girl.

2000. On CBS's *Bette*, Bette (Bette Midler) reveals that she made love to another woman, "But that was in college." She never revealed whether she enjoyed it or not. On Fox's *Dark Angel*, the characters of Cindy (Valerie Rae Miller) and Diamond (Tansele Rouse) share a kiss. Lesbians Melanie Marcus (Michelle Clunie) and Lindsay Peterson (Thea Gill) share kisses on Showtime's *Queer as Folk*. Although Sarah Jessica Parker refuses to do a nude scene on HBO's *Sex and the City*, her character, Carrie, shares an erotic kiss with Dawn (Alanis Moressette). Also on the series, Samantha (Kim Cattrell), who does nude scenes, shares a kiss with Maria (Sonja Bragen). A girl identified only as "the red-headed woman" (Colleen Azar) and Carol (Carol Baker) share a kiss on Fox's *The X-Files*.

2001. Ellen DeGeneres plays Ellen Richardson, a lesbian high school counselor on CBS's *The Ellen Show*. Also, Diane Delano plays the school's lesbian gym teacher, Bunny Hofstedder (although there is no affection shown between the two). Marcy (Lindsay Sloane) passionately kisses guest star Sarah Michelle Gellar on the WB's *Grosse Pointe*. LaTanya Richardson is Attalla "Queenie" Sims, a lesbian judge on *100 Center Street* (A&E). Caitlin (Heather Locklear) lets loose and kisses Jennifer (Denise Richards) to see what it feels like on ABC's *Spin City*. On Fox's suspenseful *24*, the tension is eased when Mandy (Mia Kirshner) and Bridget (Kim Murphy) kiss.

2002. Tiffani-Amber Thiessen plays Billie Chambers, a gorgeous lieutenant with the L.A.P.D. on Fox's *Fastlane*. In an attempt to infiltrate a female gang, Billie pretends to be a lesbian and shares a prolonged and passionate kiss with gang member Jaime Pressly. On ABC's *Less Than Perfect* supply room worker Owen Kronsky (Andy Dick) mentions that his two mothers are lesbians. Jessica (Rachel Ward) and Katie (Mischa Barton) are a lesbian couple (who also kiss) on ABC's *Once and Again*. The Fox comedy *That 80s Show* features a girl-girl kiss between Sophie (Brittany Daniel) and Katie (Tinsley Grimes). Jaime Pressly receives another kiss, this time from Tiffany Knight on the "Sensuous Cindy" episode of UPN's *The Twilight Zone*. Sonja Sohn is lesbian narcotics cop Shakima Greggs on *The Wire* (HBO).

2003. Sabrina (Rebecca DeMorney) and Catherine (Vanessa Williams) kiss on NBC's *Boomtown*. On HBO's *Carnivale*, Sophie (Clea Duvalle) and Libby (Carla Gallo) share a kiss. Lindsay Price is Jane, TV's first Asian-American bi-sexual female on the NBC comedy *Coupling*. Guest stars Melissa George (Molly) and Carly Thomas (Tabitha) share a kiss on NBC's *Friends*. Maggie (Mary McCormack) and Gail (Talia Balsam) are lesbian lovers on HBO's *K Street*. The *MTV Music Awards Show* airs on August 28th. During a dance number in which Madonna plays a sexy "groom" she first French kisses Britney Spears then Christina Aguilera. *Nip/Tuck* (FX) features kisses between Vanessa (Kate Mara) and Ridley (Sophia Bush) and Julia (Joely Richardson) and Ava (Famke Janssen). Also on the series, Roma Maffia plays Liz Cruz, a lesbian doctor. Eva (Terri J. Vaughn) and Bird (Malinda Williams) kiss on Showtime's *Soul Food*.

2004. The lesbian couple Maggie (Elizabeth Hendrickson) and Bianca (Eden Riegel) kiss on ABC's *All My Children*. Yale college student Rory Gilmore (Alexis Bledel) is a bit stunned when her friend Paris Geller (Liza Weil) kisses her on the lips to see what it feels like to kiss another girl on the WB's *Gilmore Girls*. Gina (Emilie de Raven) and Heather (Lola Glaudini) kiss on CBS's *The Handler*. Although they play sisters, Faith (Kelly Ripa) kisses Hope (Faith Ford) full on the lips on ABC's *Hope and Faith*. Faith also reveals that in high school she tested the waters and made love to fellow classmate Mandi Radner (Jenny McCarthy). Neither became lesbians. Courtney (Jessica Pare) and Katie (Kate Mara) kiss on the WB's *Jack and Bobby*. Showtime airs *The L-Word*, the first series about lesbians — their world and their lives. Mia Kirshner plays Jenny, a woman who is torn between her love for café owner Marina (Karina Lombard) and her boyfriend Tim (Eric Mabius). Kit (Pam Grier) is a musician; Dana (Erin Daniels), a tennis pro; Bette (Jennifer Beals), an art curator; Alice (Leisha Harley), a journalist; and Shane (Katherine Moennig), a hair stylist. The *L* stands for both love and lesbian and there are numerous kissing sequences. Charlene (Kristan Kalmus) and Erika (Makila Domiczky) kiss on Fox's *The North Shore* (in the pilot episode Carl [Brittany Daniel], a lesbian, is seen kissing an unnamed girl). Also on Fox, *The O.C.* features the lesbian couple of Marissa (Misha Barton) and Alex (Olivia Wilde). Over at the WB, Anna (Daniella Alonso) is bisexual; and Peyton (Hilarie Burton) and Brooke (Sophia Bush) are the lesbian couple that kiss to entice viewers on *One Tree Hill*. Sadie (Wendie Malick) is a lesbian sports agent who becomes attracted to Reba (Reba McEntire) on the WB's *Reba*. Edie (Mena Suvari) and Claire (Lauren Ambrose) kiss on HBO's *Six Feet Under*. Justine Bateman and Julia Campbell play Terry and Shelley, a married lesbian couple who are the neighbors of Bill and Judy Miller on CBS's *Still Standing*. Christine Dunford plays Lea, Holly Tyler's (Amanda Bynes) lesbian boss on *What I Like About You* (WB). Jenny McCarthy plays Lea's lover, Michelle. On Fox's *Wonderfalls*, Karen Tyler (Katie Finneran) is an immigration lawyer with Merifield, Harrison and Eldridge who is also a lesbian.

2005. Super model Janice Dickinson gives super model Tyra Banks an erotic kiss to demonstrate passion to the female contestants on *America's Next Top Model, Cycle 4* (UPN). Also on this series (Cycle 5) hopeful model Kim, a very pretty butch lesbian, shares a lip kiss with fellow straight contestant Sarah (last names of the girls are not given). A real life lesbian couple, Kit and Dot, appear on PBS's *Ask This Old House*, seeking help with a home improvement problem. The fifth season opener of UPN's *Girlfriends* reveals that Lynn Searcy (Persia White) may have lesbian tendencies. She pretended to be a lesbian to save a girl who was about to commit suicide. She lived with the girl, Jennifer (Rebecca Creskoff), and they planned to marry but Lynn broke it off. (Lynn appeared to enjoy the relationship but never admitted to making love with her.) Beth Littleford plays Carla, Joey Tribbiani's co-star (a lesbian) on his TV series "Deep Powder" on NBC's *Joey*. After a night of partying (including a visit to a lesbian club), Mary Connell (Nikki Cox) and Samantha Marquez (Vanessa Marcel), employees at the Montecito Hotel and Casino, wake up together in bed on NBC's *Las Vegas* (although it is never revealed if they made love). Also in this episode, hotel guest Nina St. James (Sharon Leil) and a girl identified only as "Pam, the butch lesbian," share a kiss. The October 13th episode of UPN's *Love, Inc.* ("Bosom Buddies") is an episode about lesbians but "all the good stuff is not seen." The story finds Love, Inc. employee Viviana (Ion Overman) escorting a lesbian client to a lesbian club. Although Viviana claims she is straight, she shares an off camera lip kiss with the girl (Jessa French) and exclaims, "I kissed a girl and I liked it." Also

in the episode, Viviana's friend, fellow employee Francine (Reagan Gomez Preston), mentions she "kissed a number of girls — but that was in college." Regina Barnes (Paula Marshall), the lesbian ER doctor on *Out of Practice* (CBS), shares a kiss with guest star Kristen Miller (as Sharon), a lesbian on the November 21 episode. Fifteen-year-old Penny (April Matson) kisses Carrie (Danica Stewart) during a school play on Fox's *Quintuplets*. On *Rome*, the HBO series set at the time of Caesar and Cleopatra, the characters of Servilla (Lindsay Duncan) and Octavia (Kerry Condon) perform an erotic lesbian love scene. Jenny McCarthy makes a guest appearance on the Pamela Anderson series *Stacked* (Fox) on November 16. The episode finds old friends Pamela and Jenny meeting again after many years. Each has had plastic surgery (breast implants) and in a rather unexpected scene, the girls feel (and jiggle) each other's breasts. Later on *Stacked*, Pamela's Skyler character, although straight, admits that she made love with other women — "I dabbled," she says. The passionate kiss shared by Tiffani-Amber Thiessen and Jaime Pressly on *Fastlane* (see 2002) is duplicated on *The Starlet* (WB). Each of the eight female contestants was paired off and had to perform a kissing scene as erotic as Tiffani and Jaime's.

2006. On the February 5 episode of ABC's *Grey's Anatomy* ("It's the End of the World"), a doctor fantasizes (and viewers see) three lesbians showering together. Fran (Fran Drescher) admits to kissing another girl when she was a teenager at summer camp on *Living with Fran* (WB).

Little People

Programs on which little people (sometimes referred to as dwarfs or midgets) are regulars or co-stars are the subjects of this entry (*The Wizard* on CBS in 1986 is the only series that starred a little person). Billy Barty and now Danny Woodburn are perhaps the most famous of these actors. This entry also contains the programs on which normal sized people play reduced height roles.

1951. Billy Barty is one of the sketch regulars on NBC's variety series *Ford Festival* (hosted by James Melton). Billy also appears as a regular in skits on NBC's *The Red Skelton Show*.

1956. Billy Barty plays Little Tom, a midget who travels with the one ring Champion Circus in the latter 19th century on *Circus Boy* (NBC/ABC).

1957. Billy Barty is a sketch regular on *Club Oasis*, an NBC variety series hosted by Spike Jones.

1958. Billy Barty plays Babby, a diminutive pool hustler who is also the snitch for private eye *Peter Gunn* (NBC episodes).

1959. An accidental exposure to a new type of rocket fuel reduces FBI agent Mel Hunter (Marshall Thompson) to a height of six inches on the syndicated *World of Giants*.

1964. Felix Silla plays Cousin Itt, a three-foot tall relative (covered with hair from head to toe) of Gomez Addams on ABC's *The Addams Family*.

1965. Michael Dunn plays Mr. Big, an evil dwarf who heads KAOS, an enemy organization bent on world domination on NBC's *Get Smart*. Michael Dunn also plays Dr. Miguelito Loveless, an evil dwarf who seeks to destroy the world on CBS's *The Wild Wild West*. In the 1979 TV movie pilot, *The Wild Wild West Revisited*, singer Paul Williams played Dr. Miguelito Loveless, Jr., a slightly taller version of his father who also seeks to rule the world.

1966. Tom, a U.S. Intelligence Maintenance Department janitor, is hit by a shrinking laser beam and recruited for the Tiny Human Underground Military Bureau to battle evil on the animated *Tom of T.H.U.M.B.*

1968. Four scientists (Jonathan Kidd, Erica Stone, Cosby Birdwell and the Guru) are reduced to microscopic size by the Combined Miniature Defense Force to battle germs on ABC's animated *Fantastic Voyage*. In a twist of fate, a solar turbulence propels a passenger plane (the *Spinthrift*) into a parallel world where the crew and passengers find themselves stranded and on the run from humans who are giants compared to their six inch height on ABC's *Land of the Giants*. Gary Conway, Heather Young and Deanna Lund head the cast. Angelo Muscat plays the Silent Butler, the dwarf servant to Number 6 on CBS's *The Prisoner*.

1971. Angelo Rossitto, Jerry Manning, Felix Silla and Hommy Stewart are among the little people who play living hats on ABC's *Lidsville*.

1973. Lennie Weinrib is the voice of Inch High, the world's smallest man, who works as a detective for the Finkerton Organization on the animated *Inch High, Private Eye* (NBC). Billy Barty and Patty Maloney play Mr. and Mrs. Stilts, dwarf circus performers with Charny's Great American Circus on the NBC pilot *Punch and Jody*. Billy Barty plays Sigmund Ooz, a sea monster that is disowned by his family for his inability to scare humans on NBC's *Sigmund and the Sea Monsters*.

1976. Angela Rossitto plays Little Mo, the shoeshine dwarf who is also the snitch for detective Tony Baretta on ABC's *Baretta*. Billy Barty appears in skits as a regular on the variety series *The Captain and Tennille* (ABC). Patty Maloney and Billy Barty play Sylvia and Lloyd, little people seeking work at the Talent Unlimited Theatrical Agency in Philadelphia on the CBS pilot *Don't Call Us*. Billy Barty plays Hugo, assistant to the mad Dr. Shrinker (who enjoys shrinking things with his inventions) on ABC's *Dr. Shrinker*.

1978. Billy Barty and Patty Maloney are regulars on NBC's variety series, *The Bay City Rollers Show*. Gary Coleman (a little person due to a kidney condition) plays Arnold Jackson, the adopted son of a Park Avenue millionaire on NBC's *Diff'rent Strokes*. The diminutive Herve Villechaize (three feet, 11 inches tall) plays Tattoo, assistant to the mysterious Mr. Roarke on ABC's *Fantasy Island*. Billy Barty plays Billy, one of several derelicts living at an inner city Los Angeles mission on the ABC pilot *Great Day*. Danny DeVito plays Louie DePalma, the nasty Sunshine Cab Company dispatcher on *Taxi* (ABC/NBC).

1979. Felix Silla plays Twiki, a three-foot tall silver robot who is the companion to William "Buck" Rogers, an astronaut propelled 500 years into the future on NBC's *Buck Rogers in the 25th Century*.

1981. Twin little people, Greg and John Rice play Ben and Beau Bernard, the landlords to TV show host Gloria Munday on ABC's *Foul Play*.

1982. Greg and John Rice host *That Quiz Show*, a syndicated game wherein players answer trivia related questions for prizes.

1983. Billy Barty plays Inch, the diminutive owner of the Shanty, a bar on the wharf on CBS's *Ace Crawford, Private Eye*. Emmanuel Lewis is Webster Long, a black child adopted by a white couple on ABC's *Webster*.

1984. Vincent Daniels (Daniel Frishman) is the diminutive D.A.'s office assistant who oversees prosecutor Dan Fielding's antics on NBC's *Night Court*.

1985. Joe Pesci is Rocky Nelson, a diminutive private detective with the Beverly Hills Patrol on NBC's *Half Nelson*.

1986. David Rappaport plays Simon McKay, a toy inventor who uses his genius to help the U.S. government solve complex cases on CBS's *The Wizard.*

1987. Luther (Cork Hubbert) is a little person who awakes to a new world in the 20th century when a spell put him, Snow White, Prince Charming and the evil Queen Lillian to sleep for 1,000 years on ABC's *The Charmings.*

1988. Nick Derringer (David Rappaport) is a diminutive private detective whose motto is "no case too small" on the ABC pilot *Nick Derringer, P.I.*

1990. Danny Woodburn plays Mickey Abbott, the easily exasperated friend of Cosmo Kramer on NBC's *Seinfeld.* Mickey is four feet tall and worked as a stand-in for child actors. He is the son of normal height parents and dates women of his own size and of normal height. ABC's *Twin Peaks* presents Michael J. Anderson as the Dream Dwarf, a mystic-like person who lived in a surreal world and spoke in an unnatural voice.

1991. When Charlie Hoover (Tim Matheson) turns 40 and he feels neglected, his tiny, pleasure-seeking alter ego, Hugh (Sam Kinison) appears to guide his life on Fox's *Charlie Hoover.*

1992. Zelda Rubinstein plays Ginny Weeden, the nosey switchboard operator to Sheriff Jimmy Brock in Rome, Wisconsin, on CBS's *Picket Fences.*

1993. Danny Woodburn plays Professor Fixel, a mad scientist who is trying to create the perfect being (but constantly fails) on the Fox pilot *Count De Clues Mystery Castle.* Diminutive detective Tom McCormick (Bill Morisette) helps Captain Mike Morgan of the Hawaiian Police Department solve crimes on the "Tropical Punch" segment of Fox's *Danger Theater.*

1997. Otli (Danny Woodburn) is an adventurer who travels with the mighty Conan the Barbarian protecting the weak from evil in an ancient time on the syndicated *Conan.*

1998. Elf Nanny (Niki Botelho) is a babysitter who cares for Wyatt, the son of witch Piper Halliwell on the WB's *Charmed.*

1999. Josh Ryan Evans plays Timothy, the "doll" of witch Tabitha Lennox (Juliet Mills) on NBC's *Passions.*

2000. Napoleon (Verne Troyer), France's diminutive leader, struggles to keep his sanity and capture the Daring Dragoon, a masked avenger who is seeking to keep the island of Pulau Pulau out of the hands of the French (1801) on the syndicated *Jack of All Trades.* Phil Fondacaro plays Roland, a dwarf Finder (locates lost things) then Equalizer (steals, then returns objects to make everything equal) on *Sabrina, the Teenage Witch* (ABC/WB; Roland also poses as Sabrina's cousin to conceal his warlock antics).

2001. Emily Resnick (Meredith Eaton) is a diminutive lawyer with the firm of Holt and Associates on CBS's *Family Law.* Aloma Wright plays Nurse Birdie and Joe Rose is Troy, a maintenance worker, both of whom are little people on NBC's *Scrubs.* Carl the Gnome (Danny Woodburn) is a dwarf con artist who helps detectives Kate Benson and Nicholas O'Malley dispose of Links (everything that is not man or beast) for the Chicago Police Department on UPN's *Special Unit 2.* Tiny Man (Kevin Thompson) is a diminutive super hero who lived in "The City" and battled crime on Fox's *The Tick.*

2004. Danny Woodburn plays Lyle Overbee, the four-foot-tall father of normal sized C.J. Barnes on ABC's *Eight Simple Rules* (Lyle had a one night stand with C.J.'s mother and abandoned her).

2005. Peter Dinklage plays Arthur Ramsey, a mathematician who is part of the government's Red Team, an agency that investigates UFO sightings on *Threshold* (CBS).

Lodges see *Clubs and Lodges*

London

A listing of series set in and around London, England.

1954. *Sherlock Holmes* (Syn.).

1955. *Inspector Fabian of Scotland Yard* (Syn.); *Scotland Yard* (Syn.).

1957. *Colonel March of Scotland Yard* (Syn.); *Dick and the Duchess* (CBS); *Saber of London* (Syn.); *Stryker of Scotland Yard* (NBC).

1958. *Dial 999* (Syn.); *The Invisible Man* (Syn.).

1960. *The Man from Interpol* (NBC); *The Third Man* (Syn.).

1961. *Danger Man* (CBS).

1962. *Fair Exchange* (CBS.

1963. *The Saint* (Syn./NBC).

1965. *Secret Agent* (CBS).

1966. *The Avengers* (ABC).

1968. *Man in a Suitcase* (ABC); *The Prisoner* (CBS); *The Ugliest Girl in Town* (ABC).

1970. *Here Come the Double Deckers* (ABC).

1971. *From a Bird's Eye View* (NBC); *Shirley's World* (ABC); *The Strange Report* (NBC).

1972. *U.F.O.* (Syn.).

1973. *My Partner the Ghost* (Syn.).

1978. *The New Avengers* (CBS).

1979. *Return of the Saint* (CBS).

1982. *Q.E.D.* (CBS).

1985. *Dempsey and Makepeace* (Syn.).

1990. *She Wolf of London* (Syn.).

2003. *Keen Eddie* (Fox).

Look-alikes

Characters on a series who look like each other — but are not twins — are the subjects of this entry. See also *Twins*.

1952. On *The Abbott and Costello Show* (Syn.), Sidney Fields plays several look-alike relatives, including a landlord, lawyer and judge.

1953. On *The Adventures of Superman* (Syn.), George Reeves plays Clark Kent, the reporter who is secretly Superman, and Boulder, a criminal made to look like Clark through plastic surgery, to learn Clark's secret. Jack Larson plays cub reporter Jimmy Olsen and Kid Collins, a thug out to steal incriminating evidence.

1954. On *Annie Oakley* (Syn.), Gail Davis plays Annie Oakley, a girl who helps Sheriff Lofty Craig up hold the law in the town of Diablo, and her outlaw double, Alias Annie Oakley. On *Father Knows Best* (CBS/NBC), Elinor Donahue plays Betty Anderson, the daughter of Jim and Margaret Anderson, and Donna Stewart, a Hollywood film star who is her exact double.

1955. On *Love That Bob* (NBC/CBS), Bob Cummings plays photographer Bob MacDonald and his grandfather, Grandpa Collins.

1957. On *Maverick* (ABC), James Garner plays gambler Bret Maverick and his father, Beauregard "Pappy" Maverick. On *Sugarfoot* (ABC), Will Hutchins plays Tom Brewster, a cowboy of the 1860s who travels from town to town helping people with his knowledge of the law. Will also played the Canary Kid, an outlaw who looked like Tom and for whom he is often mistaken.

1960. On *My Three Sons* (CBS), Fred Mac-Murray plays Steve Douglas and his look-alike cousin Fergus McBain Douglas.

1962. On *The Beverly Hillbillies* (CBS), Max Baer, Jr., plays Jethro, the nephew of hillbilly millionaire Jed Clampett, and his sister, Jethrene (voice of Linda Kaye Henning).

1963. On *The Patty Duke Show* (ABC), Patty Duke plays three roles: Patty Lane, a typical American teenage girl; her sophisticated European cousin, Cathy Lane; and Betsy Lane, Patty's glamorous Southern cousin. Also on the series, William Schallert plays Patty's father, Martin Lane, Martin's brother, Kenneth Lane (Cathy's father) and Martin's uncle Jed Lane.

1964. On *The Addams Family* (ABC), Carolyn Jones plays Morticia Addams, the wife of Gomez, and her flaky sister Ophelia Frump. On *Bewitched* (ABC), Elizabeth Montgomery plays Samantha, a witch and Serena, her fun-loving, mischievous cousin. On *The Dick Van Dyke Show* (CBS), Dick Van Dyke plays TV writer Rob Petrie and his elderly uncle, Hezekiah. *Gilligan's Island* (CBS) presents two look-alikes. Bob Denver plays the bumbling Gilligan and an unnamed agent who is sent to spy on the castaways. Tina Louise is Ginger Grant, the beautiful movie star, and Eva Grubb, a drab visitor to the island who is turned into a Ginger look-alike when she is given a makeover. On *The Munsters* (CBS), Fred Gwynne plays three roles: The Frankenstein-like gravedigger Herman Munster; his devious Cousin Charlie; and Johan, Herman's immature twin brother (his prototype).

1965. On *F Troop* (ABC), Larry Storch plays Corporal Randolph Agarn, a soldier at Fort Courage in Kansas (1860s), and his cousins El Diablo, Lucky Pierre and Dimitri Agarnoff. Also on the series, Forrest Tucker plays Sergeant Morgan O'Rourke and his father, Morgan O'Rourke, Sr., and Ken Berry is Captain Wilton Parmenter and his outlaw double, Kid Vicious. On *I Dream of Jeannie* (NBC), Barbara Eden plays three roles: Jeannie, a genie who is the slave of astronaut Tony Nelson; Jeannie II, her devious sister (who sought to steal Tony from Jeannie) and their mother, also a genie (called Mrs. Jeannie by Tony).

1966. On *The Double Life of Henry Phyfe* (ABC), Red Buttons plays mild-mannered accountant Henry Phyfe and U-31, a spy whose place Henry takes when U-31 is killed by a hit and run. On *The Man Who Never Was* (ABC), Robert Lansing plays Peter Murphy, an American espionage agent, and Mark Wainwright, the millionaire he is impersonating to protect his identity.

1967. On *The Second Hundred Years* (ABC), Monte Markham plays Luke Carpenter, a prospector frozen alive in 1900 when caught in an avalanche and thawed out in 1967 when found, and his grandson Ken Carpenter.

1969. On *I Dream of Jeannie* (NBC), in "The Case of the Vanishing Master" episode (January 6), Larry Hagman plays a Tony Nelson look-alike hired by Dr. Bellows to stand-in for the real Tony while he is on a secret mission.

1972. On *Gunsmoke* (CBS), Ken Curtis is Deputy Festus Haggen and his outlaw double, Frank Eaton. On *McMillan and Wife* (NBC), Rock Hudson is Police Commissioner Stewart McMillan and a double hired to kill him.

1976. On *The Bionic Woman* (ABC), Lindsay Wagner is Jaime Sommers and Lisa Galloway, the girl out to learn the secret of Jaime's abilities.

1977. On *Laverne and Shirley* (ABC), David L. Lander plays beer truck driver Andrew "Squiggy" Squigman and his not-so attractive sister Squendelyn Squigman. On *The Love Boat* (ABC), Gavin MacLeod plays Merrill Stubing, captain of the cruise ship *Pacific Princess* and his brothers Milo and Marshall Stubing.

1978. On *Little Women* (NBC), Eve Plumb plays Beth, the youngest (and most frail) of the March sisters. When Beth dies of a high fever, her cousin (and identical look-alike) Melissa Jane Driscoll becomes part of the cast.

1980. On *Magnum, P.I.* (CBS), John Hillerman is Jonathan Higgins, major domo of an estate owned by Robin Masters. He also plays his half-brothers Father Paddy MacGuinness and Don Luis Monqueo.

1981. On *Simon and Simon* (CBS), in addition to detective A.J. and Simon, Jameson Parker and Gerald McRaney play their cousins Orville and Wilbur Simon.

1982. On *Knight Rider* (NBC), David Hasselhoff is Michael Knight, a government agent, and his evil look-alike, Garthe Knight. On *Knots Landing* (CBS), Lisa Hartman is singer Ciji Dunn and ex con Cathy Geary.

1984. On *Hot Pursuit* (NBC), Kerri Keane is Kate Wyler, a woman framed for murder, and Kathy Ladd, the woman who framed her. On *Murder, She Wrote* (CBS), Angela Lansbury plays mystery writer Jessica Fletcher and her British cousin Emma Fletcher.

1986. On *Mama's Family* (Syn.), Vicki Lawrence plays Thelma "Mama" Harper and two look-alike roles. In "Cousin Lydia" (November 21, 1986), Vicki is also Mama's worldly cousin, Lydia. In the episode of November 11, 1988 ("My Mama, Myself"), Vicki is also the ghost of Grandma Crowley.

1989. On *Family Matters* (ABC), Jaleel White plays the nerdy Steve Urkel and his flirtatious female cousin Myrtle Urkel.

1990. On *Twin Peaks* (ABC), Sheryl Lee plays Laura Palmer, the girl whose mysterious death is being investigated by FBI agent Dale Cooper and Madeline Ferguson, Laura's cousin.

1993. On *Lois and Clark: The New Adventures of Superman* (ABC), Teri Hatcher plays *Daily Planet* reporter Lois Lane and "the Evil Lois Lane," a clone created by Lex Luthor to discover Clark Kent's secret identity. On *Walker, Texas Ranger* (CBS), Chuck Norris plays modern day Texas Ranger Cordell Walker and an Old West Texas Ranger named Hayes Cooper who looked remarkably like Cordell (in flashback sequences).

1996. On *The Steve Harvey Show* (WB), Cedric the Entertainer plays high school coach Cedric Robinson and his Grandma Puddin.

1998. On *The Lost World* (Syn.), Jennifer O'Dell plays Veronica Layton, a girl who grew up on a lost plateau forgotten by time and her mother, Abigail, the guardian of the plateau. On *V.I.P.* (Syn.), Pamela Anderson plays Vallery Irons, the owner of Vallery Irons Protection, and the criminal Joan Archer, whom Vallery calls "the Evil Me."

2005. On *Gilmore Girls* (WB), Marion Ross plays Trixie Gilmore, Lorelai Gilmore's grandmother (on her father's side) and Marilyn, her younger cousin.

Los Angeles

A listing of series set in and around Los Angeles. See also *California*.

1949: *The Life of Riley* (DuMont).

1950. *The George Burns and Gracie Allen Show* (CBS); *The Jack Benny Program* (CBS).

1951. *Boston Blackie* (Syn.); *Dragnet* (NBC).

1952. *Boss Lady* (NBC); *I Married Joan* (NBC); *My Hero* (CBS).

1953. *The Life of Riley* (NBC); *My Favorite Husband* (CBS).

1954. *Dear Phoebe* (NBC); *Hey Mulligan* (NBC); *Whirlybirds* (Syn.).

1955. *Those Whiting Girls* (CBS).

1956. *Code 3* (Syn.).

1957. *A Date with the Angels* (ABC); *Mr. Adams and Eve* (CBS); *Perry Mason* (CBS).

1958. *The George Burns Show* (CBS); *Peter Gunn* (NBC/ABC); *Rescue 8* (Syn.).

1959. *The Dennis O'Keefe Show* (CBS); *Markham* (CBS); *Mr. Lucky* (CBS); *Richard Diamond* (NBC episodes only).

1960. *Mr. Ed* (CBS); *Pete and Gladys* (CBS).

1961. *The Hathaways* (ABC); *The New Breed* (ABC); *Yes, Yes Nanette* (NBC).

1962. *I'm Dickens, He's Fenster* (ABC); *The Joey Bishop Show* (NBC); *Sam Benedict* (NBC).

1963. *Arrest and Trial* (ABC); *Burke's Law* (ABC); *Mr. Novak* (NBC); *My Favorite Martian* (CBS); *The New Phil Silvers Show* (CBS).

1964. *The Bing Crosby Show* (ABC); *The Cara Williams Show* (CBS); *Gomer Pyle, U.S.M.C.* (CBS); *Many Happy Returns* (CBS); *The Tycoon* (ABC); *Wendy and Me* (ABC).

1965. *Honey West* (ABC); *Mona McCluskey* (NBC); *My Mother the Car* (NBC).

1966. *The Felony Squad* (ABC); *The Hero* (NBC); *The Monkees* (NBC).

1967. *Dragnet* (NBC); *Good Morning, World* (CBS); *Mannix* (CBS); *The Mothers-in-Law* (NBC).

1968. *Adam-12* (NBC); *The Good Guys* (CBS); *Here's Lucy* (CBS); *Julia* (NBC); *The Mod Squad* (ABC); *The Outsider* (NBC).

1969. *The Bill Cosby Show* (NBC); *The Courtship of Eddie's Father* (ABC); *The Debbie Reynolds Show* (NBC); *The Doctors* (NBC); *The Lawyers* (NBC); *Medical Center* (CBS); *My Friend Tony* (NBC); *Room 222* (ABC).

1970. *Arnie* (CBS); *The Interns* (CBS); *Matt Lincoln* (ABC); *Nanny and the Professor* (ABC); *The Senator* (NBC); *The Storefront Lawyers* (CBS).

1971. *Cannon* (CBS); *Columbo* (NBC); *The D.A.* (NBC); *Funny Face* (CBS); *The Partners* (NBC); *The Psychiatrist* (NBC); *The Smith Family* (ABC).

1972. *Banyon* (NBC); *Emergency* (NBC); *The Rookies* (ABC); *The Sandy Duncan Show* (CBS); *Sanford and Son* (NBC); *The Sixth Sense* (ABC).

1973. *Adam's Rib* (ABC); *Barnaby Jones* (CBS); *Bob & Carol & Ted & Alice* (ABC); *Chase* (ABC); *Farraday and Company* (NBC); *The Girl with Something Extra* (NBC); *Griff* (ABC); *Here We Go Again* (ABC); *The Magician* (NBC); *The New Perry Mason* (CBS).

1974. *Chico and the Man* (NBC); *Get Christie Love* (ABC); *Harry O* (ABC); *Police Woman* (NBC); *The Rockford Files* (NBC).

1975. *The Blue Knight* (CBS); *The Bob Crane Show* (NBC); *The Cop and the Kid* (NBC); *The Invisible Man* (NBC); *Joe Forrester* (NBC); *Starsky and Hutch* (ABC); *Switch* (CBS).

1976. *Charlie's Angels* (ABC); *City of Angels* (NBC); *Holmes and Yoyo* (ABC); *Jigsaw John* (NBC); *McNaughton's Daughter* (NBC); *Quincy, M.E.* (NBC); *Viva Valdez* (ABC); *What's Happening!!* (ABC).

1977. *The Betty White Show* (CBS); *CHiPs* (NBC); *Dog and Cat* (ABC); *The Feather and Father Gang* (ABC); *Kingston Confidential* (NBC); *Lou Grant* (CBS); *Rafferty* (CBS); *Rosetti and Ryan* (NBC); *Sanford Arms* (NBC); *Sugar Time* (ABC); *Tabitha* (ABC).

1978. *David Cassidy—Man Undercover* (NBC); *The Eddie Capra Mysteries* (NBC); *Julie Farr, M.D.* (ABC); *Richie Brockelman, Private Eye* (NBC); *Sam* (CBS).

1979. *Detective School* (ABC); *Emergency* (NBC); *Flying High* (CBS); *Hart to Hart* (ABC); *House Calls* (CBS); *A New Kind of Family* (ABC); *Number 96* (NBC); *Out of the Blue* (ABC); *Paris* (CBS); *Salvage One* (ABC); *240-Robert* (ABC).

1980. *B.A.D. Cats* (ABC); *Enos* (CBS); *Sanford* (NBC); *Stone* (ABC); *Tenspeed and Brown Shoe* (ABC); *When the Whistle Blows* (ABC).

1981. *Code Red* (ABC); *The Fall Guy* (ABC); *The Greatest American Hero* (ABC); *It's a Living* (ABC); *Jessica Novak* (CBS); *Riker* (CBS); *Strike Force* (ABC); *S.W.A.T.* (ABC); *The White Shadow* (CBS).

1982. *The Devlin Connection* (NBC); *Knight Rider* (NBC); *Matt Houston* (ABC); *Philip Marlowe* (HBO); *Remington Steele* (NBC).

1983. *Automan* (ABC); *Hardcastle and McCormick* (ABC); *The Renegades* (NBC); *The Rousters* (NBC); *Ryan's Four* (ABC).

1984. *Cover Up* (CBS); *The Four Seasons* (CBS); *Hunter* (NBC); *Legmen* (NBC); *Shaping Up* (ABC).

1985. *Eye to Eye* (ABC); *First and Ten* (HBO); *Hell Town* (NBC); *Hollywood Beat* (ABC); *I Had Three Wives* (CBS); *McGruder and Loud* (ABC); *MacGyver* (ABC); *Me and Mom* (ABC); *Moonlighting* (ABC); *Small Wonder* (Syn.); *Street Hawk* (ABC); *What's Happening Now!!* (Syn); *Wildside* (CBS).

1986. *ALF* (NBC); *Downtown* (CBS); *Heart of*

the City (ABC); *L.A. Law* (NBC); *Our House* (NBC); *Side Kicks* (ABC); *What a Country* (Syn.).

1987. *Duet* (Fox); *I Married Dora* (ABC); *Karen's Song* (Fox); *Ohara* (ABC); *The Oldest Rookie* (CBS); *Once a Hero* (ABC); *Private Eye* (NBC); *Rags to Riches* (NBC); *21 Jump Street* (Fox).

1989. *Alien Nation* (Fox); *Baywatch* (NBC); *Booker* (Fox); *Hardball* (CBS); *Just in Time* (ABC); *The New Adam-12* (Syn.); *The New Dragnet* (Syn.); *Nightingales* (NBC); *Open House* (Fox); *Peaceable Kingdom* (CBS); *Wild Jack* (NBC).

1990. *Broken Badges* (CBS); *Ferris Bueller* (NBC); *Going Places* (ABC); *His and Hers* (CBS); *Max Monroe: Loose Cannon* (CBS); *Molloy* (Fox); *New Attitude* (ABC); *Normal Life* (CBS); *Shades of L.A.* (Syn.); *Sunset Beat* (ABC).

1991. *Baywatch* (Syn.); *Blossom* (NBC); *Good Sports* (CBS); *Love and Curses* (Syn.); *Pros and Cons* (ABC).

1992. *Billy* (ABC); *Bodies of Evidence* (CBS); *Camp Wilder* (ABC); *Freshman Dorm* (CBS); *The Hat Squad* (CBS); *The Jackie Thomas Show* (ABC); *Mann and Machine* (NBC); *Nightmare Café* (NBC); *Out All Night* (ABC); *Tequila and Bonetti* (CBS).

1993. *Crime and Punishment* (NBC); *Diagnosis Murder* (CBS); *Home Free* (ABC); *Open All Night* (ABC).

1994. *Burke's Law* (CBS); *Ellen* (ABC); *Good Advice* (CBS); *South Central* (Fox); *These Friends of Mine* (ABC).

1995. *Charlie Grace* (ABC); *Cybill* (CBS); *In the House* (NBC); *Murder One* (ABC).

1996. *L.A. Heat* (Syn.); *Moesha* (UPN); *Pacific Blue* (USA).

1997. *Fame L.A.* (Syn.); *Jenny* (NBC).

1998. *Buddy Faro* (CBS); *V.I.P.* (Syn.).

1999. *Angel* (WB), *Movie Stars* (WB); *Popular* (WB).

2000. *Bette* (CBS); *Daddio* (NBC); *Girlfriends* (UPN); *Grosse Pointe* (WB); *The Michael Richards Show* (NBC); *Resurrection Blvd.* (SHO); *She Spies* (Syn.); *Titus* (Fox).

2001. *Bob Patterson* (ABC); *Six Feet Under* (HBO); *Three Sisters* (NBC).

2002. *Boomtown* (NBC); *Fastlane* (Fox); *The George Lopez Show* (ABC); *Haunted* (UPN); *Hunter* (NBC); *Robbery Homicide Division* (CBS); *The Shield* (FX).

2003. *All About the Andersons* (WB); *Dragnet* (ABC); *Family Business* (SHO); *The Handler* (CBS); *I'm with Her* (ABC); *Miss Match* (NBC); *Skin* (Fox); *10–8: Officers on Duty* (ABC).

2004. *Cracking Up* (NBC); *Joey* (NBC); *LAX* (NBC); *The Second Time Around* (UPN).

2005. *The Closer* (TNT); *Eyes* (ABC); *The Inside* (Fox); *Just Legal* (WB); *Sex, Love and Secrets* (UPN); *Night Stalker* (ABC); *NUMB3RS* (CBS); *South of Nowhere* (N); *Wanted* (TNT).

2006. *Emily's Reasons Why Not* (ABC); *Heist* (NBC); *Injustice* (ABC); *The New Adventures of Old Christine* (CBS).

Love

Programs specifically revolving around the theme of love are the subjects of this entry.

1931. *TV Wedding* airs on W2XCR in Jersey City and WGSB-TV in New York City. Here on May 2, Frank DuVail married Grayce Jones in a ceremony presided over by Dr. A. Edwin Keigwin.

1946. A DuMont experiment called *Marriage A La Mode* airs on August 28 and combines romance with sales pitches. Plugs for articles sold at Wanamaker's Department Stores were hyped during s skit about a couple on the verge of divorce (John Graham, Madeline Kalleen) who find they still love each other after they meet an argumentative couple (Arthur Page, Fran Lee) seeking to buy their home after the divorce.

1949. Arlene Francis hosts *Blind Date* (ABC/NBC/DuMont), a game wherein a girl, separated from two men, must choose one for a date based on a series of prepared questions.

1954. Peter Lawford plays Phoebe Goodheart, the male advice-to-the-lovelorn columnist on NBC's *Dear Phoebe*. Live romantic dramas are broadcast by DuMont on its short-lived *Love Story*. Engaged or married couples compete in question and answer rounds for a chance at an all-expenses paid honeymoon in New York on ABC's *Manhattan Honeymoon*.

1955. Couples answer questions in an attempt to win a honeymoon in Paris on CBS's *Love Story*. Jack Smith hosts.

1957. Glenda Farrell plays Mae Sweeney, a woman with a broken heart (her husband left her for another woman) who begins a matrimonial bureau to pair off lonely hearts on the CBS pilot *The Marriage Broker*.

1958. Men and women seeking friendship are introduced to members of the opposite sex with the intent to spark a romance on ABC's *Chance for Romance*.

1961. Stories based on the joys and sorrows of love are the idea behind *Band of Gold*, an unsold CBS pilot.

1964. Bob Hope plays Horatio Lovelace, a marriage broker who peddles his ladies to prospective husbands in the Old West on the NBC special *Have Girls, Will Travel*.

1966. A young woman questions three bachelors to choose the one she would most like to date on ABC's *The Dating Game* (Jim Lange hosts). Four husband and wife teams have to predict how each mate responded to specific questions on ABC's *The Newlywed Game* (Bob Eubanks hosts).

1967. Before airtime, a computer matches three men with three women. Through a series of probe rounds, each man has to determine which girl the computer has matched him with and vice versa on *The Perfect Match* (Syn.).

1969. Comedy vignettes that tackle the ups and downs of love are the basis of ABC's *Love, American Style*. Romantic events in the lives of people living in a singles apartment house in Los Angeles as seen through the eyes of building owner Charlie Procter is the basis of the NBC pilot *Under the Yum Yum Tree*.

1971. Celebrity guests have to predict the outcome of unsuspecting individuals caught in prearranged romantic situations on CBS's *The Amateur's Guide to Love* (Gene Rayburn hosts). Jack Cassidy hosts *The Powder Room*, an NBC pilot of romantic vignettes that explore the world of love as seen through women's eyes.

1972. Lee Remick hosts *Of Men, of Women*, an ABC pilot of plays based on the trials and tribulations of love.

1973. Comedy vignettes that depict brief incidents in the lives of couples who check into Room 300 of the plush Honeymoon Suite of the Beverly Hills Hotel is the subject of two ABC pilots called *Honeymoon Suite*. Adult and contemporary variations on the theme of love are presented on NBC's *Love Story*. Stephen Boyd is the host for *Of Men, of Women*, a second ABC pilot about the many faces of love.

1974. Stories about men who fall head over heels in love with women fate did not intend them to have is the basis of the NBC pilot *Fools, Females and Fun*. Rex Harrison is the host of *Rex Harrison Presents Short Stories of Love*, an NBC pilot of romantic stories.

1977. Romantic stories set on the luxury liner *Pacific Princess* are the basis of ABC's *The Love Boat*. Gavin MacLeod is the ship's captain, Merrill Stubing.

1978. Bill Cullen hosts *The Love Experts*, a syndicated series in which four celebrities offer advice to real people on the problems of living and loving in the 1970s.

1979. Incidents in the lives of married couples are seen through the eyes of wedding photographer Bryan Fish on the NBC pilot *Marriage Is Alive and Well*. Leigh McCloskey and Cindy Grover play Billy and Joanna Baker, teenagers struggling to survive the difficult first year of marriage on CBS's *Married: The First Year*. The outrageous sexual activities of a group of people who reside at Number 96 Pacific Way in Los Angeles is the basis of NBC's *Number 96*. Romantic incidents in the lives of the guests at a secluded resort called Pleasure Cove are the focal point of the NBC pilot *Pleasure Cove*. A mysterious woman named Madge (Janis Paige) possesses the ability to make romance happen at her tropical resort, Love Island on the NBC pilot *Valentine Magic on Love Island*.

1981. Cloris Leachman plays Maggie Dale, an advice-to-the-lovelorn columnist on the NBC pilot *Advice to the Lovelorn*. Debbie Reynolds plays Sydney Chase, manager of Paradise Village, a romantic Hawaiian resort on ABC's *Aloha Paradise*. Mary Ann Mobley hosts *Wedding Day*, an NBC pilot wherein real weddings are performed on the air.

1982. Incidents in the lives of newlywed couples who spend their honeymoon at Bliss Cove Haven, an exclusive resort in the Pocono Mountains, are the basis of the ABC pilot *For Lovers Only*.

1983. Chuck Woolery hosts *The Love Connection*, a syndicated series wherein the audience selects which man should date which girl (based on pre-taped interviews with the subjects).

1984. Cary Maxwell (Anthony Franciosa) is the head of Maxwell, Ltd., an agency that helps people who deeply cared for each other but who have drifted apart find each other again on ABC's *Finder of Lost Loves*. Tawny Schneider hosts *The Love Report*, an ABC program that examines romantic problems and "presents up to the minute information on love relationships." ABC airs *The*

New Newlywed Game with Jim Lange as the host (see 1966).

1985. *Love Songs* is a daily syndicated series of music videos coupled with personal ads for singles seeking a mate. ABC airs *The New Love American Style* (see 1969), a daily series of comedy vignettes that tackle the ups and downs of love, marriage and divorce. Bob Eubanks returns as the host of the syndicated *New Newlywed Game* (see 1966).

1986. The intimate lives of couples who vacation at the Club Med resort in Ixtapa, Mexico, are revealed on the ABC pilot *Club Med.* Judy and Ben Bellin (Melinda Culea, Rex Smith) are a married couple who write an advice-to-the-lovelorn column on the ABC pilot *Dear Penelope and Peter.* In a TV rarity, a beautiful girl (Elaine Joyce) is chosen to host a game show — *The All New Dating Game* (see 1966) for syndication. Bob Goen hosts *The Perfect Match*, a syndicated game wherein husbands must determine their wives' responses to questions and vice versa.

1987. Isabel Sanford plays Isabel Scott, the manager of a debt-ridden honeymoon hotel on the syndicated pilot *Isabel Sanford's Honeymoon Hotel.* David Hull hosts *Matchmaker*, a syndicated game in which singles are paired in the hope of sparking a romance.

1989. Men are matched with women through a series of questions to see who is best for whom on the syndicated game *Straight to the Heart* (Michael Berger hosts).

1990. Eva Gabor plays Eva Hill and Hillary Bailey is her daughter Jess Hill, the operators of a San Francisco matchmaking service on the CBS pilot *Close Encounters.* Real life tear-jerking love stories are recreated on the ABC pilot *Love with a Twist* (hosted by Bruce Boxleitner). The romantic escapades of people who frequent a Manhattan hotel is the focal point of CBS's *Room for Romance.*

1991. Kristian Alfonso hosts the syndicated *Love Stories*, true tales of people who fall in love (the actual people involved appear to relate their experiences). Men are matched with women in an attempt to spark a romance on the syndicated *Studs* (Mark DeCarlo hosts).

1992. The struggles of married teenagers Dallas and Mickey Wyatt (Brooke Langton, William McNamara) to make their marriage work is the focal point of the Fox pilot *The Wyatts.*

1997. Brothers Jack and Warren Baldwin (Peter Dobson, Mitchell Whitfield) attempt to run the Miami based dating service *Head Over Heels* on UPN.

1998. Trevor Hale (Jeremy Pivan) is Cupid (the God of Love) who is stripped of his powers and sent to Earth to reunite 100 couples in order to regain his place on Mount Olympus on ABC's *Cupid.* Robert Urich plays Jim Kennedy III, the new captain of the Love Boat (now called the *Sun Princess*) on UPN's *The Love Boat: The Next Wave* (see 1977).

2003. Alicia Silverstone plays Katie Fox, a lawyer with a knack for making matches on NBC's *Miss Match.*

2005. Leslie Bibb and Paul Mark Gosselaar are a sister and brother who own a one-stop Vegas wedding chapel on the Fox pilot *Hitched.* Shannen Doherty plays Denise Johnson, a young woman with a knack for matching unlikely people with each other, but unable to find a mate for herself on the pilot episode of UPN's *Love, Inc.* In the series itself, Clea (Holly Robinson), Francine (Reagan Gomez-Preston), Viviana (Ion Overman) and Denise (Busy Phillips) are matchmakers trying to find the right man for the right woman.

Magazines see *Newspapers and Magazines; Reporters*

Magicians

Programs geared to magic and illusion is the subject of this entry.

1947. Guest magicians perform on *The Magic Carpet*, a live DuMont test program sponsored by Alexander Smith Carpets.

1949. Andre Baruch is the host of *Masters of Magic*, a live CBS series of performances by guest magicians. The program is also known as *Now You See It.*

1951. Female magician Dell O'Dell hosts *The Dell O'Dell Show*, an ABC program that spotlights guest magicians. Jerome Thor stars as *The Great Merlini*, a syndicated pilot about a master illusionist and escape artist who helps the police solve baffling crimes. Geraldine Larsen is *The Magic Lady*, the host of a syndicated program of songs and performances by guest magicians.

1952. Magician Harry Blackstone performs tricks in a three minute syndicated filler program called *Blackstone Magic Spots.*

1954. Coe Norton plays Mandrake, a master magician who uses his magic to battle evil on the syndicated *Mandrake the Magician*.

1955. Guest magicians perform on *It's Magic*, a CBS series with Paul Tripp as the host.

1957. Ernie Kovacs hosts *Festival of Magic*, an NBC special that features the magic of famous magicians (Cardini, Li King Si, June Merlin, Milbourne Christopher, Robert Harbin, Rene Septembre).

1960. Magician Mark Wilson entertains children with cartoons and feats of magic on *The Magic Land of Allakazam* (CBS/ABC).

1961. Guest magicians perform for host Don Alan on ABC's *The Magic Ranch*.

1964. Although he is a vampire, Grandpa (Al Lewis) is a master of magic who can make the impossible happen on *The Munsters* (CBS). Also trying his hand at magic is his son-in-law, Herman Munster (Fred Gwynne), who billed himself as Munster the Magnificent for his son's school talent night.

1971. An evil magician named Whoo Doo (Charles Nelson Reilly) rules Lidsville, the land of living hats on ABC's *Lidsville*.

1973. Bill Bixby plays Anthony Blake, a magician who uses the wizardry of his craft to help people on NBC's *The Magician*.

1976. Magician Doug Henning presents an hour of illusion with guest Joey Heatherton on NBC's *Doug Henning's World of Magic*.

1977. Sandy Duncan guests on the NBC special *Doug Henning's World of Magic II*.

1978. Young Arnold Jackson (Gary Coleman), the orphan adopted by a Park Avenue millionaire, fancies himself as a magician he calls the Great Arnoldo on NBC's *Diff'rent Strokes*. Magician David Copperfield hosts *The Magic of David Copperfield*, a CBS special with guest Valerie Bertinelli. Anthony Herrara plays Mandrake, a magician who uses his craft to battle evil on the NBC pilot *Mandrake*.

1979. Loni Anderson and Bill Bixby guest on *The Magic of David Copperfield II* (CBS). Vincent Price hosts *Richiardi's Chamber of Horrors*, "one of the most frightening evenings of magic ever performed on television," with illusionist Richiardi (Showtime).

1980. Barbi Benton and Bill Cosby guest on NBC's *Doug Henning's World of Magic III*. CBS airs *The Magic of David Copperfield III*. Eddie Albert hosts an hour of magic and illusion with magicians *Siegfried and Roy* (NBC).

1981. Marie Osmond guests on *Doug Henning's World of Magic IV*. Chris Kirby hosts *Like Magic*, a CBS pilot that was to spotlight guest magicians. Susan Anton and Elaine Joyce guest on CBS's *The Magic of David Copperfield IV*. Barnard Hughes plays Merlin the Magician, the centuries old sorcerer who appears in modern-day San Francisco as Max Merlin to find an apprentice on CBS's *Mr. Merlin*.

1982. NBC airs *Doug Henning's World of Magic V* and *Doug Henning's Magic on Broadway*. Orson Welles, Loni Anderson, Jaclyn Smith and Robert Guillaume host *Magic with the Stars*, a two-hour NBC special in which celebrities assist magicians.

1983. Morgan Fairchild guests on *The Magic of David Copperfield V* (CBS).

1984. *The Magic of David Copperfield VI* airs on CBS with Ricardo Montalban and Heather Thomas as guests. On NBC's *Night Court*, Harry Anderson plays Harry T. Stone, a judge deeply interested in magic (his hero is Harry Houdini).

1985. Angie Dickinson hosts *The Magic of David Copperfield VII* (CBS) with guests Teri Copley and Peggy Fleming.

1986. Alexander Blacke (Hal Linden) is a magician who teams with his father, con artist Leonard Blacke (Harry Morgan) to solve baffling crimes on *Blacke's Magic* (NBC). Ben Vereen hosts *The Magic of David Copperfield VIII ... In China*.

1987. Magician Mark Mazzarella plays the owner of the Abra Kadabra Magic Shop on the syndicated *Abra Kadabra*. Here the world of magic is explained to children via skits and magic performances. Harry Anderson presents magic and illusion on *Harry Anderson's Side Show* (NBC). Ann Jillian hosts *The Magic of David Copperfield IX ... Escape from Alcatraz* (CBS).

1988. Lisa Hartman guests on *The Magic of David Copperfield X: The Bermuda Triangle* (CBS).

1989. *The Magic of David Copperfield XI* airs on CBS with guest Emma Samms.

1990. Ricky Jay hosts *Learned Pigs and Fireproof Women*, a CBS special that highlights the performances of magicians, past and present. *The Magic of David Copperfield XII* airs on CBS. Illusionists Penn and Teller perform feats of illusion on *Penn and Teller's Don't Try This at Home* (CBS).

1991. Jane Seymour hosts *The Magic of David Copperfield XIII: Mystery on the Orient Express* (CBS).

1992. James Earl Jones hosts *The Magic of*

David Copperfield XIV: Flying ... Live the Dream (CBS).

1993. Max Maven plays Count De Clues, a magician who solves mysteries in his castle on the Fox pilot *Count De Clues Mystery Castle*. Mark Sloan (Dick Van Dyke) is a doctor at Community General Hospital who uses his fascination with magic as a therapeutic aid to children on CBS's *Diagnosis Murder*. CBS airs *The Magic of David Copperfield XV: Fires of Passion—This Time His Life Is on the Line*.

1996. Stunts by magician David Blaine appear on four ABC specials: *David Blaine: Street Magician* (1996), *David Blaine: Magic Man* (1998), *David Blaine: Frozen in Time* (2000) and *David Blaine: Fearless* (2002).

1997. Fox airs *Breaking the Code: Magic's Biggest Secrets Finally Revealed*, a series of four specials (to 1998) wherein an unknown and masked magician revealed the secrets behind illusions. On the final broadcast, the magician was revealed to be Valentino. Young Nicholas Peterson (Curtis Williams) envisions himself as a great magician (Nicholas the Great) but has yet to perfect his act on *The Parent'Hood* (WB).

2003. George Oscar Bluth (George Oscar) is a magician who prefers that his acts be called illusions not tricks on Fox's *Arrested Development* (he started the Alliance of Magicians, which blacklists magicians who reveal their secrets). Teenager Brian Miller (Taylor Ball) is a budding magician who calls himself "Miller the Magnificent" on CBS's *Still Standing*.

2005. Daredevil magician Criss Angel performs dangerous illusions on A&E's *Criss Angel Mind Freak*. Rick Hoffman plays Patrick, a magician who calls himself "Patrick, Doctor of Magicology," on ABC's *Jake in Progress*.

Maids see *Housekeepers*

Martial Arts

This entry chronicles the programs that use the martial arts as its premise.

1966. On *The Green Hornet* (ABC), Bruce Lee plays Kato, aide to the crime fighting Green Hornet, who uses his martial arts skills to battle evil.

1971. On *Longstreet* (ABC), Bruce Lee plays Li Tsung, a martial arts self defense instructor to blind insurance investigator Michael Longstreet.

1972. On *Kung Fu* (ABC), David Carradine is Kwai Chang Caine, a Shaolin priest of the 1870s who wanders across the American Frontier seeking an unknown brother (and helping people along the way).

1974. On *Men of the Dragon* (ABC pilot), Li-Teh (Robert Ito) is the owner of a karate school in Hong Kong who, with his American partners, brother and sister Jan and Lisa Kimbro (Jared Martin, Katie Saylor) use their unique skills to battle crime.

1975. On *Khan* (CBS), Khigh Dheigh is Khan, a detective with the San Francisco Police Department who uses his martial arts skills to deal with law-breakers.

1979. On *Samurai* (ABC pilot), Lee Cantrell (Joe Penny) is a half Asian, half American lawyer with the San Francisco County Prosecutor's Office who lives by the code of the Samurai and helps people who are unable to help themselves.

1982. On *Force 7* (NBC pilot), L.A.P.D. lieutenant John Legarre (Fred Dryer) organizes Force 7, a special undercover unit of martial arts experts to battle crime. The team: Cindy Miwa David (Donna Kei Benz), Sly Angelitti (Tony Longo) and Rick Nicholls (Tom Reilly).

1983. On *High Performance* (ABC), Kate Flannery (Lisa Hartman) is a martial arts expert who works as an agent for High Performance, an elite agency that tackles hazardous assignments for $5,000 a day plus expenses. On *The Last Ninja* (ABC pilot), Ken Sakura (Michael Beck) is an antique dealer who uses his martial arts abilities to battle evil as the mysterious ninja.

1984. On *The Master* (NBC), John McCallister (Lee Van Cleef) is a ninja master who, while searching for his missing daughter, helps people threatened by evil.

1986. On *Chuck Norris Karate Kommanders* (Syn.), an animated Chuck Norris is a special agent for the president of the U.S. who uses his skills as a Samurai warrior to battle evil. On *Kung Fu: The Movie* (CBS pilot), David Carradine reprises his role as Kwai Chang Caine, a Shaolin priest, in an unsuccessful attempt to revive the 1972 series. On *Sidekicks* (ABC), Jake Rizzo (Gil Gerard) is an unmarried cop and the guardian of Ernie (Ernie Reyes, Jr.), a ten-year-old karate master, who helps him solve crimes.

1987. On *Kung Fu: The Next Generation* (CBS pilot), the story finds Kwai Chang Caine (David Darlow), the great grandson of the original Caine (from 1972's *Kung Fu*), as the father of Johnny Caine (Brandon Lee). The two join forces and use their martial arts skills to battle injustice in the modern world.

1988. On *Remo Williams* (ABC pilot), Master Chiun (Roddy McDowall) is a Korean martial arts expert who teams with tough New York cop Remo Williams (Jeffrey Meek) to battle evil for CURE, a special government organization.

1992. On *Raven* (CBS), Jonathan Raven (Jeffrey Meek) is a private detective who uses his martial arts skills to battle evil in Hawaii.

1993. On *Kung Fu: The Legend Continues* (Syn.), David Carradine plays Kwai Chang Caine, the grandson of the character he played in 1972 (on *Kung Fu*). He resides in modern-day San Francisco and is the father of Peter (Chris Potter), a police detective he helps solve crimes. On *The Mighty Morphin Power Rangers* (Fox/ABC), ordinary teens are given the ability to battle evil via the martial arts and morphing powers. One series in particular, *Power Rangers: Ninja Storm* (ABC, 2003), focuses on the teens as members of the Wind Ninja Academy, a secret society that battles aliens from outer space. See *Morphing* for other series titles. On *Walker, Texas Ranger* (CBS), Chuck Norris plays Cordell Walker, a Texas Ranger who prefers to use his martial arts skills as a weapon.

1998. On *Martial Law* (CBS), Sammo Law (Sammo Hung) is a detective with the L.A.P.D. who uses his expertise in the martial arts to apprehend criminals.

1999. On *Sons of Thunder* (CBS), Trent Malloy (Jimmy Wicek) is a karate expert who helps people in trouble via his company, Thunder Investigations in Dallas, Texas.

2003. On *Black Sash* (WB), Tom Chang (Russell Wong) is a martial arts school owner who battles injustice as the mysterious Black Sash.

Matchmakers see *Love*

Mediums

This entry chronicles the programs on which mediums or psychics are featured (regulars or semi regulars), both real and portrayed.

1948. Feats of mind reading with mentalist Joseph Dunninger are coupled with the comedy of ventriloquist Paul Winchell and his dummy friend Jerry Mahoney on *Dunninger and Winchell* (CBS/NBC).

1949. Psychologist Franz J. Polgar presents demonstrations of psychic phenomena on *The Amazing Polgar* (CBS).

1950. Magic, illusion and mind reading are presented by Kuda Bux on CBS's *Kuda Bux, Hindu Mystic*.

1953. Joseph Dunninger returns to TV first in a syndicated then NBC (1954) series of mind reading demonstrations on *The Dunninger Show*. The series switched to ABC in 1956.

1958. ABC presents two series titled *E.S.P.* The first (July–August) is a game wherein two people, screened by psychiatrists, are tested to determine their degree of extra sensory perception. The second one (August) presented anthology-like stories of people endowed with E.S.P. for three weeks.

1968. Hank Stohl is the host of *The Amazing Dunninger*, a syndicated series in which mentalist Joseph Dunninger performs feats of mind reading.

1969. Master mentalist Maurice Woodruff demonstrates his powers of mind reading on *Maurice Woodruff Predicts* (Syn.). Angela Roland plays Vangie, a medium seeking to destroy the evil on the forbidding island of Maljardan in the Caribbean on *Strange Paradise* (Syn.).

1971. Mentalist Kreskin performs feats of mind reading, E.S.P. and sleight of hand on *The Amazing World of Kreskin* (Syn.).

1972. Charles Sand (Peter Haskell) is a man who possesses a special power called "The Sight," which enables him to see what others cannot on the ABC pilot *The Eyes of Charles Sand*. Gary Burghoff plays Walter O'Reilly, a private with the Mobile Army Surgical Hospital in wartime Korea who is called "Radar" for his ability to perceive what others think on CBS's *M*A*S*H*. Michael Rhodes (Gary Collins) is a professor of parapsychology at the University School in Los Angeles who possesses a sixth sense to see beyond the norm and solve cases associated with the supernatural on *The Sixth Sense* (ABC).

1973. Race car driver Tom Kovack (Leonard Nimoy) acquires mysterious occult powers (to see people in trouble) after a near-fatal crash on the NBC pilot *Baffled*. Sally Burton (Sally Field) is a young woman who possesses a high degree of E.S.P. and can read almost everyone's minds, including the most secret thoughts of her husband, John, on NBC's *The Girl with Something Extra*.

1977. Sportswriter Paul Taylor (Granville Van Dusen) possesses an inner voice that commands him to help people threatened by the occult on the CBS pilot *The World of Darkness*.

1979. Granville Van Dusen reprises his role of Paul Taylor, the sportswriter who died on the operating table and was brought back to life on the CBS pilot *The World Beyond*. The experience left Paul with a connection to the world beyond — a connection through which the dead can contact him to seek out people and protect them from evil.

1979. Rachel Longaker plays Laura Hoffman, a young girl with the ability to see the future and help people who are in trouble on the ABC special *The Girl with E.S.P.*

1983. Newspaper reporter Louis Ciconne (Louis Del Grande) possesses a gift of second sight, which he uses to help him solve crimes on the syndicated *Seeing Things*.

1987. Char (a psychic) hosts *The Extra Censory World of Char*, an ABC pilot that probes the world of E.S.P., telepathy, the paranormal and other psychic phenomena.

1990. After the horrifying murder of her family by a psychotic killer, young Sally Peters was left with a special psychic sensitivity on the NBC pilot *Chameleon in Blue*. Years later, as a criminal psychologist with the L.A.P.D., Sally (Loryn Locklin) uses her abilities to apprehend killers. Michael Burton (John DiAquino) is an L.A.P.D. cop who, after being shot, acquires a strange ability to see ghosts on the syndicated *Shades of L.A.* The shades, as John calls them, seek his help to complete unfinished business.

1993. Lyta Alexander (Patricia Tallman) is a stunning mind reader who was created by an alien race called the Vorlons as a weapon in their battle against the evil Shadows on *Babylon 5* (TNT). Barbara Eden plays Jesse Newman, a San Francisco psychotherapist who uses her powers of paranormal perception to help the police solve crimes on the NBC pilot *Visions of Murder* (Barbara starred in a second pilot, *Visions of Murder II*, in 1995).

1996. Derek Rayne (Derek DeLint) is leader of the San Francisco Legacy House, an organization that battles the occult, on *Poltergeist: The Legacy* (Showtime/Sci Fi). Derek possesses psychic abilities that he uses to help him battle the

evils of the paranormal. Ten-year-old Katherine Corrigan (Alexandra Purvis), the daughter of house psychologist Rachel Corrigan (Helen Shaver) shows promise of extraordinary psychic abilities and is often drawn into the evils that haunt the Legacy. On *The Profiler* (NBC), Ally Walker plays Samantha Walker, a forensic psychologist with the unique ability to feel for the victims of crime and understand the criminal mind (she can think in pictures and visualize the mind of a killer). Samantha is with the Violent Crimes Task Force of the FBI and was replaced in 1999 by Rachel Burke (Jamie Luner), an equally gifted profiler with psychic abilities.

2000. Frank Taylor (Matthew Fox) is a private detective who says, "I'm haunted" on UPN's *Haunted*. Frank was stabbed during a case investigation and flat lined during an operation to save his life. When revived, the experience left him with a link to the world beyond (departed souls haunt him to help them complete an earthly mission). Elmer Greentree (Bill Hobbs) is a famous medium who has formed a group of gifted individuals called *The Others* (NBC) who help people threatened by the supernatural. Others in the group are Marian Kitt (Julianne Nicholson) who can channel spirits through her body; Ellen Satori (Melissa Crider), a spirit medium; Miles Ballard (John Billingsley), a professor of folklore "who sees things that aren't there" (but can't quite interpret what he sees) and Mark Gabriel (Gabriel Macht), an impasse who can see the future.

2002. River Tam (Summer Glau) is a member of the *Serenity*, a futuristic spaceship, who possesses psychic abilities that are not yet fully developed on Fox's *Firefly*.

2003. Raven Baxter (Raven Symone) is a high school girl with limited psychic abilities (she can see several hours into the future) on *That's So Raven* (Disney). Eliza Dushku plays Tru Davies, a morgue attendant with the ability to help the dead by going back in time 24 hours to change the past on *Tru Calling* (Fox).

2004. Jess Mastriani (Catherine Scorsone) is a graduate of the FBI Training Center in Quantico who uses her psychic abilities to solve missing persons cases on *Missing* (Lifetime). Real life psychics help police solve real cases on *Psychic Detectives* (Court TV; Les Marshack narrates).

2005. Melinda Gordon (Jennifer Love Hewitt) is a young woman endowed with the ability to communicate with spirits — and help them fulfill their earthly missions on *The Ghost Whisperer* (CBS). Rebecca Locke (Rachel Nichols) is a profiler with the violent crimes unit of the FBI who uses her unique ability to apprehend criminals on *The Inside* (Fox). Allison DuBois (Patricia Arquette) is a young wife and mother who possesses the ability to see the dead and have spirits contact her on NBC's *Medium*. Allison uses her gift to help the police solve crimes. Allison's 10-year-old daughter Ariel (Sofia Vassllieva) appears to be developing the same powers (as she too has occasional dreams about horrifying events).

Men — Extraordinary

Men who are endowed with special powers or involved in situations that are out of the ordinary are the essence of this entry. See also *F.B.I. Agents, Men — Law Enforcers, Pilots, Space* and *Truckers.*

1958. A leaking chemical exposes scientist Peter Brady to an unknown substance that renders him invisible on *The Invisible Man* (Syn.; the identity of the actor playing the lead has never been revealed). David McCallum plays Daniel Weston, a scientist experimenting with laser beams who makes himself invisible (but can't reverse the process) to prove his Tele-Transportation Project works on NBC's *The Invisible Man* (1975). To make petty thief Darien Fawkes (Vincent Ventresca) do their bidding, a government scientist implants an artificial gland called Quick Silver in Darien's brain that renders him invisible on the Sci Fi Channel's *The Invisible Man* (2000. Darien assists because he needs weekly shots of a counteragent to prevent intense pain). A mysterious white "Lord of the Jungle" named Kimbar (Steve Reeves) and his chimpanzee Tamba, battle evil in Africa on the pilot *Kimbar of the Jungle.*

1959. An accidental exposure to an experimental rocket fuel affects the molecular structure of FBI agent Mel Hunter (Marshall Thompson) by reducing his height to six inches on the syndicated *World of Giants*. Don Diego de la Vega (Guy Williams) is a Spanish nobleman who takes up the cause of the weak in Old California as the masked avenger, Zorro, on ABC's *Zorro.*

1961. A white man, known only as the Phan-

tom (Roger Creed), fights for justice in Africa on the pilot *The Phantom.*

1966. Multi-millionaire Bruce Wayne (Adam West) becomes the mysterious Batman to bring criminals to justice on ABC's *Batman*. Britt Reid (Van Williams), the publisher of the *Daily Sentinel*, becomes the Green Hornet to battle crime on ABC's *The Green Hornet*. Ron Ely becomes Tarzan, Lord of the Jungle on NBC's *Tarzan.*

1967. South American rubber plantation owner Alfred (Wally Cox) fights injustice in his spare time on the CBS comedy pilot *Alfred of the Amazon*. Carter Nash (William Daniels) is a police chemist who invents a potion called Super Juice that transforms him into the heroic Captain Nice on NBC's *Captain Nice*. Stanley Beemish (Stephen Strimpell) is "a weak and droopy daffodil" who becomes "America's secret weapon against crime" when he takes a power pill on CBS's *Mister Terrific*. Jonathan Daly plays Walter, a mother dominated, clumsy jungle hero who battles evil on the CBS pilot *Walter of the Jungle.*

1968. Craig Stirling and Richard Barrett (Stuart Damon, William Gaunt) are agents for Nemesis who use their heightened senses to battle evil on NBC's *The Champions*. Denny Miller plays Tarzan, the Lord of the Jungle, on *Tarzan, the Ape Man*, a pilot filmed in 1959 but shown on TV in 1968 (February 23).

1970. Christopher George plays Ben Richards, a man with a rare blood type that prevents him from aging or catching disease on ABC's *The Immortal.*

1972. Hugh Lockwood (Hugh O'Brian), Nick Bianco (Tony Franciosa) and Christopher R. Grover (Doug McClure) are agents for the recovery service Probe who have been enhanced with super miniaturized computer implants on NBC's *Search.*

1973. Leonard Nimoy plays Tom Kovack, a race car driver who uses his powers of the occult to help people in trouble on the NBC pilot *Baffled*. A bionic operation that saves the life of astronaut Steve Austin (Lee Majors) makes him a part human, part machine agent for the government who battles evil on *The Six Million Dollar Man* (ABC).

1976. International Security Technics agent Sam Casey (Ben Murphy) is rendered invisible by a radioactive explosion on NBC's *The Gemini Man*. By wearing a special DNA stabilizer, Sam is able to control his invisibility for short periods of time. Jack Cole (Dack Rambo) is an expert criminal (learned the tricks of the trade while in prison) who uses his skills to bring white-collar criminals to justice on NBC's *Sword of Justice*.

1977. Crippled physics professor Nicholas Conrad (David Ackroyd) invents an exo-suit to enable him to walk and battle crime on the NBC pilot *Exo-Man*. Granville Van Dusen plays Paul Taylor, a sportswriter who communicates with the dead to help the living on the CBS pilot *The World of Darkness*.

1978. An accidental exposure to gamma radiation alters the DNA of scientist David Banner (Bill Bixby) and makes him capable of changing his appearance when angered on CBS's *The Incredible Hulk*. Sportswriter Paul Taylor (Granville Van Dusen) possesses the ability to communicate with unknown forces to help people threatened by evil on the CBS pilot *The World Beyond* (a revised version of *The World of Darkness*).

1979. Graduate student Peter Parker (Nicholas Hammond) is bitten by a radioactive spider and acquires the abilities of a spider on CBS's *The Amazing Spider-Man*. With the aid of FLAG (Full Latent Ability Gain), Steve Rogers (Reb Brown) becomes Captain America, a daring crusader for justice on the CBS pilot *Captain America*. David Selby plays Sir Thomas Earl, a dandy by day but the mysterious crime fighter Night Rider on the ABC pilot *The Night Rider*. Young daredevil Chris Darrow (Art Hindle) is struck by lightning, turned into a human dynamo and uses his powers to battle evil on the ABC pilot *The Power Within*.

1981. Schoolteacher Ralph Hinkley (William Katt) is chosen by aliens to battle evil on Earth as *The Greatest American Hero* (ABC). Ron Ely plays *The Seal* (NBC pilot), a man of mystery who tackles dangerous, high-risk cases.

1982. Michael Knight (David Hasselhoff) is a former police officer (Michael Long) who was given a new identity to fight evil via KITT, a Knight Industries 2000 high tech car on NBC's *Knight Rider*.

1983. Simon MacCorkindale plays Jonathan Chase, a professor at New York University who possesses the ability to transform himself into animals on *Manimal* (NBC). A lab accident renders private detective Chip Frye (Jack Blessing) to the height of six inches, making him a master of diminutive undercover work on *Small and Frye* (CBS). Darren McGavin plays Chip's partner, Nick Small.

1985. Johnny Bukowski (Mark Thomas Miller) is a rock star that can attract electricity and discharge lightning bolts. Elvin Lincoln (Kevin Peter Hall) is a scientist who injected himself with a formula that reduces his height to 12 inches. Together they help solve crimes for Humanidyne on NBC's *The Misfits of Science*. L.A.P.D. motorcycle cop Jesse Mach (Rex Smith) is chosen by federal agents to ride Street Hawk, a futuristic motorcycle designed to fight crime on ABC's *Street Hawk*.

1986. Greg Evigan plays Jack North, an astronaut whose exposure to a beam of sunlight enables him to accelerate his I.Q. on the ABC pilot *North Star*. Nick Mancuso plays a mysterious man known only as Stingray (by the black 1965 Corvette Stingray he drives) who helps people in trouble on NBC's *Stingray*. Cab driver Jeffrey Wilder (Scott Bakula) is accidentally exposed to a leaking canister of an alien substance that renders him indestructible on the ABC pilot *I-Man*.

1987. Comic book hero Captain Justice, alias Brad Steele (Jeff Lester), leaves the Comic Book World to help real people in Los Angeles on ABC's *Once a Hero*. Children's book author Nicholas Flemming (Lewis Van Bergen) avenges crimes as the mysterious Sable on ABC's *Sable*. Sam Jones plays Denny Colt, a mysterious figure who battles injustice on the ABC pilot *The Spirit*.

1988. Steve Levitt plays Donald Blake, an anthropologist who battles crime as Thor, an ancient Viking warrior on the NBC pilot *Thor*.

1990. A bolt of lightning strikes a shelf and douses police chemist Barry Allen (John Wesley Shipp) with chemicals that turns him into a crime fighter of incredible speed on CBS's *The Flash*. Ken Olandt plays Zack Stone, a cop who battles crime in a "super strong suit" that is equipped with the latest technology on the syndicated *Super Force*.

1991. Adrian Paul plays Alex Leibert, an around-the-clock vigilante known as the Owl, who helps people in trouble on the CBS pilot *The Owl*.

1992. Duncan MacLeod (Adrian Paul) is a mysterious man from a race of people called Immortals who destroys evil on the syndicated *The Highlander*. Christopher Chase (Rick Springfield) uses his talent for impersonation to help people in trouble on ABC's *Human Target*. Bob Einstein plays Super Dave Osborne, a totally incompetent stuntman who temps fate by performing incredibly dangerous stunts on Fox's *Super Dave*.

1994. Dr. Miles Hawkins (Carl Lumbly) is a crippled biophysicist who has created the Hornet, a black suit that enables him to walk and battle crime on *M.A.N.T.I.S.* (Fox). Former thief Michael Peyton (James McCaffrey) becomes the driver of *Viper*, a futuristic car he uses to fight crime on NBC's *Viper*. In the syndicated version (1997), Thomas Cole (Jeff Kaake), a former maverick CIA operative, becomes the new driver of *Viper*.

1995. Chance Harper (D.B. Sweeney), the only survivor of a devastating plane crash, teams with Lady Luck to help others on Fox's *Strange Luck*.

1996. A man known as Jarod (Michael T. Weiss) uses his talent of impersonation to help people in need on NBC's *The Pretender*. Richard Burgi plays Jim Ellison, a police detective who possesses amazing heightened senses on *The Sentinel* (Syn.).

1997. Wayne Szalinski (Peter Scolari) is a scientist for Jen Tech West Labs who uses an alien power source he found to make his inventions work on the syndicated *Honey I Shrunk the Kids: The TV Series*. Musician Johnny Domino (Matt McColm) is secretly NightMan, a crime fighter who uses a special bulletproof suit with advanced stealth capabilities on the syndicated *NightMan*.

1999. Daniel Goddard plays Dar, a man who can communicate with animals in a time when magic and nature ruled the world on the syndicated *BeastMaster*.

2000. Lorenzo Lamas plays Rafael Caine, an immortal that battles demons on the syndicated *Immortal*. Nineteenth century government agent Jack Stiles (Bruce Campbell) battles for right as the Daring Dragoon on the syndicated *Jack of All Trades*.

2001. A mysterious man known only as Lobo Fuerte (Maximo Morrone) is a masked wrestler who fights evil but never removes his mask on Fox's *Los Luchadores* (*The Wrestlers*). Brennan Mulray (Victor Webster) battles evil through enhanced DNA that allows him to generate electricity through his body and discharge bolts of electricity on the syndicated *Mutant X*.

2003. Jake Foley (Christopher Gorham) receives enhanced abilities to fight crime when he is exposed to a malfunctioning computer on *Jake*

2.0 (UPN). John Clayton, Jr., alias Tarzan (Travis Femmel) uses his unique jungle skills to avoid capture in New York City after he escapes his captors on *Tarzan* (WB).

Men — Gays see Gays (Male)

Men — Law Enforcers

Characters who are involved with law enforcement as police officers, sheriffs or private detectives are the subjects of this entry. See also *District Attorneys, F.B.I. Agents, Forensics, Women — Law Enforcers*.

1937. Sherlock Holmes (Louis Hector) and Dr. Watson (William Podmore) struggle to find a man with the odd name of Garrideb to fill the conditions of an eccentric's will on the NBC experiment *The Adventure of the Three Garridebs*.

1941. NBC adapts an episode of its radio series, *The Bishop and the Gargoyle* to TV on November 29. The episode, "The Item of the Scarlet Ace," finds a crime fighter known as the Bishop (Richard Gordon) and his assistant the Gargoyle (Ken Lynch) seeking a criminal known as the Scarlet Ace.

1948. Frank Albertson stars as Peter Hunter, a tough private detective working out of New York City on *Peter Hunter, Private Eye* (earliest known syndicated test film).

1949. Jeffrey Hall (Gordon Urquhart) is a criminologist with the Chicago Police Department on DuMont's *Chicagoland Mystery Players*. Mike Barnett (Ralph Bellamy, Frank Lovejoy) is a two-fisted private detective working out of New York City on *The Man Against Crime* (CBS/DuMont/NBC; also known as *Follow That Man*). Martin Kane (William Gargan, Lloyd Nolan, Lee Tracy) is a New York based private detective who achieves results through sheer determination on NBC's *Martin Kane, Private Eye*. Joseph Allen and Mary Lou Taylor play Jerry and Pamela North, the husband and wife who solve crimes on the NBC test film *Mr. and Mrs. North*. Marvin Miller plays Dr. Yat Fu, a curio shop owner and amateur sleuth on ABC's *Mysteries of Chinatown*. Chuck Webster plays Hannibal Cobb, an inspector with the N.Y.P.D. on ABC's *Photocrime*. The subjective camera is used to detail the investigations of a never seen lieutenant (voice of Ken Lynch) with the N.Y.P.D. on DuMont's *The Plainclothesman* (the camera becomes the eyes of the lieutenant, through which the viewer sees what he sees). On ABC's *Stand By for Crime*, Inspector Webb (Boris Aplon) investigates a case in which all the clues are given. The action is stopped prior to the conclusion to allow a guest detective to solve the case. The drama then continues to reveal the culprit. Jason Meadows and his wife Jayne (Earl Hammond, Carol Hill) are husband and wife detectives who solve crimes on the DuMont test film *Trouble, Inc.*

1950. Ellery Queen (Richard Hart, Lee Bowman, Hugh Marlowe) is a gentleman detective and writer who solves crimes to acquire story material on *The Adventures of Ellery Queen* (DuMont/ABC/Syn.). Charlie Wild (Kevin Morrison, John McQuade) is a tough New York based private investigator on *Charlie Wild, Private Detective* (CBS/ABC/DuMont). Adam Conway (Donald Curtis) is an N.Y.P.D. detective whose assignments are complicated by his wife Connie (Lynn Bari), an amateur sleuth, on *The Detective's Wife* (CBS). Ralph Byrd plays Dick Tracy, the dauntless plainclothes police detective on ABC's *Dick Tracy*. George Fame (Don DeFore) and his wife Sally (Gale Storm) are detectives who solve crimes on the ABC test film *Mystery and Mrs. Reed*. Hadley plays John Braddock, a captain with the San Francisco Police Department who solves crimes associated with con artists on *Racket Squad* (Syn./CBS). Rocky King (Roscoe Karns) is a plainclothes detective with the Homicide Division of the Manhattan 24th Precinct on DuMont's *Rocky King, Inside Detective.*

1951. Boston Blackie (Kent Taylor) is a former thief who uses his skills to help solve crimes as a private detective on the syndicated *Boston Blackie.* Jim Riland (Rusty Lane) is an N.Y.P.D. Homicide Bureau Chief who receives help in solving crimes from his daughter, Chris (Peggy Lobbin) on ABC's *Crime with Father.* Jack Webb plays Joe Friday, the no-nonsense sergeant with the L.A.P.D. on NBC's *Dragnet.* Tom Conway plays Mark Saber, a plainclothes detective with the Homicide Division of the N.Y.P.D. on ABC's *Mark Saber.* Jerry and Pamela North (Richard Denning, Barbara Britton) are a married couple who solve crimes on *Mr. and Mrs. North* (CBS/NBC). Sherlock Holmes (John Longden) and Dr.

Watson (Campbell Singer) team to solve crimes on the pilot *Sherlock Holmes.*

1952. Eddie Drake (Don Haggerty) is a private detective who receives help from Karen Gayle (Patricia Morison, Lynn Roberts), a psychologist writing a book on criminal behavior on *The Cases of Eddie Drake* (DuMont). Craig Kennedy (Donald Woods) is a criminologist who uses scientific deduction to solve crimes on the syndicated *Craig Kennedy, Criminologist.* Steve Randall (Melvyn Douglas) is a disbarred attorney turned private detective on *Hollywood Off Beat* (Syn./DuMont/CBS).

1953. Rod Cameron plays Bart Grant, a lieutenant with the N.Y.P.D. on the syndicated *City Detective.* George Raft plays George Kirby, a tough plainclothes detective with the N.Y.P.D. on *I'm the Law* (Syn.). Jimmy Hughes (Billy Redfield, Conrad Janis) is a Korean War vet who joins the N.Y.P.D. on DuMont's *Jimmy Hughes, Rookie Cop.* James Newell plays Douglas Renfrew, a Royal Canadian Mounted Policeman on *Renfrew of the Mounted* (Syn.). Mark Andrews plays Skip Taylor, a rugged private detective on the syndicated pilot *Skip Taylor.*

1954. Ben Guthrie (Warner Anderson) is a lieutenant and Matt Grebb (Tom Tully) is an inspector with the San Francisco Police Department on CBS's *The Line-Up* (also known as *San Francisco Beat*). Michael Lanyard (Louis Hayward) is a private detective known as *The Lone Wolf* (Syn.). London of the 1890s is the setting for the crime solving adventures of master detective Sherlock Holmes (Ronald Howard) and his assistant Dr. John H. Watson (H. Marion Crawford) on the syndicated *Sherlock Holmes.* Anthony Ross is Richard Hale, a detective with the Homicide Division of the N.Y.P.D. who solves crimes through one seemingly insignificant piece of evidence on *The Telltale Clue* (CBS).

1955. Jeffrey Jones (Don Haggerty) is a confidential investigator based in New York City on *The Files of Jeffrey Jones* (Syn.). Bruce Seton plays Robert Fabian, a superintendent of detectives at London's Scotland Yard on the syndicated *Inspector Fabian of Scotland Yard.* Russell Napier and Ken Henry play Duggan and Ross, inspectors with the Criminal Investigation Division of London's *Scotland Yard* (Syn.). Richard Simmons is William Preston, a sergeant with the Northwest Canadian Mounted Police during the gold rush days of the 1890s on the syndicated *Sergeant Preston of the Yukon.*

1956. Mike Hercules (Hugh Beaumont) is a tough San Francisco based detective on the ABC pilot *Alias Mike Hercules*. Broderick Crawford plays Dan Matthews, a chief of the highway patrol who is representative of any such state law enforcer on the syndicated *Highway Patrol*. Victor Beaujac (Stacy Harris) and John Conroy (Louis J. Sirgo) are homicide detectives with the New Orleans Police Department on *N.O.P.D.* (Syn.). Frank Morgan (John Bromfield) is a modern day sheriff in Cochise, Arizona, on *Sheriff of Cochise* (Syn.).

1957. Robert Beatty plays Hugh "Bulldog" Drummond, a captain with London's New Scotland Yard on the NBC pilot *Bulldog Drummond*. Police work in action is seen through the work of George Barnett (Richard Travis), the assistant sheriff of Los Angeles County, on the syndicated *Code 3*. Colonel Perceval March (Boris Karloff) is an inspector who heads D-3 (the Office of Queen's Complaints) of London's New Scotland Yard on *Colonel March of Scotland Yard* (Syn.). Donald Lam (Billy Pearson) is a shrewd investigator who is partners with the penny-pinching Bertha Cool (Beany Venuta) on the CBS pilot *Cool and Lam*. Tim Considine and Tommy Kirk play Joe and Frank Hardy, the sons of famed detective Fenton Hardy on two *Mickey Mouse Club* serials: *The Hardy Boys and the Mystery of the Applegate Treasure* and *The Mystery of Ghost Farm*. Frank Ballinger (Lee Marvin) is a special plainclothes detective with M Squad, a special division of the Chicago Police Department that handles dangerous cases on NBC's *M Squad*. Frank Lovejoy plays McGraw, a private detective who wanders from state to state minding other people's business on NBC's *Meet McGraw*. J. Carrol Naish plays Charlie Chan, the philosophical Chinese detective on *The New Adventures of Charlie Chan* (Syn.). Richard Diamond (David Janssen) is a New York (then Los Angeles) based private investigator on *Richard Diamond, Private Detective* (CBS/NBC; also known as *Call Mr. D.*). Donald Gray plays Mark Saber, a chief inspector with Scotland Yard on NBC's *Saber of London*. Rod Cameron plays Rod Blake, a chief of the Nevada state troopers on the syndicated *State Trooper*. When innocent people become the pawns of master criminals, Robert Stryker (Clifford Evans), a chief inspector for Scotland Yard, steps in on the syndicated *Stryker of Scotland Yard*. Nick and Nora Charles (Peter Lawford, Phyllis Kirk) are a married couple who solve crimes on NBC's *The Thin Man*.

1958. Michael Maguire (Robert Beatty) is a Royal Canadian Mounted Policeman assigned to study British crime detection methods at New Scotland Yard on the syndicated *Dial 999*. Ellery Queen (George Nader, Lee Phillips) solves crimes to acquire story material for his books on *The Further Adventures of Ellery Queen* (NBC). Jeff Prior (Lonny Chapman) is a tough New York based private detective on *The Investigator* (NBC). Joe Jones (Scott McKay) is a private detective based in Spain who helps Americans in trouble on *It Happened in Spain* (Syn.). Mark Stevens plays Michael Shayne, a two-fisted private detective on the NBC pilot *Michael Shayne, Detective*. Darren McGavin plays Mike Hammer, the tough detective with an eye for the ladies on *Mike Hammer* (Syn.). Dan Muldoon (John McIntire) and Jim Halloran (James Franciscus) are detectives with the Manhattan 65th Precinct on ABC's *Naked City*. Craig Stevens is Peter Gunn, a suave private detective based in Los Angeles on *Peter Gunn* (NBC/ABC). Tom Reid (Tom Hellmore) is a detective superintendent with London's Scotland Yard on the CBS pilot *Secrets of the Old Bailey*. Stuart Bailey and Jeff Spencer (Efrem Zimbalist, Jr., Roger Smith) are detectives who operate out of plush offices at 77 Sunset Strip in Hollywood, California, on ABC's *77 Sunset Strip*. Frank Morgan (John Bromfield) is a U.S. marshal stationed in Arizona on the syndicated *U.S. Marshal*.

1959. Roy Brenner (Edward Binns) is head of the Confidential Squad, a special crime-busting unit of the N.Y.P.D. on CBS's *Brenner*. Rex Randolph and Cal Calhoune (Richard Long, Andrew Duggan) are New Orleans based detectives on ABC's *Bourbon Street Beat*. Ken Clark plays Brock Callahan, a Beverly Hills private detective on the CBS pilot *Brock Callahan*. Matt Holbrook (Robert Taylor) is head of an elite team of plainclothes detectives who battle criminal elements on ABC's *The Detectives*. Tige Andrews and Adam West co-star as Lt. Johnny Russo and Sgt. Steve Nelson. Viewers are challenged to solve a capsule mystery before the intrepid Inspector Hannibal Cobb (James Craig) on the syndicated *Hannibal Cobb*. Tom Lopaka (Robert Conrad), Tracy Steele (Anthony Eisley) and Gregg MacKenzie (Grant Williams) are Honolulu based private detectives on ABC's *Hawaiian Eye*. Barney Colby (Ernie Kovacs) is a detective with an uncanny sense of smell who uses his gift to solve crimes on the CBS pilot *I Was a Bloodhound*. Ken Burns (Arthur Fleming) is the chief investigator for the William J. Burns Detective Agency on the syndicated *International Detective*. Johnny Staccato (John Cassavetes) is a jazz musician turned private detective working out of New York City on NBC's *Johnny Staccato*. Barney Ruditsky (James Gregory) is a plainclothes detective in 1920s New York City on NBC's *The Lawless Years*. Howard Finucane (Victory Jory) is a San Diego based police lieutenant on the syndicated *Manhunt*. William Reynolds plays Pete Kelly, a jazz musician in 1920s Kansas City turned unofficial detective who helps people in trouble on NBC's *Pete Kelly's Blues*. The day-to-day operations of a police station (Precinct 11) of a big city are seen through the eyes of Sergeant White (Baynes Barron) and Sgt. Stan Albertson (Henry Beckman) on the syndicated *Police Station*. Keith Andes plays Frank Dawson, the police chief of an unnamed city on the syndicated *This Man Dawson*. Nick Stone (Mike Connors) is an undercover police agent who attempts to infiltrate the mob on CBS's *Tightrope*. David Chase (Dennis Morgan) is a private detective who devises elaborate plans to solve crimes on *21 Beacon Street* (NBC).

1960. Sheriff Andy Taylor (Andy Griffith) and his deputy, Barney Fife (Don Knotts), uphold the law in the virtually crime free town of Mayberry, North Carolina, on CBS's *The Andy Griffith Show*. Mike and Bob Brannigan (Steve Dunne, Mark Roberts) are brothers who also happen to be private detectives based in Phoenix, Arizona, on *The Brothers Brannigan* (Syn.). John Hunter is a detective for the London based Eastern Insurance Company on *The Cheaters* (Syn.). Don Cory and Jed Sills (Anthony George, Doug McClure) are detectives with the San Francisco based Checkmate, Inc., on CBS's *Checkmate*. Dan Adams (Rod Cameron) is a private detective working out of San Diego's Coronado Peninsula on the syndicated *Coronado 9*. Skip Homeier plays Dan Raven, a detective lieutenant with the Hollywood sheriff's office on NBC's *Dan Raven*. Paul Duval (Charles Korvin) is a chief inspector for the International Police Force on *The Man from Interpol* (Syn.). Edmond O'Brien plays Johnny Midnight, an actor turned Manhattan private detective on the syndicated *Johnny Midnight*. Michael O'Shea plays Dan McGarry, a kind-hearted police officer on the CBS pilot *McGarry and Me* (Virginia Mayo plays his wife Kitty, the "me" of the title). Tony

Smith (Richard Wyler) is a New Scotland Yard Inspector who has been assigned to active duty with the International Police Force on NBC's *The Man from Interpol*. Richard Denning is Michael Shayne, a tough private investigator working out of Miami, Florida, on NBC's *Michael Shayne, Private Detective*. Adam Flint and Mike Parker (Paul Burke, Horace MacMahon) are detectives with the 65th Precinct of the N.Y.P.D. on ABC's *Naked City* (60 minute episodes). Philip Marlowe (Philip Carey) is a rugged private detective who wanders from state to state to solve crimes on *Philip Marlowe* (ABC). Jacques Gagnier (Gilles Pelletier) is a member of the Royal Canadian Mounted Police based in Shamattawa, Canada, on the syndicated *R.C.M.P.* Jock Mahoney plays Simon Lash, a two-fisted private detective on the pilot *Simon Lash*. Handsome detectives Dave Thorne, Ken Madison and Sandy Winfield (Lee Patterson, Van Williams, Troy Donahue) operate out of a houseboat docked at SurfSide 6 in Miami Beach, Florida, on ABC's *SurfSide 6*. Harry Lime (Michael Rennie) is a London based business tycoon who enjoys using his skills as a detective to help people on *The Third Man* (Syn.).

1961. Pete Bishop (Jerome Thor) is a rugged private detective based on San Francisco's Barbary Coast on the NBC pilot *Along the Barbary Coast*. Matthew Gower and Gus Honocek (Jack Warden, Arch Johnson) are detectives with the Metropolitan Squad of the N.Y.P.D. on ABC's *The Asphalt Jungle*. Big Jake Sloane (Andy Devine) is an elderly, jolly detective who uses common sense to solve crimes on the NBC pilot *Big Jake*. Gunther Toody and Francis Muldoon (Joe E. Ross, Fred Gwynne) are patrol car officers with the 53rd Precinct in the Bronx, New York, on NBC's *Car 54, Where Are You?* Steve Carella and Bert Kling (Robert Lansing, Ron Harper) are detectives attached to the 87th Precinct of the N.Y.P.D. on NBC's *The 87th Precinct*. Lincoln Vail (Ron Hayes) is a law enforcement officer with the Everglades County Patrol in Florida on *The Everglades* (Syn.). Steve Banks and Russ Andrews (James Philbrook, James Franciscus) are highly skilled New York based private investigators on CBS's *The Investigators*. Mike Madison and Larry Lahr (Ron Ely, Jeremy Slate) are diving instructors who moonlight as private detectives on *Malibu Run* (CBS). Lieutenant Price Adams (Leslie Nielsen) and Sergeant Vince Cavelli (John Beradino) are detectives with the elite Metro Squad of the

L.A.P.D. on ABC's *The New Breed*. Tom Smith (Audie Murphy) is a detective in 1870s Denver who uses modern (for the times) methods of analysis to apprehend criminals on *Whispering Smith* (NBC).

1962. Robert Vaughn plays A. Dunster Lowell, a Harvard-educated private detective on the NBC pilot *The Boston Terrier*. A police agent, known only as Mike (Mike Connors), infiltrates organized crime on the ABC pilot *The Expendables*. Martin Gabel plays Hercule Poirot, Agatha Christie's famous Belgian detective who uses his wit to solve crimes on the CBS pilot *Hercule Poirot*.

1963. Ben Gazzara plays Nick Anderson, a sergeant with the L.A.P.D. on ABC's *Arrest and Trial*. Robert Vaughn plays private detective A. Dunster Lowell for the second time (see 1962) on the ABC pilot *The Boston Terrier*. Amos Burke (Gene Barry) is a millionaire and a police captain with the L.A.P.D. on ABC's *Burke's Law*. J.F. Kelly (Bob Cummings) is a 1940s style private detective who puts his nose to the grindstone to solve crimes on the NBC pilot *Last of the Private Eyes*.

1964. Bill Ballin (Peter Graves) is a former police officer turned private detective who works for the Las Vegas Casino Owners Association on the NBC pilot *Las Vegas Beat*.

1965. Patrick Stone (Jeff Davis) is a not-too-bright private investigator who solves crimes quite by accident on the CBS pilot *Patrick Stone*. Paul Cameron (Mark Miller) is a London based private detective who helps distressed American tourists on the CBS pilot *The Search*.

1966. Sam Stone and Jim Briggs (Howard Duff, Dennis Cole) are detectives with the L.A.P.D. on ABC's *The Felony Squad*. John Hawk (Burt Reynolds) is a detective with the N.Y.P.D. who is part Iroquois Indian on ABC's *Hawk*. George Holloway (David Wayne) is a by-the-books private detective who often receives help from his daughters, amateur sleuths Fleming and Casey (Brooke Bundy, Barbara Hershey) on the NBC pilot *Holloways Daughters*.

1967. Ray McDonnell plays Dick Tracy, a dauntless plainclothes detective with the N.Y.P.D. on the ABC pilot *Dick Tracy*. Jack Webb returns as the no nonsense Joe Friday, a sergeant with the L.A.P.D. on NBC's *Dragnet* (see 1951). Tim Matheson and Rick Gates play Joe and Frank Hardy, the amateur detectives of investigator Fenton Hardy on the NBC pilot *The Hardy Boys*.

Johnny Corso, Mike Haines and Jeff Ward (Frank Converse, Jack Warden, Robert Hooks) are detectives with the 27th Precinct of the N.Y.P.D. on ABC's *N.Y.P.D.* Steve Ihnat plays James Paige, the captain of a large metropolitan police department on the NBC pilot *Police Story*.

1968. Pete Malloy and Jim Reed (Martin Milner, Kent McCord) are patrol car officers with the L.A.P.D. whose code is *Adam-12* (NBC). Tom Simcox plays Braddock, an investigator and partner in the Los Angeles law firm of Braddock and Tratner on the CBS pilot *Braddock*. Steve McGarrett (Jack Lord) and Danny Williams (James MacArthur) are detectives with the Five-0 branch of the Hawaiian Police Department on CBS's *Hawaii Five-0*. John McGill (Richard Bradford) is a former American intelligence agent turned London based private investigator on ABC's *Man in a Suitcase*. Joe Mannix (Mike Connors) is first a detective with the Los Angeles firm of Intertect then an independent investigator on CBS's *Mannix*. Pete Cochrane, Julie Barnes and Linc Hayes (Michael Cole, Peggy Lipton, Clarence Williams III) are young adults recruited by the L.A.P.D. as undercover agents called *The Mod Squad* (ABC). David Ross (Darren McGavin) is a embittered private detective who prefers to work alone on NBC's *The Outsider*.

1969. Deputy Police Chief Sam Danforth (Leslie Nielsen) teams with D.A. William Washburn (Hari Rhodes) to maintain the law on NBC's *The Law Enforcers*. George Maharis plays Gus Monk, a private detective who wanders from state-to-state helping people on the ABC pilot *The Monk*. John Woodruff (James Whitmore) is a private detective and criminology professor at U.C.L.A. who, with his partner Tony Novello (Enzo Ceruscio), solves crimes on NBC's *My Friend Tony*.

1970. Dan August (Burt Reynolds) is a detective lieutenant with the Santa Luisa Police Department on ABC's *Dan August*. Sam McCloud (Dennis Weaver) is a deputy marshal from Taos, New Mexico, who is studying crime detection methods under Chief Peter B. Clifford (J.D. Cannon) at New York's 27th Precinct on *McCloud* (NBC). Vanessa Smith (Yvette Mimieux) and Jonathan Croft (George Maharis) solve murders under the watchful eye of master criminologist Ethan Arcane (Ralph Bellamy) on *The Most Deadly Game* (ABC).

1971. Glenn Ford plays Sam Cade, the sheriff

of Madrid County, a southwestern community on *Cade's County* (CBS). Deputies J.J. Jackson and Arlo Pritchard (Edgar Buchanan, Taylor Lacher) assist Cade. William Conrad plays Frank Cannon, an overweight private detective working out of Los Angeles on CBS's *Cannon*. Peter Falk is Lieutenant Columbo, a shrewd and persistent detective with the L.A.P.D. on NBC's *Columbo*. Jason King, Annabelle Hurst and Stewart Sullivan (Peter Wyngarde, Rosemary Nicols, Joel Fabiani) are special operatives for Interpol on the syndicated *Department S*. Peter Lawford plays Ellery Queen, the gentleman writer and detective on the NBC pilot *Ellery Queen: Don't Look Behind You*. Stewart McMillan (Rock Hudson) is the police commissioner of San Francisco who receives help in solving crimes from his wife Sally (Susan Saint James) on NBC's *McMillan and Wife*. The bumbling Lenny Crooke (Don Adams) and the level-headed George Robinson (Rupert Crosse) are mismatched detectives with the 33rd Precinct of the L.A.P.D. on NBC's *The Partners*. Chad Smith (Henry Fonda) is a sergeant with the L.A.P.D. who is also a family man on ABC's *The Smith Family*. James McEachin plays Harry Tenafly, a detective with Hightower Investigations in Los Angeles on NBC's *Tenafly*.

1972. Robert Conrad plays Nick Carter, a turn-of-the-century private detective working out of New York City on the ABC pilot *The Adventures of Nick Carter*. Miles C. Banyon (Robert Forester) is a detective in 1937 Los Angeles on NBC's *Banyon*. Fabian Holme (Arte Johnson) is a private detective who uses his mastery of disguises to apprehend criminals on the NBC pilot *Call Holme*. Frank Farraday (Dan Dailey) and his son Steve (James Naughton) are Los Angeles based private detectives on NBC's *Farraday and Company*. Richard Widmark plays Dan Madigan, a sergeant with the 10th Precinct of the N.Y.P.D. on NBC's *Madigan*. Harry Rule, Caroline di Contini and Paul Buchet (Robert Vaughn, Nyree Dawn Porter, Tony Anholt) are private detectives who battle crime in Europe as part of an organization called *The Protectors* (Syn.). William Gillis, Terry Webster and Michael Danko (Michael Ontkean, Georg Stanford Brown, Sam Melville) are rookie police officers with Station Number 7 of the Southern California P.D. on ABC's *The Rookies*. Stewart Grainger plays Sherlock Holmes and Bernard Fox is Dr. Watson, detectives who solve baffling crimes on the ABC pilot *Sherlock Holmes:*

The Hound of the Baskervilles. Mike Stone (Karl Malden) and Steve Keller (Michael Douglas) are detectives with the San Francisco P.D. on ABC's *The Streets of San Francisco*.

1973. Buddy Ebsen plays Barnaby Jones, an L.A.-based private detective who is also an investigator for the California Meridian Insurance Company on *Barnaby Jones* (CBS). Chase Reddick (Mitchell Ryan) is a captain with the L.A.P.D. who establishes Chase, a unit that solves crimes left unsolved by other departments on NBC's *Chase*. Eddie Egan (Eugene Roche) is a former N.Y.P.D. detective who now works for the L.A.P.D. on the ABC pilot *Egan*. Wade Griffin (Lorne Greene) is a former police captain turned private detective on ABC's *Griff*. Doc Long, Jack Packard and Reggie York (David Hartman, Les Crane, Hagan Beggs) are private detectives who roam the world solving crimes on the NBC pilot *I Love a Mystery* (based on the radio series). Former FBI agent John McKinson (Stewart Whitman) runs Intertect, an international investigative agency on the ABC pilot *Intertect*. Sam Jarrett (Glenn Ford) is an ex prize fighter turned private detective who specializes in crimes associated with the fine arts on the NBC pilot *Jarrett*. Telly Savalas is Theo Kojak, a tough, no-nonsense lieutenant with the Manhattan South Precinct on *Kojak* (CBS). John Shaft (Richard Roundtree) is a hip black detective who solves baffling crimes on CBS's *Shaft*. David Toma (Tony Musante) is a detective with the New Jersey P.D. who uses his wizardry of disguises to apprehend criminals on ABC's *Toma*. Sam Wheeler and Terry Murdock (Jack Warden, Christopher Stone) are Seattle based private detectives on the ABC pilot *Wheeler and Murdock*.

1974. Thomas Banacek (George Peppard) is an insurance investigator who solves crimes to recover items on NBC's *Banacek*. Jefferson Keyes (James Farentino) is a private detective who charges $1 million a case and guarantees results (or refunds the money) on *Cool Million* (NBC). Vincent Gardenia plays Sonny Miglio, a hard-boiled city police captain who is transferred to a quiet suburban precinct on the CBS pilot *Cops*. Harry Orwell (David Janssen) is a former L.A.P.D. police officer turned private detective after being shot in the back and disabled on ABC's *Harry O*. Clint Walker plays Cal McKay, an officer with the Alaska State Police Patrol on *Kodiak* (ABC). Dan Madigan (Richard Widmark) is an embittered detective with the Manhattan 10th Precinct on NBC's *Madigan*. Paul and Nancy Roscommon (Anthony Costello, Marianne McAndrew) are newlyweds who are also police officers on the CBS pilot *Mr. and Mrs. Cop*. Robert Forster plays Nakia Parker, a Navaho Indian who is the deputy sheriff of Davis County, New Mexico, on *Nakia* (ABC). Arthur Kennedy is the sheriff, Sam Jericho, and Gloria DeHaven is Deputy Irene James. Jim Rockford (James Garner) is an ex-con turned private investigator (owner of the Rockford Private Detective Agency in Malibu Beach, California) on NBC's *The Rockford Files*.

1975. Andy Griffith plays Sam Adams, the sheriff of the small resort town of Eagle Lake on ABC's *Adams of Eagle Lake*. Brian Keith plays Lew Archer, a private detective working out of Melrose, California, on *Archer* (NBC). Roman Grey (Ron Leibman) is a Gypsy antique dealer and amateur sleuth working out of New York City on the NBC pilot *The Art of Crime*. Robert Blake plays Tony Baretta, an undercover cop with an array of disguises on ABC's *Baretta*. Barney Miller (Hal Linden) is the chief of detectives of the N.Y.P.D.'s 12th Precinct on ABC's *Barney Miller*. Other detectives in the unit include Phil Fish (Abe Vigoda), Stan Wojehowich (Max Gail), Ron Harris (Ron Glass) and Nick Yemana (Jack Soo). William Morgan, called "Bumper," (George Kennedy) is a veteran L.A.P.D. cop who still walks a beat on CBS's *The Blue Knight*. Alex Bronkov (Jack Palance) is a police lieutenant under special assignment to the mayor of Ocean City, California, on CBS's *Bronk*. Ben Logan and Mark Walters (Stacy Keach, Carl Franklin) are Miami-based police agents who tackle assignments in the Caribbean on *Caribe* (ABC). Frank Murphy (Charles Durning) is a bachelor police officer (6th Division of the L.A.P.D.) who cares for an orphaned boy named Lucas Adams (Tierre Turner) on NBC's *The Cop and the Kid*. Larry Hagman plays Dennis O'Finn, a not-too-bright private detective on the NBC pilot *The Detective*. Jim Hutton is Ellery Queen, the gentleman writer-detective (here in 1947 New York) on NBC's *Ellery Queen*. Joe Forrester (Lloyd Bridges) is a veteran cop who rejects a desk job to walk his old beat on NBC's *Joe Forrester*. Khigh Dheigh plays Khan, a Chinese detective with the San Francisco Police Department on CBS's *Khan!* Matt Helm (Anthony Franciosa) is a former government in-

telligence agent turned Los Angeles private detective on ABC's *Matt Helm*. David Robbins and his wife Mandy (John Rubinstein, Lee Kroeger) are husband and wife private detectives on the ABC pilot *Mr. and Ms.* Dave Starsky and Ken Hutchinson (Paul Michael Glaser, David Soul) are unorthodox detectives with the Metropolitan Division of the L.A.P.D. on ABC's *Starsky and Hutch*. Dave Greenberg and Bobby Hantz (Steven Keats, Alan Feinstein) are crime busting N.Y.P.D. cops called "Batman and Robin" on the CBS pilot *Super Cops*. Dan Harrelson (Steve Forrest) heads the Special Weapons and Tactics unit of the West California Police Department on ABC's *S.W.A.T.* His officers include David Kay (Rod Perry) and James Street (Robert Urich). Retired bunco cop Frank McBride (Eddie Albert) teams with ex con Pete Ryan (Robert Wagner) to beat swindlers at their own game on *Switch* (CBS).

1976. Bob Dishy plays Edward R. Ace, an eccentric private detective on the ABC pilot *Ace*. Bert D'Angelo (Paul Sorvino) is an L.A.P.D. cop whose impressive record of arrests have earned him the nickname "Superstar" on ABC's *Bert D'Angelo, Superstar*. Jake Axminster (Wayne Rogers) is a hard-boiled private detective working out of Los Angeles (1930s) on *City of Angels* (NBC). Judd Hirsch plays Dominic Delvecchio, a detective with the Washington Heights Division of the L.A.P.D. on *Delvecchio* (CBS). Alexander Holmes (Richard B. Shull) is a sergeant with the L.A.P.D. who has been teamed with Gregory Yoyonovich (John Schuck), a not quite perfected robot designed to battle crime on *Holmes and Yoyo* (ABC). John St. John (Jack Warden) is a homicide detective with the L.A.P.D. who has been nicknamed "Jigsaw" for his ability to solve complex crimes on NBC's *Jigsaw John*. Rock Hudson plays Stewart McMillan, police commissioner of San Francisco, on NBC's *McMillan* (a revamped version of *McMillan and Wife* without Sally; see 1971). Lincoln Evers (Robert Stack) is a captain who heads the Most Wanted Unit of the L.A.P.D. on ABC's *Most Wanted*. Officer Kate Manners (Jo Ann Harris) and Sgt. Charlie Nelson (Shelly Novack) are members of the unit. Frank Carey (Vic Morrow) is a former Secret Service agent turned private investigator on the CBS pilot *The P.I.* David Birney plays Frank Serpico, an undercover police officer with the 22nd Precinct of the N.Y.P.D. on *Serpico* (NBC). Tony and Shep Thomas (Jim Hager, Jon Hager) are twin police officers that pretend to be one to get the edge on investigations on the ABC pilot *Twin Detectives*.

1977. Benny Kowalski and Barney Tuscon (Terry Kiser, Tim Thomerson) are Las Vegas Police Department officers who moonlight as nightclub singer-musicians on the NBC pilot *Benny and Barney: Las Vegas Undercover*. Roy Moby (Victor French) is an old-fashioned police chief (of Clinton Corners, Georgia); Curtis Baker (Kene Holliday) is a former N.Y.P.D. officer with progressive ideas. The two constantly disagree about everything on ABC's *Carter Country*. Frank Poncherello and Jon Baker (Erik Estrada, Larry Wilcox) are motorcycle officers with the California Highway Patrol on NBC's *CHiPs*. Jack Ramsey (Lou Antonio) is a street-smart L.A.P.D. sergeant who is teamed with J.Z. Kane (Kim Basinger), a sweet and beautiful country girl who is his direct opposite on ABC's *Dog and Cat*. Joe Cleaver (Ernest Borgnine) and Bill Bundy (John Amos) are L.A.P.D. officers who work with John "Kid" Haven (Michael Shannon), a robot programmed to be the perfect law enforcer on ABC's *Future Cop*. Parker Stevenson and Shaun Cassidy play Frank and Joe Hardy, the detective sons of world famous investigator Fenton Hardy on ABC's *The Hardy Boys Mysteries*. Paul Lanigan (Art Carney), the police chief of Cameron, California, receives help in solving crimes from Rabbi David Small (Bruce Solomon), an amateur sleuth on NBC's *Lanigan's Rabbi*. Stoney Huff (Claude Akins) is a detective with the Nashville Metropolitan Police Department on *Nashville 99* (CBS). Mark Harmon plays Mike Breen, an L.A.P.D. officer who is teamed with Sam, a specially trained Labrador retriever on *Sam* (CBS).

1978. David Cassidy plays Dan Shay, an undercover agent with the L.A.P.D. on NBC's *David Cassidy — Man Undercover*. Twenty-three-year-old Richie Brockelman (Dennis Dugan) is a fledging private detective trying to make a name for himself on NBC's *Richie Brockelman, Private Eye*. Jerry Sparrow (Randy Herman) is a mailroom clerk turned detective for a large New Orleans agency on the CBS pilot *Sparrow*. Charlie Morgan and Frank Sarno (Don Johnson, Joe Bennett) are undercover cops with the 25th Precinct of a large city that is nicknamed *The Two-Five* (ABC pilot). Dan Tanna (Robert Urich) is a tough private detective with a penchant for helping beautiful women in trouble on ABC's *Vegas* (he operates out of the Desert Inn Hotel and Casino).

1979. Harry Guardino plays (No First Name) Bender, a 20-year veteran of the N.Y.P.D. who becomes the police chief of a California desert community called Tamarisk Falls on the CBS pilot *Bender*. Oscar Ramsey (Robert Conrad) is a retired boxer (called "The Duke") turned Chicago private investigator on NBC's *The Duke*. Joe Don Baker plays Earl Eischied, chief of detectives of the N.Y.P.D. on NBC's *Eischied* (Rick Alessi and Carol Wright [Vincent Bufano, Suzanne Lederer] are two of his detectives). Woodrow Paris (James Earl Jones) is a college criminology professor and a captain of the Metro Squad Division of the L.A.P.D. on *Paris* (CBS). Korean detective T.K. Yu (Johnny Yune) works with the L.A.P.D. to learn U.S. crime detection methods on the NBC pilot *Sergeant T.K. Yu*.

1980. Alex Parker (Jack Stauffer) is a private detective who uses five smart Doberman pinschers he inherited to help him solve crimes on the NBC pilot *Alex and the Doberman Gang*. Max Caulpepper (Max Baer, Jr.) is a rancher who also solves crimes as the owner of Caulpepper Security Services in Los Angeles on the NBC pilot *The Asphalt Cowboy*. Ocee James, Samantha Jensen and Nick Donovan (Steven Hanks, Michelle Pfeiffer, Asher Brauner) are officers with the Burglary Auto Detail, Commercial Auto Thefts division of the L.A.P.D. on ABC's *B.A.D. Cats*. Eddie Krowder (Flip Wilson) is a Los Angeles private detective who charges $19.95 a day plus expenses on the NBC pilot *The Cheap Detective*. Robert Fuller plays Jake Rudd, the sheriff of rural Fox County, Texas, on the CBS pilot *Jake's Way*. Thomas Magnum (Tom Selleck) is a former Naval Intelligence officer turned Hawaiian based private detective and security force for the estate of pulp writer Robin Masters on *Magnum, P.I.* (CBS). Roger Hart (Ron Moody) is a brilliant but calamity prone Scotland Yard inspector attached to the San Francisco Police Department on ABC's *Nobody's Perfect*. Dennis Weaver plays Dan Stone, a novelist who is also a homicide detective with the L.A.P.D. on *Stone* (ABC).

1981. Greg Mullavey is Fred Finger, a bumbling but tenacious detective with the San Francisco Police Department on the NBC pilot *Detective Finger, I Presume*. Grover Harding Case (Beau Kayzer) is a hard boiled New Orleans Police Department lieutenant whose unorthodox tactics have earned him the nickname of *Hardcase* (NBC pilot). "I handle the garbage — and get paid for it," says Joe Dancer (Robert Blake), a tough Los Angeles private detective on the NBC pilot *Joe Dancer*. Jim McClain (James Arness) is a 52-year-old veteran cop who is teamed with Harry Gates (Marshall Colt), a young by-the-books detective (with the San Pedro P.D.) on NBC's *McClain's Law*. William Conrad plays Nero Wolfe, gourmet, horticulturist and master criminologist who helps the police solve baffling crimes on *Nero Wolfe* (NBC). Nick Macazie (Michael Nouri) is a private detective who solves crimes with the help of three smart Doberman pinschers he inherited on the NBC pilot *Nick and the Dobermans* (a reworking of *Alex and the Doberman Gang*; see 1980). Frank Riker (Josh Taylor) is an undercover investigator for the Deputy D.A. of San Francisco on *Riker* (CBS). Jack Shannon (Kevin Dobson) is a detective lieutenant with the S-Squad Division of the San Francisco P.D. on CBS's *Shannon*. Mismatched brothers A.J. and Rick Simon (Jameson Parker, Gerald McRaney) operate the Simon and Simon Detective Agency in San Diego on CBS's *Simon and Simon* (they usually help Detective Marcel "Downtown" Brown [Tim Reid]). Sonny and Samantha Hunt (Sonny Bono, Lee Purcell) are husband and wife private detectives on the NBC pilot *Sonny and Sam*. Frank Murphy (Robert Stack) heads the Strike Force, a unit of the L.A.P.D. that tackles dangerous crimes on *Strike Force* (ABC. Rosie Johnson [Trisha Noble] and Paul Strobber [Dorian Harewood] are members of the unit). Buford Pusser (Bo Svenson) is the sheriff of McNeal County, Tennessee, who battles lawlessness with his own brand of justice — fearless determination and a large club on NBC's *Walking Tall*.

1982. William Devane plays Jake Ribideaux, a tough New Orleans detective on the NBC pilot *The Big Easy* (the nightclub at which Jake plays clarinet). Victor Isbecki and Mark Petrie (Martin Kove, Carl Lumbly) are the male detectives at the 14th Precinct of the N.Y.P.D. who work with female detectives *Cagney and Lacey* (CBS). Brian Devlin (Rock Hudson) is a former private detective turned director of the Los Angeles Performing Arts Center who helps his detective son Nick (Jack Scalia) solve crimes on *The Devlin Connection* (NBC). Efrem Zimbalist, Jr., plays Marty Malone a former police captain turned private investigator on the CBS pilot *Family in Blue*. Daniel J. Travanti heads a large cast as Captain Frank Furillo on NBC's *Hill Street Blues*. Other detectives

include Mick Belker (Bruce Weitz), Andy Renko (Charles Haid), Philip Esterhaus (Michael Conrad) and Lucy Bates (Betty Thomas). Lee Horsley plays Matt Houston, millionaire, cattle baron, playboy and private eye on ABC's *Matt Houston*. Elroy P. Lobo (Claude Akins) is the slightly dishonest sheriff of Orly County, Georgia, who dispenses his own brand of justice on NBC's *The Misadventures of Sheriff Lobo*. Frank Drebin (Leslie Nielsen) is a detective lieutenant who battles criminal elements on *Police Squad* (ABC). Remington Steele (Pierce Brosnan) is a partner with Laura Holt (Stephanie Zimbalist), the founder of Remington Steele Investigations in Los Angeles on NBC's *Remington Steele*. T.J. Hooker (William Shatner) is a veteran police officer, hardened by divorce and the shooting death of his partner on ABC's *T.J. Hooker*. Officers Stacey Sheridan (Heather Locklear), Vince Romano (Adrian Zmed) and Jim Corrigan (James Darren) work with Hooker.

1983. John Hannibal Smith (George Peppard) leads the A-Team, soldiers of fortune that use their former military skills to help people unable to turn to the police for help on NBC's *The A-Team*. Other team members are B.A. Baracus (Mr. T), Templeton Peck (Dirk Benedict) and H.M. Murdock (Dwight Schultz). Tim Conway plays Ace Crawford, an inexperienced private detective who solves crimes quite by accident on *Ace Crawford, Private Eye* (CBS). Walter Nebicher (Desi Arnaz, Jr.) battles crime for the L.A.P.D. with the help of Automan (Chuck Wagner), a hologram he created on ABC's *Automan*. Dale Robertson plays "Big" John Corbin, a Georgia County sheriff studying law detection methods with the N.Y.P.D. on the NBC pilot *Big John*. Ex cop turned private eye Andy Thorn (Nick Mancuso) teams with Florida attorney Honor Campbell (Lisa Eichhorn) to solve crimes on the ABC pilot *Feel the Heat*. Jose Perez is Antonio Perez, an inspector with the San Francisco P.D. on the NBC pilot *Inspector Perez*. Ben and George McCollum (Lewis Smith, Alan Autry) are brothers who are also Texas Rangers on the NBC pilot *Lone Star*. Mike O'Malley (Mickey Rooney) is a 1940s style detective who uses outdated methods to solve crimes on the NBC pilot *O'Malley*. Philip Marlowe (Powers Boothe) is a tough private detective working out of Los Angeles (1930s) on *Philip Marlowe, Private Eye* (HBO). Nick Ryder and Cody Allen (Joe Penny, Perry King) are struggling gumshoes that operate the Pier 56 Detective Agency (later called the Riptide Agency) in King Harbor, California, on NBC's *Riptide*. Former cop William McBride (Pat McCormick) and unorthodox psychologist Brewster "Rooster" Steele (Paul Williams) team to solve crimes on the ABC pilot *Rooster*. Douglas Hawke and Bill O'Keefe (Billy Dee Williams, Parker Stevenson) are actors seeking work while supplementing their income as private detectives on the ABC pilot *Shooting Stars*. No nonsense ex cop turned private detective Nick Small (Darren McGavin) partners with Chip Frye (Jack Blessing), a man who suffered a freak lab accident that caused him to shrink to a height of six inches on CBS's *Small and Frye*. Tom Swift (Willie Aames) is a scientific genius who teams with his cousin Linda Craig (Lori Loughlin), an amateur sleuth, to solve crimes on the ABC pilot *The Tom Swift and Linda Craig Mystery Hour*.

1984. Danny Harris (Dean Paul Martin), Grace Carpenter (Maggie Cooper) and Jeff Martin (Gregg Henry) are patrol car officers with the Prospect Division of the L.A.P.D. on the CBS pilot *The Boys in Blue*. Mac Riley and Andy Sendowski (Robert Ginty, Jeff McCracken) are former Chicago police officers now with the Criminal Investigation Unit of the Hawaiian Police Department on ABC's *Hawaiian Heat*. Rick Hunter (Fred Dryer) is a mobster's son turned honest cop with Division 122 of the L.A.P.D. on *Hunter* (NBC). Sonny Crockett and Ricardo Tubbs (Don Johnson, Philip Michael Thomas) are undercover detectives with the Vice Squad unit of the Miami Police Department on NBC's *Miami Vice*. Mike Hammer (Stacy Keach) is a tough New York private detective with an eye for the ladies and a natural instinct for violence on *Mickey Spillane's Mike Hammer* (CBS). Amos Tupper (Tom Bosley) then Mort Metzger (Ron Masak) are the sheriffs of Cabot Cove, Maine, the home of mystery writer Jessica Fletcher on CBS's *Murder, She Wrote*. Michael Nouri is Michael Spraggue, a college biology teacher and amateur sleuth on the NBC pilot *Spraggue*. Danny Wreade (Michael Beck) is an N.Y.P.D. officer who works undercover as a taxi cab driver on the NBC pilot *The Streets*. Gary Burghoff reprises his role of Walter O'Reilly from *M*A*S*H* for a CBS pilot called *W*A*L*T*E*R* wherein he joins the St. Louis Police Department to begin a new life as a rookie cop.

1985. Carl Weathers plays Harry Braker, a no nonsense lieutenant with the L.A.P.D. on the CBS pilot *Braker*. Harry Fox (Jack Warden) and his son Harrison Fox, Jr. (John Rubinstein) are San Francisco private detectives on CBS's *Crazy Like a Fox*. Press Wyman (Judd Hirsch) is a mechanical engineer who gives up a promising future to become a detective on CBS's *Detective in the House*. Robert McCall (Edward Woodward) is a former government operative turned vigilante who helps people in deep trouble on *The Equalizer* (CBS). Nick McCarren and Jack Rado (Jack Scalia, Jay Acavone) are L.A.P.D. cops who use elaborate disguises to apprehend criminals on ABC's *Hollywood Beat*. Jackson Beaudine (Victor Garber) is a private detective with three ex-wives who offer him the help he needs to solve crimes on *I Had Three Wives* (CBS). Shanna Reed (Liz), Teri Copley (Samantha) and Maggie Cooper (Mary) play the ex-wives. Malcolm MacGruder and Jenny Loud (John Getz, Kathryn Harrold) are patrol car officers who are secretly married (in defiance of departmental orders) on ABC's *MacGruder and Loud*. James Earl Jones is a private eye and Henry Darrow a police lieutenant on ABC's *Me and Mom*. Bruce Willis plays David Addison, a detective with Blue Moon Investigations in Los Angeles on ABC's *Moonlighting*. Kevin O'Brien, Florence Toland and Frank Giambone (Scott Hylands, Wanda Mason, Jeff Wincott) are among the detectives with the Toronto, Canada Police Department on CBS's *Night Heat*. Robert Lansing plays Sam Penny, a private detective one step away from bankruptcy on the CBS pilot *Sam Penny*. Patrick Evan Stark (Nick Survoy) is a tough, hard drinking Kansas City police detective on the CBS pilot *Stark*. Robert Urich plays Spenser, a Boston private detective who helps people in deep trouble on *Spenser for Hire* (ABC. Hawk [Avery Brooks], a former enforcer for the mob, assists him). Jesse Mach (Rex Smith) is a police officer with the L.A.P.D. who rides Street Hawk, a motorcycle designed to battle crime on ABC's *Street Hawk*.

1986. Dan Corbin (John Beck) is a single minded, unorthodox L.A.P.D. detective with a knack for breaking all the rules on the NBC pilot *Crazy Dan*. Michael Halsey (Cotter Smith) is a former newspaper reporter turned Washington, D.C., police detective on the CBS pilot *D.C. Cop*. Dennis Farina plays Mike Torello, a no nonsense lieutenant with the Major Crime Unit of the Chicago Police Department during the 1960s on

NBC's *Crime Story*. John Forney (Michael Nouri) is an undercover police officer with the L.A.P.D. on *Downtown* (CBS). Wes Kennedy (Robert Desiderio) is an L.A.P.D. detective struggling to cope with life after the recent death of his wife and raise his children on ABC's *Heart of the City*. Joe Bash (Peter Boyle) is an harassed police officer with the 33rd Precinct of the N.Y.P.D. who patrols a ghetto section of the city at night on *Joe Bash* (CBS). Rob Wright (Adam West) is the captain of Precinct 56, a former morgue turned stationhouse on NBC's *The Last Precinct*. Stacy Keach returns as Mike Hammer in a revised CBS version of the 1984 series called *The New Mike Hammer*. Michael Ryan (Robert Desiderio) is a lieutenant with the L.A.P.D. who receives help from his so-cialite wife Ashley (Sharon Stone) on the ABC pilot *Mr. and Mrs. Ryan*. Ed O'Neill plays Popeye Doyle, a tough, dedicated detective with the N.Y.P.D. on the NBC pilot *Popeye Doyle* (based on the feature film *The French Connection*). Sledge Hammer (David Rasche) is an unorthodox po-lice officer who dispenses his own brand of violent justice on ABC's *Sledge Hammer*. Cliff Brady (Robby Benson) is a detective with the Chicago Police Department who patrols his old neighbor-hood on *Tough Cookies* (CBS).

1987. James Cabot Barrington (Matt Salinger) is heir to a fabulous fortune and chief of the King's Bay Village Police Department on the CBS pilot *Barrington*. Dennis Franz plays Norman Buntz, a less than honorable private detective on NBC's *Beverly Hills Buntz*. Harry Hooperman (John Rit-ter) is an inspector with the San Francisco Police Department who is also the landlord of a run-down apartment building on *Hooperman* (ABC). James Reynolds and Anne Russell (Dorian Hare-wood, Mimi Kazak) are homicide detectives with the Hope Division of the L.A.P.D. on the ABC pilot *Hope Division*. Joey LaFiamma and LeVon Lundy (Michael Pare, Michael Beck) are sergeants with the Major Crime Unit of the Houston, Texas Police Department on CBS's *Houston Knights*. Jerry Orbach plays Harry McGraw, a seedy and abrasive private detective working out of Boston on *The Law and Harry McGraw* (CBS). After 25 years as the deputy chief of public relations for the L.A.P.D., Ike Porter (Paul Sorvino) quits to become a street cop on *The Oldest Rookie* (CBS). Hotshot rookie M.R. Baker (Tom O'Brien) is teamed with hard-nosed L.A.P.D. detective Jack Shake (Tom Skerritt) on the NBC pilot *On the Edge*. Tom Hanson (Johnny Depp), Judy Hoffs (Holly Robinson) and H.J. Ioke (Dustin Nguyen) are officers with the Jump Street Chapel unit of the Metropolitan Police Department on Fox's *21 Jump Street*.

1988. Bill Gillespie (Carroll O'Connor) is the police chief of Sparta, Mississippi, and Virgil Tibbs (Howard Rollins) is his chief of detectives on *In the Heat of the Night* (NBC/CBS). Michael Shane (John Terry) is an officer with the L.A.P.D. who finds true peace only when he is by himself on the ABC pilot *The Loner*. Jack Killian (Gary Cole) is a former police officer turned radio show call-in host (of "Midnight Caller") who solves crimes that result from listeners' calls on NBC's *Midnight Caller*. Salvatore Theopolis "Sonny" Spoon (Mario Van Peebles) is a smooth talking private detective who incorporates disguises to solve crimes on NBC's *Sonny Spoon*. Mr. T plays T.S. Turner, a street-smart private investigator on the syndicated *T&T*.

1989. Buddy Lee (B.L.) Stryker (Burt Rey-nolds) is a former police officer (suspended for being out of control) who now works as a private investigator in Palm Beach, Florida, on ABC's *B.L. Stryker*. Carl Winslow (Reginald VelJohn-son) is first a sergeant then a lieutenant with the Metro Division of the Chicago Police Depart-ment on *Family Matters* (ABC). Father Frank Dowling (Tom Bosley) and Sister Steve (Tracy Nelson) are a Catholic priest and nun who help Sergeant Clancy (Regina Krueger) of the Chicago Police Department solve crimes on *Father Dowl-ing Mysteries* (NBC/ABC). Veteran detective Charlie Battles (John Ashton) and his young part-ner, Joe Kaczierewicki (Richard Tyson), are with the Metro Division of the L.A.P.D. on NBC's *Hardball*. Avery Brooks plays Hawk, a Washing-ton, D.C., vigilante, who assists people desper-ately in need of help on ABC's *A Man Called Hawk* (a spinoff from *Spenser for Hire*). Gus Grant (Peter Parros) and Matt Doyle (Ethan Wayne) are patrol car officers with the L.A.P.D. on *The New Adam-12* (Syn. See also 1968). Jeff Osterhage and Bernard White play Vic Daniels and Carl Melina, detectives with the L.A.P.D. on *The New Dragnet* (Syn. See also 1951). Peter Strauss plays Peter Gunn, the two-fisted Los Angeles private investi-gator on the ABC pilot *Peter Gunn* (see also 1958). Max Jericho (John Terry) is a hard-boiled private detective working out of San Bernadino, a Cali-fornia community nicknamed *San Berdoo* (CBS pilot). Chance Reynolds (Tim Reid) is a criminologist and teacher at Georgetown University who solves crimes with the help of his wife Micki (Daphne Maxwell-Reid), a protocol aide with the State Department on *Snoops* (CBS). Tony Wolf (Jack Scalia) is a former San Francisco police sergeant who now works as an investigator for a high priced criminal attorney on *Wolf* (CBS).

1990. Beau Jack Bowman (Miguel Ferrer) is a detective with the Bay City Police Department who heads the Rubber Gun Squad, a unit of officers on psychiatric leave on CBS's *Broken Badges*. Chief Roger Kendrick (Ronny Cox), Detective Vincent La Russo (Peter Onorati) and Officer Franklin Rose (James McDaniel) are among the police officers that combine music and song with crime solving on ABC's *Cop Rock*. Dan Turner (Marc Singer) is a smooth talking, trench coat wearing, somewhat adverse to violence private detective working out of Hollywood (1947) on the syndicated pilot *Dan Turner, Hollywood Detective*. Gabriel Bird (James Earl Jones) is an ex cop turned investigator for attorney Laila Robins (Victoria Heller) on *Gabriel's Fire* (ABC). Lennie Briscoe (Jerry Orbach), Ed Greene (Jesse L. Martin), Mike Logan (Chris Noth) and Joe Fontana (Dennis Farina) are among the detectives investigating crime for the N.Y.P.D. on NBC's *Law and Order*. Shadoe Stevens plays Max Monroe, an unorthodox police detective with Precinct 157 of the L.A.P.D. on *Max Monroe: Loose Cannon* (CBS). Eduardo Cruz (Benjamin Bratt) and Paul Morrisey (Jeff Kaake) are among the members of the Northern Narcotics Bureau of the Las Vegas Police Department on NBC's *Nasty Boys*. Former Scotland Yard Inspector Maxwell Beckett (Edward Woodward) is a mystery writer who solves crimes to acquire story material for his books on *Over My Dead Body* (CBS). Parker Kane (Jeff Fahey) is a former cop with the Long Beach, California Police Department turned private detective on the pilot *Parker Kane*. Michael Burton (John DiAquino) is a cop with the Los Angeles Metro Police Department who, after being wounded in a shooting, can see ghosts on the syndicated *Shades of L.A.* (Michael helps the shades, as he calls them, complete unfinished business). Chic Chesbro (George Clooney) and Tim Kelly (Michael DeLuise) are among the motorcycle officers with the L.A.P.D. on ABC's *Sunset Beat*. Zach Stone (Ken Olandt) is a cop of the future (2020) who uses a specially equipped suit to fight

crime as a member of the 33rd Division of the Metropolitan Police Department on the syndicated *Super Force*.

1991. Brent McCord (Robert Goulet) is a former actor turned sheriff of LoMiceda County on the CBS pilot *Acting Sheriff*. Michael Chiklis plays Tony Scalia, the chief of the Eastbridge (suburban New York) Police Department on *The Commish* (ABC). Robert Ballard (Robert Guillaume), Sandy Calloway (Megan Gallagher), Richard Capparelli (Richard Libertini) and Al Buckhardt (Ron Leibman) are police detectives based at Pacific Station in Venice, California, on NBC's *Pacific Station*. Richard Cobb (Mark Harmon) is a detective with the Metropolitan Division of the Chicago Police Department who assists hearing-impaired attorney Tess Kaufman (Marlee Matlin) on *Reasonable Doubts* (NBC). Chris Lorenzo (Ron Estes) and Ruta Lee Lance (Mitzi Kapture) are detectives with the Crimes of Passion Unit of the Palm Springs, Florida Police Department on CBS's *Silk Stalkings* (refers to society murders. Detective Michael Price [Nick Kokotakis] replaced Chris. Detective Tom Ryan [Chris Potter] replaced Price). Adam Beaudreaux (Carl Weathers) is a bar owner and sergeant with the Metropolitan Police Department of a Pacific Northwest city identified as "The Beautiful Evergreen State" on the syndicated *Street Justice*. Nick Slaughter (Rob Stewart) is a disorganized, deeply in debt (to the IRS) private detective on Key Mariah in Florida on CBS's *Sweating Bullets*.

1992. Leo Burmaster and Ron Eldard star as Bill Ruskin and Danny Walsh, police officers with the Vista Valley Police Department on *Arresting Behavior*, an ABC spoof of reality cop shows. The grueling work of L.A.P.D. homicide detective Ben Carroll (Lee Horsley) is depicted on *Bodies of Evidence*, a CBS series also starring George Clooney and Kate McNeil as Detectives Ryan Walker and Nora Houghton. Mike Ragland (James Tolkan) is a captain with the 77th Precinct of the L.A.P.D. who heads what he calls *The Hat Squad* (CBS), detectives who wear black fedoras and have little respect for the law (but solve violent crimes). The viewer (called "Rookie") and Inspector Stanford Marshak (Sam McMurray) work together to solve crimes on Fox's *Likely Suspects*. Jimmy Brock (Tom Skerritt) is the police chief of Rome, Wisconsin, on CBS's *Picket Fences* Deputies Maxine Stewart (Lauren Holly) and Kenny Lacos (Costas Mandylor) assist Jimmy. Gabriel Bird (James Earl Jones) and Mitch O'Hannon (Richard Crenna) are Los Angeles private detectives who operate Bird and O'Hannon Investigations on ABC's *Pros and Cons.* Jonathan Raven (Jeffrey Meek) is a Hawaiian based private detective who uses his skills in the martial arts to battle crime on *Raven* (CBS). Charlie Street (Brian Keith) is a hard-nosed cop with the Beverly Hills Police Department on the ABC pilot *The Streets of Beverly Hills.*

1993. Sergeant Paul Gigante (Giancarlo Esposito) is half Italian and half black. Officer Wade Preston (Ron Eldard) is a white cop obsessed with African American culture. They are with the Bakersfield Police Department on Fox's *Bakersfield P.D.* Dave Brodsky (Bradley Whitford) is a private detective who owns Brodsky's Used and Hard to Find 33⅓ Record Shop and Detective Agency in San Francisco on NBC's *Black Tie Affair.* The NBC series *Crime and Punishment* presents stories from the viewpoint of criminals and then the investigations of detectives Ken O'Donnell (Jon Tenney), Annette Rey (Rachel Ticotin) and Anthony Bartoll (Carmen Argenziano). Steve Sloan (Barry Van Dyke) is a detective with the L.A.P.D. who finds help solving crimes from his father, Dr. Mark Sloan (Dick Van Dyke) on *Diagnosis Murder* (CBS). Art Giardello (Yaphet Kotto), Kay Howard (Melissa Leo) and John Munch (Richard Belzer) are among the detectives with the Homicide Division of the Baltimore, Maryland, Police Department on NBC's gritty *Homicide: Life on the Street.* Peter Caine (Chris Potter) is the son of a Shaolin priest (Kwai Chang Caine from the series *Kung Fu*) and a detective with the 101st Precinct of the Metro Division of the San Francisco Police Department on *Kung Fu: The Legend Continues* (Syn.). Walter Tatum (Bill Campbell) and Gwen Cross (Ally Walker) are private detectives based in Florida on ABC's *Moon Over Miami.* Greg Medavoy (Gordon Clapp), John Kelly (David Caruso), John Clark (Mark-Paul Gosselaar), Andy Sipowicz (Dennis Franz) and Bobby Simone (Jimmy Smits) are among the detectives attached to the 15th Detective Squad of the N.Y.P.D. on ABC's *N.Y.P.D. Blue.* Detectives J.C. Williams and Eddie Torres (Malik Yoba, Michael DeLorenzo) are undercover cops with the N.Y.P.D. on *New York Undercover* (Fox). Cody McMahon (Glenn Fry) is a former security guard for Paramount Pictures turned owner of the Beverly Hills Detective Agency on the CBS pilot *South of Sunset.* Cordell Walker (Chuck Norris)

and Jimmy Trevette (Clarence Gilyard, Jr.) are Texas Rangers dedicated to enforcing the law on *Walker, Texas Ranger* (CBS).

1994. Gene Barry reprises his role of Amos Burke (see 1963), the millionaire police captain with the L.A.P.D. who is now a police chief on *Burke's Law* (CBS). Guy Hanks (Bill Cosby) is a forensic scientist with the 15th precinct of the N.Y.P.D. on NBC's *The Cosby Mysteries.* Paul Gross plays Benton Fraser, a Canadian Mounted Policeman stationed with the Canadian Consulate in Chicago who helps the police solve crimes on *Due South* (CBS). Rob Estes plays Mike Hammer, Mickey's Spillane's tough private detective with an eye for the ladies in *Come Die with Me,* a CBS pilot that takes Mike out of New York and transplants him to Florida to solve crimes. Max Morgan (George Peppard) and his daughter Jessica (Tracy Nelson) are detectives working out of Los Angeles on the NBC pilot *The P.I.* Louis Gossett, Jr., plays Ray Alexander, a private detective and restaurant owner on two NBC pilots: *Ray Alexander: A Taste for Justice* and *Ray Alexander: A Menu for Murder* (1995). Alex Murphy (Richard Eden) is part man, part machine (fitted with a total body prosthesis, titanium skin and a computer assisted brain after he is shot) who battles crime in Delta City as *RoboCop* (Syn.). George C. Scott plays Joe Trapchek, a retired cop who serves as a special consultant to the Central Division of the Seattle Police Department on *Traps* (CBS).

1995. Charlie Grace (Mark Harmon) is a Southern California private detective who charges $300 a day and is deeply in debt on ABC's *Charlie Grace.* Newspaper reporter Frank Hardy (Colin Gray) and his younger brother, college student Joe Hardy (Paul Popowich) are also detectives who solve crimes on *The Hardy Boys* (Syn.). Tony Conetti (Tony Danza) is a detective with Precinct Number 7 of the Hoboken, New Jersey, Police Department on ABC's *Hudson Street* (the address of the precinct). Jeff Fahey plays Winston McBride, a deputy U.S. marshal on ABC's *The Marshal.* Ted Harrison (Edward Woodward) is a former chief inspector for Scotland Yard who now works as a consultant to the N.Y.P.D. on the UPN pilot *The Shamrock Conspiracy* (the series was slated to be called *The Inspector*).

1996. Brad Garrett plays Robert Barone, a sergeant then lieutenant with the N.Y.P.D. on *Everybody Loves Raymond* (CBS). Detective Jim Mc-

Carthy (John McGinley) is an N.Y.P.D. homicide detective who transfers to the suburb of Long Island hoping to find a quieter life on the ABC pilot *Long Island Fever*. Nash Bridges (Don Johnson) and Joe Dominiquez (Cheech Marin) are members of the S.I.U. (Special Investigation Unit) of the San Francisco Police Department on CBS's *Nash Bridges*. T.C. Calloway (Jim Davidson), Russ Granger (Jeff Stern) and Bobby Cruz (Mario Lopez) are members of the Santa Monica Bike Beach Patrol on *Pacific Blue* (USA).

1997. Anthony Dellaventura (Danny Aiello) is a former New York police officer turned private detective who likes happy endings to his cases on *Dellaventura* (CBS). Stacy Keach again plays Mike Hammer (see 1984), this time as a more aggressive and violent private detective operating out of New York City on the syndicated *Mike Hammer, Private Eye*. Frank Cisco (James Remar) is a former L.A.P.D. homicide detective turned owner of Total Security, a Culver City, California, based private detective organization on ABC's *Total Security*.

1998. Jimmy Doyle (Dylan Walsh), Clement Johnson (Richard T. Jones) and Hector Villanueva (Adam Rodriquez) are officers with the Brooklyn South precinct of the N.Y.P.D. on CBS's *Brooklyn South*. Buddy Faro (Dennis Farina), once the best private detective in the business, is now struggling to get his life back together again after a 20-year drinking binge on *Buddy Faro* (CBS). Dorian Gregory plays Daryl Morris and Ted King is Andrew Trudeau, inspectors with the San Francisco P.D. who help The Charmed Ones (Prue, Piper, Phoebe and Paige) battle evil on *Charmed* (WB). Sammo Law (Sammo Hung) is a detective with the L.A.P.D. who prefers to use his martial arts skills as a weapon instead of a gun on CBS's *Martial Law*. Working with Sammo are Terrell Parker (Arsenio Hall) and Louis Malone (Louis Mandylor).

1999. Elliott Stabler (Christopher Meloni), Odafi Tutuola (Ice T) and John Munch (Richard Belzer) are the male detectives attached to the Special Victims Unit (sexually offensive cases) of the N.Y.P.D. on *Law and Order: Special Victims Unit* (NBC). Sean Maher plays Ryan Caulfield, a 19-year-old Philadelphia cop who is assigned to the worst section of the city on *Ryan Caulfield: Year One* (Fox). Trent Malloy (Jimmy Wicek) is a karate expert who operates Thunder Investigations, a Dallas detective organization on CBS's *Sons of Thunder*.

2000. Zane Marinelli (Mark Raffalo) and Mike Dorigan (Derek Cecil) are police officers with the N.Y.P.D. through whose eyes a gritty view of law enforcement is presented on *The Beat* (UPN). Jack Mannion (Craig T. Nelson) is the police chief of Washington, D.C., whose goal is to clean up the worst crime rate in the nation on *The District* (CBS). Joe Noland (Roger Aaron Brown) is the Deputy Police Chief and Temple Paige (Sean Patrick Thomas) is a detective with a drug problem. Michael Richards plays Vic Nardozzo, a bumbling private investigator with the McKay Detective Agency in Los Angeles on NBC's *The Michael Richards Show*.

2001. Mike Mooney (Ed O'Neill) is a veteran detective with the N.Y.P.D.'s 11th Precinct on CBS's *Big Apple*. He investigates crimes with the help of detectives Vincent Trout (Jeffrey Pierce) and Teddy Olsen (Glynn Turman). Mike McNeil (Denis Leary) is a detective with the 21st Precinct of the N.Y.P.D. who drinks, smokes and is unfaithful to his wife on ABC's *The Job*. Vincent D'Onofrio plays Detective Robert Goren and Jamey Sheridan is Captain James Deakins, the male cops with the Criminal Intent Division of the N.Y.P.D. on *Law and Order: Criminal Intent* (NBC). Maury Chaykin plays Nero Wolfe, the overweight master criminologist, gourmet cook, horticulturist and connoisseur of fine wine on A&E's *Nero Wolfe* (see also 1981).

2002. Joel Stevens (Donnie Wahlberg) and Bobby Smith (Mykelti Williamson) are among the L.A.P.D. officers pounding a beat on NBC's *Boomtown*. Mike Olshansky (David Morse) is a former Philadelphia police officer (caught stealing money from a drug bust) who now drives a cab but uses his former training to help people on CBS's *Hack*. Dominic Purcell plays John Doe, a brilliant amnesiac who, while seeking clues to his identity, helps Detective Frank Hayes (John Marshall Jones) solve crimes on Fox's *John Doe*. Adrian Monk (Tony Shalhoub) is a brilliant but phobia ridden former San Francisco police detective turned consultant who helps the police solve crimes on *Monk* (USA. Sharona Fleming [Bitty Schram] assists Monk; Captain Leland Stottlemeyer [Ted Levine] is the police captain Monk helps). Sam Cole (Tom Sizemore) and Archie Simms (Barney Henley) are detectives with the Robbery Homicide Division of the L.A.P.D. on CBS's *Robbery Homicide Division*. Vic Mackey (Michael Chiklis) is a rogue cop who heads a strike team unit that operates under his own rules on *The Shield* (FX. Other detectives in the unit include Curtis Lemansky [Kenny Johnson], Claudette Wyms [C.C.H. Pounder] and Shane Vendrell [Walton Goggins]). William Moreland (Wendell Pierce), Lester Freeman (Clarke Peters) and Jimmy McNulty (Dominic West) are officers with the Baltimore Police Department on HBO's *The Wire*.

2003. Scotty Valens (Danny Pino), Nick Vera (Jeremy Ratchford) and Will Jeffries (Thom Barry) are the male detectives who investigate unsolved crimes on CBS's *Cold Case*. Van Ray (Peter Facinelli) and Deaquon Hayes (Bill Bellamy) are officers who work undercover for Billie Chambers (Tiffani-Amber Thiessen), head of the Candy Store, a secret unit of the L.A.P.D. on *Fastlane* (Fox). Fred Dryer reprises his role as Rick Hunter on NBC's *Hunter* (Rick is now a lieutenant and partners with Dee Dee McCall [Stepfanie Kramer] at the San Diego Police Department. See also 1984). Mark Valley plays Eddie Arlette, a New York police detective with keen instincts who is on loan to New Scotland Yard in London on Fox's *Keen Eddie*. Ed O'Neill plays a grittier Joe Friday, a lieutenant with the L.A.P.D. on ABC's *L.A. Dragnet* (see also 1951). Rico Amonte (Danny Nucci) is a rookie deputy sheriff with the L.A. County Sheriff's Department on ABC's *10–8: Officers on Duty*. Ernie Hudson plays Rico's superior and trainer Deputy John Henry Barnes.

2004. Sean Harrison (Michael Biehn) is a detective with the Hawaiian Police Department on NBC's *Hawaii*. Sean works with Detective Linah Dias (Aya Sumi Ka) and Terry Harada (Cary Tagawa) is the captain. Keith Mars (Enrico Colantoni) runs Mars Investigations in Neptune, California, on UPN's *Veronica Mars*.

2005. Jim Dunbar (Ron Eldard) is a detective with the N.Y.P.D. who was blinded by a gunshot wound but continues in active service on *Blind Justice* (ABC). Tim Daly plays Harlan Judd, the owner of Judd Risk Management, an investigative agency on *Eyes* (ABC). Ving Rhames plays Theo Kojak, a tough, no nonsense Manhattan police detective on the USA's version of *Kojak* (now black; see 1973). Jesse Stone (Tom Selleck) is a former homicide detective turned police chief of Paradise, a not so quiet New England fishing village on the CBS pilot *Stonecold*. Conrad Rose (Gary Cole) is a lieutenant with the Los Angeles Metro Squad S.W.A.T. team who has set his goal

to track down the city's 100 most wanted fugitives on *Wanted* (TNT). Jimmy McGloin (Ryan Hurst) and Carla Merced (Rashida Jones) assist Rose.

2006. Nicholas Campbell plays Dominic DaVinci, a cop turned coroner who uses his skills as a detective to help him solve crimes on *DaVinci's Inquest*. The series was produced in Canada (1998–2005) and first seen in the U.S. via syndication. Rob Estes and Orlando Jones play Inspector Sean Cole and Detective Cayman Bishop, officers with the San Francisco Police Department on ABC's *The Evidence*. Reno Wilson is Tyrese Evans and Billy Gardell is Billy O'Brien, detectives with the L.A.P.D. on NBC's *Heist*.

Mentally Disabled Characters

Characters who are regulars (or semi-regulars) on a TV series and possess a disability that challenges them mentally are the subjects of this entry. Single episode instances (guest roles on a series) are excluded.

1955. Although played strictly for laughs, Ed Norton (Art Carney) suffers from a sleep walking disorder that, among other things, enables him to eat, tour the sewers of the job he works and walk along the ledges of buildings on *The Honeymooners* (CBS).

1962. Stacey Petrie (Jerry Van Dyke), the brother of TV writer Rob Petrie, suffers from a rare type of sleepwalking that creates a complete change in personality: an extrovert when asleep, an introvert when awake.

1974. Cheryl Anders (Nicole Kallis) is the autistic daughter of police sergeant Pepper Anderson on NBC's *Police Woman*. Cheryl is cared for by Pepper and attends the Austin School for the Handicapped.

1977. Renee Taylor plays Penny, an emotionally disturbed woman who finds comfort with her therapy group on the NBC pilot *Good Penny*. Hewitt Calder (Perry Lang) is a 16-year-old mentally retarded youth who struggles to make friends with other neighborhood kids to prove he is a person too on the ABC special *Hewitt's Just Different*.

1982. Tommy Westphall (Chad Allen) is the autistic son of David Westphall, a doctor at St. Eligius Hospital in Boston on NBC's *St. Elsewhere*.

1983. Cloris Leachman plays May Lemke on *The Woman Who Willed a Miracle*, an Emmy

Award winning special. A severely retarded infant, deserted by his parents and given little hope for survival by doctors, is adopted by May, whose loving faith and devotion gave the child a chance at life.

1984. Dana Hill plays Geraldine Oxley, a mentally retarded girl on the ABC special *Welcome Home, Jellybean*. After years in an institution, Geraldine's parents decide she needs to be at home. The story depicts the havoc, humor, breakup and growth of family members as they learn to accept Geraldine, fondly called "Jellybean."

1986. Michael Countryman plays Louis, the slightly retarded adult friend of young Chip Lowell on CBS's *Kate and Allie*. Larry Drake plays Benny Stulwicz, a mentally challenged clerk for the law firm of McKenzie & Brackman on NBC's *L.A. Law*. In 1986 Amanda Plummer played Alice, Benny's mentally retarded girlfriend.

1987. ABC airs *The Kid Who Wouldn't Quit*, a special about Brad Silverman (K.C. Martel), a boy with Down syndrome who struggled to be a regular kid. The effects Alzheimer's disease has on a family are seen on the PBS special *There Were Times, Dear*. Shirley Jones, Len Cariou and Cynthia Eilbacher star.

1988. Patrick Laborteaux plays Jerome, a mentally retarded young man living in the ruthless western town of Paradise on CBS's *The Guns of Paradise*.

1989. Chris Burke plays Charles "Corky" Thatcher, a teenager with Down syndrome on ABC's *Life Goes On*. While Corky fought to become "one of the guys," and in essence did (he attended a regular school, ran for class president, held a job as a movie theater usher) he impulsively married Amanda Swanson (Andrea Friedman), a girl with the same affliction (the series ended with them struggling to make their marriage work).

1994. Sally Field plays Maggie Wyczenski, the manic depressive (bi-polar) mother of nurse Abby Lockhart on NBC's *ER*. Also on this series, Marcello Thedford plays Leon Pratt, the mentally challenged brother of Dr. Gregory Pratt.

1995. Jonathan Banks plays Jim Sugarbaker, the mentally retarded brother of Suzanne Sugarbaker, the Georgia delegate in the House of Representatives on CBS's *Women of the House*.

1996. James Gammon plays Nick Bridges, the father of San Francisco police captain Nash Bridges, who is suffering from the early stages of Alzheimer's disease on CBS's *Nash Bridges*.

1997. David Cross plays Donny DeMoreau, the brother of *Blush* magazine photographer Elliott DeMoreau on NBC's *Just Shoot Me*. Donny is a man who fakes mental illness to get out of going to work and having his family wait on him hand and foot.

2002. Tony Shalhoub is Adrian Monk, a brilliant police detective turned private investigator who suffers from a severe form of Obsessive Compulsive Disorder (manifested when his wife was killed in a car bombing while investigating a story) on *Monk* (USA).

2005. Kate Burton plays Ellis Grey, a world-famous surgeon and the mother of Seattle Grace Hospital intern Meredith Grey, who suffers from Alzheimer's disease on ABC's *Grey's Anatomy*.

2006. K Callan plays Helen, the wife of Pops, a member of a team planning the greatest robbery in history, who is suffering from Alzheimer's disease on *Heist* (NBC).

Mermaids

Half woman and half fish, a mermaid is a mythical creature of the sea that has apparently been seen by fishermen for centuries (the mermaid is perhaps best known by the feature films *Mr. Peabody and the Mermaid* with Ann Blyth playing Lenore and *Splash* with Daryl Hannah as Madison). Television mermaids are quite scarce and the only series one can attribute to being the definitive mermaid program is the animated *The Little Mermaid*.

1951. Misty Waters is TV's first mermaid, a marionette who appears on the children's series *Ozmoe* (ABC).

1952. Darla Jean Hood provides the voice for the mermaid in animated commercials for Chicken of the Sea brand tuna fish.

1960. Suzanne Turner plays Miss Minerva, a shapely mermaid who helps the good fish defeat the evils of Baron Barracuda on the syndicated *Diver Dan*.

1961. Shirley Temple plays *The Little Mermaid* in an adaptation of the fairy tale about a beautiful mermaid who yearns to become human on *The Shirley Temple Theater* (ABC).

1965. Mermaids grace the small screen on *Aqua Varieties*, an ABC special hosted by Gordon and

Sheila MacRae from the Fontainbleau Hotel in Miami Beach, Florida. Groom and Clean, a hair product for men, begins a series of live action commercials featuring the beautiful Groom and Clean Mermaid.

1968. Jeri Lynn Fraser plays a mermaid who is caught by a young boy while fishing in a river on the ABC pilot *Mike and the Mermaid.* While young Mike Malone (Kevin Brodie) can't believe his eyes, he befriends the girl and struggles to conceal her presence.

1969. The syndicated travel series *Islands in the Sun* features Minzie the Mermaid as the sailing ship *Islanda* visits tropical islands.

1974. Richard Chamberlain narrates an animated adaptation of the Hans Christian Andersen fairy tale, *The Little Mermaid,* for CBS. After saving the life of a drowning prince, a mermaid discovers love and contemplates giving up her immortal soul to experience human love.

1978. Harlee McBride plays Aqua, a beautiful mermaid with blonde hair, blue eyes, lithe legs and iridescent scales who is the daughter of a man and a mermaid on the CBS pilot *Danny and the Mermaid.* The title refers to Danny Stevens, an oceanography student who discovers her. Michelle Phillips plays Princess Nyah, the beautiful mermaid who lives in the waters surrounding the mysterious *Fantasy Island* (ABC).

1983. Pam Dawber plays a beautiful mermaid seeking to discover human love by giving up her immortal soul on *The Little Mermaid* segment of *Shelley Duvall's Fairy Tale Theater* (Showtime).

1988. Amy Yasbeck plays Madison, the beautiful mermaid from the feature film *Splash* on the ABC pilot *Splash, Too.* Here Madison, who can survive on land as long as she soaks her legs in salt water once every full moon, struggles to avoid capture by a scientist who knows she is a mermaid but can't prove it.

1989. Jodie Benson provides the voice for Ariel on the animated *The Little Mermaid* (Disney). Here Ariel is the seventh youngest daughter of King Triton. She dreams of becoming human but her father forbids it. Thus, until that time comes, Ariel frolics with her undersea friends.

1995. Although she is without the tail that distinguishes a mermaid, beautiful 15-year-old Maya (Jessica Alba) believes she is a mermaid and longs to become one on *Flipper: The New Adventures* (PAX). Maya lives on a houseboat on Dolphin Cove in Florida, has remarkable aqua abilities,

and hopes to one day return to the sea from which she believes she came.

1997. Hillary Tuck plays Amy Szalinski, the daughter of inventor Wayne Szalinski on the syndicated *Honey I Shrunk the Kids: The TV Series.* Amy is 16 years old and due to one of her father's inventions (sun block made from fish oils) was transformed into a mermaid.

2001. Rya Kihlstedt plays Marie Celeste, a beautiful (and topless) mermaid who seeks revenge on the fisherman who attempted to catch her (in Ireland) and bring her to America on HBO's *The Mermaid Chronicles: She Creature.*

2002. Alyssa Milano plays the good witch Phoebe Halliwell on *Charmed* (WB). In the episode "A Witch's Tale," Phoebe becomes a mermaid to protect Mylea (Jaime Pressly), a real mermaid being threatened by the evil Sea Hag.

2003. Bugles Snack Chips begins airing a series of commercials promoting their bugle-shaped chips. One spot features a beautiful mermaid being tossed a bugle from a man in a rowboat. The mermaid enjoys the chip; however, when the man finishes the last one, she swims away, leaving him to regret his actions. Diana (Erika Heynatz), Venus (Nikita Ager) and June (Sarah Laine) are three beautiful mermaids who become human to find the evil fisherman who killed their father on the PAX pilot *Mermaids* (had the series sold it would have focused on the sisters as they attempt to begin lives as humans).

2005. Nathalie Kelley plays Nikki, a beautiful mermaid who attempts to live life on land in Florida on a WB presentation pilot called *Mermaid* (based on the 1984 film *Splash*).

Mexican American Performers and Characters

This entry chronicles the programs on which Mexican-Americans are the stars or featured regulars. See also *Cuban American Performers and Characters, Latino Performers and Characters* and *Puerto Rican Performers and Characters.*

1950. Duncan Renaldo is the Cisco Kid, "The Robin Hood of the Old West," and Leo Carrillo is Pancho, his sidekick, on *The Cisco Kid* (Syn.). Mel Blanc plays Sy, the Mexican on *The Jack Benny Program* (CBS). Mel began the character on Jack's radio show (*The Lucky Strike Program*) and appeared in scenes that had Jack at an airport, bus or train depot. Sy had a limited vocabulary and would answer Jack's questions with "Si." He would also mention his sister, Sue (and when Jack asked what she did for a living, Sy would say "Sow").

1951. Don Diamond plays El Toro, the sidekick of frontiersman Kit Carson on *The Adventures of Kit Carson* (Syn.).

1953. Cesar Romero becomes the host of *The Chevrolet Showroom*, an ABC variety series.

1954. Natividad Vacio plays the recurring role of Fronk Smith, the gardener hired by Jim Anderson on *Father Knows Best* (NBC episodes only). Cesar Romero plays Steve McQuinn, a U.S. diplomatic courier on the syndicated *Passport to Danger*.

1957. Tony Martinez is Pepino Garcia, the hired hand who helped Amos and Luke McCoy run their San Fernando farm on *The Real McCoys* (ABC/CBS). Although of Mexican descent, Grandpa Amos considered Pepino a McCoy (but expelled him from the family when he did something wrong). When the series switched to CBS in 1962 (to 1963), Tony Martinez received billing in the opening theme (as opposed to a closing theme credit).

1959. Cesar Romero is Juan Joaquin, chief of the Mexican border police on the CBS pilot *The Caballero*. Robert Cabal plays Hey Soos, a cattle drover who worked for Gil Favor, the trail boss on CBS's *Rawhide*. Rico Rodriquez (Carlos Romero) is a deputy to Mike Dunbar, the marshal of *Wichita Town* (NBC) during the 1870s.

1961. Mel Blanc provides the voice for Speedy Gonzalez, the Mexican police officer who helped detective Dick Tracy collar criminals on the animated *Dick Tracy Show* (Syn.).

1962. Charles Bronson plays Paul Moreno, the Hispanic ranch hand on the half-million acre Garrett Ranch in Santa Fe, New Mexico, on NBC's *Empire*. Carlos Thompson plays Carlos Borella, a Mexican-American troubleshooter for an import-export company on *The Sentimental Agent* (Syn).

1963. The 1962 NBC series *Empire* is revised as *Redigo*. Charles Bronson is dropped as Jim Redigo, the former Garrett ranch foreman, becomes the owner of his own ranch in Mesa, New Mexico. Mina Martinez joins the cast as Linda, the ranch cook and Rudy Solari is her husband, Frank, a ranch hand.

1967. NBC's *High Chaparral* features several Mexican characters: Victoria Cannon (Linda Cristal), the wife of High Chaparral ranch owner "Big" John Cannon (Victoria is the daughter of Sebastian de Montoya [Frank Silvera]); Manolito de Montoya (Henry Darrow), Victoria's brother; and ranch hands Vasquero (Rodolfo Acosta) and Pedro (Roberto Contreres). Mel Blanc provides the voice of Frito Bandito, the Mexican snack foods bandit in animated commercials for Frito Lay Corn Chips (the ads were pulled two years later when the Mexican Defamation Committee objected to the stereotyped character).

1968. First season episodes of *The Doris Day Show* (CBS) feature Naomi Stevens as Juanita, the housekeeper to Buck Webb, the father of Doris Martin, a widow with two children living on a ranch in Mill Valley, California.

1969. Elena Verdugo plays Consuela Lopez, nurse to the elderly Dr. Marcus Welby on ABC's *Marcus Welby, M.D.* Elena revised her role as Consuela on the 1984 unsold pilot *The Return of Marcus Welby*.

1970. Ned Romero plays Joe Rivera, a sergeant with the Santa Luisa Police Department on *Dan August* (ABC).

1971. *Cade's County* (CBS) features Victor Campos as Rudy Davillo, a deputy to Sheriff Sam Cade. Anthony Quinn is Thomas Jefferson Alcala, the mayor of a turbulent Southwestern city on ABC's *The Man and the City*. Ramon Bieri is Barney Verick, the San Diego chief of detectives on NBC's *Sarge*.

1972. Ned Romero is Bob Ramirez, an investigator for Los Angeles district attorney Paul Ryan on *The D.A.* (NBC).

1973. Henry Darrow is Juan Hernandez, a Mexican-American detective with the Houston, Texas, police department on the NBC pilot *Hernandez, Houston P.D.* Henry Darrow is Alex Montez, the director of "Those Who Care," a mythical soap opera that stars Dick Preston (Dick Van Dyke) as Brad Fairmont on the California-based episodes of *The New Dick Van Dyke Show* (CBS; the one season revival of the Arizona-based *New Dick Van Show*, 1971–73). Chita Rivera played Connie Richardson, Dick's neighbor, the wife of Richard Richardson (Richard Dawson), the star of the TV series "Harrigan's Hooligans."

1974. Freddie Prinze plays Chico Rodriquez, the cheerful Mexican-American who worked for

Ed Brown, the cantankerous owner of a Los Angeles garage on NBC's *Chico and the Man*. In 1977, after the death of Freddie Prinze (suicide), Gabriel Melgar joined the cast for the series last season as Raul Garcia, a 12-year-old Mexican runaway taken in by Ed. Charo appeared in these episodes as Raul's Aunt Charo. ABC's *The Cowboys* features A Martinez as Cimarron, a Mexican-American teenager of the 1870s who worked with a group of orphaned children on a ranch owned by the widowed Kate Andersen. *Harry O* (ABC) features Henry Darrow as Manny Quinlan, a detective-lieutenant with the San Diego Police Department.

1975. Victor Campos is Dr. Felipe Ortega, a chief resident at Lowell Memorial Hospital on NBC's *Doctors Hospital*. Henry Darrow plays Nick Maggio, the scientist who helps Daniel Weston, an invisible man, appear visible with a special mask and hands on NBC's *The Invisible Man*. Hector Fuentes (Jose Perez) is a streetwise petty thief serving time at the Alamesa State Minimum Security Prison on ABC's *On the Rocks*.

1976. Jamie Tirelli is Orlando Lopez, the utility man for a disorganized baseball team called the Washington Americans on *Ball Four* (CBS). Rita Moreno is Rosa Dolores, the cousin of Hector Fuentes in *I'll Never Forget What's Her Name*, an ABC pilot spinoff from *On the Rocks* (see 1975). Here, Rosa and her girlfriend, Lillian (Yvonne Wilder), seek to become stars in Hollywood. Rodolfo Hoyos is Luis Valdez, a Mexican-American plumber on ABC's *Viva Valdez*. Carmen Zapata plays his wife, Sophie, with Lisa Mordente as their daughter, Connie, and James Victor, Nelson D. Cueves and Claudio Martinez as their sons Victor, Ernesto and Pepe.

1977. Erik Estrada is Frank Poncherello, the California Highway Patrol officer called "Ponch" on *CHiPs* (NBC).

1978. Paco Vela is Raul and Roseanna Christianson is Theresa, the butler and maid to the wealthy Ewing family on CBS's *Dallas*. Michael A. Salcido is Paul Sanchez, an undercover police detective with the L.A.P.D. on *David Cassidy—Man Undercover* (NBC). Although a specific ethnic background is not revealed, Ricardo Montalban (born in Mexico) plays Mr. Roarke, the mysterious owner of *Fantasy Island* (ABC). Frank LaLoggia plays Petro, a bumbling Mexican-American bellboy on the ABC pilot *Snavely*.

1979. Emilio Delgado joins the cast of *Lou Grant* (CBS) as Reuben Castillo, a reporter for the *Los Angeles Tribune* (he later becomes the national editor).

1980. Hector Elizondo plays Dan "The Bean" Delgado, a police sergeant for the San Francisco D.A.'s office on *Freebie and the Bean* (CBS).

1981. Don Cervantes plays Paco Rodriquez, a student in special education classes taught by Ralph Hinkley on *The Greatest American Hero* (ABC). Conchata Ferrell is Vangie Cruise, a bar owner on NBC's *McClain's Law*.

1982. Erica Gimpel plays Coco Hernandez, the Hispanic singer-dancer at the High School for the Performing Arts on NBC's *Fame* (in 1984, Jesse Borrego joined the cast as Jesse Velesquez, a Mexican-American student). Cesar Romero plays Miles Starling, the host of the mythical TV series "The Miles Starling Family Dance Party" on the NBC pilot *The Rainbow Girl*.

1983. NBC's *Bay City Blues* features Marco Rodriquez as Bird, the mascot for the Bluebirds baseball team. Edward Albert is Quisto Champion, son of the late Wade Champion, owner of the 200,000 acre Yellow Rose Ranch in Texas on NBC's *The Yellow Rose*.

1984. Paul Rodriquez plays Paul "Pablo" Rivera, a struggling young Los Angeles stand up comedian on ABC's *a.k.a. Pablo*. Joe Santos and Katy Jurado play his parents, Domingo and Rosa Maria; Martha Velez is his sister, Lucia, and Arnoldo Santana is Lucia's husband, Hector Del Gato.

1985. Ricardo Montalban plays Zachary Powers, the Hispanic tycoon on *The Colbys* (ABC). Lisa Antille is Lisa Flores, a young Mexican woman studying to become a U.S. citizen (while working as a maid for Henry and Muriel Rush) on *The Ted Knight Show* (the syndicated series has been retitled *Too Close for Comfort* when resyndicated with episodes of ABC's *Too Close for Comfort*). John DiAquino plays Vargas De La Costa, an expert gunsmith who helped uphold the law in the town of Wildside as a member of the Wildside Chamber of Commerce on CBS's *Wildside*.

1986. Eddie Veldez joins the cast of *The A-Team* (NBC) for its final season as Frankie Santana, the Hollywood special effects man who helped the team help people in trouble. Priscilla Lopez is Rosa Villanueva, a nurse at Manhattan General Hospital on CBS's *Kay O'Brien*. Jimmy

Smits is Victor Sifuentes, a Mexican lawyer at the Los Angeles firm of McKenzie, Brackman, Chaney and Kuzak on NBC's *Law and Order* (in 1991, A Martinez joins the cast as Hispanic attorney Daniel Morales). Henry Darrow plays Mike Rojas, a lieutenant with the L.A.P.D. on ABC's *Me and Mom*. Reni Santoni plays Ricardo Sanchez, a clothing manufacturer who moves from the barrio of East Los Angeles to fashionable Bel Air on *Sanchez of Bel Air*. Ada Maris is Maria Conchita Lopez, a Mexican immigrant studying to become a U.S. citizen on the syndicated *What a Country*.

1987. April Ortiz plays Carmen, the Hispanic maid to David Whiteman, a clothes hanger tycoon, and his family on *Down and Out in Beverly Hills* (Fox). Richard Yniquez plays Jesse Guerrea, an L.A.P.D. detective lieutenant on *Ohara* (ABC).

1988. Cheech Marin hosts *The Cheech Show*, an NBC pilot in which Cheech stars in "Party of the Week" skits with guest stars. Trinidad Silva plays Eddie, a cook in a home for troubled youths on the NBC pilot *Home Free*. Gregory Sierra is Vic Maldonado, a lieutenant with the L.A.P.D. on NBC's *Something Is Out There*. Paul Rodriguez is Tony Rivera and Eddie Velez is John Hernandez, a lawyer and a streetwise con artist who are also roommates on *Trial and Error* (CBS).

1989. Chantal Rivera-Batisse plays Melissa Santos, a beautiful Mexican-American high school student who yearns to become a dancer on NBC's *Ann Jillian*. Joe Lala plays Cito Escobar, a Mexican-American cab driver who marries Ellie Daye, the daughter of radio show host Everett Daye on NBC's *Knight and Daye*. Bernard White is Carl Montana, a plainclothes detective with the L.A.P.D. on *The New Dragnet* (Syn.). Mario Lopez is A.C. Slater, a student at Bayside High School in Palisades, California, on NBC's *Saved by the Bell*. Mario repeated his role as Slater in the spinoff series *Saved by the Bell: The College Years* (1993–94), where he is enrolled at California University.

1990. Mark Damon Espinoza is Jesse Vasquez, the Mexican-American law student on Fox's *Beverly Hills, 90210*. Paul Rodriquez plays Pedro Gomez, a bounty hunter for the Los Angeles-based Aztec Bail Bonds on *Grand Slam* (CBS). Abel Franco plays the agency owner, Al Ramirez and Lupe Ontiveros is Pedro's Grandmother Gomez.

1991. Cheech Marin stars as Chuy, a New Yorker with a dream to travel to California and make it big in show business on the Fox pilot *Culture Clash*.

1992. Arlene Taylor plays Kamala Consuelo Ricardo, a teenage Hispanic girl attending Western Pacific University in Los Angeles on *Freshman Dorm* (CBS). Cheech Marin plays Chuy Castillos, the Mexican-American chef at the Golden Palace Hotel in Miami, Florida, on *The Golden Palace* (CBS). *The Hat Squad* (CBS) features Nestor Servano as Raphael Martinez, an Hispanic orphan, adopted by Mike and Kitty Ragland, who grew up to become a cop like his father, but with a dislike for guns. Mariska Hargitay plays Angela Garcia, the widow of a slain Los Angeles police officer who is also a rookie cop on CBS's *Tequila and Bonetti*.

1993. Randy Vasquez is Marcus Gutierrez, the Mexican member of H.E.A.T. (Hemisphere Emergency Action Team), an organization that fights crime and terrorism on the syndicated *Acapulco H.E.A.T.* Tony Plana is Luke Ramirez, an Hispanic detective with the Bakersfield, California, Police Department on *Bakersfield, P.D.* (Fox). Juanita Holman (Anne Haney) is the Hispanic housekeeper for former boxer George Foster and his family on *George* (ABC). Liz Torres plays Mahalia Sanchez, the assistant manager of the Cross Roads Bus Terminal in St. Louis on *The John Larroquette Show* (NBC). Jimmy Smits is Bobby Simone, a detective with the 15th Precinct of the N.Y.P.D. on ABC's *N.Y.P.D. Blue*. Also on the series are Nicholas Turturro as Detective James Martinez and Esai Morales as Lieutenant Tony Rodriquez.

1994. Oscar Mechosa is Hector, head orderly in the psychiatric section of Riverside Hospital in Essex County, California, on *Birdland* (ABC). Jennifer Lopez is Melinda Lopez, the bartender at the luxury Hotel Malibu in Malibu Beach, California, on CBS's *Hotel Malibu*.

1995. Mark Adair Rios is Ramos, the assistant to Janos Bartok, a scientific genius of the Old West on *Legend* (UPN). Eddie Velez is Ricardo Sandoval and Wanda de Jesus is Liz Vega, reporters for Channel 3 in Los Angeles on UPN's *Live Shot*. Terry Ivens plays Elizabeth Vasquez, a doctor in Seattle on Fox's *Medicine Ball*.

1996. Leticia Robles is Maria Vallejo, a detective with the L.A.P.D. on the syndicated *L.A. Heat*. Cheech Marin is Joe Dominguez, the

Mexican-American partner of police captain Nash Bridges on CBS's *Nash Bridges*. Also cast was Jamie P. Gomez as Evan Cortez, a member of Nash's unit. Mario Lopez plays Bobby Cruz, a police officer with the Southern California Police Department on *Pacific Blue* (USA). A Martinez is Nick Cooper, an explosives expert with the Violent Crimes Task Force of the FBI on NBC's *Profiler*.

1997. Tony Plana is Luis Escobar, a member of the L.A. based Total Security, a private protection firm on ABC's *Total Security*.

1999. Mario Sanchez plays Carlos Sandoval, a martial arts expert who runs the Thunder Detective Agency in Texas on CBS's *Sons of Thunder*.

2000. Alvin Alvarez is Larry Garcia, an 11-year-old boy with a rich imagination who lives in San Antonio, Texas, on *The Brothers Garcia* (NIK). Carlos La Camara and Ana Maris are his parents, Ray and Sonia; Vaneza Leza Pitynski is his sister, Lorena; and Bobby Gonzalez and Jeffrey Licon are his brothers, George and Carlos. Michael De-Lorenzo is Carlos Santiago, a boxing champion on the Showtime series *Resurrection Blvd.* (his address in Los Angeles). Tony Plana plays his widowed father, Roberto; Nicholas Gonzalez is his younger brother, Alex; and Ruth Livier is Yolanda, his sister.

2001. *Lizzie McGuire* (Disney) features La Laine as Miranda Sanchez, the spirited best friend of Lizzie McGuire.

2002. Edward James Olmos is Jess Gonzalez, a Mexican-American barber living in East Los Angeles on *American Family* (PBS). Sonia Braga is his wife, Berta; Kurt Caceres, Constance Marie and A.J. Lamas are their children, Conrado, Nina and Cisco. Raquel Welch plays their aunt, Dora. George Lopez plays himself, a Mexican-American on ABC's *The George Lopez Show*. George is married to Angie (Constance Marie), a Cuban-American. They are the parents of Carmen (Masiela Lusha) and Max (Luis Armand Garcia). George works as the manager of the Powers Brothers Aircraft plant and Angie is a wedding planner. Life in Tucson, Arizona, is seen through the eyes of David Tiant (Pablo Santos), a 15-year-old Mexican-American on the WB's *Greetings from Tucson*. Julio Oscar Mechosa is David's father, Joaquin; Rebecca Creskoff is his mother, Elizabeth (an Irish Catholic), and Aimee Garcia is Maria, David's older sister.

2003. Yancey Arins plays Miguel Cadena, a

Mexican-American kingpin who oversees his family's drug trafficking operations on NBC's *Kingpin*. Sheryl Lee plays Marlene, his Caucasian wife and Ruben Carbajel is their son, Joey.

2005. Freddie Prinze, Jr., stars as Freddie Moreno, a chef who owns a successful restaurant in Chicago on *Freddie* (ABC). Also in the cast are Jacqueline Obradors as Sofia, his sister-in-law; Chloe Suazo as Zoey, Sofia's daughter; and Jenny Gago as his grandmother (who speaks no English; her speech is seen in captions).

Midgets see Little People

Ministers see Religious Characters

Morphing

Morphing means to change. It is a term that has been adapted by TV and motion pictures for dramatic special effects that change, most often, people into something else.

Television has been using this device since its early beginnings, although in a much more simplistic form called the dissolve (when one scene blends into another giving the illusion of a change). Every program has used it. This entry covers a selection of programs that pioneered advanced types of dissolves to the current computer generated morphing.

1952. On *My Friend Irma* (CBS), when under the sponsorship of Cool Cigarettes, star Marie Wilson is seen on the left side of the screen. As the theme plays the Cool logo (a penguin) dissolves into the scene with Marie to present the show's title, stars and sponsor, all of which dissolve in and out as needed (in very early episodes, an announcer is used to introduce the show, stars and sponsor).

1965. On *Please Don't Eat the Daisies* (NBC), to switch from scene to scene, an animated daisy appears on the screen for several seconds then dissolves to reveal the next scene.

1966. On *Batman* (ABC), like the above title, used the symbol of a bat to cover the screen then dissolve to reveal the next scene. Also, while simplistic, changes occur when Bruce Wayne and Dick Grayson use the Batpoles in Wayne Manor to automatically change from their street clothes to their crime fighting outfits as Batman and Robin. Although considered a special effect, the transporter sequences (rearranging a person's molecules to transport them from one place to another) in *Star Trek* (NBC) are an early example of morphing (disappearing in white sprinkles and reappearing the same way). This technique would prevail through all the *Star Trek* spin-offs and feature films.

1974. On *Shazam* (CBS), teenager Billy Batson becomes the mighty crime fighter Captain Marvel when he says the word "Shazam." Upon doing so, a clever dissolve is used to transform the young Billy into an older Captain Marvel.

1975. On *Isis* (CBS), schoolteacher Andrea Thomas becomes the superhero Isis when she holds a magic amulet and says "O Mighty Isis." A swirling effect is used to transform Andrea into Isis. On *Space: 1999* (Syn.), Maya, an alien from the planet Psychon, has the power of molecular transformation (she calls herself a metamorph). She can become any animal she wishes and the transformation sequences use a series of clever dissolves.

1976. Morphing became more advanced on *Wonder Woman* (ABC/CBS) when Diana Prince needed to become Wonder Woman. Diana does a twirling striptease that magically transforms her from her street clothes into the costumed Wonder Woman in a very effective series of dissolves.

1978. On *The Incredible Hulk* (CBS), effective dissolving produces the startling change for Bill Bixby as Dr. David Banner to Lou Ferrigno as the green Incredible Hulk (the reverse change is also quite effective).

1983. The term transmutation comes into being to show how Jonathan Chase can transform himself into any animal on *Manimal* (NBC). Clever dissolve editing provides believable sequences that show Jonathan becoming animals (most notably a panther or a hawk). To save on expenses, the film sequence is reversed to show the change from animal to man.

1990. On *She Wolf of London* (Syn.), Randi Wallace is a beautiful college student who becomes a hideous werewolf through excellent dissolve editing. The same techniques were used on the Fox series *Werewolf* two years earlier (here Eric Cord is bitten by a werewolf and now becomes one himself when the moon is full).

1993. On *The Mighty Morphin Power Rangers* (Fox/ABC), expert computer animation comes

into play to morph teenagers into superheroes called Power Rangers. Each Power Ranger possesses the power of a dinosaur called a Zord (which can come into being when a Ranger holds his or her special morph device into the sky and says the name of his dinosaur). If needed, the Rangers can morph their dinosaurs into one to form the gigantic Mega Zord (accomplished through miniatures and computer animation). The success of the original series led to the following spin offs, all of which used the term morphing to create Power Rangers and their Zords (later called Zeo Zords): *Power Rangers Turbo* (high tech transformable cars are used), *The Power Rangers in Space, Power Rangers Time Force, Power Rangers World Force, Power Rangers Ninja Storm* and *Power Rangers Dino Thunder*.

1994. On *The Secret World of Alex Mack* (NIK), the computer-generated sequences that change 13-year-old Alex Louise Mack from normal girl to a silvery liquid are quite effective (caused when Alex was doused with a mysterious chemical). *Viper* (NBC/Syn.). Viper, a futuristic crime-fighting car, is seen in its normal state as a 1992 red Dodge Viper. Expertly executed computer effects morph the car into the Defender, a silver car that people report as "The Phantom Vehicle."

1997. The computer-generated sequences that transform vampires from normal to fangs on *Buffy the Vampire Slayer* (WB/UPN) are quite realistic. The same holds true for the spin-off series *Angel* (WB).

1998. On *Charmed* (WB), Paige Halliwell and Leo Wyatt are White Lighters (guardians of witches) and can transport themselves from place to place by orbing (dissolving in twinkling white lights). The witch heroes, Piper, Phoebe and Paige, call demons that constantly change images Shape Shifters (accomplished through high tech computer animation).

2000. On *Sheena* (Syn.), Gena Lee Nolin plays Sheena, a white jungle goddess in Africa who possesses the power to morph and transform herself into any animal. Computer animation is used to its fullest and provides excellent girl to animal effects as well as reversal effects. Most effective, however, are the sequences in which Gena is transformed into the Darak'na, a vicious killing creature (played by Vickie Phillips and Denise Loden). The changes are so well executed that only by reading the end credits does one learn that Gena does not play the Darak'na.

2001. On *Black Scorpion* (Sci Fi), police officer Darcy Walker fights crime as the mysterious Black Scorpion. While Darcy does wear a black costume, it is her car, the Scorpion Mobile, that receives the computer's attention. She drives an orange Corvette that has a secret identity. When Darcy presses a switch, the car morphs from the Corvette into the sleek black Scorpion Mobile. Darcy can also morph (switch from her street clothes to her black Scorpion costume through a special device in her car that transmits a signal to the scorpion ring she wears). On *Witchblade* (TNT), Sara Pezzini is a police officer who wears the Witchblade, a mysterious bracelet that gives her extraordinary powers. Many effects are used but the most effective is the coat of armor the Witchblade provides to protect Darcy. It magically appears to cover her body and the effect is quite believable.

2005. Simplistic morphing returns to TV: *The Bad Girls Guide* (UPN) uses silhouettes of two girls dancing and is flashed between scenes. *Life on a Stick* (Fox) uses stills of characters then dissolves into the next scene (much like Fox's *That 70s Show*, which uses visuals of cast members to change from scene to scene). On *Stacked* (Fox), scenes before and after commercials change to black and white drawings then dissolve into live action sequences.

Native Americans see American Indian Performers and Characters

New Jersey

A listing of series set in New Jersey.
1958. *This Is Alice* (Syn).
1975. *Joe and Sons* (CBS).
1979. *Makin' It* (ABC).
1982. *No Soap Radio* (ABC); *One of the Boys* (NBC).
1989. *Charles in Charge* (CBS).
1987. *Charles in Charge* (Syn.).
1988. *Annie McGuire* (CBS); *Almost Grown* (CBS).
1989. *Dream Street* (NBC); *Live-In* (CBS).
1990. *What a Dummy* (Syn.).
1991. *Hi Honey, I'm Home* (ABC).

1992. *Stand By Your Man* (Fox); *Down the Shore* (Fox).
1995. *Bless This House* (CBS); *Hudson Street* (ABC).
1996. *Matt Waters* (CBS).
1998. *The Sopranos* (HBO).
2001. *The Ellen Show* (CBS); *That's Life* (CBS).
2003. *Like Family* (WB).
2004. *Come to Papa* (NBC).
2005. *House* (Fox); *Point Pleasant* (Fox); *Quintuplets* (Fox).
2006. *Teachers* (NBC).

New York

A listing of series set in and around New York City. Non-Manhattan locales are indicated with the program.
1948. *Barney Blake, Police Reporter* (NBC); *Off the Record* (DuMont); *Peter Hunter, Private Eye* (Syn.).
1949. *The Goldbergs* (CBS; Bronx); *Jackson and Jill* (NBC); *Martin Kane, Private Eye* (NBC).
1950. *The Adventures of Ellery Queen* (DuMont/ABC); *The Detective's Wife* (CBS); *Dick Tracy* (ABC); *The Girls* (CBS); *I Cover Times Square* (ABC); *The Peter and Mary Show* (NBC); *Rocky King, Inside Detective* (DuMont).
1951. *The Amos 'n' Andy Show* (CBS); *Crime with Father* (ABC); *The Egg and I* (CBS; Cape Flattery); *Front Page Detective* (DuMont); *Mark Saber* (ABC); *Not for Publication* (DuMont).
1952. *The Cases of Eddie Drake* (DuMont); *Heaven for Betsy* (CBS); *I Love Lucy* (CBS); *My Friend Irma* (CBS); *My Little Margie* (CBS); *Mr. and Mrs. North* (CBS); *Papa Cellini* (ABC).
1953. *Bonino* (NBC); *City Detective* (Syn.); *Jimmy Hughes, Rookie Cop* (DuMont); *Make Room for Daddy* (ABC/CBS); *Private Secretary* (CBS); *Topper* (CBS).
1954. *Duffy's Tavern* (NBC); *The Mask* (ABC); *The Plainclothesman* (DuMont).
1955. *The Honeymooners* (CBS; Brooklyn; CBS); *It's Always Jan* (CBS); *Joe and Mabel* (CBS; Manhattan and Brooklyn); *Norby* (NBC; Pearl River).
1956. *Hey Jeannie* (CBS); *Stanley* (NBC).
1957. *Decoy* (Syn.); *Richard Diamond, Private Detective* (CBS episodes, 1957–58); *The Thin Man* (NBC).
1958. *The Ann Sothern Show* (CBS); *How to*

Marry a Millionaire (Syn.); *The Investigator* (NBC); *Love That Jill* (ABC); *Mike Hammer* (Syn.); *Naked City* (ABC); *New York Confidential* (Syn.).

1959. *The Betty Hutton Show* (CBS); *Brenner* (CBS); *The D.A.'s Man* (NBC); *The Detectives* (ABC); *Johnny Staccato* (NBC); *The Lawless Years* (NBC).

1960. *Diagnosis Unknown* (CBS); *Johnny Midnight* (Syn.); *The Law and Mr. Jones* (ABC); *My Sister Eileen* (CBS); *Naked City* (ABC); *The Roaring 20s* (ABC).

1961. *The Asphalt Jungle* (ABC); *Car 54, Where Are You?* (NBC; Bronx); *The Defenders* (CBS); *The Dick Van Dyke Show* (CBS; New Rochelle); *The 87th Precinct* (NBC); *Holiday Lodge* (CBS; N.Y. State); *The Investigators* (CBS); *The Joey Bishop Show* (NBC/CBS).

1962. *The Eleventh Hour* (NBC); *Fair Exchange* (CBS; N.Y. and London); *Going My Way* (ABC); *The Nurses* (CBS); *Saints and Sinners* (NBC).

1963. *The Bill Dana Show* (NBC); *East Side/West Side* (CBS); *The Patty Duke Show* (ABC; Brooklyn Heights).

1964. *The Doctors and the Nurses* (CBS); *The Man from U.N.C.L.E.* (NBC); *Mr. Broadway* (CBS); *The Reporter* (CBS); *Valentine's Day* (ABC).

1965. *For the People* (CBS); *The Trials of O'Brien* (CBS).

1966. *Family Affair* (CBS); *The Girl from U.N.C.L.E.* (NBC); *Hawk* (ABC); *Hey Landlord!* (NBC); *Occasional Wife* (NBC); *The Pruitts of Southampton* (ABC; Long Island).

1967. *He and She* (CBS); *N.Y.P.D.* (ABC).

1969. *Mr. Deeds Goes to Town* (ABC); *The Queen and I* (CBS).

1970. *Barefoot in the Park* (ABC); *The Best of Everything* (ABC); *McCloud* (NBC); *The Odd Couple* (ABC).

1971. *All in the Family* (CBS; Queens); *Bridget Loves Bernie* (CBS).

1972. *The Corner Bar (ABC); The Don Rickles Show* (CBS; Long Island); *Madigan* (NBC); *Maude* (CBS; Tuckahoe); *The Super* (ABC).

1973. *The Corner Bar* (ABC); *Calucci's Department* (CBS); *Diana* (NBC); *Needles and Pins* (NBC); *Shaft* (CBS).

1975. *Barney Miller* (ABC); *Big Eddie* (CBS); *Doc* (CBS); *Ellery Queen* (NBC); *The Jeffersons* (CBS); *Welcome Back, Kotter* (ABC; Brooklyn).

1976. *Serpico* (NBC).

1977. *On Our Own* (CBS); *Rhoda* (CBS); *Busting Loose* (CBS); *Fish* (ABC; Brooklyn).

1978. *The Amazing Spider-Man* (CBS); *The American Girls* (CBS); *Diff'rent Strokes* (NBC); *Free Country* (ABC); *Sword of Justice* (NBC); *Taxi* (ABC/NBC); *The Ted Knight Show* (CBS); *W.E.B.* (NBC).

1979. *The Associates* (ABC); *Eischied* (NBC); *The Facts of Life* (NBC; Peekskill); *Flatbush* (CBS; Brooklyn); *13 Queens Boulevard* (ABC; Queens).

1980. *Bosom Buddies* (ABC); *Ladies' Man* (CBS); *Me and Maxx* (NBC); *The Two of Us* (CBS).

1981. *Checking In* (CBS); *Love, Sidney* (NBC); *Nero Wolfe* (NBC); *Nurse* (CBS); *Park Place* (CBS).

1982. *Baker's Dozen* (CBS); *Cagney and Lacey* (CBS); *Fame* (NBC); *Gloria* (CBS; Duchess County); *It Takes Two* (ABC); *Nine to Five* (ABC); *Silver Spoons* (NBC; Long Island).

1983. *Bare Essence* (NBC); *The Hamptons* (ABC; Long Island); *Manimal* (NBC); *Teachers Only* (NBC; Brooklyn); *We Got It Made* (NBC /Syn.).

1984. *The Cosby Show* (NBC; Brooklyn); *Double Trouble* (NBC); *Empire* (CBS); *Kate and Allie* (CBS); *Mama Malone* (CBS); *Mike Hammer* (CBS); *Night Court* (NBC); *Suzanne Pleshette Is Maggie Briggs* (CBS).

1985. *Berringer's* (NBC); *Code Name: Foxfire* (NBC); *The Equalizer* (CBS); *Foley Square* (CBS); *Growing Pains* (ABC; Long Island); *The Lucie Arnaz Show* (CBS); *Our Family Honor* (ABC).

1986. *Better Days* (CBS; Brooklyn); *Head of the Class* (ABC); *Joe Bash* (CBS); *Kay O'Brien* (CBS); *Melba* (CBS); *Nine to Five* (Syn.); *Throb* (Syn.).

1987. *Beauty and the Beast* (CBS); *The Bronx Zoo* (NBC; Bronx); *The Days and Nights of Molly Dodd* (NBC); *Everything's Relative* (CBS); *Harry* (ABC); *Leg Work* (CBS); *Mama's Boy* (NBC); *My Two Dads* (NBC); *Roxie* (CBS); *You Can't Take It with You* (Syn.; Long Island).

1988. *Annie McGuire* (CBS); *Baby Boom* (NBC); *Dear John* (NBC).

1989. *Chicken Soup* (ABC); *Gideon Oliver* (ABC); *Living Dolls* (ABC); *The Nutt House* (NBC); *One of the Boys* (NBC; Queens); *True Blue* (NBC).

1990. *Babes* (Fox); *Law and Order* (NBC); *Married People* (ABC); *Room for Romance* (CBS); *Seinfeld* (NBC); *Singer and Sons* (CBS); *Working Girl* (NBC); *Working It Out* (NBC).

1991. *Baby Talk* (ABC; Manhattan then Brooklyn); *Brooklyn Bridge* (CBS; Brooklyn); *Charlie Hoover* (Fox); *Civil Wars* (ABC); *The Commish* (ABC; Eastbridge); *Eddie Dodd* (ABC); *Herman's Head* (Fox); *Man in the Family* (NBC); *Princesses* (CBS); *Sunday Dinner* (CBS; Long Island).

1992. *Flying Blind* (Fox); *Frannie's Turn* (CBS; Staten Island); *Ghost Writer* (PBS; Brooklyn); *Love and War* (CBS); *Mad About You* (NBC); *Room for Two* (ABC).

1993. *Daddy Dearest* (Fox); *Dudley* (CBS); *Joe's Life* (ABC); *Living Single* (Fox; Brooklyn); *The Nanny* (CBS); *N.Y.P.D. Blue* (ABC); *Tribeca* (Fox); *The Trouble with Larry* (CBS).

1994. *Friends* (NBC); *The George Carlin Show* (Fox); *Madman of the People* (NBC; Brooklyn); *New York Undercover* (Fox; Harlem).

1995. *Can't Hurry Love* (CBS); *Caroline in the City* (NBC); *Central Park West* (CBS); *Cleghorn* (WB); *Fudge* (ABC); *High Society* (CBS); *Kirk* (WB); *Misery Loves Company* (Fox); *Ned and Stacey* (Fox); *News Radio* (NBC); *Pride and Joy* (NBC); *Simon* (WB); *The Single Guy* (NBC).

1996. *Common Law* (ABC); *Cosby* (CBS; Queens); *Everybody Loves Raymond* (CBS; Lynbrook); *Good Company* (CBS); *Life with Roger* (WB); *My Guys* (CBS); *Something So Right* (NBC); *Spin City* (ABC).

1997. *City Guys* (NBC); *Dellaventura* (CBS); *FX: The Series* (Syn.); *413 Hope Street* (Fox); *Just Shoot Me* (NBC); *The New Ghost Writer Mysteries* (CBS; Brooklyn); *The Parent'Hood* (WB); *Prince Street* (NBC); *The Tony Danza Show* (NBC); *Union Square* (NBC); *Veronica's Closet* (NBC).

1998. *Becker* (CBS; Bronx); *Brooklyn South* (CBS; Brooklyn); *Felicity* (WB); *Jesse* (NBC; Buffalo); *Sex and the City* (HBO); *The Single Life* (NBC); *The Wayans Bros.* (WB); *Will and Grace* (NBC).

1999. *Law and Order: Special Victims Unit* (NBC); *The Norm Show* (ABC); *Third Watch* (NBC); *Zoe, Duncan, Jack and Jane* (WB).

2000. *The Beat* (UPN); *Secret Agent Man* (UPN); *Talk to Me* (ABC); *Welcome to New York* (CBS); *Zoe* (WB).

2001. *Big Apple* (CBS); *Doc* (PAX); *The Fighting Fitzgeralds* (NBC); *Grounded for Life* (Fox/WB; Staten Island); *The Job* (ABC); *Kristen* (NBC); *Law and Order: Criminal Intent* (NBC); *Nero Wolfe* (A&E); *Witchblade* (TNT).

2002. *Bram and Alice* (CBS); *Family Affair* (WB); *The In-Laws* (NBC); *Less Than Perfect* (ABC); *The Random Years* (UPN); *What I Like About You* (WB).

2003. *A.U.S.A.* (NBC); *Less Than Perfect* (ABC); *Queens Supreme* (CBS; Queens); *Regular Joe* (ABC; Queens); *Watching Ellie* (NBC); *Whoopie* (NBC).

2004. *C.S.I.: New York* (CBS); *Kevin Hill* (UPN); *Rescue Me* (FX); *Tru Calling* (Fox); *Wonderfalls* (Fox; Niagara Falls).

2005. *Beautiful People* (ABC Family); *Blind Justice* (ABC); *Committed* (NBC); *Everybody Hates Chris* (UPN; Brooklyn); *Hot Properties* (ABC); *Jake in Progress* (ABC); *Jonny Zero* (Fox); *Law and Order: Trial By Jury* (NBC); *Living with Fran* (WB; Far Rockaway); *Related* (WB).

2006. *The Bedford Diaries* (WB); *Courting Alex* (CBS); *Four Kings* (NBC); *Love Monkey* (CBS).

News Broadcasts — Pioneering Years, 1927–1958

Instantaneous news and channels devoted entirely to news are an aspect of early television that could not even be imagined. The technology was simply not there. This entry chronicles the early newscasts and programs that paved the way for today's high tech programs and instantaneous news.

1927. On April 7th, Bell Telephone Labs in Manhattan successfully transmitted sound and picture when it broadcast a speech by Secretary of Commerce Herbert Hoover from Washington, D.C.

1928. Experimental TV station WGY broadcasts a remote pickup from Albany, New York (Governor Alfred E. Smith accepting the Democratic nomination for President on August 28th).

1932. CBS broadcasts the first political program, the Democratic National Convention.

1938. An NBC experiment to test the possibilities of remote broadcasting picks up two unexpected news stories. Cameras capture the body of a woman falling from the Time and Life Building in Manhattan and a fire at an abandoned barracks on Wards Island.

1939. Lowell Thomas reports the news as a segment of *The Variety Show*, an NBC program of music, vaudeville acts, skits and news.

1940. The Standard Oil Company of New Jersey sponsors *The Esso Newscast*, a ten- episode NBC experiment (on station W2XBS in New York) wherein William Spargrove reported the news.

1941. NBC airs *Lowell Thomas Reporting*, a simulcast of Lowell's radio program of the same title. Lowell Thomas was seated at a desk while reading the news. The only change from the radio program was that cans of the sponsor's product (Sunoco Oil) were added so the product could be seen while the commercial message was given. In August of 1941, Richard Hubbell read war news dispatches against a background of war maps on CBS's experimental series *War News*.

1943. Samuel Cuff and Kerby Cushing report the news on *Around the World in 30 Minutes*, the DuMont Network's first experimental newscast (here maps were used to help illustrate the commentary of military and political developments). Also on DuMont, Samuel Cuff commentated on the state of World War II using visual aids (maps) to illustrate the areas he was mentioning on *DuMont Varieties*.

1944. Ned Calmer delivers two 15-minute newscasts on *The CBS Studio Show*, a two-hour program of music, skits and interviews. Dick Bradley delivers the news on TV's first attempt at a daily thirty-minute newscast — *Your World Tomorrow* on DuMont.

1947. DuMont begins a regularly scheduled newscast with *Walter Compton and the News* (which originates from Washington, D.C.). NBC's *Meet the Press*, the longest running program on TV (still current in 2006) premieres. The moderators, who interview prominent people, are: Martha Roundtree (1947–52), Ned Brooks (1953–65), Lawrence E. Spevak (1966–75), Bill Monroe (1975–84), Marvin Kalb (1984–87), Chris Williams (1987–88) and Tim Russert (1988-Present).

1948. Prominent people debate topical issues on *America's Town Meeting*, an ABC series broadcast from New York's Town Hall Auditorium. George V. Denny, Jr. (and later John Daly) served as the moderator. NBC begins *The Camel News Caravan* with the news reporting of John Cameron Swayze under the sponsorship of Camel Cigarettes. Also during this time, NBC broadcasts the summer presidential conventions (anchored by John Cameron Swayze). CBS premieres *Douglas Edwards with the News* (which ran until 1962 at which time Walter Cronkite became CBS's prime early evening newscaster).

1950. Washington newspaper columnist Drew Pearson hosts *Washington Merry-Go-Round*, a news series on DuMont.

1951. Edward R. Murrow hosts *See It Now* on CBS. Murrow was responsible for leading TV news out of infancy and into maturity with this show (he took news out of the confines of a broadcast studio and into the whole wide world. The program, which ran until 1961, combined film footage and live commentary to tell news stories). CBS also has Walter Cronkite, the man who can enter a fast-breaking or complex news story and hold everything together no matter how long it takes. He hosted several news-oriented series: *You Are There, The 20th Century* and *Eyewitness to History*, as well as anchoring *The CBS Evening News*. The charm and charisma of newsmen David Brinkley and Chet Huntley became NBC's chief weapon in the ratings war against CBS (NBC's *Huntley–Brinkley Report* dislodged the powerful *Camel News Caravan* in 1956). Robert Trout, Eric Severeid and Frank McGee were among the pioneering newscasters at this time. While not as prominent as their male counterparts, women also found a place in TV news. Lisa Howard, Nancy Dickerson, Pauline Fredericks and Barbara Walters made their marks in early TV news. Over at ABC, John Daly was responsible for delivering the network's regular early evening newscast from 1949 through 1961 (at which time ABC reorganized its news department to be more competitive with CBS and NBC; DuMont had discontinued broadcasting in 1957).

1952. *The Today Show* premieres on NBC. The combination of news, weather, feature stories and light entertainment became a hit and in 2007, is still running strong as TV's longest surviving early morning series. Dave Garroway was the host and regulars included Hugh Downs, John Chancellor, Barbara Walters and Frank Blair. Newspaper columnist Walter Winchell transforms his radio news show to a TV show (which he begins with his trademark "Good evening Mr. and Mrs. North and South America and all the ships at sea"). Also in this year (and in 1956 and 1960) Walter Cronkite and Lowell Thomas anchor the CBS coverage of the presidential conventions.

1953. Edward R. Murrow hosts the pioneering *Person to Person*, a CBS series wherein Murrow visits celebrities through electronics (Murrow is seated in a studio; celebrities in their homes).

1954. CBS premieres *Face the Nation*, an in-depth analysis of the news that is still current in 2007. The hosts: Ted Koop (1954–55), Stuart Novins (1955–60), Howard K. Smith (1960–63), Martin Agronsky (1963–65), Paul Niven (1965–69), George Herman (1969–83), Leslie Stahl (1983–91), Bob Schieffer (1991–Present). CBS also airs *The Morning Show* with Jack Paar as the host and as direct competition to NBC's *Today Show* (the title changed to *Good Morning* in 1956 with Walter Cronkite as the host and eventually became *The CBS Morning Show*).

1955. *Wide Wide World* premieres on NBC. Dave Garroway hosts a program in which TV proved it could become a window on the world when it presented live pickups from various parts of the country (films were used for overseas reporting).

1956. News correspondents David Brinkley and Chet Huntley are teamed by NBC as anchors for the 1956 presidential coverage and soon afterward for their nightly newscast, *The Huntley–Brinkley Report* (their closing became a part of TV history: "Good night, Chet. Good night, David. And good night for NBC news").

1957. ABC airs *The Mike Wallace Interviews*, a series of probing news interviews and TV's first approach to hard-hitting news.

1958. David Susskind brings a new dimension to TV with *Open End*. The original concept used remote pickups for stories. When the format just didn't work, he revised it to a successful round table discussion over which he presided. Edward R. Murrow hosts the ground-breaking *Small World*, a filmed series that went to the source for its news stories — no matter where they were. From this point on, as new technology became available, television was the first to embrace it — from improving studio graphics to on-the-spot coverage to live remote pickups from any point in the world.

Newspapers and Magazines

This entry chronicles the TV characters that are associated with newspapers or magazines in a non-reporting status. For additional newspapers and magazines see *Reporters*.

1953. John Hamilton plays Perry White, the harassed editor of the Metropolis *Daily Planet* on *The Adventures of Superman* (Syn.).

1954. Peter Lawford plays Bill Hastings, a for-

mer journalism professor at U.C.L.A. who writes the "Dear Phoebe" advice-to-the-lovelorn column for the Los Angeles *Daily Star* on NBC's *Dear Phoebe*. Lily Ruskin (Spring Byington) is an advice columnist ("Tips for Housewives") for the Los Angeles *Gazette* on CBS's *December Bride*. Celeste Anders (Celeste Holm) is a former Minnesota college teacher turned writer for the New York *Express* on CBS's *Honestly, Celeste!*

1957. Wally and Beaver Cleaver (Tony Dow, Jerry Mathers) deliver newspapers for the Mayfield *Sun-Courier* on *Leave It to Beaver* (CBS/ABC). Harris Clayton (Richard Eastman) is the editor of the *Epitaph*, the newspaper of Tombstone, Arizona, on *Tombstone Territory* (ABC).

1958. Lisa Gaye plays Gwen Kirby, a writer for *Manhattan* magazine (who is also seeking a rich husband) on the syndicated *How to Marry a Millionaire*. Jefferson Drum (Jeff Richards) is a newspaper editor in the lawless gold mining town of Jubilee on NBC's *Jefferson Drum*. Adam McLean (Rex Reason) is a newspaper editor (of the Yellowstone *Sentinel*) in 1870s Dakota on *Man Without a Gun* (ABC). Dennis O'Keefe plays Dick Richards, a former attorney who is now editor of a music magazine called *Take 5* on the syndicated pilot *Night Prowl*. Chet Holliday (Tommy Farrell), the father of the mischievous nine-year-old Alice (Patty Ann Gerrity) is a writer for the *Star-Herald* in River Glen, New Jersey, on the syndicated *This Is Alice*.

1959. Dennis O'Keefe is Hal Towne, a newspaper columnist ("All About Towne") on *The Dennis O'Keefe Show* (CBS).

1960. John Michael O'Toole (Jim Backus) is the editor of the *Headline Press Service*, a newspaper fraught with problems on *The Jim Backus Show — Hot Off the Wire* (Syn.). Ruth Sherwood (Elaine Stritch) is a writer for *Manhattan* magazine who hopes to turn her hometown experience (in Columbus, Ohio) into a book on CBS's *My Sister Eileen*. Debbie Potter (Sherry Alberoni) is an eleven-year-old girl who delivers papers for the Las Palmas, California, *Gazette*, then publishes her own neighborhood gossip sheet, *The Debbie Daily* on *The Tom Ewell Show* (CBS).

1961. Bob Major (Robert Sterling) is a former editor for *The New York Times* who now publishes *The Bulletin*, the newspaper of Phippsboro, New Hampshire, on CBS's *Ichabod and Me*. Sixteen-year-old Margie Clayton (Cynthia Pepper) is editor of her high school newspaper, *The Madison Bugle*, and author of the gossip column "Through the Keyhole" on ABC's *Margie*.

1962. The stories of free-lance journalist Adam Sheppard (Lloyd Bridges) are dramatized on *The Lloyd Bridges Show* (CBS).

1963. Patty Lane (Patty Duke) is a sophomore at Brooklyn Heights High School and the editor of its newspaper, *The Bugle*, on ABC's *The Patty Duke Show*. Her father, Martin Lane (William Schallert), is the managing editor of the *New York Chronicle*.

1965. Sam Drucker (Frank Cady) owns the general store in Hooterville and publishes the community's only newspaper, *The Hooterville World Guardian* on *Green Acres* (CBS).

1969. Tom Corbett (Bill Bixby) is the editor of *Tomorrow* magazine on ABC's *The Courtship of Eddie's Father*. Jim Thompson (Don Chastain) is a sportswriter for the Los Angeles *Sun* on *The Debbie Reynolds Show* (NBC). William Windom plays John Monroe, a cartoonist for *Manhattanite* magazine on NBC's *My World … and Welcome to It*.

1970. Oscar Madison is a sports columnist for the New York *Herald* on ABC's *The Odd Couple*.

1972. Shirley Logan (Shirley MacLaine) is a photojournalist for *World Illustrated Magazine* on *Shirley's World* (ABC). In the Depression era of 1930s Virginia, John-Boy Walton (Richard Thomas) establishes his own newspaper, *The Blue Ridge Chronicle*, on *The Waltons* (CBS).

1973. Judy Evans (Nita Talbot) is the editor of *Screen World* magazine on ABC's *Here We Go Again*. Ted Harper (Ted Bessell) is the editor of *With It*, a magazine for today's people on the CBS pilot *The Ted Bessell Show*.

1974. Richie Cunningham (Ron Howard) attends Jefferson High School and works as a writer for its newspaper, *The Bugle*, on ABC's *Happy Days*. He is later a cub reporter for the Milwaukee *Journal*.

1976. Roger Thomas, called Raj (Ernest Thomas), is a student at Jefferson High School who writes for its paper, *The Gazette* on *What's Happening!!* (ABC).

1977. Tom Bradford (Dick Van Patten) is a columnist for the Sacramento *Register* on ABC's *Eight Is Enough*. R.B. Kingston (Raymond Burr) is the editor-in-chief of the Frazier News Group, a California-based organization of newspapers and TV stations on NBC's *Kingston Confidential*. Ed-

ward Asner plays Lou Grant, city editor of the Los Angeles *Tribune* on *Lou Grant* (CBS).

1979. NBC attempts two pilots called *Gossip* (about the antics of the editorial staff of a Hollywood scandal sheet called *The National Gossip*). Judy Landers and Thomas Hill star in the first pilot (June 10); John Hillerman and Dena Dietrich star in the second one (July 10).

1980. Ted Bessell plays Harry Jenkins, an accomplished womanizer and sportswriter for the San Francisco *Journal* on NBC's *Good Time Harry*. Dina Moran (Kim Cattrall) is an ambitious journalist who settles for a job as a gossip columnist for the Roper Newspaper Syndicate in California on the Operation Prime Time pilot *The Gossip Columnist*. Diana Cassidy (Diana Canova) is a columnist for the Arlington *Dispatch* in Washington, D.C., on ABC's *I'm a Big Girl Now*. Alan Thackery (Lawrence Pressman) is the lone male writer on the New York based *Women's Life* magazine on CBS's *Ladies' Man*. Louise Sorel plays the editor, Elaine Holstein. *The New Voice*, the newspaper of Boston's Lincoln High School, is the setting for a group of students preparing the paper for press on PBS's *The New Voice*. Alan Ozley (Matt McCoy) is an artist for the Essex, Connecticut, *Register*, who hopes to become a political cartoonist on the CBS pilot *Pen 'n' Inc*. Jack Ferguson and Trish Van Gordon (Desi Arnaz, Jr., Melinda Culea) are staff members at *Whacked Out*, a far-out newspaper on the NBC pilot *Whacked Out*.

1981. Fannie Flagg plays Cassie Bowman, editor of the *Sentinel*, one of two newspapers in the town of Harper Valley, Ohio, on NBC's *Harper Valley*. Tom Meechum (Christopher Stone) publishes the other paper, the *Sun*.

1982. Oscar Madison (Demond Wilson), the sloppy roommate of perfectionist Felix Unger, is a sports columnist for the New York *Herald* on ABC's *The New Odd Couple*.

1984. Jill Pembroke (Julie Cobb) is a housewife and mother who is also the theater critic for the New Jersey *Register* on CBS's *Charles in Charge*. Mickey Thompson (John Getz) is a human-interest columnist for a weekly New York newspaper called *The Island Eye* on the ABC pilot *Concrete Beat*. Cliff Penrose (Hal Linden) is the editor of *Columbus Life*, a faltering Ohio magazine on the CBS pilot *Second Edition*. Maggie Briggs (Suzanne Pleshette) is a hard news reporter for the New York *Examiner* who is transferred to feature writer for the paper's *Modern Living* section on *Suzanne Pleshette Is Maggie Briggs* (CBS).

1985. Barrie Shepherd (Jan Smithers) is a beautiful unmarried columnist who covers the singles scene for her newspaper column "The Single Life" on the ABC pilot *The Columnist.* Judy Landers plays Linda Armstrong, a gorgeous former model turned art director for *Style* magazine on the ABC pilot *Four in Love.* Mary Brennan (Mary Tyler Moore) is a former columnist for *Women's Digest* (a fashion magazine) turned consumer help line columnist for the Chicago *Eagle* on CBS's *Mary.*

1986. Tracy Bridges (Suzanne Pleshette) and Peter Cross (Nicholas Surovy) are a divorced couple who share a personal rivalry as the columnists of "Bridges to Cross" for *World Week* magazine on CBS's *Bridges to Cross.* Season Hubley plays Christine Racine, city editor of the *Sun Standard,* the daily newspaper of a locale identified only as *The City* (ABC). Shelley Hack plays Jackie Shea, author of the column "Our Kind of Town" for the Chicago *Mirror* on ABC's *Jack and Mike* (Mike, Jackie's husband, a restaurant owner, is played by Tom Mason). Jesse Witherspoon (Deidre Hall) is a photographer for the Los Angeles *Post-Gazette* on NBC's *Our House.* Balki (Bronson Pinchot) works in the mailroom of the Chicago *Chronicle* while his cousin Larry (Mark Linn-Baker) is the assistant to the city editor on ABC's *Perfect Strangers.* Ted Knight plays Henry Rush, half owner of the *Marin Bugler,* a weekly paper in Marin County, California, on *The Ted Knight Show* (Syn.).

1987. Seventh grader Caitlin Ryan (Stacie Mistysyn) is a writer for her school newspaper, *The Degrassi Digest* on *Degrassi Junior High* (Syn.). Matthew Laurance plays Ben Coleman, author of the column "True Stories" for the Los Angeles *Daily Banner* on *Duet* (Fox). Jake McCaskey (Bruce Weitz) writes the column "McCaskey" for the Manhattan *Examiner* on NBC's *Mama's Boy.* Marva (Tisha Campbell) and Rose (Kimiko Gelman) are staffers on their high school newspaper, *The Cougar* on *Rags to Riches* (NBC).

1988. Scott Kallen (Perry King) and Ben Colter (Dorian Harewood) are half brothers struggling to run a Los Angeles paper called *The Paper* on the ABC pilot *Half 'n' Half.* Patricia Kalember plays Joanna Farrell, a columnist for the *West Coast Revue* on ABC's *Just in Time.* Becca Nicholson (Eugenie Ross-Leming) is a gossip columnist for

the San Francisco *Dispatch* on NBC's *Midnight Caller.*

1989. Hannah Miller (Jamie Lee Curtis) and Marty Gold (Richard Lewis) are writers for a magazine first called *Chicago Monthly* then *Chicago Weekly* on ABC's *Anything but Love.* Becca Thatcher (Kellie Martin) is a student at Marshall High School who writes for *The Underground Marshall,* the school's alternative (and forbidden) newspaper on ABC's *Life Goes On.* Polly Cooper (Shanna Reed) is first a writer for *The Chronicle* in Oceanside, California, then the managing editor of *The Bulldog,* the paper of the Camp Hollister Marine Base in Virginia on CBS's *Major Dad.*

1990. Tom Nash (Robert Urich) is a columnist for a newspaper first called the *Chicago American* then the *Chicago Metro* on NBC's *American Dreamer.* Gabrielle Carteris plays Andrea Zuckerman, editor of the West Beverly Hills High School newspaper, *The Blaze,* on *Beverly Hills, 90210* (Fox). Lloyd Bridges plays Jonathan Turner, editor of the *Washington Capital,* a large Washington, D.C., newspaper on ABC's *Capital News.* Hal Holbrook plays Evan Evans, publisher of *The Argus,* the newspaper of the small town of *Evening Shade* (CBS). Chris Peterson (Chris Elliott) is a 30-year-old who never forgot what it is like to be a kid. He began his work career delivering newspapers for the *Pioneer Press* in Greenville, Ohio, and is still doing so on *Get a Life* (Fox). Walker Lovejoy (Brad Pitt) is a washed-up football player who returns to his hometown to work as a writer for a newspaper called *The Century Post* on *Glory Days* (Fox). Nikki Page (Jessica Lundy) is an obit writer (under the name Miss Black) for the *San Francisco Union* who yearns to become a reporter on CBS's *Over My Dead Body.*

1991. George Henderson (Bruce Davison) is a marketing executive turned publisher of a magazine called *A Better Life* on the syndicated *Harry and the Hendersons.* Clarissa Darling (Melissa Joan Hart) writes for her school newspaper, *The Thomas Tupper Times* on *Clarissa Explains It All* (NIK). Amanda Brooks (Jane Seymour) is an erotic book author who takes the job of saving the faltering *Ladies' Day* magazine by changing its name to *Passion* on the CBS pilot *Passion.* Matt Collins (Christopher McDonald) is a sports writer for the San Francisco *Examiner* on NBC's *Walter and Emily.*

1992. Liberal feminist Georgie Ann Lahti (Markie Post) was first a writer for the *Chicago*

Tribune, then the *Chicago Post* on CBS's *Hearts Afire*. In later episodes, Georgie is a reporter for the *Courier* in Clay County. Jack Stein (Jay Stein) writes the opinion column "The Steinway" for the *New York Register* on CBS's *Love and War*.

1993. Humorist Dave Barry (Harry Anderson) writes the newspaper column "Dave's World" for the Miami *Record-Dispatch* on CBS's *Dave's World*. Seamus O'Neill (Fisher Stevens) is a man who hopes to follow in the footsteps of Ernest Hemingway and begins by acquiring a job as a writer for the Key West, Florida newspaper, *The Meteor* (where Hemingway once worked) on Fox's *Key West*.

1994. Elizabeth Wakefield (Cynthia Daniel) is a writer for her high school newspaper, the Sweet Valley High *Oracle* and later its editor when she acquires a position with the Sweet Valley *Tribune* on *Sweet Valley High* (Syn.).

1995. Nora Wilde (Tea Leoni) is first a photographer, then an advice columnist for *The Comet*, a trashy tabloid that loves celebrity dirt on *The Naked Truth* (ABC). When the series switched to NBC in 1996, Nora became a reporter-columnist for a paper called *The Inquisitor*. Stacey Colbert (Debra Messing) is a columnist for *The Village Voice* in New York City on Fox's *Ned and Stacey*.

1996. Cher Horowitz (Rachel Blanchard) writes the column "Buzzline" for her high school newspaper, *The Alcott Buzz* on *Clueless* (ABC/UPN). Kyle Chandler plays Gary Hobson, a man who gets tomorrow's news today from a special edition of the Chicago *Sun-Times* on CBS's *Early Edition*. Ray Romano plays Raymond Barone, a sports columnist for New York *Newsday* on *Everybody Loves Raymond* (CBS). Mike Logan (Ted Danson) is a renowned journalist for the New York *Sun* who works for his ex-wife, Kate Montgomery (Mary Steenburgen), the editor on CBS's *Ink*. Sabrina Spellman (Melissa Joan Hart) is a beautiful witch who first writes for her high school newspaper, the West Bridge *Lantern*, then a writer for a newspaper called *The Boston Citizen* and finally a columnist for *Scorch*, a music magazine, on *Sabrina, the Teenage Witch* (ABC/WB). Susan Keane is a beautiful young columnist who pens "Suddenly Susan" for the trendy San Francisco magazine *The Gate* on NBC's *Suddenly Susan*.

1997. Jack Gallo (George Segal) publishes *Blush*, a fashion magazine based in Manhattan on *Just Shoot Me* (NBC). Slap Maxwell (Dabney Coleman) is an abrasive and crusty sports writer of the "Slap Shots" column for the *Ledger*, a Midwest newspaper on *The Slap Maxwell Story* (ABC).

1998. Prue Halliwell (Shannen Doherty) is a good witch who works as a photographer for *4-One-5*, a trendy San Francisco magazine on *Charmed* (WB). Her younger sister, Phoebe (Alyssa Milano) writes the advice column "Ask Phoebe" for the *Bay Mirror*. Carrie Bradshaw (Sarah Jessica Parker) is a sex advice columnist ("Sex and the City") for the New York *Star* on HBO's *Sex and the City*.

2000. Rory Gilmore (Alexis Bledel) is a writer for *The Franklin*, her newspaper at the prestigious Chilton High School in Connecticut. Later, when she attends Yale University, she joins the staff of its newspaper, the *Yale Daily News*, on the WB's *Gilmore Girls*.

2002. Paul Hennessey (John Ritter) is a sports columnist for the Detroit *Post* on ABC's *Eight Simple Rules for Dating My Teenage Daughter*.

2004. Tom Papa (Himself) is a writer for the *Daily Times*, a New Jersey newspaper on NBC's *Come to Papa*.

Nightclubs

This entry lists the programs that are set in, revolve around or are somehow connected to a nightclub or supper club. See also *Hotels*.

1951. Band leader Ricky Ricardo (Desi Arnaz) performs regularly at the Tropicana Club in New York City on *I Love Lucy* (CBS). In later episodes, when Ricky buys interest in the establishment, he renames it the Babalu Club (but it is also called Club Babalu and the Ricky Ricardo Babalu Club).

1952. The Chez Nikki is a plush Paris nightclub that is run by a mysterious woman named Nikki (Ilona Massey) who uses it as a front to help people in trouble on ABC's *Rendezvous*.

1953. Danny Williams (Danny Thomas) is a comedian who works nights at the Copa Club in Manhattan on *Make Room for Daddy* (ABC/CBS. CBS episodes are titled *The Danny Thomas Show*).

1955. Jan Stewart (Janis Paige) is a relatively unknown singer who performs nightly at Tony's Cellar, a Manhattan supper club on *It's Always Jan* (CBS).

1956. Willie Dante (Dick Powell) is a former gambler turned owner of Dante's Inferno, a San Francisco nightclub on *The Best in Mystery*, an

NBC series culled from the "Dante" episodes of *Four Star Playhouse*.

1958. Jane Russell plays Brandy Macreedy, a beautiful singer and hostess who becomes the owner of her late husband's supper club, Macreedy's, on the NBC pilot *Macreedy's Woman*. Mother's, a nightclub by the waterfront in Los Angeles, is the second home to private eye Peter Gunn (Craig Stevens) on *Peter Gunn* (NBC/ABC). The club later becomes Edie's when singer Edie Hart (Lola Albright) purchases the establishment. Gerald Lloyd Kookson III, better known as Kookie (Edd Byrnes) is the parking lot attendant at Dino's, the fancy supper club next to ABC's *77 Sunset Strip*.

1959. Lusti Weather (Nita Talbot) is a gorgeous entertainer (plays bongo drums, sings and dances) at the Racquet Club in the French Quarter of New Orleans on ABC's *Bourbon Street Beat*. Also seen is the prestigious and historic Absinthe House nightclub next to the offices of private detectives Rex Randolph and Cal Calhoun. A mysterious woman, known only as the Redhead (Janis Paige) owns a nightclub in Panama called the Chez Rouge (from which she helps people in trouble) on the CBS pilot *Chez Rouge*.

1960. Howard Duff plays Willie Dante, a former gambler who runs the trendy Dante's Inferno nightclub in San Francisco on NBC's *Dante*.

1963. Ethel Merman plays Maggie Brown, the owner of Maggie Brown's, a Pacific Island club for American soldiers on the CBS pilot *Maggie Brown*.

1964. Lou Ann Poovie (Elizabeth MacRae), the girlfriend of Marine private Gomer Pyle, sings at a nightclub called The Blue Bird Café in Los Angeles on *Gomer Pyle, U.S.M.C.* (CBS).

1975. Dean Martin plays himself, the owner of Dean's Place, a nightclub that spotlights new talent on the NBC pilot *Dean's Place*.

1978. Kenny Honey and his wife Lulu (Kenny Price, Lulu Roman) are the owners of Honey's, a country music nightclub in Nashville on the syndicated *Hee Haw Honeys* (a spinoff from *Hee Haw*). Gloria LeRoy plays Mary Parnell, the voluptuous owner of The Starting Gate, the nightclub over which Martin Kazinski, an ex-con turned lawyer, lives on *Raz* (CBS).

1981. Jon Bowman, a singer with the group Sha Na Na, plays Bowzer J. Bowzer, the owner of the shabby, near bankrupt nightclub Chez Bowzer on the syndicated pilot *Bowzer*.

1982. Jake Rubidoux (William Devane) is a tough private detective who plays trumpet at The Big Easy, a nightclub in the French Quarter of New Orleans on the NBC pilot *The Big Easy*. Tony, Buzz and Cowboy (Ed Marinaro, Michael Horton, Robin Strand) are private eyes who own Three Eyes, a combination nightclub and detective agency in Marina Del Rey, California on the NBC pilot *Three Eyes*.

1985. Susan Hogan plays Nicole, the owner of Nicole's Lounge, the nightclub frequented by members of the Toronto Police Department on CBS's *Night Heat*.

1988. Jonelle Allen plays a woman known only as Lulu, the owner of an after hour nightclub in New York City on the CBS pilot *After Midnight*. Some real people, some the puppets of Sid and Marty Krofft, visit the Redeye Express, a nightclub run by Ron (Ron Reagan) on the syndicated pilot *Redeye Express*.

1990. After Dark is the nightclub frequented by the regulars of Fox's *Beverly Hills, 90210*.

1992. Former blues singer Chelsea Paige (Patti LaBelle) opens her own nightclub, the trendy Club Chelsea in Los Angeles, on NBC's *Open All Night*.

1994. Model agency owner Hillary Michaels (Linda Gray) finds solace from the pressures of work at Stage 99, a retro disco on Fox's *Models Inc.* The police officers of the N.Y.P.D. frequent a nightclub called Natalie's on Fox's *New York Undercover*.

1995. Singer Lou Raymond (Lou Rawls), then the glamorous and wealthy D.J. Marco (Donna D'Errico), own Nights, a club in Los Angeles, on the syndicated *Baywatch Nights*.

1997. Johnny Domino (Matt McColm) is a jazz musician who plays sax at the House of Soul nightclub in Bay City (and is secretly the daring crime fighter NightMan) on the syndicated *NightMan*.

1998. Good witch Piper Halliwell (Holly Marie Combs) runs P-3, a trendy San Francisco nightclub, on the WB's *Charmed*.

Nudity and Sexuality

Long before cable channels like Showtime and HBO could show nudity, television had to overcome many obstacles to achieve it. Early TV is not filled with nudity, profanity or even long kissing scenes. Just the opposite; it is basically squeaky clean. It was taboo to show two people (even married) sleeping in the same bed. The word "pregnant" was forbidden and showing a woman in her bra meant instant criticism. Nudity happened in these early days — but it was all by accident. Sexuality was also restricted but not as taboo (women were allowed to be sensual but with limitations on sexual overtones and in clothing that was not too suggestive. This barrier was also broken as TV progressed). This entry chronicles the programs that paved the way for what is currently being broadcast — from accidental nudity and accidental glimpses of lingerie, to scripted nudity and lingerie shots to the evolution of sexuality as it is currently known (including the programs that sensationalize for ratings). While this entry is basically a broadcast TV history (as it is taken for granted that if it appears on cable, it is going to have nudity), pioneering cable programs are included.

1939. Up to this time TV was experimental (and basically squeaky clean) with the emphasis on trying to figure out what types of programs to broadcast. On the experimental variety program *The Cobina Wright, Jr. Show*, sexy singer Cobina Wright appeared on live TV in a strapless evening gown "that was held up by faith alone." On June 15th, NBC broadcast *The World's Fair Beauty Contest*. While beauty pageants are accepted today, in 1939 it was the first time that females competed against one another for a title ("The New York World's Fair Television Girl") and a prize (an RCA TV). It was also the first time a woman's beauty was the subject of a TV program. Despite all the problems with TV at this time (poor AM sound [FM is now used], blurry pictures and the problems linked to World War II) television did not neglect the female figure (as can be seen in the programs that follow).

1941. NBC airs *Fashion Discoveries*, the very first TV fashion show on September 18th. Models displayed the latest in women's wartime fashions.

1944. DuMont airs *The Fashion Telecast* with women modeling the latest in wartime wear on August 2nd. On November 2nd, CBS airs *Fashions of the Times*, wherein beautiful women model not only day and evening wear, but swim suits, showing more of the female figure than had previously been seen on TV. Critics too appeared to be noticing a change (on October 19th CBS

broadcast *They Were There*, a program that spotlighted five entertainers who toured the European War Front with USO camp shows. Jean Darling, one of the girls from the *Our Gang* theatrical shorts, sang a song. One critic said, "Jean has blossomed into a peachy blonde dish with a swell voice"). *The Harper's Bazaar Fashion Parade* (DuMont) was an attempt to turn the fashion magazine into a TV show with stunning girls modeling the latest dresses.

1947. CBS airs *Showroom*, a fashion program featuring beautiful girls modeling the 1947 fall line of designer Waldo of California.

1950. In 1949 Maidenform, Inc. began a series of stylized print ads advertising its sexy bras in a campaign called "I Dreamed" (" I Dreamed I Went Shopping in My Maidenform Bra" was the very first ad). In 1950 they ran one called "I Dreamed I Starred on Television in My Maidenform Bra" (a lovely girl in a long black half dress and white bra is standing to the left of the picture. On the right side is a TV set with a similar picture of her — starring on TV but seen only from the waist up). Shortly after, another bra company, Exquisite Form, took the ad one step further and used live models to advertise their line of bras on an NBC pilot called *Dear Diary*. The ads caused an outburst of criticism (you just don't show a girl in her bra on TV) and were stopped. Lingerie ads did continue on TV but with the product being displayed on mannequins or on models over a black blouse (see also 1987). Television's first accident occurs on *The George Burns and Gracie Allen Show* (CBS). On "The Nieces" episode (broadcast live), Gracie's three nieces, Geri (Geri James), Linda (Linda Plowman) and Jill (Jill Oppenheim) visit. During a skit wherein the girls are wearing very short skirts and playing space cadets, the camera captures glimpses of their panties as they bend over to enter their pretend space ship. Geri, the youngest of the girls, is later seen tugging at her waistline. Linda asks, "What's wrong?" Geri responds, "Jet number one is losing her panties." In the scene that follows, Geri falls into the nearby swimming pool and, according to an ad-lib line by George, Geri did indeed lose her panties.

1952. Marie Wilson (*My Friend Irma*), Gale Storm (*My Little Margie*) and Elena Verdugo (*Meet Millie*) begin a new process — appearing on camera in a full slip. Surprisingly, it is acceptable.

1953. Actress Faye Emerson, known for wearing low cut dresses on TV, accidentally exposes her breasts when her dress slips on live TV.

1954. The birth of a baby is shown in graphic detail on the documentary series *The Search*. Showgirls dressed in leg and breast revealing costumes appear on *The Swift Show Wagon* (NBC).

1955. Nita Talbot, in her role as Mabel Spooner on CBS's *Joe and Mabel*, appears in a full slip that shows a bit more cleavage than her 1952 counterparts.

1956. Orchestra leader Ina Ray Hutton, also known for low cut dresses, accidentally exposes her breasts while conducting her orchestra on *The Ina Ray Hutton Show* (NBC).

1957. The beautiful and busty Jayne Mansfield took the 1957 Academy Awards presentation by storm when she bent over and her low cut dress slipped to reveal her left breast on live TV. Beverly Garland, the star of the syndicated police series *Decoy*, appears in a slip. Over on CBS, the sexy Joi Lansing (38½-23-35) creates a sensation as swimsuit model Shirley Swanson on *Love That Bob* (bikinis are also seen for the first time on TV with Joi as a manufacturer's perfect model). Although the program stars David Janssen as *Richard Diamond, Private Detective* (CBS episodes only), implied sexuality is used to its fullest with a character named Sam (Mary Tyler Moore, Roxanne Brooks). Sam is Diamond's telephone answering service girl and is never fully seen. Her shapely legs and breasts (in tight sweaters or blouses) are seen in shadows and her extremely sexy voice allows the viewer to imagine her as any woman he wishes.

1959. The variety series *Playboy's Penthouse* airs in syndication with *Playboy* magazine publisher Hugh Hefner and a bevy of beautiful Playboy Bunnies serving as hostesses.

1962. While never seen by the viewing audience at the time (but since on clip shows), Soupy Sales was surprised during a skit on ABC's *The Soupy Sales Show* when he opened a door to see a totally nude woman (a joke arranged by the crew).

1964. Female models display topless swimwear (seen from the back) on *The Les Crane Show* (ABC).

1965. Girls in skimpy bikinis are seen in beach scenes on ABC's *Gidget*. Star Sally Field, however, was not as much an exhibitionist and is seen wearing a somewhat more conservative bikini. Over at NBC Barbara Eden played Jeannie, the genie on *I Dream of Jeannie*. While Barbara was allowed to show considerable cleavage (very unusual for the time), she was not permitted to show her navel (although in some scenes, it can be seen when her wide harem costume waistband slips).

1966. Provocative sexual imagery is used in the Noxzema Skin Cream TV ads "Take It Off." Here the former Miss Sweden, Gunilla Knutson, purrs "Take it off, take it all off" referring to men using the product. The ads ran until 1973.

1968. The luscious Emma Peel (Diana Rigg) appears in a sexy black bra on "The Joker" episode of ABC's *The Avengers* (the first such instance on network TV). Although nudity is not present, Goldie Hawn and Judy Carne display their figures in bikinis numerous times on *Rowan and Martin's Laugh-In* (NBC). The extremely sexy Angelique Pettyjohn appears on *Star Trek* (NBC) as Shahna, the alien in a skimpy silver costume on "The Gamesters of Triskelion" episode that created a stir for its flamboyant display of a female's figure (especially her breasts).

1969. Barbi Benton is the Bunny Hostess on *Playboy After Dark*, a syndicated variety series set at the Playboy Mansion with Hugh Hefner as the host and a bevy of Playboy Bunnies appearing on each program.

1970. Marlo Thomas chooses not to wear a bra for her character Ann Marie on ABC's *That Girl* and begins an era called "Jiggle TV." Quite risqué at the time, it is quite obvious Marlo is not wearing a bra during the show's final season.

1971. Rosemary Nicols, in her role of Interpol investigator Annabelle Hurst, appears in a sexy yellow bra and panties in the "One of Our Aircraft Is Missing" episode of the syndicated *Department S* (the first such instance in a syndicated series).

1972. Jamie Farr as Maxwell Klinger does a tour of duty in the nude (seen from the waist up) on *M*A*S*H* (CBS).

1973. During a live interview on *The Dick Cavett Show* (ABC), Barbara Hershey removes her breast from her dress to feed her infant son, Free. Valerie Perrine becomes the first woman to purposely expose her breasts on American TV on the PBS drama *Steambath*.

1974. A streaker (Robert Opal) runs across the stage while David Niven attempts to present an award on a live presentation of *The Academy Awards*. An accident occurs on CBS's *The Match Game*. A female contestant, happy to have won a chance to play the bonus round, is wearing a miniskirt and begins jumping up and down. An "oops" is placed across her bottom when the skirt rides a bit too high. Elinor Donahue appears in a white bra in a rather long scene on the "Warning All Wives" episode of NBC's *Police Woman*. A streaker strikes again, this time running across the stage of NBC's *Tonight Show Starring Johnny Carson* (it aired with the bottom half of the screen blocked out). Connie Stevens plays Kelly Williams, a Marilyn Monroe like figure, on ABC's *The Sex Symbol*. In the European version, Connie does a shower scene and exposes her breasts.

1975. In a guest appearance on "The Canterville Ghost" episode of *The Ghost Busters* (CBS), Kathy Garver is wearing a miniskirt. As she attempts to sit down, the camera catches a flash of her white panties (this scene is cut from the home video release of the series). Elizabeth Montgomery stars in the ABC TV movie *The Legend of Lizzie Borden*. While not seen here, Elizabeth's breasts are seen as she slashes a victim in added footage for the European version. Lynda Carter becomes *Wonder Woman* (ABC/CBS) and appears in a sexy bathing suit costume designed to accentuate her 38–25–37 figure.

1976. On NBC's *Captains and the Kings* miniseries, Beverly D'Angelo's breasts are seen in added footage for the European version. Farrah Fawcett, in her role as Jill Munroe, exposes her right breast and nipple when her mostly unbuttoned blouse opens to reveal more than it should on the "Angels in Chains" episode of ABC's *Charlie's Angels*. The PBS miniseries *I Claudius* looks at Roman emperors from Augustus to Nero with female nudity and sexual situations. Derek Jacobi, Sian Phillips and Brian Blessed head a large cast. On the syndicated *Mary Hartman, Mary Hartman*, the camera catches a shot of Louise Lasser (Mary Hartman) in her panties while seated at the kitchen table (scene has been cut from re-syndicated episodes). Jane Curtin, a regular on NBC's *Saturday Night Live*, rips open her blouse on live TV to reveal her bra to prove that she is sexy enough to replace Chevy Chase as the new host of the "Weekend Update" segment.

1977. An actual birth is seen on the ABC special *My Mom's Having a Baby*, wherein a nine-year-old learns about pregnancy and birth. The TV movie *Having Babies II* on ABC goes one step further and graphically shows the birth of a baby (without any negative feedback). Lovely Melinda Naud plays Dolores Crandall, an army nurse

trapped on a pink submarine during World War II, who is seen in her bra on ABC's *Operation Petticoat*. Suzanne Somers becomes part of Jiggle TV on ABC's *Three's Company* by not wearing a bra and doing what roommate Jack likes most: bouncing up and down. Bare breasted African women appear on ABC's historic *Roots* miniseries (allowed by censors for its sense of reality).

1978. Actress Jane Russell becomes the spokeswoman for the Playtex Eighteen Hour Bra. Jane, a 38C cup, pitched the bra "for us full-figured girls" (Jane wore the bra over a blouse but never directly on her skin). She continued the role until 1986. During this time (and until 1985) actress Eve Arden became the Playtex spokes-woman for the Cross Your Heart Bra. The syndicated *$1.98 Beauty Show* presents six female contestants vying for prizes. The swimsuit portion was risqué, as the bikini tops worn by some of the women were not always form fitting. CBS's *The Price Is Right* experienced an "oops" when a female contestant, running from the studio audience to be the next contestant, exposed her breasts when her blouse snapped open. Rather than re-shoot the scene, a black stripe aired across the girl's breasts.

1979. England's *The Benny Hill Show* airs in an edited version for American TV that, while still very provocative, deletes scenes of nude girls but leaves in the countless bra and panty shots. *Peek-a-Boo: The One and Only Phyllis Dixey* is a risqué PBS drama about the life of Phyllis Dixey (Lesley-Anne Downe), a British stripper of the 1930s and 40s.

1980. A teenage Brooke Shields appears in a series of very sexy, sensationalized TV ads for Calvin Klein Jeans, made even more provocative by Brooke's line "You know what comes between me and my Calvin's? Nothing." Brooke also appeared in a series of Revlon Cosmetics commercials. Julia Foster plays Moll Flanders, a 17th century woman who was married five times, was 12 years a prostitute and 12 years a thief on *Moll Flanders*, a PBS series that contains nudity and sexual situations. Nude scenes are added to the edited home video version of NBC's miniseries *Shogun*.

1981. The British produced series *Casanova* appears on select PBS stations (due to female nudity, not many stations would carry it). Frank Finlay plays the Italian lover, Casanova. Diane Lane appears topless in the role of Charity Royall on the PBS drama *Edith Wharton's Summer*. Real-life stripper Tami Roche appears nude on the HBO special *Here It Is, Burlesque*, displaying her 44–19–37 figure. It was the first time stripping was brought into living rooms (and one of the first cable programs to show nudity). Trisha Noble plays Rosie Johnson on ABC's *Strike Force*. Rosie, who is rather well built, dresses to accentuate her bosom and is seen in running sequences that made her a part of the era of Jiggle TV. Complaints stopped the running and Rosie dressed more conservatively.

1982. Rosanna Arquette appears topless in the European version (and home video release) of the NBC TV movie *The Executioner's Song*.

1983. The HBO special *Strippers* recreates the lives of famous strippers (such as Sally Randy, Josephine Baker and Gypsy Rose Lee). Nudity is seen in both rare film clips and in the reenactments.

1984. As the pay cable channels HBO and Showtime began to attract an audience, nudity and foul language also began to flourish. The instances of nudity are too numerous to list. What follows is a listing of shows (beginning with one of the first series, *Steambath*, in 1984) that have appeared on HBO and Showtime. *Bedtime, Candid Candid Camera* (topless girls used in stunts), *Carnivale, Deadwood, Dream On, First and Ten, First and 10: The Bulls Are Back, First and Ten: Training Season, The Hitchhiker, The L-Word, Oz, Queer As Folk, Red Shoe Diaries, Sex and the City, Six Feet Under, The Sopranos, Steambath, Tales from the Crypt*.

1987. Live models are used for the first time in 37 years (see 1950) to sell bras when Playtex changes the face of lingerie advertising on TV. In the years that would follow, Victoria's Secret and Fruit of the Loom would also use live models — not only to sell bras, but panties also. The Fox reality show *Cops* uses digitized distortion to hide the vital parts of people the law enforcers encounter. A bevy of beautiful women put on well coordinated wrestling matches on the syndicated *G.L.O.W.* (Gorgeous Ladies of Wrestling), a show that is an eyeful of some very beautiful, scantily dressed girls. Christina Applegate plays Kelly Bundy, the sexy dumb blonde teenager on Fox's *Married ... With Children*. Kelly's cleavage revealing blouses, short skirts and overall tramp-like appearance was sensationalized to hype the series and garner Fox ratings.

1988. Ed Flanders as Dr. Donald Westphall on

NBC's *St. Elsewhere* moons Dr. John Gideon (Ronny Cox) over his frustration with the new administration.

1989. NBC premieres *Baywatch*, a series about lifeguards (mostly female and in very sexy swimsuits). While this version raised a few eyebrows, it was not until 1991 when the series premiered in syndication that it became an enormous hit due to the bevy of gorgeous lifeguards who graced the screen each week. As the series progressed, so did the sexuality, with Pamela Anderson, Yasmine Bleeth, Gena Lee Nolin and Traci Bingham among the girls displaying their figures in tight, revealing swimwear. The series even prompted a rip off called *Son of the Beach* (a bevy of gorgeous lifeguards watched over by an out-of-shape male superior). Glynis Barber plays Jane, a beautiful undercover agent for the British government during World War II on the syndicated *Jane*. Jane has a knack for losing her dress and displaying her shapely figure in a bar and half-slip. She often manages to lose the bra and her breasts are seen (sometimes the slip is lost and she is seen in just panties). NBC airs *Nightingales*, a series about student nurses that should have been called "Lingerie Girls." The program is filled with shots of the nurses in their bra and panties and was blasted by critics for its many lingerie scenes.

1991. *The Jerry Springer Show* premieres in syndication and much digitized nudity is seen in what appears to be, for the most part, staged for broadcast (not the spontaneous nudity the viewer is led to believe). Heather McAdam plays 15-year-old Cat Margolis on NBC's *Sisters*. Cat says she likes clothes that are "stylin,'" but when at home she parades around in her bra and panties.

1992. Divorce lawyer Sydney Guilford (Mariel Hemingway) posed nude for a photographer (seen in a side view; her hands crossed over her breasts) on ABC's *Civil Wars*. Elizabeth Berkley performs a topless scene (mostly with her back to the camera although her breasts can be seen from the side) on CBS's *Raven*.

1993. Drew Barrymore plays Amy Fisher, the Long Island Lolita in the TV movie *The Amy Fisher Story*. Drew exposes her breasts in the home video version of the film. Meredith Baxter plays breast cancer victim Joyce Wadler on the CBS TV movie *My Breast*. Meredith bares her breasts in two scenes: one in the doctor's office; the other in front of a mirror. ABC's *N.Y.P.D. Blue* breaks most of the barriers and paves the way for partial nudity (and foul language) on broadcast TV. Female nudity: Amy Brenneman (Officer Janice Licaisi) shows her derriere in the first episode; Sharon Lawrence (as Sylvia Costa) shows her derriere and a side view of her breasts; Charlotte Ross (as Connie McDowell) steps out of a shower and is totally nude. Male nudity: David Caruso (as John Kelly) and Dennis Franz (Andy Sipowicz) both show tush. Brooke Shields removes her blouse to reveal her breasts in a sexy bra on the "Came the Dawn" episode of HBO's *Tales from the Crypt*.

1994. Phoebe Buffay (Lisa Kudrow) attempts to seduce Chandler (Matthew Perry) by stripping to her sexy black bra in a prolonged scene on "The One with the Vows" episode of NBC's *Friends*.

1995. The Univision series *Caliente* pushes the limits as to what a girl can wear (or not wear) on broadcast TV. The series is set at various beaches and has girls (and guys) dancing to songs. While some girls are conservative, most are not and show off their figures in very revealing bikinis (including thong bottoms). Camera shots are not skimpy either — much attention is paid to breasts and bottoms. Alyssa Milano bares her breasts in the "Caught in the Act" episode of *The Outer Limits* (USA). In a guest stint on *Late Night with David Letterman* (CBS), actress Drew Barrymore lifts her T-shirt, reveals her breasts and does a little dance atop Dave's desk as her birthday present to him. Nikki Cox plays the voluptuous Tiffany Malloy on the WB's *Unhappily Ever After*. Tiffany is beautiful and knows it. She dresses in tight, low cut blouses (revealing much cleavage) and in tight, short skirts (sitting is always a problem — but not for the WB, which used Nikki as a teenage sex symbol to attract viewers).

1996. The British produced TV movie, *The Fortunes and Misfortunes of Moll Flanders* airs on PBS's *Masterpiece Theater*. In it actress Alex Kingston appears totally nude in a story about the amoral Moll Flanders. Fran Drescher shows her shapely figure in a black bra and half-slip on *The Nanny* (CBS). Helen Shaver appears in her bra and panties in "The Town Without Pity" episode of *Poltergeist: The Legacy* (Showtime/Sci Fi) when she escapes from a Victorian village and her era's outer clothes vanish. Julia Louis-Dreyfus creates a sensation on NBC's *Seinfeld* when an antique button pops off her character, Elaine's, blouse and exposes her breasts in a very sexy low cut bra. In another instance, Elaine distributes a Christmas card picture of herself without realizing that her blouse is open and her nipple is exposed. "The Caddy" episode of *Seinfeld* introduces Brenda Strong as Sue Ellen Mischke, heiress to the O'Henry Candy Bar fortune, who is called "The Braless Wonder" by Elaine because "she never wears a bra." Elaine tried to remedy the situation and bought her one — which Sue Ellen wore without a blouse and created havoc when she walked down the street.

1997. On NBC's *Just Shoot Me*, Maya Gallo (Laura San Giacomo) appears in a very sexy gown that happens to be see-through. Her "vital parts" are digitized [blurred] in the episode "The Emperor." In "The Apology" episode of NBC's *Seinfeld*, Jerry's girlfriend Melissa (Kathleen McClellan) parades around Jerry's apartment in the nude (camera shots manage to capture her breasts being obstructed by furniture). This same technique was used on a number of other shows, like the WB's *What I Like About You*, when two of the main characters wind up at a nude ranch instead of a dude ranch.

1998. Angelina Jolie does full frontal nudity in *Gia*, a sexually graphic HBO movie about the life of Gia Marie Carangi, a top fashion model of the 1970s (the film set the pace for considerable nudity on the many other premium cable channel movies that would follow). Pamela Anderson plays Vallery Irons, the head of a protection agency on the syndicated *V.I.P.* Pamela shows considerable cleavage and wears many tops that are see through and allow the viewer to see her array of sexy bras.

1999. Singer Lil' Kim exposes her left breast (although a medallion covers her nipple) when she falls out of the purple dress she is wearing on *The MTV Music Awards*.

2000. Although Gena Lee Nolin shows considerable cleavage in her role as *Sheena* (Syn.), she does not perform the nude scenes of the creature she morphs into, the Darak'na (topless scenes played by Vickie Phillips and Denise Loden).

2002. Tyra Banks is one of several models seen in TV ads for Victoria's Secret lingerie. Fruit of the Loom and Playtex, with its new half-size bras, begin to appear on TV also (and all using live models). The bare breast of a dead girl is shown on CBS's *C.S.I.: Crime Scene Investigation*. Singer-actress Courtney Love appears on *Late Night with David Letterman* (March 17th) and to everyone's surprise flashes her breasts during a performance of the song "Danny Boy" (her breasts were digitized [blurred] when the program aired).

2003. Ashlie Brillault plays Kate Sanders on the Disney Channel's *Lizzie McGuire*. In the episode "Kate's Birthday," the camera catches a shot of 13-year-old Kate's white panties as she sits down on a sofa. Camryn Manheim wears a see-through outfit that shows off her maternity lingerie on ABC's *The Practice*. Loni Anderson displays her 36-24-36 figure by showing considerable cleavage on UPN's *The Mullets*. Rich girls Paris Hilton and Nicole Richie attempt to experience *The Simple Life* (Fox). Scenes with Paris showing skin (no bras, open blouses, short skirts) are blurred for broadcast. On the "Joan's Birthday Suit" episode of *Girlfriends*, Joan (Tracee Ellis Ross) bares it all (black bars across her vital parts) on a nude beach. The Spike TV animated series *Stripperella* features Pamela Anderson as Erotica Jones, a beautiful stripper who shows even more cleavage than Pamela shows on *V.I.P.* (see 1998). Erotica calls herself a "Double D Cup superhero" and battles crime as the mysterious Stripperella. In a locker room scene on ABC's *10-8: Officers on Duty*, Jamie Luner (as Deputy Ryan Layne) is seen in a red bra.

2004. During half-time on the CBS telecast of the Super Bowl (Feb. 1st) Janet Jackson's bustier costume is torn by singer Justin Timberlake during a performance, exposing Janet's right breast (her nipple is covered by a medallion she had been wearing). Requirements on UPN's *America's Next Top Model* found the female hopefuls involved in the following shoots: modeling sexy bras and panties; modeling skimpy bathing suits; and posing topless (the girls were allowed to place their hands across their breasts). On *Charmed* (WB), Lady Godiva (Kristen Miller) is conjured up from the past and is seen supposedly nude (but covered by her long blonde hair). At the end of the episode, "The Bare Witch Project," Phoebe (Alyssa Milano) appears as Lady Godiva in the nude to make a statement about breast-feeding in public. While trying on a dress, Angie Lopez (Constance Marie) exposes herself in a sexy white bra in a prolonged scene on ABC's *The George Lopez Show*. *Hope and Faith* (ABC) sensationalizes the plot of a young girl getting her first bra. When young Hayley (Macey Cruthird) feels she needs a bra, her older sister Sydney (Megan Fox) decides to get her one — one that is padded and far too big for her (her Aunt Faith [Kelly Ripa] re-

marks, "Nice rack Hayley," when she sees Hayley wearing the bra). This subject matter was handled much more sensitively on such shows as *Who's the Boss?* (Alyssa Milano), *Lizzie McGuire* (Hilary Duff) and *Degrassi Junior High* (Sarah Ballingall). On CBS's *Joan of Arcadia*, Joan (Amber Tamblyn) finds herself in an embarrassing situation when she exits the girls' locker room in her purple panties. Nicollette Sheridan plays Edie, one of ABC's *Desperate Housewives*, who enjoys showing much cleavage and washing her car half naked. Also on this series, the prim and proper Bree (Marcia Cross) seduces her husband in a sexy red bra and panties while the adulteress Gabrielle (Eva Longoria) is seen in multiple lingerie shots (mostly in a lacy black bra). Teri Hatcher, housewife Susan, appears totally nude (although her "vital parts" are obstructed by shrubbery) when she accidentally locks herself out of the house after taking a shower. On *Tripping the Rift*, the Sci Fi Channel computer animated series, the beautiful and sexy Six of One, science officer on the *Jupiter 42*, is seen totally nude (but only in the pilot episode; Terry Farrell provided the voice).

2005. Although it did not occur on American television, accidents can happen elsewhere. While performing a song on German TV, Mariah Carey's loose fitting dress slipped and revealed her breasts. In a stunt to promote her series *Desperate Housewives*, Nicollette Sheridan appears in a provocative scene in which she is seen nude from the back in a teaser on *ABC's Monday Night Football*. On UPN's *America's Next Top Model* (2005 edition), the female contestants engage in a topless photo shoot (digitized for broadcast) and in the same episode model-photographer Janice Dickinson lip kisses one of the female model hopefuls. Also on this series (fall 2005 edition), hopeful model Jayla parades around topless in the model's living quarters (scene blurred for broadcast). On ABC's *Blind Justice*, a dead prostitute is seen totally nude, lying face down. Police department computer whiz Angela Montenegro (Michaela Conlin) flashes her breasts at the airport to get an information clerk's attention on Fox's *Bones*. Jennifer Love Hewitt strips to a very sexy cleavage-revealing black bra on "The Homecoming" episode of her series *Ghost Whisperer*. The Playboy Bunnies, in much more revealing outfits than had been seen in 1959 and 1969 (see dates) appear with Hugh Hefner on *The Girls*

Next Door, an E! series that looks at the life of the Playboy magazine publisher. Katherine Heigl, in her role as Isabel, strips to her blue bra and panties on ABC's *Grey's Anatomy*. ABC's *Jake in Progress* gives the viewer two unexpected events: A teenage girl stepping out of a shower and seen nude from the side and back; series co-star Wendie Malick, in her role as Jake's pregnant boss, in a red bra and panties. Broadcast networks become a bit bolder when NBC broadcasts the November 7th, 1960s flashback episode of *Las Vegas* ("Everything Old Is You Again") without an advisory (normally, an advisory for partial nudity precedes the program). Here casino hostess Samantha Marquiz (Vanessa Marcil) removes her bra to reveal her breasts in a side view (with her arm strategically placed to conceal her nipple); however, when the scene switches to a front view, her bra magically appears to cover most of her breasts. Later in this episode, Lorraine (guest star Jessica Sonneborn), removes her bra to reveal the latest development in plastic surgery — breast implants (Lorraine is seen from the back [unhooking her bra] then in front [shoulders up] but in a side view, the camera catches a bit more of her breast than was noticed at the time of filming and her right nipple is digitally blurred for broadcast). Fran Drescher again shows her sexy figure in a black bra (see 1996) on the WB's *Living with Fran*. On NBC's *Medium*, a girl clad only in a skimpy bikini bottom, steps out of a hot tub but places her hand over her breasts to conceal them from the camera; her barely covered derriere however, is photographed as she exits the room. Prior to its airing on October 31st, the WB heavily promoted "The Naked Truth" episode of its series *Related*. The promos showed Rose Sorrelli (Laura Breckenridge), the youngest of four sisters, taking off her blouse (seen from the shoulders up) to appear "totally nude" in a stage play. The episode itself showed this scene plus a split second blurred long shot of Rose on stage (nothing was actually seen). This gimmick (to attract viewers) was used several times before, most notably for the first time in 1977 on *Eight Is Enough* (Nancy Bradford [Dianne Kay] appearing topless in a stage play, but only seen from the shoulders up) and on *Nash Bridges* (with Cassidy Bridges [Jodi Lynn O'Keefe] appearing topless in a play but only seen from the shoulders up). The Fox series *Stacked* doesn't refer so much to the bookstore where Skyler (Pamela Anderson)

works, but to her breasts (34D) that she proudly displays in tight, low cut blouses. Lori Loughlin, in her role as Ava on the WB's *Summerland*, appears not only in bikinis, but in an extended bra sequence also. On NBC's *Surface* ("Episode 7") Lake Bell strips to a very revealing bra and panties in an extended scene that gives the viewer an eye full of Lake's gorgeous figure. Tyra Banks leads the parade of beautiful models displaying sexy and revealing lingerie on *The Victoria's Secret Fashion Show* (CBS and UPN). Farrah Arnold (Molly Stanton), the fraternal twin sister of Mitchee (Sara Gilbert) is a lingerie model for Arnold Undergarments and shows considerable skin modeling her work clothes — sexy bras and panties on the WB's *Twins*. On the March 14th episode of *America's Next Top Model* (Cycle 6; UPN), several of the thirteen hopeful models appear topless in a hot tub (although the girls attempt to cover their breasts with their hands, not every effort is successful and blurring is used to cover the nude scenes). The March 23rd episode of ABC's *American Inventor* showcases a girl named Gina and her invention, "One Tug Removable Lingerie for Women." To demonstrate, a girl dressed in a red ribbon-like bra and skimpy white panties, pulls on a string and instantly becomes naked. Horizontal bars labeled "Censored" appear across her vital parts; the panel rejected the idea. Gabrielle (Eva Longoria) appears nude (seen from the back) performing exercises; and Susan (Teri Hatcher) strips to a very sexy bra and panties for an MRI on ABC's *Desperate Housewives*.

2006. On *America's Next Top Model* (CW; Cycle 7), the first episode has hopeful models posing nude for a topless shoot (tastefully done, but there are a number of blurred breast and bottom scenes). Also on this series, hopeful model Caridee's dress slips and exposes her left breast (blurred for broadcast). On *Pepper Dennis* (WB), Pepper (Rebecca Romijn) strips to a revealing blue bra and panties in the episode of May 23rd. Life among the tribes of the remote regions of Ethiopia is explored on *Tribal Life*, a Travel Channel series, that although rated PG, shows bare-breasted women. On *The Tyra Banks Show* (Syn.), in the episode "Model Search Round-Up," full figure potential models appear topless for a photo shoot (breasts are blurred for broadcast).

Nuns see *Religious Characters*

Nurses see *Women — Nurses* (see also *Doctors*)

Opera

This entry chronicles the operas and operettas that have been broadcast on TV from 1939 to 2003. Operatic segments broadcast on the series *Omnibus* have been excluded.

1939. NBC televises *The Pirates of Penzance*, an operetta by Gilbert and Sullivan on June 20th. Ray Heatherton and Margaret Daum star.

1940. *Grand Opera* airs on NBC (March 10th) from Radio City under the auspices of the New York Metropolitan Opera Company. The program features songs from *The Barber of Seville, Carmen, Rigoletto* and *Pagliacci*. Performers include Lucia Albanese, Richard Bonelli and Hilda Burke.

1944. The DuMont experimental program *Here's Click* presents Met Opera star Gerhard Peschner in an excerpt from *The Barber of Seville*. The Gilbert and Sullivan opera, *H.M.S. Pinafore*, is broadcast by NBC (August 13th). It features Cecil Carol, Joseph DeStefano and the Light Opera Theater Chorus.

1945. *Comedians*, an adaptation of the opera *Pagliacci* by Leoncavallo, airs on NBC (August 26th). However, due to a musicians strike at the time, the cast had to lip-sync the songs to recordings of the opera by Benamico Gigli and the La Scala Opera Stars. Lyle Bettger, Marjorie Hess and William Horne are among the performers.

1949. Gian-Carlo Menotti's comic operetta, *The Old Maid and the Thief* airs on NBC (March 16th). Marie Powers plays a man-hungry old maid who falls for a handsome thief (Norman Young).

1950. The NBC Opera Company comes to television (from radio) as *The NBC Opera Theater* with its premiere presentation, Kurt Weill's *Down in the Valley* with Marian Bell as its star. This opera, and the ones that follow, are sung in English to enable the viewing audience to understand them. The other presentations are: *Carmen* (with Vera Bryner; the program marks the first presentation of an opera broadcast in color); *Dialogues of the Carmelites* (Leontyne Price, Rosemary Kulhman); *Die Fledermaus* (Adele Bishop);

Don Giovanni (Leontyne Price); *Gianti Schicci* (Jan Handzlik); *Hansel and Gretel* (David Lloyd, Virginia Haskin); *Madame Butterfly* (Cio Cio San); *The Magic Flute* (Leontyne Price); *Pagliacci* (Paul Frank); *Tales of Hoffman* (George Britton); *Tosca* (Mario Cavaradossi); and *The Would-Be Gentleman* (Charlotte Rae).

1951. The Christmas operetta, *Amahl and the Night Visitors* airs on NBC's *Hallmark Hall of Fame* (December 24th). Chet Allen plays Amahl, a crippled boy who joins the Three Wise Men as they journey to Bethlehem on the eve of the first Christmas. The operetta was written especially for television by Gian-Carlo Menotti and was restaged five times: April 13, 1952, December 20, 1953, December 19, 1954, December 2, 1955 and December 24, 1958. New versions were produced in 1968 (December 25th) and 1978 (December 24th).

1953. Giovanni Martinelli hosts *Opera Cameos*, a DuMont series that presents condensed versions of popular operas. The series *Opera vs. Jazz* appears on ABC. Nancy Kenyon hosts a musical symposium in which two guests discuss and perform operatic arias and standard tunes.

1955. NBC broadcasts *The Chocolate Soldier*, a comic opera based on George Bernard Shaw's 1894 play *Arms and the Man*. Eddie Albert stars as Bumerli, the soldier who carries chocolate in his holsters instead of guns, and his efforts to court Nadine (Rise Stevens), a woman who is engaged to a man she does not love. Nelson Eddy and Gale Sherwood star in *The Desert Song*, an NBC operetta about a Robin Hood-like character and his efforts to win the heart of a woman engaged to another man. *The Grand Waltz*, an operetta by Moss Hart, tells of Johann Strauss, Jr. (Keith Andes) and his attempts to overcome the machinations of his father (Henry Sharpe) who is jealous of his son's ability to compose waltzes. A prince (Barry Sullivan) courts a widow (Anne Jeffreys) in the hope of using her money to restore his country's empty treasury on the NBC operetta *The Merry Widow*. A young woman (Patrice Munsel) attempts to change the mind of a man (Alfred Drake) who wants nothing to do with marriage on the NBC comic opera *Naughty Marietta*.

1957. A greedy family attempts to frame a rich relative to acquire his wealth on the NBC operetta *The Yeoman of the Guard*. Alfred Drake and Celeste Holm star.

1960. Greed rears its ugly head when, on Christmas Eve in 1849, a miner claims to have found large gold nuggets on the NBC opera *The Golden Child*. Jerome Hines, Patricia Neway and Brenda Lewis star.

1963. Gian-Carlo Menotti composes *Labyrinth*, an original opera for NBC (the first such opera written expressly for TV and one in which every trick known to TV is used for its visual effects. The story follows a newlywed couple [John Reardon, Judith Raskin] as they become lost in the endless corridors of a big hotel).

1968. Gian-Carlo Menotti's Christmas operetta *Amahl and the Night Visitors* is restaged for the seventh time (see 1951) with Kurt Yaghijian as Amahl.

1972. Dominique Tirmont and Elaine Manchef star in *Les Brigands*, a PBS opera set in 19th century Italy that centers on bandits who masquerade as escorts to rob a duke.

1978. The eighth staging of the Christmas operetta *Amahl and the Night Visitors* airs on NBC (see 1951) with Robert Sapolisky as Amahl.

1985. PBS airs *The Compleat Gilbert and Sullivan*, a series of three two-hour operas. *Ruddigore*, the first presentation, stars Vincent Price, Sandra Dugdale and Keith Michell in a story about a lord's efforts to cancel a curse that compels him to commit a crime each day or die. The second opera, *The Sorcerer*, stars Clive Revill and Nan Christie in a story about a sorcerer who casts a love spell on an entire village. Reginald Bunthorne and Sandra Dugdale star in the final presentation, *Patience*, the tale of a foppish poet and his love for a charming dairymaid.

1986. On the PBS special *Placido Domingo Sings Zarzuela!* Grand Opera star Placido Domingo and Spain's Antologia de al Zarzuela (a touring company) perform some of Spain's most tuneful operettas.

1998. PBS airs the San Francisco Opera Company production of Tennessee Williams' *A Streetcar Named Desire* with Renee Fleming as Blanche DuBois and Rodney Gilfrey as Stanley Kowalski.

1999. Real life couple Roberto Alagna and Angela Gheorghiu star as Romeo and Juliet in an operatic adaptation of Shakespeare's *Romeo and Juliet* (PBS).

2000. Archival clips and new musical sequences are used to tell the story of African Americans in opera (from the time of legendary Paul Robeson) on *Aida's Brothers and Sisters: Black Voices in Opera*

(PBS). Featured are Jessye Norman, Simon Estes, Miriam Anderson and Leontyne Price. PBS airs *Candide*, a musical that combines elements of a Broadway show with an operetta to tell the story of a professor (Thomas Allen) and his love for a student (Kristin Chenoweth).

2001. The Houston Grand Opera Company performs Louisa Mae Alcott's *Little Women* on PBS. Stephanie Novacek plays Jo March with Margaret Lloyd as Amy, Stacey Tappan as Beth and Joyce Didonato as Meg.

2003. Joseph McManners and Mairead Carlin star in *The Little Prince*, a PBS opera about a young boy who relates encounters with solitary inhabitants of other planets.

2005. Natalie Desay and Laurent Naouri star in *The Nightingale* (PBS), an operatic adaptation of the Hans Christian Anderson fairy tale that combines computer animation with the live performances and music of the Opera National de Paris under the direction of James Conlin.

Philadelphia

A listing of series set in and around Philadelphia, Pennsylvania. Other locales are listed after the network indication.

1970. *The Young Rebels* (ABC).

1976. *Gibbsville* (NBC); *The Tony Randall Show* (ABC/CBS).

1978. *Rollergirls* (NBC; Pittsburgh).

1979. *Angie* (ABC).

1980. *Grand* (NBC); *Skag* (NBC; Pittsburgh).

1985. *Mr. Belvedere* (ABC; Beaver Falls).

1986. *Amen* (NBC); *Gung Ho* (ABC; Pittsburgh).

1987. *Sweet Surrender* (NBC); *The Pursuit of Happiness* (ABC).

1988. *The Van Dyke Show* (CBS).

1990. *Equal Justice* (ABC; Pittsburgh); *Shannon's Deal* (NBC); *You Take the Kids* (CBS; Pittsburgh).

1991. *Teech* (CBS).

1993. *Boy Meets World* (ABC); *Family Album* (CBS).

1994. *Sirens* (ABC; Pittsburgh).

1995. *Hope and Gloria* (NBC; Pittsburgh); *Maybe This Time* (ABC).

1996. *Brotherly Love* (NBC).

1999. *Katie Joplin* (WB); *Reunited* (UPN; Pittsburgh); *Ryan Caulfield: Year One* (Fox).

2000. *Queer as Folk* (Showtime; Pittsburgh); *Strong Medicine* (Lifetime).
    2001. *American Dreams* (NBC); *Philly* (ABC).
    2002. *Hack* (CBS).
    2003. *Happy Family* (NBC); *Cold Case* (CBS).
    2004. *The Big House* (NBC).

Physically Disabled Performers and Characters

This entry lists characters with a physical disability who appear as regulars on a program. Individual episodes of a series are excluded.
    1946. Ernest Jones, a one-legged golf pro, becomes the first known person with a handicap to appear on TV. He did so on the DuMont interview program *Look Who's Here* on April 28th. Earlier in the year (January 30th) CBS broadcast an experimental drama called *Sorry Wrong Number* with Mildred Natwick playing an invalid woman who overhears a murder plot on the telephone, then seeks to get help — unaware that she is the intended victim.
    1950. CBS airs a second version of *Sorry Wrong Number* in a color experiment on January 8th. Meg Mundy plays a crippled woman who overhears her own murder plot on the telephone.
    1951. Susan Peters, a real life crippled woman (paralyzed from the waist down) plays herself, an attorney in the town of Martinville, Ohio, on the NBC serial *Miss Susan*.
    1955. Dennis Weaver plays Chester Goode, the crippled (right leg) deputy to Marshal Matt Dillon in Dodge City, Kansas, on *Gunsmoke* (CBS).
    1956. Robert Newton plays Long John Silver, a pirate of the 1700s who is missing his left leg (walked with a peg leg and crutch) on *The Adventures of Long John Silver* (Syn.). The NBC series *Noah's Ark* features Vic Rodman as Dr. Sam Rinehart, an aging veterinarian confined to a wheelchair.
    1957. Walter Brennan plays Amos McCoy, the elderly, cantankerous head of the McCoy family (farmers) who walked with a limp on *The Real McCoys* (ABC/CBS). Donald Gray plays Mark Saber, a one-armed former inspector with Scotland Yard turned private detective on NBC's *Saber of London*.
    1960. James McCallion plays Mi Taylor, a ranch hand who helps Velvet Brown (Lori Martin) train her horse King, for the Grand National

Steeplechase on NBC's *National Velvet*. Mi was a former jockey who broke his leg when he was thrown from a horse. The injury healed but left him with a limp. David McLean plays Tate (no other name given), a one-armed gunfighter of the Old West on NBC's *Tate*. Tate lost the use of his arm in an explosion during the Civil War; he now supports that arm in a black leather casing.
    1963. Bill Raisch plays Fred Johnson, the mysterious one-armed man who killed the wife of Dr. Richard Kimble (David Janssen) and is now running from Kimble's endless pursuit of him on ABC's *The Fugitive*.
    1964. Dick York, who played the role of Darrin Stevens on ABC's *Bewitched* for five years, had to relinquish the role due to a severe back injury he sustained in 1959 during the filming of the movie *They Came to Cordura* (a railroad handcar fell on him).
    1965. Leonard Strong plays the Claw, the evil Chinese head of KAOS, the enemy of secret Agent Maxwell Smart on the NBC episodes of *Get Smart*. Because of his accent, the Claw had to correct people who said his name — "Claw, not Craw."
    1967. Raymond Burr plays Robert T. Ironside, a Chief of Detectives with the San Francisco Police Department who, after being shot and crippled (confined to a wheelchair), is made a special consultant to the Police Commissioner on NBC's *Ironside*.
    1968. Patrick Newell plays Mother, the crippled superior of Ministry agents John Steed and Tara King on the last season episodes of ABC's *The Avengers*. Mother (no other name given), is a cripple (injured during service) who, although confined to a wheelchair, is able to walk with the aid of straps suspended from the ceiling.
    1973. Todd Crespi plays Dennis Pomeroy, the wheelchair bound son of columnist Max Pomeroy, the information man to magician Anthony Blake on NBC's *The Magician*. Steve Austin (Lee Majors), a former astronaut who is now an agent for the O.S.I. (Office of Scientific Information), received two bionic legs, an arm and an eye after he was severely injured in the crash of a test plane on ABC's *The Six Million Dollar Man*.
    1974. David Janssen plays Harry Orwell, a former San Diego police officer turned private detective after a shooting disabled him (shot in the back) on ABC's *Harry O*.
    1975. Dina Ousley plays Ellen Bronkov, the

crippled (in a car accident that killed her mother) daughter of Lt. Alex Bronkov on *Bronk* (CBS).

1976. Jaime Sommers (Lindsay Wagner) is a former tennis pro who works as an agent for the O.S.I. (Office of Scientific Information) to repay the government for saving her life by replacing her legs, arm and inner ear after a serious parachuting accident on *The Bionic Woman* (ABC/ NBC).

1977. David Ackroyd plays Dr. Nicholas Conrad, a crippled college physics professor who is able to walk via an exo-suit he developed that revitalizes his limbs (to fight crimes) on the NBC pilot *Exo-Man*. Ellen Corby, who plays Esther Walton on *The Waltons* (CBS), suffered a stroke in real life. When she returned to the series her character suffered from aphasia (speech difficulty) as well as walking difficulty.

1979. During the 1979–80 season of *Dallas* (CBS), Southfork ranch hand Dusty Farlow (Jared Martin) suffered a plane crash injury that confined him to a wheelchair. Torgue (Ji-Tu Cumbuka) is an agent for the government organization UNIT who has a metal right hand (upon which he can attach various weapons) on NBC's *A Man Called Sloane*.

1981. Geri Jewell plays Geri Warner, an aspiring standup comedian with cerebral palsy (real life also) on NBC's *The Facts of Life* (Geri is the cousin of the snobbish Blair Warner, a student at the Eastland School for Girls). On *McClain's Law* (NBC), James Arness plays Jim McClain, a detective with an injured leg. Lionel Smith plays Aaron MacRae, a wheelchair bound attorney for the Legal Aid Society in New York on CBS's *Park Place*. The NBC pilot *Skyward Christmas* (based on the feature film *Skyward*) focuses on the life of 16-year-old paraplegic Julie Ward (Suzanne Gilstrap). The pilot story is quite moving: Julie's efforts to survive when a plane crash strands her in the wilderness during Christmas.

1983. Melanie Watson joins the cast of NBC's *Diff'rent Strokes* as Kathy Gordon, the crippled classmate of Arnold Jackson.

1986. V.H. Adderly (Winston Rekert) is a government agent (for the Department of Miscellaneous Affairs) with an injured left hand (over which he wears a black leather glove) on CBS's *Adderly*.

1987. Annie Hartung (Madlyn Rhue) is a wheelchair bound police officer (suffers from multiple sclerosis) on CBS's *Houston Knights*. Jim

Byrnes plays Lifeguard, the crippled employee of the FBI's Organized Crime Bureau on CBS's *Wiseguy*.

1988. Although she has no character name, Charlotte Price can be seen in background scenes as the wheelchair bound gopher on CBS's *Murphy Brown*. Phil Akin plays Norton Drake, a wheelchair bound computer genius that works for the Blackwood Project (battles aliens) on the syndicated *War of the Worlds*. Drake calls his voice-activated wheelchair Gertrude.

1989. Jon Cypher plays Major General Marcus Gray, the Marine base commander of Camp Hollister in Virginia, who suffers from an injured leg and needs to use a wheelchair on *Major Dad* (CBS). After an acid bomb horribly disfigures his face, Paul Cain (Leigh Lawson) pretends to be dead to avenge crimes as *The Dark Avenger* (CBS pilot).

1990. In the last spinoff from *The Brady Bunch*, Bobby Brady (Michael Lookinland) becomes paralyzed from the waist down after a racing car accident on *The Bradys* (CBS). Damon Wayans plays Clark Bent, a newspaper mailroom clerk who avenges crime as Handi-Man, a physically challenged super hero (cerebral palsy-like symptoms) on *In Living Color* (Fox).

1991. Real life wheelchair bound physical fitness instructor Maria Serraro hosts a cable-syndicated program called *Everyone Can Exercise*, wherein she devises exercises for the handicapped.

1992. Jim Byrnes plays Joe Dawson, a member of a secret society known as the Watchers (monitors a race of people called Immortals) on *Highlander: The Series* (Syn.) Joe has an injured leg and walks with the aid of a cane.

1993. Madlyn Rhue joins the cast of CBS's *Murder, She Wrote* as Jean O'Neill, the crippled Cabot Cove librarian who suffers from multiple sclerosis.

1994. On NBC's *ER*, Laura Innes plays Dr. Kerry Weaver, who suffers from Congenital Hip Dysphasia (causes her to walk with a limp). Chandler Bing (Matthew Perry) is one of NBC's *Friends*. He is missing the little pinky toe from his right foot due to Monica's carelessness. (She dropped a large chopping knife onto the floor while preparing a Thanksgiving dinner. His friend, Ross Geller, calls him "Sir Limps a Lot" while he is recuperating.) Carl Lumbly plays Dr. Miles Hawkins, a scientist paralyzed from the waist down (shot in the back) who can walk (and battle crime) by an exoskeleton he created called *M.A.N.T.I.S.* (Fox), a Mechanically Automated Neuro Transmitter Interactive System that gives him a bug-like appearance. Dorian Harewood plays Julian Wilkes, a scientist (confined to a wheelchair) who developed *Viper*, a high tech crime-fighting car of the future on *Viper* (NBC/Syn.).

1996. Psychotherapist Louie Lundregen (Louie Anderson) is assisted by Helen (Nancy Becker-Kennedy), a wheelchair bound HMO worker on CBS's *The Louie Show*. While not mentioned on his series *Spin City* (ABC), Michael J. Fox was diagnosed with Parkinson's disease in 1991. In syndication each episode contains a 30 second public service announcement concerning the disease (Michael appears in each with various cast members).

1997. Deanna Milligan plays Laurie Jarvis, an ex cop who suffered a spinal injury that crippled her on the syndicated *NightMan*. Laurie had experimental spinal surgery and with the aid of an energizer suit she created, she can walk and avenge crimes as the head of a company called Woman Trouble ("I help women in trouble"). Harold Perrineau, Jr. plays Augustus Hill, a wheelchair bound convict who narrates stories of prison life at the Oswald State Correctional Facility on HBO's *Oz*.

1998. Jim Byrnes reprises his role of Joe Dawson, the crippled Watcher of Immortals, on the syndicated *Highlander: The Raven*. Diane Delano plays Miss Roberta "Bobbi" Glass, the tough teacher at John F. Kennedy High School who is missing a finger on her right hand on the WB's *Popular*.

1999. Patrick Warburton provides the voice of Joe, the wheelchair bound (paraplegic) friend of Peter Griffin on the animated *Family Guy* (Fox). Jed Bartlet (Martin Sheen) is the President of the United States who suffers from MS on NBC's *The West Wing*. Sara Rue plays Breeny Kennedy, a wheelchair bound high school girl on *Zoe, Duncan, Jack and Jane* (WB).

2000. Kathy Baker plays Meredith Peters, a teacher at Boston's Winslow High School who is missing her right hand (claims from a gardening accident) on Fox's *Boston Public* (she originally wore a hook, then a prosthetic hand). Robert David Hall plays Dr. Robbins, a double amputee (in real life also) who walks with crutches on CBS's *C.S.I.: Crime Scene Investigation* (he works

in the coroner's office of the Las Vegas P.D.). On Fox's *Dark Angel*, Logan Cale (Michael Weatherly) is a cyber journalist with a spinal injury that makes him incapable of walking (he is later able to walk somewhat when he receives a blood transfusion from Max Guevara [Jessica Alba], the title character who has genetically enhanced blood). Stephen Lang plays Fred Johnson, the one-armed man who killed the wife of Dr. Richard Kimble (Tim Daly) and who is now on the run as Kimble seeks to find him on CBS's *The Fugitive*. Two physically challenged characters are presented on Fox's *Malcolm in the Middle*. Stevie Kenarben (Craig Lamar Traylor) is a boy with asthma who is also wheelchair bound and a close friend of Malcolm. Malcolm's older brother Francis attends a military school run by the tormenting Commander Edwin Spangler (David von Bargen). Spangler limps, has a black patch over his left eye, a hook for a right hand and missing fingers on his left hand (he wears a black glove). The *Baywatch* rip-off series, FX's *Son of the Beach*, features Steven Ryan as Professor Milosevic, a former lifeguard who is now wheelchair bound (boating accident) and seeking revenge on the man he believes caused the accident — overweight lifeguard Notch Johnson.

2001. Chandra Wilson plays Claudia, the klutzy wheelchair bound assistant to Bob Patterson, a self-help guru on ABC's *Bob Patterson*. Living downstream from a toxic dump creates the Oblong family, cartoon characters on the WB's *The Oblongs*. Bob (Will Ferrell), the father, has no arms or legs; his wife, Pickles (Jean Smart) is bald (wears a wig); their daughter Beth (Jeannie Elias) has a strange growth on the right side of her head; twin sons Biff and Chip (Jason and Randy Sklar) share three legs; youngest son Milo (Pamela Segall) has one eye and one strand of hair on his head. On UPN's *Special Unit 2*, Richard Gant plays Richard Page, a captain (missing his right hand) who commands a unit of the Chicago Police Department that battles unearthly creatures.

2002. Dina Meyer plays Barbara Gordon, alias the crime fighting Batgirl in New Gotham City on the WB's *Birds of Prey*. Barbara was crippled when she was shot by the evil Joker (he snuck into her apartment and shot her when she stepped out of the shower). She is a teacher at New Gotham High School and now avenges crime as Oracle (she can walk but with difficulty, when she wears a special costume she created that makes her partially mobile). Daryl "Chill" Mitchell plays Eli Cartwright Goggins III, the crippled (wheelchair bound) manager of the Stuckyville Bowling Alley on NBC's *Ed*. Charles Durning plays Henry Hoskins, an elderly Superior Court Judge who is also wheelchair bound on *First Monday* (CBS). On *JAG* (NBC/CBS), Patrick Laborteaux plays Bud Roberts, a legal clerk (later a lawyer) for the Judge Advocate General (defends military personnel), who lost his right leg when he stepped on a land mine in Afghanistan.

2003. Jason Ritter plays Kevin Giraldi, the brother of Joan (the girl who sees and speaks to God) on CBS's *Joan of Arcadia*. Kevin was crippled in a car accident (wheelchair bound) but is hopeful he will walk again despite the negative opinions of his doctors. Mitch Longley plays Mitch, a wheelchair bound security room employee at the Montecito Casino on NBC's *Las Vegas*. Christopher Reeve, who suffered a horse riding accident that left him paralyzed, appears on several episodes of the WB's *Smallville* as Dr. Virgil Swann, a scientist who befriends young Clark Kent.

2004. Grant Albrecht plays Leonard Gilesi, the wheelchair bound medical examiner on *C.S.I.: New York* (CBS). Hugh Laurie is Gregory House, a maverick, anti-social doctor who walks with a limp (result of a heart attack) on Fox's *House*. Terry O'Quinn plays John Locke, wheelchair bound for four years after an accident, who finds he can suddenly walk after the plane on which he was traveling crash lands on a mysterious island on ABC's *Lost*.

2005. Ron Renço Lee plays Todd, the wheelchair bound friend of Marni (Jennifer Finnegan) on NBC's *Committed*. Buster Bluth (Tony Hale), the brother of Bluth Company executive Michael Bluth (Jason Bateman), suffers an accident in third season episodes when he loses his hand to a seal.

Pilot Film Series

One pilot film series, *Preview Tonight*, opened with these words: "Each year, many of the new shows developed for television fail to make the network schedules even though they are entertaining and well produced. Tonight's pilot film is one of these. We invite you behind the scenes to see what you think of (name of pilot) on *Preview Tonight*." This entry chronicles the series (and the

pilot films that aired) that were once a part of early TV (broadcast during the summer months as a means of original programming). Pilot films (called test films before 1951) were an aspect of television until 1996 when costs prohibited, in most cases, filming a complete episode (segments or presentation pilots became the norm and not meant for broadcast). Stand-alone pilot films (those not broadcast on a series) are not included in this entry (too numerous to list).

1949: Program Playhouse (DuMont). Test films: *Federal Agent, Hands of Murder, Roscoe Karns and Inky Poo, The Timid Soul, Trouble, Inc.*

1956: Sneak Preview (NBC). Pilots: *Calling Terry Conway, Carolyn, Just Plain Folks, Real George.*

1958: Decision (NBC). Pilots: *Indemnity, Man Against Crime, Man on a Raft, The Virginian.*

1960: Comedy Spot (CBS). Pilots: *Coogan's Reward, Full Speed Anywhere, Head of the Family* (pilot for *The Dick Van Dyke Show*), *Meet the Girls, The Sky's the Limit, Tom, Dick and Harry* and *Welcome to Washington*. **New Comedy Showcase** (CBS). Pilots: *Johnny Come Lately, They Went Thataway, The Trouble with Richard, You're Only Young Once.*

1961: Preview Theater (NBC). Pilots: *Five's a Family, Happily Ever After, Harry's Business, Heave Ho Harrigan, I Married a Dog, Innocent Jones, Miss Bishop, Picture Window, Shore Leave.*

1962: Comedy Spot (CBS). Pilots: *For the Love of Mike, Life with Virginia, The Soft Touch.*

1963–1967: Vacation Playhouse (CBS). The *Lucy Show* summer replacement. Pilots: *Alfred of the Amazon, All About Barbara, The Apartment House, An Apartment in Rome, At Your Service, The Barbara Rush Show, The Bean Show, Bravo Duke, Charlie Angelo, Come a Running, Down Home, The Eve Arden Show, The First Hundred Years, For the Love of Mike, Frank Merriwell, The Freewheelers, The Ginger Rogers Show, The Good Old Days, The Graduation Dress, Heaven Help Us, Hey Teacher, Hide and Seek* (the pilot for *Glynis*), *His Model Wife, The Hoofer, Hooray for Hollywood, Hooray for Love, The Human Comedy, I and Claudie, I Love My Doctor, The Jimmy Durante Show, The Jones Boys, Life with Virginia, Love Is a Lion's Roar, Low Man on the Totem Pole, Luke and the Tenderfoot, McGhee, The McGonigle, Maggie Brown, Mickey and the Contessa, The Mighty O, Mimi, My Boy Googie, My Lucky Penny, My Son the*

Doctor, Off We Go, Octavius and Me, Papa G.I., Patrick Stone, Poor Mr. Campbell, Satan's Waitin,' The Soft Touch, Swingin' Together, Sybil, Three on an Island, Three Wishes, The Two of Us, Where's There's Smokey, You're Only Young Twice.

1965: The General Foods Summer Playhouse (CBS). Pilots: *Acres and Pains, Adventures of a Model, Kibbee Hates Fitch, Mr. Belvedere, Sally and Sam, Starr First Baseman, Take Him—He's All Yours, Young in Heart.*

1966: Preview Tonight (ABC). Pilots: *The Cliff Dwellers, Great Bible Adventures, Pursue and Destroy, Roaring Camp* and *Somewhere in Italy, Company B.* **Summer Fun** (ABC). Pilots: *Baby Crazy, Little Leatherneck, McNab's Lab, Meet Me in St. Louis, The Pirates of Flounder Bay, Thompson's Ghost.*

1968: Premiere (CBS). Pilots: *Call to Danger, Crisis, Higher and Higher: Attorneys at Law, Operation Greasepaint, Out of the Blue, The Search, A Walk in the Night.*

1969: Summer Theater (NBC). Pilots: *The Best Years, Doc, The Flim-Flam Man, Harper Valley, U.S.A.* and *Pioneer Spirit.*

1970: Comedy Preview (ABC). Pilots: *The Murdocks and the McClays, Prudence and the Chief, Three for Tahiti.* **Monday Theater** (NBC). Pilots: *The Boys, The Kowboys, Me and Benjy, Run, Jack, Run and Southern Fried.*

1971: Comedy Playhouse (CBS). Pilots: *Eddie, Elke, My Wives Jane, Shepherd's Flock.*

1974: Just for Laughs (ABC). Pilots: *Ann in Blue, The Barbara Eden Show; Ernie, Madge and Artie; The Life and Times of Barney Miller* (the pilot for *Barney Miller*).

1975: Comedy Theater (NBC). Pilots: *Ace, The Bureau, The Cheerleaders.*

1976: ABC Tuesday Night Pilot Film (ABC). Pilots: *Charo and the Sergeant, Flatbush/Avenue J, Rear Guard.* **Comedy Time** (NBC). Pilots: *Daughters, Look Out World, The Natural Look.*

1977: Comedy Time (NBC). Pilots: *Daughters, Look Out World, The Natural Look.*

1987: The CBS Summer Playhouse (CBS). Pilots: *Barrington, Changing Patterns, Day to Day, The Infiltrator, King of the Building, Kingpins, Kung Fu: The Next Generation, Mabel and Max, Mickey and Nora, Puppetman, Sirens, Sons of Gunz, The Time of Their Lives, Traveling Man.*

Pilots (Aviators)

This entry chronicles the characters involved with airplanes, helicopters, jets or other flying equipment. The listing also includes series featuring stewardesses. See also *Space* (for space ship pilots).

1950. Ding Howe (Richard Denning) is a World War II U.S. Air Force fighter pilot who heads a small group of pilots called the Flying Tigers on the syndicated *Ding Howe and the Flying Tigers.*

1951. Dell Conway (Eric Fleming, Ed Peck) is a former World War II Air Force pilot turned chief pilot for the L.A. based Flying Tigers airline on DuMont's *Major Dell Conway of the Flying Tigers.* Sky King (Kirby Grant) is a former World War II naval aviator turned owner of the Flying Crown Ranch who uses his plane, the *Songbird,* to maintain law and order in Grover City, Arizona on *Sky King* (CBS).

1952. Terry Lee (John Baer) is a pilot for Air Cathay, a small cargo airline based in Singapore on *Terry and the Pirates* (Syn.).

1953. Major Dell Conway (Art Fleming) is a U.S. Fighter Squadron pilot based in China during World War II on *Major Dell Conway of the Flying Tigers* (a syndicated reworking of the 1951 DuMont series).

1954. Chuck Martin and P.T. Moore (Kenneth Tobey, Craig Hill) are pilots for Whirlybirds, Inc., a California based helicopter charter service on the syndicated *Whirlybirds.*

1958. General George C. Kenney, USAF (Ret.) hosts *Flight,* a syndicated series of true stories based on the files of the U.S. Air Force. Dean Fredericks plays *Steve Canyon* (NBC), a Lieutenant Commander who is also a trouble-shooter for the U.S. Air Force. James Stewart hosts *Cowboy Five-Seven,* an NBC pilot about and starring the men and women of the Strategic Air Command. Greg Graham (Richard Denning) is an American doctor based in Australia who uses his plane to help those far removed from society on *The Flying Doctor* (Syn.). Scott Brady plays *Johnny Nighthawk* (CBS pilot), the adventurous owner of a one-plane airline. The adventures of American fliers during World War II were to be the subject of *Skyfighters,* a syndicated pilot starring Brian Kelly and Joe Flynn. The experiences of the men and women of the U.S. Air Force were to be the focal point of *Strategic Air Command,* an NBC pilot starring Kerwin Matthews.

1960. The experiences of the pilots and crew of the Blue Angels, four precision U.S. Naval jets, are seen on *The Blue Angels* (Syn.). Dennis Cross and Mike Galloway star. Sandy Wade and Zack Malloy (William Reynolds, James Philbrook) are the owners of a Grumman Goose, a cargo seaplane that comprises the one plane Lato Airlines on the island of Ambowina (off Sumatra) on ABC's *The Islanders*. Doug McClure and Ross Martin play Josh Holt and Danny Wallace, foul-up trainees at the Naval Air Force Base in Pensacola, Florida on the CBS pilot *The Sky's the Limit*.

1961. Bob Carson (Bob Cummings) is a freelance pilot based in Palm Springs, California on *The New Bob Cummings Show*. Bob owns the never marketed Aero Car (a car that could be converted into a plane in ten minutes. Its inventor could never get it mass-produced and Bob flew the prototype model). Called "The most danger-packed show on television" because "every aerial maneuver is real," *Ripcord* (Syn.) told of Jim Buckley and Ted McKeever (Ken Curtis, Larry Pennell), sky diving instructors for Ripcord, Inc., a sky diving school and charter service.

1962. Alan Garrett (Nigel Patrick) is the head of Airline Security International, a London-based airline crime detection team on the syndicated *Zero One*.

1965. John Cassavetes plays Lee Harmon, a World War I Air Corps pilot who flies by his own rules on the NBC pilot *The Fliers*.

1967. The puppet series *Captain Scarlet and the Mysterons* presents five female pilots called Angels: Destiny Angel (voice of Liz Morgan), Harmony Angel (Shin-Lian), Melody Angel (Sylvia Anderson), Rhapsody Angel (Liz Morgan) and Symphony Angel (Jana Hill). Lee Ragdon, Buggs Middle and Rippy Sloane (George Hamilton, John Craig, Warren Berlinger) are trouble-prone student fliers who help people in trouble on the ABC pilot *The Hellcats*.

1969. Mike and Carol Wilson are a husband and wife who own Skyhawks, Inc., an air transport and rescue service on the ABC animated series *Skyhawks*.

1970. Lloyd Bridges plays Jim Conrad, manager of a large airport on NBC's *San Francisco International Airport*. Spud Barrett (Tim Conway) is the inept pilot of the *Lucky Linda*, a decrepit plane that comprises Triple A Airlines on *The Tim Conway Show* (CBS).

1971. Millie Grover and Maggie Ralston (Millicent Martin, Pat Finley) are stewardesses for the London based International Airlines on NBC's *From a Bird's Eye View*.

1973. Jim Watkins (Jerry Anderson) is the pilot of *The Spirit*, a 737 jet that is owned by Anthony Blake on NBC's *The Magician*.

1974. Gil Foley and Don Burdick (Dirk Benedict, Jim McMullan) are helicopter pilots (of Chopper One) for the West California Police Department on ABC's *Chopper One*.

1975. In addition to her stunning good looks, Diana Prince (Lynda Carter), alias Wonder Woman, has the ability to fly her invisible plane and go undetected on *Wonder Woman* (ABC/CBS).

1976. William Windom plays Gregory Heck, a World War I Air Corps Colonel who heads Aero Squadron 35, a group of inferior fliers on the CBS pilot *Heck's Angels*. Cass Garrett (Christopher Stone) is a charter pilot for Spencer Aviation on CBS's *Spencer's Pilots*.

1978. Jenny, Mitch and Toby (Lauren Tewes, John Bennett Perry, Carl Anderson) are U.S. Air Force medical technicians assigned to airlift assignments on the syndicated pilot *Aeromeds*. Robert Conrad plays Major Gregory "Pappy" Boyington, a daring World War II air ace and leader of the VMF 214 Black Sheep on NBC's *Black Sheep Squadron* (originally titled *Baa Baa Black Sheep*). Pam Bellagio (Kathryn Witt), Lisa Benton (Connie Sellecca) and Marcy Bower (Patricia Klous) are stewardesses for Sun West Airlines on CBS's *Flying High*.

1980. T.C. Calvin (Roger E. Mosley) is a former Golden Gloves boxer turned owner of Island Hoppers, a helicopter charter service in Hawaii on *Magnum, P.I.* (CBS).

1982. Jake Cutter (Stephen Collins) is a cargo pilot (of a plane he calls *Cutter's Goose*) on the South Pacific island of Bora Gora (1938) on ABC's *Tales of the Gold Monkey*.

1984. Stringfellow Hawke (Jan-Michael Vincent) is the pilot of *Airwolf*, an awesome attack helicopter (see *Gadgets*) that he uses to battle criminal elements for the government on CBS's *Airwolf*. Also on the series, Ernest Borgnine plays Dominic Santini, pilot and owner of the Santini Air Charter Service; and Jean Bruce Scott plays Caitlin O'Shaughnessy, a pilot for Santini Air (formerly a helicopter pilot for the Texas Highway Patrol, Aerial Division). Frank Chaney

(James Farentino) heads the Blue Thunder unit of the L.A.P.D. that incorporates a state of the art helicopter on ABC's *Blue Thunder*. Irene Gorley (Tracy Scoggins) is a beautiful young woman who runs Cupid Eyes Tours, a helicopter sightseeing service in Hawaii on *Hawaiian Heat* (ABC).

1985. Gil Gerard plays David Montgomery, manager of a large airport on the ABC pilot *International Airport*.

1987. When the USA network acquired *Airwolf* from CBS (see 1984) the format changed to focus on the helicopter's new pilot, Jason Locke (Anthony Sherwood), as he performed missions for the government (Stringfellow had been injured in an explosion and was unable to fly the copter).

1988. John Denver plays Jim Clayton, a former FBI agent turned bush pilot in Alaska for Annakin Air Charter, on the CBS pilot *Higher Ground*.

1990. Maggie O'Connell (Janine Turner) is the owner of the one plane O'Connell Air Taxi Service in Cicely, Alaska, on CBS's *Northern Exposure*. Joe Hackett (Tim Daly) and his brother Brian (Steve Weber) run Sandpiper Air, a one-plane airline based at the Tom Nevers Field in Nantucket on *Wings* (NBC).

1991. Sally Monroe (Shannon Tweed) is a former stewardess for Air Canada who begins her own one-plane airline, Slick Air, on *Fly by Night* (CBS).

1992. Jeff Carlyle (Sami Chester) pilots the *Wing*, a high tech black plane that resembles the wings of an airliner, for Chris Chance, the man who impersonates people to protect them, on *The Human Target* (ABC).

1995. Tess Jameson (Rose Jackson), Maggie Reynolds (Kristin Bauer) and Leonora Zwick (Christine Estabrook) are stewardesses for Regency Airlines on Fox's *The Crew*.

1997. Bill Kelly (James Brolin) heads the Sea Dragons, a unit of U.S. Air Force pilots on *Pensacola: Wings of Gold* (Syn.).

1998. *Sky One* is a large plane that serves as the base of operations for Kyle Stewart (Brixton Karnes), the head of the crime fighting *Team Knight Rider* (Syn.).

2000. Matt Cutter (John Allen Nelson) is the owner of Cutter Enterprises, a land and air safari service in Africa on *Sheena* (Syn.).

2004. Harley Random (Heather Locklear) is the manager of Los Angeles International Airport on NBC's *LAX*.

Politics

Programs with political overtones are the subjects of this entry. For information on the programs on which the actual Presidents of the United States appear see *Presidential Appearances*.

1945. Stephen Courtleigh plays Abraham Lincoln on NBC's *Abraham Lincoln in Illinois*, a three-part adaptation of the Broadway play by Robert E. Sherwood. Mary Michaels co-stars as his wife, Mary Todd Lincoln.

1954. Thomas Mitchell plays Thomas Russell, the mayor of the small American town of Springdale on *Mayor of the Town* (Syn.).

1955. Clem Waters (Herb Shriner) is a midwestern lawyer with ambitions of becoming the governor of his state on the NBC pilot *Meet the Governor*. John Peoples (Paul Maxey) is the jovial mayor of New City, California on *The People's Choice* (CBS). Also on the series, Socrates Miller (Jackie Cooper), John's son-in-law, is a 5th District Councilman in later episodes.

1958. Claudette Colbert plays Elizabeth Harper, a newly elected Congresswoman beginning her career in Washington, D.C. on the NBC pilot *The Claudette Colbert Show* (also known as *Welcome to Washington*).

1962. The theatrical film, *The Farmer's Daughter*, is adapted to TV (NBC) on *Theater '62*. Lee Remick plays Katrin Holstrom, a Swedish farm girl who comes to work as a housekeeper for Congressman Glen Morley (Peter Lawford) in Washington, D.C. Fess Parker plays Eugene Smith, a country politician struggling to adjust to the norms of Capitol life in Washington, D.C. on ABC's *Mr. Smith Goes to Washington*.

1963. Inger Stevens plays Katy Holstrom, a Minnesota farm girl who becomes the governess to the children of widowed Washington, D.C. Congressman Glen Morley (William Windom) on *The Farmer's Daughter* (ABC). Andrew Jackson Tyree (Edgar Buchanan) and his son Boford (Phil Alford) are *The Tyrees of Capitol Hill* (CBS pilot), Senate Page Boys.

1964. Jason Robards plays Abraham Lincoln and Kate Reid is Mary Todd Lincoln on *The Hall-*

mark Hall of Fame presentation of *Abe Lincoln in Illinois* (NBC). Richard Crenna plays James Slattery, politician, lawyer and minority leader in the state legislature who crusades against government injustice on *Slattery's People* (CBS).

1968. Comedian Pat Paulsen runs for President of the United States in a mock campaign (begun as a series of skits on *The Smothers Brothers Comedy Hour*) on the CBS special *Pat Paulsen for President*.

1969. Political life is satirized on *The Governor and J.J.*, a CBS series about William Drinkwater (Dan Dailey), the governor of an unidentified state, and his beautiful 23-year-old daughter Jennifer Jo (Julie Sommars), better known as J.J.

1970. Nancy Smith (Renne Jarrett), the daughter of the President of the United States, marries Adam Hudson (John Fink), an Iowa veterinarian on *Nancy*, an NBC series that focuses on their attempts to live a life that is more public than private. Hal Holbrook plays Hays Stowe, a progressive politician who attempts to meet and understand the people he represents on *The Bold Ones: The Senator* (NBC).

1971. Anthony Quinn plays Thomas Jefferson Alcala, the mayor of an unnamed New Mexico city, who strays from political office to mix with the people on ABC's *The Man and the City*.

1972. Carroll O'Connor plays John P. Wintergreen, a presidential candidate who runs on a platform of silver linings and love on the CBS special *Of Thee I Sing*.

1975. Fred Stuthman plays Abraham Lincoln in *The Case Against Milligan*, an historic CBS special about President Lincoln's suspension of the Constitutional right of habeas corpus during the Civil War. Karen Angelo (Karen Valentine) is an idealistic staff worker for Open America, a Capitol Hill citizen's lobby in Washington, D.C. on ABC's *Karen*. The 1858 Lincoln-Douglas Debates (the issue of slavery) are recreated on *The Rivalry*, a *Hallmark Hall of Fame* (NBC) special with Arthur Hill as Abraham Lincoln and Charles Durning as Stephen Douglas.

1976. A profile of four generations of an historic American family, the Adams, is profiled on *The Adams Chronicles* (PBS). The family produced two U.S. Presidents and a Secretary of State. It stars George Grizzard, Kathryn Walker and William Daniels. Michael Keaton plays Lenny Wolfe, President Jimmy Carter's joke writer on *All's Fair*, a CBS series that centers on the relationship between newspaper columnist Richard Barrington III (Richard Crenna) and Charlotte Drake (Bernadette Peters), a beautiful photojournalist. Rudy Jordache (Peter Strauss) is an ambitious U.S. Senator on ABC's *Rich Man, Poor Man*. Peter Strauss continues the role in *Rich Man, Poor Man Book II*.

1978. Joe Kelly (Jack Albertson) is a former political science professor turned U.S. Senator who tries to practice what he taught — honest government — on *Grandpa Goes to Washington* (NBC).

1979. Olivia Cole and Leslie Uggams star as Maggie Rogers and her daughter Lillian, White House maids who served U.S. Presidents from William Howard Taft to Dwight D. Eisenhower on NBC's *Backstairs at the White House*. Robert Guillaume plays Benson DuBois, butler to Gene Gatling, the governor of Capitol City on ABC's *Benson* (Benson is the budget director of the state in later episodes). David Huddleston plays Michael Cooper, the kindly mayor of a small midwestern town on NBC's *Hizzoner*. Cleavon Little plays Matthew Dugan, a fledgling congressman on the unaired series *Mr. Dugan* (pulled by CBS after it was found to be offensive to black congressmen).

1980. The 201st Bob Hope special, *Bob Hope for President* (NBC) finds Bob lampooning the political system as he begins a mythical campaign to run for the President of the U.S.

1981. Joyce Van Patten plays Barbara Thatcher, the Deputy Chief of Staff of the U.S. Embassy on Bulba, a tiny island in the Indian Ocean on the ABC pilot *Bulba*.

1982. The problems that befall a royal family are the subject of the NBC pilot *Fit for a King*. Dick Van Patten stars as King Alfred of Brailand (a mythical European kingdom) with Katherine Helmond as his wife, Queen Mary Ella.

1984. Barry Bostwick plays *George Washington* (CBS) in a miniseries that chronicles the life of the first President of the U.S. Patty Duke also stars as Martha Washington. The personalities and politics of Capitol Hill are satirized on *Washingtoon*, a Showtime pilot about Bob Forehead (Thomas Galloway), a TV announcer turned political candidate seeking a congressional seat. Anne Lockhart plays his wife, Ginger; Christina Applegate is their daughter, Sally.

1985. Patty Duke plays Julia Mansfield, the first woman president of the U.S. on ABC's *Hail* *to the Chief.* Ted Bessell is her husband, First Gentleman Oliver Mansfield. Royal families and commoners are satirized on *Royal Match*, a CBS pilot set in the kingdom of Crescenda that is ruled by King Edmond (John Moulder-Brown) and his American wife Susan (Haviland Morris).

1986. Barry Bostwick recreates his role as George Washington on *George Washington II: The Forging of a Nation*, a continuation of the 1984 CBS miniseries, that focuses on the nine years from the Constitutional Ratification Convention in Virginia in 1788 to the inauguration of the second President, John Adams in 1797. Patty Duke also reprises her role as Martha Washington. Twenty-five-year-old college graduate Cal Burke (Kevin Hooks) runs for and is elected mayor of an unidentified crisis-ridden city on ABC's *He's the Mayor*.

1987. Laurence Luckinbill portrays the 36th President in a monologue that recalls LBJ's rise in politics on the PBS special *Lyndon Johnson*. Former Wisconsin governor Sam Tresch (George C. Scott) becomes the 43rd President of the U.S. on Fox's *Mr. President*. Carlin Glynn plays his wife, First Lady Meg Tresch.

1988. Christopher Lloyd plays President for Life Paul Joseph Domino, a deposed South Seas island ruler who now runs a coin operated laundry in Rego Park, Queens (New York) on the unaired CBS series *The Dictator* (the victim of a writer's strike). HBO's *Tanner '88* is a political satire that follows the campaign trail of Jack Tanner (Michael Murphy), a congressman who runs for President. Cynthia Nixon co-stars as his daughter, Alex Tanner.

1989. TV kid show host (of "Hobo Ed") Ed Hobart (Ed Begley, Jr.) finds a new career as a city councilman when he replaces his wife Carol (Wendie Malick) during her maternity leave on the CBS pilot *The Ed Begley, Jr. Show*.

1991. Jim Doyle (James Garner) is a 7th District City Councilman (unnamed city) who feels he needs to pull scams to live ("I can't survive on what they pay me in this burg") on NBC's *Man of the People*. Lauren Tom plays Judy Song, liaison to widowed San Francisco politician Philip Harte (George Hamilton) on the CBS pilot *Our Song*. Martha Katzenberg (Haviland Morris) and Jim Smith (George Newborn) are speechwriters for the President of the U.S. on the NBC pilot *Word of Mouth*.

1992. Strobe Smith (George Gaynes) is a se-

nile, conservative Southern Senator who is married to the beautiful (and much younger) Mary Fran (Mary Ann Mobley) but having a secret affair with his office secretary, Dee Dee Star (Beth Broderick) on CBS's *Hearts Afire*. A look at a dysfunctional political family occurs on NBC's *The Powers That Be*. John Forsythe heads the cast as Senator William Powers, a liberal Democrat, with Holland Taylor as his wife, Margaret and Valerie Mahaffey as their daughter, Caitlin, the wife of wimpy Congressman Theodore Van Horne (David Hyde Pierce).

1994. When his wife, Marjorie Litchfield (Helen Shaver) becomes the first woman President of the U.S., Frank (Kevin Dunn) assumes the role of *First Gentleman* (CBS pilot). Frank is a police officer who still upholds the law. Henry Winkler plays Monty Richardson, the politically right wing host of "Right Speak with Monty Richardson" on Channel 35 in Long Island (New York) on Fox's *Monty*.

1995. Following the death of her husband, Ray, Suzanne Sugarbaker (Delta Burke) fills his seat as the Georgia delegate in the House of Representatives on CBS's *Women of the House*.

1996. Barry Bostwick plays Randall Winston, the mayor of New York City on ABC's *Spin City*.

1998. A look at the administration of Abraham Lincoln (Dann Florek) is seen through the eyes of Desmond Pfeiffer (Chi McBride), a highbrow English butler on *The Secret Life of Desmond Pfeiffer* (UPN).

1999. NBC's *The West Wing* presents a look at presidential politics in the nation's capital. Martin Sheen stars as President Jeb Bartlet with Stockard Channing as his wife Abbey.

2001. Jerome Daggett (David Alan Grier) is a Secret Service agent assigned to protect the President of the U.S. (David Rasche) his wife, Judith Whitman (Delta Burke), and their daughter Camilla (Lea Mareno Young) on NBC's *DAG*. A parody of the George W. Bush administration is seen on *That's My Bush!*, a Comedy Central series starring Timothy Bottoms as President George W. Bush and Carrie Quinn Dolan as his wife, Laura.

2003. Nathan Lane plays Charlie Lawrence, an actor who moves from New York to Washington, D.C. to become a congressman on CBS's *Charlie Lawrence*. Josh Brolin plays William Sterling, a California state senator struggling to adjust to the norms of Capitol Hill on *Mister Sterling* (NBC).

2004. Michael Murphy reprises his role as Jack Tanner (see 1988) on *Tanner on Tanner*, a spoof of politics as Congressman Jack Tanner runs for president. Cynthia Nixon reprises her role as Alex, Jack's daughter, now a documentary filmmaker.

2005. Mackenzie Allen (Geena Davis), the Vice President of the U.S., becomes the first woman president when she replaces the dying current president on ABC's *Commander-in-Chief*. Andrew James Allen plays her ambitious husband, Horace.

Presidential Appearances

This entry chronicles the television appearances of United States Presidents on non-political programs (presidential news conferences, addresses to the nation, conventions and inaugurations are excluded except for historic first presentations). The appearances of the following Presidents are listed: Herbert Hoover (31st President, 1929–1933), Franklin D. Roosevelt (32nd President, 1933–1945), Harry S. Truman (33rd President, 1945–1953), John F. Kennedy (35th President, 1961–1963), Lyndon B. Johnson (36th President, 1963–1969), Richard M. Nixon (37th President, 1969–1974), Gerald Ford (38th President, 1974–1977), Jimmy Carter (39th President, 1977–1981), Ronald Reagan (40th President, 1981–1989), George H.W. Bush (41st President, 1989–1993), Bill Clinton (42nd President, 1993–2001), George W. Bush (43rd President, 2001-Current).

1927. On April 27th, Bell Telephone Laboratories televises a speech by then Secretary of Commerce Herbert Hoover. Two firsts occurred: the complete transmission of sound and picture and long distance video broadcasting (between New York and Washington, D.C.).

1932. CBS broadcasts the first political campaign, a show by the Democratic National Committee on October 11th.

1939. President Franklin Delano Roosevelt speaks at the opening ceremonies of the New York World's Fair (from Flushing, Queens) on April 30th.

1940. The Republican National Committee Convention is broadcast by NBC.

1945. President Harry S. Truman makes his first live TV appearance at the Navy Day Special in Central Park (New York) on October 27th.

1949. NBC broadcasts the first Presidential Inaugural (of Harry S. Truman's second term) in January.

1950. Former first lady Eleanor Roosevelt hosts *Today with Mrs. Roosevelt*, an NBC series in which she interviews guests and answers questions submitted by viewers.

1954. President Dwight D. Eisenhower appears on *Light's Diamond Jubilee*, a four-network celebration (ABC, CBS, DuMont, NBC) of the 75th anniversary of the invention of the light bulb.

1955. Dwight D. Eisenhower becomes the first president to give a news conference (on January 19th that is filmed and edited for broadcast). Eisenhower also becomes the first president to be seen in color on June 7th when he addresses the graduating class at the West Point Military Academy. An intimate glimpse of former President Herbert Hoover is seen on *Conversations with Herbert Hoover* with newsman Ron Henle conducting the interview.

1960. Howard K. Smith conducts the first televised presidential debates between Senator John F. Kennedy and Vice President Richard M. Nixon. Seventy-six year old Former First Lady Eleanor Roosevelt is honored on *Eleanor Roosevelt's Diamond Jubilee Plus One*, an NBC special on which Former President Franklin D. Roosevelt, Senator John F. Kennedy and Vice President Richard M. Nixon appear. John F. Kennedy appears as a guest on *The Jack Paar Show* (NBC). Garry Moore hosts *The Right Man*, a TV special that reviews the presidential campaigns and gimmicks used to attract voters.

1961. On January 25th, John F. Kennedy presents TV's first live presidential news conference (prior to this, the conferences were filmed and edited for broadcast).

1962. Marilyn Monroe appears in a very sexy dress to sing, "Happy Birthday, Mr. President" on *The Presidential Birthday Bash* for John F. Kennedy. First Lady Jacqueline Kennedy reveals the White House treasures on *The White House Tour*, a special broadcast by ABC, CBS and NBC.

1964. John F. Kennedy's book, *Profiles in Courage*, is made into an NBC TV series of the same name. The syndicated *Decisions: The Conflicts of Harry S. Truman*, covers historic events of the Truman years in Washington. Former President Dwight D. Eisenhower chats with newsman Eric Severeid about suggested changes on presidential succession procedures on *CBS Reports: The Crisis in Presidential Succession*. On the CBS special *D-*

Day Plus 20, Walter Cronkite accompanies Dwight D. Eisenhower as he returns to Normandy to recall the invasion that took place 20 years earlier during World War II.

1966. President Lyndon B. Johnson conducts a tour of his Texas ranch on the special *Lyndon B. Johnson's Texas*.

1970. President Richard M. Nixon appears on *Rowan and Martin's Laugh-In* (and even says the show's historic catch phrase, "Sock It to Me").

1971. Governor Ronald Reagan appears as a guest on *The Carol Burnett Show* (CBS).

1972. Governor Ronald Reagan appears on *The Sonny and Cher Comedy Hour* and *The Tonight Show Starring Johnny Carson*.

1973. President Richard Nixon appears on the special, *The American Film Institute Salute to John Ford*.

1974. Governor Ronald Reagan appears on the special, *The American Film Institute Salute to James Cagney*.

1977. President Richard Nixon appears on *The David Frost Interviews*. President Elect Jimmy Carter and Vice President Walter Mondale are saluted on CBS's *Inaugural Eve Gala Performance*.

1981. President Ronald Reagan appears in a pre-taped message on *The 53rd Academy Awards* presentation. Ronald Reagan and his wife Nancy appear on *The Kennedy Center Honors: A Celebration of the Performing Arts* (also on the 1982, 83, 84, 85, 86, 87 and 1988 broadcasts). Ronald Reagan appears as himself on *NBC White Paper: The First Hundred Days*, which examines his first four months in office. Former President Gerald R. Ford appears on *Bob Hope's All Star Celebration: The Opening of the Gerald R. Ford Presidential Museum*.

1983. Former President Gerald Ford and his wife appear in a cameo at a carousel ball on ABC's *Dynasty*.

1982. President Ronald Reagan and First Lady Nancy Reagan appear on *Christmas in Washington*, a celebration of the holidays from the White House (also on the 1983, 84, 85, 86, 87 and 1988 broadcasts).

1986. Ronald Reagan is honored on *The All Star Party for Dutch Reagan*. Former President Lyndon B. Johnson dances on the TV special *Madonna: The Virgin Tour*.

1987. President Ronald Reagan and his wife Nancy appear on *In Performance at the White House*, a PBS special celebrating the music of Richard Rogers and Lorenz Hart.

1988. Ronald Reagan appears on the TV special *America's Tribute to Bob Hope*. The special *In Performance at the White House* salutes Broadway with an appearance by Ronald and Nancy Reagan.

1989. President George H. W. Bush. and his wife Barbara appear on *Christmas in Washington* (also on the 1989, 90, 91, 92, 93 and 1994 broadcasts). Ronald Reagan appears on the TV special *The Disney-M-G-M Studio's Theme Park Opening*. Newly elected President George H. W. Bush and his wife Barbara are given a lavish party on CBS's *Presidential Inaugural Gala*.

1992. Bill Clinton appears on *The Arsenio Hall Show* (playing his saxophone).

1993. The TV special *Bob Hope: The First 90 Years* features appearances by Ronald Reagan and Richard Nixon. Show business celebrities honor newly elected President Bill Clinton and his wife Hillary on CBS's *Presidential Inaugural Gala*.

1994. Gerald Ford appears on the TV special *A Gala for the President at Ford's Theater*.

1995. Ronald Reagan is interviewed on *Inside the White House* and makes a guest appearance on the syndicated documentary series *The History of Rock and Roll* (Episode 6: "My Generation").

1996. George W. Bush appears on the TV special *Vote for Me: Politics in America*.

2000. George W. Bush appears on *A&E Biography: Son Also Rises* and on *Saturday Night Live: Presidential Bash 2000*.

2002. George W. Bush and his wife Laura appear on *The Kennedy Center Honors: A Celebration of the Performing Arts*.

2003. The National Geographic special, *The FBI: 100 Years of Hope and Honor* features an appearance by George W. Bush.

2004. Former Presidents Bill Clinton and Jimmy Carter appear on the political satire series *Tanner on Tanner*. George W. Bush and his wife Laura appear on *The Kennedy Center Honors: A Celebration of the Performing Arts*.

Priests see *Religious Characters*

Prison

This entry chronicles the programs set at a prison (includes characters who work as parole officers).

1950. Paul Kelly plays Clinton T. Duffy, the warden of San Quentin Prison in California, on the pilot *Warden Duffy of San Quentin*. The program was set to focus on life inside the prison.

1956. Pat O'Brien plays Pat Duggan, a parole chief who strives to help rehabilitate young parolees just out of prison on the NBC pilot *Parole Chief*.

1963. Sam Morrison (Robert Webber) is a warden with liberal ideas who is attempting to bring modern techniques to the prison system on the pilot *The Warden*.

1965. Colonel Robert Hogan (Bob Crane) heads a group of World War II Allied prisoners being held captive in Germany at Stalag 13 on CBS's *Hogan's Heroes*.

1967. The success of *Hogan's Heroes* led NBC to develop a pilot called *Campo 44*, a World War II comedy about the American and British prisoners of war. Philip Abbott and Jim Dawson star.

1975. Wilbur Poindexter (Logan Ramsey) is the warden of Alamesa State Minimum Security Prison on ABC's *On the Rocks*. Tony LoBianco plays Pete Mackey, an ex-con who serves as a paraprofessional deputy parole agent while on parole himself on the NBC pilot *A Shadow in the Streets*.

1980. A harsh view of life in a women's prison (the Wentworth Detention Center) in Melbourne, Australia, is presented on the syndicated *Prisoner: Cell Block H*. Erica Davidson (Patsy King) is the Warden. *Willow B: Women in Prison* is an ABC pilot about life in a women's prison (the El Camino Institution for Women). Norma Donaldson plays the warden, Mrs. McCallister.

1982. Andy Driscoll (James Naughton) is a street wise, caring Boston parole officer on the CBS pilot *Parole*. Eddie Murphy (Michael Keaton) is a parole officer with the Department of Correction and Rehabilitation who believes in a psychological approach to dealing with his charges on CBS's *Report to Murphy*.

1985. Stephen Elliott plays Robert McShane, warden of the Riverdale Correctional Facility, and Jean Smart is his deputy warden, Dr. Allison Brody, on HBO's *Maximum Security*.

1987. Ned Sheffield (John Getz) is the Deputy Superintendent of a large maximum-security prison in the small community of Mariah on ABC's *Mariah*. A comical look at prison life is seen through the eyes of Vicki Springer (Julia Campbell), an inmate (convicted of shop lifting) at the Bass Women's Prison in Wisconsin on *Women in Prison* (Fox).

1989. Lorraine Toussaint plays Cheryl Woolrich, the warden of *Camp California* (ABC pilot), the nickname for a posh, minimum-security prison for white-collar criminals.

1991. A look at life in a women's prison called *Women's State Prison* is seen on the syndicated *Dangerous Women*. The large cast includes Katherine Justice, Lynn Hamilton and Melanie Vincz as prisoners Rita Jones, Cissie Johnson and Crystal Fox.

1997. A gritty, harsh look at life in a men's prison is presented on *Oz*, an HBO series set at the Oswald State Penitentiary. Among the prisoners (in a very large cast) are Granville Adams as Zahir Arif, J.K. Simmons as Vernon Wangler and Steven Wishnoff as Tony Masters.

2005. In a plot twist on normal prison dramas, Michael Scofield (Wentworth Miller) gets himself arrested (bank robbery) and sent to the Fox River State Prison to break his brother, Lincoln Burrows (Dominic Purcell), out of prison (and save him from Death Row) on Fox's *Prison Break*. Second season episodes focus on Michael and Lincoln as fugitives when they escape from prison.

Prostitutes

This entry chronicles the programs on which prostitutes (or hookers, ladies of the evening or call girls) are regularly featured characters. Single episode appearances (such as Mary Beth Lacey and Chris Cagney posing as hookers to catch a killer on *Cagney and Lacey*) are excluded.

1972. Lesley Ann Warren plays Mae, an Old West lady of the evening who poses as one of *The Daughters of Joshua Cabe* (ABC pilot) to help a fur trapper win a homesteading claim.

1974. Conchata Ferrell and Jeannie Linero play April and Suzy, prostitutes who reside in a decaying Maryland residence called *Hot l Baltimore* (ABC; the *e* in the hotel sign has burned out).

1975. Brooke Adams takes over the role of Mae, the lady of the evening hired by fur trapper Joshua Cabe to pose as one of his daughters on the ABC pilot *The Daughters of Joshua Cabe Return* (this time to win the title to a farm).

Bernadette Peters plays the beautiful but not-too-bright Doris, a model turned actress who often sells her body for money (she hates being called a hooker) on the NBC pilot *The Owl and the Pussycat*.

1979. Dena Dietrich plays Billie Barkley, a former madam seeking to reestablish her relationship with her estranged daughter, Sharon (Amy Johnston) on the NBC pilot *But Mother!*

1980. Margaret Laurance plays Anne Mason, a fashion model arrested for prostitution and now serving time at the Wentworth Women's Detention Center in Australia on the syndicated *Prisoner: Cell Block H*.

1981. Stella Stevens plays Lute Mae Sanders, a high priced call girl who runs Lute Mae's, a brothel in Truro County on NBC's *Flamingo Road*. Cristina Raines plays Lane Ballou, Lute Mae's top girl. Jesse Wells is Gwen, the prostitute Danny Dallas falls for on *Soap* (ABC).

1982. Maggie McCulloch (Priscilla Barnes) is a doctor and the owner of a brothel in the lawless (1860s) town of Sweetwater, Missouri, on the ABC pilot *The Wild Women of Chastity Gulch*. Maggie inherited the brothel and its prostitutes from her late aunt. Phyllis Elizabeth Davis and Morgan Brittany play the main prostitutes, Sugar and Laine.

1987. Mamie Van Doren plays Minnie, the owner of a brothel on HBO's comedy series, *The Glory Years* (Donna Denton plays Gina, Minnie's top call girl). Antoinette Byron plays Bonnie Harper, a lesbian who is also a prostitute (now serving time in jail for soliciting) on Fox's *Women in Prison*.

1988. Karen Colosky (Marg Helgenberger), who prefers to be called K.C., is a high priced call girl ($100 an hour) in Vietnam at the time of the war on ABC's *China Beach* (the armed forces rest and recreation facility). Milla Jovovich plays TV's youngest prostitute, the gorgeous 13-year-old Katie Hamilton on CBS's *Paradise* (Katie was raised by her mother, Sarah, the owner of Zack's Traveling Social Club, to become a high-priced prostitute — an idea, borrowed in part, from Brooke Shields' 1977 feature film *Pretty Baby*).

1991. Crystal Fox (Melanie Vincz) is a blonde, 24-year-old prostitute addicted to wearing miniskirts (and arrested many times for soliciting) on the syndicated *Dangerous Women*. Romy Walthall plays Rita, receptionist to Congressman Jim Doyle on NBC's *Man of the People*. Rita is a prostitute (arrested several times) and trying to give up her old lifestyle.

1992. Jade O'Keefe (Lisa Hartman) is a stunning, high priced call girl who is trying to turn her life around on CBS's *2000 Malibu Road* (the address of a house she shares with two girlfriends).

1993. Gigi Rice plays Carlie Watkins, a gorgeous, high priced prostitute ($300 a night) whose "office" is the Rain Check Room Bar in St. Louis on *The John Larroquette Show* (NBC). Jennifer Tilly plays Savannah Summer, a beautiful high priced prostitute ($100 an hour) who is proud of what she does ("It was a lifelong dream of mine since childhood") on Fox's *Key West*.

2001. Veronica (Enya Flack), better known as Tender Lovin',' is a streetwalker trying to turn her life around as the owner of a fashion boutique on *Black Scorpion* (Sci Fi). Inara Sera (Morena Baccaren) is a futuristic prostitute (called a companion). She is a member of the *Serenity*, a Firefly class transport vehicle, and acts as the ship's ambassador to open the door of communication between the various planets on Fox's *Firefly*.

Psychiatrists

This entry lists the programs that star or feature characters as psychiatrists, psychologists or psychotherapists. See also *Doctors, Women — Nurses*.

1952. Dr. Karen Gayle (Patricia Morison, Lynn Roberts) is a Manhattan based psychiatrist who assists private detective Eddie Drake (Don Haggerty) to acquire material for a book she is writing on abnormal human behavior on *The Cases of Eddie Drake* (DuMont). Psychologist Lee Graham hosts an advice program presented in a manner that is understandable to the layman on *A Letter to Lee Graham*.

1955. Thomas Wilson (Steve Dunne) is a child psychologist with a knack for solving the problems of children other than his own on CBS's *Professional Father*.

1958. Psychologist Dr. Joyce Brothers comes to TV in 1958 with her first advice series, *Dr. Joyce Brothers* over New York station WRCA (now WNBC). Her informal look into the world of psychology and discussions on the problems that confront many people were presented in terms that could be understood by the layman. Her other series (all syndicated): *Consult Dr. Brothers* (1961), *Tell Me, Dr. Brothers* (1964), *Appointment with Dr. Brothers* (1969) and *Living Easy* (1973).

1962. Theodore Bassett, Paul Graham and L. Richard Starke (Wendell Corey, Jack Ging, Ralph Bellamy) are New York based psychiatrists on NBC's *The Eleventh Hour*.

1963. Eduard Franz plays Dr. Edward Raymer, director of the psychiatric clinic at York Hospital in Los Angeles on ABC's *Breaking Point*.

1964. Roger Corder (Herbert Lom) is a London based psychiatrist who incorporates the newest techniques to help people in deep emotional distress on *The Human Jungle* (Syn.).

1968. Dr. Frank Chandler (Carl Betz) is the head of the Crisis Clinic of the Los Angeles Board of Welfare, an around-the-clock psychiatric service on the CBS pilot *Crisis*.

1970. Vince Edwards plays Matt Lincoln, a psychiatrist who practices preventive psychiatry (treating a patient before deep emotional problems arise) on ABC's *Matt Lincoln* (in the pilot film, *Dial Hot Line*, Vince Edwards plays the role as Dr. David Leopold). Louis Jourdan plays David Sorell, a psychiatrist who investigates crimes involving the supernatural on the NBC pilot *Ritual of Evil*.

1971. James Whitman (Roy Thinnes) is a young Los Angeles psychiatrist who practices the new but controversial techniques of therapy on NBC's *The Psychiatrist*.

1972. Bob Newhart plays Dr. Robert Hartley, a Chicago based psychologist on *The Bob Newhart Show* (CBS). Allan Arbus plays the recurring role of Major Sidney Freedman, the U.S. Army psychiatrist who finds the staff of the 4077 Mobile Army Surgical Hospital (in Korea during the war) a gold mine of psychological problems on CBS's *M*A*S*H*. The session between psychiatrist Paul Bernard (Chris Wiggins) and his female patients is seen on a daily basis on *Paul Bernard—Psychiatrist* (Syn.).

1977. Zohra Lambert plays Dr. Sarah Allgood, a psychiatrist who, like her name, tries to help people as a member of the Rosewood State Psychiatric Center on the ABC pilot *Mixed Nuts*.

1978. Dr. Stephen Strange (Peter Hooten) is a psychiatrist at New York's Eastside Hospital who is also a sorcerer capable of controlling the elements of the universe on the CBS fantasy pilot *Doctor Strange*. David McKay (Robert Reed) is a former vice squad detective turned private practice psychiatrist who teaches psychology at Westwood University in Los Angeles and is devoted to helping children and teenagers in trouble on NBC's *Operation: Runaway*.

1979. Steve Arizzio (Alan Feinstein) is a Los Angeles-based psychologist who specializes in tracking down runaway children on NBC's *The Runaways*.

1982. Paul Williams plays Brewster Steele, a rather short, unorthodox psychologist with the L.A.P.D., who is nicknamed *Rooster* (ABC pilot). Carrie Jessup (Karen Valentine) is a clinical psychologist (at the Willow View Home for Children) who uses her dog, Skeezer, as a therapeutic aid on the NBC pilot *Skeezer*.

1983. Frasier Crane (Kelsey Grammer) is a psychiatrist who is also a regular at the Boston bar *Cheers* (NBC; the character was later spun-off into his own show, *Frasier*. See 1993). Frasier was married to Lilith Sternin (Bebe Neuwirth), a psychiatrist at Boston Memorial Hospital.

1984. Sex therapist Dr. Ruth Westheimer offers advice to couples and singles on the syndicated *Dr. Ruth* Jessica Hayden (Lindsay Wagner) is a beautiful police psychiatrist with the Behavioral Science Department of the Metro Division of the San Francisco P.D. on ABC's *Jessie*.

1985. Alan Thicke plays Jason Seaver, a psychiatrist who moves his practice from Long Island General Hospital to his home on ABC's *Growing Pains*. Kate and Elliott Weston (Beth Howland, Geoffrey Bowes) are a neurotic married couple that share a psychiatric practice on the ABC pilot *It Takes Two*. Jane Lucas (Lucie Arnaz) is a psychologist that hosts a radio call-in advice program on *The Lucie Arnaz Show* (CBS). Psychiatrist Joseph Braeden (Mike Farrell) and psychoanalyst Elizabeth Bolger (Maureen Stapleton) are doctors who share adjoining offices in Manhattan on the NBC pilot *Private Sessions*.

1988. Marie Teller (Michael Learned), Sam Garrison (Josef Sommer) and Art Makter (Michael Jeter) are doctors attached to the Garrison Center Psychiatric Clinic on ABC's *Hothouse*. Ellen Ludlow (Nancy Youngblut) is a futuristic psychiatrist who has been assigned to *Mars: Base One* (CBS pilot) to help homesick earthlings adjust to life on another planet.

1989. Brooke Adams plays Meg Robbins, a gorgeous, single psychologist who hosts a daily radio call-in advice program in Chicago on the ABC pilot *A Girl's Life*. Abigail McIntyre (Mary

4

Gross) is a psychiatrist in Covington, a small town whose major industry is eggs, on the CBS pilot *The People Next Door*.

1990. Dr. Ruth Westheimer plays Dr. Ruth Engelhof, a psychology professor at Blake University on the ABC pilot *Dr. Ruth's House*. Doug Lambert (Martin Mull) and his ex-wife Regina Hewitt (Stephanie Faracy) are psychologists who counsel married couples in adjoining offices on *His and Hers* (CBS).

1993. Frasier Crane (Kelsey Grammer) is a psychiatrist who hosts "The Frasier Crane Show," a radio call-in advice program in Seattle on NBC's *Frasier*. David Hyde Pierce plays Niles Crane, Frasier's brother, a private practice psychiatrist. Christine Winters (Sydney Walsh) and Steven Mitchell (Richard Lewis) are rival psychologists who share a Manhattan office on Fox's *Daddy Dearest*. Barbara Eden plays Jesse Newman, a widowed psychotherapist who possesses a paranormal power of perception that entangles her in homicide investigations on the NBC pilot *Visions of Murder*. A second pilot aired in 1994 (*Visions of Murder II*).

1992. Norman Lloyd plays Dr. Frederick Marcus, a psychiatrist whose brief counseling sessions with the dysfunctional Kramer family precedes each episode of NBC's *Home Fires*.

1994. Dr. Brian McKenzie (Brian Dennehy) is the Chief of Psychiatry at Riverside Hospital in Essex County on ABC's *Birdland*.

1995. Susan Gardner (Mia Cottet) is a psychotherapist who lives in Beverly Hills, shares an apartment with two girlfriends and fears growing older on the WB's *First Time Out*.

1996. Louie Anderson plays Louie Lundregan, a mishap prone psychoanalyst on *The Louie Show* (CBS). Rachel Corrigan (Helen Shaver) is a psychologist who tries to explain the unnatural as a member of the San Francisco Legacy House on *Poltergeist: The Legacy* (Showtime/Sci Fi).

1999. B.D. Wong plays George Huang, a psychiatrist with the N.Y.P.D. on NBC's *Law and Order: Criminal Intent*.

2002. Psychologist Phil McGraw offers advice to singles, engaged and married couples on the syndicated *Dr. Phil*. Peggy Fowler (Rae Dawn Chong) is a psychiatrist who assists Declan Dunn (Adrian Pasdar), a man who investigates so-called miracles, on *Mysterious Ways* (PAX).

Psychics see *Mediums*

Puerto Rican Performers and Characters

This entry contains the programs on which a Puerto Rican actor is the star or a featured regular. See also *Cuban American Performers and Characters; Latino Performers and Characters; Mexican American Performers and Characters*.

1967. Alejandro Rey plays Carlos Ramirez, a wealthy playboy who owns the Casino Carlos, a discotheque in San Juan, Puerto Rico on *The Flying Nun* (ABC).

1972. Gregory Sierra plays Julio Fuentes, junk dealer Fred Sanford's neighbor on NBC's *Sanford and Son*. A young Puerto Rican boy named Santiago (Reuben Figueroa) sets out to build a ship and sail it on the lake in New York's Central Park on the ABC special *Santiago's Ark*.

1973. Carmen Lopez (Carmen Zapata) is a widow who works as the housekeeper to a rich Bel Air, California, family (the owners of the Stuffy Toy Company) on the ABC pilot *Carmen*.

1974. Jose and Raul (Jose Perez, Raul Julia) are the fumbling owners of the Ace Moving and Hauling Service on the CBS pilot *Aces Up*. Singer Tony Orlando and his backup group Dawn (Telma Hopkins, Joyce Vincent Wilson) perform on the CBS variety series *Tony Orlando and Dawn*.

1975. Chano Amenguale (Gregory Sierra) is a detective with the 12th Precinct of the N.Y.P.D. on ABC's *Barney Miller*. Hector Fuentes (Jose Perez) is an inmate at the Alamessa Minimum Security Prison on ABC's *On the Rocks*. Jeremiah Salt (Mel Stewart) is black and the owner of a window washing service. His daughter, Nadine (Sharon Brown) is married to Pepe (Frank LaLoggia), a Puerto Rican Jeremiah dislikes for marrying his daughter, but whom he takes on as a partner on the CBS pilot *Salt and Pepe*. Young Santiago (Ruben Figueroa) from the 1972 special *Santiago's Ark* journeys from New York to California by car to become the New York delegate at the Young American Continental Congress on the ABC special *Santiago's America*.

1976. Liz Torres joins the cast of *All in the*

Family (CBS) as Teresa Betancourt, a nurse who becomes a boarder in the home of Archie and Edith Bunker. Rosa Dolores (Rita Moreno) is a young woman with a dream of becoming a star in Hollywood on the ABC pilot *I'll Never Forget What's Her Name*. Abraham "Popi" Rodriguez (Hector Elizando) is a widower, working as a handyman and raising two sons on CBS's *Popi*.

1978. Gregory Sierra plays Tony Menzies, the head of the poorly equipped Adult Emergency Services Hospital on Hudson Street in New York City on ABC's *A.E.S. Hudson Street*. Panchito Gomez plays Gaucho Campos, an errand boy who is saving his money to help his mother fulfill a dream of leaving New York's Barrio and returning to Puerto Rico on the ABC special *Gaucho*. Rita Moreno plays Marie Costanza, the owner of a Pennsylvania hotel fraught with problems on the CBS pilot *The Rita Moreno Show*.

1979. Jose and Raul (Abraham Alvarez, Joe Rosario) are the bus boys hired by bar owner Archie Bunker on CBS's *Archie Bunker's Place*. Alfonso Ribiero plays Willie, a 12-year-old boy living in Harlem on *Oye, Willie* (PBS)

1980. Dan Delgado, nicknamed "the Bean" (Hector Elizondo), and Tom "Freebie" Walker (Tom Mason) are police sergeants who work for the San Francisco D.A. on *Freebie and the Bean* (CBS). Ginny Ramirez (Maria O'Brien) is a young woman who lives in an apartment complex at Number 96 Pacific Way in Los Angeles and hoping for a career in show business on NBC's *Number 96*.

1981. Trinidad Silva plays Jesus Martinez, gang leader of the Diablos in the worst neighborhood of an unnamed city on NBC's *Hill Street Blues*. Despite the large cast, there are no Puerto Rican police officers (Rene Enriquez, who plays Officer Ray Calletano, is Colombian, not Puerto Rican).

1982. Coco Hernandez (Erica Gimpel) is a hopeful singer and dancer who attends the High School for the Performing Arts in New York City on NBC's *Fame*. When the series left NBC for syndication in 1983, Jesse Borrego joined the cast as hopeful dancer Jesse Valesquez.

1983. Luis Avalos and Yvonne Wilder play Jesse and Linda Rodriquez, an Hispanic couple on ABC's *Condo*. Corporal Grace Pavlik (Rachel Ticotin) and Private Georgio Lucas (Eddie Velez) are military personnel with the peacetime Army's 88th Airborne Division at Fort Geller in Texas on NBC's *For Love and Honor*. Jose Perez plays An-

tonio Perez, an inspector with the Homicide Division of the San Francisco P.D. on the NBC pilot *Inspector Perez*.

1984. Paul Rodriguez plays Paul Rivera, known as Pablo to his family, who is struggling to make his mark as a standup comedian on *A.K.A. Pablo* (ABC). Joe Santos and Katy Juardo play his parents, Domingo and Rosa Maria Rivera. Jose Perez plays God, who appears as steambath attendant Morty, on the Showtime series *Steambath* (sort of a purgatory where souls wait before moving on).

1985. Tony Orlando plays Tony Castillo, a social worker at the Keystone Community Center in Brooklyn, New York, on the NBC pilot *The Center*. Ada Maris plays Tony's girlfriend, Selena Cruz.

1986. Hector Martinez (Robert Beltran) is a former gang member who, after becoming a lawyer, returns to his old neighborhood to help its people on the CBS pilot *The Family Martinez*. Rosana DeSoto plays Diana Olmos, the waitress at Al's Grill, an inner city eatery and newsstand on *The Redd Foxx Show*. Rita Moreno plays Rita Barnes, a businesswoman who operates Rita's Toys from her Manhattan apartment on the CBS pilot *Rita*. Ricardo Sanchez is a clothing salesman who moves his family from the Los Angeles Barrio to posh Bel Air on *Sanchez of Bel Air* (USA).

1987. Renee and George Corliss (Rita Moreno, Paul Dooley) are a middle-aged couple seeking a new meaning to life after their children leave home on the NBC pilot *Empty Nest*. Geraldo Rivera hosts *Geraldo,* a daily syndicated discussion series. Richard Yniquez plays Jesse Guerrera, a detective with the L.A.P.D. on ABC's *Ohara*. Ramon Franco plays Alberto Ruiz and Miguel A. Nunez, Jr., is Marcus Taylor, soldiers with Bravo Company on a 12-month tour of Vietnam on CBS's *Tour of Duty*.

1988. The CBS series *Trial and Error* follows the lives of two friends: John Hernandez (Eddie Velez), a lawyer, and Tony Rivera (Paul Rodriguez), a street schemer.

1989. Chantal Rivera-Batisse plays Melissa Santos, a beautiful but conceited student at Marvel High School on NBC's *Ann Jillian*. Rita Moreno plays Kimberly, the ex-wife of private detective B.L. Stryker (Burt Reynolds) who is now married to the wealthy but elderly Clayton Baskin (Abe Vigoda) on ABC's *B.L. Stryker*. Joe Lala plays Cito Escobar, a Puerto Rican cab driver who is married to Eleanor (Lela Ivey), the Caucasian daughter of crusty radio show host Everett Daye (Mason Adams) on NBC's *Knight and Daye*.

1990. Pedro Gomez (Paul Rodriguez) is a bounty hunter who works for Aztec Bail Bonds on *Grand Slam* (CBS). Abel Franco plays Pedro's boss, Al Ramirez.

1991. Maria Trent (Maria Rangel) is a Puerto Rican high school teacher and battered wife who killed her abusive husband and is now serving time in prison on the syndicated *Dangerous Women*. Geraldo Rivera hosts *Now It Can Be Told*, a syndicated interview/discussion series. Rita Moreno is Alexandra Stone, manager of the Rolling Hills Country Club in Chicago on *Top of the Heap* (Fox).

1992. Gaby Fernandez (Mayteana Morales) and her brother Alex (David Lopez) are the Puerto Rican members of the grammar school kids who solve mysteries with the help of an entity named *Ghost Writer* (PBS).

1994. Rita Moreno plays Angie Corea, the housekeeper to Guy Hanks (Bill Cosby), a forensic scientist with the N.Y.P.D. on *The Cosby Mysteries* (NBC). Lisa Vidal plays Lt. Sandy Lopez of the Chicago Fire Department on NBC's *ER*. Eddie Torres (Michael DeLorenzo) and Nina Moreno (Lauren Velez) are detectives with the Fourth Precinct of the N.Y.P.D. on Fox's *New York Undercover*. Lisa Vidal plays Eddie's wife, Carmen, on the series.

1996. Movie and TV special effects artist Rollie Tyler (Cameron Daddo) uses trickery to help the police nab felons, receiving help from Angie Ramirez (Christina Cox) on the syndicated *FX: The Series*.

1997. Lili Arquelo (Rosalyn Sanchez) is a young woman struggling to make her dream of becoming a dancer a reality on the syndicated *Fame — L.A.*

1998. Luis Antonio Ramos plays Billy Hernandez, a weatherman on a local Los Angeles TV news show anchored by Brian Benben on CBS's *The Brian Benben Show*.

1999. Rosalyn Sanchez plays Kim Veras, a young Philadelphia police woman on Fox's *Ryan Caulfield: Year One*. Lisa Vidal plays Sandra Morales, a paramedic with Squad 55 of the New York City Fire Department on NBC's *Third Watch*.

2000. The adventures of the young Garcia brothers, Larry (Alvin Alvarez), George (Bobby Gonzalez) and Carlos (Jeffrey Licon) are depicted on Nickelodeon's *The Brothers Garcia*

2001. Magda Ramirez (Lisa Vidal) is a police woman with the Central Division of the San Francisco P.D. on Lifetime's *The Division*. Taina Morales (Christina Vidal) is a teenager at the Manhattan School of the Arts on *Taina* (NICK).

2003. Luis Gus plays Luis, the owner of Park Avenue Donuts in East Harlem on Fox's *Luis*. Diana-Maria Riva plays his ex-wife, Isabella, and Jacqueline DeSantis is their daughter, Marlena.

2005. Lizette Carrion is Esmeralda DelRio, a private in Iraq during the war on *Over There* (TNT).

2006. Jimmy Smits is the nation's first Hispanic President, Matthew Santos, on *The West Wing* (NBC).

Puppets and Marionettes

This entry lists the programs that star or feature puppets, dummies (wooden), marionettes and ventriloquists. See also *Children's Programs*.

1931. CBS airs TV's first puppet program, *Punch and Judy* (about a henpecked husband who is constantly battered by his domineering wife).

1944. On June 6th the National Peanut Council aired *The Peanut Is a Serious Guy* on DuMont to promote the nutritional value of the peanut. The story finds Mr. Peanut (a double jointed peanut puppet) asking the program's host [Maria Gambarelli] to revise the peanut's image so it is not thought of as a circus and ballgame snack). To do so, two recipes were given — for a peanut milk shake and a peanut cake.

1945. Ventriloquist Shirley Reid and her dummy Bedelia (who portrays Shirley's younger sister) star on *Bedelia*, a CBS test program that revolves around the antics of the mischievous Bedelia.

1947. The puppet Howdy Doody and his human assistant Buffalo Bob Smith operate a circus in Doodyville on NBC's *Howdy Doody*. Other puppets include Phineas T. Bluster, the Flubadub and Dilly Dally. Fran Allison is the host and Burr Tillstrom the puppeteer and voice actor on *Kukla, Fran and Ollie* (NBC/ABC), a children's series set at the Kuklapolitan Theater. Puppets include Ollie the Dragon, Kukla the boy, Beulah Witch and

Mercedes Rabbit. Ventriloquist Paul Winchell and his dummy friends Jerry Mahoney and Knucklehead Smiff host *Winchell and Mahoney*, an NBC children's series set at Jerry Mahoney's Club House.

1948. Wendy Barrie and her puppet assistant, Oky Doky, host game contests for children and performances by juvenile artists on *The Adventures of Oky Doky* (DuMont). Hope and Morey Bunin provide the puppet voices on *Lucky Pup*, a CBS series about an evil magician (Foodini) and his efforts to acquire the $5 million inheritance of a dog (Lucky Pup). The puppet Oky Doky appears on *Tots, Tweens and Teens*, television's first infomercial (or paid programming), a thirty-minute plug for Macy's Department Stores' 1948 fall line of clothes for children and teenagers. Ventriloquist Jimmy Nelson and his dummy Danny O'Day, appear as regulars on *Texaco Star Theater* (NBC, with Milton Berle as the host) and also in costume (gas station attendants) as pitchmen for Texaco Gasoline.

1949. Ventriloquist Shirley Dinsdale and her dummy Judy Splinters, host *Judy Splinters*, an NBC series that relates the antics of the very mischievous Judy Splinters. Jimmy Scribner plays Sleepy Joe, a lovable Uncle Remus type of character whose stories to a young girl (Gayle Scribner) are seen performed by puppets on ABC's *Sleepy Joe*. Spanish ventriloquist Senor Wences appears regularly on *The Milton Berle Show* (NBC) and *Toast of the Town* (CBS) with his two most famous puppets: Johnny (painted on his closed fist. Eyes are painted on the index finger; a mouth on the thumb) and Pedro, the head in a box ("Are you all right Pedro," Senor would ask. "S'alright," Pedro would respond).

1950. Ross Jones provides the voice of Cyclone Malone, a fearless western hero (puppet) on *The Adventures of Cyclone Malone* (Syn.). Ventriloquist Al Robinson and his dummy, Alkali Ike, host a program of puppet antics on CBS's *Alkali Ike*. Buffalo Billy is a young adventurer (puppet) who journeys west with a wagon train on *The Buffalo Billy Show* (CBS). Ventriloquist Edgar Bergen and his wooden pals, Charlie McCarthy and Mortimer Snerd, attempt to bring their popular radio program to TV on the CBS pilot *The Charlie McCarthy Show* (which revolves around Charlie's antics). Newton Figg (marionette) is the kindly proprietor of a general store in Figg Center on ABC's *Hold 'er Newt*. The Bil and Cora Baird Puppets star on *Life with Snarky Parker*, a CBS series about Deputy Sheriff Snarky Parker and his

efforts to maintain the law in the town of Hot Rock (Heathcliffe is his horse). Helen York is the voice of Paddy, a pelican puppet whose adventures unfold through comic strip drawings on ABC's *Paddy the Pelican*. Yarns told by Johnny Coons and ventriloquist Jennifer Holt and her life-size dummy Panhandle Pete, unfold in a cartoon story format on NBC's *Panhandle Pete and Jennifer*. Paul Winchell and his dummy pal Jerry Mahoney host *The Paul Winchell and Jerry Mahoney Show*, an NBC series for children set at the Jerry Mahoney Club. The freckle-faced little boy Rootie Kazootie (puppet) welcomes children to his clubhouse on NBC's *Rootie Kazootie*. Todd Russell hosts and other puppets include Gala Poochie Pup, El Squeako the Mouse and Polka Dottie, Rootie's girlfriend. The mischievous Froggie the Gremlin, a rubber frog toy that is often mistaken for a puppet, appears on NBC's *Smilin' Ed McConnell and His Buster Brown Gang* (later with Andy Devine as the host on *Andy's Gang*). A young boy named Beany and his pet sea serpent Cecil find adventure with Captain Horatio, skipper of the boat *Leakin' Lena* on the syndicated puppet series *Time for Beany* (the animated *Beany and Cecil Show* appeared in 1961). The lives of the puppets that live on Candy Cane Lane in a magical wonderland are seen on ABC's *Uncle Mistletoe and His Adventures*.

1951. Patches, an orphaned hobo boy, and his friend Wacky Rabbit (puppets) find excitement on the road on *The Adventures of Patches* (Syn.). The mishaps of the evil magician Foodini and his assistant Pinhead unfold on the puppet series *Foodini the Great* (ABC). Electronic marionettes perform on *Ozmoe*, an ABC series about a monkey (Ozmoe), a leprechaun (Roderick Dhon't), a mermaid (Misty Waters), a caterpillar (Horatio), Throckmorton the Sea Serpent and Sam the Clam. CBS's *The Whistling Wizard* follows the adventures of a young boy (J.P.) who falls into an enchanted well and reappears in the fantasy kingdom of the Land of Beyond.

1952. While walking through an enchanted forest, a young boy (Blinky) is transformed into a marionette and transported to a land of puppets on *The Adventures of Blinky*, a syndicated series that follows his efforts to become human again. The antics of Jimmy Morton, the dummy of ventriloquist Skeets Minton, are showcased on CBS's *All Aboard*. Police detective Fearless Fosdick upholds the law on NBC's *Fearless Fosdick*, a puppet series based on the character created by Al Capp. Willie the Worm, the puppet of ventriloquist Warren Wright, hosts 1920s and 30s theatrical comedy shorts on *Junior High Jinks* (CBS). The Miles Laboratories figure Speedy Alka Seltzer (red hair, blue eyes, Alka Seltzer mid section) becomes an advertising icon with the slogan "Plop plop, fizz fizz, oh what a relief it is." The ads ended in 1964. Paul Winchell and Jerry Mahoney host *What's My Name*, an NBC game wherein players have to guess the name of a famous celebrity from clues provided by Paul and Jerry.

1953. Ventriloquist Jimmy Nelson and Farfel, the dog of his dummy Danny O'Day, star in a series of commercials for Nestle's Chocolate Mix (after the tag line, "Nestle's makes the very best," is said, Farfel responds in a slow voice "Choclate"). The Bil and Cora Baird Puppets are featured on *The Bil Baird Show*, a CBS variety series for children. Miniature musicals are presented on *Bobo Hobo and His Traveling Troupe*, a syndicated series with Brett Morrison as the voice of the puppet Bobo Hobo. Ventriloquist Shari Lewis hosts *Facts 'n' Fun*, a local New York (WNBT) series for children with her hand puppets Lamb Chop and Charlie Horse. Amateur inventor Ernest P. Duckweather (Wright King) communicates with the people (puppets) of Jupiter through interplanetary TV he invented on *Johnny Jupiter* (DuMont/ABC). Puppets include Johnny Jupiter, B-12 and Reject the Robot.

1954. Jimmy Weldon and his talkative duck puppet, Webster Webfoot, host *Funny Boners*, an NBC game in which children perform stunts for prizes. Paul Winchell and Jerry Mahoney host *Jerry Mahoney's Clubhouse*, an NBC program of comedy and games for children. Shari Lewis and her puppets Lamb Chop, Charlie Horse and Hush Puppy star on *Shari and Her Friends*, a local New York (WPIX) series for children. Johnny Coons and his dummy George host stories, old theatrical shorts and skits for children on *Uncle Johnny Coons* (CBS/NBC).

1955. Bob Keeshan is *Captain Kangaroo* (CBS), a kindly man who invites children into the Treasure House for stories, cartoons and sketches. He is assisted by Mr. Green Jeans (Lumpy Brannum) and puppets include Mr. Moose and Mr. Rabbit. Josie Carey is the host and Fred Rogers the puppeteer and voice artist on *The Children's Corner*, a NBC series that uses puppets to instill learning abilities in children. Puppets included King Friday XIII, X the Owl, Daniel S. Tiger, Henrietta the Pussycat and Grandpere the Skunk. Comedian Soupy Sales hosts *The Soupy Sales Show*, an ABC children's program of skits that feature the hand puppets White Fang, Black Tooth (dogs), Pookie the whistling lion, and Hippie the hippopotamus. Paul Winchell and Jerry Mahoney host *Toyland Express*, a children's series on ABC.

1956. Paul Winchell and Jerry Mahoney host *Circus Time*, an ABC series of circus variety acts.

1957. The adventures of an animated clay boy (Gumby) and his horse Pokey, are presented on *Gumby* (NBC). Shari Lewis hosts two series for NBC with her puppets Lamb Chop, Hush Puppy and Charlie Horse: *Shariland* (songs and skits for kids) and *Hi Mom* (advice and entertainment geared to young mothers). Paul Winchell and Jerry Mahoney host the ABC variety series *The Paul Winchell Show*.

1959. Art Carney appears with the Bil and Cora Baird Puppets on two NBC specials: *Art Carney Meets Peter and the Wolf* (May 3rd) and *Art Carney Meets the Sorcerer's Apprentice* (April 5th). ABC's *Willie Wonderful* is a puppet series about a young boy who travels with a circus.

1960. Frank Freda plays Diver Dan, a fearless ocean explorer who protects the good fish (puppets) from the evil Baron Barracuda and his sidekick Trigger Fish on the syndicated *Diver Dan*. Shari Lewis, Lamb Chop and Charlie Horse host a program of entertainment geared to children on NBC's *The Shari Lewis Show*. Paul Winchell, Jerry Mahoney and Knucklehead Smiff provide entertainment for the small fry at Jerry Mahoney's Clubhouse on ABC's *The Paul Winchell Show*.

1961. The process of Animagic (giving life to marionettes) is used to tell the story of Pinocchio, his father, Gepetto, and friend Jiminy Crickett on the syndicated *New Adventures of Pinocchio*.

1962. A process called Supermarionation (giving life to marionettes) is used for the first time on *Supercar*, a syndicated adventure about Mike Mercury, driver of a futuristic crime-fighting car.

1963. Paul Winchell and Jerry Mahoney host *Cartoonsville*, an ABC series that features "Sheriff Saddle Head," "Goodie the Gremlin" and "Scatt Katt." Steve Zodiak is a member of the futuristic Galaxy Patrol and pilots the space ship *Fireball XL-5*, a syndicated marionette series filmed in Supermarionation. Rowlf, the hound dog Muppet, becomes a regular on the ABC variety series *The Jimmy Dean Show*. Captain Larry Dart and the members of the Galasphere Patrol (marionettes) protect the earth from alien invaders on the syndicated *Planet Patrol*. The Italian mouse puppet Topo Gigio (created and operated in part by Maria Perego) appears almost regularly on *Toast of the Town* (later called *The Ed Sullivan Show*) and converses with host Ed Sullivan.

1964. The Podrecia Piccolli Theater Marionettes provide interpretations of musical masterpieces on *The Colorful World of Music* (Syn.).

1965. The Pillsbury Company introduces (and maintains through the present) the Poppin Fresh Pillsbury Doughboy, a rubber doll-like figure that represents the company's line of refrigerated dough products (from biscuits to cookies). Troy Tempest, a member of the World Aquanaut Security Patrol, is the captain of the submarine *Stingray*, and battles injustice on the syndicated marionette adventure *Stingray*. Paul Winchell and Jerry Mahoney star on *Winchell and Mahoney Time*, a syndicated series of skits and game contests for children.

1966. Soupy Sales hosts *The Soupy Sales Show*, a syndicated series of skits set at Soupy's house and featuring the antics of his two large dogs (seen only as paw puppets) White Fang and Black Tooth.

1967. The marionette series *Captain Scarlet and the Mysterons* presents the adventures of Spectrum agent Captain Scarlet as he battles the evil Mysterons, residents of the planet Mars, who have waged a war on Earth. "Welcome to my neighborhood" is heard for the first time on *Mr. Rogers' Neighborhood*, an NET (then PBS) series with Fred Rogers as the gentle host of a world where everything is fun for children aged three to eight years. Puppets (voiced by Fred) appear alongside the show regulars and guests.

1968. Life-size puppets Fleegle, Bingo, Drooper and Snorky host *The Banana Splits Adventure Hour* (NBC), a series of live action segments and cartoons. Jeff Tracy heads International Rescue, an elaborate organization of search and rescue equipment on the marionette adventure *Thunderbirds* (Syn.).

1969. An array of Sid and Marty Krofft puppets appear on *H.R. Pufnstuf* (NBC/ABC), a fantasy about young Jimmy's (Jack Wild) adventures on Living Island and his battle against the evil Witchiepoo (Billie Hayes). Kermit the Frog, Miss Piggy, the Cookie Monster, Elmo and dozens of other Muppets created by Jim Henson come to

TV on a regular basis on *Sesame Street*, an educational series for children on PBS (originally NET — National Educational Television — stations).

1970. Four human-formed insects (Harmony, Joy, Courage and I.Q.) protect Tranquility Forest from the evil Benita Bizarre (Martha Raye) on *The Bugaloos*, an NBC series featuring the Sid and Marty Krofft Puppets. The success of *Sesame Street* prompts ABC to air the first Muppet TV special, *Tales from Muppetland*. The Muppets recreate the story of "Cinderella" with Kermit the Frog as the storyteller and Belinda J. Montgomery as Cinderella.

1971. Comedian Danny Kaye and puppets brought to life by Animagic combine to present the fairy tale "The Emperor's New Clothes" on the CBS special *The Enchanted World of Danny Kaye*. Paul Winchell and Jerry Mahoney host *Runaround*, an NBC series of game contests for children. Young Mark's (Butch Patrick) adventures in a land of living hats unfold on *Lidsville* (ABC/NBC), a series that features the Sid and Marty Krofft Puppets.

1972. Willie Tyler and his dummy Lester appear on *The Merv Griffin Show* and become regulars on *Rowan and Martin's Laugh-In* (1972) and the hosts of *The ABC Weekend Special* (1981).

1973. Emu, the large puppet bird of ventriloquist Rod Hull, tells of his adventures traveling from Australia to England (where the series was taped) on the syndicated *It's Rod Hull and Emu*.

1974. Sherlock Squirrel and Flap the Bird are the puppets that inhabit *The Magic Garden*, a syndicated series for children hosted by Carole Demas and Paula Janis (and originally broadcast locally in New York on WPIX-TV). Carol Corbett is the host and Rags the puppet her assistant on *The Patchwork Family*, a CBS series broadcast on its owned and operated stations, for children (composed of songs, skits and games). Floyd Vivino and his puppet Oogie host *The Uncle Floyd Show*, a local New Jersey series (WBBT) of outlandish comedy skits aimed more for adults than children. The program had a brief syndicated run in 1982 and left the air in 1986.

1975. Mr. Bill, an-inches tall, down-trodden clay figure, lives in a world where he falls prey to every imaginable pitfall (namely to the squashing of Mr. Hand [Vance DeGeneres, Dave Deirckson]) on NBC's *Saturday Night Live*. In 1986 Peter Scolari played Mr. Bill (in costume) on the HBO pilot *Mr. Bill's Real Life Adventures*. Here Mr. Sluggo (Mike McManus) plagues Mr. Bill. ABC airs *The Muppet Show*, a pilot featuring Jim Henson's Muppets that failed to become a network series (although it did become a syndicated series in 1976 featuring Kermit the Frog as the host and Miss Piggy as his co-host). On the pilot a Muppet named Nigel served as the host while Kermit and Miss Piggy only had a cameo appearance. Shari Lewis plays herself, the human station manager to the puppet-run TV network, the Bearly Broadcasting Company on *The Shari Show*.

1976. The Sid and Marty Krofft Puppets are featured on *Far Out Space Nuts*, a CBS series about NASA crewmen Junior and Barney (Bob Denver, Chuck McCann) and their adventures in outer space when they accidentally launch a rocket ship. The *New Howdy Doody Show* premieres in syndication (see 1947). Buffalo Bob Smith and the puppet Howdy Doody host a program of songs, stories and skits for children.

1977. Jay Johnson plays Chuck Campbell, an insecure member of the eccentric Campbell family, who needs to speak through his dummy Bob on ABC's *Soap*.

1978. Life-size puppets Honey (voice of Udana Power) and Sis (Wendy McKenzie) host *The Hanna-Barbera Happiness Hour*, an NBC pilot of music, songs and comedy skits featuring characters created by Sid and Marty Krofft (creators of such series as *Sigmund and the Sea Monsters*, *Lidsville*, *The Bugaloos* and *H.R. Pufnstuf*).

1979. Various aspects of the adult world are related to children via the puppets who inhabit an establishment called *Gigglesnort Hotel* (Syn.).

1980. The puppet B.B. Beagle heads a cast of 51 puppets who perform in comedy skits with guests on the syndicated pilot *The B.B. Beagle Show*. Henry Rush (Ted Knight) is a cartoonist who uses his hand puppet, Cosmic Cow, for inspiration when drawing his comic strip ("Cosmic Cow") on ABC's *Too Close for Comfort*.

1981. Wayland Flowers and his puppet, Madame, perform a comedy concert taped at Manhattan's Grand Finale Club on the Showtime special *Madame in Manhattan*.

1982. The HBO special *Blockheads* features performances by the country's top ventriloquists (including Jay Johnson, Chris Kirby and Willie Tyler). Wayland Flowers is the voice and puppeteer of Madame on *Madame's Place*, a syndicated series about a former movie star who hosts

her own talk show from her fabulous Hollywood mansion.

1983. The activities of the residents of Fraggle Rock come to life in the guise of Jim Henson's Muppets on HBO's *Fraggle Rock*. Characters are the fun-loving Fraggles, the diminutive Doozers and the gargantuan Gorgs (who enjoy munching on Fraggles).

1984. John Wheeler plays Clipper, the human editor of a newspaper run by puppets, on *The Kid-a-Littles*, a syndicated series that relates learning experiences to children.

1985. An old hickory tree in a magical forest is home to Nutso and Shirl, squirrel puppets who relate aspects of the world to children on the syndicated *Hickory Hideout*.

1986. An alien named Gordon Schumway, better known as Alf (electronic puppet; voice of Paul Fusco), becomes the live-in houseguest of the Tanner family when his space ship crashes into their garage on NBC's *ALF*. In 1890s London famed detective Sherlock Holmes attempts to duplicate himself but fails when a three-foot version of him appears (Sherlock Jones). Holmes ships his creation to the FBI in New York but the crate is delivered to a woman in Texas. The crate is placed in an attic and forgotten. In 1986 young Brian Hudson (Chad Sheets) and his dog Procter (a puppet) discover the crate, open it and befriend the diminutive Sherlock Jones (a puppet). The PBS series *Sherlock Jones and Procter Watson* follows the trio as they solve mysteries. Life-size puppets from England's Spitting Image Workshop are made to look like celebrities and incorporated in three NBC pilots called *Spitting Image*. The first pilot (August 30th), titled "Down and Out in the White House," finds Sylvester Stallone as the new President of the U.S. The second pilot (January 14, 1987), called "The Ronnie and Nancy Show," has First Lady Nancy Reagan attempting to throw a surprise anniversary party for hubby Ron. The final pilot (March 26, 1987), "The 1987 Movie Awards," finds Leonard Nimoy plotting to win an Oscar.

1987. Harry the Rabbit and the Professor are two of the puppets who live at the Abra Kadabra Magic Shop on *Abra Kadabra*, a syndicated series that explains the world of magic to children. Buddy Lembeck (Willie Aames), the not-too-bright friend of Charles (Scott Baio) on the syndicated *Charles in Charge*, has a hand puppet he calls Handie. Puppets that resemble celebrities and politicians frequent a Washington pub called *D.C. Follies*, a syndicated series with Fred Willard as Fred the Bartender and the puppets of Sid and Marty Krofft. Joey Gladstone (David Coulier) is a standup comedian and cartoon voice impersonator who hosts "The Ranger Joe Show" with his puppet Mr. Woodchuck on ABC's *Full House*. Dana Woodrow (Wendy Crewson) is the producer of "In the Lion's Den," a puppet show on KPLA-TV that stars Maynard the Lion on the CBS pilot *In the Lion's Den*. Fred Newton plays Gary, the hand puppet on *Dragon Time*, a local kids' show on WGRF-TV in Madison, Wisconsin on the CBS pilot *Puppetman*.

1988. Tinky Winky, Dipsy, Laa-Laa and Po are the Teletubbies, alien-like creatures who live in Tellytubby Land and have TV screens in their stomachs. They sing, dance and entertain children on PBS's *The Teletubbies*.

1989. Skits and songs with Jim Henson's Muppets and adaptations of medieval fairy tales from the Story Teller (John Hurt) combine on *The Jim Henson Hour* (NBC). The eerie Crypt Keeper (voice of John Kassir) is an electronic marionette that hosts weird stories on HBO's *Tales from the Crypt*.

1990. Jay Johnson plays Stanley Jones, a sergeant with the Bay City Police Department who, due to the pressures of work, has retreated to a ventriloquist's world where he now communicates through his dummy, Officer Danny on CBS's *Broken Badges*. Thirty-year-old paper delivery boy Chris Peterson (Chris Elliott) has a ventriloquist's dummy he calls Mr. Poppy on *Get a Life* (Fox). Buster "Buzz" Brannigan (voice of Loren Freeman) is a ventriloquist's dummy that magically comes to life after being inherited by his ventriloquist's relatives on the syndicated *What a Dummy* (Buzz is full of wise cracks, mischievous and can't resist a straight line).

1991. Leslie Nielsen is the anchorman on a news show populated by the puppet creations of Sid and Marty Krofft on the ABC pilot *ABC Presents Krofft Late Night*. Spex, Nit and Truk are three clay figures that come to life (via a meteor) to help Cheryl Singer (Kathleen Beller) a beautiful junior detective for the Carl Stalling Detective Agency solve crimes on the ABC pilot *The Danger Team*. Dinosaurs speak and work like humans on ABC's *Dinosaurs*. The focus is on Earl Sinclair, his wife Fran, and their children Char-

lene, Robbie and Baby Sinclair, who live in 60,000,000 B.C.

1992. Barney is a purple dinosaur that, with his puppet friends Baby Bob and B.J., relates songs, stories and games for children on *Barney and Friends* (PBS). Shari Lewis and her puppets Lamb Chop, Charlie Horse and Hush Puppy host a potpourri of songs, stories and games for children on PBS's *Lamb Chop's Play-a-Long*. A four-foot, 1300-year-old dragon (an electronic marionette voiced by Ronn Lucas) falls into the backyard of the Stevens family when he is hit by lightning. He is found by young Jessica (Rhea Silver-Smith) and becomes a member of the family on CBS's *Scorch*. On NBC's *Seinfeld* viewers see Mr. Marbles, the ventriloquist's dummy of Kramer.

1993. *Toby the Terrier and His TV Pals* is a syndicated puppet pilot about Toby Terrier (voice of Kevin Carlson), a dog who runs WOOF, a TV station "that has gone to the dogs" (canine puppets).

1995. Lewis Kiniski (Ryan Stiles) uses the sock puppet Professor Von Sock to help get him out of tight spots on *The Drew Carey Show* (ABC). Mr. Floppy (voice of Bobcat Goldthwait) is a puppet that becomes real to help guide the pathetic life of Jack Malloy (Geoff Pearson) on the WB's *Unhappily Ever After*.

1996. When N.Y.P.D. sergeant Robert Barone (Brad Garrett) teaches traffic school he uses his dummy, Traffic Cop Timmie, on *Everybody Loves Raymond* (CBS). Bobut is a baby (electronic puppet) who believes he is the center of the universe on ABC's *Aliens in the Family*. Nick Bakay provides the voice for Salem Saberhagen (electronic puppet), a warlock turned into a cat for attempting to take over the world on *Sabrina, the Teenage Witch* (ABC/WB).

1998. A large brown bear (named Bear) and a group of puppets relate learning experiences to children on *Bear in the Big House* (Disney). Lynsey McLeod is Belle, a young woman who entertains a group of children at her magic cottage with songs and stories on *Sing Me a Song* (Syn.). Puppets are Harmony the Cat; Louis and Carol, the bookworms; and Big Book, the old talking book.

1999. A puppet animation process called Fomation is used to give life to Thurgood Stubbs (voice of Eddie Murphy), the maintenance engineer of the 13-story Hilton-Jacobs Building in the Projects on *The PJ's* (Fox/WB). Loretta Devine is the voice of Muriel, Thurgood's wife.

2000. Children learn how to read on *Between the Lions*, a PBS series with library lion puppets Theo and Cleo, their sister Leona and brother Lionel. Stuart Devenie plays Governor Croque, the wimpy brother of France's Napoleon Bonaparte on the syndicated *Jack of All Trades*. Croque rules the island of Pulau Pulau in the East Indies (1801) and finds courage from his hand puppet Mr. Nippers.

2002. Three point two million puppets that prefer to be called "Fabricated Americans" live in the U.S. (as stated in the opening theme to Fox's *Greg the Bunny*). Greg (voice of Dan Milano) lives with a human, Jim Bender (Seth Green) and works as one of the regulars on the TV show "Sweet Knuckle Junction" (where Jim is the producer).

2005. Bear (from 1998's *Bear in the Big House*) returns to TV with his puppet pals to help children learn their morning routines on *Breakfast with Bear* (Disney). John Tartaglia plays Johnny T., a young man who retreats to a secluded area of the woods to find solitude but encounters woodland sprite puppets (Ginger and Basil) on *Johnny and the Sprites* (Disney).

Rabbis see *Religious Characters*

Reality Programs

Before they were tagged reality programs, series featuring real people were called human-interest programs. This entry chronicles these pioneering programs that are, for the most part, long forgotten, from 1931 through 1992. After this date the genre was virtually extinct. In 1999 ABC aired *Who Wants to Be a Millionaire* and launched a whole new era now identified as reality programs. The list that follows is a generous sampling of the numerous reality shows that have been broadcast on cable and broadcast TV from 2000 through 2005: *Ambush Makeover, American Idol, American Idol, Jr., America's Most Talented Kids, America's Next Swimsuit Model, America's Next Top Model, The Amazing Race, Anna Nicole Smith, The Apprentice, The Bachelor, The Bachelorette, Big Brother, The Biggest Loser, Brat Camp, Chasing Farrah, Celebrity Mole, Cold Turkey, The Complex: Malibu, The Contender, Design Invasion, Dog Eat Dog, Extreme Fakeover, Extreme Makeover, Extreme Makeover: Home Edition, Fame, Fear Factor, For Love or Money, Greed, Hell's Kitchen, High School Reunion, I Married a Princess, I'm a Celebrity, The Law Firm, Lie Detector, Meet Mr. Mom, The Mole, My Kind of Town, Nanny 911, The Next Great Chef, The Next Great Champ, The Osbornes, The Player, Queer Eye for the Straight Girl, Queer Eye for the Straight Guy, The Real Gilligan's Island, Renovate My Family, The Simple Life, RU (Are You) The Girl, So You Think You Can Dance, Super Nanny, The Starlet, Studio 7, The Surreal Life, Trading Spouses: Meet Your New Mommy, Vacation Swap, Who Wants to Marry My Dad, Wife Swap, The Will*.

1931. On May 21st television-engineer Frank DuVail married Grayce Jones in a ceremony presided over by Dr. Edwin Keigwin. TV's first wedding (and reality program) was televised by New York experimental station WGBS and Jenkins Laboratory station W2XCR in Jersey City.

1943. Captain John J. Cronin, head of the N.Y.P.D., hosts *The Bureau of Missing Persons*, a DuMont experiment in which the name, age, description and picture of a missing person are given to the home audience in the hope that someone may have information to help the police solve a case.

1946. Gil Fates conducts live interviews with people who pass by Vanderbilt Avenue and 42nd Street in New York City on the CBS test program *All Around Town*. NBC adapts its radio series *People Are Funny* to TV in a test program that features people performing stunts for prizes. New talent discoveries perform on *Tele Varieties*, a live NBC test program hosted by Tommy Farrell.

1948. Undiscovered talent performs with the hope of discovery on *Arthur Godfrey's Talent Scouts*. People caught in prearranged situations by hidden cameras are the subject of *Candid Camera*, one of TV's most prolific series. Allen Funt, the creator, hosted the series on ABC (1948–49; 1951–56), CBS (1949–51; 1960–67; 1990; 1997–2000), in syndication (1974–80; 1991–92) and on PAX (2001–02). Allen's son, Peter, hosted the PAX series from 2002–05. Johnny Thompson hosts *Club 7*, an ABC series that spotlights new talent discoveries. The radio series *Major Bowes and His Original Amateur Hour* is adapted to TV as *Ted Mack and His Original Amateur Hour* (DuMont/NBC/ABC/CBS), a program that features undiscovered talent.

1949. Robert L. Ripley hosts *Believe It or Not*, an NBC series of unusual but true stories. Amateur talent performs on *Doorway to Fame*, a DuMont series hosted by Johnny Olsen. Johnny Downs hosts undiscovered talent on CBS's *Manhattan Showcase*. Bud Collyer is the host of *Talent Jackpot*, a DuMont series that spotlights new talent.

1950. Arlene Francis hosts *By Popular Demand*, a CBS series that spotlights amateur talent. Bandleader Horace Heidt seeks new talent discoveries on CBS's *The Horace Heidt Show*. New talent acts look for stardom on *Lights, Camera, Action!*, an NBC series hosted by Walter Woolf King. Amateur talent acts perform on *The Show Goes On* (CBS) in the hope of receiving bookings from talent buyers who are present (Robert Q. Lewis hosts). Peter Lind Hayes and Mary Healy host *Star of the Family*, a CBS talent search wherein performers are selected from letters written by family members. Aspiring entertainers perform on *The Vim Talent Search*, an NBC program hosted by Skitch Henderson. "Wherever it is. Whatever it is. At home or around the world, you see it here, *You Asked for It*." Art Baker then Jack Smith host a program wherein viewer requests for unusual entertainment acts are presented through films (DuMont/ABC).

1951. Mike Wallace and Biff Cobb host *All Around Town*, a CBS series that presents interviews with people from all walks of life. Actual wedding ceremonies are televised from a chapel in New York City on *Bride and Groom* (CBS/NBC; Byron Palmer and Robert Paige are among the hosts). Henry Morgan hosts a showcase for unusual talent acts on *Henry Morgan's Great Talent Hunt* (NBC). Undiscovered talent acts compete seeking possible stardom — and one week's tax on a million dollars — on *Live Like a Millionaire* (CBS/ABC). John Nelson and Jack McCoy are the hosts.

1952. New talent acts perform against the background of a carnival on *The M&M Candy Carnival* (CBS) with host Barry Cossell. Tony Bartlett and Bob Cunningham host *Welcome Travelers* (NBC/CBS), a series on which people visiting Chicago are asked their impressions of the city. Good Samaritans are honored and awarded prizes for their unselfish acts of kindness on CBS's *Wheel of Fortune* (Todd Russell hosts).

1953. Women are given makeovers, including a new wardrobe, to make the average woman a

Glamour Girl (NBC; Harry Babbitt hosts). Female talent scouts present their choices for stardom on NBC's *Ladies' Choice*. Johnny Dugan is the host. ABC's *Talent Patrol* first presented performances by military personnel, then by civilian talent. Steve Allen, Bud Collyer and Richard Hayes served as the hosts.

1954. Jack Douglas is the host of *I Search for Adventure*, a syndicated series that depicts the sometimes hazardous things people will do for excitement. Real people perform stunts (sometimes humiliating) in return for prizes on NBC's *People Are Funny*. Art Linkletter is the host.

1957. Ben Alexander plays "The Man," who interviews people he meets on the street on the ABC pilot *People*.

1959. *Dick Clark's World of Talent* (ABC) presents performances by young hopefuls followed by a discussion of their merits with a professional guest panel. People from all walks of life appear on ABC's *Hobby Lobby* to discuss their hobbies. Cliff Arquette is the host.

1960. Celebrities present undiscovered talent on *Celebrity Talent Scouts*, a CBS series hosted by Sam Levinson.

1962. Jack Douglas hosts *Across the Seven Seas*, a syndicated series that depicts the customs and cultures of people from around the world. Jim Backus, Merv Griffin and Art Linkletter host *Hollywood Talent Scouts*, a CBS series on which celebrities present their talent discoveries. Red Rowe hosts *Tell It to the Camera*, a CBS series wherein ordinary people speak directly into a camera and reveal their thoughts.

1967. Dick Stewart, Wink Martindale and Paul Petersen are the hosts of *Dream Girl of '67*, a daily ABC series in which 20 girls (five per day) compete in contests of beauty, charm and talent. Weekly winners return to compete for the title of "Dream Girl of '67."

1968. College students possessing talent perform on *Your All American College Show*. Dennis James, Rich Little and Arthur Godfrey host the syndicated series.

1969. Art Linkletter hosts *The Lid's Off*, a syndicated series of interviews with people from all walks of life.

1972. Dave Garroway hosts *The CBS Newcomers*, a showcase for undiscovered talent.

1973. The PBS cinema-verite portrait of the Loud family (parents William and Patricia and their children Kevin, Lance, Michele, Delilah and

Grant) of Santa Barbara, California are profiled on *An American Family*.

1976. Acts ranging from professional to just plain awful perform on *The Gong Show* (NBC) with Chuck Barris as the host.

1978. Professional and amateur acts perform on *The Chuck Barris Rah-Rah Show* (NBC), an extension of his *Gong Show*. Rip Taylor hosts a weekly talent hunt to find the one woman who possesses talent, beauty and charm on the syndicated *$1.98 Beauty Show*. Winners not only achieve the title of "The $1.98 Beauty of the Week," but also the top prize — $1.98 — in cash! Jackson Beck narrates *Lifeline*, an unscripted NBC series that follows the day-to-day lives of various doctors on and off the job.

1979. College students perform their original material on the CBS pilot *The All American College Show* (hosted by Jaye P. Morgan). People who, after reaching the zenith of their careers, fell from those heights, then fought their way back to the top, are profiled on *Comeback*, a syndicated series hosted by James Whitmore. Real but sometimes unusual people are profiled on NBC's *Real People* (hosted by Sarah Purcell).

1980. Joe Namath is the host of *All American Pie*, an ABC pilot that was set to showcase the adventures of ordinary people at work and play. Four exceptionally bright people compete in very challenging mental and physical contests on *The Krypton Factor*, an ABC series hosted by Dick Clark. Cathy Lee Crosby and John Davidson are the hosts of *That's Incredible*, an ABC series that profiles unusual people and strange phenomena.

1981. Ordinary people speak their minds on subjects that concern them on the NBC pilot *It's Only Human* with Allen Funt as the host. Peter Billingsley is among the child hosts of *Real Kids*, an NBC pilot that spotlights the abilities of children. Barbara Feldon hosts *Real Life Stories*, a CBS pilot that examines crises that occur in real life families. Real couples are married on the air on the NBC pilot *Wedding Day* (Mary Ann Mobley hosts). Rich Little hosts *You Asked for It*, a syndicated update of the 1950 series that fulfills the unusual requests of viewers.

1982. Actual crimes are reenacted to illustrate crime prevention tips and increase viewer awareness of potential crime situations on ABC's *Counterattack: Crime in America* (George Kennedy hosts). Cyndy Garvey and Gary Collins host *Suc-*

cess: It Can Be Yours, an ABC pilot that recounts the stories of people who overcame adversity to achieve success.

1983. People are given the opportunity to substantiate any claim by means of a polygraph test on the syndicated *Lie Detector*. F. Lee Bailey hosts and most notable of the subjects was adult film actress Linda Lovelace who proved on the air that she was forced into pornography (a contention she long held but could never prove).

1984. The private lives of celebrities and people of great wealth are profiled on the syndicated *Lifestyles of the Rich and Famous* (Robin Leach hosts). Ordinary people are challenged to perform outrageous tasks for laughs on the syndicated *People Are Funny* (Flip Wilson hosts). The comical side of human nature is revealed as ordinary people react to unusual situations on ABC's *People Do the Craziest Things* (Bert Convy hosts).

1985. Children caught in prearranged situations by hidden cameras react on *Candid Kids*, an NBC pilot hosted by Allen Funt. Actress Shawn Weatherly appears as herself as she devotes one year of her life to the greatest adventure of her life: documenting the mysteries of the sea on NBC's *Ocean Quest*.

1986. Ken Howard hosts *Dream Girl U.S.A.*, a syndicated beauty contest in which four girls compete in weekly contests of beauty, charm, talent, figure and form for the title *Dream Girl of 1987*.

1988. John Walsh hosts *America's Most Wanted*, a weekly Fox series that reveals the facts behind criminal cases in the hope that someone in the viewing audience possesses the information necessary to bring the culprits to justice.

1989. Camera crews are placed in police cars to capture the action as crimes are investigated and suspects apprehended on *Cops*, a Fox series narrated by Harry Newman. Mike Pitta hosts *Hidden Videos*, a Fox series that captures the results of people caught in prearranged situations by hidden cameras.

1992. People who have overcome life-threatening situations, sudden tragedies or a unique adventure are profiled on *Against All Odds*, an NBC pilot hosted by Lindsay Wagner.

Religious Characters (God, ministers, nuns, priests, rabbis)

This entry chronicles the men and women who serve God in capacities as Catholic priests and nuns, Jewish Rabbis and Protestant, Lutheran and Episcopalian ministers. See also *Angels, The Devil* and *Religious Programs.*

1955. Dramas based on the men of the clergy are the basis of ABC's anthology *Crossroads.*

1956. Dennis O'Keefe plays Charles Parker, a soft-touch minister whose kind heart causes more trouble than he can handle on the NBC pilot *It's Always Sunday.*

1962. Father Charles O'Malley (Gene Kelly) is a Catholic priest with progressive ideas at St. Dominic's Parish in New York City on *Going My Way* (ABC). Leo G. Carroll plays Father Fitzgibbon, the elder conservative priest.

1967. Sister Bertrille (Sally Field) is a Catholic nun assigned to the Convent San Tanco in San Juan, Puerto Rico, who uses her ability to fly (when strong gales strike her nun's habit) to help the people of her poor community on ABC's *The Flying Nun.*

1971. Robert Sampson is Father Michael Fitzgerald, a priest at the Immaculate Heart Church on CBS's *Bridget Loves Bernie.* Father Samuel Patrick Cavanaugh (George Kennedy) is a Catholic priest at St. Aloysius parish in San Diego on NBC's *Sarge* (Sarge, as he is called, was a cop who became a priest after his wife was killed by a bullet meant for him). Kenneth Mars plays Jack Shepherd, a retired football player turned minister of the Cypress Bay Union Church on the CBS pilot *Shepherd's Flock.*

1972. The younger Rabbi Miller (Bert Convy) clashes with the elder Rabbi Mossman (Howard Da Silva) over their temple's affairs on the CBS pilot *Keep the Faith.* William Christopher plays First Lieutenant Father Francis Mulcahy, the chaplain at the 4077th Mobile Army Surgical Hospital in Korea during the war on CBS's *M*A*S*H.* John Ritter plays Reverend Matthew Fordwicke, the minister in Jefferson County, Virginia (1930s) on *The Waltons* (CBS).

1974. Falsely accused of murder, Old West gunfighter Ernie Parsons (Marjoe Gortner) flees from justice and poses as a minister to find the man responsible for framing him on the ABC pilot *The Gun and the Pulpit.* Dabbs Greer plays

Robert Alden, the reverend in Walnut Grove on Plum Creek, Minnesota, on *Little House on the Prairie* (NBC).

1975. Tom Holvak (Glenn Ford) is a minister in Bensfield, Tennessee (1933) who is struggling to feed his family and maintain the faith of his congregation on *The Family Holvak* (NBC). Julie Harris plays his wife Elizabeth.

1976. The ABC pilot *Father O Father* focuses on the clash between Father Flicker (Iggie Wolfington), the conservative pastor of Saints Peter and Paul Church in Boston, and Father Morgan (Dennis Dugan), his liberal assistant. Sparky Marcus plays the Reverend Jimmy Jo Jeeter, the child minister in Fernwood, Ohio, on the syndicated *Mary Hartman, Mary Hartman.*

1977. David Small (Bruce Solomon) is a rabbi at the Temple Beth Halell Synagogue in Cameron, California, who helps police chief Paul Lanigan (Art Carney) solve crimes on NBC's *Lanigan's Rabbi.*

1978. The conservative Catholic priest Dan Cleary (McLean Stevenson) clashes with streetwise nun Sister Agnes (Priscilla Lopez) on how to run a mission to help the people of their community on *In the Beginning* (CBS). Pam Dawber plays Terri Morgan, a former gang leader (of the Velvet Knuckles Gang) who becomes a Catholic nun (to prevent children from turning to a life of crime) on the ABC pilot *Sister Terri.*

1979. Barnard Hughes plays Father John Brown, an eccentric Manhattan priest and pastor of St. Eustacious Church who has a knack for solving crimes on the NBC pilot *Sanctuary of Fear* (originally titled "Girl in the Park" and slated to be called "Father Brown, Detective"). Christopher Lloyd joins the cast of *Taxi* (ABC/NBC) as Jim Ignatowski, a spaced-out cab driver who is also an ordained minister in the Church of the Peaceful (Jim is also called Reverend Jim).

1981. Gale Gordon plays the Abbott and Charlie Callas, Guy Marks and Graham Jarvis are Brothers Charles, Hush and Virgil on *Bungle Abbey*, an NBC pilot about the monks assigned to the San Fernando Abbey founded by Brother Bungle. Merlin Olsen plays John Murphy, an 1870s frontiersman who pretends to be a priest to care for the orphaned children of the Gold Hill School on NBC's *Father Murphy.* Grady Nutt plays Grady Williams, a minister at the Rockwell Community Church in Rockwell, Tennessee, on the NBC pilot *The Grady Nutt Show*. Father Peter Matthews (Fred McCarren) is a young Episcopal priest just beginning his duties at the 4th Street Church in Manhattan on the NBC pilot *Saint Peter*.

1982. Kenneth More plays Father John Brown, a Catholic priest who dabbles as an amateur sleuth on PBS's *Father Brown*.

1985. The Reverend Billy Joe Bickerstaff (Richard Paul) is the minister who disapproves of Julia Mansfield as the first woman president of the United States and is seeking to oust her on ABC's *Hail to the Chief*. Father Noah Rivers (Robert Blake) is an ex-con turned Catholic priest and pastor of St. Dominic's Church in a tough East Los Angeles neighborhood called *Hell Town* (NBC). Among the nuns of the parish are Mother Maggie (Natalie Core), Sister Indigo (Vonetta McGee) and Sister Anastasia, called Sister Angel Cakes (Isabel Grandin).

1986. Ernest Frye (Sherman Hemsley) is deacon of the First Community Church in Philadelphia. Reuben Gregory (Clifton Davis) is the church's newly appointed reverend. The two clash over church policy on NBC's *Amen*. John Short plays Charles Cavanaugh, Jr., a Catholic priest at Our Lady of Perpetual Sorrow Church on *The Cavanaughs* (CBS).

1988. Leon Russom plays Reverend Paul Dirkson, a Lutheran minister on the NBC pilot *Down Delaware Road*. Frank Bonner is Father Robert Hargis, the priest in charge of St. Augustine's High School on *Just the Ten of Us* (ABC).

1989. Father Frank Dowling (Tom Bosley) and Sister Steve (Tracy Nelson) of St. Michael's Church in Chicago are a Catholic priest and nun with a knack for solving crimes on *Father Dowling Mysteries* (NBC/ABC). Incidents in the lives of Catholic priests are the basis of ABC's *Have Faith*. Joel Higgins stars as Monsignor Joseph MacKenzie with Stephen Furst as Father Gabriel. Tom Bower plays Father Jim, pastor of a church in a tough inner city that houses the Knights, a community watch group, on ABC's *Knight Watch*. Sister Katherine Lambert, called Sister Kate (Stephanie Beacham) is the head of Redemption House, a Catholic residence for orphaned children on *Sister Kate* (NBC).

1990. Richard Libertini plays Father Angelo Lombardi, a Catholic priest at St. Helen's Church and host of the TV talk show "Voice of the People" on NBC's *The Fanelli Boys*.

1991. Jonathan Frain (Mark Harmon) is a Catholic priest on a leave of absence (to sort out personal problems) who helps people via his call-in radio program, "True Confessions," on the CBS pilot *Original Sins*.

1994. Sister Michael (Delta Burke) is a Mother Superior (of the St. Claire Convent in Los Angeles) and the daughter of a famous mystery writer who helps the police solve crimes on the CBS pilot *Sister Michael Wants You*. Eddie Bracken plays Father Burke, a Catholic priest in the small town of Oak Bluff (a suburb of Chicago) on NBC's *Winnetka Road*.

1995. Patty Duke plays Hannah Miller, a reverend at the Lakeview Church who helps troubled souls on NBC's *Amazing Grace*.

1996. Stephen Collins plays Eric Camden, a Protestant minister in Glen Oak, California on the WB's *7th Heaven*. He is married to Annie (Catherine Hicks) and the father of seven children. His daughter, Lucy (Beverley Mitchell), hopes to follow in his footsteps.

1997. Brad Sullivan and Kevin Anderson are priests at St. Thomas Church in Chicago on *Nothing Sacred* (ABC).B.D. Wong plays Father Ray Mukada, the chaplain at Oswald State Prison on HBO's *Oz*. Dan Aykroyd plays Reverend Mike Weber, pastor of St. Stephen's Episcopal Church who is struggling to raise four children after the death of his wife on ABC's *Soul Man*.

1999. Zotoh Zhann (Virginia Robyn Hey) is a futuristic female priest (called a Pa'u) from the planet Devlin (where she evolved from a plant) on *Farscape* (Sci Fi).

2002. Brooke Dillman plays Sister Brenda, "The Weather Nun" on WWEN TV, Channel 11 on NBC's *Good Morning, Miami*.

2003. George Dzundza plays Father Tom Gizelak, a Catholic priest and confidant to Mike Olshansky (David Morse), the ex-cop turned cab driver who helps people in trouble on CBS's *Hack*. Hector Elizondo plays Father Jose Silva, a friend of Ranata Malone, the host of a TV cooking show on *Mama Malone* (CBS).

2005. Sister Joespha Montafiore (Natascha McElhone) is a Catholic nun who investigates religious phenomena (seeking to find the reborn Jesus Christ) on *Revelations* (NBC).

2006. Aidan Quinn plays Reverend Daniel Webster, a priest who turns to an incarnation of Jesus Christ to help him deal with personal and professional problems on *The Book of Daniel* (NBC).

Religious Programs

This entry lists the programs with religious overtones or those relating to God. TV preachers are excluded from the listing (those that buy airtime to raise money for their particular causes. These include TV's most popular preacher, the Reverend Billy Graham [who began his Evangelist crusade in 1953], Jerry Falwell, Reverend Ike, Pat Robertson, Jimmy Swaggert and Jim and Tammy Faye Bakker of the PTL Club). See also *Angels, The Devil, Holiday Specials* (for Christmas and Easter programs), and *Religious Characters*.

1945. Robert Shaw's Collegiate Chorus performs hymns while House Jameson tells the story of Easter over religious paintings and scripture readings on the Easter Eve (March 31st) special *The Story of Easter* (NBC).

1948. Guests appear in religious stories on the CBS Sunday morning series *Lamp Unto My Feet*.

1951. The NBC Sunday morning series *Frontiers of Faith* is an anthology series that devotes its half-hours to Catholics (*The Catholic Hour*), Protestants (*Frontiers of Faith*) and the Jewish (*The Eternal Light*).

1952. Actor Charles Laughton reads selections from the Bible (as well as from classic and modern stories) on *This Is Charles Laughton* (Syn.). Dramas that examine contemporary moral problems and their solutions are broadcast on the syndicated *This Is the Life*.

1953. Bishop Fulton J. Sheen makes TV history on *Life Is Worth Living* (ABC/DuMont), a weekly series of sermons on morality that captivated audiences and even put a dent into ratings champ Milton Berle's NBC series. Also during this time Dr. Norman Vincent Peale, a best-selling pastor, advocated positive thinking on his series *What's Your Trouble*.

1954. Celebrity guests appear on *Look Up and Live*, a CBS Sunday morning series of religious dramas.

1956. Several nuns are faced with a dilemma when a baby is left on their convent doorstep and they are asked to care for it on *The Cradle Song*, an NBC *Hallmark Hall of Fame* presentation. Evelyn Varden and Judith Anderson star.

1957. Incidents from the Bible are seen in a series of vignettes as a Sunday school teacher preaches to her students on *The Green Pastures*, an NBC *Hallmark Hall of Fame* presentation.

The program is set in the deep South and features an all black cast: Estelle Hemsley as the teacher, Mrs. Beshee; William Warfield as DeLaud; Eddie "Rochester" Anderson as Noah; Earle Hyman as Adam; and Frederick O'Neal as Moses.

1959. On February 8th NBC aired *The Third Commandment*, the pilot for a proposed series based on The Ten Commandments. The initial episode tells of an embittered writer who violates the Third Commandment ("Thou Shalt Not Take the Name of Thy Lord in Vain") by abandoning his principals and striving for success at any cost. Arthur Kennedy and Anne Francis star.

1960. Top Hollywood stars appear on *Insight*, a religious anthology produced by the Paulist Fathers.

1961. *Give Us Barabbas* is an NBC *Hallmark Hall of Fame* presentation that explores the reason for Pontius Pilate (Dennis King) to free the thief Barabbas (James Daly) and crucify Jesus Christ.

1963. Animated clay figures Davy Hanson and his dog Goliath learn religious lessons about life on the syndicated *Davy and Goliath*.

1966. Hugh O'Brian plays Joseph on "Seven Rich Years ... And Seven Lean," the NBC pilot episode for a proposed series based on stories from the Bible called *Great Bible Adventures*.

1968. The Battle of Issus is recreated on *Alexander the Great*, the pilot episode for a series based on stories from the Bible. Here Alexander (William Shatner) and his Greek forces battle the invading Persian army.

1972. The Biblical story of Salome (Ludmilla Tcherina), a daughter of Herod, and her lust for and the ultimate destruction of John the Baptist (Jean Paul Zehnocker) is dramatized on the PBS drama *Salome*.

1973. God appears in the guise of a Puerto Rican steambath attendant (Jose Perez) on *Steambath*, a PBS special where souls wait before moving on.

1975. Burt Lancaster plays Moses on *Moses the Lawgiver*, an NBC miniseries drawn from the Book of Exodus that follows Moses as he defies the Egyptian Empire to deliver Jews from their enslavement and lead them to the Promised Land.

1976. The life of the Biblical warrior David (Timothy Bottoms) is dramatized on the two-part NBC drama, *The Story of David*.

1977. Robert Powell stars as Jesus Christ in the Biblical retelling of his life on the NBC miniseries *Jesus of Nazareth*. Olivia Hussey plays Mary and Yorgo Voyagis is Joseph.

1978. NBC airs *The Greatest Heroes of the Bible*, a collection of stories from the Old Testament: *Abraham's Sacrifice, David and Goliath, Joseph in Egypt, Samson and Delilah, Sodom and Gomorrah, The Story of Moses, The Story of Noah* and *The Ten Commandments*. Victor Jory narrates. Nancy Walker plays God on *Human Feelings*, an NBC pilot in which She seeks six righteous people to save a world She is fed up with.

1979. *Mary and Joseph: A Story of Faith* is an NBC Biblical drama about Mary (Blanche Baker) and Joseph (Jeff East), the parents of Jesus Christ, and the events that led to his birth. *The 13th Day: The Story of Esther* is the pilot for a potential series of Biblical dramas (ABC). The initial presentation tells the story of Esther (Olivia Hussey), the Jewish girl who is forced to become the reluctant queen to the King of Persia.

1981. An old book gives young Chris and his friend Joy the ability to see events depicted in the Bible on *Superbook*, a syndicated cartoon featuring the voices of Billie Lou Watt and Peter Fernandez.

1984. The allegorical series *Steambath*, about life in the hereafter, premieres on Showtime. Jose Perez plays God as Morty, the washroom attendant at a steambath where souls remain on a waiting list between this world and the next. The rising conflict between the Jewish Zealots, the early Christians and the Roman Empire are depicted on *A.D.*, an NBC miniseries with Ava Gardner, John Houseman, Jennifer O'Neill and Ben Vereen heading a very large cast. The ABC Easter special *The Fourth Wiseman* tells of Artaban (Martin Sheen), a prosperous doctor who sells his possessions to buy three precious stones to present to the Christ Child on the eve of the Nativity.

1986. *God, the Universe and Hot Fudge Sundaes* is a tender CBS drama about faith. Roxana Zal plays Alfie Newton, a young girl who attempts to understand why God chose to make her sister Frances (Melanie Gaffin) terminally ill and bound to a wheelchair.

1988. Aaron Miller and his wife Sarah (Merlin Olsen, Belinda J. Montgomery) are an Amish family who leave Pennsylvania for California and struggle to adjust to a life that contradicts their religious ways on *Aaron's Way* (NBC).

1990. A very sick boy (Chris Demetral) facing an operation dreams he is the helper of Mordachai (Bernie Kopell), a magician in ancient Jerusalem, on the syndicated special *The Magic Boy's Easter*. When the boy learns that Jesus can heal the sick, he begins a journey to find him — a journey that gives him the courage to face his operation when he awakens. Audrey Messner hosts *Sonshiny Day*, a syndicated religious-oriented series of songs, stories and skits for children.

2000. Psychologist Peggy Fowler (Rae Dawn Chong) and anthropologist Declan Dunn (Adrian Pasdar) investigate miracles on *Mysterious Ways* (PAX).

2001. Richard Kiley and Jean Simmons narrate *Mysteries of the Bible*, a syndicated series that investigates the best known stories from the Bible: *Abraham, Biblical Angels, Cain and Able, Heaven and Hell, Jesus — Holy Child, The Puzzle of Revelation* and *Herod the Great*.

2003. God appears as various people — from young girls to janitors — to relay messages to 16-year-old Joan Girardi (Amber Tamblyn), a girl He has chosen to perform minor miracles on *Joan of Arcadia*. Paul Callan (Skeet Urich) is an investigator for the Catholic Church who seeks the truth behind supposed miracles on ABC's *Miracles*.

2004. Willie Aames plays Miles Peterson, a deeply religious man who uses the power of the scriptures to battle evil as the armor-clad Bible Man, a cable syndicated series designed to teach children the Bible.

2005. A nun, Sister Josepha Montafiore (Natascha McElhone) and a physicist (Bill Pullman) seek to find the real Jesus Christ just before the start of Armageddon on *Revelations* (NBC).

2006. Garrett Dillahaunt plays Jesus Christ, the heavenly visitor who appears to Episcopal minister Daniel Webster (Aidan Quinn) to help guide his life on *The Book of Daniel* (NBC). The biblical tale of Moses as he returns to Egypt to free the Hebrews from slavery is dramatized on the ABC miniseries *The Ten Commandments*. The large cast features Dougray Scott as Moses; Naveen Andrews as Menerith; Claire Bloom as Rani; Omar Sharif as Jethro; and Hannah Taylor-Gordon as Rachel.

Reporters

This entry chronicles the TV characters who

work on newspapers, magazines or TV shows as reporters. For additional newspapers and magazines see *Newspapers*.

1945. Ruth Ford plays Ann Williams, a crime reporter for the *Morning Express*, a New York newspaper on *Diary of Death*, a TV adaptation of the CBS radio series *Crime Photographer* (the title refers to Casey [Oliver Thorndike]).

1948. Gene O'Donnell plays Barney Blake, a New York City police reporter on *Barney Blake, Police Reporter* (NBC).

1949. Hildy Johnson (Mark Roberts) is a reporter for the Center City *Examiner* on *The Front Page* (CBS).

1950. Steve Wilson (Patrick McVey, Mark Stevens) and Lorelei Kilbourne (Margaret Hayes, Mary K. Wells, Jane Nigh, Trudy Wroe, Julie Stevens) are crime reporters for *The Illustrated Press* on *Big Town* (CBS/NBC). Evelyn Ankers plays Bombay Fay, the beautiful American reporter covering World War II in China for *The Bombay News* on *Ding Howe of the Flying Tigers* (Syn.). Johnny Warren (Harold Huber) is a Broadway newspaper reporter-columnist on ABC's *I Cover Times Square*.

1951. Jan Miner plays Ann Williams, a crime reporter for the New York *Morning Express*, on *Crime Photographer* (CBS; the title refers to Casey [Richard Carlyle, Darren McGavin]). Robert Cannon and Helen Davis (Jerome Thor, Sydna Scott) are foreign correspondents for the Consolidated News Service while Steve Powers (Robert Arden) is a correspondent for the Amalgamated News Service on the syndicated *Dateline Europe*. Edmund Lowe plays David Chase, a New York newspaper reporter and amateur sleuth on Du-Mont's *Front Page Detective*. William Adler (then Jerome Cowan) plays Collins, a reporter for the New York *Ledger* on DuMont's *Not for Publication* (also known as *Reporter Collins*).

1952. Kay Foster (Mary Shipp) is a reporter for the New York *Globe* who shares an apartment with the scatterbrained Irma Peterson (Marie Wilson) on *My Friend Irma* (CBS).

1953. Clark Kent (George Reeves), alias Superman, and Lois Lane (Phyllis Coates, Noel Neill) are crime reporters for the Metropolis *Daily Planet* on *The Adventures of Superman* (Syn.).

1954. Celeste Anders (Celeste Holm) is a former college teacher struggling to become a reporter for the New York *Express* on *Honestly, Celeste!* (CBS). Michael Powers and Patricia Bennett

(James Daly, Ann Preville) are foreign correspondents for *Associated News* on the syndicated *Overseas Adventures*.

1956. Dean Evans (George Brent), Katherine Wells (Mercedes McCambridge) and Dan Miller (Dane Clark) are reporters for *Trans Globe News* on ABC's *Wire Service*.

1958. Lee Tracy plays Lee Cochran, a tough New York newspaper reporter-columnist on the syndicated *New York Confidential*. Walter Winchell plays himself, a crime reporter for the New York *Daily Mirror* on *The Walter Winchell File* (ABC).

1960. Dan Duryea plays Barnaby Hooke, a newspaper reporter who investigates murders on the CBS pilot *Confidentially Yours*. Glenn Evans (Rod Taylor) is a foreign correspondent for *World Wide News* on ABC's *Hong Kong*. Johnny Martin (Jack Carson) is a TV newscaster who will go to any lengths to get a story on the CBS pilot *Johnny Come Lately*. Tim Rourke (Jerry Paris) is a reporter-photographer for the Miami *Tribune* on NBC's *Michael Shayne*. Pat Garrett and Scott Norris (Donald May, Rex Reason) are crime reporters for the *Daily Record* in New York City during the 1920s on *The Roaring 20s* (ABC).

1961. Ben Gregory and Paul Templin (Barry Coe, Brett Halsey) are free-lance magazine reporters based in Hawaii on ABC's *Follow the Sun*. Innocent Jones (Chris Warfield) is a free-lance magazine reporter who becomes personally involved in the stories he covers on the NBC pilot *Innocent Jones*. Racket reporter Paul Marino (Stephen McNally) seeks to expose the underworld on ABC's *Target: The Corruptors*.

1962. Floyd Gibbons (Scott Brady) is a World War I combat correspondent turned investigative reporter battling corruption in 1930s Chicago on the ABC pilot *Floyd Gibbons, Reporter*. Nick Alexander (Nick Adams) is a reporter for the New York *Bulletin* on NBC's *Saints and Sinners*.

1963. Tim O'Hara (Bill Bixby) is a reporter for the Los Angeles *Sun* on *My Favorite Martian* (CBS).

1964. Griswold Knight (Roger Smith) is a newspaper reporter who uses unorthodox methods to acquire stories on the NBC pilot *Knight's Gambit*. Harry Guardino plays Danny Taylor, a crime reporter for the New York *Globe* on *The Reporter* (CBS).

1965. Pat Buttram plays Hardy Madison, the editor of a small town newspaper, *The Freedom*

Press on the CBS pilot *Down Home*. Sam Drucker (Frank Cady) is the reporter, columnist and publisher of the *Hooterville World Guardian*, the paper of rural Hooterville on *Green Acres*.

1966. Britt Reid (Van Williams) is a newspaper publisher (of the *Daily Sentinel*) who is secretly *The Green Hornet* (ABC). Donald Hollinger (Ted Bessell) is the boyfriend of Anne Marie (Marlo Thomas) and a columnist for *Newsday* magazine on ABC's *That Girl*.

1968. Doris Martin (Doris Day) is first a secretary, then general news reporter for *Today's World* magazine on *The Doris Day Show* (CBS). Burt Reynolds plays Pete Lassiter, an investigative reporter for *Contrast* magazine on the CBS pilot *Lassiter*. Glenn Howard (Gene Barry) is the publisher of *Crime Magazine* and owner of Howard Publications on NBC's *Name of the Game*. Dan Farrell (Robert Stack) and Jeff Dillon (Tony Franciosa) uncover the story material.

1974. Darren McGavin plays Carl Kolchak, a reporter for the Chicago based Independent News Service on *Kolchak: The Night Stalker* (ABC).

1975. Shirley Jones plays Jenny Dolan, a glamorous newspaper reporter for the *New World Journal* on the NBC pilot *The Lives of Jenny Dolan*. Jackie Cooper plays Pete Campbell, a reporter for KONE-TV, Channel 1 in Southern California on ABC's *Mobile One*.

1976. Brenda Starr (Jill St. John) is a crusading reporter for the *Daily Flash* who risks her life to get stories on the NBC pilot *Brenda Starr*. Laurie and Judy (Deidre Hall, Judy Strangis) are reporters of *Newsmaker* magazine and secretly the crime-fighting *Electra Woman and Dyna Girl* (ABC). Events in the lives of the people of the 1940s mining town of Gibbsville, Pennsylvania, are seen through the eyes of Ray Whitehead (Gig Young), a reporter for the *Courier* on NBC's *Gibbsville*.

1977. Mike Andros (James Sutorius) is an investigative reporter for the *Forum*, a crusading New York newspaper on *The Andros Targets* (CBS). Jack McGee (Jack Colvin) is a reporter for the *National Register* who is trying to prove that Dr. David Banner is really the green *Incredible Hulk* (CBS). A mousy newspaper reporter named Feeney (Don Knotts) encounters mishaps as he goes about getting stories on the syndicated pilot *Front Page Feeney*.

1978. Rebecca Thompkins and Amy Wardell (Priscilla Barnes, Debra Clinger) are reporters for the TV newsmagazine *The American Report* on *The American Girls* (CBS).

1979. Sherry Jackson plays Brenda Starr, the beautiful reporter for the *Daily Flash* who risks her life to acquire stories on the syndicated pilot *Brenda Starr, Reporter*. Natalie Greene (Mindy Cohn) is a student at the Eastland School for Girls who works as a reporter for the *Peekskill Press* on *The Facts of Life* (NBC). Kate Mulgrew plays Kate Columbo, the wife of the famed police Lieutenant Columbo, and a journalist for the *Weekly Advertiser* in San Fernando, California, who uses her amateur sleuthing skills to solve crimes on *Mrs. Columbo* (NBC). When *Mrs. Columbo* was cancelled, Kate Mulgrew was Kate Callahan, now divorced from the lieutenant, but still a reporter (now for the *Valley Advocate*) on NBC's *Kate Loves a Mystery*. Susan Williams (Susan Anton) is a reporter-photographer for the New York *Dispatch* on *Stop Susan Williams* (a segment on NBC's *Cliffhangers*).

1980. Stephanie Faracy plays Stephanie Burke, a reporter and host of *L.A.L.A.*, a local Los Angeles TV morning series on the CBS pilot *Stephanie*. Stockard Channing plays Susan Goodenow, a consumer advocate reporter for *The Big Ripoff* on KXLA-TV in West Hollywood on *The Stockard Channing Show*.

1981. Ryan Fitzpatrick (Dick Smothers) is an on-the-air reporter for KSFB-TV's *Newsline 3* in San Francisco, and Bones Howard (Tom Smothers) is his cameraman on NBC's *Fitz and Bones*. Helen Shaver plays Jessica Novak, an on-the-air reporter for *Close-Up News* on KLA-TV, Channel 6 in Los Angeles on *Jessica Novak* (CBS).

1982. Janet Eilber plays Kate Bennett, an investigative reporter for the News Six Team in Los Angeles on the ABC pilot *This Is Kate Bennett*. Reporter-photographers Louie and Buzz (Alan Arkin, Rick Casorla) find mishaps as they seek stories for the scandal sheet *Muck* on the NBC pilot *Two Guys from Muck*.

1983. Amanda Allen (Melinda Culea) is a reporter for the Los Angeles *Courier-Express* who acquires stories by helping military fugitives the A-Team help people in trouble on *The A-Team* (NBC). In later episodes, Marla Heasley (as Tawnia Baker) replaces Amy when she is transferred overseas. Louis Ciconne (Louis Del Grande) is a reporter for the Toronto *Gazette* in Canada who uses his gift of second sight to acquire stories on the syndicated *Seeing Things*. Kate Simpson and

Sam Dillon (Morgan Brittany, David Birney) are among a large staff of reporters for *Glitter,* "The hottest celebrity magazine on the newsstands," on ABC's *Glitter.* Lew Farley (Max Gail) is a reporter for the Los Angeles *Gazette* on CBS's *The Whiz Kids.*

1985. Maggie Seaver (Joanna Kearns) is a former researcher for *Newsweek* magazine who now works as a reporter for the Long Island (New York) *Daily Herald* on ABC's *Growing Pains* (Maggie later works as a reporter for *Action News* on Channel 19). Elizabeth Bailey (Shanna Reed) is a reporter for the Los Angeles *Chronicle* and one of the three ex-wives of private detective Jack Beaudine (Victor Garber) on *I Had Three Wives* (CBS). Nick Fox and James Mackey (Nicholas Campbell, Stoney Jackson) are investigative reporters for *Newspoint* magazine on ABC's *The Insiders.* Tom Kirkwood (Allan Royal) is a crime reporter for the Toronto, Canada *Eagle* who writes the column *Night Heat* (CBS). Edgar Benedek (Dennis Dugan) and Jonathan MacKenzie (Trevor Eve) are reporters for the *National Register* who investigate mysterious happenings on ABC's *The Shadow Chasers.*

1986. Madeline Kahn plays Violet Kingsley, an investigative consumer reporter who dons various disguises to get her stories for WGGK-TV, Channel 8's *The Bushnell Report* on the ABC pilot *Chameleon* (George Wyner plays George Bushnell, the show host). Amanda Reed and Jason West (Dorothy Parke, Booth Savage) are reporters for *Crime World* magazine on CBS's *Hot Shots.* Chris Nichols (Caroline McWilliams) is an American magazine reporter for *News Today* magazine who is stationed at the Moscow Bureau in the USSR on the ABC pilot *Moscow Bureau.*

1987. Sarah Powell (Josie Davis) is a teenager who does free-lance reporting for the New Brunswick (New Jersey) *Herald* on the syndicated *Charles in Charge.* Blake Calisher (Wendy Crewson) of the City Wire Service and Andy Omart (Michael Murphy) of *The Morning Express* cover the activities of the California Metro Police Department on CBS's *Hard Copy.*

1988. Before Clark Kent (John Haymes Newton, Gerard Christopher), alias Superboy, moved to Metropolis to become a reporter for the *Daily Planet,* he attended Schuster University and worked for the school newspaper, *The Herald,* on *The Adventures of Superboy* (Syn). CBS's *Murphy Brown* presents several investigative reporters for

the TV newsmagazine *F.Y.I.:* Murphy Brown (Candice Bergen), Corky Sherwood (Faith Ford), Frank Fontana (Joe Regalbuto) and Jim Dial (Charles Kimbrough).

1990. Earl Brattigan (Bruce Greenwood) is a journalist for the *Post-Dispatch* who has a basement office and gets the worst assignments possible on the NBC pilot *Dead End Brattigan.*

1991. Cheryl Pollak plays Sarah Parker, the researcher for KQSF-TV reporter Jim Malone (William Russ) on the ABC pilot *Bay City Story.* Gaby Fernandez (Mayteana Morales) and Tina Nuen (Tran-Ahn Tran) are reporters for their grammar school (the Hurston School) newspaper, *The Hurston Herald* on *Ghost Writer* (PBS). Julie Robbins (Julie Brown) is a celebrity reporter for the TV show *Inside Scoop* on the NBC pilot *The Julie Brown Show.*

1992. Pierce Brosnan plays Reid Wilde, a reporter for *Auto World* magazine who lives the stories he covers on the NBC pilot *Running Wilde.*

1993. Matthew Perry plays Matthew Bailey, a reporter for the *Beach Cities News Advertiser* in San Diego on ABC's *Home Free.* Clark Kent (Dean Carter) and Lois Lane (Teri Hatcher) are reporters for the Metropolis *Daily Planet* on *Lois and Clark: The New Adventures of Superman* (ABC).

1995. Elizabeth Montgomery plays Edna Buchanan, a Pulitzer Prize-winning reporter for the Miami *Tribune* on the CBS pilot *Deadline for Murder: From the Files of Edna Buchanan.* Ann Jillian plays Frances Hampton-Smith, a reporter for *News Watch* on Channel 6 in Los Angeles on the NBC pilot *Fast Company.* Jane Curtin plays Susan Baker, a community affairs reporter for a Los Angeles paper called the *L.A. Paid Reader* on the ABC pilot *Mystery Dance.*

1997. Camela Gorrick (Charlotte Sullivan) and Emily Robson (Erica Luttrell) are 13-year-old girls who write for their school newspaper, *The Rattler* (at the Jesse Owens Junior High School in Brooklyn, N.Y.) on *The New Ghost Writer Mysteries* (CBS).

1999. Samantha McPherson (Carly Pope) is a reporter for *The Zapruder Reporter*, the paper of John F. Kennedy High School on the WB's *Popular.*

2000. Wallace Benton (Oliver Platt) is a journalism professor whose students help him investigate crimes for the New York *Ledger* on NBC's *Deadline.*

2001. Melvin Frohike (Tom Braidwood), Richard Langly (Dean Hayland) and John Byers (Bruce Harwood) are *The Lone Gunmen* (Fox), publishers of *The Lone Gunman*, a Maryland based newsletter designed to expose injustice. Chloe Sullivan (Allison Mack) is a reporter for her school newspaper, *The Torch* (at Smallville High) on the WB's *Smallville*.

2002. Tucker Burns (Chad Willett) is a reporter who covers bizarre stories for a tabloid called *The Chronicle* (Sci Fi).

2003. Wanda Hawkins (Wanda Sykes) is a TV reporter who does the street interviews for her segment "Wanda at Large" on WHDC-TV, Channel 11 in Washington, D.C. on Fox's *Wanda at Large*.

2005. Carl Kolchak (Stuart Townsend) and Perri Reed (Gabrielle Union) are reporters who investigate bizarre crimes for the Los Angeles *Beacon* on *The Night Stalker* (ABC).

2006. Rebecca Romijn is Pepper Dennis, a bubbly but mishap-prone television news reporter for station WEIE in Chicago on *Pepper Dennis* (WB).

Restaurants

This entry chronicles the programs set at restaurants, cafes, coffee shops, diners and taverns. See also *Bars*.

1949. Staff and clientele problems plague Studs Turkel (himself), the owner of the Chicago based Stud's Place restaurant on *Stud's Place* (NBC/ABC).

1952. On CBS's *I Love Lucy*, Lucy and Ricky Ricardo (Lucille Ball, Desi Arnaz) attempt to run a diner called A Little Bit of Cuba while their friends Fred and Ethel Mertz (William Frawley, Vivian Vance) run a diner called A Big Hunk of America. An Italian immigrant named Pasquale (Alan Reed, Thomas Gomez) runs a restaurant called Pasquale's Spaghetti Palace in Chicago's Little Italy on *Life with Luigi* (CBS).

1955. Matt Dillon (James Arness), the Marshal of Dodge City, Kansas (1860s) enjoys a meal at Del Monico's Café on CBS's *Gunsmoke*. While not seen eating there, Ralph Kramden (Jackie Gleason) frequently mentions the Hong Kong Gardens as his favorite eatery on *The Honeymooners* (CBS).

1956. Cab driver Joe Spartan (Larry Blyden) frequents Mac's Coffee Shop ("The Waldorf As-

toria of coffee shops") in Brooklyn, New York on *Joe and Mabel* (CBS).

1958. Dan Troop (John Russell), Marshal of Laramie, Wyoming (1880s), enjoys a meal at the Blue Bonnet Café on ABC's *Lawman*. Tito and Amelia (Ricardo Montalban, Lita Milan) are restaurant owners in Havana who help people in trouble on the NBC pilot *Tonight in Havana*.

1959. John Vivyan plays *Mr. Lucky*, an entrepreneur who owns the *Fortuna*, a yacht he runs as a floating gambling hall then supper club on *Mr. Lucky* (CBS).

1960. Andy Taylor (Andy Griffith), the Sheriff of Mayberry, North Carolina, enjoys meals at the Junction Café on *The Andy Griffith Show* (CBS). Foreign correspondent Glenn Evans (Rod Taylor) enjoys a meal at the Golden Dragon Café on ABC's *Hong Kong*. Peter Porter and his wife Gladys (Harry Morgan, Cara Williams) frequent Petroni's Restaurant on *Pete and Gladys* (CBS).

1966. Hopeful actress Ann Marie (Marlo Thomas) dines at Nino's Restaurant in Manhattan on *That Girl* (ABC). Also on the series Ann's father, Lou Marie (Lew Parker) owns the La Parisienne Restaurant in Brewster, New York. Professional bodyguard Thomas Hewitt Cat (Robert Loggia) frequents the Casa Del Gato restaurant on *T.H.E. Cat* (NBC).

1968. Bert Gramus and his wife Claudia (Herb Edelman, Joyce Van Patten) struggle to make a living as the owners of Bert's Diner in Los Angeles on *The Good Guys* (CBS).

1972. Sam and Sophie Steinberg (Harold J. Stone, Bibi Osterwald) own Steinberg's Delicatessen in Manhattan on *Bridget Loves Bernie* (CBS). Jason Walton (John Walmsley), the second oldest son of John and Olivia Walton, plays guitar at the Dew Drop Inn on *The Waltons* (CBS).

1973. Ex-football quarterback Jerry Standish (Dick Gautier) owns the Polynesia Paradise Café on *Here We Go Again* (ABC).

1974. Papa Caruso's Restaurant in Los Angeles is the favorite eatery of Christie Love (Teresa Graves), an undercover police woman on ABC's *Get Christie Love*. Private detective Jim Rockford (James Garner) enjoys a meal at a roadside diner called Casa Tacos on NBC's *The Rockford Files*. A widow named Flo (Della Reese) operates a San Pedro café called Flo's Place on the NBC pilot *Twice in a Lifetime*.

1975. Ernie and Adelle (Wynn Irwin, Fannie

245   RESTAURANTS

Flagg) are a married couple who run Ernie's Truck Stop on the NBC pilot *Home Cooking*.

1976. Mel's Diner is a less-than-fashionable roadside diner in Phoenix, Arizona, that is run by Mel Sharples (Vic Tayback), a man who believes he makes the world's best chili on *Alice* (CBS). Joe and Angela Dumpling (James Coco, Geraldine Brooks) are the overweight owners of the Dumplings Luncheonette on the ground floor of the Bristol Oil Company on NBC's *The Dumplings*. Della Reese plays Flo, the owner of *Flo's Place* (NBC pilot), a small dockside hotel and restaurant. Frank DeFazio (Phil Foster), the father of Laverne (Penny Marshall) owns the Pizza Bowl (combination bowling alley and pizzeria) on ABC's *Laverne and Shirley*. Also on the series, beer truck driver Squiggy (David L. Lander) inherits a restaurant from his late uncle Lazlo and renames it Dead Lazlo's Place.

1977. John Ritter plays Jack Tripper on ABC's *Three's Company*. He begins as a cooking student at the Los Angeles Technical School. In 1980 he becomes a chef at Angelino's Restaurant and in 1984 opens his own eatery, Jack's Bistro.

1978. The Trucker's Paradise is a truck stop run by Goober Pyle (George Lindsey) and his sister Pearl Pyle (Leigh French) on the CBS pilot *Goober and the Trucker's Paradise*.

1979. Angie Falco (Donna Pescow) is a waitress at the Liberty Coffee Shop in Philadelphia on ABC's *Angie*. The Country Comfort Trucker's Stop in Bowlin County, Georgia, is the favorite eatery of trucker B.J. McKay (Greg Evigan) on NBC's *B.J. and the Bear*. In second season episodes, the bar-restaurant Phil's Disco in Los Angeles becomes the hangout.

1980. Ma's Place, run by Ma (LaWanda Page) is the favorite eatery of Nick, Ocee and Samantha, undercover cops on *B.A.D. Cats* (ABC). Above the Top is a posh 13th floor Los Angeles restaurant that features "Sky High Dining" on ABC's *It's a Living*. Susan Sullivan, Ann Jillian, Crystal Bernard, Louise Lasser, Barrie Youngfellow and Sheryl Lee Ralph are among the stars playing waitresses.

1982. Donna Seigel plays Dora, a waitress at an eatery called Tony's Coffee Shop in Los Angeles on the HBO pilot *All Night Radio*. Larry, Darryl and Darryl (William Sanderson, Tony Papenfuss, John Volstad) are three unkempt brothers who run the Minuteman Café in Vermont on CBS's *Newhart*.

1983. The Falls Point Diner in Baltimore, Ohio, is the gathering place for a group of men each week on the CBS pilot *Diner*. Paul Reiser and James Spader head the cast. Rolly Hutton (Cleavon Little) and Cookie Porter (Lyman Ward) are ex-cons struggling to keep on the straight and narrow as waiters in an unnamed diner owner by a woman named Marge (Carole Cooke) on the CBS pilot *Now We're Cookin'.'*

1984. The private detectives of the Riptide Detective Agency in California enjoy meals at the Straightaways Restaurant on NBC's *Riptide*.

1985. Former government operative Robert McCall (Edward Woodward) frequents O'Phelan's Restaurant in Manhattan on *The Equalizer* (CBS). Johnnie Baylor (Dorothy Lyman) is a single mother who works as a waitress at the Blue Moon Café on the NBC pilot *Heart's Island*. Housekeeper Lynn Belvedere (Christopher Hewett) cares for the Owens family and enjoys snacks at Donut World on ABC's *Mr. Belvedere*. Susan Hogan plays Nicole, the owner of Nicole's Lounge, the local eatery for the detectives of CBS's *Night Heat*.

1986. A group of laid off Pennsylvania steel workers help a young woman named Annie (Annie Potts) open a restaurant on the ABC pilot *Hearts of Steel*. Stefan Popalardo (Reuven Bar-Yotam) is a senior citizen who runs The Last Word, a restaurant for the young-at-heart on the NBC pilot *The Last Word*. Redd Foxx plays Al Hughes, the cantankerous, widowed owner of Al's Grill, a coffee shop and newsstand on *The Redd Foxx Show* (ABC).

1987. Lillian (Ellen Travolta), the mother of college student Charles, runs The Yesterday Café in New Jersey on the syndicated *Charles in Charge*.

1988. Kate McCarron (Isabella Hofmann) runs Kate's Place, a Manhattan restaurant on NBC's *Dear John*. Maureen (Betty Thomas) and Estelle (Deborah Rush) are sisters who run Ma's Place, a restaurant in rural Ohio on the ABC pilot *Home Again*. Bill Gillespie (Carroll O'Connor), the police chief of Sparta, Mississippi, frequents the Magnolia Café on *In the Heat of the Night* (NBC/CBS). Phil's Bar and Grill, owned by Phil (Pat Corley) is the watering hole for the staff of the TV news show, *F.Y.I.* on *Murphy Brown* (CBS). The Lunch Box in Lanford, Ohio, is a roadside eatery run by Roseanne Conner (Roseanne) on ABC's *Roseanne*. Nick and Hillary Tattinger (Stephen Collins, Blythe Danner) are a married couple who run Tattinger's, an upscale Manhattan restaurant on NBC's *Tattinger's*.

1989. Ann Jillian plays Ann McNeil, the manager of Aunt Betty's Coffee and Bean Shop on NBC's *Ann Jillian*. Rachel Crawford (Telma Hopkins) runs a diner called Rachel's Place on *Family Matters* (ABC). George Clooney plays Ben Braddock, a former prospector (in Silverberg, California, 1902) who opens a restaurant in a train depot for pioneers on the CBS pilot *Hot Prospects*. Drew Thatcher (Bill Smitrovich) runs the Glen Brook Diner with the help of his wife Libby (Patti LuPone) on ABC's *Life Goes On*.

1990. Holly Baker (Margaret Welsh) owns The Baker's Corner Diner, the favorite eatery of newspaper columnist Tom Nash on *American Dreamer*. Whoopi Goldberg plays Brenda, the owner of the Bagdad Café, a rundown diner, hotel and truck stop in the one building town of Bagdad in the Mojave Desert on *Bagdad Café* (CBS). Ponder Blue (Ossie Davis) runs Blue's Barbecue Villa, the local diner hangout in Evening Shade, Arkansas on CBS's *Evening Shade*. Salinger's Sea Food Restaurant in San Francisco is the eatery inherited by the five Salinger children after their parents are killed in a car accident on Fox's *Party of Five*. Neve Campbell heads the cast. Monk's Café in Manhattan is the hangout for Jerry Seinfeld and his friends, George, Kramer and Elaine on NBC's *Seinfeld*. Harold Gould plays Nate Singer, a widower who operates *Singer and Sons* (CBS), a New York Deli. Loretta Devine plays Loretta, hostess at the Café Jacques in Ponca City, Oklahoma on *Sugar and Spice* (CBS). Tail o' the Pup is the favorite eatery of Chic Chesbro (George Clooney), a motorcycle cop for the L.A.P.D. on ABC's *Sunset Beat*.

1991. Frankie Reed (Julianne Phillips) runs a restaurant called Sweet 16 on NBC's *Sisters*.

1992. Josephine Austin (Madge Sinclair) runs a Los Angeles restaurant called the Angel City Grill on ABC's *Pros and Cons*.

1993. Los Angeles police detective Steve Sloan (Barry Van Dyke) and Dr. Jesse Travis (Charlie Schlatter) of Community General Hospital, are partners in an eatery called Bar-B-Q Bob's (also seen as BBQ Bob's) in the Fonatine Mall on *Diagnosis Murder* (CBS). Frasier Crane (Kelsey Grammer) and his brother Niles (David Hyde Pierce) frequent the Café Nervosa on NBC's *Frasier*. They also attempted to open their own eatery, The Happy Brothers Restaurant, but

failed. Sanitation engineer Roc Emerson (Charles S. Dutton) enjoys coffee and cake at the Depot (originally called The Landfill), the café next to the sanitation depot on Fox's *Roc*.

1994. Gerald Krepple (Jim J. Bullock) is the harassed manager of a trendy eatery on the syndicated *Boogie's Diner*. Holly Aldridge (Valerie Bertinelli) is a young American woman who manages the Café Americain, a famous Paris eatery on NBC's *Cafe Americain*. Monica Geller (Courteney Cox) is head chef at Alesandro's Restaurant on NBC's *Friends*. She and her friends (Rachel, Phoebe, Ross, Joey and Chandler) hang out at a coffee shop called Central Perk (where Rachel [Jennifer Aniston] worked as a waitress). Connie Drego (Stephanie Hodge) and her daughter Madeline (Jennifer Aniston) run Drego's Oasis, a roadside diner and motel on *Muddling Through* (CBS). Twin sisters Tia and Tamera (Tia and Tamera Mowry) are waitresses at the Rocket Burger on *Sister, Sister* (ABC/WB). Tia later works as a counter girl at Book 'Em Joe, a coffee shop in the mall. Kelly LaRue (Carol Alt) is a gorgeous girl who runs the Scuttlebutt Bar and Grill on Paradise Island in Florida on the syndicated *Thunder in Paradise*.

1995. The Coffee Dog Café is a small Pennsylvania eatery run by Julia Wallace (Marie Osmond) and her mother, Shirley (Betty White) on *Maybe This Time* (ABC). John Williams, called Pops (John Witherspoon) is the owner of Pop's Joint, a diner in the lobby of a hotel on *The Wayans Bros.* (WB). Drew Carey and his friends hang out at the Warsaw Tavern, a bar-restaurant on *The Drew Carey Show* (ABC). Cartoonist Caroline Duffy (Lea Thompson) enjoys a meal at Remo's Restaurante on NBC's *Caroline in the City*.

1996. Willie Goode (Sherman Hemsley) is a reformed con artist who owns Willie's Chili, a diner on UPN's *Goode Behavior*.

1997. Ally McBeal (Calista Flockhart) and her co-workers from the law firm of Cage and Fish enjoy meals at Jasper's Restaurant on *Ally McBeal* (Fox). Robin Riker plays Nicole Moran, the owner of Nicole's, a restaurant frequented by Home Court Publishing House employee Ben Stevenson (Gregory Hines) on *The Gregory Hines Show* (CBS).

1998. The rude and obnoxious doctor, John Becker (Ted Danson) frequents Reggie's Diner in the Bronx on CBS's *Becker*. Dean and DeLuca's is a Manhattan restaurant managed by Javier Quintata (Ian Gomez) on *Felicity* (WB). The Lighthouse is a seafood restaurant in California that is owned by Peter Collins (Ed Blatchford) on the syndicated *Malibu, Ca.* Peter also owns the Surf Shack, a beachside eatery.

1999. The Crashdive Café in New Mexico is the eatery frequented by the regulars of UPN's *Roswell.* Zoe Bean (Selma Blair) and her friends frequent the Café 'n Pastries in Manhattan on *Zoe, Duncan, Jack and Jane* (WB). In second season episodes, titled *Zoe*, Zoe is the manager of the Ching Hi Chinese Restaurant.

2000. Lorelai Gilmore (Lauren Graham) and her daughter Rory (Alexis Bledel) are coffee junkies who find Luke's Diner in Stars Hollow, Connecticut the perfect hangout on the WB's *Gilmore Girls.* Joan Clayton (Tracee Ellis Ross) and her friends lunch at Skia's, a trendy restaurant on UPN's *Girlfriends.* In 2004, Joan opens her own bar-restaurant, The J-Spot. Frank DeLucca (Paul Sorvino) and his wife Dolly (Ellen Burstyn) own Cucina DeLucca's, an Italian restaurant in New Jersey on *That's Life* (CBS).

2001. Real life chef Emeril Lagasse plays himself, a chef at the Culinary Network who often goes against the wishes of his producer Trish O'Connell (Tricia O'Kelley) to get his show on the air on NBC's *Emeril.*

2002. The Jade Swan Restaurant is the eatery frequented by the regulars on the syndicated *Once a Thief.*

2003. Dancing Zorba's Greek Restaurant is the featured eatery on *My Big Fat Greek Life*, a CBS series based on the feature film *My Big Fat Greek Wedding.* Raven Baxter (Raven Symone) is the daughter of a chef who, as strange as it may seem, rarely eats at her father's diner, The Chill Grill, on *That's So Raven* (Disney). Tru Davies (Eliza Dushku), the girl who can go back in time 24 hours to change events, enjoys meals at the Standard Diner in Manhattan on *Tru Calling* (Fox).

2005. Bradley Cooper plays Jack Bourdain, the head chef of the Nolita Restaurant, an upscale New York eatery on *Kitchen Confidential* (Fox). Valerie Tyler (Jennie Garth) and her partner Lauren (Leslie Grossman) open a bakery called Sugar Babies Bakery on *What I Like About You* (WB). Val's younger sister, Holly (Amanda Bynes), enjoys meals at the Liberty Café in Manhattan.

2006. In 2003, when *All of Us* premiered on UPN, the gorgeous Neesee James (LisaRaye McCoy) operated a successful catering company. When a fire destroyed her business, she opened a trendy restaurant called Neesee's. Mitch Crumb (Ben Savage) is a Hollywood film writer who returns to his home town (Connecticut) to help his family run their restaurant, the Stonehouse Grill, on *Crumbs* (ABC).

Rescue

This entry chronicles the programs on which highly trained people risk their lives to help people in trouble or in precarious situations.

1954. The work of paramedics with the Los Angeles County Fire Department is brought to life for the first time on *Alarm*, a syndicated series starring Richard Arlen and J. Pat O'Malley.

1957. Frank Lovejoy plays Ed McCook, an inspector for the Chicago Fire Department on the CBS pilot *Chicago 212.*

1958. The work of the L.A. County Fire Department's Rescue 8 Division is seen through the work of paramedics Wes Cameron and Skip Johnson (Jim Davis, Lang Jeffries) on the syndicated *Rescue 8.*

1965. Firefighting is played for laughs on *Kibbee Hates Fitch*, a CBS pilot with Don Rickles as Russell Kibbee, captain of Hook and Ladder Company 23 of the New York Fire Department, and Lou Jacobi as Arthur Fitch, a fire lieutenant who is jealous of Kibbee's promotion to captain.

1966. Soupy Sales plays an inefficient but eager fireman who is trying to please his brother in law, the fire chief, on the CBS comedy pilot *Where There's Smokey.*

1968. The marionette adventure *Thunderbirds* (syndicated) presents the search and rescue operations of Jeff Tracy, the head of International Rescue, a futuristic organization that uses highly advanced equipment to rescue people.

1971. Firefighters and doctors work together on *Emergency!*, an NBC series starring Robert Fuller and Bobby Troup as Drs. Kelly Brackett and Joe Early. Julie London is Nurse Dixie McCall and Kevin Tighe and Randolph Mantooth are paramedics Roy DeSoto and John Gage (with Squad 51 of the L.A. County Fire Department).

1973. Kevin Tighe and Randolph Mantooth repeat their roles in animated form on *Emergency Plus 4*, an NBC series in which they receive assistance from four children (Sally, Matt, Jason and Randy) in rescue operations. The collie Lassie becomes the leader of the Rescue Force, a group of animals that assist Ben Turner (voice of Ted Knight) and his rescue team on the animated ABC series *Lassie's Rescue Rangers*.

1974. James Drury plays Spike Ryerson, captain of Engine Company 23 of the Los Angeles County Fire Department on *Firehouse* (ABC). The rescue operations of the Sierra National Park Rangers are seen through the experiences of Rangers Tim Cassidy, Julie Beck and Jack Moore (James Richardson, Susan Foster, Robert Hogan) on NBC's *Sierra*.

1975. Firefighting is again played for laughs on *Where's the Fire?*, an ABC pilot about the antics of the men of Engine Company 22. Dave Ketchum stars as Captain O'Hara.

1977. Wiley Starrett and Buzz Wizzer (Bruce Fairbarin, David Gilliam) are officers with the Search and Rescue Division of the Los Angeles Harbor Patrol on the CBS pilot *Bravo Two* (their boat code). Walt Robinson and Rick Wilson (Tom Simcox, James Houghton) head Emergency Services, an organization that combines police, fire and ocean rescue services into the Code R Rescue Service (based off Channel Island in Southern California) on *Code R* (CBS). Kent McCord plays William Stone, the operator of a one-man fire rescue station in Pine Valley, California on the NBC pilot *Pine Canyon Is Burning*. Widower Bob Donell (Michael J. Reynolds) and his children, Kate (Donann Calvin) and Jim (Michael Tough) own the Alpha Ranch in Texas and use animals for difficult rescue missions on NBC's *Search and Rescue: The Alpha Team*.

1979. The work of John Gage and Roy DeSoto (Randolph Mantooth, Kevin Tighe) is revised (see 1972), as they become visiting paramedics with the 87th Rescue Unit of the San Francisco Fire Department on *Emergency!* (NBC). The search and rescue operations of the 240-Robert Division of the Los Angeles County Sheriff's Emergency Services Department are profiled on *240-Robert* (ABC). Mark Harmon and Joanna Cassidy star as Deputies T.R. Applegate and Morgan Wainwright.

1981. ABC revises *240-Robert* with Pamela Hensley replacing Joanna Cassidy as Deputy Sandy Harper. Haley Green (Martina Deignan) becomes the first female firefighter with the Los Angeles County Fire Department (Battalion 6, Station 1) on ABC's *Code Red*. Lorne Greene stars as Fire Captain Joe Rorchek.

1982. Although ABC's *Star of the Family* features Kathy Maisnik as Jennie Lee Krebs, a 16-year-old girl who aspires to be a singer, the series also revolves around her father, Buddy Lee Krebbs (Brian Dennehy), a captain of Fire Company 64 of the Southern California Fire Department.

1988. Robert Conrad plays Jesse Hawkes, head of High Mountain Rangers, a rescue organization based in the Sierra Nevadas near Lake Tahoe on *High Mountain Rangers* (CBS).

1989. The work of the Emergency Services Unit of the N.Y.P.D., Truck One Division is depicted on NBC's *True Blue*. Timothy Van Patten, Ally Walker and Eddie Velez star.

1990. Gregory Harrison plays Jack Taylor, a widower, the father of four children (Allison, Brian, Steve and Jeff) and the captain of the E.R.F.D. (Eagle Ridge Fire Department) in California on *The Family Man* (CBS). The Harlem Eastside Lifesaver Program, H.E.L.P. for short, is an emergency New York City unit of paramedics, cops and firemen on ABC's *H.E.L.P.* Wesley Snipes, John Mahoney and David Caruso star. Jim Carrey plays Fire Marshal Bill, a firefighter who demonstrates what not to do to avoid injury — but becomes the victim of his demonstrations on the Fire Marshal Bill segments of Fox's *In Living Color*.

1995. James Brolin plays Reese Wheeler, head of the Steep Mountain Ranger Group, a band of men and women who risk their lives to rescue people on ABC's *Extreme*. Elizabeth Gracen, Brooke Langton and Justin Lazard co-star. Robert Conrad plays Tooter Campbell, head of the Bear Valley Search and Rescue team in California's Sierra Nevada Mountains on NBC's *High Sierra Search and Rescue*. Dee Wallace and Brittany Powell co-star. Stan Kelly (Peter Boyle) is the chief of Battalion 6 of Engine Company 31, Ladder 7, the busiest firehouse in Philadelphia on the ABC pilot *Philly Heat*. Mary Mara and Ving Rhames co-star as Laura Walker and DeWitt Wardlaw.

1999. Mike Bell (Victor Browne), Kathleen Ryan (Marjorie Monagham) and Christian Kane (Wick Lobo) are paramedics with Task Force 77 of the L.A. County Fire Department on the WB's *Rescue 77*. The rescue operations of Squad 55 of the New York Fire Department are depicted on NBC's *Third Watch* (between 3 P.M. and 11 PM.). Coby Bell, Cara Buono, Nia Longand and Anthony Ruivivar head a large cast.

2004. The work of the men and women of the Engine Company 62 Fire House of the New York Fire Department is dramatized on *Rescue Me* (FX). Denis Leary stars as Tommy Gavin, the featured firefighter.

Ringmasters see *Circus and Carnivals*

Robots

This entry chronicles the programs on which a robot or android is featured as a regular or recurring character. See also *Computers—Extraordinary*.

1949. Tobor (robot spelled backwards) is a robot that fights evil on *Captain Video and His Video Rangers* (DuMont). Tobor was originally an evil robot built by Dr. Pauli to destroy Captain Video ("The Guardian of the Safety of the World"). He was captured by the Captain and reprogrammed for good.

1953. Mr. McTavish is the robot created by Professor Horatio Hinkle on *The Adventures of Superman* (Syn.). Reject the Robot is an inhabitant of the planet Jupiter who has befriended Ernest P. Duckweather, the Earthling who invented interplanetary television on *Johnny Jupiter* (DuMont/ABC/Syn.). Reject is seen in two versions: a small marionette when on Jupiter; life size when he comes to Earth to help Johnny.

1955. Tobor the Robot (see 1949) reappears on *Here Comes Tobor*, a pilot in which Tobor is teamed with a highly intelligent boy (Tommy) to battle evil.

1962. Jean VanderPyl provides the voice for Rosie, the robotic maid (from the U-Rent-A-Bot Maid Service) to the futuristic Jetson family on the animated ABC series *The Jetsons*.

1963. Astro Boy and his sister Astro Girl are robots built by Dr. Boynton and Dr. Elefun to battle evil on the animated Japanese series *Astro Boy* (Syn.). Robert the Robot is the pilot of the futuristic space ship *Fireball XL-5* (NBC).

1964. Julie Newmar plays Rhoda, a beautiful U.S. Air Force robot (the prototype for a project to send robots into outer space) on *My Living Doll*. Rhoda appears as the ultimate female but is mentally immature. She is assigned to psychia-

trist Dr. Bob McDonald (Bob Cummings) to mold her character and create a real woman.

1965. Dick Gautier plays Hymie, a once evil robot that has been reprogrammed for good (to battle the evils of KAOS) on the NBC episodes of *Get Smart*. An environmental control robot called simply Robot (voice of Dick Tufeld) is a member of the *Jupiter II*, an Earth ship that is *Lost in Space* (CBS). Robot defends itself with electrical charges and does not like to be overworked ("I need eight hours rest like other robots").

1966. An indestructible robot named Gigantor and his 12-year-old master Tommy Sparks battle evil on the animated series *Gigantor* (Syn.).

1968. Giant Robot (as it is called) and its controller, young Johnny Sokko, battle evil as members of Unicorn on the Japanese series *Johnny Sokko and His Flying Robot* (Syn.).

1969. Goldar is a 50-foot gold robot created by Earth scientists to battle the evil alien Rodak on the syndicated *Space Giants*. Also built were Silva, Goldar's wife, and Gam, their gold son.

1973. The British series *Doctor Who* appears on American television for the first time. Here a Time Lord, called the Doctor (Tom Baker), battles evil throughout the universe. He faces numerous enemies, most notably the cone-like robots the Daleks (famous for their metallic tone — "Ex-ter-min-ate, ex-ter-min-ate") and the Cybermen, a race of deadly robots. The Doctor also has a mechanical dog he calls K-9. Steve Austin (Lee Majors) is considered a cyborg, part man, part machine, after a bionic operation saved his life (replacing his legs, arm and eye) on *The Six Million Dollar Man* (ABC).

1976. Jaime Sommers (Lindsay Wagner) is considered a cyborg (part woman, part machine) after a bionic operation saves her life (replacing her legs, arm and inner ear) on *The Bionic Woman* (ABC/NBC). Also on the series (ABC episodes only) are the Fembots, beautiful but evil female robots seeking to destroy Jaime and her bionic counterpart, Steve Austin, "The Six Million Dollar Man" (see 1973). John Schuck plays Gregory "YoYo" Yoyonovich, a prototype robot (for a project to create the perfect crime fighter) who is not yet perfected on ABC's *Holmes and Yoyo* (the title refers to Alexander Holmes [Richard B. Shull], the L.A.P.D. officer assigned to work with Yoyo).

1977. John "Kid" Haven (Michael Shannon) is a secret L.A.P.D. android programmed to be the perfect police officer on *Future Cop* (ABC).

Donald Moffat plays Rem, a 24th century robot that fled his programmed society (the City of Domes) to live free in an outside world called Serenity on *Logan's Run* (CBS). *Mystery Island* is a live action segment of the CBS cartoon *The Skatebirds*. Here, scientists Chuck Kelly and Sue Corwin (Stephen Parr, Lynne Marie Johnson) are stranded on a mysterious island with Pops (voice of Frank Welker), a sophisticated robot they protect from Dr. Strenge (Michael Kermotan), an evil scientist who needs Pops to complete his machines of mass destruction. Robert Shields and Lorene Yarnell play the Clinkers, clumsy robots living in suburbia in skits on the variety series *Shields and Yarnell* (CBS). Peepo is a 38th century robot who helps Commander Gampu (Jonathan Harris) train cadets for space exploration on *Space Academy* (CBS). Craig Richard Nelson plays Earl, the robot butler to Elaine and Vance Keefer, a futuristic couple on the ABC pilot *Stick Around*. Also on the program is Andy (Andy Kaufman), the robot who raised Elaine (Nancy New) but who is now outdated and prone to breakdowns.

1978. Lucifer (voice of Jonathan Harris) is a sinister robot who, with the deadly Cylon robots (of the Cylon Empire), seeks to destroy the Earthlings aboard the giant battleship *Galactica* on ABC's *Battlestar Galactica*. Also on the series, a robot called Muffit (a cross between a bear and a dog) is the pet to young Boxey (Noah Hathaway) on the *Galactica*. Bobby Porter plays Andy, the cowardly robot crewmember of a U.G.S.P. (United Galaxy Sanitation Patrol) space ship on NBC's *Quark*. A space age Moe, Larry and Curly (the Three Stooges) are reconstructed as robots from the finest parts available to battle evil on the animated series *The Three Robotic Stooges* (CBS).

1979. NBC's *Buck Rogers in the 25th Century* features Twiki (Felix Silla), the silver robot aide to Buck Rogers, and Crichton (voice of Jeff Davis), a robot who refuses to believe that he is man-made. Frances Kaskadden (Eugenie Ross-Leming) is a scientist at the eerie Blacke Foundation who has created Bram Shelley (Christian Marlowe), a cyborg who is not perfected on NBC's *Highcliffe Manor*. *Whitney and the Robot* is a syndicated series in which cab driver Whitney (Whitney Rydbeck) and 4-U-2 (Buddy Douglas), a robot from the planet Zeda, team to explore aspects of the world for children.

1980. Cassandra Peterson (as the Dance Hall Girl), Alex Kubik (the Gunfighter) and Edward Coch, Jr. (Gunfighter's opponent) are three of the robots (seen in the opening theme) created by Simon Quaid (James Wainwright) for a futuristic adult playground called Westworld. Quaid, however goes *Beyond Westworld* (CBS) when he programs his robots for evil. Seeking to stop him is Delos Corporation agent John Moore (Jim McMullan).

1981. Rich Little plays Miles Fenton, a widowed computer engineer who builds robots to help him raise his children on the ABC pilot *Nuts and Bolts*. Victor is his caustic, sophisticated robot; Primo is the caring, out-of-date robot; and Beeper is a vacuum cleaning robot.

1982. Stephen Moore provides the voice of Marvin, a paranoid robot on *The Hitchhiker's Guide to the Galaxy* (PBS).

1983. Don Adams provides the voice for Inspector Gadget, a dim-witted, bumbling bionic crime fighter (half human, half contraption) for the Metro City Police Force on the animated *Inspector Gadget* (Syn.). Richie Adler (Matthew Laborteaux) is a computer genius (built his own computer [Ralph] and robot [Herman]) that helps authorities solve crimes on *The Whiz Kids* (CBS).

1984. Futuristic android pilots Fi and Fum (Ruth Buzzi, Jim Nabors) seek a way to return to their planet (ZR-3) when their space ship becomes lost in time on *The Lost Saucer*. To protect 23rd century Earth from the evil Shadow (ruler of the planet Umbra), Rob Simmons, a scientist with the Galaxy Patrol, constructs an army of robots (Bort, Tur, Beau, Crunch, and Ono) to battle him on the animated series *The Mighty Orbots* (Syn.). The Roboz is a robot created by Murray Bozinski (Thom Bray), an inventor who also works as a private detective on NBC's *Riptide*. The battle for good over evil is seen on *The Transformers*, a syndicated animated series about the AutoBots, residents of the planet Zobitron, as they attempt to stop a race of deadly robots (the Decepitrons) from controlling the universe. Super-powered robot Voltron, a member of the Space Explorers, battles the evils of King Zarcer, ruler of the Planet of Doom, on the animated series *Voltron — Defender of the Universe* (Syn.).

1985. Sarah Jane Smith (Elisabeth Sladen) is a journalist who uses her robotic dog, K-9, to help her solve crimes on the syndicated pilot *K-9 and Company* (Sarah Jane was one of the traveling companions of Doctor Who [see 1973]. He gave

Sarah his dog as a parting gift). Nova (Amanda Wyss) is a beautiful android that helps Hal Sterling and his family avoid capture when they are mysteriously transported to a parallel universe on *Otherworld* (CBS). Rick Hunter and his assistant Linay battle alien robots as members of Veratech on the syndicated animated series *Robotech*. Steller and Oops are robots that need to be charged by human love as they help humans in need on the syndicated cartoon *Robotman*. Tiffany Brissette plays Vicki (Voice Input Child Identicate), a very pretty 10-year-old girl who happens to be a robot on *Small Wonder* (Syn.). Vicki was created by Ted Lawson to help handicapped children. Vicki is not yet perfected and lives with Ted and his family while she learns to be a real girl. Charles Rocket plays D-5-B, a super human android that can think for itself and learn from experience on the CBS pilot *Steel Collar Man*.

1986. An earthling named Crystal Kane and her robotic allies, the Centurions (Max Ray, Jake Rockwell, Ace McCloud), battle the enemies of the Earth (Doc Terror and Hacker) on the syndicated cartoon *The Centurions*. Wendy Kilbourne plays Lisa Hampton, a beautiful android specifically designed to battle crime on the ABC pilot *Condor* (the agency for which she was created). A concoction of items evolved into Conky, the robot owned by Pee Wee Herman on *Pee Wee's Playhouse* (CBS).

1987. Brent Spiner plays Lieutenant Commander Data, a futuristic robot that is a Starfleet officer on the syndicated *Star Trek: The Next Generation*.

1988. Daniel Butler is Willie, the homemade robot on *Hey Verne, It's Ernest* (CBS). B.O.B. (Marty Polio) is an environmental robot that has been assigned to the pioneering Ludlow family as they attempt to colonize the planet Mars on the CBS pilot *Mars: Base One*. Elaine Giftos plays Katara, a beautiful killing android from the planet Qar'to on the syndicated *War of the Worlds*. Although the Katara storyline was dropped when the second season began, her mission was to save the Earth by destroying the invading Mortex aliens. If successful, the Earth would then become a feeding ground for her people.

1989. The nerdy Steve Urkel (Jaleel White) is a child genius who created a robot in his own image (the Urkelbot) and an android in the image of his girlfriend, Laura Winslow (the Laurabot) on ABC's *Family Matters*. An uncontrollable alien

named Jesse (Martin Kove) is sentenced to Earth as punishment to help people on *Hard Time on Planet Earth* (CBS). He is monitored by Control, his robotic parole officer. The robots Tom Servo and Crow are forced to watch awful B-movies of the past on *Mystery Science Theater 3000* (Comedy Central/Sci Fi). The characters, including the show's host, Joel Hodgson (then Mike Nelson) are seen in a theater setting at the bottom of the screen (watching the movie along with the TV audience). Rachel Morgan (Joanna Going) is the Marshal of Icarus, a planet with hostile inhabitants, who is struggling to uphold the peace with the help of her android, Cray (Jeremy Flynn) on the CBS science fiction pilot *Outpost*. High school nerd Screech Powers (Dustin Diamond) has built his own operating robot, Kevin, on NBC's *Saved by the Bell*.

1990. Naomi Fisher (Catherine Mary Stewart) is a doctor on a quest to help Daniel, a highly sophisticated robot, find his creator on the ABC pilot *Project Tin Man* (Daniel was created to be the perfect soldier by the government. However, when his moral program rejected killing, he was ordered destroyed. Daniel escaped and befriended Naomi when he hid in her car and she helped him avoid capture from the agents who want him back).

1992. Eve Edison (Yancy Butler) is a beautiful android created for the L.A.P.D. to be the perfect cop on NBC's *Mann and Machine*. Eve is the prototype for a project called "The Protector" and has been assigned to Detective Bobby Mann (David Andrews) to monitor her activities.

1993. Jack McGee plays Doc, a human with a number of synthetic parts (heart, liver, knee, arm) who works as a flight engineer and is called "Tin Man" by his crewmates on *Space Rangers* (CBS).

1994. Richard Eden plays Alex Murphy, a police officer in Delta City who, after being shot multiple times, is saved through a cybernetic operation that gives him a total body prosthesis, titanium skin and a computer-assisted brain that turns him into the crime-fighting *RoboCop* (Syn.). Kim Cattrall plays Delilah, a beautiful U.S. government undercover agent who is half android (literally rebuilt by scientists to save her life after she was brutally beaten by thugs) on the ABC pilot *Running Delilah*. Sullivan Walker plays Yale, the cyborg on NBC's *Earth 2*.

1996. A robot called Pimpbot (distinguished by its frankfurter-like head) appears on NBC's late night talk show, *Conan O'Brien*. While not the star of the show, the robot does interact with some guests. Anik Marten plays T.H.E.L.M.A. (Techno Human Emulating Machine), a female android on *Space Cases* (NIK).

1997. Before *Buffy the Vampire Slayer* switched networks (from the WB to UPN), Sarah Michelle Gellar also played Buffy's robot double, the Buffy Bot, a remarkable life-like android that the good witch Willow programmed with Buffy's qualities (including her fighting abilities) to convince demons that Buffy was still alive (on the WB it appeared that Buffy died in a battle, hence the need for the robot. On UPN, Buffy was reborn and the robot deactivated).

1998. Julia Pennington plays A.N.I. (Android Nursing Interface), a 23rd century robotic nurse on NBC's *Mercy Point*. Nikki Franco (Natalie Raitano) is a beautiful but very violent girl who works for Vallery Irons Protection on the syndicated *V.I.P.* Nikki loves firearms and explosives and has a robotic bomb-sniffing dog she calls Rex.

1999. Rusty (voice of Pamela Segall), a robotic boy with artificial intelligence, and Dwayne Hunter (Jonathan Cook), a lieutenant who wears a robotic exo-skeleton called Big Guy, team to battle evil on the animated *Big Guy and Rusty the Robot Boy* (Fox). Bender (voice of John D. Maggio) is a futuristic robot built for bending things but who also smokes, drinks and steals on the animated Fox series *Futurama*. Karl Pruner plays Ian Farve, an android that is a member of the Citizens Protective Bureau (in the year 2070) on *Total Recall* (Showtime).

2000. Mauser (Patrick Kake) is a robotic reactor engineer who battles the aliens (Baileys) seeking to take over the Earth on the syndicated *Cleopatra 2525*. Also on the series Cleopatra (Jennifer Sky), a member of the Flagship team battling the Baileys, has a mechanical dog named Mr. Pants Two (after her dog as a child). The Sci Fi Channel's *Lexx* features Robot Head 790 (voice of Jeffrey Hirschfield), a robotic drone that was zapped by a love machine (he is now gay), his head severed from his body (placed on a running board) and is now "a confused junk head" that travels from planet to planet on the space ship *Lexx*.

2002. On NBC's *Friends*, actor Joey Tribbiani (Matt Le Blanc) acquires a job on the TV series "Mac and Cheese" as Mac, the human assistant to the robotic cop Cheese.

2003. Jenny (voice of Janice Kawaye) is a super powered robot "with a super sensitive teenage heart" who protects the Earth from evil on the animated *My Life as a Teenage Robot* (NIK).

2004. A teenager named Chris receives help in defending his utopian world of Shuggazoom (from the evil Skeleton King) from five high tech androids on the animated ABC Family series *Super Robot Monkey Team Hyperforce Go!* Gus (voice of Maurice LaMarche) is a cynical robot who works as the engineer on the space ship *Bob* and is often mistaken for being gay (but he says he is not) on *Tripping the Rift* (Sci Fi).

San Francisco *(see also California)*

A listing of series set in San Francisco. See also *California Settings* and *Los Angeles Settings*.

1949. *Mama* (CBS); *Mysteries of Chinatown* (ABC); *One Man's Family* (NBC).

1954. *The Line-Up* (CBS; also known as *San Francisco Beat*).

1956. *The Brothers* (CBS).

1957. *The Californians* (NBC); *Have Gun—Will Travel* (CBS).

1960. *Checkmate* (CBS); *Dante* (NBC).

1962. *The Lucy Show* (CBS).

1967. *Ironside* (NBC).

1968. *The Doris Day Show* (CBS).

1970. *San Francisco International Airport* (NBC).

1971. *McMillan and Wife* (NBC).

1972. *The Streets of San Francisco* (ABC).

1974. *Amy Prentiss* (NBC).

1975. *Fay* (NBC); *Phyllis* (CBS).

1976. *The Barbary Coast* (ABC); *McMillan* (NBC);

1979. *The Curse of Dracula* (NBC); *Trapper John, M.D.* (CBS).

1980. *Freebie and the Bean* (CBS); *Goodtime Harry* (NBC); *Nobody's Perfect* (ABC); *Too Close for Comfort* (ABC).

1981. *Fitz and Bones* (NBC); *Foul Play* (ABC); *Mr. Merlin* (CBS); *Shannon* (CBS).

1983. *Hotel* (ABC).

1984. *Crazy Like a Fox* (CBS); *Jessie* (ABC); *Partners in Crime* (NBC).

1985. *Double Dare* (CBS); *Sara* (NBC).

1986. *My Sister Sam* (CBS).

1987. *Full House* (ABC); *Hooperman* (ABC).

1988. *Brother's Keeper* (NBC).

1989. *Christine Cromwell* (ABC); *Wolfe* (CBS).

1990. *Over My Dead Body* (CBS).
1991. *Good and Evil* (ABC).
1993. *Black Tie Affair* (NBC).
1994. *All American Girl* (ABC); *Party of Five* (Fox).
1995. *Partners* (Fox).
1996. *Nash Bridges* (CBS); *Poltergeist: The Legacy* (Sci Fi); *Suddenly Susan* (NBC).
1997. *Crisis Center* (NBC); *Dharma and Greg* (ABC).
1998. *Charmed* (WB).
2001. *The Division* (Lifetime).
2002. *Girl's Club* (Fox); *Half and Half* (UPN); *Just Cause* (PAX).
2003. *Abby* (UPN); *Black Sash* (WB); *The Mullets* (UPN); *Presidio Med* (CBS); *That's So Raven* (Disney).
2004. *Monk* (USA).
2005. *Killer Instinct* (Fox); *Twins* (WB).

Scatterbrained Women see Women — "Dumb Blonds"; Women — Scatterbrained

Schools see Teachers

Secret Agents see Espionage

Senior Citizens

This entry concerns itself with characters (stars, regulars or recurring) who are sixty years of age and over. Single episode guest appearances are excluded as this numbers in the thousands (for example, the one time only appearance of the parents of a husband or wife).

1947. Dayton Allen provides the voice of Phineas T. Bluster (a marionette), an old man who opposes people having fun on *Howdy Doody* (NBC).
1950. Real life seniors discuss issues on *Life Begins at 80* (ABC/DuMont/NBC). Jack Barry is the host.
1951. Amanda Randolph plays Mama, the always yelling, nagging mother of Ruby, the wife of George "Kingfish" Stevens, on *The Amos 'n' Andy Show* (CBS).

1952. Cliff Arquette, famous for his elder hillbilly character, Charley Weaver, appears on the series *Dave and Charlie* on NBC (about old timer Charley's friendship with unemployed file clerk Dave Willock). Cliff's character would appear on many shows, including as the host of ABC's *Hobby Lobby* in 1959 and as a semi-regular on NBC's *Hollywood Squares* in the 1960s and 70s. Stanley Andrews plays the Old Ranger, the host of western dramas on the syndicated *Death Valley Days*. Gloria Gordon is Mrs. O'Reilly, the owner of Mrs. O'Reilly's Boarding House, the residence of Irma Peterson on *My Friend Irma* (CBS). Gertrude Hoffman is Clarissa Odetts, the 82-year-old, young-at-heart neighbor of Margie Albright on *My Little Margie* (CBS/NBC). Also on the series, Clarence Kolb plays George Honeywell, the owner of Honeywell and Todd Investments, the company for which Margie's father, Vern, works. Margaret Davis is the owner of Mrs. Davis's Rooming House, the residence of schoolteacher Connie Brooks on *Our Miss Brooks* (CBS).
1953. Ernest Truex plays Frank Dimmer, the grandfather of young Jamison John Francis McHummer (Brandon DeWilde) on *Jamie* (ABC). Thurston Hall plays Humphrey Schuyler, a bank president and Cosmo Topper's boss on *Topper* (CBS).
1954. Spring Byington is Lily Ruskin, a widow who works as a newspaper advice columnist on *December Bride* (CBS). George Cleveland plays George Miller, called Gramps, the grandfather of Jeff Miller, the owner of *Lassie* (CBS; also known as *Jeff's Collie*).
1955. Milburn Stone is Galen Adams, the doctor in 1860s Dodge City, Kansas, who, as the series progressed, became a senior citizen on *Gunsmoke* (CBS).
1957. Burt Mustin is Mr. Finley, the crusty neighbor of Gus and Vickie Angel on *A Date with the Angels* (ABC). Burt Mustin plays Gus, the old fire station chief Beaver (Jerry Mathers) visits on *Leave It to Beaver* (CBS/ABC). Amos McCoy (Walter Brennan) is the cantankerous head of the McCoy family ("He roars like a lion but he's gentle as a lamb") on *The Real McCoys* (ABC/CBS). Also on the series, Andy Clyde plays Amos's friend and neighbor, George MacMichael, and Madge Bake is George's sister, Flora. Marion Lorne is Myrtle Banford, the rich, elderly widow and co-owner of the Banford and Bascomb Department

Store on NBC's *Sally* (Joan Caulfield plays Sally, Myrtle's friend, a salesgirl at the store).

1958. Ernest Truex is Jason Maculey and Reta Shaw his wife Flora, the managers of the Bartley House Hotel in New York City on *The Ann Sothern Show* (CBS). John Beamer (Ed Wynn) is a widower and retired businessman who cares for his orphaned granddaughters, Midge and Laurie, on *The Ed Wynn Show* (NBC).

1959. George and Martha Wilson (Joseph Kearns, Sylvia Field) are the neighbors of Dennis Mitchell, the very mischievous young boy on *Dennis the Menace* (CBS). Doris Packer is Clarissa Osborne, the wealthy but snobbish mother of the spoiled rotten Chatsworth Osborne, Jr. on *Dobie Gillis* (CBS).

1960. Frances Bavier plays Aunt Bee, housekeeper to Sheriff Andy Taylor and his son Opie on *The Andy Griffith Show* (CBS). Buddy Flower (Frank Aletter) is an investment broker who lives with his two spinster aunts, Violet and Iris (Enid Markey, Doro Merande), on *Bringing Up Buddy* (CBS). Pat O'Brien plays James Harrigan, Sr., a lawyer who is partners with his son, James, Jr., on *Harrigan and Son* (ABC). Spring Byington is Melinda Gray, a baby sitter for the Westwood Baby Sitters Service in California on the pilot *Here Comes Melinda*. Larry Keating is Roger Addison and Edna Skinner is his younger wife Kay, the neighbors of Wilbur and Carol Post on *Mister Ed* (Syn/CBS). Also on the series, Leon Ames plays Gordon Kirkwood, the Posts neighbor in later episodes, with Florence MacMichael, as his a bit younger wife, Winnie. William Frawley plays William Michael Francis Aloysius O'Casey, affectionately called "Bub," the father-in-law of Steve Douglas on *My Three Sons* (ABC). CBS episodes feature William Demarest as Charles O'Casey, Bub's brother, the former merchant marine who cares for Steve and his family and is called Uncle Charlie.

1961. Sam Jaffe is David Zorba, the elderly doctor who is idolized by neurosurgeon *Ben Casey* (ABC). Raymond Massey is Dr. Leonard Gillespie, the senior physician at Blair General Hospital on *Dr. Kildare* (NBC). Donald Foster is Herbert Johnson and Norma Varden his wife, Harriet, the elderly friends of maid Hazel Burke on NBC episodes of *Hazel*. First season episodes of *The Joey Bishop Show* (NBC) feature Madge Blake as the widowed mother of public relations man Joey Barnes (Joey Bishop). Sarah Green

(Gertrude Berg) is a widow who fulfills a life long dream by attending college on *Mrs. G. Goes to College* (CBS). Newlyweds Dick and Penny Cooper (Dick Sargent, Jody Warner) live with her parents, Barney and Mildred Hogan (Chick Chandler, Elizabeth Fraser) and her grandparents, Charley and Lovey Hackett (Jack Kirkwood, Cheerio Meredith) on *One Happy Family* (NBC).

1962. Irene Ryan plays Daisy Moses, called Granny, the mother-in-law of backwoods millionaire Jed Clampett on *The Beverly Hillbillies* (CBS). Octavius and Hallie Todd (Dub Taylor, Loie Bridge) are a retired couple who spend their time traveling from trailer court to trailer court on the CBS pilot *Octavius and Me*. Ed McMahon becomes Johnny Carson's sidekick and over the years turns senior citizen on NBC's *Tonight Show Starring Johnny Carson*.

1963. Cathleen Nesbitt is Agatha Morley, the mother of Congressman Glen Morley on *The Farmer's Daughter* (ABC). Bea Benaderet plays Kate Bradley, a widow who runs the Shady Rest Hotel in Hooterville on *Petticoat Junction* (CBS). Also on the series, Edgar Buchanan plays her uncle, Joe Carson, the somewhat lazy hotel manager.

1964. Blossom Rock plays Grandmamma Addams, the mother of the eccentric Gomez Addams, on *The Addams Family* (ABC). Also on the series, Margaret Hamilton is Esther Frump, the mother of Gomez's wife, Morticia. Agnes Moorehead and Maurice Evans play Endora and Maurice, the powerful witch parents of Samantha on *Bewitched* (ABC). Also on the series, Marion Lorne is Aunt Clara, the lovable but senile witch; and Mabel Albertson is Phyllis Stevens and Robert F. Simon (then Roy Roberts) is Frank Stevens, the parents of Darrin Stevens, the mortal who married Samantha. Edward Everett Horton plays Mr. Fenwick, the elderly head of Fenwick Diversified Industries on *The Cara Williams Show* (CBS). Jim Backus and Natalie Schafer play Thurston and Lovey Howell, "the millionaire and his wife" who are stranded on a South Pacific island after a shipwreck on *Gilligan's Island* (CBS). Jimmy Durante plays Jimmy Bannister, a former entertainer who would like his grandson, Eddie, to follow in his footsteps, on the CBS pilot *The Jimmy Durante Show*. Al Lewis is Count Dracula, better known as Grandpa, the father of Lily Munster on *The Munsters* (CBS). Also on the series, John Carradine plays Mr. Gateman, Herman Munster's elderly employer at the Gateman, Goodbury and Graves Funeral Parlor. Walter Brennan is Walter Andrews, the 65-year-old head of the Thunder Holding Corporation in Los Angeles on *The Tycoon* (ABC).

1965. Hank Patterson is Fred Ziffel and Barbara Pepper (then Fran Ryan) is his wife Doris, the elderly farmers on *Green Acres* (CBS). Also on the series, Frank Cady plays Sam Drucker, the owner of the general store; Pat Buttram is Eustace Haney, Hooterville's own con artist; and Eleanor Audley is Eunice Douglas, the mother of Oliver Douglas, the man who bought a run down farm called Green Acres. General Martin Peterson (Barton MacLane) then General Winfield Schaefer (Vinton Hayworth) are Major Anthony Nelson's commanding officers at NASA on *I Dream of Jeannie* (NBC). Elsa Lanchester is Miss Culver, the principal of the Foster School for Girls on *The John Forsythe Show* (NBC). Edmond O'Brien (then Dan O'Herlihy) plays Will Varner, the powerful (and deceitful) owner of the Varner Bank in Frenchman's Bend, Mississippi, on *The Long Hot Summer* (ABC). Arthur Treacher becomes the sidekick to talk show host Merv Griffin on *The Merv Griffin Show* (Syn.).

1966. Alan Napier plays Alfred Pennyworth, the butler to Bruce Wayne, alias the crime fighting Batman on *Batman* (ABC). Andrew and Grandma Hanks (Douglas V. Fowley, Ruth McDevitt) are the gun-toting parents of Henrietta Hanks (Ann Sheridan), a woman of 1870s Colorado who helps maintain the peace on *Pistols 'n' Petticoats* (CBS). Lew Parker and Rosemary DeCamp play Lou and Helen Marie, the parents of hopeful actress Ann Marie on *That Girl* (ABC). Also on the series, Mabel Albertson and Frank Faylen are Mildred and Bert Hollinger, the parents of Don Hollinger, Ann's boyfriend.

1967. Bob Steele plays Trooper Duffy, a survivor of the Alamo who is soldier at Fort Courage, Kansas (1860s) on *F Troop* (ABC). Walter Brennan plays Will Sonnett, an ex-Confederate cavalry scout seeking his son, James, a wanted gunman, on *The Guns of Will Sonnett* (ABC). Arthur O'-Connell is Edwin Carpenter, a father who is 33 years older than his father on ABC's *The Second Hundred Years* (Edwin's father, Luke [Monte Markham], was frozen alive in an avalanche in 1900. He was found and thawed out in 1967. He remained unchanged for 67 years, thus making him appear young although he is technically 100 years old).

1968. Lloyd Nolan plays Morton Chegley, head doctor at the Inner Aero Space Center on *Julia* (NBC). Arte Johnson plays Tyrone F. Horneigh, the "dirty old man" who seeks the affections of the spinster Gladys Ormphby (Ruth Buzzi) on *Rowan and Martin's Laugh-In* (NBC).

1969. Nightclub comedian Danny Williams (Danny Thomas) and his wife Kathy (Marjorie Lord) become grandparents when their daughter Terry has a son (Michael) on *Make Room for Granddaddy* (ABC; an update of *Make Room for Daddy*). Robert Young plays Marcus Welby, an elderly doctor who cares for his patients on *Marcus Welby, M.D.* (ABC). Oren Hayes (Pat O'Brien), Nash Crawford (Walter Brennan) and George Agnew (Chill Wills) are retired Texas Rangers who roam throughout the Old West upholding the law on the ABC pilot *The Over-the-Hill Gang*. Ralph Bellamy is Baylor Carlyle, head of the wealthy Carlyle family on ABC's *The Survivors*. Walter Brennan plays Andy Pruett, the father-in-law of English professor Michael Endicott on *To Rome with Love* (CBS).

1970. Barry Sullivan plays Jason Braddock, an aging and dying billionaire who is seeking a new lease on life by acquiring the blood of Ben Richards, a man whose blood grants him immunity to old age on *The Immortal* (ABC). Nash Crawford, Jason Fitch and George Agnew (Walter Brennan, Edgar Buchanan, Chill Wills) are retired Texas Rangers who right wrongs on the ABC pilot *The Over-the-Hill Gang Rides Again*.

1971. Edgar Buchanan is J.J. Jackson, a deputy sheriff to Sheriff Sam Cade on CBS's *Cade's County*. Jack Albertson plays Andrew Sellers, an aging doctor in the town of Dixon Mills, Canada, on the syndicated *Dr. Simon Locke*.

1972. The Relationship between a teenage boy (Richie) and his grandfather is depicted on the pilot *Grandpa and Richie*. John Marley plays Grandfather and Scott Jacoby is Richie. Bob Barker becomes the host of *The Price Is Right* (CBS) and over the years becomes the oldest person to host a game show. Fred Sanford (Red Foxx) is the cantankerous, 65-year-old owner of the Sanford and Son junkyard, a business he considers to be his empire on NBC's *Sanford and Son*. Will Geer and Ellen Corby are Zeb and Esther Walton, the parents of John Walton on CBS's *The Waltons*. Also on the series, Helen Kleeb and Mary Jackson play Mamie and Emily Baldwin, the elderly sisters who are famous for their home-brewed liquor tonic "Papa's Recipe."

1973. Barnaby Jones (Buddy Ebsen) is an elderly Los Angeles private detective who never lets age get in the way of his solving a crime on *Barnaby Jones* (CBS). Ruth McDevitt plays Emily Cowles, an elderly columnist for the Independent News Service on *Kolchak: The Night Stalker* (ABC). Malcolm Atterbury plays Jonas Paine, the cantankerous owner of a company called Paines Pure Pickles on *Thicker Than Water* (ABC). Shirley Booth plays Grace Sherwood, a widow who meets (and falls in love with) Herbert Morrison (J. Pat O'Malley), an equally elderly widower on *A Touch of Grace* (ABC).

1974. Ed Brown (Jack Albertson) is the honest but cynical owner of a Los Angeles garage on *Chico and the Man* (NBC). Mary Wickes and Arthur Space play Ma and Pa, an elderly couple trying to enjoy their golden years in suburban Chicago on the CBS pilot *Ma and Pa*. Joseph Rockford (Robert Donley), called "Rocky," is a retired truck driver and the father of private detective Jim Rockford on *The Rockford Files* (NBC). Helen Hayes and Mildred Natwick play Ernestine and Gwendolyn Snoop, elderly sisters who are also eccentric mystery writers on *The Snoop Sisters* (NBC). On the ABC animated cartoon, *These Are the Days*, Henry Jones provides the voice of Jeff Day, the owner of the Day General Store in the town of Elmsville (1900s).

1975. Tom Ewell is Billy Truman, the elderly house detective at the King Edward Hotel on ABC's *Baretta*. Abe Vigoda plays Phil Fish, a past retirement detective with the 12th Precinct of the N.Y.P.D. on *Barney Miller* (ABC). Max Sherman (Larry Best) is a crusty, caustic Jewish widower who is also young at heart on the CBS pilot *Grandpa Max*. Zara Cully plays Olivia Jefferson, the mother of pompous George Jefferson on *The Jeffersons* (CBS). Ned Cooper and Jenny Ludlow (Charles Lane, Florida Friebus) are widowed seniors who decide to live together when they find they can't survive alone on their social security incomes on the CBS pilot *Love Nest*. Victor Killian plays Raymond Larkin, the senile grandfather (always asking "Where's the peanut butter?") on *Mary Hartman, Mary Hartman* (Syn.). Harry Morgan is Colonel Sherman Potter, head of the 4077 Mobile Army Surgical Hospital on *M*A*S*H* (CBS). Nanette Fabray is Kathryn Romano, the mother of the liberated Ann Romano

on *One Day at a Time* (CBS). Jane Rose is Audrey Dexter, the elderly mother-in-law of Phyllis Lindstrom on *Phyllis* (CBS). Burt Mustin plays Audrey's second husband, Arthur Lanson. Also on the series, Jack Elam plays Van Horn, the park wino. Nate Rosenthal and Henry Jones (Ned Glass, George Kirby) are retired widowers sharing a low rent apartment (and trying to get along with each other) on the CBS pilot *Rosenthal and Jones*.

1976. Lucas Flannery (Red Buttons) and Samuel Quilt (Harold Gould) are seniors who live together but can never agree on anything on the NBC pilot *Flannery and Quilt*. *Grady*, the *Sanford and Son* spinoff, features Whitman Mayo as Grady Wilson, the senior citizen who moves from Los Angeles to Santa Monica to live with his daughter Ellie Marshall and her husband Hal.

1977. Detective Phil Fish (Abe Vigoda), from *Barney Miller*, and his wife Bernice (Florence Stanley) become the host parents to a group of street-smart kids on *Fish* (ABC). In the original pilot, *Fish and Bernice* (ABC, 1975), Doris Belack played the role of Bernice. Dr. Jules Bedford (Danny Thomas) is a gruff but lovable doctor working on New York's Lower East Side on *The Practice* (NBC). Willie Clark and Al Lewis (Red Buttons, Lionel Stander) are retired vaudevillian comics who share an apartment and struggle to get along with each other on the NBC pilot *The Sunshine Boys*.

1978. Jack Gilford is Grandpa Hollyhock, the blind and somewhat senile grandfather of Ginger-Nell Hollyhock on ABC's *Apple Pie*. Jack Albertson plays Joe Kelly, a retired political science professor who becomes a U.S. Senator on *Grandpa Goes to Washington* (NBC). Elizabeth Kerr plays Cora Hudson, the grandmother of Mindy McConnell on *Mork and Mindy*. Also on the series, Mindy and Mork the alien produce an alien baby named Mearth. The baby (Jonathan Winters) is a senior citizen who grows younger with time. Professor Charles Kingsfield (John Houseman) is a brilliant contract law professor at a prestigious Northwestern university on *The Paper Chase* (CBS). John Houseman would repeat the role on Showtime's *The Paper Chase: The Second Year* (1983), *The Paper Chase: The Third Year* (1985) and *The Paper Chase: The Graduation Year* (1986), Sylvia Sidney (then Carol Bruce) play Lillian "Mama" Carlson, the stern head of radio station *WKRP in Cincinnati* (CBS).

1979. The CBS series *Dallas* presents several

older Americans: John Ewing, called Jock (Jim Davis) and his wife Eleanor (Barbara Bel Geddes, Donna Reed), the parents of the evil J.R. Ewing; and Willard "Digger" Barnes (David Wayne, Keenan Wynn), the father of Pamela Barnes, the girl who marries J.R.'s younger brother, Bobby. Denver Pyle plays Uncle Jesse Duke, patriarch of the Duke family of Hazzard County, Georgia, on *The Dukes of Hazzard* (CBS). Henry Alder (Fred Stuthman) is the father of radio talk show host Larry Alder on *Hello Larry* (NBC). Lionel Stander plays Max, chauffeur, housekeeper, cook and dear friend to Jonathan and Jennifer Hart, the couple who love solving crimes, on *Hart to Hart* (ABC). Mickey Rooney plays Oliver Nugent, a 66-year-old retiree who moves in with his grandson and struggles to live with the younger generation on *One of the Boys* (NBC). Stanley and Helen Roper (Norman Fell, Audra Lindley) are a retired couple who settle into a new home and struggle to adjust to a new life after selling the apartment house they ran on *Three's Company* on the spinoff series *The Ropers*. On *Three's Company*, Don Knotts joins the cast as Ralph Furley, the new landlord who considers himself a playboy and all around swinger. Elsa Lanchester plays Mamma Hockheiser, a senile widow whose demands are wrecking havoc on her family on the ABC pilot *Where's Poppa?*

1980. Redd Foxx continues his role as Fred Sanford (from *Sanford and Son*; see 1972), the irascible Watts junkman, on *Sanford* (NBC).

1981. Tom Ewell plays Jerome "Doc" Kullens, the intoxicated town doctor in Copper Creek, Montana (1865) on *Best of the West* (ABC). Wilford Hyde-White plays Dr. Goodfellow, the elderly science officer aboard the *Searcher*, a ship that is exploring the universe on *Buck Rogers in the 25th Century* (NBC). Angela Channing (Jane Wyman) is the head of the powerful Channing family, the owners of the Falcon Crest vineyards in California's Napa Valley on *Falcon Crest* (CBS). John Hoyt plays Stanley Kanisky, the elderly father of police chief Carl Kanisky on *Gimme a Break* (NBC). Eddie Albert plays Vincent Slattery, a retired businessman trying to find a peaceful life after moving into a retirement village called Paradise Park on the NBC pilot *Living in Paradise*. Milo Hoots (Noah Beery, Jr.), Reuben Milton (Scatman Crothers), Daisy "Boots" Duffy (Maxine Stuart) and Joe Malcheski (Mike Mazurki) are senior citizens fed up with crime

who ban together to battle it as the Grey Gang on the NBC pilot *Revenge of the Grey Gang*.

1982. Sidney Clute plays Paul LaGuardia, a detective with the 14th Precinct of the N.Y.P.D. on *Cagney and Lacey* (CBS). Nicholas Colasanto is Ernie Pantusso, a bartender at the Boston bar Cheers on NBC's *Cheers* (until 1985). Burgess Meredith plays Dr. Willard Adams, an aging veterinarian on *Gloria* (CBS). Billie Bird is Anna, the senile mother of Assistant D.A. Molly Quinn on *It Takes Two* (ABC). Although much younger than the character she plays, Vicki Lawrence is Thelma Harper, a feisty, cantankerous widow living in Raytown on *Mama's Family* (NBC/Syn.). Helen Martin is Pearl Shay, the eldest resident at 227, a tenement building in Washington, D.C. on *227* (NBC). Henry Darrow plays Don Diego de la Vega, an aging nobleman who once fought injustice as Zorro, who is now retired and teaching his son, Don Carlos (Paul Regina) to become the new Zorro on CBS's *Zorro and Son*.

1983. Harold Gould plays Jonas Foot, a recent widower who, after 40 years of marriage, moves in with his newlywed son and his wife on *Foot in the Door* (CBS).

1984. NBC's *The Cosby Show* presents several seniors: Earle Hyman and Clarice Taylor as Russell and Anna Huxtable, the parents of pediatrician Cliff Huxtable (Bill Cosby); and Joe Williams and Ethel Ayler as Al and Carrie Hanks, the parents of Cliff's wife, Claire (Phylicia Rashad). Doris Roberts plays Ethel Connelly, an independent widow who takes in a young ex con named Jeri Monroe (Deborah Malone) to help guide her life on the NBC pilot *Me and Mrs. C.* In 1986, NBC ran a short-lived series based on the pilot called *Me and Mrs. C.* with Peg Murray as Ethel Conklin and Misha McK as Gerri Kilgore. George Gaynes is Henry Warnimont, a 60-year-old gruff photographer who is the guardian of Punky Brewster, an adorable orphan on *Punky Brewster* (NBC). Maxine Stuart plays Amanda Earp, the mother of Wyatt Earp III, a descendant of the famous Old West lawman who is also a bounty hunter on *The Rousters* (NBC). Harold Gould and Frances Sternhagen play Ben and Millie Sprague, the parents of Doris Winger, a mother with two children (her husband ran off with his secretary) on *Under One Roof* (NBC).

1985. Barbara Stanwyck plays Constance Colby, matriarch of the powerful and wealthy Colby family on ABC's *The Colbys*. Blanche Devereaux (Rue McClanahan), Rose Nylund (Betty White), Dorothy Zbornak (Bea Arthur) and Sophia Petrillo (Estelle Getty) are senior citizens who share a home in Florida on *The Golden Girls* (NBC). In the series spinoff, *The Golden Palace* (1992, CBS), Blanche, Rose and Sophia attempt to run a hotel called the Golden Palace (Dorothy had married and moved away). Mary Martin and Mildred Natwick play Zora and May Hardcastle, amateur sleuths on the ABC pilot *Hardcastle, Hardcastle and McCormick* (a proposed spinoff from *Hardcastle and McCormick*).

1986. Marilla and Matthew Cuthbert (Colleen Dewhurst, Richard Farnsworth) are an elderly brother and sister who adopt Anne Shirley, the feisty red-haired orphan girl on *Anne of Green Gables* (PBS). Leonard Blacke (Harry Morgan) is a semi-retired con artist who helps his magician son, Alexander Blacke (Hal Linden), solve crimes on *Blacke's Magic* (NBC). Francis Cavanaugh (Barnard Hughes) is the 72-year-old head of the Cavanaugh Construction Company and the oldest living member of the family on *The Cavanaughs* (CBS). Alice Ghostley is Bernice Clifton, an elderly, somewhat senile friend of interior decorator Julia Sugarbaker on *Designing Women* (CBS). Jack Elam plays Alvin "Bully" Stevenson, the uncle of the wealthy L.K. McGuire on NBC's *Easy Street*. Andy Griffith plays Ben Matlock, a brilliant criminal defense attorney working out of Atlanta, Georgia on *Matlock* (NBC/ABC). Binnie Byrd Baylor (Sylvia Sidney), Bill MacGregor (Jeff Corey), Excell Dennis (Scatman Ccrothers) and Alice Blair (Teresa Wright) are among the seniors living at the Evening Star Retirement Home on *Morning Star/Evening Star* (CBS). Angela Lansbury plays Jessica Fletcher, a mystery writer who lives in Cabot Cove, Maine on *Murder, She Wrote* (CBS). Also on the series, William Windom plays the town doctor, Seth Hazlett, and Tom Bosley is the sheriff, Amos Tupper. Russell Lawrence (William Schallert) is the father of Frances Lawrence, better known as Gidget, on *The New Gidget*, a syndicated update of the 1965 series *Gidget*. The *Leave It to Beaver* update, *The New Leave It to Beaver* (TBS) finds June Cleaver (Barbara Billingsley), the mother of Wally and Beaver, now a widow and a member of the Mayfield City Council. Jake Hatton (Danny Thomas) is a show business veteran who moves in with his nephew, Don, to help him care for his brothers and sisters after their parents are killed in

a car accident on the syndicated *One Big Family*. Wilford Brimley plays Gus Witherspoon, a 65-year-old, set in his ways widower who works part time as a blacksmith on NBC's *Our House*. Also on the series, Gerald S. O'Loughlin plays Joe Kaplan, Gus's friend. Redd Foxx plays Al Hughes, the cantankerous owner of Al's Grill, a newsstand/coffee shop on *The Redd Foxx Show* (ABC). Harry Morgan plays Martin Vanderhof, a retired advertising man and head of a somewhat dysfunctional family on the syndicated *You Can't Take It with You*.

1987. James Callahan plays Walter Powell, a retired naval officer and member of the John Paul Jones Society for Retired Naval Men on *Charles in Charge* (Syn.). Hughes Whitney Lennox is the elderly owner of the architecture firm that employs Peter Farrell, a widower with two children on *I Married Dora* (ABC). Geraldine Fitzgerald plays Mabel Oberdine, a 70-year-old show business veteran who takes struggling actress Maxine Tanner (Mary B. Ward) under her wing on the CBS pilot *Mabel and Me*. Jimmy Bryce (Robert Loggia) and Mayo Dunlap (Robert Prosky) are retired cops who work as consultants to the police department on the ABC pilot *Old Dogs*. Eve Shipley (Peggy Cass) is a 1930s gun moll serving a life sentence for murder on Fox's *Women in Prison*. Marjorie Lord (then Jo deWinter) play Joyce Holden, the mother of Ken Holden; and David Doyle is Frank, the father of Ken's wife Georgia on NBC's *Sweet Surrender* (the parents lend a helping hand to the newlywed couple). Robert Stack hosts *Unsolved Mysteries*, an NBC series that explores the facts behind stories that have remained unsolved.

1988. The Dunes Retirement Resort in Arizona is the home to Ed and Trudie Pepper (Alan Young, Glynis Johns), a retired couple on *Coming of Age* (CBS). Also living at the resort are Dick Hale and his wife Ginny (Paul Dooley, Phyllis Newman). Carroll O'Connor plays Bill Gillespie, the police chief of Sparta, Mississippi, on *In the Heat of the Night* (NBC/CBS). Lucille Barker (Lucille Ball) and Curtis McGibbon (Gale Gordon) are seniors who are also partners in the M&B Hardware Store on *Life with Lucy* (ABC). Colleen Dewhurst plays Avery Brown and Darren McGavin is Bill Brown, the parents of news journalist *Murphy Brown* (CBS). Howard Morton plays Count Dracula, alias Grandpa Munster, the centuries old vampire on *The Munsters Today*.

1989. Luther Van Dam (Jerry Van Dyke) is

the assistant coach of the Minnesota State University Screaming Eagles football team on *Coach* (ABC). Estelle "Mama" Winslow (Rosetta Le Noir) is the mother of Chicago police officer Carl Winslow on *Family Matters* (ABC). Hank Knight (Jack Warden) and Everett Daye (Mason Adams) are the hosts of "Knight and Daye," a morning radio program on station KLOP in San Diego on NBC's *Knight and Daye*. Regis Philbin turns senior citizen on the syndicated talk show *Live with Regis and Kathy Lee* (with Kathy Lee Gifford; later with Kelly Ripa on *Live with Regis and Kelly*). Cloris Leachman plays Edwina Nutt, the elderly and eccentric owner of a hotel called *The Nutt House* (NBC). Don Porter plays Charles Palmer, the elderly head of the fabulously wealthy but eccentric Palmer family on the CBS pilot *Old Money*. S. Monroe Shamsky (Bill Macy), Susannah Somerset (Betty Garrett) and Debbie Whitmire (June Lockhart) are among the seniors living at *Somerset Gardens* (ABC pilot), a large condo development in San Diego.

1990. Hal Holbrook plays newspaper publisher Evan Evans, the father of Ava Newton on *Evening Shade* (CBS). Also on the series is Ponder Blue (Ossie Davis), the owner of the diner, Blue's Barbecue Villa; and Harlan Eldridge (Charles Durning), the town doctor (at Evening Shade Hospital), who is married to a much younger woman, Merleen (Ann Wegeworth). Robert Mitchum plays Joe Whitaker, a long-lost relative of a family of five orphaned children on *A Family for Joe* (NBC). Bob Elliott and Elinor Donahue play Fred and Gladys Peterson, the parents of Chris Peterson (Chris Elliott), a 30-year-old who still believes he is a kid on *Get a Life* (Fox). John Randolph is Harris Weldon, the elderly owner of the Grand Piano Works in the town of Grand, Pennsylvania, on NBC's *Grand*. Gloria DeHaven plays Ruth Egan and Doris Roberts is Bea Morina, seniors who live in a retirement village on Sweet Street in New Jersey on the NBC pilot *The Ladies of Sweet Street*. Phil Bruns (then Barney Martin) and Liz Sheridan play Morty and Helen Seinfeld, the parents of comedian Jerry Seinfeld on NBC's *Seinfeld*. Also on the series, Jerry Stiller and Estelle Harris play Frank and Estelle Costanza, the parents of Jerry's friend George Costanza, and Len Lesser is Jerry's Uncle Leo. Abraham Simpson (voice of Dan Castellaneta) is the elderly father of the dim-witted Homer Simpson on the animated Fox series *The Simpsons*. Georgann Johnson is Charlotte O'Neill, the 64-

year-old, snobbish mother of lawyer Rosie O'Neill on *The Trials of Rosie O'Neill* (CBS).

1991. Marion Ross and Louis Zorich play Sophie and Jules Berger, Jewish grandparents in 1950s Brooklyn, New York, on *Brooklyn Bridge* (CBS). Jonathan Winters plays William "Gunny" Davis, the father of schoolteacher Dwight Davis on *Davis Rules* (ABC/CBS). Florence Stanley is the voice of Ethyl Phillips, the 72-year-old, wheelchair-bound mother of Fran Sinclair on ABC's *Dinosaurs*. Andrew Emerson (Carl Gordon) is a retired train porter and the father of garbage man Roc Emerson on *Roc* (Fox). Alfonso Royal (Redd Foxx) and his wife Victoria (Della Reese) are a couple married for 47 years who are now looking forward to their golden years on *The Royal Family* (CBS). James Coburn is Robert Fox, an aging secret agent called *The Silver Fox* (ABC pilot). Wesley Hodges (William Schallert), called Border Hodges, rents a basement room in the home of Millicent Torkelson on NBC's *The Torkelsons*. Brian Keith and Cloris Leachman play Walter and Emily Collins, a couple married for 38 years who are now looking forward to their golden years on NBC's *Walter and Emily*.

1992. Sheriff Cody McPherson (Richard Farnsworth) and his deputy Bill Huntoon (Wilford Brimley) are elderly peace officers who uphold the law in Twilight, a small rural town in Utah on *The Boys of Twilight* (CBS). George Gaynes plays Strobe Smithers, a senile Washington, D.C., Senator who is married to a gorgeous younger woman (Mary Fran) but cheats behind her back on *Hearts Afire* (CBS).

1993. The relationship between an obnoxious father, Al Mitchell (Don Rickles) and his demure son, Steve Mitchell (Richard Lewis) is put to the test as Al feels he has to be a part of his son's life on *Daddy Dearest* (Fox). Also on the series, Barney Martin plays Pete Peters, Al's friend. Mark Sloan is a doctor at Community General Hospital in Los Angeles who delights in solving crimes on CBS's *Diagnosis Murder*. John Mahoney plays Martin Crane, the father of psychiatrists Frasier and Niles Crane on NBC's *Frasier*. Renee Taylor plays Sylvia Fine, the mother of Fran Fine, the nanny to the children of Broadway producer Maxwell Sheffield on *The Nanny* (CBS). Also on the series, Steve Lawrence plays Fran's father, Morty Fine; and Ann Guilbert is Fran's senile grandmother, Yetta Rosenberg. C.D. Parker (Noble Willingham) is the owner of C.D.'s Bar and Grill, the hangout for Texas Ranger Cordell Walker and his friends on *Walker, Texas Ranger* (CBS).

1994. Eileen Heckart plays "Mother" Emma Buchanan, a 70-year-old meddling mother-in-law on *The Five Mrs. Buchanans* (CBS; the title refers to her and her son's four wives. One of her daughters-in-law, Alexandra [Judith Ivey] sums Emma up best: "The woman would qualify for sainthood if it was not for one little thing — she's a bitch"). Chance Wayne (Dennis Weaver), Robert Smith (Robert Guillaume), Akira Mochizuka (Pat Morita) and John Dolan (James Coburn) are old timers who form the Greyhounds to do what the police don't — catch criminals on the CBS pilot *The Greyhounds*. Gil Jones (Ed Asner) is a former stock car racer who now runs the Thunder Alley Garage in Indiana on *Thunder Alley* (ABC).

1995. Beulah Carey (Marion Ross) is the mother of Wilford-Louder department store employee Drew Carey on *The Drew Carey Show*. Also on the ABC series, Nan Martin plays the elderly owner of the department store, Mrs. Louder. Neb Langston (James Earl Jones) is a former cop, now a widower, who moves in with his son and his wife (Ron and Maggie) and their children (Charlie and David) on *Under One Roof* (CBS). Betty White plays Shirley Sullivan, a widow who lives with her daughter, Julia, and helps her run the family business, the Coffee Dog Café, on ABC's *Maybe This Time*.

1996. Bill Cosby plays Hilton Lucas, a downsized baggage handler for National West Airlines on *Cosby* (CBS). He lives in Queens, New York, with his wife Ruth (Phylicia Rashad) and is not enjoying his golden years, as he was forced to leave a job he loved. Frank and Marie Barone (Peter Boyle, Doris Roberts) are the over-caring parents of Raymond and Robert Barone on *Everybody Loves Raymond* (CBS). Also on the series, Fred Willard and Georgia Engel play Hank and Pat MacDougall, the parents of Amy (Monica Horan), the girl who marries Robert Barone (Brad Garrett); and Robert Culp and Katherine Helmond play Warren and Lois Whalen, the parents of Debra (Raymond's wife). James Gammon plays Nick Bridges, the father of San Francisco police inspector *Nash Bridges* (CBS).

1997. Episodes of *Columbo* (produced as ABC TV movies) feature Peter Falk as the famed sleuth, Lieutenant Columbo, who, while not specifically stated on the program, is working past retirement.

Mitchell Ryan and Susan Sullivan are Edward and Kitty Montgomery, the wealthy parents of Greg Montgomery, the lawyer who married the slightly daffy Dharma Finkelstein on ABC's *Dharma and Greg*. George Segal is Jack Gallo, the 60-year-old publisher of *Blush*, a fashion magazine for women on *Just Shoot Me* (NBC). Jerry Van Dyke plays Jerry Beauchamp, the grandfather of Steve, the teen who receives help from his guardian angel on ABC's *Teen Angel*. Ed McMahon plays Charlie Dickerson, the host of *Breakfast with Charlie* on KOGD-TV in Minneapolis on *The Tom Show* (WB).

1998. Jerry Stiller plays the loud and obnoxious Arthur Spooner, the father of Carrie Heffernan on *The King of Queens* (CBS). Michael Sinelinkoff is Professor Arthur Sommerlee, an explorer stranded on a strange plateau on *The Lost World* (Syn.). Shelly Morrison plays Rosie, the abused maid to the wealthy and snobbish Karen Walker on *Will and Grace* (NBC).

1999. Tyne Daly is Maxine Gray, the mother of Judge Amy Gray on *Judging Amy* (CBS). Mrs. Avery (puppet; voice of Ja'net DuBois) is an elderly woman called "the dried-up old gargoyle" by her building super, Thurgood Stubbs, on *The PJ's* (Fox/WB). Dominic Chianese is Corrado Soprano, Jr., better known as Uncle Junior, the son of Italian immigrants who became a member of the DiMeo crime family and led the way for his descendants to become members of the New Jersey underworld on *The Sopranos* (HBO). Regis Philbin hosts *Who Wants to Be a Millionaire*, a prime time game show that offered a top prize of $1 million. Regis is also the host of *Live with Regis and Kelly* (Kelly Ripa) and hosts NBC's *America's Got Talent* (2006).

2000. Marion Ross plays Trixie Gilmore, the grandmother of Lorelai Gilmore on the WB's *Gilmore Girls*. Bill Hobbs plays Elmer Greentree, an 83-year-old paranormal who helps people threatened by the supernatural on *The Others* (NBC). Stacy Keach is Ken Titus, an abusive, obnoxious, beer-drinking, woman-chasing father on *Titus* (Fox).

2001. Brian Dennehy is Pop "Fitz" Fitzgerald, a retired fireman who lives with his family on *The Fighting Fitzgeralds* (NBC). Eileen Albertoni Dow plays Harriet Krump, the somewhat senile grandmother (hides food; always repeats herself) and Dabbs Greer is Fred Stage, a gruff grandfather with all his facilities on *Maybe It's Me* (WB). Jo

Marie Payton provides the voice of Grandma "Suga Mama," the feisty grandmother of 14-year-old Penny Proud on the Disney animated series *The Proud Family*. Jerry Adler plays Sam Stewart, the father of writer Matt Stewart on the WB's *Raising Dad*.

2003. Jessica Walter is Lucille Bluth, the pampered and spoiled wife of Bluth Company founder George Bluth (Jeffrey Tambor) on *Arrested Development* (Fox). Jim Egan (James Garner) is the father of school nurse Cate Hennessey on ABC's *Eight Simple Rules*. J. Anthony Brown plays Ed "Pops" Ward, a senior citizen who doesn't believe in age, has an eye for the opposite sex and does what he pleases on the WB's *Like Family*. David McCallum plays Dr. Donald Mallard, a forensic medical examiner on *Navy NCIS* (CBS). Holland Taylor plays Evelyn Harper, the mother of Charlie and Alan Harper on CBS's *Two and a Half Men*. Also on the series, Conchata Ferrell plays Berta, Charlie's housekeeper.

2004. Betty White is Cynthia Piper, a legal clerk on ABC's *Boston Legal*. Denny Crane (William Shatner) is a senior partner in the law firm of Crane, Poole and Schmitt on ABC's *Boston Legal*. Alan Alda plays the elderly Senator Arnold Vinick on NBC's *The West Wing*.

2005. Donald Sutherland is Nathan Templeton, the Speaker of the House under the presidency of Mackenzie Allen on *Commander in Chief* (ABC). Tom Poston plays Clown (no other name given), a retired vaudeville clown who lives in the closet of an apartment rented by a young woman (Marni) on NBC's *Committed* (Clown came packaged with the apartment). Judd Hirsch plays Alan Epps, the father of brilliant math instructor Charlie Epps on *NUMB3RS* (CBS).

2006. Martin Landau is Sol Goldman, a forensic doctor with the San Francisco Police Department on *The Evidence* (ABC). Seymour Cassel is Pops, an elderly thief who is part of a group that plans to rob three jewelry stores at the same time on NBC's *Heist*. Dick Van Dyke is Jonathan Maxwell, a criminology professor who also solves crimes on *Murder 101* (Hallmark Channel).

Series Based on Films

This entry lists the TV series that have been adapted from theatrical films. Certain titles, like

Dr. Kildare, *The Saint* and *Ellery Queen*, are based on the radio series, not the film series. See also *Films Based on Television Series* and *Series Based on Radio Programs*.

1948. *Hopalong Cassidy* (Syn.).

1949. *Mama* (CBS; based on *I Remember Mama*).

1953. *Life with Father* (CBS); *Flash Gordon* (Syn.).

1954. *That's My Boy* (CBS).

1955. *Casablanca* (ABC); *Commando Cody, Sky Marshal of the Universe* (NBC; based on the theatrical serial *King of the Rocket Men*); *King's Row* (ABC).

1956. *Broken Arrow* (CBS); *My Friend Flicka* (CBS).

1957. *The New Adventures of Charlie Chan* (Syn.). *Wagon Train* (based on *Wagon Master*).

1958. *How to Marry a Millionaire* (Syn.).

1959. *Mr. Lucky* (CBS); *Pete Kelly's Blues* (NBC).

1960. *My Sister Eileen* (CBS); *National Velvet* (NBC); *The Third Man* (Syn.).

1961. *Father of the Bride* (CBS); *Margie* (ABC).

1962. *Going My Way* (ABC); *Mr. Smith Goes to Washington* (ABC); *My Sister Eileen* (CBS); *Room for One More* (ABC; based on *The Easy Way*).

1963. *The Farmer's Daughter* (ABC); *The Greatest Show on Earth* (ABC).

1964. *Flipper* (NBC); *No Time for Sergeants* (ABC); *Peyton Place* (ABC); *Twelve O'clock High* (ABC); *Voyage to the Bottom of the Sea* (ABC).

1965. *Gidget* (ABC); *The Long Hot Summer* (ABC); *Mr. Roberts* (NBC); *Please Don't Eat the Daisies* (NBC); *Tammy* (ABC); *The Wackiest Ship in the Army* (NBC).

1966. *Daktari* (CBS; based on *Clarence, the Cross-Eyed Lion*), *King Kong* (ABC); *The Man Who Never Was* (ABC); *The Rounders* (ABC); *Shane* (ABC); *Tarzan* (NBC).

1967. *Hondo* (ABC); *Journey to the Center of the Earth* (ABC); *Maya* (NBC).

1968. *Blondie* (CBS); *Cowboy in Africa* (ABC; based on *Africa — Texas Style*); *Fantastic Voyage* (ABC).

1969. *The Courtship of Eddie's Father* (ABC); *The Pink Panther* (NBC).

1970. *Barefoot in the Park* (ABC); *The Best of Everything* (ABC); *The Odd Couple* (ABC).

1971. *Anna and the King* (CBS; based on *The King and I*).

1972. *Around the World in 80 Days* (NBC);

Madigan (NBC); *M*A*S*H* (CBS); *The Waltons* (based on *Spencer's Mountain*).

1973. *Adam's Rib* (ABC); *Bob & Carol & Ted & Alice* (ABC).

1974. *Born Free* (NBC); *The Cowboys* (ABC); *Planet of the Apes* (CBS).

1975. *Return to the Planet of the Apes* (NBC).

1976. *Popi* (CBS); *Serpico* (NBC).

1977. *How the West Was Won* (ABC); *The Life and Times of Grizzly Adams* (NBC); *Logan's Run* (CBS); *Operation Petticoat* (ABC).

1978. *The Godzilla Power Hour* (NBC; based on *Godzilla*).

1979. *The Bad News Bears* (CBS).

1980. *Beyond Westworld* (CBS; based on *Westworld*); *Freebie and the Bean* (CBS); *From Here to Eternity* (NBC).

1981. *Foul Play* (ABC); *Harper Valley* (NBC); *Private Benjamin* (CBS); *Walking Tall* (NBC).

1982. *Herbie the Love Bug* (CBS); *9 to 5* (ABC/Syn.); *Seven Brides for Seven Brothers* (CBS).

1983. *Casablanca* (NBC); *Gun Shy* (CBS; based on *The Apple Dumpling Gang*).

1984. *Blue Thunder* (ABC); *The Four Seasons* (CBS).

1985. *Home Town* (CBS; based on *The Big Chill*).

1986. *Fast Times* (CBS; based on *Fast Times at Ridgemont High*); *Starman* (ABC).

1987. *Down and Out in Beverly Hills* (Fox); *Friday the 13th: The Series* (Syn.); *Gung Ho* (ABC); *Nothing in Common* (NBC).

1988. *Baby Boom* (NBC); *Dirty Dancing* (CBS); *The Dirty Dozen: The Series* (Fox); *Freddy's Nightmares: A Nightmare on Elm Street: The Series* (Syn.); *The War of the Worlds* (Syn.).

1989. *The Absent Minded Professor* (NBC); *Alien Nation* (Fox).

1990. *Attack of the Killer Tomatoes* (Fox); *Bagdad Café* (CBS); *Ferris Bueller* (*NBC; based on Ferris Bueller's Day Off*); *Swamp Thing* (USA); *Uncle Buck* (CBS).

1991. *Baby Talk* (ABC; based on *Look Who's Talking*); *Back to the Future* (CBS); *Eddie Dodd* (ABC; based on *True Believer*); *Working Girl* (NBC).

1992. *Bill and Ted's Excellent Adventures* (Fox); *Highlander: The Series* (Syn.); *The Little Mermaid* (Disney); *The Young Indiana Jones Chronicles* (ABC; based on *Indiana Jones*).

1993. *A League of Their Own* (CBS).

1994. *RoboCop* (Syn.); *Weird Science* (USA).

1995. *Dumb and Dumber* (ABC); *The Mask* (CBS).

1996. *Clueless* (ABC/UPN).

1997. *Buffy the Vampire Slayer* (WB/UPN); *Conan* (Syn.); *La Femme Nikita* (U.S.A.); *FX: The Series* (Syn.); *Honey I Shrunk the Kids: The TV Series* (Syn.); *Stargate SG-1* (Sci Fi).

1998. *BeastMaster* (Syn); *The Lost World* (Syn.).

2000. *Kong: The Animated Series* (Syn; based on *King Kong*); *Soul Food* (Showtime).

2003. *Lilo and Stitch: The Series* (Disney); *My Big Fat Greek Life* (CBS; based on *My Big Fat Greek Wedding*).

2005. *Barber Shop* (Showtime).

Series Based on Radio Programs

This entry lists the TV series that were adapted from radio programs. See also *Films Based on Television Series* and *Series Based on Movies*.

1947. *Juvenile Jury* (NBC).

1948. *Arthur Godfrey's Talent Scouts* (CBS); *Break the Bank* (ABC); *Candid Camera* (ABC/CBS; based on *Candid Microphone*); *The Chesterfield Supper Club* (NBC); *Stop Me if You've Heard This One* (NBC); *Ted Mack and His Original Amateur Hour* (DuMont; based on *Major Bowes and His Original Amateur Hour*); *The Texaco Star Theater* (NBC; based on *The Milton Berle Show*); *Toast of the Town* (CBS; based on *The Ed Sullivan Show*); *Who Said That?* (NBC).

1949. *The Aldrich Family* (NBC); *Believe It or Not* (NBC); *Blind Date* (ABC); *The Clock* (CBS); *Easy Aces* (DuMont); *Famous Jury Trials* (DuMont); *Garroway at Large* (NBC; based on *The Dave Garroway Show*); *The Goldbergs* (CBS); *Hopalong Cassidy* (Syn.); *It Pays to Be Ignorant* (CBS); *Johnny Olsen's Rumpus Room* (DuMont; based on *Rumpus Room*); *Kay Kyser's Kollege of Musical Knowledge* (NBC); *Ladies Be Seated* (ABC); *Leave It to the Girls* (NBC); *The Life of Riley* (DuMont); *Lights Out* (NBC); *The Lone Ranger* (ABC); *Lum and Abner* (CBS); *The Man Against Crime* (CBS); *The Martin and Lewis Show* (NBC; based on *The Dean Martin and Jerry Lewis Show*); *Martin Kane, Private Eye* (NBC); *One Man's Family* (NBC); *The O'Neills* (NBC); *Quiet, Please* (ABC); *The Quiz Kids* (NBC); *Silver Theater* (CBS); *Starring Boris Karloff* (ABC); *Stop the Music* (ABC); *Suspense* (CBS); *20 Questions* (NBC).

1950. *The Alan Young Show* (CBS); *Beulah* (CBS); *Big Town* (CBS); *Beat the Clock* (CBS);

0

The Bob Hope Show (NBC); *The Breakfast Club* (ABC); *Buck Rogers in the 25th Century* (ABC); *By Popular Demand* (CBS); *Can You Top This?* (ABC); *Charlie Wild, Private Detective* (CBS); *The Cisco Kid* (Syn.); *Dick Tracy* (ABC); *Ellery Queen* (DuMont); *Escape* (CBS); *The First Hundred Years* (CBS); *The George Burns and Gracie Allen Show* (CBS); *The Jack Benny Program* (CBS/NBC). *The Kate Smith Hour* (NBC); *Life Begins at 80* (ABC); *The Lux Video Theater* (CBS; based on *The Lux Radio Theater*); *The Perry Como Show* (CBS); *Robert Q's Matinee* (CBS; based on *The Robert Q. Lewis Show*); *Sing It Again* (CBS); *Smilin' Ed Mc-Connell and His Buster Brown Gang* (NBC); *So You Want to Lead a Band* (NBC); *Songs for Sale* (CBS); *You Bet Your Life* (NBC); *Your Hit Parade* (NBC).

1951. *The Amazing Mr. Malone* (CBS); *The Amos 'n' Andy Show* (CBS); *The Bickersons* (Syn.); *The Bob and Ray Show* (NBC); *Boston Blackie* (Syn.); *Bride and Groom* (CBS); *Crime Photographer* (CBS); *City Hospital* (ABC); *A Date with Judy* (ABC); *Down You Go* (DuMont); *Dragnet* (NBC); *Front Page Detective* (Syn.); *The Hallmark Hall of Fame* (NBC); *The March of Time* (ABC); *Mark Saber* (ABC; based on *Inspector Mark Saber*); *Meet Corliss Archer* (CBS); *Mr. District Attorney* (Syn.); *The Red Skelton Show* (NBC/CBS); *The Roy Rogers Show* (NBC); *Sky King* (CBS); *Strike it Rich* (CBS); *Tales of Tomorrow* (ABC); *Wild Bill Hickok* (Syn.).

1952. *The Abbott and Costello Show* (Syn.); *The Adventures of Ozzie and Harriet* (ABC); *Arthur Godfrey Time* (CBS); *Cavalcade of America* (NBC); *Claudia: The Story of a Marriage* (NBC; based on *Claudia and David*); *Dangerous Assignment* (Syn.); *Death Valley Days* (Syn.); *Double or Nothing* (CBS); *Ford Theater* (NBC); *Gangbusters* (NBC); *The Guiding Light* (CBS); *House Party* (NBC); *Information Please* (CBS); *Life with Luigi* (CBS); *Meet Millie* (CBS); *Mr. and Mrs. North* (CBS); *My Friend Irma* (CBS); *My Little Margie* (CBS); *Our Miss Brooks* (CBS); *Terry and the Pirates* (Syn.); *Topper* (CBS; based on *The Adventures of Topper*).

1953. *The Adventures of Superman* (Syn.); *Colonel Humphrey Flack* (DuMont); *Dr. I.Q.* (ABC); *The Dunninger Show* (Syn.); *Ethel and Albert* (NBC); *I Led Three Lives* (Syn; based on *I Was a Communist for the FBI*); *The Life of Riley* (NBC); *Meet Mr. McNutley* (CBS); *My Favorite Husband* (CBS); *My Son Jeep* (ABC); *Name That Tune* (NBC); *Peter Potter's Juke Box Jury* (ABC; based on *Juke Box Jury*); *Quick As a Flash* (ABC); *Philip Morris Playhouse* (CBS); *Renfrew of the Mounted* (Syn.); *Valiant Lady* (CBS); *You Are There* (CBS).

1954. *Breakfast in Hollywood* (NBC); *Captain Midnight* (CBS); *December Bride* (CBS); *Duffy's Tavern* (NBC); *Earn Your Vacation* (CBS); *Father Knows Best* (CBS); *The Halls of Ivy* (CBS); *Inner Sanctum Mysteries* (Syn.); *The Joe Palooka Story* (Syn.); *The Liberace Show* (Syn.); *The Line-Up* (CBS); *The Lone Wolf* (Syn.); *The Marriage* (NBC); *Mayor of the Town* (Syn.); *Portia Faces Life* (CBS); *The Road of Life* (CBS); *The Spike Jones Show* (NBC); *The Whistler* (Syn.).

1955. *The Damon Runyon Theater* (CBS); *The Falcon* (Syn.); *Gunsmoke* (CBS); *Joe and Mabel* (CBS); *Jungle Jim* (Syn.); *The Lawrence Welk Show* (ABC); *Screen Director's Playhouse* (NBC); *Sergeant Preston of the Yukon* (Syn.); *The $64,000 Question* (CBS; based on *Take It or Leave It*).

1956. *The Dinah Shore Show* (NBC); *Dr. Christian* (Syn.); *The Man Called X* (Syn.); *Queen for a Day* (NBC); *Red Ryder* (Syn.).

1957. *Blondie* (NBC); *Richard Diamond, Private Detective* (CBS/NBC); *The Thin Man* (NBC; based on *The Adventures of the Thin Man*).

1958. *Counterspy* (Syn.); *Kitty Foyle* (NBC); *The Kraft Music Hall* (NBC); *Steve Canyon* (NBC); *Young Dr. Malone* (NBC).

1959. *The Bell Telephone Hour* (NBC); *Bold Venture* (Syn.); *Fibber McGee and Molly* (NBC); *Hobby Lobby* (ABC); *Pete Kelly's Blues* (NBC); *Philip Marlowe* (ABC).

1960. *Michael Shayne* (NBC).

1962. *Our Man Higgins* (ABC; based on *It's Higgins, Sir*)

1963. *The Saint* (Syn.).

1965. *Green Acres* (CBS; based on *Granby's Green Acres*).

1966. *The Green Hornet* (ABC); *Hawaii Calls* (Syn.).

1972. *Bridget Loves Bernie* (CBS; based on *Abie's Irish Rose*).

Note: Several radio series were based on television shows. These include: *The Adventures of Rin Tin Tin, Have Gun—Will Travel, I Love Lucy, Space Patrol* and *Tom Corbett, Space Cadet*.

Sex see *Nudity and Sexuality*

Shakespeare

This entry chronicles the plays by William Shakespeare that have been adapted to TV as stand alone performances. Excerpts, such as those broadcast on series like *Omnibus*, have been excluded (as have modern interpretations of the Bard's plays; for example, *Romeo and Juliet on Ice* [a 1983 ice ballet with Dorothy Hamill] and *Kiss Me Kate* [a 1958 musical based on *Taming of the Shrew* with Patricia Morison and Alfred Drake]).

1944. *Romeo and Juliet* (DuMont). Dennis Osborn (Romeo), Helen Zampiella (Juliet).

1947. *Twelfth Night* (NBC). Anne Burr (Viola), Vaughn Taylor (Sir Andrew).

1948. *Romeo and Juliet* (NBC). Douglas Moppert (Romeo), Eleanore Chapin (Juliet).

1951. *Macbeth* (CBS; on *Studio One*). Charlton Heston (Romeo), Judith Evelyn (Juliet).

1953. *Hamlet* (NBC; on *The Hallmark Hall of Fame*). Maurice Evans (Hamlet), Sarah Churchill (Ophelia).

1954. *King Richard III* (NBC; on *The Hallmark Hall of Fame*). Maurice Evans (King Richard), Sarah Churchill (Queen). *Macbeth* (NBC; on *The Hallmark Hall of Fame*). Maurice Evans (Macbeth), Dame Judith Anderson (Lady Macbeth). *Romeo and Juliet* (NBC; on *Kraft Theater*). Liam Sullivan (Romeo), Susan Strasberg (Juliet).

1956. *Taming of the Shrew* (NBC; on *The Hallmark Hall of Fame*). Lilli Palmer (Katherine), Maurice Evans (Petruchio).

1957. *Romeo and Juliet* (NBC; on *Kraft Theater*). John Neville (Romeo), Claire Bloom (Juliet). *Twelfth Night* (NBC; on *The Hallmark Hall of Fame*). Piper Laurie (Viola), Rosemary Harris (Olivia).

1959. *Hamlet* (CBS; on *The DuPont Show of the Month*). John Neville (Hamlet); John Humphrey (Laertes).

1960. *Macbeth* (NBC; on *The Hallmark Hall of Fame*). Maurice Evans (Macbeth), Dame Judith Anderson (Lady Macbeth). *The Tempest* (NBC; on *The Hallmark Hall of Fame*). Maurice Evans (Prospero), Lee Remick (Miranda).

1961. *An Age of Kings* (Syn. series). The British Broadcasting Repertory Company performs Shakespeare's plays that chronicle the English Kings. David Williams and Sean Connery head the cast.

1964. *Spread of the Eagle* (Syn. series). The Roman plays of William Shakespeare are dramatized: *Antony and Cleopatra, Coriolanus* and *Julius Caesar*. Performers include Peter Cushing, Mary Morris and Keith Michell.

1967. *Romeo and Juliet* (Syn; on *Play of the Month*). Hywel Bennett (Romeo), Kika Markham (Juliet).

1969. *Julius Caesar* (Syn; on *Play of the Month*). Robert Stephens (Julius Caesar), Edward Woodward (Cassius).

1970. *Hamlet* (NBC; on *The Hallmark Hall of Fame*). Richard Chamberlain (Hamlet), Michael Redgrave (Poloneus). *Macbeth* (Syn; on *Play of the Month*). Eric Porter (Macbeth), Janet Suzman (Lady Macbeth).

1971. *A Midsummer's Night Dream* (Syn; on *Play of the Month*). Robert Stephens (Oberon), Eileen Atkins (Titania), Lynn Redgrave (Helena).

1972. *The Merchant of Venice* (Syn; on *Play of the Month*). Charles Gray (Antonio), Frank Finlay (Shylock), Maggie Smith (Portia).

1975. *King Lear* (Syn; on *Play of the Month*). Michael Hordern (King Lear), Angela Down (Cordella). *Macbeth* (PBS; on *Classic Theater*). Eric Porter (Macbeth), Janet Suzman (Lady Macbeth).

1978–1985. PBS airs *BBC Television Shakespeare*, a series of 37 Shakespeare plays that were broadcast in the U.S. over a seven-year period. The plays are presented here in broadcast order: **1978:** *Romeo and Juliet* (Patrick Ryecart as Romeo; Rebecca Saire as Juliet), *King Richard II* (Charles Gray as Duke of York; John Gielgud as John of Gaunt), *As You Like It* (Helen Mirren as Rosalind; Richard Easton as Duke Frederick). **1979:** *Julius Caesar* (Charles Gray as Julius Caesar; Virginia McKenna as Portia), *Measure for Measure* (Kenneth Colley as Duke Vincentio; Kate Nelligan as Isabella), *King Henry VIII* (John Stride as King Henry; Julian Glover as Duke of Buckingham), *King Henry IV, Part 1* (John Finch as King Henry, Anthony Quayle as Sir John Falstaff), *King Henry IV, Part 2* (same cast), *King Henry V* (David Gwillim as King Henry; Derek Hollis as Duke of York). **1980:** *Twelfth Night* (Alec McCowen as Malvolio; Sinead Cusack as Olivia), *The Tempest* (Michael Hordern as Prospero; Pippa Guard as Miranda), *Hamlet, Prince of Denmark* (Derek Jacobi as Hamlet, Lalla Ward as Ophelia), *The Taming of the Shrew* (John Cleese as Petruchio; Susan Penhaligon as Bianca),

The Merchant of Venice (John Rhys-Davies as Salerno; Gemma Jones as Portia). **1981:** *All's Well That Ends Well* (Celia Johnson as Countess of Rousillon; Ian Charleson as Bertram), *The Winter's Tale* (Jeremy Kemp as King Leontes; Anna Calder-Marshall as Queen Hermione), *Timon of Athens* (John Fortune as the Poet; Jonathan Pryce as Timon), *Antony and Cleopatra* (Colin Blakely as Antony; Jane Lapotaire as Cleopatra), *Othello* (Anthony Hopkins as Othello; Penelope Wilton as Desdemona), *Troilus and Cressida* (Anton Lesser as Troilus; Suzanne Burden as Cressida), *A Midsummer's Night Dream* (Estelle Kohler as Hippolyta; Pippa Guard as Hermia). **1982:** *King Lear* (Michael Hordern as King Lear; Penelope Walton as Regan), *The Merry Wives of Windsor* (Miranda Foster as Anne Page; Prunella Scales as Margaret Page). **1983:** *King Henry VI, Part 1* (Peter Benson as King Henry; Julia Foster as Margaret of Anjou), *King Henry VI, Part 2* (same cast), *King Henry VI, Part 3* (same cast), *The Tragedy of King Richard III* (Ron Cook as King Richard; Julia Foster as Queen Margaret), *Cymbeline* (Richard Johnson as Cymbeline; Helen Mirren as Princess Imogen), *Macbeth* (Nicol Williamson as Macbeth; Jane Lapotaire as Lady Macbeth), *The Comedy of Errors* (Roger Daltrey as Dromio of Syracuse; Marsha Fitzalan as Luce), *The Two Gentlemen of Verona* (Frank Barrie as Sir Eglamour; Tessa Peake-Jones as Julia). **1984:** *The Tragedy of Coriolanus* (Alan Howard as Coriolanus; Joss Ackland as Menenius), *The Life and Death of King John* (Leonard Rossiter as King John; Claire Bloom as Constance), *Pericles, Prince of Tyre* (Michael Gwilym as Pericles; Juliet Stevenson as Thaisa), *Much Ado About Nothing* (Cherie Lunghi as Beatrice; Robert Lindsay as Benedict). **1985:** *Love's Labour's Lost* (Jenny Agutter as Rosaline; Jonathan Kent as Ferdinand), *Titus Andronicus* (Trevor Peacock as Titus; Anna Calder-Marshall as Lavinia).

Shows within Shows

This entry chronicles the programs in which the main characters are involved in two situations — their private lives and their job when it involves a TV or radio program. The listing shows the original program, the star, and the program within a program.

1958. *How to Marry a Millionaire* (Syn.). Greta Hanson (Lori Nelson) is the hostess of a game show called *Go for Broke*.

1960. *Head of the Family* (CBS; the pilot for *The Dick Van Dyke Show*). Rob Petrie (Carl Reiner) is head writer for the TV variety series *The Alan Sturdy Show*.

1961. *The Dick Van Dyke Show* (CBS). Rob Petrie (Dick Van Dyke) is head writer of the variety series, *The Alan Brady Show*.

1962. *The Joey Bishop Show* (NBC/CBS). Joey Barnes (Joey Bishop) is host of the talk-variety series *The Joey Barnes Show*.

1966. *The Hero* (NBC). Sam Garrett (Richard Mulligan) is the star of the western series *Jed Clayton, U.S. Marshal*.

1967. On *Good Morning World* (CBS), Dave Lewis and Larry Clark (Joby Baker, Ronnie Schell) host the morning radio program *The Lewis and Clark Show* in Los Angeles. On *He and She* (CBS), Oscar North (Jack Cassidy) is the star of the TV series *Jetman*.

1970. *The Mary Tyler Moore Show* (CBS). Mary Richards (Mary Tyler Moore) works as the assistant producer of the WJM-TV "Six O'clock News Program" in Minneapolis.

1971. *The New Dick Van Dyke Show* (CBS). Dick Preston (Dick Van Dyke) is the host of *The Dick Preston Show*, a talk-variety program on KXIU-TV in Phoenix; later, when the series switches formats to Tarzana, California, Dick plays Dr. Brad Fairmont on the TV soap opera *Those Who Care*.

1973. *The Barbara Eden Show* (ABC pilot). Barbara Norris (Barbara Eden) stars on the TV soap opera *All My Tomorrows*.

1975. *Mobile One* (ABC). Pete Campbell (Jackie Cooper) is a reporter for KONE-TV, Channel 1 in Southern California.

1977. On *The Betty White Show* (CBS), Joyce Whitman (Betty White) is the star of the TV series *Undercover Woman*. On *Tabitha* (ABC), Tabitha Stevens (Lisa Hartman), the daughter of Samantha Stevens (*Bewitched*), is a young witch who works as a production assistant for KXLA-TV in Los Angeles.

1979. On *Hello, Larry* (NBC), Larry Alder (McLean Stevenson) is the host of *Hello, Larry* (later *The Larry Alder Show*), a call-in radio program in Portland, Oregon. On *The Mary Tyler Moore Comedy Hour* (CBS), Mary McKinnon (Mary Tyler Moore) is the star of the comedy series *The Mary McKinnon Show*. On *The Paul Wil-*

liams Show (NBC pilot), Paul Hamilton (Paul Williams) plays a Martian on the KFAP-TV (Denver) kid show *Marvin the Martian*.

1980. *The Stockard Channing Show* (CBS). Susan Goodenow (Stockard Channing) works as a reporter on the KXLA-TV show *The Big Ripoff*.

1981. On **Foul Play** (ABC), Gloria Mundy (Deborah Raffin) is the host of *Gloria's World*, a kid show on KSF-TV in San Francisco. On *Jessica Novak* (CBS), Jessica Novak (Helen Shaver) is an on-the-air reporter for *Close-Up News* on KLA-TV in Los Angeles. On *Stephanie* (CBS pilot), Stephanie Burke (Stephanie Faracy) is the host of *L.A.L.A.*, a morning program on KXLA-TV. On *The Two of Us* (CBS), Nan Gallagher (Mimi Kennedy) is the host of the New York-based *Mid-Morning Manhattan* TV show. On *Two the Hard Way* (CBS pilot), Veronica Moorehead (Marlyn Mason) plays Erin Bolton, the star of the daytime soap opera *Paradise Lost*.

1982. On *Family Ties* (NBC), Steven Keaton (Michael Gross) is the manager of WKS, Channel 3, a PBS station in Columbus, Ohio. On *Madame's Place* (Syn.), the puppet Madame hosts *Madame's Place*, a late night talk show, from her Hollywood mansion. On *The Rainbow Girl* (NBC pilot), Ann Jordan (Ann Jillian) appears as the Rainbow Girl on *The Miles Starling Family Dance Party*, a local TV show on Channel 66 in New York City.

1983. On *Buffalo Bill* (NBC), Bill Bittinger (Dabney Coleman) is the egotistical, sharp-tongued host of *The Buffalo Bill Show* on WBFL-TV in Buffalo, New York. On *Goodnight, Beantown* (CBS), Matt Cassidy and Jennifer Barnes (Bill Bixby, Mariette Hartley) are the co-anchors of Boston's "Evening News" program.

1984. On *Domestic Life* (CBS), Martin Crane (Martin Mull) is a commentator on Seattle's *Domestic Life Report* on KMR-TV. On *The Duck Factory* (NBC), Skip Tarkenton (Jim Carrey) is a young artist on *The Dippy Duck Show*, a cartoon series produced by Buddy Winkler Productions. On *Mama Malone* (CBS), Ranata Malone (Lila Kaye) hosts *Cooking with Mama Malone*, a TV show broadcast from her Brooklyn home.

1985. On *The Lucie Arnaz Show* (CBS), Dr. Jane Lucas (Lucie Arnaz) is a psychologist who co-hosts with Larry Love (Todd Waring) the radio advice program *The Love and Lucas Show*. On *Mr. Belvedere* (ABC), George Owens is the sports anchor of *Metro News* on WBN-TV in Pittsburgh.

1986. *All Is Forgiven* (NBC). Paula Russell (Bess Armstrong) is the producer of the TV soap opera *All Is Forgiven*.

1987. On *Full House* (ABC), Danny Tanner (Bob Saget) is the host of *Wake Up, San Francisco* on KTMB-TV, Channel 8; Joey Gladstone (Dave Coulier) is the star of *The Ranger Joe Show*, a kid program on Channel 8. On *Max Headroom* (ABC), Edison Carter (Matt Frewer) is a reporter for the futuristic TV Network 23.

1988. On *Murphy Brown* (CBS), Murphy Brown (Candice Bergen) is the head journalist who reports the news on *F.Y.I.*, a Washington, D.C.-based newsmagazine series.

1989. On *Coach* (ABC), football coach Hayden Fox (Craig T. Nelson) is the host of the sports talk program *The Hayden Fox Show* on KCCY-TV in Minnesota. His wife, Christine (Shelley Fabares) hosts *Wake Up, Minneapolis* (later *Coach's Corner*, a sports post-game show). On *A Fine Romance* (ABC), Louisa Phillips (Margaret Whitton) and Michael Trent (Christopher Cazenove) are the hosts of *Ticket to Ride*, a TV travel series. On *Starting Now* (CBS pilot), Felicia Kent (Cecilia Hart) is the star of a TV soap opera called *Gossamer Glen*.

1990. *The Fresh Prince of Bel Air* (NBC), Hilary Banks (Karyn Parsons) is the host of the talk-interview series *Hilary*. On *Going Places* (ABC), Alexandra Burton (Heather Locklear) is the head writer on the TV series *Here's Looking at You* (later, a talk program called *The Dick Roberts Show*). On *Good Sports* (CBS), Gayle Roberts (Farrah Fawcett) and Bobby Tannen (Ryan O'Neal) host *Sports Central*, on the All Sports Cable Network. On *Molloy* (Fox), thirteen-year-old Molloy Martin (Mayim Bialik) is the star of the kid show *Wonderland* on KQET-TV in Beverly Hills. On *The Sinbad Show* (Fox), David Bryan (Sinbad) hosts the TV show *It's Science Time*.

1991. On *Home Improvement* (ABC), Tim "The Tool Man" Taylor (Tim Allen) hosts *Tool Time*, a local home improvement program sponsored by Binford Tools. On *The Julie Brown Show* (NBC pilot), Julie Robbins (Julie Brown) is a celebrity reporter on the TV series *Inside Scoop*. On *Rewrite for Murder* (CBS pilot), Carolyn Hudson (Pam Dawber) is the writer and creator of the TV series *Miss Markham Mysteries*.

1992. On *Martin* (Fox), Martin Payne (Martin Lawrence) is the host of the radio call-in program *The Martin Payne Show,* then the TV show *On the Street.* On *On the Air* (ABC), Lester Guy (Ian Buchanan) is a washed-up movie actor who stars on *The Lester Guy Show* for the Zoblotnick Broadcasting Corporation. On *Room for Two* (ABC), Jill Kurland (Patricia Heaton) is the producer of *Wake Up, New York,* an early morning program for WXOR-TV.

1993. *Frasier* (NBC). Frasier Crane (Kelsey Grammer) is a psychiatrist who hosts the call-in program *The Frasier Crane Show* on KACL radio in Seattle.

1994. *Monty* (Fox). Monty Richards (Henry Winkler) is the politically right wing host the TV talk show *Right Speak with Monty Richardson.*

1995. On *The Bonnie Hunt Show* (CBS), Bonnie Kelly (Bonnie Hunt) works in the newsroom of *TV News Now* on WBDC-TV in Chicago. On *The George Wendt Show* (CBS), George Coleman (George Wendt) and his brother Daniel (Pat Finn) are the hosts of an auto advice radio program called *The Coleman Brothers.* On *Hope and Gloria* (NBC), Hope Davidson (Cynthia Stevenson) is the producer of *The Dennis Dupree Show* on Channel 5 in Pittsburgh (the title refers to Hope's best friend Gloria, played by Jessica Lundy). On *A Whole New Ballgame* (ABC), Brett Spooner (Corbin Bernsen) is a baseball player who provides commentary ("Brett Spooner on Sports") for *Live at Five,* a news program on WPLP-TV in Milwaukee

1997. On *Hiller and Diller* (ABC), Ted Hiller (Kevin Nealon) and Ned Diller (Richard Lewis) write the TV teen sitcom *The Katie Show.* On *The Tom Show* (WB), Tom Amross (Tom Arnold) produces *Breakfast with Charlie* on KOGD-TV in St. Paul, Minnesota.

2001. *One on One* (UPN). Flex Washington (Flex Alexander) is the host of *The Flex Files,* a sports show on WYNX-TV in Baltimore.

2002. On *Greg the Bunny* (Fox), Greg the Bunny (voice of Dan Milano) is a puppet who lives with a human, Jimmy Bender (Seth Green), and stars on the kid TV show *Sweet Knuckle Junction.* On *Life with Bonnie* (ABC), Bonnie Molloy (Bonnie Hunt) is a wife, mother and the host of an early morning TV show called *Morning Chicago.*

2003. On *All of Us* (UPN), Robert James (Duane Martin) is the host of *Mr. L.A.,* a man-about-town talk program on KJSB-TV in Los Angeles. On *A Minute with Stan Hooper* (Fox), Norm

MacDonald plays Stan Hooper, a TV commentator who closes each episode of the TV show *Newsline* with his "Minute" segments about life. On *Rock Me Baby* (UPN), Jimmy Cox (Dan Cortese) and Carl (Carl Anthony Payne) co-host the radio call-in program *The Jimmy and Carl Show* on station KHOR. On *Wanda at Large* (Fox), Wanda Hawkins (Wanda Sykes) is a correspondent for *The Beltway,* a discussion show on WHDC-TV in Washington, D.C. On *Will and Grace* (NBC), Jack McFarland (Sean Hayes) acquires a job as a producer at Out TV, a gay network.

2004. On *Joey* (NBC), Joey Tribbiani (Matt Le Blanc) is the star of a TV series called *Deep Powder.* On *Listen Up* (CBS), Jason Alexander is Tony Kleinman, the host of a TV sports show called *Listen Up.*

2005. *Hope and Faith* (ABC). Faith Fairfield (Kelly Ripa), the former star of the soap opera *The Sacred and the Sinful,* now works as the weather girl on Channel 13's *Good Day Glen Falls* TV show.

Sitcoms — Pioneering Years, 1936–1960

Of all the genres on TV, situation comedies, called sitcoms, are the most prolific. This entry chronicles the early years of the sitcom, from its beginnings in 1936, to its establishment as solid entertainment in 1960.

1936. Eddie Albert and Grace Brandt star in *The Honeymooners,* an NBC series (adapted from radio) about a young married couple and their varied misadventures.

1939. Vaudeville comic Pinky Lee and two unidentified assistants perform in various comedy sketches on NBC's *Pinky and Company.*

1941. NBC adapts its radio series, *The Parker Family,* to TV with Taylor Holmes and Violet Henning as the parents of a not-so-typical family. Leon Janney and Mitzi Gould play their children, Richard and Nancy Parker.

1947. Sandra Barkin plays a happy-go-lucky college coed during the 1920s on the DuMont test film, *The Gay Coed* (referring to a girl who is happy and carefree). Marital misadventures abound on *Mary Kay and Johnny* (DuMont/NBC/CBS), a series based on the experiences of real life marrieds Mary Kaye and Johnny Stearns.

1948. The comic dialogue between Colonel

Lemuel Q. Stoopnagle (F. Chase Taylor) and the people who drop by his home forms the basis of the CBS test film *Colonel Stoopnagle's Stoop*. Day to day events in the lives of George Payne (John Harvey, Ed Holmes) and his wife Laraine (Julie Parrish, Elaine Stritch) as they raise their son John (David Anderson) is the focus of *Growing Paynes* (DuMont). DuMont premiered *Off the Record*, a series about a New York radio disc jockey (Zero Mostel) and his man Friday (Joey Faye) that also became one of TV's first short-lived series (canceled after two episodes). A young lady named Ruthie (Ruth Gilbert) struggles to impress a man named Richard (Philip Reed) who wants nothing to do with her on *Ruthie on the Telephone*, a CBS series that uses a split screen effect (accomplished by mirrors) to show Ruthie at home while she talks to Richard (at his office) on the telephone. Hiram Sherman is featured in a variety of skits on the NBC test film *That's Our Sherman*. NBC adapts the radio series *The Goldbergs* to TV in a test film called *Whistle, Daughter, Whistle* that focuses on the lives of two Jewish families, the Goldbergs and the Blooms. Gertrude Berg stars as Molly Goldberg.

1949. Robert Casey plays Henry Aldrich, Mary Malone is his sister, Mary, and House Jameson and Lois Wilson are their parents, Sam and Alice on *The Aldrich Family*, a NBC adaptation of its radio series about the comic incidents that befall the family. Comic incidents in the lives of newlyweds John and Barbara Gay (portraying themselves) form the basis of the syndicated comedy *Apartment 3-C*. Life with Molly Goldberg (Gertrude Berg) and her Bronx family is seen on CBS as *The Goldbergs*, a second adaptation of the radio series (see 1948) that becomes a weekly series. NBC adapts its radio series, *Vic and Sade* to TV as *The Gook Family,* a test film with Frank Dane as Vic, Bernadine Flynn as Sade and Dick Conan as their son Rush, a not-so-typical family living in Crooper, Illinois. A kind hearted bumbler (Hank McCune) attempts (but always fails) to achieve success on *The Hank McCune Show* (NBC). Paul and Grace Hartman play themselves, a married couple in the small town of Forrest Heights on *The Hartmans* (NBC). Elizabeth Cote is Betsy and Mary Best is Mary, friends seeking Broadway careers on *Heavens to Betsy* (NBC). There is no musical background, no audience laugh track and limited scene changes, but NBC's *Jackson and Jill* is a pleasant visit with Jackson and

Jill Jones (Todd Karns, Helen Chapman), a young couple struggling to cope with the first years of marriage. Chester Riley (Jackie Gleason) is a good natured but mishap prone riveter (for Stevenson Aircraft) who is struggling to cope with life on *The Life of Riley* (DuMont). Chester Lauck and Norris Goff play Lum Edwards and Abner Peabody, the owners of the Jot 'em Down General Store in Pine Ridge, Arkansas, on *Lum and Abner* (CBS). San Francisco in 1910 is the setting for *Mama*, a CBS adaptation of the motion picture *I Remember Mama* about the Hansons, a Norwegian family. Eldest daughter Katrin (Rosemary Rice, Iris Mann) recalls life with Mama (Peggy Wood), Papa (Judson Laire), sister Dagmar (Robin Morgan, Toni Campbell) and brother Nels (Dick Van Patten). Incidents in the lives of newlywed couples living side by side in a New York apartment building forms the basis of NBC's *Mixed Doubles*. Bill Idelson and Ada Friedman play Bill and Ada Abbott; Eddie Firestone and Rhoda Williams are Eddy and Elaine Coleman. *Roscoe Karns and Inky Poo* is a DuMont test film about a middle class family man (Roscoe Karns) whose conscience, seen in the form of a clown named Inky Poo (Curtis Wheeler), helps him solve problems. Charlie Ruggles plays himself, the head of a family on ABC's *The Ruggles*. Erin O'Brien Moore is his wife, Margaret, and Margaret Kerry, Judy Nugent, Tommy Bernard and Jimmy Hawkins are their children Sharon, Donna, Chuck and Donald. Ernest Truex is Casper Milquetoast, a gentle man who is constantly plagued by life's misfortune on the NBC test film *The Timid Soul*. Events in the life of the Eggleston family are seen weekly on *Wesley*, a CBS series starring Frankie Thomas, Sr., Mona Thomas and Donald Devlin. Sam and Virginia Wren play themselves, a young couple coping with the first years of marriage on *Wren's Nest* (ABC).

1950. Ethel Waters (then Hattie McDaniel and Louise Beavers) plays Beulah, maid to the Henderson family on *The Beulah Show* (CBS). Fred Robbins and Barbara Belben play a young couple coping with married life on the NBC serialized comedy pilot *Dear Diary*. The comic escapades of Hildy Johnson (Mark Roberts), a small town newspaper reporter, are depicted on *The Front Page* (CBS). The hectic life of comedian George Burns and his scatterbrained wife Gracie Allen are depicted on *The George Burns and Gracie Allen Show* (CBS). The comic escapades of Cornelia

Otis Skinner (Bethel Leslie, Gloria Stroock), a hopeful actress, and her friend Emily Kimbrough (Mary Malone), a would-be writer, are depicted on *The Girls* (CBS). The ABC pilot *In the Doghouse* features the comic spats between a husband and wife (George O'Hanlon, Joan Dolan). The title refers to the literal doghouse the husband winds up in after a spat. The chaotic home and working life of comedian Jack Benny is depicted on *The Jack Benny Program* (CBS/NBC). Comedian Joey Faye performs in various skits on the CBS experimental series *Joey Faye's Frolics*. Menasha Skulnik plays Menasha, the Jewish manager of a small restaurant on the NBC pilot *The Magnificent Menasha*. Peter Lind Hayes and Mary Healy play themselves, a show business couple who entertain celebrities from their New Rochelle home on *The Peter and Mary Show* (NBC). One man's approaches to solving everyday problems are comically depicted by Cliff Norton on *The Public Life of Cliff Norton* (NBC). Jack Lemmon plays Harold, a misadventure prone actor on *That Wonderful Guy* (ABC). Simplistic comic events are depicted on *Trouble with Father*, an ABC series starring Stu Erwin as the principal of Hamilton High School, June Collyer as his wife, June, Ann Todd (then Merry Anders) as their daughter Joyce, and Sheila James as younger daughter Jackie.

1951. Amos Jones (Alvin Childress), Andrew Halt Brown (Spencer Williams, Jr.) and George "Kingfish" Stevens (Tim Moore) are African American friends struggling to cope with life in Harlem on *The Amos 'n' Andy Show* (CBS). Arnold Stang plays Billy Bean, a clumsy soda jerk in a small town corner drugstore on *The Billy Bean Show* (ABC). Patricia Crowley (then Mary Lynn Beller) plays Judy Foster, a pretty high school girl with a knack for finding trouble on *A Date with Judy* (ABC). A husband plagued by the antics of his wife as she attempts to break into show business forms the basis of *I Love Lucy* (CBS). Lucille Ball plays the wife, Lucy Ricardo, and Desi Arnaz her husband, Ricky. Radio and movie comedienne Joan Davis plays herself on *Let's Join Joanie*, a CBS pilot about a clumsy salesgirl who works in a store called Hats By Anatole. Corliss Archer (Lugene Sanders) is a small town high school girl with a penchant for finding trouble on *Meet Corliss Archer* (CBS). Ralph Charm (Maurice Copeland) and his wife Abby (Fern Parsons, Betty Arnold) are a married couple who run a mail order

business that caters to collectors of household gadgets on *Those Endearing Young Charms* (NBC). Babs Smith (Peggy Ann Garner, Marcia Henderson) and Frances Smith (Peggy French) are *Two Girls Named Smith* (ABC), cousins who have come to New York (from Nebraska) to further their dreams: Babs, a singer; Frances, a fashion designer. Jackie Kelk plays Alexander Bobbin, a recent high school graduate encountering mishap as he attempts to establish himself in the business world on *Young Mr. Bobbin* (NBC).

1952. Bud Abbott and Lou Costello play themselves, out-of-work comedians living day by day, taking whatever jobs Bud can find for Lou on *The Abbott and Costello Show* (Syn.). Events in the day-to-day lives of the Nelson family: parents Ozzie and Harriet and their children Dave and Ricky are seen on *The Adventures of Ozzie and Harriet*. Lynn Bari plays Gwen F. Allen, TV's first female boss as the owner of the Hillendale Homes Construction Company in California on *Boss Lady* (DuMont/NBC). Cliff Arquette plays his famous Charley Weaver hillbilly character as the friend to unemployed file clerk Dave Willock on *Dave and Charley* (NBC). Eddie Mayehoff plays *Doc Corkle* (NBC), a short-lived (three episode) series about a dentist beset with financial problems. The comic struggles that make up a marriage are seen through the experiences of Peter Bell (Jack Lemmon), an assistant New York toy store buyer, and his wife Betsy (Cynthia Stone), a secretary turned homemaker, on *Heaven for Betsy* (CBS). Joan Davis is Joan Stevens, the wacky wife of Judge Bradley Stevens (Jim Backus) on *I Married Joan* (NBC). Eddie Albert plays Larry Tucker, a fumbling but good-natured shoe store clerk on *Leave It to Larry* (CBS). Luigi Basco (J. Carrol Naish, Vito Scotti) is an Italian immigrant struggling to begin a new life in Chicago as the owner of an antique shop on *Life with Luigi* (CBS). Millie Bronson (Elena Verdugo) is a young Manhattan secretary who is secretly in love with her boss, Johnny Boone, Jr. (Ross Ford) on *Meet Millie* (CBS). Wally Cox is Robinson J. Peepers, a timid schoolteacher at Jefferson Junior High School in Jefferson City on *Mister Peepers* (NBC). Irma Peterson (Marie Wilson) is a beautiful but dumb blonde who possesses a keen knack for complicating life for all concerned on *My Friend Irma* (CBS). Bob Cummings plays Robert S. Beanblossom, a carefree salesman for the Thackery Realty Company on *My Hero* (CBS). *My Little Margie*

(CBS/NBC) presents events in the life of 50-year-old Vernon Albright (Charles Farrell) and his unpredictable 21-year-old daughter Margie (Gale Storm). The day-to-day happenings of an Italian American family form the basis of Papa Cellini (ABC). Tito Virolo and Carol DeAngelo head the cast.

1953. Ezio Pinza is Babbo Bonino, a widowed opera singer who gives up his career to spend time with his six children on *Bonino* (NBC). A young boy's efforts to readjust to life after the death of his parents when he moves in with relatives is the focal point of *Jamie* (ABC). Brandon DeWilde stars as Jamie McHummer. Comedienne Jean Carroll plays an average American housewife on *The Jean Carroll Show* (ABC) with Alan Carney as her husband and Lynn Loring as their daughter. William Bendix becomes Chester A. Riley, the mishap-prone riveter on NBC's *The Life of Riley*. Betty White is Elizabeth White and Del Moore her husband Alvin, newlyweds struggling to survive the first years of marriage on *Life with Elizabeth* (DuMont). Life in 1900 New York City is seen through the eyes of Clarence Day (Leon Ames), a man who refuses to accept the progress of a changing world on *Life with Father* (CBS). *Make Room for Daddy* (ABC/CBS) stars Danny Thomas as nightclub comedian Danny Williams. Jean Hagen was his first wife, Margaret; Marjorie Lord his second wife, Kathy. Marge and Jeff Green (themselves) are a newlywed couple coping with life on *Marge and Jeff* (DuMont). Ray McNutley (Ray Milland) is a drama professor at the all-girl Lynn Haven College on CBS's *Meet Mr. McNutley*. Young bank executive George Cooper (Barry Nelson) struggles to cope with life with his scatterbrained wife Liz (Joan Caulfield, Vanessa Brown) on *My Favorite Husband* (CBS). Martin Houston plays Jeep Allison, the mischievous son of a doctor in Glen Falls on *My Son Jeep* (ABC). ABC's *Pride of the Family* presents comical events in the lives of the Morrison family: Albie (Paul Hartman), advertising head of a small town newspaper, his wife Catherine (Fay Wray), and their children Ann and Albie, Jr. (Natalie Wood, Bobby Hyatt). Henpecked bank vice president Cosmo Topper (Leo G. Carroll) finds his life turned upside down when he becomes haunted by the ghosts of George and Marion Kerby (Robert Sterling, Ann Jeffreys) on *Topper* (CBS). Events in the life of Raymond Wallace (Ray Bolger), a song and dance

man who arrives moments before a performance, unfold on *Where's Raymond?* (ABC). Young Kevin Acton (Ronnie Walker) reminisces about his childhood in Ludlow, Kentucky on ABC's *Wonderful John Acton*. Harry Holcombe plays his father, John, and Virginia Dwyer is his mother, Julia.

1954. A levelheaded wife named Blondie (Pamela Britton) and her scatterbrained husband Dagwood (Hal LeRoy) form the basis for laughs on the syndicated *Blondie*. Peter Lawford plays Bill Hastings, an ex-college professor who works as Phoebe Goodheart, the advice-to-the-lovelorn columnist on the Los Angeles *Daily Blade* on *Dear Phoebe* (NBC). Spring Byington is Lily Ruskin, a young-at-heart widow on *December Bride* (CBS). Ed Gardner plays Archie, a con artist who manages the rundown *Duffy's Tavern* (NBC) for the never-seen Mr. Duffy. Paul Gilbert is Duke London, a former prizefighter turned nightclub owner on *The Duke* (NBC). Life in the small town of Springfield is seen through the activities of the Anderson family: parents Jim and Margaret (Robert Young, Jane Wyatt) and their children Betty, Bud and Kathy (Elinor Donahue, Billy Gray, Lauren Chapin). Throckmorton P. Gildersleeve (Willard Waterman) is the water commissioner of Summerfield and the bachelor uncle of two children, Marjorie and Leroy (Stephanie Griffin, Roland Keith) on *The Great Gildersleeve* (Syn.). Life at the mythical Ivy College in Ivy, U.S.A. is seen through the eyes of its president William Todhunter Hall (Ronald Colman) on *The Halls of Ivy* (CBS). Events in the life of Mickey Mulligan (Mickey Rooney), a page at the fictitious International Broadcasting Company in Los Angeles, unfold on *Hey Mulligan* (NBC). Minnesota farm girl Celeste Anders (Celeste Holm) struggles to acquire journalism experience as a reporter for the New York *Examiner* on *Honestly, Celeste*. Denny David and Steve Connors (Michael O'Shea, William Bishop) attempt to better their position in life on NBC's *It's a Great Life*. Bob MacDonald (Bob Cummings) is a suave and sophisticated photographer and ladies' man trying to avoid the paths of matrimony on *Love That Bob* (NBC/CBS). Events in the lives of the close-knit Marriott family are depicted on *The Marriage* (NBC). Real life husband and wife Hume Cronyn and Jessica Tandy play Ben and Liz Marriott with Susan Strasberg and Malcolm Broderick as their children Emily and Peter. Ann Baker plays Corliss Archer, a pretty high school girl with a knack for finding trouble on *Meet Corliss Archer*, a syndicated version of the 1951 series. Ann Sothern plays Susie McNamara, a stage actress turned secretary to theatrical agent Pete r Sands (Don Porter) on *Private Secretary* (CBS). Ray McNutley (Ray Milland) is a drama professor at Comstock University, a coed college on *The Ray Milland Show* (CBS; a revised version of 1953's *Meet Mr. McNutley*). Jarrin' Jack Jackson (Eddie Mayehoff) is a former college athlete who is attempting to turn his near-sighted, asthma prone, bookworm son, Jack, Jr. (Gil Stratton, Jr.) into an image of his former self on *That's My Boy* (CBS). Willy Dodger (June Havoc) is a lawyer encountering mishap in the small town of Renfrew, New Hampshire, on *Willy* (CBS). Cicero P. Sweeney (Charlie Ruggles) is a teller of tale tales who owns the general store in the town of Mapleton on *The World of Mr. Sweeney* (NBC).

1955. Ethel and Albert Arbuckle (Peg Lynch, Alan Bunce) are a married couple coping with life in the small town of Sandy Harbor on *Ethel and Albert* (NBC/CBS/ABC). Cecil Kellaway plays Grandpa Sycamore, the head of an eccentric family on the NBC pilot *The Fabulous Sycamores*. The struggles that make up a marriage are played for laughs on *The Honeymooners*, a CBS series in which Jackie Gleason is Ralph Kramden, a bus driver whose good intentions for wife Alice (Audrey Meadows), always backfire. Hopeful nightclub singer Janis Stewart (Janis Paige) struggles to make her dreams become a reality on *It's Always Jan* (CBS). The efforts of Mabel Spooner (Nita Talbot) to convince her reluctant to get married boyfriend Joe Sparton (Larry Blyden) that she would make the perfect wife forms the basis of *Joe and Mabel* (CBS). The NBC pilot, *The Life of Vernon Hathaway* tells of Vernon Hathaway (Alan Young), a meek watch repairman who daydreams himself into exciting adventures. The humorous incidents that befall Pearson Norby (David Wayne), his wife Helen (Joan Lorring) and their children Diane and Hank (Susan Holloran, Evan Elliott) unfold on *Norby* (NBC). Socrates "Sock" Miller (Jackie Cooper) is a Bureau of Fish and Wildlife ornithologist who hopes to become a lawyer on *The People's Choice* (CBS). Phil Silvers stars as Master Sergeant (and master con artist) Ernest Bilko, a soldier at Camp Freemont in Roseville, Kansas on *The Phil Silvers Show*

(CBS; originally titled *You'll Never Get Rich*). Thomas Wilson (Steve Dunne) is a child psychologist who is a success at the office but a hopeless failure at home when it comes to his family on *Professional Father* (CBS). Aspiring actress Kim Tracy (Virginia Gibson) struggles to make her mark in the movie capital on *So This Is Hollywood* (NBC). Hal March and Tom D'Andrea are reluctant privates struggling to complete their hitch in the army as *The Soldiers* (NBC). Margaret and Barbara Whiting play themselves, a singer and hopeful actress, on *Those Whiting Girls* (CBS). Janis Carter, Barbara Gayelord and Jeannie Johnson are misadventure-prone career girls on *Three Girls* (ABC). CBS revises *Willy* (see 1954) with June Havoc as Willy Dodger, legal counselor for the Bannister Vaudeville Company in New York City.

1956. Mild-mannered newspaper proofreader Hiram Holiday (Wally Cox) finds mishaps on a trip around the world on *The Adventures of Hiram Holiday* (NBC). Harvey and Gilmore Box (Gale Gordon, Bob Sweeney) are enthusiastic but inexperienced brothers who are attempting to run a photography studio in San Francisco on *The Brothers* (CBS). Celeste Holm plays Carolyn Daniels, an actress who becomes the guardian of three children after the death of her best friend on the NBC pilot *Carolyn*. Retired film star Charlie Farrell plays himself, the owner of the Racquet Club resort in Palm Springs, California, on *The Charlie Farrell Show* (CBS). Newly arrived in New York from Scotland, Jeannie MacLennan (Jeannie Carson) struggles to adjust to life on *Hey, Jeannie* (CBS). The home and show business life of writer Cy Howard and his beautiful Hungarian wife Zsa Zsa (Zsa Zsa Gabor) are the focal point of the NBC pilot *Just Plain Folks*. George O'Hanlon is George Gidley, a meek shoe clerk on the NBC pilot *Real George*. Buddy Hackett plays Stanley Peck, the disorganized, non-aggressive manager of a New York hotel lobby newsstand on NBC's *Stanley*.

1957. Joan Shawlee is Aggie, an American fashion buyer encountering mishaps in England on *Aggie* (Syn.). Bentley Gregg (John Forsythe) is a playboy attorney whose life suddenly changes when he takes in his orphaned niece Kelly (Noreen Corcoran) on *Bachelor Father* (CBS/NBC/ABC). Arthur Lake is Dagwood Bumstead, a bumbling architect whose wife, Blondie (Pamela Britton) has to resolve the situations he causes on

Blondie (NBC). Hectic events in the lives of marrieds Gus and Vickie Angel (Bill Williams, Betty White) are the focus of ABC's *A Date with the Angels*. Dick Starrett (Patrick O'Neill) is a London-based insurance claims detective who receives help in solving cases from Jane (Hazel Court), his wife, a British Duchess on *Dick and the Duchess* (CBS). Wally and Beaver Cleaver (Tony Dow, Jerry Mathers) are the well-meaning but mischievous children of Ward and June Cleaver (Hugh Beaumont, Barbara Billingsley) on *Leave It to Beaver* (CBS/ABC). Professional dancers Marge and Gower Champion (themselves) attempt to enjoy a quiet life despite their hectic schedules on *The Marge and Gower Champion Show* (CBS). The home and working lives of Howard Adams and Eve Drake (Howard Duff, Ida Lupino), a happily married show business couple, unfold on *Mr. Adams and Eve* (CBS). Amos McCoy (Walter Brennan), his grandson Luke (Richard Crenna) and Luke's wife Kate (Kathy Nolan) struggle to begin new lives as farmers in San Fernando on *The Real McCoys* (ABC/CBS). Joan Caulfield plays Sally Truesdale, a traveling companion to the elderly Myrtle Banford (Marion Lorne) on *Sally* (NBC).

1958. Ann Sothern is Katy O'Connor, the assistant manager of the Bartley House Hotel in New York City on *The Ann Sothern Show* (CBS). Comedian George Burns turns theatrical producer after his wife Gracie Allen retires on *The George Burns Show* (NBC). Loco Jones (Barbara Eden), Mike Page (Merry Anders) and Greta Lindquist (Lori Nelson) are three beautiful women seeking to find happiness with a rich man on *How to Marry a Millionaire* (Syn.). Rival all-girl modeling agency owners Jack Gibson and Jill Johnson (Robert Sterling, Anne Jeffreys) scheme to outdo each other and become the number one agency in Manhattan on ABC's *Love That Jill*. Yvonne Craig is Suzanne Stacey, a beautiful marriage-minded young girl seeking the proper man — one that she likes as well as her disapproving father, John (Patric Knowles) on the CBS pilot *Papa Said No*. The 1957 series *Sally* is revised slightly to focus on Sally (Joan Caulfield) as a salesgirl in the department store owned by Myrtle Banford (Marion Lorne). Patty Ann Gerrity is Alice Holliday, a mischievous nine-year-old girl on *This Is Alice* (Syn.).

1959. Jack Carson plays Augie Adams, a good-natured toy salesman on the NBC pilot *Another Day, Another Dollar*. Betty Hutton is Goldie Appleby, the guardian of three motherless children on *The Betty Hutton Show* (CBS; also known as *Goldie*). Dennis O'Keefe is Hal Towne, a newspaper columnist (of "All About Towne") on *The Dennis O'Keefe Show* (CBS). Jay North is Dennis Mitchell, the very mischievous young boy on *Dennis the Menace* (CBS). *Fibber McGee and Molly* (NBC) becomes one of the last radio programs to make the transition to TV. Here patient wife Molly McGee (Cathy Lewis) struggles to cope with the antics of husband Fibber (Bob Sweeney), an amateur inventor and expert liar. Navy personnel are satirized on *Hennessey*, a CBS series starring Jackie Cooper as Lt. Chick Hennessey, a doctor assigned to the San Diego Naval base. Maggie Randall (Patricia Crowley) is a debutante who lives with her Aunt Caroline (Lurene Tuttle) and her brother Eric (Elliott Reid) on the NBC pilot *I Remember Caviar*. The Randalls are broke (lost their money through bad investments) and must now learn to live a much simpler life. Bill Harris (William Demarest) is a music publisher struggling to keep Harris Publishing from going bankrupt on NBC's *Love and Marriage*. Dobie Gillis (Dwayne Hickman) is a teenage ladies' man, a high school student and the son of a cheap father, who finds it difficult to romance the ladies on *The Many Loves of Dobie Gillis* (CBS). Marie Pepperdine (Marie Wilson) is a sweet mailroom clerk (for the Pontifore Dress Company) who yearns to become a model on the CBS pilot *Miss Pepperdine*. Torey Peck (Patricia McCormack) is a mischievous 12-year-old girl who prefers to remain a tomboy rather than face the world as a young lady on *Peck's Bad Girl* (CBS). Pamela Blake (Brigid Bazlen) is a pretty 15-year-old girl who is struggling to make the transition from tomboy to young lady on *Too Young to Go Steady* (NBC).

1960. Patricia Crowley plays Maggie Randall on *All in the Family*, a sequel to the 1959 pilot *I Remember Caviar*. Here Maggie (Patricia Crowley) and her Aunt Caroline (Lurene Tuttle) have established an interior decorating business as a means of regaining their wealth after losing their money to bad investments. Events in the small town of Mayberry, North Carolina, are seen through the eyes of Sheriff Andy Taylor (Andy Griffith) and his deputy, Barney Fife (Don Knotts) on *The Andy Griffith Show* (CBS). A French girl named Angel (Annie Farge), newly married to architect John Smith (Marshall Thompson), struggles to adjust to the American way of life on *Angel* (CBS). Bachelor Buddy Flower (Frank Aletter) finds his life plagued by his meddlesome aunts, Violet and Iris (Enid Markey, Doro Merande) on *Bringing Up Buddy* (CBS). Bill and Babs Hooten (Mark Miller, Joanne Dru) are a couple fed up with city life who move to New Mexico, purchase a dude ranch (Guestward Ho) and struggle to make it a success on *Guestward Ho* (ABC). The father and son legal team of James Harrigan, Sr. (Pat O'Brien) and James, Jr. (Roger Perry) defend clients on *Harrigan and Son* (ABC). Carl Reiner is TV writer Rob Petrie; Barbara Britton is his wife, Laura; and Gary Morgan is their son Richie on *Head of the Family*, the CBS pilot for *The Dick Van Dyke Show*. John Michael O'Toole (Jim Backus) is a newspaper editor struggling to keep his paper, the *Headline Press*, afloat on *The Jim Backus Show — Hot Off the Wire* (Syn.). The CBS comedy pilot *McGarry and Me* follows incidents in the life of Don McGarry (Michael O'Shea), a kind hearted policeman, and his wife Kitty (Virginia Mayo). Janis Paige is Maisie Ravier, a beautiful showgirl who works the small nightclub circuit on the CBS pilot *Maisie* (based on the 1940s Ann Sothern theatrical films). The CBS pilot *Meet the Girls* finds three beautiful women seeking rich husbands: Maybelle Perkins (Mamie Van Doren), a model called "The Shape"; Lacey Sinclair (Gale Robbins), an ad executive called "The Face"; and Josephine Dunning (Virginia Field), a department store buyer known as "The Brain." Ruth and Eileen Sherwood (Elaine Stritch, Shirley Boone) are sisters living in New York's Greenwich Village and seeking to further their careers as a writer and a singer on *My Sister Eileen*. Steve Douglas (Fred McMurray) is a widower struggling to raise three children (Mike, Robbie and Chip) on *My Three Sons* (ABC/CBS). Insurance salesman Peter Porter (Harry Morgan) finds life complicated by the antics of his wife Gladys (Cara Williams) on *Pete and Gladys* (CBS). Peter and Mary Lindsey (Peter Lind Hayes, Mary Healy) are a show business couple who move from New York to Connecticut to find a quieter life on *Peter Loves Mary* (NBC). Paul Morgan (Tab Hunter), creator of the comic strip "Bachelor at Large," is a playboy who lives the strips he creates on *The Tab Hunter Show* (NBC). Real estate salesman Tom Potter (Tom Ewell) finds his life complicated by the women in his life — his wife Fran (Marilyn Erskine), their daughters Debbie, Carol and Cissy (Sherry Alberoni, Cindy Robbins, Eileen Chesis) and Irene Brady (Mabel Albertson), his mother-in-law, on *The Tom Ewell Show* (CBS).

Soap Operas — Pioneering Years, 1945–1970

Dramas, presented in a serialized format to provide a break for the housewife from her daily chores, began on radio over 70 years ago with such shows as *Dan Harding's Wife* (1936), *Ma Perkins* (1933) and *One Man's Family* (1933). This type of programming easily made the transition from radio to television with the 1936 serial *Big Sister* becoming TV's first soap opera in 1945.

By the mid-1930s laundry detergents (such as Lux Soap Flakes, Tide, Oxydol and White King Granulated Soap Flakes) began sponsoring these program, which soon became known as soap operas.

1945. CBS adapts its radio series *Big Sister* to TV, but due to the limitations of the new medium at the time, it airs with only four characters in a story about Ruth and Hope (Mercedes McCambridge, Ann Shepherd), sisters who live in the town of Glen Falls. Shortly after the premiere of *Big Sister* on October 9th, CBS aired *Three Houses*, a simple serial about three families who live next to each other in the same neighborhood. Bonnie Baker and Martin Milner star in what is TV's first attempt at its own soap opera (as opposed to borrowing from radio).

1946. *Faraway Hill* premieres on DuMont and tells the story of a woman (Flora Campbell) seeking to escape the memories of her past after her husband's death.

1947. Patricia Wheel stars on *A Woman to Remember*, a DuMont serial about the hostilities and tension that exist behind the scenes of a radio soap opera.

1949. NBC enters the market with *One Man's Family*, an adaptation of its radio series about the wealthy Barbour family of San Francisco. Bert Lytell and Marjorie Gateson star. Vera Allen plays fashion designer Peggy O'Neill on *The O'Neills* (DuMont). A mother (Alma Platto) struggles to raise her fatherless children on NBC's second soap opera, *These Are My Children*.

1950. *Fairmeadows, U.S.A.* (NBC) tells the dramatic story of an American family living in a small town. Howard St. John and Ruth Matheson star. Young marrieds Chris and Connie Thayer (Jimmy Lydon, Anne Sargent) cope with life on *The First Hundred Years* (CBS). Newspaper editor Cleate Weathers (Frank Dane) presents portraits of the people who live in a small town on *Hawkins Falls, Population 6200* (NBC). *Mama Rosa*, an ABC serial about an Italian American family, is broadcast live in Los Angeles and seen on kinescope in other areas of the country.

1951. Susan Peters plays herself, a handicapped lawyer, on NBC's *Miss Susan*. The lives of two sisters, Vanessa Dale Sterling (Peggy McCay) and Meg Dale Harper (Jean McBride) are serialized on *Love of Life* (CBS). Events in the life of Joanne Barron (Mary Stewart) unfold on *Search for Tomorrow* (CBS).

1952. Joan McCracken is Claudia Naughton, a naïve 18-year-old girl who is married to architect David Naughton (Hugh Riley), a slightly older man, on *Claudia: The Story of a Marriage* (NBC; based on the radio serial *Claudia and David*). The dramatic story of the Bauer family is brought to life on *The Guiding Light* (CBS), an adaptation of its 1937 serial that is still current in 2006. Four part stories that dramatize the joys and sorrows of men are presented on *One Man's Experience* (DuMont). DuMont also airs *One Woman's Experience*, serialized stories about women.

1953. Life in a small town is seen through the experiences of marrieds Wayne and Nancy Bennet (Don Gibson, Paula Houston) on *The Bennets* (NBC). Judy Fielding (Sallie Brophy) is a young woman struggling to break the tradition of her wealthy family and marry outside her social scale on *Follow Your Heart* (NBC). Poco Thurman (Phyllis Hill) is a young woman fraught with romantic heartaches on *Three Steps to Heaven* (NBC). Helen Emerson (Nancy Coleman) is a woman who, despite financial strain, is struggling to raise her children on *Valiant Lady* (CBS).

1954. Dramatic events in the life of Reverend Richard Dennis (William Smith) form the basis of *A Brighter Day* (CBS). Louise Albritton is Margaret Malone, a middle-aged actress in New York City, on *Concerning Miss Marlowe* (CBS). Young marrieds Laurie and Zachary James (Patricia Barry, Val DuFour) face a new life together on *First Love* (NBC). Hopeful singer Juliet Goldwin

(Lela Martin) leaves her home in Maine to further her career in New York on *Golden Windows* (NBC). Eve Allen (Ann Burr) is a doctor faced with a dilemma: remain in her small hometown and continue running her late uncle's practice or leave to fulfill her dream of a large city practice on *The Greatest Gift* (NBC). Portia Manning (Fran Carlon) is an attorney and mother struggling to divide her time between work and family on *Portia Faces Life* (CBS; also known as *The Inner Flame*). The dramatic story of Dr. Jim Brent (Don McLaughlin) and his wife Joycelyn (Virginia Dwyer) unfold on *The Road of Life* (CBS). Events in the lives of the Ames family come into focus on *The Secret Storm* (CBS). Scott Forbes is John Adams, a general practitioner and criminologist on *The Seeking Heart* (CBS). Julie Byron (Patricia Sully) is a newspaper proofreader who longs to become a reporter on *A Time to Live* (NBC). Constance Ford is Lynn Sherwood, a fashion designer struggling to make her mark on the world on *Woman with a Past* (CBS).

1955. Life in the small town of Bay City is seen through the eyes of Jim Bradley (Logan Field) on *A Date with Life* (NBC). Gloria Lucas appears as Linda Porter, the host of serialized dramas based on stories in leading women's magazines, on *Way of the World* (NBC).

1956. The lives of the Hughes and Lowell families are explored on *As the World Turns* (CBS). The lives of ordinary people driven by intense feeling and difficult circumstances are seen on *The Edge of Night* (CBS/ABC).

1958. Events in the lives of the Frasiers, a prestigious family living in the town of Strathfield, are seen on *From These Roots* (NBC). Kitty Foyle (Kathleen Murray) is a young girl "just discovering life" on NBC's *Kitty Foyle*. Laura Manning (Patricia Benoit) is the assistant principal of Bolton High School; she is divorced, the mother of a young son and romantically involved with a married man on *Today Is Ours* (NBC). William Prince is Dr. Jerry Malone, the head of Valley Hospital, on *Young Dr. Malone* (NBC).

1959. Philip Abbott is John Collier, a defense attorney on *The House on High Street*, an NBC series based on actual records of the Los Angeles Domestic Relations Court.

1960. The problems faced by the first Cape Canaveral astronauts and their courageous wives are dramatized on *Clear Horizon* (CBS). Gary Donovan (Robert Fortier) is a wanderer who remains in one place only long enough to earn the resources he needs to continue his travels on *Full Circle* (CBS). John Beal is Dr. Lewis on *The Road to Reality*, an ABC serial that dramatizes what happens at a group therapy session.

1962. Jim and Helen Lee (Michael Keene, Esther Ralston) are the parents of five daughters (Ann, Marjorie, Barbara, Jane and Mary) on *Our Five Daughters* (NBC).

1963. The town of Indian Hill is the setting for the story of John P. Abbott (Addison Richards), an elder lawyer, and Ben Jerrod (Michael Ryan), his young assistant, on *Ben Jerrod* (NBC). Hope Memorial Hospital is the setting for a look at the private and working lives of medical professionals on *The Doctors* (NBC). Intimate glimpses into the lives of the doctors and nurses at General Hospital are explored on ABC's *General Hospital*.

1964. Dramatic incidents in the lives of the Matthews and Randolph families are the basis of *Another World* (NBC). The secret lives and hidden dreams of the people of the small New England town of Peyton Place come into view on "the continuing story of *Peyton Place*" (ABC). The dramatic story of three married couples, the Garretts, Reynoldses and Gilroys, unfold on *The Young Married* (ABC). Peggy McCay and Lee Meriwether star.

1965. "Like sands through the hour glass, so are *The Days of Our Lives*," that an NBC serial set in Salem, Massachusetts, that focuses on the life of Dr. Thomas Horton (Macdonald Carey), a professor of medicine at University Hospital, and his family. "No matter how dark the night, there is always a new dawn to come. The sun is but a *Morning Star*," an NBC drama about Kathy Elliott (Elizabeth Perry), a model caught in the intrigue and excitement of high fashion. "We're young but never too young to set this whole world spinning" is said in the opening theme to *Never Too Young*, an ABC serial about the young people who hang out at Alfie's Café on Malibu Beach in California. Tony Dow and Tommy Rettig star. Liz Thorpe and Gail Lucas (Mary Fickett, Melinda Plank) are nurses at Alden General Hospital on *The Nurses* (ABC). The dramatic story of Lisa Hughes (Eileen Fulton) as she struggles to adjust to life after a deeply affecting divorce is seen on *Our Private World*, a CBS prime time soap opera spinoff from its daytime *As the World Turns*. *Scarlett Hill*, TV's first syndicated soap opera, tells the dramatic story of Kate Russell (Beth Lockerbie),

the owner of the Russell Boarding House in Scarlett Hill, New York, and her rebellious teenage daughter Ginny (Lucy Warner).

1966. A beautiful young woman named Victoria Winters (Alexandra Moltke) finds her life in constant danger, especially from the vampire Barnabas Collins (Jonathan Frid), when she moves from New York to Maine to care for young David Collins (David Henesy) on *Dark Shadows* (ABC).

1967. The lives and romantic interludes of a group of people living in San Francisco form the basis of *Love Is a Many Splendored Thing* (CBS).

1968. The dramatic story of Arthur Adams (Conrad Fowkes), a lawyer living in a small Midwestern town, is depicted on NBC's *Hidden Faces*. The lives of two families are dramatized on ABC's *One Life to Live*: The Woleks, first generation Americans struggling for a position on top of the social ladder, and the Lords, an established family entrenched in the dominant social and economic milieu.

1969. The private and professional lives of the people of Bancroft, a small college community beset by contemporary crises, is depicted on *Bright Promise* (NBC). Supernatural occurrences, voodoo and the undead are seen on the syndicated *Strange Paradise*, the story of Jean Paul Desmond (Colin Fox), a man who brings his wife Erica (Tudi Wiggins) back from the dead, and of Erica's attempts to possess the body of Holly Marshall (Sylvia Feigel) so she can be born again. The struggles and emotional problems faced by the wealthy Carlyle family are dramatized on *The Survivors*, an ABC prime time serial starring Ralph Bellamy as Baylor Carlyle, Lana Turner as Tracy Carlyle and George Hamilton as Duncan Carlyle. The conflicts and tensions that divide the close-knit Hathaway family are dramatized on *Where the Heart Is* (CBS).

1970. April Morrison (Julie Mannix), Linda Warren (Patricia McCormack) and Kim Jordan (Kathy Glass) are secretaries at Key Publishing in New York and struggling to fulfill their dreams on *The Best of Everything* (ABC). NBC's *Somerset*, a spinoff from *Another World*, tells the dramatic story of three families: The Grants, Lucases and Delaneys.

Note: Many soap operas both daytime and primetime have since been televised. Additional daytime soaps include *The Bold and the Beautiful*, *Passions*, *Port Charles*, *Return to Peyton Place*, *Rit-*

uals, *Ryan's Hope, Texas* and *The Young and the Restless*. Prime time soaps include *Beacon Hill, Dallas, Dynasty, Falcon Crest, Flamingo Road, King's Crossing, Knots Landing, Melrose Place, The O.C., Savannah* and *The Yellow Rose*.

Although considered daytime programs, soap operas did introduce some interesting firsts. *The Guiding Light, Kitty Foyle, One Man's Family, Valiant Lady* and *Young Doctor Malone* all made successful transitions from radio to TV. *Scarlett Hill* (1965) was the first soap opera made especially for syndication (sold to local stations; *Strange Paradise* [1969], *The Life and Times of Eddie Roberts* [1980], *Young Lives* [1981] and *Rituals* [1984] are the others). The 1970 NBC pilot *The Shameful Secrets of Hastings Corners* became the first attempt to spoof soap operas (this was followed by the syndicated *Mary Hartman, Mary Hartman* [1976], and *Forever Fernwood* and *Soap*, both in 1977).

Big Sister (1945) became not only TV's first soap opera but also the first for CBS and the first one to be broadcast as a half hour (most soaps that followed were 15 minutes long). *Faraway Hill* in 1946 was the DuMont Network's first serial. NBC entered the picture in 1949 with *One Man's Family* and ABC was last with *Mama Rosa* in 1950. NBC experimented with color broadcasting on *Ben Jerrod*. *The Guiding Light* (1958) and *The House on High Street* (1959) experimented with primitive videotape broadcasting. *The Nurses* (1965) was the first soap to be continued from a non-soap prime time series (also called *The Nurses*). *Somerset* (1970) was the first soap to be spun off from another soap (*Another World*). *The Edge of Night* (1956) was the first soap to introduce murder, mystery and crime-solving, while *Dark Shadows* (1966) was the first to introduce horror — from vampires and werewolves to a Frankenstein-like creation called Adam. It is also the only serial to receive a prime time revival (1991). *Our Private World* (1965) became the first prime time soap to be based on an afternoon serial (*As the World Turns*). *Never Too Young* (1965) was the first soap to be geared to a younger audience (teenagers) as opposed to the prior adult-themed dramas. *Peyton Place* (1964) and *The Best of Everything* (1970) were the only soaps based on theatrical films (*Love Is a Many Splendored Thing* borrows the film title, not the storyline). *Another World* became the first hour serial (1975), then the first 90-minute soap (1979; it switched back to 60 minutes in 1980).

Dallas is considered the first program to introduce the cliffhanger in 1980 with the season finale episode, "Who Shot J.R.?" NBC's *Miss Susan* (1951) is not only the first soap opera to feature a handicapped person (spinal injury to star Susan Peters) but the first series to star such a person.

Space

Television easily captured the imaginations of young and old alike with programs set in outer space or on planets other than Earth. Programs dealing with these topics are chronicled here.

1949. *Captain Video and His Video Rangers* (DuMont). TV's first space adventure with Richard Coogan (then Al Hodge) as Captain Video, "The Guardian of the Safety of the World." He pilots a ship first called the *X-9*, then the *Galaxy*.

1950. On *Buck Rogers in the 25th Century* (ABC), Kem Dibbs (then Robert Pastine) is Buck Rogers, a 20th century man who is placed in a state of suspended animation by a mysterious gas, then awakened 500 years later to battle futuristic evil with Lt. Wilma Deering (Lou Prentis) of the Earth Defense League. On *Space Patrol* (ABC), "Missions of daring in the name of interplanetary justice" are the assignments of Buzz Corry (Ed Kemmer), the commander-in-chief of the Space Patrol, an Earth-based organization responsible for the safety of the United Planets. Buzz piloted the *Battlestar 100*, *Terra IV* and *Terra V*. On *Tom Corbett, Space Cadet* (CBS/ABC/NBC/DuMont), Tom Corbett (Frankie Thomas) is a cadet at Space Academy, a 24th century celestial police force. Tom, although a cadet, pilots the space ship *Polaris*.

1953. On *Flash Gordon* (Syn.), Flash Gordon (Steve Holland) and his assistant Dale Arden (Irene Champlin) are members of the 23rd century Galactic Bureau of Investigation, an organization that battles aliens. Flash pilots the ship *Sky Flash II*. On *Rod Brown of the Rocket Rangers* (CBS), Rod Brown (Cliff Robertson) is a member of the Rocket Rangers, a 22nd century defense organization that battles interplanetary evil. He pilots a ship called *Beta*.

1954. On *Rocky Jones, Space Ranger* (Syn.), Rocky Jones (Richard Crane) is chief of the Space rangers, a 21st century organization established to safeguard the planets of a united solar system from alien invaders. Rocky and his assistant, the beautiful Vena Ray (Sally Mansfield), first piloted the *Orbit Jet,* then the *Silver Moon.*

1955. On *Captain Z-Ro* (Syn.), Captain Z-Ro (Roy Steffens) is a mysterious scientist who has invented a time machine that allows him to go back in time — to learn from the past to learn for the future. He also pilots a space ship called *ZX-99.* On *Commando Cody, Sky Marshal of the Universe* (NBC), a mysterious scientist known only as Commando Cody (Judd Holdren), works for an undisclosed organization that battles alien invaders. While Cody does not have a ship, he does have his Rocket Flying Suit, which enables him to travel through space.

1959. *Men Into Space* (CBS). William Lundigan is Edward McCauley, an Air Force Colonel attempting to further the U.S. Space Program.

1962. *Space Angel.* Scott McCloud is an agent for the Interplanetary Space Force on this syndicated animated series.

1963. *Planet Patrol.* Larry Dart is an agent for the Galasphere Patrol, an interplanetary police force, on this syndicated marionette adventure.

1965. *Lost in Space* (CBS). The Robinson family, headed by parents John and Maureen (Guy Williams, June Lockhart), struggle to return to Earth after their ship, the *Jupiter II,* is sabotaged and lost in space.

1966. On *Space Ghost* (CBS), Gary Owens is the voice of Space Ghost, an interplanetary crime fighter on this animated series. On *Space Kiddettes* (NBC), space age youngsters battle celestial evil in this animated Saturday morning series. On *Star Trek* (NBC), James Tiberius Kirk (William Shatner) captains the U.S.S. *Enterprise NCC-1701.* He holds the record for being the youngest captain (at age 34) in Starfleet history. Also on board: Mr. Spock (Leonard Nimoy), the emotionless Vulcan Science Officer; Lt. Uhura (Nichelle Nichols), the African American Communications Officer (her name, translated from Swahili, means Freedom); Leonard McCoy (DeForest Kelley), called Bones, the chief medical officer; and Montgomery Scott (James Doohan), called Scotty, the chief engineer.

1967. *Captain Scarlet and the Mysterons* (Syn.) Captain Scarlet, a top agent for Spectrum, a futuristic Earth defense organization, fights to protect Earth from the inhabitants of Mars (the Mysterons) on this marionette series.

1972. On *Josie and the Pussycats in Outer Space* (CBS cartoon, the Josie and the Pussycats rock

group find adventure when they are accidentally launched into space. On *U.F.O.* (Syn), Edward Stryker (Ed Bishop), the commander of S.H.A.D.O. (Supreme Headquarters Alien Defense Organization) protects the Earth from outer space visitors; on the moon, the gorgeous Gay Ellis (Gabrielle Drake) commands the Moon Base Alpha tracking station.

1973. On *Doctor Who* (Syn.), Tom Baker plays the Doctor, a traveler in time and space who battles evil wherever he finds it. The Doctor travels in his TARDIS (Time and Relative Dimensions in Space), a time machine that resembles a British police call box (a telephone booth). The Doctor is from the planet Gallifrey and travels with Earth journalist Sarah Jane Smith (Elisabeth Sladen), whom he met during a story she was covering. The series began in England in 1963 with Doctor Number 1 (William Hartnell). It was first seen in the U.S. with Tom Baker (Doctor Number 4). On *The Starlost* (Syn.), a ship called *The Starlost* and its three-member crew, Devon, Rachel and Garth (Keir Dullea, Gay Rowan, Robin Ward), seek a Class Six star to save the Earth from destruction.

1974. *Star Trek* (NBC). William Shatner, Leonard Nimoy, Nichelle Nichols, DeForest Kelley, James Doohan and George Takei recreate their roles from the original 1966 *Star Trek* in this animated update of the filmed series.

1975. On *Far Out Space Nuts* (CBS), Barney and Junior (Chuck McCann, Bob Denver) accidentally launch a NASA rocket and become lost in space on this Saturday morning series. On *The Lost Saucer* (ABC), androids Fi and Fum (Ruth Buzzi, Jim Nabors) are universe explorers lost in time on this live action Saturday morning series. On *Space: 1999* (Syn.), Helena Russell (Barbara Bain) is a doctor with Space Services and attached to the Moon Base Alpha Medical Center on the moon. John Koenig (Martin Landau) is a noted astronaut responsible for the success of the U.S. space missions and is now the commander of Moon Base.

1977. *Space Academy* (CBS). Jonathan Harris is Gampu, the commander of the Nova Blue Team, a futuristic group of young cadets who safeguard the universe.

1978. On *Battlestar Galactica* (ABC), Adama (Lorne Greene) is the commander of *Galactica,* a gigantic battle starship in the seventh millennium of time. Captain Apollo (Richard Hatch) is Adama's oldest son, head of the Galactica Fighter Squadron. Starbuck (Dirk Benedict) is Adama's younger son, a colonial warrior and ace Viper pilot (Vipers are the small ships that protect the *Galactica* from alien foes). On *The Galaxy Goofups* (NBC), Yogi Bear and Huckleberry Hound become members of the Celestial Police Force on this animated series. On *Quark* (NBC), Adam Quark (Richard Benjamin) is the captain of a United Galaxy Sanitation Patrol ship in the year 2226. His mission is to pick up the trash (space baggies) of the United Planets. He is assisted by Jean/Gene (Tim Thomerson), a transmute (possesses male and female chromosomes), who is the chief engineer; Betty I and Betty II (Tricia and Cyb Barnstable), twins (one is a clone but Adam is not sure which one) who are second in command; and Ficus (Richard Kelton), the chief science officer, a plant from the planet Vegeton. On *Space Force* (CBS), William Edward Phipps is Irving Hinkley, the commander of a crew of astronauts assigned to a remote military space station on this unsold pilot.

1979. On *Buck Rogers in the 25th Century* (NBC), William "Buck" Rogers (Gil Gerard) is a U.S. Air Force test pilot who was suspended in time for 500 years (due to a mixture of gases in his ship, the *Ranger III*). He awoke in the 25th century to battle evil with Lt. Wilma Deering (Erin Gray), as a member of the Earth Defense Force. On *Casper and the Angels* (NBC), Casper the Friendly Ghost becomes the futuristic guardian of Minnie and Maxi, 21st century Space Patrol women, on this animated series. On *Jason of Star Command* (CBS), Craig Littler is Jason, a pilot for the futuristic police station, Star Command on this live action Saturday morning series. On *Star Struck* (CBS), McCallister's Midway Inn is an orbiting way station between Earth and Pluto that is run by the McCallister family. Their experiences with the alien visitors are the basis of this unsold pilot that stars Beeson Carroll, Tania Myren and Meegan King.

1981. *Space Stars* (NBC). A group of futuristic heroes battle evil in outer space on this animated series; the heroes include Space Ghost, the Herculoids and Kid Comet and the Teen Force.

1983. *He-Man and the Masters of the Universe* (Syn.). The mighty warrior He-Man (voice of George DiCenzo) struggles to protect the universe from the evils of Skeletor on the animated series.

1985. *She-Ra: Princess of Power* (Syn.). Melendy Britt is the voice of She-Ra, Princess of the planet Eternia, as she struggles to safeguard it from the evil Horda on this animated series.

1986. *The Silverhawks* (Syn.). Five Earthlings (Jonathan Quick, Emily and Will Hart, Bluegrass and The Copper Kid) are transformed into the Silverhawks (beings who are part human, part metal to withstand the pressures of space) to battle the evil Monstar on this animated pilot.

1987. *Star Trek: The Next Generation* (Syn.). Jean-Luc Picard (Patrick Stewart) commands the Galaxy class starship, U.S.S. *Enterprise*, with William Ryker (Jonathan Frakes) as his second-in-command. Also on board: Beverly Crusher (Gates McFadden), the chief medical officer; and Geordi LaForge (LeVar Burton), the chief engineer.

1988. *Mars: Base One* (CBS). An Earth family, led by Doug and Ellen Ludlow (Tim Thomerson, Nancy Youngblut), attempt to colonize the planet Mars on this unsold comedy pilot.

1989. *Outpost* (CBS). A young woman, Marshal Rachel Morgan (Joanna Going) attempts to maintain law and order on her volatile planet, Icarus, on this unsold pilot.

1993. On *Babylon 5* (TNT), Elizabeth Lockley (Tracy Scoggins) is the captain of *Babylon 5*, a futuristic star ship. John Sheridan (Bruce Boxleitner) is the ship's former captain who is now president of the Alliance (an organization that protects member planets). Susan Ivanova (Claudia Christian) is second in command on *Babylon 5*. On *Space Rangers* (CBS), John Boon (Jeff Kaake) is a Federal Space Ranger who captains *Ranger 377*, a battle star ship. Also on board: Jo Jo (Marjorie Monaghan), a beautiful alien from a planet where men are wimps; Doc (Jack McGee), the ship's repairman; and Zylyn (Cary-Hiroyuki Tagawa), an alien from the planet Grakka. On *Star Trek: Deep Space Nine* (Syn.), Benjamin Sisko (Avery Brooks) is the commanding officer of the space station Deep Space Nine complex (also captain of the Starfleet space ship U.S.S. *Defiant NX-74205*). Ezri Dax (Nicole deBoer) is the station counselor; and Jadzia Dax (Terry Farrell) is the science officer.

1994. *Earth 2* (NBC). A group of Earth colonists attempt to colonize an alien, hostile planet to create a new world for children who are being stricken with illness on an over-polluted Earth. Debrah Farentino, Jessica Steen, Joey Zimmerman and Clancy Brown star.

1995. *Star Trek: Voyager* (UPN). Kathryn Janeway (Kate Mulgrew) captains the U.S.S. starship *Voyager NCC-7465*. Also on board is Tuvok

(Tim Russ) the Vulcan science officer; B'Elanna Torres (Roxann Dawson), the chief engineer; and Seven of Nine (Jeri Ryan), a woman rescued by Kathryn from the evil Borg Collective, who now serves wherever she is needed.

1996. *Homeboys in Outer Space* (UPN). Ty Walker (Flex Alexander) and Morris Clay (Darryl M. Bell) are 25th century planet hoppers (looking for work) who pilot a star ship called *Space Hoopty*.

1999. *Crusade* (Sci Fi), Matthew Gideon (Gary Cole) is captain of the space ship *Excalibur*, on a crusade to save the Earth by finding a cure for the deadly Drakh Plague. On *Farscape* (Sci Fi), an American astronaut, John Crichton (Ben Browder) and his crew of aliens, including Chiana (Gigi Edgely), Aeryn Sun (Claudia Black) and Zotah Zhaan (Virginia Robyn Hey), are freedom fighters battling evil in outer space.

2000. On *Andromeda* (Syn.), Dylan Hunt (Kevin Sorbo) is captain of the Systems Commonwealth battleship *Andromeda Ascendant*. Also on board: Beka Valentine (Lisa Ryder), the former captain of the salvage ship *Eureka Maru*, who now serves as the first officer; Trance Gemini (Laura Bertram), an alien who is the Avatar of the Sun (a balance between light and dark) who works at various jobs; and Rommie (Lexa Doig), a beautiful hologram who controls the ship. On *Lexx* (Sci Fi), Stanley H. Twiddle (Brian Downey) is the self-appointed captain of the *Lexx*, a space ship that cruises through the Dark Zone in a futuristic time. He is a coward and accomplishes things by accident. Also on board: Zev Bellringer (Eva Haberman, Xenia Seeberg), a gorgeous girl who is part cluster lizard, and Kai (Michael McManus), an undead assassin who is eager to learn about other life forms.

2001. *Star Trek: Enterprise* (UPN). Jonathan Archer (Scott Bakula) is the commander of the first Star Fleet space ship, *Enterprise NX-01*. Also on board are T'Pol (Jolene Blalock), a gorgeous Vulcan who serves as the science officer; Hoshi Sato (Linda Park), the communications officer; and Travis Mayweather (Anthony Montgomery), the chief engineer.

2002. *Firefly* (Fox). Malcolm Reynolds (Nathan Fillion) pilots the *Serenity*, a transport vessel with a crew of renegades who manage to stay just one step ahead of the law.

2003. *Battlestar Galactica* (Sci Fi). A revival of the 1978 series. William Adama (Edward James Olmos) is the commander of the battle star ship *Galactica*. His son, Apollo (Jamie Bamber) heads the Viper defense fleet; and Starbuck (Katee Sackhoff) is now a woman and an ace Viper pilot.

2006. *Doctor Who* (Sci Fi). The original *Doctor Who* series (see 1973) is revised with Christopher Eccleston as the time traveling alien Time Lord, the Doctor, and Billie Piper as his Earth girl traveling companion, Rose Tyler.

Spectaculars see *Variety and Drama Spectaculars*

Speech Impaired Characters

This entry chronicles characters who are unable to speak or have difficulty talking (and who appear as regulars on a program).

1951. Andy Devine plays Jingles P. Jones, the shrill-voiced deputy to U.S. Marshal James Butler Hickok on the syndicated *Wild Bill Hickok*. Andy was later the host of *Andy's Gang*, an NBC series for children in 1955. Andy suffered a childhood accident that affected his speech.

1955. Ernie Kovacs portrays a character named Eugene on *The Ernie Kovacs Show* (NBC). Eugene never speaks and is always seen in skits involving video and audio effects (for example, pouring a glass of water and having it come out of the pitcher on an angle or in loud pouring sounds).

1957. Gene Sheldon plays Bernardo, the deaf mute servant of Don Diego de la Vega, alias *Zorro* (ABC).

1961. Gena Rowlands plays Teddy Carella, the deaf mute wife of N.Y.P.D. detective Steve Carella, on *The 87th Precinct* (NBC).

1968. Angelo Muscat is the Silent Butler, the non-speaking servant to Number 6, the prisoner (CBS) of a resort village from which there is no escape, on *The Prisoner*.

1977. Lou Ferrigno plays *The Incredible Hulk* (CBS). Although he does not speak, Lou suffers from a partial hearing loss that affects his speech.

1988. David Beecroft plays Eric Bolan, a detective left with a whisper of a voice after he is stabbed in the throat, on the CBS pilot *Silent Whisper*.

1989. Karron Graves plays Katie Larson, the daughter of marine research scientist Michael Lar-

son on *Dolphin Cove* (CBS). Katie suffered a traumatic shock in a car accident that killed her
mother and left her unable to speak. Her inability to speak gives Katie a special affinity with the
dolphins her father is studying — a situation that
he cannot explain. Travis Fine is Ike McSwain, a
mute (a result of Scarlet Fever) who works as a
Pony Express rider for the Overland Express on
The Young Riders (ABC).

1991. Brooke Theiss is Caroline Sandler, a
teenage girl who is unable to speak on ABC's *Good
and Evil*. Caroline suffered a traumatic shock
when her father died under mysterious circumstances.

1997. Robert McRay plays Zzeben, a mute
gladiator who teams with the warrior Conan to
battle injustice on *Conan* (Syn.). Peter MacNichol is John Gage, senior partner in the Boston law
firm of Cage and Fish, who suffers from a stuttering problem, on *Ally McBeal*.

1998. Oris Orhuero is Rongar, a mute sailor
who travels with the mighty Sinbad on *The Adventures of Sinbad* (Syn.). John Lehr plays John
Warner, Jr., the brother of nursing student Jesse
Warner, who refuses to speak until he finds a more
efficient use of the English language, on NBC's
Jesse.

1999. Pepe Serna provides the voice for
Sanchez (Fomation puppet), a promising opera
star whose passion for cigarettes forces him to
speak with a throat microphone on *The PJ's*
(Fox/WB).

2000. Lou Ferrigno, who speaks with a slight
speech impediment, plays himself as the next-
door neighbor of Doug and Carrie Heffernan on
The King of Queens.

Stage Shows see Broadway

Stock Car Racers

Characters who race cars for a living or just for
fun are the subjects of this entry.

1961. *Straightaway* (ABC). Scott Ross and
Clipper Hamilton (Brian Kelly, John Ashley) are
mechanics who own the Straightaway Garage and
become involved with professional drivers and
racers.

1962. *Tack Reynolds* (ABC pilot). Michael
Parks plays Tack Reynolds, a stock car racer who

travels the racecar circuit and helps people in trouble along the way.

1967. *Speed Racer* (Syn.). The animated adventures of a daring young racecar driver (of the Mark
5) are depicted on this Japanese series dubbed in
English.

1969. *Hot Wheels* (ABC cartoon). Automotive
safety is seen through the experiences of the members of the Hot Wheels Racing Club.

1970. *Southern Fried* (NBC pilot). Lonnie
Allen (John Neilson) is a not-too-bright stock car
racer whose big heart is also his biggest shortcom-
ing when people try to take advantage of him.

1979. *The Dukes of Hazzard* (CBS). Bo and
Luke Duke (John Schneider, Tom Wopat) are
cousins who race their car, the *General Lee*, in various competitions in and around Hazzard County,
Georgia, while at the same time trying to overcome the evils of county commissioner Boss
Hogg. Although not a racer in the typical sense,
Daisy (Catherine Bach), Bo and Luke's cousin,
drives a souped-up Jeep (*Dixie*).

1980. *The Georgia Peaches* (CBS pilot). Dusty
Tyree (Dirk Benedict) is a Treasury agent who
poses as a stock car racer. He is teamed with
Lorette Peach (Tanya Tucker), a mechanic who
owns the Georgia Peaches Garage, and her sister
Sue Lynn Peach (Terri Nunn), a country and western singer, ordinary citizens who have been recruited by the government to work with Dusty.

1981. *Stockers* (NBC pilot). J.T. Spangler (Terry
Bradshaw) and Curtis Witlock (Mel Tillis) are
stock car racers hoping to win the Daytona 500 by
competing in as many races as possible to qualify.

1983. *Six Pack* (NBC pilot). Brewster Baker
(Don Johnson) is a stock car racer and the
guardian of five parentless children (whom he
found when they were attempting to strip his car).

1990. *Checkered Flag* (ABC pilot). Andrew
Valiant (Pernell Roberts) is the head of the Valiant
Racing Team, an auto-racing club based in
Riverdale, California. Alexis Cross (Carrie Hamil-
ton) is the chief mechanic, and Alan Blondel and
Mike Reardon (Christian Bocher, Rob Estes), the
drivers.

Super Heroes

Characters who possess extraordinary powers,
either human or alien, by normal means or by
artificial assistance, are the subjects of this entry.

See also *Kids — Extraordinary, Men — Extraordinary* and *Women — Extraordinary.*

1953. An alien, from the planet Krypton, becomes newspaper reporter Clark Kent, his cover for his true identity as Superman (George Reeves), the hero of Metropolis on *The Adventures of Superman* (Syn.).

1958. In a takeoff on the Superman character, actors dressed in dog costumes perform on the pilot *The Adventures of Superpup*. Here Bark Bent (Billy Curtis), a reporter for the *Daily Beagle*, is secretly Superpup, the hero of Metropolis.

1961. Before Clark Kent (John Rockwell) became a reporter for the Metropolis *Daily Planet*, he attended Smallville High School. Here, on the pilot *The Adventures of Superboy*, Clark battles evil as a teenager called Superboy.

1964. Shoeshine Boy (voice of Wally Cox) is a humble dog who, when the need arises, becomes the mighty Underdog, an heroic crime fighter on *The Underdog Show* (NBC/CBS cartoon).

1965. The syndicated *Marvel Super Heroes* presents serialized animated adaptations of five of its comic book characters: Captain America, The Incredible Hulk, Iron Man, The Mighty Thor and Sub Mariner. *Captain America* relates Steve Rogers' battle as Captain America against the Red Skull, America's enemy during World War II. Dr. Bruce Banner is "belted by gamma rays" and becomes *The Incredible Hulk*, a menacing but good creature who combats the villainous Leader (who has a gamma ray mutated brain). Tony Stark and his electronic alter ego, *Iron Man*, battle saboteurs, in particular, the megalomaniac Mandarin. Dr. Donald Blake finds the ancient hammer of the Thunder god Thor and through its magical powers becomes the crime fighting *Mighty Thor*. Namor, the Prince of the Deep, battles the enemies of the lost city of Atlantis on *Sub Mariner*.

1966. Bruce Wayne (Adam West) and his youthful ward Dick Grayson (Burt Ward) battle villains in Gotham City as Batman and Robin on ABC's *Batman*. In 1968 Yvonne Craig joins the cast as librarian Barbara Gordon, alias Batgirl. Newspaper publisher Britt Reid (Van Williams) and his valet Kato (Bruce Lee) battle criminal elements as *The Green Hornet* (ABC). Bud Collyer provides the voice of Clark Kent, alias Superman, the hero of Metropolis, on the animated CBS series *The New Adventures of Superman*.

1967. When their rocket ship enters a strange radioactive belt, four people acquire amazing powers on *The Fantastic Four* (ABC cartoon). Reed Richards can stretch like taffy; his wife, Sue, can become invisible at will; Ben Grimm becomes the Thing, a beast with incredible strength; and Johnny Storm is the Human Torch. Aquaman is an Aquarian born of an Atlantian mother and a human father (a lighthouse keeper) who protects the lost kingdom of Atlantis from evil on *The Superman-Aquaman Hour*, an animated CBS series that combines 1966's *The New Adventures of Superman* with *Aquaman* cartoons. Carter Nash (William Daniels) is a mild-mannered police chemist who invents super juice, a liquid that transforms him into *Captain Nice* (NBC), a daring crime fighter in Big Town, U.S.A. When a U.S. government scientist invents a power pill, the Bureau of Special Projects chooses gas station attendant Stanley Beemish (Stephen Strimpell) to test it and become *Mr. Terrific* (CBS), a daring but bumbling crime fighter. Central High School student Peter Parker is bitten by a radioactive spider and soon after absorbs the proportionate powers and abilities of a spider to become the crime fighting *Spider Man* (ABC cartoon).

1968. Yvonne Craig plays Barbara Gordon, alias Batgirl, on *Batgirl*, a pilot that failed to feature the character in her own companion series to ABC's *Batman* (the female crime fighter joined the *Batman* cast shortly after). Batman and Robin are seen in animated form and join Superman on *The Batman-Superman Hour* (CBS). *Batman* replaces the *Aquaman* segment from the 1967 *Superman-Aquaman Hour*. Ellie Wood Walker plays Diana Prince, alias Wonder Woman, on *Wonder Woman*, a pilot that presents a pretty but vain crime fighter ("who has the strength of Hercules, the wisdom of Athena, the speed of Mercury, and who thinks she has the beauty of Aphrodite").

1973. *The Super Friends* premieres on ABC and unites a number of animated characters as members of the Justice League of America. Battling crime are Batman and Robin, Superman, Wonder Woman, Aquaman and Marvin, Wendy and Wonder Dog. Steve Austin (Lee Majors) uses the bionic abilities of his legs, arm and eye (received during a bionic operation to save his life after a test plane crash) to battle crime for the government on *The Six Million Dollar Man* (ABC).

1974. Billy Batson (Michael Gray) is a teenager chosen by the immortal elders (Solomon, Hercules, Achilles, Zeus, Atlas and Mercury) to become Captain Marvel, a daring crime fighter on *Shazam!* (CBS). Cathy Lee Crosby is Diana Prince, alias Wonder Woman, an immortal Amazon who leaves her home on Paradise Island to battle evil on the ABC pilot *Wonder Woman.*

1975. Andrea Thomas (JoAnna Cameron) is a high school science teacher who becomes the crime fighter Isis through the powers of an amulet she found while on an expedition in Egypt on *Isis* (CBS).

1976. Jaime Sommers (Lindsay Wagner) is a young woman whose life is saved following a parachuting accident by a bionic operation that replaces her legs, arm and inner ear with powerful synthetic parts on *The Bionic Woman* (ABC/NBC). Jaime uses her abilities to battle crime for the government. Laurie and Judy (Deidre Hall, Judy Strangis) are reporters who become the crime fighting *Electra Woman and Dyna Girl* (ABC) through the power of Crime Scope, a computer complex. Diana Prince, alias Wonder Woman (Lynda Carter), leaves the serenity of her home on Paradise Island to battle Nazis during World War II (ABC), then criminals in the modern world (CBS) on *Wonder Woman* (also called *The New, Original Wonder Woman* and *The New Adventures of Wonder Woman*).

1977. Adam West and Burt Ward provide the voices for their animated counterparts, Batman and Robin, on *The New Adventures of Batman* (CBS). Joining them are Batgirl, alias Barbara Gordon (voice of Melendy Britt) and Batmite the mouse (Lennie Weinrib). *The New Fantastic Four* cartoon airs on NBC (see 1967). While testing a rocket, three scientists acquire amazing powers. Reed Richards becomes the plastic-skinned Mr. Fantastic; Sue, his wife, is the Invisible Girl; and Ben Grimm, the powerful Thing. The character of Johnny Storm was dropped in favor of Herbie the Robot.

1978. Nicholas Hammond is Peter Parker, a reporter for the New York *Bugle* who is bitten by a radioactive spider and endowed with spider abilities to battle crime on *The Amazing Spider-Man.* While experimenting with gamma rays Dr. Bruce Banner (Bill Bixby) is exposed to an overdose of radiation. His DNA changes and when he becomes angered or enraged he transforms into the green Hulk (Lou Ferrigno) on *The Incredible Hulk* (CBS), a frightening creature that actually helps people in trouble.

1979. Reb Brown is Steve Rogers, Jr., the son of the famous World War II crime fighter Captain America, who uses his father's potion, FLAG (Full Latent Ability Gain), to battle current day crime on the CBS pilot *Captain America.* While in her father's lab Jessica Drew is bitten by a poisonous spider. To save her, Dr. Drew injects her with an experimental spider serum. The serum endows Jessica with special spider powers that she uses to battle crime on *Spider-Woman* (ABC cartoon).

1980. Batman and Robin battle crime on *Batman and the Super Seven,* an animated NBC series that also features *Isis and the Freedom Force* (Isis, Hercules, Merlin, Sinbad, Super Samurai), *Manta and Moray* (underwater crime fighters), *Superstretch and Microwoman* (shapeshifters) and *Web Woman* (a girl endowed by aliens with the power of all insects).

1981. Ralph Hinkley (William Katt) is a schoolteacher chosen by aliens to battle crime in a special suit as *The Greatest American Hero* (ABC). *Spider-Man and His Amazing Friends* is an NBC cartoon that also relates the crime fighting adventures of Angelica Jones, alias Fire Star, and a Mutant X-Men character called Ice Man.

1982. The animated adventures of the Incredible Hulk and Spider-Man are combined on NBC's *The Incredible Hulk and the Amazing Spider-Man.*

1983. Holly Hathaway (Mary Ellen Stuart) is a young woman with all the humanitarian qualities aliens are seeking to battle crime on *The Greatest American Heroine,* an ABC pilot that failed to pick up where *The Greatest American Hero* left off (with Ralph's identity becoming known and the aliens needing a new crime fighter).

1987. Brad Steele (Jeff Lester), a schoolteacher who is actually Captain Justice, leaves Comic Book World to battle crime in the real world (Los Angeles) on *Once a Hero* (ABC).

1988. Clark Kent (John Haymes Newton, Gerard Christopher) is a journalism student at Schuster University who secretly battles crime as *Superboy* (Syn.). Later episodes find Clark as an intern at the Bureau of Extra-Normal Matters in Florida. The series is also called *The Adventures of Superboy.* While exploring a cave, anthropologist Donald Blake (Steve Levitt) finds the ancient hammer of the Viking warrior Thor (the god of Thunder). Thor (Eric Kramer) appears before Blake and attaches himself to Donald. When Blake needs help he holds the hammer, says the name "Oden" (Thor's father), and Thor appears to battle evil on the NBC pilot *Thor.*

1990. Barry Allen (John Wesley Shipp) suffers a chemical accident that gives him incredible speed that enables him to battle crime in Central City as *The Flash* (CBS).

1992. Batman and Robin's animated fight against crime is continued on *Batman: The Animated Series* (Fox). Mystique, Banshee, Storm and Beast, the genetically engineered mutants of Professor Xavier, battle evil for the benefit of mankind on *The X-Men* (Fox cartoon).

1993. Clark Kent, alias Superman (Dean Cain), returns to battle crime in Metropolis as a reporter for the *Daily Planet* on *Lois and Clark: The New Adventures of Superman.* The ABC series also features Teri Hatcher as Clark's girlfriend, reporter Lois Lane.

1994. Kevin Sorbo plays Hercules, the half human, half mortal son of Zeus, the King of the Gods, who uses his strength to battle injustice on the syndicated *Hercules: The Legendary Journeys.* Dr. Miles Hawkins (Carl Lumbly) is a biochemist who battles crime in Port Columbia via a black exo-skeleton suit that gives him a bug-like appearance on Fox's *M.A.N.T.I.S.* (Mechanically Augmented Neuro Transmitter Interception System). Fox revises the character of Peter Parker, the reporter who acquires the powers of a spider on the animated *Spider-Man.*

1995. Xena (Lucy Lawless) is a beautiful warrior based on the legends of Greek and Roman mythology who battles evil to help the oppressed on *Xena: Warrior Princess* (Syn.).

1996. Jubilee (Heather McComb), Buff (Suzanne Davis), Refrax (Randall Slavin), Mondo (Bumper Robinson), Skin (Augustine Rodriquez) and Monet (Amarilis) are teenagers who possess a mutant X-factor that produces bizarre powers that they use to battle evil on the Fox pilot *Generation X.* Lou Ferrigno reprises his role as the Hulk on *The Incredible* Hulk, a UPN animated series that follows Bruce Banner as he battles evil as the green Hulk. Timothy Daly provides the voice of Clark Kent, alias Superman, the visitor from the planet Krypton who battles evil in Metropolis on the animated *Superman* (WB).

1997. When Dick Grayson, alias Robin, leaves Batman to fight evil as Nightwing, teenager Tim Drake becomes the new Robin, the Boy Wonder, the aide to Bruce Wayne, alias Batman, on the animated WB series *Batman Gotham Knights.* Johnny Domino (Matt McColm) is a jazz musician who is secretly *NightMan* (Syn), a daring

crime fighter who helps the police battle evil in Bay City.

1999. The animated WB series *Batman Beyond,* finds Ted McGinnis battling the evil Derek Powell, the new ruler of Gotham City, as the mysterious Dark Night. Fox's animated series, *Spider-Man Unlimited,* continues Peter Parker's battle against evil as the mysterious *Spider-Man.*

2000. Night Crawler, Shadowcast, Rogue, Wolverene, Cyclops and Jean Grey are students of Professor Xavier's Institute for Gifted Children who battle evil on *X-Men Evolution* (WB cartoon).

2001. Darcy Walker (Michelle Lintel) is a detective with the 21st Precinct in Angel City who is secretly Black Scorpion, a daring crime fighter who uses the power of her scorpion ring to enhance her physical abilities on *Black Scorpion* (Sci Fi). The WB pilot *Electra Woman and Dyna Girl* revises the 1976 series with Markie Post as Electra Woman and Anne Steadman as Dyna Girl, crusaders who use the power of electricity to battle evil. Clark Kent (Tom Welling), alias Superboy, returns to TV on the WB's *Smallville.* Here Clark is a student at Smallville High School just discovering his powers (which he uses to solve bizarre incidents that result from the people who come in contact with Kryptonite, the remnant fragments of his home planet, which has since been destroyed by its sun). An unknown man (Patrick Warburton), dressed in a blue latex body suit with exaggerated muscles and twitching antennae, battles evil in The City as *The Tick* (Fox).

2002. *The Birds of Prey* (WB) is set in New Gotham City and presents the crime fighting exploits of Helena Kyle (Ashley Scott), the daughter of Batman and Cat Woman; Barbara Gordon (Dina Meyers), a teacher who is secretly Batgirl; and Dinah Lance (Rachel Skarsten), a 16-year-old girl with amazing telekinetic powers.

2003. The animated adventures of Peter Parker, alias Spider-Man, are revised by MTV for *Spider-Man 2003* with Neal Patrick Harris as the voice of the crime fighter. Pamela Anderson is the voice of Erotica Jones, alias *Stripperella* (Spike TV cartoon), a well-endowed stripper who uses her sexuality to battle evil as "a Double D Cup Superhero."

2004. The WB animated series *The Batman* details the work of Bruce Wayne before he became a legend as Batman in Gotham City.

The Supernatural

Programs that deal with the occult, strange phenomena, urban legends and incidents that are attributed to the supernatural are the focus of this entry.

1950. Elements of the supernatural are presented on *Tales of the Black Cat*, a syndicated anthology series hosted by James Monks.

1951. Futuristic tales with elements of the supernatural are presented on *Tales of Tomorrow*, an ABC anthology series.

1958. Dramas based on incredible but true phenomena are the subject of *The Veil*, an anthology series hosted by Boris Karloff.

1959. Dramas based on events that are strange, frightening and unexplainable in terms of normal human experience are the subject of *One Step Beyond*, an ABC anthology series hosted by John Newland. Elements of the unnatural occur on *The Twilight Zone*, a CBS anthology series with Rod Serling as the host. In 1985 a new version of *The Twilight Zone* appeared on CBS with Charles Aidman as the host. And in 2002 on UPN, Forest Whitaker hosted a revised version of the original series called *The Twilight Zone*.

1961. The legend of Frankenstein is dramatized on the initial presentation of *Tales of Frankenstein*, an unsold pilot that was to dramatize stories based on urban legends. Elements of the supernatural appear on *Thriller*, an NBC anthology series hosted by Boris Karloff. Roald Dahl is the host of *Way Out*, a series of supernatural-based tales on CBS.

1963. Elements of the supernatural occur on *The Outer Limits*, an ABC anthology series. The series was revised in 1995 on Showtime as *The Outer Limits*.

1965. David Mathews (Karl Held) is a government agent who investigates strange happenings on the NBC pilot *The 13th Gate*.

1966. Joan Bennett plays Elizabeth Collins Stoddard, the head of a family whose lives are immersed in the supernatural, on the ABC daytime soap opera *Dark Shadows*.

1967. Barnaby Cross (Kerwin Matthews) is a university professor who dabbles in the occult on the NBC pilot *Ghost Breaker*.

1969. Investigating the supernatural is not only a hobby but the job of Jonathan Fletcher (Kerwin Matthews) on the ABC pilot *In the Dead of Night*. The cowardly dog Scooby-Doo and his human assistants, Freddy, Shaggy, Daphne and Velma, attempt to solve supernatural-based crimes on the animated CBS series *Scooby-Doo, Where Are You?* Voodoo and the undead are the subjects of *Strange Paradise*, a syndicated soap opera about Erica Desmond (Tudi Wiggins), a woman brought back from the dead and who now seeks to live again by possessing the body of young Holly Marshall (Sylvia Feigel).

1971. Stories of the occult and the supernatural are hosted by Rod Serling on NBC's *Night Gallery*.

1972. Supernatural tales are the subject of *Circle of Fear*, an NBC anthology series. Michael Rhodes (Gary Collins) is a professor of parapsychology at the University School who investigates people threatened by ghosts and solves crimes linked to the supernatural on *The Sixth Sense* (ABC).

1973. Roy Thinnes plays David Norliss, a writer who investigates crimes associated with unnatural situations, on the NBC pilot *The Norliss Tapes*.

1974. Carl Kolchak (Darren McGavin) is a reporter for the Independent News Service who investigates stories involving unearthly creatures on *Kolchak: The Night Stalker* (ABC).

1977. Paul Taylor (Granville Van Dusen) is a writer who investigates cases associated with unnatural happenings on the CBS pilot *The World of Darkness*.

1978. Dr. Stephen Strange (Peter Hooten) is a psychiatrist who uses his abilities as a sorcerer to battle evil on the CBS pilot *Doctor Strange*. Lou Ferrigno plays *The Incredible Hulk* (CBS), the alter ego of Dr. Bruce Banner, a scientist exposed to an overdose of gamma radiation that altered his DNA and now, when he becomes angered or enraged, he turns into the green Hulk. True stories of psychic happenings are showcased on *The Next Step Beyond* with John Newland as the host. Lee Purcell plays The Girl, an evil female possessed of supernatural powers, who seeks to destroy people on the NBC pilot *Stranger in Our House*. Granville Van Dusen returns as Paul Taylor, the writer who investigates matters that can't be explained in normal terms on the CBS pilot *The World Beyond*.

1981. Tales of the supernatural were the premise behind the syndicated pilot *Tales of the Haunted*.

1982. Skip Miller and Harold Van Couver (Jeff

Altman, Donovan Scott) investigate unusual phenomena for B.O.O.O. (The Beardsley Office of Occult Occurrences) on the ABC pilot *Scared Silly.*

1984. Stories that delve into the opposite world of reality, the supernatural side of life are presented on the syndicated anthology series *Tales from the Darkside.*

1985. Occult book writer Benny Benedek (Dennis Dugan) investigates strange happenings on *Shadow Chasers* (ABC).

1987. Alex West (Bud Cort) is the man who inherits the Norman Bates legacy—the Bates Motel (from the film *Psycho*) and its supernatural happenings—on the NBC pilot *Bates Motel.* Micki Foster (Louise Robey) and Ryan Dallion (John D. LeMay) seek to retrieve cursed antiques before they kill their owners on *Friday The 13th: The Series.*

1988. Robert Englund plays Freddy Kruger, a mass murderer who escaped punishment by the legal system, but not from irate citizens who burned him to death. His evil spirit has returned to haunt the dreams of people on *Freddy's Nightmares—A Nightmare on Elm Street the Series* (Syn.). The syndicated anthology *Monsters* presents just that—strange stories of unearthly happenings.

1990. Horror novelist Anthony Strack (Anthony Perkins) is a man who must contend with the unnatural happenings in his home on the Fox pilot *The Ghost Writer.*

1991. NBC revises *Dark Shadows* (see 1966) with Jean Simmons as Elizabeth Collins Stoddard, the head of a family involved with the supernatural. Associated Press reporter Jack Mann (Brett Cullen) teams with ER nurse Annalisse Summer (Chelsea Field) and Dr. Linus (William Sadler) to stop the Omen, an evil entity that seeks to release unspeakable horror on the world on the NBC pilot *The Omen.* A lab accident turns Dr. Alec Holland into a creature called *Swamp Thing* (USA), a man who is part plant and protects the swamplands from evil.

1992. Two young boys, Marshall Teller and Simon Holmes (Omri Katz, Justin Shenkarow), attempt to prove that the unnatural exists in their town of *Eerie, Indiana* (NBC). The mysterious Blackie (Robert Englund) is the proprietor of The All Night Café, a seemingly innocent-looking establishment that can alter people's lives on NBC's *Nightmare Café.*

1995. Mitch Buchannon (David Hasselhoff), Ryan McBride (Angie Harmon) and Garner Ellerbee (Greg Alan Williams) are private detectives who investigate crimes associated with the unnatural on *Baywatch Nights* (a syndicated spinoff from *Baywatch*).

1996. Derek Rayne (Derek DeLindt) and a group of gifted associates help people threatened by unknown forces on *Poltergeist: The Legacy* (Showtime).

1998. The 1992 series *Eerie, Indiana* is revised by Fox as *Eerie Indiana: The Other Dimension* with Marshall Taylor and Stanley Hope (Bill Switzer, Daniel Clark) encountering unnatural occurrences.

1999. The syndicated series *BeastMaster* presents several demons that live in a time when magic and nature ruled the world. Curupira (Emilie DeRaven) rules the forests. She is incredibly strong, has blonde hair and a normal flesh face, but she is green from the neck down. Her feet are backwards and to kiss her means death (she drains life forces). Iara (Samantha Healy) is an enchanting demon who is as beautiful as Curupira but is evil and seeks to rule the forest world. She has the power of the mist (a white, fog-like mist to trap her victims) and derives strength from water. The Apparition (Leah Purcell), called "The Demon of the Burning Forests," is "a Hell on Earth" and "rules in the Dark Ways" (receives her powers from the Rulers of Darkness).

2000. A group of gifted people, headed by Elmer Greentree (Bill Hobbs), help people threatened by the supernatural on *The Others* (NBC). On the syndicated *Sheena*, Sheena (Gena Lee Nolin) is a beautiful 25-year old jungle goddess who protects her adopted homeland from evil. She is also capable of becoming the Darak'na ("Shadow" in English), a vicious, cat-like creature with razor sharp claws, to battle evil ("because evil doesn't fight fair").

2001. Ethan Embry plays Derek Barnes, a computer whiz kid who runs www.freakylinks. com, a website dedicated to uncovering the dark truths behind urban legends on *Freakylinks* (Fox). Assisting Derek are Chloe Tanner (Lisa Sheridan), Jason Tatum (Karim Prince) and Lani Williams (Lizette Carrion). Nick O'Malley (Michael Landers) and Alice Benson (Alexandra Lee) are detectives with Special Unit 2, a secret branch of the Chicago Police Department that investigates cases involving Links (anything that is not man or beast) on *Special Unit 2* (UPN).

2003. Grim Reapers seek the souls of people moments before they are destined to die on *Dead Like Me* (Showtime). The Reapers include Georgie (Ellen Muth), Rube (Mandy Patinkin), Roxy (Jasmine Guy) and Daisy (Laura Harris).

2005. ABC revises 1974's *Kolchak: The Night Stalker* as *Night Stalker* with Stuart Townsend as Carl Kolchak, now a reporter for the Los Angeles *Beacon* who investigates cases involving unnatural circumstances. Dean and Sam Winchester (Jensen Ackles, Jared Padalecki) are brothers who travel the country seeking to destroy the creatures of urban legends on *Supernatural* (WB). Mysterious, hungry sea creatures suddenly appear and cause concern for a group of people secretly seeking to discover what they are and where they came from before a panic occurs on *Surface* (NBC). Lake Bell stars as Dr. Laura Daughtery with Jay R. Ferguson as Richard Connelly and Carter Jenkins as Miles Bennett

Talking Animals and Machines

This entry chronicles the live action programs on which the main characters are talking animals or machines. Animated cartoons are excluded. See also *Puppets* (for additional talking animals) and *Computers — Extraordinary* (for machines).

1955. Events that befall Bureau of Fish and Wildlife ornithologist Sock Miller are seen and commented on by Cleo (voice of Mary Jane Croft), his basset hound on *The People's Choice* (CBS).

1958. Actors dressed as dogs perform on *The Adventures of Superpup*, a Superman parody pilot about *Daily Bugle* reporter Bark Bent (Billy Curtis), alias Superpup, and his colleague Pamela Poodle (Ruth Delfino), a reporter constantly in danger.

1960. Alan "Rocky" Lane provides the voice for Mister Ed, the talking horse of architect Wilbur Post on *Mister Ed* (Syn/CBS).

1965. Lawyer Dave Crabtree is shocked to discover that the 1928 Porter he purchases is his reincarnated mother Abigail (speaks through the car's radio; voice of Ann Sothern), who has returned to guide his life on *My Mother the Car* (NBC).

1970. Voice over dubbing is used to convey the adventures of Lancelot Link, a fumbling chimpanzee who works for A.P.E. (the Agency to Prevent Evil) on *Lancelot Link, Secret Chimp* (ABC).

1972. The children's series *The New Zoo Revue* features the talking animals Charlie the Owl (Sharon Baird), Freddie the Frog (Yanco Inone) and Henrietta Hippo (Thomas Cari).

1973. Pete Richards is the host of the kiddie show in which he incorporates a talking bear named Barney (voice of Shepard Menkin) to improve ratings on the CBS pilot *Barney and Me*.

1974. On NBC's *Land of the Lost*, Enik (Walker Edmiston) is an intelligent lizard, called a Sleestak, who befriends the Marshall family (Rick, Will and Holly), the humans trapped in a prehistoric lost world. Humans are subservient and intelligent apes rule Earth in the year 3085 on *Planet of the Apes* (CBS). Galen (Roddy McDowall) is the ape seeking to further his knowledge about humans; Zaius (Booth Coleman) is the ape leader who opposes Galen's research.

1976. Dr. Calvin Campbell is a veterinarian whose life is complicated by McDuff (voice of Jack Lester), the ghost of a sheep dog who appears and speaks only to him on *McDuff, the Talking Dog* (NBC). Susan, Barry and C.C. are teenagers who drive Schlep Car, a conglomeration of junk parts that becomes the amazing Wonderbug (voice of Frank Welker) when its magic horn is activated on *Wonderbug* (ABC).

1979. Man as seen through the eyes of dogs (actors in costume) is presented on the NBC pilot *A Dog's Life*. Barney Martin stars as McGurk with Beej Johnson as Iris and Sherry Lynn as Camille.

1982. William Daniels provides the voice for KITT, the Knight Industries 2000 super high tech car that Michael Knight uses to battle crime on *Knight Rider* (NBC; see *Gadgets* for additional information).

1984. After young Arthur Cane (Ross Harris) reads the inscription on an old amulet ("If all you care about is you the next thing you see under a full moon is what you will be"), he becomes a dog when that is what he sees on the ABC special *The Dog Days of Arthur Cane*. Arthur reverts back to himself when he learns about caring for others. Ed Weinberger provides the voice for Mr. Smith, an orangutan who, after drinking a chemical solution, develops an I.Q. of 256 and the ability to speak on NBC's *Mr. Smith*.

1985. Sarah Jane Smith is a freelance journalist who solves crimes with the help of K-9 (voice of John Leeson), a robotic dog on *K-9 and Com-*

pany, a syndicated pilot spinoff from *Doctor Who* (where Sara Jane was the traveling companion to the Tom Baker Doctor Who).

1986. Ralph (voice of Evan Richards) is a mouse (dimensional animation) who lives in a hole in the wall at the Mountain View Inn on the ABC special *The Mouse and the Motorcycle*. One day Ralph sees a toy motorcycle, and his adventures as he rides the bike are depicted. In the sequel, *Runaway Ralph* (1988), Ralph's adventures as he ventures outside the inn are depicted when he feels he is not appreciated by his family and runs away. *Ralph S. Mouse* (1991), the final installment, finds Ralph befriending a human boy named Ryan.

1987. On the CBS special *A Mouse, a Mystery and Me*, mystery writer Jill Darcy and her detective mouse Alex (voice of Donald O'Connor) seek to find the culprits responsible for kidnapping a department store Santa Claus.

1988. The adventures shared by young Eric Gillman and Jeepers (voice of David Garrison), the dog he can telepathically communicate with, are depicted on the ABC pilot *Mutts*.

1990. Earl Sinclair, his wife Fran, and their children Robbie, Charlene and Baby Sinclair are dinosaurs who live in a world where they talk, work and are superior to humans on ABC's *Dinosaurs*. Robert McKay is a police detective who receives help in solving crimes from his late partner, Stanley Poochinski, who has come back as an English bulldog (voice of Peter Boyle) on the NBC pilot *Poochinski*.

1991. ABC's revival of NBC's *Land of the Lost* (see 1974) finds the Porter family (Tom, Anne and Kevin) stranded in a world forgotten by time and on the run from Shung (Tom Allard), an intelligent lizard-like creature who seeks to control the Land of the Lost. Crystal, Merv and Petey are cats who voice their thoughts on the people with whom they live on the CBS pilot *Claws*. The thoughts of a burrito loving police dog named Tequila (voice of Brad Sanders) are heard by viewers as he helps his human partner, Detective Nico Bonetti, solve crimes on *Tequila and Bonetti* (CBS).

1994. Heidi Leich is the voice of a high tech 1969 Ford Mustang that is used by brothers Jake and Will McQueen to battle evil on the syndicated pilot *Knight Rider 2010*.

1996. Salem Saberhagen (voice of Nick Bakay) is a former warlock, now serving a 100 year sentence as a black cat for attempting to take over the world, on *Sabrina, the Teenage Witch* (ABC/WB).

1997. Team Knight Rider is a crime-fighting unit of the Foundation for Law and Government that incorporates five operatives and five special talking cars on *Team Knight Rider* (Syn.). Kyle Stewart, the head of the team, drives Dante (voice of Tom Kane), a Ford Expedition Sport Utility Vehicle (it is also the liaison between the human team members and their cars). Jenny Andrews drives Domino (Nia Valdaros), a Ford Mustang GT convertible; Erica West rides a motorcycle named Kat (Andrea Beutner); Duke DePalma has Beast (Kerrigan Mahan), a Ford F-150 truck; and Trek Sanders has Plato (John Kissir), a highly intelligent motorcycle.

1998. Jerome Ehlers is Tribune, the lizard-like creature who befriends the members of the Challenger Expedition (who are stranded on a plateau forgotten by time) on *The Lost World* (Syn.).

2001. The *Lexx* is a powerful spaceship that is also a weapon of destruction (it can destroy entire planets). It talks (voice of Tom Gallant) to its crew (Zev, Kai, Stanley), has a bug-like appearance and needs to devour planets for energy on *Lexx* (Sci Fi).

2002. Frank Scott (Michael Brandon) and his two sons, Karl and David (Erik Von Detter, Shiloh Strong), crash land in a world where talking dinosaurs live side by side with humans on *Dinotopia* (ABC).

2004. *Father of the Pride*, an NBC computer animated sitcom, follows the lives of the lions who perform for magicians Seigfried and Roy. John Goodman is the voice of the main lion, Larry, with Cheryl Hines as his wife Kate, the white lioness. On *Tripping the Rift* (Sci Fi), John Melendez provides the voice of Space Ship Bob, the neurotic computer that pilots the *Jupiter 42*.

Taxi Cabs

Characters who either own their own cabs or work for someone else are the subjects of this entry.

1951. Amos Jones and Andrew H. Brown (Alvin Childress, Spencer Williams, Jr.) own the Fresh Air Taxi Cab Company of America, Inc., a one-car company in Harlem on *The Amos 'n' Andy Show* (CBS).

1955. Joe Sparton (Larry Blyden) is a Brooklyn-based independent cab driver who keeps a picture of his girlfriend Mabel Spooner above his rear view mirror on *Joe and Mabel* (CBS).

1956. Al Murray (Allen Jenkins) is a New York cab driver who is also the guardian of Jeannie MacLennan, a girl newly arrived in America from Scotland on *Hey, Jeannie!* (CBS).

1969. Vito Scotti plays Gino Mancini, a con artist who runs Gino's Taxi Stand in Rome, Italy, on CBS's *To Rome with Love.*

1971. Archie Bunker (Carroll O'Connor), a dock foreman for the Prendergast Tool and Dye Company in Queens, New York, moonlights as a cab driver on *All in the Family* (CBS).

1972. Bernie Steinberg (David Birney) is an independent Jewish cab driver who is in love with Bridget Fitzgerald (Meredith Baxter), a Catholic schoolteacher, on *Bridget Loves Bernie* (CBS).

1974. Keith Anderson (Ben Masters), the man who marries Thelma Evans, the daughter of James and Florida Evans, drives a taxi for the Windy City Cab Company on *Good Times* (CBS).

1976. Pat McCormick is Eddie Shaughnessey, the crusty dispatcher for the Morgan Cab Company in Chicago on the NBC pilot *Shaughnessey.*

1977. Greg Antonacci plays Vinnie Mordabito, a 24-year-old New York City cab driver on CBS's *Busting Loose.* Nick Malloy (Ben Masters) is a cab driver in an unnamed inner city on NBC's *Muggsy* (the title refers to his half-sister, Margaret, called Muggsy).

1978. Louie DePalma (Danny DeVito) is the nasty Sunshine Cab Company dispatcher on *Taxi* (ABC/NBC). Alex Reiger, Elaine Nardo, Jim Ignatowski and Tony Banta are among the cabbies who work for the Manhattan company. *The Hallmark Hall of Fame* (NBC) airs *Taxi*, an original TV play about the conversation between a taxi cab driver (Martin Sheen) and his passenger (Eva Marie Saint).

1983. Saul Rubinek plays Dusty, a Los Angeles cab driver who longs to become a detective on the NBC pilot *Dusty.*

1984. Michael Beck is Danny Wreade, an N.Y.P.D. officer who works undercover as a taxi cab driver on the NBC pilot *The Streets.*

1989. Cito Escobar (Joe Lala) is an independent cab driver in San Diego on NBC's *Knight and Daye.* Elya Baskin plays Yuri, a Manhattan cab driver who earns extra money by selling photographs of the Emergency Services Unit of the N.Y.P.D. performing rescue operations on NBC's *True Blue.*

1994. On NBC's *Friends*, Phoebe Buffay (Lisa Kudrow) turns a failed catering business van into a taxi business called Relax-A-Ride (a cab with a massage table in the back) that also fails. George O'Grady (George Carlin) is a nasty New York cab driver who has been exposed for bilking customers on *The George Carlin Show* (Fox).

2002. Mike Olahansky (David Morse) is an ex cop (caught stealing money during a drug bust) who has become a driver for the Victory Taxi Company on CBS's *Hack.*

Teachers

This entry chronicles the programs on which a teacher (or principal or headmaster) is the star or a featured regular. Institution names are included where possible.

1950. Stu Erwin (himself) is a teacher turned principal of Alexander Hamilton High School on *Trouble with Father* (ABC).

1952. Robinson J. Peepers (Wally Cox) is a timid and mild mannered biology instructor and his friend, Harvey Weskitt (Tony Randall), is the outgoing English teacher at Jefferson Junior High School on *Mister Peepers* (NBC). Connie Brooks (Eve Arden) is the romantic English teacher and Philip Boynton (Robert Rockwell) her heart throb, the shy biology instructor at Madison High School on *Our Miss Brooks* (CBS). (In last season episodes, Connie becomes a teacher at Mrs. Nestor's Private Elementary School.)

1953. Ray McNutley (Ray Milland) is a drama professor at the all-girl Lynnhaven College on *Meet Mr. McNutley* (CBS).

1954. Dr. William Todhunter Hall is the president of Ivy College who resides at Number One Faculty Row in Ivy, U.S.A., on *The Halls of Ivy* (CBS). *Meet Mr. McNutley* is revised as *The Ray Milland Show* (CBS) with Ray Milland as a drama professor at Comstock, a coeducational university.

1959. William Schallert plays Leander Pomfritt, an English teacher first at Central High School, then at S. Peter Pryor Junior College on *Dobie Gillis* (CBS).

1960. Gene Evans plays Otis Stockett, a schoolmaster in the rough and tumble town of Wichita, Kansas, during the 1870s on the NBC pilot *The Frontiersman.*

1961. Jan Clayton plays Ella Bishop, a dedicated English teacher in a small midwestern college on the NBC pilot *Miss Bishop* (based on the feature film *Cheers for Miss Bishop*). Sir Cedric Hardwicke is Professor Crayton, a strict instructor at a college that resembles the University of Southern California on *Mrs. G Goes to College* (CBS).

1963. Joseph Howe (Jason Evers) is an English professor at Channing University, a mythical Midwestern coeducational college on ABC's *Channing*. John Novak (James Franciscus) is a tough-minded idealist who teaches English at Jefferson High School in Los Angels on *Mr. Novak* (NBC).

1964. Dwayne Hickman plays Joe Hannon, the only male teacher in an elementary school dominated by females on the CBS pilot *Hey Teacher*.

1965. John Foster (John Forsythe) is a former U.S. Air Force major who becomes the headmaster of his late aunt's school, the Foster School for Girls, in San Francisco on *The John Forsythe Show* (NBC).

1969. Pete Dixon (Lloyd Haynes) is a black American history instructor and Alice Johnson (Karen Valentine) is a student teacher at Walt Whitman High School in Los Angeles on ABC's *Room 222*. Michael Endicott (John Forsythe) is an English professor at the American School in Rome, Italy, on *To Rome with Love* (CBS).

1970. Andy Thompson (Andy Griffith) is a former teacher turned head of Concord, a small, private coeducational California high school on *Headmaster* (CBS).

1971. Mike Srivic (Rob Reiner) is a liberal (called a "Meathead" by his father-in-law, Archie Bunker) who instructs at an unnamed New York college on *All in the Family* (CBS). James Howard (Jimmy Stewart) is an anthropology professor at Josiah Kessel College in Easy Valley, California, on *The Jimmy Stewart Show* (NBC). Sandy Stockton (Sandy Duncan) is a student teacher at U.C.L.A. and a part-time actress for the Prescott Advertising Agency on *Funny Face* (CBS). The series was revised in 1972 as *The Sandy Duncan Show* with Sandy still a student teacher but employed as a secretary at the Quinn and Cohen Advertising Agency.

1972. Anna Owens (Samantha Eggar) is an American schoolteacher hired by the King of Siam (Yul Brynner) to educate his children and introduce them to Western Culture on *Anna and the King* (CBS; based on *The King and I*). Emily Hartley (Suzanne Pleshette), the wife of psychologist Bob Hartley, is first a third grade teacher at Gorman Elementary School, then the vice principal of Tracy Grammar School on *The Bob Newhart Show* (CBS). Bridget Fitzgerald (Meredith Baxter) is a Catholic school fourth grade teacher at the Immaculate Heart Academy in Manhattan on *Bridget Loves Bernie* (CBS). Joanna Pettet plays Kate Stewart, the first female faculty member at an all male boarding school, on the CBS pilot *Miss Stewart, Sir*.

1974. Melissa Gilbert plays Laura Ingalls, the daughter of Charles and Caroline Ingalls, who becomes a teacher at the Plum Creek School in Walnut Grove, Minnesota, on *Little House on the Prairie* (NBC). Lucas Tanner (David Hartman) is an English teacher at Harry S. Truman Memorial High School in Webster Groves, Missouri, on NBC's *Lucas Tanner*. Marion McMasters (Jack Cassidy) is a gentle schoolteacher from Boston who confronts the difficulties of frontier life when he comes to teach in the early 1900s settlement town of Sweetwater, Arizona, on the syndicated pilot *McMasters of Sweetwater*. Paul Cameron (Hari Rhodes) is an idealistic American exchange teacher in London on the CBS pilot *To Sir with Love* (based on the feature film).

1975. Gabe Kotter (Gabriel Kaplan) is a former Sweathog (nickname for a special education student) who returns to teach at his old school, James Buchanan High in Brooklyn, New York, on *Welcome Back, Kotter* (ABC).

1976. Sara Yarnell (Brenda Vaccaro) is a young woman who leaves what she considers a dull existence in Philadelphia to teach school out west (in the town of Independence) on *Sara* (CBS).

1977. Susan Dey plays Jane Benson, a young, pretty grammar school teacher who is unsure about romantic relationships on *Loves Me, Loves Me Not*.

1978. John Houseman is Professor Charles Kingsfield, Jr., a brilliant contract law instructor at an unidentified Northeastern university on *The Paper Chase* (CBS). John Houseman continued the role on *The Paper Chase: The Second Year* (1983), *The Paper Chase: The Third Year* (1985) and *The Paper Chase: The Graduation Year* (1986; all on Showtime). Ken Howard plays Ken Reeves, a former pro basketball player turned coach at Carver High School in Los Angeles, on *The White Shadow* (CBS).

1979. Dorothy Banks (Dorothy Loudon) is a former Broadway star turned music and drama teacher at Connecticut's Hannah Hartley School for Girls on *Dorothy* (CBS). Jean Brodie (Geraldine McEwan) is a vain and eccentric teacher at the Marcia Blaine School for Girls in Scotland during the 1930s on *The Prime of Miss Jean Brodie* (PBS).

1980. Eddie Roberts (Renny Temple) is an anthropology professor at Cranpool College in Anaheim, California, on *The Life and Times of Eddie Roberts* (Syn.).

1981. Annie Cooper (Melinda Culea) is a young college graduate who is just beginning her career as a history teacher in an unnamed grammar school on the NBC pilot *Dear Teacher*. Philip Malley (Stephen Nathan) is an amateur inventor and science professor at Rutledge University in Riverside County on the CBS pilot *The Wonderful World of Philip Malley*.

1982. Lydia Grant (Debbie Allen), the dance instructor, and Benjamin Shorofsky (Albert Hague), the music professor, are among the teachers at the New York High School for the Performing Arts on NBC's *Fame*. Harry Barnes (James Naughton), Sara Canover (Ally Mills) and Jack Felspar (Graham Jarvis) are among the teachers at the problem-plagued Franklin High School in St. Louis, Missouri, on *Making the Grade* (NBC). Winfrop Dingleman (Basil Hoffman) is the principal of Weemawee Central High School on CBS's *Square Pegs*. Diana Swanson (Lynn Redgrave) is a teacher at the mythical Millard Fillmore High School in Los Angeles on NBC's *Teachers Only*.

1983. Kene Holliday plays Don Kingman, a teacher at U.S. Grant High School on the CBS pilot *The Best of Times*. Tony Dow is Pete Kinney, the principal, and Dawn Wells, Miss Lori Lee, a teacher, at Excelsior Union High School in Indiana, on the NBC pilot *High School, U.S.A.* NBC revises *Teachers Only* (1982) with Lynn Redgrave as Diana Swanson, now a teacher at Arnold Wilson High School in Brooklyn, New York. Diana Muldaur is Claire Shelton, the principal of the Pepperidge Preparatory School for Girls, on the ABC pilot *Too Good to Be True*.

1984. NBC revises its 1983 pilot *High School, U.S.A.* with Rick Nelson as Peter Kinney, the principal at Excelsior Union High School. Teachers include Melody Anderson as Cindy Franklin and Jerry Mathers as Mr. Sirota. Joanne Braithwaite (Gretchen Corbett) is a new teacher at John

F. Kennedy High School in Ventura, California, on the CBS pilot *Things Are Looking Up*.

1985. Janet Eilber is Joanne Braithwaite, an English teacher at John F. Kennedy High School in Southern California on NBC's *The Best of Times* (based on the 1984 CBS pilot *Things Are Looking Up*). Dorothy Zbornak (Bea Arthur) is a substitute teacher for the Florida Public School System on NBC's *The Golden Girls*.

1986. On *Anne of Green Gables* (PBS), Megan Follows plays Anne Shirley, an orphaned girl who becomes a teacher at the Avonlea Public School on Prince Edward Island in Canada. She is later a teacher at the Kingspoint Ladies College. Valerie Arnold (Blair Brown) and Dr. Julius Pepper (Richard Lawson) are among the teachers at Harrington High School on the ABC pilot *The Faculty*. Merlin Olsen plays Buddy Landau, a coach at the Charles Lindberg Elementary School on NBC's *Fathers and Sons*. Ray Walston is Arnold Hand, a strict teacher at California's Ridgemont High School on *Fast Times*, a CBS series based on the movie *Fast Times at Ridgemont High*. Charlie Moore (Howard Hesseman) teaches a group of brilliant students in the Honors Program at Fillmore High School in New York City on ABC's *Head of the Class*. Paul Cook (Jeffrey Tambor) is an acerbic English professor at Kenyon College who uses his dry wit and fast thinking to deal with life after an accident cost him his sight on *Mr. Sunshine* (ABC).

1987. Joe Danzig (Ed Asner) is a tough but dedicated teacher who becomes the principal of the unruly Benjamin Harrison High School in the Bronx, New York, on *The Bronx Zoo* (NBC). Kathleen Beller and Kathryn Harrold co-star as teachers Mary Caitlin Callahan and Sara Newhouse. Dwayne Wayne (Kardeem Hardison) is a student at Hillman College in Georgia who later becomes a math teacher on *A Different World* (NBC). David Hanley (Brian Keith) is a senior history professor at John Marshall University in Philadelphia on *The Pursuit of Happiness* (ABC).

1988. Henry Crawford (Harry Anderson) is a physics professor at Medford College who is noted for his strange inventions (like Flubber, a rubberlike substance) on NBC's *The Absent Minded Professor* (based on the feature film). John Lacey (Judd Hirsch) is an English teacher at the Drake Prep School in New York City on NBC's *Dear John*. Hayley Mills plays Carrie Bliss, a teacher at J.F.K. Junior High School in Indianapolis, Indiana, on *Good Morning, Miss Bliss* (Disney). Graham Lubbock (Bill Kirchenbauer) is the father of eight children and the athletic director at Saint Augustine's Catholic High School in Eureka, California, on *Just the Ten of Us* (ABC). Robert Randall (Lyle Alzado) is a teacher at Ridgedale Prep, a private school for rich kids, who moonlights as a wrestler called "The Masked Maniac" on *Learning the Ropes* (Syn.). After graduating from Langley College, Blair Warner (Lisa Whelchel) becomes the headmistress of her high school alma mater, the Eastland School for Girls in Peekskill, New York, on the NBC pilot *The Lisa Whelchel Show* (a proposed spinoff from the last episode of *The Facts of Life*). Michael Fields (Michael McKean) is a high-powered New York publisher who quits his job to return to his hometown of Barrington (New England) to become the headmaster of Oakmont, the boarding school he attended as a child, on the NBC pilot *Oakmont*. Kevin Keegan (Sam Robards) is a journalism teacher at Franklin Delano Roosevelt High School who changes the concept of the school's newspaper (the *Kangaroo Courier*) from printed to video journalism (over the school's TV system) on *TV 101* (CBS).

1989. Tracy Nelson plays Sister Steve, a Catholic nun who teaches at Saint Michael's Elementary School and helps Father Frank Dowling (Tom Bosley) solve crimes on *Father Dowling Mysteries* (NBC/ABC). Louis Gossett, Jr., is Gideon Oliver, an anthropology professor at New York's Columbia University, who helps the police solve crimes on *Gideon Oliver* (ABC). Richard Belding (Dennis Haskins) is a former student then teacher at Bayside High School in Palisades, California, who now works as its principal on *Saved by the Bell* (NBC). Chance Reynolds (Tim Reid) is a criminology teacher at Georgetown University in Washington, D.C., who helps the police solve crimes on *Snoops* (CBS).

1990. Donna Breedlove (Nancy Valen) is an English teacher and John Deerborn the history teacher at Cordell Hull High School on NBC's *Hull High*. Grace Musso (Melanie Chartoff) is a former student then teacher at Santo Domingo High School in California who is now its stern principal on *Parker Lewis Can't Lose* (Fox). Joy Capadeluca (Joy Behar) is the vice principal at Nelson Rockefeller Junior High School who is struggling to cope with student and faculty problems on the CBS pilot *The Rock*. Ellen Davis-Freeman (Stephanie Faracy) is a substitute ele-

mentary school teacher at Cortez Junior High School in Baltimore on *True Colors* (Fox).

1991. Dwight Ulysses Davis (Randy Quaid) is a math, history and science teacher who is also the principal of Pomahac Elementary School in Seattle, Washington, on *Davis Rules* (ABC/CBS). Otis Drexell (Dabney Coleman) "is a drifter who failed in the business world and crawled out of some sewer grate to teach his amoral poison to impressionable children" at the Grantwood Avenue School in Cleveland on *Drexell's Class* (Fox). David Gibson (Phill Lewis), called "Teech," is a black music instructor at Winthrop Academy, an all-white boarding school on *Teech* (CBS).

1992. Billy MacGregor (Billy Connolly), a former teacher at Fillmore High School in New York City, now teaches at Berkeley Community College in California on ABC's *Billy*. Mark Cooper (Mark Curry) is a substitute teacher at Oakridge High School in Oakdale, California, on *Hanging with Mr. Cooper* (ABC). Dr. Alice Davis (June Chadwick) is a teacher of internal medicine at Croft University on ABC's *Going to Extremes*. Dr. Henry Croft (Roy Dotrice) established the college as a last resort on the island of Jantique (which he calls "One Happy Island") for students to attend a medical school when no one else wanted them. Caroline McWilliams is Dorothy Loomis, headmistress of the Crawford Academy for Girls (which also allows male enrollment) on the CBS pilot *Just One of the Girls*.

1993. William Daniels plays George Fenney, a teacher at John Adams High School in Philadelphia on *Boy Meets World* (ABC).

1994. Nineteen year old Christy Huddleston (Kellie Martin) teaches at Miss Alice Henderson's Mission School in the poor community of Cutter Gap, Tennessee (1912), on *Christy* (CBS). Lauren Lee Smith plays Christy in a PAX remake of the series in 2000.

1996. Alphonse Hall (Wallace Shawn) and Miss Geist (Twink Caplan) are the featured teachers at the posh Bronson Alcott High School in Beverly Hills on *Clueless* (ABC/UPN). Meredith Baxter is Flynn Sullivan, vice principal of Hamilton Junior High School ("Guiding young people through puberty since 1936") on *The Faculty* (ABC). Matt Waters (Montel Williams) is a science teacher at Bayview High School who is determined to make a difference in the lives of his students on *Matt Waters* (CBS). Nick Freno (Mitch Mullany) is an out-of-work actor who substitutes as an English teacher at the Gerald R. Ford Middle School on *Nick Freno, Licensed Teacher* (WB). Malcolm McDowell is Stephen Pynchon, a tough professor at the prestigious university where widow Pearl Caraldo (Rhea Perlman) has just enrolled on CBS's *Pearl*. Willard Kraft (Martin Mull) is the harassed principal of Westbridge High School, the Massachusetts school attended by *Sabrina, the Teenage Witch* (ABC). Steve Hightower (Steve Harvey) is a former singer with a group called the High Tops who is now the music teacher at Booker T. Washington High School in Chicago on *The Steve Harvey Show* (WB). Dick Solomon (John Lithgow) is an alien from the Home Planet who teaches quantum physics at Pendleton University in Ohio as his cover to study life on Earth on *Third Rock from the Sun* (NBC).

1997. Karen Noble (Marcella Lowery) is a teacher (later principal) at Manhattan High School in New York City on *City Guys* (NBC). Robert Peterson (Robert Townsend) is a professor at New York University on *The Parent'Hood* (WB).

1999. Jo Bhaer (Michelle Renee Thomas), one of the four March sisters (from the book *Little Women*), runs the Plumfield School for Boys in 1860s Concord, Massachusetts, on *Little Men* (PAX). Stanley Oglevee (Dorien Wilson) is a professor at Santa Monica Junior College on *The Parkers* (UPN). Sydney Fox (Tia Carrere) is a beautiful professor of ancient studies at Trinity College who takes assignments to recover lost artifacts on behalf of the university on *Relic Hunter* (Syn.).

2000. Steven Harper (Chi McBride), Lauren Davis (Jessalyn Gilsig), Scott Gruber (Anthony Herald) and Harvey Lipschultz (Fyvush Finkel) are among the teachers trying to make a difference at Winslow High School on *Boston Public* (Fox).

2001. Matt Stewart (Bob Saget) teaches creative writing at Great Barrington High School in Massachusetts on *Raising Dad* (WB). Joan Gallagher (Joan Cusack) calls herself "a low maintenance dependable girl" who teaches at Chicago High School on *What About Joan* (ABC).

2003. Patrick Owen (David Sutcliffe) is an English teacher at Center High School in San Francisco and dating glamorous film star Alex Burton on *I'm with Her* (ABC). Mary Steenburgen plays Helen Girardi, an art teacher at Arcadia High School on *Joan of Arcadia* (CBS).

2005. Jeff Cahill (Justin Bartha) is an English teacher at Filmore High School in New Jersey on NBC's *Teachers*. Other teachers are Alice (Sarah Alexander), Tina (Sarah Shahi) and Calvin (Deon Richmond).

Teen After-School Hangouts

Adults have their bars, taverns, cafes and restaurants, but teenagers are restricted to (at least on TV) their after school eateries. This entry is an overall review of the places teens frequent at the end of their school day. See also *Adolescence* and *Teenagers*.

1951. *A Date with Judy* (ABC). Judy Foster and her boyfriend Oogie Pringle hang out at the Coke Parlor (later called Scully's Soda Fountain).

1954. *Father Knows Best* (CBS/NBC). Betty Anderson, the eldest child of Jim and Margaret Anderson, frequents The Malt Shop.

1957. On *Bachelor Father* (CBS/NBC/ABC), Kelly Gregg, the niece of attorney Bentley Gregg, and her friends Ginger and Howard call Bill's Malt Shop home. On *The Real McCoys* (ABC), Valley High School student Hassie McCoy hangs out at The Malt Shop (later called The Soda Fountain).

1958. *The Donna Reed Show* (ABC). Mary Stone, the eldest child of Donna and Alex Stone, enjoys meals at The Blue Lantern and soft drinks as Kelsey's Malt Shop (later the hangout for Mary's brother Jeff).

1959. *Dobie Gillis* (CBS). Charlie Wong's Ice Cream Parlor (which features 31 flavors of ice cream) is the favorite hangout of high school student Dobie Gillis and his friend Maynard G. Krebs.

1961. *Margie* (ABC). Crawford's Ice Cream Parlor is the hangout for Margie Clayton, a girl who lives in the small town of Madison during the 1920s.

1963. *The Patty Duke Show* (ABC). Patty Lane and her cousin Cathy Lane enjoy sodas at The Shake Shop (later called Leslie's Ice Cream Parlor).

1965. *Gidget* (ABC). Frances Lawrence, called Gidget, attends Westside High School, and she and her best friend Larue enjoy hamburgers and sodas at The Shaggy Dog (later called The Shake Shop and Pop's).

1969. *The Brady Bunch* (ABC). Marcia and

Greg, the eldest of the Brady children, hang out at The Pizza Parlor.

1970. *The Partridge Family* (ABC). Keith and Laurie Partridge, the eldest of the Partridge children, enjoy snacks at The Taco Stand. Younger brother Danny enjoys treats at The Sweet Shoppe.

1974. *Happy Days* (ABC). Arnold's Drive-In is the after school hangout for Richie Cunningham and his friends.

1978. *Diff'rent Strokes* (NBC). Brothers Willis and Arnold Jackson enjoy after school snacks at Hamburger Heaven (later called The Hamburger Hut).

1979. *California Fever* (CBS). Rick's Place is the beach eatery frequented by Westside High School students Vince, Laurie and Russ.

1986. On *A Different World* (NBC), the students at Hillman College in Georgia frequent a diner called The Pit. On *Fast Times* (CBS), the Cattle Burger, where high school students Linda Barrett and Stacy Hamilton work, is also the hangout for students at Ridgemont High School.

1987. On *Charles in Charge* (Syn.), Jamie, Sarah and Adam Powell frequent Sid's Pizza Parlor (later called The Yesterday Café). On *Degrassi Junior High* (Syn.), a hamburger joint called 13 Busy Place is the hangout for the school's students. On *Out of This World* (Syn.), the Goodie Goodie is the soda shop hangout of Evie Garland, a high school student who is part earthling and part alien (Anterian).

1988. On *Just the Ten of Us* (ABC), Danny's Pizza Parlor is the hangout of the Lubbock sisters, Wendy, Marie, Connie and Cindy (who also perform there as the singing Lubbock Babes). On *Learning the Ropes* (Syn.), the Burger Palace is the hangout for high school students Ellen and Mark Randall.

1989. On *Family Matters* (ABC), Eddie Winslow, his sister Laura and their nerdy friend Steve Urkel, hangout at LeRoy's (a burger joint) that is later rebuilt as Rachel's Place. On *Saved by the Bell* (NBC), the Max is the hangout for the students at Bayside High School (Zack, Kelly, Jessie, Lisa, Slater and Screech).

1990. On *Beverly Hills, 90210* (Fox), high school students Brenda and Brandon Walsh find The Peach Pit the perfect eatery (a diner). In later episodes, when they graduate high school, the nightclub After Dark becomes the hangout. On *Ferris Bueller* (NBC), high school student Ferris Bueller hangs out at Danny's Pizza Parlor. On The

Fresh Prince of Bel Air ((NBC), Will Smith and his cousin Carlton Banks hang out at an eatery called The Peacock Stop. On *Parker Lewis Can't Lose* (Fox), Parker Lewis and his "buds" Mikey and Jerry frequent The Atlas Diner.

1991. *Step by Step* (ABC/CBS). The 50s Café and The Burger Barn are the hangouts for Dana and Karen Foster and Alicia and J.T. Lambert — kids related by marriage.

1992. *California Dreams* (NBC). Sharkey's is the beach eatery frequented by the students of Pacific Coast High School (in particular students Jenny, Tiffany, Sly, Jake and Matt).

1994. On *Someone Like Me* (NBC), twelve-year-old Gaby Stepjack and her friends hang out at The Park Recreation Center. On *Sister, Sister* (ABC/WB), twins Tia and Tamera enjoy a meal at The Rocket Burger (high school) and The Cellar (college).

1996. On *City Guys* (NBC), the New York Diner is the after school hangout for Manhattan High School students Chris Anderson and Jamal Grant. On *Clueless* (ABC/UPN), the Koffee House is the hangout for rich girlfriends Cher Horowitz, Dee Davenport and Amber Mariens. On *Moesha* (UPN), Moesha Mitchell and her friends find food at The Den the perfect place to relax after school. On *Sabrina, the Teenage Witch* (ABC/WB), Sabrina Spellman and her friends hang out at The Slicery. In later episodes it's The Coffee Shop (later Hilda's Coffee Shop) and finally Eve's Diner. On *Sweet Valley High* (Syn.), twin sisters Elizabeth and Jessica Wakefield hang out at The Beach Café.

1997. *Buffy the Vampire Slayer* (WB/UPN). The Bronz (then The Grotto) are the hangouts for Sunnydale High School student (and vampire slayer) Buffy Summers and her friends.

1998. On *Malibu, Ca.* (Syn.), the Surf Shack, a beach eatery, is a hangout run by surfer dude Murray Updike. On *One World* (NBC), the Warehouse, managed by teen Marcie Blake, is the hangout for the students at South Beach High School. On *Popular* (WB), Brooke, Samantha and Mary are students at Kennedy High School in California who hang out at The Coffee Shop after school. On *Smart Guy* (WB), the Dawgburger is the favorite eatery of Piedmont High School student T.J. Henderson, a 12-year-old with an I.Q. of 180.

2001. On *All About Us* (NBC), high school friends Alicia Elliott, Christina Castelli, Nikki

Merrick and Sierra Jennings hang out at The Loft. On *Lizzie McGuire* (Disney), a fancy eatery called The Digital Bean is the after school hangout for 13-year-old Lizzie McGuire and her friends Miranda and Gordo. On *What I Like About You* (WB), Holly Tyler and her friends enjoy a meal at The Liberty Café.

Teenagers

This entry chronicles the programs that star or feature teenagers. See also *Adolescence, Children — Extraordinary* and *Twins*.

1949. The mischievous Henry Aldrich (Robert Casey, Richard Tyler, Henry Girard, Kenneth Nelson, Bobby Ellis) and his friend Homer Brown (Jackie Kelk, Robert Barry, Jackie Grimes) are teens who live in the small town of Centerville but manage to find big trouble on *The Aldrich Family* (NBC). Also on the series is Henry's sister, Mary (Mary Malone, June Dayton). Rosalie (Arlene McQuade) and Sammy (Larry Robinson, Tom Taylor) are the children of a wise Jewish mother, Molly Goldberg, on *The Goldbergs* (CBS). Gloria Winters and Lanny Rees play Babs and Junior, the children of the mishap prone Chester A. Riley and his wife Peg on *The Life of Riley* (DuMont with Jackie Gleason as Chester). In 1953, when NBC revised the series with William Bendix in the title role, Lugene Sanders and Wesley Morgan played Babs and Junior. Katrin Hanson (Rosemary Rice, Iris Mann) recalls her life with her "little sister Dagmar [Robin Morgan, Toni Campbell], my big brother Nels [Dick Van Patten]" but most of all her mother, Marta, and father, Lars on *Mama* (CBS).

1950. Joyce Erwin (Ann Todd, Merry Anders) is the eldest child of high school principal Stu Erwin and his wife June on *Trouble with Father* (ABC).

1951. Judy Foster (Patricia Crowley, Mary Lynn Beller) is an attractive high school girl with a knack for finding trouble on *A Date with Judy* (ABC). Over at CBS, Corliss Archer (Lugene Sanders) is also a pretty high school girl whose unpredictable nature constantly gets her into trouble on *Meet Corliss Archer*. Dick Jones plays Dick West, the teenage sidekick to the Range Rider, a daring defender of justice in the Old West on *The Range Rider* (Syn.).

1952. Ricky and David Nelson, the children of Ozzie and Harriet Nelson, play themselves from pre-teen to teen to young adults on *The Adventures of Ozzie and Harriet* (ABC).

1953. Clarence Day, Jr. (Steve Terrell, Ralph Reed), is the eldest son of turn-of-the-century New York Wall Street banker Clarence Day, Sr., and his wife Vinnie on *Life with Father*. Their other children on the CBS series: Whitney (Ronald Keith), John (Freddie Lesiton, Malcolm Cossell) and Harlan Day (Harvey Grant). Teresa, called Terry (Sherry Jackson, Penny Parker), is the eldest child of nightclub comedian Danny Williams and his wife Margaret on *Make Room for Daddy* (ABC). Natalie Wood plays Ann Morrison and Bobby Hyatt is her younger brother Albie, Jr., the children of small town newspaper advertising head Albie Morrison, Sr., and his wife Catherine, on *Pride of the Family* (ABC).

1954. Andrew, Doris and Edward (Van Dyke Parks, Lenka Peterson, Conrad Janis) are the eldest children of Babbo Bonino, a widowed opera singer on NBC's *Bonino*. Also on the series, Jerry, Francesca and Carlos (Chet Allen, Gaye Huston, Oliver Andes) are Babbo's younger offspring. Betty and Bud Anderson (Elinor Donahue, Billy Gray) are the teenage children of insurance salesman Jim Anderson and his wife Margaret on *Father Knows Best* (CBS/NBC). Marjorie and Leroy Forrester (Stephanie Griffin, Ronald Keith) are the wards of Throckmorton P. Gildersleeve, the water commissioner of Sommerfield on *The Great Gildersleeve* (Syn.). Ann Baker plays Corliss Archer, the high school girl with a knack for finding trouble on *Meet Corliss Archer*, a syndicated revival of the 1951 CBS series. Gil Stratton, Jr., plays Jack Jackson, Jr., the near-sighted, bookworm, adverse to sports son of Jarrin' Jack, Sr., a former college athlete who is seeking to turn his son into another him on *That's My Boy* (CBS).

1955. Chuck MacDonald (Dwayne Hickman) is a teenager who hopes to follow in the footsteps of his uncle, Bob (Bob Cummings), a ladies' man and fashion photographer, on *Love That Bob* (NBC/CBS). Annette Funicello, Darlene Gillespie, Bobby Burgess and Lonny Burr are the principal teenaged Mouseketeers who sing, dance and entertain children on *The Mickey Mouse Club* (ABC).

1957. Noreen Corcoran is Kelly Gregg, the pretty, obedient and slightly mischievous niece of bachelor attorney Bentley Gregg on *Bachelor Father* (CBS/NBC/ABC). Judy Graves (Carol Lynley) is an imaginative teenage girl with a knack for involving herself in and attempting to solve the problems of others on the CBS pilot *Junior Miss*. Hassie and Little Luke McCoy (Lydia Reed, Michael Winkelman) are the siblings of Luke McCoy and cared for by Luke and his wife Kate after their parents' death on *The Real McCoys* (ABC).

1958. Muriel Davis plays Jane Edwards, the teenage daughter of a former military man (Bart Edwards), who dons a disguise to battle evil in a small border town between California and Mexico on the pilot *El Coyote*. Shelley Fabares plays Mary, the eldest child of Dr. Alex Stone and his wife Donna on *The Donna Reed Show* (ABC).

1959. Dwayne Hickman is Dobie Gillis and Bob Denver, Maynard G. Krebs, high school students struggling to find their place in life on *Dobie Gillis* (CBS). Pamela Blake (Brigid Bazlen) is a pretty 15-year-old girl struggling to make the transition from tomboy to young lady on *Too Young to Go Steady* (NBC).

1960. Maggie Bradley (Margaret O'Brien) is the daughter of a famous acting couple who finds mishaps after moving from New York to Connecticut on the CBS pilot *Maggie*. Mike, Robbie and Chip Douglas (Tim Considine, Don Grady, Stanley Livingston) are the teenage sons of widower Steve Douglas (Fred MacMurray) on *My Three Sons* (ABC/CBS).

1961. Susan Silo is April Fleming, the daughter of a famous acting couple who yearns to become an actress and make a name for herself on the CBS pilot *Always April*. Candy Moore plays Chris Carmichael, the teenage daughter of the scatter-brained Lucy Carmichael on *The Lucy Show*. Also on the CBS series, Jimmy Garrett plays Chris's younger brother Jerry. Margie Clayton (Cynthia Pepper) is a teenage girl growing up (and finding trouble) in the small New England town of Madison during the 1920s on *Margie* (ABC). Also on the series are Penny Parker as Maybell Jackson and Tommy Ivo as Heywood Botts, friends of Margie. Jacklyn O'Donnell and Bobby Diamond are Nancy and Buddy, the children of Hollywood writer Dan McGovern and his wife Nanette on *Yes, Yes Nanette* (NBC).

1962. Patty Walker (Lynn Loring) is an American teenager who resides with the Finch family in London to attend the Royal Academy of Dramatic Arts. Heather Finch (Judy Carne) is a British girl who resides with the Walker family in New York to experience the American way of life. Their par-

ents agreed to the arrangement to allow the girls to follow their dreams on *Fair Exchange* (CBS). Michael Burns plays Howie Macauley, the 14-year-old brother of college student Wes Macauley on *It's a Man's World* (NBC). Judy (voice of Jane Webb) and her younger brother Elroy (Daws Butler) are the children of George and Jane Jetson, a futuristic space couple on *The Jetsons* (ABC cartoon). Candy Moore is Virginia Carol, a very pretty girl with a penchant for solving other people's problems on the CBS pilot *Life with Virginia*. Roberta Shore plays Betty Garth, the daughter of Henry Garth, a widowed judge who owns the Shiloh Ranch in 1880s Wyoming on *The Virginian*. Also on the NBC series, Randy Boone plays Randy, Henry's son, and Diane Roter is Jennifer, Henry's orphaned niece.

1963. Patty Duke plays Patty and Cathy Lane, look-alike cousins who are as different as night and day on *The Patty Duke Show* (ABC). Billie Jo Bradley (Jeannine Riley, Gunilla Hutton, Meredith MacRae) and her sisters Bobbie Jo (Pat Woodell, Lori Saunders) and Betty Jo (Linda Kaye Henning) are the gorgeous daughters of Kate Bradley, a widow who runs the Shady Rest Hotel in the town of Hooterville on *Petticoat Junction* (CBS).

1964. Carol Faylen plays Joyce, the 15-year-old, not inclined for schoolwork daughter of Bing Collins, a former singer, and his wife Ellie, on *The Bing Crosby Show*. Also on the ABC series, Diane Sherry plays Janice, Joyce's younger sister. Homer Macauley (Timmy Rooney) is a 13-year-old boy who becomes the man of the house after his father's death on the CBS pilot *The Human Comedy*. Karen Scott (Debbie Watson) is a beautiful high school girl with an uncontrollable penchant for mischief on *Karen* (NBC; originally broadcast as a segment of *90 Bristol Court*). Beverley Owen (then Pat Priest) plays Marilyn Munster, the plain, unattractive member of a family who resemble movie monsters of the 1930s on *The Munsters* (CBS).

1965. Alec Tate (Dean Jones) is a brilliant scientist and a swinging bachelor who finds his life turned upside down when he is forced to raise his 15-year-old sister Bunny (Robyn Millan) after the death of their parents on the CBS pilot *The Dean Jones Show*. Sally Field is 15½-year-old Frances Lawrence, a high school girl who is in love with the world of surfing on *Gidget* (ABC). Marta Kristen and Angela Cartwright are Judy and Penny Robinson, the teenage children of John and Maureen Robinson, members of a family that are *Lost in Space* (CBS). Tammy Tarleton (Debbie Watson) is a backwoods Louisiana Bayou girl struggling to adjust to a new life when she acquires a job as a secretary on *Tammy* (ABC).

1966. Catherine Davis (Kathy Garver), called Cissy, is a 15-year-old girl who comes from Indiana to New York to live with her bachelor uncle Bill Davis (Brian Keith) after the death of her parents on *Family Affair* (CBS). Fleming and Casey (Brooke Bundy, Barbara Hershey) are teenage sleuths who help their father, private detective George Holloway, solve crimes on the NBC pilot *Holloway's Daughters.* Mlor (Mary Grace) is a gorgeous prehistoric cave girl and the daughter of Gronk and his wife Shad on *It's About Time* (CBS). Also on the series, Pat Cardi plays Mlor's younger brother Breer. Diane Sherry plays Nancy, the teenage daughter of Frank Johnson, a TV writer who tries to get with the times but just can't manage on the ABC pilot *The Man in the Square Suit.* Clayt and Kathleen Monroe (Michael Anderson, Jr., Barbara Hershey) are the eldest children of Albert and Mary Monroe and the last hope of a future for them and their younger siblings (Amy, Jefferson and Fennimore) after their parents drown and they attempt to establish a homeland in 1875 Wyoming on *The Monroes* (ABC). Michael Burns plays Rod Ryan, a 16-year-old who looks older than he actually is, who joins the Army Air Corps (World War II) on the CBS pilot *Off We Go.* Rod quickly advances to the rank of colonel and is placed in charge of a small base in England.

1967. Eunice (Lori Martin), Norm (Tony Dow) and Randy (Tim Matheson) are among the teenagers who flock to the beach in Southern California each weekend for two days of fun in the sun on the NBC pilot *Weekend.*

1968. Sue and Noah Wells (Susanne Haworth, Rodney Pearlman) are the children of John Wells, a freelance writer and skipper of the schooner *Seaspray* on *The Adventures of the Seaspray* (Syn.). Kim and Craig (Lucie Arnaz, Desi Arnaz, Jr.) are the children of Lucille Carter, a widow who works as a secretary for the Unique Employment Agency on *Here's Lucy* (CBS).

1969. Nancy, Kim and Charlotte (Brooke Bundy, Robyn Millan, Susan Joyce) are the daughters of the widowed Walter Randolph on the NBC pilot *The Best Years.* Alison Endicott (Joyce Menges) is the eldest daughter of Michael Endicott, a professor at the American School in Italy on *To Rome with Love.* Also on the CBS series, Susan Neher and Melanie Fullerton play Alison's younger sisters, Penny and Pokey.

1970. Stephanie Steele and Del Russell are Andrea and Richard, the children of Arnie and Lillian Nuvo on CBS's *Arnie.* Joy, Harmony and I.Q. (Caroline Ellis, Wayne Laryea, John McIndoe) are human-looking teenage insects who protect Tranquility Forest from evil on *The Bugaloos* (NBC). Josie, Melody and Valerie (voices of Janet Waldo, Jackie Joseph, Barbara Pariot) are teenage girls who encounter misadventures as they travel around the world performing as the rock group *Josie and the Pussycats* (CBS cartoon). Keith and Laurie Partridge (David Cassidy, Susan Dey) are a brother and sister who are members of the singing *Partridge Family* (ABC). Their younger siblings are Danny, Tracy and Chris.

1971. Charlie (Paul Petersen) and his younger sister Dodie (Debi Storm) are the children of Peter Stefan, a widowed doctor who marries a beautiful German girl named Elke (Elke Sommer) on the CBS pilot *Elke.* Michael Shea is Lucas and Angela Powell is his younger sister Annie, the children of TV talk show host Dick Preston and his wife Jenny on *The New Dick Van Dyke Show* (CBS). Pebbles Flintstone (voice of Sally Struthers), the daughter of Fred and Wilma, and Bamm Bamm Rubble (Jay North), the son of Barney and Betty, are teenagers who attend Bedrock High School on *Pebbles and Bamm Bamm*, an animated CBS spin off from *The Flintstones.* Cindy, Bob and Brian (Darleen Carr, Ron Howard, James-Michael Wixted) are the children of L.A.P.D. detective sergeant Chad Smith and his wife Betty on *The Smith Family* (ABC). Ron Russell hosts *Visual Girl*, a syndicated program geared to teenage girls that concentrates on exercise, makeup and skin care.

1972. Billy Williams (Stephen Cottier) is a teenage boy growing up amid the challenge of the land around Lake Huron in Ontario, Canada, on the syndicated *Adventures in Rainbow Country.*

1974. Vincent Van Patten plays Paul Apple, the eldest child of George and Barbara Apple, a city couple who now live in the small town of Appleton, Iowa, on *Apple's Way* (CBS). Also on the series are Paul's younger siblings, Patricia (Franny Michel, Kristy McNichol) and Cathy (Patti Cohoon). *The Cowboys* (ABC) are a group of children who help Kate Andersen, the widowed owner of the Longhorn Ranch in Spanish Wells,

New Mexico (1870s), run her spread. They are: Sam (Robert Carradine), Cimarron (A Martinez), Homer (Kerry McLane), Steve (Clint Howard), Jim (Sean Kelly), Hardy (Mitch Brown) and Weedy (Clay O'Brien). J.J. Evans (Jimmie Walker), a teenage ladies' man who calls himself "The Ebony Prince," and Thelma Evans (Bern-Nadette Stanis), a high school student with aspirations to become an actress, are the children of Florida and James Evans on CBS's *Good Times*. Life in 1950s Milwaukee is seen through the experiences of several teenagers on ABC's *Happy Days*: Richie Cunningham (Ron Howard), his friends Potsie (Anson Williams) and Ralph (Donny Most) and in later episodes, as she grows from pre-teen to teen, Richie's sister Joanie (Erin Moran). Jaytee, Cindy and Terry (Alan Abelew, Trish Soodik, Kimberly Beck) are the featured students at Harry S. Truman Memorial High School on *Lucas Tanner* (NBC). Seventeen-year-old Doobie Wheeler (Mark Hamill) and his younger siblings Boo and T.J. (Karen Oberdiear, Tony Becker) are the children of Zack Wheeler, a lazy good for nothing who, after deserting his children after the death of his wife, returns to sponge off them on *The Texas Wheelers* (ABC).

1975. Dina Ousley is Ellen Bronkov, the daughter of Alex Bronkov, a widowed lieutenant who works under special assignment for the mayor of Ocean City, California, on *Bronk* (CBS). Lance Kerwin plays Ramey, the eldest child of Reverend Tom Holvak and his wife Elizabeth on *The Family Holvak*. Also on the NBC series, Elizabeth Cheshire plays Ramey's younger sister Julie Mae. Mark and Nick (Barry Miller, Jimmy Baio) are the sons of Joe Vitalie, a widowed sheet metal worker on *Joe and Sons* (CBS). Julie and Barbara Cooper (Mackenzie Phillips, Valerie Bertinelli) are the somewhat rebellious daughters of liberal Ann Romano (Bonnie Franklin) on *One Day at a Time* (CBS). Vincent Van Patten and Leif Garrett play John and Endy, the sons of Peter Karris, a widowed photographer who travels around the country in a mobile home on *Three for the Road* (CBS). Vinnie Barbarino (John Travolta), Juan Epstein (Robert Hegyes), Freddie "Boom Boom" Washington (Lawrence Hilton-Jacobs) and Arnold Horshack (Ron Palillo) are the Sweathogs (nickname for special education students) at James Buchanan High School in Brooklyn, New York, on *Welcome Back, Kotter* (ABC). Michael Platt (Jerry Houser) and his younger siblings Andrew

(Devon Scott) and Kenny (Willie Aames) are the bright and sassy children of attorney George Platt and his wife Liz on *We'll Get By* (CBS). Kimberly Beck and Steve Burns are Robin and Tom Andrews, the children of underwater photographer Steve Andrews and his marine biologist wife Kate on *The Westwind* (NBC).

1976. Philip McKeon plays Tommy, the son of waitress Alice Hyatt, on CBS's *Alice*. Snowy (Kathleen Cody), B.J. (Debbie Zipp) and Beverly (Teresa Medaris) are three fun-loving, small town high school girls on the NBC pilot *The Cheerleaders*. B.J. (Susan Lawrence), Brad (Ted Eccles) and Gordie (Jeff McKay) are teenagers who have been reduced to the height of six inches by a mad scientist and trapped on a remote island on *Dr. Shrinker* (ABC). Brother and singing teenage singing sensations Donny and Marie Osmond host a weekly program of music, songs and comedy on *Donny and Marie* (ABC). Leticia Lawrence, better known as Buddy (Kristy McNichol), and Willie (Gary Frank) are the teenage children of attorney Doug Lawrence and his wife Kate on *Family*. Also on the ABC series is Quinn Cummings as Annie Cooper, the adopted daughter of Doug and Kate. Sonia and Sasha (Caroline Kava, Matthew Barry) are the children of Ivan Petrovsky, headwaiter at the Hotel Metropole in Moscow, Russia, on *Ivan the Terrible* (CBS). P.T., Bugs, Doomsday and Doc (Steve Bonino, Cosie Costa, Biff Warren, John Lansing) are teenage agents for the Civilian Authority for the Protection of Everybody, Regardless on *The Kids from C.A.P.E.R.* (NBC). Debralee Scott plays Cathy Schumway, the very pretty but very promiscuous sister of the neurotic Mary Hartman on *Mary Hartman, Mary Hartman* (Syn.). Life in an unnamed inner city is seen through the eyes of Margaret Malloy (Sarah MacDonnell), a pretty 13-year-old girl who has the street name "Muggsy" on NBC's *Muggsy*. Connie and Victor Valdez (Lisa Mordente, James Victor) and their younger siblings Ernesto and Pepe (Nelson D. Cuevas, Claudio Martinez) are the children of Luis and Sophie Valdez, a hard working Mexican-American couple on *Viva Valdez* (ABC). Roger Thomas (Ernest Thomas), Dwayne Clemens (Haywood Nelson) and Freddie "Rerun" Stubbs (Fred Berry) are three friends who attend Jefferson High School in Southern California on ABC's *What's Happening!!* Debra Winger plays Drucilla, alias Wonder Girl, the 15-year-old sister of Diana Prince, the heroic *Won-*

der Woman (ABC). Susan, Barry and C.C. (Carol Anne Seflinger, David Levy, John Anthony Bailey) are teenagers who own Wonderbug, a car that possesses amazing abilities on *Wonderbug* (ABC).

1977. Kathy, Nick, Arthur and Mountain Man (Sherry Hursey, James Canning, Bill Douglas, Gary Epp) are teens from varying backgrounds who scheme, dream and plan their futures together on the CBS pilot *Best Friends*. Michael Constantine plays Dominick, a widowed father struggling to raise three beautiful daughters — Cookie, Diane and Terry (Judy Landers, Olivia Barash, Robin Graves) — on the NBC pilot *Daughters*. Tom Bradford (Dick Van Patten) is the father of eight children, five of whom are teenagers — Joanie (Laurie Walters), Nancy (Dianne Kay), Elizabeth (Connie Needham), Tommy (Willie Aames) and Susan (Susan Richardson) — on ABC's *Eight Is Enough*. Chrissy, Caroline and Andy (Vicky Dawson, Kathy Jo Kelly, William McMillan) are the children of Julie Matthews, a young widow who moves from the suburbs to New York City to begin a new life on the CBS pilot *The Four of Us*. Lance Kerwin plays James Hunter, a student at Bunker Hill High School in Boston on NBC's *James at 15* (later titled *James at 16*). Bonnie Lou (Bonnie Ebsen) and her brother Junior (Patrick J. Petersen) are the children of Jasper and Venus Kallikak, a rural couple who run a gas station in Nowhere, California, on *The Kallikaks* (NBC). Melinda, Mark and Jimmy (Julie Anne Haddock, Johnny Doran, K.C. Martel) are the children of Mike and Jane Mulligan. Polly, Stevie, Adam and Kimmy (Lory Walsh, Suzanne Crough, Chris Ciampa, Sunshine Lee) are the children of Steve and Kathy Freeman (Mike's sister and brother-in-law). When Steve and Kathy are killed in a plane crash the families become one on *Mulligan's Stew* (NBC). Dirt, Bogen, Teddy, Evel and Pantsface (John Cassissi, Jimmy Baio, Pierre Daniel, Moosie Drier, David Arnott) are teens who hang together and call themselves the Supreme Machine on the ABC pilot *Sheehy and the Supreme Machine* (the title refers to Jack Sheehy, the maintenance man in the building in which the teens live).

1978. Caitlin O'Heaney plays Anna Marie Hollyhock, the teenage daughter of the eccentric Ginger Nell and Fast Eddie on *Apple Pie* (ABC). Kimberly Drummond (Dana Plato) is the daughter of millionaire Philip Drummond, and Willis Jackson (Todd Bridges), his adopted son on

NBC's *Diff'rent Strokes*. Scott Baio plays Frankie, the wise cracking 15-year-old brother of Las Vegas showgirl Angie Viola on *Who's Watching the Kids?* (NBC). Sixteen-year-old Molly Foster (Linda Purl) marries 18-year-old David Beaton (Roger Kern) and together set out to make a new life for themselves in the Dakota Territory of the 1870s on *The Young Pioneers* (ABC).

1979. Debralee Scott is Marie Falco, the sister of Angie Falco, the waitress at the Liberty Coffee Shop in Pennsylvania on *Angie*. Also on the ABC series Tammy Lauren plays Hilary Benson, the daughter of Joyce Benson, the sister of the doctor (Brad Benson) Angie later marries. The loud-mouthed and bigoted Archie Bunker cares for Stephanie Mills (Danielle Brisebois) and her cousin Billie Bunker (Denise Miller) after the passing of his wife Edith on *Archie Bunker's Place* (CBS). Steve Guttenberg plays Billy Fisher, a 19-year-old who prefers his colorful fantasies to life's realities on *Billy* (CBS). Suzi Cooper (Mary Crosby), Mary Lee (Amy Johnson) and Isabel (Susan Gotton) are among the members of the college sorority Gamma Delta Iota on NBC's *Brothers and Sisters*. Members of the Pi Nu Fraternity of the Larry Crandall College are Checko (Chris Lemmon), Stanley (John Cutler) and Ronald (Randy Brooks). Vince (James Vincent McNichol), Laurie (Michele Tobin) and Ross (Marc McClure) are best friends who attend West Side High School and hangout together at Sunset Beach on CBS's *California Fever*. Sandi (Heather Thomas), Melba (Jillian Kesner), Hope (Tracey Phillips) and Maria (Alexa Kenin) are among the students at the all-girl Baxter University in Connecticut on *Co-Ed Fever* (CBS). Blair Warner (Lisa Whelchel), Jo Polniaszek (Nancy McKeon), Tootie Ramsey (Kim Fields) and Natalie Green (Mindy Cohn) are students at the East School for Girls in Peekskill, New York, on *The Facts of Life* (NBC). Susan Swift plays 13-year-old Kelly and Dana Hill is her younger sister, Courtney, children cared for by their father Charlie Featherstone while their mother attends an out of state law school on the CBS pilot *Featherstone's Nest*. The problems facing a black family are realistically portrayed on *Harris and Company*, an NBC series about widowed mechanic Mike Harris and his five children: Juanita (Lia Jackson), Liz (Renee Brown), David (David Hubbard), Tommy (Eddie Singleton) and Richard (Dian Turner). Ruthie (Kim Richards) and Diane (Donna

Wilkes, Krista Errickson) are the teenage daughters of widower Larry Alder (McLean Stevenson), the host of the radio call-in program *Hello, Larry* (NBC) in Portland, Oregon. Maggie (Melissa Sherman) and Steve (Christopher Knight) are the eldest children of Joe Wabash, a painter, and his wife Katie on *Joe's World*. The NBC series also features their younger children: Jimmy, Linda and Rick Wabash (Michael Sharrett, Missy Francis, Ari Zelter). Seventeen-year-old Bridget MacKenzie (Lory Walsh), her 16-year-old brother Kevin (Shawn Stevens) and their younger siblings, Celia, Michael and Timothy (Randi Kiger, Sean Marshall, Keith Mitchell), are orphans cared for by their adopted uncle, Cuda Webster, a fisherman in Hawaii on *The MacKenzies of Paradise Cove* (ABC). Carol Munday (Linda Cook) and Cidra Hopnagel (Jayne Modean), better known as Ducky, are best friends who attend San Francisco High School on the NBC pilot *Me and Ducky*. Chris and Laura Richards (Clark Brandon, Olivia Barash) are orphaned teens who live with their Aunt Marion but looked over by an angel named Random on ABC's *Out of the Blue*.

1980. Molly, Rosie and Meg (Lory Walsh, Robin Dearden, Lori Lowe) are the daughters of Max Caulpepper, a widowed detective on the NBC pilot *The Asphalt Cowboy*. Vickie, Jimmy, Miles and Beethoven (Elissa Leeds, Paul Provenza, Charles Fleischer, Jay Fenichel) are Boston-based teens struggling to make it in the world of rock music as the group *Blue Jeans* (ABC pilot). Dave, Mike, Cyril and Moocher (Shaun Cassidy, Tom Wiggins, Thom Bray, Jackie Earle Haley) are high school grads attempting to find their place in the world on *Breaking Away* (ABC). Susan Elliot and Stephen Myers are Susan and Bradley, the children of Global Canning Company employee Sal Ugily and his wife, Verna, on the ABC pilot *The Ugily Family*. Also on the series is Lory Walsh as Bambi Bing, the bubbly teenage daughter of Henry and Babs Bing, the Ugily's neighbors.

1981. Julie Piekarski, Crispin Glover, Jill Schoelen and Nicholas Coppola are real life teens who perform in various skits geared to teenagers on the ABC variety pilot *The Best of Times*. Sandy (Penelope Sudrow), Kris (Lisa Lindren), Heather (Heather Hobbs), Chubby (Paul Jarnagin, Jr.) and Fred (Rusty Gilligan) are among the children stranded on a deserted island when their plane crashes en route to Hawaii on the NBC pilot *Crash Island*. Katie and Julie (Kari Michaelsen, Lauri Hendler) are the teenage daughters of gruff police chief Carl Kanisky on *Gimme a Break* (NBC). Jenn Thompson plays Dee, the daughter of flamboyant Angel Glow Cosmetics salesgirl Stella Johnson on *Harper Valley*. Also on the NBC series is Suzi Dean as Scarlett Taylor, the very spoiled daughter of city attorney Bobby Taylor and his wife Wanda. Karen Chase and her brother Craig (Ally Sheedy, Michael Spound) are students at Hancock High School on the ABC pilot *Homeroom*. Ivy Miller (Lisa Freeman) and her best friends Annie Monahan (Nancy Cartwright) and Janey Zerneck (Deena Freeman) are prankish high school girls on the ABC pilot *In Trouble*. Janet Julian and Brett Cullen play Laura and Matt, the children of John Tyree, the owner of a salvage boat service in Florida on the CBS pilot *Key Tortuga*. Girl crazy teenager Zack Rogers (Clark Brandon) becomes the apprentice to the legendary Merlin the Magician (who has resurfaced in modern times a gas station owner Max Merlin) to learn the art of sorcery on *Mr. Merlin* (CBS). Andy, Joey and Jonah (Christopher Barnes, Richard Moore, Chris Dobbs) are mischievous students at Buckminster's, a co-ed boarding school on the CBS pilot *Rise and Shine*. The problems faced by teenagers in today's world are the focal point of the syndicated serial pilot *Young Lives*. Heidi Holicker, Emily Banks and Joey Seifers head a large cast. Carolyn McCuen and Heywood Nelson host *That Teen Show*, a syndicated program of information geared to teenagers.

1982. Buzz Ryan (Jimmy Baio), George Knight (Peter Frechette) and Alfred Webster (John P. Navin, Jr.) are the main cadets at the Stone Military Academy on the NBC pilot *The Academy*. Melora Hardin is Christy, the daughter of Dr. Matt Jennings, the head of a marine research center off California's Catalina Island on the CBS pilot *Catalina Sea Lab*. Alex and Mallory Keaton (Michael J. Fox, Justine Bateman) are the teenage children of Steven and Elyse Keaton on NBC's *Family Ties*. As the series progressed, younger daughter Jennifer (Tina Yothers) blossomed into a beautiful teenage girl. Claudia Wells is Julie, the eldest child of Susan McLane, a widow who marries Jim Douglas, a former racecar driver who now runs the Famous Driving School and also owns Herbie, the magical Volkswagen on *Herbie the Love Bug* (CBS). The pilot *Little Darlings* is adapted from the feature film and relates the activities of tough teen girl Angel Bright (Pamela Segall) and her rich, pampered friend Farris Whitney (Tammy Lauren). Dey Young and John Calvin are Sis and Junior Gooseberry, the almost normal offspring of Bronco and Betty Gooseberry, a less-than-intellectual couple on the HBO pilot *Sitcom*. Heather and Duffy Akins (Jennifer Runyon, Billy Warlock) and their younger siblings Rebel, Hank and Tad (Bubba Dean, Von Martin, Leaf Phoenix) are orphans (their parents killed in a car crash) who are cared for by racecar driver Brewster Baker on the NBC pilot *Six Pack* (based on the feature film). Patty Green and Lauren Hutchinson (Sarah Jessica Parker, Amy Linker) are best friends who attend Weemawee Central High School on CBS's *Square Pegs*. Jennie Lee Krebs (Katy Maisnik) is a 16-year-old girl struggling up the rocky road to stardom as a teenage singer on *Star of the Family* (ABC).

1983. Katy Kurtzman plays Allison Sidney Harrison, a high school girl and amateur sleuth who helps her father, David, a private detective, solve crimes on the NBC pilot *Allison Sidney Harrison*. Tracey Gold plays Susan Barnes, the 13-year-old daughter of Boston TV anchorwoman Jennifer Barnes on *Goodnight, Beantown* (CBS). Pete Falcone (Robert Romanus), Robin DuPree (Krista Errickson) and Patti Eubanks (Hallie Todd) are among the students at U.S. Grant High School on the CBS pilot *The Best of Times*. Dana Hill plays Gussie Mapes, a teenage girl who helps her stepfather, Dan Brannigan, raise her younger siblings Theresa and Logan (Rebecca Sweet, Brett Johnson) after the death of her mother on the CBS pilot *Brannigan and Mapes*. Melora Hardin plays Tess, the daughter of Annie Benjamin. Her younger siblings are Sam and Toby (Martin Hewitt, Jonathan Hall Kovacs). James Spader is Jake, the son of Kevin Nichols. Annie and Kevin, both divorced, marry and begin a new life together on *Family Tree* (NBC). John P. Navin, Jr., plays Joey Elliott, a teenager whose life is guided by the ghost of Jennifer Farrell, a one time glamorous movie star on *Jennifer Slept Here* (NBC). Tony Becker plays Odell "Kudzu" DuBose, a teenage boy who lives in the small town of Bypass, North Carolina, and hopes to become a writer on the CBS pilot *Kudzu*. Karin Argoud and Eric Brown play Sonia and Buzz Harper, the children of Quick Keys locksmith Vinton Harper on *Mama's Family* (NBC). Taryn Blake and Laurie Casswell (Daryl Hannah, Alexandra Paul) are high fashion mod-

els on the ABC pilot *Paper Dolls* (in the 1984 series that followed, Nicollette Sheridan plays Taryn and Terry Farrell is Laurie). Richie (Matthew Laborteaux), Alice (Andrea Elson), Jeremy (Jeffrey Jacquet) and Ham (Todd Porter) are computer savvy high school students on *The Whiz Kids* (CBS).

1984. Boone Sawyer (Thomas Byrd) is a 17-year-old growing up in Trinity, Tennessee (1953), who hopes to become a singer but faces opposition from his parents (who want him to become a mechanic in the family owned gas station) on NBC's *Boone*. Denise and Theo Huxtable (Lisa Bonet, Malcolm-Jamal Warner) are the teen children of Cliff and Clair Huxtable on *The Cosby Show* (NBC). Megan Follows plays Didi Crane, the pretty, fashion conscious daughter of TV commentator Martin Crane and his wife Candy on *Domestic Life* (CBS). Allison and Kate Foster (Jean and Liz Sagal) are the twin 18-year-old daughters of Art Foster, the owner of a gym on NBC's *Double Trouble*. Julie and Matt Burton (Tricia Cast, Jason Bateman) are the children of widowed legal secretary Eileen Burton on *It's Your Move* (NBC). On *Kate and Allie* (CBS), Ari Meyers plays Emma, the daughter of Kate McArdle, a travel agency employee, and Allison Smith is Jennie, the daughter of Jill of all trades Allie Lowell. Allie is also the mother of Chip, a pre-teen boy (Frederick Koehler). Shannon (Claudia Wells) and her younger brother Timothy (R.J. Williams) are the children of Kate Halloran, a widow who is part owner of the near bankrupt H&W Garment Industry on *Off the Rack* (ABC). Spencer Winger (Chad Lowe) is a slightly offbeat, girl-crazy 16-year-old boy who excels in finding trouble on *Spencer* (NBC). Jenny Beck (then Jennifer Cooke) plays Elizabeth Maxwell, a star child (born of an Earth mother and an alien father), who is the only hope the world has in its battle against aliens on *V* (NBC). Doug (Jeffrey Rogers), Karen (Anne Howard) and Jeanie (Janeen Best) are among the teenagers who find adventure and romance at the local shopping mall in St. Louis on the NBC pilot *Young Hearts*.

1985. Mia Braithwaite (Beth Ehlers), Giselle Kraft (Tammy Lauren), Joy Villa Franco (Melora Hardin) and Neil Troutman (David Packer) are among the students at John F. Kennedy High School in Southern California on *The Best Times* (NBC). Fran Robinson is Lauren and Kristoff St. John and Jaleel White are her younger brothers

Charlie, Jr., and Robert, the children Chicago Department of Highways employee Charlie Richmond and his wife Diana, on *Charlie and Company* (CBS). Deborah, Todd and Dunc (Mandy Ingber, Meeno Peluce, R.J. Williams) are the children of private detective Press Wyman and his wife Diane, a schoolteacher, on *Detective in the House* (CBS). Mike and Carol Seaver (Kirk Cameron, Tracey Gold) are the teenage children of Jason and Maggie Seaver on *Growing Pains* (ABC). Lucy Mansfield (Quinn Cummings) and her younger brother Willie (Taliesin Jaffe) are the children of Julia Mansfield, the first woman president of the United States, on *Hail to the Chief* (ABC). Kevin and Heather Owens (Rob Stone, Tracy Wells) are the children of TV sports anchor George Owens and his wife Marsha on *Mr. Belvedere*. Gina, Trace and Smith (Jonna Lee, Tony O'Dell, Chris Hebert) are the children of Hal and June Sterling, a family engulfed by a time warp and transported to a hostile world that resembles Earth, on *Otherworld* (CBS).

1986. Lynn Tanner (Andrea Elson) and her younger brother Brian (Benji Gregory) are the children of Willie and Kate Tanner, the couple who opened their home to Gordon Schumway, an alien who crashed into their garage and is now stranded on *ALF* (NBC). Brian McGuire (Raphael Sbarge) is a teen who, after his parents divorce, is sent to live with his grandfather on *Better Days* (CBS). Allie and Jamie (Virginia Keehne, Noah Hathaway) are teenage sleuths who help their grandfather, retired police detective Sam Donahue, solve crimes on the ABC pilot *The Case Busters*. Karla Montana plays Anita Martinez, the 16-year-old sister of Hector Martinez, a former gang member turned lawyer on the CBS pilot *The Family Martinez*. Linda Barrett (Claudia Wells), Stacy Hamilton (Courtney Thorne-Smith) and Jeff Spicoli (Dean Cameron) are the main teens who attend California's Ridgemont High School on *Fast Times* (CBS, based on the film *Fast Times at Ridgemont High*). Robin Givens, Khrystyne Haje, Dan Frischman and Dan Schneider play Darlene, Simone, Arvid and Dennis, the main students in an Honors program at Fillmore High School in New York City on ABC's *Head of the Class*. Christina Applegate plays Robin Kennedy and Jonathan Ward is her brother, Kevin, the children of widowed L.A.P.D. detective Wes Kennedy on *Heart of the City* (ABC). Rebecca Schaeffer is Patti Russell, the 16-year-old sister of photographer Samantha Russell and her new roommate when she comes to live with her on *My Sister Sam* (CBS). Sydney Penny plays Danni Collins, the niece of Frances "Gidget" Lawrence (now married to Jeff Griffin) and a second-generation lover of the beach and surfing on *The New Gidget* (Syn.). Marianne (Anastasia Fielding), Kate (Alison McMillan), Brian (Michael DeLuise) and Roger (Gabriel Damon) are the siblings of Don Hastings, a police officer who takes on the responsibility of caring for them after their parents' death on *One Big Family* (Syn.). Molly and David Witherspoon (Shannen Doherty, Chad Allen) are the teenage children of widowed photographer Jessie Witherspoon on NBC's *Our House*. Betsy Bleil, Stapp Beaton, Chandra Wilson, Veronica Rosas and Wiley Wiggins are the main children who play adult roles on *The Perkins Family*, a PBS series that features teens and adolescents in all roles. Pamela Segall plays Toni Rutledge, a very pretty 15-year-old girl and potential jailbird who finds a chance at life when Al Hughes, a cantankerous widower, takes her under his wing on *The Redd Foxx Show* (ABC). Jack Randall is the natural son of David and Lori Randall. Amy (Katie O'Neill), Sam (Ke Huy Quan) and Sally (Natasha Bobo) are Jack's adopted siblings on CBS's *Together We Stand* (later titled *Nothing Is Easy*). Danny, Dorothy and Rosie (Billy Warlock, Marissa Mendenhall, Shana O'Neil) are the children of Pete Seltzer. Kathleen and Frank (Mary Kohnert, Ricky Stout) are the offspring of Frank Manley. Frank, a widower, and Pete, divorced, move in with their bachelor friend, Chick, to save on expenses on the ABC pilot *2½ Dads*. David Hogan (Jason Bateman) is the teenage son of Valerie and Michael Hogan on NBC's *Valerie*. When the series switched titles to *The Hogan Family* (1987), David's younger brothers, Willie and Mark (Danny Ponce, Jeremy Licht), became teenagers and attended Clifton High School with Mark. Teens find fun and romance at the local shopping mall on the NBC pilot *Young Hearts*. Jeffrey Rogers and Anne Howard play the featured teens, Doug and Karen Fettis (brother and sister).

1987. Laura (Cami Cooper), Zan (Hayley Carr) and Jimmy (Joel Carlson) are the children of Ben Madison and his second wife Meg, a former Broadway star, on the NBC pilot *Act II*. Molly McCue (Royana Black) is a 14-year-old girl with the mind of Sherlock Holmes who helps police detective Jack Wilder (Paul Sorvino) solve crimes on the PBS pilot *Almost Partners*. Jamie and Sarah Powell (Nicole Eggert, Josie Davis) are the teenage daughters of Ellen and Robert Powell on the syndicated *Charles in Charge*. Tracy Nelson and Michael Sharrett play Susan and Kelly, the teenage children of Will and Maggie Costigan, a couple burdened with problems on the ABC pilot *Home*. Juliette Lewis is Kate, a gorgeous but very naïve 13-year-old girl who lives in a fantasy world of her own dreams on *I Married Dora* (ABC). Kelly Bundy (Christina Applegate) is the beautiful but flaky daughter of Al and Peggy Bundy on *Married ... With Children* (Fox; as the series progressed, Kelly's brother Bud [David Faustino] became a would-be teenage ladies' man). Cynthia Tresch (Maddie Corman) and her brother Nick (Andre Gower) are the children of Sam and Meg Tresch, the president of the United States and his wife, the First Lady on *Mr. President* (Fox). Hilary Van Dyke plays Marilyn Munster, a beautiful 17-year-old girl who is considered quite unattractive by her movie monster-like family on *The Munsters Today* (Syn.). Also on the series, Jason Marsden plays Marilyn's cousin, Eddie Munster, a 16-year-old werewolf. Benjamin Baxter, called Beans (Jonathan Ward), is a very unusual 17-year-old boy. He is a courier for the Network, a postal service for the secret agencies of the U.S. government on *The New Adventures of Beans Baxter* (Fox). Maureen Flannigan plays Evie Garland, a high school girl who is half earthling and half alien (Anterian) on *Out of This World* (Syn.). Lynne Holly (Faith Ford), Scott (Bruce Norris) and Gwen (Penelope Ann Miller) are teens that work the popcorn concession at the Majestic Theater, a movie palace in Kansas City on *The Popcorn Kid* (CBS). In an attempt to refine his flamboyant, girl-chasing playboy image, frozen food king Nick Foley (Joseph Bologna) adopts and struggles to cope with three tough, streetwise teenage girls: Diane (Bridget Michele), Rose (Kimiko Gelman) and Marva (Tisha Campbell) on NBC's *Rags to Riches*.

1988. Chazz Russell (Matthew Perry) is a girl-crazy teen who works at Zorro Burger fast food on *Boys Will Be Boys* (Fox). Soleil Moon Frye plays Tyler McKay, a very pretty 13-year-old girl who is struggling to adjust to life at Appomattox, a very strict military academy on the ABC pilot *Cadets*. Louanne Ponce plays Isabel, the daughter of Linda Tidmunk and her estranged husband "Cowboy" Joe Cutler (who has returned to reclaim his family) on the ABC pilot *Cowboy Joe*. Marie, Wendy, Cindy and Connie (Heather Langenkamp, Brooke Theiss, Jamie Luner, JoAnn Willette) are the teenage children of high school coach Graham Lubbock and his wife Elizabeth on *Just the Ten of Us* (ABC). Ellen Randall (Nicole Stoffman) and her brother Mark (Yannick Bisson) are the children of Robert Randall, a schoolteacher who moonlights as a wrestler on *Learning the Ropes* (Syn.). Sara and Davy (Gennie James, Jaime McEnnan) are children who, after the death of their mother, are sent to Kenya, East Africa, to live with their estranged father, Dr. Charles Marston, on the CBS pilot *My Africa*. Andrew Clements (Jerry O'Connell) is a teenager who, after being exposed to gamma rays, acquires superhuman abilities to battle evil as his hero, Ultraman, on *My Secret Identity* (Syn.). Mijin Hong and Becky LeGrande are among the hosts of *Over 17 Not Admitted*, a Fox pilot that reports on topics of interest to teenagers. Miranda Marshack (Royana Black) is a shy and awkward 14-year-old girl who is struggling to cope with life after her mother deserts her and her father on *Raising Miranda* (CBS). Becky Conner (Lecy Goranson, Sarah Chalke) and her sister Darlene (Sara Gilbert) are the defiant daughters of Roseanne and Dan Conner on ABC's *Roseanne*. Joey Thorn (Lisa Rieffel) and her younger brothers Chad and Edmond (Adam Bisek, Jesse Tendler) are the children of the snobbish Sloan Thorn and his wife Ginger on *The Thorns* (ABC). Colin Quinn and Ahmet Zappa host *2 Hip 4 TV*, an NBC pilot of items of interest to teenagers. Karen and Wayne Arnold (Olivia D'Abo, Jason Hervey) are the teenage children of Jack and Norma Arnold on *The Wonder Years* (ABC).

1989. Lisa Rieffel plays Lucy McNeal, the 15-year-old daughter of Ann McNeil, the manager of Aunt Betty's Coffee and Bean Shop in Marvel California on NBC's *Ann Jillian*. Jim and Kevin (James MacDonald, David Arnott) are high school students struggling to maintain their B grades while moonlighting as bounty hunters on the CBS pilot *B-Men*. Eddie and Laura Winslow (Darius McCrary, Kellie Shaygne Williams) are the children of Chicago police officer Carl Winslow and his wife Harriette on ABC's *Family Matters*. Also on the series is Steve Urkel (Jaleel White), the nerd with an unrelenting crush on Laura. Sasha Mitchell plays Jeffrey Willis, a 16-year-old who works as a Cabana Boy at the El

Flamingo, a beach club on Long Island (N.Y.) on the ABC pilot *The Flamingo Kid* (based on the feature film). Jessica (Alyson Hannigan), Robb (Paul Scherner) and Gene (Edan Gross) are the children of a divorced attorney (Thomas J. Harper) who are watched over by Winnie Goodwin, a very pretty but slightly ditzy witch on *Free Spirit* (ABC). Attractive 15-year-old Becca Thatcher (Kellie Martin) is a bright high school girl who strives for straight A grades but feels her slowly developing figure is her greatest downfall on ABC's *Life Goes On*. Danny and Peter Matthews (Chris Young, David Moscow) are the teenage sons of a working couple who are looked after by Lisa Wells (Lisa Patrick), a beautiful live-in nanny on CBS's *Live-In*. Charlie Briscoe (Leah Remini), Emily Franklin (Halle Berry), Caroline Weldon (Deborah Tucker) and Martha Lambert (Alison Elliott) are gorgeous 16-year-old models on ABC's *Living Dolls*. Elizabeth and Robin Cooper (Marissa Ryan, Nicole Dubuc) are the teenage daughters of Polly Cooper, a widow who marries a tough marine sergeant (John MacGillis) on *Major Dad* (CBS). NBC's *Saved by the Bell* presented a number of teens at Bayside High School in Palisades, California, over the course of its eleven-year run. The following is a chronological listing of the principal teen stars: *1989–93:* Zack Morris (Mark-Paul Gosselaar), Kelly Kapowski (Tiffani-Amber Thiessen), Jesse Spano (Elizabeth Berkley), Lisa Turtle (Lark Voorhies), A.C. Slater (Mario Lopez) and Screech Powers (Dustin Diamond). *1992–93:* Leanna Creel joins the cast as Tori Scott. *1993–94:* Vickie Needleman (Bonnie Russavage), Lindsay Warner (Natalia Cigliuti), Megan Jones (Bianca Lawson), Scott Erickson (Robert Sutherland), Weasel Wyzell (Isaac Lindsky), Tommy DeLucca (Jonathan Angel). *1994–95:* Rachel Meyers (Sarah Lancaster), Brian Keller (Christian Oliver), Bobby Wilson (Spankee Rogers). *1995–96:* Maria Lopez (Samantha Becker), Ryan Parker (Richard Lee Jackson), R.J. Collins (Salim Grant). *1996–97:* Katie Peterson (Lindsey McKeon), Nicky Farina (Ben Gould), Eric Little (Anthony Harrell). *1997–98:* Ashley Lyn Cafagna joins the cast as student Liz Miller; Rachel (from 1994) is dropped. *1998–2000:* Tom Wade Huntington joins the cast as Tony Dillon; Ryan (from 1995) is dropped. April (Erin Reed), Freddie (Hannah Cutrona), Hilary (Pamela Segall) and Todd (Jason Priestley) are the main orphaned children residing at Redemption

House, a Catholic residence run by *Sister Kate* (NBC). Corin Nemec plays Alan Hoffstetter, a 17-year-old high school student who finds he can interact with various TV characters when he flips through the channels on the CBS pilot *What's Alan Watching?*

1990. Rachel Nash (Chay Lentin) is the pretty, always having boy problems daughter of widowed newspaper columnist Tom Nash on *American Dreamer* (NBC). Lillian Pinkerton (Hayley Brown) is a very pretty 13-year-old freshman who is struggling to fit into a new life at school where she is the tallest girl (five feet, eight inches) on the ABC pilot *Beanpole*. Brenda and Brandon Walsh (Shannen Doherty, Jason Priestley) are fraternal twins who attend West Beverly Hills High School on *Beverly Hills, 90210*. Also on the Fox series are their friends Kelly Taylor (Jennie Garth), Donna Martin (Tori Spelling), Steve Sanders (Ian Ziering) and Andrea Zuckerman (Andrea Carteris). Ericka (Jennie Garth), Christy (Alison Sweeney) and Bart (David Thomas) are the children of waitress Barbara McCray. Amanda (Shawnee Smith), Laird (Byron Thomas) and Barlow (Eric Foster) are the children of attorney Roger Gibbons. The eight become a family when Barbara and Roger marry on *Brand New Life* (NBC). Louanne Ponce plays Penny, the daughter of Liz Gianni, a widow who is a city manager on CBS's *City*. Thirteen-year-old Katie Larson, the daughter of marine scientist Michael Larson, finds an affinity with dolphins after a traumatic shock (the death of her mother in a car accident) makes her unable to speak on *Dolphin Cove* (CBS). Mia Kirshner plays Sophie Martineck, a teenage girl who teams with brothers Max and Chris Townsend (Jacob Tierney, Joe Roncetti) to destroy vampires on *Dracula: The Series* (Syn.). Holly Bankston (Juliette Lewis), her brother Nick (Dick Lascher) and their younger siblings Mary (Jessica Player) and Chris (Ben Savage) are cared for by Joe Whitaker (Robert Mitchum), a homeless man the kids "adopted" to pose as their uncle so they could remain a family after their parents' deaths in a plane crash on *A Family for Joe* (NBC). Ferris Bueller (Charlie Schlatter) is a carefree high school student who seems to get away with everything on NBC's *Ferris Bueller* (based on the film *Ferris Bueller's Day Off*). Ferris's sister, Jeannie (Jennifer Aniston) is beautiful, vicious and nasty (and proud of it) and longs for the day Ferris will get caught. Will Smith (himself), a Philadelphia teen headed for trouble, is sent to live with his aunt and uncle in Bel Air in the hopes of getting straightened out on *The Fresh Prince of Bel Air*. Also on the NBC series are his teenage cousins Hilary (Karyn Parsons), Carlton (Alfonso Riberio) and Ashley (Tatyana M. Ali). Staci Keanan plays Lindsay Bowen, a very pretty teenage girl who is best friends with Alexandra Burton, a TV writer on *Going Places* (ABC). Camilla Croft (Cheryl Pollak), D.J. Cameron (Kristin Dattilo) and Cody Rome (Harold Pruett) are the featured 16-year-old students attending *Hull High* (NBC). Annie and Kevin Porter (Jennifer Drugan, Robert Gavin) are engulfed by a time warp while in their camper with their father, Tom, and transported to a world of prehistoric creatures on *Land of the Lost* (ABC). Thirteen-year-old Kelly Callahan (Jenna Von Oy) and her 10-year-old sister Tracey (Alexis Caldwell) are the children of Boston utility gasman Lenny Callahan and his wife Shelly on *Lenny* (CBS). Life's ups and downs are seen through the eyes of Marshall Brightman (Joshua Rifkind), a high school student on *The Marshall Chronicles* (ABC). Mayim Bialik plays Molly Martin, a pretty 13-year-old professional actress who stars on the TV series "Wonderland" on *Molloy*. Also on the Fox series is Jennifer Aniston as Courtney, Molloy's gorgeous 16-year-old sister who is totally devoted to herself. Katie (Brigid Conley Walsh) is the daughter of Ellen Davis. Terry and Adam (Claude Brooks, Adam Jeffries) are the children of Ron Freeman. The children become a family when their parents marry on *True Colors* (Fox). Tia Russell (Dah-ve Chodan) is a 16-year-old girl who claims she has the technical skill to become a model right now ("I can walk and wear lip gloss at the same time") but also faces tough times at home as she is cared for by her late father's irresponsible bother Buck on *Uncle Buck* (CBS; based on the feature film). Raymond Kirkland (Dante Beze) is 18 and thinks he's pretty; Lorette (Caryn Ward) is 13 and desperately wants breasts to become popular. They are the children of hard working parents Nell and Michael Kirkland on *You Take the Kids* (CBS). Rodney Barnes (Jared Rushton) is a 14-year-old boy who receives help in coping with life from his idol, comedian Rodney Dangerfield, on the NBC pilot *Where's Rodney?* Jodie Stuart (Robin Lange) is the 17-year-old daughter of David Stuart, a divorced freelance photographer on *Working It Out* (NBC).

1991. Jeremy Jackson plays Hobie, the son of lifeguard Mitch Buchannon and his ex-wife, Gayle, on *Baywatch* (Syn). *The Belles of Bleecker Street* is an ABC pilot about Lindsay Alexander and Jo Jo Martinez (Melissa Clayton, Barbara Gonzalez), 13-year-old best friends who live on Bleecker Street in Manhattan. Charlotte and Kitty (Sara Marx, Courtney Peldon) are the teenage children of Rachel Flax (Shera Danese), a very sexy but flamboyant mother on the CBS pilot *Big Girls Don't Cry* (based on the feature film *Mermaids*). Blossom Russo (Mayim Bialik) and her brother Joey (Joey Lawrence) are the teenage children of divorced musician Nick Russo on NBC's *Blossom*. Also featured on the series is Jenna Von Oy as Six LeMeure, Blossom's fun-loving girlfriend. Melissa Joan Hart plays Clarissa Darling, a very pretty and energetic 13-year-old girl who speaks directly to the audience "to explain all the stuff that goes on around here" (her home in Baxter Beach, Florida) on *Clarissa Explains It All* (NIK). Carol-Ann Plante plays Sarah Henderson, a 16-year-old teen beauty who believes that she is the only normal member of a family that lives with a Big Foot named Harry on the syndicated *Harry and the Hendersons*. The well-endowed Babs Nielsen (Julie Benz), the daughter of Honey and Lloyd Nielsen, is a 1950s TV sitcom character transported to the 1990s (via the Sitcom Relocater Program) and struggling to adjust to a new life on *Hi Honey, I'm Home* (ABC). Dana and Kate Foster (Staci Keanan, Angela Watson) are the teenage daughters of widowed hair stylist Carol Foster (Suzanne Somers). Alicia and J.T. Lambert (Christine Lakin, Brandon Call) are the children of divorced contractor Frank Lambert (Patrick Duffy). Frank and Carol marry and their different as night and day children must learn to live with each other on ABC's *Step by Step*. Dorothy Jane Torkelson (Olivia Burnette) is a very sweet 14-year-old girl who lives in Pyramid Corners, Oklahoma, and hopes to one day find "a life of poetry, romance and beauty" on *The Torkelsons* (NBC).

1992. Bill Preston (Evan Richards) and Ted Logan (Christopher Kennedy) are teens who travel through time to ensure the future of their excellent society, San Demas, California, in the year 2692 on *Bill and Ted's Excellent Adventures* (Fox). Life in 1956 Brooklyn, New York, is seen through the eyes of Alan Silver (Danny Gerard), a 14-year-old Jewish boy, and his Catholic girlfriend Katie Monahan (Jenny Lewis) on *Brook-*

lyn Bridge (CBS). Jenny Garrison (Heidi Noelle Lenhart), Tiffany Smith (Kelly Packard), Tony Wickes (William James Jones), Samantha Woo (Jennie Kwan), Sly Winkle (Michael Cade) and Jake Sommers (Jay Anthony Franke) are members of a soft rock group called *California Dreams* (NBC). Brody and Melissa Wilder (Jerry O'Connell, Meghann Haldeman) are the brother and sister of Ricky Wilder (Mary Page Keller), a nurse who is caring for them after the death of their parents on *Camp Wilder* (ABC). Scott Melrod (Tobey Maguire) is a teenager who escapes real life by daydreaming he is a cool guy instead of a geek on *Great Scott* (Fox). Libby Kramer (Nicole Eggert) is a beautiful 18-year-old girl who believes her parents want her to always remain their little girl; Jesse (Jarrod Paul), her 14-year-old brother, is obsessed with driving. They are the children of Ted and Anne Kramer, a couple with numerous problems on NBC's *Home Fires*. Allie (Hayley Tyrie) and Adam (Rider Strong) are the children of Sam McGuire, a veterinarian who is married to TV show star Julie Carlisle on *Julie* (ABC). Parker Lewis (Corin Nemec) is an enterprising high school student who comes out on top no matter what happens to him on *Parker Lewis Can't Lose* (Fox). Parker's 13-year-old sister, Shelly Ann (Maia Brewton), lives for the day she can get the goods on Parker and expose him. Kimberly Brock (Holly Marie Combs) is the 16-year-old daughter of Rome, Wisconsin, sheriff Sam Brock and his wife Jill on CBS's *Picket Fences*. The series also features Kimberly's younger siblings Matthew and Zachary (Justin Shenkarow, Adam Wylie). Thirteen-year-old Jessica Stevens (Rhea Silver-Smith) is a girl who possesses a most unusual pet — Scorch, a 100-year-old fire breathing dragon — on *Scorch* (CBS). Jennifer Love Hewitt plays Bernadette Moody. Bradley Pierce and Matthew Brooks are her brothers Dillon and Carter, the children of Bob Moody and his wife Helen on *Shaky Ground* (Fox). Joey Adams plays Mona Williams, an absolutely gorgeous 17-year-old girl who has an unrelenting crush on Vinnie Verducci (Matt LeBlanc), an older man who is trying to avoid Mona's advances (she is underage and her father owns a gun shop) on *Vinnie and Bobby* (Fox; Bobby [Robert Torti] is Vinnie's roommate).

1993. Molly (Brittany Murphy) and Gregory (Jason Marsden) are called "Beelzebub" and "Mephistopheles" by their father, attorney Brian Morgan, for all the trouble they cause on *Almost Home* (NBC). Morgan Nagler is Amy Gennaro, the 14-year-old daughter of househusband Joe Gennaro and his wife Sandy, a Temp Jobs employee on *Joe's Life* (ABC). The Fox series *The Mighty Morphin Power Rangers* tells the story of ordinary teenagers who are endowed with special powers by aliens to battle evil from outer space. Among the stars are Austin St. James, Thuy Trang, Amy Jo Johnson, Walter Jones and David Yost. Maggie Sheffield (Nicolle Tom) is the 14-year-old daughter of Broadway producer Maxwell Sheffield and cared for by her nanny Fran Fine on *The Nanny* (CBS). Angela Goethals plays Angela Doolan, a natural born tennis player who is struggling to balance her life between practices, matches and high school on ABC's *Phenom*. Judith Light is Angela's mother, Diane; Ashley Johnson is Angela's younger sister, Mary Margaret; and Todd Louiso is Angela's older brother, Brian.

1994. Franny, Harry and Zeke (Jennifer Love Hewitt, Seth Green, Ryan O'Donohue) are the children of Sam Byrd, a widowed college professor who is attempting to start a new life for his family in Hawaii after the death of his wife on *The Byrds of Paradise* (ABC). Alicia Levitch plays Nicki, "a 14-year-old budding bombshell" and the daughter of Denise Lerner, an architect, and her husband Jonathan on *Family Album* (CBS). Fifteen-year-old Liberty High School student Angela Chase (Claire Danes) struggles to cope with friends, family and first loves despite her gloomy and narrow outlook on life on ABC's *My So-Called Life*. Bailey Salinger (Scott Wolf) and his sister Julia (Neve Campbell) are students at Grant High School in San Francisco on Fox's *Party of Five*. Alexandra Mack, called Alex (Larisa Oleynik), is a 13-year-old girl who acquires extraordinary powers when she is exposed to a chemical called GC 161 on *The Secret World of Alex Mack*. Also on the Nickelodeon series is Meredith Bishop as Annie, Alex's 16-year-old sister and the only other person who knows her secret. Tia Landry (Tia Mowry) and Tamera Campbell (Tamera Mowry) are identical twins, separated at birth, who are reunited 14 years later to become sisters again on *Sister, Sister* (ABC/WB). Nikki Cox plays Samantha Stepjak, a gorgeous 16-year-old high school student who believes being beautiful will solve all of life's problems on NBC's *Someone Like Me*. Sam Collins (Matthew Lawrence), Sydney Forrester (Robin Mary Florence) and Amp (Troy

Slaten) are teenagers who attend North Valley High School on *The Super Human Samurai Syber Squad* (Syn.). Sam heads a band called Teen Samurai and due to a freak accident (shocked by his computer) he can enter the computer realm to battle evil as Servo. Elizabeth and Jessica Wakefield (Cynthia and Brittany Daniel) are gorgeous twins who attend Sweet Valley High School on the syndicated *Sweet Valley High*. Mike and Trevor (Jason Marsden, Josh Stoppelwerth) and their twin sisters Charlotte and Emily (Tiffany and Kathryn Lubran) are the children of Tom Graham, a welder who dreams of building a farmhouse, and his wife Dorothy on *Tom* (CBS).

1995. Jenny and Brian (Marguerite Moreau, Justin Garms) are the children of Hannah Miller, pastor of the Lakeview Church on *Amazing Grace* (NBC). NBC's *Hang Time* is a teen comedy set at Deering High School. Principal focus is on Julie Conner (Danielle Deutscher), the only girl on the varsity basketball team; Samantha Morgan (Hillary Tuck), the team manager (her dream is to become a coach), and Mary Beth Pepperton (Megan Parlen), a beautiful material girl and the daughter of rich parents. *Time Well Spent* is an ABC pilot about Kenny, Lloyd and Bobby (Ryan Phillips, Johnny Strong, Alexis Cruz), friends who attend Harry S. Truman High School. Nikki Cox plays Tiffany Malloy, a stunning teenage girl who knows she is beautiful and uses that to her best advantage to get what she wants on *Unhappily Ever After* (WB). On the other hand, Tiffany's brother Ryan (Kevin Connelly) is quite naïve and in his own words, "a loser girls find completely repulsive."

1996. Cher Horowitz (Rachel Blanchard), Dee Davenport (Stacey Dash) and Amber Mariens (Elisa Donovan) are three beautiful, rich friends who attend the posh Bronson Alcott High School in Beverly Hills on *Clueless* (ABC/UPN; based on the feature film). Brandy Norwood plays Moesha Mitchell, a 15-year-old high school girl who hopes to become a journalist on *Moesha* (UPN). Veronica (Veronica Blume), Peg (Brooke Burns) and Max (Paulo Benedeti) are teens who work together at a marine life park in Florida on the syndicated *Out of the Blue*. Sabrina Spellman (Melissa Joan Hart) is a pretty 16-year-old witch who is just discovering and learning how to use her powers on *Sabrina, the Teenage Witch* (ABC/WB). Mary (Jessica Beal), Matt (Brian Watson) and Lucy (Beverley Mitchell) are the

teenage children of Reverend Eric Camden and his wife Annie on the WB's *7th Heaven*. As the series progressed, younger children Simon (David Gallagher) and Ruthie (Mackenzie Rosman) also became teenagers. Marnette Patterson plays Nicole and Emily Ann Lloyd is her younger sister Sarah, the children of a blended family when their three times divorced father, Jack, marries Carly, a twice divorced woman on NBC's *Something So Right*.

1997. Ashley Dupree (Terri Conn), Tony Gifford (Richard Cox) and Cassidy Cartwright (Wendi Kenyan) are among the students at Breaker High School who are spending a semester at sea on *Breaker High* (UPN). Sarah Michelle Gellar is 16-year-old Buffy Summers, a girl called "The Chosen One," who fights vampires and other unearthly creatures on *Buffy the Vampire Slayer* (WB/UPN). Buffy's 14-year-old sister, Dawn (Michelle Trachtenberg), joins the cast in 2000. Chris Anderson (Scott Whyte) and Jammal Grant (Wesley Jonathan) are the *City Guys* (NBC), students at Manhattan High School in New York City. Amy (Hillary Tuck) and her younger brother, near genius Nicholas (Thomas Dekker), are the offspring of inventor Wayne Szlinski and his wife Diane, an attorney, on *Honey I Shrunk the Kids: The TV Series* (Syn.). Zaria Peterson (Reagan Gomez-Preston) is the studious daughter of college professor Robert Peterson and his wife Geri on *The Parent'Hood* (WB). Camela (Charlotte Sullivan), Emily (Erica Luttrell) and Strick (Kristian Ayre) solve minor crimes with the help of an entity called Ghost Writer on *The New Ghost Writer Mysteries* (CBS). Teenager Steve Beauchamp (Corbin Allred) finds he has a guardian angel when his late friend Marty De-Polo (Mike Damus) returns to guide his life on *Teen Angel* (ABC).

1998. Whitney (Angelica Chitwood), Erin (Bethany Santiago), Brian (James Serbel) and Robert (Adam Ward) are teens who learn about science through practical demonstrations on the syndicated *Algo's Factory*. Dawson Leery (James Van Der Beek), Josephine Potter (Katie Holmes), Jennifer Lindley (Michelle Williams) and Joshua Jackson (Pacey Witter) are teens struggling through adolescence in the small coastal town of Capeside near Boston on *Dawson's Creek* (WB). The transformation of Felicity Porter (Keri Russell) from teen to young woman is seen on *Felicity* (WB) as she moves from the West Coast to

New York to attend college. Karen and Dave Blake are a childless couple who are the adoptive parents of five children on NBC's *One World*: Jane (Arroyn Lloyd), Ben (Bryan Kirkwood), Marcie (Alisa Reyes), Sue (Michelle Krusiec) and Neil (Harvey Silver). Life in 1970s Wisconsin is seen through the eyes of Eric Foreman (Topher Grace), Donna Pincietti (Laura Prepon), Michael Kelso (Ashton Krutcher) and Fez (Wilmer Valderrama), four friends on *That 70s Show* (Fox).

1999. Seventeen-year-old Hope Harrison (Maggie Lawson) considers herself to be cool. Anne (Shawna Waldron), her 16-year-old sister, is extremely bright while 14-year-old sister C.J. (Andi Eystad) is a bit kooky and a bit irresponsible. They are the children of Nate Harrison, a widowed high school basketball coach on *Family Rules* (UPN). Amanda Bynes is the host and star of *The Amanda Show*, a series of skits geared to children (NIK). *Freaks and Geeks* is an NBC sitcom that focuses on the lives of a group of less-than-popular teenagers in 1980s Detroit. Becky Ann Baker, James Franco, Sammi Levine and Seth Rogen head a large cast. Scott and Jason Collins (Trevor Merszei, Jason Hayes) are brothers who work as waiters for their father, Peter, the owner of the Lighthouse, a seafood restaurant in California on the syndicated *Malibu, Ca.* Marnette Patterson plays Lori Harden, the glamorous daughter of action film star Reese Harden on *Movie Stars* (WB). Paige Whitney (Natalia Cigliuti) is a gorgeous 16-year-old South Beach, Florida, high school girl who yearns to be a model on ABC's *Odd Man Out.* Also on the series are Erik Von Detten as Andrew, Paige's brother (the only male in an all-female house), and her younger sisters Elizabeth (Marina Malota) and Val (Vicki Davis), all the children of single mother Julia Whitney. Countess Vaughn plays Kim Parker, a student at Santa Monica Junior College (the same college being attended by her mother Nikki), on *The Parkers* (UPN). Also featured is Jenna Von Oy as Stevie Van Lowe, Kim's best friend. The WB's *Popular* revolves around the escapades of a group of students at John F. Kennedy High School in Los Angles. Samantha McPherson (Carly Pope), a reporter for the school newspaper; Brooke McQueen (Leslie Bibb), a cheerleader; Mary Cherry (Leslie Grossman), the spoiled daughter of a rich mother; Nicole Julian (Tammy Lynn Michaels), "the daughter of a knocked-up 16-year-old cheerleader who gave birth to me in the rest room of a

greasy spoon"; Sugar Daddy (Ron Lester), a heavy set Caucasian who has immersed himself in black culture; and Lily Esposito (Tamara Mello), an insecure girl who wishes people will like her. Essence Atkins is Yvette Henderson, a bright and beautiful high school girl, and Jason Weaver is her less intelligent brother, Marcus, the siblings of T.J., a 12-year-old genius on *Smart Guy* (WB). The relationship between four close high school friends in New York City is the focus of the WB's *Zoe, Duncan, Jack and Jane.* Selma Blair stars as Zoe Bean, with David Moscow as Duncan Milch, Michael Rosenberg as Jack Cooper and Azure Skye as Jane Cooper, Jack's sister.

2000. Alexis Bledel plays Rory Gilmore, the 16-year-old, obedient, addicted to coffee, straight A student of single mom Lorelai Gilmore (Lauren Graham) on *Gilmore Girls* (WB). Francis (Christopher Kennedy Masterson) is the troublesome son of Hal and Lois on *Malcolm in the Middle.* Also featured on the Fox series are Malcolm (Frankie Muniz), the intellectual brother; Reese (Justin Berfield), the brother who can find trouble anywhere; and Dewey (Erik Per Sullivan), the sly and cunning brother. Riley Veatch (Katherine Towne) is a 16-year-old girl who is aware that she is a character on a TV series and comments on and off camera about the situations that arise on *M.Y.O.B.* (NBC). Cheyenne (JoAnna Garcia) and Kyra (Scarlett Pomers) are the children of single mother Reba Hart on *Reba* (WB).

2001. The close friendship between four Belmont High School friends is the focal point of NBC's *All About Us.* Alecia Alcott (Alecia Elliott) hates confrontation and hopes to become a singer; Christine Castelli (Alicia Lagano) excels in sports, especially basketball; Nikki Merrick (Marieh Delfino) is self-centered and has a positive attitude about everything; and Sierra Jennings (Crystal Grant) is a careful planner and teen feminist activist. Ren Stevens (Christy Carlson Romano) is a very pretty 15-year-old girl who is not only smart but also obsessed with being perfect on *Even Stevens* (Disney). The series also features Shai LaBeouf as Louis Stevens, Ren's conniving younger brother. Lily Finnerty (Lynsey Bartilson) is a 14-year-old student at St. Finian's High School who is a bit defiant and believes in flaunting her sexuality to get what she wants on *Grounded for Life* (Fox/WB; when Lily turned 16 she lost her virginity in a storyline that sent the wrong message to teenage viewers, as it appeared to advocate teenage sex). Lizzie McGuire (Hilary Duff) and her friends Miranda (La Laine) and Gordo (Adam Lamberg) are 13-year-old students at Eldridge Elementary School and facing the ups and downs of life as they prepare for high school on *Lizzie McGuire* (Disney). Fifteen-year-old Molly Stage (Reagan Dale Neis) lives in Rhode Island, attends Wicketstown High School, is an expert at chess and believes she is the only normal one in her eccentric family on *Maybe It's Me* (WB). Claire Kyle (Jazz Raycole, Jennifer Freeman) and the lesser intelligent Michael Kyle, Jr. (George O. Gore II) are the teenage children of Michael and Jay Kyle on ABC's *My Wife and Kids*. Fourteen-year-old Breanna Barnes (Kyla Pratt) is a cheerleader at McKinley High School who hopes to become an actress on UPN's *One on One*. Fourteen-year-old Penny Proud (voice of Kyla Pratt) is a girl struggling to live a normal life despite an over protective father (Oscar), an over loving mother (Trudy), an all-knowing grandmother, and her mischievous siblings, twins Bee Bee and Cee Cee on the animated *Proud Family* (Disney). Sarah Stewart (Kat Denning) is a student at Great Barrington High School in Massachusetts and holds a job at a bookstore called Pulp 'n' Fiction on *Raising Dad* (WB).

2002. Seventeen-year-old Meg Pryor (Brittany Snow) and her friend Roxanne (Vanessa Lengies) are students at East Catholic High School in Philadelphia during the 1960s on *American Dreams* (NBC). Also featured is Sarah Ramos as Patty Pryor, Meg's 13-year-old sister. Bridget Hennessey (Kaley Cuoco) and her sister Kerry (Amy Davidson) are the daughters of Paul and Cate Hennessey on ABC's *Eight Simple Rules for Dating My Teenage Daughter* (like *Grounded for Life* [see 2001] a 16-year-old girl lost her virginity. Here it was Kerry, but the wrong message was not sent. Kerry regretted what she did and made sure the message got across). Ephram Brown (Gregory Smith) and his younger sister Delia (Vivien Cardone) are the children of Andrew Brown, a doctor who relocates to Everwood, Colorado, after the death of his wife in a car accident to begin a new life on *Everwood* (WB). Caitlin Wachs plays Sigourney Davis, better known as Cissy, the bright 13-year-old girl who comes to live with her bachelor uncle, Bill Davis (Gary Cole) after the death of her parents on *Family Affair* (WB; see also 1966). Carmen Lopez (Marsiela Lusha) is a very pretty 16-year-old girl who

likes things her way and is eager to grow up and become a woman on *The George Lopez Show* (ABC). Life in a multicultural family living in Tucson, Arizona, is seen through the eyes of David Tiant (Pablo Santos), the 15-year-old son of Joaquin and Elizabeth Tiant on *Greetings from Tucson*. Also on the WB series is Sara Paxton as Sarah, Pablo's neighbor and girlfriend. Kim Possible (voice of Christy Carlson Romano) is a high school girl struggling to live a normal life while at the same time risking her life to save the world from villains on the animated *Kim Possible* (Disney). Renee Olstead is Lauren, the vivacious daughter of Bill and Judy Miller, and Taylor Ball is Brian, her boarding on genius brother on *Still Standing* (CBS). Adorable 14-year-old Holly Tyler (Amanda Bynes) struggles to cope with life in New York City while living with her older sister Valerie (Jennie Garth) on *What I Like About You* (WB).

2003. Sydney (Nicole Paggi, Megan Fox) and Hayley (Macey Cruthird) are the children of Charlie Shanoski, a dentist, and his wife Hope, the sister of soap star Faith Fairfield, on ABC's *Hope and Faith*. Also on the series is Justin (Paulie Litt), Hope's younger son. Joan Girardi (Amber Tamblyn) is a 16-year-old high school girl God has chosen to perform minor miracles on *Joan of Arcadia* (CBS). Also on the series are Kevin (Jason Ritter), her older brother, and Luke (Michael Welsh), her younger sibling. Danika (Megalyn Echikunwoke) is the teenage daughter of Ed and Tanya Ward. Her younger brother is Bobby (B.J. Mitchell). They live with Diane Farr, Tanya's best friend, and her teenage son Keith (J. Mack Slaughter) on the WB's *Like Family*. Kate Redding (Brooke Harmon) is a teenager girl who, with her younger siblings Sarah (Eliza Taylor Cotter) and Nicholas (Nicholas Donaldson) are zapped into a video game and become lost in a world of pirates and mysterious islands on *Pirate Islands* (Fox). Margo Harshman is Brooke Franklin, an alluring 15-year-old girl who is being watched over by her older brother Kurt (Joseph Lawrence) while their parents are away on *Run of the House* (WB). Josie Trent (Emma Taylor Isherwood) is a student at Blake Holsey High School where students excel in science and where strange phenomena occur on *Strange Days at Blake Holsey High* (NBC). San Francisco teen Raven Baxter (Raven Symone) is a girl with psychic abilities that allow her to see brief events in the future on *That's So Raven* (Disney).

2004. Sam, T.J., Kyle and Chris (Andrew Eiden, Jason Dolley, Evan Ellingson, Erik Von Detten) are the unpredictable children of Nick Savage, a single father with little control over them on *Complete Savages* (ABC). Fourteen-year-old Darcy Fields (Sara Paxton) struggles to adjust to a new life on a rural working farm in the town of Bailey when her actress mother, Victoria, leaves the glamorous Hollywood life behind her on *Darcy's Wild Life* (NBC). ABC's *Desperate Housewives* presents several teens: Andrea Bowen as Julie, the daughter of single mother Susan Mayer; Joy Lauren and Shawn Pyfrom as Danielle and Andrew, the offspring of Bree and Rex Van DeKamp; and Cody Kasch as Zack, the son of the series narrator, Mary Alice Young, the housewife who committed suicide and now looks back on her friends on Wisteria Lane. Drake Parker (Drake Bell) and Josh Nichols (Josh Peck) are stepbrothers (Audrey, Drake's mother, married Walter, Josh's father) who find trouble everywhere on *Drake and Josh* (NIK). Sex-on-the-mind teenagers living in Seattle is the focal point of ABC's *Life as We Know It*. Among the teens are Dino Whitman (Sean Faris), Ben Conner (Jon Foster) and Jonathan Fields (Chris Lowell). Megan (Daniella Monet) and her less intelligent brother Mickey (Will Rothaar) are the children of TV show host Tony Kleinman and his wife Dana on *Listen Up* (CBS). Phil and Pim (Ricky Ullman, Amy Bruckner) are the children of Lloyd and Barbara Diffy, a futuristic family (from the year 2121) who are stranded in the present time due to a malfunctioning time machine on *Phil of the Future* (Disney). Penny (April Matson), Paige (Sarah Wright), Patton (Ryan Pinkston), Parker (Jake McDorman) and Pearce (Johnny Lewis) are the 15-year-old quintuplets of Bob and Carol Chase on *Quintuplets* (Fox). Kay Panabaker plays Nikki Westerly and Nick Benson and Jesse McCartney are her brothers, Nick and Bradin, orphans who come to live with their aunt Ava Gregory in California after the death of their parents on *Summerland* (WB). Veronica Mars (Kristen Bell) is a stunningly beautiful 16-year-old Neptune High School student who works as a detective for her father, Keith, the owner of Mars Investigations on UPN's *Veronica Mars*.

2005. Life in Brooklyn, New York, as seen through the eyes of comedian Chris Rock when he was 13 years old (Tyler James Williams) is the focal point of *Everybody Hates Chris*. The UPN series also features Chris's younger siblings, Tonya (Imani Hakim) and Drew (Teaquam Richmond), all the children of Julius and Rochelle Rock. Jackson (Johnny Pacer), Daley (Hallee Hirsh), Melissa (Kristy Wu), Taylor (Lauren Storm) and Lex (Allen Alvarado) are among the teenagers stranded on a desolate island after their plane is struck by lightning and forced to crash land on *Flight 29 Down* (NBC). Chloe Suazo is Zoey, the 13-year-old daughter of Sophia Moreno, the divorced sister of restaurant owner Freddie Moreno on ABC's *Freddie*. The carefree Derek (Michael Seater) and the drama queen Casey (Ashley Leggat) find mishaps when Derek's father George Venturi marries Casey's mother, Norma McDonald on *Life with Derek* (Disney). Misti Traya plays Allison, the very pretty 16-year-old daughter of Fran Reeves, an interior decorator who is dating a younger man (Riley) on *Living with Fran*. Also on the WB series is Ben Feldman as Josh, Fran's medical school drop out son. Sadie (Charlotte Arnold) is a brainy teenage girl who attempts to use her knowledge of animal behavior to solve problems on *Naturally Sadie* (Disney). Life among a group of teens in the small town of Palmetto Pointe is the focus of *Palmetto Pointe*, the inaugural series for I-TV (Independent Television), a new broadcast network. Among the teens are Melinda Gale (Nina Repeta), Callie O'Connor (Amanda Baker), Logan James (Brent Lovell) and Lacy Timberline (Madison Weidberg). Spencer and Glen Carlin (Gabrielle Christian, Chris Hunter), the teenage children of Arthur and Paula Carlin, attempt to adjust to a new life in California after relocating from Ohio on *South of Nowhere* (The N [Noggin]). Brenda Song plays London Tipton, the spoiled daughter of the owner of the Tipton Hotel on *The Suite Life of Zack and Cody*. Also on the Disney series is Ashley Tisdale as Maddie, the hotel's teenage gift shop clerk. Kaylee DeFer is Hillary and Kyle Sullivan is Larry, the teen children of Dave and Vicky on *The War at Home* (Fox). Hillary is the normal high school girl; Larry appears to be a cross dresser and is believed by his parents to be gay. Jamie Lynn Spears plays Zoey Brooks, a teenage girl who becomes the first female student to enroll in the previously all male Pacific Coast Academy on *Zoey 101* (NIK).

Television Firsts

Over the course of 80 years television has produced many firsts, a number of which can be found in the various entries in this book. This entry is a condensed listing of many of those firsts, placed here as an important document on the history of television.

1925. Moving pictures are broadcast over radio station WNOF in Washington, D.C., by television pioneer Francis C. Jenkins.

1926. A weather map is broadcast from the Jenkins Labs in Washington, D.C. (over radio station WNAA), to the National Weather Bureau in Washington.

1927. Comedian Milton Berle appears in very primitive TV transmissions as does the image of the cartoon character Felix the Cat. It is also at this time that the first political broadcast occurs: Secretary of Commerce Herbert Hoover's speech is simulcast (over radio and TV) from Washington, D.C., on April 7. The event also marks the first known simulcast of a radio and TV broadcast (also the first remote news cast).

1928. The Bell Telephone Labs experiments with outdoor broadcasting on July 12. *The Queen's Messenger* by J. Hartley Masters is the first stage play to be broadcast on TV by station WGY in Schenectady, New York.

1931. Kate Smith becomes the first singer to appear on TV when she helps CBS launch its inaugural TV station, W2XAB, on July 21. *Half-Hour on Broadway* (August 1) becomes the first musical variety series; *Punch and Judy* (August 18) becomes the first puppet series; and *Musical Miniatures* (August 27) becomes the first comedy variety series to air. Also on this date, CBS premieres the first anthology series *The Television Ghost* (referring to an unseen narrator).

1932. The first drama series, *Character Slants*, premieres on CBS (June 30). The network also broadcasts the first political campaign (the Democratic National Convention) on October 11.

1936. Jack Kirkland and Erskine Caldwell star in *Tobacco Road*, the first dramatic monologue (NBC, July 7). The first comedy series, *The Honeymooners*, premieres on NBC on September 21. The program, adapted from the radio series, stars Eddie Albert and Grace Brandt.

1938. *Return of the Scarlet Pimpernel* becomes the first motion picture to be broadcast on TV (over NBC's New York station W2XBS).

1939. Ethel Waters becomes the first known black performer to appear on TV on NBC's *Variety Over the Air* (June 14) wherein she performs a scene from the Broadway play *Mamba's Daughters* (the program is also known as *The Ethel Waters Show*). The Walt Disney theatrical cartoon, *Donald's Cousin Gus*, is the first known cartoon to air on TV. *The Pirates of Penzance*, broadcast by NBC, becomes the first opera to be performed on TV. President Franklin Delano Roosevelt speaks at the opening ceremonies of the New York World's Fair. NBC airs TV's first beauty pageant, *The World's Fair Beauty Contest*. NBC also airs TV's first western, *Missouri Legend* and a Los Angeles station broadcasts the first soap opera locally called *Vine Street*.

1940. On March 6 NBC/RCA and United Airlines experimented with lightweight TV equipment by spot telecasting from an airplane. A scene of New York City was telecast from a height of 2,000 feet. The Ringling Brothers and Barnum & Bailey Circus, broadcast by CBS from Madison Square Garden, becomes the first telecast of a circus on TV.

1941. CBS broadcasts a 20-minute over-the-air color broadcast using its mechanical wheel system (which eventually lost out to RCA's development of the color picture tube). The NBC experiment *Bottlenecks of 1941* inaugurates commercial broadcasting on American TV. On July 1, NBC broadcast the first sponsored programs (contained within the *Bottlenecks* program): *Lowell Thomas Reporting, Truth or Consequences* and *Uncle Jim's Question Bee*. Sunoco Oil and Ivory Soap became TV's pioneering sponsors. CBS airs the first children's series, *Jack and the Beanstalk*. NBC airs the first game show, *Play the Game*.

1943. DuMont airs its first game show, *Let's See*; CBS broadcasts its first game show, *The Missus Goes a Shopping*.

1944. NBC produces *Miracle at Blaise*, the first TV program about a war (World War II) that was still under way at the time (see *World War II*). World famous clown Emmett Kelly appears on TV for the first time on *Side Show*.

1945. NBC broadcasts the first miniseries, *The Black Angel*, which was shown over four nights, with Mary Patton, Phil Foster and Richard Keith. ABC airs its first game show, *King's Record Shop*. *Folksay* is the first ballet to be performed on TV (on CBS). The Macy's Thanksgiving Day Parade is broadcast on television for the first time. President Harry S. Truman makes his first live TV appearance at the Navy Day Special in New York's Central Park. *The Queen Was in the Kitchen* becomes the first TV program to feature cooking.

1946. Ernest Jones, a one-legged golf pro, becomes the first handicapped person to appear on TV on the interview program *Look Who's Here* (DuMont). Live action is mixed with animation for the first time on *Shorty* (see *Cartoons* for information).

1948. Sex symbol Marilyn Monroe, a struggling actress at the time, makes her TV debut (paid $10) on a local Los Angeles program called *Yer Ole Buddy*. DuMont airs the first infomercial (although not called this at the time; it was just a special broadcast), a 30-minute plug for the kid line of clothes at Macy's Department Store on *Tots, Tweens and Teens.*

1949. NBC broadcasts the first presidential inaugural (of Harry S. Truman's second term).

1950. Live models are used to advertise bras (for Exquisite Form) for the first time on TV. Objections immediately ended the campaign and it would not be until 1987 that live models were once again used to advertise lingerie. ABC experiments with color broadcasting with its ill-fated CTI system (a modified black and white RCA TV).

1951. Anna May Wong is the first Oriental to star in a series about an Asian on DuMont's *The Gallery of Mme. Liu Tsong. The Cisco Kid* is the first series to be filmed in color (although broadcast in black and white). CBS inaugurates commercial broadcasting with a five-city hookup (New York, Philadelphia, Baltimore, Washington and Boston).

1952. *I Love Lucy* is the first series to deal with the issues of pregnancy and to show, as much as was permitted at the time, a pregnant woman on TV.

1953. Accidental nudity occurs on TV for the first time when actress Faye Emerson, known for wearing low cut gowns, slips out of her dress and exposes her breasts on live TV.

1954. The birth of a baby is shown in somewhat graphic detail (for the time) on the series *The Search.* Although simplistic, TV's first catfight occurs on *I Love Lucy* when Lucy Ricardo attempts to make wine and gets into a brawl with a fellow grape crusher (in 1980, TV's first real cat fight occurs between Joan Collins and Linda Evans in the pond on *Dynasty*).

1955. Dwight D. Eisenhower becomes the first president to give a news conference; several months later (on June 7) he becomes the first president to be seen in color when he addresses the cadets at West Point. *Entertainment 1955* becomes the first color program to be broadcast from NBC's new Burbank studios.

1956. Teenage heartthrob Elvis Presley creates a sensation when he appears on *The Ed Sullivan Show* (but because of his swiveling hips, he is only seen from the waist up).

1960. The first televised presidential debates are seen between Senator John F. Kennedy and Vice President Richard M. Nixon. Wilma Flintstone becomes the first animated character to experience pregnancy on *The Flintstones.*

1962. Luke and Kate McCoy become the first married couple to be seen sleeping in the same bed (as opposed to twin beds separated by a night table) on *The Real McCoys.*

1964. The Beatles create a worldwide sensation when they appear on American TV for the first time on *The Ed Sullivan Show.*

1965. On October 24, NBC becomes the first network to begin a thirty-minute nightly newscast with *The Huntley-Brinkley Report.*

1966. *Star Trek* premieres on NBC and later raises eyebrows when Captain Kirk and Lieutenant Uhura (William Shatner, Nichelle Nichols) inaugurate TV's first interracial kiss.

1971. The controversial *All in the Family* premieres on CBS. While noted for a number of things, like bigotry, adult topics and bathroom humor, the series was also the first to deal with the issues of rape and menopause in graphic terms.

1973. Valerie Perrine is the first actress to purposely expose her breasts on TV in the PBS special *Steambath.*

1975. *The Jeffersons* presents TV's first interracial couple — Tom Willis (white) and his wife, Helen (black).

1977. Though not between lesbians, the first girl/girl lip kiss occurs between Penny Marshall and Cindy Williams on *Laverne and Shirley* (see Lesbians). The actual birth of a baby is shown — in all its graphic detail — on the TV movie *Having Babies II.*

1978. Actress Jane Russell becomes the first celebrity to endorse and star in a series of commercials for the Playtex 18 Hour Bra.

1981. *Here It Is, Burlesque,* an HBO special,

brings nudity into the living room with the show's star, stripper Tami Roche.

1987. Playtex changes the face of lingerie advertising when it incorporates live models to once again sell lingerie (see 1950). Alex Trebek, Meredith MacRae and Richard Simmons host *VTV* (Value Television), the first game show (syndicated) to offer home viewers merchandise at greatly reduced prices (via a toll free number)

1993. Broadcast TV allows a nude scene (breasts) for the CBS TV movie *My Breast* (wherein Meredith Baxter plays a victim of breast cancer).

1998. Full frontal nudity is seen for the first time via Angelina Jolie on the HBO TV movie *Gia*.

1999. John Carpenter becomes the first person to win TV's largest cash prize (at the time) — $1 million on *Who Wants to Be a Millionaire*.

2004. Ken Jennings wins $2,520,200 on *Jeopardy*, making him the highest cash winner ever on TV (Ken won the money over a 75-day reign as champion from June 2 to November 30).

2002. Kelly Clarkson becomes the first *American Idol*.

2005. On November 21, Maria Wenglinsky becomes the first woman to win more than $122,000 on *Jeopardy* (a non-tournament record).

Time Travel

This entry chronicles the programs on which time travel is an essential part of the premise.

1952. *Captain Z-Ro* (Syn.). A mysterious man known only as Captain Z-Ro (Roy Steffins) created an elaborate computer that permitted time travel (via the Lectric Chamber) when the Cycle Reactor was activated ("which cracks the fourth dimension and ejects us back into time").

1953. *Space Patrol* (ABC). Three years after its premiere in 1950, time travel was introduced and has been accomplished through a magnetic time drive (that was installed in a rocket ship called the *XRC* [Experimental Rocket Ship]). It was first used to travel from the series 30th century setting to Earth in the year 1956.

1959. *Peabody's Improbable History* (ABC). Animated smart dog (Mr. Peabody) and his boy assistant (Sherman) travel back in time via the Way Back Machine.

1966. *The Time Tunnel* (ABC). Tic Toc Base

in Arizona is the secret government locale for the Time Tunnel, a 7½ billion dollar experiment concerned with time travel. Massive atomic turbines and elaborate computers enable man to travel through time. Before a subject is sent in time he must take a radioactive bath to enable the tunnel engineers to track him through a magnetic fix. The system suffers from one serious flaw: it cannot retrieve a traveler once he is sent into time — "yesterday, today or a million years from now."

1973. *Doctor Who* (Syn.). Time Lords on the planet Gallifrey are concerned with time travel and have developed a futuristic time machine called a TARDIS (Time and Relative Dimensions in Space). Its original shape is a metal cabinet with a sliding door. However, once activated it has the ability to disguise itself in the surroundings in which it lands. The Time Lord viewers see is called Doctor Who and his TARDIS has a malfunction that is stuck in the guise of a 1960s police call booth (a telephone booth). The Time Lords accomplished time travel through a source of power called the Eye of Harmony, a large black stone that contains awesome forces.

1976. *Time Travelers* (ABC pilot). Scientists Clinton Earnshaw (Sam Groom) and Jeff Adams (Tom Hallick) created a time machine that enables them to travel back in time to learn from the past to help for the future.

1979. *Time Express* (CBS). A special train called the Time Express takes people back in time to alter important moments in their pasts. Subjects, selected by an unseen person (the head of the line), receive a ticket and board at Union Station, Gate 6, Track 13 in California.

1981. *Through the Magic Pyramid* (NBC pilot). Bobby Tutt (Christopher Daniel Barnes) is a young boy who can travel through time via a magic pyramid he received as a birthday gift. By holding the crystal and concentrating, Bobby can transport himself into any period in time.

1982. *Voyagers!* (NBC). Phineas Bogg (Jon-Erik Hexum) is a Voyager, a traveler in time who helps correct history's mistakes. While not explained in the actual series, the altered home video release, *Voyager from the Unknown*, explains that Bogg was born on the planet Voyager, where its inhabitants are concerned with time travel. Such travel is made possible by a hand held Omni, a link to a massive computer complex that allows time travel and monitors Voyagers as they do their jobs.

1989. *Quantum Leap* (NBC). Quantum Leap is a secret government project concerned with time travel. It was created by Sam Beckett (Scott Bakula) and is run by a massive computer complex he calls Ziggy. A subject enters the Acceleration Chamber and leaps (travels) within thirty years of his or her own lifetime. Sam's purpose for building Ziggy was to go back in time to correct history's mistakes "to make right what was once wrong."

1991. *Back to the Future* (CBS cartoon). An adaptation of the *Back to the Future* movies that follows Doc Brown (Christopher Lloyd) and Marty McFly (David Kaufman) as they use their time traveling car, the DeLorean, to help people in need.

1992. *Bill and Ted's Excellent Adventures* (Fox). In the year 2692 time travel has been accomplished and San Demas, California, has based its philosophy on the wisdom of "The Two Great Ones," Bill and Ted (Evan Richards, Christopher Kennedy), teenagers who travel through time. The lessons Bill and Ted learn (their "excellent adventures") become the philosophy of San Demas. Time travel is accomplished by the Circuits of Time Phone Booth (activated by dialing the number 7560).

1993. *Time Traxx* (Syn.). Trans-Time Research and Experimentation (Traxx for short) is a futuristic government project concerned with time travel. A subject can travel in time with the aid of a TXP pill (which aligns a person's molecules to the delta wave transmissions of the Traxx computers thus enabling the transfer of molecules). At present the body can only withstand two doses of TXP, thus the limit is one round trip.

1994. *A.J.'s Time Travelers* (Fox). A magic disk transports A.J. Molloy (John Patrick White) to the *Carious*, a time traveling space ship that can witness history as it happens. The ship is controlled by B.I.T. (Back In Time), the navigator (played by Patty Maloney).

1995. *Sliders* (Fox). College student Quinn Mallory (Jerry O'Connell) accidentally discovers time travel while experimenting with an anti gravity device that creates a circle of power that is actually an interdimensional portal to Earth but in different dimensions and times. To use the portal, one jumps into the wormhole-like entrance and slides between the different earths.

1998. *7 Days* (UPN). A NSA (National Security Agency) project called Back Step allows

Frank Parker (Jonathan LaPaglia) to enter a ball-like time machine and travel back in time seven days to change events before they effect the future.

2000. *Sabrina, the Teenage Witch* (WB). The Lost in Time Clock is a magical timepiece that helps travels lost in time — people seeking to go back to correct a mistake in their lives. The clock is in the possession of Hilda Spellman (Caroline Rhea), the aunt of Sabrina, the Teenage Witch.

2003. *Tru Calling* (Fox). Tru Davies (Eliza Dushku) is a young woman with an amazing ability to travel back in time one day to change the past in order to change the future. Tru does not know how or why she has the ability but it is activated when a dead person (she works for the coroner) calls from beyond and asks for her help.

2005. *Time Warp Trio* (NBC cartoon). A magic book, given to 10-year-old Joel by his magician uncle, enables him and his friends Sam and Fred to travel back in time when they wish upon it.

2006. *Doctor Who* (Sci Fi). A new version of *Doctor Who* (see 1973) with Christopher Eccleston as the time traveling Time Lord from the planet Gallifrey who battles evil wherever he finds it.

Transsexuals

This entry concerns itself with those individuals who feel they are trapped in the wrong body and seek a means to become the other sex. See also *Gays* and *Lesbians*.

1977. Linda Gray plays Linda Markland, a former man who is a gorgeous woman on *All That Glitters*, a syndicated series that focuses on a society where women are the workers and men the housekeepers and secretaries.

1978. Tim Thomerson is Jean/Gene, chief engineer on a United Galaxy Sanitation Patrol ship in the 23rd century. Jean/Gene is a transmute and possesses a full set of female and male chromosomes. Jean/Gene unpredictably switches genders (via voice and actions but always appears as a male).

1986. You would never know by looking at her but the gorgeous Mel Brubaker (Randi Brooks) was once a man and now works as a police officer on NBC's *The Last Precinct*.

1992. Nataliji Nogolich plays Louise Talbot, the transsexual schoolteacher at Rome High School on CBS's *Picket Fences*.

1993. The PBS series *Tales of the City* features Olympia Dukakis as Anna, a transsexual landlady.

1995. Carlotta Chang plays Azure C. (a.k.a. Lee Chen), a female transsexual super model on *The City* (ABC).

1999. Julie Caitlin Brown is Nicki, the old boyhood chum of Dr. John Becker who is now a woman on *Becker* (CBS).

2000. On *Ally McBeal* (Fox), Lisa Edelstein plays Cindy McCauliff, a transsexual client of the law firm of Cage and Fish. Jenny McCarthy is Brandi, an old school chum of Dennis Finch who was once a guy but is now a gorgeous woman on NBC's *Just Shoot Me*.

2002. The CBS TV movie *The Education of Max Bickford* finds Helen Shaver as a transsexual college professor Erica Bettis. Showtime airs *Soldier Girl*, a true story about a G.I. named Barry Winchell (Troy Garity) who was beaten to death in 1999 by other soldiers when they became enraged over his dating transsexual nightclub performer Calpernia Addams (Lee Pace). At this same time HBO airs *Normal* with Tom Wilkinson as Roy Applewood, a factory worker who contemplates going from man to woman.

2004. Famke Janssen plays Ava Moore, a male to female transsexual on *Nip/Tuck* (FX).

Truckers

Programs centered on trucks and their drivers are the focus of this entry.

1956. J. Pat O'Malley plays a dispatcher who introduces tales about truckers on the anthology pilot *The Long Highway*.

1958. "Cannonball" Mike Malone (Paul Birch) is a seasoned truck driver for the C&A Transport Company in Canada, and Jerry Austin (William Campbell) is his younger partner on *Cannonball* (Syn.).

1973. Veteran trucker Sonny Pruett (Claude Akins) and his college educated younger partner, Will Chandler (Frank Converse) ride an 18-wheeler and, as they transport cargo, help people in trouble along the way on *Movin' On* (NBC).

1979. B.J. McKay (Greg Evigan) and his simian companion Bear, ride an 18-wheeler and haul anything legal anywhere for $1.50 a mile plus

expenses on *B.J. and the Bear*. In second season episodes B.J. establishes a trucking company (Bear Enterprises) and acquires seven lady truckers: Jeannie Campbell (Judy Landers), Samantha Smith (Barbra Horan), Callie Everett (Linda McCullough), Cindy Grant (Sherilyn Wolter), Angie Cartwright (Sheila DeWindt) and twins Teri and Geri Garrison (Candi and Randi Brough). Flatbed Annie (Annie Potts) and Ginny "Sweetie Pie" La Rosa (Kim Darby) are lady truckers who drive a 1978 blue and white Sturdy Built Super Liner on the CBS pilot *Flatbed Annie and Sweetie Pie*.

1982. While the NBC series *Knight Rider* features KITT, a crime fighting car of the future, it also features Goliath, a seemingly indestructible truck that has been programmed to destroy KITT.

1983. Carol Lee Shepherd (Mary Davis Duncan) and Daytona (Will Bledsoe) are a clean-living sister and brother who work for their father Cannonball Shepherd (Don Collier), the owner of the Good Shepherds Towing Service on the NBC pilot *Highway Honeys*. Also featured is Kirstie Alley as Draggin' Lady, a trucker for the corrupt Apocalypse Towing Service.

1988. A mysterious U.S. government agent, known only as the Highwayman (Sam J. Jones), battles crime and corruption in a high tech 18-wheeler along the highways, byways and fringe areas of the country on *The Highwayman* (NBC).

2000. Chance Bowman (Lucky Vanous) is the driver of an aerodynamic blue Kenworth T-2000 Advanced Technology truck designed by Katherine Spencer (Lisa Thornhill) that the government uses to battle crime on *18 Wheels of Justice* (TNN).

Twins

This entry chronicles the programs that star or feature twins (either real twins or one performer playing both roles). Infant twins playing a single role (for example, Erin and Diane Murphy playing Tabitha on *Bewitched*) are excluded. See also *Look-alikes*.

1947. Bob Smith provides the voice for the puppet Howdy Doody and his twin brother, Double Doody, on *Howdy Doody* (NBC).

1949. Judy Nugent and Jimmy Hawkins are Donna and Donald, the twins of Charlie and Margaret Ruggles on *The Ruggles* (ABC).

1950. Arlene and Ardell Terry, "The Singing Teenage Twins," perform regularly on *Toni Twin*

Time, a variety series sponsored by Toni Home Permanents (CBS).

1954. The Campbell Soup Company introduces its mascots, the chubby cherub twins for its series of soup commercials.

1957. Gail Stone and Karen Greene play Jenny and Mary, the twin daughters of traveling lecturer Liza Hammond on *The Eve Arden Show* (CBS).

1959. "Double your pleasure, double your fun with Doublemint, Doublemint Gum," is heard for the first time on TV as Wrigley Chewing Gum inaugurates its Doublemint commercials featuring twins. Twins include Jayne and Joan Boyd, Brittany and Cynthia Daniel, Trish and Cyb Barnstable, Jean and Meghan Delaney and Jean and Liz Sagal.

1960. Charles Bateman plays Rick January, a town marshal of the Old West, and his twin brother, Ben January, a frontier doctor, on *Two Faces West* (Syn.).

1962. Dack and Dirk Rambo play Dack and Dirk Massey, the twin sons of children's book author Christine Massey on *The New Loretta Young Show* (CBS).

1963. Ginger Rogers plays Margaret and Elizabeth Harcourt, twin sisters (an artist and a fashion designer) who help each other in times of need on the CBS pilot *The Ginger Rogers Show*.

1964. Fred Gwynne plays Herman Munster, a Frankenstein-like clone, and his twin brother Charlie Munster on *The Munsters* (CBS).

1965. Joe and Jeff Fithian play Tracy and Trevor, the twin sons of college professor Jim Nash and his wife Joan on *Please Don't Eat the Daisies* (NBC).

1966. Johnny Whitaker and Anissa Jones are Jody and Buffy Davis, twins who live with their Uncle Bill Davis after the death of their parents in a car accident on *Family Affair* (CBS). Keith and Kevin Schultz play Jefferson and Fennimore Monroe, twins called "Big Twin" and "Little Twin," the children of Albert and Mary Monroe on *The Monroes* (ABC).

1970. Hal Linden plays Corey and Morey Honker, the twin sons of Ta Ta Honker, head of the powerful Honker family, a family that hides many shameful secrets on the soap opera pilot spoof *The Shameful Secrets of Hastings Corners* (NBC).

1974. Twins Leah and Sophie Pennington (Tannis G. Montgomery, Denise Nickerson) are not only sisters but also best friends on the CBS pilot *If I Love You, Am I Trapped Forever?*

1976. Martin Mull plays Garth Gimble, the neighbor of Mary Hartman, and his twin brother, Barth Gimble, on *Mary Hartman, Mary Hartman* (Syn.). Tony and Shep Thomas (Jim and Jon Hager) are twin police officers who use their ability to fool people by pretending to be one on the ABC pilot *Twin Detectives*.

1978. Trish and Cyb Barnstable play twins Betty I and Betty II, the co-pilots of a United Galaxy Sanitation ship captained by Adam Quark on *Quark* (NBC).

1979. Candi and Randi Brough play Teri and Geri Garrison, waitresses at Phil's Disco who also work as truckers for B.J. McKay on *B.J. and the Bear* (NBC). Sorrell Booke is the dishonest Jefferson Davis Hogg and his honest brother Abraham Lincoln Hogg on *The Dukes of Hazzard* (CBS). Candi and Randi Brough also play Daphne and Yvonne, dance hall girls on the CBS pilot *More Wild Wild West*.

1981. Greg and John Rice play Ben and Beau Bernard, twin landlords (of the building in which TV show host Gloria Munday lives) on *Foul Play* (ABC).

1982. Greg and John Rice host *That Quiz Show*, a short-lived syndicated game show.

1984. Danny Kramer and Thomas Tulak play Elvis and Jesse, the twin terror sons of Carla, the nasty waitress at the Boston bar *Cheers* (NBC). Jean and Liz Sagal play Allison and Kate Foster, the twin 18-year-old daughters of Art Foster, a widower who runs a gym, on *Double Trouble* (NBC). Ann and Tom Edison (Marnie McPhail, Andrew Sabiston) are teenaged twin sleuths who apply scientific principles to solve crimes on *The Edison Twins* (Disney).

1985. Tracy Scoggins and Maxwell Caulfield are twins Monica and Myles Colby on *The Colbys* (ABC).

1986. Danny Ponce and Jeremy Licht play Willie and Mark Hogan, the twin sons of Valerie and Mike Hogan on *Valerie* (NBC; later titled *The Hogan Family*). Sara and Jamie Werner (Bridget and Tiffany Despar) are the twin daughters of attorney Judy Werner on the ABC pilot *Hardesty House*.

1987. Angela and Maureen Deiseach are Erica and Heather Farrell, identical teenage twins who attend Degrassi Junior High School in Canada on *Degrassi Junior High* (Syn.).

1989. Tom Bosley plays Father Frank Dowling, a Catholic parish priest, and his twin brother, a con artist named Blaine Dowling, on *Father Dowling Mysteries* (NBC/ABC). NBC airs the pilot *The Parent Trap* with Hayley Mills as twins Sharon and Susan. Sharon is single; Susan is the mother of teenage triplets — Lisa, Jesse and Megan (Leanna, Monica and Joy Creel). Stories were to focus on the lives of the triplets.

1990. Shannen Doherty and Jason Priestley play 16-year-old fraternal twins Brenda and Brandon Walsh on *Beverly Hills, 90210* (Fox). The 1990 episodes of *The Bill Cosby Show* feature Jessica Vaughn as Winnie and Gary Gray as Nelson, the twins of Sondra and Elvin.

1992. The Hurry Up Twins (Raleigh and Raymond Friend) appear weekly on "The Lester Guy Show," a ZBC (Zoblotnick Broadcasting Corporation) series starring washed-up movie actor Lester Guy on ABC's *On the Air.*

1993. Blake and Alan Tuomy-Wilhoit play Nick and Alex, the twin children of Jesse and Rebecca Katsopolis on ABC's *Full House.*

1994. Lisa Kudrow plays Phoebe Buffay, a massage therapist, and her slightly off-the-wall twin sister Ursula, a waitress at Riff's Bar on NBC's *Friends.* Tia and Tamera Mowry play Tia Landry and Tamera Campbell, twins separated at birth who are reunited 14 years later by chance at a mall on *Sister, Sister* (ABC/WB). Gabe and Sam (Ian Bottiglier, Carl Michael Lindner) are the fraternal twin sons of Gene Bergman, an advertising man and his wife Annie on *Something Wilder* (NBC). Elizabeth and Jessica Wakefield (Cynthia and Brittany Daniel) are identical 16-year-old twins who are as different as day and night on *Sweet Valley High* (Syn.). Jessica is a bit flaky and cares for fashion and makeup; Elizabeth is sentimental and studious. Tiffany and Kathryn Lubran play Charlotte and Emily Graham, the identical twin daughters of Tom Graham, a welder, and his wife Dorothy, on *Tom* (CBS). Roma Downey plays Monica, an Angel of good, and her evil twin named Monique, a demon who causes human misery on *Touched by an Angel* (CBS).

1995. Mary Kate and Ashley Olsen play themselves, eight-year-old sleuths and the twin daughters of Terry and Jack Olsen, dolphin researchers at Sea World in Florida on the ABC pilot *The Adventures of Mary Kate and Ashley.* Lori Singer plays Sidney Bloom, a computer whiz who discovers the fifth level of reality (the ability to enter a cyber realm); and Tracey Needham is her twin sister Samantha Bloom on *VR.5* (Fox).

1996. Sawyer and Sullivan Sweeten play Michael and Jeffrey, the twin sons of sportswriter Raymond Barone and his wife Debra on *Everybody Loves Raymond* (CBS). Lorenzo and Nicholas Brino are Sam and David, the twin sons of Reverend Eric Camden his wife Annie on *7th Heaven* (WB). Michael Easton plays the dual role of Guy McCain, a college professor and his twin brother Booth on *Two* (Syn.).

1998. Melissa Joan Hart plays Sabrina, a good teenage witch, and her Other Realm evil twin sister Katrina on *Sabrina, the Teenage Witch* (ABC/WB). Mary Kate and Ashley Olsen play Mary Kate and Ashley Burke, identical 12-year-old twins who are complete opposites on *Two of a Kind* (ABC). Ashley is glamorous and addicted to fashion; Mary Kate is a tomboy and in love with sports.

1999. Azure Skye is Jane Cooper and Michael Rosenbaum is Jack, her fraternal twin brother, students at Fielding High School in Manhattan on *Zoe, Duncan, Jack and Jane* (WB).

2000. Alvin Alvarez and Vaneza Leza Pitynski are 11-year-old Mexican-American twins Larry and Lorena Garcia on *The Brothers Garcia* (NIK).

2001. Eric and Steve Cohen are the Dancing Twins, the characters seen at Jasper's Restaurant, the favorite eatery of Ally McBeal and her coworkers on *Ally McBeal* (Fox). Cindy and Mindy Stage (Daniella and Deanna Canterman) are "sweet faced little terrors," the twin daughters of Jerry and Mary Stage on *Maybe It's Me* (WB). Mary Kate and Ashley Olsen play Riley and Chloe Carlson, fun-loving teenage twins living in California on *So Little Time* (Fox Family).

2002. Diane and Elaine Klimaszewski are the Coors Light Beer Twins seen in commercials for Coors Light Beer. Buffy and Jody Davis (Sasha Pieterse, Jimmy Pinchak) are six-year-old twins who live with the uncle, Bill Davis, after their parents' death on *Family Affair* (WB).

2003. Michael and Lindsay Bluth (Jason Bateman, Portia DeRossi) are fraternal twins on Fox's *Arrested Development.* Michael is responsible and runs the family business (Bluth Enterprises); Lindsay is a bit flaky and is married to Tobias Funke, a would-be actor. Also on the series, Jeffrey Tambor plays George Bluth, the head of Bluth Enterprises, and his twin brother Oscar (a crook). Antique furniture appraisers Leigh and

Leslie Keno host *Find*, a PBS series dealing with antiques. Diane and Elaine Klimaszewski appear as the Twin Hostesses on *Steve Harvey's Big Time Challenge* (WB).

2005. Caitlin Wachs and Matt Lanter play Rebecca and Horace, the twin children of Mackenzie Allen, the first woman president of the United States on *Commander in Chief* (ABC). Brent and Shane Kinsman play Preston and Porter, the twin sons of Lynette and Tom Scavo on ABC's *Desperate Housewives*. Dylan and Cole Sprouse play Zack and Cody Martin, the 12-year-old twins of lounge singer Cary Martin on *The Suite Life of Zack and Cody* (Disney; the title refers to the Tipton Hotel, where the twins live). Farrah Arnold (Molly Stanton) is blonde, beautiful and dumb (takes after her mother). She works as a lingerie model at her parents' company (Arnold Undergarments) with her brunette sister Mitchee (Sara Gilbert), a brilliant designer (takes after her father). The girls are twins, but look little like each other on *Twins* (WB). Tia and Tamera Mowry play witches Alex and Camryn on *Twitches*, a Disney pilot in which the twins must use their powers to save the world from evil.

Vampires

A listing of the programs starring or featuring creatures of the night called Vampires. See also *Horror, The Supernatural, Werewolves* and *Witches*.

1954. Maila Nurmi, better known as Vampira (a girl who dresses and wears makeup to resemble a sexy female vampire), came to light in Los Angles in 1954 when a local station (Channel 7) hired her to host its late night series of horror movies. She became an instant hit. Vampira, "The Queen of Horror," is perhaps best known as the Vampire Girl in the film *Plan 9 from Outer Space* (Maila based her costume on the Charles Addams cartoon character Morticia Addams of "The Addams Family").

1964. Although played for laughs, Lily Munster (Yvonne DeCarlo) and her father, Count Dracula (Al Lewis), better known as Grandpa, are non-human feeding vampires on *The Munsters* (CBS).

1966. Horror comes to daytime TV with the premiere of ABC's *Dark Shadows* and its main character, the vampire Barnabas Collins (Jona-

than Frid). There were also ghosts, witches, a werewolf, and a Frankenstein-like creation called Adam (Robert Rodan).

1976. Wax museum figure Dracula (Henry Polic II) comes to life to help criminology student Walt (Fred Grandy) battle crime on *The Monster Squad* (NBC).

1979. Kurt Von Helsing (Stephen Johnson) seeks to destroy the evil Count Dracula (Michael Nouri) who is posing as a European History professor at South Bay College in San Francisco on *The Curse of Dracula* (NBC). Judd Hirsch is Dracula, one of the monsters fearing Halloween will not occur on the ABC special *The Halloween That Almost Wasn't*.

1980. Big D (Dracula) and his son, Drak, Jr., battle the evil Dr. Dred and Vampira on the animated CBS series *Drak Pack*. Dick Shawn and Carol Lawrence are Vladimir and Sonia Dracula, a vampire couple that now live in the Bronx, New York (after angry villagers forced them from their home in Transylvania), on the ABC pilot *Mr. and Mrs. Dracula*.

1983. The vampire Roland Keats (Paul Kreppell) is a resident of the spooky apartment house at 13 Thirteenth Avenue in New York City on the CBS pilot *13 Thirteenth Avenue*.

1988. *The Munsters Today* (Syn.) presents an update of the 1964 series with Lee Meriwether as the female vampire, Lily Munster, and Howard Morton as her father, Count Dracula, better known as Grandpa.

1989. Rick Springfield plays Nick Knight, a vampire who uses his special powers to solve crimes as a police officer on the CBS pilot *Nick Knight*.

1990. Geordie Johnson is Alexander Lucard, the most sophisticated and the most dangerous vampire of his breed, who is seeking to spread his evil ways on *Dracula: The Series* (Syn.).

1991. NBC revises *Dark Shadows* (see 1966) with Ben Cross as Barnabas Collins, a modern-day vampire in Collinsport, Maine.

1992. The 1989 pilot *Nick Knight* is revived as the CBS series *Forever Knight* with Geraint Wyn Davies as Nicholas Knight, a vampire for the Toronto Police Department, who uses his extraordinary powers as a vampire to battle crime.

1993. Max Maven is Count De Clues, a vampire-like magician who lives in a strange castle on the Fox pilot *Count De Clues Mystery Castle*.

1996. Fox premieres *Kindred: The Embraced*, a

short-lived series about the life and loves of a society of vampires in San Francisco. Kelly Rutherford, Stacy Haiduck, C. Thomas Howell and Jeff Kober head a large cast.

1997. Unearthly creatures dispensed from a Hellmouth in Sunnydale, California, are destroyed by Buffy Summers (Sarah Michelle Gellar), a 16-year-old-girl who is the Chosen One (a Slayer) on *Buffy the Vampire Slayer*. Recurring vampires include Angel (David Boreanaz), Spike (James Marsters), Drusilla (Juliet Landau) and the Master (Mark Metcalf), an ancient, powerful vampire.

1999. *The Buffy the Vampire* spinoff *Angel* premieres on the WB with David Boreanaz as Angel, a vampire with a soul who battles demons. James Marsters recreates his role as the vampire Spike on the WB series.

2002. Count Blah (voice of Drew Massey) is one of the "living" puppets (a vampire) who stars on the children's series "Sweetknuckle Junction" on the Fox series *Greg the Bunny*.

2006. Kirk "Sticky Fingaz" Jones is Blade, a half human, half immortal modern-day vampire hunter on *Blade: The Series* (Spike TV), an adaptation of the film series.

Variety and Drama Spectaculars

Before lavish and one time only programs were commonly called specials, they were known as spectaculars (to attract viewers). This novelty wore off as the 1960s approached. This entry covers those one time only programs that were broadcast as spectaculars from 1939 to 1960. See also *Broadway and Stage Shows* and *Variety Programs* (for the series that were broadcast along side these spectaculars).

1939. Flora Campbell plays Jane Eyre, the orphan girl who becomes the governess to Adele, the ward of Edward Rochester, on *Jane Eyre* (NBC). The progression of the four March sisters in 1880s Massachusetts is seen in an NBC adaptation of the Louisa May Alcott book, *Little Women*. Joanna Post, Flora Campbell, Frances Reid and Joyce Arling star. NBC adapts the Robert Louis Stevenson story *Treasure Island* to TV with Dennis Hoey as the pirate Long John Silver and Billy Redfield as his young ward, Jim Hawkins. NBC's *When a Nightingale Sang in Berkeley Square* tells the story of Ralph Loyalty (Anthony Cooper), an

ex con trying to go straight, who is duped into robbing a bank.

1940. The Robert Louis Stevenson story *Dr. Jekyll and Mr. Hyde* is adapted by NBC with Dennis Hoey as Henry Jekyll, the doctor who invents a serum that transforms him into the hideous Edward Hyde.

1944. Ann Andrews, Alice Fleming and Roberta Henderson star in *When We Are Married*, an NBC adaptation of the British stage play about a couple, married 25 years, who suddenly learn that the person who married them was not legally ordained.

1945. Dorothy Emery, Margaret Hayes and Frances Lee star in *Little Women*, a second NBC adaptation of the story by Louisa May Alcott (see 1939). When miserly skinflint Herman Grubb (John Souther) refuses to let his nightclub staff have Christmas Eve off, he receives a visit from a man, dressed in fashion typical of the 1870s, who changes Grubb's mind. The stranger is revealed to be Charles Dickens (Grandon Rhoades), the author of *A Christmas Carol*, when a hatcheck girl, who asked for his autograph, looks at the signature. The NBC program was called *A Strange Christmas Dinner*.

1946. Vaughn Taylor plays Mr. Mergenthwirker, a reporter for a small town newspaper who is assisted by a group of invisible pixes who speak only to him on *Mr. Mergenthwirker's Lobblies* (NBC). Songs, dances and skits based on vaudeville routines are presented on *Window Shade Revue* (NBC). Maxine Barnett, Lillian Carroll and Bibi Osterwald perform.

1947. John Becker and Mary Alice Moore star on *This Time Next Year*, an NBC fantasy about a Southern politician with a dream to build a monument to the Confederacy that will outshine Grant's Tomb.

1948. NBC airs *Great Catherine*, a romantic adventure about an empress (Gertrude Lawrence) and a British sea captain (David Wayne). DuMont airs *Holiday in Spring*, a musical celebration of the spring of 1948. Adelaide Hawley narrates. George Jessel hosts *Holiday Star Revue*, a two-hour variety outing starring Morey Amsterdam, Connee Boswell, Phil Silvers and Paul and Grace Hartman. CBS airs *The March of Dimes Fashion Show*, the first televised benefit for the March of Dimes. John Conte, Judy Holliday, Gloria Swanson, Kim Hunter and Basil Rathbone appear. Morey Amsterdam hosts *The Morey Am-*

sterdam Show, a two-hour New Year's Eve program welcoming 1949. The Three Stooges appear on the program. Carl McDonald hosts *Television Symphony*, the first broadcast of a symphony orchestra (under the direction of Eugene Ormandy) on TV (CBS). On August 10 the ABC TV network is launched with New York station WJZ (now WABC) in a lavish program (4hrs. 37 min.) of music songs and comedy. Skip Farrell hosts *U.S. Treasury Salutes*, a program of music and songs designed to assist in the post–World War II bond drive.

1949. CBS airs *The March of Dimes Benefit Show* with Shirley Booth, Henry Fonda, Sondra Deel and the music of Ray Bloch and His Orchestra. The music, songs and comedy of vaudeville are recreated on the NBC production of *On the Two a Day* with Jackie Gleason, Pat Harrington and Elaine Stritch.

1950. Walt Disney ventures into TV for the first time on NBC (12/25) with *One Hour in Wonderland*, a program of live performances and highlights from Disney cartoons. Walt Disney served as the host. NBC also airs *Show of the Year*, a 2½-hour variety outing for the benefit of cerebral palsy sufferers. Milton Berle served as the host.

1951. NBC airs *Irving Berlin's Salute to America,* a musical salute to the U.S. by composer Irving Berlin.

1953. CBS celebrates the fiftieth anniversary of the Ford Motor Company in a lavish 2-hour presentation on *The Ford 50th Anniversary Show*. Eddie Fisher, Ethel Merman, Frank Sinatra and Rudy Vallee are among the guests.

1954. The fantasy world of Toyland comes to life as Tommy Tucker (Dennis Day) tries to romance the lovely Joan Piper (Ellen Barrie) against the wishes of the evil Silas Barnaby (Jack E. Leonard) on *Babes in Toyland* (NBC). Fading movie star Gale Joy (Marilyn Maxwell) finds she has not been forgotten when she accompanies a college student to his junior prom on the NBC musical *Best Foot Forward*. NBC airs *Fanfare*, a lavish color production of music and songs with Steve Allen, Frank Sinatra and Judy Holliday. French ballerina Jean Marie ("The Parisian Pixie") stars in three love stories set at various times in American history on *The Follies of Suzy* (NBC). Ann Sothern plays Liza Elliott, a plain, insecure magazine editor whose psychotic dreams propel her into a world where she is beautiful and

in charge of her life on NBC's *Lady in the Dark*. ABC, CBS. DuMont and NBC air *Light's Diamond Jubilee*, a celebration of the 75th anniversary of Thomas Edison's invention of the light bulb. Lauren Bacall, Walter Brennan, Dorothy Dandridge, Helen Hayes, Joseph Cotten and Kim Novak are among the guests who appear. NBC broadcasts two variety shows starring Mary Martin on the same day (March 29th): *Magic with Mary Martin* and *Music with Mary Martin*. *Operation Entertainment* is an NBC program that salutes the many show business personalities who gave their time and service to the U.S.O. (United Serviceman's Organization) during World War II and the Korean War. Terry Moore, Pat O'Brien, Bob Hope and Danny Kaye are among the performers who appear. Betty Hutton plays Cindy, a beautiful rodeo queen on the most lavish production of 1954, the NBC musical *Satins and Spurs*.

1955. Gillian Barber plays Alice, the young girl who enters a magical fantasy land when she follows the white rabbit on *Alice in Wonderland* (NBC). Milton Berle hosts *The Big Time*, a lavish NBC program of music, songs and comedy. Eddie Albert plays Martin Barrett, a Connecticut man who suffers a head injury and is propelled back in time to sixth century England and the Court of King Arthur on *A Connecticut Yankee* (NBC). Jose Ferrer is Cyrano de Bergerac, the 17th century French nobleman, and Claire Bloom is Roxane, the girl he is attempting to court on *Cyrano de Bergerac* (NBC). *Dearest Enemy* (NBC) is an adaptation of the Rodgers and Hart musical about a group of American Revolutionary women who help the Continental Army by making ammunition. Anne Jeffreys and Robert Sterling star. Nelson Eddy plays Pierre Birbeau, a governor's son in French Morocco who is secretly the Red Shadow, a Robin Hood-like character on *The Desert Song* (NBC). Fred Allen hosts *Entertainment 1955*, a lavish color program from NBC's new Burbank studios. Jeannie Carson plays Heidi, the orphaned Swiss girl on *Heidi*, an NBC adaptation of the Johanna Spyri story. Nat King Cole, Debbie Reynolds, Eddie Fisher and Ella Fitzgerald are among the performers who appear on *I Hear America Singing* (CBS). David Wayne is the emcee for *The Judy Garland Show*, a CBS program that spotlights the singing talents of Judy Garland. Judy Holliday and Frank Sinatra star on *Kaleidoscope*, a fast-paced program of music and songs (CBS). French entertainer

Maurice Chevalier headlines a variety outing with the backing of the Charles Sanford Orchestra on *The Maurice Chevalier Show* (NBC). Patrice Munsel plays Marietta D'Altena, an Italian countess who seeks the hand of the pirate Dick Warrington (Alfred Drake) in marriage on *Naughty Marietta* (NBC). Singer Patti Page captures the spotlight on *The Patti Page Premiere Party Show* (NBC). Mary Martin plays Peter Pan, the boy who never grew up, and his adventures with the Darling children on *Peter Pan* (NBC). Mary Martin would recreate the role on NBC in two additional presentations in 1956 and 1960. Judy Holliday, Tyrone Power and Kay Starr perform on *Promenade*, a lavish variety outing on NBC. Greer Garson makes her dramatic TV debut as Elena Krug, the wife of a psychiatrist who finds she still loves an old flame on *Reunion in Vienna* (NBC). Art Linkletter hosts *Show Biz*, a lavish program that traces the art of music and comedy from the early days of vaudeville to present day 1955. Ethel Barrymore narrates *Svengali and the Blonde* (NBC), the story of Trilby (Carol Channing), a girl who is transformed into a great singer by Svengali (Basil Rathbone), a hypnotist with magical powers. Singer Harry Belafonte and dancers Marge and Gomer Champion are spotlighted on *Three for Tonight* (CBS). Janet Parker plays Ginger Carol, a tomboyish girl who decides to join the all male football team at her school on the CBS comedy *Time Out for Ginger*. Perry Como, Pat Carroll and Buddy Hackett are among the performers who appear on *Variety*, a potpourri of music and songs on NBC.

1956. Jayne Mansfield and Hal March star in *The Bachelor* (NBC), a comedy about a ladies' man's efforts to remain single. The aquatic skills of Esther Williams are showcased on the NBC special *The Esther Williams Aqua Spectacular*. Opera and concert artists perform on *Festival of Music*, a lavish NBC production featuring Roberta Peters, Jan Peerce, Rise Stevens and Isaac Stern. Tony Randall hosts *Heaven Will Protect the Working Girl*, an NBC salute to the working woman with Janet Blair, Tammy Grimes and Nancy Walker. Hal March plays flamboyant confidence man Harrison Floy on the NBC musical comedy *High Button Shoes*. The ghost of a Dutch girl (Julie Andrews) appears to help a man (Bing Crosby) save his mountain from people seeking to buy it on *High Thor* (CBS). Doretta Morrow and Keith Andes star in *Holiday* (NBC),

a musical in which a schoolteacher falls for an embezzler. Joel Grey plays Jack, the poor farm boy who trades the family cow for magic beans, and his adventures when he climbs the beanstalk that grows from those beans on *Jack and the Beanstalk* (NBC). Judy Garland performs songs she has never sung in public on *The Judy Garland Show* (CBS). A young couple (Peter Marshall, Helen O'Connell) meet and fall in love while visiting New York City on *Manhattan Tower* (NBC). Alfred Drake plays Marco Polo, the 13th century traveler in a musical chronicle of his journeys on *Marco Polo* (NBC). Tony Bennett and Ethel Merman are among the performers who appear on *The Music of Gershwin*, an NBC salute to composer George Gershwin. Imogene Coca hosts *Panorama*, a fast paced series of music, songs and comedy skits (NBC). Dan Dailey, Helen Gallagher and Gale Sherwood star in *Paris in the Springtime* (NBC), the story of a dancer who becomes involved with two women. Art Linkletter hosts *Sonja Henie's Holiday on Ice*, an NBC color production featuring ice skating star Sonja Henie. Jimmy Durante hosts *Spotlight*, an NBC program that showcases the many talents of the versatile comedian. Bankrupt theatrical producer Oscar Jaffe (Orson Welles) seeks to sign movie star Lily Garland (Betty Grable) to an exclusive contract to recoup his loses on the CBS production of *Twentieth Century*. Cole Porter's song writing career is celebrated on *You're the Top* (CBS) with Louis Armstrong, Bing Crosby, Dorothy Dandridge and Shirley Jones among the guests.

1957. Julie Andrews plays Cinderella in a musical adaptation the classic fairy tale by Rodgers and Hammerstein on *Cinderella* (CBS). Bing Crosby hosts *The Edsel Show* (CBS), a program of music and songs sponsored by the Ford Motor Company, in an effort to promote what would become one of the biggest flops in automotive history, the 1958 Edsel. Kirk Douglas hosts *The General Motors 50th Anniversary Show* (NBC), a star studded salute to General Motors on the occasion of its 50th birthday. Ann Sothern hosts *Holiday in Las Vegas* (NBC), a musical revue from the gambling capitol. Carol Lynley plays Judy Graves, a vivacious teenage girl with a knack for finding trouble on *Junior Miss* (CBS). Mickey Rooney plays George M. Cohen, writer, producer, playwright, dancer and songwriter on the NBC musical *Mr. Broadway*. Van Johnson plays the Pied Piper, a wanderer who uses his magical flute to rid the town of Hamelin of rodents on *The Pied Piper of Hamelin* (NBC). Mickey Rooney plays Pinocchio, the wooden boy who comes to life to please his creator, Geppetto (Burl Ives), a lonely toy maker on *Pinocchio* (NBC). Artists signed by RCA records perform on *The RCA Victor Gallery of Stars*. Vaughn Monroe hosts the NBC program. Tyrone Power and Brandon DeWilde host a salute to the 75th anniversary of the Standard Oil Company of New Jersey on *The Standard Oil Anniversary Show* (NBC). Comedian Ed Wynn is honored on the occasion of his fifty-fifth year in show business on *Texaco Command Performance* (NBC). A second Texaco program was broadcast two months later honoring Ethel Merman. Timex watches sponsors four programs (1957–59) that feature performances by jazz musicians on *The Timex All-Star Jazz Show*. The four hosts were Steve Allen, Garry Moore, Hoagy Carmichael and Jackie Gleason.

1958. Sal Mineo plays *Aladdin* (CBS) in an Arabian Knights tale about a boy (Aladdin), his genie (Cyril Ritchard) and a beautiful princess (Anna Maria Alberghetti). Dancer Fred Astaire performs on *An Evening with Fred Astaire*, a CBS program of music, songs and dancing (in 1959 Fred was host to *Another Evening with Fred Astaire* on CBS). A tennis star (Maurice Evans) marries a woman (Rosemary Harris) for money then plots to have her killed on *Dial "M" for Murder* (NBC). Actress Ginger Rogers performs with guests the Ritz Brothers on *The Ginger Rogers Show*, a CBS variety outing. Red Buttons and Barbara Cook play Hansel and Gretel, a brother and sister who find unknown danger from a witch they encounter in the woods on *Hansel and Gretel* (NBC). Dedicated drinker Elwood P. Dowd (Art Carney) finds companionship from Harvey, a six-foot tall white rabbit that only he can see on *Harvey* (CBS). Phil Silvers hosts *Phil Silvers on Broadway*, a revue of the current Broadway shows (CBS). Walter Pidgeon, Laraine Day and Patty Duke star in *Swiss Family Robinson*, an NBC adventure about a family's efforts to survive on a desolate island after a shipwreck. Rosalind Russell and Jacqueline McKeever star as Ruth and Eileen Sherwood, sisters seeking fame and fortune in New York City on *Wonderful Town* (CBS). An aristocrat (Yvonne Furneaux) falls for a gypsy (Richard Burton), a man beneath her social scale on *Wuthering Heights* (CBS). Shirley Jones and Donald O'Connor star in *The Red Mill* (CBS), a

musical comedy (narrated by Harpo Marx) about a small Dutch town and the effects its enchanted red mill has on its people.

1959. Claudette Colbert stars as Sister Benedict, a nun who tries to convince a millionaire to help save their decaying parochial school on *The Bells of St. Mary's* (CBS). Jerry Lewis plays Joey Robbins, the son of a show business family who seeks to break tradition (become a singer) and strike out on his own as a comedian on *The Jazz Singer* (NBC). Tab Hunter, Jane Powell, Jeanne Crane and Patty Duke star in *Meet Me in St. Louis*, a musical about a family in turn-of-the-century St. Louis. Writer Charles Strickland (Sir Laurance Olivier) deserts his family to pursue a career as an artist on *The Moon and Sixpence* (NBC). Rosalind Russell hosts *The Rosalind Russell Show*, a lavish musical revue that traces the changes in show business over the years. A governess (Ingrid Bergman) struggles to protect a young girl (Alexandra Wayne) and her brother (Hayward Morse) from a spirit who is seeking to possess them on *The Turn of the Screw* (NBC). Ten people are summoned to a desolate house and taunted by an unknown voice that accuses them of murder, then sets out to kill each one of them on *Ten Little Indians*. Nina Foch, Barry Jones and Valerie French star in the NBC adaptation of the Agatha Christie story.

1960. Debbie Reynolds hosts *A Date with Debbie*, a music and songfest on ABC. The talents of singer, dancer and comedian Donald O'Connor are showcased on *The Donald O'Connor Special* (NBC). Esther Williams performs in water and on dry land on the NBC special *Esther Williams at Cypress Gardens*. Boris Karloff hosts *Hollywood Sings* (NBC), a review of Hollywood movie musicals. Andy Williams plays *The Man in the Moon* on an NBC musical in which he comes down to earth to tour America. Maureen O'Hara plays Mrs. Minerva in a TV adaptation of the novel by Jan Struther about the effects of World War II on a family that live in a small English town. Nanette Fabray plays Sally, a waitress who refuses to marry, hoping instead to make her dreams of becoming famous a reality on *So Help Me, Aphrodite*, an NBC musical written especially for TV. Five men, lost in the Himalayas after a plane crash, stumble upon a paradise on earth on *Shangri-La* (NBC). Claude Rains and Richard Basehart star. Pat Carroll, Jackie Gleason and Shirley Jones star on *Step on the Gas* (CBS), a series of skits that spoofs driving in America. The music of the 1940s is recalled on *The Swingin' Singin' Years*, an NBC program hosted by Ronald Reagan. Dave Garroway hosts *The Talent Scouts Program* (NBC), a showcase for undiscovered talent. Art Carney is featured on *Three in One*, an NBC program of three one-act plays ("A Pound on Demand," "Where the Cross Is Made" and "Red Peppers").

Variety Programs — Pioneering Years, 1930–1960

Programs of music, songs and comedy are one of the earliest forms of TV entertainment. They began with the earliest experiments and have survived over the decades. This entry chronicles the variety program from its beginnings in 1930 to its establishment as a solid entertainment form in 1960. See also *Broadway and Stage Shows* and *Variety and Drama Spectaculars*.

1930. Harry Hershfield hosts *Variety Show*, an experimental Jenkins Laboratories program that explored the possibilities of home reception. George Jessel, Benny Rubin and Diana Seaby were among the performers who appeared on TV's first variety show.

1938. Dennis James hosts *Television Roof*, a DuMont experimental series that presents performances by top name personalities.

1939. All NBC productions: *The Albert and Josephine Butler Program* (dancing). *The Cobina Wright, Jr. Show* (songs). *Ireene Wicker Sings. The Jack Cole Dancers. The Lucy Monroe Program* (songs). *The Marie Eve, George Lloyd Show* (songs). *The NBC Revue* (variety acts). *Night Club Revue* (songs and conga dancing). *Total Eclipse* (songs with black entertainer Howard Reed). *Variety Over the Air* (George Hicks hosts). *The Variety Show* (Helen Lewis hosts). *The Vaudeville Show* (Dorothy Gish hosts).

1940. *The Benjamin David Revue* (named after the producer) is a series of variety acts hosted by Alan Holt (NBC).

1941. The CBS series *Dancing Lessons* features dancers from the Arthur Murray Dance Studio teaching viewers how to dance. Singer-actress Tamara performs in English, Russian and Spanish on *Tamara* (CBS). Performers from the vaudeville stage appear on *The Vaudeville Show* (CBS).

1942. Jazz musicians (including Woody Herman, Eddie Condon and Pee Wee Russell) perform on *Men at Work* (CBS).

1943. Night club entertainers perform on *Café Television*, a DuMont program that was dubbed "Night clubbing for television." Music, songs and dramatic vignettes are presented on *DuMont Varieties*.

1944. Variety acts perform in a situated house party setting on *At Home* (CBS). A mixed bag of entertainment (songs, music, skits) is presented on *The CBS Studio Show* (later called *The Columbia Television Workshop*). The Compton Advertising Agency creates and sponsors *The Compton Tele Show*, a DuMont program of music, songs and comedy. Country and western entertainers perform on *Country Style* (DuMont) with Patty Adair and Peggy Ann Ellis as the hosts. Orchestra leader Fred Waring and His Pennsylvanians perform on *Fred Waring's Pleasure Time* (DuMont). Variety acts perform on *Here's Click*, a program hosted by Danton Walker and sponsored by *Click* magazine. Ballet dancing is performed on *Rhythm* (CBS). Variety acts perform on DuMont's *Television Canteen* and its *Theater House* series. Pianist-comedian Victor Borge hosts *The Victor Borge Show* on CBS. Eddie Dowling hosts *Wide Horizons*, a DuMont program of variety acts and dramatic skits. Radio station WOR in New York is used to broadcast a TV signal for *WOR Television Varieties* (DuMont; Bob Emery hosts).

1945. Don McNeill hosts *The Breakfast Club* (DuMont), a prime time TV version (8:00 P.M.) of the morning radio program (which features music, talk and songs). Billy Rose hosts *On Stage Everybody* (DuMont), a series of entertainment acts.

1946. The A.E. Rittenhouse Company (makers of Rittenhouse Chimes) sponsors *Chime Time*, an ABC program of songs by Jean Tighe and the Gay Moods Quintet. Don McNeill hosts *Don McNeill's Dinner Club*, a program of music, songs and chatter (later titled *Don McNeill's TV Club*). Entertainers from the Roaring 20s perform the music and songs of that era on *Memories with Music* (NBC). Vera Massey hosts *Poetry and Music* on DuMont. Red Benson hosts variety acts on *The Red Benson Show* (DuMont). Diane Courtney hosts the NBC test program *Song and Dance*. Tommy Farrell is the host for *Tele Varieties*, an NBC test program that spotlights new talent discoveries. The various styles of dancing are showcased on *The Valerie Bettis Dancers* (CBS). Songs and skits based on vaudeville are performed on *Window Shade Revue* (NBC).

1947. Radcliffe Hall hosts *Dancing on Air*, a CBS test program in which the Fred Astaire Instructors demonstrate various dance steps. Country and western entertainers perform on *Midwestern Hayride* (Syn.). Jack Kilty hosts *Musical Merry-Go-Round*, an NBC series of music and songs.

1948. Ralph Dunne is Captain Billy Bryant, the host of *Captain Billy's Mississippi Music Hall* (CBS). Swing music with Orson Bean as the host is presented on *The Chamber Music Society of Lower Basin Street* (ABC/NBC). Adrienne Meyerberg hosts *Champagne and Orchids*, a program of music and songs on DuMont. Perry Como hosts the Chesterfield cigarette sponsored program *The Chesterfield Supper Club* on NBC. Maggi McNellis hosts *The Crystal Room*, an ABC series of music and songs. Dennis James and Dagmar (Jennie Lewis) star on *Dennis James' Carnival*, a program of music and songs on CBS. Music and songs are performed on *The Earl Wrightson Show* (ABC). A casual program of music and songs is presented with host Kyle MacDonnell on NBC's *For Your Pleasure*. French singer Gabrielle hosts her own series, *Gabrielle*, on ABC. Kyle MacDonnell hosts *Girl About Town*, a live NBC show in which entertainment is presented from various New York nightclubs. Music and songs are performed at the Shufflebottom General Store, a Southern establishment that sponsors a Wednesday evening get-together on *Kobb's Corner* (CBS). Singer Lanny Ross hosts *The Lanny Ross Show* on NBC. Carole Coleman hosts *Make Mine Music* on CBS. Music and comedy is set against the background of the Silver Swan Café on *The Morey Amsterdam Show* (CBS/DuMont). Henry Morgan hosts *On the Corner*, an ABC series of acts culled from the "Vaudeville" section of *Variety* magazine. Country and western acts perform on *Saturday Night Jamboree* (NBC). Roberta Quinlan hosts *Song and Dance Time* on NBC. Various American cities are saluted through music on *The Swift Show Wagon* with host Horace Heidt (NBC; sponsored by Swift and Company foods). Orchestra leader Ted Steele performs on his own series, *The Ted Steele Show* (NBC/DuMont/CBS). Milton Berle hosts TV's first successful variety series, *The Texaco Star Theater*, on NBC. Broad-

way columnist Ed Sullivan introduces variety acts from all over the world on *Toast of the Town* (CBS; later titled *The Ed Sullivan Show*). Aspiring talent performs on *Ted Mack and the Original Amateur Hour* (DuMont/ABC/CBS). Excerpts from Broadway shows are presented on *Tonight on Broadway* (CBS). Variety acts from New York's Village Barn Night Club in Greenwich Village are presented on *Village Barn* (NBC). Music and songs performed against the background of a cruise ship are presented on *Welcome Aboard* (NBC). Ralph Vincent hosts *You're Invited*, an ABC series that spotlights performances by guests.

1949. Sylvie St. Claire hosts *Café de Paris*, a DuMont series of music and songs set against the background of a Paris nightclub. Variety programs tailored to the talents of its guest hosts are seen on *Cavalcade of Stars* (DuMont). Ford Bond hosts *Cities Services Band of America* featuring the music of the 48-piece Band of America (NBC). Music, songs and comedy are combined on *The Cliff Edwards Show* (CBS). Joe Rosenfeld and Joe Bushkin host music and comedy on *A Couple of Joes* (ABC). Vincent Lopez hosts a program of music and songs from New York's Hotel Taft on *Dinner Date with Vincent Lopez* (DuMont). Comedian Ed Wynn brings his unique vaudeville-style humor to television on *The Ed Wynn Show* (NBC). Faye Emerson hosts *15 with Faye*, a daily 15-minute program of music, songs and interviews. Ole Olsen and Chick Johnson host *Fireball Fun for All*, an NBC series of music, comedy and song. Delora Bueno hosts *Flight to Rhythm* (DuMont). Jazz musicians perform on *Floor Show* (NBC/CBS). Fred Waring and his orchestra perform on *The Fred Waring Show* (CBS). Frank Fontaine hosts *Front Row Center*, a DuMont program that features performances by Broadway stars. Dave Garroway hosts a relaxed program of music, chatter and songs on *Garroway at Large* (NBC). The music and songs of the early 1890s is presented on *Gay 90s Revue* (ABC). Earl Wrightson hosts *The Goodyear Revue*, an ABC program of music and comedy sponsored by Goodyear. Peter Lind Hayes and Mary Healy host *Inside U.S.A. with Chevrolet*, a CBS program of variety acts sponsored by Chevrolet. Jack Carter hosts *Jack Carter and Company*, an ABC series of songs and comedy. *Jacques Fray's Music Room* airs on ABC and features performances by aspiring talent. Music, songs and game contests are presented on

Johnny Olsen's Rumpus Room (DuMont). Members of the show business fraternity the Lambs Club, perform on *The Lambs Gambol* (NBC). Lynne Barrett hosts *Melody, Harmony, Rhythm* (NBC). Mindy Carson hosts her own series, *Mindy Carson Sings* (NBC). Roberta Quinlan and Morton Downey host the Mohawk carpet sponsored *Mohawk Showroom* (NBC). Johnny Hill hosts ABC's *Music in Velvet*. Singer Paul Arnold hosts his own CBS series *The Paul Arnold Show*. Orchestra leader Paul Whiteman hosts *Paul Whiteman's Saturday Night Revue* (ABC). June Browne hosts *Penthouse Sonata* (ABC). Minstrel acts are performed on *Pick and Pat* (ABC). Beverly Fite hosts *Quadrangle*, a CBS series of music and songs that is also known as *Campus Corner*. Bandleader Ray Knight hosts *The Ray Night Revue* (ABC). Singer Roberta Quinlan hosts her own series *The Roberta Quinlan Show* on NBC. Aspiring talent perform against a school house setting on DuMont's *School House* (Kenny Delmar hosts). Singer Dolores Marshall hosts *Serenade*, an ABC series featuring the George Barnes Trio. Original cast members perform songs from Broadway shows on *Show Business, Inc.* (NBC). Music and songs with Dolores Marshall and Joanelle Jones are presented on *Sing-Co-Pation* (ABC). Singer Sonny Kendis hosts his own CBS series, *The Sonny Kendis Show*. Helen Lee hosts a program of songs on NBC's *Sunday Date*. Sandy Buckert plays a merchant sailor whose recollections about his experiences in South America are seen on *Tropic Holiday* (NBC). Eddie Hubbard hosts *Vaudeo Varieties*, a live program of entertainment acts on ABC. George Givot is the host for *Versatile Varieties*, an NBC program of performances by guest acts. Classical and semi-classical concerts are performed on *Voice of Firestone* (NBC/ABC; hosted by John Daly and sponsored by Firestone Tire and Rubber Company). *The Wayne King Show* (NBC) presents music and songs from Chicago. Barbara Marshall hosts NBC's *Words and Music*.

1950. Variety programs are tailored to the talents of guest hosts on *The All Star Revue* (NBC). Bob Hope begins a series of variety specials that would run until 1993. Morey Amsterdam, Jack E. Leonard and Jerry Lester host *Broadway Open House*, TV's first late night (11:00 P.M. to Midnight) series of music and comedy. Music and songs with Jim Dimitri is presented on *Chez Paree Revue* (DuMont). Singer Ginny Simms hosts *Club Celebrity* on NBC. Programs tailored to the talents

of specific hosts are seen on *The Colgate Comedy Hour* (NBC). Jack Haley hosts *Ford Star Revue* on NBC. Frank Sinatra performs songs on *The Frank Sinatra Show* (CBS). Music, songs and chatter with Garry Moore appear on *The Garry Moore Show* (CBS). Pianist Hazel Scott performs on *The Hazel Scott Show* (DuMont). Russ Morgan and his orchestra perform on *In the Morgan Manner* (ABC). Music and comedy acts perform on *The Jack Carter Show* (NBC). An informal music and comedy session is presented on *Jamboree* (DuMont). Singer-pianist Joan Edwards performs on *The Joan Edwards Show* (DuMont). Music and songs with John Conte are presented on *John Conte's Little Show* (NBC/ABC). Singer Kate Smith comes to TV on her own afternoon program, *The Kate Smith Hour* (NBC). Novelty acts are presented on *The Ken Murray Show* (CBS). Husband and wife singers Jimmy and Rita Carroll perform on DuMont's *Mr. and Mrs. Carroll*. Ben Alexander hosts the Roma Wines sponsored *Party Time at Club Roma* (NBC). Music and songs with Betty Furness are presented on *Penthouse Party* (ABC). Singer Perry Como comes to CBS on *The Perry Como Show*. Comedy is mixed with music on *The Ransom Sherman Show* (NBC). Carol Reed hosts NBC's *Rendezvous with Music*. *Robert Q's Matinee*, hosted by singer Robert Q. Lewis, airs on CBS. Scenes from Broadway plays are performed by original cast members on *Showtime, U.S.A.* (ABC). Variety acts chosen from various New York nightclubs are seen on *The S.S. Holliday* (DuMont). Georgia Lee hosts *Stage Two Revue*, an ABC series of music and songs. Satire mixes with music on *Three's Company*, a CBS series starring Stan Freeman, Martha Wright and Judy Lynn. Guest composers perform on *Tin Pan Alley TV* with Johnny Desmond as the host. Arlene and Ardell Terry, "The singing teenage twins," perform on *Toni Twin Time* with host Jack Lemmon (CBS; sponsored by Toni home hair care products). Singer Beverly Fite appears with Cliff "Ukulele" Ike on CBS's *Ukulele Ike*. Bandleader Vaughn Monroe performs on *The Vaughn Monroe Show* (CBS). Danny O'Neal hosts an hour of music from Chicago on *Windy City Jamboree* (DuMont). The top songs of the week are performed on *Your Hit Parade* (NBC). Sid Caesar hosts *Your Show of Shows*, a lavish series of music and comedy presentations (NBC).

1951. Laraine Day hosts *Daydreaming with Laraine*, an ABC series of music and chatter.

Singer Dinah Shore headlines her own NBC series on *The Dinah Shore Chevy Show* (sponsored by Chevrolet). The performances of a group of entertainers at a summer theater are seen through the eyes of the stage manager (Don Ameche) on *Don's Musical Playhouse* (ABC). Singer Frances Langford teams with actor Don Ameche for songs and skits on *The Frances Langford–Don Ameche Show* (ABC). Violinist Marguerite Hamilton and actor John Conte team for music and songs on *The Feminine Touch* (ABC). James Melton hosts a series of entertainment acts on *Ford Festival* (NBC; sponsored by Ford cars). Edgar Guest and Rachel Stevenson host *A Guest in Your House*, an NBC series of music and poetry. Bandleader Freddy Martin hosts *The Hazel Bishop Show*, an NBC series sponsored by Hazel Bishop Cosmetics. The homespun philosophy of comedian Herb Shriner is presented alongside variety acts on *Herb Shriner Time* (ABC). Music and comedy is coupled with comedy on *The Jerry Colonna Show* (ABC). Singers Johnny Johnston and Rosemary Clooney team for a daily CBS songfest on *The Johnny Johnston Show*. Kate Smith brings her afternoon series to prime time on *The Kate Smith Evening Hour* (NBC). Wayne Howell hosts *The Left Over Revue*, a variety outing that replaced *Broadway Open House* (see 1950). Singer Mel Torme performs on *The Mel Torme Show* (CBS). Kay Westfall performs on a live show from Chicago on *Oh, Kay!* (ABC). Ballerina Patricia Bowman performs live on *The Patricia Bowman Show* (CBS). Singer Dotty Mack is the featured regular on *The Paul Dixon Show*, a weekly series of music and songs (ABC/DuMont). Songs from Jim McKay and his guests air on *The Real McKay* (CBS). George DeWitt hosts *Seven at Eleven*, a live NBC variety series broadcast from New York at 11:00 P.M. Bob Carroll, Buddy Greco and Johnny Andrews perform on NBC's *Songs at Twilight*. Music associated with different tropical ports is featured each week on *The S.S. Telecruiser* (ABC). Aspiring talent performs on *Stage Entrance* (DuMont) with host Earl Wilson. Alexandra Gray hosts *This Is Music*, a DuMont series in which the hit songs of famous recording artists are pantomimed through lip-synching. Songs are built around an accompanist (Pinky Lee) who falls in love with a nightclub singer (Vivian Blaine, then Martha Stuart) on *Those Two* (NBC). Peggy Lee and Mel Torme host *TV's Top Tunes*, a CBS series that features renditions of popular songs. Hugh

Downs and Nancy Wright host an afternoon program of music and songs on *Your Luncheon Date* (DuMont).

1952. A daily program of music and songs is presented on *The Al Pearce Show* (CBS). Mindy Carson and Connie Russell perform songs on NBC's *Club Embassy*. Jennie Lewis, better known as the glamorous Dagmar, hosts entertainment acts by members of the U.S. Armed forces on *Dagmar's Canteen* (NBC). Country and western entertainers perform on *The Eddy Arnold Show* (CBS/NBC). Music and comedy with Jackie Gleason is presented on *The Jackie Gleason Show* (CBS). Singer Jane Froman hosts performances by the men and women of the U.S. Armed services on *Jane Froman's U.S.A. Canteen* (CBS). Singer Johnny Dugan performs on the Hollywood-based *Johnny Dugan Show* (NBC). Jerry Lester hosts *The Saturday Night Dance Party* on NBC. Patti Page performs weekly on *The Scott Music Hall*, a CBS series sponsored by the Scott Paper Company. Undiscovered talent performs on *U.S. Royal Showcase*, an NBC series hosted by George Abbott and Jack Carson (and sponsored by the U.S. Rubber Company).

1953. Singer Eddie Fisher performs on his own series, *Coke Time with Eddie Fisher* (NBC). Dave Garroway hosts a casual program of music, songs and chatter on *The Dave Garroway Show* (NBC). Dotty Mack and a cast pantomime the songs of famous singers on *The Dotty Mack Show* (DuMont/ABC). Actor Eddie Albert hosts a series of music and song performances on *The Eddie Albert Show* (CBS). Interviews are coupled with music and songs on *Faye and Skitch* (NBC) with hosts Faye Emerson and Skitch Henderson. Singer-actress Gloria DeHaven performs on *The Gloria DeHaven Show* (ABC). Comedy, coupled with music and songs, is presented on *The Jerry Lester Show* (ABC). Skits are coupled with music on *The Larry Storch Show* (CBS). Pianist Liberace headlines a program of music on the syndicated *Liberace*. Elliott Lawrence and Tony Mattola host *Melody Street*, a DuMont program in which popular songs are pantomimed. Slapstick comedy is combined with music on *The Milton Berle Show* (NBC). Orchestras from Frank Dailey's Meadowbrook in Cedar Grove, New Jersey, perform on *Music from Meadowbrook* (ABC). Robert Trendler hosts *The Music Show*, an unsponsored hour of music from Chicago (DuMont). Guest artists perform on *Nothing But the Best* (NBC; Eddie Albert hosts). Sid Caesar is the New York host and Jack Carter the Chicago host on *The Saturday Night Revue*, an NBC program that presents variety acts from all over the world. Civilian and military talent perform on *Stars on Parade* (DuMont). Country and western entertainers perform on *The Strawhatters*, a DuMont series hosted by Johnny Olsen and Virginia Graham. Teresa Brewer and Mel Torme host *Summertime U.S.A.*, a twice-weekly CBS program of music and songs. Performances by vaudeville entertainers are presented on *The Vaudeville Show* (ABC). Lesser-known performers are spotlighted on *Your Chevrolet Showroom* (ABC; hosted by Cesar Romero).

1954. The Ames Brothers (Ed, Vic, Joe and Gene) perform songs with the backup of the Harry Geller Orchestra on the syndicated *Ames Brothers Show*. Orson Bean is the host and Polly Bergen the vocalist on *The Blue Angel*, a CBS series broadcast from the Blue Angel Nightclub in New York City. Donald O'Connor headlines his own variety series, *The Donald O'Connor Show*, on NBC. The Harry Zimmerman Orchestra provides backing for violinist Florian Zabach on *The Florian Zabach Show* (CBS). Frankie Laine appears with singer Connie Haines on *The Frankie Laine Show* (Syn.; later titled *Frankie Laine Time* on CBS). Comedian George Gobel is host to his own program of music and comedy on *The George Gobel Show* (NBC). Guy Lombardo and His Royal Canadians orchestra perform on the syndicated *Guy Lombardo and His Royal Canadians*. Ilona Massey hosts a program of music and songs set against the background of a Continental supper club on *The Ilona Massey Show* (DuMont). Comedy skits are mixed with music on *The Jack Carson Show* (NBC). The Milton DeLugg Trio backs singer Jane Pickens on *The Jane Pickens Show* (ABC). The Paul Weston Orchestra provides backing for singer Jo Stafford on *The Jo Stafford Show* (CBS). The syndicated *Les Paul and Mary Ford Show* features songs by the married couple. Martha Wright and Ralph Mooney host *Let's Dance*, a live hour of ballroom dancing (ABC). Slapstick comedy mixes with music on *The Martha Raye Show* (NBC). Packard Automobiles sponsors singer Martha Wright on *The Martha Wright Show* (ABC; also known as *The Packard Showroom*). Stan Freeman hosts *Melody Tour* (ABC), a look at the world via music. Country and western artists perform at a ranch setting

on the syndicated *Pee Wee King's Flying Ranch*. Acts from the Apollo Theater in Harlem are presented on *Showtime at the Apollo* (Syn.; hosted by Willie Bryant). The Henry Sylvern Orchestra accompanies Merv Griffin and Betty Lynn on *Song Snapshots on a Summer Holiday* (CBS). Spike Jones and the City Slickers perform their outlandish lampoons of famous songs on *The Spike Jones Show* (CBS). Elvis Presley was the emcee for six occasions on *Stage Show*, a CBS series hosted by Tommy and Jimmy Dorsey. Texaco Gasoline sponsors *The Texaco Star Theater* with Jimmy Durante as the host (NBC). Steve Allen becomes the first host of *The Tonight Show* on NBC (Ernie Kovacs, Jack Paar and Johnny Carson would become later hosts). The David Rose Orchestra provides backing for singer Tony Martin on *The Tony Martin Show* (NBC). Julius La Rosa hosts *TV's Top Tunes*, a CBS series that presents renditions of famous songs. Bandleader Vaughn Monroe performs on *The Vaughn Monroe Show* (NBC).

1955. Country and western artists perform on *The Grand Ole Opry* (ABC). Music mixes with comedy on *Here's the Show* (NBC; hosted by Jonathan Winters and Ransom Sherman). Music and skits are presented on *The Jan Murray Show* (NBC). Songs, skits and interviews are presented on *The Johnny Carson Show* (CBS). Country and western artists perform on *Jubilee, U.S.A.*, an ABC series hosted by Red Foley. Singer Julius La Rosa performs on *The Julius La Rosa Show* (NBC). Lawrence Welk and his Champagne Music Makers begin a long ABC run (to 1971) as well as in syndication (1971–83) on *The Lawrence Welk Show*. Frank Sinatra performs off-camera introductions for pianist Matt Dennis on *The Matt Dennis Show* (NBC). Slapstick comedy is combined with music and songs on *The Milton Berle Show* (NBC). The various fields of music are explored with Stan Kenton on *Music '55* (CBS). Singer Patti Page headlines her own syndicated series on *The Patti Page Show*. Country and western artists perform on *The Pee Wee King Show* (ABC). The Mitchell Ayres Orchestra provides backing for singer Perry Como on *The Perry Como Show* (NBC). Army talent performs on *Soldier Parade* (NBC). Horace Heidt and his orchestra salute various American cities on *The Swift Show Wagon* (NBC; sponsored by Swift Foods). Slim Pickens hosts *Talent Varieties*, an ABC series that features performances by country and western artists. Singers perform daily on *Ted Mack's Mati-*

nee (NBC). Music and songs are presented with a country-western accent on *The Tennessee Ernie Ford Show* (NBC). Popular music and songs are presented on *This Is Your Music*, a syndicated series hosted by Byron Palmer.

1956. The Benny Payne Trio accompanies singer Billy Daniels on *The Billy Daniels Show* (ABC). Music and songs from the Great White Way are presented on *Chevrolet on Broadway* (NBC; hosted by Gisele MacKenzie). Harry Zimmerman and his orchestra accompany Dinah Shore on *The Dinah Shore Show* (NBC). Country and western artists perform on NBC's *Eddy Arnold Time*. Pianist Frankie Carle headlines a CBS series called *Frankie Carle Time*. The Van Alexander Orchestra accompany singer Gordon MacRae on *The Gordon MacRae Show* (NBC). Female orchestra Ian Ray Hutton and a bevy of beautiful girls entertain on *The Ina Ray Hutton Show* (NBC). The Joel Herron Orchestra backs Singer Jaye P. Morgan on *The Jaye P. Morgan Show* (ABC). Faye Emerson hosts *Of All Things*, a summer series of music and songs on CBS. Singer Patti Page also hosts a summer series of music and songs on *The Patti Page Show* (NBC). Bandleader Ray Anthony headlines his own series on *The Ray Anthony Show* (Syn/ABC). Western singer Foy Willing and the Riders of the Purple Sage perform songs about cowboys and the west on the variety pilot *The Riders of the Purple Sage*. Vocalist Helen O'Connell joins Russ Morgan on *The Russ Morgan Show* (CBS). Singer Snooky Lanson is featured on his own program, *The Snooky Lanson Show* (NBC). Steve Allen brings his brand of humor to TV on *The Steve Allen Show*. The NBC series features Don Knotts, Louis Nye and Tom Poston. Singer Tony Bennett appears with the Spellbinders on *The Tony Bennett Show* (NBC). Tutti Camarata and his orchestra provide backing for singer Vic Damone on *The Vic Damone Show* (CBS). Bandleader Vincent Lopez performs on his own series, *The Vincent Lopez Show* (CBS). Newspaper columnist Walter Winchell hosts performances by guests on *The Walter Winchell Show* (NBC). Music and songs set against the background of New York's Greenwich Village are seen on *Washington Square* (NBC; hosted by Ray Bolger).

1957. Teenagers dance to music on *American Bandstand* (ABC) with Dick Clark as the host. Andy Williams and June Valli team for a songfest on *The Andy Williams–June Valli Show* (NBC).

Guest artists perform on *Club Oasis* (NBC). Don Sherwood hosts *Club 60*, a live color program of music and songs on NBC. The Buddy Bregman Orchestra accompanies singer Eddie Fisher on *The Eddie Fisher Show* (NBC). Music and songs are mixed with anthology-like dramas on *The Frank Sinatra Show* (ABC). Comedian George Gobel hosts a program of light comedy and music on *The George Gobel Show* (NBC). Vocalist Gisele MacKenzie is supported by the Axel Stordahl Orchestra on *The Gisele MacKenzie Show* (NBC). Singer Guy Mitchell receives accompaniment by the Van Alexander Orchestra on *The Guy Mitchell Show* (NBC). Singer Helen O'Connell is supported by the David Rose Orchestra on *The Helen O'Connell Show* (NBC). The Pete King Orchestra backs singer Kay Starr on the syndicated *Kay Starr Show*. Mort Lindsey and his orchestra provide backup for singer Pat Boone on *The Pat Boone Show* (ABC). Metropolitan Opera soprano Patrice Munsel headlines a program of music and songs on *The Patrice Munsel Show* (ABC). Vic Schoen and his orchestra provide accompaniment for singer Patti Page on *The Patti Page Show* (CBS). Singer Polly Bergen receives backup from the Luther Henderson, Jr. Orchestra on *The Polly Bergen Show* (NBC). Western film star Tex Ritter hosts a syndicated program of country and western music on *Ranch Party*. Nelson Riddle and his orchestra provide musical backing for Rosemary Clooney on *The Rosemary Clooney Show* (NBC). The lyrics to songs are rolled across the bottom of the screen to enable viewers to sing along on CBS's *Sing Along*. Xavier Cugat and his orchestra perform music featuring the Continental Sound on *The Xavier Cugat Show*. The NBC series also features singer Abbe Lane.

1958. Edie Adams, Janet Blair and John Raitt host a warm weather program of music and songs on *The Chevy Summer Show* (NBC). Rock and Roll personalities perform on *The Dick Clark Saturday Night Beechnut Show* (ABC; sponsored by Beechnut Chewing Gum). Garry Moore hosts a relaxed program of music, songs and comedy on *The Garry Moore Show* (CBS). Former stripper Gypsy Rose Lee hosts an informal program of music and talk on *The Gypsy Rose Lee Show* (Syn.). The Kraft Foods Company sponsors a weekly program of lavish music and songs on *The Kraft Music Hall* (NBC). Milton Berle, Perry Como and Dave King are the hosts. The Orchestra of Gordon Robinson provides musical backing for pianist Liberace on *The Liberace Show* (ABC). Vic Schoen and his orchestra perform with Patti Page on *The Patti Page Show* (ABC). Peter Lind Hayes and his wife Mary Healy perform popular songs with the backing of the Bert Farber Orchestra on *The Peter Lind Hayes Show* (ABC). Orchestra leader Sammy Kaye hosts a program of soothing music on *Sammy Kaye's Music from Manhattan* (ABC).

1959. Jack Kane and his orchestra provide the backing for Andy Williams on *The Andy Williams Show* (CBS). Revlon Cosmetics is the sponsor and Barbara Britton the host of *The Big Party for Revlon*, a CBS series in which guests gather at a pre-selected celebrity's home for an informal party. Country and western artists perform on the syndicated *Country Style, U.S.A.* Top name entertainers perform on the NBC pilot *Frances Langford Presents*. Alex Houston and His Texas Wildcats accompany country and western singer George Hamilton IV on *The George Hamilton IV Show* (ABC). Byron Morrow and his orchestra provide musical backing for Jimmie Rodgers on *The Jimmie Rodgers Show* (NBC). The Glenn Osser Orchestra performs on ABC's *Music for a Summer Night*. The music industry's top artists appear on *The Music Shop* (NBC). ABC's *Oh, Boy* presents performances by country and western artists. Jaye P. Morgan, Tony Bennett and Teresa Brewer perform on *Perry Presents*, the NBC summer replacement for *The Perry Como Show*. Colin Male hosts *This Is Music*, a revised version of the 1951 series in which a cast pantomimes recordings of famous artists.

1960. Neil Hefti and his orchestra accompany singer Kate Smith on *The Kate Smith Show* (CBS). Glenn Osser and his orchestra perform on *Music for a Spring Night* (ABC). Skating personalities appear on *Music on Ice* (NBC; hosted by Johnny Desmond). The top names in music are presented on the NBC pilot *NBC Saturday Prom* with host Merv Griffin. Country and western artists perform on *The Porter Wagoner Show* (Syn.). Revlon Cosmetics sponsors the *Revlon Revue* (CBS), a series tailored to the talents of its guest hosts. Spike Jones and the City Slickers host a summer program of music and songs on *The Spike Jones Show* (CBS).

Ventriloquists see *Puppets and Marionettes*

Vietnam War see *War — Korea, Vietnam and Iraq*

Visually Impaired Characters

Characters who are blind or who have difficulty seeing are the subjects of this entry. Single episode (guest) appearances are excluded.

1955. Alec Templeton, a blind pianist, hosts his own variety series called *Alec Templeton Time* on DuMont.

1957. Boris Karloff plays Colonel Perceval March, a British inspector with Scotland Yard, who wears a patch over his left eye on the syndicated *Colonel March of Scotland Yard*. Jack Elam plays the role of Toothy Thompson, the sidekick to Tom Brewster on ABC's *Sugarfoot*. Jack has an immobile eye (the result of a fight at the age of 12). His other series are *The Dakotas* (1963), *The Texas Wheelers* (1974), *Struck by Lightning* (1979), *Detective in the House* (1985) and *Easy Street* (1986).

1964. Jim Backus provides the voice for Quincy Magoo, a crusty, nearsighted and almost blind old man who plays various historical figures on the animated *Famous Adventures of Mr. Magoo* (NBC). Jim also provided Magoo's voice in a series of theatrical cartoons that have been seen on TV in syndication.

1965. Joe Brooks is Private Vanderbilt, the nearly blind lookout (for Indians) at Fort Courage in 1860s Kansas on *F Troop* (ABC). As a child Peter Falk lost sight in his right eye after an operation. In his first series, *The Trials of O'Brien* (CBS), he plays New York lawyer Daniel J. O'Brien but no mention is made of his vision problem.

1966. Douglas V. Fowley plays Andrew Hanks, the almost blind father of Henrietta Hanks, a woman who upholds the peace in the town of Wretched, Colorado (1871) on *Pistols 'n' Petticoats* (CBS). Performer Sammy Davis, Jr., has a glass left eye as the result of a car accident in 1955. Sammy has appeared on many TV shows and starred on *The Sammy Davis, Jr. Show* (1966) and on *Sammy and Company* (1975).

1971. Peter Falk plays the intrepid Lieutenant Columbo of the L.A.P.D. on *Columbo* (NBC) but no mention is made of his artificial right eye. James Franciscus is Michael Longstreet, an insurance investigator for Great Pacific Casualty who was blinded in an explosion but continues in his capacity on ABC's *Longstreet*. Michael receives help from his braille teacher, Nikki (Marlyn Mason), and his martial arts instructor, Li Tsung (Bruce Lee). Comedian Marty Feldman is known for his huge bulging eyes, the result of a hyperactive thyroid and a botched operation after a car accident. Marty starred on *The Marty Feldman Comedy Machine* in 1971.

1972. Keye Luke plays Master Po, the blind Shaolin priest, on *Kung Fu* (ABC). Master Po helped guide the life of Kwai Chang Caine, a young orphan who would grow up to become a Shaolin priest and wander across the American frontier of the 1870s. Sandy Duncan plays Sandy Stockton, a student teacher at U.C.L.A. who (in real life) is blind in her left eye (a result of an eye operation during the filming of her 1971 series *Funny Face*). After recovering Sandy played the same role on *The Sandy Duncan Show* (CBS). In 1986 she would star on *The Hogan Family* (NBC), but no mention is ever made of her vision problem.

1974. Melissa Sue Anderson plays Mary Ingalls, the daughter of Charles and Caroline Ingalls, on *Little House on the Prairie* (NBC). Scarlet Fever claimed Mary's eyesight when she was a teenager. She attended the Sleepy Eye School for the Blind where she fell in love with and married Adam Kendall (Linwood Boomer), her blind instructor who, through a freak accident, later regained his sight.

1976. Eileen (Jewel Blanch) is a blind teenage girl who is dating Jeff (Leigh McCloskey), a sighted boy. To strengthen their relationship, Jeff spends one day blindfolded on the ABC special *Blind Sunday*.

1978. Jack Gilford is Grandpa Hollyhock, a senile blind man who applied for the position of grandfather when the lonely Ginger Nell Hollyhock advertised for a family on *Apple Pie* (ABC). Warren Oates plays Rooster Cogburn, a crusty, one-eyed, hard-drinking Old West Marshal on the ABC pilot *True Grit: A Further Adventure* (based on the feature film *True Grit*).

1979. Bill Quinn plays Edgar Van Ranseleer, the elderly blind patron of bar owner Archie Bunker on *Archie Bunker's Place* (CBS).

1980. Susan Bigelow plays Karen Alexander, a sighted woman who is married to Jonathan (Philip Levien), a blind jingles writer on the CBS pilot *Love at First Sight*.

1982. CBS revises the above pilot with Philip Levien as Jonathan Grant, a blind jingles writer for the Fame Advertising agency, and his sighted wife Karen (Susan Bigelow).

1984. Alex Cord plays Michael Archangel, the government agent (wears an eye patch) Stringfellow Hawke helps on CBS's *Airwolf*. River Phoenix stars as Brian Ellsworth, a teenager struggling to cope with the problems of dyslexia on the ABC special *Backwards: The Riddle of Dyslexia*. Theo (Malcolm-Jamal Warner), the eldest son of Cliff and Clair Huxtable, suffers from dyslexia on *The Cosby Show* (NBC).

1985. Dana Elcar, who played the role of Peter Thornton, the Director of Field Operations for the Phoenix Foundation, on *MacGyver* (ABC), developed glaucoma in 1989. His character was revised to include the medical condition.

1986. Jeffrey Tambor plays Paul Stark, an acerbic English professor at Kenyon College who is blind but uses his dry wit and fast thinking to deal with problems on *Mr. Sunshine* (ABC).

1987. Ken Page plays Joe Tyson, alias "Cheesecake" (for his love of strawberry cheesecake), the blind computer whiz on *Sable* (ABC). Joe provides information to Jon Sable, a man who battles crime as the mysterious Sable. LeVar Burton is Lieutenant Geordi La Forge, a member of Starfleet, who is blind but can see via a prosthetic VISOR (Visual Input Sensory Optical Reflector) on *Star Trek: The Next Generation* (Syn.). Chuck Connors plays the evil Janos Skorzeny, a sea captain (with a black patch over his left eye) who was also a werewolf on Fox's *Werewolf*.

1989. Rex Smith plays Matt Murdock, a blind lawyer who fights crime as the mysterious Dare Devil on the CBS pilot *Dare Devil* (as a teenager Matt was exposed to a radioactive liquid that blinded him but gave him extraordinary powers including amplified sense which allows him to function as well as a sighted person). Mark Blankfield plays Freddy, the almost blind elevator operator in a New York hotel called *The Nutt House* (NBC).

1990. Robert Shayne is Reggie, the blind newsstand operator who knows (and keeps) the secret of Barry Allen — he is the crime fighter known as *The Flash* (CBS). Wendy Robie plays Nadine Hurley, a woman who wears an patch over her left eye and is a resident of the strange community of *Twin Peaks* (ABC).

1991. Mark Blankfield is George, the blind

(and clumsy) university psychiatrist who is in love with Genny (Margaret Whitton), the biochemist who experiments on herself on ABC's *Good and Evil*.

1992. Tracey Walter plays Blinky Watts, the visually impaired sound effects director on the mythical "The Lester Guy Show" on ABC's *On the Air*. Blinky suffers from Bozeman Syndrome and sees 26 times more than the normal person. Ivory Oceans plays Roosevelt "King" Cole, the blind publisher of the *Meteor*, a Key West, Florida, newspaper on Fox's *Key West*.

1993. David Duchovny is Fox Mulder, an FBI agent who investigates strange phenomena but who is also color blind on *The X-Files* (Fox).

1994. Eddie Bracken plays Father Burke, the blind Catholic priest in Oak Bluff, Illinois, on NBC's *Winnetka Road*.

1995. David James Elliott plays Lt. Commander Harmon Rabb, Jr., a navy pilot who suffers from night blindness on *JAG* (NBC/CBS).

1996. Shanesia Davis-Williams is Marissa Clark, the blind bookkeeper for Gary Hobson, the owner of McGinty's Bar, who receives tomorrow's newspaper today on CBS's *Early Edition*.

1998. Alex Desert is Jake Malinak, the blind man who runs the newsstand inside Reggie's Diner on *Becker* (CBS). Dee Jay Daniels plays Michael, the young son of Darryl Hughley who suffers from dyslexia on *The Hughleys* (ABC/UPN).

1999. Jamey Sheridan, who plays Captain James Deakins on NBC's *Law and Order: Criminal Intent*, wears an eye patch (at times) due to Bell's Palsy, a condition that causes facial muscles to weaken and become paralyzed.

2000. Daniel von Bargen is Commandant Edwin Spangler, the headmaster of the military academy the mischievous Francis (the son of Hal and Lois) attends on *Malcolm in the Middle* (Fox). Edwin wears a patch over his left eye (he is also missing his right hand, wears a black glove on his left hand and walks with a limp). John Aylward plays Albert McGonagle, a blind paranormal whose visions enable him to see ghosts on *The Others* (NBC).

2002. Jason O'Mara is A.B. Stiles, a CIA agent who suffers from color blindness on *The Agency* (CBS). Max (Luis Armand Garcia), the young son of George and Angie Lopez, suffers from dyslexia (the same affliction George had) on *The George Lopez Show* (ABC). Dominic Purcell is John Doe,

a man with an exceptional I.Q. but is color blind on Fox's *John Doe*.

2005. Ron Eldard plays Jim Dunbar, an NYPD detective who was blinded after being shot but remains active on the force on ABC's *Blind Justice*.

War — Civil War see The Civil War

War — Korea, Vietnam, Iraq

This entry lists the specific programs dealing with the U.S. involvement on the Korean, Vietnam and Iraqi battlefields. See also *The Civil War, War — World War II*.

1972. *M*A*S*H* airs on CBS. The 4077th Mobile Army Surgical Hospital, located about five miles from the Korean War front, is the setting for a gritty look at the lives of the doctors and nurses in wartime. Alan Alda as the nonconformist Dr. Benjamin Franklin Pierce, and Loretta Swit as the strictly military army nurse, Major Margaret Houlihan, head the large cast. Other regulars include Larry Linville (Major Frank Burns), Wayne Rogers (Trapper John McIntire), Mike Farrell (B.J. Hunnicutt), McLean Stevenson (Colonel Henry Blake) and Harry Morgan (Colonel Sherman Potter).

1977. CBS airs *Handle with Care*, a pilot about a group of army nurses assigned to a M*A*S*H unit on the Korean War front. Mary Jo Catlett plays Major Charlotte Hinkley, the head of the unit. Marlyn Mason and Didi Conn play nurses Liz Baker and Jackie Morse.

1978. *The Fighting Nightingales* is a CBS pilot that stars Adrienne Barbeau as Major Kate Steele, the head of a combat weary unit of nurses stationed in Korea during the war.

1979. Myron, Billy, Carmine and Rick (Bo Kaprall, Donald Petrie, Richard Dimitri, Richard Lewis) are Vietnam Army Reservists assigned to combat training as part of the 416th Medical Detachment Supply Distribution Team, the U.S. Army's smallest and most confused unit on the CBS pilot *The 416th*.

1980. *The Six O'clock Follies* (NBC) is set during the Vietnam War (Saigon, 1967). The setting is the Armed Forces Vietnam Network, a TV station that produces the AFVN news and sports on a six o'clock program called "The Follies." Joby

Baker heads the cast as Colonel Harvey Marvin. A.C. Weary plays Sam Paige, the newscaster and Aarika Wells is Candi Le Roy, the weathergirl.

1981. The ABC pilot *Fly Away Home* is set in South Vietnam (1968) and presents a view of the war as seen through the eyes of Carl Danton (Bruce Boxleitner), a war correspondent for the TBC-TV Network.

1987. A grueling portrait of the horrors of war is presented by CBS on *Tour of Duty*. Here viewers follow the members of Bravo Company as they serve a 12-month tour of duty in Vietnam in 1967. Terrence Knox heads the large cast as Sergeant Zeke Anderson. Others in the cast are Ramon Franco (Pvt. Alberto Ruiz), Tony Becker (Capt. Danny Percell) and Miguel Nunez, Jr. (Pvt. Marcus Taylor). HBO airs *Vietnam War Story*, a series of stark reality war stories based on the actual experiences of Vietnam vets. The stories, which are very graphic, are not suitable for broadcast television and feature different stars and stories.

1988. Colleen McMurphy (Dana Delany) and Cherry White (Nan Woods) are trauma nurses with the U.S. Army's 510th Evac Hospital on China Beach in Da Nang at the height of the Vietnam War on *China Beach* (ABC). A bittersweet look at life in Vietnam during the war is seen through the eyes of Matt Thompson (Jeffrey Nordling), a young combat photographer on the NBC pilot *Shooter*.

2005. A U.S. army unit struggling through its first tour of duty in Iraq is the focus of *Over There*, a gritty FX series starring Luke McFarlane (Pvt. Chris Silas), Erik Palladino (Sgt. Chris Silas), Nicki Ajcox (Pvt. Brenda Mitchell) and Lizette Carrion (Pfc. Esmeralda Del Rio).

War—World War II

This entry chronicles the programs that deal with the Second World War. See also *The Civil War* and *The Korean, Vietnam and Iraqi Wars*.

1944. The time is June 6. The place is Brooklyn, New York. A young woman (Lesley Woods) is about to spend $275 on a fur coat when she meets a soldier named Casey (Joseph Julian). While talking the girl learns first hand of Casey's horrifying war experiences on the battlefront. The girl is drawn to tears as she listens. Before leaving Casey convinces the girl to use her money for

something more important — war bonds. The audience then learns that Casey has been killed in action in France and that his ghost was used to convey a message — support the war. Although the NBC program was used to sell war bonds, it is also TV's first attempt to relate a view of a war that was actually being fought at the time. DuMont airs the World War II drama, *Miracle at Blaise* on August 22. Here Claire Luce played a mysterious American girl who risks her life to help the French underground battle Nazis. *Two Soldiers* airs on NBC on October 27. It is adapted from the story by William Faulkner and shows the effects the outbreak of Word War II has on a simple mountain family in Tennessee. Three CBS experimental programs called *Women in Wartime* also relay the tragedies of World War II. Beth Blackwell hosts the first program (November 16) wherein two dramas are presented. The first deals with a group of women facing the difficulties of preparing meals and acquiring clothing due to the wartime restrictions. The second story shows how maps in a war zone can save the lives of soldiers. "Christmas Without Tinsel" is the subject of the second program (December 14). Keith Woodner hosts a story about the Christmas season and how the women of G.I.s left behind cope with the holidays. Beth Blackwell hosts the last program (April 18, 1945) and introduces a wartime love story about two underground workers (Ann Shepherd, William Hollenbeck) who fall in love and marry and are suddenly separated when the girl is sent on a dangerous mission.

1945. NBC adapts the World War II radio play *Beachhead at Louie's* to TV on September 16. The story is set at Louie's, a popular European bar that is frequented by American servicemen who find it a place to relax and work out their problems. Joseph Marion, Jay Norris and Emily Ross star. DuMont airs *The Town Crier of Chung King*, a drama about the Chinese underground and the efforts of two brothers (Jay Gorlin, George Kahn) and their sister (Joan Danton) to infiltrate the Japanese supply lines and blow up their links. NBC adapts the Norman Corwin radio play *Untitled* to TV on May 24. It tells the rather unsettling story of Hank Peters (Michael Everett), a deceased serviceman who rises from his resting place on the battlefield to tell the audience how he came to be there.

1950. Richard Denning plays Ding Howe, head of the Flying Tigers, a group of American volunteers who fly daring missions against the Japanese on the syndicated *Ding Howe and the Flying Tigers*.

1952. The U.S. Naval operations during World War II are seen via archival film footage on *Victory at Sea*, an NBC documentary narrated by Leonard Graves.

1953. Art Fleming plays Major Dell Conway, head of the Third Pursuit Squadron, a group of American volunteers (part of General Chenault's Gallant Fighters) who fly missions to destroy Japanese Zeros on *Major Dell Conway of the Flying Tigers* (Syn.).

1955. While not totally devoted to World War II, the CBS anthology *Navy Log* dramatizes incidents in the lives of the men who served with the Navy during the war and after.

1956. Incidents in the lives of the Allied Forces battle against Rommel's Afrika Korps are seen on ABC's *Combat Sergeant*. Michael Thomas and Cliff Clark star as Sergeant Nelson and General Harrison. Films that recount the history of Britain's Royal Air Force during World War II are seen on the syndicated *War in the Air*.

1957. Merle Oberon is a foreign correspondent whose reports show the role the French Foreign Legion played during the North African Campaign during World War II on *Assignment: Foreign Legion* (CBS). True stories of Americans in combat are seen on the syndicated anthology series *The Big Attack* (also known as *Citizen Soldier*). Ron Rondell plays Frank Hawthorne, an agent of the O.S.S. (Office of Strategic Services) during World War II on *O.S.S.* (ABC).

1959. Brian Kelly and Joe Flynn star on *Skyfighters*, a syndicated pilot about a group of American flyers stationed in the European Theater of War. *War Correspondent* is a CBS pilot for an anthology series that was to relate the experiences of correspondents covering World War II in various parts of the world.

1961. The war activities of the men of K Company (Second Platoon of the U.S. Infantry) from their D-Day landing to victory one year later is seen on ABC's *Combat!* Rick Jason stars as Lt. Gil Hanley with Vic Morrow as Sgt. Chip Saunders.

1962. The Navy and World War II are satirized on ABC's *McHale's Navy*. Ernest Borgnine plays Quinton McHale, a lieutenant who commands Squadron 19 and P.T. Boat 73 on the South Pacific island of Taratupa. He commands a group of misfit sailors and is the target of Wallace B. Bing-

hamton (Joe Flynn), a captain who feels McHale and his "band of cutthroats" is ruining his life and seeks a way to get him transferred. Dick Powell stars as Colonel Luke Harper on *Squadron*, an NBC pilot about the combat activities and emotional problems of the men of an Air Force unit.

1963. The key battles and campaigns of World War II are traced through films on the syndicated *Battleline* (narrated by Jim Bishop). William Reynolds plays Conley Wright, a war correspondent (assigned to the 36th Infantry of the American Fifth Army) who reports the actions of men in combat on ABC's *The Gallant Men*. Van Williams plays Lt. Dave Cameron, the head of a group of Marines during World War II on the ABC pilot *The Leathernecks*. Britain's naval battles during World War II are depicted on the syndicated documentary *Sea War*.

1964. *Broadside*, the *McHale's Navy* spinoff focuses on the comical activities of four beautiful WAVES assigned to the motor pool on the South Pacific island of New Caledonia: Lt. Anne Morgan (Kathleen Nolan) and Privates Molly McGuire (Lois Roberts), Roberta Love (Joan Staley) and Selma Kowalski (Sheila James). A filmed history of the British and American participation in the Second World War is seen on the syndicated *Great War* (narrated by Sir Michael Redgrave). Robert Lansing is General Frank Savage, the head of the American 918th B-17 Bomber Squadron in England during World War II on *Twelve O'clock High* (ABC).

1965. John Gavin is Commander Dan Talbot and John Larch is Captain Ben Foster, the men in charge of a convoy of 200 heavily armed American ships slowly heading toward England on NBC's *Convoy*. Tony Randall plays Willie Coogan, a war correspondent who dislikes covering battles but does so because he has to on the CBS pilot *Coogan's Reward*. Major Simon Butcher (Jack Warden) captains the *Kiwi*, a two-masted 1871 schooner that has been incorporated by U.S. Army Intelligence to pose as a neutral Swedish vessel (to roam the South Pacific and observe Japanese movements) on *The Wackiest Ship in the Army* (NBC; based on the feature film).

1966. David March (Robert Goulet), an agent for Blue Light Control, renounces his American citizenship and poses as a traitor to join the ranks of the German High Command (to destroy it from within) on ABC's *Blue Light*. Attorneys Frank Whittaker (Peter Graves) and David Young

(Bradford Dillman) of the Judge Advocate General's Office defend American military personnel on ABC's *Court-Martial*. Franklin Shepherd, Nicholas Gage and Jean-Gaston Andre (Don Francks, John Leyton, Marino Mase) are Allied agents who infiltrate enemy lines to sabotage and discredit the Germans under the code name *Jericho* (CBS). Rod Ryan (Michael Burns) is a 16-year-old boy who looks older than he appears, joins the Air Force, quickly moves up the ranks and is assigned to a small base in England on the ABC pilot *Off We Go*. The experiences of the officers and crew of a U.S. naval submarine during World War II are depicted on the ABC pilot *Pursue and Destroy*. Van Williams stars as Lt. Commander Russ Enright. Sam Troy (Christopher George) is the head of the Rat Patrol, a squadron of four desert allies assigned to harass and demoralize Rommel's Afrika Korps on *The Rat Patrol* (ABC). Robert Reed is Lt. John Leahy, the head of a fouled-up infantry squadron cut off from its battalion command on the ABC pilot *Somewhere in Italy ... Company B*.

1967. Ron Harper is Lt. Craig Garrison, the head of a group of four convicts (chosen from various federal pens) who demoralize German troops in Europe on ABC's *Garrison's Gorillas*. Avery Schreiber and Jack Burns plays Spivak and Minihane, members of a ragtag entertainment unit assigned to tour the Normandy Combat Zone on the CBS pilot *Operation Greasepaint*.

1973. An Air Force base staffed by an assortment of odd people is the focus on the ABC pilot *Catch-22* (based on the feature film). Richard Dreyfuss stars as Captain Yossarian with Dana Elcar as Colonel Cathcart. Stu Gilliam and Hilly Hicks star as Carter "Sweet" Williams and Jed Brooks, members of the 5050th Quartermaster Trucking Company of the U.S Third Army's Red Ball Express, a mostly black unit that delivers supplies to the front lines on *Roll Out!* (CBS). The history of World War II is traced from the rise of Hitler to Allied victory on the syndicated documentary *The World at War* (narrated by Sir Laurence Olivier).

1976. Robert Conrad plays Major Gregory "Pappy" Boyington, a daring air ace and commander of the VMF 214 Black Sheep, a squadron of misfit pilots on NBC's *Baa Baa Black Sheep* (later titled *The Black Sheep Squadron*). Betty, Cookie, Paula, Lizard and Alice (Michele Lee, Susan Lanier, Pat Finley, Alice Playten, Mary Jo

Catlett) are female communications officers who become stranded on an all-male army base when their plane crashes on the NBC pilot *Over and Out*. Lou Jacobi, Cliff Norton and Eddie Foy, Jr., star on *Rear Guard*, an ABC pilot about an American Civil Defense volunteer group during World War II. The insanity of war is seen through the eyes of battle-weary G.I.s spending World War II in the muddy trenches of Italy on the ABC pilot *SNAFU* (Situation Normal, All Fouled Up). Tony Roberts and James Cromwell star.

1977. *The Banana Company* (CBS pilot) is the nickname for a group of combat correspondents who go to outrageous lengths to acquire stories. Ron Masak, Ted Gehring and John Reilly star. ABC produces three pilots called *McNamara's Band* with John Byner as Johnny McNamara, the leader of a group of ex-cons who are recruited to perform hazardous assignments behind enemy lines. In the first pilot (May 14), Johnny and the team (Zoltan, Gaffney, Frankie, Milgrim and Aggie) are ex-cons; the second pilot (December 5), the team, dubbed "The Dirty One-Third of a Dozen," are misfit police officers (the character of Milgrim has been replaced by Milano); the final pilot (June 10, 1978) has the team as "cuckoo" ex–New York police officers. Dolores Crandell (Melinda Naud), Edna Hayward (Yvonne Wilder), Barbara Duran (Jamie Lee Curtis), Ruth Colfax (Dorrie Thompson) and Claire Reid (Bond Gideon) are five army nurses stranded on a pink submarine (the *Sea Tiger*) commanded by Matthew Sherman (John Astin) on *Operation Petticoat* (ABC).

1978. Shelly Alhern (James Whitmore, Jr.) and Ted Brinkerhoff (Tom Selleck) are U.S. Army captains who pose as gypsies to tackle dangerous assignments behind enemy lines in Germany on the CBS pilot *The Gypsy Warriors*. ABC revises *Operation Petticoat* (see 1977) as *The New Operation Petticoat*, wherein the submarine *Sea Tiger* is assigned to duty as a sea going ambulance. Sam Heller (Robert Hogan) is the captain, and Melinda Naud, Jo Ann Pflug and Hilary Thompson are the nurses (Dolores Crandall, Katherine O'Hara and Betty Wheeler).

1980. Peter Buchanan (Kenneth Gilman) and John Vitella (Jonathan Banks) are members of a squad of servicemen who serve as "mop up" troops during the Italian Campaign on the CBS pilot *The G.I.'s*. In England in 1939, Jackie Scott (Mariette Hartley) recruits five nurses to secretly perform missions behind enemy lines on the NBC pilot *The Secret War of Jackie's Girls*. Lee Purcell, Ann Dusenberry, Tracy Brooks Swope and Caroline Smith play the nurses, Casey, Donna, Zimmy, Patti and Maxine.

1983. Robert Mitchum, Ali McGraw, Jan-Michael Vincent and Ralph Bellamy head a large cast on *The Winds of War*, an epic ABC miniseries that relates the events that led up to Pearl Harbor.

1988. In an attempt to infiltrate enemy lines in Europe, the U.S. Army recruits a group of military convicts to form a suicide mission unit called the Dirty Dozen on *The Dirty Dozen: The Series* (Fox; based on the feature film). Ben Murphy stars as Lieutenant Danko with John Slattery as Dylan Leeds and Jon Tenney as Janos Feke. *War and Remembrance* (ABC), the sequel to 1983's *The Winds of War*, depicts the attack on Pearl Harbor and America's entrance into the Second World War. Robert Mitchum, Jane Seymour, Victoria Tennant and Sharon Stone star.

1989. Bob Hope, Maxene Andrews, Frances Langford and Mel Blanc are among the guests who appear on *Entertaining the Troops*, a PBS special that uses archival footage to salute the performers who gave of their time to entertain the troops in war zones.

2001. The story of the Easy Company of the U.S. Army Airborne Paratroop Division and their missions in World War II France during Operation Over Lord are depicted on HBO's *Band of Brothers*. Damian Lewis, Donnie Walberg and Ron Livingston head a large cast.

Washington, D.C.

A listing of series set in and around Washington, D.C. (Washington state locales are indicated with the program).

1950. *Treasury Men in Action* (ABC).
1953. *Pentagon U.S.A.* (CBS).
1962. *Mr. Smith Goes to Washington* (ABC).
1963. *The Farmer's Daughter* (ABC).
1964. *Slattery's People* (CBS).
1965. *The F.B.I.* (ABC); *Get Smart* (NBC).
1966. *The Double Life of Henry Phyfe* (ABC); *The Green Hornet* (ABC); *Mr. Terrific* (CBS).
1968. *Here Come the Brides* (ABC; Seattle); *It Takes a Thief* (ABC).
1970. *The Silent Force* (ABC).
1971. *O'Hara, U.S. Treasury* (CBS).

1972. *Cool Million* (NBC); *The Delphi Bureau* (ABC); *Search* (NBC); *Temperatures Rising* (ABC).
1973. *The New Temperatures Rising Show* (ABC).
1974. *That's My Mama* (ABC).
1975. *Karen* (ABC); *Wonder Woman* (ABC/CBS).
1976. *All's Fair* (CBS); *Ball Four* (CBS).
1978. *Baby, I'm Back* (CBS); *Grandpa Goes to Washington* (NBC).
1981. *Today's F.B.I.* (ABC).
1983. *Mr. Smith* (NBC); *Scarecrow and Mrs. King* (CBS).
1984. *Domestic Life* (CBS); *Rituals* (Syn.).
1985. *Hail to the Chief* (ABC); *227* (NBC).
1986. *One Big Family* (Syn.).
1987. *Mr. President* (Fox); *The New Adventures of Beans Baxter* (Fox); *A Year in the Life* (NBC).
1988. *Murphy Brown* (CBS).
1989. *FM* (NBC); *Snoops* (CBS).
1991. *Good and Evil* (ABC); *Harry and the Hendersons* (Syn.; Seattle).
1992. *Hearts Afire* (CBS); *The Powers That Be* (NBC).
1993. *Frasier* (NBC; Seattle).
1995. *University Hospital* (Syn.).
1998. *Smart Guy* (WB).
1999. *The West Wing* (NBC).
2000. *DAG* (NBC/CBS); *The District* (CBS); *Level 9* (UPN).
2002. *John Doe* (Fox; Seattle); *Sue Thomas, F.B.Eye* (PAX).
2003. *Charlie Lawrence* (CBS); *Jake 2.0* (UPN); *Mister Sterling* (NBC); *Wanda at Large* (Fox).
2005. *Bones* (Fox); *Commander in Chief* (ABC); *E-Ring* (NBC); *Grey's Anatomy* (ABC; Seattle).

Werewolves

A listing of programs that feature or star beings that, under a full moon, become a wolf-like creature.

1964. Butch Patrick plays Edward Wolfgang Munster, the pre-teen werewolf son of Herman and Lily Munster on *The Munsters*.

1966. In addition to the vampire Barnabas Collins, *Dark Shadows* (ABC) features Alex Stevens as the werewolf who prowls the grounds of the Collinwood estate.

1976. Wax museum figure Bruce W. Wolf (Buck Kartalian), alias the Wolfman, comes to life to help criminology student Walt (Fred Grandy) battle crime on *The Monster Squad* (NBC).

1978. Sherman Fangsworth, called "Fang," is a teenager who changes into a werewolf under a full moon on the CBS animated series *Fang Face*.

1979. Jack Riley is the Wolfman, who with Dracula and Frankenstein, attempts to save his favorite holiday on the ABC special *The Halloween That Almost Wasn't*.

1980. The son of the Wolfman, Wolfman, Jr. (called Howler), joins Dracula, Jr., to battle the evil Dr. Dred on the animated CBS series *Drak Pack*.

1983. Robert Harper is Marv Hoberman, a werewolf who resides at a monsters-only apartment house in New York City on the CBS pilot *13 Thirteenth Avenue*.

1985. Knowl Johnson plays Walt Cribbens, a 13-year-old boy who inherits his family's affliction. He becomes a friendly werewolf for periods of two minutes at a time on the ABC special *The Adventures of a Two Minute Werewolf*.

1986. Townsend Coleman is the voice of Scott Howard, the teenager who becomes a werewolf when the moon is full on *Teen Wolf: The Animated Series*, an adaptation of the feature film *Teen Wolf*.

1987. John J. York plays Eric Cord, a college student seeking to end his curse, transformations into a werewolf, by destroying the original bloodline of the creature that bit him on *Werewolf* (Fox).

1988. The syndicated *The Munsters Today* presents an update of the 1964 series with Jason Marsden as Edward Wolfgang Munster, the werewolf son of Herman and Lily Munster.

1990. Randi Wallace (Kate Hodge) is a beautiful college coed who, while studying in England, is bitten by a werewolf and cursed to become a hideous demon under the full moon on *She Wolf of London* (Syn.; later titled *Love and Curses*).

1999. Tommy Dawkins (Brandon Quinn) is a high school student who is bitten by a werewolf, then becomes one himself when he encounters stressful situations on *Big Wolf on Campus* (Syn.).

Westerns

Once a prolific form of TV entertainment, the western is now a fond memory of a time long gone. This entry chronicles the western programs that have aired from 1948 through 2005.

1948. William Boyd plays Hopalong Cassidy, a rancher (owner of the Bar 20 Ranch) who battles injustice wherever he finds it on *The Gene Autry Show* (Syn.).

1949. "With his faithful Indian companion Tonto, the daring and resourceful Masked Rider of the Plains led the fight for law and order in the early west. Return with us now to those thrilling days of Yesteryear — the Lone Ranger rides again!" was said in the introduction to *The Lone Ranger* (ABC). Clayton Moore (then John Hart) plays the Lone Ranger (John Reid) with Jay Silverheels as Tonto.

1950. A marshal (Russell Hayden then Eddie Dean) and his deputy (Roscoe Ates) uphold the law in the ruthless town of Gunsight Pass on *The Marshal of Gunsight Pass* (ABC).

1951. "Here's romance ... Here's adventure ... Here's O. Henry's famous Robin Hood of the Old West, the Cisco Kid" was said to introduce *The Cisco Kid* (Syn.) with Duncan Renaldo as Cisco and Leo Carrillo as his sidekick Pancho. Gene Autry (himself), the Singing Cowboy, and his partner Pat Buttram (himself) fight for right on *The Gene Autry Show* (Syn.). "... And who could be more at home on the range than the Range Rider with his thrilling adventures, rivaling those of Davy Crockett, Buffalo Bill and other pioneers of this wonderful country of ours" was said to introduce Jock Mahoney as *The Range Rider* (Syn.), a daring defender of range justice, and his sidekick Dick West (Dick Jones), "The All-American boy." Roy Rogers, "The King of the Cowboys," and Dale Evans, "Queen of the West," uphold the law on *The Roy Rogers Show* (NBC).

1952. Pat Gallagher and Stoney Crockett (Russell Hayden, Jackie Coogan) are U.S. government undercover agents who patrol the west of the 1880s on the syndicated *Cowboy G-Men*. The Old Ranger (Stanley Andrews) introduces stories of the people who lived, worked and journeyed throughout California during the latter 1880s on the syndicated *Death Valley Days*. Ronald Reagan (1964–67), Robert Taylor (1967–69) and Dale Robertson (1969–72) were the other hosts. U.S. Marshal James Butler, better known as Wild Bill Hickok (Guy Madison) and his partner, Jingles P. Jones (Andy Devine) battle injustice in the west of the 1870s on the syndicated *Wild Bill Hickok*.

1953. CBS airs *Action in the Afternoon*, a daily,

live series about the citizens of Huberle, Montana, during the 1890s. Jack Valentine and Elaine Watts head the cast. Cattle rancher Red Ryder (Jim Bannon) and his Indian companion Little Beaver (himself) uphold the law in the Painted Valley in the Colorado Rockies on the pilot *Red Ryder*.

1954. Female sharpshooter Annie Oakley (Gail Davis) helps Deputy Lofty Craig (Brad Johnson) uphold the law In Diablo County, Arizona, on *Annie Oakley* (Syn.).

1955. Jack Carson plays Lamar Kendall, a self-appointed judge who struggles to uphold the law in Arroyo, New Mexico, on the NBC pilot *Arroyo*. A view of the west as seen through the eyes of the Indian is presented on *Brave Eagle: Chief of the Cheyenne*, a CBS series starring Keith Larsen as Brave Eagle. A lawman, Buffalo Bill, Jr. (Dick West), is helped and hindered by his younger sister Calamity (Nancy Gilbert), as he attempts to uphold the peace on the syndicated *Buffalo Bill, Jr.* Curley Bradley (himself) plays Marshal Bradley, a law enforcer who sings, but also uses his wits, rather than guns, to capture outlaws on the pilot *Curley Bradley, the Singing Marshal*. Walter Coy narrates stories depicting the hardships faced by pioneers as they journeyed west during the 19th century on *Frontier* (CBS). Marshal Matt Dillon (James Arness) and his deputy, Chester Goode (Dennis Weaver) uphold the law in Dodge City, Kansas, on *Gunsmoke* (CBS). Ken Curtis plays Matt's deputy, Festus Haggen, in later episodes. Edgar Buchanan plays Roy Bean, the self-appointed judge of Langtry, Texas, who fought to uphold the law in "America's most lawless region" on *Judge Roy Bean* (Syn.). Hugh O'Brian is Wyatt Earp, "brave, courageous and bold," a U.S. Marshal (first in Dodge City, Kansas, then Tombstone, Arizona) on *The Life and Legend of Wyatt Earp* (ABC). Marshal Steve Donovan (Douglas Kennedy) and his deputy Rusty Lee (Eddy Waller) uphold the law on the ruthless frontier of the mid 1800s on the syndicated *Steve Donovan, Western Marshal*.

1956. Christopher "Kit" Carson (Bill Williams) and his Mexican sidekick El Toro (Don Diamond) fight for justice on *The Adventures of Kit Carson* (Syn.). U.S. Army captain and Indian Agent Tom Jeffords (John Lupton) and Cochise (Michael Ansara), Chief of the Apache, struggle to maintain a broken arrow (peace between the white man and the Indian) on *Broken Arrow* (ABC). Clint Walker

is Cheyenne Bodie, a frontier scout learned in both the ways of the white man and the Cheyenne Indian, who is looking for a place to settle down on *Cheyenne* (ABC). "From out of the west ... *Dick Powell's Zane Grey Theater*," a CBS series of western dramas hosted by Dick Powell. Leon Ames plays John Cooper, a circuit-riding judge of the Old West on the syndicated *Frontier Judge*. Alan "Rocky" Lane plays Red Ryder and Louis Letteri is Little Beaver, his Navaho companion, ranchers who battle for right on the syndicated *Red Ryder*. Matt Clark (Jim Davis) and Frankie Adams (Mary Castle) are detectives for the Southwestern Railroad who strive to keep the line safe on *Stories of the Century* (Syn; in later episodes, Kristine Miller replaces Mary Castle as Jonesy Jones).

1957. Gene Barry is Barclay "Bat" Masterson, a wandering law enforcer, "known for his marching cane and derby hat," on *Bat Masterson* (NBC). The life and times of the officers of the American Fifth Cavalry during the 1870s are depicted on *Boots and Saddles*. The syndicated series stars Jack Pickard as Captain Shank Adams and Patrick McVey as Luke Cummings, the scout. Dion Patrick (Adam Kennedy) then Matt Wayne (Richard Coogan) attempt to establish a system of law and order in 1850s San Francisco on *The Californians* (NBC). Government undercover agent Christopher Colt (Wade Preston) poses as a salesman for the Colt .45 repeater to battle frontier lawlessness on *Colt. 45* (ABC; Chris is replaced by Donald May as Sam Colt, Jr., in later episodes). "Have Gun — Will Travel. Wire Paladin, Carlton Hotel, San Francisco" reads the card of Paladin (Richard Boone), a fast gun for hire who helps people in need on *Have Gun — Will Travel* (CBS). Bret and Bart Maverick (James Garner, Jack Kelly) are brothers and gentlemen gamblers who roam the west of the 1860s seeking rich prey on *Maverick* (ABC). John Payne plays Vint Bonner, a wandering ex-gunfighter (known as "The Six Gun") who helps people in trouble on *The Restless Gun* (NBC/ABC). In the original CBS pilot, John Payne plays the role as Britt Ponsett. Will Hutchins is Tom Brewster, a wandering cowboy who is studying law and sides with right against wrong on *Sugarfoot* (ABC). Dramas based on the files of the Texas Rangers are seen on ABC's *Tales of the Texas Rangers*. Willard Parker and Harry Lauter star as Rangers Jace Pearson and Clay Morgan. "Gold is what we carry, stop we don't dare, for Wells Fargo must get it there," said the theme to *The Tales of Wells Fargo*, an NBC series with Dale Robertson as Jim Hardie, an agent-troubleshooter for the gold transporting company. *Epitaph* newspaper editor Harris Clayton (Richard Eastman) struggles to establish peace through the power of the press in Arizona on *Tombstone Territory* (ABC). Texas Ranger Hoby Gilman (Robert Culp) seeks wanted outlaws in the west of the 1870s on *Trackdown* (CBS). The saga of a wagon train's journey from the Midwest to California in the 1800s is presented on *Wagon Train* (NBC/ABC). Ward Bond played the original wagon master, Seth Adams; John McIntire replaced him as Chris Hale.

1958. Abby Dalton plays Myra Belle Shirley, alias Belle Starr, a lawless woman of the Old West who, despite her reputation as "The Bandit Queen," helps people in trouble on the CBS pilot *Belle Starr*. Sallie Brophy is Annie O'Connell, a young widow struggling to operate a hotel in Buckskin, Montana, on *Buckskin* (NBC). Events in the growth of Cimarron City, Oklahoma, during the 1890s are seen through the eyes of cattle baron Matthew Rockford (George Montgomery) on *Cimarron City* (NBC). Robert Loggia is Elfego Baca, a sheriff then lawyer (a man said to have nine lives) who battles for justice in Socorro County, New Mexico, on *Elfego Baca* (ABC). The role of a doctor during the early settlement days of the 20th century are seen through the eyes of Bill Baxter (Rex Allen), a doctor in Rising Springs, Arizona, on the syndicated *Frontier Doctor*. Jeff Richards plays Jefferson Drum, a newspaper publisher attempting to establish peace through the power of the press in the lawless gold mining town on Jubilee (1850s) on *Jefferson Drum* (NBC). John Russell is Dan Troop, the Marshal of 1870s Laramie, Wyoming, on *Lawman* (ABC). Peter Brown plays his deputy, Johnny McKay. Adam MacLean (Rex Reason) attempts to establish peace through the power of his newspaper, the Yellowstone *Sentinel* in the Dakotas of the 1870s on *Man Without a Gun* (ABC). Rancher Lucas McCain (Chuck Connors), the fastest man with a .44–40 hair trigger action rifle, and his young son Mark (Johnny Crawford) attempt to build a new life for themselves in North Fork, New Mexico, on *The Rifleman* (ABC). Following the surrender at Appomattox, Union officers Jim Flagg and Buck Sinclair (Kent Taylor, Peter Whitney) and a Confederate lieutenant, Colin Kirby (Jan Merlin)

team to roam the West on *The Rough Riders* (ABC). Bill Longley (Rory Calhoun) is a wandering ex-gunfighter who wanders throughout 1860s Texas helping people in trouble on *The Texan* (CBS). Tom Tryon plays John Slaughter, "The man who made 'em do what they oughta 'cause if they didn't they die," the sheriff of Friotown, Texas, on *Texas John Slaughter* (ABC). Stories based on the files of the Arizona Rangers (limited by law to 26 men) are seen through the experiences of Captain Tom Rynning (Tris Coffin) on the syndicated *26 Men*. Steve McQueen plays Josh Randall, a bounty hunter of the 1870s on *Wanted: Dead or Alive* (CBS).

1959. Steve Forrest plays Chris Hody, an Old West bounty hunter on the CBS pilot *Ballad for a Bad Man*. Peter Breck is Clay Culhane, a lawyer in Latigo, New Mexico, on *Black Saddle* (ABC). Ben Cartwright (Lorne Greene) and his sons Adam (Pernell Roberts), Hoss (Dan Blocker) and Little Joe (Michael Landon) struggle to maintain their Ponderosa ranch on *Bonanza* (NBC). Ty Hardin is Bronco Layne, an ex–Confederate captain who helps people as he wanders across Texas (1860s) on *Bronco* (ABC). Cesar Romero plays Juan Joaquin, a chief of the border police in the early west on the CBS pilot *The Caballero*. Marshal Simon Fry (Henry Fonda) and his deputy Clay McCord (Allen Case) uphold the law in Silver City, Arizona (1880s), on *The Deputy* (NBC). Earl Holliman is Sundance, an ex-gunfighter turned owner of the Hotel De Paree, the 1870s west's most colorful gathering place (in George Town, Colorado) on *Hotel De Paree* (CBS). William Joyce plays Johnny Guitar, a singing cowboy who roams throughout the west on the CBS pilot *Johnny Guitar*. Don Durant is Johnny Ringo, an ex-gunfighter turned sheriff of Velardi, Arizona (1870s), on *Johnny Ringo* (CBS). John Smith and Robert Fuller play Slim Sherman and Jess Harper, ranchers who also operate a swing station (stage depot) for the Great Overland Stage Lines in Wyoming on *Laramie* (NBC). Michael Ansara is Sam Buckhart, a U.S. Marshal who is also an Indian struggling to maintain the peace between his people and the white man on *Law of the Plainsman* (NBC). Robert Rockwell plays Sam Logan, an investigator for the Blackhawk Insurance Company during the lawless 1870s on *The Man from Blackhawk* (ABC). Mark Miller is Ward Pendleton, a bank examiner in the Old West on the CBS pilot *The Man from Denver*. Jean Willes is Megan Francis, the owner of the Outrider House, a combination saloon, hotel and gambling hall in Ellsworth, Kansas, on the CBS pilot *The Outrider*. The saga of a cattle drive from San Antonio, Texas, to Sedalia, Kansas (1860s), is seen through the eyes of trail boss Gil Favor (Eric Fleming) and ramrod Rowdy Yates (Clint Eastwood) on *Rawhide* (CBS). Lloyd Nolan plays Orville Darrow, an aging sheriff in the town of Donegan on the CBS pilot *Six Guns for Donegan*. Scott Brady plays Shotgun Slade, a detective of the Old West who possesses a unique two-barreled shotgun on the syndicated *Shotgun Slade*. Joel McCrea plays Mike Dunbar, the marshal of Wichita Town, Kansas (1870s), on *Wichita Town* (NBC). Brian Keith is Dave Blassingame, a wandering cowboy of the Old West on the CBS pilot *Winchester*.

1960. Tom Keene plays the Tucson Kid, an insurance company investigator who goes undercover to solve crimes in the west on the pilot *The Adventures of the Tucson Kid*. Vic Morrow plays the mysterious Lassiter, a man who seems to come from out of nowhere to help people in trouble on the NBC pilot *The Avenger*. Ed Nelson plays a man known only as Kirk, the owner of the Garden of Eden Gambling House that is built half on the border of New Mexico and half on the border of Arizona on the CBS pilot *Border Town*. Fess Parker plays Jonathan West, a fighting man with principals (called "Preach") on the CBS pilot *The Code of Jonathan West*. Gene Evans is Otis Stockett, an Old West schoolteacher in the town of Wichita, Kansas, on the NBC pilot *The Frontiersman*. Frank Lovejoy plays Judge Parker, a man who is struggling to uphold the law in the town of Fort Smith, Kansas (1870s), on the NBC pilot *The Hanging Judge*. The apprehension of outlaws is seen through the eyes of Frank Caine (Barton MacLane), the marshal of Stillwater, Oklahoma (1890s), on *The Outlaws* (NBC). Fred Thomas (William Bendix) and Frank Flippen (Doug McClure) are engineers attempting to establish a route for the Overland Stage Lines from Missouri to California (1860s) on the syndicated *Overland Trail*. Mike and Chris Reno (Ben Cooper, Jim Beck) are brothers who are also co-sheriffs of a small but growing town on the CBS pilot *The Reno Brothers*. Wayne Rogers and Robert Bray play Luke Perry and Simon Kane, drivers for the Overland Stage Lines (1860s), on *Stagecoach West* (ABC). The relationship between Sheriff Pat Gar-

rett (Barry Sullivan) and William Bonny, alias Billy the Kid (Clu Gulager), is explored on *The Tall Man* (NBC). David McLean plays Tate, an ex-gunfighter with an injured right arm who sides with justice against criminal elements on NBC's *Tate*. A satire of the Old West is seen through the experiences of Black Ace Barton (James Westerfield), "the meanest gunfighter in the Old West," on the CBS pilot *They Went Thataway*. Brian Keith plays Dave Blassingame, a wandering cowboy of the 1890s who helps people in trouble on *The Westerner* (NBC). Jason Evers plays Pitcarin, a wandering two-fisted cowboy of the early west on NBC's *Wrangler* (the first western to be video taped).

1961. A man, known only as Cord (Tony Young) is a U.S. Cavalry undercover agent who poses as a gunfighter to apprehend criminals wanted by the army on *Gunslinger* (CBS). Guy Madison plays Jericho, an undercover agent for the Attorney General, who helps people wrongly accused of crimes on the CBS pilot *Jericho*. Burt Reynolds is Branch Taylor, a happy-go-lucky drifter who takes any job he can find on the CBS pilot *The Man from Everywhere*. Fess Parker is Charles Russell, an artist, sculptor, writer and cowboy who helps people in trouble on the CBS pilot *Russell*. Claude Akins is Sam Hill, a traveling blacksmith of legendary strength who roams throughout the west of the 1860s with only a knife and a hammer on the NBC pilot *Sam Hill*. Charles Bateman plays Ben January, a doctor, and his twin brother, Rick, the marshal of Gunnison (1860s) on the syndicated *Two Faces West*.

1962. Ben Thompson (Claude Akins), Frank Burling (Jay Lanin) and Myles Ree (Christopher King) are bickering U.S. Cavalry scouts stationed at Fort Stillwater (1890s) on the NBC pilot *Outpost*. The shaping of Wyoming during the 1880s is seen through the eyes of a man called The Virginian (James Drury), foreman of the Shiloh Ranch in Medicine Bow on NBC's *The Virginian*. The original pilot aired on NBC in 1958.

1963. Michael Ansara plays Adam MacKenzie, a doctor who travels throughout the Old West on the NBC pilot *Adam MacKenzie, Frontier Doctor*. Larry Ward plays Frank Regan, a U.S. Marshal in the post–Civil War Dakota Territory on ABC's *The Dakotas*. Jeffrey Hunter plays Temple Houston, a circuit-riding attorney who defends people unjustly accused of crimes before circuit-riding judges in the post–Civil War west on *Tem-*

ple *Houston* (NBC). The hardships faced by the Beaver Patrol, a wagon train of settlers destined for California (1849) are seen through the eyes of a 12-year-old boy (Jaimie McPheeters) on *The Travels of Jaimie McPheeters* (ABC; Kurt Russell plays Jaimie). Neb Jackman (Peter Whitney) and his not-too-bright sons Haslam (Conlan Carter) and Bo (John Craig) attempt to uphold the law in the town of Pair-O-Dice on the ABC pilot *Which Way'd They Go?*

1964. John Gavin plays Harrison Destry, the peace-loving son of a famous lawman (Tom Destry) who roams the west seeking to find the man who framed him for a murder on *Destry* (ABC). Ron Hayes plays Duncan McIvor, a lieutenant who heads the Dog Troop, a group of misfit Old West soldiers on the ABC pilot *The Dog Troop*.

1965. The struggles of the Barkley family to maintain their ranch in the San Joaquin Valley (1870s) are seen on *The Big Valley* (ABC). Barbara Stanwyck plays Victoria Barkley, the head of the family, with Richard Long, Peter Breck, Linda Evans and Lee Majors as her children Jarrod, Nick, Audra and Heath. Chuck Connors plays Jason McCord, the only known survivor of the Battle of Bitter Creek, who is believed to have run during a battle with the Comanche Indians, and has been branded a coward. He now roams the west of the 1870s seeking to clear his name on NBC's *Branded*. Ken Berry plays Wilton Parmenter, a cavalry captain who is assigned to a group of misfit soldiers at Fort Courage in Kansas (1860s) on *F Troop* (ABC). Reese Bennett, Chad Cooper and Joe Riley (Neville Brand, Peter Brown, William Smith) are Texas Rangers who, despite their constant bickering, manage to get the job done on *Laredo* (NBC). Chris Jones and Allen Case are Jesse and Frank James, the outlaw brothers who, in this series, avenge the death of their mother (by railroad officials) by striking the Great Western Railroad and returning stolen property to their rightful owners on *The Legend of Jesse James* (ABC). Lloyd Bridges is William Colton, a disillusioned Civil War officer who heads west after Appomattox to search for the meaning of life on *The Loner* (CBS). Robert Horton is Shenandoah, a man without a memory, who is searching for his identity on *A Man Called Shenandoah* (ABC).

1966. Jack Lord plays Jab Heller, a gunslinger who fights for right on the NBC pilot *Above the*

Law. Dale Robertson is Ben Calhoun, a high stakes gambler who wins the near-bankrupt Buffalo Pass, Scalplock and Defiance Railroad in a poker game and then struggles to keep it running on ABC's *Iron Horse*. Five children struggle to establish a life for themselves in Wyoming (1875) after their parents drown while crossing a river on *The Monroes* (ABC). Michael Anderson, Jr., and Barbara Hershey star as the eldest children Clayt and Kathleen Monroe. The gun-toting Hanks family maintains the law in Wretched, Colorado, during the 1860s on CBS's *Pistols 'n' Petticoats*. Ann Sheridan heads the cast as Henrietta Hanks. A family of homesteaders (the Prides), struggle to begin a new life in Lawrence County, Kansas (1860s), on *The Road West.* Starring on the NBC series are Barry Sullivan as Ben Pride, Kathryn Hays as Elizabeth Pride, Andrew Prine as Tim Pride and Brenda Scott as Midge Pride. Jim McMullan plays a man known only as Cain, a gunslinger who joins U.S. Marshal Walker (Richard Bradford) to help maintain the law in Roaring Camp, a California town struck by gold fever on the ABC pilot *Roaring Camp*. A drifter, known only as Shane (David Carradine), attaches himself to the homesteading Starrett family to help them maintain their ranch on *Shane* (ABC).

1967. Stuart Whitman plays Jim Crown, a U.S. Marshal in 1880s Cimarron City, Oklahoma, on *Cimarron Strip* (CBS). Ex Cavalry scout Will Sonnett (Walter Brennan) and his grandson Jeff Sonnett (Dack Rambo) begin a quest to find Jeff's father, James, a wanted killer who deserted his family, on *The Guns of Will Sonnett* (ABC). Leif Erickson is John Cannon, the head of a family struggling to maintain their ranch, the High Chaparral, in Tucson, Arizona (1870s), on *The High Chaparral* (NBC). Ralph Taeger plays Hondo Lane, a U.S. Army troubleshooter attempting to solve the conflict between settlers and the Apache Indians over the prospect of land (Arizona, 1860s), on *Hondo* (ABC). Wayne Maunder plays General George Armstrong Custer, the commander of the Seventh Labor Battalion at Fort Henry in Kansas (1860s) on *The Legend of Custer* (ABC). Tim Conway is Rango, a fumbling Texas Ranger (stationed in Deep Wells, Texas) who accomplishes things quite by accident on ABC's *Rango. Sheriff Who?* is an NBC pilot that is set in the town of Blood, Texas, and relates the efforts of its citizens to find a sheriff who will live long enough to defeat the town boss, Evil Roy Slade (John Astin).

1968. Murdock Lancer (Andrew Duggan) and his sons Scott and Johnny (Wayne Maunder, James Stacy) struggle to maintain their 100,000-acre timberland ranch (Lancer) during the lawless 1870s (San Joaquin, California) on *Lancer* (CBS). Earl Corey (Don Murray), an uprooted Virginia aristocrat, and Jamal David (Otis Young), an ex-slave freed by the Proclamation, team to become bounty hunters on *The Outcasts* (ABC). Van Williams plays Dave Barrett, sheriff of the ruthless gold mining town of Rimfire on the ABC pilot *Rimfire*.

1969. Oren Hayes (Pat O'Brien), Nash Crawford (Walter Brennan) and George Agnew (Chill Wills) are retired Texas Rangers who roam the west righting wrongs on the ABC pilot *The Over-the-Hill Gang*. The same performers repeated their roles in the sequel 1970 pilot *The Over-the-Hill Gang Rides Again*.

1970. Smitty, Matthew, Zack and Sweetwater (Joy Bang, Boomer Castleman, Michael Martin, Jamie Carr) are four Old West flower children who travel from town to town helping people in trouble on the NBC pilot *The Kowboys*. The *Virginian* spinoff, *The Men from Shiloh* (NBC), tells the story of four men and their efforts to maintain the Shiloh Ranch in Medicine Bow, Wyoming: The Virginian (James Drury), Alan MacKenzie (Stewart Granger), Trampas (Doug McClure) and Roy Tate (Lee Majors).

1971. In an attempt to receive amnesty outlaws Jed "Kid" Curry (Ben Murphy) and Hannibal Hayes (Peter Duel, Roger Davis) pose as Thaddeus Jones and Joshua Smith and seek to stay out of trouble for 12 months to earn full pardons on *Alias Smith and Jones* (ABC). NBC airs two pilots called *Cat Ballou* (on September 5 and September 6) about an unorthodox Old West heroine as she attempts to start a school in the town of Wolf City, Wyoming. Lesley Ann Warren plays Cat Ballou in the first pilot; Jo Ann Harris is Cat in the second pilot. Roselle and Clare Bridgeman (Belinda J. Montgomery, Tim Matheson) are newlyweds struggling to begin a new life on the ruthless frontier on the NBC pilot *Lock, Stock and Barrel*. James Garner plays Nichols (no other name), the sheriff of Nicholas, Arizona (named after his founding family), on NBC's *Nichols*. Clint Walker is Dave Harmon, a tough U.S. Marshal, on the ABC pilot *Yuma*.

1972. Clint Walker plays Kincaid, an Old West bounty hunter who enjoys tracking down outlaws

but who also gives them a choice — "ride in the saddle or across it" on the ABC pilot *The Bounty Man*. ABC airs *The Daughters of Joshua Cabe*, the first of three pilots about a fur trapper who hires three shady ladies to pose as his daughters to win a homesteading claim and their efforts to keep it once they acquire it. Buddy Ebsen plays Joshua Cabe with Karen Valentine, Lesley Ann Warren and Sandra Dee as his daughters Charity, Mae and Ada. The second pilot, *The Daughters of Joshua Cabe Return* (1975) has Dan Dailey as Joshua Cabe with Ronne Troup, Christina Hart and Brooke Adams as his daughters Ada, Charity and Mae. The final pilot, *The New Daughters of Joshua Cabe* (1976) finds John McIntire as Joshua Cabe and Liberty Williams, Rene Jarrett and Lezlie Dalton as his daughters Charity, Ada and Mae. John Astin is Evil Roy Slade, the most wanted man in the west in the comical NBC pilot *Evil Roy Slade* (a reworking of the 1967 pilot *Sheriff Who?*). Richard Boone is Hector "Hec" Ramsey, an ex-gunfighter turned law enforcer (in New Prospect, Oklahoma, 1901) on NBC's *Hec Ramsey*.

1973. Wagon Master Callahan (Forrest Tucker) attempts to get his passengers to the Promised Land despite the actions of his fumbling trail scout Dusty (Bob Denver) on the syndicated *Dusty's Trail*. Young newlyweds Roselle and Clare Bridgeman (Sally Field, Tim Matheson) attempt to begin a new life in the 1890s west on the NBC pilot *Hitched* (a remake of 1971's *Lock, Stock and Barrel*). Joanna Pettet is Margaret Sergeant, a young widow with two children (Sarah and Jeremy) who struggles to establish a home in 1876 Wyoming on the ABC pilot *Pioneer Woman*.

1974. A range cook named Mr. Nightlinger (Moses Gunn) and seven children help widowed rancher Kate Andersen (Diana Douglas) maintain her spread (the Longhorn Ranch) in Spanish Wells, New Mexico, on *The Cowboys* (ABC). Sally Ferguson (Jeanette Nolan), an aging collector of prairie junk, and Cyrus Pike (Dack Rambo), a young outlaw she considers her son, head for the gold hills of California on *Dirty Sally* (CBS). Marjoe Gortner plays Ernie Parsons, an Old West gunfighter who poses as a preacher to find the man responsible for framing him for a murder on the ABC pilot *The Gun and the Pulpit*.

1975. Louis Gossett, Jr., plays Black Bart, a black sheriff in the bigoted town of Paris, Arizona, on the CBS pilot *Black Bart*. Cliff Potts plays

Nevada Smith, a half-breed gunslinger who enforces law and order on the NBC pilot *Nevada Smith* (based on the feature film).

1976. Don Meredith is Banjo Hackett, an easy-going traveler of the Old West on the NBC pilot *Banjo Hackett: Roamin' Free*. Morgan and Quentin Baudine (Kurt Russell, Tim Matheson) are brothers who begin a dangerous journey to find their sister, Patricia, who was kidnapped by Cheyenne Indians on *The Quest* (NBC).

1977. The saga of the Macahan family as they attempt to establish a new life on the Great Plains (1860s) is the focus of ABC's *How the West Was Won*. James Arness, Eva Marie Saint and Bruce Boxleitner head a large cast. Rod Taylor plays Evan Thorpe, the head of a family of pioneers heading from Illinois to Oregon on *The Oregon Trail* (NBC). Jenny Cullen (Yvette Mimieux) and Clint Kirby (Gil Gerard) are 1890s law enforcers on the NBC pilot *Ransom for Alice* (wherein they attempt to end a white slavery ring).

1978. Netty Booth (Karen Valentine) is a beautiful New England newspaper reporter who journeys west to seek fame and fortune by writing of her experiences on the ABC pilot *Go West Young Girl*. Suzanne Pleshette is Kate Bliss, a turn-of-the century private detective on the ABC pilot *Kate Bliss and the Ticker Tape Kid*. Kathleen Lloyd is Kate Lacy, a pretty, level-headed cowgirl and Debra Feuer is Queenie, her tomboyish, gun-toting sister on the NBC pilot *Lacy and the Mississippi Queen*. Charles Frank plays Ben Maverick, the son of Beau Maverick (Roger Moore from the series *Maverick*) who, like his father is a wandering, fast-talking gambler on the CBS pilot *The New Maverick* (in 1979 the pilot became the CBS series *Young Maverick*). Warren Oates is Rooster Cogburn, a one-eyed, hard-drinking Old West lawman on the ABC pilot *True Grit: A Further Adventure* (based on the film *True Grit*). Lacey (Christine DeLisle), Liz (Susan Bigelow) and Shiloh (Elyssa Davalos) are undercover agents in the early 1900s west on the ABC pilot *Wild and Wooly*.

1979. John Beck plays Frank "Buckshot" O'-Connor, a U.S. Army colonel who heads the 10th Cavalry, a mostly black unit that has been nicknamed *The Buffalo Soldiers* (NBC pilot). The Old West is satirized on the CBS pilot *The Dooley Brothers*, wherein Garrett Brown and Robert Pierce play George and Bill Dooley, bumbling brothers who uphold the law despite the fact they can't shoot, ride or rope. Jeff Osterhage plays John Golden, a legendary gunfighter who wears a gold outfit and a carries a gold-plated seven-barrel gun on the NBC pilot *The Legend of the Golden Gun*.

1981. Joel Higgins plays Sam Best, the marshal of Copper Creek, Montana (1865), on ABC's *Best of the West*. Carlene Watkins plays his wife, Elvira. James Garner reprises his role as Bret Maverick (see *Maverick*, 1957), a wandering gambler who finally settles down as the owner of the Lazy Ace Ranch and the Red Ox Saloon in the town of Sweetwater, Arizona, on *Bret Maverick* (NBC). Cindy Pickett plays Mary Breydon, a widow who runs the Cherokee Station, a stopover for the Overland Express Stage Lines, on the CBS pilot *The Cherokee Trail*. Jeff Osterhage and Larry Gelman play Andy Bennett and Bill Cavanaugh, members of the Houston Division of the Texas Rangers on the NBC pilot *The Texas Rangers*.

1982. Priscilla Barnes is Maggie McCulloch, a doctor in the town of Sweetwater, Missouri (1860s), who is also the owner of a brothel (which she inherited from a late aunt) on the ABC pilot *The Wild Women of Chastity Gulch*.

1983. Amos and Theodore (Tim Thomerson, Geoffrey Lewis) are two inept Old West outlaws who befriend two children, Celia and Clovis (Bridgette Andersen, Keith Mitchell), and together form the Apple Dumpling Gang to help people in trouble on *Gun Shy*, a CBS series based on the Disney feature *Tales of the Apple Dumpling Gang*.

1984. Stella Stevens plays Nellie Wilder, a widow and the mother of three daughters (Sarah, Brianne and Missy) who inherits the job of sheriff of Wilder, New Mexico, after her husband's death on the NBC pilot *No Man's Land*.

1985. William Smith plays Brodie Hollister, a fast gun who heads the Chamber of Commerce, an elite law enforcement organization that upholds the law in Wildside, California (1880s), on *Wildside* (CBS).

1987. Alex McArthur plays Duell McCall, a man of principle who roams the west of yesteryear helping people in trouble along the way while attempting to clear himself of a false murder charge on the NBC pilot *Desperado*. John Bennett Perry is Sam Hatch, the sheriff of Independence, Missouri, a somewhat peaceful town of the 1880s on the NBC pilot *Independence*. Lee Horsley plays Ethan Allen Cord, an ex-gunfighter struggling to raise his late sister's children (Claire, Joseph, Ben and George) in the ruthless mining town of Paradise on *The Guns of Paradise* (CBS; also known as *Paradise*). Curtis Long (John Terlesky) is a tough deputy marshal assigned to apprehend the bad guys in New Mexico during the 1870s on the ABC pilot *Longarm*.

1989. U.S. Marshal Jack Craddock (Richard Comar) and Canadian Mountie Clive Bennett (John Brennan) work together to keep the peace in Bordertown, a ruthless town on the U.S.-Canadian border (1880s) on *Bordertown* (CBN). The CBS miniseries *Lonesome Dove* tells the story of Augustus McCrae and Woodrow Call (Robert DuVall, Tommy Lee Jones), former Texas Rangers who run cattle and live in the town of Lonesome Dove. This led to the follow-up miniseries *Return to Lonesome Dove* and two cable syndicated Canadian series *Lonesome Dove: The Series* (1994) and *Lonesome Dove: The Outlaw Years* (1995). The series is set in the town of Curtis Wells and follows the romance and eventual marriage of Newt Call (Scott Bairstow) and Hannah Peale (Christina Hirt) despite the objections of Clay Mosby (Eric McCormack), a man who also loves Hannah. *The Outlaw Years* is set two years after the death of Hannah and follows events in Newt's life, now a bounty hunter. The experiences of the young men who ride for the Russell, Majors and Waddell Pony Express Company (1860s) are depicted on ABC's *The Young Riders*. Anthony Zerbe, Ty Miller, Stephen Baldwin and Josh Brolin star.

1991. Bruce Campbell plays Brisco County, Jr., a college educated bounty hunter and visionary of the early 1890s who is looking forward to the new century on *The Adventures of Brisco County, Jr.* (Fox).

1993. Jane Seymour plays Michaela Quinn, a doctor in the town of Colorado Springs (1860s) and the guardian of Colleen, Matthew and Brian, the children of a late friend, on *Dr. Quinn, Medicine Woman* (CBS). Brad Johnson is Ned Blessing, an ex-gunfighter turned law enforcer of Plum Creek, Texas, on *Ned Blessing: The Story of My Life and Times* (CBS).

1995. Ernest Pratt (Richard Dean Anderson) is a dime novelist who, with the help of Janos Bartok (John de Lancie), an ingenious inventor, assumes the identity of his fictional literary hero, Nicodemus Legend, to help people in trouble on *Legend* (UPN).

2001. The 1959 series *Bonanza* is revised by PAX as *Ponderosa* (the name of the Cartwrights'

ranch). Daniel Hugh Kelly plays Ben Cartwright, with Matt Carmody, Drew Powell and Jared DaPeris as his sons Adam, Hoss and Little Joe.

2003. The WB revises the 1949 *Lone Ranger* series with Chad Michael Murray as the Masked Rider of the Plains and Nathaniel Arcand as Tonto, his Indian companion, on the unsold pilot *The Lone Ranger* (here the Ranger's real name is Luke Hartman, not John Reid as in the original series).

2004. HBO's *Deadwood* depicts the California town during the lawless gold rush days of the late 1840s. The adult series (nudity, foul language) stars Robert Carradine as Wild Bill Hickok, Robin Weigert as Calamity Jane and Ian McShane as Al Swearengen.

2005. The settling of the west, as seen through the experiences of Wheeler family, is presented on *Into the West* (TNT). The very large cast includes Matthew Settle as Jacob Wheeler; Rachel Cook as Claire Wheeler; Rebecca Jenkins as Susannah Wheeler; and Keri Russell as Naomi Wheeler (see also the 2005 entry on *American Indian*).

Witches

This entry chronicles the programs in which a witch (or sorceress) is the star or featured character.

1949. The Kuklapolitan puppet, Beulah Witch (operated and voiced by Burr Tillstrom), becomes the first witch to appear on TV. Beulah follows the traditions of a Halloween witch and is rather unattractive.

1963. Wendy the Good Witch is adapted from the Harvey comic books and appears on TV as a segment of *The New Casper Cartoon Show* (ABC). The animated Wendy lived with her aunts, Thelma, Velma and Zelma and traveled on her flying broom.

1964. Elizabeth Montgomery becomes TV's first live witch on ABC's *Bewitched*. Samantha was beautiful thus dispensing the theory that all witches are ugly. She was married to a mortal (Darrin Stevens) and was the daughter of two powerful witches, Endora and Maurice. As the series progressed, Samantha and Darrin became the parents of a witch (Tabitha) and a warlock (Adam).

1966. Lara Parker plays Angelique, a beautiful and extremely sexy witch who also became TV's first evil witch on ABC's *Dark Shadows*. Angelique sought only one thing, to win the love of the vampire Barnabas Collins, and would destroy anything that stood in her way.

1969. *Sabrina, the Teenage Witch* (voice of Jane Webb) becomes a segment of the animated series *The Archie Comedy Hour* (CBS). Appearing with Sabrina is her pet cat Salem. Billie Hayes plays Miss Witchiepoo, a good witch who resides on Living Island on *H.R. Pufnstuf* (NBC).

1970. Martha Raye plays Benita Bizarre, an evil witch who is seeking to rule Tranquility Forest on *The Bugaloos* (NBC). Juliet Mills is Phoebe Figalilly, a beautiful but mysterious woman who is assumed to be a good witch (or an angel) as she has the ability to spread love and joy on ABC's *Nanny and the Professor*.

1971. Barbara Minkus plays Gertel the Witch on *Curiosity Shop*, an ABC series that explains aspects of the world to children. The animated character of Sabrina is spun off from *The Archie Comedy Hour* into her own series with Jane Webb as the voice of *Sabrina, the Teenage Witch* (CBS).

1973. Erica Scheimer provides the voice for Miss Tickle, a schoolteacher with magical powers that she uses to help good defeat evil on the animated ABC series *Mission Magic*.

1976. Yvette Mimieux plays Gillian Holroyd, a beautiful young witch who works with her aunt, Enid (Doris Roberts), a sorceress in a Manhattan curio shop, on the NBC pilot *Bell, Book and Candle* (adapted from the feature film of the same title). Liberty Williams is Tabitha Stevens, a witch (the daughter of Samantha and Darrin from *Bewitched*) who is now 24 years old and working as an editorial associate on *Trend* magazine in San Francisco on the ABC pilot *Tabitha*. Bruce Kimmel plays her warlock brother Adam.

1977. Jane Webb provides the voice for Sabrina the teenage witch on the animated NBC series *Super Witch*. Lisa Hartman becomes Tabitha, the daughter of Samantha and Darrin (from *Bewitched*), on *Tabitha*, an ABC series that finds the young witch as a production associate at KXLA-TV in Los Angeles. David Ankrum plays her brother Adam, a warlock.

1978. Peter Hooten plays Stephen Strange, a New York psychiatrist at Eastside Hospital who is in reality a sorcerer, a magical champion of good over evil on the CBS pilot *Dr. Strange*.

1979. Barbara Cason is Agnes, a good witch who helps a young boy (Jonathan) and his mag-

ical pony (Tony) help children in trouble on the syndicated *Tony the Pony*.

1981. Margaret Phillips plays Alice Sommers, a mysterious woman is believed to be a witch but her real essence is never revealed on the CBS gothic serial pilot *Castle Rock*.

1982. Kim Cattrall is Amanda Tucker, a witch who uses her powers to help her detective husband Rick (Art Hindle) solve crimes on the CBS pilot *The Good Witch of Laurel Canyon*. CBS cast Catherine Hicks as Amanda Tucker and Tim Matheson as her husband Rick in a reworking of *The Good Witch of Laurel Canyon* that became the series *Tucker's Witch*.

1983. Randi Brooks plays Bethel, a beautiful, seductive and evil witch on *Wizards and Warriors* (CBS). Ilene Graff is Melinda York, a pretty witch who lives in an apartment with other unearthly beings on the CBS pilot *13 Thirteenth Avenue*.

1986. Diana Rigg is Miss Hardbottom, headmistress at Miss Cackle's International Academy for Witches. Mildred Hubble (Fairuza Balk) is a young girl struggling to pass her courses and become a full-fledged witch on the HBO special *The Worst Witch*.

1987. Judy Parfait plays Queen Lillian, a vain, evil witch from the Snow White fairy tale, who mellows somewhat when she, Snow White and Prince Charming (Snow's husband) are transported to modern times on ABC's *The Charmings*. Lillian still seeks to become the fairest of all but is not as prone to cast spells as she once was. Rue McClanahan plays Avarissa, an evil witch on the NBC special *The Wickedest Witch*. When Avarissa fails to commit enough dastardly deeds she is banished to an underground kingdom beneath Ohio and ordered to make an innocent child commit a despicable act.

1989. Corinne Bohrer plays Winnie Goodwin, a 300-year-old good witch who performs good deeds on ABC's *Free Spirit* (where she is the guardian of the children of a divorced attorney). The Masterson family is profiled on the NBC comedy pilot *A Little Bit Strange*. Ben, the father (Michael Warren), is a widowed sorcerer; Margaret, his mother (Myra J), is a mind reader; Tasha (Cherie Johnson), his daughter, is a witch; and T.J. (Shawn Skie), his son, is a warlock.

1991. Lysette Anthony plays the beautiful but evil witch Angelique on *Dark Shadows*, the NBC revision of the 1966 series. Angelique, like before, will destroy anything that stands in her way of acquiring the love of the vampire Barnabas Collins.

1992. Pat Carroll provides the voice of Ursula, the evil witch who lives at the bottom of the sea on *The Little Mermaid* (Disney). Also on the series is Morgana, Ursula's equally evil sister. Alex, Jane and Sukie (Julia Campbell, Ally Walker, Catherine Mary Stewart) are three beautiful witches who live in the town of Eastwick on the NBC pilot *The Witches of Eastwick* (based on the feature film). One night the witches decide to conjure up the perfect man; what they get is Darryl Van Horne (Michael Siberry), the Devil himself. The proposed series was to focus on the witches as they seek to send the trouble-making Darryl back to Hell.

1996. Melissa Joan Hart plays Sabrina Spellman, a beautiful 16-year-old witch who is part mortal and part witch and just learning to use her powers on *Sabrina, the Teenage Witch* (ABC/WB). Also on the series are her teachers, her aunts Hilda and Zelda (Caroline Rhea, Beth Broderick). In 2001 episodes, Barbara Eden plays the role of the Spellman family head, Great Aunt Irma.

1997. Alyson Hannigan plays Willow Rosenberg, a high school girl who is just discovering her powers of witchcraft (and who later becomes an all-powerful witch) on *Buffy the Vampire Slayer* (WB/UPN).

1998. Jacqueline Collen plays Maeve, a beautiful sorcerer's apprentice who travels with the mighty sailor Sinbad on *The Adventures of Sinbad*. Monika Schnarre plays a woman known only as the Sorceress, a captivating female who is capable of "keeping the world from sinking into darkness" on the syndicated *BeastMaster*. Also on the series is Dylan Bierk as the New Sorceress, a woman as beautiful as Monika but not quite as developed in the art of sorcery. Shannen Doherty, Alyssa Milano and Holly Marie Combs play Prue, Phoebe and Piper Halliwell, good witches who use the Power of Three to battle demons on the WB's *Charmed*. Rose McGowan joined the cast in 2001 as Paige Matthews, a half sister to Prue, Piper and Phoebe, when Shannen Doherty chose to leave the series. In the fall of 2005 Kaley Cuoco joined the cast as Billie, a very sexy teenage witch who bonds with Phoebe, Paige and Piper to learn her craft. Marnie Cromwell (Kimberly J. Brown) is a 13-year-old girl who is adjusting to the fact that she is a witch on *Halloween Town* (Disney). Helping Marnie learn her craft is her Aunt Aggie

(Debbie Reynolds), a full-fledged witch. Both characters appeared in two additional Disney productions: *Halloween Town II: Kalbar's Revenge* (2001, wherein the witches attempt to stop an evil being from destroying Halloween Town), and *Halloween Town III: Halloween High* (2004, wherein Marine becomes a freshman in high school).

1999. Juliet Mills plays Tabitha Lenox, an evil witch who resides in the seaside community of Harmony on NBC's *Passions*. Timmy (Josh Ryan Evans), a doll she brings to life, assists Tabitha in her bidding. Emily Hart provides the voice for Sabrina Spellman on *Sabrina: The Animated Series*. Here Sabrina is 12 years old and already a witch (as compared to the live action series, *Sabrina, the Teenage Witch*, where Melissa Joan Hart was 16 years old and just discovering her powers as a witch). Salem, Sabrina's cat is present as are her aunts Hilda and Zelda (voice of Melissa Joan Hart) but as teenagers, not adults.

2002. The Fox pilot *Eastwick* is an extension of the feature film *The Witches of Eastwick* (also a pilot; see 1992). Alex, Jane and Sukie (Marcia Cross, Kelly Rutherford, Lori Loughlin) are now the mothers of 15-year-old warlock sons: Adam (Sukie's son; Chris Evans), Dakota (Jane's son; Riley Smith) and Simon (Alex's son; Jonathan Bennett). The proposed series was to follow the adventures of the three warlocks.

2004. Darcy, Icy and Stormy (voices of Caren Manual, Lisa Ortiz, Suzy Myers) are evil witches who attend the Cloud Tower School of Magic on the animated Fox series *Winx Club* (the witches seek only to create havoc by casting spells).

2005. Tia and Tamera Mowry play Alex Fielding and Camryn Barnes, witch twins, separated at birth, who are reunited by chance 21 years later to use their powers to save their parallel world of Coventry from evil on the Disney pilot *Twitches*. Will, Irma, Taranee, Cornelia and Hay are teenage witches who protect the world from evil on the animated series *W.I.T.C.H.* (ABC).

Women — "Dumb Blondes"

There are blondes who are beautiful and highly intelligent (like Jennifer Marlowe [Loni Anderson] on *WKRP in Cincinnati*) and there are blondes who are beautiful and naïve (like Wendy

Conway [Connie Stevens] on *Wendy and Me*). This entry concerns itself with the Wendy Conways of the world — the gorgeous blondes who try to be like other women but find being blonde (and dumb) is really more fun. See also *Scatterbrained Women* (some women don't have to be blonde to be dumb).

1952. Marie Wilson as Irma Peterson of CBS's *My Friend Irma* is television's first dumb blonde (a character she carried over from the radio series of the same title). Irma is sweet, feminine and beautiful but so naïve that she constantly bounces back and forth from the fine line that separates genius from insanity. She works as a secretary and it was said that "while Mother Nature gave other girls brains and cleverness, she slipped Irma a Mickey."

1958. Barbara Eden plays Loco Jones on the syndicated *How to Marry a Millionaire*. While not a total ditz, Loco is very naïve when it comes to world affairs (she prefers her world of comic book trivia). She works as a fashion model, looks absolutely fabulous in a dress and because of her hour glass figure was voted by her high school class as "The one to go further with less than anyone else." Barbara Nichols plays Ginger, a buxom blonde who is quite naïve but whose fabulous figure gets her jobs as a fashion model on *Love That Jill* (ABC).

1959. Marie Wilson plays Marie Pepperdine, a beautiful but dizzy mailroom clerk who hopes to become a fashion model on the CBS pilot *Miss Pepperdine*. Jean Carson plays Rosemary Zandt, a waitress at the Pelican Club in Manhattan on *The Betty Hutton Show* (CBS). Rosemary, like Marie, is brilliant one moment, a total airhead the next.

1962. The lovely Marie Wilson stars in *The Soft Touch*, a charming CBS pilot in which she plays Ernestine McDougal, the dizzy daughter of a loan company owner who believes her misguided feminine intuition is better than collateral in determining the recipients of loans.

1964. Connie Stevens plays Wendy Conway, a girl who never knows what she is going to say next (even after she says it) on ABC's *Wendy and Me*. Wendy is a former airline stewardess and married to an airline pilot (Jeff) who enjoys being a housewife. Meeting Wendy means an eyeful of beauty but an instant headache if you begin a conversation with her or ask her for help (and asking Wendy for help "is like being lost in the desert for four days and then having someone give you a glass of sand").

1967. Elaine Joyce plays Carol Chase, a ditzy secretary for the Oglethorpe Realty Company on the CBS pilot *Carol*. Goldie Hawn is Sandy Kramer, the pretty, energetic and ditzy dancer on CBS's *Good Morning World*.

1968. Goldie Hawn brings her bubbly dumb blonde character to NBC's *Rowan and Martin's Laugh-In* where she displays her slender figure in a bikini and in miniskirts in party scenes where she is the butt of dumb blonde jokes (she also forgets what she is saying even when she knows what she wants to say).

1970. Jackie Joseph provides the voice for Melody, a singer with the rock group Josie and the Pussycats on the animated *Josie and the Pussycats* (CBS; also for the sequel series *Josie and the Pussycats in Outer Space* in 1972). Melody is a pretty blonde who is also dense and often the only one who understands what she says. Being naïve is her strong point as the dumb things she does not only get the group into troublesome situations, but out with relative ease.

1971. Diane Nyland plays Tracy Young, a young wife who always sets out to do the right thing but somehow manages to complicate matters with her ineffable sense of logic on the syndicated *Trouble with Tracy*.

1973. Candace Azzara is Shirley Balukis, a very pretty but not very bright blonde whose good intentions always spell trouble for her boss at the unemployment office on NBC's *Calucci's Department*.

1974. Melodie Johnson plays Pamela Stevens, a beautiful but dizzy criminologist whose "brilliance" helps the police solve crimes on the NBC pilot *Ready and Willing*.

1975. Bernadette Peters is Doris, a beautiful, not-too-bright model and actress who is always in need of money on the NBC pilot *The Owl and the Pussycat* (Doris says she is in between last names and hasn't found the right one yet and when things get bad, she ventures into prostitution). Misty Rowe plays Maid Marian, the romantic interest of Robin Hood on ABC's *When Things Were Rotten*. This Maid Marian, however, is not the demure, conservative girl from the legend; she is a sexy, naïve and bosom-revealing "dingbat" who seems to relish in the fact that her beauty gives her a power over men (namely Robin's fumbling Merry Men).

1977. Suzanne Somers plays Chrissy Snow, a buxom, sweet and trusting secretary on ABC's

Three's Company. Chrissy's naïveté makes her appear dumb (she does do idiotic things because she acts first and thinks later).

1978. Janelle Price plays Wanda, the gorgeous but dizzy co-host of *The Cheap Show*, a syndicated game hosted by Dick Martin. Judy Landers plays Angie Turner, a gorgeous but ditzy showgirl who also works as the secretary to private detective Dan Tanna on ABC's *Vegas.* Angie is not a great typist or note taker but she is captivating and the main reason why Dan keeps her on.

1981. Connie Stevens plays Mary Carol Fitz-simmons, a gorgeous housewife whose well-meaning intentions always backfire on the ABC pilot *Harry's Battles.* Judy Landers also retains her dumb blonde image for NBC's *B.J. and the Bear.* Judy plays Jeannie Campbell, a shapely girl whose 37C-34-36 figure has earned her the nickname of "Stacks." Stacks drives an 18-wheeler and is so sweet and trusting that despite the dumb things she does, you can't help but love her.

1982. Judy Landers again plays a dumb blonde, this time Sara Joy Pitts, the stunningly beautiful niece of Hollywood has-been Madame on the syndicated *Madame's Place.* Sara Joy is from a small town and has come to Hollywood "to become a star like my Auntie Madame." Other than displaying her stunning figure in bosom-revealing tops and short shorts, Sara Joy really never got to pursue her dream.

1983. Teri Copley plays Mickey MacKenzie, a stunning Marilyn Monroe–like girl who is trying to shed her image as a dumb blonde and prove she is capable of anything on NBC's *We Got It Made.* A revised version of the series appeared in syndication (1987) with Teri Copley reprising her role as Mickey MacKenzie, this time as a bit more intelligent blonde bombshell (36-24-34) who earns a living as a housekeeper.

1984. Teresa Ganzel plays Shirley Jurwalski, a gorgeous but ditzy topless Las Vegas ice skater who inherits an animation studio after the death of her husband on NBC's *The Duck Factory.*

1985. Michele Matheson plays Angela, the pretty but kooky blonde girlfriend of Heather Owens on ABC's *Mr. Belvedere.* Angela is not very outgoing but smart in her own way. She treasures not only her friendship with Heather but her hanger collection. She feels her only assets are "that I'm blonde and pretty."

1987. Christina Applegate plays 16-year-old Kelly Bundy, a very smart dumb blonde on Fox's

Married ... With Children. Kelly is a sexy teenager who knows how to manipulate men to get what she wants. She appears naïve at times but also very smart at other times (usually as the result of doing something so stupid that it turns out for the best). She treads the fine line that separates genius from insanity and loves to dress in miniskirts and bosom-revealing tops. As her father, Al, often wonders when he talks to her, "Is there anybody home up there?" Jean Kasem plays Loretta Tortelli, a tall, beautiful airhead who hopes to become a Las Vegas showgirl on NBC's *The Tortellis.* Like other dumb blondes, Loretta's naïveté always makes things right. You don't have to be a woman to be a dumb blonde. You can be a beautiful 13-year-old girl like Juliette Lewis as Kate Farrell on ABC's *I Married Dora.* Kate knows she is beautiful and likes "to dress hot" (short skirts, tight blouses) "and go to the local mall to drive shoe salesmen crazy." Kate sometimes appears to be living in her own world but always manages to get out of a scrape when her senses kick in. Judy Landers plays another dumb blonde on the syndicated *Rock Candy.* Here she is Sherrie Waverly, a singer with a band called Rock Candy. She is gorgeous, naïve and doesn't realize how sexy she is. She has many boyfriends but says, "I don't know why. I guess they like my singing."

1988. Brooke Theiss plays 17-year-old Wendy Lubbock, one of eight children on ABC's *Just the Ten of Us.* Wendy has the distinction of being the airhead of the family. She enjoys shopping at the mall and claims "attitude gets me men. I think I'm beautiful. I fool people. I'm not as perfect as you think I am. I've got fat ankles" (which she calls "my shame"). Ashley Crow plays Mickey Castle, the pretty but batty secretary to scientific genius Austin James on ABC's *Probe.* Mickey has had several jobs but has always had to quit "because my boss thinks I can do my job better in the nude." Austin has a photographic memory and really doesn't need Mickey but he keeps her around because her unpredictability challenges his mind.

1993. Jennifer Blanc plays Tiffany, a girl who believes being pretty is the only asset she has on NBC's *The Mommies.* Tiffany says, "People say I'm an airhead" and she has an annoying (to others) habit of giggling at everything.

1998. Priscilla Lee Taylor plays Tracee Banks, a gorgeous, busty blonde on the syndicated *Mal-*

ibu, Ca. Tracee loves to dress in pink and believes she is "the most beautiful girl in Malibu and California and the whole U.S. of A. except for alien chicks who may appear on *Star Trek.*" Tracee is an actress and plays a bikini-clad surgeon on the mythical TV series *Malibu Hospital.*

2002. Kaley Cuoco plays teenager Bridget Hennessey on ABC's *Eight Simple Rules.* While not a total airhead, Bridget is the smartest of the dumb blondes listed in this entry. She is beautiful like the others but she often thinks before she acts, making her not quite the dumb blonde. However, when she doesn't think before she acts, she is what Archie Bunker of *All in the Family* would call a "dingbat." Her sister, Kerry (Amy Davidson), a redhead, is often jealous of Bridget because her dumbness always makes her appear smart.

2003. Kelly Ripa plays Faith Fairfield, a total dumb blonde, on ABC's *Hope and Faith.* Faith is extremely naïve (you would never think she went to school) and is the dumbest of the dumb blondes ever to appear on TV (she believes, for example, that singer Glen Campbell makes Campbell's Soups; that Sally Field [whom she calls Sally Fields] is the woman behind the line of Mrs. Fields cookies). Faith believes she is bright and doesn't realize what she says is often misconstrued by others as totally idiotic. Because of this she doesn't realize what she does and often creates chaotic situations for her family, especially her sister Hope (Faith Ford). Paris Hilton and Nicole Richie are best friends in real life who are not only beautiful and rich but the stars of Fox's reality series *The Simple Life.* While it is obvious Paris and Nicole are putting on the dumb blonde act (it is supposed to be a reality series) they do it so convincingly that people fall for their act and go out of their way to help them in their tasks for the show (taking Paris and Nicole away from the high life to experience the working life).

2004. Sarah Wright plays Paige Chase, an adorable but ditzy 15-year-old on Fox's *Quintuplets.* Paige lives in her own world. She strives to be alluring, is not work oriented and is called "Bimbo the Clown" by her sister Penny. Paige loves to wear low cut blouses but her mother fears her going to the mall "because the air conditioning gives her chest colds." Her mother also doesn't like it when Paige wears white and eats pizza— "White and tomato sauce don't match."

2005. Molly Stanton plays Farrah Arnold, a stunning lingerie model who is rather naïve and incapable of thinking for herself on *Twins* (WB). Farrah has an intelligent sister, Mitchee (Sara Gilbert), and became famous by modeling the Breast-O Change-O Bra ("Makes any woman a goddess"). Farrah's mother, Lee (Melanie Griffith) is also a dumb blonde.

Women — Extraordinary

Women who possess special powers or are involved in situations that are out of the ordinary are the essence of this entry. See also *F.B.I. Agents, Mediums, Robots, Witches* and *Women — Law Enforcers.*

1950. Margaret Garland (then Patricia Ferris) plays Dr. Joan Drake, an instructor at Space Academy, on *Tom Corbett, Space Cadet* (CBS/ABC/NBC/DuMont). Joan was beautiful, intelligent and capable of defending herself. She was, in the 1950s, the first role model for girls in the viewing audience.

1952. Ilona Massey plays Nikki, a beautiful but mysterious woman (supposedly engaged in underground activities during World War II) who now owns a nightclub in Paris and helps people in trouble on ABC's *Rendezvous.*

1953. Gail Davis plays sharpshooter Annie Oakley, a western heroine for girls on the syndicated *Annie Oakley.* Irene Champlin plays Dale Arden, a brilliant futuristic scientist and aid to space hero Flash Gordon on the syndicated *Flash Gordon.*

1954. Ella Raines becomes Janet Dean, TV's first nurse (private duty in New York City), on the syndicated *Janet Dean, Registered Nurse.*

1955. Sheena (Irish McCalla) is a white jungle goddess who protects her adopted African homeland from evil on the syndicated *Sheena, Queen of the Jungle.*

1958. Abby Dalton plays Belle Starr, the Bandit Queen of the Old West, who, despite her outlaw reputation, fights for right on the CBS pilot *Belle Starr.* Jane Edwards (Muriel Davis) is the daughter of a ranch owner who battles crime as a mysterious, costumed figure called *El Coyote* (pilot).

1966. Diana Rigg plays Emma Peel, a woman who is not only beautiful and highly intelligent but also well versed in the martial arts who battles evil on ABC's *The Avengers*. Linda Thorson replaced her in 1968 as Tara King, an equally beautiful girl who helps John Steed battle injustice.

1968. Yvonne Craig joins the cast of ABC's *Batman* as Barbara Gordon, alias the daring Batgirl, a crusader for justice in Gotham City. Sharron Macready (Alexandra Bastedo) is a woman who uses her heightened senses to battle crime on NBC's *The Champions*.

1971. Two pilots titled *Cat Ballou* aired on NBC. In the first one (September 5), Leslie Ann Warren plays Catherine "Cat" Ballou, a rancher, schoolteacher and Old West heroine. JoAnn Harris plays Cat in the second pilot on September 6. Annabelle Hurst (Rosemary Nicols) is a beautiful and gifted woman with extraordinary crime-solving skills on the syndicated *Department S*.

1975. Schoolteacher Andrea Thomas (JoAnna Cameron) acquires a magic amulet that transforms her into Isis, a champion of Justice on *Isis* (CBS). The beautiful Amazon Diana Prince (Lynda Carter) leaves her home on the secluded Paradise Island to battle evil in America on *Wonder Woman* (ABC/CBS).

1976. Lindsay Wagner plays Jaime Sommers, a government agent (for the O.S.I.) who uses her bionic limbs (arm, legs) to battle evil on *The Bionic Woman* (ABC/NBC). Newspaper reporters Laurie and Judy (Deidre Hall, Judy Strangis) are secretly *Electra Woman and Dyna Girl* (ABC), crime fighters who use the power of electricity to foil evil.

1978. Joanna Lumley plays Purdy, a British government agent who uses her skills in the martial arts and firearms to battle villains on *The New Avengers* (CBS).

1980. Securities Hazards Expert Lavinia Kean (Cornelia Sharpe) is a female James Bond who tackles extremely dangerous assignments on the CBS pilot *S*H*E*.

1982. Modesty Blaise (Ann Turkel), a former criminal turned mysterious adventurer, helps people in distress on the ABC pilot *Modesty Blaise*.

1983. Martial arts and weapons expert Kate Flannery (Lisa Hartman) uses her skills as an agent for High Performance, an agency that tackles extremely dangerous assignments on ABC's *High Performance*. Newspaper reporter Sandy Martinson (Alexa Hamilton) touches a spilled chemical solution, becomes invisible, and uses her newfound gift to solve crimes on the NBC pilot *The Invisible Woman*.

1985. Patty Duke plays Julia Mansfield, the first woman president of the United States on ABC's *Hail to the Chief*. Terri MacLaine (Jenny Seagrove) is a novelist who solves crimes for story material on the ABC pilot *In Like Flynn*. Actress Shawn Weatherly is chosen to devote one year of her life "to the greatest adventure of her life" by documenting the myths, mysteries and monsters of the seas on NBC's *Ocean Quest*.

1986. Nikki Blake (Patricia Charbonneau) is a forensics and computer expert who risks her life to battle international crime on the NBC pilot *C.A.T. Squad*. A second pilot about the Counter Assault Tactics (C.A.T.) Squad was made in 1988 with Deborah Van Valkenburgh as Nikki Pappas. Mary Ellen Stuart plays Holly Hathaway, a young woman chosen by aliens to battle evil on Earth on *The Greatest American Heroine*, an ABC pilot that was to pick up where *The Greatest American Hero* left off when Ralph Hinkley was exposed as being the super crime fighter.

1987. Police department secretary Jennifer Cameo (Sela Ward) dispenses justice at night as the mysterious crime fighter Cameo on the NBC pilot *Cameo by Night*. Justice Department secretary Carly Fox (Daphne Ashbrook) poses as a top agent to recruit people in trouble (with a promise to help them with their government woes) to help her solve crimes on the NBC pilot *Carly's Web*.

1989. Jane (Glynis Barber) is a girl who battles the enemies of the free world during World War II with the only weapon she has — her sexuality, on *Jane* (Syn.).

1991. Cheryl Singer (Kathleen Beller) is a beautiful bookkeeper who longs to be a detective. Fate brings Cheryl in contact with Spex, Truk and Nit, miniature clay figures brought to life by a meteor and saved by Cheryl. Cheryl takes on the role of detective and with the help of her clay figures solves crimes on the ABC pilot *The Danger Team*.

1992. Ione Skye plays Eleanor Covington, a member of the 14th century Grey clan on ABC's *Covington Cross*. Eleanor is an expert with a cross bow and can defend herself as she struggles to protect her home from evil.

1993. Ashley Coddington (Catherine Oxenberg) and Catherine Pascal (Alison Armitage) are the top female agents of H.E.A.T. (Hemisphere Emergency Action Team) on the syndicated *Acapulco H.E.A.T.* Ashley was formerly with MI-6 and is an explosives and martial arts expert.

Catherine, who likes to be called Cat, is a cunning thief and expert pickpocket.

1994. Helen Shaver plays Marjorie Litchfield, the first female president of the United States on the CBS pilot *The First Gentleman* (refers to her husband, Frank). A beautiful model known only as Lex (Famke Janssen) fights crime as the mysterious Lady X on the Fox pilot *Model by Day*.

1995. Lucy Lawless is Xena and Renee O'Connor is her traveling companion, Gabrielle, warriors who did not exist but are adapted from the legends of ancient Greek and Roman mythology on the syndicated *Xena: Warrior Princess*.

1997. Buffy Summers (Sarah Michelle Gellar) is a very special 16-year-old girl. She is the Chosen One, the one girl in the world with the ability to fight the unnatural (namely vampires) on *Buffy the Vampire Slayer* (WB/UPN). Nikita Wirth (Peta Wilson) is a highly skilled and deadly operative for Section One, an anti terrorist operation on USA's *La Femme Nikita*.

1998. Elizabeth Gracen plays Amanda, a mysterious woman from a race called Immortals, who battles evil in the modern-day world on the syndicated *Highlander: The Raven*. Veronica Layton (Jennifer O'Dell), Marguerite Krux (Rachel Blakely) and Finn (Lara Cox) are the women of the syndicated *The Lost World*. Veronica grew up on the Plateau, a land forgotten by time. She managed to survive its perils (dinosaurs, hostile tribes) since she lost her parents 10 years ago (she is now 22). Marguerite is a member of an expedition trapped on the Plateau. She lusts for wealth, is a skilled fighter and an expert shot. Finn is a girl from the future (100 years) who is also trapped on the Plateau. She is fearless and an expert with a cross bow. Vallery Irons (Pamela Anderson) is a girl with no special skills who heads Vallery Irons Protection on the syndicated *V.I.P.* Vallery does contribute glamour to the series but it is two of her operatives, Nikki Franco (Natalie Raitano) and Tasha Dexter (Molly Culver), who are exceptional. Nikki is a member of the Franco crime family (from which she has distanced herself). She is an expert shot and feels bullets and guns are the only way to deal with criminals. Tasha is a ruthless former CIA double agent, KGB operative and member of the Israeli Army who uses her vast knowledge of the military to accomplish a goal.

1999. Kim Taylor (Angie Everhart), Victoria Correra (Traci Bingham) and Eva Kiroff (Eva Halina) are the female members of Dream (Dangerous Reconnaissance Emergency Action Missions) on the syndicated *The Dream Team*. Kim is tough. She is a former member of the FBI Hostage Rescue Team who is bitter because she could not become a Navy SEAL (women were not permitted at the time). Victoria is an explosives expert and was a former Freedom Fighter. Eva is a world-class gymnast who also worked as a spy for the Russian KGB. She has knowledge of foreign operatives and can get into places without being detected. Tia Carrere plays Sydney Fox, a college professor who battles unscrupulous characters as she seeks ancient relics on the syndicated *Relic Hunter*. Sydney is a martial arts expert and knows how to use her sexuality for distraction when the need arises.

2000. Cleopatra (Jennifer Sky), Hel (Gina Torres) and Sarge (Victoria Pratt) are members of a resistance force battling to reclaim the Earth from aliens on the syndicated *Cleopatra 2525*. Other than her sexy dress and her ability to scream, cry and whimper, Cleopatra has no special skills. Hel (short for Helen) is a skilled fighter who is careful in her approach to battling the enemy. Sarge (real name Rose) was a former soldier with the Black Watch who is impulsive and plunges into violent confrontations without thinking first. Max Guevara (Jessica Alba) is a genetically enhanced girl who fights evil but lives by her own set of rules on Fox's *Dark Angel*. Annette O'Toole and Jordana Spiro play Dottie and Brandi Thorson, a mother and daughter team of bounty hunters on USA's *Huntress* (Aleska Palladino played Brandi in the pilot). Kate Hodge plays Anne Price, a former FBI agent with a remarkable arrest record who heads Level 9, a state-of-the-art government agency that solves the cases other agencies cannot on UPN's *Level 9*. Angela Dotchin plays Emilia Smythe Rothschild, a scientific British secret agent who seeks to keep the island of Pulau Pulau from the French expansion of 1801 on the syndicated *Jack of All Trades*. Dona Alvarado (Tessie Santiago) is a young woman who poses as a lady of leisure but secretly helps the people of Old California when necessary as *The Queen of Swords* (Syn.). Gena Lee Nolin plays Sheena, a white jungle goddess who protects her adopted homeland of Africa from evil on the syndicated *Sheena*.

2001. Jennifer Garner plays Sydney Bristow, a highly skilled and deadly agent for the CIA on ABC's *Alias*. Michelle Lintel plays Darcy Walker, a police officer who secretly avenges crimes as the mysterious Black Scorpion on the Sci Fi Channel's *Black Scorpion*. Maria Valentine (Sarah Carter) is a young woman who defeats the forces of evil as an up and coming enmascarada (masked wrestler) on the Fox series *Los Luchadores* (*The Wrestlers*). Shalimar Fox (Victoria Pratt) and Emma DeLauro (Lauren Lee Smith) are young women with enhanced DNA that gives them extraordinary powers as crime fighters on the syndicated *Mutant X*. Francesca Hunt plays Rebecca Fogg, cousin of the famed Phileas Fogg (from the book *Around the World in 80 Days*) and British Secret Service agent who battles the evils of the 19th century League of Darkness on *The Secret Adventures of Jules Verne* (Sci Fi). Liz Vassey plays Captain Liberty, a beautiful super hero hired by the U.S. government to be a symbol of good but who also battles evil on Fox's *The Tick*. Sara Pezzini (Yancy Butler) is a police officer that is chosen by unknown forces to wield the Witchblade, a mysterious bracelet with a mind of its own that compels her to battle evil on TNT's *Witchblade*.

2002. Helena Kyle (Ashley Scott), the daughter of Batman and Cat Woman, battles evil as Huntress in New Gotham City on the WB's *Birds of Prey*. Assisting Helena is Barbara Gordon (Dina Meyers), a teacher at New Gotham High School who is secretly Batgirl. Cassie McBain (Natasha Henstridge), D.D. Cummings (Kristen Miller) and Shane Phillips (Natashia Williams) are She Spies, government agents who battle crime and corruption on the syndicated *She Spies*. Cassie is an expert con artist; D.D. is a computer whiz; Shane is a master thief.

2004. Eliza Dushku plays Tru Davies, a young woman with the unique ability to help the dead by going back in time to save them on Fox's *Tru Calling*. Jaye Tyler (Caroline Dhavernas) is a 24-year-old woman who receives cryptic messages from inanimate objects that tell her how to help others on Fox's *Wonderfalls*.

2005. Geena Davis plays Mackenzie Allen, a wife and mother who is also the first female president if the U.S. on ABC's *Commander-in-Chief*. Cathy Davis (Lea Thompson) is a wife and mother who secretly solves crimes for the U.S. government on *Jane Doe* (Hallmark Channel)

Women — Law Enforcers

This entry chronicles the women who work as either private detectives or police officers. See also *F.B.I. Agents, Forensics* and *Lawyers*.

1949. Carol Hill (Jayne Meadows) is TV's first female detective. She operates an agency called Trouble, Inc. with her husband Jason (Earl Hammond) on the DuMont test film *Trouble, Inc.* Although technically not a detective, Pamela North (Mary Lou Taylor), the wife of private detective turned publisher Jerry North (Joseph Allen, Jr.), believes she has the instincts of one and goes about solving crimes on the NBC test film *Mr. and Mrs. North*.

1950. Sally Fame (Gale Storm) and her husband, George (Don DeFore), are detectives who strive to solve crimes on the ABC test film *Mystery and Mrs.*

1952. *Mr. and Mrs. North* returns to TV (CBS /NBC) with Barbara Britton as Pamela North, the woman with a knack for stumbling upon and solving crimes. Richard Denning plays her husband, Jerry.

1957. Bertha Cool (Beany Venuta) is a penny-pinching, shrewd detective who operates the Cool and Lam Private Detective Agency with Donald Lam (Billy Pearson) on the CBS pilot *Cool and Lam*. Beverly Garland plays Patricia "Casey" Jones, a courageous New York City police woman on the syndicated *Decoy*. Nora Charles (Phyllis Kirk), the wife of former detective Nick Charles (Peter Lawford) enjoys solving the crimes she stumbles upon on *The Thin Man* (NBC).

1959. Melody Lee Mercer (Arlene Howell) is a receptionist at the New Orleans investigative firm of Randolph and Calhoun who does part time investigative work on ABC's *Bourbon Street Beat*. While not a licensed detective, the beautiful Cricket Blake (Connie Stevens), a singer at the Hawaiian Village Hotel in Honolulu, becomes an amateur sleuth when needed to help her private detective friends on ABC's *Hawaiian Eye*.

1962. Barbara Stanwyck plays Agatha Stewart, a lieutenant with the Chicago Police Department's Bureau of Missing Persons on the ABC pilot *The Seekers*. Barbara repeated the character on a second pilot, also called *The Seekers*, in 1963 that also failed to become a series.

1965. Anne Francis plays Honey West, the extremely sexy owner of a detective agency (H. West and Company) who incorporates the latest in scientific gadgetry on ABC's *Honey West*.

1966. Fleming and Casey Holloway (Brooke Bundy, Barbara Hershey) are the teenage daughters of a private detective who help their father solve crimes on the NBC pilot *Holloway's Daughters*.

1968. Peggy Lipton plays Julie Barnes, a special undercover agent for the L.A.P.D. on ABC's *The Mod Squad*.

1970. Yvette Mimieux plays Vanessa Smith, a criminologist who solves cases of the most deadly nature, murder, on ABC's *The Most Deadly Game*.

1972. Caroline di Contini (Nyree Dawn Porter) is a Contessa who is also a member of the Protectors, a European-based organization of private detectives who battle crimes on *The Protectors* (Syn.). Hildegarde Withers (Eve Arden) is a retired schoolteacher and amateur sleuth who helps the police solve crimes on the ABC pilot *A Very Missing Person*.

1973. Tracy Fleming (Donna Mills) is an undercover police officer who poses as the bait to nab criminals on the ABC pilot *The Bait*.

1974. Jessica Walter plays Amy Prentiss, a chief of detectives with the San Francisco Police Department on NBC's *Amy Prentiss*. Ann Neal (Penny Fuller) is an N.Y.P.D. sergeant assigned to a four-woman unit designed to watch over schools, families and merchants on the ABC pilot *Ann in Blue*. Cindy Weintraub is Terry Munson, an undercover police officer with the Anti Crime Unit of the N.Y.P.D., on *Baker's Dozen* (CBS). Shelley Winters plays Rose Winters, a private detective working out of Los Angeles, on the CBS pilot *Big Rose*. Teresa Graves is Christie Love, a gorgeous undercover police officer with the L.A.P.D., on ABC's *Get Christie Love*. Paul and Nancy Roscommon (Anthony Costello, Marianne McAndrew) are a husband and wife who are also police officers on the CBS pilot *Mr. and Mrs. Cop*. Pepper Anderson (Angie Dickinson) is a former model turned sergeant for the Criminal Conspiracy Division of the L.A.P.D. on NBC's *Police Woman* (in the pilot episode, broadcast on NBC's *Police Story*, Angie played the role as vice squad detective Lisa Beaumont). Ernestine and Gwendolyn Snoop (Helen Hayes, Mildred Natwick) are elderly and eccentric mystery writers who solve crimes to acquire story material on NBC's *The Snoop Sisters*.

1975. The life of rookie L.A.P.D. police officer Dana Hill (JoAnn Pflug) is explored on the NBC pilot *Dana Hill*. John Rubinstein and Lee Kroeger play David and Mandy Robbins, a husband and wife team of private detectives on the ABC pilot *Mr. & Ms.*

1976. Sabrina Duncan (Kate Jackson), Jill Munroe (Farrah Fawcett) and Kelly Garrett (Jaclyn Smith) are former police officer turned private detectives for the mysterious Charlie Townsend on ABC's *Charlie's Angels*. Kris Munroe (Cheryl Ladd), Tiffany Welles (Shelley Hack) and Julie Rogers (Tanya Roberts) were future Angels. Jo Ann Harris plays Kate Manners, an officer with the Most Wanted unit of the L.A.P.D. on ABC's *Most Wanted*.

1977. Randi Oakes, Brianne Leary and Tina Gayle play Bonnie Clark, Sindy Cahill and Kathy Linehan, officers for the California Highway Patrol on NBC's *CHiPs*. J.Z. Kane (Kim Basinger) is a beautiful, easy-going police officer that is teamed with tough L.A.P.D. sergeant Jack Ramsey (Lou Antonio) on ABC's *Dog and Cat*. Pamela Sue Martin (then Janet Louise Johnson) plays Nancy Drew, the beautiful daughter of a criminal attorney who solves crimes on ABC's *The Nancy Drew Mysteries*. Barbara Eden plays Elizabeth Stonestreet, a woman who becomes a private detective after the death of her police officer husband to keep his beliefs about law and order alive on the NBC pilot *Stonestreet: Who Killed the Centerfold Model?*

1978. Jackie Clifton and Darlene Shilton (Sarina Grant, Anna L. Pagan) are roommates and police officers with California's West Valley Precinct on the ABC pilot *Jackie and Darlene*. Suzanne Pleshette plays Kate Bliss, an early 20th century detective on the ABC pilot *Kate Bliss and the Ticker Tape Kid*.

1979. Kate Hudson (Brenda Vaccaro) is a divorced police officer with a young daughter who heads a male unit of detectives on *Dear Detective* (CBS). Suzanne Lederer plays Carol Wright, a detective under Chief Earl Eischied on NBC's *Eischied*. Jennifer Hart (Stefanie Powers) and her husband Jonathan (Robert Wagner) are a wealthy couple who enjoy solving crimes on *Hart to Hart* (ABC). Kate Columbo (Kate Mulgrew), the wife of Lieutenant Columbo, becomes a newspaper reporter who solves crimes on NBC's *Mrs. Columbo* (later titled *Kate Loves a Mystery*. Here Kate resumes her maiden name of Callahan when she divorces the lieutenant). Jennifer Palmero and Cotton Gardner (Marcia Strassman, Colette Blonigan) are an experimental team of female patrol car officers whose beat are the streets of Hollywood on the ABC pilot *The Nightingales*.

1980. Samantha Jensen (Michelle Pfeiffer) is a member of the Burglary Auto Detail, Commercial Auto Thefts Division of the L.A.P.D. on ABC's *B.A.D. Cats*. Heather Fern (Rebecca Reynolds) and Caroline Capoty (Lorrie Mahaffey) are detectives for Texas International, a two-bit investigative firm on the NBC pilot *The Eyes of Texas*. A second pilot was made a year later with Heather Thomas as Caroline Capoty. Michelle Phillips and Tanya Roberts play Casey Hunt and Britt Blackwell, detectives with the San Francisco P.D., on the ABC pilot *Ladies in Blue*. Jennifer Dempsey (Cassie Yates) is a detective with the 22nd Precinct of the San Francisco P.D. on *Nobody's Perfect* (ABC).

1981. Chris Cagney (Loretta Swit, Meg Foster, Sharon Gless) and Mary Beth Lacey (Tyne Daly) are detectives with the Manhattan 14th Precinct on CBS's *Cagney and Lacey*. Debra Feuer plays Jane Ryan, an officer with the New Orleans P.D. on the NBC pilot *Hardcase*. Momma Sykes (Esther Rolle) is a hotel housekeeper with sleuthing abilities who solves crimes on the NBC pilot *Momma the Detective*. Paula Woods (Jayne Kennedy) and Melanie Mitchell (Cindy Morgan) are former traffic cops turned plainclothes detectives with the Ocean City, California P.D. on the NBC pilot *Mitchell and Woods*. The characters of Melanie Mitchell and Paula Woods are revised by Trisha Townsend and Barbara Stock and seen as motorcycle cops on the "Ponch's Angels" episode of *CHiPs* (a pilot spinoff for a new version of *Mitchell and Woods*). Trisha Noble plays Rosie Johnson, a sergeant with the Strike Force Unit of the L.A.P.D., who handles dangerous cases on ABC's *Strike Force*.

1982. Cindy Weintraub plays Terry Munson, an officer with the Anti Crime Unit of the N.Y.P.D. on CBS's *Baker's Dozen*. Caroline McWilliams plays Cass Malloy, a wife and mother who, after the untimely death of her husband, replaced him as the sheriff of Burr County on the CBS pilot *Cass Malloy*. Cassie Holland (Angie Dickinson) is a Los Angeles private detective who uses her expertise as a former criminologist to solve crimes on *Cassie and Company* (NBC). Alexandra Brewster (Sharon Gless) is an inspector

with the Palms City, California P.D. on the NBC pilot *Palms Precinct*. Laura Holt (Stephanie Zimbalist) is a woman of class who operates Remington Steele Investigations on NBC's *Remington Steele*. Stacey Sheridan (Heather Locklear) and Victoria Taylor (April Clough) are patrol car officers with a California city identified only as L.C. on ABC's *T.J. Hooker*. Lynn Taylor (Ellen Regan), the only female rookie cop in a class of 25, begins her duties on the NBC pilot *The 25th Man (Ms.)*.

1983. Roxanne Caldwell (Heather McNair) is an officer with the L.A.P.D. on ABC's *Automan*. Melody Anderson plays Brooke McKenzie, a detective with the N.Y.P.D. on NBC's *Manimal*. Laura Ireland (Tovah Feldshuh) is an avid mystery fan and owner of a bookstore (Murder Ink) who helps her detective husband solve crimes on the CBS pilot *Murder Ink*. Barbara Brady (Bess Armstrong) is a Los Angeles–based private detective who charges $200 a day, packs a .38 and is a fan of old detective movies on the CBS pilot *This Girl for Hire*. Linda Craig (Lori Loughlin) is a young detective who helps her scientific genius cousin, Tom Swift solve crimes on the ABC pilot *The Tom Swift and Linda Craig Mystery Hour*.

1984. Stepfanie Kramer and D.D. Howard play Tracy and Jean, private detectives working out of Southern California on the NBC pilot *Four Eyes*. Dee Dee McCall (Stepfanie Kramer), Joann Molinski (Darlanne Fluegel) and Christine Novack (Lauren Lane) are detectives with the L.A.P.D. who were also partners (over the course of the series) with Rick Hunter (Fred Dryer) on NBC's *Hunter*. Carole Stanwyck (Lynda Carter) and Sydney Kovak (Loni Anderson) are the ex-wives of a detective agency owner who inherit his company (The Caulfield Detective Agency) after his death to become *Partners in Crime* (NBC).

1985. Glynis Barber plays Harriet Makepeace, a sergeant with London's New Scotland Yard, who is teamed with New York exchange cop James Dempsey on the syndicated *Dempsey and Makepeace*. Stephanie Faracy plays Tracy Doyle, a slightly off-center Jill of all trades who solves crimes on ABC's *Eye to Eye*. Dani Starr (Sharon Stone) is a detective with the L.A.P.D. Hollywood Station, Vice Squad Division, on the ABC pilot *Hollywood Sarr*. Jamie Rose plays Katy Mahoney, a detective with the Chicago Metro P.D. Violent Crimes Unit, who is herself extremely violent when it comes to catching criminals on ABC's *Lady Blue*. Jenny Loud (Kathryn Harrold) is a patrol car officer who is secretly married to Malcolm McGruder (in defiance of departmental orders) on ABC's *McGruder and Loud*. Kate Morgan (Lisa Eilbacher) is a beautiful criminologist who teams with her wealthy mother, Zena Hunnicutt (Holland Taylor), to solve crimes on *Me and Mom* (ABC). Maddie Hayes (Cybill Shepherd) is a beautiful but penniless ex-model who runs Blue Moon Investigations on ABC's *Moonlighting*. Deborah Adair plays Zoey Martin, a private investigator who uses the latest scientific technology on the ABC pilot *Zoey*.

1986. Toni Adams (Sydney Walsh) is a former district attorney turned New York–based private detective on the CBS pilot *Adams Apple*. Mary Crosby plays Bonnie Raines, an officer with the L.A.P.D. on the NBC pilot *Crazy Dan*. Jessica Fletcher (Angela Lansbury) is a former schoolteacher turned mystery novelist who solves crimes on *Murder, She Wrote* (CBS). Dori Doreau (Anne-Marie Martin) is an officer with an unidentified police department who is a top martial arts expert on ABC's *Sledge Hammer*. Elizabeth Pena plays Connie Rivera, an officer with the Chicago Police Department, on CBS's *Tough Cookies*.

1987. Linda Hamilton plays Catherine Chandler, an investigator for the Manhattan D.A.'s office, on CBS's *Beauty and the Beast*. Janet Gunn replaced her as N.Y.P.D. Detective Diana Bennett. Christina Towne (Peggy Smithhart) is a private investigator who runs the Two of Diamonds, Confidential Investigations, with her partner Miles Devitt (Nicholas Campbell) on CBS's *Diamonds*. Fionnula Flannagan plays Guyla Cook, a lieutenant with the Metro California P.D. on CBS's *Hard Copy*. Mary Frann plays Harriet Quayle, a gorgeous Australian private detective who makes New York City her base of operations on the CBS pilot *Harry*. Barbara Bosson is Captain Celeste Stern and Sydney Walsh is Detective McNeil, law enforcers with the San Francisco Police Department on ABC's *Hooperman*. Anne Russell (Mimi Kuzak) is an officer with the Hope Division Precinct of the L.A.P.D. on the ABC pilot *Hope Division*. Joanne Beaumont (Robyn Douglass) is a lieutenant with the Major Crimes Unit of the Houston P.D. on CBS's *Houston Knights*. Claire McCarron (Margaret Colin) is an assistant D.A. who quits her job to become her own boss as the head of McCar-

ron Investigations on *Leg Work* (CBS). Catherine Keene plays Cricket Sideris, a detective with the L.A.P.D. on ABC's *Ohara*. Hildy Granger (Suzanne Somers) becomes the sheriff of Lakes County, Nevada, when she replaces her late husband on *She's the Sheriff* (Syn.). The mishaps that occur when the Metropolitan P.D. teams married officer Cheryl Kelly (Loretta DeVine) with single officer Franny Aronson (Dinah Manoff) are the basis of the CBS pilot *Sirens*. Judy Hoffs (Holly Robinson) is a youthful looking cop who infiltrates high schools and battles juvenile crime on *21 Jump Street* (Fox).

1988. Patricia Charbonneau plays Dakota Goldstein, a former operative with the National Securities Agency who now works as a plainclothes detective with the L.A.P.D. on the ABC pilot *Dakota's Way*. Kristol McNichol plays Barbara Weston, an officer (then sergeant) with the Miami P.D. on NBC's *Empty Nest*. Satin Carlyle (Lisa Cutter) is an undercover agent and troubleshooter who solves crimes for Interpol on the NBC pilot *Lovers, Partners and Spies*.

1989. Ally Walker plays Jessica Haley, an officer with the N.Y.P.D. Emergency Services Unit on NBC's *True Blue*.

1990. Officer Judy Tingreedies (Eileen Davidson) is a Rambo-like motorcycle cop who is currently on leave because of her addiction to danger on CBS's *Broken Badges*. Victoria Principal plays Claire Moreno, a former police officer turned investigator for the Los Angeles D.A.'s office, on the ABC pilot *Just Life*. Sydney Elizabeth Kells (Valerie Bertinelli) is an investigator for the Los Angeles law firm of Fenton, Benton and Sloane on CBS's *Sydney*.

1991. Mary Mara plays Nancy Kraus, a detective who investigates cases involving the rich and famous in New York on the CBS pilot *Empire City*. Pam Dawber plays Carolyn Hudson, creator of the TV series "Miss Markham Mysteries," who solves crimes to get story material on the CBS pilot *Rewrite for Murder*. Rita Lee Lance (Mitzi Kapture) is an officer with the Crimes of Passion Unit of the Palm Springs, Florida, Police Department on CBS's *Silk Stalkings*. Tyler Layton replaced Rita as Detective Holly Rawlins (who was later replaced by Janet Gunn as Detective Cassandra St. John).

1992. Anita Wellman King (Robin Givens) and Dorothy Paretsky (Pamela Gidley) are detectives with the Homicide Division of Chicago's Violent

Crimes Unit on *Angel Street* (CBS). Angie Dickinson plays Angie Martin, a lieutenant who heads an all male unit of L.A.P.D. officers on the ABC pilot *Angie the Lieutenant*. Nora Houghton (Kate McNeil) is a detective with the Westside Division of the L.A.P.D. on CBS's *Bodies of Evidence*. Eve Madison (Yancy Butler) is an alluring sergeant with the L.A.P.D. who happens to be a robot (created by the Artificial Intelligence Program) designed to battle crime on NBC's *Mann and Machine*. Maxine Stewart, called Max (Lauren Holly), is a deputy sheriff in the small town of Rome, Wisconsin, on *Picket Fences* (CBS). Cybill Shepherd plays Stormy Weathers, a confidential private investigator based in Venice, California, on the ABC pilot *Stormy Weathers*. Mariska Hargitay plays Angela Garcia, a rookie police officer on CBS's *Tequila and Bonetti*.

1993. Rachel Ticotin plays Annette Rey and Lisa Darr is Jan Sorenson, police detectives on NBC's *Crime and Punishment*. S. Epatha Merkerson plays Lieutenant Anita Van Buren on NBC's *Law and Order*. Jill Kirkendall (Andrea Thompson), Janice Licalsi (Amy Brenneman), Diane Russell (Kim Delaney), Laura Murphy (Bonnie Sommerville) and Rita Ortiz (Jacqueline Obradors) are the female officers attached to the 15th Detective Squad on ABC's *N.Y.P.D. Blue*. Patti D'Arbanville plays Virginia Cooper, a lieutenant with the N.Y.P.D., on *New York Undercover* (Fox). The daily adventures of rookie police officers Sarah Berkezchuk (Jayne Brook), Molly Whelan (Liza Snyder) and Lynn Stanton (Adrienne-Joi Johnson) are the focal point of ABC's *Sirens*. In the syndicated version (1994) Jayne Hertmeyer replaces Jayne Brook as Officer Jessica Jaworski.

1994. Kate Jackson plays Arly Hanks, a former New York private detective turned police chief of a small Arkansas town (Maggoty), on the CBS pilot *Arly Hanks Mysteries*. Jessie Morgan (Tracy Nelson) is an aspiring artist who joins her father, private detective Max Morgan, on cases on the ABC pilot *The P.I.* Jacqueline Samuda plays Isabella Vargas, a detective with a police precinct called the Two-Five, on the ABC pilot *Police File*. Brett Robin (Linda Purl) heads Robin's Nest, a nightclub that doubles as a private detective organization on the syndicated *Robin's Hoods*. Her female operatives are McKenzie Magnuson (Claire Yarlett), Stacey Wright (Julie McCullough), Maria Alvarez (Mayte Vilan) and Anastasia Beckett (Jennifer Campbell). Rose Phillips

(Karen Sillas) is the only "guy" in an all male squad room of a Pacific Northwest P.D. on CBS's *Under Suspicion*.

1995. Ryan McBride (Angie Harmon) is a private detective based in California on the syndicated *Baywatch Nights*. Kelly McGillis plays Meala McGann, a lieutenant with the Cleveland Police Department who is in charge of a task force designed to battle corruption on the ABC pilot *Dark Eyes*. Susan Baker (Jane Curtin) is a bored housewife and amateur sleuth who offers her services (via newspaper ads) as a detective on the ABC pilot *Mystery Dance*. Tracy Ryan plays 21-year-old sleuth Nancy Drew in a new version of the 1977 series called simply *Nancy Drew* (here Nancy is a college student who solves crimes). Lisa Vidal plays Consuela Muldoon, a dedicated N.Y.P.D. homicide detective who prefers to work alone, on the ABC pilot *Off Broadway*.

1996. Cory McNamara (Paula Trickey), Monica Harper (Shanna Moakler) and Jamie Strickland (Amy Hunter Cornelius) are motorcycle cops with the Santa Monica Beach Patrol on U.S.A.'s *Pacific Blue*.

1997. Jayne Hertmeyer plays Brianna Branca, a lieutenant with the Bay City Police Department, on the syndicated *NightMan*. Mariska Hargitay is Nina Echeverria, an undercover cop with the Intelligence Squad of the N.Y.P.D. (based on Prince Street in Manhattan) on *Prince Street* (NBC). Cameron Westlake (Heather Medway) is a patrol car officer with the Metro City Police Department on the syndicated *Viper*.

1998. Anne-Marie Kersey (Yancy Butler) and Nora Valentine (Klea Scott) are officers with the Brooklyn South Precinct of the N.Y.P.D. on CBS's *Brooklyn South*. Dana Dickson (Tammy Lauren) and Grace Chen (Kelly Hu) are detectives with the L.A.P.D. on CBS's *Martial Law*. Yasmine Bleeth joins the cast of *Nash Bridges* (CBS) as Caitlin Cross, a beautiful internal affairs inspector with the Special Investigative Unit of the San Francisco P.D. Nia Peeples joins the cast of *Walker Texas, Ranger* (CBS) as Sydney Cook, a Texas Ranger with the Department of Public Safety, who is well versed in the martial arts.

1999. Mariska Hargitay plays Olivia Benson, a detective who investigates sex based crimes for the N.Y.P.D.'s Special Victims Unit on NBC's *Law and Order: S.V.U.* Gina Gershon plays Glenn Hall, the operator of a high-tech private detective agency in Santa Monica on ABC's *Snoops*.

Dana Plant (Paula Marshall) and Roberta Young (Paula Jai Parker) assist her.

2001. Darcy Walker (Michelle Lintel) is a police officer with the 21st Precinct of Angel City who is secretly the mysterious crime fighter *Black Scorpion* (Sci Fi Channel). Jinny Exstead (Nancy McKeon), Kate McCafferty (Bonnie Bedelia) and Magda Ramirez (Lisa Vidal) are among the female officers who risk their lives to enforce the law in San Francisco on Lifetime's *The Division*. Kathryn Erbe plays Alexandra Eames, a detective with the N.Y.P.D. on NBC's *Law and Order: Criminal Intent*. Alexondra Lee plays Kate Benson, a detective who investigates cases that involve unnatural phenomena, on UPN's *Special Unit 2*. Sara Pezzini (Yancy Butler) is a detective with the 11th Precinct of the N.Y.P.D. who wields the mysterious Witchblade (giving her crime fighting powers) on *Witchblade* (TNT).

2002. Wilhelmina Chambers, called Billie (Tiffani-Amber Thiessen), is an L.A.P.D. lieutenant who heads the Candy Store, a secret warehouse of seized weapons and cars that she uses on cases on Fox's *Fastlane*. Jayne Brook plays Jamie Avery, a lieutenant with the Seattle Police Department on *John Doe* (Fox). While not a detective in the real sense, nurse Sharona Fleming (Bitty Schram) finds herself helping paranoid detective Adrian Monk solve crimes on *Monk* (USA). Maggie Lawson plays Nancy Drew, a college student who solves crimes on the ABC pilot *Nancy Drew*. Klea Scott plays Sonya Robbins, a detective with the L.A.P.D. on CBS's *Robbery Homicide Division*. Glenn Close is Captain Monica Rawling and C.C.H. Pounder is Detective Claudette Wyms on *The Shield* (FX).

2003. Lily Rush (Kathryn Morris) solves crimes that have remained unsolved for years for the Philadelphia P.D. on *Cold Case* (CBS). Carla Gugino plays Karen Sisco, a tough and seductive U.S. Marshal on ABC's *Karen Sisco*. Elena Mocias (Roselyn Sanchez) is a deputy under Lieutenant Joe Friday (Ed O'Neill) on ABC's *L.A. Dragnet*. Ryan Layne (Jamie Luner) and Christina Vidal (Gabrielle Lopez) are deputies with the Los Angeles County Sheriff's Office on ABC's *10–8: Officers on Duty*. Sarah Wayne Callie plays Jane Porter, an N.Y.P.D. detective who breaks the law by helping an escaped prisoner (Tarzan) evade capture on the WB's *Tarzan*. Joely Fisher plays Zoey Busick, a fraud investigator, on Lifetime's *Wild Card*.

2004. Kristen Bell plays Veronica Mars, a captivating high school student in Neptune, California, who helps her detective father solve crimes on UPN's *Veronica Mars*.

2005. Marisol Nichols plays Karen Bettancourt, a detective with the N.Y.P.D.'s 8th Precinct on *Blind Justice* (ABC). Kyra Sedgwick plays Brenda Leigh Johnson, a CIA trained detective who handles sensitive, high profile murder cases on *The Closer* (TNT). Nora Gage (Gracelle Beauvais-Nilon) is a Primary Investigator and Meg Brando (A.J. Langer) a street investigator for Judd Risk Management on ABC's *Eyes*. Marguerite Moreau plays Rachel Lyford, a detective with the Deviant Crime Unit of the San Francisco P.D. on *The Gate* (Fox). Samantha Kinsey (Kellie Martin) is an amateur sleuth and owner of the Mystery Woman's Bookstore who solves crimes on *Mystery Woman* (Hallmark Channel).

2006. Michele Hicks is Amy Sykes, a no-nonsense detective with the L.A.P.D. on NBC's *Heist*.

Women — Nurses

This entry chronicles the programs on which nurses are the star or featured regular. See also *Doctors*.

1952. Patricia Benoit plays Nancy Remington, a school nurse at Jefferson Junior High School in Jefferson City on NBC's *Mister Peepers*.

1954. Ella Raines plays Janet Dean, a private duty nurse working in New York City on the syndicated *Janet Dean, Registered Nurse*

1959. Martha Hale (Abby Dalton) is a military nurse assigned to the San Diego Naval Base on *Hennessey* (CBS).

1961. Maggie Graham (Bettye Ackerman) is a nurse at County General Hospital on ABC's *Ben Casey*. Annie Brenner (Peggy Cass) is a dedicated but mishap-prone nurse on the NBC pilot *Call Me Annie*. Lee Kurty plays Zoe Lawton, a nurse at Blair General Hospital on *Dr. Kildare* (NBC).

1962. Liz Thorpe and Gail Lucas (Shirl Conway, Zina Bethune) are dedicated nurses at New York's Alden General Hospital on *The Nurses* (CBS; the title switched to *The Doctors and the Nurses* in 1964).

1965. ABC adapts the CBS series *The Nurses* to a daytime serial of the same name with Mary

Fickett as Liz Thorpe and Melinda Plank as Gail Lucas.

1968. Diahann Carroll plays Julia Baker, a nurse with the Los Angeles Inner Aero Space Health Center on *Julia* (NBC).

1969. Mary Treen plays Nurse Tillie, assistant to the elderly Dr. Jason Fillmore, on the NBC pilot *Doc*. Elena Verdugo plays Kathleen Faverty, nurse to Drs. Marcus Welby and Steven Kiley in Santa Monica, California, on ABC's *Marcus Welby, M.D.* Audrey Totter is Eve Wilcox, a nurse at the University Medical Center in Los Angeles, on *Medical Center* (CBS).

1971. Nuala Fitzgerald plays Louise Wynn, nurse to Drs. Andrew Sellers and Simon Locke on the syndicated *Dr. Simon Locke*.

1972. Marge Nelson (Barbara Barrie) and Ann Linden (Jean Fowler) are nurses with the Los Angeles Code 3 Emergency Medical Division of the U.C.L.A. Medical Center on the pilot *Code 3*. Loretta Swit plays Margaret Houlihan, the head nurse at the 4077th Mobile Army Surgical Hospital in Korea during the war on *M*A*S*H* (CBS). Michelle Johnson (Kate Jackson) is a nurse in Hope, a rural California community on the ABC pilot *The New Healers*. Susan Foster, Heather Young, Lori Saunders and Judy Pace play Kathi, Lu Ann, Maria and Gail, student nurses on the CBS pilot *Oh Nurse!* Mary Ellen Walton (Judy Norton-Taylor), the eldest daughter of John and Olivia Walton, is a county nurse in 1930s Jefferson County, Virginia, on *The Waltons* (CBS). Marsha Mason plays Marsha Lord, a nurse at Blair General Hospital on the syndicated *Young Dr. Kildare*.

1973. Ann Carlisle (Joan Van Ark), Ellen Turner (Nancy Fox) and Mildred McInerney (Reva Rose) are nurses stationed at Capital General Hospital in Washington, D.C., on ABC's *Temperatures Rising*.

1974. ABC revises the above title with Jennifer Darling as Wendy Winchester, a nurse at Capital General Hospital on *The New Temperatures Rising Show*.

1975. Mary Wickes plays Beatrice Tully, nurse to Dr. Joe Bogert on CBS's *Doc*. Connie Kimbrough (Elisabeth Brooks) is a nurse at Memorial General Hospital on *Doctors Hospital* (NBC).

1976. Dottie Dickson (Katherine Cannon), Sue Webster (Brianne Leary), Nancy Gilmore (Nancy Conrad) and Ann Wilson (Leslie Charleson) are army nurses stationed on Bella La

Cava in the South Pacific during World War II on NBC's *The Black Sheep Squadron* (originally titled *Baa Baa Black Sheep*). Audrey Lindley plays Janet Scott, nurse to Dr. Joe Bogert of the New York Westside Community Clinic on *Doc* (CBS). Liz Baker and Jackie Morse (Marlyn Mason, Didi Conn) are nurses with an all female M*A*S*H unit during the Korean War on the CBS pilot *Handle with Care*.

1977. Dolores Crandall (Melinda Naud), Barbara Duran (Jamie Lee Curtis), Edna Howard (Yvonne Wilder), Ruth Colfax (Dorrie Thompson) and Claire Reid (Bond Gideon) are World War II army nurses stranded on the U.S.S. *Sea Tiger*, a pink submarine on ABC's *Operation Petticoat*.

1978. Rosa Santiago (Rosa Soto) and Rhonda Todd (Julienne Wells) are nurses with the Adult Emergency Services Hospital on Hudson Street in New York on ABC's *A.E.S. Hudson Street*. Annie Flynn (Barrie Youngfellow) is a nurse who hopes to become a doctor on the CBS pilot *Annie Flynn*. Adrienne Barbeau plays Major Kate Steele, the head of a combat weary unit of nurses stationed in Korea during the war, on the CBS pilot *The Fighting Nightingales*. Katherine O'Hara (Jo Ann Pflug), Dolores Crandall (Melinda Naud) and Betty Wheeler (Hilary Thompson) are the World War II nurses stranded on the pink submarine, the U.S.S. *Sea Tiger*, on *The New Operation Petticoat* (ABC).

1979. Eddie Benton (a female) plays Diane Curtis, a nurse at City Hospital in California, on *Doctors Private Lives* (NBC). Beth Jacobs plays Nancy McMillan, a nurse at Kensington General Hospital in Los Angeles, on *House Calls* (CBS). Gloria "Ripples" Brancusi (Christopher Norris [a female]), Clara "Starch" Willoughby (Mary McCarty) and Ernestine Shoop (Madge Sinclair) are nurses at San Francisco Memorial Hospital on *Trapper John, M.D.* (CBS).

1980. Priscilla Barnes joins the cast of *Three's Company* as Terri Alden, a nurse at Wilshire Memorial Hospital in Los Angeles.

1981. Michael Learned plays Mary Benjamin, a middle-aged widow attempting to begin a new life as head nurse at New York's Grant Memorial Hospital on *Nurse* (CBS). Hattie Winston, Bonnie Hellman and Hortensia Colorado play nurses Toni Gillette, Penny Brooks and Betty La Sada on the series.

1983. Hannah Hertelendy plays Florence Hudson, a nurse at Wilshire Memorial Hospital in Los Angeles on ABC's *Ryan's Four*. Sandy Burns (Jane Kaczmarek), Julie McPhail (Melinda Culea), Shirley Daniels (Ellen Bry) and Helen Rosenthal (Christina Pickles) are among the nurses at St. Eligius Hospital in Boston on NBC's *St. Elsewhere*. Jayne Modean and Eileen Heckert play Jane Hooter and Agnes Decker, nurses attached to the Medstar Trauma Center of the McKee General Hospital in Los Angeles, on *Trauma Center* (ABC). Ruth O'Malley (Barbara Rhoades) and Abby McGee (D.D. Howard) are nurses with the Venice Medical Center in California on the ABC pilot *Venice Medical*.

1984. Corinne Bohrer, Lynne Moody and Conchata Ferrell play Cory Smith, Julie Williams and Joan Thor, nurses with Chicago's Clark Street Hospital on CBS's *E/R*.

1986. Rosa Villanueva (Priscilla Lopez) is a nurse at Manhattan General Hospital on CBS's *Kay O'Brien*.

1988. Colleen McMurphy (Dana Delany) is one of many nurses stationed at China Beach, the U.S. Armed Forces R&R Facility in Vietnam during the war on *China Beach* (ABC). Cherry White (Nan Woods) and Lila Garreau (Concetta Tomei) are the other principal nurses. Laverne Todd (Park Overall) is the nurse-receptionist to Harry Weston, a pediatrician at the Community Medical Center in Florida on NBC's *Empty Nest*. Julie Ronnie plays Alice Swanson, the featured nurse on *Heart Beat* (ABC). Incidents in the lives of student nurses Bridget (Susan Walters), Thea (Britta Phillips), Samantha (Chelsea Field) and Becky (Kristy Swanson) are related in the NBC pilot *Nightingales*.

1989. Samantha (Chelsea Field), Allyson (Kim Urich), Bridget (Susan Walters) and Becky (Kristy Swanson) are the student nurses whose lives are profiled on *Nightingales*, an NBC series based on the 1988 pilot (see above). NBC's *13 East* also explores the lives of nurses. Here, Maggie Doyle (Diana Bellamy), Kelly Morrison (Barbara Isenberg) and Monique Roberts (Jan Cobler) at a hospital called 13 East.

1991. Sandy Miller (Stephanie Hodge), Anne Roland (Arnetia Walker), Gina Cuevas (Ada Maris) and Julie Milbury (Mary Jo Keenan) are among the nurses at the Community Medical Center (3rd Floor West) in Miami Beach, Florida, on NBC's *Nurses*. Eleanor Emerson (Ella Joyce) is a nurse attached to Wing C of Harbor Hospital in Baltimore on *Roc* (Fox).

1992. Ricky Wilder (Mary Page Keller) is a nurse (hospital or doctor affiliation not given) on ABC's *Camp Wilder*. Rachel Gunn (Christine Ebersole) is a middle-aged nurse at Little Innocents Hospital who is called "The Iron Nightingale" on Fox's *Rachel Gunn, R.N.*

1994. Julianne Margulies plays Carol Hathaway and later Linda Cardellini is Samantha Taggart, the featured nurses on NBC's *ER*.

1995. Chelsea Noble plays Elizabeth Waters, a nurse at New York's St. Bernard's Hospital, on the WB's *Kirk*. Hudson Leick, Rebecca Cross and Hillary Danner are student nurses Tracy Stone, Megan Peterson and Jamie Fuller at *University Hospital* (Syn.).

1998. Jesse Warner (Christina Applegate) is a young divorcee and student nurse at the Student Health Center in Buffalo, New York on NBC's *Jesse*. Jesse is divorced, the mother of a young son and works at her father's bar to make ends meet.

2003. Katey Sagal plays Cate Hennessey, a mother who is also a nurse (first at an unnamed hospital; then at Liberty High School in Michigan) on ABC's *Eight Simple Rules*.

Women — Scatterbrained

A girl doesn't have to be a blonde to be dumb. She can be a redhead, a brunette or even a raven-haired beauty and still do things associated with being a dumb blonde. This entry chronicles the scatterbrained women of TV, the non-blondes who complicate life for all concerned. See also *Women — Dumb Blondes*.

1949. Jane Ace, playing herself, the wife of writer Goodman Ace, is television's first scatterbrained woman on *Easy Aces* (DuMont). Jane means well but her ineffable sense of logic causes her to act before she thinks, thus making Goodman the recipient of her misguided good intentions.

1950. Butterfly McQueen (then Ruby Dandridge) plays Oriole, the totally scatterbrained friend of Beulah, a maid on *The Beulah Show* (CBS). Oriole is TV's first flaky black character. She knows everything about nothing and just thinking about something can cause chaos if she follows through on it. Gracie Allen plays herself, the wife of comedian George Burns, on *The George Burns and Gracie Allen Show* (CBS). Gracie is TV's quintessential scatterbrained woman. She has a

knack for totally confusing people and complicating the simplest of situations — all of which are
resolved by George before a particular episode
ends.

1951. Lucille Ball plays Lucy Ricardo, the wife
of Cuban bandleader Ricky Ricardo (Desi Arnaz)
on *I Love Lucy* (CBS). Lucy yearns for a career in
show business but Ricky won't allow it. Her efforts
to change Ricky's mind by doing things that seem
logical to her but create minor disasters when she
acts upon them place Ricky in the situation of re-
solving all the chaos she causes. Comedienne Joan
Davis plays herself, a scatterbrained salesgirl at a
store called Hats By Anatole on the CBS pilot *Let's
Join Joanie*.

1952. In *I Married Joan* (NBC), Joan Davis,
as Joan Stevens, the wife of Judge Bradley Stevens
(Jim Backus), best sums up a scatterbrained
woman (pretending to be an item on an auction
block): "I have here a wife. Due to circumstances
beyond her control, this wife is losing its owner.
Now, what am I bid for this wife? This is no ordinary wife. This one's a real goof. This wife is
unconditionally guaranteed to louse things up."
Joan always means well but her good intentions in-
evitably backfire (even her fortune cookies are
against her — "When you opened this cookie you
read the fortune we put in it. But when you
opened your mouth, you stuck your foot in it").

1955. Mabel Spooner (Nita Talbot) is a beautiful, marriage-mined young woman who borders
on being a bit scatterbrained on *Joe and Mabel*
(CBS). Mabel is in love with Joe Sparton (Larry
Blyden), a man who is not ready for marriage.
Mabel's efforts to change Joe's mind sets off an
inner hormone that makes her do crazy things —
things that seem natural to her but wacky to
everyone else.

1958. When the U.S. space program requires a
person to become the first human in space, a computer chooses Joan Jones (Joan Davis), a dental
technician from Hot Springs, Arkansas, on the
CBS pilot *Joan of Arkansas*. What that computer
didn't know is that Joan is a bit scatterbrained and
her attempts to become an astronaut were to be the
focal point of the series.

1961. Lucille Ball plays Lucy Carmichael, a
widow and the mother of two children, Chris and
Jerry, on *The Lucy Show* (CBS). Lucy lives off a
small pension and to supplement her income devises harebrained schemes to acquire additional
money. Naturally, with Lucy, the schemes always

backfire but in the end seem to work out for the
best.

1962. "When strange things are looking to
happen, somebody gives them Gladys's address,"
say Peter Porter (Harry Morgan) about his wife
Gladys (Cara Williams), a scatterbrained housewife on *Pete and Gladys* (CBS). Pete, who always
becomes the innocent victim of his wife's antics,
is apparently the only one who can undo Gladys's
misguided good intentions and return the situation to normal.

1963. Glynis Johns plays Glynis Granville, a
mystery writer on *Glynis* (CBS). Glynis appears
to be a normal woman — until she stumbles upon
a crime and loses all sense of logic as she goes
about trying to solve it. It is usually her attorney
husband, Keith (Keith Andes), who comes to the
rescue. Pamela Britton plays Lorelei Brown, a
pretty but slightly dizzy widow (famous for her
fudge brownies) who runs a small rooming house,
on *My Favorite Martian* (CBS).

1964. Joan Staley plays Roberta Love, a Navy
WAVE stationed on the South Pacific island of
New Caledonia during World War II, on *Broadside* (ABC). Roberta is assigned to the motor pool,
is a bit scatterbrained and her well-meaning intentions often backfire, leaving it up to her superior,
Lt. Anne Morgan (Kathleen Nolan), to resolve.
Cara Wilton (Cara Williams) is a file clerk at Fenwick Diversified Industries who knows she is a bit
scatterbrained and has devised a filing system that
only she can understand to protect her job on *The
Cara Williams Show* (CBS). Cara's good intentions always backfire and it is her husband, Frank
(Frank Aletter), who resolves the chaotic situations that develop.

1965. Karen Scott (Debbie Watson) is a beautiful 16-year-old girl on NBC's *Karen*. She is the
youngest of the scatterbrained females listed here
and her overeagerness causes her to do things
(usually to help people) that always backfire and
make her seem like a scatterbrain. However, un-
like the other females listed here, Karen's senses
kick in when she realizes what is happening and
she can usually resolve the chaos she has caused.

1966. Tammy Ward (Tammy Grimes) is
young, beautiful and single. She is also heir to a
fabulous fortune but is unable to touch it until
she turns thirty on *The Tammy Grimes Show*
(ABC). In the meantime, Tammy works as a cus-
tomer services officer in a bank and, to finance
her expensive tastes, devises elaborate and wacky

schemes to get her hands on some of that money — all of which fail and cause nothing but trouble.

1967. Paula Hollister (Paula Prentiss) is an employee of the Manhattan Tourist Aid Society who has a heart of gold but a knack for totally confusing people with her ineffable sense of logic on *He and She* (CBS).

1968. Lucille Ball plays yet another scatterbrained woman, this time Lucille Carter on *Here's Lucy* (CBS). Lucille is a widow, the mother of two children (Kim and Craig) and works as a secretary for her Uncle Harry, the owner of the Unique Employment Agency. Whether she means to or not, Lucille's attempts to improve her situation in life (or impress her boss) always backfire and require Harry's intervention to straighten things out.

1971. Millie Grover (Millicent Martin) is a stewardess for the London-based International Airlines on *From a Bird's Eye View* (NBC). Millie is a bit on the scatterbrained side but eager to please everyone — an eagerness that often backfires and involves her and her company in embarrassing situations. Millie works with Maggie Ralston (Pat Finley), a level-headed girl who not only becomes involved in Millie's antics, but resolves the problems that result.

1979. Sydney Goldsmith plays Coral, a waitress at the Juice Bar at the Fountain of Youth Health Spa in Beverly Hills, on *Stockard Channing in Just Friends* (CBS). Coral is black, beautiful and a scatterbrain. Like the women before her, her good intentions always backfire and involve people in embarrassing situations.

1980. On *The Stockard Channing Show* (CBS), Sydney Goldsmith plays Earline Cunningham, a sexy but dimwitted receptionist at Los Angeles TV station KXLA. Earline is impressed by people she believes have class (like her friend Susan, who eats pizza with a knife and fork) and tries to impress people with stories she reads in gossip papers.

1981. Jerry Martin (Dean Jones) is a level-headed husband who is struggling to cope with and solve the problems that result from Louise (Diane Stilwell), his pretty but totally scatterbrained wife on the ABC pilot *I Love Her Anyway!*

1982. Mallory Keaton (Justine Bateman), the second born child of Steven and Elyse Keaton, is a very pretty 16-year-old girl who is bright in her own way but has a hard time relaxing, which gives her a scatterbrained appearance on *Family Ties* (NBC).

1984. Chelsea Field plays Barbara Myer, supervisor of the Just Temporary Employment Agency on the NBC pilot *Only Temporary*. Barbara has a ditsy sister named Nicole (Christine Mellor) and Nicole has an equally empty-headed girlfriend named Torie (Lisa Kudrow). The proposed series was to relate Barbara's efforts to resolve the situations that result when Nicole and Torie set out to do something.

1985. Tracy Doyle (Stephanie Faracy) is a Jill of all trades, including a private detective, on ABC's *Eye to Eye*. Tracy is also a bit off the wall, forgetful and attracts trouble like a magnet.

1990. Karyn Parsons plays Hilary Banks, a stunningly beautiful black girl who is also a flake on *The Fresh Prince of Bel Air* (NBC). Hilary is rich and totally self-absorbed and very naïve when it comes to world affairs. She does things without thinking and is seeking a glamorous job so that when people ask what she does for a living she can see them turn green with envy.

1991. Lillian Abernathy (Carol Kane) is the flaky secretary to newspaper columnist Tom Nash (Robert Urich) on *American Dreamer* (NBC). Lillian is not so much a scatterbrain by her actions, but more by what she says (for example, "I know my marriage was over when my husband said, 'It's over,'" or "I once attended a bachelor party. I jumped out of the cake").

2005. Jennifer Tilly plays Crystal, a beautiful but ditzy brunette who, despite her silliness, is so lovable that her boyfriend, the older and divorced Dr. Stuart Barnes (Henry Winkler), can't help but love her on *Out of Practice* (CBS).

Note: While not specifically categorized as dumb blondes or scatterbrained, men can also share the same symptoms as women when it comes to doing dumb things. Over the years TV has had its scatterbrained men, the most notable of which are as follows. Arthur Lake is the bumbling, seemingly simple-minded architect Dagwood Bumstead on *Blondie* (NBC, 1954). Alan Reed is Clifton Finnegan, "a subnormal chowder head; a dope; a low grade moron" (the compliments of his friend Archie the bartender) on NBC's *Duffy's Tavern* (1954). Will Hutchins later plays Dagwood Bumstead in a revised version of the series also called *Blondie* (CBS, 1968). Joey Lawrence plays Joey Russo, a teenager who is quite dense (he believes, for example, that the earth is the other side of the sun) on *Blossom* (NBC, 1991). Chris Stacy is King Hollis Weed, "a hulking dimwit" who often says, "I'm as dumb as a post," on *Flesh 'n' Blood* (NBC, 1991). Shawn Harrison is Waldo, a dim-witted, if not dense high school student on ABC's *Family Matters* (1995). Kevin Connolly plays Ryan Malloy, a naïve and scatterbrained high school student on the WB's *Unhappily Ever After* (1995).

Index

A&E Biography: Son Also Rises Presidential Appearances (2000)

A.D. Religious Programs (1984)

A.E.S. Hudson Street Doctors (1978), Latino American (1978), Puerto Rican (1978), Women — Nurses (1978)

A.J.'s Time Travelers Time Travel (1994)

a.k.a. Pablo Mexican American (1984), Puerto Rican (1984)

A.U.S.A. Lawyers (2003), New York (2003)

Aaron's Way Adolescence (1988), Religious Programs (1988)

The Abbott and Costello Cartoon Show Cartoons (1966)

The Abbott and Costello Show Animals (1952), California (1952), Hotels (1952), Look-alikes (1952), Series Based on Radio Programs (1952), Sitcoms (1952)

Abby San Francisco (2003)

The ABC Afternoon Playhouse Drama (1973)

The ABC Afterschool Special Drama (1972)

ABC Album Drama (1953)

ABC Presents Krofft Late Night Puppets (1991)

ABC Stage '67 Drama (1966)

ABC Tuesday Night Pilot Film Pilot Film Series (1976)

The ABC Weekend Special Puppets (1972)

ABC's Monday Night Football Nudity (2005)

ABC's Wide World of Entertainment Drama (1967)

Abe Lincoln in Illinois Broadway (1945), Politics (1964)

Abie's Irish Rose Series Based on Radio Programs (1972)

About Faces Game Shows (1960)

Above the Law Westerns (1966)

Abra Kadabra Magicians (1987), Puppets (1987)

Abraham Religious Programs (2001)

Abraham Lincoln in Illinois Politics (1945)

Abraham's Sacrifice Religious Programs (1978)

The Absent Minded Professor Series Based on Films (1989), Teachers (1988)

The Academy Teenagers (1982)

The Academy Awards Nudity (1974)

Acapulco Adventurers (1961)

Acapulco H.E.A.T. Government Agents (1993), Mexican American (1993), Women — Extraordinary (1993)

Accidental Family California (1967)

According to Jim Adolescence (2001), American Indian (2001)

Ace Men — Law Enforcers (1976)

Ace Crawford, Private Eye Little People (1983), Men — Law Enforcers (1983)

Aces Up Puerto Rican (1974)

The Acquittal Broadway (1952)

Acres and Pains Country Folk (1965), Pilot Film Series (1965)

Across the Seven Seas Reality Programs (1962)

Act II Teenagers (1987)

Acting Sheriff Men — Law Enforcers (1991)

Action in the Afternoon Westerns (1953)

Action News Reporters (1985)

Action Tonight Drama — Repeat Series (1957)

Actor's Studio Drama (1949)

Actors in the Making Drama (1945)

Adam and Eva Broadway (1952)

Adam MacKenzie, Frontier Doctor Doctors (1963), Westerns (1963)

Adam-12 Cars (1968), Los Angeles (1968), Men — Law Enforcers (1968)

Adams Apple Women — Law Enforcers (1986)

The Adams Chronicles Politics (1976)

Adams of Eagle Lake Men — Law Enforcers (1975)

Adam's Rib Lawyers (1973), Los Angeles (1973), Series Based on Films (1973)

Adamsburgh, U.S.A. Judges (1963)

The Addams Family Adolescence (1964), Films Based on Television Series (1991), Housekeepers (1964), Latino American (1965), Lawyers (1964), Little People (1964), Look-alikes (1964), Senior Citizens (1964)

Adderly Physically Disabled (1986)

The Admirable Crichton Broadway (1968)

Adorn Playhouse Drama — Repeat Series (1958)

Adventure, Inc Adventurers (2002)

The Adventure of the Three Garridebs Men — Law Enforcers (1937)

Adventure Theater Drama — Repeat Series (1961)

The Adventurer Espionage (1972)

Adventures in Paradise Adventurers (1959), Beaches (1959), Hotels (1959)

Adventures in Rainbow Country Teenagers (1972)

The Adventures of a Jungle Boy Adolescence (1957), Africa (1957), Children — Extraordinary (1957)

Adventures of a Model Pilot Film Series (1965)

The Adventures of a Two Minute Werewolf Werewolves (1985)

The Adventures of Black Beauty Animals (1972)

The Adventures of Blinky Puppets (1952)

The Adventures of Brisco County, Jr. Westerns (1991)

The Adventures of Captain Hartz Adventurers (1952)

The Adventures of Champion Adolescence (1955), Animals (1955)

The Adventures of Colonel Flack Con Artists (1953)

The Adventures of Con Sawyer and Hucklemary Finn Adolescence (1985)

The Adventures of Cyclone Malone Puppets (1950)

The Adventures of Ellery Queen Men — Law Enforcers (1950), New York (1950)

The Adventures of Fu Manchu Asian American (1950)

The Adventures of Hiram Holiday Adventurers (1956) Sitcoms (1956)

The Adventures of Hoppity Hopper from Foggy Bogg Cartoons (1962)

The Adventures of Jim Bowie Adventurers (1956), Historical Settings (1956)

The Adventures of Jimmy Neutron: Boy Genius Adolescence (2002), Geniuses (2002)

The Adventures of Jonny Quest Cartoons (1964)

The Adventures of Kit Carson Mexican American (1951), Westerns (1956)

The Adventures of Long John Silver Historical Settings (1956), Latino

American (1955), Physically Disabled (1956)

The Adventures of Mary Kate and Ashley Adolescence (1995), Twins (1995)

The Adventures of Nick Carter Men — Law Enforcers (1972)

The Adventures of Noah Beery, Jr. Adventurers (1954)

The Adventures of Oky Doky Puppets (1948)

The Adventures of Ozzie and Harriet Series Based on Radio Programs (1952), Sitcoms (1952), Teenagers (1952)

The Adventures of Patches Puppets (1951)

The Adventures of Pollyanna Adolescence (1982)

The Adventures of Pow Wow American Indian (1957), Cartoons (1957)

The Adventures of Rin Tin Tin Animals (1954), Series Based on Radio Programs (1972)

The Adventures of Robin Hood Historical Settings (1955)

The Adventures of Rocky and Bullwinkle Films Based on Television Series (2000)

Adventures of Sinbad Adventurers (1998)

The Adventures of Sinbad Speech Impaired (1998), Witches (1998)

The Adventures of Sir Francis Drake Historical Settings (1962), Latino American (1962)

The Adventures of Superboy Aliens (1953), Reporters (1988), Super Heroes (1961), Super Heroes (1988)

The Adventures of Superman Aliens (1953), Look-alikes (1953), Newspapers (1953), Reporters (1953), Robots (1953), Series Based on Radio Programs (1953), Super Heroes (1953)

The Adventures of Superpup Animals (1958), Super Heroes (1958), Talking Animals and Machines (1958)

The Adventures of the Sea Hawk Adventurers (1959)

The Adventures of the Seaspray Adventurers (1968), Australia (1968), Beaches (1968), Teenagers (1968)

The Adventures of the Thin Man Series Based on Radio Programs (1957)

The Adventures of the Tucson Kid Westerns (1960)

The Adventures of Topper Series Based on Radio Programs (1952)

The Adventures of William Tell Historical Settings (1957)

Adventuring with the Chopper African American (1976)

Advice to the Lovelorn Love (1981)

Aeromeds Pilots (1978)

The Affairs of China Smith Adventurers (1952)

Africa — Texas Style Series Based on Films (1968)

The African Patrol Africa (1957)

After Midnight Nightclubs (1988)

Against All Odds Reality Programs (1992)

Against the Law Boston (1990), Lawyers (1990)

An Age of Kings Shakespeare (1961)

The Agency Visually Impaired (2002)

Aggie Sitcoms (1957)

Ah! Wilderness Broadway (1959)

Aida's Brothers and Sisters: Black Voices in Opera Opera (2000)

Ain't Misbehavin' Broadway (1982)

Airwolf California (1984), Gadgets (1984), Pilots (1984), Pilots (1987), Visually Impaired (1984)

Al Haddon's Lamp Genies(1955)

The Al Pearce Show Variety Programs (1952)

Aladdin Variety and Drama Spectaculars (1958)

Aladdin and His Wonderful Lamp Fairy Tales (1982)

The Alan Brady Show Shows within Shows (1961)

Alan King's Thanksgiving Special Holiday Specials (1980)

The Alan Young Show Series Based on Radio Programs (1950)

Alarm Rescue (1954)

The Alaskans Adventurers (1959), Historical Settings (1959)

The Albert and Josephine Butler Program Variety Programs (1939)

The Alcoa Hour Drama (1955)

Alcoa Premiere Drama (1955)

The Alcoa-Goodyear Theater Drama (1955

The Aldrich Family Series Based on Radio Programs (1949), Sitcoms (1949), Teenagers (1949)

Alec Templeton Time Visually Impaired (1955)

Alex and the Doberman Gang Men — Law Enforcers (1980), Men — Law Enforcers (1981)

Alexander the Great Religious Programs (1968)

ALF Aliens (1986), Los Angeles (1986), Puppets (1986), Teenagers (1986)

The Alfred Hitchcock Hour Drama (1955)

Alfred Hitchcock Presents Drama (1955), Drama (1985)

Alfred of the Amazon Adventurers (1967), Men — Extraordinary (1967), Pilot Film Series (1963–1967)

Algo's Factory Teenagers (1998)

Ali Baba and the 40 Thieves Fairy Tales (1958)

Alias Espionage (2001), Women — Extraordinary (2001)

Alias Mike Hercules Men — Law Enforcers (1956)

Alias Smith and Jones Westerns (1971)

Alice Arizona (1976), Bars (1980), Hotels (1978), Restaurants (1976), Teenagers (1976)

Alice in Wonderland Broadway (1955), Fairy Tales (1955), Variety and Drama Spectaculars (1955)

Alien Nation Aliens (1989), Los Angeles (1989), Series Based on Films (1989)

Aliens for Breakfast Aliens (1995)

Aliens in the Family Aliens (1996), Aviators (1996), California (1996), Puppets (1996)

Alkali Ike Puppets (1950)

All Aboard Puppets (1952)

All About Barbara Pilot Film Series (1963–1967)

All About the Andersons Adolescence (2003), Los Angeles (2003)

All About Us Teen After-School Hangouts (2001), Teenagers (2001)

The All American College Show Reality Programs (1979)

All American Girl Asian American (1994), San Francisco (1994)

All American Pie Reality Programs (1980)

All Around Town Reality Programs (1946), Reality Programs (1951)

All in the Family African American (1971), African American (1975), Bars (1971), Cross Dressers (1976), New York (1971), Puerto Rican (1976), Sitcoms (1960), Taxi Cabs (1971), Teachers (1971), Television Firsts (1971), Women — "Dumb Blondes" (2002)

All Is Forgiven Shows within Shows (1986)

All My Children Lesbians (1983), Lesbians (2004)

All My Clients Are Innocent Lawyers (1962)

All My Tomorrows Shows within Shows (1973)

The All New Dating Game Love (1986)

All Night Radio Restaurants (1982)

All of Us Adolescence (2003), Restaurants (2006), Shows within Shows (2003)

All Souls Bars (2001), Boston (2001), Doctors (2001)

The All Star Party for Dutch Reagan Presidential Appearances (1986)

The All Star Revue Variety Programs (1950)

All That Glitters F.B.I. Agents (1984), Transsexuals (1977)

Allison Sidney Harrison Teenagers (1983)

All's Fair Politics (1976), Washington, D.C. (1976)

All's Well That Ends Well Shakespeare (1981)

Ally McBeal Asian American (1998), Boston (1997), Lawyers (1997), Lesbians (1997), Restaurants (1997), Transsexuals (2000), Twins (2001)

Almost American Immigrants (1981)

Almost Grown New Jersey (1988)

Almost Heaven Angels (1978)

Almost Home Housekeepers (1993), Teenagers (1993)

Almost Partners Children — Extraordinary (1987), Teenagers (1987)

Aloha Paradise Beaches (1981), Hawaii (1981), Love (1981)

Along the Barbary Coast Men — Law Enforcers (1961)

Alright Already Florida (1997)

The Alvin Show Cartoons (1961)

Always April Teenagers (1961)

Amahl and the Night Visitors Holiday Specials (1951), Opera (1951), Opera (1968), Opera (1978)

Amanda Fallon Doctors (1972)

The Amanda Show Adolescence (1997), Teenagers (1999)

Amanda's Hotels (1983)

The Amateur's Guide to Love Love (1971)

The Amazing Adventures of Tumblin' Tim Children's Program (1945), Clowns (1945)

The Amazing Dunninger Mediums (1968)

Amazing Grace Religious Characters (1995), Teenagers (1995)

The Amazing Mr. Malone Lawyers (1951), Series Based on Radio Programs (1951)

The Amazing Polgar Mediums (1949)

The Amazing Spider-Man Men — Extraordinary (1979), New York (1978), Super Heroes (1978)

Amazing Stories Drama (1985)

The Amazing Tales of Hans Christian Andersen Drama (1954), Fairy Tales (1954)

The Amazing Three Cartoons (1967)

The Amazing World of Kreskin Mediums (1971)

Amen Cars (1986), Philadelphia (1986), Religious Characters (1986)

American Bandstand Variety Programs (1957)

The American Dance Machine Presents a Celebration of Broadway Dance Broadway (1981)

The American Dream Adolescence (1981)

American Dreamer Newspapers (1990), Restaurants (1990), Teenagers (1990), Women — Scatterbrained (1991)

American Dreams Chicago (1981), Historical Settings (2002), Philadelphia (2001), Teenagers (2002)

The American Embassy Cross Dressers (2002)

American Eyes Asian American (1990)

American Family Mexican American (2002)

An American Family Reality Programs (1973)

The American Film Institute Salute to James Cagney Presidential Appearances (1974)

The American Film Institute Salute to John Ford Presidential Appearances (1973)

The American Girls New York (1978), Reporters (1978)

American Gothic Ghosts (1995)

American Idol Television Firsts (2002)

American Inventor Nudity (2005)

American Justice Devil (1995)

American Latino TV Latino American (2004)

The American Report Reporters (1978)

Americana Game Shows (1947)

Americans Civil War (1961)

America's Funniest Home Videos Cuban American (1992)

America's Most Wanted Reality Programs (1988)

America's Next Top Model Lesbians (2004), Nudity (2004), Nudity (2005)

America's Town Meeting News Broadcasts (1948)

America's Tribute to Bob Hope Presidential Appearances (1988)

Ames Brothers Show Variety Programs (1954)

Amos Burke, Secret Agent Espionage (1965)

The Amos 'n' Andy Show African American (1951), Hotels (1951), New York (1951), Senior Citizens (1951), Series Based on Radio Programs (1951), Sitcoms (1951), Taxi Cabs (1951)

Amy and the Angel Angels (1982)

The Amy Fisher Story Nudity (1993)

Amy Prentiss Adolescence (1974), San Francisco (1974), Women — Law Enforcers (1974)

Anastasia Broadway (1967)

And Beautiful, II African American (1970)

Anderson and Company Adolescence (1969)

Andromeda Aliens (2000), Computers — Extraordinary (2000), Space (1999)

The Andros Targets Reporters (1977)

The Andy Griffith Show Adolescence (1960), Cars (1960), Country Folk (1960), Judges (1960), Men — Law Enforcers (1960), Restaurants (1960), Senior Citizens (1960), Sitcoms (1960)

Andy Richter Controls the Universe Chicago (2003)

Andy Williams and the NBC Kids Easter in Rome Holiday Specials (1987)

Andy Williams and the NBC Kids Search for Santa Holiday Specials (1985)

The Andy Williams Christmas Show Holiday Specials (1967), Holiday Specials (1968), Holiday Specials (1971), Holiday Specials (1974)

The Andy Williams Christmas Special Holiday Specials (1973)

Andy Williams' Early New England Christmas Holiday Specials (1982)

The Andy Williams–June Valli Show Variety Programs (1957)

The Andy Williams New Year's Eve Special Holiday Specials (1963)

The Andy Williams Show Variety Programs (1959)

Andy's Gang Children's Program (1955), Puppets (1950), Speech Impaired (1951)

Angel Los Angeles (1999), Morphing (1997: Buffy the Vampire Slayer), Sitcoms (1960), Vampires (1999)

Angel in the Pawnshop Broadway (1952)

Angel Street Bars (1992), Broadway (1952), Chicago (1992), Women — Law Enforcers (1992)

Angela Anaconda Adolescence (1999)

Angels Don't Marry Broadway (1946)

Angie Philadelphia (1979), Restaurants (1979), Teenagers (1979)

Angie the Lieutenant Women — Law Enforcers (1992)

Animal Atlas Animals (2004)

Animal Crack-Ups Animals (1987)

Animal Kingdom Animals (1968)

Animal Secrets Animals (1966)

Animal World Animals (1969)

Animals, Animals, Animals Animals (1976)

Animals Are the Funniest People Animals (1983)

Ann in Blue Women — Law Enforcers (1974)

Ann Jillian California (1989), Mexican American (1989), Puerto

Rican (1989), Restaurants (1989), Teenagers (1989)

The Ann Sothern Show Hotels (1958), New York (1958), Senior Citizens (1958), Sitcoms (1958)

Anna and the King Asian American (1971), Series Based on Films (1971), Teachers (1972)

Anne Frank: The Whole Story Broadway (2001)

Anne of Avonlea Canada (1988)

Anne of Green Gables Canada (1986), Senior Citizens (1986), Teachers (1986)

Annette Housekeepers (1958)

Annie Broadway (1999)

Annie Flynn Women — Nurses (1978)

Annie Get Your Gun Broadway (1957), Broadway (1967)

Annie McGuire New Jersey (1988), New York (1988)

Annie Oakley Arizona (1954), Fairy Tales (1985), Look-alikes (1954), Westerns (1954), Women — Extraordinary (1953)

Another Day Adolescence (1978)

Another Day, Another Dollar Sitcoms (1959)

Another Evening with Fred Astaire Variety and Drama Spectaculars (1958)

Another Language Broadway (1939), Broadway (1946)

Another Man's Shoes Adolescence (1984)

Another World Soap Operas (1964), Soap Operas (1970), Soap Operas (Note)

The Answer Man Game Shows (1946)

Answer Yes or No Game Shows (1950)

The Antagonists District Attorneys (1991)

Antony and Cleopatra Shakespeare (1964), Shakespeare (1981)

Anybody Can Play Game Shows (1958)

Anyone Can Win Game Shows (1953)

Anything But Love Chicago (1989), Newspapers (1989)

Anything Goes Broadway (1950), Broadway (1954)

Anywhere, U.S.A. Doctors (1952)

Apartment 3-C Sitcoms (1949)

The Apartment House Pilot Film Series (1963–1967)

An Apartment in Rome Pilot Film Series (1963–1967)

Applause Broadway (1973)

The Apple Dumpling Gang Series Based on Films (1983)

Apple Pie Historical Settings (1978), Senior Citizens (1978), Teenagers (1978), Visually Impaired (1978)

Apple's Way Teenagers (1974)

Appointment for Adventure Drama (1955)

Appointment with Dr. Brothers Psychiatrists (,)

Aqua Varieties Mermaids (1965)

Aquaman Super Heroes (1967), Super Heroes (1968)

The Aquanauts Adventurers (1961), Beaches (1960)

Archer Men — Law Enforcers (1975)

Archie Bunker's Place Bars (1971), Puerto Rican (1979), Teenagers (1979), Visually Impaired (1979)

The Archie Comedy Hour Cartoons (1969), Witches (1969), Witches (1971)

Are You Afraid of the Dark? Drama (1992), Drama (1999)

Are You Now or Have You Ever Been Broadway (1980)

Arena District Attorneys (1964)

Arlene Dahl's Playhouse Drama (1953)

Arliss Asian American (1995)

Arly Hanks Mysteries Women — Law Enforcers (1994)

Arms and the Man Opera (1955)

The Army Show Con Artists (1998)

Arnie Los Angeles (1970), Teenagers (1970)

Around the World in 80 Days Series Based on Films (1972), Women — Extraordinary (2001)

Around the World in 30 Minutes News Broadcasts (1943)

Arrest and Trial Lawyers (1963), Los Angeles (1963), Men — Law Enforcers (1963)

Arrested Development California (2003), Magicians (2003), Senior Citizens (2003), Twins (2003)

Arresting Behavior Men — Law Enforcers (1992)

Arroyo Judges (1955), Westerns (1955)

Arsenic and Old Lace Broadway (1949), Broadway (1952), Broadway (1955), Broadway (1962), Broadway (1969)

The Arsenio Hall Show Presidential Appearances (1992)

Art and Mrs. Bottle Broadway (1939)

Art Carney Meets Peter and the Wolf Puppets (1959)

Art Carney Meets the Sorcerer's Apprentice Puppets (1959)

The Art Ford Show Game Shows (1951)

The Art of Crime Men — Law Enforcers (1975)

The Arthur Godfrey Thanksgiving Special Holiday Specials (1963)

Arthur Godfrey Time Series Based on Radio Programs (1952)

Arthur Godfrey's Talent Scouts Reality Programs (1948), Series Based on Radio Programs (1948)

As Is Broadway (1986)

As the World Turns Soap Operas (1956), Soap Operas (1965), Soap Operas (Note)

As You Like It Shakespeare (1978)

Ask Me Another Game Shows (1952)

Ask This Old House Lesbians (2005)

The Asphalt Cowboy Men — Law Enforcers (1980), Teenagers (1980)

The Asphalt Jungle Men — Law Enforcers (1961), New York (1961)

Assassin Espionage (1986)

Assignment: Earth Aliens (1968)

Assignment: Foreign Legion War — World War II (1957)

Assignment: Munich Espionage (1972)

Assignment: Underwater Adolescence (1960), Adventurers (1960), Beaches (1960)

Assignment: Vienna Espionage (1972)

The Associates Lawyers (1979), New York (1979)

Astro Boy Cartoons (1963), Robots (1963)

At Ease Camps (1983), Con Artists (1983)

At Home Variety Programs (1944)

At Your Service Pilot Film Series (1963–1967)

The A-Team Cars (1983), Men — Law Enforcers (1983), Mexican American Performers (1983), Reporters (1983)

The Atom Ant/Secret Squirrel Show Cartoons (1965)

Attack of the Killer Tomatoes Series Based on Films (1990)

Audubon Wild Life Theater Animals (1971)

Aunt Jenny's Real Life Stories Drama (1945)

Automan Los Angeles (1983), Men — Law Enforcers (1983), Women — Law Enforcers (1983)

The Avenger Westerns (1960)

The Avengers Cars (1966), Espionage (1966), Films Based on Television Series (1998), Nudity (1968), Physically Disabled (1968), Women — Extraordinary (1966)

The Awakening Land Lesbians (1978)

Award Theater Drama — Repeat Series (1958)

B.A.D. Cats Los Angeles (1980), Men — Law Enforcers (1980), Restaurants (1980), Women — Law Enforcers (1980)

The B.B. Beagle Show Puppets (1980)

B.J. and the Bear Animals (1979),

Restaurants (1979), Truckers (1979), Twins (1979), Women — "Dumb Blondes" (1981)

B.L. Stryker Florida (1989), Men — Law Enforcers (1989), Puerto Rican (1989)

Baa Baa Black Sheep Pilots (1978), War — World War II (1976), Women — Nurses (1976)

Babes New York (1990)

Babes in Toyland Fairy Tales (1954), Fairy Tales (1960), Holiday Specials (1954), Holiday Specials (1986), Variety and Drama Spectaculars (1954)

Baby Bob Aviators (2003), California (2002)

Baby Boom Aviators (1988), New York (1988), Series Based on Films (1988)

Baby Crazy Aviators (1966), Pilot Film Series (1966)

The Baby Game Aviators (1967)

Baby, I'm Back Adolescence (1978), Washington, D.C. (1978)

Baby Makes Five Adolescence (1983)

Baby on Board Aviators (1988)

Baby Talk Aviators (1991), New York (1991), Series Based on Films (1991)

Babylon 5 Latino American (1994), Mediums (1993), Space (1993)

The Bachelor Variety and Drama Spectaculars (1956)

Bachelor at Law Lawyers (1973)

Bachelor Father Asian American (1957), California (1957), Cars (1957), Housekeepers (1957), Lawyers (1957), Sitcoms (1957), Teen After-School Hangouts (1957), Teenagers (1957)

Back the Fact Game Shows (1953)

Back to the Future Series Based on Films (1991), Time Travel (1991)

Back Together Ghosts (1984)

Backstairs at the White House Politics (1979)

Backwards: The Riddle of Dyslexia Visually Impaired (1984)

The Bad Girl's Guide Chicago (2005)

The Bad News Bears Adolescence (1979), Series Based on Films (1979)

Baffled Mediums (1973), Men — Extraordinary (1973)

Bagdad Café Hotels (1990), Restaurants (1990), Series Based on Films (1990)

The Baileys of Balboa Beaches (1964), California (1964)

The Bait Women — Law Enforcers (1973)

Baker's Dozen New York (1982), Women — Law Enforcers (1974), Women — Law Enforcers (1982)

Bakersfield California (1993)

Bakersfield, P.D. Latino American (1993), Men — Law Enforcers (1993), Mexican American (1993)

Balance Your Budget Game Shows (1952)

Ball Four Mexican American (1976), Washington, D.C. (1976)

Ballad for a Bad Man Westerns (1959)

Baltimore Baltimore (1975)

Banacek Boston (1972), Men — Law Enforcers (1974)

The Banana Company War — World War II (1977)

The Banana Splits Adventure Hour Cartoons (1968), Puppets (1968)

Band of Brothers War — World War II (2001)

Band of Gold Love (1961)

Banjo Hackett: Roamin' Free Westerns (1976)

Banyon Historical Settings (1977), Los Angeles (1972), Men — Law Enforcers (1972)

Bar Girls Lawyers (1990)

The Barbara Eden Show Shows within Shows (1973)

Barbara Mandrell's Christmas ... A Family Reunion Holiday Specials (1986)

The Barbara Rush Show Pilot Film Series (1963–1967)

Barbara Stanwyck Presents Drama (1956)

The Barbara Stanwyck Theater Drama (1960)

The Barbary Coast Government Agents (1976), San Francisco (1976)

The Barber of Seville Opera (1944)

The Barber of Seville, Carmen, Rigoletto Opera (1940)

Barber Shop Series Based on Films (2005)

A Barbi Doll for Christmas Holiday Specials (1978)

Bare Essence New York (1983)

Barefoot in the Park African American (1970), Broadway (1982), Latino American (1970), New York (1970), Series Based on Films (1970)

Baretta African American (1975), Cars (1975), Little People (1976), Men — Law Enforcers (1975), Senior Citizens (1975)

The Barker Broadway (1952)

Barnaby Jones Los Angeles (1973), Men — Law Enforcers (1973), Senior Citizens (1973)

Barney and Friends Puppets (1992)

Barney and Me Animals (1973), Talking Animals and Machines (1973)

Barney Blake, Police Reporter New York (1948), Reporters (1948)

Barney Google, Beetle Bailey Cartoons (1963)

Barney Miller African American (1975), Men — Law Enforcers (1975), New York (1975), Pilot Film Series (1974), Puerto Rican (1975), Senior Citizens (1975), Senior Citizens (1977)

The Barretts of Wimpole Street Broadway (1955)

Barrier Reef Australia (1971)

Barrington Men — Law Enforcers (1987), Pilot Film Series (1987)

Baryshnikov in Hollywood Ballet (1982)

Baryshnikov on Broadway Ballet (1980)

The Bat Broadway (1952)

Bat Masterson Westerns (1957)

Bates Motel Hotels (1987), The Supernatural (1987)

Batfink Cartoons (1966)

Batgirl Super Heroes (1968)

Batman Cars (1966), Children — Extraordinary (1966), Films Based on Television Series (1966), Films Based on Television Series (2006), Gadgets(1966), Housekeepers (1966), Men — Extraordinary (1966), Morphing (1966: Batman), Senior Citizens (1966), Super Heroes (1966), Super Heroes (1968), Women — Extraordinary (1968)

The Batman Super Heroes (2004)

Batman and the Super Seven Super Heroes (1980)

Batman Beyond Super Heroes (1999)

Batman Gotham Knights Super Heroes (1997)

Batman: The Animated Series Super Heroes (1992)

The Batman-Superman Hour Super Heroes (1968)

Battery Park Latino American (2001)

Battle of the Ages Game Shows (1952)

Battleline War — World War II (1963)

Battlestar Galactica Aliens (1978), Aliens (2005), Robots (1978), Space (1978), Space (2003)

Battlestar 100 Space (1950)

Bay City Blues California (1983), Mexican American (1983)

The Bay City Rollers Show Little People (1978)

Bay City Story Reporters (1991)

Bay Mirror Newspapers (1998)

Baywatch Beaches (1989), Beaches (1999), Beaches (2000), Los Angeles (1989), Los Angeles (1991), Nudity (1989), Physically Disabled (2000), Teenagers (1991), The Supernatural (1995)

Baywatch Hawaii Beaches (1999), Hawaii (1999)

Baywatch Nights California (1995), Nightclubs (1995), The Supernatural (1995), Women — Law Enforcers (1995)

BBC Television Shakespeare Shakespeare (1978)

The Beach Girls Beaches (2005)

The Beach Patrol Beaches (1979)

The Beachcomber Beaches (1961)

Beachhead at Louie's War — World War II (1945)

Beacon Hill Boston (1975), Historical Settings (1975), Soap Operas (Note)

The Beagles Cartoons (1966)

The Bean Show Pilot Film Series (1963–1967)

Beanpole Teenagers (1990)

Beantown Boston (1983)

Beany and Cecil Show Cartoons (1961), Puppets (1950)

Bear in the Big House Puppets (1998), Puppets (2005)

Bearcats! Adventurers (1971), Cars (1971), Historical Settings (1971)

BeastMaster Animals (1999), Men — Extraordinary (1999), Series Based on Films (1998), The Supernatural (1999), Witches (1998)

The Beat Men — Law Enforcers (2000), New York (2000)

Beat the Clock Game Shows (1950), Series Based on Radio Programs (1950)

The Beatles Cartoons (1965)

Beautiful People New York (2005)

Beauty and the Beast Fairy Tales (1958), Fairy Tales (1982), New York (1987), Women — Law Enforcers (1987)

Becker Doctors (1998), New York (1998), Restaurants (1998), Transsexuals (1999), Visually Impaired (1998)

Becky Sharpe Broadway (1949)

Bedelia Puppets (1945)

The Bedford Diaries New York (2006)

Bedtime Lesbians (1996), Nudity (1984)

Behind Closed Doors Drama (1959), Espionage (1958)

Belafonte, New York African American (1960)

Believe It or Not Drama (1949), Drama (1950), Reality Programs (1949), Series Based on Radio Programs (1949)

Bell, Book and Candle Witches (1976)

The Bell Telephone Hour Series Based on Radio Programs (1959)

Belle Starr Westerns (1958), Women — Extraordinary (1958)

The Belles of Bleecker Street Teenagers (1991)

The Bells of St. Mary's Variety and Drama Spectaculars (1959)

Ben Casey Doctors (1961), Senior Citizens (1961), Women — Nurses (1961)

Ben Jerrod Soap Operas (1963), Soap Operas (Note)

Bender Men — Law Enforcers (1979)

The Benjamin David Revue Variety Programs (1940)

Benji, Zax and the Alien Prince Aliens (1983)

The Bennets Soap Operas (1953)

Benny and Barney: Las Vegas Undercover Men — Law Enforcers (1977)

The Benny Hill Show Nudity (1979)

Benson Adolescence (1979), African American (1977), Politics (1979)

The Bernie Mac Show Adolescence (2003), California (2001)

Berringer's Latino American (1984), New York (1985)

Bert D'Angelo, Superstar Men — Law Enforcers (1976)

The Best Christmas Pageant Ever Holiday Specials (1983)

The Best Defense Lawyers (1995)

Best Foot Forward Broadway (1952), Variety and Drama Spectaculars (1954)

Best Friends Teenagers (1977)

The Best in Mystery Drama — Repeat Series (1954), Nightclubs (1956)

The Best of Broadway Broadway (1954)

The Best of Everything New York (1970), Series Based on Films (1970), Soap Operas (1970), Soap Operas (Note)

Best of the West Adolescence (1987), Senior Citizens (1981), Westerns (1981)

The Best of Times Teachers (1983), Teachers (1985), Teenagers (1981), Teenagers (1983)

Best Seller Drama (1976)

The Best Times Teenagers (1985)

The Best Years Pilot Film Series (1969), Teenagers (1969)

Bette Gays (2000), Lesbians (2000), Los Angeles (2000)

Better Days New York (1986), Teenagers (1986)

A Better Life Newspapers (1991)

The Betty Crocker Show Cooking (1950)

The Betty Hutton Show Adolescence (1959), New York (1959), Sitcoms (1959), Women — "Dumb Blondes" (1959)

The Betty White Show Los Angeles (1977), Shows within Shows (1977)

Between Brothers Chicago (1997)

Between the Lions Puppets (2000)

Beulah Adolescence (1950), African American (1950), Housekeepers (1950), Series Based on Radio Programs (1950), Sitcoms (1950), Women — Scatterbrained (1950)

The Beverly Hillbillies California (1962), Cars (1962), Country Folk (1962), Films Based on Television Series (1993), Look-alikes (1962), Senior Citizens (1962)

Beverly Hills Buntz California (1987), Men — Law Enforcers (1987)

A Beverly Hills Christmas Holiday Specials (1987)

Beverly Hills, 90210 Lesbians (1990), California (1990), Mexican American (1990), Newspapers (1990), Nightclubs (1990), Teen After-School Hangouts (1990), Teenagers (1990), Twins (1990)

Bewitched Adolescence (1964), Cars (1964), Connecticut (1964), Films Based on Television Series (2005), Look-alikes (1964), Physically Disabled (1964), Senior Citizens (1964), Shows within Shows (1977), Witches (1964), Witches (1976), Witches (1977)

Beyond Westworld Robots (1980), Series Based on Films (1980)

Beyond Witch Mountain Adolescence (1982), Aliens (1982)

Biblical Angels Religious Programs (2001)

The Bickersons Bars (1951), Series Based on Radio Programs (1951)

Bid 'n' Buy Game Shows (1958)

Biff Baker, U.S.A. Espionage (1952)

Big Apple Bars (2001), Men — Law Enforcers (2001), New York (2001)

The Big Attack Drama (1957), War — World War II (1957)

The Big Brain Geniuses (1963)

The Big Chill Series Based on Films (1985)

The Big Comfy Couch Clowns (1992)

Big Daddy African American (1973)

Big Deals Con Artists (1991)

The Big Easy Men — Law Enforcers (1982), Nightclubs (1982)

Big Eddie Adolescence (1975), New York (1975)

The Big Five Adolescence (1983)

Big Foot and Wild Boy Children — Extraordinary (1977)

Big Game Game Shows (1958)

Big Girls Don't Cry Teenagers (1991)

Big Guy and Rusty the Robot Boy Robots (1999)

Big Hawaii Beaches (1977), Hawaii (1977)

The Big House Philadelphia (2004)

Big Jake Men — Law Enforcers (1961)

Big John Men — Law Enforcers (1983)

Big John, Little John Adolescence (1976)

The Big Party for Revlon Variety Programs (1959)

The Big Payoff Game Shows (1951)

The Big Ripoff Reporters (1980), Shows within Shows (1980)

Big Rose Women — Law Enforcers (1974)

Big Shamus, Little Shamus Hotels (1979)

Big Shots in America Immigrants (1985)

Big Sister Soap Operas (1945), Soap Operas (Note)

Big Story Drama (1949)

The Big Time Variety and Drama Spectaculars (1955)

The Big Top Clowns (1950)

Big Town Reporters (1950), Series Based on Radio Programs (1950)

The Big Valley California (1965), Housekeepers (1965), Lawyers (1965), Westerns (1965)

Big Wave Dave's Beaches (1993), Hawaii (1993)

Big Wolf on Campus Werewolves (1999)

The Big World of Little Adam Cartoons (1964)

The Bil Baird Show Puppets (1953)

Bill and Ted's Excellent Adventures California (1992), Series Based on Films (1992), Teenagers (1992), Time Travel (1992)

Bill Cosby Does His Own Thing African American (1968)

The Bill Cosby Show Los Angeles (1969)

The Bill Cosby Special African American (1968)

The Bill Cosby Special Or? African American (1968)

The Bill Dana Show Hotels (1963), Latino American (1963), New York (1963)

Billy Los Angeles (1992), Teachers (1992), Teenagers (1979)

The Billy Bean Show Sitcoms (1951)

The Billy Daniels Show Variety Programs (1956)

Billy Rose's Playbill Drama (1951)

Bing Crosby and the Sounds of Christmas Holiday Specials (1971)

The Bing Crosby Christmas Show Holiday Specials (1962), Holiday Specials (1970)

The Bing Crosby Show Los Angeles (1964), Teenagers (1964)

Bing Crosby's Merrie Olde Christmas Holiday Specials (1977)

Bing Crosby's Sun Valley Christmas Holiday Specials (1973)

Bing Crosby's White Christmas Holiday Specials (1976)

The Bionic Woman Animals (1977), California (1976), Cars (1976), Government Agents (1976), Look-alikes (1976), Physically Disabled (1976), Robots (1976), Super Heroes (1976), Women — Extraordinary (1976)

Birdland Mexican American (1994), Psychiatrists (1994)

Birdman and the Galaxy Trio Cartoons (1967)

Birds of Prey Bars (2001), Children — Extraordinary (2002), Physically Disabled (2002),Super Heroes (2002), Women — Extraordinary (2002)

The Bishop and the Gargoyle Men — Law Enforcers (1941)

The Bishop Misbehaves Broadway (1952)

The Black Angel Television Firsts (1945)

The Black Arrow Fairy Tales (1960)

Black Bart African American (1975), Westerns (1975)

The Black Robe Judges (1949)

Black Saddle Hotels (1959), Lawyers (1959), Westerns (1959)

Black Sash Martial Arts (2003), San Francisco (2003)

Black Scorpion Prostitutes (2001), Super Heroes (2001), Women — Extraordinary (2001), Women — Law Enforcers (2001)

The Black Sheep Fairy Tales (1960)

The Black Sheep Squadron War — World War II (1976), Women — Nurses (1976)

Black Tie Affair Asian American (1993), Men — Law Enforcers (1993), San Francisco (1993)

Blacke's Magic Magicians (1986), Senior Citizens (1986)

Blackstone Magic Spots Magicians (1952)

Blade: The Series Vampires (2006)

Blansky's Beauties Adolescence (1977), American Indian (1977), American Indian (1978), Asian American (1977), Hotels (1977), Las Vegas Settings (1977)

Bless This House Adolescence (1995), New Jersey (1995)

Blind Alley Broadway (1952)

Blind Alleys Asian American (1985)

Blind Date Love (1949), Series Based on Radio Programs (1949)

Blind Justice Animals (2005), Men — Law Enforcers (2005), New York (2005), Nudity (2005), Visually Impaired (2005), Women — Law Enforcers (2005)

Blind Sunday Visually Impaired (1976)

Blithe Spirit Broadway (1946), Broadway (1956), Broadway (1966), Ghosts (1946), Ghosts (1956), Ghosts (1966)

Blockheads Puppets (1982)

Blondie Adolescence (1968), Series Based on Films (1968), Series Based on Radio Programs (1957), Sitcoms (1954), Sitcoms (1957), Women — Scatterbrained (Note)

Bloomer Girl Broadway (1956)

Blossom California (1991), Los Angeles (1991), Teenagers (1991), Women — Scatterbrained (Note)

The Blue and the Gray Civil War (1982)

The Blue Angel Variety Programs (1954)

The Blue Angels Pilots (1960)

Blue Jeans Teenagers (1980)

The Blue Knight Los Angeles (1975), Men — Law Enforcers (1975)

Blue Light War — World War II (1966)

The Blue Ribbon Christmas Eve Musical Holiday Specials (1952)

The Blue Ridge Chronicle Newspapers (1972)

Blue Skies Adolescence (1988)

Blue Thunder Pilots (1984)

Blush Mentally Disabled (1997), Newspapers (1997), Senior Citizens (1997)

B-Men Teenagers (1989)

Bob Chicago (1992), Robots (2004)

Bob & Carol & Ted & Alice Adolescence (1973), Los Angeles (1973), Series Based on Films (1973)

The Bob and Ray Show Series Based on Radio Programs (1951)

The Bob Crane Show Doctors (1975), Los Angeles (1975)

The Bob Hope Christmas Show Holiday Specials (1952, 1953, 1954, 1955, 1956, 1957, 1958, 1959, 1960, 1961, 1962, 1963, 1964, 1965, 1966, 1967, 1968, 1969, 1970, 1971, 1972, 1973, 1974, 1975, 1976, 1977, 1980, 1981, 1982, 1985).

The Bob Hope Christmas Show — A Snow Job in Florida Holiday Specials (1987)

The Bob Hope Chrysler Theater Drama (1963)

Bob Hope for President Politics (1980)

Bob Hope: The First 90 Years Presidential Appearances (1993)

Bob Hope's All Star Celebration: The Opening of the Gerald R. Ford Presidential Museum Presidential Appearances (1981)

Bob Hope's All-Star Christmas Holiday Specials (1978)

Bob Hope's Bagful of Christmas Cheer Holiday Specials (1986)

Bob Hope's Christmas Cheer from Saudi Arabia Holiday Specials (1990)

Bob Hope's Christmas in Hawaii Holiday Specials (1989)

Bob Hope's Christmas Party Holiday Specials (1975)

Bob Hope's Cross Country Christmas Show Holiday Specials (1990)

Bob Hope's Four Star Christmas Fiesta Holiday Specials (1990)

Bob Hope's Merry Christmas Show Holiday Specials (1983)

Bob Hope's 1990 Christmas Show Holiday Specials (1990)

Bob Hope's USO Christmas from the Persian Gulf: Around the World in Eight Days Holiday Specials (1988)

The Bob New Cummings Show California (1961)

The Bob Newhart Show Chicago (1972), Psychiatrists (1972), Teachers (1972)

Bob Patterson Bars (2001), Los Angeles (2001), Physically Disabled (2001)

Bob Villa's Home Again Cuban American (1978)

Bobo Hobo and His Traveling Troupe Puppets (1953)

Bodies of Evidence Los Angeles (1992), Men — Law Enforcers (1992), Women — Law Enforcers (1992)

Body and Soul Doctors (2002)

The Bold and the Beautiful Soap Operas (Note)

The Bold Ones Doctors (1969)

The Bold Ones: The Lawyers Lawyers (1969)

The Bold Ones: The Senator Politics (1970)

Bold Venture Hotels (1959), Series Based on Radio Programs (1959)

Bonanza Adolescence (1972), Asian American (1959), Color Broadcasting (1957-1965), Housekeepers (1959), Westerns (1959), Westerns (2001)

Bones F.B.I. Agents (2005), Forensics(2005), Nudity (2005), Washington, D.C. (2005)

Bonino Housekeepers (1953), New York (1953), Sitcoms (1953), Teenagers (1954)

The Bonnie Hunt Show Chicago (1995), Shows within Shows (1995)

The Bontempis Cooking (1952)

Boogie's Diner Restaurants (1994)

The Book of Daniel Asian American (2006), Gays (2006), Religious Characters (2006), Religious Programs (2006)

Book of Magic Adolescence (1979)

Booker Los Angeles (1989)

Boomtown Lesbians (2003), Los Angeles (2002), Men — Law Enforcers (2002)

The Boondocks Adolescence (2005)

Boone Historical Settings (1983), Teenagers (1984)

Boots and Saddles Westerns (1957)

The Borden Television Theater Drama (1947)

Border Town Westerns (1960)

Bordertown Westerns (1989)

Boris and Natasha Films Based on Television Series (1992)

The Boris Karloff Mystery Playhouse Drama (1949)

Born Free Africa (1974), Animals (1974), Series Based on Films (1974)

Born to the Wind American Indian (1982)

Born Yesterday Broadway (1956)

Bosom Buddies Cross Dressers (1980), Hotels (1980), New York (1980)

Boss Lady California (1952), Los Angeles (1952), Sitcoms (1952)

Boston Blackie Los Angeles (1951), Men — Law Enforcers (1951), Series Based on Radio Programs (1951)

Boston Common Boston (1996)

Boston Legal Boston (2004), Lawyers (2004), Senior Citizens (2004)

Boston Public Bars (2000), Boston (2000), Physically Disabled (2000), Teachers (2000)

The Boston Terrier Men — Law Enforcers (1962), Men — Law Enforcers (1963)

Bottlenecks Television Firsts (1941)

Bottlenecks of 1941 Television Firsts (1941)

The Bounder Con Artists (1984)

The Bounty Man Westerns (1972)

Bourbon Street Beat Men — Law Enforcers (1959), Nightclubs (1959), Women — Law Enforcers (1959)

The Bourgeois Gentleman Broadway (1945)

Bowzer Nightclubs (1981)

Boy Meets World Philadelphia (1993), Teachers (1993)

The Boy Who Left Home Fairy Tales (1982)

The Boys Pilot Film Series (1970)

The Boys in Blue Men — Law Enforcers (1984)

The Boys of Twilight Senior Citizens (1992)

Boys Will Be Boys Teenagers (1988)

Bozo the Clown Children's Program (1959), Clowns (1959)

Bozo's Big Top Circus Children's Program (1959)

Bozo's Big Top Circus Show Clowns (1959)

Bozo's Circus Children's Program (1959)

Bozo's Place Clowns (1959)

Bracken's World California (1969)

Braddock Men — Law Enforcers (1968)

The Brady Bunch Adolescence (1969), Films Based on Television Series (1995), Housekeepers (1969), Physically Disabled (1990)

The Bradys Physically Disabled (1990)

Brains and Brawn Game Shows (1958)

Braker Men — Law Enforcers (1985)

Bram and Alice New York (2002)

Brand New Life California (1989), Teenagers (1990)

Branded Westerns (1965)

Brannigan and Mapes Adolescence (1983), Teenagers (1983)

Brat Camp Camps (2005)

Brave Eagle: Chief of the Cheyenne Adolescence (1955), American Indian (1955), Westerns (1955)

Bravo Duke Pilot Film Series (1963–1967)

Bravo Two Rescue (1977)

Break the Bank Game Shows (1948), Game Shows (1956), Series Based on Radio Programs (1948)

Break the $250,000 Bank Game Shows (1956)

Breaker High Teenagers (1997)

The Breakfast Club Series Based on Radio Programs (1950), Variety Programs (1945)

Breakfast in Hollywood Series Based on Radio Programs (1954)

Breakfast Time Cooking (1953)

Breakfast with Bear Puppets (2005)

Breakfast with Charlie Senior Citizens (1997), Shows within Shows (1997)

Breaking Away Teenagers (1980)

Breaking Point Psychiatrists (1963)

Breaking the Code: Magic's Biggest Secrets Finally Revealed Magicians (1997)

Breezly and Sneezly Cartoons (1964)

The Bremen Town Musicians Fairy Tales (1977)

Brenda Starr Reporters (1976)

Brenda Starr, Reporter Reporters (1979)

Brenner Men — Law Enforcers (1959), New York (1959)

Bret Maverick Arizona (1981), Bars (1981), Westerns (1981)

The Brian Benben Show Gays (1998), Latino American (1998), Puerto Rican (1998)

The Brian Keith Show Beaches

(1972), Doctors (1973), Hawaii (1972)

Bride and Groom Reality Programs (1951), Series Based on Radio Programs (1951)

Bridges to Cross Newspapers (1986)

Bridget Loves Bernie New York (1971), Religious Characters (1971), Restaurants (1972), Series Based on Radio Programs (1972), Taxi Cabs (1972), Teachers (1972)

Brief Encounter Broadway (1961), Broadway (1974)

Brigadoon Broadway (1966)

Bright Promise Soap Operas (1969)

A Brighter Day Soap Operas (1954)

Brilliant Benjamin Boggs Geniuses (1966)

Brimstone Devil (1998)

Bring 'Em Back Alive Historical Settings (1982)

Bringing Up Buddy California (1960), Senior Citizens (1960), Sitcoms (1960)

Broadside Beaches (1964), War—World War II (1964), Women—Scatterbrained (1964)

Broadway Broadway (1952), Broadway (1955)

The Broadway of Lerner and Loewe Broadway (1962)

Broadway Open House Variety Programs (1950), Variety Programs (1951)

Broadway Sings the Music of Jule Styne Broadway (1989)

Broadway: The American Musical Broadway (2004)

Broadway TV Theater Broadway (1952)

Broadway's Lost Treasures Broadway (2003)

Brock Callahan Men—Law Enforcers (1959)

Broken Arrow American Indian (1956), Arizona (1956), Series Based on Films (1956), Westerns (1956)

Broken Badges American Indian (1990), California (1990), Los Angeles (1990), Men—Law Enforcers (1990), Puppets (1990), Women—Law Enforcers (1990)

Bronco Westerns (1959)

Bronk California (1975), Men—Law Enforcers (1975), Physically Disabled (1975), Teenagers (1975)

The Bronx Zoo New York (1987), Teachers (1987)

Brooklyn Bridge Historical Settings (1992), New York (1991), Senior Citizens (1991), Teenagers (1991)

Brooklyn South Latino American (1997), Men—Law Enforcers (1998), New York (1998), Women—Law Enforcers (1998)

Brother Rat Broadway (1939)

Brotherly Love Philadelphia (1996)

Brothers Gays (1984)

The Brothers San Francisco (1956), Sitcoms (1956)

Brothers and Sisters Teenagers (1979)

The Brothers Brannigan Arizona (1960), Men—Law Enforcers (1960)

The Brothers Garcia Mexican American (2000), Puerto Rican (2000), Twins (2000)

Brother's Keeper San Francisco (1988)

The Buccaneers Adventurers (1956)

Buck James American Indian (1987), Doctors (1987)

Buck Rogers in the 25th Century Aliens (1979), Little People (1979), Robots (1979), Senior Citizens (1981), Series Based on Radio Programs (1950), Space (1950), Space (1979)

Buckaroo 500 Children's Program (1963)

Buckskin Hotels (1958), Westerns (1958)

Buddy Faro Los Angeles (1998), Men—Law Enforcers (1998)

Buffalo Bill Shows within Shows (1983)

Buffalo Bill, Jr. Adolescence (1955), Westerns (1955)

The Buffalo Bill Show Shows within Shows (1983)

The Buffalo Billy Show Puppets (1950)

Buffalo Dreams American Indian (2005)

The Buffalo Soldiers Westerns (1979)

Buffy the Vampire Slayer California (1997), Children—Extraordinary (2000), Lesbians (1997), Robots (1997), Series Based on Films (1997), Teen After-School Hangouts (1997), Teenagers (1997), Vampires (1997), Witches (1997), Women—Extraordinary (1997)

The Bugaloos Puppets (1970), Teenagers (1970), Witches (1970)

The Bugs Bunny Easter Special Holiday Specials (1977)

The Bugs Bunny Show Cartoons (1960)

Bugs Bunny Thanksgiving Diet Holiday Specials (1979)

Bugs Bunny's Looney Christmas Tales Holiday Specials (1979)

The Buick Circus Hour Clowns (1951)

The Building Bars (1992), Chicago (1993), Hotels (1993)

Bulba Politics (1981)

The Bulldog Newspapers (1989)

Bulldog Drummond Men—Law Enforcers (1957)

The Bullwinkle Show Cartoons (1964)

Bunco Con Artists (1977)

Bungle Abbey Religious Characters (1981)

The Bureau Espionage (1976), F.B.I. Agents (1996)

The Bureau of Missing Persons Reality Programs (1943)

Burke's Law Cars (1963), Espionage (1965), Housekeepers (1963), Los Angeles (1963), Los Angeles (1994), Men—Law Enforcers (1963), Men—Law Enforcers (1994)

The Burl Ives Thanksgiving Special Holiday Specials (1968)

Burlesque Broadway (1949), Broadway (1952), Broadway (1955)

Bus Stop Broadway (1982), District Attorneys (1961)

The Buster Brown TV Show with Smilin' Ed McConnell and His Buster Brown Gang Children's Program (1950)

Bustin' Loose Housekeepers (1987)

Busting Loose New York (1977), Taxi Cabs (1977)

But Mother! Prostitutes (1979)

Butch and Billy and Their Bang Bang Western Movies Cartoons (1961)

The Butter and Egg Man Broadway (1939)

By Popular Demand Reality Programs (1950), Series Based on Radio Programs (1950)

Bye Bye Birdie Broadway (1995)

The Byrds of Paradise Beaches (1989), Hawaii (1994), Teenagers (1994)

C.A.T. Squad Women—Extraordinary (1986)

C.P.O. Sharkey California (1976), Latino American (1975)

C.S.I.: Crime Scene Investigation Forensics (2000), Hearing Impaired Characters (2000), Las Vegas Settings (2000), Nudity (2002), Physically Disabled (2000)

C.S.I.: Miami Florida (2002), Forensics (2002)

C.S.I.: New York Forensics (2004), New York (2004), Physically Disabled (2004)

The Caballero Mexican American (1959), Westerns (1959)

The Cabot Connection Espionage (1981)

Cade's County American Indian (1971), Men—Law Enforcers (1971), Mexican American (1971), Senior Citizens (1971)

Cadets Teenagers (1988)

Caesar and Cleopatra Broadway (1956), Broadway (1976)

Cafe Americain Restaurants (1994)

Café De Paris Variety Programs (1949)

Café Television Variety Programs (1943)

Cagney and Lacey Latino American (1986), Men — Law Enforcers (1982), New York (1982), Senior Citizens (1982), Women — Law Enforcers (1981)

Cain and Able Religious Programs (2001)

Cain's Hundred F.B.I. Agents (1961)

Caliente Beaches (1995), Nudity (1995)

California Dreams Asian American (1994), Beaches (1992), California (1992), Cuban American (1992), Teen After-School Hangouts (1992), Teenagers (1992)

California Fever Beaches (1979), Teen After-School Hangouts (1979), Teenagers (1979)

The Californians San Francisco (1957), Westerns (1957)

Call Her Mom Housekeepers (1972)

Call Holme Men — Law Enforcers (1972)

Call Me Annie Women — Nurses (1961)

Call Mr. D. Men — Law Enforcers (1957)

Call to Danger Government Agents (1961, 1968, 1973, 1988)

Call to Glory Historical Settings (1984)

Calling Dr. Storm, M.D Doctors (1977)

Calling Terry Conway Hotels (1956)

Calucci's Department Latino American (1973), New York (1973), Women — "Dumb Blondes" (1973)

Calvin and the Colonel Cartoons (1961)

The Camel News Caravan News Broadcasts (1948)

Camel News Caravan News Broadcasts (1951)

Camelot Broadway (1982)

Cameo by Night Women — Extraordinary (1987)

Cameo Theater Drama — Repeat Series (1959)

Camp California Camps (1989), Prison (1989)

Camp Grizzly Camps (1980)

Camp Runamuck Camps (1965)

Camp Wilder Adolescence (1992), California (1992), Camps (1993), Los Angeles (1992), Teenagers (1992), Women — Nurses (1992)

Camp Wilderness Camps (1980)

Campo 44 Camps (1967), Prison (1967)

Campus Corner Variety Programs (1949)

Can You Top This? Game Shows

(1950), Series Based on Radio Programs (1950)

Candid Camera Films Based on Television Series (1970), Reality Programs (1948), Series Based on Radio Programs (1948)

Candid Kids Reality Programs (1985)

Candid Microphone Series Based on Radio Programs (1948)

Candida Broadway (1983)

Candide Opera (2000)

Candlelight Broadway (1952)

Cannon Los Angeles (1971), Men — Law Enforcers (1971)

Cannonball Truckers (1958)

Can't Hurry Love New York (1995)

Capital News Newspapers (1990)

Captain America Men — Extraordinary (1979), Super Heroes (1965), Super Heroes (1979)

The Captain and Tennille Little People (1976)

Captain Billy's Mississippi Music Hall Variety Programs (1948)

Captain Brassbound's Conversion Broadway (1960)

Captain David Grief Adventurers (1957)

Captain Gallant of the Foreign Legion Adolescence (1955)

Captain Kangaroo Children's Program (1955), Children's Program (1964), Clowns (1955), Puppets (1955)

Captain Midnight Series Based on Radio Programs (1954)

Captain Nice Men — Extraordinary (1967), Super Heroes (1967)

Captain Safari of the Jungle Patrol Adventurers (1955), Children's Program (1955)

Captain Scarlet and the Mysterons Pilots (1967), Puppets (1967), Space (1967)

Captain Video and His Video Rangers Aliens (1949), Films Based on Television Series (1949), Gadgets (1949), Robots (1949), Space (1949)

Captain Z-Ro Space (1955), Time Travel (1952)

Captains and the Kings Nudity (1976)

Capture Animals (1965)

Car 54, Where Are You? Films Based on Television Series (1994), Men — Law Enforcers (1961), New York (1961)

The Cara Williams Show Los Angeles (1964), Senior Citizens (1964), Women — Scatterbrained (1964)

Caribe African American (1975), Florida (1975), Men — Law Enforcers (1975)

Carly's Web Women — Extraordinary (1987)

Carmen Color Broadcasting (1951), Opera (1950), Puerto Rican (1973)

Carnival Drama — Repeat Series (1953)

Carnivale Lesbians (2003), Nudity (1984)

Carol Women — "Dumb Blondes" (1967)

The Carol Burnett Show Cross Dressers (1967), Presidential Appearances (1971)

Carol for Another Christmas Holiday Specials (1964)

Caroline in the City New York (1995), Restaurants (1995)

Carolyn Sitcoms (1956)

Carousel Broadway (1967)

The Carpenter's at Christmas Holiday Specials (1977)

Carrie Williams, Justice of the Peace Judges (1956)

Carter Country African American (1977), Men — Law Enforcers (1977)

Cartoon-O Game Shows (1950)

Cartoon Theater Cartoons (1948)

Cartoonsville Cartoons (1963), Puppets (1963)

Casablanca Bars (1955), Series Based on Films (1955), Series Based on Films (1983)

Casanova Nudity (1981)

The Case Against Milligan Politics (1975)

The Case Busters Teenagers (1986)

The Cases of Eddie Drake Men — Law Enforcers (1952), New York (1952), Psychiatrists (1952)

Casey at the Bat Fairy Tales (1985)

Casey Jones Adolescence (1957)

Cash and Carry Game Shows (1946)

Casper and the Angels Space (1979)

Casper the Friendly Ghost Cartoons (1953), Ghosts (1953)

Casper's First Christmas Holiday Specials (1979)

Cass Malloy Adolescence (1982), Women — Law Enforcers (1982)

Cassie and Company Latino American (1982), Women — Law Enforcers (1982)

The Castaways on Gilligan's Island Beaches (1964)

Castle Rock Ghosts (1981), Witches (1981)

The Cat and the Canary Broadway (1960)

Cat Ballou American Indian (1971), Westerns (1971), Women — Extraordinary (1971)

Cat on a Hot Tin Roof Broadway (1976), Broadway (1984)

Catalina Sea Lab Teenagers (1982)

Catch 22 War — World War II (1973)

The Catholic Hour Religious Programs (1951)
Cats Broadway (1998)
The Cattanooga Cats Cartoons (1969)
Cavalcade of America Drama (1952), Series Based on Radio Programs (1952)
Cavalcade of Stars Variety Programs (1949)
The Cavanaughs Boston (1986), Religious Characters (1986), Senior Citizens (1986)
Cavender Is Coming Angels (1962)
The CBS Cartoon Theater Cartoons (1956)
The CBS Evening News News Broadcasts (1951)
The CBS Morning Show News Broadcasts (1954)
The CBS Newcomers Reality Programs (1972)
CBS Reports: The Crisis in Presidential Succession Presidential Appearances (1964)
The CBS Schoolbreak Special. Gays (1987), Lesbians (1993)
The CBS Studio Show News Broadcasts (1944), Variety Programs (1944)
The CBS Summer Playhouse Pilot Film Series (1987)
CBS Tele-Talkie Drama (1932)
Celanese Theater Drama (1951)
Celebrity Playhouse Drama — Repeat Series (1956)
Celebrity Talent Scouts Reality Programs (1960)
The Center Puerto Rican (1985)
Center Stage Drama — Repeat Series (1954)
Central Park West New York (1995)
The Centurions Robots (1986)
Chain Letter Devil (1989)
Chalk One Up for Johnny Beaches (1962)
The Chamber Music Society of Lower Basin Street Variety Programs (1948)
Chameleon Con Artists (1986), Reporters (1986)
Chameleon in Blue Mediums (1990)
Champagne and Orchids Variety Programs (1948)
The Champions Men — Extraordinary (1968), Women — Extraordinary (1968)
Chance for Romance Love (1958)
Chance of a Lifetime Game Shows (1950)
Chan-Ese-Way, The Frugal Gourmet, Daisy Cooks Cooking (1970)
Change at 125th Street African American (1974)
Changing Patterns Pilot Film Series (1987)

Channing Teachers (1963)
Character Slants Television Firsts (1932)
Charade Quiz Game Shows (1947)
Charge Account Game Shows (1960)
The Charles Boyer Theater Drama (1953)
Charles in Charge Adolescence (1984), Housekeepers (1984), New Jersey (1987), New Jersey (1989), Newspapers (1984), Puppets, Reporters (1987), (1987), Restaurants (1987), Senior Citizens (1987), Teen After-School Hangouts (1987), Teenagers (1987)
Charley's Aunt Broadway (1983)
Charlie and Company Chicago (1985), Teenagers (1985)
Charlie Angelo Angels (1962), Pilot Film Series (1963–1967)
A Charlie Brown Christmas Cartoons (1965), Holiday Specials (1965)
A Charlie Brown Thanksgiving Holiday Specials (1973)
The Charlie Farrell Show California (1956), Sitcoms (1956)
Charlie Grace Los Angeles (1995), Men — Law Enforcers (1995)
Charlie Hoover Little People (1991), New York (1991)
Charlie Lawrence Politics (2003), Washington, D.C. (2003)
The Charlie McCarthy Show Puppets (1950)
Charlie Wild, Private Detective Men — Law Enforcers (1950), Series Based on Radio Programs (1950)
Charlie's Angels Cars (1976), Films Based on Television Series (2000), Los Angeles (1976), Nudity (1976), Women — Law Enforcers (1976)
Charlotte Light and Dark Geniuses (2001)
Charmed Angels (1998), Little People (1998), Men — Law Enforcers (1998), Mermaids (2002), Newspapers (1998), Nightclubs (1998), Nudity (2004), San Francisco (1998), Witches (1998)
The Charmings California (1987), Fairy Tales (1987), Little People (1987), Witches (1987)
Charo and the Sergeant Latino American (1976)
Chase Los Angeles (1973), Men — Law Enforcers (1973)
The Chatterbox Asian American (1995)
The Cheap Detective Men — Law Enforcers (1978)
The Cheap Show Women — "Dumb Blondes" (1978)
The Cheaters Broadway (1980), Men — Law Enforcers (1960)

Check It Out Canada (1986)
Checkered Flag Stock Car Racers (1990)
Checking In Hotels (1981), Latino American (1981), New York (1981)
Checkmate Men — Law Enforcers (1960), San Francisco (1960)
The Cheech Show Mexican American (1988)
The Cheerleaders Teenagers (1976)
Cheers Bars (1982), Boston (1982), Psychiatrists (1983), Senior Citizens (1982), Twins (1984)
Cheers for Miss Bishop Teachers (1961)
The Cheese Champ Broadway (1939)
The Cherokee Trail Westerns (1981)
Chester the Pup Children's Program (1950)
The Chesterfield Supper Club Series Based on Radio Programs (1948), Variety Programs (1948)
Chevrolet on Broadway Variety Programs (1956)
The Chevrolet Showroom Mexican American (1953)
Chevrolet Tele-Theater Drama (1948)
Chevy Mystery Show Drama — Repeat Series (1960)
The Chevy Summer Show Variety Programs (1958)
Cheyenne American Indian (1955), Westerns (1956)
Chez Paree Revue Variety Programs (1950)
Chez Rouge Nightclubs (1959)
Chicago Hope Chicago (1994), Doctors (1994), Gays (1994), Latino American (1994)
Chicago Story Chicago (1982), District Attorneys (1981)
The Chicago Teddy Bears Chicago (1971), Historical Settings (1971)
Chicago 212 Rescue (1957)
Chicagoland Mystery Players Chicago (1949), Men — Law Enforcers (1949)
Chicken Soup New York (1989)
Chicken Soup for the Soul Drama (1999)
Chico and the Man African American (1974), Los Angeles (1974), Mexican American (1974), Senior Citizens (1974)
The Children's Corner Children's Program (1955)
The Children's Hour Children's Program (1949), Children's Program (1951), Puppets (1955)
Children's Sketch Book Children's Program (1950)
A Child's Christmas in Wales Holiday Specials (1987)
Chime Time Variety Programs (1946)
China Beach Prostitutes (1988),

War — Korea, Vietnam, Iraq (1988), Women — Nurses (1988)

CHiPs California (1977), Los Angeles (1977), Men — Law Enforcers (1977), Mexican American (1977), Women — Law Enforcers (1977), Women — Law Enforcers (1981)

The Chisholms American Indian (1979)

The Chocolate Soldier Opera (1955)

Choose Up Sides Children's Program (1956)

Chopper One California (1974), Pilots (1974)

Choreotones African American (1946), Ballet (1946)

Chris and the Magical Drip Adolescence (1981)

Christine Cromwell Lawyers (1989), San Francisco (1989)

Christmas Around the World Holiday Specials (1976)

Christmas Calendar Holiday Specials (1988)

A Christmas Carol Holiday Specials (1945, 1947, 1948, 1951, 1954, 1982), Holiday Specials (1947), Variety and Drama Spectaculars (1945)

A Christmas Dream Holiday Specials (1984)

Christmas in Disneyland Holiday Specials (1976)

Christmas in Washington Holiday Specials (1982, 1983, 1984, 1985, 1986, 1987, 1988, 1989, 1990), Presidential Appearances (1982, 1989)

Christmas Legends of Nashville Holiday Specials (1982)

A Christmas Memory Holiday Specials (1966)

A Christmas Present Holiday Specials (1948)

Christmas Snow Holiday Specials (1986)

A Christmas Song Holiday Specials (1950)

Christmas Special ... With Love, Mac Davis Holiday Specials (1979)

Christmas Star Time with Leonard Bernstein Holiday Specials (1959)

Christmas with Lorne Greene Holiday Specials (1966)

Christmas with the Bing Crosbys Holiday Specials (1972), Holiday Specials (1974)

Christmas with the Stars Holiday Specials (1953)

Christy Country Folk (1994), Teachers (1994)

The Chronicle Newspapers (1989), Reporters (2002)

The Chuck Barris Rah-Rah Show Reality Programs (1978)

Chuck Norris Karate Kommanders Martial Arts (1986)

Cimarron City Westerns (1958)

Cimarron Strip Westerns (1967)

Cinderella Ballet (1957), Ballet (1981), Fairy Tales (1957), Fairy Tales (1977), Fairy Tales (1982), Variety and Drama Spectaculars (1957)

Circle African American (1960)

The Circle Family Adolescence (1982), Hotels (1982)

Circle of Fear Drama (1973), The Supernatural (1972)

Circus Boy Clowns (1956), Little People (1956)

Circus Time Puppets (1956)

The Cisco Kid Color Broadcasting (1950), Mexican American (1950), Series Based on Radio Programs (1950), Television Firsts (1951), Westerns (1951)

Cissie Country Folk (1960)

Cities Services Band of America Variety Programs (1949)

Citizen Soldier War — World War II (1957)

City Cuban American (1990), Teenagers (1990)

The City Newspapers (1986), Transsexuals (1995)

City Detective Men — Law Enforcers (1953), New York (1953)

City Guys Latino American (1997), New York (1997), Teachers (1997), Teen After-School Hangouts (1996), Teenagers (1997)

City Hospital Doctors (1951), Series Based on Radio Programs (1951)

City of Angels Historical Settings (1976), Los Angeles (1976), Men — Law Enforcers (1976)

Civil Wars Lawyers (1991), New York (1991), Nudity (1992)

Clarence, the Cross-Eyed Lion Series Based on Films (1966)

Clarissa Explains It All Florida (1991), Newspapers (1991), Teenagers (1991)

Class of '61 Civil War (1992)

Classic Theater Shakespeare (1975)

Classic This Old House Cuban American (1978)

The Claudette Colbert Show Politics (1958)

Claudia: The Story of a Marriage Series Based on Radio Programs (1952), Soap Operas (1952)

Claws Talking Animals and Machines (1991)

Clear Horizon Soap Operas (1960)

Cleghorn New York (1995)

Cleopatra 2525 Robots (2000), Women — Extraordinary (2000)

Click Variety Programs (1944)

The Cliff Dwellers Pilot Film Series (1966)

The Cliff Edwards Show Variety Programs (1949)

Cliffhangers Reporters (1979)

The Cliffwood Avenue Kids Adolescence (1977)

Climax Broadway (1952), Drama (1954)

Cloak of Mystery Drama — Repeat Series (1965)

The Clock Drama (1949), Series Based on Radio Programs (1949)

Close Encounters Love (1990)

Close Ties Broadway (1983)

Close to Home Lawyers (2005)

Close-Up News Reporters (1981), Shows within Shows (1981)

The Closer Los Angeles (2005), Women — Law Enforcers (2005)

Clown Alley Clowns (1966)

Clownaround Clowns (1972)

Club Celebrity Variety Programs (1950)

Club Embassy Variety Programs (1952)

Club Med Beaches (1986), Love (1986)

Club Oasis Little People (1957), Variety Programs (1957)

Club 7 Reality Programs (1948)

Club 60 Color Broadcasting (1957-1965), Variety Programs (1957)

Clue You In Adolescence (1985)

Clueless California (1996), Series Based on Films (1996), Teachers (1996), Teen After-School Hangouts (1996), Teenagers (1996)

Clyde Crashcup Cartoons (1961)

Coach Bars (1989), Florida (1995), Senior Citizens (1989), Shows within Shows (1989)

Coach's Corner Shows within Shows (1989)

The Cobina Wright, Jr. Show Nudity (1939), Variety Programs (1939)

Coconut Downs Hotels (1991)

Code Name: Eternity Aliens (2000)

Code Name: Foxfire Espionage (1985), Government Agents (1985), Housekeepers (1985), New York (1985)

Code Name: Heraclitus Espionage (1967)

The Code of Jonathan West Westerns (1960)

Code R California (1977), Rescue (1977)

Code Red Los Angeles (1981), Rescue (1981)

Code 3 Doctors (1972), Los Angeles (1956), Men — Law Enforcers (1957), Women — Nurses (1972)

Co-Ed Fever Teenagers (1979)

Coke Time with Eddie Fisher Variety Programs (1953)

The Colbys Mexican American (1985), Senior Citizens (1985), Twins (1985)

Cold Case Men — Law Enforcers (2003), Philadelphia (2003), Women — Law Enforcers (2003)

The Colgate Comedy Hour Variety Programs (1950)

Colonel Bleep Cartoons (1957)

Colonel Humphrey Flack Series Based on Radio Programs (1953)

Colonel Humphrey J. Flack Con Artists (1953)

Colonel March of Scotland Yard Men — Law Enforcers (1957), Visually Impaired (1957)

Colonel Stoopnagle's Stoop Country Folk (1948), Sitcoms (1948)

The Colorful World of Music Puppets (1964)

Colossus Immigrants (1963)

Colt .45 Westerns (1957)

The Columbia Television Workshop Variety Programs (1944)

Columbo Cars (1971), Los Angeles (1971), Men — Law Enforcers (1971), Senior Citizens (1997), Visually Impaired (1971)

The Columnist Newspapers (1985)

Combat! War — World War II (1961)

Combat Sergeant War — World War II (1956)

Come a Running Doctors (1963), Pilot Film Series (1963–1967)

Come Back to the Five and Dime, Jimmy Dean, Jimmy Dean Broadway (1983)

Come Blow Your Horn Broadway (1981)

Come Die with Me Men — Law Enforcers (1994)

Come to Papa New Jersey (2004), Newspapers (2004)

Comeback Reality Programs (1979)

Comedians Opera (1945)

Comedy of Horrors Ghosts (1981), Hotels (1981)

The Comedy of Errors Shakespeare (1983)

Comedy Playhouse Drama — Repeat Series (1958), Pilot Film Series (1971)

Comedy Preview Pilot Film Series (1970)

Comedy Spot Pilot Film Series (1960), Pilot Film Series (1962)

Comedy Spotlight Drama — Repeat Series (1961)

Comedy Theater Pilot Film Series (1975)

Comedy Time Pilot Film Series (1976), Pilot Film Series (1977)

Coming of Age Arizona (1988), Senior Citizens (1988)

Commander in Chief Politics (2005), Senior Citizens (2005), Twins

(2005), Washington, D.C. (2005), Women — Extraordinary (2005)

Commando Cody, Sky Marshal of the Universe Aliens (1955), Series Based on Films (1955), Space (1955)

The Commish Men — Law Enforcers (1991), New York (1991)

Committed Clowns (2005), New York (2005), Physically Disabled (2005), Senior Citizens (2005)

Common Law Latino American (1996), New York (1996)

The Compleat Gilbert and Sullivan Opera (1985)

Complete Savages Teenagers (2004)

The Compton Tele Show Variety Programs (1944)

Conan Little People (1997), Series Based on Films (1997), Speech Impaired (1997)

Conan O'Brien Robots (1996)

Concentration Game Shows (1958)

Concerning Miss Marlowe Soap Operas (1954)

Concrete Beat Newspapers (1984)

Concrete Cowboys Adventurers (1981)

Condo Latino American (1983), Puerto Rican (1983)

Condor Robots (1986)

The Coneheads Aliens (1983)

Confidentially Yours Reporters (1960)

Conflict Drama (1956)

A Conflict of Interest Broadway (1980)

A Connecticut Yankee Variety and Drama Spectaculars (1955)

Consult Dr. Brothers Psychiatrists (,)

Consumer Quiz Game Shows (1946)

Continental Cookery Cooking (1966)

Conversations with Herbert Hoover Presidential Appearances (1955)

Conviction District Attorneys (2006)

Convoy War — World War II (1965)

Coogan's Reward War — World War II (1965)

Cooking with Mama Malone Shows within Shows (1984)

Cool and Lam Men — Law Enforcers (1957), Women — Law Enforcers (1957)

Cool McCool Cartoons (1966)

Cool Million Men — Law Enforcers (1974), Washington, D.C. (1972)

The Cop and the Kid Adolescence (1975), African American (1975), Los Angeles (1975), Men — Law Enforcers (1975)

Cop Rock Gays (1990), Men — Law Enforcers (1990)

The Copperhead Broadway (1945)

Cops Men — Law Enforcers (1974), Nudity (1987), Reality Programs (1989)

Corey for the People District Attorneys (1977)

The Corn Is Green Broadway (1956)

The Corner Bar Bars (1972), Bars (1973), Gays (1972), New York (1972), New York (1973)

Coronado 9 Men — Law Enforcers (1960)

Cos African American (1976)

Cos: The Bill Cosby Special African American (1968)

Cosby Bars (1996), New York (1996), Senior Citizens (1996)

The Cosby Mysteries Housekeepers (1994), Men — Law Enforcers (1994), Puerto Rican (1994)

The Cosby Show Adolescence (1984), Doctors (1984), New York (1984), Senior Citizens (1984), Teenagers (1984), Twins (1984), Visually Impaired (1984)

Cosmopolitan Drama (1951)

Cosmopolitan Theater Drama (1951)

Cotton Club '75 African American (1975)

Count De Clues Mystery Castle Little People (1993), Magicians (1993), Vampires (1993)

The Count of Monte Cristo Historical Settings (1956)

Counterattack: Crime in America Reality Programs (1982)

Counterpoint Drama — Repeat Series (1952), Drama — Repeat Series (1954)

Counterspy Espionage (1958), Series Based on Radio Programs (1958)

A Country Christmas Holiday Specials (1980), Holiday Specials (1981)

The Country Girl Broadway (1974)

Country Style Variety Programs (1944)

Country Style, U.S.A. Variety Programs (1959)

County General Doctors (1962)

A Couple of Joes Variety Programs (1949)

Coupling Asian American (2003), Lesbians (2003)

Courageous Cat Cartoons (1961)

The Court Judges (2002)

The Court of Last Resort Lawyers (1957)

Courthouse Lesbians (1995)

Courting Alex New York (2006)

Court-Martial War — World War II (1966)

The Courtship of Eddie's Father Adolescence (1969), Asian American (1969), Housekeepers (1969), Los Angeles (1969), Newspapers (1969), Series Based on Films (1969)

Covenant Devil (1985)

Cover Girls Government Agents (1977)

Cover Up Espionage (1984), Los Angeles (1984)

Covington Cross Historical Settings (1992), Women — Extraordinary (1992)

Cowboy Five-Seven Pilots (1958)

Cowboy G-Men Espionage (1952), Westerns (1952)

Cowboy in Africa Africa (1967), American Indian (1967), Animals (1967), Series Based on Films (1968)

Cowboy Joe Teenagers (1988)

The Cowboys African American (1974), Mexican American (1974), Series Based on Films (1974), Teenagers (1974), Westerns (1974)

Cowboys and Injuns American Indian (1950)

Coyote Waits American Indian (2002)

Cracking Up Los Angeles (2004)

The Cradle Song Religious Programs (1956)

Craig Kennedy, Criminologist Men — Law Enforcers (1952)

Craig's Wife Broadway (1952)

Crash Corrigan's Ranch Children's Program (1950)

Crash Island Beaches (1981), Teenagers (1981)

Crazy Dan Men — Law Enforcers (1986), Women — Law Enforcers (1986)

Crazy for You Broadway (1999)

Crazy Like a Fox Con Artists (1984), Men — Law Enforcers (1985), San Francisco (1984)

Creative Cookery Cooking (1951)

The Crew Pilots (1995)

Crime and Punishment Latino American (1993), Los Angeles (1993), Men — Law Enforcers (1993), Women — Law Enforcers (1993)

Crime Magazine Reporters (1968)

Crime Photographer Bars (1951), Reporters (1945), Reporters (1951), Series Based on Radio Programs (1951)

Crime Quiz Drama (1944)

Crime Story Chicago (1986), Historical Settings (1986), Men — Law Enforcers (1986)

Crime with Father Men — Law Enforcers (1951), New York (1951)

Crimes of Passion Judges (1976)

Criminal at Large Broadway (1952)

Criminal Minds F.B.I. Agents (2005)

Crisis Drama — Repeat Series (1971), Pilot Film Series (1968), Psychiatrists (1968)

Crisis Center Latino American (1997), San Francisco (1997)

Criss Angel Mind Freak Magicians (2005)

Crossing Jordan Bars (2001), Forensics(2001)

Crossroads Drama (1953), Religious Characters (1955)

Crowfoot American Indian (1995)

Crown Theater with Gloria Swanson Drama (1953)

Crumbs Gays (2006), Restaurants (2006)

Crunch and Des Adventurers (1955)

Crusade Space (1999)

The Crusader Adventurers (1955)

A Crystal Christmas Holiday Specials (1987)

The Crystal Room Variety Programs (1948)

Culture Clash Mexican American (1991)

Cupid Love (1998)

Curiosity Shop Witches (1971)

Curley Bradley, the Singing Marshal Westerns (1955)

The Curse of Dracula San Francisco (1979), Vampires (1979)

Curtain's Up Broadway (1985)

Cutter to Houston Doctors (1983)

Cutter's Goose Pilots (1982)

Cybill Los Angeles (1995)

Cymbeline Shakespeare (1983)

Cyrano de Bergerac Variety and Drama Spectaculars (1955)

D-Day Plus 20 Presidential Appearances (1964)

The D.A. Los Angeles (1971), Mexican American (1972)

The D.A.'s Man District Attorneys (1959), New York (1959)

D.C. Cop Men — Law Enforcers (1986)

D.C. Follies Puppets (1987)

D.E.A. Government Agents (1990)

D.H.O. Doctors (1973)

Daddio Los Angeles (2000)

Daddy Dearest New York (1993), Psychiatrists (1993), Senior Citizens (1993)

Daddy's Girl Adolescence (1973), Adolescence (1979)

Dads Adolescence (1987)

Daffy Duck's Easter Show Holiday Specials (1980)

Daffy Duck's Thanks-for-Giving Special Holiday Specials (1980)

DAG Politics (2001), Washington, D.C. (2000)

Dagmar's Canteen Variety Programs (1952)

Daisy Fuentes Cuban American (1992)

The Dakotas Visually Impaired (1957), Westerns (1963)

Dakota's Way Women — Law Enforcers (1988)

Daktari Africa (1966), Series Based on Films (1966)

Dallas Cars (1978), Mexican American (1978), Physically Disabled (1979), Senior Citizens (1979), Soap Operas (Note)

The Damon Runyon Theater Drama (1955), Series Based on Radio Programs (1955)

Dan August California (1970), Men — Law Enforcers (1970), Mexican American (1970)

Dan Raven California (1960), Men — Law Enforcers (1960)

Dan Turner, Hollywood Detective Men — Law Enforcers (1990)

Dana Hill Women — Law Enforcers (1975)

The Dancing Bandit Hearing Impaired Characters (1995)

Dancing Lessons Variety Programs (1941)

Dancing on Air Variety Programs (1947)

The Dancing Princesses Fairy Tales (1982)

Danger Drama (1950)

Danger Man Espionage (1961)

The Danger Team Puppets (1991), Women — Extraordinary (1991)

Danger Theater Little People (1993)

Dangerous Assignment Government Agents (1952), Series Based on Radio Programs (1952)

The Dangerous Christmas of Red Riding Hood Holiday Specials (1965)

Dangerous Curves Bars (1992)

Dangerous Women Latino American (1991), Prison (1991), Prostitutes (1991), Puerto Rican (1991)

Daniel Boone Adolescence (1964), American Indian (1964), Historical Settings (1964)

Danny and the Mermaid Mermaids (1978)

The Danny Thomas Hour Drama (1967)

The Danny Thomas Show Latino American (1961), Nightclubs (1953)

Dante Nightclubs (1960), San Francisco (1960)

Darcy's Wild Life Teenagers (2004)

Dare Devil Visually Impaired (1989)

Dark Adventure Drama (1953)

Dark Angel Lesbians (2000), Physically Disabled (2000), Women — Extraordinary (2000)

The Dark Avenger Physically Disabled (1989)

Dark Eyes Women — Law Enforcers (1995)

Dark Justice Judges (1991)

Dark of Night Drama (1952)

Dark Shadows Ghosts (1966), Ghosts (1991), Soap Operas

(1966), Soap Operas (Note), The Supernatural (1966), The Supernatural (1991), Vampires (1966), Vampires (1991), Werewolves (1966), Witches (1966), Witches (1991)

Dark Skies Aliens (1996)

Dark Victory Broadway (1952)

Darkroom Drama (1981)

Dastardly and Muttley in Their Flying Machines Cartoons (1969)

A Date with Debbie Variety and Drama Spectaculars (1960)

A Date with Judy Adolescence (1951), Series Based on Radio Programs (1951), Sitcoms (1951), Teen After-School Hangouts (1951), Teenagers (1951)

A Date with Life Soap Operas (1955)

A Date with the Angels Los Angeles (1957), Senior Citizens (1957), Sitcoms (1957)

Dateline Europe Reporters (1951)

The Dating Game Love (1966)

Daughters Teenagers (1977)

The Daughters of Joshua Cabe Prostitutes (1972), Westerns (1972)

The Daughters of Joshua Cabe Return Prostitutes (1975), Westerns (1972)

Dave and Charley Senior Citizens (1952), Sitcoms (1952)

The Dave Garroway Show Series Based on Radio Programs (1949), Variety Programs (1953)

Dave's World Florida (1993), Newspapers (1993)

David and Goliath Religious Programs (1978)

David Blaine: Fearless Magicians (1996)

David Blaine: Frozen in Time Magicians (1996)

David Blaine: Magic Man Magicians (1996)

David Blaine: Street Magician Magicians (1996)

David Cassidy – Man Undercover Los Angeles (1978), Men — Law Enforcers (1978), Mexican American (1978)

The David Frost Interviews Presidential Appearances (1977)

The David Niven Theater Drama (1959)

DaVinci's Inquest Men — Law Enforcers (2006)

Davis Rules Asian American (1991), Senior Citizens (1991), Teachers (1991)

Davy and Goliath Religious Programs (1963)

Davy Crockett, Indian Fighter American Indian (1954)

Davy Crockett American Indian (1954), Historical Settings (1954)

Davy Crockett at the Alamo American Indian (1954)

Dawson's Creek Teenagers (1998)

Day in Court Judges (1958)

Day to Day Pilot Film Series (1987)

Daydreaming with Laraine Variety Programs (1951)

The Days and Nights of Molly Dodd New York (1987)

The Days of Our Lives Soap Operas (1965)

DEA: Special Task Force Latino American (1990)

Dead End Brattigan Reporters (1990)

Dead Like Me Devil (2003), The Supernatural (2003)

Deadline Drama (1959), Reporters (2000)

Deadline for Murder: From the Files of Edna Buchanan Reporters (1995)

Deadwood Nudity (1984), Westerns (2004)

The Dean Jones Show Geniuses (1965), Teenagers (1965)

The Dean Martin and Jerry Lewis Show Series Based on Radio Programs (1949)

The Dean Martin Christmas Special Holiday Specials (1980)

Dean Martin's Christmas in California Holiday Specials (1975), Holiday Specials (1977)

Dean's Place Nightclubs (1975)

Dear Detective Adolescence (1979), Women — Law Enforcers (1979)

Dear Diary Nudity (1950), Sitcoms (1950)

Dear John Con Artists (1988), New York (1988), Restaurants (1988), Teachers (1988)

Dear Penelope and Peter Love (1986)

Dear Phoebe Los Angeles (1954), Love (1954), Newspapers (1954), Sitcoms (1954)

Dear Teacher Teachers (1981)

Dearest Enemy Broadway (1955), Variety and Drama Spectaculars (1955)

Death of a Salesman Broadway (1966)

Death Takes a Holiday Broadway (1952)

Death Valley Days Drama (1952), Senior Citizens (1952), Series Based on Radio Programs (1952), Westerns (1952)

The Debbie Reynolds Show Los Angeles (1969), Newspapers (1969)

December Bride Newspapers (1954), Senior Citizens (1954), Series Based on Radio Programs (1954), Sitcoms (1954)

Decision Pilot Film Series (1958)

Decisions: The Conflicts of Harry S.

Truman Presidential Appearances (1964)

Decoy New York (1957), Nudity (1957), Women — Law Enforcers (1957)

The Defender Lawyers (1961)

The Defenders Lawyers (1961), New York (1961)

Degrassi Junior High Adolescence (1987), Canada (1987), Newspapers (1987), Nudity (2004), Teen After-School Hangouts (1987), Twins (1987)

The Dell O'Dell Show Magicians (1951)

The Della Reese African American (1970)

Dellaventura Bars (1997), Men — Law Enforcers (1997), New York (1997)

The Delphi Bureau Espionage (1972), Geniuses (1972), Washington, D.C. (1972)

Delta Bars (1992)

Delta House Historical Settings (1979)

Delvecchio Men — Law Enforcers (1976)

Demi-Tasse Tales Drama — Repeat Series (1953)

Dempsey and Makepeace Women — Law Enforcers (1985)

The Dennis Dupree Show Shows within Shows (1995)

Dennis James' Carnival Variety Programs (1948)

The Dennis O'Keefe Show Housekeepers (1959), Los Angeles (1959), Newspapers (1959), Sitcoms (1959)

Dennis the Menace Adolescence (1959), Adolescence (1987), Senior Citizens (1959), Sitcoms (1959)

Department S Men — Law Enforcers (1971), Nudity (1971), Women — Extraordinary (1971)

The Deputy Arizona (1959), Westerns (1959)

Deputy Dawg Cartoons (1960)

The Desert Song Opera (1955), Variety and Drama Spectaculars (1955)

Designing Women Senior Citizens (1986)

The Desilu Playhouse Drama (1957)

Desperado Westerns (1987)

The Desperate Hours Broadway (1967)

Desperate Housewives Gays (2005, 2006), Latino American (2004), Nudity (2004, 2005), Teenagers (2004), Twins (2005)

Destry Westerns (1964)

Detect and Collect Game Shows (1946)

The Detective Men — Law Enforcers (1975)
Detective Finger, I Presume Men — Law Enforcers (1981)
Detective in the House Men — Law Enforcers (1985), Teenagers (1985), Visually Impaired (1957)
Detective School Latino American (1979), Los Angeles (1979)
The Detectives Men — Law Enforcers (1959), New York (1959)
The Detective's Wife Men — Law Enforcers (1950), New York (1950)
The Devil and Daniel Webster Broadway (1960)
The Devil's Disciple Broadway (1955)
The Devlin Connection Los Angeles (1982), Men — Law Enforcers (1982)
Dharma and Greg Lawyers (1997), San Francisco (1997), Senior Citizens (1997)
Diagnosis: Danger Doctors (1963)
Diagnosis Murder Cars (1993), Doctors (1993), Los Angeles (1993), Magicians (1993), Men — Law Enforcers (1993), Restaurants (1993), Senior Citizens (1993)
Diagnosis Unknown Doctors (1960), New York (1960)
The Diahann Carroll Show African American (1971), African American (1976)
Dial Hot Line Psychiatrists (1970)
Dial "M" for Murder Variety and Drama Spectaculars (1958)
Dial 999 Men — Law Enforcers (1958)
Dialogues of the Carmelites Opera (1950)
Diamond Head Espionage (1977)
The Diamond Head Game Hawaii (1975)
Diamonds Women — Law Enforcers (1987)
Diana African American (1971), New York (1973)
The Diary of Anne Frank Broadway (1967), Broadway (1980)
Diary of Death Reporters (1945)
Dick and the Duchess Sitcoms (1957)
The Dick Clark Saturday Night Beechnut Show Variety Programs (1958)
Dick Clark's Rockin' New Year's Eve Holiday Specials (1972)
Dick Clark's World of Talent Reality Programs (1959)
The Dick Powell Show Drama (1961)
Dick Powell's Zane Grey Theater Westerns (1956)
Dick Tracy Adolescence (1967), Men — Law Enforcers (1950, 1967), New York (1950), Series Based on Radio Programs (1950)

The Dick Tracy Show Mexican American (1961)
The Dick Van Dyke Show Adolescence (1961), Cars (1963), Lookalikes (1964), New York (1961), Shows within Shows (1961), Sitcoms (1961)
Dick Wittington and His Cat Fairy Tales (1958)
The Dictator Politics (1988)
A Different World Teachers (1987), Teen After-School Hangouts (1986)
Diff'rent Strokes Adolescence (1978), Hotels (1978), Housekeepers (1978), Little People (1978), Magicians (1978), New York (1978), Physically Disabled (1983), Teen After-School Hangouts (1978), Teenagers (1978)
The Dinah Shore Chevy Show Variety Programs (1951)
The Dinah Shore Show Color Broadcasting (1957-1965), Series Based on Radio Programs (1956), Variety Programs (1956)
Diner Restaurants (1983)
Ding Dong School Children's Program (1952)
Ding Howe and the Flying Tigers Pilots (1950), Reporters (1950), War — World War II (1950)
Dinner Date with Vincent Lopez Variety Programs (1949)
Dinosaurs Aviators (1991), Bars (1991), Historical Settings (1991), Puppets (1990, 1991), Senior Citizens (1990), Senior Citizens (1991), Talking Animals and Machines (1990)
Dinotopia Talking Animals and Machines (2002)
Dione Lucas' Cooking School Cooking (1948)
Dirty Dancing Latino American (1988), Series Based on Films (1988)
The Dirty Dozen: The Series Series Based on Films (1988), War — World War II (1988)
Dirty Sally Country Folk (1973), Westerns (1974)
Discovery Children's Program (1963)
Disneyland American Indian (1954)
The Disney-M-G-M Studio's Theme Park Opening Presidential Appearances (1989)
Disney's Christmas on Ice Holiday Specials (1990)
The District Bars (2000), Men — Law Enforcers (2000), Washington, D.C. (2000)
Diver Dan Mermaids (1960), Puppets (1960)
The Division Puerto Rican (2001),

San Francisco (2001), Women — Law Enforcers (2001)
Divorce Court Judges (1957)
Divorce Hearing Judges (1958)
Dobie Gillis Geniuses (1959), Senior Citizens (1959), Teachers (1959), Teen After-School Hangouts (1959), Teenagers (1959)
Doc Doctors (1969), Doctors (2001), Latino American (1975), New York (1975), New York (2001), Pilot Film Series (1969), Women — Nurses (1969), Women — Nurses (1975), Women — Nurses (1976)
Doc and Gladys Celebrate Holiday Specials (1977)
Doc Corkle Sitcoms (1952)
Doc Elliot Doctors (1973)
The Doctor Doctors (1952)
Dr. Christian Doctors (1956), Series Based on Radio Programs (1956)
Doctor, Doctor Bars (1989), Doctors (1989)
Doctor Dolittle Cartoons (1970)
Doctor Domingo Cuban American (1974), Doctors (1974)
Dr. Fad Asian American (1988)
Dr. Fu Manchu Asian American (1950)
Dr. Hudson's Secret Journal Doctors (1954)
Doctor I.Q Game Shows (1953), Series Based on Radio Programs (1957)
Dr. Jekyll and Mr. Hyde Variety and Drama Spectaculars (1940)
Dr. Joyce Brothers Psychiatrists (,)
Dr. Kildare Doctors (1961), Senior Citizens (1961), Women — Nurses (1961)
Dr. Mike Doctors (1959)
Dr. Paradise Beaches (1988)
Dr. Phil Psychiatrists (2002)
Dr. Quinn, Medicine Woman Adolescence (1993), American Indian (1993), Doctors (1993), Westerns (1993)
Dr. Ruth Psychiatrists (1984)
Dr. Ruth's House Psychiatrists (1990)
Dr. Seuss' How the Grinch Stole Christmas Holiday Specials (1966)
Dr. Shrinker Little People (1976), Teenagers (1976)
Dr. Simon Locke Canada (1971), Senior Citizens (1971), Women — Nurses (1971)
Doctor Strange Psychiatrists (1978), The Supernatural (1978), Witches (1978)
Dr. Vegas Doctors (2004), Hotels (2004), Las Vegas Settings (2004)
The Doctor Was a Lady Doctors (1958)
Doctor Who Aliens (1973), Robots (1973), Space (1973), Space

(2006), Talking Animals and Machines (1985), Time Travel (1973), Time Travel (2006)

The Doctors Doctors (1969), Los Angeles (1969), Soap Operas (1963)

The Doctors and the Nurses Doctors (1964), New York (1964), Women — Nurses (1962)

Doctors Hospital Doctors (1975), Mexican American (1975), Women — Nurses (1975)

Doctors Private Lives Women — Nurses (1979)

The Doctors Wilde Animals (1987)

Dodo — The Kid from Outer Space Cartoons (1965)

Dog and Cat Cars (1977), Los Angeles (1977), Men — Law Enforcers (1977), Women — Law Enforcers (1977)

The Dog Days of Arthur Cane Talking Animals and Machines (1984)

The Dog Troop Westerns (1964)

A Dog's Life Animals (1979), Talking Animals and Machines (1979)

Dollar a Second Game Shows (1953)

A Doll's House Broadway (1959)

Dolphin Cove Australia (1989), Speech Impaired (1989), Teenagers (1990)

The Dom DeLuise Show California (1987)

Domestic Life Adolescence (1984), Shows within Shows (1984), Teenagers (1984), Washington, D.C. (1984)

The Don Ameche Theater Drama — Repeat Series (1958)

Don Giovanni Opera (1950)

The Don Ho Show Hawaii (1976)

Don McNeill's Dinner Club Variety Programs (1946)

Don McNeill's TV Club Variety Programs (1946)

Don Quixote Ballet (2001)

The Don Rickles Show New York (1972)

The Donald O'Connor Show Variety Programs (1954)

The Donald O'Connor Special Variety and Drama Spectaculars (1960)

Donald's Cousin Gus Cartoons (1939), Television Firsts (1939)

The Donna Reed Show Teen After-School Hangouts (1958), Teenagers (1958)

Donny and Marie Teenagers (1976)

The Donny and Marie Christmas Special Holiday Specials (1979)

The Donovan Affair Broadway (1939)

Don's Musical Playhouse Variety Programs (1951)

Don't Call Me Charlie Country Folk (1962)

Don't Call Us Little People (1976)

Doogie Howser, M.D. California (1989), Doctors (1989), Geniuses (1989)

The Dooley Brothers Westerns (1979)

The Door with No Name Espionage (1951), Espionage (1952)

Doorway to Danger Espionage (1952)

Doorway to Fame Reality Programs (1949)

The Doris Day Show Adolescence (1968), California (1968), House-keepers (1968), Mexican American (1968), Reporters (1968), San Francisco (1968)

Doris Day's Best Friends Animals (1985)

Dorothy Adolescence (1979), Connecticut (1979), Teachers (1979)

Dorothy Hamill in Romeo and Juliet on Ice Ballet (1983)

Dotto Game Shows (1958)

The Dotty Mack Show Variety Programs (1953)

Double Agent Government Agents (1987)

Double Dare San Francisco (1985)

The Double Life of Henry Phyfe Espionage (1966), Look-alikes (1966), Washington, D.C. (1966)

Double or Nothing Game Shows (1952), Series Based on Radio Programs (1952)

Double Trouble New York (1984), Teenagers (1984), Twins (1984)

Doug Henning's Magic on Broadway Magicians (1982)

Doug Henning's World of Magic Magicians (1976)

Doug Henning's World of Magic II Magicians (1977)

Doug Henning's World of Magic III Magicians (1980)

Doug Henning's World of Magic IV Magicians (1981)

Doug Hennings's World of Magic V Magicians (1982)

Douglas Edwards with the News News Broadcasts (1948)

Douglas Fairbanks, Jr. Presents Drama (1953)

Dow Hour of Great Mysteries Drama (1960)

Down and Out in Beverly Hills Housekeepers (1987), Mexican American (1987), Series Based on Films (1987)

Down Delaware Road Religious Characters (1988)

Down Home Pilot Film Series (1963–1967), Reporters (1965)

Down in the Valley Opera (1950)

Down the Shore Beaches (1992), New Jersey (1992)

Down You Go Game Shows (1951),

Series Based on Radio Programs (1951)

Downtown Los Angeles (1986), Men — Law Enforcers (1986)

Dracula: The Series Teenagers (1990), Vampires (1990)

Dragnet Films Based on Television Series (1954), Films Based on Television Series (1987), Los Angeles (1951), Los Angeles (1967), Los Angeles (2003), Men — Law Enforcers (1951), Men — Law Enforcers (1967), Series Based on Radio Programs (1951)

The Dragon Asian American (2001)

Drak Pack Vampires (1980), Werewolves (1980)

Drake and Josh Teenagers (2004)

Dramatic Moments Drama (1932)

Draw to Win Game Shows (1952)

Dream Girl Broadway (1955)

Dream Girl of '67 Reality Programs (1967)

Dream Girl of 1987 Reality Programs (1986)

Dream Girl U.S.A. Reality Programs (1986)

Dream Keeper American Indian (2003)

Dream On Nudity (1984)

Dream Street New Jersey (1989)

The Dream Team Women — Extraordinary (1999)

The Drew Carey Show Cars (1995), Cross Dressers (1995), Latino American (1995), Puppets (1995), Restaurants (1995), Senior Citizens (1995)

Drexell's Class Teachers (1991)

Droodles Game Shows (1954)

The Drunkard Broadway (1982)

The Duck Factory Shows within Shows (1984), Women — "Dumb Blondes" (1984)

Dudley Latino American (1993), New York (1993)

Dudley Do-Right Films Based on Television Series (1999)

The Dudley Do-Right Show Cartoons (1969)

Due South Men — Law Enforcers (1994)

Duet Adolescence (1987), Los Angeles (1987), Newspapers (1987)

Duffy Animals (1977)

Duffy's Tavern Bars (1954), New York (1954), Series Based on Radio Programs (1954), Sitcoms (1954)

The Duke Chicago (1979), Men — Law Enforcers (1979), Sitcoms (1954)

Duke Ellington's Sophisticated Ladies Broadway (2005)

The Dukes of Hazzard Cars (1979), Con Artists (1979), Films Based on Television Series (2005), Senior Citizens (1979), Stock Car Racers (1979), Twins (1979)

Dumb and Dumber Series Based on Films (1995)

The Dumb Waiter Broadway (1987)

DuMont Beepstakes Game Shows (1946)

DuMont Varieties Game Shows (1943), News Broadcasts (1953), Variety Programs (1943)

The Dumplings Restaurants (1976)

Dundee and the Culhane Lawyers (1967)

Dunninger and Winchell Mediums (1948)

The Dunninger Show Mediums (1953), Series Based on Radio Programs (1953)

The DuPont Show of the Month Drama (1957), Shakespeare (1959)

The DuPont Show of the Week Drama (1957)

Dusty Taxi Cabs (1983)

Dusty's Trail Westerns (1973)

Dweebs Geniuses (1995)

Dynasty Gays (1981), Presidential Appearances (1983), Soap Operas (Note), Television Firsts (1954)

E.S.P. Drama (1958), *Mediums* (1958)

E/R Doctors (1984), Latino American (1984), Women — Nurses (1984)

The Earl Wrightson Show Variety Programs (1948)

Early Edition Bars (1996), Chicago (1996), Newspapers (1996), Visually Impaired (1996)

Earn Your Vacation Game Shows (1954), Series Based on Radio Programs (1954)

Earth 2 Robots (1994), Space (1994)

Earthbound Aliens (1982)

The Earthlings Aliens (1982)

East Side/West Side New York (1963)

The Easter Bunny Is Comin' to Town Holiday Specials (1977)

Easter Parade of Stars Holiday Specials (1954)

The Easter Promise Holiday Specials (1975)

Eastwick Witches (2002)

Easy Aces Series Based on Radio Programs (1949), Women — Scatterbrained (1949)

Easy Street California (1986), Cars (1986), Senior Citizens (1986), Visually Impaired (1957)

The Easy Way Series Based on Films (1962)

Ebony, Ivory and Jade Government Agents (1979)

Ed Lawyers (2000), Physically Disabled (2002)

The Ed Begley, Jr. Show Politics (1989)

The Ed Sullivan Show Puppets (1963), Series Based on Radio Programs (1948), Television Firsts (1956), Television Firsts (1964), Variety Programs (1948)

Ed Sullivan's Broadway Broadway (1973)

The Ed Wynn Show Senior Citizens (1958), Variety Programs (1949)

Eddie Con Artists (1970)

The Eddie Albert Show Variety Programs (1953)

The Eddie Capra Mysteries Adolescence (1978), Lawyers (1978), Los Angeles (1978)

Eddie Dodd Lawyers (1991), New York (1991), Series Based on Films (1991)

The Eddie Fisher Show Color Broadcasting (1957-1965), Variety Programs (1957)

The Eddy Arnold Show Variety Programs (1952)

Eddy Arnold Time Variety Programs (1956)

The Edge of Night Soap Operas (1956), Soap Operas (Note)

The Edison Twins Twins (1984)

Edith Wharton's Summer Nudity (1981)

The Edsel Show Variety and Drama Spectaculars (1957)

The Education of Max Bickford Transsexuals (2002)

Eerie Indiana: The Other Dimension The Supernatural (1998)

Eerie, Indiana The Supernatural (1992), The Supernatural (1998)

Egan Men — Law Enforcers (1973)

The Egg and I Country Folk (1951), New York (1951)

Eight Is Enough Adolescence (1977), California (1977), Cars (1977), Lawyers (1977), Newspapers (1977), Nudity (2005), Teenagers (1977)

Eight Simple Rules Little People (2004), Newspapers (2002), Senior Citizens (2003), Teenagers (2002), Women — "Dumb Blondes" (2002), Women — Nurses (2003)

18 Wheels of Justice Truckers (2000)

The Eighth Man Cartoons (1965)

The 87th Precinct Hearing Impaired Characters (1961), Men — Law Enforcers (1961), New York (1961), Speech Impaired (1961)

Eischied Men — Law Enforcers (1979), New York (1979), Women — Law Enforcers (1979)

Eisenhower and Lutz Lawyers (1988)

El Coyote Teenagers (1958), Women — Extraordinary (1958)

Eleanor Roosevelt's Diamond Jubilee Plus One Presidential Appearances (1960)

Electra Woman and Dyna Girl Gadgets (1976), Reporters (1976), Super Heroes (1976), Super Heroes (2001), Women — Extraordinary (1976)

The Eleventh Hour New York (1962), Psychiatrists (1962)

Elfego Baca Latino American (1957), Latino American (1958), Lawyers (1958), Westerns (1958)

The Elgin Hour Drama (1954)

Elke Teenagers (1971)

Ellen Gays (1995), Lesbians (1994), Los Angeles (1994)

The Ellen Burstyn Show Baltimore (1986)

The Ellen Show Lesbians (2001), New Jersey (2001)

Ellery Queen Historical Settings (1975), Men — Law Enforcers (1975), New York (1975), Series Based on Radio Programs (1950)

Ellery Queen: Don't Look Behind You Men — Law Enforcers (1971)

Elly and Jools Ghosts (1988)

Elvis Historical Settings (1990)

Emerald Point NAS California (1983)

Emergency Los Angeles (1972), Los Angeles (1979), Rescue (1971), Rescue (1979)

Emergency Plus 4 Rescue (1973)

Emeril Restaurants (2001)

Emeril Live Cooking (1970)

Emily's Reasons Why Not Asian American (2006), Gays (2006), Los Angeles (2006)

Emmy Lou Fairy Tales (1960)

The Emperor's New Clothes Fairy Tales (1958), Fairy Tales (1982)

Empire Mexican American (1962), Mexican American (1963), New York (1984)

Empire City Women — Law Enforcers (1991)

Empty Nest Florida (1988), Puerto Rican (1987), Women — Law Enforcers (1988), Women — Nurses (1988)

The Enchanted Cottage Broadway (1952)

The Enchanted World of Danny Kaye Puppets (1971)

Encore Theater Drama — Repeat Series (1956)

Encounter Drama (1958)

Encyclopedia Brown — The Boy Detective Children — Extraordinary (1989)

Enos Los Angeles (1980)

Entertaining the Troops War — World War II (1989)

Entertainment 1955 Color Broadcasting (1955), Television Firsts (1955), Variety and Drama Spectaculars (1955)

Equal Justice District Attorneys (1990), Philadelphia (1990)

The Equalizer Cars (1985), Men — Law Enforcers (1985), New York (1985), Restaurants (1985)

ER Chicago (1994), Doctors (1994), Lesbians (1994), Mentally Disabled (1994), Physically Disabled (1994), Puerto Rican (1994), Women — Nurses (1994)

E-Ring Washington, D.C. (2005)

The Ernie Kovacs Show Gays (1955), Speech Impaired (1955)

Ernie, Madge and Artie Ghosts (1974), Pilot Film Series (1974)

The Errol Flynn Theater Drama (1957)

Escapade Espionage (1978)

Escape Drama (1950), Drama (1973), Drama (1981), Series Based on Radio Programs (1950)

Escape from Alcatraz Magicians (1987)

Espionage Drama (1963), Espionage (1963)

The Esso Newscast News Broadcasts (1940)

The Esther Williams Aqua Spectacular Variety and Drama Spectaculars (1956)

Esther Williams at Cypress Gardens Variety and Drama Spectaculars (1960)

The Eternal Light Religious Programs (1951)

Ethel and Albert Series Based on Radio Programs (1953), Sitcoms (1955)

The Ethel Barrymore Theater Drama (1956)

The Ethel Waters Show African American (1939), Television Firsts (1939)

Eve Bars (2003), Florida (2003)

The Eve Arden Show Adolescence (1957), Housekeepers (1957), Pilot Film Series (1963–1967), Twins (1957)

Evel Knievel Adventurers (1971)

Even Stevens California (2001), Geniuses (2001), Teenagers (2001)

Evening Shade Adolescence (1990), Doctors (1990), Lawyers (1990), Newspapers (1990), Restaurants (1990), Senior Citizens (1990)

An Evening with Fred Astaire Variety and Drama Spectaculars (1958)

The Everglades Beaches (1961), Florida (1961), Men — Law Enforcers (1961)

Everwood Teenagers (2002)

Everybody Hates Chris New York (2005), Teenagers (2005)

Everybody Loves Raymond Adolescence (1996), Men — Law Enforcers (1996), New York (1996), Newspapers (1996), Puppets (1996), Senior Citizens (1996), Twins (1996)

Everyone Can Exercise Physically Disabled (1991)

Everything's Relative New York (1987)

The Evidence Men — Law Enforcers (2006), Senior Citizens (2006)

Evil Roy Slade Westerns (1972)

The Evil Touch Australia (1973), Drama (1973)

Exclusive Drama (1960)

The Executioner's Song Nudity (1982)

Exo-Man Men — Extraordinary (1977), Physically Disabled (1977)

Expedition: Danger Adventurers (1985)

The Expendables Men — Law Enforcers (1962)

Exploring Children's Program (1962)

Expose Government Agents (1963)

The Extra Censory World of Char Mediums (1987)

Extreme Rescue (1995)

Eye to Eye Los Angeles (1985), Women — Law Enforcers (1985), Women — Scatterbrained (1985)

Eye Witness Drama (1953)

Eyes Gays (2005), Lawyers (2005), Los Angeles (2005), Men — Law Enforcers (2005), Women — Law Enforcers (2005)

The Eyes Have It Game Shows (1948)

The Eyes of Charles Sand Mediums (1972)

The Eyes of Texas Women — Law Enforcers (1980)

Eyewitness to History News Broadcasts (1951)

F Troop Look-alikes (1965), Senior Citizens (1967), Visually Impaired (1965), Westerns (1965)

The F.B.I. Washington, D.C. (1965)

The Fabulous Dr. Fable Doctors (1973)

The Fabulous Sycamores Sitcoms (1955)

Face of Danger Drama — Repeat Series (1965)

Face the Nation News Broadcasts (1954)

The Faceless Man Government Agents (1966)

Face-to-Face Game Shows (1946)

Facts 'n' Fun Puppets (1953)

The Facts of Life Adolescence (1988), Housekeepers (1979), New York (1979), Physically Disabled (1981), Reporters (1979), Teachers (1988), Teenagers (1979)

The Faculty Teachers (1986), Teachers (1996)

Fair Exchange New York (1962), Teenagers (1962)

Fairmeadows, U.S.A. Soap Operas (1950)

Fairy Tale Theater Drama (1982), Fairy Tales (1982)

Faith Baldwin's Theater of Romance Drama (1951)

The Falcon Adventurers (1955), Series Based on Radio Programs (1955)

Falcon Crest California (1981), Housekeepers (1981), Senior Citizens (1981), Soap Operas (Note)

The Fall Guy Bars (1981), Cars (1981), Los Angeles (1981)

Fallen Angels Drama (1993)

Fame Mexican American (1982), New York (1982), Puerto Rican (1982), Teachers (1982)

Fame L.A. Latino American (1997), Los Angeles (1997), Puerto Rican (1997)

Family Adolescence (1976), California (1976), Housekeepers (1976), Lawyers (1976), Teenagers (1976)

Family Affair Color Broadcasting (1966), Housekeepers (1966, 2002), New York (1966, 2002), Teenagers (1966, 2002)

Family Album Philadelphia (1993), Teenagers (1994)

Family Business Los Angeles (2003)

A Family for Joe Senior Citizens (1990), Teenagers (1990)

Family Genius Geniuses (1949)

Family Guy Physically Disabled (1999)

The Family Holvak Historical Settings (1975), Religious Characters (1975), Teenagers (1975)

Family in Blue Men — Law Enforcers (1982)

Family Law California (1999), Lawyers (1999), Little People (2001)

The Family Man Adolescence (1990), California (1990), Rescue (1990)

The Family Martinez Latino American (1986), Puerto Rican (1986), Teenagers (1986)

Family Matters Adolescence (1989), Cars (1989), Chicago (1989), Look-alikes (1989), Men — Law Enforcers (1989), Restaurants (1989), Robots (1989), Senior Citizens (1989), Teen After-School Hangouts (1989), Teenagers (1989), Women — Scatterbrained (Note)

Family Rules Teenagers (1999)

Family Ties Adolescence (1982), Ohio (1982), Shows within Shows (1982), Teenagers (1982), Women — Scatterbrained (1982)

Family Tree Hearing Impaired Characters (1983), Teenagers (1983)

The Famous Adventures of Mr. Magoo Cartoons (1964), Visually Impaired (1964)

Famous Jury Trials Drama (1949), Series Based on Radio Programs (1949)

The Fanelli Boys Bars (1990), Religious Characters (1990)

Fanfare Drama — Repeat Series (1959), Variety and Drama Spectaculars (1954)

Fang Face Werewolves (1978)

The Fantastic Four Cartoons (1967), Super Heroes (1967)

Fantastic Journey Aliens (1977), Cartoons (1968)

Fantastic Voyage Little People (1968), Series Based on Films (1968)

Fantasy Island Angels (1978), Beaches (1978), Devil (1978), Little People (1978), Mermaids (1978), Mexican American (1978)

Far Out Space Nuts Aliens (1975), Puppets (1976), Space (1975)

Faraway Hill Soap Operas (1946), Soap Operas (Note)

Fare Enough Game Shows (1946)

The Farebrand Broadway (1952)

The Farmer's Daughter Adolescence (1963), Housekeepers (1963), Politics (1962), Politics (1963), Senior Citizens (1963), Series Based on Films (1963), Washington, D.C. (1963)

Farraday and Company Los Angeles (1973), Men — Law Enforcers (1972)

Farrell: For the People Lawyers (1982)

Farscape Aliens (1999), Religious Characters (1999)

Fashion Discoveries Nudity (1941)

The Fashion Telecast Nudity (1944)

Fashions of the Times Nudity (1944)

Fast Company Reporters (1995)

Fast Times Series Based on Films (1986), Teachers (1986), Teen After-School Hangouts (1986), Teenagers (1986)

Fastlane Lesbians (2002), Lesbians (2005), Los Angeles (2002), Men — Law Enforcers (2003), Women — Law Enforcers (2002)

Fat Albert Christmas Special Holiday Specials (1977)

Father Brown Religious Characters (1982)

Father Dowling Mysteries Chicago (1989), Housekeepers (1989),

Men — Law Enforcers (1989), Religious Characters (1989), Teachers (1989), Twins (1989)

Father Knows Best Look-alikes (1954), Mexican American (1954), Series Based on Radio Programs (1954), Teen After-School Hangouts (1954), Teenagers (1954)

Father Murphy Religious Characters (1981)

Father O Father Religious Characters (1976)

Father of the Bride Series Based on Films (1961)

Father of the Pride Talking Animals and Machines (2004)

Father on Trial Judges (1972)

Fathers and Sons Adolescence (1986), Teachers (1986)

The Favor Ghosts (1944)

Favorite Story Drama (1952)

Fawlty Towers Hotels (1977), Housekeepers (1977)

The Fawn Fairy Tales (1960)

Fay San Francisco (1975)

Faye and Skitch Variety Programs (1953)

FBI Code 98 F.B.I. Agents (1962)

The FBI: 100 Years of Hope and Honor Presidential Appearances (2003)

Fear and Fancy Drama (1953)

Fearless Fly Cartoons (1965)

Fearless Fosdick Puppets (1952)

The Feather and Father Gang Con Artists (1977), Lawyers (1977), Los Angeles (1977)

Feather Your Nest Game Shows (1954)

Featherstone's Nest Adolescence (1979), Teenagers (1979)

Federal Agent F.B.I. Agents (1949), Pilot Film Series (1949)

Feel the Heat Men — Law Enforcers (1983)

Felicity Gays (1998), Latino American (1998), New York (1998), Restaurants (1998), Teenagers (1998)

Felix the Cat Cartoons (1960)

The Felony Squad Color Broadcasting (1966), Los Angeles (1966), Men — Law Enforcers (1966)

Female of the Species Drama (1957)

The Feminine Touch Variety Programs (1951)

Ferris Bueller Los Angeles (1990), Series Based on Films (1990), Teen After-School Hangouts (1990), Teenagers (1990)

The Fess Parker Show Adolescence (1974)

Festival of Magic Magicians (1957)

Festival of Music Variety and Drama Spectaculars (1956)

Festival of Stars Drama — Repeat Series (1956)

Fibber McGee and Molly Adolescence (1959), Series Based on Radio Programs (1959), Sitcoms (1959)

Fifth of July Gays (1982)

15 with Faye Variety Programs (1949)

The 53rd Academy Awards Presidential Appearances (1981)

The Fighting Fitzgeralds Bars (2001), New York (2001), Senior Citizens (2001)

The Fighting Nightingales War — Korea, Vietnam, Iraq (1978), Women — Nurses (1978)

The Files of Jeffrey Jones Men — Law Enforcers (1955)

Find Twins (2003)

Finder of Lost Loves Love (1984)

A Fine Romance Shows within Shows (1989)

Fireball Fun for All Variety Programs (1949)

Fireball XL-5 Puppets (1963), Robots (1963)

Fired Up Cross Dressers (1997)

Firefly. Mediums (2002), Prostitutes (2001), Space (2002)

Firehouse African American (1973), Rescue (1974)

Fireside Theater Drama (1949)

The Firm Lawyers (1983)

First and Ten Los Angeles (1985), Nudity (1984)

First and Ten. The Bulls Are Back Nudity (1984)

First and Ten: Training Season Nudity (1984)

The First Bill Cosby Special African American (1968)

First Easter Rabbit Holiday Specials (1978)

The First Gentleman Politics (1994), Women — Extraordinary (1994)

The First Hundred Years Pilot Film Series (1963–1967), Series Based on Radio Programs (1950), Soap Operas (1950)

First Impressions Adolescence (1988)

First Love Soap Operas (1954)

First Monday Judges (2002), Physically Disabled (2002)

First Person Singular Drama (1953)

First Time Out California (1995), Latino American (1995), Psychiatrists (1995)

The First Year Broadway (1946)

Fish Adolescence (1977), New York (1977), Senior Citizens (1977)

Fish and Bernice Senior Citizens (1977)

Fit for a King Politics (1982)

Fitz and Bones Reporters (1981), San Francisco (1981)

Five Fingers Espionage (1959)
The Five Mrs. Buchanans Senior Citizens (1994)
Five's a Family Pilot Film Series (1961)
The Flamingo Kid Teenagers (1989)
Flamingo Road Cuban American (1981), Florida (1981), Prostitutes (1981), Soap Operas (Note)
Flannery and Quilt Senior Citizens (1976)
The Flash Men — Extraordinary (1990), Super Heroes (1990), Visually Impaired (1990)
Flash Gordon Aliens (1953), Series Based on Films (1953), Space (1953), Women — Extraordinary (1953)
Flatbed Annie and Sweetie Pie Truckers (1979)
Flatbush New York (1979)
Die Fledermaus Opera (1950)
Flesh 'n' Blood Baltimore (1991), District Attorneys (1991), Women — Scatterbrained (Note)
Flesh and Blood Broadway (1968)
The Flex Files Shows within Shows (2001)
The Fliers Pilots (1965)
Flight Pilots (1958)
Flight 29 Down Teenagers (2005)
Flight to Rhythm Latino American (1949), Variety Programs (1949)
The Flim-Flam Man Con Artists (1969), Pilot Film Series (1969)
Flintstone Kids Adolescence (1986)
The Flintstones Adolescence (1960), Adolescence (1986), Cars (1960), Cartoons (1960), Films Based on Television Series (1966), Films Based on Television Series (1994), Historical Settings (1960), Teenagers (1971), Television Firsts (1960)
The Flip Wilson Show African American (1970), Cross Dressers (1970)
Flipper Adolescence (1964), Animals (1964), Animals (1995), Beaches (1964), Beaches (1995), Florida (1964), Series Based on Films (1964)
Flipper: The New Adventures Animals (1964), Animals (1995), Beaches (1995), Florida (1995), Mermaids (1995)
Flo Bars (1980)
Flo's Place African American (1976), Restaurants (1976)
Floor Show Variety Programs (1949)
The Florian Zabach Show Variety Programs (1954)
Floyd Gibbons, Reporter Reporters (1962)
Flukey Luke Cartoons (1965)
Fly Away Home War — Korea, Vietnam, Iraq (1981)

Fly by Night Bars (1991), Canada (1991), Pilots (1991)
Flying Blind New York (1992)
The Flying Doctor Australia (1959), Pilots (1958)
Flying High Los Angeles (1979), Pilots (1978)
The Flying Nun Puerto Rican (1967), Religious Characters (1967)
FM Washington, D.C. (1989)
Foley Square District Attorneys (1986), Latino American (1984), New York (1985)
Folksay Ballet (1945), Television Firsts (1945)
The Follies of Suzy Variety and Drama Spectaculars (1954)
Follow That Man Men — Law Enforcers (1949)
Follow the Leader Game Shows (1953)
Follow the Sun Adventurers (1961), Beaches (1960), Hawaii (1960), Reporters (1961)
Follow Your Heart Soap Operas (1953)
Foodini the Great Puppets (1951)
Fools, Females and Fun Love (1974)
Foot in the Door Senior Citizens (1983)
Footlight Theater Drama (1952)
For Love and Honor Puerto Rican (1983)
For Love or Money Broadway (1952), Game Shows (1958)
For Lovers Only Love (1982)
For the Defense Lawyers (1954)
For the Love of Mike Doctors (1962), Pilot Film Series (1962), Pilot Film Series (1963–1967)
For the People District Attorneys (1965), New York (1965)
For Your Pleasure Variety Programs (1948)
Force 7 Martial Arts (1982)
The Ford 50th Anniversary Show Variety and Drama Spectaculars (1953)
Ford Festival Little People (1951), Variety Programs (1951)
Ford Star Revue Variety Programs (1950)
Ford Theater Series Based on Radio Programs (1952)
The Ford Theater Hour Broadway (1949)
Foreign Intrigue Espionage (1954)
Foreign Legionnaire Adolescence (1955)
Forest Rangers American Indian (1964), Canada (1965)
Forever Fernwood Ohio (1977), Soap Operas (Note)
Forever Knight Canada (1992), Vampires (1992)

Fort Figueroa Latino American (1988)
Fortune Dane California (1986)
The Fortune Hunter Broadway (1939), Broadway (1952)
The Fortunes and Misfortunes of Moll Flanders Nudity (1996)
Foul Play Little People (1981), San Francisco (1981), Series Based on Films (1981), Shows within Shows (1981), Twins (1981)
Four Eyes Women — Law Enforcers (1984)
413 Hope Street Latino American (1997), New York (1997)
The 416th War — Korea, Vietnam, Iraq (1979)
Four in Love Newspapers (1985)
Four Kings New York (2006)
The Four of Us Teenagers (1977)
The Four Seasons Los Angeles (1984), Series Based on Films (1984)
Four Star Playhouse Drama (1952), Nightclubs (1956)
The 4400 Aliens (2004)
The Fourth Annual Victoria's Secret Fashion Show Angels (1999)
The Fourth Wise Man Holiday Specials (1985)
The Fourth Wiseman Religious Programs (1984)
Fraggle Rock Puppets (1983)
Frances Langford Presents Variety Programs (1959)
The Frances Langford–Don Ameche Show Variety Programs (1951)
Frank Merriwell Pilot Film Series (1963–1967)
The Frank Sinatra Show Drama (1957), Variety Programs (1950), Variety Programs (1957)
Frank's Place Boston (1987)
Frankenstein Jr. and the Impossibles Cartoons (1966)
Frankie and Annette: The Second Time Around Housekeepers (1978)
Frankie Avalon's Easter Special Holiday Specials (1969)
Frankie Carle Time Variety Programs (1956)
The Frankie Laine Show Variety Programs (1954)
Frankie Laine Time Variety Programs (1954)
Frannie's Turn Cuban American (1992), New York (1992)
Frasier Bars (1993), Housekeepers (1993), Psychiatrists (1983, 1993), Restaurants (1993), Senior Citizens (1993), Shows within Shows (1993), Washington, D.C. (1993)
Freaks and Geeks Teenagers (1999)
Freakylinks The Supernatural (2001)
The Fred Waring Show Variety Programs (1949)

Fred Waring's Pleasure Time Variety Programs (1944)

Freddie Chicago (2005), Mexican American (2005), Teenagers (2005)

Freddy's Nightmares: A Nightmare on Elm Street the Series Drama (1988), Series Based on Films (1988), The Supernatural (1988)

Free Country Immigrants (1978), New York (1978)

Free Spirit Connecticut (1989), Housekeepers (1989), Teenagers (1989), Witches (1989)

Freebie and the Bean District Attorneys (1980), Mexican American (1980), Puerto Rican (1980), San Francisco (1980), Series Based on Films (1980)

Freedom Rings Game Shows (1953)

Freeman African American (1976), Ghosts (1976)

The Freewheelers Pilot Film Series (1963–1967)

The French Chef Cooking (1963), Cooking (1970)

The French Connection Men — Law Enforcers (1986)

The Fresh Prince of Bel Air California (1990), Housekeepers (1990), Judges (1990), Shows within Shows (1990), Teen After-School Hangouts (1990), Teenagers (1990), Women — Scatterbrained (1990)

Freshman Dorm Los Angeles (1992), Mexican American (1992)

Friday the 13th: The Series Devil (1987), Series Based on Films (1987), The Supernatural (1987)

Friends Adolescence (1979), Asian American (2004), Cross Dressers (1997), Lesbians (1994), Lesbians (2003), New York (1994), Nudity (1994), Physically Disabled (1994), Restaurants (1994), Robots (2002), Taxi Cabs (1994), Twins (1994)

The Frog Prince Fairy Tales (1977)

From a Bird's Eye View Pilots (1971), Women — Scatterbrained (1971)

From Here to Eternity American Indian (1980), Beaches (1980), Hawaii (1980), Historical Settings (1980), Latino American (1979), Series Based on Films (1980)

From These Roots Soap Operas (1958)

The Front Page Broadway (1945), Broadway (1952), Broadway (1970), Reporters (1949), Sitcoms (1950)

Front Page Detective New York (1951), Reporters (1951), Series Based on Radio Programs (1951)

Front Page Feeney Reporters (1977)

Front Page Story Drama (1959)

Front Row Center Drama (1955), Variety Programs (1949)

Frontier Drama (1955), Westerns (1955)

Frontier Doctor Arizona (1958), Doctors (1958), Westerns (1958)

Frontier Judge Judges (1956), Westerns (1956)

Frontier Justice Drama — Repeat Series (1958)

Frontierland Latino American (1958)

Frontiers of Faith Religious Programs (1951)

The Frontiersman Teachers (1960), Westerns (1960)

Frosty the Snowman Holiday Specials (1969), Holiday Specials (1976)

Frosty's Winter Wonderland Holiday Specials (1976), Holiday Specials (1979)

F-Troop American Indian (1965)

Fudge Adolescence (1995), New York (1995)

The Fugitive Films Based on Television Series (1993), Physically Disabled (1963), Physically Disabled (2000)

Full Circle Soap Operas (1960)

Full House Adolescence (1987), Aviators (1987), Cars (1987), Puppets (1987), San Francisco (1987), Twins (1993)

Fun for '51 Holiday Specials (1950)

The Funky Phantom Ghosts (1971)

Funny Boners Children's Program (1954), Puppets (1954)

The Funny Bunny Children's Program (1954)

Funny Face Hotels (1971), Los Angeles (1971), Teachers (1971), Visually Impaired (1972)

The Funny Manns Children's Program (1961)

The Furst Family of Washington African American (1973)

The Further Adventures of Ellery Queen Men — Law Enforcers (1958)

The Further Adventures of Spin and Marty Camps (1955)

Fury Adolescence (1955), Animals (1955)

Futurama Robots (1999)

Future Cop Men — Law Enforcers (1977), Robots (1977)

The Fuzz Brothers African American (1973)

FX: The Series New York (1997), Puerto Rican (1996), Series Based on Films (1997)

The G.E. College Bowl Game Shows (1959)

The G.I.'s War — World War II (1980)

G.L.O.W. Nudity (1987)

Gabriel's Fire Chicago (1990), Lawyers (1990), Men — Law Enforcers (1990)

Gabrielle Variety Programs (1948)

A Gala for the President at Ford's Theater Presidential Appearances (1994)

The Galaxy Goofups Space (1978)

The Gallant Men War — World War II (1963)

The Gallery of Mme. Liu Tsong Asian American (1951), Television Firsts (1951)

The Galloping Gourmet Cooking (1969)

Gamble on Love Game Shows (1954)

Gangbusters Drama (1951), Drama (1952), Series Based on Radio Programs (1952)

A Garfield Christmas Holiday Specials (1987)

Garfield's Thanksgiving Special Holiday Specials (1989)

Garrison's Gorillas War — World War II (1967)

Garroway at Large Series Based on Radio Programs (1949), Variety Programs (1949)

The Garry Moore Show Variety Programs (1950), Variety Programs (1958)

The Gary Coleman Show Angels (1982)

The Gate Cuban American (1996), Newspapers (1996), Women — Law Enforcers (2005)

Gaucho Puerto Rican (1978)

Gavilan Beaches (1982), California (1982), Latino American (1983)

Gay 90s Revue Variety Programs (1949)

The Gay Coed Sitcoms (1947)

Gemini Broadway (1982)

The Gemini Man Men — Extraordinary (1976)

The Gene Autry Show Animals (1951), Westerns (1951)

The General Electric Theater Clowns (1955), Drama (1953)

General Electric True Drama (1962)

The General Foods Summer Playhouse Pilot Film Series (1965)

General Hospital Soap Operas (1963)

The General Motors 50th Anniversary Show Variety and Drama Spectaculars (1957)

Generation X Super Heroes (1996)

Gentle Ben Adolescence (1967), Animals (1967), Florida (1967)

George Mexican American (1993)

George and Margaret Broadway (1952)

The George Burns and Gracie Allen Show California (1950), Los Angeles (1950), Nudity (1950), Series

Based on Radio Programs (1950), Sitcoms (1950), Women — Scatterbrained (1950)

George Burns Comedy Week Drama (1985)

George Burns Early, Early, Early Christmas Show Holiday Specials (1981)

The George Burns Show Los Angeles (1958), Sitcoms (1958)

The George Carlin Show Bars (1992), New York (1994), Taxi Cabs (1994)

The George Gobel Show Color Broadcasting (1957-1965), Variety Programs (1954), Variety Programs (1957)

The George Hamilton IV Show Variety Programs (1959)

The George Lopez Show Bars (2002), Cars (2002), Los Angeles (2002), Mexican American (2002), Nudity (2004), Teenagers (2002), Visually Impaired (2002)

George M! Broadway (1970)

George of the Jungle Cartoons (1967), Films Based on Television Series (1997)

The George Sanders Mystery Theater Drama (1957)

George Washington Politics (1984)

George Washington II: The Forging of a Nation Politics (1986)

The George Wendt Show Shows within Shows (1995)

The Georgia Peaches Government Agents (1980), Stock Car Racers (1980)

Gerald McBoing Boing Cartoons (1956)

Geraldo, Puerto Rican (1987)

Get a Life Newspapers (1990), Puppets (1990), Senior Citizens (1990)

Get Christie Love African American (1974), Los Angeles (1974), Restaurants (1974), Women — Law Enforcers (1974)

Get Smart Cars (1965), Espionage (1965), Espionage (1995), Gadgets(1965), Little People (1965), Physically Disabled (1965), Robots (1965), Washington, D.C. (1965)

Getting By Adolescence (1993), Chicago (1993)

Getting Together Adolescence (1971)

Ghost Game Shows (1952)

The Ghost and Mrs. Muir Adolescence (1968), Ghosts (1968), Housekeepers (1968)

Ghost Breaker Ghosts (1967), The Supernatural (1967)

The Ghost Busters Ghosts (1975), Ghosts (1986), Nudity (1975)

Ghost of a Chance Ghosts (1980)

The Ghost of Thomas Kemp Ghosts (1979)

Ghost Story Drama (1972), Ghosts (1973)

Ghost Whisperer Ghosts (2005), Mediums (2005), Nudity (2005)

Ghost Writer Adolescence (1992), Children — Extraordinary (1992), Ghosts (1992), Latino American (1992), New York (1992), Puerto Rican (1992), Reporters (1991)

The Ghost Writer Ghosts (1990), The Supernatural (1990)

Gia Nudity (1998), Television Firsts (1998)

The Giant Step Children's Program (1956)

Gianti Schicci Opera (1950)

Gibbsville Historical Settings (1976), Philadelphia (1976), Reporters (1976)

Gideon Oliver New York (1989), Teachers (1989)

Gideon's Crossing Boston (2000), Latino American (2001)

Gidget Beaches (1965), California (1965), Nudity (1965), Senior Citizens (1986), Series Based on Films (1965), Teenagers (1965)

Gift of the Magi. Holiday Specials (1958)

Gigantor Cartoons (1966), Robots (1966)

Gigglesnort Hotel Puppets (1979)

Gilligan's Island Beaches (1964), Beaches (2004), Color Broadcasting (1966), Geniuses (1964), Look-alikes (1964), Senior Citizens (1964)

Gilmore Girls Asian American (2000), Connecticut (2000), Housekeepers (2000), Lesbians (2004), Look-alikes (2005), Newspapers (2000), Restaurants (2000), Senior Citizens (2000), Teenagers (2000)

Gimme a Break Adolescence (1981), California (1981), Senior Citizens (1981), Teenagers (1981)

The Gin Game Broadway (1981), Broadway (2003)

The Ginger Rogers Show Pilot Film Series (1963–1967), Twins (1963), Variety and Drama Spectaculars (1958)

Girl About Town Variety Programs (1948)

A Girl, a Guy and a Pizza Place Boston (1998)

Girl Crazy Broadway (1999)

The Girl from U.N.C.L.E Espionage (1966), Gadgets(1966), New York (1966)

The Girl with E.S.P. Mediums (1979)

The Girl with Something Extra Los Angeles (1973), Mediums (1973)

Girl's Club San Francisco (2002)

A Girl's Life Psychiatrists (1989)

Girlfriends Bars (2005), Gays (2003, 2004), Lawyers (2000), Lesbians (2005), Los Angeles (2000), Nudity (2003), Restaurants (2000)

The Girls New York (1950), Sitcoms (1950)

Girls Club Lawyers (2002)

The Girls Next Door Nudity (2005)

The Gisele MacKenzie Show Variety Programs (1957)

Give Us Barabbas Religious Programs (1961)

Gladys Knight and the Pips African American (1975)

Gladys Knight and the Pips Midnight Train to Georgia African American (1974)

Glamour Girl Reality Programs (1953)

The Glass Menagerie Broadway (1966), Broadway (1973)

Glencannon Adventurers (1958)

Glitter Reporters (1983)

Gloria New York (1982), Senior Citizens (1982)

The Gloria DeHaven Show Variety Programs (1953)

Glory Days Newspapers (1990)

Glory of Easter Holiday Specials (1989)

The Glory Years Prostitutes (1987)

Glynis Lawyers (1963), Pilot Film Series (1963–1967), Women — Scatterbrained (1963)

Go for Broke Shows within Shows (1958)

The Go Go Gophers American Indian (1968), Cartoons (1968)

Go Lucky Game Shows (1951)

Go West Young Girl Westerns (1978)

God, the Devil and Bob Devil (2000)

God, the Universe and Hot Fudge Sundaes Religious Programs (1986)

Godzilla Series Based on Films (1978)

The Godzilla Power Hour Series Based on Films (1978)

Going Bananas Animals (1984)

Going My Way Housekeepers (1962), New York (1962), Religious Characters (1962), Series Based on Films (1962)

Going Places Los Angeles (1990), Shows within Shows (1990), Teenagers (1990)

Going to Extremes Latino American (1992), Teachers (1992)

The Goldbergs Hotels (1949), New York (1949), Series Based on Radio Programs (1949), Sitcoms

(1948), Sitcoms (1949), Teenagers (1949)

The Golddiggers Broadway (1952)

The Golden Child Opera (1960)

The Golden Girls Florida (1985), Hotels (1992), Senior Citizens (1985), Teachers (1985)

The Golden Palace Florida (1992), Hotels (1992), Mexican American (1992), Senior Citizens (1985)

Golden Windows Soap Operas (1954)

Goldie Sitcoms (1959)

Goldilocks and the Three Bears Fairy Tales (1982)

Gomer Pyle, U.S.M.C. Los Angeles (1964), Nightclubs (1964)

The Gong Show Reality Programs (1976)

Goober and the Trucker's Paradise Restaurants (1978)

Good Advice Los Angeles (1994)

Good and Evil San Francisco (1991), Speech Impaired (1991), Visually Impaired (1991), Washington, D.C. (1991)

Good Company New York (1996)

The Good Guys Beaches (1968), Los Angeles (1968), Restaurants (1968)

Good Heavens Angels (1976)

Good Life Chicago (1994)

The Good Life Housekeepers (1971)

Good Morning , Miami Cuban American (2001), Florida (2002), Religious Characters (2002)

Good Morning, Miss Bliss Adolescence (1988), Teachers (1988)

Good Morning, World Los Angeles (1967), Shows within Shows (1967), Women — "Dumb Blondes" (1967)

The Good Old Days Pilot Film Series (1963–1967)

Good Penny Mentally Disabled (1977)

Good Sports Los Angeles (1991), Shows within Shows (1990)

Good Time Harry Newspapers (1980)

Good Times Adolescence (1974), African American (1972), African American (1974), Chicago (1974), Hotels (1974), Taxi Cabs (1974), Teenagers (1974)

The Good Witch of Laurel Canyon Witches (1982)

Goodbye Doesn't Mean Forever Adolescence (1982)

The Goodbye Girl Adolescence (1982)

Goode Behavior Con Artists (1986), Restaurants (1996)

Goodnight, Beantown Boston (1983), Shows within Shows (1983), Teenagers (1983)

Goodtime Girls Historical Settings (1980)

Goodtime Harry San Francisco (1980)

The Goodyear Revue Variety Programs (1949)

Goodyear Theater Drama — Repeat Series (1956)

The Gook Family Sitcoms (1949)

Goosebumps Drama (1995)

The Gordon MacRae Show Variety Programs (1956)

Gossip Newspapers (1979)

The Gossip Columnist Newspapers (1980)

The Gourmet Cooking (1969)

The Gourmet Club Cooking (1958)

The Governor and J.J. Housekeepers (1969), Politics (1969)

Grace Under Fire Adolescence (1993), Cars (1993)

The Graduation Dress Pilot Film Series (1963–1967)

Grady Adolescence (1975), African American (1975), California (1975), Senior Citizens (1976)

The Grady Nutt Show Religious Characters (1981)

The Gramercy Ghost Broadway (1952)

Granby's Green Acres Series Based on Radio Programs (1965)

Grand Philadelphia (1980), Senior Citizens (1990)

The Grand Ole Opry Variety Programs (1955)

Grand Opera Opera (1940)

Grand Slam Mexican American (1990), Puerto Rican (1990)

The Grand Waltz Opera (1955)

Grandpa and Richie Senior Citizens (1972)

Grandpa Goes to Washington Politics (1978), Senior Citizens (1978), Washington, D.C. (1978)

Grandpa Max Senior Citizens (1975)

The Gray Ghost Civil War (1957)

Great Adventure Drama (1963)

Great Bible Adventures Pilot Film Series (1966), Religious Programs (1966)

Great Catherine Variety and Drama Spectaculars (1948)

Great Day Little People (1978)

The Great Defender Boston (1995), Latino American (1995), Lawyers (1995)

Great Ghost Tales Drama (1961), Ghosts (1961)

The Great Gildersleeve Housekeepers (1954), Sitcoms (1954), Teenagers (1954)

The Great Merlini Magicians (1951)

The Great Mysteries of Hollywood Drama (1981)

Great Scott Teenagers (1992)

Great War War — World War II (1964)

The Greatest American Hero Los Angeles (1981), Men — Extraordinary (1981), Mexican American (1981), Super Heroes (1981), Super Heroes (1983), Women — Extraordinary (1986)

The Greatest American Heroine Super Heroes (1983), Women — Extraordinary (1986)

The Greatest Gift Soap Operas (1954)

The Greatest Heroes of the Bible Religious Programs (1978)

The Greatest Man on Earth Game Shows (1952)

The Greatest Show on Earth Series Based on Films (1963)

Green Acres Animals (1965), Con Artists (1965), Country Folk (1965), Newspapers (1965), Reporters (1965), Senior Citizens (1965), Series Based on Radio Programs (1965)

The Green Felt Jungle District Attorneys (1965)

The Green Hornet Asian American (1966), Cars (1966), Housekeepers (1966), Martial Arts (1966), Men — Extraordinary (1966), Reporters (1966), Series Based on Radio Programs (1966), Super Heroes (1966), Washington, D.C. (1966)

The Green Pastures Religious Programs (1957)

Greetings from Tucson Arizona (2002), Mexican American (2002), Teenagers (2002)

Greg the Bunny Puppets (2002), Shows within Shows (2002), Vampires (2002)

The Gregory Hines Show Restaurants (1997)

Grey's Anatomy Asian American (2005), Doctors (2005), Lesbians (2006), Mentally Disabled (2005), Nudity (2005), Washington, D.C. (2005)

The Greyhounds Senior Citizens (1994)

Griff Los Angeles (1973), Men — Law Enforcers (1973)

Grindl Housekeepers (1963)

Grosse Pointe Lesbians (2001), Los Angeles (2000)

Grounded for Life Bars (2002), New York (2001), Teenagers (2001), Teenagers (2002)

Growing Pains Adolescence (1985), Cars (1985), New York (1985), Psychiatrists (1985), Reporters (1985), Teenagers (1985)

Growing Paynes Housekeepers (1948), Sitcoms (1948)

Grownups Lesbians (1999)

Gruen Guild Playhouse Drama (1951)

The Guardian Lawyers (2000)

The Guardsman Broadway (1952, 1955)

Guess Again Game Shows (1951)

Guess What Happened? Game Shows (1952)

Guess What? Game Shows (1952)

Guess Who's Coming to Dinner? African American (1975)

Guest in the House Broadway (1952)

A Guest in Your House Variety Programs (1951)

Guestward Ho Adolescence (1960), American Indian (1960), Hotels (1960), Sitcoms (1960)

The Guiding Light Series Based on Radio Programs (1952), Soap Operas (1952), Soap Operas (Note)

Guilty or Not Guilty District Attorneys (1966)

Gulf Playhouse Drama (1952)

Gumby Puppets (1957)

The Gun and the Pulpit Religious Characters (1974), Westerns (1974)

Gun Shy Adolescence (1982), Series Based on Films (1983), Westerns (1983)

Gung Ho Asian American (1987), Philadelphia (1986), Series Based on Films (1987)

Gunn Films Based on Television Series (1967)

The Guns of Paradise Adolescence (1988), American Indian (1988), Mentally Disabled (1988), Prostitutes (1988)

The Guns of Will Sonnett Senior Citizens (1967), Westerns (1967)

Gunslinger Westerns (1961)

Gunsmoke American Indian (1962), Bars (1955), Doctors (1955), Hotels (1955), Look-alikes (1972), Physically Disabled (1955), Restaurants (1955), Senior Citizens (1955), Series Based on Radio Programs (1955), Westerns (1955)

The Gus of Paradise Westerns (1987)

Guy Lombardo and His Royal Canadians Variety Programs (1954)

Guy Lombardo's New Year's Party Holiday Specials (1954)

The Guy Mitchell Show Variety Programs (1957)

Guys and Dolls: Off the Record Broadway (1992)

The Gypsy Rose Lee Show Variety Programs (1958)

The Gypsy Warriors War — World War II (1978)

H.E.L.P. Rescue (1990)

H.M.S. Pinafore Opera (1944)

H.R. Pufnstuf Puppets (1969), Puppets (1978), Witches (1969)

Hack Men — Law Enforcers (2002), Philadelphia (2002), Religious Characters (2003), Taxi Cabs (2002)

Hagen Housekeepers (1980)

Haggis Baggis Game Shows (1958)

Hail to the Champ Children's Program (1951)

Hail to the Chief Housekeepers (1985), Latino American (1984), Politics (1985), Religious Characters (1985), Teenagers (1985), Washington, D.C. (1985), Women — Extraordinary (1985)

Half 'n' Half Newspapers (1988)

Half and Half Gays (2002), San Francisco (2002)

Half-Hour on Broadway Broadway (1931), Television Firsts (1931)

Half Nelson California (1984), Little People (1985)

Half-Hour Theater Drama (1953)

Half-Pint Party Children's Program (1951)

The Hallmark Hall of Fame Angels (1969), Drama (1951), Hearing Impaired Characters (1958), Holiday Specials (1951), Opera (1951), Politics (1964, 1975), Religious Programs (1961, 1956), Series Based on Radio Programs (1951), Shakespeare (1953, 1954, 1956, 1957, 1960, 1970), Taxi Cabs (1978)

The Hallmark Hall of Fame Christmas Special Holiday Specials (1959)

The Halloween That Almost Wasn't Vampires (1979), Werewolves (1979)

Halloween Town Witches (1998)

Halloween Town II: Kalbar's Revenge Witches (1998)

Halloween Town III: Halloween High Witches (1998)

The Halls of Ivy Housekeepers (1954), Series Based on Radio Programs (1954), Sitcoms (1954), Teachers (1954)

Hamlet Shakespeare (1953), Shakespeare (1959), Shakespeare (1970)

Hamlet, Prince of Denmark Shakespeare (1980)

The Hamptons New York (1983)

Handle with Care Drama (1954), War — Korea, Vietnam, Iraq (1977), Women — Nurses (1976)

The Handler F.B.I. Agents (2003), Lesbians (2004), Los Angeles (2003)

Hands of Destiny Drama (1949)

Hands of Murder Drama (1949), Pilot Film Series (1949)

Hands of Mystery Drama (1949)

Hang Time Teenagers (1995)

Hanging In Housekeepers (1979)

The Hanging Judge Judges (1960), Westerns (1960)

Hanging with Mr. Cooper Adolescence (1993), California (1992), Teachers (1992)

Hank Adolescence (1965)

The Hank McCune Show Sitcoms (1949)

The Hanna-Barbera Happiness Hour Puppets (1978)

Hannah Montana Adolescence (2006)

Hannibal Cobb Men — Law Enforcers (1959)

Hansel and Gretel Fairy Tales (1958), Fairy Tales (1977), Fairy Tales (1982), Opera (1950), Variety and Drama Spectaculars (1958)

Happily Ever After Pilot Film Series (1961)

Happy Aviators (1960), Hotels (1960)

Happy Birthday Broadway (1956), Children's Program (1947)

Happy Days Adolescence (1974), Asian American (1977), Cars (1974), Historical Settings (1970), Historical Settings (1974), Newspapers (1974), Teen After-School Hangouts (1974), Teenagers (1974)

The Happy Face Murders Forensics(1999)

Happy Family Philadelphia (2003)

The Happy Journey Broadway (1939)

Hard Copy California (1987), Reporters (1987), Women — Law Enforcers (1987)

Hard Knocks Ghosts (1981)

Hard Time on Planet Earth Aliens (1989), Robots (1989)

Hardball Los Angeles (1989), Men — Law Enforcers (1989)

Hardcase Men — Law Enforcers (1981), Women — Law Enforcers (1981)

Hardcastle, Hardcastle and McCormick Senior Citizens (1985)

Hardcastle and McCormick Judges (1983), Los Angeles (1983)

Hardesty House Twins (1986)

The Hardy Boys Adolescence (1957), Men — Law Enforcers (1967), Men — Law Enforcers (1995)

The Hardy Boys and the Mystery of the Applegate Treasure Men — Law Enforcers (1957)

The Hardy Boys Mysteries Housekeepers (1977), Men — Law Enforcers (1977)

The Harlem Globetrotters Cartoons (1970)

The Harlem Globetrotters on Gilligan's Island Beaches (1964)

The Harlem Globetrotters Popcorn

Machine African American (1974)

Harper Valley Newspapers (1981), Series Based on Films (1981), Teenagers (1981)

Harper Valley U.S.A. Pilot Film Series (1969)

The Harper's Bazaar Fashion Parade Nudity (1944)

Harrigan and Son Lawyers (1960), Senior Citizens (1960), Sitcoms (1960)

Harris Against the World California (1964)

Harris and Company Teenagers (1979)

Harry Con Artists (1987), New York (1987), Women — Law Enforcers (1987)

Harry and Lena African American (1970)

Harry and the Hendersons Newspapers (1991), Teenagers (1991), Washington, D.C. (1991)

Harry Anderson's Side Show Magicians (1987)

Harry O Los Angeles (1974), Men — Law Enforcers (1974), Mexican American (1974), Physically Disabled (1974)

Harry's Battles Women — "Dumb Blondes" (1981)

Harry's Business Pilot Film Series (1961)

Hart to Hart Cars (1979), Housekeepers (1979), Los Angeles (1979), Senior Citizens (1979), Women — Law Enforcers (1979)

The Hartmans Sitcoms (1949)

Harts of the West American Indian (1993)

Harvey Broadway (1958), Broadway (1971), Variety and Drama Spectaculars (1958)

The Hasty Heart Broadway (1952), Broadway (1983)

The Hat Squad Los Angeles (1992), Men — Law Enforcers (1992), Mexican American (1992)

A Hatful of Rain Broadway (1968)

The Hathaways Animals (1961), Housekeepers (1961), Los Angeles (1961)

Haunted Ghosts (2002), Los Angeles (2002), Mediums (2000)

The Haunted Trailer Ghosts (1977)

The Haunting of Harrington House Ghosts (1981)

Have a Heart Game Shows (1955)

Have Faith Religious Characters (1989)

Have Girls, Will Travel Love (1964)

Have Gun — Will Travel Asian American (1957), Hotels (1957), San Francisco (1957), Series Based

on Radio Programs (1972), Westerns (1957)

Have I Got a Christmas for You Holiday Specials (1977)

Have Mercy Adolescence (1992)

Have You Ever Tried Talking to Patty? Hearing Impaired Characters (1986)

Having Babies II Nudity (1977), Television Firsts (1977)

Hawaii Beaches (2004), Hawaii (2004), Men — Law Enforcers (2004)

Hawaii Calls Hawaii (1966), Series Based on Radio Programs (1966)

Hawaii Five-0 Asian American (1968), Beaches (1968), Cars (1968), Hawaii (1968), Men — Law Enforcers (1968)

Hawaiian Eye Beaches (1959), Hawaii (1959), Hotels (1959), Men — Law Enforcers (1959), Women — Law Enforcers (1959)

Hawaiian Heat Asian American (1984), Beaches (1984), Hawaii (1984), Men — Law Enforcers (1984), Pilots (1984)

Hawk American Indian (1966), African American (1966), Men — Law Enforcers (1966), New York (1966)

Hawkeye American Indian (1994)

Hawkeye and the Last of the Mohicans American Indian (1957)

Hawkins Lawyers (1973)

Hawkins Falls, Population 6200 Soap Operas (1950)

Hay Fever Broadway (1939)

Hazel Adolescence (1961), Color Broadcasting (1957-1965), Housekeepers (1961), Housekeepers (1965), Senior Citizens (1961)

The Hazel Bishop Show Variety Programs (1951)

The Hazel Scott Show Variety Programs (1950)

Hazzard's People Lawyers (1976)

He and She New York (1967), Shows within Shows (1967), Women — Scatterbrained (1967)

Head of the Class Game Shows (1960), Latino American (1986), New York (1986), Teachers (1986), Teenagers (1986)

Head of the Family Shows within Shows (1960), Sitcoms (1960)

Head Over Heels Bars (1997), Florida (1997), Gays (1997), Love (1997)

Headmaster Teachers (1970)

The Healers Doctors (1974)

Hear No Evil Hearing Impaired Characters (1982)

Heart Beat{en}Doctors (1989), Lesbians (1988), Women — Nurses (1988)

Heart of the City Los Angeles (1986), nforcers (1986), Teenagers (1986)

Heartbreak House Broadway (1985)

Hearts Afire Lesbians (1992), Newspapers (1992), Politics (1992), Senior Citizens (1992), Washington, D.C. (1992)

Hearts Are Wild Hotels (1992), Las Vegas Settings (1992)

Heart's Island Restaurants (1985)

Hearts of Steel Restaurants (1986)

Heat of Anger Lawyers (1972)

Heave Ho Harrigan Pilot Film Series (1961)

Heaven and Hell Religious Programs (2001)

Heaven for Betsy New York (1952), Sitcoms (1952)

Heaven Help Us Angels (1994), Ghosts (1967), Latino American (1994), Pilot Film Series (1963–1967)

Heaven on Earth Angels (1979), Angels (1981)

Heaven Sent Angels (1981)

Heaven Will Protect the Working Girl Variety and Drama Spectaculars (1956)

Heavens to Betsy Sitcoms (1949)

Hec Ramsey Westerns (1972)

Heck's Angels Pilots (1976)

The Heckle and Jeckle Show Cartoons (1955)

The Hector Heathcote Show Cartoons (1963)

Hedda Gabler Broadway (1963)

Hee Haw Nightclubs (1978)

Hee Haw Honeys Nightclubs (1978)

Heidi Variety and Drama Spectaculars (1955)

Heist Los Angeles (2006), Men — Law Enforcers (2006), Mentally Disabled (2006), Senior Citizens (2006), Women — Law Enforcers (2006)

The Helen O'Connell Show Variety Programs (1957)

Hell Town Cars (1985), Los Angeles (1985), Religious Characters (1985)

The Hellcats Pilots (1967)

Hello Larry Senior Citizens (1979), Shows within Shows (1979), Teenagers (1979)

The Help Florida (2004), Housekeepers (2004)

He-Man and the Masters of the Universe Space (1983)

Hennessey California (1959), Sitcoms (1959), Women — Nurses (1959)

Henry Fonda Presents the Star and the Story Drama (1954)

Henry Hamilton, Graduate Ghost Ghosts (1984)

Henry Morgan's Great Talent Hunt Reality

Herb Shriner Time Variety Programs (1951)

Herbie, the Love Bug Cars (1982), Series Based on Films (1982), Teenagers (1982)

Hercule Poirot Men — Law Enforcers (1962)

Hercules: The Legendary Journeys Super Heroes (1994)

The Herculoids Cartoons (1967)

Here Come the Brides Historical Settings (1968), Washington, D.C. (1968)

Here Come the Double Deckers Adolescence (1970)

Here Comes Melinda Senior Citizens (1960)

Here Comes the Grump Cartoons (1969)

Here Comes Tobor Geniuses (1955), Robots (1955)

Here It Is, Burlesque Nudity (1981), Television Firsts (1981)

Here We Go Again Adolescence (1973), California (1973), Los Angeles (1973), Newspapers (1973), Restaurants (1973)

Hereafter Devil (1975)

Here's Click Opera (1944), Variety Programs (1944)

Here's Looking at You Shows within Shows (1990)

Here's Lucy Los Angeles (1968), Teenagers (1968), Women — Scatterbrained (1968)

Here's the Show Variety Programs (1955)

Herman's Head Bars (1991), Lesbians (1991), New York (1991)

Hernandez, Houston P.D. Mexican American (1973)

Herndon and Me Geniuses (1983)

The Hero Los Angeles (1966), Shows within Shows (1966)

Herod the Great Religious Programs (2001)

He's the Mayor Politics (1986)

Hewitt's Just Different Mentally Disabled (1977)

Hey Dude Arizona (1989), Camps (1989)

Hey Verne, It's Ernest Robots (1988)

Hey Jeannie New York (1956), Sitcoms (1956), Taxi Cabs (1956)

Hey Landlord! Hotels (1966), New York (1966)

Hey Mack Hotels (1957)

Hey Mulligan Los Angeles (1954), Sitcoms (1954)

Hey Teacher Pilot Film Series (1963–1967), Teachers (1964)

Hi Honey, I'm Home New Jersey (1991), Teenagers (1991)

Hi Mom Puppets (1957)

Hiawatha Fairy Tales (1958)

Hickey vs. Anybody Lawyers (1976)

Hickory Hideout Puppets (1985)

Hidden Faces Soap Operas (1968)

Hidden Videos Reality Programs (1989)

Hide and Seek Pilot Film Series (1963–1967)

High Button Shoes Variety and Drama Spectaculars (1956)

The High Chaparral Arizona (1967), Westerns (1967)

High Chaparral Mexican American (1967)

High Feather Camps (1980)

High Finance Game Shows (1956)

High Low Game Shows (1957)

High Mountain Rangers American Indian (1988), Rescue (1988)

High Performance Martial Arts (1983), Women — Extraordinary (1983)

High School, U.S.A. Teachers (1983), Teachers (1984)

High Sierra Search and Rescue Rescue (1995)

High Society New York (1995)

High Thor Broadway (1956), Variety and Drama Spectaculars (1956)

Highcliffe Manor Housekeepers (1979), Latino American (1979), Robots (1979)

Higher and Higher, Attorneys at Law Lawyers (1968), Pilot Film Series (1968)

Higher Ground Pilots (1988)

Highlander: The Raven Physically Disabled (1998), Women — Extraordinary (1998)

Highlander: The Series Men — Extraordinary (1992), Physically Disabled (1992), Series Based on Films (1992)

Highway Honeys Truckers (1983)

Highway Patrol Men — Law Enforcers (1956)

Highway to Heaven Angels (1984), Cars (1984)

The Highwayman Truckers (1988)

Hill Street Blues Latino American (1981), Men — Law Enforcers (1982), Puerto Rican (1981)

The Hillbilly Bears Cartoons (1968)

Hiller and Diller Adolescence (1997), Shows within Shows (1997)

His and Hers Adolescence (1984), Los Angeles (1990), Psychiatrists (1990)

His Honor, Homer Bell Housekeepers (1955), Judges (1956)

His Model Wife Pilot Film Series (1963–1967)

The History of Rock and Roll Presidential Appearances (1995)

Hitched Love (2005), Westerns (1973)

The Hitchhiker Drama (1983), Nudity (1984)

The Hitchhiker's Guide to the Galaxy Aliens (1982), Robots (1982)

Hizzoner Housekeepers (1979), Politics (1979)

Hobby Lobby Reality Programs (1959), Senior Citizens (1952), Series Based on Radio Programs (1959)

The Hogan Family Teenagers (1986), Twins (1986), Visually Impaired (1972)

Hogan's Heroes African American (1965), Camps (1965), Prison (1965), Prison (1967)

Hokey Wolf Cartoons (1958)

Hold 'er Newt Puppets (1950)

Hold Me Broadway (1981)

Hold That Camera Game Shows (1950)

Hold That Note Game Shows (1957)

Holiday Variety and Drama Spectaculars (1956)

Holiday Hotel Hotels (1950)

Holiday in Las Vegas Variety and Drama Spectaculars (1957)

Holiday in Spring Variety and Drama Spectaculars (1948)

Holiday Lodge Hotels (1961), New York (1961)

Holiday Star Revue Variety and Drama Spectaculars (1948)

Holloway's Daughters Men — Law Enforcers (1966), Teenagers (1966), Women — Law Enforcers (1966)

Hollywood Beat American Indian (1985), Los Angeles (1985), Men — Law Enforcers (1985)

Hollywood Junior Circus Clowns (1951)

Hollywood Off Beat Lawyers (1953), Men — Law Enforcers (1952)

Hollywood Opening Night Drama (1951)

Hollywood Sarr Women — Law Enforcers (1985)

Hollywood Screen Test Drama (1948)

Hollywood Showcase Drama — Repeat Series (1966)

Hollywood Sings Variety and Drama Spectaculars (1960)

Hollywood Squares Senior Citizens (1952)

Hollywood Talent Scouts Reality Programs (1962)

Hollywood Television Theater Drama (1970)

Holmes and Yoyo Los Angeles (1976), Men — Law Enforcers (1976), Robots (1976)

Home Teenagers (1987)

Home Again Cuban American (1978), Restaurants (1988)

Home Cooking. Restaurants (1975)

The Home Court Chicago (1995), Judges (1995)

Home Fires Psychiatrists (1992), Teenagers (1992)

Home Free Los Angeles (1993), Mexican American (1988), Reporters (1993)

The Home Front Historical Settings (1991)

Home Improvement Cars (1991), Shows within Shows (1991)

Home on the Range Cooking (1948)

Home Town Series Based on Films (1985)

Homeboys in Outer Space Space (1996)

Homemaker's Exchange Cooking (1950)

Homeroom Teenagers (1981)

Homicide: Life on the Street Baltimore (1993), Men — Law Enforcers (1993)

Hondo American Indian (1967), Arizona (1967), Series Based on Films (1967), Westerns (1967)

Honestly, Celeste! Newspapers (1954), Reporters (1954), Sitcoms (1954)

Honey I Shrunk the Kids: The TV Series Geniuses (1997), Lawyers (1997), Men — Extraordinary (1997), Mermaids (1997), Series Based on Films (1997), Teenagers (1997)

Honey West Gadgets(1965), Hotels (1965), Los Angeles (1965), Women — Law Enforcers (1965)

Honeymoon Suite Hotels (1973), Love (1973)

The Honeymooners Films Based on Television Series (2005), Hotels (1955), Mentally Disabled (1955), New York (1955), Sitcoms (1936), Sitcoms (1955), Television Firsts (1936)

Hong Kong Asian American (1960), Reporters (1960), Restaurants (1960)

The Hoofer Pilot Film Series (1963–1967)

Hooperman Gays (1987), Men — Law Enforcers (1987), San Francisco (1987), Women — Law Enforcers (1987)

Hooray for Hollywood Pilot Film Series (1963–1967)

Hooray for Love Pilot Film Series (1963–1967)

Hopalong Cassidy Series Based on Films (1948), Series Based on Radio Programs (1949)

Hope and Faith Lesbians (2004), Nudity (2004), Ohio (2003), Shows within Shows (2005), Teenagers (2003), Women — "Dumb Blondes" (2003)

Hope and Gloria Philadelphia

(1995), Shows within Shows (1995)

Hope Division Men — Law Enforcers (1987), Women — Law Enforcers (1987)

The Horace Heidt Show Reality Programs (1950)

Hot Beaches (1995)

Hot l Baltimore Baltimore (1975), Hotels (1975), Prostitutes (1974)

Hot Properties Latino American (2005), New York (2005)

Hot Prospects Restaurants (1989)

Hot Pursuit Look-alikes (1984)

Hot Shots Reporters (1986)

Hot Wheels Cartoons (1969), Stock Car Racers (1969)

Hotel Hotels (1983), San Francisco (1983)

Hotel Broadway Hotels (1949)

Hotel Cosmopolitan Hotels (1957)

Hotel De Paree Hotels (1959), Westerns (1959)

Hotel Malibu Beaches (1994), Hotels (1994), Mexican American (1994)

Hothouse Psychiatrists (1988)

Hotpoint Holiday Holiday Specials (1949)

Hour Glass Drama (1952)

Hour of Stars Drama — Repeat Series (1958)

House Doctors (2004), New Jersey (2005), Physically Disabled (2004)

House Calls Los Angeles (1979), Women — Nurses (1979)

House of Buggin Latino American (1995)

The House of Seven Gables Fairy Tales (1960)

House of Style Cuban American (1992)

The House on High Street Judges (1959), Soap Operas (1959), Soap Operas (Note)

House Party Series Based on Radio Programs (1952)

The House Without a Christmas Tree Holiday Specials (1972)

Houston Knights Latino American (1987), Men — Law Enforcers (1987), Physically Disabled (1987), Women — Law Enforcers (1987)

How Do You Rate? Game Shows (1958)

How the West Was Won Series Based on Films (1977), Westerns (1977)

How to Marry a Millionaire Hotels (1958), New York (1958), Newspapers (1958), Series Based on Films (1958), Shows within Shows (1958), Sitcoms (1958), Women — "Dumb Blondes" (1958)

Howdy Doody American Indian (1947), Children's Program (1947), Clowns (1947), Puppets (1947),

Senior Citizens (1947), Twins (1947)

The Huckleberry Hound Show Cartoons (1958)

Hudson Street Men — Law Enforcers (1995), New Jersey (1995)

Hughie Broadway (1981)

The Hughleys Adolescence (1998), California (1998), Cars (1998), Visually Impaired (1998)

Hull High Teachers (1990), Teenagers (1990)

The Human Comedy Pilot Film Series (1963–1967), Teenagers (1964)

The Human Factor Doctors (1992)

Human Feelings Religious Programs (1978)

The Human Jungle Psychiatrists (1964)

Human Target Men — Extraordinary (1992)

The Human Target Pilots (1992)

Hunter Australia (1968), Espionage (1977), Los Angeles (1984), Los Angeles (2002), Men — Law Enforcers (1984), Men — Law Enforcers (2003), Women — Law Enforcers (1984)

The Hunter Cartoons (1960), Espionage (1952)

The Huntley-Brinkley Report News Broadcasts (1951, 1956), Television Firsts (1965)

Huntress Women — Extraordinary (2000)

Hurdy Gurdy Historical Settings (1967)

Hurricane Sam Adolescence (1990), Geniuses (1990)

Husbands California (1978)

I and Claudie Con Artists (1964), Pilot Film Series (1963–1967)

I Believe in Christmas Holiday Specials (1977)

I Claudius Nudity (1976)

I Cover Times Square New York (1950), Reporters (1950)

I Dream of Jeannie Color Broadcasting (1966), Films Based on Television Series (2006), Florida (1965), Genies(1965), Look-alikes (1965), Look-alikes (1969), Nudity (1965), Senior Citizens (1965)

I Had Three Wives California (1985), Latino American (1984), Los Angeles (1985), Men — Law Enforcers (1985), Reporters (1985)

I Hear America Singing Variety and Drama Spectaculars (1955)

I Led Three Lives Espionage (1953), Series Based on Radio Programs (1953)

I Like It Here Broadway (1952)

I Love a Mystery Men — Law Enforcers (1973)

I Love Her Anyway! Women — Scatterbrained (1981)

I Love Lucy Adolescence (1953), Cuban American (1951), Hotels (1952), New York (1952), Nightclubs (1951), Restaurants (1952), Series Based on Radio Programs (1972), Sitcoms (1951), Television Firsts (1952), Television Firsts (1954), Women — Scatterbrained (1951)

I Love My Doctor Doctors (1962), Pilot Film Series (1963–1967)

I-Man Government Agents (1986)

I Married a Dog Pilot Film Series (1961)

I Married Dora Hotels (1987), Housekeepers (1987), Immigrants (1987), Latino American (1987), Los Angeles (1987), Senior Citizens (1987), Teenagers (1987), Women — "Dumb Blondes" (1987)

I Married Joan Judges (1952), Los Angeles (1952), Sitcoms (1952)

I Remember Caviar Sitcoms (1959), Sitcoms (1960)

I Remember Mama Immigrants (1949), Series Based on Films (1949), Sitcoms (1949)

I Search for Adventure Adventurers (1954), Reality Programs (1954)

I Spy African American (1965), Color Broadcasting (1966), Espionage (1956), Espionage (1965)

I Was a Bloodhound Men — Law Enforcers (1959)

I Was a Communist for the FBI Series Based on Radio Programs (1953)

I Was an MTV V.J Cuban American (1992)

Ichabod and Me Housekeepers (1961), Newspapers (1961)

I'd Rather be Calm Bars (1982)

The Ida Lupino Theater Drama (1956)

If I Had a Million Drama (1973)

If I Lost You, Am I Trapped Forever? Twins (1974)

If Men Played Cards As Women Do Broadway (1936), Broadway (1945)

I'll Never Forget What's Her Name Mexican American (1976), Puerto Rican (1976)

The Ilona Massey Show Variety Programs (1954)

I'm a Big Girl Now Adolescence (1980), Newspapers (1980)

I'm Dickens, He's Fenster Los Angeles (1962)

I'm the Law Men — Law Enforcers (1953)

I'm with Her Los Angeles (2003), Teachers (2003)

I-Man Men — Extraordinary (1986)

The Immortal Men — Extraordinary (2000)

The Imperial Grand Band Hotels (1975)

In Common Game Shows (1954)

In Like Flynn Women — Extraordinary (1985)

In Living Color Clowns (1990), Cross Dressers (1990), Gays (1990), Physically Disabled (1990), Rescue (1990)

In Performance at the White House Presidential Appearances (1988)

In the Beginning Adolescence (1978), Latino American (1978), Religious Characters (1978)

In the Dead of Night Ghosts (1969), The Supernatural (1969)

In the Doghouse Sitcoms (1950)

In the Heat of the Night Men — Law Enforcers (1988), Restaurants (1988), Senior Citizens (1988)

In the House Adolescence (1995), Los Angeles (1995)

In the Kelvinator Kitchen Cooking (1947)

In the Lion's Den Puppets (1987)

In the Morgan Manner Variety Programs (1950)

In Trouble Teenagers (1981)

The Ina Ray Hutton Show Nudity (1956), Variety Programs (1956)

Inaugural Eve Gala Performance Presidential Appearances (1977)

Inch High, Private Eye Little People (1973)

Inconceivable Asian American (2005)

The Incredible Hulk Hearing Impaired Characters (1978), Men — Extraordinary (1978), Speech Impaired (1977), Super Heroes (1965, 1978), The Supernatural (1978)

The Incredible Hulk and the Amazing Spider-Man Super Heroes (1982)

The Incredible Ida Early Angels (1987)

Indemnity, Man Against Crime, Man on a Raft, The Virginian Pilot Film Series (1958)

The Indian Captive Fairy Tales (1960)

The Infiltrator Pilot Film Series (1987)

Information Please Game Shows (1950), Series Based on Radio Programs (1952)

Inherit the Wind Broadway (1965)

Injustice Lawyers (2006), Los Angeles (2006)

The In-Laws New York (2002)

The Inner Flame Soap Operas (1954)

The Inner Sanctum Drama (1954)

Innocent Jones Pilot Film Series (1961), Reporters (1961)

The Inquisitor Newspapers (1995)

The Inside Bars (2005), F.B.I. Agents (2005), Los Angeles (2005), Mediums (2005)

Inside O.U.T. Government Agents (1971)

Inside Scoop Reporters (1991), Shows within Shows (1991)

Inside the White House Presidential Appearances (1995)

Inside U.S.A. with Chevrolet Variety Programs (1949)

The Insiders Reporters (1985)

Insight Religious Programs (1960)

The Inspector Men — Law Enforcers (1995)

Inspector Fabian of Scotland Yard Men — Law Enforcers (1955)

Inspector Gadget Robots (1983)

Inspector Mark Saber Series Based on Radio Programs (1951)

Inspector Perez Men — Law Enforcers (1983), Puerto Rican (1983)

Instant Family Adolescence (1977)

International Airport Pilots (1985)

International Detective Men — Law Enforcers (1959)

The Interns African American (1970), Doctors (1970), Los Angeles (1970)

Intertect Men — Law Enforcers (1973)

Into the West American Indian (2005), Westerns (2005)

Intrigue Government Agents (1988)

The Invaders Aliens (1967)

Invasion Aliens (2005)

The Investigator Men — Law Enforcers (1958), New York (1958)

The Investigators Men — Law Enforcers (1961), New York (1961)

The Invisible Man Los Angeles (1975), Men — Extraordinary (1958), Mexican American (1975)

The Invisible Woman Women — Extraordinary (1983)

The Ireene Wicker Show Children's Program (1946)

Ireene Wicker Sings Variety Programs (1939)

Ireene Wicker's Story Time Children's Program (1953)

Iron Chef Cooking (1970)

Iron Horse Westerns (1966)

Iron Man Super Heroes (1965)

Ironside African American (1967), Physically Disabled (1967), San Francisco (1967)

Irving Berlin's Salute to America, Variety and Drama Spectaculars (1951)

Isabel Sanford's Honeymoon Hotel Hotels (1987), Love (1987)

Isis California (1975), Super Heroes (1975), Women — Extraordinary (1975)

Isis and the Freedom Force Super Heroes (1980)

Island Son Beaches (1990), Doctors (1990), Hawaii (1990)

Island Sons Beaches (1987)

The Islander Beaches (1978), Hotels (1978)

The Islanders Asian American (1960), Beaches (1960), Pilots (1960)

Islands in the Sun Beaches (1969), Mermaids (1969)

It Could Be You Game Shows (1958)

It Had to Be You Boston (1993)

It Happened in Spain Latino American (1958), Men — Law Enforcers (1958)

It Pays to Advertise Broadway (1952)

It Pays to Be Ignorant Series Based on Radio Programs (1949)

It Pays to Be Married Game Shows (1955)

It Takes a Thief Con Artists (1968), Washington, D.C. (1968)

It Takes Two District Attorneys (1982), Doctors (1982), New York (1982), Psychiatrists (1985), Senior Citizens (1982)

It's a Bird, It's a Plane, It's Superman Broadway (1975)

It's a Boy Broadway (1952)

It's a Gift Game Shows (1946)

It's a Great Life Sitcoms (1954)

It's a Living Los Angeles (1981), Restaurants (1980)

It's a Man's World Teenagers (1962)

It's a Miracle Drama (1998)

It's About Time Game Shows (1954), Historical Settings (1966), Teenagers (1966)

It's All Relative Bars (2003), Boston (2003), Gays (2003)

It's Always Jan Hotels (1955), New York (1955), Nightclubs (1955), Sitcoms (1955)

It's Always Sunday Religious Characters (1956)

It's Higgins, Sir Series Based on Radio Programs (1962)

It's Magic Magicians (1955)

It's News to Me Game Shows (1951)

It's Only Human Reality Programs (1981)

It's Rod Hull and Emu Puppets (1973)

It's Science Time Shows within Shows (1990)

It's the Easter Beagle, Charlie Brown Holiday Specials (1974)

It's Your Move California (1984), Teenagers (1984)

Ivan the Terrible Cuban American (1976), Hotels (1976), Teenagers (1976)

Ivanhoe Historical Settings (1957)

I've Got a Secret Game Shows (1952)

Jack and Bobby Lesbians (2004)

Jack and Mike Chicago (1986), Newspapers (1986)

Jack and the Beanstalk Children's Program (1941), Fairy Tales (1941), Fairy Tales (1967), Fairy Tales (1982), Television Firsts (1941), Variety and Drama Spectaculars (1956)

The Jack Benny Christmas Special Holiday Specials (1966)

The Jack Benny Program African American (1950), California (1950), Cars (1950), Housekeepers (1950), Los Angeles (1950), Mexican American (1950), Series Based on Radio Programs (1950), Sitcoms (1950)

The Jack Carson Show Variety Programs (1954)

Jack Carter and Company Variety Programs (1949)

The Jack Carter Show Variety Programs (1950)

The Jack Cole Dancers Variety Programs (1939)

Jack Frost Holiday Specials (1980)

Jack of All Trades Bars (2000), Cross Dressers (2000), Little People (2000), Men — Extraordinary (2000), Puppets (2000), Women — Extraordinary (2000)

The Jack Paar Show Presidential Appearances (1960)

Jackie and Darlene Women — Law Enforcers (1978)

Jackie Gleason and His American Scene Magazine Bars (1962)

The Jackie Gleason Show Variety Programs (1952)

The Jackie Thomas Show Los Angeles (1992)

Jack's Place Bars (1992)

Jackson and Jill New York (1949), Sitcoms (1949)

The Jacksons African American (1976)

Jacques Fray's Music Room Variety Programs (1949)

Jacques Pepin: Fast Food My Way Cooking (1970)

JAG Physically Disabled (2002), Visually Impaired (1995)

Jake 2.0 Men — Extraordinary (2003), Washington, D.C. (2003)

Jake and the Fatman Beaches (1988), California (1987), District Attorneys (1987), Hawaii (1988)

Jake in Progress Magicians (2005), New York (2005), Nudity (2005)

Jake Lassiter: Justice on the Bayou Lawyers (1995)

Jake's Way Men — Law Enforcers (1980)

Jambo Animals (1969), Children's Program (1969)

Jamboree Variety Programs (1950)

James at 15 Boston (1977), Teenagers (1977)

James at 16 Boston (1978), Teenagers (1977)

James Beard Cooking (1963)

The James Boys Adolescence (1982)

Jamie Adolescence (1953), Senior Citizens (1953), Sitcoms (1953)

The Jamie Foxx Show Hotels (1996)

The Jan Murray Show Variety Programs (1955)

Jane Nudity (1989), Women — Extraordinary (1989)

Jane Doe Women — Extraordinary (2005)

Jane Eyre Variety and Drama Spectaculars (1939)

Jane Froman's U.S.A. Canteen Variety Programs (1952)

The Jane Pickens Show Variety Programs (1954)

The Jane Wyman Theater Drama (1956)

Janet Dean, Registered Nurse Women — Extraordinary (1954), Women — Nurses (1954)

Janie Broadway (1952)

Jarrett Men — Law Enforcers (1973)

Jason of Star Command Space (1979)

The Jaye P. Morgan Show Variety Programs (1956)

The Jazz Singer Broadway (1952), Variety and Drama Spectaculars (1959)

Jean Arthur Show California (1966)

The Jean Arthur Show Lawyers (1966)

The Jean Carroll Show Sitcoms (1953)

Jeannie Genies (1973)

Jed Clayton, U.S. Marshal Shows within Shows (1966)

Jeff Corwin Unleashed Animals (2004)

The Jeff Foxworthy Show Adolescence (1995)

Jeff's Collie Senior Citizens (1954)

Jefferson Drum Newspapers (1958), Westerns (1958)

The Jeffersons African American (1971), African American (1975), Housekeepers (1976), New York (1975), Senior Citizens (1975), Television Firsts (1975)

Jekyll and Hyde Broadway (2005)

Jennifer Slept Here California (1983), Ghosts (1983), Teenagers (1983)

Jenny California (1997), Los Angeles (1997)

Jenny Kissed Me Broadway (1952)
Jeopardy Geniuses (2002), Television Firsts (2004), Television Firsts (2005)
Jeremiah of Jacob's Neck Ghosts (1976)
Jericho Color Broadcasting (1966), War — World War II (1966), Westerns (1961)
The Jerry Colonna Show Variety Programs (1951)
The Jerry Lester Show Variety Programs (1953)
Jerry Mahoney's Clubhouse Puppets (1954)
The Jerry Springer Show Nudity (1991)
Jesse Cars (1998), New York (1998), Speech Impaired (1998), Women — Nurses (1998)
Jessica Novak Los Angeles (1981), Reporters (1981), Shows within Shows (1981)
Jessie Psychiatrists (1984), San Francisco (1984)
Jesus Christ, Superstar Broadway (2001)
Jesus — Holy Child Religious Programs (2001)
Jesus of Nazareth Religious Programs (1977)
The Jetsons Adolescence (1962), Cartoons (1962), Robots (1962), Teenagers (1962)
Jetsons: The Movie Films Based on Television Series (1990)
Jigsaw John Los Angeles (1976), Men — Law Enforcers (1976)
Jim and Judy in Teleland Cartoons (1953)
The Jim Backus Show — Hot Off the Wire Newspapers (1960), Sitcoms (1960)
The Jim Henson Hour Puppets (1989)
The Jimmie Rodgers Show Variety Programs (1959)
The Jimmy Dean Show Puppets (1963)
The Jimmy Durante Show Pilot Film Series (1963–1967), Senior Citizens (1964)
Jimmy Hughes, Rookie Cop Men — Law Enforcers (1953), New York (1953)
The Jimmy Stewart Show Teachers (1971)
The Jo Stafford Show Variety Programs (1954)
The Joan Edwards Show Variety Programs (1950)
Joan of Arcadia Angels (2003), Nudity (2004), Physically Disabled (2003), Religious Programs (2003), Teachers (2003), Teenagers (2003)

Joan of Arkansas Women — Scatterbrained (1958)
Joanie Loves Chachi Chicago (1983)
The Job Men — Law Enforcers (2001), New York (2001)
Joe and Mabel New York (1955), Nudity (1955), Restaurants (1956), Series Based on Radio Programs (1955), Sitcoms (1955), Taxi Cabs (1955), Women — Scatterbrained (1955)
Joe and Sons New Jersey (1975), Teenagers (1975)
Joe Bash Men — Law Enforcers (1986), New York (1986)
Joe Dancer Men — Law Enforcers (1981)
The Joe DiMaggio Show Children's Program (1950)
Joe Forrester Los Angeles (1975), Men — Law Enforcers (1975)
The Joe Palooka Story Series Based on Radio Programs (1954)
Joe's Life New York (1993), Teenagers (1993)
Joe's World Teenagers (1979)
Joey Asian American (2004), Lesbians (2005), Los Angeles (2004), Shows within Shows (2004)
The Joey Bishop Show Housekeepers (1962), Los Angeles (1962), New York (1961), Senior Citizens (1961), Shows within Shows (1962)
Joey Faye's Frolics Sitcoms (1950)
John Conte's Little Show Variety Programs (1950)
John Curry's Ice Dancing Broadway (1981)
The John Davidson Christmas Show Holiday Specials (1976), Holiday Specials (1977)
John Denver and the Muppets: A Christmas Together Holiday Specials (1980)
John Denver's Rocky Mountain Christmas Holiday Specials (1975)
John Doe Geniuses (2002), Men — Law Enforcers (2002), Visually Impaired (2002), Washington, D.C. (2002), Women — Law Enforcers (2002)
The John Forsythe Show California (1965), Senior Citizens (1965), Teachers (1965)
John Forsythe's World of Survival Animals (1987)
John Grin's Christmas Holiday Specials (1986)
The John Larroquette Show Bars (1993), Mexican American (1993), Prostitutes (1993)
John Schneider's Christmas Holiday Holiday Specials (1983)
Johnny and the Sprites Puppets (2005)
Johnny Appleseed Fairy Tales (1985)

Johnny Belinda Broadway (1955), Broadway (1958), Broadway (1967), Broadway (1982), Hearing Impaired Characters (1955), Hearing Impaired Characters (1958), Hearing Impaired Characters (1967)
The Johnny Carson Show Variety Programs (1955)
The Johnny Cash 10th Anniversary Christmas Special Holiday Specials (1985)
A Johnny Cash Christmas Holiday Specials (1979), Holiday Specials (1980)
A Johnny Cash Christmas 1983 Holiday Specials (1983)
The Johnny Cash Christmas Show Holiday Specials (1977)
Johnny Cash: Christmas on the Road Holiday Specials (1984)
Johnny Cash's Christmas in Scotland Holiday Specials (1981)
Johnny Cash — A Merry Memphis Christmas Holiday Specials (1982)
Johnny Come Lately Pilot Film Series (1960), Reporters (1960)
Johnny Dugan Show Variety Programs (1952)
Johnny Guitar Westerns (1959)
The Johnny Johnston Show Variety Programs (1951)
Johnny Jupiter Aliens (1953), Puppets (1953), Robots (1953)
Johnny Midnight Asian American (1960), Housekeepers (1960), Latino American (1960), Men — Law Enforcers (1960), New York (1960)
Johnny Nighthawk Pilots (1958)
Johnny Olsen's Rumpus Room Series Based on Radio Programs (1949), Variety Programs (1949)
Johnny Ringo Arizona (1959), Westerns (1959)
Johnny Sokko and His Flying Robot Robots (1968)
Johnny Staccato Men — Law Enforcers (1959), New York (1959)
The Jones Boys Pilot Film Series (1963–1967)
Jonny Zero New York (2005)
Joseph in Egypt Religious Programs (1978)
Joseph Schildkraut Presents Drama (1954)
Josephine McCarthy Cooking (1953)
Joshua's World Doctors (1980), Housekeepers (1980)
Josie and the Pussycats Cartoons (1970), Films Based on Television Series (2001), Teenagers (1970), Women — "Dumb Blondes" (1970)
Josie and the Pussycats in Outer Space Women — "Dumb Blondes" (1970)
Journey to the Center of the Earth

Cartoons (1967), Series Based on Films (1967)
Journey to the Unknown Drama (1968)
Journey's End Broadway (1983)
Jubilee, U.S.A. Variety Programs (1955)
Judd for the Defense Lawyers (1967)
The Judge Judges (1963), Judges (1986)
Judge Alex Judges (2005)
The Judge and Jake Wyler Judges (1972)
Judge Dee in the Monastery Murders Judges (1974)
Judge Hatchett Judges (2004)
Judge Joe Brown Judges (1998)
Judge Judy Judges (1996)
Judge Mathis Judges (1999)
Judge Mills Lane Judges (1997)
Judge Roy Bean Color Broadcasting (1955), Judges (1955), Westerns (1955)
Judge Wopner's Animal Court Judges (1997)
Judging Amy Connecticut (1999), Judges (1999), Senior Citizens (1999)
Judgment Day Devil (1981), Judges (1981)
The Judy Garland Show Variety and Drama Spectaculars (1955), Variety and Drama Spectaculars (1956)
Judy Splinters Puppets (1949)
The Juggler of Notre Dame Holiday Specials (1982)
Juke Box Jury Series Based on Radio Programs (1953)
Julia Adolescence (1968), African American (1968), Los Angeles (1968), Senior Citizens (1968), Women — Nurses (1968)
Julie Housekeepers (1992), Teenagers (1992)
Julie Andrews ... The Sound of Christmas Holiday Specials (1987)
The Julie Brown Show Reporters (1991), Shows within Shows (1991)
Julie Farr, M.D. Doctors (1978), Los Angeles (1978)
Julius Caesar Shakespeare (1964), Shakespeare (1969), Shakespeare (1979)
The Julius La Rosa Show Variety Programs (1955)
The June Allyson Show Drama (1959)
June Moon Broadway (1940)
Jungle Jim Adventurers (1955), Africa (1955), Animals (1955), Series Based on Radio Programs (1955)
Junior High Jinks Children's Program (1952), Puppets (1952)
Junior Miss Teenagers (1957), Vari-

ety and Drama Spectaculars (1957)
Junior Rodeo Children's Program (1952)
Just Cause Lawyers (2002), San Francisco (2002)
Just Desserts Angels (1992)
Just for Laughs Pilot Film Series (1974)
Just in Time Los Angeles (1989), Newspapers (1988)
Just Legal Lawyers (2005), Los Angeles (2005)
Just Life Women — Law Enforcers (1990)
Just One of the Girls Teachers (1992)
Just Our Luck California (1983), Genies(1983)
Just Plain Folks Sitcoms (1956)
Just Shoot Me Lesbians (1997), Mentally Disabled (1997), New York (1997), Newspapers (1997), Nudity (1997), Senior Citizens (1997), Transsexuals (2000)
Just the Ten of Us Adolescence (1988), California (1988), Prison (1988), Religious Characters (1988), Teachers (1988), Teen After-School Hangouts (1988), Teenagers (1988), Women — "Dumb Blondes" (1988)
Justice Judges (1953), Judges (1954), Judges (1956)
Justice of the Peace Judges (1959)
Justin Case Ghosts (1988)
Juvenile Jury Children's Program (1947), Series Based on Radio Programs (1947)

K Street Lesbians (2003)
K-9 Animals (1991)
K-9 and Company Robots (1985), Talking Animals and Machines (1985)
K-9000 Animals (1989)
Kaleidoscope Variety and Drama Spectaculars (1955)
The Kallikaks California (1977), Country Folk (1977), Teenagers (1977)
Kangaroo Courier Teachers (1988)
Kangaroos in the Kitchen Animals (1982)
Karen Adolescence (1964), California (1964), Politics (1975), Teenagers (1964), Washington, D.C. (1975), Women — Scatterbrained (1965)
Karen Sisco Florida (2003), Women — Law Enforcers (2003)
Karen's Song Los Angeles (1987)
Kate Adolescence (1979)
Kate and Allie Adolescence (1984), Mentally Disabled (1986), New York (1984), Teenagers (1984)
Kate Bliss and the Ticker Tape Kid

Westerns (1978), Women — Law Enforcers (1978)
Kate Brasher California (2001)
Kate Loves a Mystery Reporters (1979), Women — Law Enforcers (1979)
Kate McShane Lawyers (1975)
The Kate Smith Evening Hour Variety Programs (1951)
The Kate Smith Hour Series Based on Radio Programs (1950), Variety Programs (1950)
The Kate Smith Show Variety Programs (1960)
Katie Joplin Philadelphia (1999)
Kay Kyser's Kollege of Musical Knowledge Series Based on Radio Programs (1949)
Kay O'Brien Doctors (1986), Mexican American (1986), New York (1986), Women — Nurses (1986)
Kay Starr Show Variety Programs (1957)
Kaz Nightclubs (1978)
Keen Eddie Men — Law Enforcers (2003)
Keep It in the Family Game Shows (1957)
Keep Talking Game Shows (1958)
Keep the Faith Religious Characters (1972)
Keeper of the Wild Animals (1977)
Keeping Up with the Joneses African American (1972)
Kelly's Kids Adolescence (1974), African American (1974), Asian American (1973)
Ken Burns' Civil War Civil War (1990)
The Ken Murray Show Variety Programs (1950)
The Kennedy Center Honors: A Celebration of the Performing Arts Presidential Appearances (2004)
Kenny and Dolly: A Christmas To Remember Holiday Specials (1984)
Kentucky Jones Adolescence (1964), Asian American (1964)
Kevin Hill New York (2004)
Key Club Playhouse Drama — Repeat Series (1956)
Key Tortuga Adventurers (1981), Teenagers (1981)
Key West Bars (1993), Cuban American (1993), Florida (1993), Newspapers (1993), Prostitutes (1993), Visually Impaired (1992)
Khan! Asian American (1975), Martial Arts (1975), Men — Law Enforcers (1975)
Kibbee Hates Fitch Pilot Film Series (1965), Rescue (1965)
The Kick-In Broadway (1952)
Kid Gloves Children's Program (1951)
Kid Power Adolescence (1972)

The Kid Who Wouldn't Quit Mentally Disabled (1987)

The Kid with the Broken Halo Angels (1982)

The Kida-Littles Puppets (1984)

Kids 2 Kids Adolescence (1981)

Kids and Company Children's Program (1951)

The Kids from C.A.P.E.R. Teenagers (1976)

Kids Incorporated Adolescence (1985)

Kids' Biz Adolescence (1986)

The Kidsong TV Show Adolescence (1987)

Kiernan's Kaleidoscope Children's Program (1949)

Killer Instinct San Francisco (2005)

Kim Fairy Tales (1960)

Kim Possible Teenagers (2002)

Kimba, the White Lion Cartoons (1966)

Kimbar of the Jungle Men — Extraordinary (1958)

Kind Lady Broadway (1952)

Kindred: The Embraced Vampires (1996)

The King and I Series Based on Films (1971), Teachers (1972)

The King and Odie Cartoons (1960)

King Features Trilogy Cartoons (1963)

King Henry IV, Part 1 Shakespeare (1979)

King Henry IV, Part 2 Shakespeare (1979)

King Henry V Shakespeare (1979)

King Henry VI, Part 1 Shakespeare (1983)

King Henry VI, Part 2 Shakespeare (1983)

King Henry VI, Part 3 Shakespeare (1983)

King Henry VIII Shakespeare (1979)

King Kong Series Based on Films (1966), Series Based on Films (2000)

The King Kong Show Cartoons (1966)

King Lear Shakespeare (1975), Shakespeare (1982)

King Leonardo and His Short Subjects Cartoons (1960)

King Midas Fairy Tales (1960)

King of Diamonds Adventurers (1961)

King of Kensington Canada (1977)

The King of Queens Hearing Impaired Characters (2000), Senior Citizens (1998), Speech Impaired (2000)

King of the Building Hotels (1987), Pilot Film Series (1987)

King of the Hill American Indian (1997)

King of the Road Hotels (1978)

King of the Rocket Men Series Based on Films (1955)

King Richard II Shakespeare (1978)

King Richard III Shakespeare (1954)

The King with Eight Daughters Fairy Tales (1977)

King's Crossing California (1982), Soap Operas (Note)

King's Party Line Game Shows (1946)

King's Record Shop Game Shows (1945), Television Firsts (1945)

King's Row Historical Settings (1955), Series Based on Films (1955)

Kingpin Mexican American (2003)

Kingpins Pilot Film Series (1987)

Kingston Confidential Los Angeles (1977), Newspapers (1977)

Kirk Adolescence (1995), New York (1995), Women — Nurses (1995)

Kismet Broadway (1967)

Kiss Me, Kate Broadway (1958), Broadway (1968), Broadway (2000)

Kitchen Confidential Restaurants (2005)

Kitty Foyle Series Based on Radio Programs (1958), Soap Operas (1958)

Klondike Adventurers (1960), Historical Settings (1960), Hotels (1960)

Klondike Kat Cartoons (1965)

The Klowns Clowns (1970)

Knight and Daye California (1989), Mexican American (1989), Puerto Rican (1989), Senior Citizens (1989), Taxi Cabs (1989)

Knight Rider California (1982), Cars (1982), Gadgets(1982), Lookalikes (1982), Los Angeles (1982), Men — Extraordinary (1982), Talking Animals and Machines (1982), Truckers (1982)

Knight Rider 2010 Talking Animals and Machines (1994)

Knight Watch Latino American (1988), Religious Characters (1989)

Knight's Gambit Reporters (1964)

Knots Landing California (1979), Cars (1979), Look-alikes (1982), Soap Operas (Note)

Kobb's Corner Variety Programs (1948)

Kodak Request Performance Drama — Repeat Series (1955)

Kodiak American Indian (1974), Men — Law Enforcers (1974)

Kojak Latino American (1989), Men — Law Enforcers (1973), Men — Law Enforcers (2005)

Kolchak: The Night Stalker Chicago (1974), Reporters (1974), Senior Citizens (1973), The Supernatural (1974), The Supernatural (2005)

Kong: The Animated Series Series Based on Films (2000)

Korg, 70,000 B.C. Historical Settings (1974)

Koska and His Family Adolescence (1973)

The Kowboys Pilot Film Series (1970), Westerns (1970)

The Kraft Music Hall Series Based on Radio Programs (1958), Variety Programs (1958)

The Kraft Mystery Theater Drama (1961)

Kraft Presents Jim Henson's "The Christmas Toy" Holiday Specials (1986)

The Kraft Suspense Theater Color Broadcasting (1957-1965), Drama (1963)

Kraft Television Theater Broadway (1952), Drama (1947)

Kraft Theater Shakespeare (1954), Shakespeare (1957)

Krazy Kat Cartoons (1963)

Kristen New York (2001)

The Krypton Factor Geniuses (1981), Reality Programs (1980)

Kuda Bux Mediums (1950)

Kudzu Teenagers (1983)

Kukla, Fran and Ollie Puppets (1947)

The Kuklapolitan Easter Show Holiday Specials (1955)

Kung Fu Asian American (1972), Martial Arts (1972), Martial Arts (1987), Martial Arts (1993), Men — Law Enforcers (1993), Visually Impaired (1972)

Kung Fu: The Legend Continues Martial Arts (1993), Men — Law Enforcers (1993)

Kung Fu: The Movie Martial Arts (1986)

Kung Fu: The Next Generation Martial Arts (1987), Pilot Film Series (1987)

L.A. Dragnet Asian American (2003), District Attorneys (2003), Latino American (2004), Men — Law Enforcers (2003), Women — Law Enforcers (2003)

L.A. Heat Los Angeles (1996), Mexican American (1996)

L.A. Law District Attorneys (1986), Lawyers (1984), Lesbians (1986), Los Angeles (1986), Mentally Disabled (1986)

La Femme Nikita Lesbians (1998), Series Based on Films (1997), Women — Extraordinary (1997)

La Route Est Dure Gays (1972)

La Sylphide Ballet (1972)

Labyrinth Opera (1963)

Lacy and the Mississippi Queen Westerns (1978)

Ladies Be Seated Game Shows

(1945), Game Shows (1946), Series Based on Radio Programs (1949)

Ladies Before Gentlemen Game Shows (1951)

Ladies in Blue Women — Law Enforcers (1980)

The Ladies of Sweet Street Senior Citizens (1990)

Ladies' Choice Reality Programs (1953)

Ladies' Day Newspapers (1991)

Ladies' Man Adolescence (1980), California (1999), New York (1980), Newspapers (1980)

Lady Blue Cars (1985), Chicago (1985), Latino American (1984), Women — Law Enforcers (1985)

Lady in the Dark Broadway (1952), Broadway (1981), Variety and Drama Spectaculars (1954)

Lady Luck Angels (1973)

The Lady Next Door Children's Program (1949)

Lamb Chop's Play-a-Long Puppets (1992)

The Lambs Gambol Variety Programs (1949)

Lamp Unto My Feet Religious Programs (1948)

Lancelot Link, Secret Chimp Animals (1970), Talking Animals and Machines (1970)

Lancer Westerns (1968)

The Land of Green Ginger Fairy Tales (1958)

Land of Hope Immigrants (1976)

The Land of Oz Fairy Tales (1960)

Land of the Giants Adolescence (1968), African American (1968), Little People (1968)

Land of the Lost Adolescence (1974), Talking Animals and Machines (1991), Teenagers (1990)

Landon, Landon & Landon Ghosts (1980)

Lanigan's Rabbi California (1977), Men — Law Enforcers (1977), Religious Characters (1977)

The Lanny Ross Show Variety Programs (1948)

Laramie Adolescence (1959), Westerns (1959)

Laredo Westerns (1965)

The Lark Broadway (1957)

The Larry Storch Show Variety Programs (1953)

Las Vegas Hotels (2003), Las Vegas Settings (2003), Lesbians (2005), Nudity (2005), Physically Disabled (2003)

Las Vegas Beat Men — Law Enforcers (1964)

Las Vegas Gambit Las Vegas Settings (1980)

The Las Vegas Show Las Vegas Settings (1967)

Lash of the West Children's Program (1951)

Lassie Adolescence (1964), Animals (1954), Senior Citizens (1954)

Lassie: The New Beginning Animals (1954)

Lassie's Rescue Rangers Rescue (1973)

Lassiter Reporters (1968)

The Last Chance Café Angels (1986)

The Last Ninja Martial Arts (1983)

The Last of Mrs. Cheney Broadway (1952)

Last of the Wild Animals (1974)

Last of the Mohicans American Indian (1957), Historical Settings (1957)

Last of the Private Eyes Men — Law Enforcers (1963)

The Last Precinct Men — Law Enforcers (1986), Transsexuals (1986)

The Last Resort Hotels (1979)

The Last Word Restaurants (1986)

Late Night with David Letterman Nudity (1995), Nudity (2002)

LatiNation Latino American (2004)

The Latino Laugh Festival Cuban American (1992)

Laugh Line Game Shows (1959)

Laughter in Paris Ghosts (1946)

Laura Broadway (1955), Broadway (1968)

Laurie Hill Doctors (1992)

Laverne and Shirley California (1980), Historical Settings (1976), Hotels (1976), Lesbians (1977), Look-alikes (1977), Restaurants (1976), Television Firsts (1977)

The Law and Harry McGraw Boston (1987), Men — Law Enforcers (1987)

The Law and Mr. Jones Lawyers (1960), New York (1960)

Law and Order District Attorneys (1990), Latino American (1995), Men — Law Enforcers (1990), Mexican American (1986), New York (1990), Women — Law Enforcers (1993)

Law and Order: Criminal Intent District Attorneys (2001), Men — Law Enforcers (2001), New York (2001), Psychiatrists (1999), Visually Impaired (1999), Women — Law Enforcers (2001)

Law and Order: S.V.U. Women — Law Enforcers (1999)

Law and Order: Special Victims Unit District Attorneys (1999), Men — Law Enforcers (1999), New York (1999)

Law and Order: Trial by Jury District Attorneys (2005), New York (2005)

The Law Enforcers Men — Law Enforcers (1969)

Law of the Plainsman American Indian (1959), Hotels (1959), Westerns (1959)

Lawbreaker Drama (1963)

The Lawless Years Historical Settings (1959), Men — Law Enforcers (1959), New York (1959)

Lawman Bars (1958), Hotels (1958), Restaurants (1958), Westerns (1958)

The Lawrence Welk Show Series Based on Radio Programs (1955), Variety Programs (1955)

The Lawyers Los Angeles (1969)

LAX Los Angeles (2004), Pilots (2004)

Lazy Town Adolescence (2004)

A League of Their Own Historical Settings (1993), Series Based on Films (1993)

Learned Pigs and Fireproof Women Magicians (1990)

Learning the Ropes Teachers (1988), Teen After-School Hangouts (1988), Teenagers (1988)

The Leathernecks War — World War II (1963)

Leave It to Beaver Adolescence (1957), Adolescence (1986), Cars (1957), Films Based on Television Series (1997), Newspapers (1957), Senior Citizens (1957), Senior Citizens (1986), Sitcoms (1957)

Leave It to Larry Sitcoms (1952)

Leave It to the Girls Series Based on Radio Programs (1949)

The Left Over Revue Variety Programs (1951)

Leg Work Cars (1987), New York (1987), Women — Law Enforcers (1987)

Legend African American (1946), Mexican American (1995), Westerns (1995)

The Legend of Custer American Indian (1967), Westerns (1967)

The Legend of Jesse James Westerns (1965)

The Legend of Lizzie Borden Nudity (1975)

The Legend of Silent Night Holiday Specials (1968)

The Legend of Sleepy Hollow Fairy Tales (1958), Fairy Tales (1985)

The Legend of the Golden Gun Westerns (1979)

Legend of the Lone Ranger Films Based on Television Series (1991)

Legmen Los Angeles (1984)

Legs American Indian (1978)

Lenny Adolescence (1990), Teenagers (1990)

Leo and Liz in Beverly Hills California (1986)

Les Brigands Opera (1972)

Les Paul and Mary Ford Show Variety Programs (1954)

Less Than Perfect Lesbians (2002), New York (2002), New York (2003)

The Lester Guy Show Shows within Shows (1992)

Let's Dance Game Shows (1946), Variety Programs (1954)

Let's Join Joanie Sitcoms (1951), Women — Scatterbrained (1951)

Let's Play Reporter Game Shows (1946)

Let's See Game Shows (1943), Television Firsts (1943)

Let's Take a Trip Children's Program (1955)

The Letter Broadway (1952)

A Letter to Lee Graham Psychiatrists (1952)

Letter to Loretta Drama (1953)

Level 9 F.B.I. Agents (2000), Washington, D.C. (2000), Women — Extraordinary (2000)

Lewis and Clark Adolescence (1981), Bars (1981)

Lexx Aliens (2000), Gays (2002), Robots (2000), Space (1999), Talking Animals and Machines (2001)

Liberace Variety Programs (1953)

The Liberace Show Series Based on Radio Programs (1954), Variety Programs (1958)

The Lid's Off Reality Programs (1969)

Lidsville Adolescence (1971), Genies(1971), Little People (1971), Magicians (1971), Puppets (1971)

Lie Detector Reality Programs (1983)

The Lieutenant California (1963), Camps (1963)

The Life and Death of King John Shakespeare (1984)

The Life and Legend of Wyatt Earp Arizona (1955), Westerns (1955)

The Life and Times of Barney Miller Pilot Film Series (1974)

The Life and Times of Eddie Roberts California (1980), Soap Operas (Note), Teachers (1980)

The Life and Times of Grizzly Adams American Indian (1977), Animals (1977), Historical Settings (1977), Series Based on Films (1977)

Life As We Know It Teenagers (2004)

Life Begins at 80 Senior Citizens (1950), Series Based on Radio Programs (1950)

Life Goes On Mentally Disabled (1989), Newspapers (1989), Restaurants (1989), Teenagers (1989)

Life Is Worth Living Religious Programs (1953)

The Life of Riley Los Angeles (1949, 1953), Series Based on Radio Programs (1949, 1953), Sitcoms (1949, 1953), Teenagers (1949)

The Life of Vernon Hathaway Sitcoms (1955)

Life with Bonnie Shows within Shows (2002)

Life with Derek Teenagers (2005)

Life with Elizabeth Sitcoms (1953)

Life with Father Historical Settings (1953), Housekeepers (1953), Series Based on Films (1953), Sitcoms (1953), Teenagers (1953)

Life with Lucy Senior Citizens (1988)

Life with Luigi Chicago (1952), Immigrants (1952), Restaurants (1952), Series Based on Radio Programs (1952), Sitcoms (1952)

Life with Roger New York (1996)

Life with Snarky Parker Puppets (1950)

Life with Virginia Pilot Film Series (1962), Pilot Film Series (1963–1967), Teenagers (1962)

Lifeline Reality Programs (1978)

Lifestyles of the Rich and Famous Reality Programs (1984)

Light's Diamond Jubilee Presidential Appearances (1954), Variety and Drama Spectaculars (1954)

Lights Out Drama (1949), Drama (1972), Series Based on Radio Programs (1949)

Lights, Camera, Action! Reality Programs (1950)

Like Family New Jersey (2003), Senior Citizens (2003), Teenagers (2003)

Like Magic Magicians (1981)

Likely Suspects Men — Law Enforcers (1992)

Li'l Abner Broadway (1967), Broadway (1971), Country Folk (1967), Country Folk (1971)

Li'l Abner in Dog Patch Today Broadway (1978), Country Folk (1978)

The Lilli Palmer Theater Drama (1956)

Lilo and Stitch: The Series Series Based on Films (2003)

Line of Fire F.B.I. Agents (2003)

The Line-Up Men — Law Enforcers (1954), San Francisco (1954), Series Based on Radio Programs (1954)

Linus the Lionhearted Cartoons (1964)

Lippy the Lion Cartoons (1962)

The Lisa Whelchel Show Adolescence (1988), Teachers (1988)

Listen Up Shows within Shows (2004), Teenagers (2004)

A Little Bit Strange Witches (1989)

Little Darlings Camps (1982), Teenagers (1982)

The Little Drummer Boy Holiday Specials (1967)

The Little Drummer Boy, Book II Holiday Specials (1976)

The Little Foxes Broadway (1956)

Little House on the Prairie Adolescence (1974), Adolescence (2005), Historical Settings (1974), Historical Settings (2005), Religious Characters (1974), Teachers (1974), Visually Impaired (1974)

The Little Lame Prince Fairy Tales (1958)

Little Leatherneck Pilot Film Series (1966)

Little Lulu Adolescence (1978)

Little Men Adolescence (1999), Fairy Tales (1960), Historical Settings (1999), Teachers (1999)

The Little Mermaid Fairy Tales (1960), Fairy Tales (1974), Fairy Tales (1982), Mermaids (1961), Mermaids (1974), Mermaids (1983), Mermaids (1989), Series Based on Films (1992), Witches (1992)

The Little People Beaches (1972), Doctors (1973)

The Little Prince Opera (2003)

Little Red Riding Hood Fairy Tales (1977), Fairy Tales (1982)

Little Roguefort Cartoons (1956)

Little Shots Adolescence (1983)

Little Vic Animals (1977)

Little Women Ballet (1976), Historical Settings (1971), Historical Settings (1979), Look-alikes (1978), Opera (2001), Variety and Drama Spectaculars (1939), Variety and Drama Spectaculars (1945)

The Littlest Angel Angels (1969), Holiday Specials (1969)

The Littlest Hobo Animals (1964)

Live Like a Millionaire Reality Programs (1951)

Live Shot Mexican American (1995)

Live with Regis and Kathy Lee Senior Citizens (1989)

Live with Regis and Kelly Senior Citizens (1989)

Live-In Housekeepers (1989), New Jersey (1989), Teenagers (1989)

The Lively Lady Adventurers (1960)

The Lives of Jenny Dolan Reporters (1975)

Living Dolls New York (1989), Teenagers (1989)

Living Easy Psychiatrists (,)

The Living End African American (1972), African American (1973)

Living in Paradise Senior Citizens (1981)

Living Single New York (1993)

Living with Fran Gays (2005), Lesbians (2006), New York (2005), Nudity (2005), Teenagers (2005)

Lizzie McGuire Mexican American (2001), Nudity (2003), Nudity (2004), Teen After-School Hangouts (2001), Teenagers (2001)

The Lloyd Bridges Show Drama (1963), Newspapers (1962)

Lloyd Bridges Water World Beaches (1972)

Lock Up Lawyers (1959)

Lock, Stock and Barrel Westerns (1971), Westerns (1973)

The Log of the Black Pearl Adventurers (1975)

Logan's Run Robots (1977), Series Based on Films (1977)

Lois and Clark: The New Adventures of Superman Aliens (1953), Look-alikes (1993), Reporters (1993), Super Heroes (1993)

Lola Lawyers (1990)

The Lone Gunmen Cars (2001), Reporters (2001)

The Lone Ranger American Indian (1949), American Indian (2003), Animals (1949), Color Broadcasting (1956), Films Based on Television Series (1956), Films Based on Television Series (1991), Series Based on Radio Programs (1949), Westerns (1949), Westerns (2003)

The Lone Ranger and the City of Gold Films Based on Television Series (1956)

Lone Star Men — Law Enforcers (1983)

The Lone Wolf Men — Law Enforcers (1954), Series Based on Radio Programs (1954)

The Loner Men — Law Enforcers (1988), Westerns (1965)

Lonesome Dove Westerns (1989)

Lonesome Dove: The Outlaw Years Westerns (1989)

Lonesome Dove: The Series Westerns (1989)

Long Day's Journey into Night Broadway (1973)

The Long Highway Truckers (1956)

The Long Hot Summer Senior Citizens (1965), Series Based on Films (1965)

Long Island Fever Men — Law Enforcers (1996)

Longarm Westerns (1987)

Longstreet Animals (1971), Asian American (1971), Martial Arts (1971), Visually Impaired (1971)

Look Drama (1945)

Look Back in Anger Broadway (1981)

Look Photo Quiz Game Shows (1953)

Look Up and Live Religious Programs (1954)

Look Who's Here Physically Disabled (1946), Television Firsts (1946)

Look Who's Talking Series Based on Films (1991)

The Loretta Young Theater Drama (1954)

Lost Adolescence (2004), Asian American (2004), Beaches (2004), Physically Disabled (2004)

Lost in Space Adolescence (1965), Aliens (1965), Geniuses (1965), Robots (1965), Space (1965), Teenagers (1965)

The Lost Saucer Aliens (1975), Robots (1984), Space (1975)

Lost Treasure Adventurers (1971)

The Lost World Historical Settings (1998), Look-alikes (1998), Senior Citizens (1998), Series Based on Films (1998), Talking Animals and Machines (1998), Women — Extraordinary (1998)

Lou Grant Los Angeles (1977), Mexican American (1979), Newspapers (1977)

The Louie Show Physically Disabled (1996), Psychiatrists (1996)

Love, American Style Adolescence (1974), Drama (1969), Love (1969)

Love and Curses Los Angeles (1991), Werewolves (1990)

Love and Marriage Sitcoms (1959)

Love and War Bars (1992), New York (1992), Newspapers (1992)

Love at First Sight Visually Impaired (1980)

The Love Boat Adolescence (1977), Latino American (1977), Look-alikes (1977), Love (1977)

The Love Boat: The Next Wave Latino American (1998), Love (1998)

The Love Connection Love (1983)

The Love Experts Love (1978)

Love, Inc. Lesbians (2005), Love (2005)

Love Is a Lion's Roar Pilot Film Series (1963–1967)

Love Is a Many Splendored Thing Soap Operas (1967), Soap Operas (Note)

Love Monkey New York (2006)

Love Nest Senior Citizens (1975)

Love of Life Soap Operas (1951)

Love on a Rooftop Color Broadcasting (1966)

The Love Report Love (1984)

Love Songs Love (1985)

Love Stories Love (1991)

Love Story Drama (1954), Drama (1973), Love (1954), Love (1955), Love (1973)

Love, Sidney Adolescence (1981), Gays (1981), New York (1981)

Love That Bob California (1955),

Look-alikes (1955), Nudity (1957), Sitcoms (1954), Teenagers (1955)

Love That Jill New York (1958), Sitcoms (1958), Women — "Dumb Blondes" (1958)

Love Thy Neighbor African American (1973), California (1973)

Love with a Twist Love (1990)

Lovers, Partners and Spies Women — Law Enforcers (1988)

Loves a Mystery Adolescence (1979)

Love's Labour's Lost Shakespeare (1985)

Loves Me, Loves Me Not Teachers (1977)

Loving Cuban American (1992)

Low Man on the Totem Pole Pilot Film Series (1963–1967)

Lowell Thomas Reporting News Broadcasts (1941)

Lucas Tanner Adolescence (1974), Teachers (1974), Teenagers (1974)

Los Luchadores Men — Extraordinary (2001), Women — Extraordinary (2001)

The Lucie Arnaz Show New York (1988), Psychiatrists (1985), Shows within Shows (1985)

Lucky Letters Game Shows (1950)

Lucky Partners Game Shows (1958)

Lucky Pup Puppets (1948)

The Lucky Strike Program Mexican American (1950)

The Lucy Monroe Program Variety Programs (1939)

The Lucy Show Connecticut (1962), Pilot Film Series (1963–1967), San Francisco (1962), Teenagers (1961), Women — Scatterbrained (1961)

The Lucy-Desi Comedy Hour Cuban American (1951)

Luis Puerto Rican (2003)

Luke and the Tenderfoot Con Artists (1965), Pilot Film Series (1963–1967)

Lum and Abner Country Folk (1949), Series Based on Radio Programs (1949), Sitcoms (1949)

The Lux Radio Theater Series Based on Radio Programs (1950)

The Lux Video Theater Broadway (1957), Drama (1950), Series Based on Radio Programs (1950)

The L-Word Cross Dressers (2003), Lesbians (2004), Nudity (1984)

Lyndon B. Johnson's Texas Presidential Appearances (1966)

Lyndon Johnson Politics (1987)

M Squad Chicago (1957), Men — Law Enforcers (1957)

M Station: Hawaii Beaches (1980)

The M&M Candy Carnival Reality Programs (1952)

*M*A*S*H* Bars (1972), Camps

(1972), Cross Dressers (1972), Doctors (1972), Mediums (1972), Men — Law Enforcers (1984), Nudity (1972), Psychiatrists (1972), Religious Characters (1972), Senior Citizens (1975), Series Based on Films (1972), War — Korea, Vietnam, Iraq (1972), Women — Nurses (1972)

M.A.N.T.I.S. Men — Extraordinary (1994), Physically Disabled (1994), Super Heroes (1994)

M.Y.O.B California (2000), Teenagers (2000)

Ma and Pa Senior Citizens (1974)

Mabel and Max Pilot Film Series (1987)

Mabel and Me Senior Citizens (1987)

Mac Davis Holiday Specials (1977)

The Mac Davis Christmas Show Holiday Specials (1981)

The Mac Davis Christmas Special Holiday Specials (1975)

The Mac Davis Christmas Special ... When I Grow Up Holiday Specials (1976)

Mac Davis — I'll Be Home for Christmas Holiday Specials (1980)

The Mac Davis Special: The Music of Christmas Holiday Specials (1983)

Mac Davis's Christmas Odyssey: Two Thousand and Ten Holiday Specials (1978)

MacGruder and Loud Men — Law Enforcers (1985)

Macbeth Shakespeare (1951), Shakespeare (1954), Shakespeare (1960), Shakespeare (1970), Shakespeare (1975), Shakespeare (1983)

MacGyver Cars (1985), Geniuses (1985), Los Angeles (1985), Visually Impaired (1985)

The MacKenzies of Paradise Cove Beaches (1979), Teenagers (1979)

Macreedy's Woman Nightclubs (1958)

Mad About You Bars (1992), Lesbians (1996), New York (1992)

Madame Butterfly Opera (1950)

Madame in Manhattan Puppets (1981)

Madame's Place California (1982), Cars (1982), Housekeepers (1982), Latino American (1982), Puppets (1982), Shows within Shows (1982), Women — "Dumb Blondes" (1982)

Madeline Fairy Tales (1960)

Madigan Men — Law Enforcers (1972), Men — Law Enforcers (1974), New York (1972), Series Based on Films (1972)

Madman of the People New York (1994)

Madonna: The Virgin Tour Presidential Appearances (1986)

Mady Christians' Ode to Liberty Broadway (1940)

Maggie Teenagers (1960)

Maggie Brown Nightclubs (1963), Pilot Film Series (1963–1967)

The Magic Boy's Easter Religious Programs (1990)

The Magic Carpet Magicians (1947)

The Magic Clown Children's Program (1949), Clowns (1949)

The Magic Cottage Children's Program (1949)

The Magic Fishbone Fairy Tales (1958)

The Magic Flute Opera (1950)

The Magic Garden Puppets (1974)

A Magic Garden Christmas Holiday Specials (1981)

The Magic Lady Children's Program (1951), Magicians (1951)

The Magic Land of Allakazam Children's Program (1960), Magicians (1960)

Magic Mongo Genies (1977)

The Magic of David Copperfield Magicians (1978)

The Magic of David Copperfield II Magicians (1979)

The Magic of David Copperfield III Magicians (1980)

The Magic of David Copperfield IV Magicians (1981)

The Magic of David Copperfield V Magicians (1983)

The Magic of David Copperfield VI Magicians (1984)

The Magic of David Copperfield VII Magicians (1985)

The Magic of David Copperfield VIII ... In China Magicians (1986)

The Magic of David Copperfield IX Magicians (1987)

The Magic of David Copperfield X: The Bermuda Triangle Magicians (1988)

The Magic of David Copperfield XI Magicians (1989)

The Magic of David Copperfield XII Magicians (1990)

The Magic of David Copperfield XIII: Mystery on the Orient Express Magicians (1991)

The Magic of David Copperfield XIV: Flying ... Live the Dream Magicians (1992)

The Magic of David Copperfield XV: Fires of Passion — This Time His Life Is on the Line Magicians (1993)

The Magic Ranch Magicians (1961)

The Magic Slate Children's Program (1950)

Magic Vault Drama (1952)

Magic with Mary Martin Variety and Drama Spectaculars (1954)

Magic with the Stars Magicians (1982)

The Magician Cars (1973), Los Angeles (1973), Magicians (1973), Physically Disabled (1973), Pilots (1973)

The Magilla Gorilla Show Cartoons (1964)

Magnavox Theater Drama (1950)

The Magnificent Menasha Sitcoms (1950)

The Magnificent Yankee Broadway (1965)

Magnum, P.I Bars (1980), Beaches (1980), Cars (1980), District Attorneys (1980), Hawaii (1980), Housekeepers (1980), Look-alikes (1980), Men — Law Enforcers (1980), Pilots (1980)

Maisie Sitcoms (1960)

Major Bowes and His Original Amateur Hour Reality Programs (1948), Series Based on Radio Programs (1948)

Major Dad Adolescence (1989), California (1989), Newspapers (1989), Physically Disabled (1989), Teenagers (1989)

Major Dell Conway of the Flying Tigers Pilots (1951), Pilots (1953), War — World War II (1953)

Make Me Laugh Game Shows (1959)

Make Mine Music Variety Programs (1948)

Make Room for Daddy Adolescence (1953), African American (1953), Hotels (1953), Housekeepers (1953), Latino American (1961), New York (1953), Nightclubs (1953), Senior Citizens (1969), Sitcoms (1953), Teenagers (1953)

Make Room for Granddaddy Adolescence (1971), Senior Citizens (1969)

Make the Connection Game Shows (1955)

Makin' It New Jersey (1979)

Making the Grade Teachers (1982)

Malcolm and Eddie Bars (1996)

Malcolm in the Middle Adolescence (2000), Geniuses (2000), Physically Disabled (2000), Teenagers (2000), Visually Impaired (2000)

Malibu Beach Party Beaches (1989)

Malibu, Ca. California (1988), Restaurants (1998), Teenagers (1999), Women — "Dumb Blondes" (1998)

Malibu Road California (1991)

Malibu Run Adventurers (1961), Beaches (1961), California (1961), Men — Law Enforcers (1961)

Malibu U Beaches (1967), California (1967)

Mama Historical Settings (1949), Immigrants (1949), San Francisco (1949), Series Based on Films (1949), Sitcoms (1949), Teenagers (1949)

Mama Malone Latino American (1984), New York (1984), Religious Characters (2003), Shows within Shows (1984)

Mama Rosa Soap Operas (1950), Soap Operas (Note)

Mama's Boy New York (1987), Newspapers (1987)

Mama's Family Bars (1982), Cars (1982), Look-alikes (1986), Senior Citizens (1982), Teenagers (1983)

Mamba's Daughters African American (1939), Television Firsts (1939)

Man Against Crime Lawyers (1958)

The Man Against Crime Men — Law Enforcers (1949), Series Based on Radio Programs (1949)

Man and Superman Broadway (1956)

The Man and the City Mexican American (1971), Politics (1971)

A Man Called Flintstone Films Based on Television Series (1966)

A Man Called Hawk Men — Law Enforcers (1989)

A Man Called Shenandoah Westerns (1965)

A Man Called Sloane Espionage (1979), Physically Disabled (1979)

The Man Called X Espionage (1956), Series Based on Radio Programs (1956)

The Man from Atlantis Aliens (1977), Latino American (1977)

The Man from Blackhawk Westerns (1959)

The Man from Denver Westerns (1959)

The Man from Everywhere Westerns (1961)

The Man from Interpol Men — Law Enforcers (1960)

The Man from U.N.C.L.E. Cars (1964), Color Broadcasting (1966), Espionage (1966), Gadgets(1964), New York (1964)

Man in a Suitcase Men — Law Enforcers (1968)

Man in the Family New York (1991)

The Man in the Moon Variety and Drama Spectaculars (1960)

The Man in the Square Suit Teenagers (1966)

Man of the People Con Artists (1991), Politics (1991), Prostitutes (1991)

Man on a String Government Agents (1972)

The Man Who Came to Dinner Broadway (1952), Broadway (1972), Broadway (2000)

The Man Who Fell to Earth Aliens (1977)

The Man Who Never Was Espionage (1966), Look-alikes (1966), Series Based on Films (1966)

The Man with the Power Aliens (1977)

Man Without a Gun Newspapers (1958), Westerns (1958)

Mancuso, FBI Bars (1989), The FBI (1989)

Mandrake Magicians (1978)

Mandrake the Magician Magicians (1954)

Manhattan Newspapers (1958), Newspapers (1960)

Manhattan Honeymoon Love (1954)

Manhattan Showcase Reality Programs (1949)

Manhattan Tower Variety and Drama Spectaculars (1956)

Manhunt Men — Law Enforcers (1959)

Manhunter Historical Settings (1974)

Manimal Men — Extraordinary (1983), New York (1983), Women — Law Enforcers (1983)

Mann and Machine Los Angeles (1992), Robots (1992), Women — Law Enforcers (1992)

Mannix African American (1968), Cars (1967), Los Angeles (1967), Men — Law Enforcers (1968)

Manta and Moray Super Heroes (1980)

Many Happy Returns Los Angeles (1964)

The Many Loves of Dobie Gillis Sitcoms (1959)

Marblehead Manor Housekeepers (1987), Latino American (1987)

The March of Dimes Benefit Show Variety and Drama Spectaculars (1949)

The March of Dimes Fashion Show Variety and Drama Spectaculars (1948)

The March of Time Series Based on Radio Programs (1951)

Marco Polo Variety and Drama Spectaculars (1956)

Marcus Welby, M.D. California (1969), Doctors (1969), Mexican American (1969), Senior Citizens (1969), Women — Nurses (1969)

The Marge and Gower Champion Show Sitcoms (1957)

Marge and Jeff Sitcoms (1953)

Margie Historical Settings (1961), Newspapers (1961), Series Based on Films (1961), Teen After-School Hangouts (1961), Teenagers (1961)

Mariah Prison (1987)

The Marie Eve, George Lloyd Show Variety Programs (1939)

Marine Boy Cartoons (1966)

The Mark of Zorro Films Based on Television Series (1998)

Mark Saber Men — Law Enforcers (1951), New York (1951), Series Based on Radio Programs (1951)

Markham Lawyers (1959), Los Angeles (1959)

The Marriage Series Based on Radio Programs (1954), Sitcoms (1954)

Marriage a la Mode Love (1946)

The Marriage Broker Love (1957)

Marriage Is Alive and Well Love (1979)

The Marriage Proposal Broadway (1940)

Married ... With Children Cars (1987), Chicago (1987), Nudity (1987), Teenagers (1987), Women — "Dumb Blondes" (1987)

Married People Bars (1991), Lawyers (1990), New York (1990)

Married: The First Year Love (1979)

Mars: Base One Psychiatrists (1988), Robots (1988), Space (1988)

The Marshal Men — Law Enforcers (1995)

The Marshal of Gunsight Pass Westerns (1950)

The Marshall Chronicles Teenagers (1990)

The Martha Raye Show Variety Programs (1954)

The Martha Wright Show Variety Programs (1954)

Martial Law Asian American (1998), Martial Arts (1998), Men — Law Enforcers (1998), Women — Law Enforcers (1998)

Martin Cross Dressers (1992), Shows within Shows (1992)

The Martin and Lewis Show Series Based on Radio Programs (1949)

Martin Kane, Private Eye Men — Law Enforcers (1949), New York (1949), Series Based on Radio Programs (1949)

The Martin Payne Show Shows within Shows (1992)

The Marty Feldman Comedy Machine Visually Impaired (1971)

Marvel Super Heroes Cartoons (1965), Super Heroes (1965)

Mary Newspapers (1985)

Mary and Joseph: A Story of Faith Religious Programs (1979)

The Mary Hartline Show Children's Program (1951)

Mary Hartman, Mary Hartman Adolescence (1977), Bars (1977), Gays (1977), Hearing Impaired Characters (1976), Lesbians (1977), Nudity (1976), Ohio (1976), Religious Characters

(1976), Senior Citizens (1975), Teenagers (1976), Twins (1976)

Mary Kate and Ashley in Action Adolescence (2001)

Mary Kay and Johnny Sitcoms (1947)

The Mary McKinnon Show Shows within Shows (1979)

The Mary Tyler Moore Comedy Hour Shows within Shows (1979)

The Mary Tyler Moore Show Adolescence (1975), Bars (1970), Clowns (1970), Hotels (1970), Shows within Shows (1970)

The Mask Lawyers (1954), New York (1954), Series Based on Films (1995)

Mason Adolescence (1977)

Masquerade Fairy Tales (1971), Government Agents (1983)

Masquerade Party Game Shows (1952)

Massarati and the Brain Geniuses (1982)

Massine's Ballet Ballet (1945)

The Master Martial Arts (1984)

Masterpiece Playhouse Drama (1950)

Masterpiece Theater Drama (1970), Nudity (1996)

Masters of Magic Magicians (1949)

The Match Game, Nudity (1974)

Matchmaker Love (1987)

Matinee Theater Color Broadcasting, Drama (1955)

Matlock Lawyers (1986), Senior Citizens (1986)

The Matt Dennis Show Variety Programs (1955)

Matt Helm Cars (1975), Lawyers (1975), Men — Law Enforcers (1975)

Matt Houston Cars (1982), Los Angeles (1982), Men — Law Enforcers (1982)

Matt Lincoln Los Angeles (1970), Psychiatrists (1970)

Matt Waters Latino American (1996), New Jersey (1996), Teachers (1996)

Maude African American (1972), Housekeepers (1972), New York (1972)

The Maurice Chevalier Show Variety and Drama Spectaculars (1955)

Maurice Woodruff Predicts Mediums (1969)

Maverick Con Artists (1957), Films Based on Television Series (1994), Look-alikes (1957), Westerns (1957), Westerns (1978), Westerns (1981)

Max Headroom Shows within Shows (1987)

Max Monroe: Loose Cannon Los Angeles (1990), Men — Law Enforcers (1990)

Maximum Security Prison (1985)

May Eve Broadway (1939)

Maya Animals (1967), Series Based on Films (1967)

Maybe It's Me Senior Citizens (2001), Teenagers (2001), Twins (2001)

Maybe This Time Adolescence (1995), Philadelphia (1995), Restaurants (1995), Senior Citizens (1995)

Mayberry, R.F.D Adolescence (1968), Housekeepers (1968)

Mayor of the Town Housekeepers (1954), Politics (1954), Series Based on Radio Programs (1954)

The Mazurka Fairy Tales (1977)

McAllister American Indian (1988)

McClain's Law California (1981), Men — Law Enforcers (1981), Mexican American (1981), Physically Disabled (1981)

McCloud Men — Law Enforcers (1970), New York (1970)

McCoy Con Artists (1975)

McDuff, the Talking Dog Adolescence (1976), Talking Animals and Machines (1976)

McGarry and Me Men — Law Enforcers (1960), Sitcoms (1960)

McGhee Pilot Film Series (1963–1967)

McGhee and Me Adolescence (1994)

The McGonigle Pilot Film Series (1963–1967)

McGruder and Loud Los Angeles (1985), Women — Law Enforcers (1985)

McHale's Navy Asian American (1963), Beaches (1962), Beaches (1964), Films Based on Television Series (1965), War — World War II (1962), War — World War II (1964)

McHale's Navy Joins the Air Force Films Based on Television Series (1965)

McKeever and the Colonel Adolescence (1963)

McLeish and the Kid Adolescence (1975)

McLeod's Daughters Australia (2005)

McMasters of Sweetwater Teachers (1974)

McMillan Housekeepers (1976), Men — Law Enforcers (1976), San Francisco (1976)

McMillan and Wife Cars (1971), Housekeepers (1971), Look-alikes (1972), Men — Law Enforcers (1971), San Francisco (1971)

McNab's Lab Pilot Film Series (1966)

McNamara's Band War — World War II (1977)

McNaughton's Daughter District Attorneys (1976), Los Angeles (1976)

McShane District Attorneys (1986)

Me and Benjy Adolescence (1970), Pilot Film Series (1970)

Me and Buttons Adolescence (1972)

Me and Ducky Teenagers (1979)

Me and Maxx Adolescence (1980), New York (1980)

Me and Mom Los Angeles (1985), Men — Law Enforcers (1985), Mexican American (1986), Women — Law Enforcers (1985)

Me and Mrs. C. Senior Citizens (1984)

Me and the Chimp Animals (1971)

The Me Nobody Knows Broadway (1980)

Measure for Measure Shakespeare (1979)

Medic Doctors (1954)

Medical Center Doctors (1969), Los Angeles (1969), Women — Nurses (1969)

Medical Investigation Forensics (2004)

Medical Story Doctors (1975), Drama (1975)

Medicine Ball Doctors (1995), Mexican American (1995)

Medicine Man Con Artists (1962)

Medium Adolescence (2005), Arizona (2005), District Attorneys (2005), Ghosts (2005), Mediums (2005), Nudity (2005)

Meego Aliens (1997)

Meet Corliss Archer Series Based on Radio Programs (1951), Sitcoms (1951), Sitcoms (1954), Teenagers (1951), Teenagers (1954)

Meet McGraw Men — Law Enforcers (1957)

Meet Me in St. Louis Pilot Film Series (1966), Variety and Drama Spectaculars (1959)

Meet Millie Hotels (1952), Nudity (1952), Series Based on Radio Programs (1952), Sitcoms (1952)

Meet Mr. McNutley Series Based on Radio Programs (1953), Sitcoms (1953, 1954)), Teachers (1953, 1954))

Meet the Girls Pilot Film Series (1960), Sitcoms (1960)

Meet the Governor Politics (1955)

Meet the Press News Broadcasts (1947)

Meet Your Match Game Shows (1952)

The Mel Torme Show Variety Programs (1951)

Melba New York (1986)

The Melba Moore–Clifton Davis Show African American (1972)

Melody Street Variety Programs (1953)

Melody Tour Variety Programs (1954)

Melody, Harmony, Rhythm Variety Programs (1949)

Melrose Place Bars (1992), Gays (1992), Hotels (1994), Lesbians (1996), Soap Operas (Note)

The Member of the Wedding Broadway (1958), Broadway (1982)

Memories with Music Variety Programs (1946)

Men Lawyers (1989)

Men at Law Lawyers (1970)

Men at Work Variety Programs (1942)

The Men from Shiloh Westerns (1970)

Men in White Doctors (1945)

Men Into Space Space (1959)

Men of Annapolis Drama (1957)

Men of the Dragon Martial Arts (1974)

The Merchant of Venice Shakespeare (1972), Shakespeare (1980)

Mercy Point Robots (1998)

Mermaid Mermaids (2005)

The Mermaid Chronicles: She Creature Mermaids (2001)

Mermaids Mermaids (2003), Teenagers (1991)

Merman on Broadway Broadway (1959)

Merry Christmas from the Bing Crosbys Holiday Specials (1975)

Merry Christmas from the Grand Ole Opry Holiday Specials (1979)

Merry Christmas Land Holiday Specials (1947)

Merry Christmas, with Love Julie Holiday Specials (1979)

The Merry Widow Ballet (2000), Opera (1955)

The Merry Wives of Windsor Shakespeare (1982)

Merv Griffin and the Christmas Kids Holiday Specials (1973)

The Merv Griffin Show Puppets (1972), Senior Citizens (1965)

Messing Prize Party Game Shows (1948)

Miami Undercover Florida (1961), Hotels (1961)

Miami Vice Cuban American (1984), Films Based on Television Series (2006), Florida (1984), Latino American (1984), Men — Law Enforcers (1984)

The Michael Richards Show Los Angeles (2000), Men — Law Enforcers (2000)

Michael Shayne Florida (1960), Reporters (1960), Men-Law Enforcers (1960), Series Based on Radio Programs (1960)

Michael Shayne, Detective Men — Law Enforcers (1958)

The Michaels in Africa Animals (1958)

The Michele Lee Show Hotels (1974)

Mickey Asian American (1964), California (1964), Hotels (1964)

Mickey and Nora Lawyers (1987), Pilot Film Series (1987)

Mickey and the Contessa Pilot Film Series (1963–1967)

The Mickey Mouse Club Adolescence (1955), Camps (1955), Children's Program (1955), Teenagers (1955)

Mickey Spillane's Mike Hammer Men — Law Enforcers (1984)

Mickie Finn's Historical Settings (1966)

Micro Woman and Super Stretch Super Heroes (1980)

Microcops Aliens (1989)

Midnight Caller Men — Law Enforcers (1988), Newspapers (1988)

Midnight Mystery Drama (1957)

A Midsummer's Night Dream Shakespeare (1971), Shakespeare (1981)

Midwestern Hayride Variety Programs (1947)

The Mighty Hercules Cartoons (1960)

The Mighty Heroes Cartoons (1966)

The Mighty Morphin Power Rangers Aliens (1993), Children — Extraordinary (2003), Martial Arts (1993), Teenagers (1993)

The Mighty Mouse Playhouse Cartoons (1955)

The Mighty O Pilot Film Series (1963–1967)

The Mighty Orbots Robots (1984)

Mighty Thor Super Heroes (1965)

Mike and the Mermaid Mermaids (1968)

Mike Douglas Christmas Special Holiday Specials (1969)

Mike Hammer Cars (1984), Men — Law Enforcers (1958), New York (1958), NewYork (1984)

Mike Hammer, Private Eye Men — Law Enforcers (1997)

The Mike Wallace Interviews News Broadcasts (1957)

A Milestone in Television Cartoons (1940)

The Milky Way Broadway (1939)

The Millionaire Drama (1955)

The Milton Berle Show Cross Dressers (1948), Puppets (1949), Series Based on Radio Programs (1948), Variety Programs (1953), Variety Programs (1955)

The Milton the Monster Cartoon Show Cartoons (1965)

Mimi Pilot Film Series (1963–1967)

Mindy Carson Sings Variety Programs (1949)

A Minute with Stan Hooper Gays (2003), Shows within Shows (2003)

Miracle at Blaise Ghosts (1944), Television Firsts (1944), War — World War II (1944)

Miracle on 34th Street Holiday Specials (1955, 1959, 1973)

Miracle Pets Animals (2002)

The Miracle Worker Broadway (1957), Broadway (1979), Broadway (2000)

Miracles Latino American (2003), Religious Programs (2003)

The Misadventures of Sheriff Lobo Men — Law Enforcers (1982)

Misery Loves Company New York (1995)

The Misfits of Science Children — Extraordinary (1985), Men — Extraordinary (1985)

Miss America Pageant Hearing Impaired Characters (1994)

Miss Bishop Pilot Film Series (1961), Teachers (1961)

Miss Jones Lawyers (1991)

Miss Match Los Angeles (2003), Love (2003)

Miss Pepperdine Sitcoms (1959), Women — "Dumb Blondes" (1959)

Miss Stewart, Sir Housekeepers (1972), Teachers (1972)

Miss Susan Physically Disabled (1951), Soap Operas (1951), Soap Operas (Note)

Miss Winslow and Son Aviators (1979)

Missing F.B.I. Agents (2003), Mediums (2004)

Missing Persons Chicago (1993), Latino American (1993)

Mission Magic Witches (1973)

Mission: Impossible African American (1966), Espionage (1966), Espionage (1988), Films Based on Television Series (1996)

The Mississippi Lawyers (1983)

Missouri Legend Television Firsts (1939)

The Missus Goes-a-Shopping Game Shows (1943, 1947), Television Firsts (1943)

Mr. Adams and Eve Los Angeles (1957), Sitcoms (1957)

Mr. and Mrs. Carroll Variety Programs (1950)

Mr. and Mrs. Cop Men — Law Enforcers (1974), Women — Law Enforcers (1974)

Mr. and Mrs. Dracula Vampires (1980)

Mr. and Mrs. North Broadway (1946), Men — Law Enforcers (1949), Men — Law Enforcers

(1951), New York (1952), Series Based on Radio Programs (1952), Women — Law Enforcers (1949), Women — Law Enforcers (1952)

Mr. and Mrs. Ryan Men — Law Enforcers (1986)

Mr. and Ms. Men — Law Enforcers (1975)

Mr. & Ms. Women — Law Enforcers (1975)

Mr. Arsenic Drama (1952)

Mr. Belvedere Adolescence (1985), Housekeepers (1985), Philadelphia (1985), Pilot Film Series (1965), Restaurants (1985), Shows within Shows (1985), Teenagers (1985), Women — "Dumb Blondes" (1985)

Mr. Bevis Angels (1960)

Mr. Bill's Real Life Adventures Puppets (1975)

Mr. Black Drama (1949)

Mr. Boogedy Ghosts (1986)

Mr. Broadway New York (1964), Variety and Drama Spectaculars (1957)

Mr. Citizen Drama (1955)

Mr. Deeds Goes to Town Country Folk (1969), New York (1969)

Mr. District Attorney District Attorneys (1951), Series Based on Radio Programs (1951)

Mr. Dugan Politics (1979)

Mister Ed Cars (1960), Espionage (1965), Senior Citizens (1960), Talking Animals and Machines (1960)

Mr. Ed Los Angeles (1960)

Mr. Garland Asian American (1960)

Mr. Glencannon Takes All Adventurers (1953), Adventurers (1958)

Mr. Imagination Children's Program (1949)

Mr. Jericho Con Artists (1970)

Mr. Kruger's Christmas Holiday Specials (1980)

Mr. L.A. Shows within Shows (2003)

Mr. Lucky Latino American (1959), Los Angeles (1959), Restaurants (1959), Series Based on Films (1959)

Mr. Magoo Cartoons (1963)

Mr. Mayor Children's Program (1964)

Mr. Mergenthwirker's Lobblies Variety and Drama Spectaculars (1946)

Mr. Merlin Children — Extraordinary (1981), Magicians (1981), San Francisco (1981), Teenagers (1981)

Mr. Novak Los Angeles (1963), Teachers (1963)

Mr. O'Malley Angels (1959)

Mister Peepers Sitcoms (1952), Teachers (1952), Women — Nurses (1952)

Mr. President Politics (1987), Teenagers (1987), Washington, D.C. (1987)

Mr. Roberts Broadway (1984), Series Based on Films (1965)

Mr. Rogers' Neighborhood Children's Programs (1967), Puppets (1967)

Mr. Smith Talking Animals and Machines (1984)

Mr. Smith Washington, D.C. (1983)

Mr. Smith Goes to Washington Country Folk (1962), Politics (1962), Series Based on Films (1962), Washington, D.C. (1962)

Mister Sterling Politics (2003), Washington, D.C. (2003)

Mr. Sunshine Teachers (1986), Visually Impaired (1986)

Mr. T and Tina Adolescence (1976), Chicago (1976)

Mister Terrific Men — Extraordinary (1967)

Mr. Terrific Super Heroes (1967), Washington, D.C. (1966)

Mr. Tutt Lawyers (1958)

Mr. Wizard Children's Program (1951)

Mitchell and Woods Women — Law Enforcers (1981)

Mixed Doubles Sitcoms (1949)

Mixed Nuts Psychiatrists (1977)

Mme. Liu Tsong Asian American (1951)

The Mob Squad African American (1968)

Mobile Medics Doctors (1977)

Mobile One Reporters (1975), Shows within Shows (1975)

Moby Dick and the Mighty Mightor Cartoons (1967)

The Mod Squad Cars (1968), Films Based on Television Series (1999), Los Angeles (1968), Men — Law Enforcers (1968), Women — Law Enforcers (1968)

Model by Day Women — Extraordinary (1994)

Models Inc. Nightclubs (1994)

Modern Living Newspapers (1984)

Modern Men Bars (2006)

Modern Romances Drama (1954)

Modesty Blaise Espionage (1982), Women — Extraordinary (1982)

Moe's World Ghosts (1992)

Moesha Los Angeles (1996), Teen After-School Hangouts (1996), Teenagers (1996)

Mohawk Showroom Variety Programs (1949)

Moll Flanders Nudity (1980)

Molloy California (1990), Los Angeles (1990), Shows within Shows (1990), Teenagers (1990)

Mom and Dad Can't Hear Me Hearing Impaired Characters (1978)

Moment of Decision Drama — Repeat Series (1957)

Moment of Fear Drama — Repeat Series (1960)

Momma the Detective Women — Law Enforcers (1981)

The Mommies Adolescence (1993), Women — "Dumb Blondes" (1993)

Mona Hotels (1987)

Mona McCluskey Los Angeles (1965)

Monday Theater Pilot Film Series (1970)

The Monk Men — Law Enforcers (1969)

Monk Men — Law Enforcers (2002), Mentally Disabled (2002), San Francisco (2004), Women — Law Enforcers (2002)

The Monkees Cars (1966), Los Angeles (1966)

The Monroes American Indian (1966), Teenagers (1966), Twins (1966), Westerns (1966)

The Monster Squad Vampires (1976), Werewolves (1976)

Monsters Drama (1988), The Supernatural (1988)

The Montefuscos Connecticut (1975)

Montgomery's Summer Stock Drama (1953)

Monty Politics (1994), Shows within Shows (1994)

Monty Nash Espionage (1971)

The Moon and Sixpence Variety and Drama Spectaculars (1959)

A Moon for the Misbegotten Broadway (1974)

Moon Over Miami Florida (1993), Men — Law Enforcers (1993)

Moonlight Broadway (1952)

Moonlighting Los Angeles (1985), Men — Law Enforcers (1985), Women — Law Enforcers (1985)

More Wild Wild West Twins (1979)

The Morey Amsterdam Show Variety and Drama Spectaculars (1948), Variety Programs (1948)

Mork and Mindy Aliens (1978), Cars (1978), Hotels (1978), Senior Citizens (1978)

Morning Chicago Shows within Shows (2002)

Morning Court Judges (1960)

The Morning Show News Broadcasts (1954)

Morning Star Soap Operas (1965)

Morning Star/Evening Star Senior Citizens (1986)

Moscow Bureau Reporters (1986)

Moses the Lawgiver Religious Programs (1975)

The Most Deadly Game Men — Law Enforcers (1970), Women — Law Enforcers (1970)

Most Wanted Men — Law Enforcers

(1976), Women — Law Enforcers (1976)

Mother Goose Fairy Tales (1958)

Mother, Juggs and Speed Doctors (1978)

Mother's Day Game Shows (1958)

The Mothers-in-Law Cuban American (1951), Los Angeles (1967)

Motor Mouse Cartoons (1970)

A Motown Merry Christmas Holiday Specials (1987)

The Mouse and the Motorcycle Talking Animals and Machines (1986)

The Mouse That Roared Cross Dressers (1966)

A Mouse, a Mystery and Me Talking Animals and Machines (1987)

Movie Land Quiz Game Shows (1948)

Movie Stars Adolescence (1999), California (1999), Los Angeles (1999), Teenagers (1999)

Movin' On Truckers (1973)

Moya Aliens (1999)

Mrs. Columbo Adolescence (1979), Reporters (1979), Women — Law Enforcers (1979)

Mrs. G. Goes to College Senior Citizens (1961), Teachers (1961)

The MTV Music Awards Nudity (1999)

The MTV Music Awards Show Lesbians (2003)

The MTV Top 20 Countdown Cuban American (1992)

Much Ado About Nothing Shakespeare (1984)

Muddling Through Hotels (1994), Restaurants (1994)

Muggy Doo Cartoons (1965)

Muggsy Taxi Cabs (1977), Teenagers (1976)

The Mullets Nudity (2003), San Francisco (2003)

Mulligan's Stew California (1977), Teenagers (1977)

Munster Go Home Films Based on Television Series (1966)

The Munsters Adolescence (1964), Films Based on Television Series (1966), Look-alikes (1964), Magicians (1964), Senior Citizens (1964), Teenagers (1964), Twins (1964), Vampires (1964), Werewolves (1964)

The Munsters Today Adolescence (1964), Teenagers (1987), Vampires (1988), Werewolves (1988)

A Muppet Family Christmas Holiday Specials (1987)

The Muppet Show Puppets (1975)

Murder Ink Women — Law Enforcers (1983)

Murder One Los Angeles (1995)

Murder 101 Senior Citizens (2006)

Murder, She Wrote Look-alikes

(1984), Men — Law Enforcers (1984), Physically Disabled (1993), Senior Citizens (1986), Women — Law Enforcers (1986)

The Murdocks and the McClays Country Folk (1970), Pilot Film Series (1970)

Murphy Brown Cars (1988), Housekeepers (1988), Physically Disabled (1988), Reporters (1988), Restaurants (1988), Senior Citizens (1988), Shows within Shows (1988), Washington, D.C. (1988)

Murphy's Law Asian American (1988)

Music '55 Variety Programs (1955)

Music for a Spring Night Variety Programs (1960)

Music for a Summer Night Variety Programs (1959)

Music from Meadowbrook Variety Programs (1953)

Music in Velvet Variety Programs (1949)

The Music Man Broadway (2003)

The Music of Gershwin Variety and Drama Spectaculars (1956)

Music on Ice Variety Programs (1960)

The Music Shop Variety Programs (1959)

The Music Show Variety Programs (1953)

Music with Mary Martin Variety and Drama Spectaculars (1954)

Musical Chairs African American (1975), Game Shows (1955)

Musical Comedy Tonight Broadway (1981)

Musical Merry-Go-Round Variety Programs (1947)

Musical Miniatures Television Firsts (1931)

Mutant X Geniuses (2001), Men — Extraordinary (2001), Women — Extraordinary (2001)

Mutts Talking Animals and Machines (1988)

Mutual of Omaha's Wild Kingdom Animals (1963)

My Africa Teenagers (1988)

My Big Fat Greek Life Chicago (2003), Restaurants (2003), Series Based on Films (2003)

My Big Fat Greek Wedding Restaurants (2003), Series Based on Films (2003)

My Boy Googie Adolescence (1967), Pilot Film Series (1963–1967)

My Breast Nudity (1993), Television Firsts (1993)

My Darling Judge Judges (1961)

My Father the Clown Clowns (1987)

My Favorite Husband California (1953), Los Angeles (1953), Series

Based on Radio Programs (1953), Sitcoms (1953)

My Favorite Martian Aliens (1963), Hotels (1963), Los Angeles (1963), Reporters (1963), Women — Scatterbrained (1963)

My Friend Flicka Animals (1956), Color Broadcasting (1956), Series Based on Films (1956)

My Friend Irma Adolescence (1952), Hotels (1952), New York (1952), Nudity (1952), Reporters (1952), Senior Citizens (1952), Series Based on Radio Programs (1952), Sitcoms (1952), Women — "Dumb Blondes" (1952)

My Friend Tony Los Angeles (1969), Men — Law Enforcers (1969)

My Guys New York (1996)

My Hero Los Angeles (1952), Sitcoms (1952)

My Life as a Teenage Robot Robots (2003)

My Little Margie African American (1952), Hotels (1952), New York (1952), Nudity (1952), Senior Citizens (1952), Series Based on Radio Programs (1952), Sitcoms (1952)

My Living Doll Robots (1964)

My Lucky Penny Pilot Film Series (1963–1967)

My Mom's Having a Baby Nudity (1977)

My Mother the Car Adolescence (1965), Los Angeles (1965), Talking Animals and Machines (1965)

My Partner the Ghost Ghosts (1973)

My Secret Identity Adolescence (1988), Canada (1988), Children — Extraordinary (1988), Lesbians (1988), Teenagers (1988)

My Sister Eileen Hotels (1960), New York (1960), Newspapers (1960), Series Based on Films (1960), Series Based on Films (1962), Sitcoms (1960)

My Sister Hank Adolescence (1972)

My Sister Sam San Francisco (1986), Teenagers (1986)

My So-Called Life Gays (1992), Latino American (1994), Teenagers (1994)

My Son Jeep Series Based on Radio Programs (1953), Sitcoms (1953)

My Son the Doctor Doctors (1966), Pilot Film Series (1963–1967)

My Three Angels Holiday Specials (1954)

My Three Sons Adolescence (1960), Adolescence (1970), Color Broadcasting (1966), Housekeepers (1960), Look-alikes (1960), Senior Citizens (1960), Sitcoms (1960), Teenagers (1960)

My True Story Drama (1950)

My Two Dads Adolescence (1987), New York (1987)

My Wife and Kids Adolescence (2001), Connecticut (2001), Geniuses (2002), Teenagers (2001)

My World and Welcome to It Adolescence (1969), Connecticut (1969), Newspapers (1969)

Mysteries of Chinatown Asian American (1949), Men — Law Enforcers (1949), San Francisco (1949)

Mysteries of the Bible Religious Programs (2001)

The Mysterious Two Aliens (1982)

Mysterious Ways Psychiatrists (2002), Religious Programs (2000)

Mystery Drama (1980)

Mystery and Mrs Men — Law Enforcers (1950), Women — Law Enforcers (1950)

Mystery Chef Cooking (1949)

Mystery Dance Reporters (1995), Women — Law Enforcers (1995)

Mystery Island Robots (1977)

The Mystery of Ghost Farm Men — Law Enforcers (1957)

Mystery Science Theater 3000 Robots (1989)

Mystery Woman Women — Law Enforcers (2005)

N.O.P.D. Men — Law Enforcers (1956)

N.Y.P.D. Men — Law Enforcers (1967), New York (1967)

N.Y.P.D. Blue District Attorneys (1993), Gays (2000), Lesbians (1994), Lesbians (1995), Men — Law Enforcers (1993), Mexican American (1993), New York (1993), Nudity (1993), Women — Law Enforcers (1993)

Naked City Men — Law Enforcers (1958), Men — Law Enforcers (1960), New York (1958), New York (1960)

The Naked Gun: From the Files of the Police Squad Films Based on Television Series (1988)

The Naked Truth Newspapers (1995)

Nakia American Indian (1974), Men — Law Enforcers (1974)

Name of the Game Reporters (1968)

Name That Tune Game Shows (1953), Series Based on Radio Programs (1953)

The Name's the Same Game Shows (1951)

Nancy Politics (1970)

Nancy Drew Women — Law Enforcers (1995), Women — Law Enforcers (2002)

The Nancy Drew Mysteries Women — Law Enforcers (1977)

The Nancy Walker Show California (1976), Gays (1976)

The Nanny Adolescence (1993), Housekeepers (1996), New York (1993), Nudity (1996), Senior Citizens (1993), Teenagers (1993)

Nanny and the Professor Adolescence (1970), Housekeepers (1970), Los Angeles (1970), Witches (1970)

Nash Bridges Angels (1996), Cars (1996), District Attorneys (1996), Gays (1996), Lesbians (1997), Men — Law Enforcers (1996), Mentally Disabled (1996), Mexican American (1996), Nudity (2005), San Francisco (1996), Senior Citizens (1996), Women — Law Enforcers (1998)

Nashville 99 Men — Law Enforcers (1977)

Nasty Boys Latino American (1990), Men — Law Enforcers (1990)

The Nat King Cole Show African American (1956)

The National Gossip Newspapers (1979)

National Register Reporters (1977), Reporters (1985)

National Velvet Adolescence (1960), Animals (1960), Physically Disabled (1960), Series Based on Films (1960)

Native American Programs Westerns (2005)

Naturally Sadie Teenagers (2005)

Naughty Marietta Opera (1955), Variety and Drama Spectaculars (1955)

Navy Log War — World War II (1955)

Navy NCIS Forensics (2003), Senior Citizens (2003)

NBC Action Playhouse Drama — Repeat Series (1971)

NBC Adventure Theater Drama — Repeat Series (1971)

NBC Comedy Theater Drama — Repeat Series (1971)

The NBC Family Christmas Party Holiday Specials (1982)

The NBC Opera Theater Opera (1950)

The NBC Revue Variety Programs (1939)

NBC Saturday Prom Variety Programs (1960)

NBC White Paper: The First Hundred Days Presidential Appearances (1981)

Nearly Departed Ghosts (1989)

Ned and Stacey New York (1995), Newspapers (1995)

Ned Blessing: The Story of My Life and Times American Indian (1993), Westerns (1993)

Needles and Pins New York (1973)

Nero Wolfe Men — Law Enforcers (1981), Men — Law Enforcers

(2001), New York (1981), New York (2001)

The Nervous Wreck Broadway (1952)

Nestor, the Long-Eared Christmas Donkey Holiday Specials (1977)

Nettie Broadway (1945)

Nevada Smith Westerns (1975)

Never Too Young Soap Operas (1965), Soap Operas (Note)

The New Adam-12 Los Angeles (1989), Men — Law Enforcers (1989)

The New Addams Family Adolescence (1998), Housekeepers (1998), Latino American (1998)

The New Adventures of Batman Super Heroes (1977)

The New Adventures of Beans Baxter Children — Extraordinary (1987), Espionage (1987), Teenagers (1987), Washington, D.C. (1987)

The New Adventures of Charlie Chan Asian American (1957), Men — Law Enforcers (1957), Series Based on Films (1957)

The New Adventures of Huckleberry Finn American Indian (1968), Cartoons (1968), Historical Settings (1968)

The New Adventures of Old Christine Los Angeles (2006)

New Adventures of Pinocchio Puppets (1961)

The New Adventures of Spin and Marty Camps (1955)

The New Adventures of Superman Super Heroes (1966), Super Heroes (1967)

The New Adventures of Wonder Woman Super Heroes (1976)

The New Adventures of Zorro Latino American (1957)

The New Andy Griffith Show Adolescence (1972)

New Attitude Los Angeles (1990)

The New Avengers Espionage (1978), Women — Extraordinary (1978)

The New Bill Cosby Show African American (1972)

The New Bob Cummings Show Pilots (1961)

The New Breed Los Angeles (1961), Men — Law Enforcers (1961)

The New Casper Cartoon Show Ghosts (1953), Witches (1963)

New Comedy Showcase Pilot Film Series (1960)

The New Daughters of Joshua Cabe Westerns (1972)

The New Dick Van Dyke Show Adolescence (1969), Arizona (1971), Mexican American (1973), Shows within Shows (1971), Teenagers (1971)

The New Dragnet Los Angeles

(1989), Men — Law Enforcers (1989), Mexican American (1989)

The New Fantastic Four Super Heroes (1977)

The New Ghost Writer Mysteries Children — Extraordinary (1997), Ghosts (1997), New York (1997), Reporters (1997), Teenagers (1997)

The New Gidget Beaches (1986), Senior Citizens (1986), Teenagers (1986)

The New Healers Doctors (1972), Women — Nurses (1972)

New Howdy Doody Show Puppets (1976)

A New Kind of Family Los Angeles (1979)

The New Land Adolescence (1974), Immigrants (1974)

The New Lassie Adolescence (1989), Animals (1954)

The New Leave It to Beaver Adolescence (1986), Senior Citizens (1986)

The New Loretta Young Show Adolescence (1962), Connecticut (1962), Twins (1962)

The New Love, American Style Drama (1985), Love (1985)

The New Maverick Westerns (1978)

The New Mickey Mouse Club Adolescence (1977)

The New Mike Hammer Men — Law Enforcers (1986)

The New Newlywed Game Love (1984)

New Newlywed Game Love (1985)

The New Odd Couple Newspapers (1982)

The New Operation Petticoat War — World War II (1978), Women — Nurses (1978)

The New, Original Wonder Woman Super Heroes (1976)

The New People Beaches (1969)

The New Perry Mason District Attorneys (1957(2005), Lawyers (1973), Los Angeles (1973)

The New Phil Silvers Show Con Artists (1963), Los Angeles (1963)

The New Temperature's Rising Show African American (1973), Doctors (1974), Washington, D.C. (1973), Women — Nurses (1973)

The New Three Stooges Cartoons (1966)

The New Voice Newspapers (1980)

A New Year's Eve Party with Guy Lombardo and His Royal Canadians Holiday Specials (1954)

New York Confidential New York (1958), Reporters (1958)

New York Undercover Men — Law Enforcers (1993), New York (1994), Nightclubs (1994), Puerto Rican (1994), Women — Law Enforcers (1993)

The New Zoo Revue Talking Animals and Machines (1972)

Newhart Country Folk (1982), Hotels (1982), Restaurants (1982)

The Newlywed Game Love (1966)

News Radio New York (1995)

The Next Step Beyond Drama (1978), The Supernatural (1978)

Nichols Arizona (1971), Bars (1971), Historical Settings (1971), Westerns (1971)

Nichols and Dymes Government Agents (1981)

Nick and the Dobermans Men — Law Enforcers (1981)

Nick Derringer, P.I. Little People (1988)

Nick Freno, Licensed Teacher Teachers (1996)

Nick Knight Vampires (1989), Vampires (1992)

Night Cap Broadway (1952)

Night Club Revue Variety Programs (1939)

Night Court Asian American (1984), Cars (1984), Judges (1965), Judges (1984), Lawyers (1984), Little People (1984), Magicians (1984), New York (1984)

Night Gallery Drama (1970), The Supernatural (1971)

Night Heat Canada (1985), Men — Law Enforcers (1985), Nightclubs (1985), Reporters (1985), Restaurants (1985)

Night Must Fall Broadway (1952)

The Night of January 16th Broadway (1952)

Night Prowl Newspapers (1958)

The Night Rider Men — Extraordinary (1979)

Night Stalker Los Angeles (2005), The Supernatural (2005)

The Night Stalker Reporters (2005)

Night Visions Drama (2001)

The Nightingale Fairy Tales (1958), Fairy Tales (1982), Opera (2005)

Nightingales Latino American (1989), Los Angeles (1989), Nudity (1989), Women — Nurses (1988), Women — Nurses (1989)

The Nightingales Women — Law Enforcers (1979)

NightMan Men — Extraordinary (1997), Nightclubs (1997), Physically Disabled (1997), Super Heroes (1997), Women — Law Enforcers (1997)

Nightmare Drama (1958)

Nightmare Café Angels (1992), Los Angeles (1992), The Supernatural (1992)

Nightmare Classics Drama (1989)

Nightmare Room Drama (2001)

Nightmares and Dreamscapes: Short Stories by Stephen King Drama (2006)

Nikki Hotels (2000), Las Vegas Settings (2000)

905-Wild Animals (1975)

9 to 5 Latino American (1982), Series Based on Films (1982)

Nine to Five New York (1982), New York (1986)

90 Bristol Court California (1964), Teenagers (1964)

Nip/Tuck Florida (2003), Lesbians (2003), Transsexuals (2004)

No Man's Land Westerns (1984)

No Soap, Radio Hotels (1982), New Jersey (1982)

No Time for Sergeants Series Based on Films (1964)

No Warning Drama (1958)

Noah's Ark Animals (1957), Physically Disabled (1956)

Noble Quest Asian American (1991)

Nobody's Perfect Men — Law Enforcers (1980), San Francisco (1980), Women — Law Enforcers (1980)

Norby Adolescence (1955), New York (1955), Sitcoms (1955)

The Norliss Tapes The Supernatural (1973)

Norm Bars (1999), Latino American (1999)

The Norm Show Latino American (1999), New York (1999)

Normal Transsexuals (2002)

Normal Life Los Angeles (1990)

Normal, Ohio Gays (2000)

Norman Corwin Presents Drama (1971)

North and South Civil War (1985), Civil War (1986)

North and South, Book II Civil War (1986)

The North Shore Hawaii (2004), Hotels (2004), Lesbians (2004)

North Star Geniuses (1986), Men — Extraordinary (1986)

Northern Exposure American Indian (1990), Bars (1990), Doctors (1990), Gays (1990), Lesbians (1990), Pilots (1990)

Northwest Passage American Indian (1958), Color Broadcasting (1957-1965), Historical Settings (1958)

Not for Publication New York (1951), Reporters (1951)

Nothing But the Best Variety Programs (1953)

Nothing But the Truth Broadway (1952), Game Shows (1956)

Nothing in Common Chicago (1987), Series Based on Films (1987)

Nothing Is Easy Asian American (1986), Teenagers (1986)

Nothing Sacred Religious Characters (1997)

Now It Can Be Told Puerto Rican (1991)

Now We're Cookin.' Restaurants (1983)

Now You See It Magicians (1949)

Number 13 Demon Street Devil (1962)

Number 96 Los Angeles (1979), Love (1979), Puerto Rican (1980)

NUMB3RS Geniuses (2005), Los Angeles (2005), Senior Citizens (2005)

The Nunundaga American Indian (1977)

Nurse New York (1981), Women — Nurses (1981)

The Nurses Doctors (1964), New York (1962), Soap Operas (1965), Soap Operas (Note), Women — Nurses (1962), Women — Nurses (1965)

Nurses Florida (1991), Latino American (1991), Women — Nurses (1991)

The Nutcracker Ballet (1958), Holiday Specials (1958)

Nuts and Bolts Robots (1981)

The Nutt House Hotels (1989), New York (1989), Senior Citizens (1989), Visually Impaired (1989)

The O. Henry Playhouse Drama (1957)

The O.C. California (2003), Lesbians (2004), Soap Operas (Note)

Oakmont Teachers (1988)

The Oblongs Physically Disabled (2001)

Occasional Wife New York (1966)

Ocean Quest Reality Programs (1985), Women — Extraordinary (1985)

O'Connor's Ocean Lawyers (1960)

Octavius and Me Pilot Film Series (1963–1967), Senior Citizens (1962)

The Odd Couple Broadway (1981), Hotels (1970), New York (1970), Newspapers (1970), Series Based on Films (1970)

Odd Man Out Florida (1999), Teenagers (1999)

Of All Things Variety Programs (1956)

Of Men, of Women Love (1972), Love (1973)

Of Thee I Sing Broadway (1972), Politics (1972)

Off Broadway Women — Law Enforcers (1995)

Off the Rack Teenagers (1984)

Off the Record Sitcoms (1948)

Off to See the Wizard Drama (1967)

Off We Go Pilot Film Series (1963–1967), Teenagers (1966), War — World War II (1966)

Oh, Boy Variety Programs (1959)

Oh Coward! Broadway (1980)

Oh Grow Up Gays (1999), Lawyers (1999)

Oh, Kay! Variety Programs (1951)

Oh Nurse! Women — Nurses (1972)

Oh, Those Bells California (1962)

Ohara Asian American (1987), Los Angeles (1987), Mexican American (1987), Puerto Rican (1987), Women — Law Enforcers (1987)

O'Hara, United States Treasury Government Agents (1971), Washington, D.C. (1971)

O.K. Crackerby California (1965)

The O'Keefe's Geniuses (2003)

Oklahoma Broadway (1999)

Old Dogs. Senior Citizens (1987)

The Old Maid and the Thief Opera (1949)

Old Money Senior Citizens (1989)

The Old Knickerbocker Music Hall Game Shows (1948)

The Oldest Rookie Los Angeles (1987), Men — Law Enforcers (1987)

The Oldsmobile Music Theater Drama (1959)

Oliver Beene Adolescence (2003), Historical Settings (2004)

O'Malley Men — Law Enforcers (1983)

The Omen The Supernatural (1991)

On Borrowed Time Broadway (1957)

On Our Own New York (1977)

On Stage Everybody Variety Programs (1945)

On the Air Shows within Shows (1992), Twins (1992), Visually Impaired (1992)

On the Corner Variety Programs (1948)

On the Edge Men — Law Enforcers (1987)

On the Rocks African American (1975), Mexican American (1975), Mexican American (1976), Prison (1975), Puerto Rican (1975)

On the Street Shows within Shows (1992)

On the Town Broadway (1993)

On the Town in Concert Broadway (1993)

On the Two a Day Variety and Drama Spectaculars (1949)

On Trial Judges (1948), Judges (1955), Judges (1957), Judges (1978), Judges (1994)

On Your Account Game Shows (1954)

On Your Way Game Shows (1953)

Onawandah Fairy Tales (1960)

Once a Hero Los Angeles (1987), Men — Extraordinary (1987), Super Heroes (1987)

Once a Thief Con Artists (2002), Restaurants (2002)

Once and Again Lesbians (2002)

Once Upon a Brothers Grimm Fairy Tales (1977)

Once Upon a Christmas Time Holiday Specials (1959)

Once Upon a Fence Children's Program (1952)

Once Upon a Mattress Broadway (1964), Broadway (1972), Broadway (2005)

Once Upon a Midnight Dreary Ghosts (1979)

Once Upon a Spy Espionage (1980)

Once Upon an Easter Time Holiday Specials (1954)

One Big Family Senior Citizens (1986), Teenagers (1986), Washington, D.C. (1986)

One Day at a Time Adolescence (1984), Bars (1975), Hotels (1975), Senior Citizens (1975), Teenagers (1975)

The $1.98 Beauty Show Reality Programs (1978)

1–800-Missing F.B.I. Agents (2003)

One Happy Family Senior Citizens (1961)

One Hour in Wonderland Holiday Specials (1950), Variety and Drama Spectaculars (1950)

100 Center Street Judges (1984), Latino American (1984), Lesbians (2001)

The 100 Lives of Black Jack Savage Geniuses (1991), Ghosts (1991), Latino American (1991)

The $100,000 Big Surprise Game Shows (1956)

One Touch of Venus Broadway (1955)

One Life to Live Soap Operas (1968)

One Man's Experience Soap Operas (1952)

One Man's Family San Francisco (1949), Series Based on Radio Programs (1949), Soap Operas (1949), Soap Operas (Note)

One Minute from Broadway Hotels (1956)

One Minute Please Game Shows (1954)

One of the Boys Cuban American (1989), New Jersey (1982), New York (1989), Senior Citizens (1979)

One on One Baltimore (2001), Shows within Shows (2001), Teenagers (2001)

One Step Beyond Drama (1959), Drama (1978), The Supernatural (1959)

One Sunday Afternoon Broadway (1949), Broadway (1951), Broadway (1952), Broadway (1957), Broadway (1959)

One Tree Hill Lesbians (2004)

One, Two, Three—Go! Children's Program (1961)

One West Waikiki Beaches (1994), Doctors (1994), Forensics(1994), Hawaii (1994)

One Woman's Experience Soap Operas (1952)

One World Asian American (1998), Cuban American (1998), Florida (2001), Teen After-School Hangouts (1998), Teenagers (1998)

The O'Neills Series Based on Radio Programs (1949), Soap Operas (1949)

Only Temporary Women—Scatterbrained (1984)

Open All Night California (1981), Los Angeles (1993), Nightclubs (1992)

Open End News Broadcasts (1958)

Open House Housekeepers (1989), Los Angeles (1989)

Opening Night Drama—Repeat Series (1958)

Opera Cameos Opera (1953)

Opera vs. Jazz Opera (1953)

Operation Entertainment Variety and Drama Spectaculars (1954)

Operation Greasepaint Pilot Film Series (1968), War—World War II (1967)

Operation Petticoat Nudity (1977), Series Based on Films (1977), War—World War II (1977), War—World War II (1978), Women—Nurses (1977)

Operation: Runaway Psychiatrists (1978)

The Oregon Trail Westerns (1977)

The Orient Express Drama (1953)

Original Sins Religious Characters (1991)

The Orphan and the Dude African American (1975)

Orson Welles' Great Mysteries Drama (1973)

O.S.S. War—World War II (1957)

Othello Shakespeare (1981)

The Others Mediums (2000), Senior Citizens (2000), The Supernatural (2000), Visually Impaired (2000)

Otherworld Robots (1985), Teenagers (1985)

Our Family Honor New York (1985)

Our Five Daughters Soap Operas (1962)

Our House Los Angeles (1986), Newspapers (1986), Senior Citizens (1986), Teenagers (1986)

Our Man Flint Espionage (1976), Government Agents (1976)

Our Man Higgins Adolescence (1962), Housekeepers (1962), Series Based on Radio Programs (1962)

Our Miss Brooks Films Based on Television Series (1956), Hotels (1952), Senior Citizens (1952), Series Based on Radio Programs (1952), Teachers (1952)

Our Private World Soap Operas (1965), Soap Operas (Note)

Our Song Asian American (1991), Politics (1991)

Our Street African American (1971)

Our Time Historical Settings (1985)

Our Town Broadway (1950), Broadway (1955), Broadway (1959), Broadway (1977)

Out All Night Los Angeles (1992)

Out of Practice Doctors (2005), Lesbians (2005), Women—Scatterbrained (2005)

Out of the Blue Adolescence (1979), Aliens (1968), Angels (1979), Chicago (1979), Florida (1995), Housekeepers (1979), Los Angeles (1979), Pilot Film Series (1968), Teenagers (1979), Teenagers (1996)

Out of the Inkwell Clowns (1961)

Out of This World Aliens (1987), California (1987), Teen After-School Hangouts (1987), Teenagers (1987)

Out There Drama (1951)

The Outcasts African American (1968), Westerns (1968)

The Outer Limits Drama (1963), Drama (1995), Lesbians (1995), Nudity (1995), The Supernatural (1963)

The Outlaw Years Westerns (1989)

The Outlaws Westerns (1960)

Outpost Robots (1989), Space (1989), Westerns (1962)

The Outrider Westerns (1959)

The Outside Man Government Agents (1977)

The Outsider Los Angeles (1968), Men—Law Enforcers (1968)

Outward Bound Broadway (1952)

Over 17 Not Admitted Teenagers (1988)

Over and Out War—World War II (1976)

Over My Dead Body Cars (1990), Men—Law Enforcers (1990), Newspapers (1990), San Francisco (1990)

Over There Puerto Rican (2005), War—Korea, Vietnam, Iraq (2005)

Overland Trail Westerns (1960)

Overseas Adventures Reporters (1954)

The Over-the-Hill Gang Senior Citizens (1969), Westerns (1969)

The Over-the-Hill Gang Rides Again Senior Citizens (1970), Westerns (1969)

Owen Marshall, Counselor at Law Lawyers (1971)

The Owl Men—Extraordinary (1991)

The Owl and the Pussycat Prostitutes (1975), Women—"Dumb Blondes" (1975)

Oye, Willie Puerto Rican (1979)

Oz Gays (1997), Latino American (1997), Nudity (1984), Physically Disabled (1997), Prison (1997), Religious Characters (1997)

Ozmoe Mermaids (1951), Puppets (1951)

The P.I. Men—Law Enforcers (1976), Men—Law Enforcers (1994), Women—Law Enforcers (1994)

P.S.I. Luv U California (1991), Con Artists (1991)

Pacific Blue Los Angeles (1996), Men—Law Enforcers (1996), Mexican American (1996), Women—Law Enforcers (1996)

Pacific Station California (1991), California (1999), Men—Law Enforcers (1991)

The Packard Showroom Variety Programs (1954)

Paddy the Pelican Puppets (1950)

Pagliacci Opera (1940), Opera (1945), Opera (1950)

Pajama Tops Broadway (1983)

Palace Guard Hotels (1991)

Pall Mall Playhouse Drama—Repeat Series (1955)

Palmerstown, U.S.A. Historical Settings (1980)

Palmetto Pointe Teenagers (2005)

Palms Precinct Women—Law Enforcers (1982)

Panama Hattie Broadway (1952)

Panhandle Pete and Jennifer Puppets (1950)

Panic Drama (1957)

Panorama Variety and Drama Spectaculars (1956)

Papa Cellini New York (1952)

Papa G.I Asian American (1964), Pilot Film Series (1963–1967)

Papa Said No Sitcoms (1958)

The Paper Chase Lawyers (1978), Senior Citizens (1978), Teachers (1978)

The Paper Chase: The Graduation Year Lawyers (1978), Senior Citizens (1978), Teachers (1978)

The Paper Chase: The Second Year Lawyers (1978), Senior Citizens (1978), Teachers (1978)

The Paper Chase: The Third Year Lawyers (1978), Senior Citizens (1978), Teachers (1978)

Paper Dolls Teenagers (1983)

Paper Moon Adolescence (1975),

Cars (1974), Con Artists (1974), Historical Settings (1974)
Paradise Adventurers (1984), American Indian (1988), Prostitutes (1988), Westerns (1987)
Paradise Lost Shows within Shows (1981)
Paragon Playhouse Drama — Repeat Series (1953)
The Parent Trap Twins (1989)
The Parent'Hood Adolescence (1997), Magicians (1997), New York (1997), Teachers (1997), Teenagers (1997)
Paris Los Angeles (1979), Men — Law Enforcers (1979)
Paris in the Springtime Variety and Drama Spectaculars (1956)
Park Place Lawyers (1980), New York (1981), Physically Disabled (1981)
The Parker Family Sitcoms (1941)
Parker Kane Men — Law Enforcers (1990)
Parker Lewis Can't Lose California (1990), Teachers (1990), Teen After-School Hangouts (1990), Teenagers (1992)
The Parkers Gays (1999), Teachers (1999), Teenagers (1999)
Parole Prison (1982)
Parole Chief Prison (1956)
Partners Doctors (1993), Lawyers (1995), San Francisco (1995)
The Partners Los Angeles (1971), Men — Law Enforcers (1971)
Partners in Crime San Francisco (1984), Women — Law Enforcers (1984)
The Partridge Family Adolescence (1970), Cars (1970), Teen After-School Hangouts (1970)
Partridge Family Teenagers (1970)
Party Line Game Shows (1947)
Party of Five Adolescence (1994), Lesbians (1999), Restaurants (1990), San Francisco (1994), Teenagers (1994)
Party Time at Club Roma Variety Programs (1950)
Passion Broadway (1996), Newspapers (1991)
The Passion of Dracula Broadway (1980)
Passions Little People (1999), Soap Operas (Note), Witches (1999)
Passport to Danger Adventurers (1954), Mexican American (1954)
The Pat Boone and Family Easter Special Holiday Specials (1979)
The Pat Boone Family Christmas Special Holiday Specials (1979)
The Pat Boone Show Variety Programs (1957)
Pat Paulsen for President Politics (1968)

The Patchwork Family Puppets (1974)
Patience Opera (1985)
The Patrice Munsel Show Variety Programs (1957)
The Patricia Bowman Show Variety Programs (1951)
Patrick Stone Men — Law Enforcers (1965), Pilot Film Series (1963–1967)
The Patriots Broadway (1963)
The Patsy Broadway (1952)
The Patti Page Premiere Party Show Variety and Drama Spectaculars (1955)
The Patti Page Show Variety Programs (1955), Variety Programs (1956), Variety Programs (1957), Variety Programs (1958)
The Patty Duke Show Housekeepers (1963), Look-alikes (1963), New York (1963), Newspapers (1963), Teen After-School Hangouts (1963), Teenagers (1963)
The Paul Arnold Show Variety Programs (1949)
Paul Bernard — Psychiatrist Psychiatrists (1972)
The Paul Dixon Show Variety Programs (1951)
The Paul Lynde Show Lawyers (1972)
Paul Sand in Friends and Lovers Boston (1972)
The Paul Williams Show Shows within Shows (1979)
Paul Whiteman's Saturday Night Revue Variety Programs (1949)
The Paul Winchell and Jerry Mahoney Show Puppets (1950)
The Paul Winchell Show Puppets (1957), Puppets (1960)
Paula Stone's Toy Shop Children's Program (1955)
Payne Hotels (1999), Latino American (1999)
Peaceable Kingdom Animals (1909), Los Angeles (1989)
The Peanut Is a Serious Guy Puppets (1944)
Pearl Teachers (1996)
The Pearl Bailey African American (1971)
Pebbles and Bamm Teenagers (1971)
Peck's Bad Girl Adolescence (1959), Sitcoms (1959)
Pecos Bill, King of the Cowboys Fairy Tales (1985)
The Pee Wee King Show Variety Programs (1955)
Pee Wee King's Flying Ranch Variety Programs (1954)
Pee Wee's Playhouse Genies (1986), Robots (1986)
Peek-a-Boo: The One and Only Phyllis Dixey Nudity (1979)
The Peg Leg Pirate Fairy Tales (1960)

Peking Encounter Asian American (1982)
Pen 'n' Inc Newspapers (1980)
The Pendulum Drama — Repeat Series (1956)
Penn and Teller's Don't Try This at Home Magicians (1990)
Penny Penguin Cartoons (1965)
Penny to a Million Game Shows (1955)
Pensacola: Wings of Gold Bars (1997), Florida (1996), Pilots (1997)
Pentagon U.S.A. Washington, D.C. (1953)
Penthouse Party Variety Programs (1950)
Penthouse Sonata Variety Programs (1949)
People Reality Programs (1957)
People Are Funny Game Shows (1946), Game Shows (1954), Reality Programs (1946), Reality Programs (1954), Reality Programs (1984)
People Do the Craziest Things Reality Programs (1984)
The People Next Door Psychiatrists (1989)
The People's Choice Politics (1955), Sitcoms (1955), Talking Animals and Machines (1955)
People's Court Judges (1981)
The People's Court of Small Claims Judges (1958)
Pepper Dennis Nudity and Sexuality (2006), Reporters (2006)
The Pepsi Cola Playhouse Drama (1953)
The Perfect Match Love (1967), Love (1986)
Perfect Strangers Chicago (1986), Hotels (1986), Newspapers (1986)
Pericles, Prince of Tyre Shakespeare (1984)
The Perils of Penelope Pitstop Cartoons (1969)
The Perkins Family Teenagers (1986)
The Perry Como Christmas Show Holiday Specials (1964, 1966, 1968, 1974)
The Perry Como Christmas Special Holiday Specials (1986)
The Perry Como Show Color Broadcasting (1957-1965), Series Based on Radio Programs (1950), Variety Programs (1950), Variety Programs (1955), Variety Programs (1959)
The Perry Como Thanksgiving Special Holiday Specials (1965), Holiday Specials (1966)
Perry Como's Christmas in Australia Holiday Specials (1976)
Perry Como's Christmas in England Holiday Specials (1984)

Perry Como's Christmas in Hawaii Holiday Specials (1985)

Perry Como's Christmas in Mexico Holiday Specials (1975)

Perry Como's Christmas in New York Holiday Specials (1983)

Perry Como's Christmas in the Holy Land Holiday Specials (1980)

Perry Como's French-Canadian Christmas Holiday Specials (1982)

Perry Como's Olde English Christmas Holiday Specials (1977)

Perry Mason District Attorneys (1957), Lawyers (1957), Los Angeles (1957)

Perry Presents Variety Programs (1959)

Person to Person News Broadcasts (1953)

The Persuaders! Adventurers (1971), Judges (1971)

Pet Keeping with Marc Morrone Animals (2003)

Pet Set Animals (1971)

Pete and Gladys Los Angeles (1960), Restaurants (1960), Sitcoms (1960), Women — Scatterbrained (1962)

Pete Kelly's Blues Bars (1959), Historical Settings (1959), Men — Law Enforcers (1959), Series Based on Films (1959), Series Based on Radio Programs (1959)

The Peter and Mary Show New York (1950), Sitcoms (1950)

Peter Gunn Films Based on Television Series (1967), Little People (1958), Los Angeles (1958), Men — Law Enforcers (1958), Men — Law Enforcers (1989), Nightclubs (1958)

Peter Hunter, Private Eye Men — Law Enforcers (1948), New York (1948)

The Peter Lind Hayes Show Variety Programs (1958)

Peter Loves Mary Adolescence (1960), Connecticut (1960), Sitcoms (1960)

Peter Pan Broadway (1955), Broadway (1956), Broadway (1960), Broadway (1976), Color Broadcasting (1956), Fairy Tales (1955), Variety and Drama Spectaculars (1955)

The Peter Potamus Show Cartoons (1964)

Peter Potter's Juke Box Jury Series Based on Radio Programs (1953)

The Petrified Forest Broadway (1955)

Petrocelli Lawyers (1974)

Petticoat Fever Broadway (1945)

Petticoat Junction Country Folk (1963), Hotels (1963), Senior Citizens (1963), Teenagers (1963)

Peyton Place Hearing Impaired Characters (1965), Series Based on Films (1964), Soap Operas (1964), Soap Operas (Note)

The Phantom Men — Extraordinary (1961)

Phenom Teenagers (1993)

Phil of the Future Teenagers (2004)

Phil Silvers on Broadway Variety and Drama Spectaculars (1958)

The Phil Silvers Show Camps (1955), Con Artists (1955), Films Based on Television Series (1991), Sitcoms (1955)

The Philadelphia Story Broadway (1950), Broadway (1952), Broadway (1959)

Philco Television Playhouse Broadway (1949), Drama (1948)

Philip Marlowe Los Angeles (1982), Men — Law Enforcers (1960), Series Based on Radio Programs (1959)

Philip Marlowe, Private Eye Men — Law Enforcers (1983)

Philip Morris Playhouse Drama (1953), Series Based on Radio Programs (1953)

Philly Latino American (2001), Lawyers (2000), Philadelphia (2001)

Philly Heat Rescue (1995)

The Phoenix Aliens (1982)

Photocrime Drama (1945), Men — Law Enforcers (1949)

Photon Aliens (1986)

Phyllis Adolescence (1975), Latino American (1975), San Francisco (1975), Senior Citizens (1975)

Piaf Broadway (1982)

Pick and Pat Variety Programs (1949)

Picket Fences Adolescence (1992), Hearing Impaired Characters (1995), Latino American (1992), Lesbians (1993), Little People (1992), Men — Law Enforcers (1992), Teenagers (1992), Transsexuals (1992), Women — Law Enforcers (1992)

Picture Window Pilot Film Series (1961)

The Pied Piper Fairy Tales (1982)

The Pied Piper of Hamelin Variety and Drama Spectaculars (1957)

Pine Canyon Is Burning Rescue (1977)

The Pink Panther Show Cartoons (1969)

Pinky and Company Sitcoms (1939)

Pinocchio Fairy Tales (1982), Variety and Drama Spectaculars (1957)

Pinocchio's Christmas Holiday Specials (1980)

Pioneer Spirit Pilot Film Series (1969)

Pioneer Woman Westerns (1973)

The Pioneers Drama — Repeat Series (1964)

Pip the Piper Children's Program (1961)

Pippi Longstocking Adolescence (1961), Adolescence (1988), Children — Extraordinary (1961), Children — Extraordinary (1985), Fairy Tales (1960)

Pirate Islands Australia (2003), Beaches (2003), Children — Extraordinary (2003), Teenagers (2003)

The Pirates of Flounder Bay Pilot Film Series (1966)

The Pirates of Penzance Opera (1939), Television Firsts (1939)

Pistols 'n' Petticoats American Indian (1966), Senior Citizens (1966), Visually Impaired (1966), Westerns (1966)

Pitfall Drama (1955)

Pixie and Dixie Cartoons (1958)

The PJ's Puppets (1999), Senior Citizens (1999), Speech Impaired (1999)

Placido Domingo Sings Zarzuela! Opera (1986)

The Plainclothesman Men — Law Enforcers (1949), New York (1954)

Plan 9 from Outer Space Vampires (1954)

Planet of the Apes Series Based on Films (1974), Talking Animals and Machines (1974)

Planet Patrol Puppets (1963), Space (1963)

Play of the Month Shakespeare (1967), Shakespeare (1969), Shakespeare (1970), Shakespeare (1971), Shakespeare (1972), Shakespeare (1975)

The Play of the Week Drama (1960)

Play the Game Game Shows (1941), Game Shows (1946), Television Firsts (1941)

Play Your Hunch Game Shows (1958)

Playboy After Dark Nudity (1969)

Playboy's Penthouse Nudity (1959)

Players Latino American (1997)

Playhouse 90 Drama (1956)

Playhouse of Mystery Drama — Repeat Series (1957)

Playhouse of Stars Drama (1952), Drama — Repeat Series (1960)

Playwrights '55 Drama (1955)

Plaza Suite Broadway (1982), Broadway (1987)

Please Don't Eat the Daisies Adolescence (1965), Series Based on Films (1965), Twins (1965)

Please Stand By Adolescence (1978)

Pleasure Cove Hotels (1979), Love (1979)

Plymouth Playhouse Drama (1953)

Poetry and Music Variety Programs (1946)

Point Pleasant Devil (2005), New Jersey (2005)

Poison Ivy Camps (1985)

Police File Women — Law Enforcers (1994)

Police Squad Films Based on Television Series (1988), Men — Law Enforcers (1982)

Police Station Men — Law Enforcers (1959)

Police Story Drama (1952), Drama (1973), Men — Law Enforcers (1967), Women — Law Enforcers (1974)

Police Surgeon Canada (1972), Doctors (1972)

Police Woman Los Angeles (1974), Mentally Disabled (1974), Nudity (1974), Women — Law Enforcers (1974)

The Polly Bergen Show Variety Programs (1957)

Poltergeist: The Legacy Adolescence (1996), Mediums (1996), Nudity (1996), Psychiatrists (1996), San Francisco (1996), The Supernatural (1996)

Ponderosa Westerns (2001)

Poochinski Talking Animals and Machines (1990)

Poor Devil African American (1973(1998), Devil (1973)

Poor Mr. Campbell Pilot Film Series (1963–1967)

The Popcorn Kid Teenagers (1987)

Popeye Doyle Men — Law Enforcers (1986)

Popeye the Sailor Cartoons (1962)

Popi Adolescence (1976), Puerto Rican (1976), Series Based on Films (1976)

Popular Latino American (1999), Lesbians (1999), Los Angeles (1999), Physically Disabled (1998), Reporters (1999), Teen After-School Hangouts (1998), Teenagers (1999)

The Porky Pig Show Cartoons (1964)

Port Charles Soap Operas (Note)

The Porter Waggoner Show Variety Programs (1960)

Portia Faces Life Series Based on Radio Programs (1954), Soap Operas (1954)

The Possessed Angels (1977)

The Powder Room Love (1971)

Power Rangers Dino Thunder Morphing (1993)

The Power Rangers in Space Morphing (1993)

Power Rangers: Ninja Storm Martial Arts (1993), Morphing (1993)

Power Rangers Time Force Morphing (1993)

Power Rangers Turbo Morphing (1993)

Power Rangers World Force Morphing (1993)

The Power Within Men — Extraordinary (1979)

The Powers of Matthew Star Aliens (1982)

The Powers That Be Housekeepers (1992), Politics (1992), Washington, D.C. (1992)

The Practice Boston (1997), District Attorneys (1997), Lawyers (1997), Nudity (2003), Senior Citizens (1977)

Premiere Pilot Film Series (1968)

The Presidential Birthday Bash Presidential Appearances (1962)

Presidential Inaugural Gala Presidential Appearances (1989), Presidential Appearances (1993)

Presidio Med Doctors (2002), San Francisco (2003)

The Pretender Men — Extraordinary (1996)

The Pretenders Government Agents (1988)

Pretty Baby Prostitutes (1988)

Preview Theater Pilot Film Series (1961)

Preview Tonight Pilot Film Series (1966)

The Price Broadway (1971)

The Price Is Right Game Shows (1956), Nudity (1978), Senior Citizens (1972)

Pride and Joy New York (1995)

Pride of the Family Sitcoms (1953), Teenagers (1953)

The Primary English Class Immigrants (1977)

The Prime of Miss Jean Brodie Teachers (1979)

Primus Adventurers (1971)

The Prince and the Pauper Fairy Tales (1960)

Prince Planet Cartoons (1966)

Prince Street Latino American (1997), New York (1997), Women — Law Enforcers (1997)

The Princess and the Goblins Fairy Tales (1960)

The Princess and the Pea Fairy Tales (1982)

The Princess Who Had Never Laughed Fairy Tales (1982)

Princesses New York (1991)

Prison Break Prison (2005)

The Prisoner Cars (1968), Little People (1968), Speech Impaired (1968)

Prisoner: Cell Block H Australia (1980), Lesbians (1980), Prison (1980), Prostitutes (1980)

Private Benjamin Camps (1981), Series Based on Films (1981)

Private Eye Historical Settings (1987), Los Angeles (1987)

Private Secretary Hotels (1953), New York (1953), Sitcoms (1954)

Private Sessions Psychiatrists (1985)

Probe Geniuses (1988), Women — "Dumb Blondes" (1988)

Producer's Showcase Drama (1954)

Professional Father Adolescence (1955), Psychiatrists (1955), Sitcoms (1955)

Profiler Adolescence (1996), F.B.I. Agents (1996), Mediums (1996), Mexican American (1996)

Profiles in Courage Presidential Appearances (1964)

Program Playhouse Pilot Film Series (1949)

Project Tin Man Robots (1990)

Project UFO Aliens (1978)

Projection Room Drama (1952)

Pros and Cons Con Artists (1986), Los Angeles (1991), Men — Law Enforcers (1992), Restaurants (1992)

Protect and Surf Beaches (1989)

The Protectors Men — Law Enforcers (1972), Women — Law Enforcers (1972)

The Proud Family Senior Citizens (2001)

Proud Family Teenagers (2001)

Prudence and the Chief American Indian (1970), Pilot Film Series (1970)

Prudential Family Playhouse Drama (1950)

Prudential Playhouse Broadway (1951)

The Pruitts of Southampton New York (1966)

The Psychiatrist Los Angeles (1971), Psychiatrists (1971)

Psychic Detectives Mediums (2004)

Psycho Hotels (1987), The Supernatural (1987)

Public Defender Lawyers (1954)

The Public Life of Cliff Norton Sitcoms (1950)

Pud's Prize Party Children's Program (1952)

Pulitzer Prize Playhouse Drama (1950)

Pulse of the City Drama (1952)

Pump Boys and Dinettes Broadway (1983)

Pump Boys and Dinettes on Television Broadway (1983)

Punch and Jody Little People (1973)

Punch and Judy Puppets (1931), Television Firsts (1931)

Punky Brewster Adolescence (1984), Chicago (1984), Senior Citizens (1984)

Puppetman Pilot Film Series (1987), Puppets (1987)

Purlie Broadway (1981)

Pursue and Destroy Pilot Film Series (1966), War — World War II (1966)

Pursuit Drama (1958)

The Pursuit of Happiness Chicago (1995), Lawyers (1995), Philadelphia (1987), Teachers (1987)

Puss 'n' Boots Fairy Tales (1982)

The Puzzle of Revelation Religious Programs (2001)

Pygmalion Broadway (1963)

Q.E.D. Game Shows (1951), Geniuses (1982), Historical Settings (1982)

Q.T. Hush Cartoons (1960)

Quadrangle Variety Programs (1949)

Quantum Leap Time Travel (1989)

Quark Aliens (1978), Cross Dressers (1978), Robots (1978), Space (1978), Twins (1978)

Que Pasa, U.S.A.? Cuban American (1975)

The Queen and I Con Artists (1969), New York (1969)

Queen for a Day Game Shows (1956), Series Based on Radio Programs (1956)

The Queen of Swords California (2000), Historical Settings (2000), Latino American (2000), Women — Extraordinary (2000)

Queen Supreme Judges (2003)

The Queen Was in the Kitchen Cooking (1945), Television Firsts (1945)

The Queen's Messenger Broadway (1928), Television Firsts (1928)

Queens Supreme New York (2003)

Queer as Folk Gays (2000), Lesbians (2000), Nudity (1984), Philadelphia (2000)

Queer Eye for the Straight Girl Gays (2005)

Queer Eye for the Straight Guy Gays (2003)

The Quest American Indian (1976), Westerns (1976)

Quick and Quiet Ghosts (1981)

Quick as a Flash Game Shows (1953), Series Based on Radio Programs (1953)

Quick on the Draw Game Shows (1952)

Quiet, Please Drama (1949), Series Based on Radio Programs (1949)

Quiller: Night of the Father Espionage (1975)

Quiller: The Price of Violence Espionage (1975)

Quincy, M.E. Cars (1976), Forensics (1976), Los Angeles (1976)

Quintuplets Lesbians (2005), New

Jersey (2005), Teenagers (2004), Women — "Dumb Blondes" (2004)

The Quiz Kids Game Shows (1945), Series Based on Radio Programs (1949)

Quizzing the News Game Shows (1948)

The R.C.A. Thanksgiving Show Holiday Specials (1948)

R.C.M.P. Men — Law Enforcers (1960)

R.U.R Broadway (1952)

Rachel Gunn, R.N. American Indian (1992), Women — Nurses (1992)

Racket Squad Con Artists (1950), Men — Law Enforcers (1950)

Rackets Are My Racket Con Artists (1947)

Radio City Matinee Cooking (1946)

Radio City Music Hall at Christmas Time Holiday Specials (1967)

Rafferty Doctors (1977), Los Angeles (1977)

Raggedy Ann and Andy in the Great Santa Claus Caper Holiday Specials (1978)

Rags to Riches Historical Settings (1987), Los Angeles (1987), Newspapers (1987), Teenagers (1987)

The Rainbow Girl Mexican American (1982), Shows within Shows (1982)

The Rainbow Review Color Broadcasting (1950)

The Rainmaker Broadway (1982)

Raising Dad Adolescence (2001), Senior Citizens (2001), Teachers (2001), Teenagers (2001)

Raising Miranda Teenagers (1988)

Ralph S. Mouse Talking Animals and Machines (1986)

Ramar of the Jungle Adventurers (1952), Africa (1952)

Ramona Adolescence (1988), Canada (1988)

Ranch Party Variety Programs (1957)

The Random Years New York (2002)

The Range Rider Teenagers (1951), Westerns (1951)

Rango American Indian (1967), Westerns (1967)

Ransom for Alice Westerns (1977)

The Ransom Sherman Show Variety Programs (1950)

Rapunzel Fairy Tales (1958), Fairy Tales (1982)

The Rat Patrol War — World War II (1966)

Raven Bars (1992), Beaches (1996), Hawaii (1996), Martial Arts (1992), Men — Law Enforcers (1992), Nudity (1992)

Rawhide Mexican American (1959), Westerns (1959)

Ray Alexander: A Menu for Murder Men — Law Enforcers (1994)

Ray Alexander: A Taste for Justice Men — Law Enforcers (1994)

The Ray Anthony Show Variety Programs (1956)

The Ray Bradbury Theater Drama (1986)

The Ray Milland Show Sitcoms (1954), Teachers (1954)

The Ray Night Revue Variety Programs (1949)

The RCA Victor Gallery of Stars Variety and Drama Spectaculars (1957)

Ready and Willing Women — "Dumb Blondes" (1974)

Real George Sitcoms (1956)

The Real Ghost Busters Ghosts (1986)

Real Ghosts Ghosts (1995)

The Real Gilligan's Island Beaches (2004)

Real Kids Reality Programs (1981)

Real Life Stories Reality Programs (1981)

The Real McCoys Adolescence (1962), Cars (1957), Country Folk (1957), Mexican American (1957), Physically Disabled (1957), Senior Citizens (1957), Sitcoms (1957), Teen After-School Hangouts (1957), Teenagers (1957), Television Firsts (1962)

The Real McKay Variety Programs (1951)

Real People Reality Programs (1979)

Really Weird Tales Drama (1986)

Rear Guard War — World War II (1976)

Reasonable Doubts Bars (1991), Chicago (1991), Hearing Impaired Characters (1991), Men — Law Enforcers (1991)

Reba Adolescence (2001), Lesbians (2004), Teenagers (2000)

Rebecca Broadway (1952)

Rebel Gun Fairy Tales (1960)

Reckoning Drama — Repeat Series (1959)

The Recovery Room Bars (1985)

The Red Benson Show Variety Programs (1946)

The Red Mill Variety and Drama Spectaculars (1958)

Red Ryder American Indian (1953), American Indian (1956), Series Based on Radio Programs (1956), Westerns (1953), Westerns (1956)

Red Shoe Diaries Drama (1992), Nudity (1984)

The Red Skelton Show Con Artists (1950), Country Folk (1951), Little People (1951), Series Based on Radio Programs (1951)

Red Skelton's Christmas Dinner Holiday Specials (1982)

The Redd Foxx Hour African American (1977)

The Redd Foxx Show Puerto Rican (1986), Restaurants (1986), Senior Citizens (1986), Teenagers (1986)

Redeye Express Nightclubs (1988)

Redigo Hotels (1963), Mexican American (1963)

Regular Joe New York (2003)

Related New York (2005), Nudity (2005)

Relativity Lesbians (1995)

Relentless American Indian (1977)

Relic Hunter Adventurers (1998), Teachers (1999), Women — Extraordinary (1999)

The Reluctant Dragon Fairy Tales (1960)

The Reluctant Dragon and Mr. Toad Cartoons (1970)

The Reluctant Spy Espionage (1962)

Remember WENN Historical Settings (1996)

Remington Steele Cars (1982), Hotels (1982), Los Angeles (1982), Men — Law Enforcers (1982), Women — Law Enforcers (1982)

Remo Williams Government Agents (1988), Martial Arts (1988)

Rendezvous Nightclubs (1952), Women — Extraordinary (1952)

Rendezvous Hotel Hotels (1979)

Rendezvous with Music Variety Programs (1950)

Renegade Adventurers (1960), American Indian (1992)

The Renegades Latino American (1983), Los Angeles (1983)

Renfrew of the Mounted Canada (1953), Men — Law Enforcers (1953), Series Based on Radio Programs (1953)

The Reno Brothers Westerns (1960)

Reno English Lawyers (1956)

Report to Murphy Prison (1982)

The Reporter New York (1964), Reporters (1964)

Reporter Collins Reporters (1951)

Rescue 77 Bars (1999), Rescue (1999)

Rescue 8 Los Angeles (1958), Rescue (1958)

Rescue from Gilligan's Island Beaches (1964)

Rescue Me New York (2004), Rescue (2004)

The Restless Gun Westerns (1957)

Resurrection Blvd. Los Angeles (2000), Mexican American (2000)

Return Engagement Drama — Repeat Series (1953)

The Return of Ben Casey Doctors (1987)

The Return of Charlie Chan Asian American (1979)

The Return of Long John Silver Fairy Tales (1960)

The Return of Marcus Welby Doctors (1984), Mexican American (1969)

Return of the Saint Adventurers (1979)

Return of the Scarlet Pimpernel Television Firsts (1938)

Return to Lonesome Dove Westerns (1989)

Return to Peyton Place Soap Operas (Note)

Return to the Planet of the Apes Series Based on Films (1975)

Reunion in Vienna Variety and Drama Spectaculars (1955)

Reunited Philadelphia (1999)

Revelations Religious Characters (2005), Religious Programs (2005)

Revenge of the Grey Gang Senior Citizens (1981)

Revlon Mirror Theater Drama (1953)

Revlon Revue Variety Programs (1960)

Rewrite for Murder Shows within Shows (1991), Women — Law Enforcers (1991)

Rex Harrison Presents Short Stories of Love Drama (1974), Love (1974)

Rheingold Theater Drama (1955)

Rhoda Hotels (1974), Latino American (1974), New York (1977)

Rhythm Variety Programs (1944)

Rich Man Politics (1976)

Rich Man, Poor Man Politics (1976)

The Richard Boone Show Drama (1963)

Richard Diamond, Private Detective Los Angeles (1959), Men — Law Enforcers (1957), New York (1957), Nudity (1957), Series Based on Radio Programs (1957)

The Richard Pryor Show African American (1977)

Richiardi's Chamber of Horrors Magicians (1979)

Richie Brockelman, Private Eye Los Angeles (1978), Men — Law Enforcers (1978)

Richie Rich Films Based on Television Series (1994)

Riders in the Sky American Indian (1991)

The Riders of the Purple Sage Variety Programs (1956)

The Rifleman American Indian (1959), Bars (1958), Hotels (1958), Westerns (1958)

The Right Man Presidential Appearances (1960)

Right or Rewrite Game Shows (1946)

Riker District Attorneys (1981), Los Angeles (1981), Men — Law Enforcers (1981)

Rimfire Westerns (1968)

Rin Tin Tin, K-9 Cop Animals (1988)

The Ringling Brothers and Barnum & Bailey Clown College 20th Anniversary Clowns (1988)

Rip Van Winkle Fairy Tales (1958), Fairy Tales (1982)

Ripcord Pilots (1961)

Riptide Adventurers (1965), California (1984), Geniuses (1983), Men — Law Enforcers (1983), Restaurants (1984), Robots (1984)

Riptide, Inc Adventurers (1965)

Rise and Shine Teenagers (1981)

Risko Lawyers (1976)

Rita Puerto Rican (1986)

The Rita Moreno Show Hotels (1978), Latino American (1976), Puerto Rican (1978)

Ritual of Evil Psychiatrists (1970)

Rituals Soap Operas (Note), Washington, D.C. (1984)

The Rivalry Politics (1975)

Riverboat Historical Settings (1959)

Riviera Hotels (1987)

The Road of Life Series Based on Radio Programs (1954), Soap Operas (1954)

The Road Runner Show Cartoons (1968)

The Road to Reality Soap Operas (1960)

The Road West Westerns (1966)

The Roads to Freedom Gays (1972)

Roaring Camp Pilot Film Series (1966), Westerns (1966)

The Roaring 20s Historical Settings (1960), New York (1960), Reporters (1960)

The Robber Bridegroom Broadway (1980)

Robbery Homicide Division Los Angeles (2002), Men — Law Enforcers (2002), Women — Law Enforcers (2002)

Robert Herridge Theater Drama (1960)

Robert Montgomery Presents Drama (1950), Drama (1953)

Robert Montgomery Presents Your Lucky Strike Theater Drama (1950)

The Robert Q. Lewis Show Series Based on Radio Programs (1950)

Robert Q's Matinee Series Based on Radio Programs (1950), Variety Programs (1950)

Robert Shaw's Christmas Holiday Specials (1988)

Roberta Broadway (1958), Broadway (1969)

The Roberta Quinlan Show Variety Programs (1949)

Robin's Hoods Women — Law Enforcers (1994)

Robinson Crusoe Beaches (1964)

RoboCop Men — Law Enforcers

(1994), Robots (1994), Series Based on Films (1994)

Robotech Robots (1985)

Robotman Robots (1985)

Roc Baltimore (1991), Bars (1991), Restaurants (1993), Senior Citizens (1991), Women — Nurses (1991)

The Rock Teachers (1990)

A Rock and a Hard Place Con Artists (1981)

Rock Candy Women — "Dumb Blondes" (1987)

Rock Hopper Espionage (1984)

Rock Me Baby Shows within Shows (2003)

A Rock 'n' Roll Christmas Holiday Specials (1988)

Rockabye the Infantry Con Artists (1963)

Rocket Robin Hood Cartoons (1967)

The Rockford Files Cars (1974), Los Angeles (1974), Men — Law Enforcers (1974), Restaurants (1974), Senior Citizens (1974)

Rocky and His Friends Films Based on Television Series (1992), Films Based on Television Series (2000)

Rocky Jones, Space Ranger Aliens (1954), Space (1954)

Rocky King, Inside Detective Men — Law Enforcers (1950), New York (1950)

Rod Brown of the Rocket Rangers Space (1953)

Rodney Adolescence (2004)

Roger Ramjet Cartoons (1965)

The Rogues Con Artists (1964)

Roll Out! African American (1973), War — World War II (1973)

The Roller Girls American Indian (1978)

Rollergirls Philadelphia (1978)

Romantic Interlude Drama — Repeat Series (1955)

Rome Lesbians (2005)

Romeo and Juliet Ballet (1948), Opera (1999), Shakespeare (1944), Shakespeare (1948), Shakespeare (1954), Shakespeare (1957), Shakespeare (1967), Shakespeare (1978)

Romper Room Children's Program (1953)

The Rookies African American (1972), Los Angeles (1972), Men — Law Enforcers (1972)

Room for One More Adolescence (1962), Series Based on Films (1962)

Room for Romance Adolescence (1990), Love (1990), New York (1990)

Room for Two New York (1992), Shows within Shows (1992)

Room Service Broadway (1952)

Room 222 Los Angeles (1969), Teachers (1969)

Roomies Geniuses (1987)

Rooster Men — Law Enforcers (1983), Psychiatrists (1982)

Rootie Kazootie Children's Program (1950), Puppets (1950)

Roots African American (1977), Nudity (1977)

Roots: The Next Generations, African American (1977)

The Ropers Adolescence (1977), California (1979), Senior Citizens (1979)

The Rosalind Russell Show Variety and Drama Spectaculars (1959)

Roscoe Karns and Inky Poo Clowns (1949), Pilot Film Series (1949), Sitcoms (1949)

Roseanne Adolescence (1988), Gays (1988), Lesbians (1988), Restaurants (1988), Teenagers (1988)

The Rosemary Clooney Show Variety Programs (1957)

Rosenthal and Jones African American (1975), Senior Citizens (1975)

Rosetti and Ryan Lawyers (1977), Los Angeles (1977)

Roswell Aliens (1999), Latino American (1999), Restaurants (1999)

The Rough Riders Westerns (1958)

The Rounders Series Based on Films (1966)

The Rousters Los Angeles (1983), Senior Citizens (1984)

Route 66 Adventurers (1960), Adventurers (1993), Cars (1960)

Rowan and Martin's Laugh-In Nudity (1968), Presidential Appearances (1970), Puppets (1972), Senior Citizens (1968), Women — "Dumb Blondes" (1968)

Roxie New York (1987)

The Roy Rogers Show American Indian (1951), Animals (1951), Cars (1951), Series Based on Radio Programs (1951), Westerns (1951)

Royal Canadian Mounted Police Canada (1960)

The Royal Family Broadway (1952), Senior Citizens (1991)

Royal Match Politics (1985)

Ruddigore Opera (1985)

Rudolph, the Red-Nosed Reindeer Holiday Specials (1964)

Rudolph's Shiny New Year Holiday Specials (1976)

The Ruff and Ready Show Cartoons (1957)

The Ruggles Adolescence (1949), Sitcoms (1949), Twins (1949)

Rumpelstiltskin Fairy Tales (1958), Fairy Tales (1982)

Rumpus Room Series Based on Radio Programs (1949)

Run Pilot Film Series (1970)

Run and Southern Fried Pilot Film Series (1970)

Run, Joe, Run Animals (1974)

Run of the House Teenagers (2003)

Runaround Puppets (1971)

Runaway Ralph Talking Animals and Machines (1986)

The Runaways Psychiatrists (1979)

Running Delilah Robots (1994)

Running Wilde Reporters (1992)

The Russ Morgan Show Variety Programs (1956)

Russell Westerns (1961)

Ruthie on the Telephone Sitcoms (1948)

Rx for the Defense Doctors (1973), Lawyers (1973)

Ryan Caulfield: Year One Men — Law Enforcers (1999), Philadelphia (1999), Puerto Rican (1999)

Ryan's Four Doctors (1983), Los Angeles (1983), Women — Nurses (1983)

Ryan's Hope Soap Operas (Note)

S*H*E Espionage (1980), Women — Extraordinary (1980)

S.R.O. Playhouse Drama — Repeat Series (1957)

The S.S. Holliday Variety Programs (1950)

The S.S. Telecruiser Variety Programs (1951)

S.W.A.T. California (1975), Los Angeles (1981), Men — Law Enforcers (1975)

Saber of London Men — Law Enforcers (1957), Physically Disabled (1957)

Sable Chicago (1987), Men — Extraordinary (1987), Visually Impaired (1987)

Sabrina Witches (1969)

Sabrina: The Animated Series Witches (1999)

Sabrina, the Teenage Witch Adolescence (1999), Latino American (2001), Little People (2000), Newspapers (1996), Puppets (1996), Talking Animals and Machines (1996), Teachers (1996), Teen After-School Hangouts (1996), Teenagers (1996), Time Travel (2000), Twins (1998), Witches (1971), Witches (1996), Witches (1999)

The Saddle Club Adolescence (2005)

Safari Tracks Animals (2006)

Sailor of Fortune Adventurers (1957)

The Saint Adventurers (1963), Adventurers (1979), Cars (1963), Films Based on Television Series (1997), Series Based on Radio Programs (1963)

St. Elsewhere Doctors (1982), Mentally Disabled (1982), Nudity (1988), Women — Nurses (1983)

Saint Peter Religious Characters (1981)

Saints and Sinners New York (1962), Reporters (1962)

Salanthiel Harris African American (1976)

Sally Senior Citizens (1957), Sitcoms (1957), Sitcoms (1958)

Sally and Sam Doctors (1965), Pilot Film Series (1965)

Salome Religious Programs (1972)

Salt and Pepe African American (1975), Puerto Rican (1975)

Salty Adolescence (1974), Animals (1974)

Salvage 1 Cars (1979), Los Angeles (1979)

Sam Animals (1977), Los Angeles (1978), Men — Law Enforcers (1977)

Sam Benedict Lawyers (1962), Los Angeles (1962)

Sam Hill Westerns (1961)

Sam Penny Men — Law Enforcers (1985)

Sammy and Company African American (1975), Visually Impaired (1966)

Sammy and His Friends African American (1965)

The Sammy Davis, Jr. Show African American (1966), Visually Impaired (1966)

The Sammy Davis, Jr. Special African American (1965)

Sammy Kaye's Music from Manhattan Variety Programs (1958)

Samson and Delilah Religious Programs (1978)

Samson and Goliath Cartoons (1967)

Samurai Martial Arts (1979)

San Berdoo Men — Law Enforcers (1989)

San Francisco Beat Men — Law Enforcers (1954), San Francisco (1954)

San Francisco International Airport Pilots (1970), San Francisco (1970)

The San Pedro Beach Bums Beaches (1977)

Sanchez of Bel Air Mexican American (1986), Puerto Rican (1986)

Sanctuary of Fear Religious Characters (1979)

Sandy Dreams Children's Program (1950)

The Sandy Duncan Show Hotels (1971), Los Angeles (1972), Teachers (1971), Visually Impaired (1972)

Sanford Los Angeles (1980), Senior Citizens (1980)

Sanford and Son Adolescence (1975),

African American (1972), African American (1975), Los Angeles (1972), Puerto Rican (1972), Senior Citizens (1972), Senior Citizens (1976), Senior Citizens (1980)

Sanford Arms Adolescence (1977), African American (1977), Hotels (1977), Los Angeles (1977)

Santa Bear's First Christmas Holiday Specials (1986)

Santa Claus Is Comin' to Town Holiday Specials (1970)

Santiago's America Puerto Rican (1975)

Santiago's Ark Puerto Rican (1972), Puerto Rican (1975)

Sara Adolescence (1976), Lawyers (1985), San Francisco (1985), Teachers (1976)

Sarge Mexican American (1971), Religious Characters (1971)

Satan's Waitin Devil (1964)

Satins and Spurs Variety and Drama Spectaculars (1954)

The Saturday Evening Post Con Artists (1939)

The Saturday Night Dance Party Variety Programs (1952)

Saturday Night Jamboree Variety Programs (1948)

Saturday Night Live Aliens (1983), Hearing Impaired Characters (1975), Nudity (1976), Puppets (1975)

Saturday Night Live: Presidential Bash 2000 Presidential Appearances (2000)

The Saturday Night Revue Variety Programs (1953)

Savannah Soap Operas (Note)

Saved by the Bell California (1989), Mexican American (1989), Robots (1989), Teachers (1989), Teen After-School Hangouts (1989), Teenagers (1989)

Saved by the Bell: The College Years Mexican American (1989)

Say It with Acting Game Shows (1950)

Scalpels Doctors (1980)

Scamps Adolescence (1982)

Scarecrow and Mrs. King Adolescence (1983), Cars (1983), Espionage (1983), Washington, D.C. (1983)

Scared Silly Ghosts (1982), The Supernatural (1982)

Scarlett Hill Soap Operas (1965), Soap Operas (Note)

Scary Tales Drama (1986)

Scat Cat Cartoons (1963)

Schaefer Century Theater Drama (1952)

Scheherazade Ballet (1945)

The Schlitz Playhouse of Stars Drama (1951)

School House Variety Programs (1949)

Science Fiction Theater Drama (1955)

Scooby-Doo Films Based on Television Series (2002)

Scooby-Doo, Where Are You? Cartoons (1969), Clubs (1997), Films Based on Television Series (2002), Ghosts (1969), The Supernatural (1969)

Scorch Connecticut (1992), Latino American (2001), Newspapers (1996), Puppets (1992), Teenagers (1992)

Scotland Yard Men — Law Enforcers (1955)

The Scott Music Hall Variety Programs (1952)

Scout's Safari Animals (2003)

Screen Director's Playhouse Drama (1955), Series Based on Radio Programs (1955)

Scrooge's Rock 'n' Roll Christmas Holiday Specials (1984)

Scrubs Doctors (2001), Latino American (2001), Little People (2001)

Sea Hawk Adventurers (1959)

Sea Hunt Adventurers (1957), Adventurers (1987), Beaches (1957), Beaches (1986)

Sea Quest DSV Latino American (1993)

Sea War War — World War II (1963)

The Seal Men — Extraordinary (1981)

Search Gadgets (1972), Men — Extraordinary (1972), Washington, D.C. (1972)

The Search Men — Law Enforcers (1965), Nudity (1954), Pilot Film Series (1968), Television Firsts (1954)

Search and Rescue: The Alpha Team Canada (1977), Rescue (1977)

Search for Tomorrow Soap Operas (1951)

Searcher Senior Citizens (1981)

Season's Greetings — An Evening with John Williams and the Boston Pops Orchestra Holiday Specials (1988)

Seasonal Differences Holiday Specials (1987)

Seaway Canada (1965)

The Second Bill Cosby Special African American (1968)

Second Chance Angels (1987), California (1987)

Second Edition Newspapers (1984)

The Second Half Chicago (1993), Latino American (1993)

The Second Hundred Years California (1967), Look-alikes (1967), Senior Citizens (1967)

The Second Time Around Los Angeles (2004)

The Secret Adventures of Jules Verne Historical Settings (2001), Women — Extraordinary (2001)

Secret Agent Espionage (1965)

Secret Agent Man Espionage (2000), New York (2000)

Secret File, U.S.A. Espionage (1954)

The Secret Life of Desmond Pfeiffer Politics (1998)

The Secret Storm Soap Operas (1954)

The Secret War of Jackie's Girls War — World War II (1980)

The Secret World of Alex Mack California (1994), Children — Extraordinary (1994), Geniuses (1994), Teenagers (1994)

Secrets of the Old Bailey Men — Law Enforcers (1958)

See It Now News Broadcasts (1951)

See What You Know Game Shows (1946)

Seeing Things Canada (1983), Mediums (1983), Reporters (1983)

The Seekers Women — Law Enforcers (1962)

The Seeking Heart Soap Operas (1954)

Seinfeld Cars (1990), Gays (1995), Hotels (1990), Lesbians (1990), Little People (1990), New York (1990), Nudity (1996), Nudity (1997), Restaurants (1990), Senior Citizens (1990)

The Senator Los Angeles (1970)

Sense and Nonsense Game Shows (1952)

The Sentimental Agent Adventurers (1962), Mexican American (1962)

The Sentinel Cars (1996), Men — Extraordinary (1996)

Separate Tables Broadway (1983)

Serenade Variety Programs (1949)

Sergeant Bilko Films Based on Television Series (1991)

Sergeant Preston of the Yukon Animals (1955), Canada (1955), Historical Settings (1955), Men — Law Enforcers (1955), Series Based on Radio Programs (1955)

Sergeant T.K. Yu Asian American (1979), Men — Law Enforcers (1979)

Serpico Men — Law Enforcers (1976), New York (1976), Series Based on Films (1976)

Sesame Street Children's Program (1969), Hearing Impaired Characters (1976), Latino American (1969), Puppets (1969), Puppets (1970)

Seven Arts Quiz Game Shows (1947)

Seven at Eleven Variety Programs (1951)

Seven Brides for Seven Brothers California (1982), Series Based on Films (1982)

7 Days Time Travel (1998)

Seven Keys to Baldpate Broadway (1946), Broadway (1952)

The Seven Wishes of a Rich Kid Genies(1979)

1775 Bars (1992), Hotels (1992)

7th Heaven Adolescence (1996), California (1996), Religious Characters (1996), Teenagers (1996), Twins (1996)

Seventh Heaven Broadway (1952)

77 Sunset Strip California (1958), Men — Law Enforcers (1958), Nightclubs (1958)

Sex and the City Lesbians (1998), Lesbians (2000), New York (1998), Newspapers (1998), Nudity (1984)

Sex, Love and Secrets Los Angeles (2005)

The Sex Symbol Nudity (1974)

Shades of L.A. Ghosts (1990), Los Angeles (1990), Mediums (1990), Men — Law Enforcers (1990)

The Shadow Chasers Reporters (1985), The Supernatural (1985)

A Shadow in the Streets Prison (1975)

Shadow of the Cloak Espionage (1951)

Shaft African American (1973), Men — Law Enforcers (1973), New York (1973)

Shaky Ground Teenagers (1992)

The Shaman's Last Raid American Indian (1975)

The Shameful Secrets of Hastings Corners Soap Operas (Note), Twins (1970)

The Shamrock Conspiracy Men — Law Enforcers (1995)

Shane Series Based on Films (1966), Westerns (1966)

Shangri-La Variety and Drama Spectaculars (1960)

Shannon Men — Law Enforcers (1981), San Francisco (1981)

Shannon's Deal Latino American (1990), Lawyers (1990), Philadelphia (1990)

Shaping Up Los Angeles (1984)

Shari and Her Friends Puppets (1954)

The Shari Lewis Show Puppets (1960)

The Shari Show Puppets (1975)

Shariland Puppets (1957)

Shaughnessey Taxi Cabs (1976)

Shazam Children — Extraordinary (1974), Super Heroes (1974)

Shazzan! Cartoons (1967), Genies(1967)

She Spies Cars (2000), Los Angeles (2000), Women — Extraordinary (2002)

She Wolf of London Werewolves (1990)

Sheehy and the Supreme Machine Teenagers (1977)

Sheena Africa (2000), Films Based on Television Series (1984), Nudity (2000), Pilots (2000), The Supernatural (2000), Women — Extraordinary (2000)

Sheena, Queen of the Jungle Africa (1955), Animals (1955), Women — Extraordinary (1955)

The Sheik Ballet (1982)

Shell Game California (1987), Con Artists (1987)

Shelley Duvall's Bedtime Stories Drama (1992)

Shelley Duvall's Fairy Tale Theater Mermaids (1983)

Shelley Duvall's Tall Tales and Legends Drama (1985), Fairy Tales (1985)

Shenanigans Children's Program (1964)

Shepherd's Flock Religious Characters (1971)

She-Ra: Princess of Power Space (1985)

The Sheriff of Cochise Arizona (1956), Men — Law Enforcers (1956)

Sheriff Who? Westerns (1967), Westerns (1972)

Sherlock Holmes Historical Settings (1954), Men — Law Enforcers (1951), Men — Law Enforcers (1954)

Sherlock Holmes: The Hound of the Baskervilles Men — Law Enforcers (1972)

Sherlock Jones and Procter Watson Puppets (1986)

She's the Sheriff Adolescence (1987), Women — Law Enforcers (1987)

The Shield Los Angeles (2002), Men — Law Enforcers (2002), Women — Law Enforcers (2002)

Shields and Yarnell Robots (1977)

Shining Time Station American Indian (1989)

The Shirley Temple Theater Fairy Tales (1960), Mermaids (1961)

Shirley Temple's Storybook Fairy Tales (1958)

Shirley's World Newspapers (1972)

Shivers Ghosts (1989)

Shogun Nudity (1980)

Shooter War — Korea, Vietnam, Iraq (1988)

Shooting Stars Men — Law Enforcers (1983)

Shore Leave Pilot Film Series (1961)

Short Story Theater Drama (1952)

Short, Short Drama Drama (1952)

Shorty Cartoons (1946), Television Firsts (1946)

Shotgun Slade Westerns (1959)

Show Biz Variety and Drama Spectaculars (1955)
Show Business, Inc. Variety Programs (1949)
The Show Goes On Reality Programs (1950)
Show of the Year Variety and Drama Spectaculars (1950)
Showboat African American (1946), Ballet (1946)
The Showoff Broadway (1946), Broadway (1952), Broadway (1955)
Showroom Nudity (1947)
Showtime at the Apollo African American (1954), Variety Programs (1954)
Showtime, U.S.A. Variety Programs (1950)
Side Show Clowns (1944), Television Firsts (1944)
Sidekicks Adolescence (1986), Asian American (1986), Con Artists (1974), Los Angeles (1986), Martial Arts (1986)
Sidney Shorr Gays (1981)
Siegfried and Roy Magicians (1980)
Sierra Rescue (1974)
Sigmund and the Sea Monsters Adolescence (1973), Beaches (1973), Genies (1973), Little People (1973)
The Silent Force African American (1970), F.B.I. Agents (1970), Washington, D.C. (1970)
Silent Mouse Holiday Specials (1988)
Silent Whisper Speech Impaired (1988)
Silk Stalkings Florida (1991), Men — Law Enforcers (1991), Women — Law Enforcers (1991)
Silver Fox Espionage (1991), Senior Citizens (1991)
Silver Spoons Adolescence (1982), New York (1982)
Silver Theater Series Based on Radio Programs (1949)
The Silverhawks Space (1986)
Simon New York (1995)
Simon and Simon California (1981), Look-alikes (1981), Men — Law Enforcers (1981)
Simon Lash Men — Law Enforcers (1960)
The Simple Life Nudity (2003), Women — "Dumb Blondes" (2003)
The Simpsons Adolescence (1990), Bars (1990), Clowns (1990), Senior Citizens (1990)
Sinbad Adventurers (1967)
The Sinbad Show Bars (1993), Latino American (1993), Shows within Shows (1990)
Sinbad, Jr. Cartoons (1961)
Sing Along Variety Programs (1957)

Sing Along with Mitch African American (1961)
Sing-Co-Pation Variety Programs (1949)
Sing It Again African American (1949), Series Based on Radio Programs (1950)
Sing Me a Song Puppets (1998)
Singer and Sons New York (1990), Restaurants (1990)
The Singing Lady Children's Program (1948), Fairy Tales (1946)
The Single Guy Asian American (1995), New York (1995)
The Single Life New York (1998)
Sirens Philadelphia (1994), Pilot Film Series (1987), Women — Law Enforcers (1987), Women — Law Enforcers (1993)
Sirota's Court African American (1976), Judges (1976), Lawyers (1976)
Sister Kate Religious Characters (1989), Teenagers (1989)
Sister Michael Wants You Religious Characters (1994)
Sister, Sister Restaurants (1994), Teen After-School Hangouts (1994), Teenagers (1994), Twins (1994)
Sister Terri Religious Characters (1978)
Sisters Chicago (1991), District Attorneys (1990), Lesbians (1993), Nudity (1991), Restaurants (1991)
Sit or Miss Game Shows (1950)
Sitcom Teenagers (1982)
Six Feet Under Gays (2001), Geniuses (2001), Latino American (2001), Lesbians (2004), Los Angeles (2001), Nudity (1984)
Six Guns for Donegan Westerns (1959)
The Six Million Dollar Man California (1973), Government Agents (1973), Men — Extraordinary (1973), Physically Disabled (1973), Robots (1973), Super Heroes (1973)
The Six O'clock Follies War — Korea, Vietnam, Iraq (1980)
Six Pack Stock Car Racers (1983), Teenagers (1982)
6 RMS RIV VU Broadway (1974)
The Sixth Sense Los Angeles (1972), Mediums (1972), The Supernatural (1972)
The $64,000 Challenge Game Shows (1956)
The $64,000 Question Game Shows (1955), Game Shows (1956), Series Based on Radio Programs (1955)
Skag Bars (1980), Philadelphia (1980)
The Skatebirds Robots (1977)

Skeezer Animals (1982), Psychiatrists (1982)
Sketch Book Drama (1953)
Skin Los Angeles (2003)
The Skin of Our Teeth Broadway (1955)
Skinflint Holiday Specials (1979)
Skinwalkers American Indian (2002)
Skip Taylor Men — Law Enforcers (1953)
Skippy, the Bush Kangaroo Adolescence (1969), Animals (1969), Australia (1969)
Sky King Arizona (1951), Pilots (1951), Series Based on Radio Programs (1951)
Skyfighters Pilots (1958), War — World War II (1959)
Skyhawks Cartoon (1969), Pilots (1969)
The Sky's the Limit Game Shows (1954), Pilot Film Series (1960), Pilots (1960)
Skyward Christmas Physically Disabled (1981)
The Slap Maxwell Story Newspapers (1997)
Slattery's People Latino American (1964), Politics (1964), Washington, D.C. (1964)
Sledge Hammer Men — Law Enforcers (1986), Women — Law Enforcers (1986)
Sleeping Beauty Ballet (1955), Ballet (1987), Fairy Tales (1958, 1977, 1982)
Sleepy Joe Puppets (1949)
Slezak and Son Con Artists (1960)
Sliders Time Travel (1995)
The Slightly Fallen Angel Angels (1959)
Small and Frye Men — Extraordinary (1983), Men — Law Enforcers (1983)
The Small Fry Club Children's Program (1947)
Small Wonder Adolescence (1985), Los Angeles (1985), Robots (1985)
Small World News Broadcasts (1958)
Smallville Aliens (1953), Physically Disabled (2003), Reporters (2001), Super Heroes (2001)
Smart Guy Adolescence (1998), Geniuses (1998), Teen After-School Hangouts (1998), Teenagers (1999), Washington, D.C. (1998)
Smart Guys Con Artists (1988)
Smilin' Ed McConnell and His Buster Brown Gang Puppets (1950), Series Based on Radio Programs (1950)
Smilin' Ed McConnell and His Gang American Indian (1951), Children's Program (1950)
Smilin' Through Broadway (1952)
The Smith Family Los Angeles

(1971), Men — Law Enforcers (1971), Teenagers (1971)

Smokey Joe's Café Broadway (2005)

The Smokey the Bear Show Cartoons (1969)

The Smothers Brothers Comedy Hour Politics (1968)

The Smothers Brothers Show Angels (1965)

SNAFU War — World War II (1976)

Snagglepuss Cartoons (1958)

Snavely Hotels (1978), Housekeepers (1978), Mexican American (1978)

Sneak Preview Pilot Film Series (1956)

Sniff Animals (1988)

The Snooky Lanson Show Variety Programs (1956)

The Snoop Sisters Senior Citizens (1974), Women — Law Enforcers (1974)

Snoops Men — Law Enforcers (1989), Teachers (1989), Washington, D.C. (1989), Women — Law Enforcers (1999)

Snoopy — the Musical Broadway (1988)

The Snow Queen Fairy Tales (1982)

Snow White and the Seven Dwarfs Fairy Tales (1982)

So Help Me, Aphrodite Variety and Drama Spectaculars (1960)

So Little Time Twins (2001)

So This Is Hollywood California (1955), Lesbians (1955), Sitcoms (1955)

So You Want to Lead a Band Series Based on Radio Programs (1950)

Soap African American (1977), Connecticut (1977), Gays (1977), Housekeepers (1977), Latino American (1980), Lesbians (1977), Prostitutes (1981), Puppets (1977), Soap Operas (Note)

Social Studies Housekeepers (1990)

Sodom and Gomorrah Religious Programs (1978)

The Soft Touch Pilot Film Series (1962), Women — "Dumb Blondes" (1962)

Soldier Girl Transsexuals (2002)

Soldier of Fortune Latino American (1997)

Soldier Parade Variety Programs (1955)

The Soldiers Sitcoms (1955)

Soldiers of Fortune Adventurers (1955)

Someone Like Me Adolescence (1994), Teen After-School Hangouts (1994), Teenagers (1993), Teenagers (1994)

Somerset Soap Operas (1970), Soap Operas (Note)

Somerset Gardens Senior Citizens (1989)

Something Is Out There Mexican American (1988)

Something So Right New York (1996), Teenagers (1996)

Something Wilder Twins (1994)

Somewhere in Italy, Company B Pilot Film Series (1966), War — World War II (1966)

Son of the Beach Beaches (2000), Nudity (1989), Physically Disabled (2000)

Song and Dance Variety Programs (1946)

Song and Dance Time Variety Programs (1948)

Song Snapshots on a Summer Holiday Variety Programs (1954)

Songs at Twilight Variety Programs (1951)

Songs for Sale Series Based on Radio Programs (1950)

Sonja Henie's Holiday on Ice Variety and Drama Spectaculars (1956)

The Sonny and Cher Comedy Hour Presidential Appearances (1972)

Sonny and Sam Men — Law Enforcers (1981)

The Sonny Kendis Show Variety Programs (1949)

Sonny Spoon District Attorneys (1988), Men — Law Enforcers (1988)

Sons and Daughters California (1974)

Sons of Gunz Pilot Film Series (1987)

Sons of Thunder Martial Arts (1999), Men — Law Enforcers (1999), Mexican American (1999)

Sonshiny Day Religious Programs (1990)

The Sopranos New Jersey (1998), Nudity (1984), Senior Citizens (1999)

The Sorcerer Opera (1985)

Sorry, Wrong Number Color Broadcasting (1950), Physically Disabled (1946), Physically Disabled (1950)

Soul Food Lesbians (2003), Series Based on Films (2000)

Soul Man Religious Characters (1997)

Soul Train African American (1971)

The Sounds of Christmas Eve Holiday Specials (1973)

The Sounds of Home Civil War (1960)

The Soupy Sales Show Nudity (1962), Puppets (1955), Puppets (1966)

South Beach Con Artists (1993), Florida (2006), Hotels (2006)

South Central Los Angeles (1994)

South of Nowhere Teenagers (2005)

South of Sunset Men — Law Enforcers (1993)

South Pacific Broadway (2001)

Southern Fried Stock Car Racers (1970)

Space Academy Aliens (1977), Robots (1977), Space (1977)

Space Angel Cartoons (1962), Space (1962)

Space Cases Robots (1996)

Space Force Space (1978)

Space Ghost Cartoons (1966), Space (1966)

Space Giants Robots (1969)

Space Hoopty Computers — Extraordinary (1996), Space (1996)

Space Kiddettes Cartoons (1966), Space (1966)

Space: 1999 Aliens (1975), Space (1975)

Space Patrol Aliens (1950), Series Based on Radio Programs (1972), Space (1950), Time Travel (1953)

Space Rangers Aliens (1993), Robots (1993), Space (1993)

Space Stars Space (1981)

Sparrow Men — Law Enforcers (1978)

A Special Anne Murray Christmas Holiday Specials (1981)

Special Unit 2 Chicago (2001), Little People (2001), Physically Disabled (2001), The Supernatural (2001), Women — Law Enforcers (2001)

Speed Racer Cartoons (1967), Stock Car Racers (1967)

Spencer Teenagers (1984)

Spencer's Mountain Series Based on Films (1972)

Spencer's Pilots California (1976), Pilots (1976)

Spenser: For Hire Boston (1985), Cars (1985), Men — Law Enforcers (1985)

Spider-Man Cartoons (1969), Super Heroes (1967), Super Heroes (1994), Super Heroes (1999)

Spider-Man and His Amazing Friends Super Heroes (1981)

Spider-Man 2003 Super Heroes (2003)

Spider-Man Unlimited Super Heroes (1999)

Spider-Woman Super Heroes (1979)

Spies Espionage (1987)

The Spike Jones Show Series Based on Radio Programs (1954), Variety Programs (1954), Variety Programs (1960)

Spin and Marty Camps (1955)

Spin City Bars (1996), Gays (1996), Lesbians (2001), New York (1996), Physically Disabled (1996), Politics (1996)

Spitting Image Puppets (1986)

Splash Mermaids (1988), Mermaids (2005)

Splash, Too Mermaids (1988)

Split Personality Game Shows (1959)
Spotlight Drama (1954), Variety and Drama Spectaculars (1956)
Spotlight on the Stars Drama — Repeat Series (1958)
Spotlight Playhouse Drama — Repeat Series (1955)
Spraggue Men — Law Enforcers (1984)
Spread of the Eagle Shakespeare (1964)
Spunky and Tadpole Cartoons (1958)
Squadron War — World War II (1962)
Square Pegs Teachers (1982), Teenagers (1982)
Stacked Cars (2005), Lesbians (2005), Nudity (2005)
Stage Door Broadway (1939), Broadway (1948), Broadway (1952), Broadway (1955)
Stage Entrance Variety Programs (1951)
Stage 7 Drama (1955)
Stage Show Variety Programs (1954)
Stage 13 Drama (1950)
Stage Two Revue Variety Programs (1950)
Stagecoach West Westerns (1960)
Stand by for Crime Men — Law Enforcers (1949)
Stand by Your Man New Jersey (1992)
The Standard Oil Anniversary Show Variety and Drama Spectaculars (1957)
Stanley Hotels (1956), New York (1956), Sitcoms (1956)
Star Crossed Aliens (1985)
Star Maidens Aliens (1977)
Star of the Family California (1982), Latino American (1982), Reality Programs (1950), Rescue (1982), Teenagers (1982)
Star Struck Space (1979)
Star Tonight Drama (1955)
Star Trek African American (1966), Asian American (1966), Morphing (Star Trek), Nudity (1968), Space (1966), Space (1974), Television Firsts (1966), Women — "Dumb Blondes" (1998)
Star Trek: Deep Space Nine Aliens (1993), Gadgets, Lesbians (1995), Space (1993)
Star Trek Enterprise Aliens (2001), Asian American (2001), Gadgets, Space (2001)
Star Trek: The Motion Picture Films Based on Television Series (1979)
Star Trek: The Next Generation Aliens (1987), Gadgets, Robots (1987), Space (1987), Visually Impaired (1987)
Star Trek: Voyager Aliens (1995),

American Indian (1995), Gadgets, Space (1995)
Stargate SG-1 Aliens (1997), Gadgets (1997), Series Based on Films (1997)
Stark Men — Law Enforcers (1985)
The Starlet Lesbians (2005)
Starlight Theater Drama (1950)
The Starlost Space (1973)
Starman Aliens (1986), Series Based on Films (1986)
Starr First Baseman Pilot Film Series (1965)
Starring Boris Karloff Drama (1949), Series Based on Radio Programs (1949)
Stars on Parade Variety Programs (1953)
Stars Over Hollywood Drama (1950)
Starsky and Hutch African American (1975), Cars (1975), Films Based on Television Series (2004), Hotels (1975), Los Angeles (1975), Men — Law Enforcers (1975)
Starstruck Hotels (1979)
Starting Now Shows within Shows (1989)
Stat! Doctors (1973), Latino American (1991)
State Trooper Men — Law Enforcers (1957)
The Statler's Christmas Present Holiday Specials (1986)
Steambath Broadway (1973), Nudity (1973), Nudity (1984), Puerto Rican (1984), Religious Programs (1973), Religious Programs (1984), Television Firsts (1973)
Steel Collar Man Robots (1985)
Step by Step Cars (1991), Teen After-School Hangouts (1991), Teenagers (1991)
Step on the Gas Variety and Drama Spectaculars (1960)
Stephanie Reporters (1980), Shows within Shows (1981)
Stephen King's IT Clowns (1990)
Stephen King's Kingdom Hospital Doctors (2004)
Stephen Sondheim's Putting It Together: A Musical Revue Broadway (2005)
The Steve Allen Show Latino American (1956), Variety Programs (1956)
Steve Canyon Pilots (1958), Series Based on Radio Programs (1958)
Steve Donovan, Western Marshal Westerns (1955)
The Steve Harvey Show Cars (1996), Chicago (1996), Cross Dressers (1996), Look-alikes (1996), Teachers (1996)
Steve Harvey's Big Time Challenge Gays (2003), Twins (2003)

Stick Around Robots (1977)
Still Standing Adolescence (2003), Lesbians (2004), Magicians (2003), Teenagers (2002)
Stingray Cars (1986), Men — Extraordinary (1986), Puppets (1965)
Stockard Channing in Just Friends California (1979), Women — Scatterbrained (1979)
The Stockard Channing Show California (1980), Reporters (1980), Shows within Shows (1980), Women — Scatterbrained (1980)
Stockers Stock Car Racers (1981)
Stone Los Angeles (1980), Men — Law Enforcers (1980)
Stonecold Men — Law Enforcers (2005)
The Stones California (2004)
Stonestreet: Who Killed the Centerfold Model? Women — Law Enforcers (1977)
Stop Me If You've Heard This One Game Shows (1948), Series Based on Radio Programs (1948)
Stop Susan Williams Reporters (1979)
Stop the Music Series Based on Radio Programs (1949)
The Storefront Lawyers California (1970), Lawyers (1970), Los Angeles (1970)
Stories of the Century Westerns (1956)
Stormy Weathers Women — Law Enforcers (1992)
The Story Behind the Song Drama (1957)
Story for Americans Drama (1952)
The Story of— Drama (1962)
The Story of Christmas Holiday Specials (1963)
The Story of David Religious Programs (1976)
The Story of Easter Holiday Specials (1945), Religious Programs (1945)
The Story of Moses Religious Programs (1978)
The Story of Noah Religious Programs (1978)
Story Theater Drama (1949), Fairy Tales (1971)
The Storybook Squares Children's Program (1969)
The Storyteller Drama (1987)
Straight to the Heart Love (1989)
Straightaway Stock Car Racers (1961)
Stranded Beaches (1966), Beaches (1976)
The Strange Christmas Dinner Holiday Specials (1945), Variety and Drama Spectaculars (1945)
Strange Days at Blake Holsey High Children — Extraordinary (2002), Teenagers (2003)

Strange Interlude Broadway (1988)
Strange Luck Men — Extraordinary (1995)
Strange Paradise Beaches (1969), Mediums (1969), Soap Operas (1969), Soap Operas (Note), The Supernatural (1969)
Strange Stories Drama (1956)
Strange True Stories Drama (1982)
The Stranger Angels (1954)
Stranger in Our House The Supernatural (1978)
Strategic Air Command Pilots (1958)
The Strawberry Blonde Broadway (1959)
The Strawhatters Variety Programs (1953)
Street Hawk Gadgets(1985), Los Angeles (1985), Men — Extraordinary (1985), Men — Law Enforcers (1985)
Street Justice Bars (1991), Men — Law Enforcers (1991)
A Streetcar Named Desire Broadway (1984), Opera (1998)
The Streets Men — Law Enforcers (1984), Taxi Cabs (1984)
The Streets of Beverly Hills Men — Law Enforcers (1992)
The Streets of San Francisco Men — Law Enforcers (1972), San Francisco (1972)
Strike Force California (1981), Los Angeles (1981), Men — Law Enforcers (1981), Nudity (1981), Women — Law Enforcers (1981)
Strike It Rich Game Shows (1951), Series Based on Radio Programs (1951)
The Strip Hotels (1999), Las Vegas Settings (1999)
Stripperella Gadgets(2003), Nudity (2003), Super Heroes (2003)
Strippers Nudity (1983)
Strong Medicine Doctors (2000), Philadelphia (2000)
Struck by Lightning Visually Impaired (1957)
Stryker of Scotland Yard Men — Law Enforcers (1957)
The Stu Erwin Show African American (1950)
Stubby Pringle's Christmas Holiday Specials (1978)
Studio '57 Drama (1954)
Studio One Drama (1948), Shakespeare (1951)
Studs Love (1991)
Stud's Place Chicago (1949), Restaurants (1949)
Stump the Authors Game Shows (1946)
Style and Substance Gays (1998)
Sub Mariner Cartoons (1965), Super Heroes (1965)

Subu and the Magic Ring Genies (1957)
Success: It Can Be Yours Reality Programs (1982)
Suddenly Susan Bars (1996), Cuban American (1996), Hotels (1996), Newspapers (1996), San Francisco (1996)
Sue Thomas, F.B. Eye Animals (2002), F.B.I. Agents (2002), Hearing Impaired Characters (2002), Washington, D.C. (2002)
Sugar and Spice California (1990), Restaurants (1990)
Sugar Hill Times African American (1949)
Sugar Time Los Angeles (1977)
Sugarfoot Lawyers (1957), Lookalikes (1957), Visually Impaired (1957), Westerns (1957)
The Suite Life of Zack and Cody Asian American (2005), Boston (2005), Hotels (2005), Teenagers (2005), Twins (2005)
Summer Beaches (1984)
Summer Fun Pilot Film Series (1966)
Summer Theater Pilot Film Series (1969)
Summerland Beaches (2004), Nudity (2005), Teenagers (2004)
Summertime U.S.A. Variety Programs (1953)
Sunday Date Variety Programs (1949)
Sunday Dinner Lawyers (1991), New York (1991)
Sunday in the Park with George Broadway (1986)
Sunday in Town Ballet (1954)
Sunday Mystery Drama — Repeat Series (1961)
Sunset Beat Los Angeles (1990), Men — Law Enforcers (1990), Restaurants (1990)
Sunshine Adolescence (1975), Canada (1975)
The Sunshine Boys Senior Citizens (1977)
The Super New York (1972)
Super Carrier Latino American (1988)
Super Chicken Cartoons (1967)
Super Circus Clowns (1949)
Super Cops Men — Law Enforcers (1975)
Super Dave Asian American (1992), Men — Extraordinary (1992)
Super Force Men — Extraordinary (1990), Men — Law Enforcers (1990)
The Super Friends Super Heroes (1973)
Super Ghost Game Shows (1952)
Super Human Samurai Syber Squad Children — Extraordinary (1994), Teenagers (1994)

Super President Cartoons (1967)
Super Robot Monkey Team Hyperforce Go! Robots (2004)
The Super Six Cartoons (1966)
Super Witch Witches (1977)
Superbook Religious Programs (1981)
Superboy Aliens (1953), Super Heroes (1988)
Supercar Puppets (1962)
Superior Court Judges (1986)
Superman Films Based on Television Series (2006), Super Heroes (1996)
The Superman–Aquaman Hour Super Heroes (1967, 1968)
Supernatural Ghosts (2005), The Supernatural (2005)
Sure as Fate Drama (1950)
Surface Nudity (2005), The Supernatural (2005)
SurfSide 6 Beaches (1960), Florida (1960), Hotels (1960), Latino American (1960), Men — Law Enforcers (1960)
Survivor Beaches (2000)
The Survivors Senior Citizens (1969), Soap Operas (1969)
Susan's Show Children's Program (1957)
Suspect Broadway (1952)
Suspense Drama (1949), Series Based on Radio Programs (1949)
Suspense Playhouse Drama — Repeat Series (1971)
Suspense Theater on the Air Drama (1981)
Suspicion Drama (1957)
Suzanne Pleshette Is Maggie Briggs New York (1984), Newspapers (1984)
Svengali and the Blonde Variety and Drama Spectaculars (1955)
Swamp Thing Series Based on Films (1990), The Supernatural (1991)
Swan Lake Ballet (1998), Ballet (2005)
Sweating Bullets Bars (1991), Florida (1991), Men — Law Enforcers (1991)
Sweeney Todd Broadway (1982)
Sweet Justice Lawyers (1994)
Sweet Surrender Adolescence (1987), Philadelphia (1987), Senior Citizens (1987)
Sweet Valley High Newspapers (1994), Teen After-School Hangouts (1996), Teenagers (1994), Twins (1994)
The Swift Show Wagon Variety Programs (1948), Variety Programs (1955)
The Swingin' Singin' Years Variety and Drama Spectaculars (1960)
Swingin' Together Pilot Film Series (1963–1967)
Swiss Family Robinson Adolescence

(1975), Beaches (1975), Historical Settings (1975), Variety and Drama Spectaculars (1958)

The Swiss Family Robinson Beaches (1976), Historical Settings (1976)

Switch Con Artists (1975), Los Angeles (1975), Men — Law Enforcers (1975)

The Sword of Freedom Historical Settings (1957)

Sword of Justice Latino American (1978), Men — Extraordinary (1976), New York (1978)

Sybil Angels (1965), Pilot Film Series (1963–1967)

Sydney Bars (1990), Women — Law Enforcers (1990)

Sylvan in Paradise Hotels (1986)

T&T Lawyers (1988), Men — Law Enforcers (1988)

T.H.E. Cat Color Broadcasting (1966), Latino American (1966), Restaurants (1966)

T.J. Hooker California (1982), Men — Law Enforcers (1982), Women — Law Enforcers (1982)

The Tab Hunter Show California (1960), Sitcoms (1960)

Tabitha Los Angeles (1977), Shows within Shows (1977), Witches (1976), Witches (1977)

Tack Reynolds Stock Car Racers (1962)

Tag the Gag Game Shows (1951)

Taina Puerto Rican (2001)

Take a Good Look Game Shows (1959)

Take a Guess Game Shows (1953)

Take 5 Newspapers (1958)

Take Him — He's All Yours Pilot Film Series (1965)

Take It or Leave It Series Based on Radio Programs (1955)

Take Two: Living the Movies Cuban American (1992)

The Tale of the Frog Prince Fairy Tales (1982)

Talent Jackpot Reality Programs (1949)

Talent Patrol Reality Programs (1953)

The Talent Scouts Program Variety and Drama Spectaculars (1960)

Talent Varieties Variety Programs (1955)

Tales from Muppetland Puppets (1970)

Tales from the Crypt Drama (1989), Nudity (1984), Nudity (1993), Puppets (1989)

Tales from the Darkside Drama (1984), The Supernatural (1984)

Tales of Frankenstein Drama (1961), The Supernatural (1961)

Tales of Hoffman Opera (1950)

Tales of Morpheus Drama (1953)

Tales of Mystery Drama (1954)

Tales of the Apple Dumpling Gang Adolescence (1982), Westerns (1983)

Tales of the Black Cat Drama (1950), The Supernatural (1950)

Tales of the City Drama (1953), Transsexuals (1993)

Tales of the Gold Monkey Bars (1982), Beaches (1982), Historical Settings (1982), Hotels (1982), Pilots (1982)

Tales of the Haunted Drama (1981), The Supernatural (1981)

Tales of the Texas Rangers Westerns (1957)

Tales of the Unexpected Drama (1977), Drama (1979)

Tales of the Unknown Drama (1954)

Tales of the Vikings Historical Settings (1960)

Tales of the Wizard of Oz Cartoons (1961)

Tales of Tomorrow Drama (1951), Series Based on Radio Programs (1951), The Supernatural (1951)

The Tales of Wells Fargo Westerns (1957)

Talk to Me New York (2000)

The Tall Man Westerns (1960)

Tallahassee 7000 Florida (1961)

Tamara Variety Programs (1941)

Taming of the Shrew Broadway (2000), Shakespeare (1956, 1980)

Tammy Country Folk (1965), Series Based on Films (1965), Teenagers (1965)

The Tammy Grimes Show Color Broadcasting (1966), Women — Scatterbrained (1966)

Tanner '88 Politics (1988)

Tanner on Tanner Politics (2004), Presidential Appearances (2004)

Target Drama (1951)

Target: The Corrupters F.B.I. Agents (1961), Reporters (1961)

Taro, Giant of the Jungle Cartoons (1969), Chicago (1969)

Tarzan Africa (1966), Men — Extraordinary (1966), Men — Extraordinary (2003), Series Based on Films (1966), Women — Law Enforcers (2003)

Tarzan, the Ape Man Men — Extraordinary (1968)

Tate Physically Disabled (1960), Westerns (1960)

Tattinger's Restaurants (1988)

Taxi Bars (1978), Immigrants (1978), Little People (1978), New York (1978), Religious Characters (1979), Taxi Cabs (1978)

Teachers New Jersey (2006), Teachers (2005)

Teachers Only New York (1983), Teachers (1982), Teachers (1983)

Teahouse of the August Moon Broadway (1962)

Team Knight Rider Pilots (1998), Talking Animals and Machines (1997)

The Ted Bessell Show Newspapers (1973)

The Ted Knight Show Housekeepers (1985), Mexican American (1985), New York (1978), Newspapers (1986)

Ted Mack and the Original Amateur Hour Reality Programs (1948), Series Based on Radio Programs (1948), Variety Programs (1948)

Ted Mack's Matinee Variety Programs (1955)

The Ted Steele Show Variety Programs (1948)

Teech Asian American (1991), Philadelphia (1991), Teachers (1991)

Teen Angel Angels (1997), Senior Citizens (1997), Teenagers (1997)

Teen Wolf Werewolves (1986)

Teen Wolf: The Animated Series Werewolves (1986)

Tele Pun Game Shows (1948)

Tele Tales for Children Children's Program (1945)

Tele Varieties Reality Programs (1946), Variety Programs (1946)

Telephone Time Drama (1956)

The Teletubbies Puppets (1988)

Television Canteen Variety Programs (1944)

The Television Ghost, Drama (1931), Television Firsts (1931)

Television Roof Variety Programs (1938)

Television Symphony Variety and Drama Spectaculars (1948)

Tell It to the Camera Reality Programs (1962)

Tell Me, Dr. Brothers Psychiatrists (,)

The Teller and the Tale Drama (1985)

Teller of Tales Drama (1950)

The Telltale Clue Men — Law Enforcers (1954)

Temple Houston Westerns (1963)

Temperature's Rising African American (1972), Doctors (1973), Washington, D.C. (1972), Women — Nurses (1972)

The Tempest Shakespeare (1960), Shakespeare (1980)

Temple Houston Lawyers (1963)

The Ten Commandments Religious Programs (1978), Religious Programs (2006)

10-8: Officers on Duty Los Angeles (2003), Men — Law Enforcers (2003), Nudity (2003), Women — Law Enforcers (2003)

Ten Little Indians Variety and Drama Spectaculars (1959)

The Ten of Us Women — "Dumb Blondes," (1988), Teenagers (1988)

Tenafly African American (1973), Men — Law Enforcers (1971)

Tenko Camps (1985)

The Tennessee Ernie Ford Show Variety Programs (1955)

Tennessee Ernie Ford's White Christmas Holiday Specials (1972)

Tennessee Tuxedo and His Tales Cartoons (1963)

Tenspeed and Brown Shoe Cars (1980), Con Artists (1980), Los Angeles (1980)

Tequila and Bonetti Adolescence (1992), Los Angeles (1992), Mexican American (1992), Talking Animals and Machines (1991), Women — Law Enforcers (1992)

The Terrible Clocksman Fairy Tales (1960)

Terror Drama (1952)

Terry and the Pirates Asian American (1952), Pilots (1952), Series Based on Radio Programs (1952)

Terrytoon Circus Clowns (1956)

Texaco Command Performance Variety and Drama Spectaculars (1957)

Texaco Presents Bob Hop's Comedy Christmas Special Holiday Specials (1976)

The Texaco Star Theater Cross Dressers (1948), Puppets (1948), Series Based on Radio Programs (1948), Variety Programs (1948), Variety Programs (1954)

The Texan Westerns (1958)

Texas Soap Operas (Note)

Texas John Slaughter Westerns (1958)

Texas Justice Judges (2002)

The Texas Rangers Westerns (1981)

The Texas Wheelers Teenagers (1974), Visually Impaired (1957)

The Thanksgiving Treasure Holiday Specials (1973)

The Thanksgiving Visitor Holiday Specials (1968)

That 80s Show California (2002), Historical Settings (2002), Lesbians (2002)

That Girl American Indian (1966), Color Broadcasting (1966), Nudity (1970), Reporters (1966), Restaurants (1966), Senior Citizens (1966)

That Quiz Show Little People (1982), Twins (1982)

That 70s Show Historical Settings (1998), Lodges (1998), Morphing (1998), Teenagers (1998)

That Teen Show Teenagers (1981)

That Wonderful Guy Sitcoms (1950)

That's Incredible Reality Programs (1980)

That's Life Bars (2000), New Jersey (2001), Restaurants (2000)

That's My Boy Ohio (1954), Series Based on Films (1954), Sitcoms (1954), Teenagers (1954)

That's My Bush! Politics (2001)

That's My Mama African American (1974), Washington, D.C. (1974)

That's Our Sherman Sitcoms (1948)

That's So Raven Mediums (2003), Restaurants (2003), San Francisco (2003), Teenagers (2003)

Theater Broadway (1952)

Theater '58 Drama — Repeat Series (1958)

Theater '59 Drama — Repeat Series (1959)

Theater House Variety Programs (1944)

Theater Macabre Drama (1970)

Theater '60 Drama (1960)

Theater '62 Politics (1962)

Theater Time Drama — Repeat Series (1957)

There Shall Be No Light Broadway (1957)

There Were Times, Dear Mentally Disabled (1987)

These Are My Children Soap Operas (1949)

These Are the Days Adolescence (1974), Senior Citizens (1974)

These Friends of Mine Lesbians (1994), Los Angeles (1994)

They Stand Accused Judges (1949)

They Went Thataway Pilot Film Series (1960), Westerns (1960)

They Were There Nudity (1944)

Thicker Than Water Senior Citizens (1973)

A Thief of Time American Indian (2002)

Thieves Baltimore (2000), Con Artists (2001)

The Thin Man Cars (1957), Men — Law Enforcers (1957), New York (1957), Series Based on Radio Programs (1957), Women — Law Enforcers (1957)

Things Are Looking Up Teachers (1984), Teachers (1985)

The Third Bill Cosby Special African American (1968)

The Third Commandment Religious Programs (1959)

The Third Man Men — Law Enforcers (1960), Series Based on Films (1960)

Third Rock from the Sun Aliens (1996), Ohio (1996), Teachers (1996)

Third Watch Latino American (1999), New York (1999), Puerto Rican (1999), Rescue (1999)

13 East Bars (1989), Women — Nurses (1979)

The 13 Ghosts of Scooby-Doo Ghosts (1985)

13 Thirteenth Avenue Vampires (1983), Werewolves (1983), Witches (1983)

The 13th Chair Broadway (1952)

The 13th Day: The Story of Esther Religious Programs (1979)

The 13th Gate Government Agents (1965), The Supernatural (1965)

Thirty Minute Meals with Rachael Ray Cooking (1970)

thirtysomething Gays (1990)

This Girl for Hire Women — Law Enforcers (1983)

This Is Alice New Jersey (1958), Newspapers (1958), Sitcoms (1958)

This Is Charles Laughton Religious Programs (1952)

This Is Galen Drake Children's Program (1957)

This Is Kate Bennett Reporters (1982)

This Is Music Variety Programs (1951), Variety Programs (1959)

This Is the Life Religious Programs (1952)

This Is Your Music Variety Programs (1955)

This Man Dawson Men — Law Enforcers (1959)

This Old House Cuban American (1978)

This Thing Called Love Broadway (1952)

This Time Next Year Variety and Drama Spectaculars (1947)

Thompson's Ghost Ghosts (1966), Pilot Film Series (1966)

Thor Men — Extraordinary (1988)

The Thorns Housekeepers (1986), Teenagers (1988)

Those Endearing Young Charms Sitcoms (1951)

Those Fabulous Clowns Clowns (1984)

Those Two Variety Programs (1951)

Those Whiting Girls Los Angeles (1955), Sitcoms (1955)

Those Who Care Shows within Shows (1971)

Three Con Artists (1998)

Three Cornered Moon Broadway (1952)

Three Eyes Nightclubs (1982)

The Three Flames Show African American (1949)

Three for Danger Adventurers (1967)

Three for Tahiti Beaches (1970), Pilot Film Series (1970)

Three for the Road Teenagers (1975)

Three for Tonight Variety and Drama Spectaculars (1955)

Three Girls Sitcoms (1955)

Three Houses Soap Operas (1945)

Three in One Variety and Drama Spectaculars (1960)

The Three Little Pigs Fairy Tales (1982)

Three Men on a Horse Broadway (1952)

The Three Musketeers Historical Settings (1956)

Three of a Kind Bars (1989)

Three on an Island Pilot Film Series (1963–1967)

The Three Robotic Stooges Robots (1978)

Three Sisters Bars (2001), Los Angeles (2001)

Three Steps to Heaven Soap Operas (1953)

333 Montgomery Lawyers (1960)

Three Wishes Genies (1963), Genies (2005), Pilot Film Series (1963–1967)

Three's a Crowd California (1984)

Three's Company Bars (1977), California (1977), Gays (1977), Hotels (1977), Housekeepers (1980), Latino American (1977), Nudity (1977), Restaurants (1977), Senior Citizens (1979), Variety Programs (1950), Women — "Dumb Blondes" (1977), Women — Nurses (1980)

Threshold Aliens (2005), Little People (2005)

Thriller Drama (1960), Drama (1967), The Supernatural (1961)

Throb Adolescence (1986), New York (1986)

Through the Crystal Ball Children's Program (1949)

Through the Magic Pyramid Time Travel (1981)

Thumbelina Fairy Tales (1982)

Thunder Adolescence (1972), Animals (1977)

Thunder Alley Adolescence (1994), Senior Citizens (1994)

Thunder Boat Row Beaches (1989)

Thunder in Paradise Adolescence (1994), Beaches (1994), Florida (1994), Hotels (1994), Restaurants (1994)

Thunderbirds Films Based on Television Series (2004), Puppets (1968), Rescue (1968)

Tic Tac Dough Game Shows (1956)

The Tick Latino American (2001), Little People (2001), Super Heroes (2001), Women — Extraordinary (2001)

Ticket to Ride Shows within Shows (1989)

Tie This Game Shows (1946)

Tiger! Tiger! Animals (1969)

Tightrope Men — Law Enforcers (1959)

The Tim Conway Show Pilots (1970)

Time Express Time Travel (1979)

Time for Beany Puppets (1950)

Time for Fun Clowns (1955)

The Time of Their Lives Pilot Film Series (1987)

Time Out for Ginger Variety and Drama Spectaculars (1955)

Time Remembered Broadway (1961)

A Time to Live Soap Operas (1954)

Time Travelers Time Travel (1976)

Time Traxx Time Travel (1993)

The Time Tunnel Time Travel (1966)

Time Warp Trio Time Travel (2005)

Time Well Spent Teenagers (1995)

The Timex All-Star Jazz Show Variety and Drama Spectaculars (1957)

The Timid Soul Pilot Film Series (1949), Sitcoms (1949)

Timon of Athens Shakespeare (1981)

Tin Pan Alley TV Variety Programs (1950)

Tin Tin Cartoons (1961)

Tintypies Broadway (2005)

The Tiny Tree Holiday Specials (1977)

Titus Los Angeles (2000), Senior Citizens (2000)

Titus Andronicus Shakespeare (1905)

To Rome with Love Adolescence (1969), Hotels (1969), Senior Citizens (1969), Taxi Cabs (1969), Teachers (1969), Teenagers (1969)

To Sir with Love African American (1974), Teachers (1974)

To Tell the Truth Game Shows (1956)

To the Ladies Broadway (1942)

To the Queen's Taste Cooking (1948)

Toast of the Town Puppets (1949), Puppets (1963), Series Based on Radio Programs (1948), Variety Programs (1948)

Tobacco Road Television Firsts (1936)

Toby the Terrier and His TV Pals Puppets (1993)

Today Is Ours Soap Operas (1958)

The Today Show Animals (1952), News Broadcasts (1952, 1954)

Today with Mrs. Roosevelt Presidential Appearances (1950)

Today's F.B.I F.B.I. Agents (1982), Washington, D.C. (1981)

Together We Stand Asian American (1986), Teenagers (1986)

Tom California (1964), Pilot Film Series (1960), Teenagers (1994), Twins (1994)

Tom and Huck Fairy Tales (1960)

The Tom and Jerry Show Cartoons (1966)

Tom Corbett, Space Cadet Aliens (1950), Gadgets (1950), Series Based on Radio Programs (1972), Space (1950), Women — Extraordinary (1950)

The Tom Ewell Show Adolescence (1960), Newspapers (1960), Sitcoms (1960)

Tom of T.H.U.M.B. Little People (1966)

The Tom Show Senior Citizens (1997), Shows within Shows (1997)

Tom Slick Cartoons (1967)

The Tom Swift and Linda Craig Mystery Hour Geniuses (1983), Men — Law Enforcers (1983), Women — Law Enforcers (1983)

Tom Terrific Cartoons (1957)

Toma Men — Law Enforcers (1973)

Tomahawk Historical Settings (1957)

Tombstone Territory Arizona (1957), Bars (1957), Newspapers (1957), Westerns (1957)

Tomfoolery Cartoons (1970)

The Tommy Seven Show Clowns (1960)

Toni Twin Time Twins (1950), Variety Programs (1950)

Tonight at 8:30 Broadway (1952)

Tonight in Havana Restaurants (1958)

Tonight on Broadway Variety Programs (1948)

The Tonight Show Variety Programs (1954)

The Tonight Show Starring Johnny Carson Nudity (1974), Presidential Appearances (1972), Senior Citizens (1962)

Tony Awards Broadway (2003)

The Tony Bennett Show Variety Programs (1956)

The Tony Danza Show Latino American (1997), New York (1997)

The Tony Martin Show Variety Programs (1954)

Tony Orlando and Dawn Puerto Rican (1974)

The Tony Randall Show Housekeepers (1976), Judges (1976), Philadelphia (1976)

Tony the Pony Adolescence (1979), Witches (1979)

Too Close for Comfort Mexican American (1985), Puppets (1980), San Francisco (1980)

Too Good to Be True Con Artists (1994), Teachers (1983)

Too Young to Go Steady Sitcoms (1959), Teenagers (1959)

Tootsie Hippodrome Children's Program (1952)

Top Cat Cartoons (1961)

Top Dollar Game Shows (1958)

Top of the Heap Chicago (1991), Puerto Rican (1991)

Top Secret Government Agents (1952), Government Agents (1978)

Topper Ghosts (1950), Ghosts (1952), Ghosts (1979), House-keepers (1953), New York (1953), Senior Citizens (1953), Series Based on Radio Programs (1952), Sitcoms (1953)

Topper Returns Ghosts (1973)

Topsy Turvey Quiz Game Shows (1946)

The Torch Reporters (2001)

The Torkelsons Senior Citizens (1991), Teenagers (1991)

The Tortellis Las Vegas Settings (1987), Women — "Dumb Blondes" (1987)

Tosca Opera (1950)

Total Eclipse African American (1939), Variety Programs (1939)

Total Recall Robots (1999)

Total Security California (1997), Men — Law Enforcers (1997), Mexican American (1997)

Tots, Tweens and Teens Puppets (1948), Television Firsts (1948)

A Touch of Grace Senior Citizens (1973)

Touche Turtle Cartoons (1962)

Touched By an Angel Angels (1994), Cars (1994), Twins (1994)

Tough Cookies Chicago (1986), Latino American (1986), Men — Law Enforcers (1986), Women — Law Enforcers (1986)

Tour of Duty Puerto Rican (1987), War — Korea, Vietnam, Iraq (1987)

The Town Crier of Chung King War — World War II (1945)

Toyland Express Puppets (1955)

The Tracey Ullman Show Gays (1987)

Trackdown Westerns (1957)

Tracker Aliens (2001), Bars (2001), Chicago (2001)

Traffic Court Judges (1958)

The Tragedy of Coriolanus Shake-speare (1984)

The Tragedy of King Richard III Shakespeare (1983)

The Trailblazers Camps (1952)

Trails West Drama — Repeat Series (1958)

The Transformers Robots (1984)

The Trap Drama (1950)

Trapper John, M.D. San Francisco (1979), Women — Nurses (1979)

Traps Men — Law Enforcers (1994)

Trauma Center California (1983), Doctors (1983), Women — Nurses (1983)

Traveling Man Adventurers (1987), Pilot Film Series (1987)

The Travels of Jaimie McPheeters Adolescence (1963), Westerns (1963)

Treasure Hunt Game Shows (1956)

Treasure Island Variety and Drama Spectaculars (1939)

Treasury Men in Action Government Agents (1950), Washington, D.C. (1950)

Trial and Error Mexican American (1988), Puerto Rican (1988)

Trial by Jury Judges (1989)

The Trial of Mary Dugan Broadway (1952)

The Trials of O'Brien Lawyers (1965), New York (1965), Visually Impaired (1965)

The Trials of Rosie O'Neill California (1990), Cars (1990), Lawyers (1990), Senior Citizens (1990)

Tribal Life Nudity and Sexuality (2006)

Tribeca Drama (1993), New York (1993)

Tripping the Rift Clowns (2004), Nudity (2004), Robots (2004), Talking Animals and Machines (2004)

Troilus and Cressida Shakespeare (1981)

Tropic Holiday Variety Programs (1949)

Trouble, Inc. Men — Law Enforcers (1949), Women — Law Enforcers (1949)

Trouble with Father Adolescence (1950), African American (1950), African American (1952), Sitcoms (1950), Teachers (1950), Teenagers (1950)

The Trouble with Larry New York (1993)

The Trouble with Richard Pilot Film Series (1960)

Trouble with Tracy Canada (1971), Women — "Dumb Blondes" (1971)

Tru Calling Mediums (2003), New York (2004), Restaurants (2003), Time Travel (2003), Women — Extraordinary (2004)

True Believer Series Based on Films (1991)

True Blue New York (1989), Rescue (1989), Taxi Cabs (1989), Women — Law Enforcers (1989)

True Colors Baltimore (1990), Teach-ers (1990), Teenagers (1990)

True Confessions Drama (1986)

True Grit Visually Impaired (1978), Westerns (1978)

True Grit: A Further Adventure Visu-ally Impaired (1978), Westerns (1978)

True Life Stories Drama (1981)

The True Meaning of Christmas Hol-iday Specials (1988)

True Story Drama (1957)

The Truth About Alex Gays (1987)

Truth or Consequences Game Shows

(1941), Game Shows (1943), Game Shows (1950)

Try and Do It Game Shows (1948)

Tucker's Witch California (1982), Witches (1982)

Turbo: A Power Rangers Movie Films Based on Television Series (1997)

Turn of Fate Drama (1957)

The Turn of the Screw Variety and Drama Spectaculars (1959)

Turn to a Friend Game Shows (1953)

Turner and Hooch Animals (1990)

The Turning Point Drama (1953)

Turning Point Drama (1958)

Tutor the Turtle Cartoons (1960)

TV 101 Teachers (1988)

TV Auction Game Shows (1954)

TV General Store Game Shows (1953)

TV Reader's Digest Drama (1955)

TV Sound Stage Drama (1953)

TV Wedding Love (1931)

TV's Top Tunes Variety Programs (1951), Variety Programs (1954)

Twas the Night Before Christmas Holiday Specials (1974), Holiday Specials (1977)

Twelfth Night Shakespeare (1947), Shakespeare (1957), Shakespeare (1980)

Twelve O'clock High Series Based on Films (1964), War — World War II (1964)

The Twentieth Century Broadway (1952, 1956), Variety and Drama Spectaculars (1956)

20th Century–Fox Hour Drama (1955)

20 Questions Series Based on Radio Programs (1949)

26 Men Arizona (1958), Westerns (1958)

The 25th Man Women — Law En-forcers (1982)

24 Lesbians (2001)

Twenty-One Game Shows (1956)

21 Beacon Street Boston (1959), Men — Law Enforcers (1959)

21 Jump Street Los Angeles (1987), Men — Law Enforcers (1987), Women — Law Enforcers (1987)

2½ Dads Teenagers (1986)

Twice in a Lifetime Angels (1999), Restaurants (1974)

Twigs Broadway (1975), Broadway (1982)

Twilight Theater Drama — Repeat Series (1958)

The Twilight Zone Angels (1960, 1962), Drama (1959, 1985, 2002), Lesbians (2002), The Supernat-ural (1959)

Twin Detectives Men — Law En-forcers (1976), Twins (1976)

Twin Peaks American Indian (1990),

Films Based on Television Series (1992), Little People (1990), Lookalikes (1990), Visually Impaired (1990)

Twin Peaks: Fire Walks with Me Films Based on Television Series (1992)

Twins Gays (2005), Housekeepers (2005), Nudity (2005), San Francisco (2005), Twins (2005), Women — "Dumb Blondes" (2005)

Twitches Twins (2005), Witches (2005)

Two Twins (1996)

Two and a Half Men Adolescence (2003), California (2003), Housekeepers (2003), Senior Citizens (2003)

Two Boys Adolescence (1970)

Two Faces West Twins (1960), Westerns (1961)

The Two-Five Men — Law Enforcers (1978)

Two for the Money Game Shows (1952)

Two for the Road Fairy Tales (1960)

The Two Gentlemen of Verona Shakespeare (1983)

Two Girls Named Smith Sitcoms (1951)

Two Guys Boston (1998)

Two Guys from Muck Reporters (1982)

2 Hip 4 TV Teenagers (1988)

227 Senior Citizens (1982), Washington, D.C. (1985)

240-Robert California (1979), California (1981), Los Angeles (1979), Rescue (1979), Rescue (1981)

Two in Love Game Shows (1954)

Two Marriages Adolescence (1983)

The Two Mrs. Carrols Broadway (1952)

Two of a Kind Adolescence (1998), Chicago (1998), Twins (1998)

The Two of Us Adolescence (1981), Housekeepers (1981), New York (1980), Pilot Film Series (1963–1967), Shows within Shows (1981)

Two Soldiers War — World War II (1944)

Two the Hard Way Shows within Shows (1981)

2000 Malibu Road Prostitutes (1992)

Two's Company African American (1973)

The Tycoon Los Angeles (1964), Senior Citizens (1964)

The Tyra Banks Show Nudity and Sexuality (2006)

The Tyrees of Capitol Hill Politics (1963)

U.C.: Undercover Government Agents (2001)

UFO Aliens (1972)

U.F.O. Space (1972)

U.S. Marshal Arizona (1957), Men — Law Enforcers (1958)

U.S. Royal Showcase Variety Programs (1952)

The U.S. Steel Hour Drama (1953)

U.S. Treasury Salutes Variety and Drama Spectaculars (1948)

The Ugily Family Teenagers (1980)

The Ugliest Girl in Town Cross Dressers (1968)

The Ugly Duckling Cartoons (1940)

Ukulele Ike Variety Programs (1950)

Ultraman Aliens (1967)

Ultraman Aliens (1967)

Ultraman: Towards the Future Aliens (1967)

The Uncle Al Show Children's Program (1958)

Uncle Buck Chicago (1990), Series Based on Films (1990), Teenagers (1990)

The Uncle Floyd Show Puppets (1974)

Uncle Jim's Question Bee Game Shows (1941), Television Firsts (1941)

Uncle Johnny Coons Puppets (1954)

Uncle Miltie's Christmas Party Holiday Specials (1950)

Uncle Miltie's Easter Party Holiday Specials (1951)

Uncle Mistletoe and His Adventures Puppets (1950)

Uncommon Women and Others Broadway (1978)

Under One Roof Senior Citizens (1984), Senior Citizens (1995)

Under Suspicion Women — Law Enforcers (1994)

Under the Yum Yum Tree Love (1969)

Undercover Cats (1991), Espionage (1991), Government Agents (1991)

Undercurrent Drama — Repeat Series (1955)

The Underdog Show Cartoons (1964), Super Heroes (1964)

The Unexpected Drama (1952)

The Unexplained Drama (1956)

Unhappily Ever After California (1995), Gays (1995), Ghosts (1995), Lesbians (1995), Nudity (1995), Puppets (1995), Teenagers (1995), Women — Scatterbrained (Note)

Union Square Latino American (1997), New York (1997)

The Unit Government Agents (2006)

Unit 4 Government Agents (1981)

United States Adolescence (1980)

University Hospital Washington, D.C. (1995), Women — Nurses (1995)

Unk and Andy Children's Program (1950)

Unsolved Mysteries Senior Citizens (1987)

Unsub Forensics (1989)

Untamed World Animals (1969)

Untitled Ghosts (1945), War — World War II (1945)

The Untouchables American Indian (1959), American Indian (1993), Chicago (1959), Chicago (1993), Government Agents (1959), Government Agents (1993), Historical Settings (1959), Historical Settings (1993)

Up to No Good Con Artists (1991)

Uptown Jubilee African American (1949)

Urban Angel Canada (1991), Latino American (1991)

Urban Latino TV Latino American (2002)

V Aliens (1984), Teenagers (1984)

V.I.P. Cars (1998), Hotels (1998), Look-alikes (1998), Los Angeles (1998), Nudity (1998), Nudity (2003), Robots (1998), Women — Extraordinary (1998)

Vacation Playhouse Pilot Film Series (1963–1967)

Valentine Magic on Love Island Beaches (1980), Love (1979)

Valentine's Day Asian American (1964), Housekeepers (1964), New York (1964)

Valerie Teenagers (1986)

The Valerie Bettis Dancers Variety Programs (1946)

Valiant Lady Series Based on Radio Programs (1953), Soap Operas (1953)

The Van Dyke Show Philadelphia (1988)

Vanities Broadway (1981)

Vanity Fair Broadway (1949), Broadway (1961)

Variety Variety and Drama Spectaculars (1955), Variety Programs (1948)

Variety Over the Air African American (1939), Television Firsts (1939), Variety Programs (1939)

The Variety Show News Broadcasts (1939), Variety Programs (1939)

Variety Show Variety Programs (1930)

Vaudeo Varieties Variety Programs (1949)

The Vaudeville Show Variety Programs (1939), Variety Programs (1941), Variety Programs (1953)

The Vaughn Monroe Show Variety

Programs (1950), Variety Programs (1954)

Vegas American Indian (1978), Cars (1978), Hotels (1978), Las Vegas Settings (1978), Men — Law Enforcers (1978), Women — "Dumb Blondes" (1978)

The Veil Drama (1958), The Supernatural (1958)

Velvet Espionage (1984), Government Agents (1984)

The Velvet Glove Broadway (1952)

Venice Medical Women — Nurses (1983)

The Verdict Is Yours Judges (1958)

Veronica Mars California (2004), Cars (2004), Men — Law Enforcers (2004), Teenagers (2004), Women — Law Enforcers (2004)

Veronica's Closet Gays (1997), New York (1997)

Versatile Varieties Variety Programs (1949)

A Very Merry Cricket Holiday Specials (1973)

A Very Missing Person Women — Law Enforcers (1972)

Vic and Sade Sitcoms (1949)

The Vic Damone Show Variety Programs (1956)

The Victor Borge Show Variety Programs (1944)

Victor/Victoria Broadway (1995)

Victoria Regina Broadway (1961)

The Victoria's Secret Fashion Show Nudity (2005)

Victory Beaches (1945), Hotels (1945)

Victory at Sea War — World War II (1952)

Video Chef Cooking (1952)

Video Village Children's Program (1961), Game Shows (1960)

Video Village Junior Children's Program (1961)

Vietnam War Story Drama (1987), War — Korea, Vietnam, Iraq (1987)

Village Barn Variety Programs (1948)

The Village Greene Broadway (1952)

The Vim Talent Search Reality Programs (1950)

The Vincent Lopez Show Variety Programs (1956)

Vine Street Television Firsts (1939)

Vinnie and Bobby Chicago (1992), Hotels (1992), Teenagers (1992)

Violet Adolescence (1992)

Viper Cars (1994), Chicago (1994), Gadgets (1994), Men — Extraordinary (1994), Physically Disabled (1994), Women — Law Enforcers (1997)

The Virginian Color Broadcasting (1957-1965), Teenagers (1962), Westerns (1962), Westerns (1970)

The Vise Drama (1954)

Vision On Hearing Impaired Characters (1973)

Visions Drama (1976)

Visions of Murder Mediums (1993), Psychiatrists (1993)

Visions of Murder II Mediums (1993), Psychiatrists (1993)

Visual Girl Teenagers (1971)

Viva Valdez Los Angeles (1976), Mexican American (1976), Teenagers (1976)

Voice of Firestone Variety Programs (1949)

Voltron — Defender of the Universe Robots (1984)

Volume One Drama (1949)

Vote for Me: Politics in America Presidential Appearances (1996)

Voyage to the Bottom of the Sea Series Based on Films (1964)

Voyager from the Unknown Time Travel (1982)

Voyagers! Adolescence (1982), Time Travel (1982)

VR.5 Geniuses (1995), Twins (1995)

W.E.B. New York (1978)

The Wackiest Ship in the Army Series Based on Films (1965), War — World War II (1965)

The Wacky Races Cartoons (1968)

Wagon Train Country Folk (1963), Westerns (1957)

Waikiki Beaches (1980)

Wait Until Dark Broadway (1982)

Waldo Animals (1960)

A Walk in the Night Pilot Film Series (1968)

Walker, Texas Ranger American Indian (1993), Bars (1991), Cars (1993), District Attorneys (1993), Look-alikes (1993), Martial Arts (1993), Men — Law Enforcers (1993), Senior Citizens (1993), Women — Law Enforcers (1998)

Walkin' Walter African American (1977)

Walking Tall Adolescence (1981), Men — Law Enforcers (1981), Series Based on Films (1981)

Wally Gator Cartoons (1962)

Wally Western Cartoons (1962)

The Walt Disney Christmas Show Holiday Specials (1951)

Walt Disney Presents Latino American (1958)

Walt Disney's Wonderful World of Color Color Broadcasting (1957-1965)

*W*A*L*T*E*R* Men — Law Enforcers (1984)

Walter and Emily Newspapers (1991), Senior Citizens (1991)

Walter Compton and the News News Broadcasts (1947)

Walter of the Jungle Men — Extraordinary (1967)

The Walter Winchell File Drama (1957), Reporters (1958)

The Walter Winchell Show Variety Programs (1956)

The Waltons Cars (1972), Historical Settings (1972), Newspapers (1972), Physically Disabled (1977), Religious Characters (1972), Restaurants (1972), Senior Citizens (1972), Series Based on Films (1972), Women — Nurses (1972)

Wanda at Large Reporters (2003), Shows within Shows (2003), Washington, D.C. (2003)

Wanted Drama (1955), F.B.I. Agents (1955), Los Angeles (2005), Men — Law Enforcers (2005)

Wanted: Dead or Alive Westerns (1958)

War and Remembrance War — World War II (1988)

The War at Home Teenagers (2005)

War Correspondent War — World War II (1959)

War in the Air War — World War II (1956)

War News News Broadcasts (1941)

War of the Worlds American Indian (1988), Physically Disabled (1988), Robots (1988)

The War of the Worlds Series Based on Films (1988)

The War Widow Lesbians (1976)

The Warden Prison (1963)

Warden Duffy of San Quentin Prison (1950)

Warner Bros. Presents Drama (1956)

Was in the Kitchen Cooking (1945)

Washington Capital Newspapers (1990)

Washington Merry-Go-Round News Broadcasts (1950)

Washington Square Variety Programs (1956)

Washingtoon Politics (1984)

Watching Ellie New York (2003)

Waterfront California (1954)

Way of the World Drama (1955), Soap Operas (1955)

Way Out Drama (1960), The Supernatural (1961)

The Wayans Bros. Latino American (1995), New York (1998), Restaurants (1995)

The Wayne King Show Variety Programs (1949)

We Got it Made Housekeepers (1983), New York (1983), Women — "Dumb Blondes" (1983)

We Take Your Word Game Shows (1950)

The Web Drama (1950), Drama (1957)

Web Woman Super Heroes (1980)

Webster Little People (1983)
Wedding Day Love (1981), Reality Programs (1981)
Weekend Beaches (1967), Teenagers (1967)
Weird Science Genies (1994)
Welcome Aboard Variety Programs (1948)
Welcome Back, Kotter African American (1975), Hotels (1975), New York (1975), Teachers (1975), Teenagers (1975)
Welcome Home, Jellybean Mentally Disabled (1984)
Welcome to New York New York (2000)
Welcome to Paradise Adventurers (1984)
Welcome to Washington Pilot Film Series (1960), Politics (1958)
Welcome Travelers Reality Programs (1952)
We'll Get By Teenagers (1975)
We'll Take Manhattan American Indian (1968)
Wendy and Me Los Angeles (1964), Women — "Dumb Blondes" (1964)
Wendy Wu: Homecoming Warrior Asian American (2006)
Werewolf Morphing (1990: She Wolf of London), Visually Impaired (1987), Werewolves (1987)
Wesley Adolescence (1949), Sitcoms (1949)
West Coast Revue Newspapers (1988)
The West Point Story Drama (1956)
The West Wing Physically Disabled (1999), Politics (1999), Puerto Rican Performers (2006), Senior Citizens (2004), Washington, D.C. (1999)
Western Theater Drama — Repeat Series (1958)
The Westerner Westerns (1960)
The Westerners Drama — Repeat Series (1965)
Westinghouse Summer Theater Drama (1951)
Westside Medical Doctors (1977)
The Westwind Adventurers (1975), Beaches (1975), Teenagers (1975)
Westworld Series Based on Films (1980)
Whacked Out Newspapers (1980)
What a Country Immigrants (1986), Los Angeles (1986), Mexican American (1986)
What a Dummy Adolescence (1990), New Jersey (1990), Puppets (1990)
What About Joan Chicago (2001), Teachers (2001)
What Do You Have in Common? Game Shows (1954)
What Do You Say to a Naked Lady? Films Based on Television Series (1970)

What Happened? Game Shows (1952)
What Have You Got to Lose? Game Shows (1953)
What I Like About You Lesbians (2004), New York (2002), Nudity (1997), Restaurants (2005), Teen After-School Hangouts (2001), Teenagers (2002)
What If I'm Gay? Gays (1987)
What Really Happened to the Class of '65? Historical Settings (1977)
What Will They Think of Next? Game Shows (1948)
What's Alan Watching? Teenagers (1989)
What's Going On? Game Shows (1954)
What's Happened to Elaine? Ghosts (1973)
What's Happening Now!! Los Angeles (1985)
What's Happening!! African American (1976), Los Angeles (1976), Newspapers (1976), Teenagers (1976)
What's in a Word? Game Shows (1954)
What's It For? Game Shows (1957)
What's My Line? Game Shows (1950)
What's My Name Puppets (1952)
What's the Story? Game Shows (1951)
What's Your Bid? Game Shows (1953)
What's Your Trouble Religious Programs (1953)
Wheel of Fortune Reality Programs (1952)
Wheeler and Murdock Men — Law Enforcers (1973)
When a Nightingale Sang in Berkeley Square Variety and Drama Spectaculars (1939)
When the Whistle Blows Los Angeles (1980)
When Things Were Rotten Historical Settings (1975), Women — "Dumb Blondes" (1975)
When We Are Married Broadway (1940), Variety and Drama Spectaculars (1944)
Where the Heart Is Soap Operas (1969)
Where There's Smokey Rescue (1966)
Where Was I? Game Shows (1953)
Where's Huddles? Cartoons (1970)
Where's Poppa? Senior Citizens (1979)
Where's Raymond? Sitcoms (1953)
Where's Rodney? Teenagers (1990)
Where's the Fire?, Rescue (1975)
Where's There's Smokey Pilot Film Series (1963–1967)
Which Way'd They Go? Westerns (1963)
Whiplash Australia (1961), Historical Settings (1961)

The Whirlybirds California (1954)
Whirlybirds Los Angeles (1954), Pilots (1954)
Whispering Smith Historical Settings (1961), Men — Law Enforcers (1961)
Whistle, Daughter, Whistle Sitcoms (1948)
The Whistler Drama (1954), Series Based on Radio Programs (1954)
Whistling in the Dark Broadway (1952)
The Whistling Wizard Puppets (1951)
The White House Tour Presidential Appearances (1962)
The White Shadow Los Angeles (1981), Teachers (1978)
Whitney and the Robot Robots (1979)
The Whiz Kids Geniuses (1983), Reporters (1983), Robots (1983), Robots (1987), Teenagers (1983)
Who Do You Trust? Game Shows (1956)
Who Pays? Game Shows (1959)
Who Said That? Game Shows (1948), Series Based on Radio Programs (1948)
Who Wants to Be a Millionaire Senior Citizens (1999), Television Firsts (1999)
A Whole New Ballgame Shows within Shows (1995)
Whoopi Hotels (2003), Housekeepers (2003)
Whoopie New York (2003)
Who's the Boss? Adolescence (1984), Cars (1984), Connecticut (1984), Game Shows (1954), Housekeepers (1984), Nudity (2004)
Who's There? Game Shows (1953)
Who's Watching the Kids? Adolescence (1978), American Indian (1978), Hotels (1978), Las Vegas Settings (1978), Teenagers (1978)
Who's Whose? Game Shows (1951)
Why? Game Shows (1952)
Wichita Town Mexican American (1959), Westerns (1959)
The Wickedest Witch Witches (1987)
Wide Horizons Variety Programs (1944)
Wide Wide World News Broadcasts (1955)
Wild About Animals Animals (2004)
Wild and Wooly Westerns (1978)
Wild Bill Hickok Series Based on Radio Programs (1951), Speech Impaired (1951), Westerns (1952)
Wild Card Women — Law Enforcers (2003)
Wild Cargo Animals (1963)
Wild Jack Los Angeles (1989)
Wild Oats Chicago (1994)
The Wild Swans Fairy Tales (1958)

The Wild Wild West Espionage (1965), Films Based on Television Series (1999), Gadgets(1965), Little People (1965)

The Wild Wild West Revisited Little People (1965)

Wild, Wild World of Animals Animals (1973)

The Wild Women of Chastity Gulch Prostitutes (1982), Westerns (1982)

Wildest Dreams Adolescence (1988)

The Wilds of Ten Thousand Islands Beaches (1978)

Wildside Los Angeles (1985), Mexican American (1985), Westerns (1985)

Will and Grace Gays (1998), Hotels (1998), Housekeepers (2000), Lawyers (1998), Lesbians (1998), New York (1998), Senior Citizens (1998), Shows within Shows (2003)

Will the Real Jerry Lewis Please Sit Down Cartoons (1970)

Willie Wonderful Puppets (1959)

Willow B: Women in Prison Prison (1980)

Willy Lawyers (1954), Lawyers (1955), Sitcoms (1954), Sitcoms (1955)

Win with a Winner Game Shows (1958)

Winchell and Mahoney Puppets (1947)

Winchell and Mahoney Time Puppets (1965)

Winchester Westerns (1959)

Window Shade Revue Variety and Drama Spectaculars (1946), Variety Programs (1946)

Windows Drama (1955)

The Winds of War War — World War II (1983), War — World War II (1988)

Windy City Jamboree Variety Programs (1950)

Wingo Game Shows (1958)

Wings Bars (1990), Pilots (1990)

Winky Dink and You Cartoons (1953), Cartoons (1969)

Winner Take All Game Shows (1948)

Winnetka Road Religious Characters (1994), Visually Impaired (1994)

Winnie the Pooh Fairy Tales (1960)

The Winter's Tale Shakespeare (1981)

Winterset Broadway (1945), Broadway (1959)

Winx Club Witches (2004)

The Wire Baltimore (2002), Lesbians (2002), Men — Law Enforcers (2002)

Wire Service Reporters (1956)

Wiseguy Cuban American (1990), F.B.I. Agents (1987), Latino

American (1990), Physically Disabled (1987)

W.I.T.C.H. Witches (2005)

Witchblade Ghosts (2001), New York (2001), Women — Extraordinary (2001), Women — Law Enforcers (2001)

The Witches of Eastwick Witches (1992), Witches (2002)

The Witching Hour Broadway (1952)

Within the Law Broadway (1952)

Without a Trace F.B.I. Agents (2002)

Wives and Lovers California (1978)

The Wizard Geniuses (1986), Government Agents (1986), Little People (1986)

The Wizard of Oz Cartoons (1961), Drama (1967)

Wizards and Warriors Witches (1983)

WKRP in Cincinnati Nudity (2003), Senior Citizens (1978)

Wodehouse Playhouse Drama (1977)

Wolf Men — Law Enforcers (1989), San Francisco (1989)

A Woman to Remember Soap Operas (1947)

The Woman Who Willed a Miracle Mentally Disabled (1983)

Woman with a Past Soap Operas (1954)

The Women Broadway (1955), Broadway (2005)

Women in Prison Lesbians (1987), Prostitutes (1987), Senior Citizens (1987)

Women in Wartime War — World War II (1944)

Women of the House Mentally Disabled (1995), Politics (1995)

Wonder Woman Gadgets (1975), Nudity (1975), Pilots (1975), Super Heroes (1968, 1974, 1976), Teenagers (1976), Washington, D.C. (1975), Women — Extraordinary (1975)

The Wonder Years Adolescence (1988), Cars (1988), Teenagers (1988)

Wonderbug Talking Animals and Machines (1976), Teenagers (1976)

Wonderfalls Bars (2004), Lesbians (2004), New York (2004), Women — Extraordinary (2004)

Wonderful John Acton Adolescence (1953), Historical Settings (1953), Sitcoms (1953)

Wonderful Town Broadway (1958), Variety and Drama Spectaculars (1958)

The Wonderful World of Philip Malley Teachers (1981)

Wonderland Shows within Shows (1990)

Woobinda — Animal Doctor Animals (1978), Australia (1978)

The Woody Woodpecker Show Cartoons (1957)

WOR Television Varieties Variety Programs (1944)

Word of Mouth Politics (1991)

Words and Music Variety Programs (1949)

Working Broadway (1981)

Working Girl New York (1990), Series Based on Films (1991)

Working It Out Adolescence (1990), Hotels (1990), New York (1990), Teenagers (1990)

The World at War War — World War II (1973)

The World Beyond Mediums (1979), Men — Extraordinary (1978), The Supernatural (1978)

The World of Darkness Mediums (1977), Men — Extraordinary (1977), Men — Extraordinary (1978), The Supernatural (1977)

World of Giants Little People (1959), Men — Extraordinary (1959)

The World of Mr. Sweeney Sitcoms (1954)

The World's Fair Beauty Contest Nudity (1939), Television Firsts (1939)

The Worst Witch Witches (1986)

The Would-Be Gentleman Opera (1950)

Wrangler Westerns (1960)

Wren's Nest Sitcoms (1949)

The Wrestlers Men — Extraordinary (2001), Women — Extraordinary (2001)

The Wright Verdicts Lawyers (1995)

Wuthering Heights Broadway (1952), Variety and Drama Spectaculars (1958)

The Wyatts Love (1992)

The Xavier Cugat Show Latino American (1957), Variety Programs (1957)

Xena: Warrior Princess Lesbians (1995), Super Heroes (1995), Women — Extraordinary (1995)

The X-Files Aliens (1993), Films Based on Television Series (1998), Lesbians (2000), Visually Impaired (1993)

The X-Men Super Heroes (1992)

X-Men Evolution Super Heroes (2000)

Yakky Doodle Duck Cartoons (1958)

Yancy Derringer American Indian (1958), Historical Settings (1959)

Yappie and Yahooey Cartoons (1964)

A Year at the Top Devil (1977)

A Year in the Life Chicago (1987), Washington, D.C. (1987)

The Year Without a Santa Claus Holiday Specials (1974)

The Yellow Rose American Indian (1983), Mexican American (1983), Soap Operas (Note)

The Yeoman of the Guard Opera (1957)

Yer Ole Buddy Television Firsts (1948)

Yes Virginia, There Is a Santa Claus Holiday Specials (1974)

Yes, Dear Adolescence (2000)

Yes, Yes Nanette Los Angeles (1961), Teenagers (1961)

Yogi Bear Cartoons (1958)

Yogi Bear's All-Star Christmas Caper Holiday Specials (1982)

You Are There Drama (1953), Series Based on Radio Programs (1953)

You Asked for It Reality Programs (1950), Reality Programs (1981)

You Bet Your Life Game Shows (1950), Series Based on Radio Programs (1950)

You Can't Take It with You Broadway (1945), Broadway (1979), New York (1987), Senior Citizens (1986)

You Gotta Start Somewhere American Indian (1977)

You Take the Kids Philadelphia (1990), Teenagers (1990)

You Wish Genies (1997)

You'll Never Get Rich Con Artists (1955), Sitcoms (1955)

Young Again Angels (1986)

The Young and the Restless Soap Operas (Note)

Young Blades Cross Dressers (2004)

Young Dan'l Boone African American (1977), American Indian (1977), Historical Settings (1977)

Young Doctor Malone Soap Operas (Note)

Young Dr. Kildare Doctors (1972), Women — Nurses (1972)

Young Dr. Malone Series Based on Radio Programs (1958), Soap Operas (1958)

Young Guy Christian Espionage (1979)

Young Hearts Teenagers (1984), Teenagers (1986)

Young in Heart Housekeepers (1965), Pilot Film Series (1965)

The Young Indiana Jones Chronicles Series Based on Films (1992)

The Young Lawyers Lawyers (1970)

Young Lives Soap Operas (Note), Teenagers (1981)

The Young Marrieds Soap Operas (1964)

Young Maverick Westerns (1978)

Young Mr. Bobbin Sitcoms (1951)

The Young Pioneers Children — Extraordinary (1978), Historical Settings (1978), Teenagers (1978)

The Young Rebels African American (1970), Philadelphia (1970)

The Young Riders American Indian (1989), Speech Impaired (1989), Westerns (1989)

Your All American College Show Reality Programs (1968)

Your Chevrolet Showroom Variety Programs (1953)

Your Hit Parade Color Broadcasting (1957-1965), Series Based on Radio Programs (1950), Variety Programs (1950)

Your Jeweler's Showcase Drama (1952)

Your Lucky Clue Game Shows (1952)

Your Luncheon Date Variety Programs (1951)

Your Play Time Drama (1954)

Your Show of Shows Variety Programs (1950)

Your Show Time Drama (1949)

Your Surprise Store Game Shows (1952)

Your Uncle Dudley Broadway (1952)

Your World Tomorrow News Broadcasts (1944)

You're Invited Variety Programs (1948)

You're on Your Own Game Shows (1956)

You're Only Young Once Pilot Film Series (1960)

You're Only Young Twice Pilot Film Series (1963–1967)

You're the Top Variety and Drama Spectaculars (1956)

Yuma Westerns (1971)

The Zack Files Children — Extraordinary (2001)

Zane Grey Theater Drama (1956)

Zero One Pilots (1962)

Zoe New York (2000), Restaurants (1999)

Zoe, Duncan, Jack and Jane Lesbians (1999), New York (1999), Physically Disabled (1999), Restaurants (1999), Teenagers (1999), Twins (1999)

Zoey Women — Law Enforcers (1985)

Zoey 101 Teenagers (2005)

Zorro California (1959), Films Based on Television Series (1998), Hearing Impaired Characters (1957), Historical Settings (1959), Latino American (1957), Men — Extraordinary (1959), Speech Impaired (1957)

Zorro and Son California (1983), Hearing Impaired Characters (1983), Historical Settings (1982), Latino American (1957), Senior Citizens (1982)